D1429843

CAPTAIN MARVEL
CAROL DANVERS
THE Ms. MARVEL YEARS

CAPTAIN MARVEL
CAROL DANVERS
THE Ms. MARVEL YEARS

WRITER: **BRIAN REED**

MS. MARVEL SPECIAL: STORYTELLER
PENCILER: **GIUSEPPE CAMUNCOLI**
INKER: **LORENZO RUGGIERO**
COLORIST: **ANDRES MOSSA**

MS. MARVEL #35-37
PENCILER: **PATRICK OLLIFFE**
INKERS: **SERGE LaPOINTE** WITH
KRIS JUSTICE (#35) & **LIVESAY** (#37)
COLORIST: **CHRIS SOTOMAYOR**

MS. MARVEL #38
ARTIST: **REBEKAH ISAACS**
COLORIST: **CHRIS SOTOMAYOR**

MS. MARVEL #39-40, #42, #44 & #46
ARTIST & COLORIST: **SANA TAKEDA**
PENCILER (#40 PP.1-3 & 17-22): **LUKE ROSS**
COLORIST (#40 PP.1-3 & 17-22): **ROB SCHWAGER**
SPECIAL THANKS TO AKI YANAGI

MS. MARVEL #41 & #43
ARTIST: **SERGIO ARIÑO**
COLORISTS: **EMILY WARREN** &
CHRISTINA STRAIN (#41)
AND **IKARI STUDIO** (#43)

MS. MARVEL #45
ARTIST: **PHIL BRIONES**
COLORIST: **IKARI STUDIO**

MS. MARVEL #47
ARTISTS: **MIKE McKONE** (PP.1-12 & 14-15),
ROBERTO DI SALVO (PP.13 & 16-19)
& **DEREC DONOVAN** (PP.20-22)
COLORIST: **CHRIS SOTOMAYOR**

MS. MARVEL #48-50
ARTIST & COLORIST: **SANA TAKEDA**
ARTIST (#49 PP.12-17, #50 PP.1-3 & 17-22):
BEN OLIVER
COLORIST (#49 PP.12-17, #50 PP.1-3 & 17-22):
VERONICA GANDINI

MS. MARVEL #50: "PROTECTOR"
PENCILER: **MICHAEL RYAN**
COLORIST: **VERONICA GANDINI**

SIEGE: SPIDER-MAN
ARTIST: **MARCO SANTUCCI**
COLORIST: **CHRIS SOTOMAYOR**

LETTERERS: **BLAMBOT's NATE PIEKOS** (STORYTELLER), **DAVE SHARPE** (#35-50)
& **VC's JOE CARAMAGNA** (SIEGE: SPIDER-MAN)

COVER ART:

GIUSEPPE CAMUNCOLI, LORENZO RUGGIERO & ANDRES MOSSA (STORYTELLER)
ED McGUINNESS, DEXTER VINES & RAIN BEREDO (#35)
PHIL JIMENEZ & CHRIS CHUCKRY (#36-38)
MIKE DEODATO JR. & RAIN BEREDO (#39)
SANA TAKEDA (#40-46 & #48-50)
PASQUAL FERRY & FRANK D'ARMATA (#47)
MARKO DJURDJEVIĆ (SIEGE: SPIDER-MAN)

ASSISTANT EDITORS: **TOM BRENNAN** & **RACHEL PINNELAS**
EDITORS: **STEPHEN WACKER, BILL ROSEMANN** & **TOM BRENNAN**
EXECUTIVE EDITOR: **TOM BREVOORT**

COLLECTION EDITOR: **MARK D. BEAZLEY** ▪ ASSISTANT EDITOR: **CAITLIN O'CONNELL** ▪ ASSOCIATE MANAGING EDITOR: **KATERI WOODY**
ASSOCIATE MANAGER, DIGITAL ASSETS: **JOE HOCHSTEIN** ▪ SENIOR EDITOR, SPECIAL PROJECTS: **JENNIFER GRÜNWALD**
VP PRODUCTION & SPECIAL PROJECTS: **JEFF YOUNGQUIST** ▪ RESEARCH: **JOHN RHETT THOMAS** ▪ LAYOUT: **JEPH YORK** ▪ PRODUCTION: **JOE FRONTIRRE**
BOOK DESIGNER: **JAY BOWEN** ▪ SVP PRINT, SALES & MARKETING: **DAVID GABRIEL**

EDITOR IN CHIEF: **C.B. CEBULSKI** ▪ CHIEF CREATIVE OFFICER: **JOE QUESADA** ▪ PRESIDENT: **DAN BUCKLEY** ▪ EXECUTIVE PRODUCER: **ALAN FINE**

CAPTAIN MARVEL: CAROL DANVERS — THE MS. MARVEL YEARS VOL. 3. Contains material originally published in magazine form as MS. MARVEL #35-50, MS. MARVEL SPECIAL: STORYTELLER ONE-SHOT and SIEGE: SPIDER-MAN #1. First printing 2018. ISBN 978-1-302-91563-6. Published by MARVEL WORLDWIDE, INC., a subsidiary of MARVEL ENTERTAINMENT, LLC. OFFICE OF PUBLICATION: 135 West 50th Street, New York, NY 10020. Copyright © 2018 MARVEL. No similarity between any of the names, characters, persons, and/or institutions in this magazine with those of any living or dead person or institution is intended, and any such similarity which may exist is purely coincidental. **Printed in the U.S.A.** DAN BUCKLEY, President, Marvel Entertainment; JOHN NEE, Publisher; JOE QUESADA, Chief Creative Officer; TOM BREVOORT, SVP of Publishing; DAVID BOGART, SVP of Business Affairs & Operations, Publishing & Partnership; DAVID GABRIEL, SVP of Sales & Marketing, Publishing; JEFF YOUNGQUIST, VP of Production & Special Projects; DAN CARR, Executive Director of Publishing Technology; ALEX MORALES, Director of Publishing Operations; DAN EDINGTON, Managing Editor; SUSAN CRESPI, Production Manager; STAN LEE, Chairman Emeritus. For information regarding advertising in Marvel Comics or on Marvel.com, please contact Vit DeBellis, Custom Solutions & Integrated Advertising Manager, at vdebellis@marvel.com. For Marvel subscription inquiries, please call 888-511-5480. **Manufactured between 10/26/2018 and 11/27/2018 by LSC COMMUNICATIONS INC., KENDALLVILLE, IN, USA.**

10 9 8 7 6 5 4 3 2 1

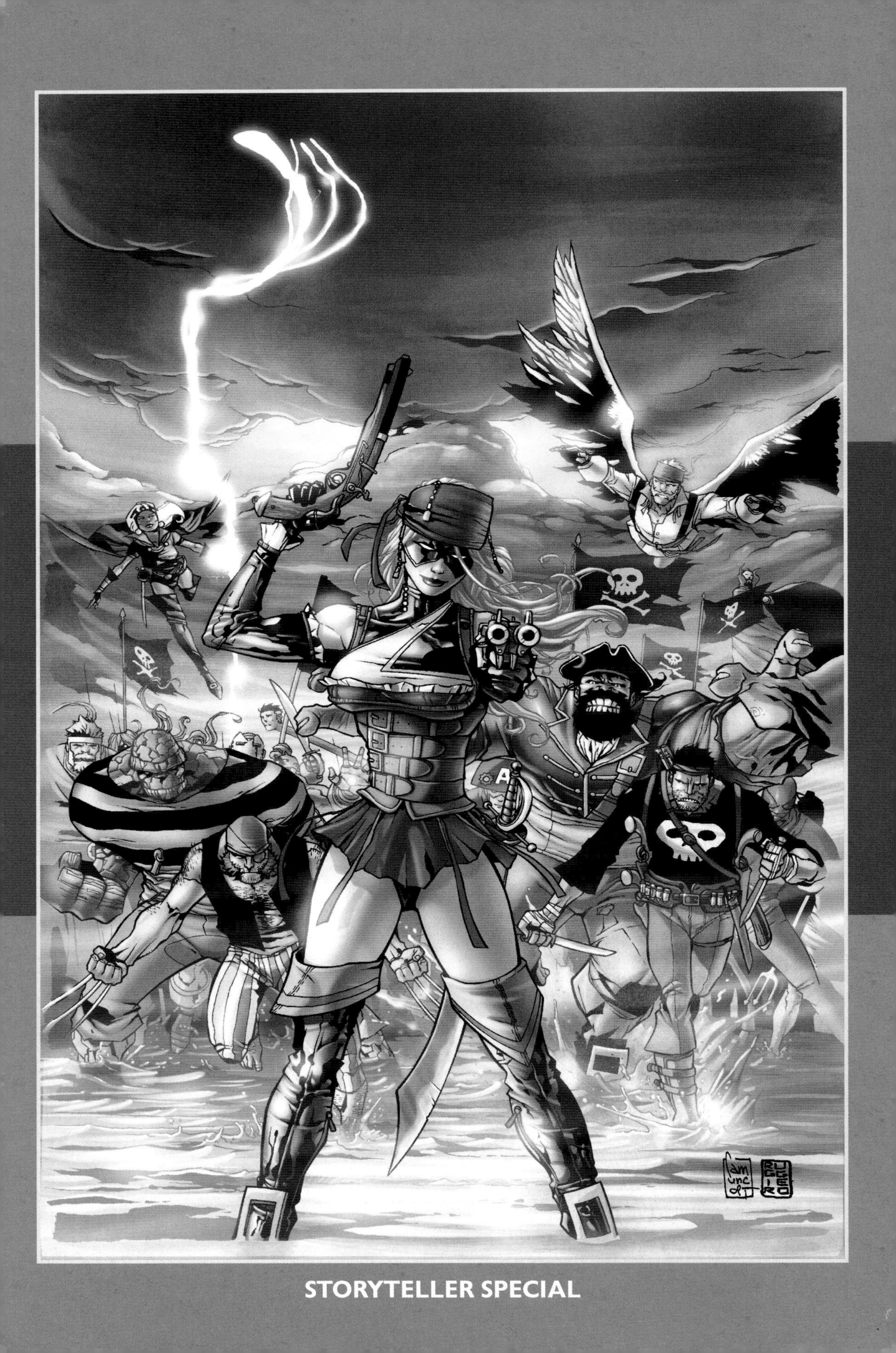

STORYTELLER SPECIAL

In a brilliant flash of light, former U.S. Air Force pilot Carol Danvers was transformed by alien Kree DNA-altering technology, becoming the hard-hitting, high-flying Ms. Marvel!

MS. MARVEL

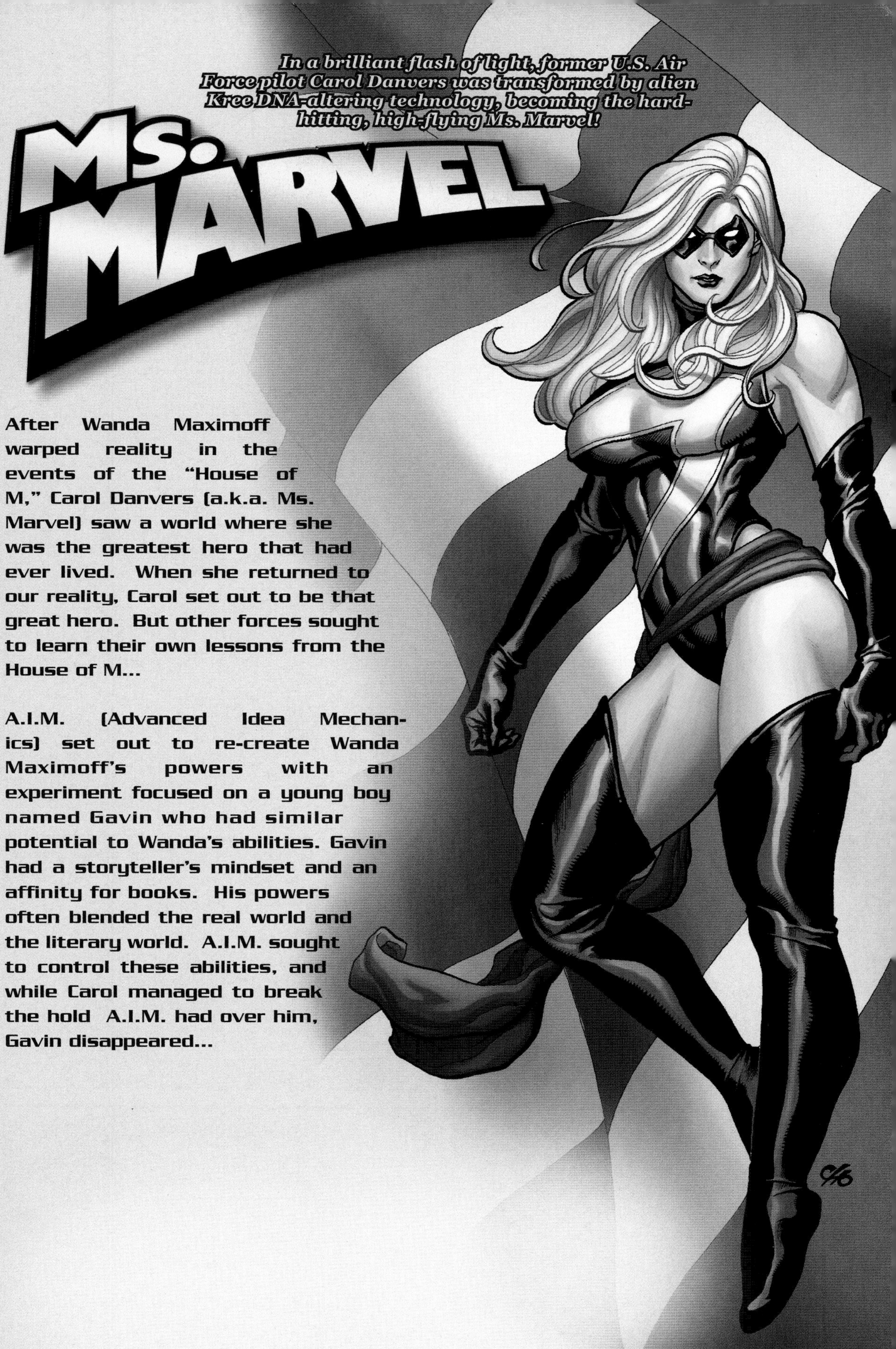

After Wanda Maximoff warped reality in the events of the "House of M," Carol Danvers (a.k.a. Ms. Marvel) saw a world where she was the greatest hero that had ever lived. When she returned to our reality, Carol set out to be that great hero. But other forces sought to learn their own lessons from the House of M...

A.I.M. (Advanced Idea Mechanics) set out to re-create Wanda Maximoff's powers with an experiment focused on a young boy named Gavin who had similar potential to Wanda's abilities. Gavin had a storyteller's mindset and an affinity for books. His powers often blended the real world and the literary world. A.I.M. sought to control these abilities, and while Carol managed to break the hold A.I.M. had over him, Gavin disappeared...

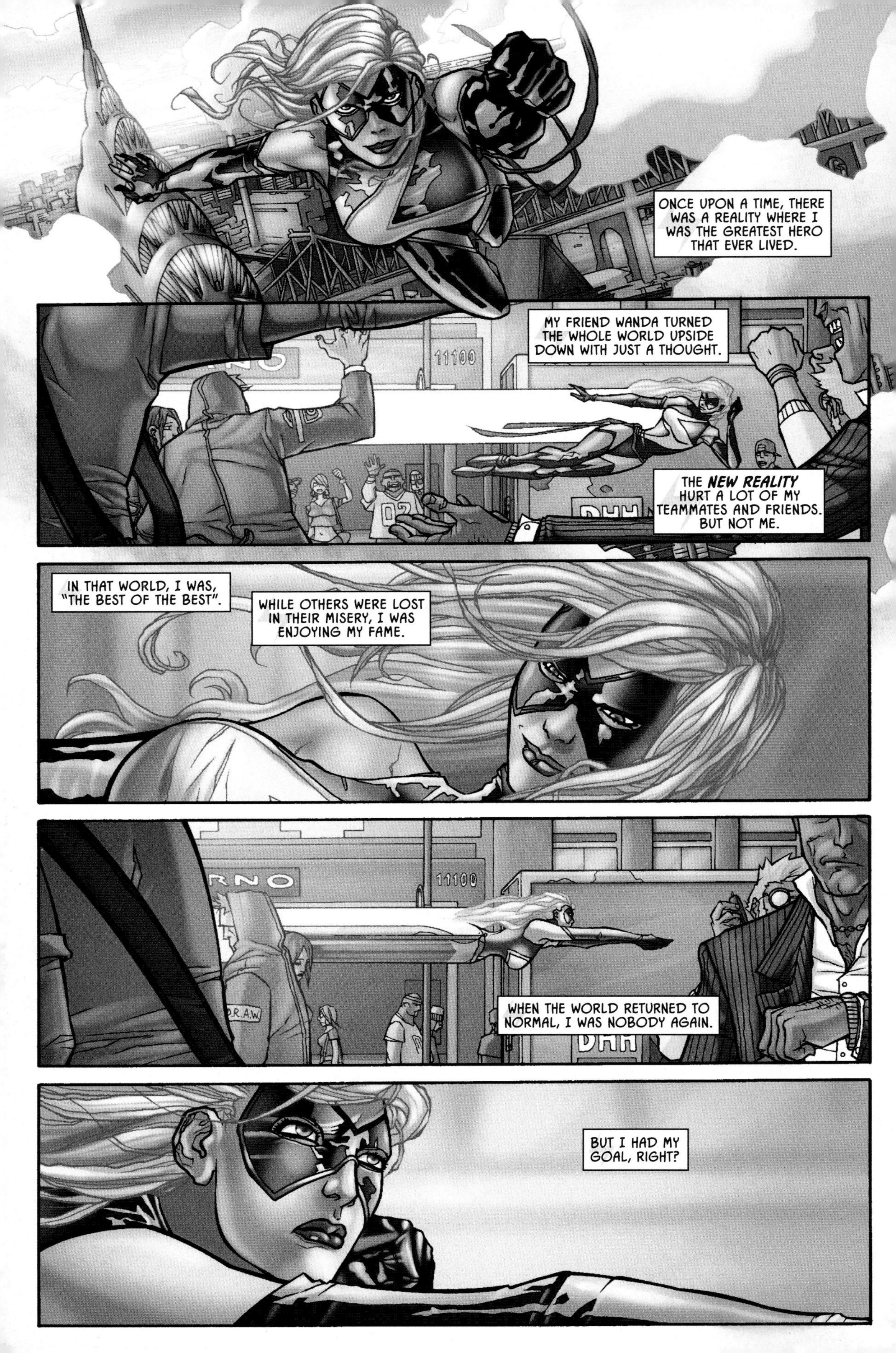
ONCE UPON A TIME, THERE WAS A REALITY WHERE I WAS THE GREATEST HERO THAT EVER LIVED.
MY FRIEND WANDA TURNED THE WHOLE WORLD UPSIDE DOWN WITH JUST A THOUGHT.
THE NEW REALITY HURT A LOT OF MY TEAMMATES AND FRIENDS. BUT NOT ME.
IN THAT WORLD, I WAS, "THE BEST OF THE BEST".
WHILE OTHERS WERE LOST IN THEIR MISERY, I WAS ENJOYING MY FAME.
WHEN THE WORLD RETURNED TO NORMAL, I WAS NOBODY AGAIN.
BUT I HAD MY GOAL, RIGHT?

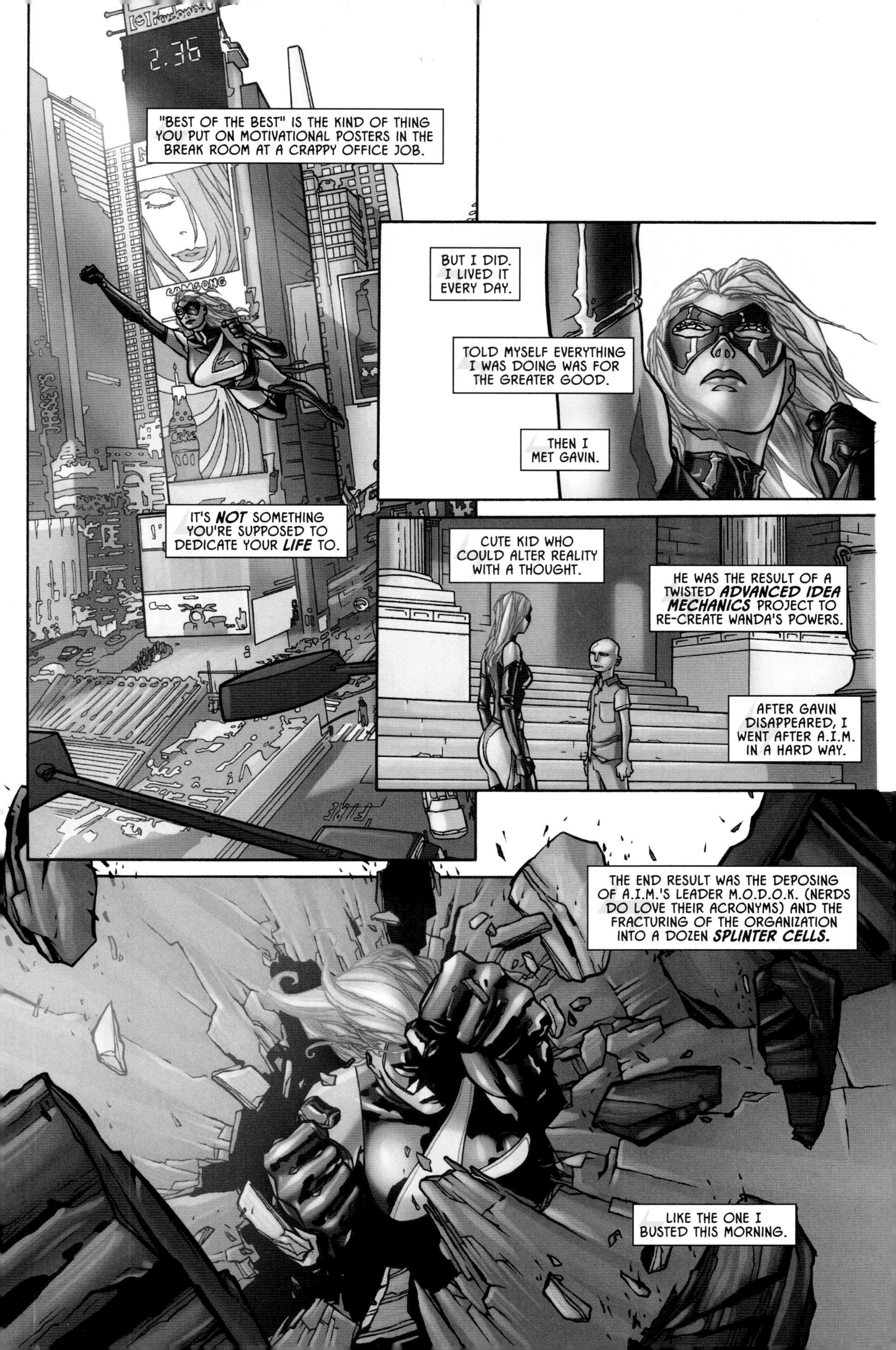
"BEST OF THE BEST" IS THE KIND OF THING YOU PUT ON MOTIVATIONAL POSTERS IN THE BREAK ROOM AT A CRAPPY OFFICE JOB.
IT'S NOT SOMETHING YOU'RE SUPPOSED TO DEDICATE YOUR LIFE TO.
BUT I DID. I LIVED IT EVERY DAY.
TOLD MYSELF EVERYTHING I WAS DOING WAS FOR THE GREATER GOOD.
THEN I MET GAVIN.
CUTE KID WHO COULD ALTER REALITY WITH A THOUGHT.
HE WAS THE RESULT OF A TWISTED ADVANCED IDEA MECHANICS PROJECT TO RE-CREATE WANDA'S POWERS.
AFTER GAVIN DISAPPEARED, I WENT AFTER A.I.M. IN A HARD WAY.
THE END RESULT WAS THE DEPOSING OF A.I.M.'S LEADER M.O.D.O.K. (NERDS DO LOVE THEIR ACRONYMS) AND THE FRACTURING OF THE ORGANIZATION INTO A DOZEN SPLINTER CELLS.
LIKE THE ONE I BUSTED THIS MORNING.

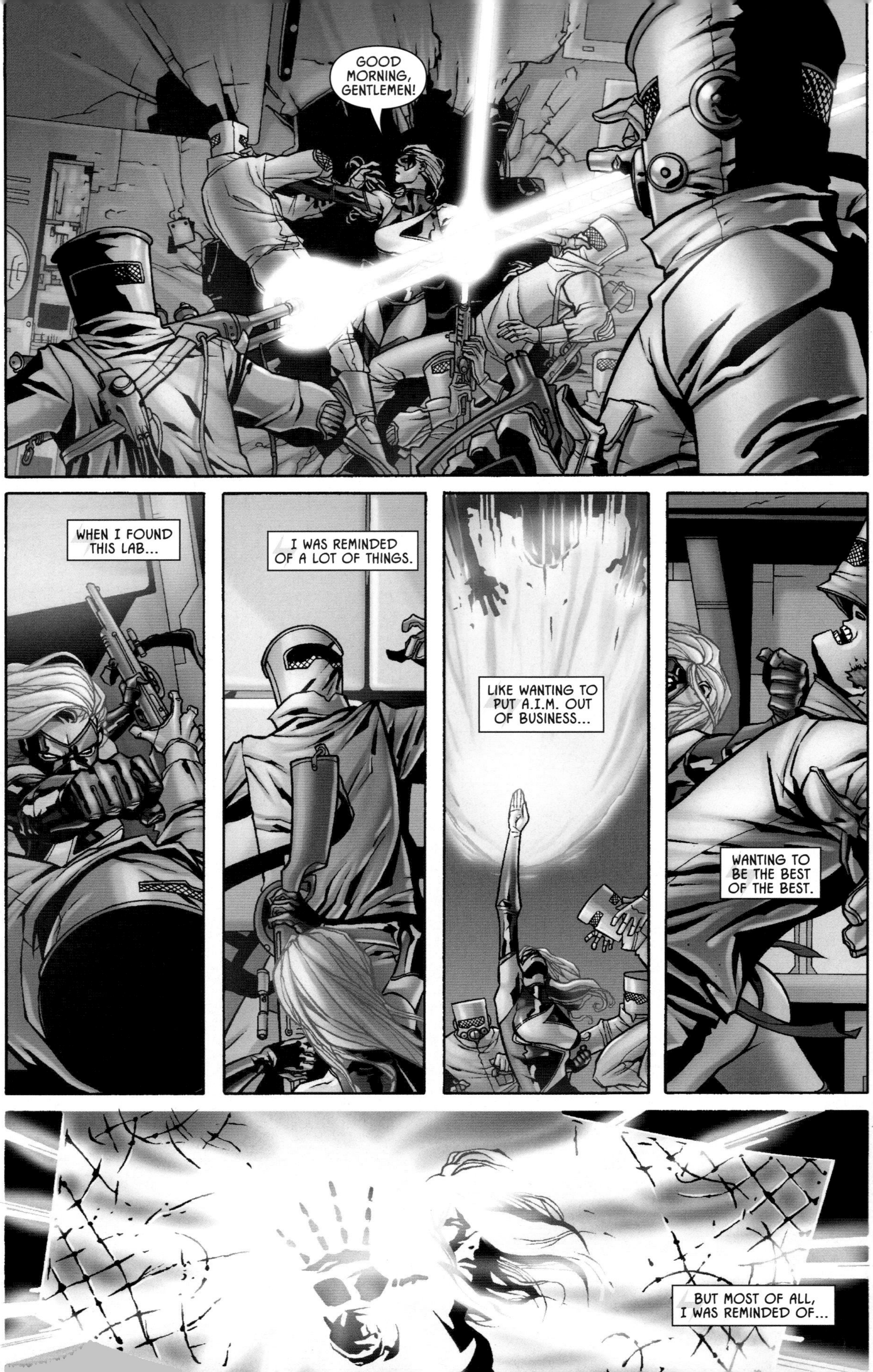
GOOD MORNING, GENTLEMEN!
WHEN I FOUND THIS LAB...
I WAS REMINDED OF A LOT OF THINGS.
LIKE WANTING TO PUT A.I.M. OUT OF BUSINESS...
WANTING TO BE THE BEST OF THE BEST.
BUT MOST OF ALL, I WAS REMINDED OF...

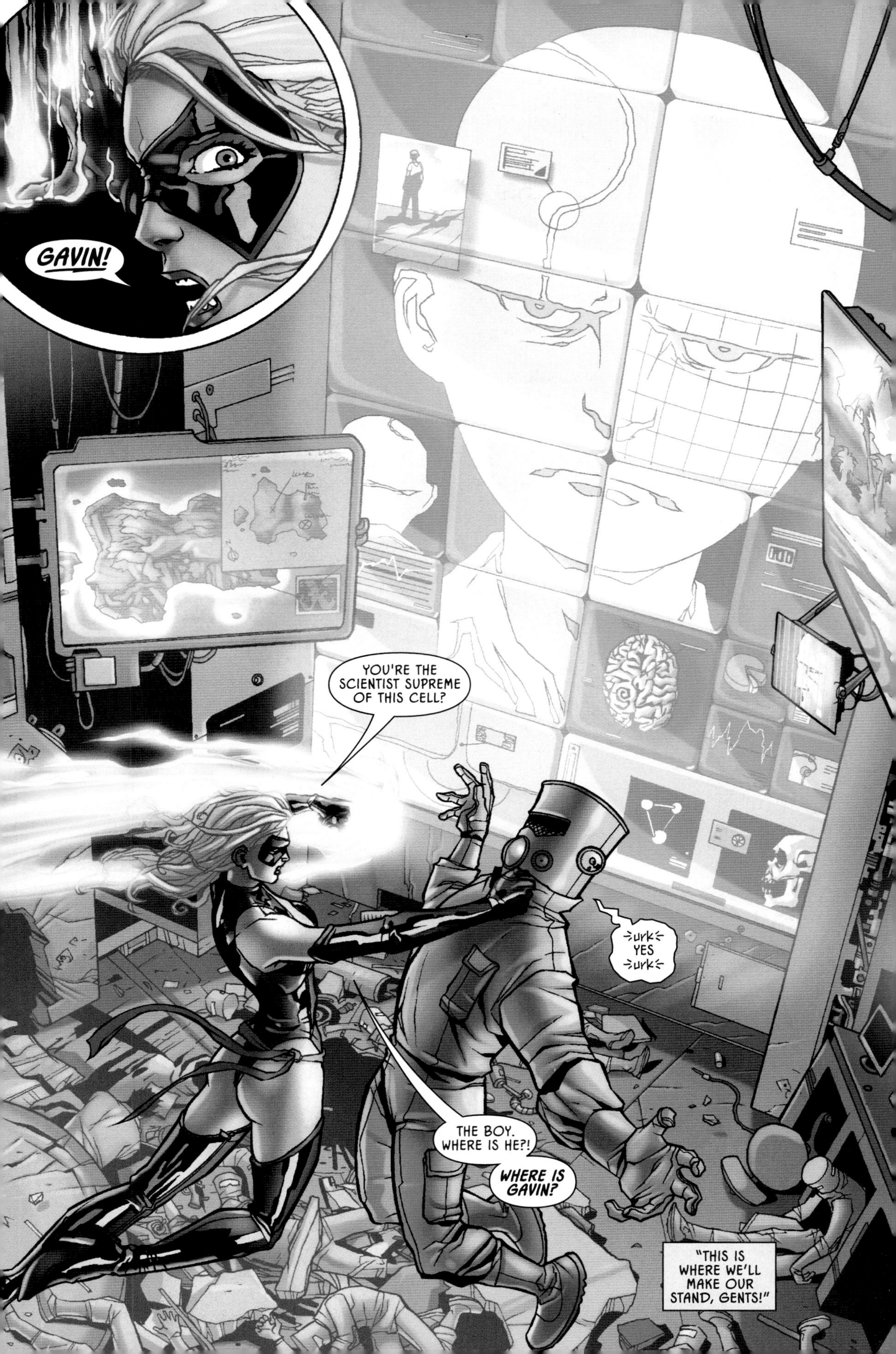
GAVIN!
YOU'RE THE SCIENTIST SUPREME OF THIS CELL?
=urk= YES =urk=
THE BOY. WHERE IS HE?!
WHERE IS GAVIN?
"THIS IS WHERE WE'LL MAKE OUR STAND, GENTS!"

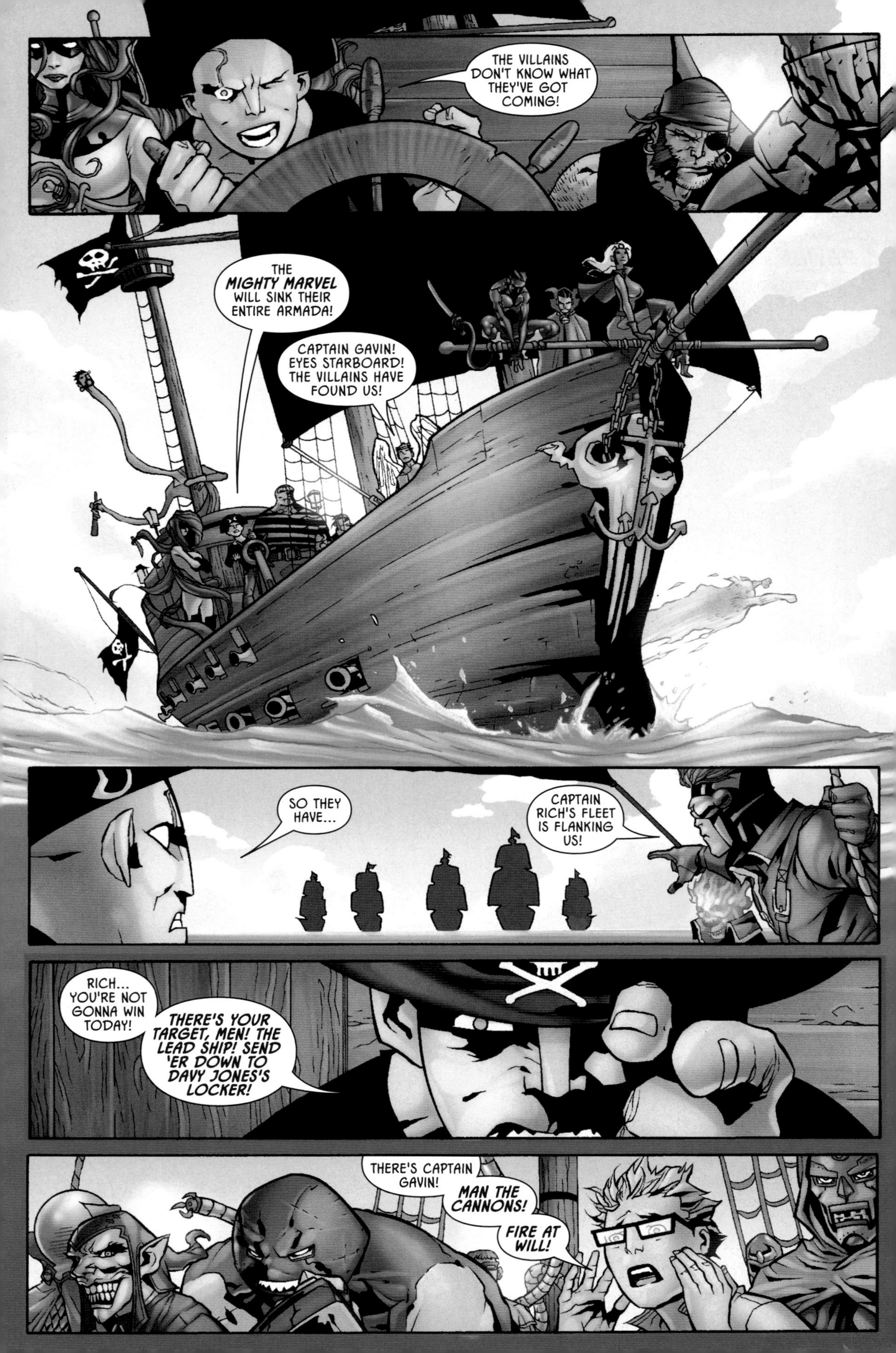
THE VILLAINS DON'T KNOW WHAT THEY'VE GOT COMING!
THE ***MIGHTY MARVEL*** WILL SINK THEIR ENTIRE ARMADA!
CAPTAIN GAVIN! EYES STARBOARD! THE VILLAINS HAVE FOUND US!
SO THEY HAVE...
CAPTAIN RICH'S FLEET IS FLANKING US!
RICH... YOU'RE NOT GONNA WIN TODAY!
THERE'S YOUR TARGET, MEN! THE LEAD SHIP! SEND 'ER DOWN TO DAVY JONES'S LOCKER!
THERE'S CAPTAIN GAVIN!
MAN THE CANNONS!
FIRE AT WILL!

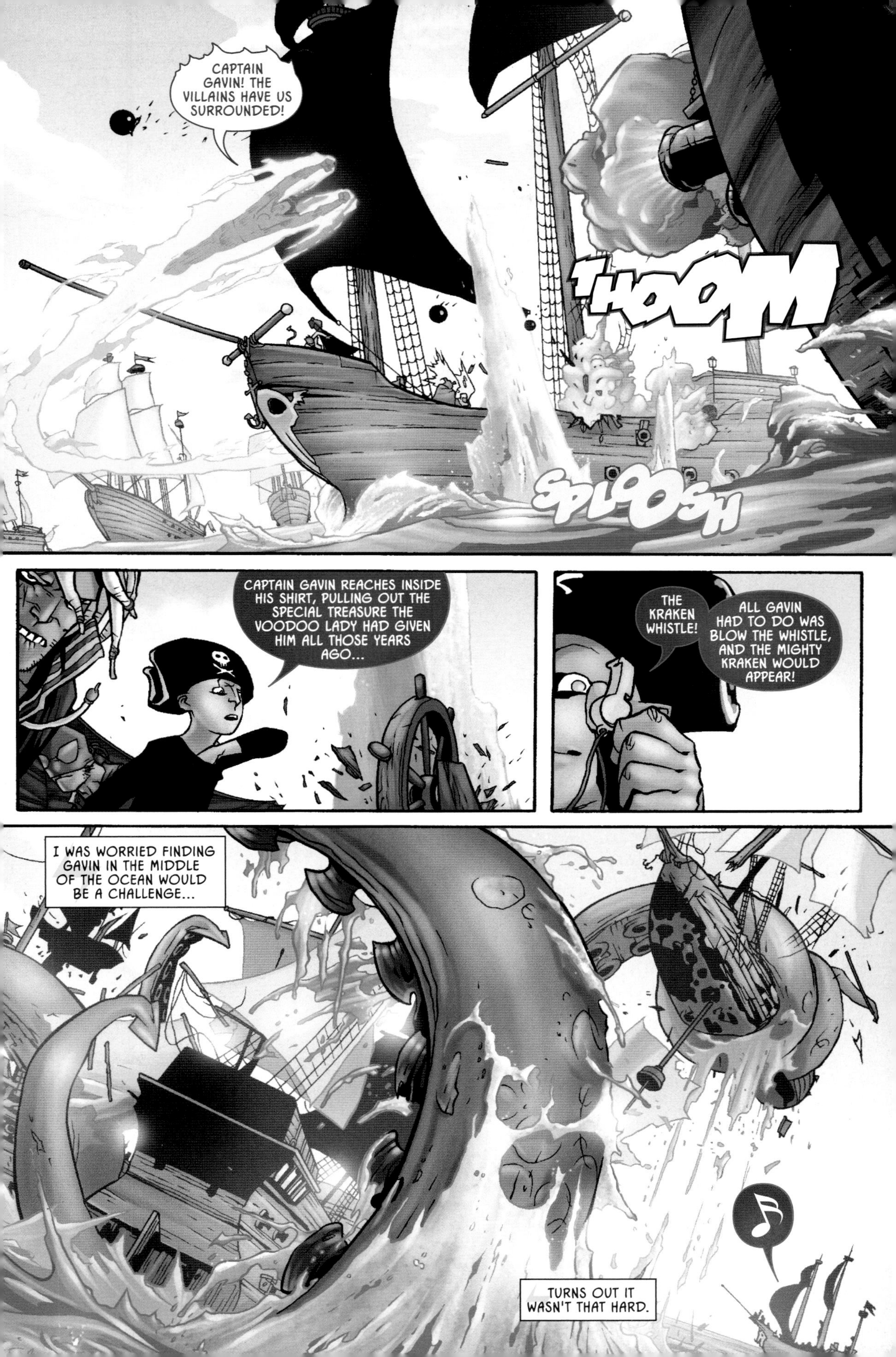
CAPTAIN GAVIN! THE VILLAINS HAVE US SURROUNDED!
THOOM
SPLOOSH
CAPTAIN GAVIN REACHES INSIDE HIS SHIRT, PULLING OUT THE SPECIAL TREASURE THE VOODOO LADY HAD GIVEN HIM ALL THOSE YEARS AGO...
THE KRAKEN WHISTLE!
ALL GAVIN HAD TO DO WAS BLOW THE WHISTLE, AND THE MIGHTY KRAKEN WOULD APPEAR!
I WAS WORRIED FINDING GAVIN IN THE MIDDLE OF THE OCEAN WOULD BE A CHALLENGE...
TURNS OUT IT WASN'T THAT HARD.

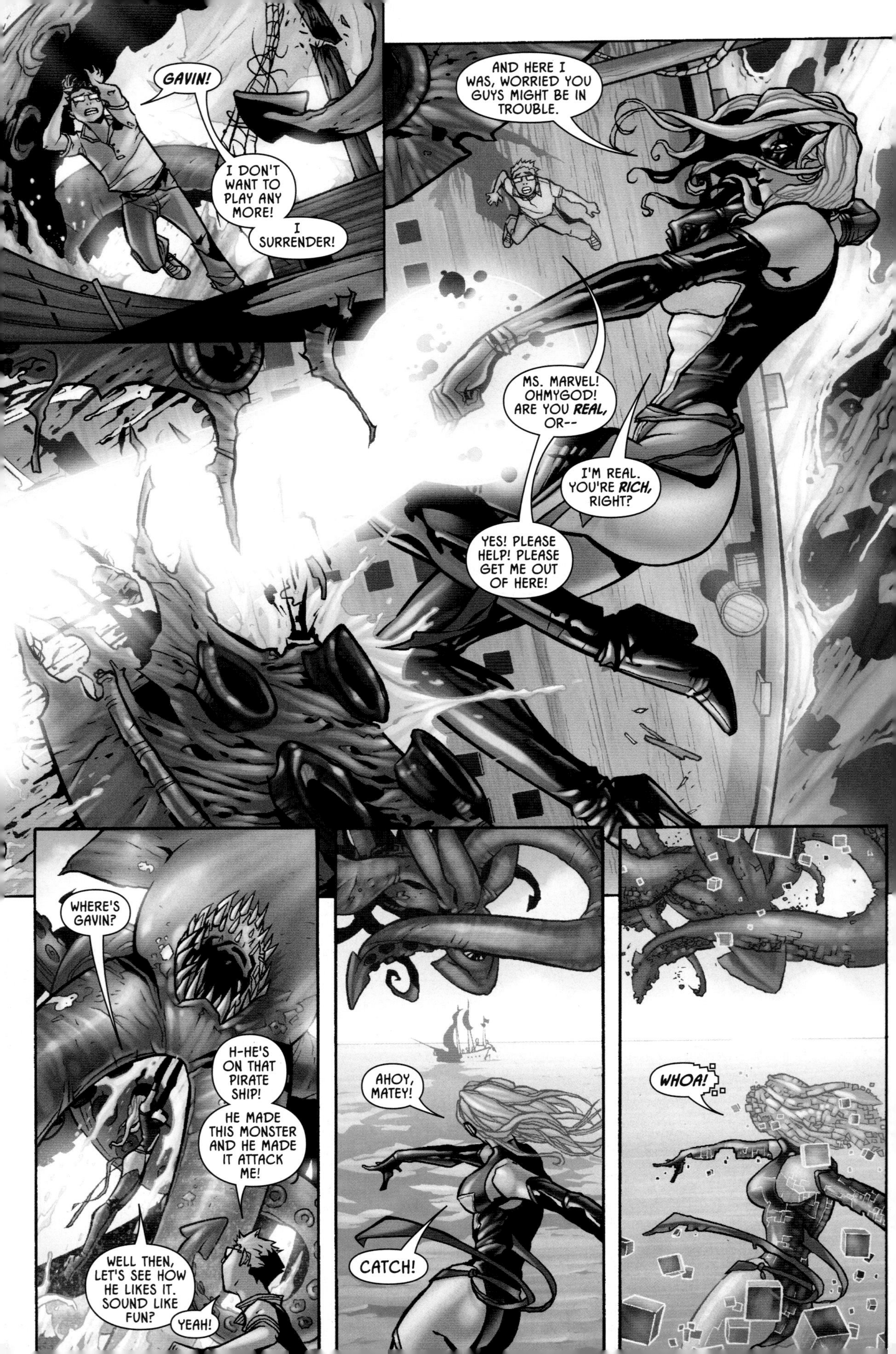

GAVIN!
I DON'T WANT TO PLAY ANY MORE!
I SURRENDER!
AND HERE I WAS, WORRIED YOU GUYS MIGHT BE IN TROUBLE.
MS. MARVEL! OHMYGOD! ARE YOU REAL, OR--
I'M REAL. YOU'RE RICH, RIGHT?
YES! PLEASE HELP! PLEASE GET ME OUT OF HERE!
WHERE'S GAVIN?
H-HE'S ON THAT PIRATE SHIP!
HE MADE THIS MONSTER AND HE MADE IT ATTACK ME!
WELL THEN, LET'S SEE HOW HE LIKES IT. SOUND LIKE FUN?
YEAH!
AHOY, MATEY!
CATCH!
WHOA!

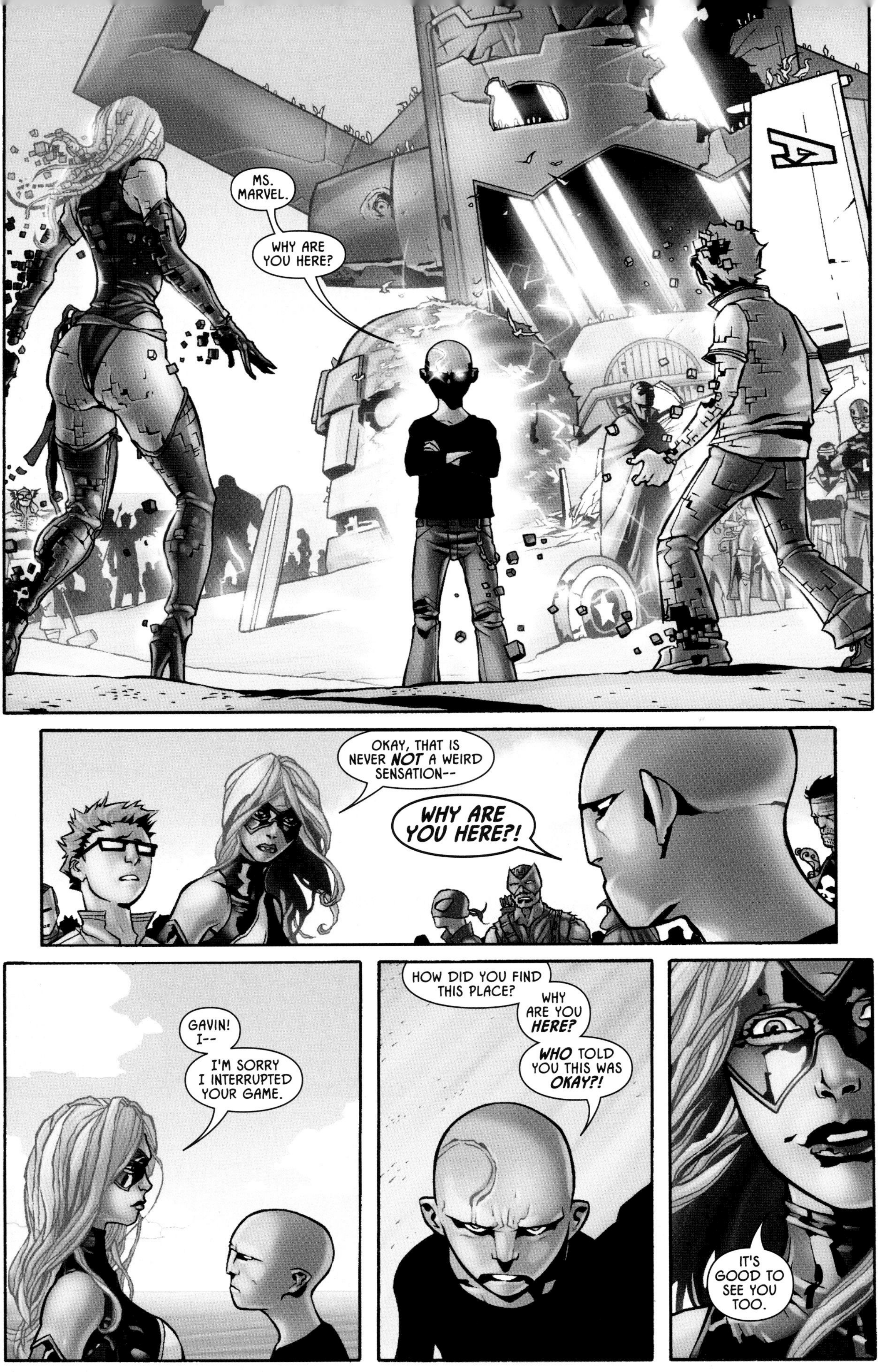
MS. MARVEL.
WHY ARE YOU HERE?
OKAY, THAT IS NEVER NOT A WEIRD SENSATION--
WHY ARE YOU HERE?!
GAVIN! I--
I'M SORRY I INTERRUPTED YOUR GAME.
HOW DID YOU FIND THIS PLACE?
WHY ARE YOU HERE?
WHO TOLD YOU THIS WAS OKAY?!
IT'S GOOD TO SEE YOU TOO.

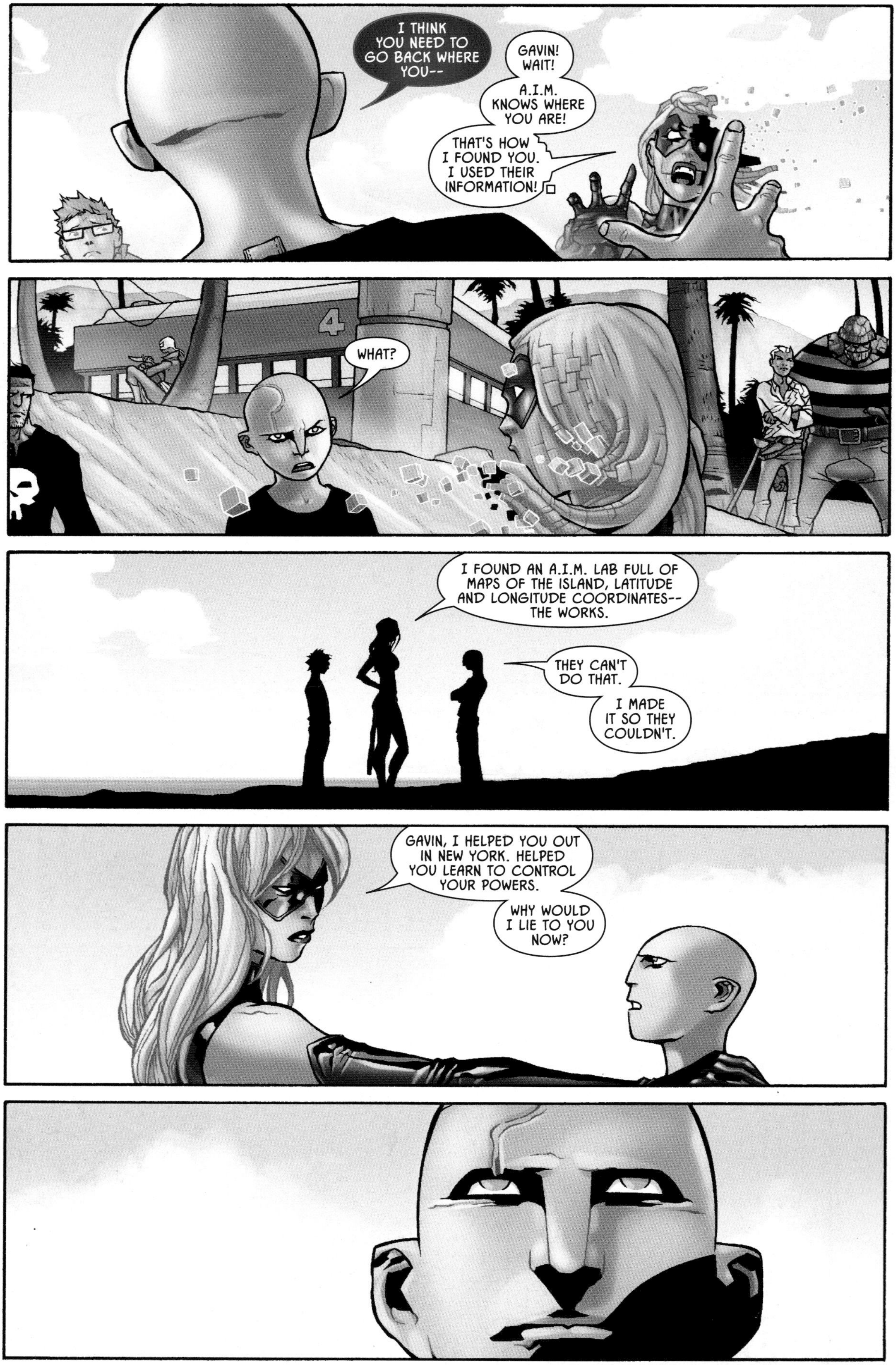
I THINK YOU NEED TO GO BACK WHERE YOU--
GAVIN! WAIT!
A.I.M. KNOWS WHERE YOU ARE!
THAT'S HOW I FOUND YOU. I USED THEIR INFORMATION!
WHAT?
I FOUND AN A.I.M. LAB FULL OF MAPS OF THE ISLAND, LATITUDE AND LONGITUDE COORDINATES-- THE WORKS.
THEY CAN'T DO THAT.
I MADE IT SO THEY COULDN'T.
GAVIN, I HELPED YOU OUT IN NEW YORK. HELPED YOU LEARN TO CONTROL YOUR POWERS.
WHY WOULD I LIE TO YOU NOW?

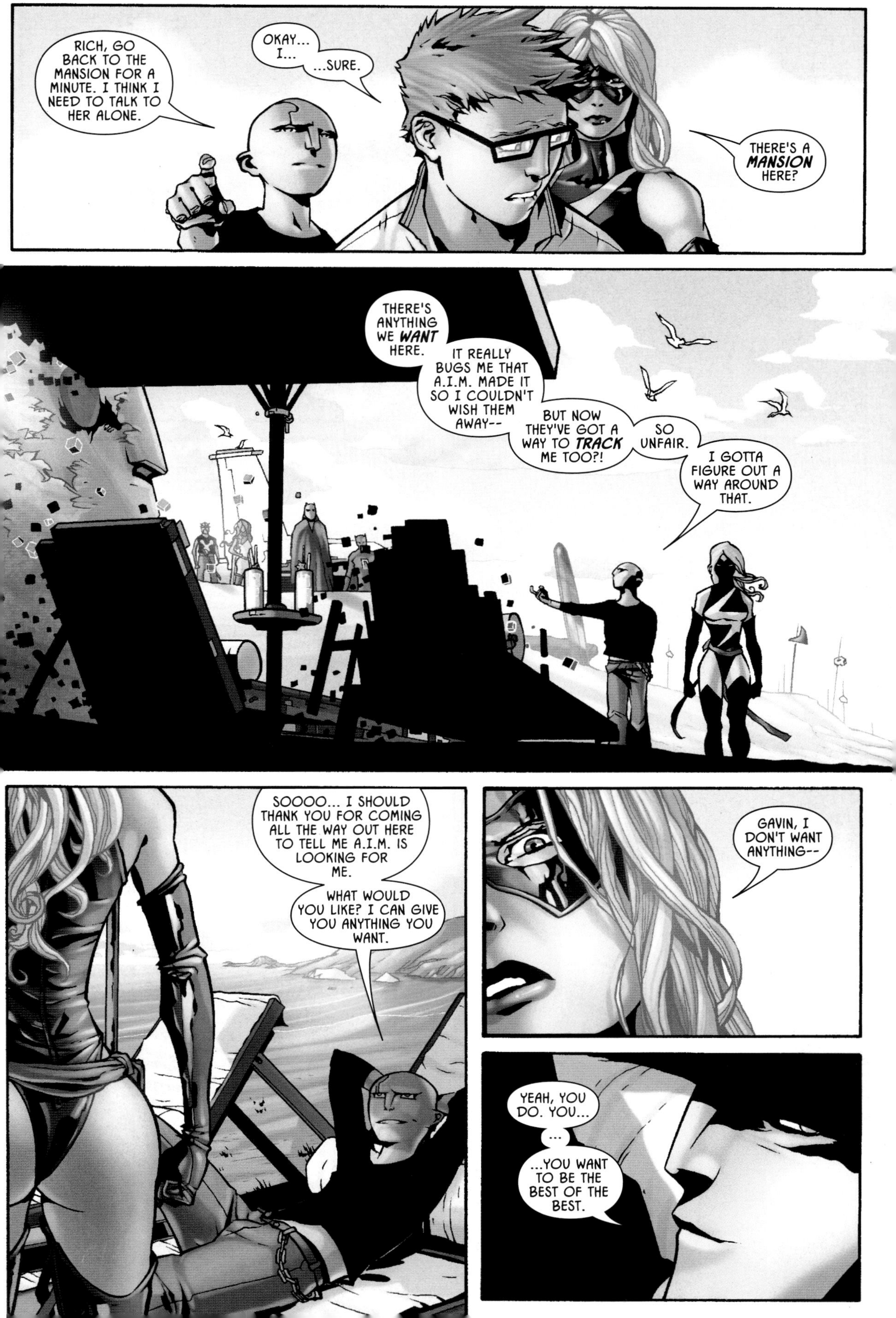
RICH, GO BACK TO THE MANSION FOR A MINUTE. I THINK I NEED TO TALK TO HER ALONE.
OKAY... I...
...SURE.
THERE'S A ***MANSION*** HERE?
THERE'S ANYTHING WE ***WANT*** HERE.
IT REALLY BUGS ME THAT A.I.M. MADE IT SO I COULDN'T WISH THEM AWAY--
BUT NOW THEY'VE GOT A WAY TO ***TRACK*** ME TOO?!
SO UNFAIR.
I GOTTA FIGURE OUT A WAY AROUND THAT.
SOOOO... I SHOULD THANK YOU FOR COMING ALL THE WAY OUT HERE TO TELL ME A.I.M. IS LOOKING FOR ME.
WHAT WOULD YOU LIKE? I CAN GIVE YOU ANYTHING YOU WANT.
GAVIN, I DON'T WANT ANYTHING--
YEAH, YOU DO. YOU...
...
...YOU WANT TO BE THE BEST OF THE BEST.

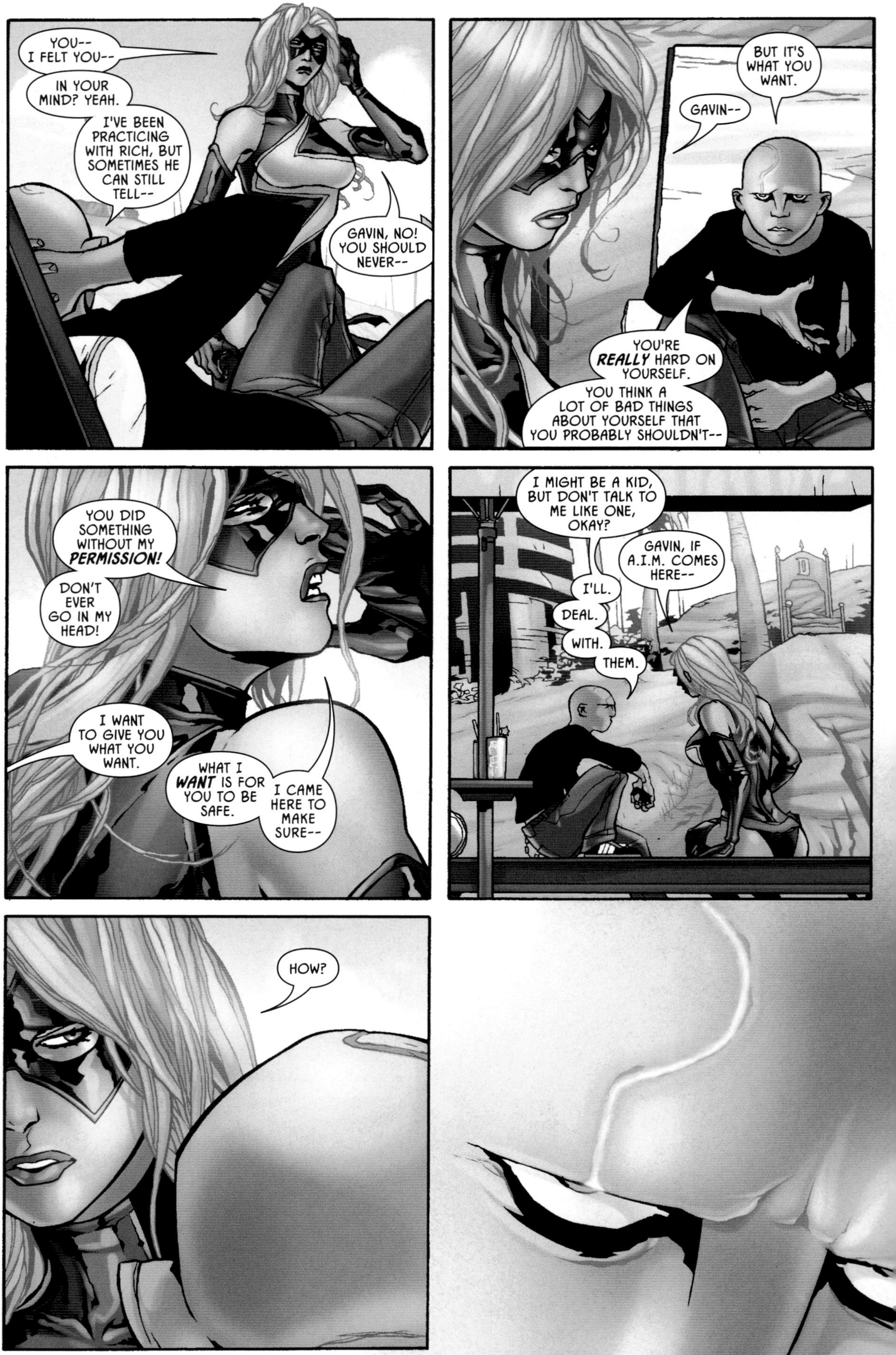
YOU-- I FELT YOU--
IN YOUR MIND? YEAH.
I'VE BEEN PRACTICING WITH RICH, BUT SOMETIMES HE CAN STILL TELL--
GAVIN, NO! YOU SHOULD NEVER--
BUT IT'S WHAT YOU WANT.
GAVIN--
YOU'RE REALLY HARD ON YOURSELF.
YOU THINK A LOT OF BAD THINGS ABOUT YOURSELF THAT YOU PROBABLY SHOULDN'T--
YOU DID SOMETHING WITHOUT MY PERMISSION!
DON'T EVER GO IN MY HEAD!
I WANT TO GIVE YOU WHAT YOU WANT.
WHAT I WANT IS FOR YOU TO BE SAFE.
I CAME HERE TO MAKE SURE--
I MIGHT BE A KID, BUT DON'T TALK TO ME LIKE ONE, OKAY?
GAVIN, IF A.I.M. COMES HERE--
I'LL.
DEAL.
WITH.
THEM.
HOW?

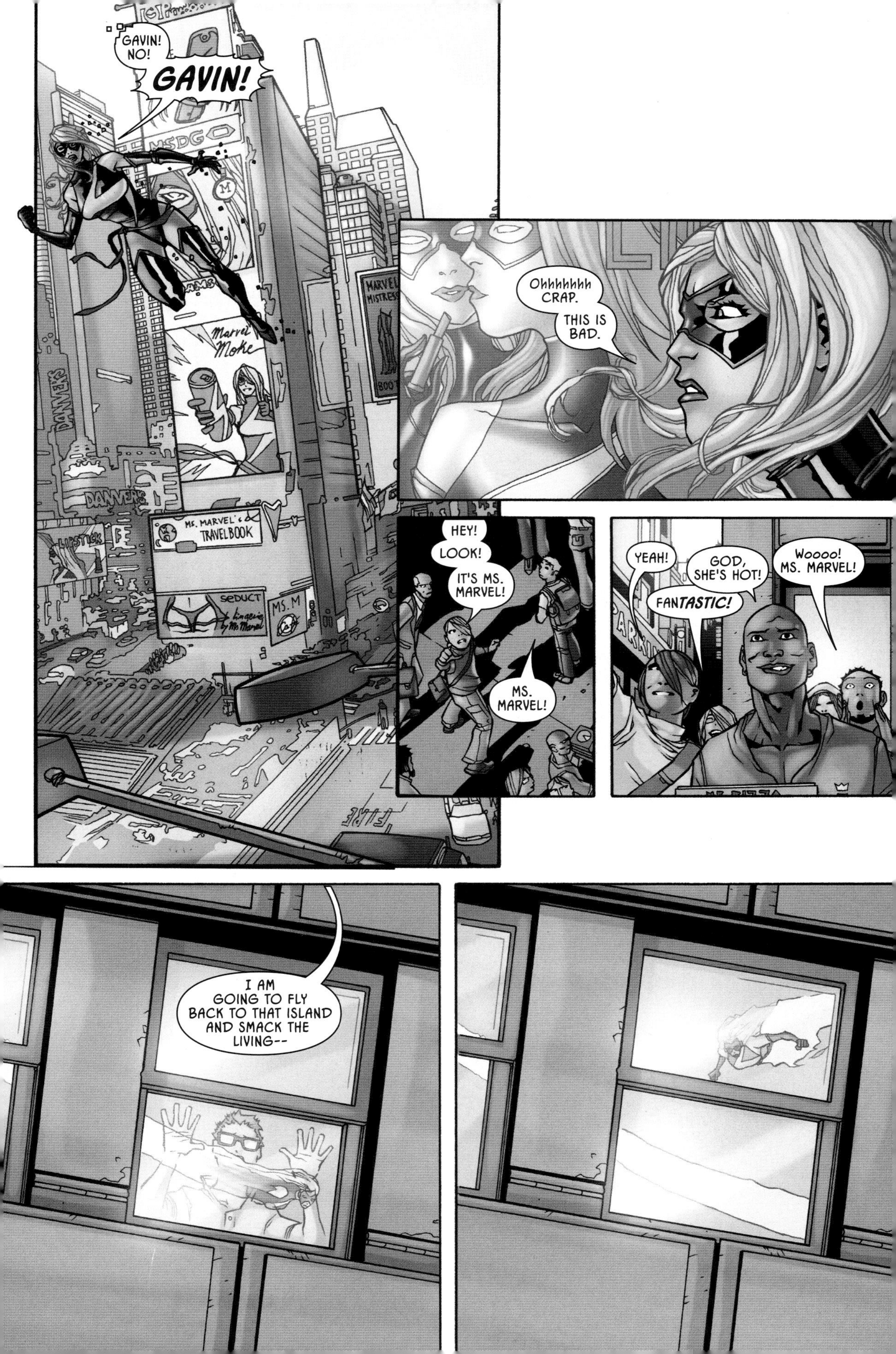
GAVIN! NO!
GAVIN!
MSDG
Marvel Moke
MARVEL MISTRESS
DANVERS
MS. MARVEL's TRAVELBOOK
LIPSTICK
SEDUCT
MS. M
Ohhhhhhh CRAP.
THIS IS BAD.
HEY!
LOOK!
IT'S MS. MARVEL!
MS. MARVEL!
YEAH!
GOD, SHE'S HOT!
Woooo! MS. MARVEL!
FANTASTIC!
I AM GOING TO FLY BACK TO THAT ISLAND AND SMACK THE LIVING--

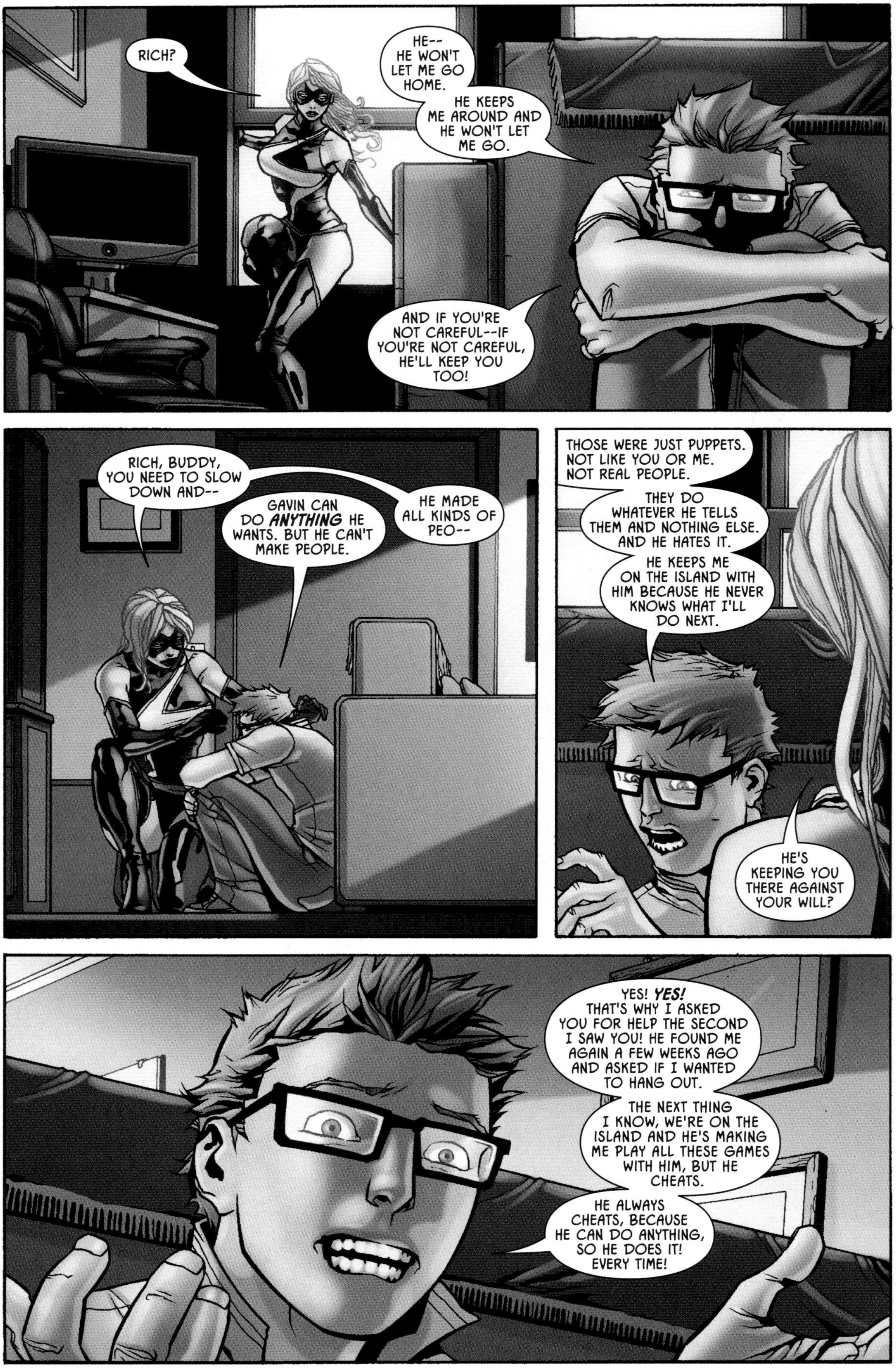
RICH?
HE-- HE WON'T LET ME GO HOME.
HE KEEPS ME AROUND AND HE WON'T LET ME GO.
AND IF YOU'RE NOT CAREFUL--IF YOU'RE NOT CAREFUL, HE'LL KEEP YOU TOO!
RICH, BUDDY, YOU NEED TO SLOW DOWN AND--
GAVIN CAN DO **ANYTHING** HE WANTS. BUT HE CAN'T MAKE PEOPLE.
HE MADE ALL KINDS OF PEO--
THOSE WERE JUST PUPPETS. NOT LIKE YOU OR ME. NOT REAL PEOPLE.
THEY DO WHATEVER HE TELLS THEM AND NOTHING ELSE. AND HE HATES IT.
HE KEEPS ME ON THE ISLAND WITH HIM BECAUSE HE NEVER KNOWS WHAT I'LL DO NEXT.
HE'S KEEPING YOU THERE AGAINST YOUR WILL?
YES! ***YES!*** THAT'S WHY I ASKED YOU FOR HELP THE SECOND I SAW YOU! HE FOUND ME AGAIN A FEW WEEKS AGO AND ASKED IF I WANTED TO HANG OUT.
THE NEXT THING I KNOW, WE'RE ON THE ISLAND AND HE'S MAKING ME PLAY ALL THESE GAMES WITH HIM, BUT HE CHEATS.
HE ALWAYS CHEATS, BECAUSE HE CAN DO ANYTHING, SO HE DOES IT! EVERY TIME!

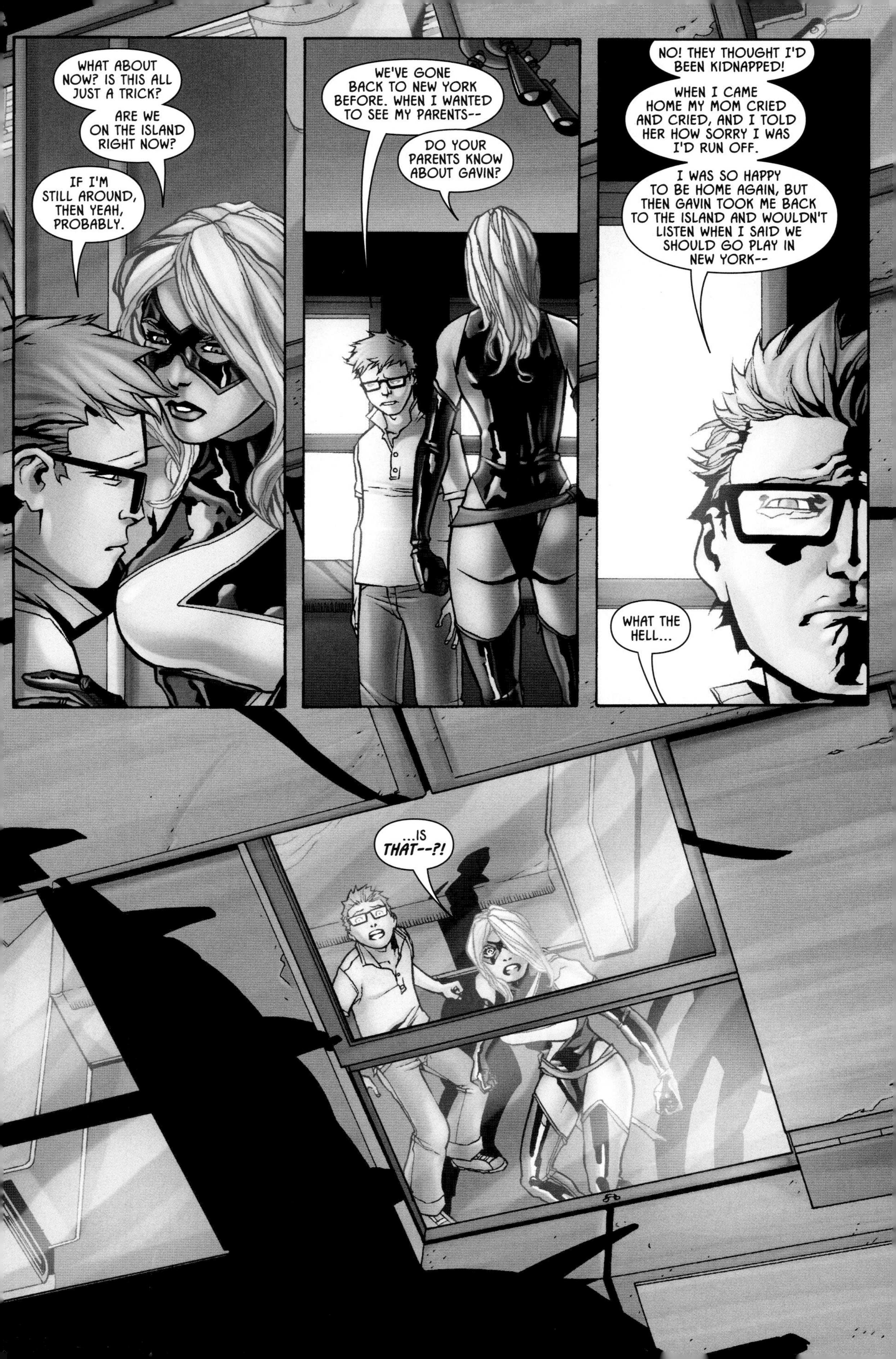
WHAT ABOUT NOW? IS THIS ALL JUST A TRICK?
ARE WE ON THE ISLAND RIGHT NOW?
IF I'M STILL AROUND, THEN YEAH, PROBABLY.
WE'VE GONE BACK TO NEW YORK BEFORE. WHEN I WANTED TO SEE MY PARENTS--
DO YOUR PARENTS KNOW ABOUT GAVIN?
NO! THEY THOUGHT I'D BEEN KIDNAPPED!
WHEN I CAME HOME MY MOM CRIED AND CRIED, AND I TOLD HER HOW SORRY I WAS I'D RUN OFF.
I WAS SO HAPPY TO BE HOME AGAIN, BUT THEN GAVIN TOOK ME BACK TO THE ISLAND AND WOULDN'T LISTEN WHEN I SAID WE SHOULD GO PLAY IN NEW YORK--
WHAT THE HELL...
...IS *THAT*--?!

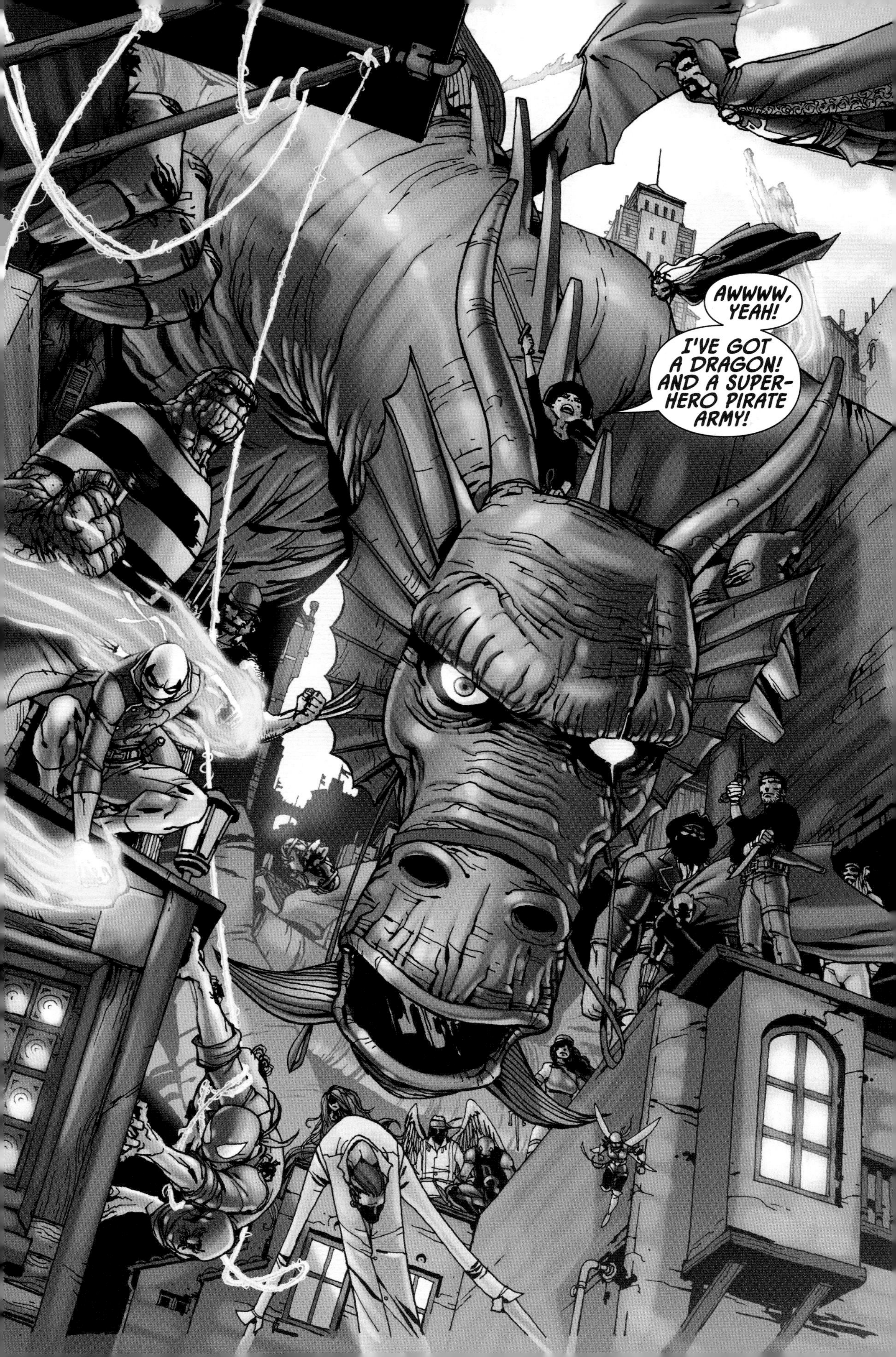
AWWWW, YEAH!
I'VE GOT A DRAGON! AND A SUPER-HERO PIRATE ARMY!

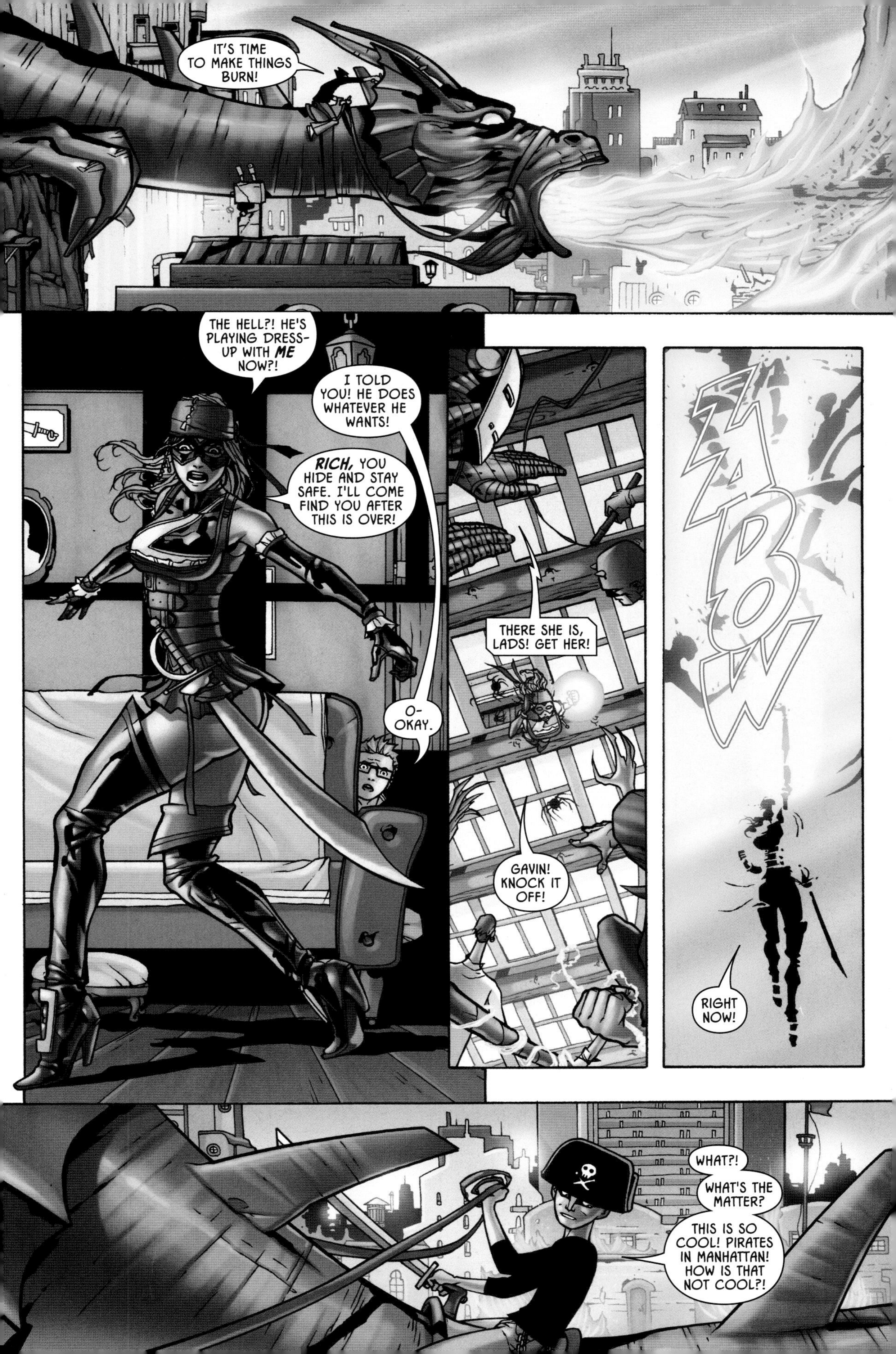
IT'S TIME TO MAKE THINGS BURN!
THE HELL?! HE'S PLAYING DRESS-UP WITH ME NOW?!
I TOLD YOU! HE DOES WHATEVER HE WANTS!
RICH, YOU HIDE AND STAY SAFE. I'LL COME FIND YOU AFTER THIS IS OVER!
O-OKAY.
THERE SHE IS, LADS! GET HER!
GAVIN! KNOCK IT OFF!
ZZBOW
RIGHT NOW!
WHAT?!
WHAT'S THE MATTER?
THIS IS SO COOL! PIRATES IN MANHATTAN! HOW IS THAT NOT COOL?!

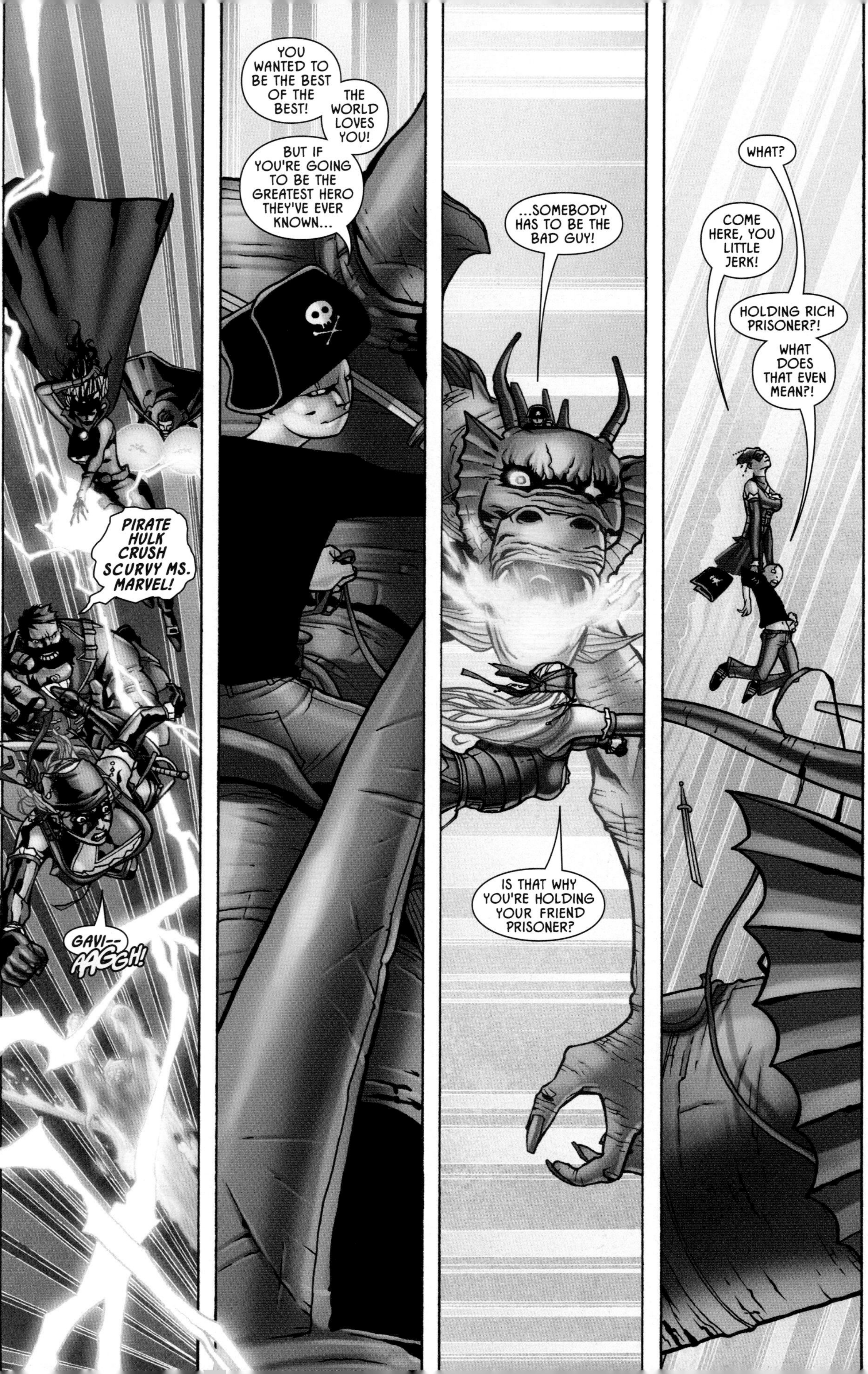
PIRATE HULK CRUSH SCURVY MS. MARVEL!
GAVI--AAGGH!
YOU WANTED TO BE THE BEST OF THE BEST!
THE WORLD LOVES YOU!
BUT IF YOU'RE GOING TO BE THE GREATEST HERO THEY'VE EVER KNOWN...
...SOMEBODY HAS TO BE THE BAD GUY!
IS THAT WHY YOU'RE HOLDING YOUR FRIEND PRISONER?
WHAT?
COME HERE, YOU LITTLE JERK!
HOLDING RICH PRISONER?!
WHAT DOES THAT EVEN MEAN?!

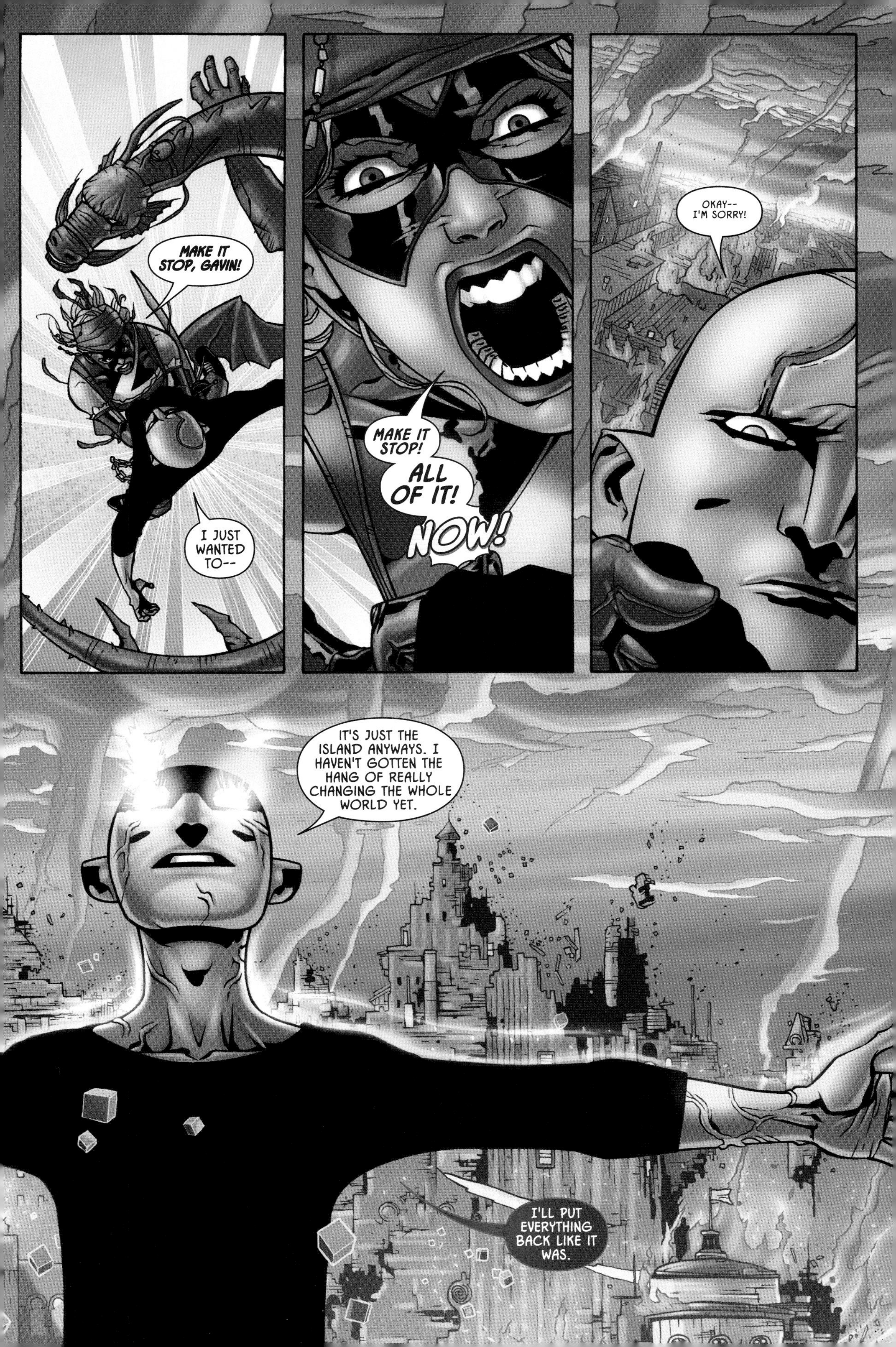
MAKE IT STOP, GAVIN!
I JUST WANTED TO--
MAKE IT STOP!
ALL OF IT!
NOW!
OKAY-- I'M SORRY!
IT'S JUST THE ISLAND ANYWAYS. I HAVEN'T GOTTEN THE HANG OF REALLY CHANGING THE WHOLE WORLD YET.
I'LL PUT EVERYTHING BACK LIKE IT WAS.

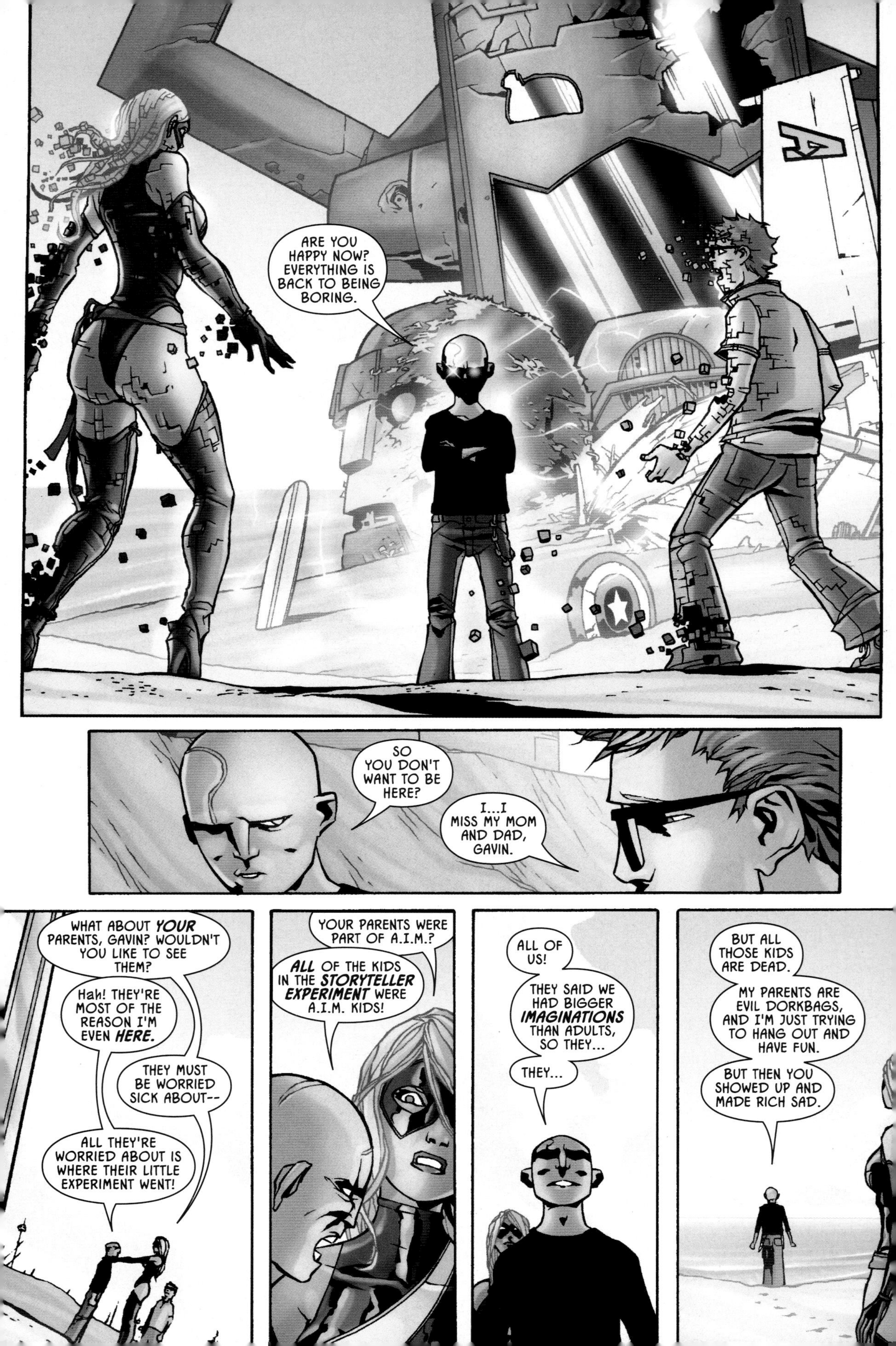
ARE YOU HAPPY NOW? EVERYTHING IS BACK TO BEING BORING.
SO YOU DON'T WANT TO BE HERE?
I...I MISS MY MOM AND DAD, GAVIN.
WHAT ABOUT YOUR PARENTS, GAVIN? WOULDN'T YOU LIKE TO SEE THEM?
Hah! THEY'RE MOST OF THE REASON I'M EVEN HERE.
THEY MUST BE WORRIED SICK ABOUT--
ALL THEY'RE WORRIED ABOUT IS WHERE THEIR LITTLE EXPERIMENT WENT!
YOUR PARENTS WERE PART OF A.I.M.?
ALL OF THE KIDS IN THE STORYTELLER EXPERIMENT WERE A.I.M. KIDS!
ALL OF US!
THEY SAID WE HAD BIGGER IMAGINATIONS THAN ADULTS, SO THEY...
THEY...
BUT ALL THOSE KIDS ARE DEAD.
MY PARENTS ARE EVIL DORKBAGS, AND I'M JUST TRYING TO HANG OUT AND HAVE FUN.
BUT THEN YOU SHOWED UP AND MADE RICH SAD.

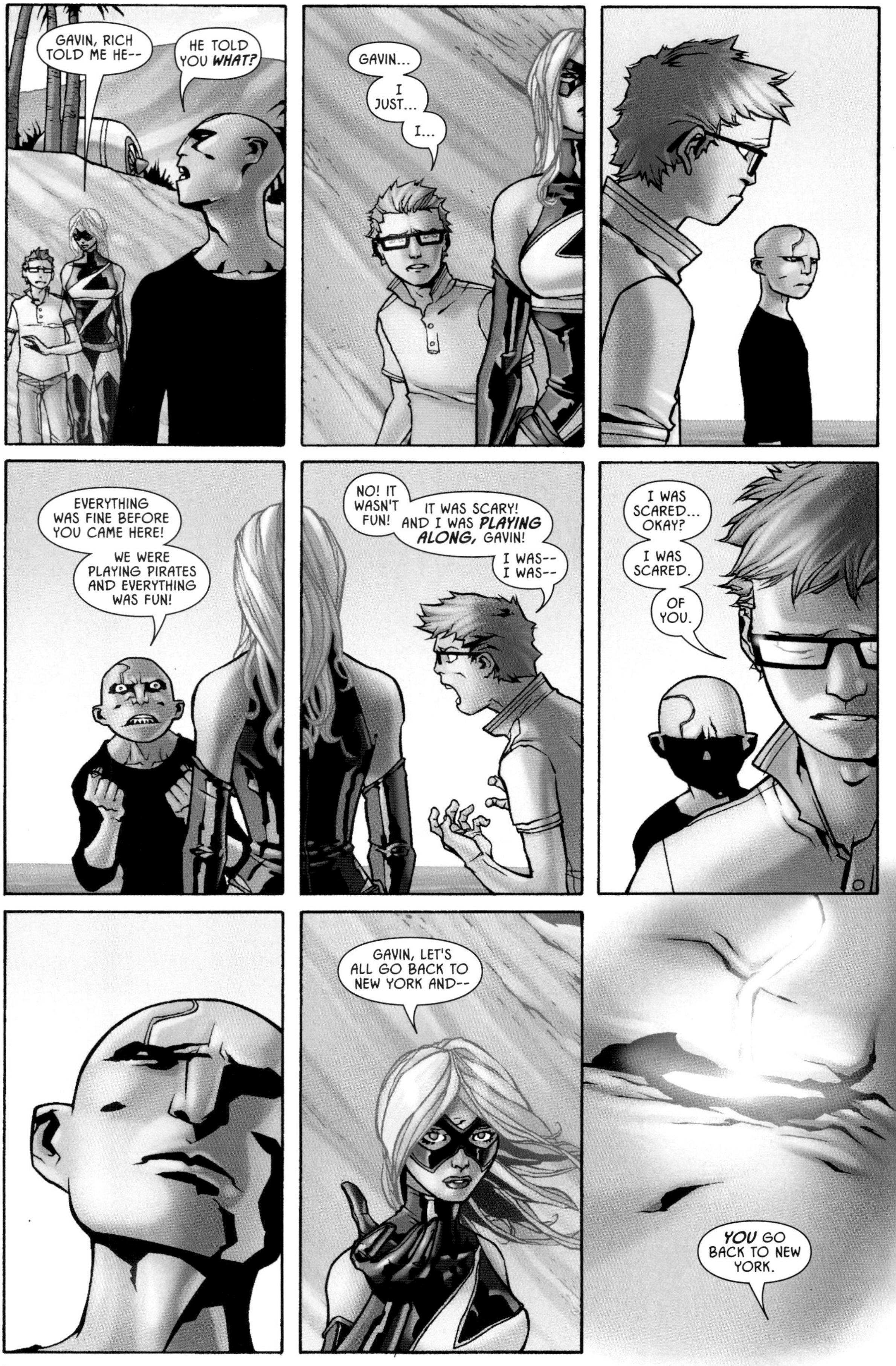
GAVIN, RICH TOLD ME HE--
HE TOLD YOU **WHAT?**
GAVIN...
I JUST...
I...
EVERYTHING WAS FINE BEFORE YOU CAME HERE!
WE WERE PLAYING PIRATES AND EVERYTHING WAS FUN!
NO! IT WASN'T FUN!
IT WAS SCARY! AND I WAS **PLAYING ALONG,** GAVIN!
I WAS-- I WAS--
I WAS SCARED... OKAY?
I WAS SCARED.
OF YOU.
GAVIN, LET'S ALL GO BACK TO NEW YORK AND--
YOU GO BACK TO NEW YORK.

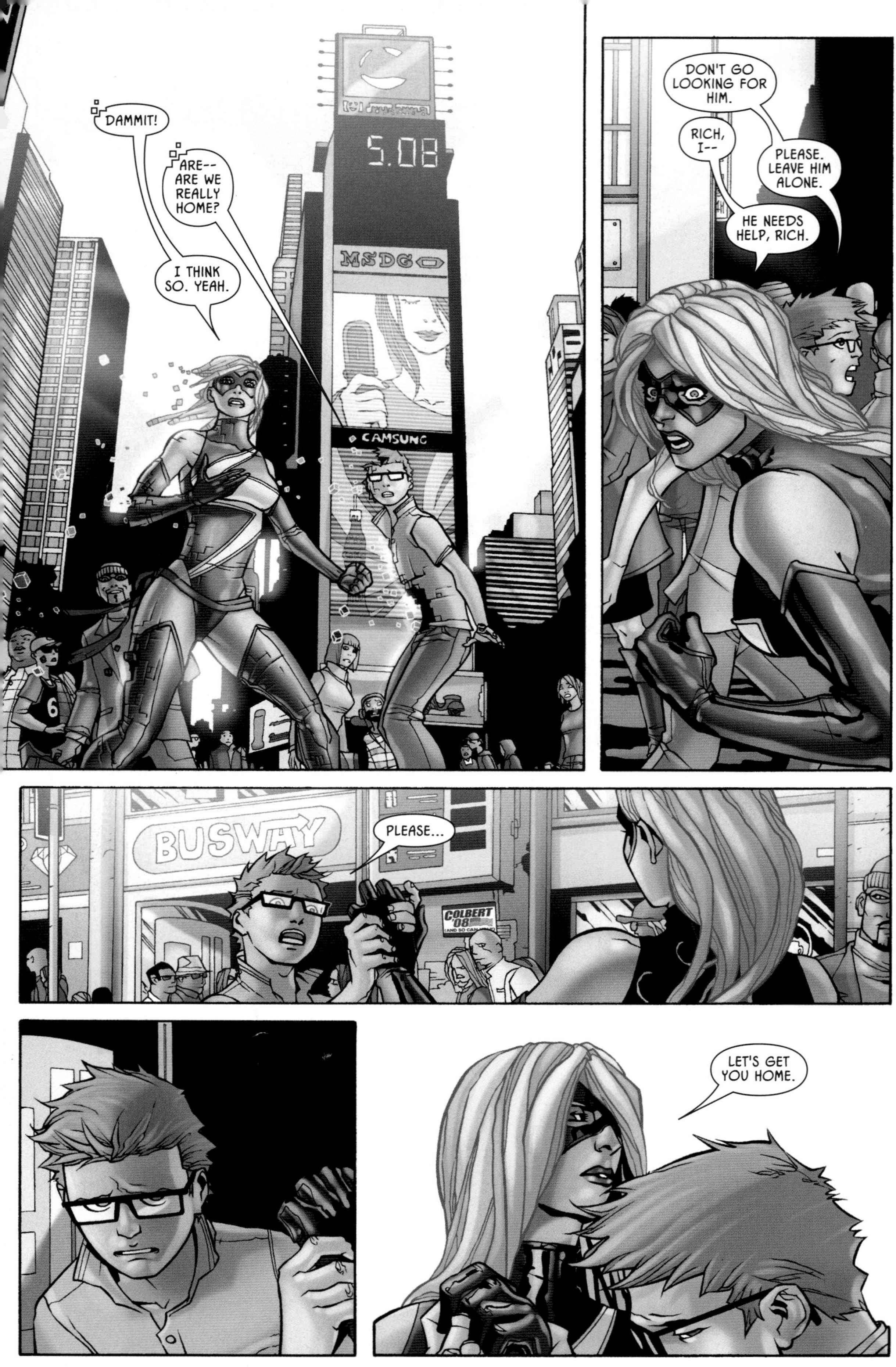
DAMMIT!
ARE--
ARE WE REALLY HOME?
I THINK SO. YEAH.
5.08
MSDG
CAMSUNG
DON'T GO LOOKING FOR HIM.
RICH, I--
PLEASE. LEAVE HIM ALONE.
HE NEEDS HELP, RICH.
BUSWAY
PLEASE...
COLBERT '08
LET'S GET YOU HOME.

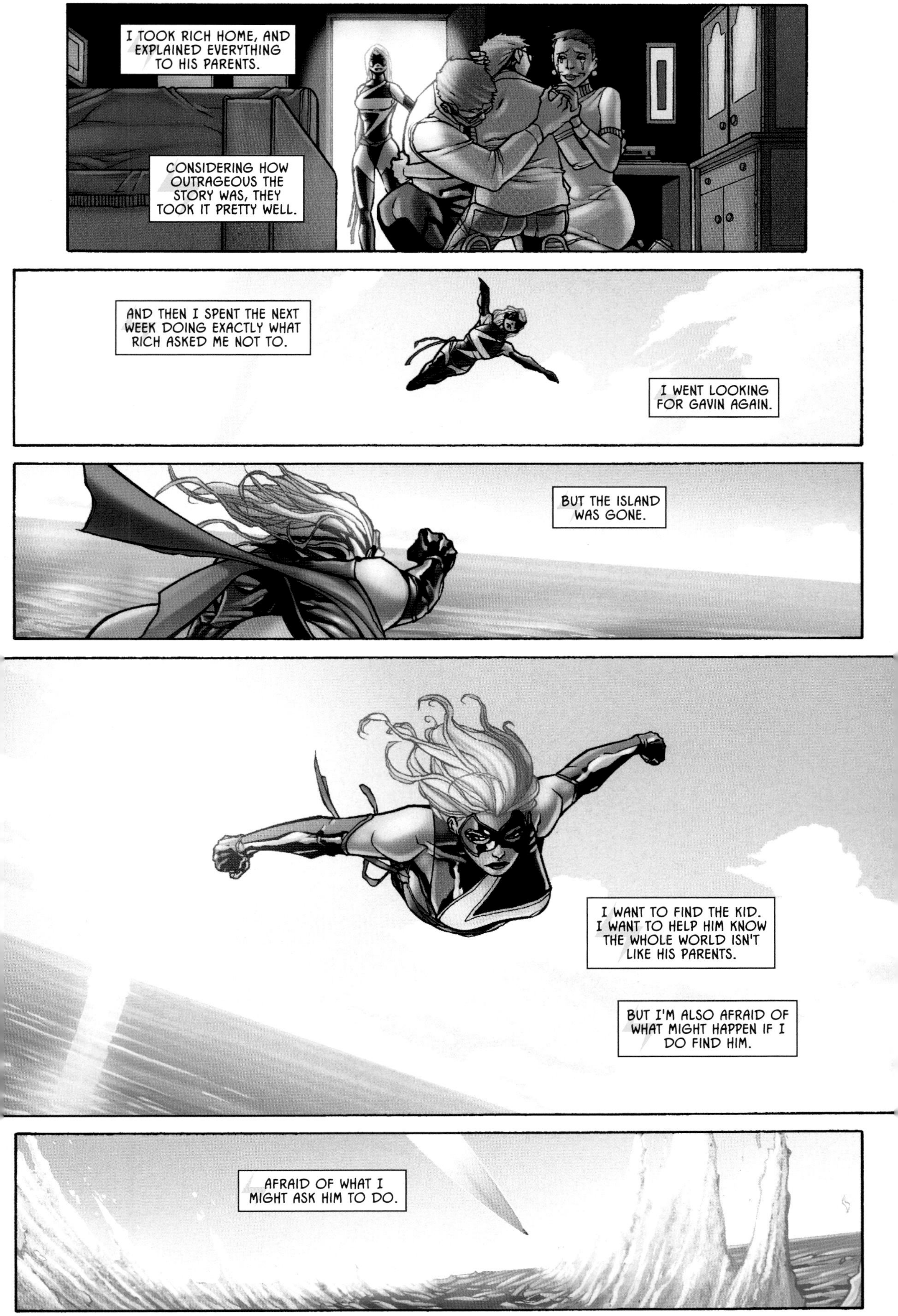
I TOOK RICH HOME, AND EXPLAINED EVERYTHING TO HIS PARENTS.
CONSIDERING HOW OUTRAGEOUS THE STORY WAS, THEY TOOK IT PRETTY WELL.
AND THEN I SPENT THE NEXT WEEK DOING EXACTLY WHAT RICH ASKED ME NOT TO.
I WENT LOOKING FOR GAVIN AGAIN.
BUT THE ISLAND WAS GONE.
I WANT TO FIND THE KID. I WANT TO HELP HIM KNOW THE WHOLE WORLD ISN'T LIKE HIS PARENTS.
BUT I'M ALSO AFRAID OF WHAT MIGHT HAPPEN IF I DO FIND HIM.
AFRAID OF WHAT I MIGHT ASK HIM TO DO.

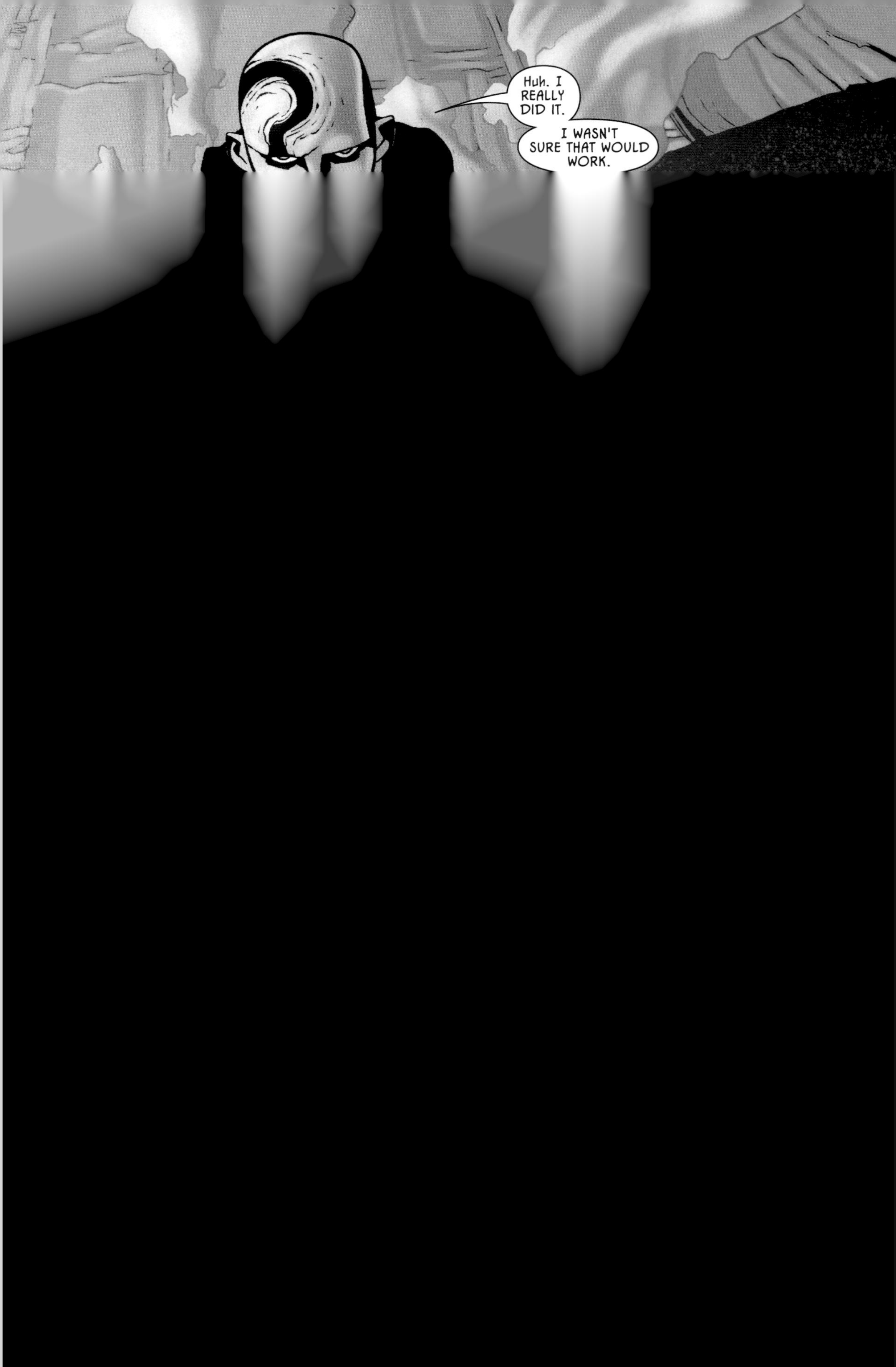
Huh. I REALLY DID IT.
I WASN'T SURE THAT WOULD WORK.

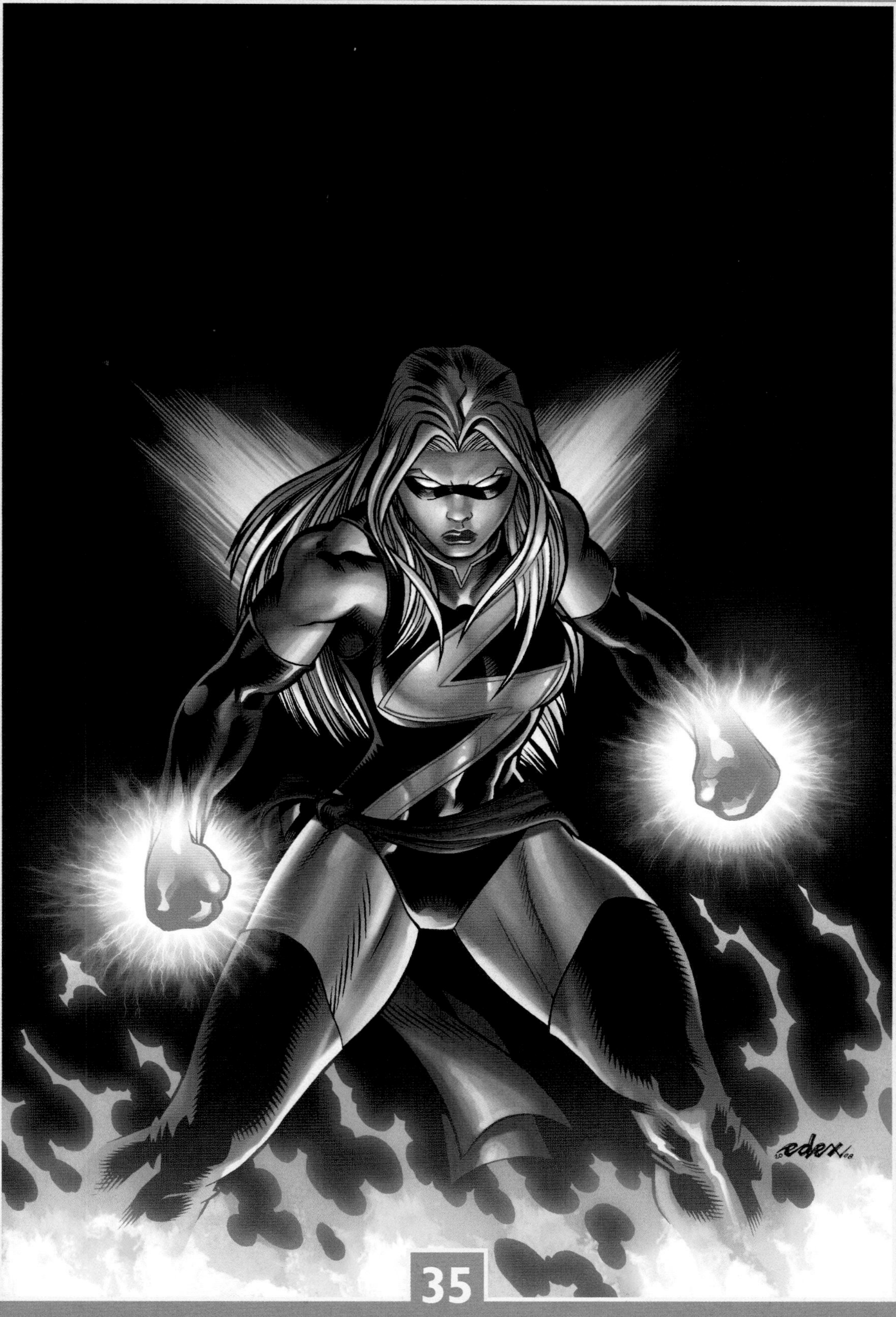

35

THE DEATH OF MS. MARVEL, PART 1 OF 3

PREVIOUSLY IN MS. MARVEL

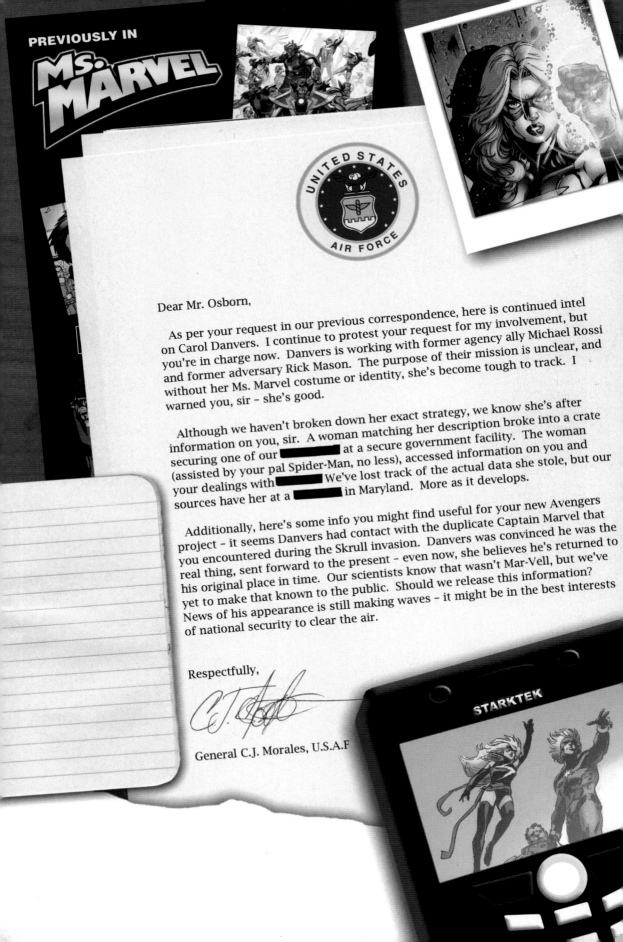

UNITED STATES AIR FORCE

Dear Mr. Osborn,

As per your request in our previous correspondence, here is continued intel on Carol Danvers. I continue to protest your request for my involvement, but you're in charge now. Danvers is working with former agency ally Michael Rossi and former adversary Rick Mason. The purpose of their mission is unclear, and without her Ms. Marvel costume or identity, she's become tough to track. I warned you, sir – she's good.

Although we haven't broken down her exact strategy, we know she's after information on you, sir. A woman matching her description broke into a crate securing one of our [redacted] at a secure government facility. The woman (assisted by your pal Spider-Man, no less), accessed information on you and your dealings with [redacted] We've lost track of the actual data she stole, but our sources have her at a [redacted] in Maryland. More as it develops.

Additionally, here's some info you might find useful for your new Avengers project – it seems Danvers had contact with the duplicate Captain Marvel that you encountered during the Skrull invasion. Danvers was convinced he was the real thing, sent forward to the present – even now, she believes he's returned to his original place in time. Our scientists know that wasn't Mar-Vell, but we've yet to make that known to the public. Should we release this information? News of his appearance is still making waves – it might be in the best interests of national security to clear the air.

Respectfully,

General C.J. Morales, U.S.A.F

STARKTEK

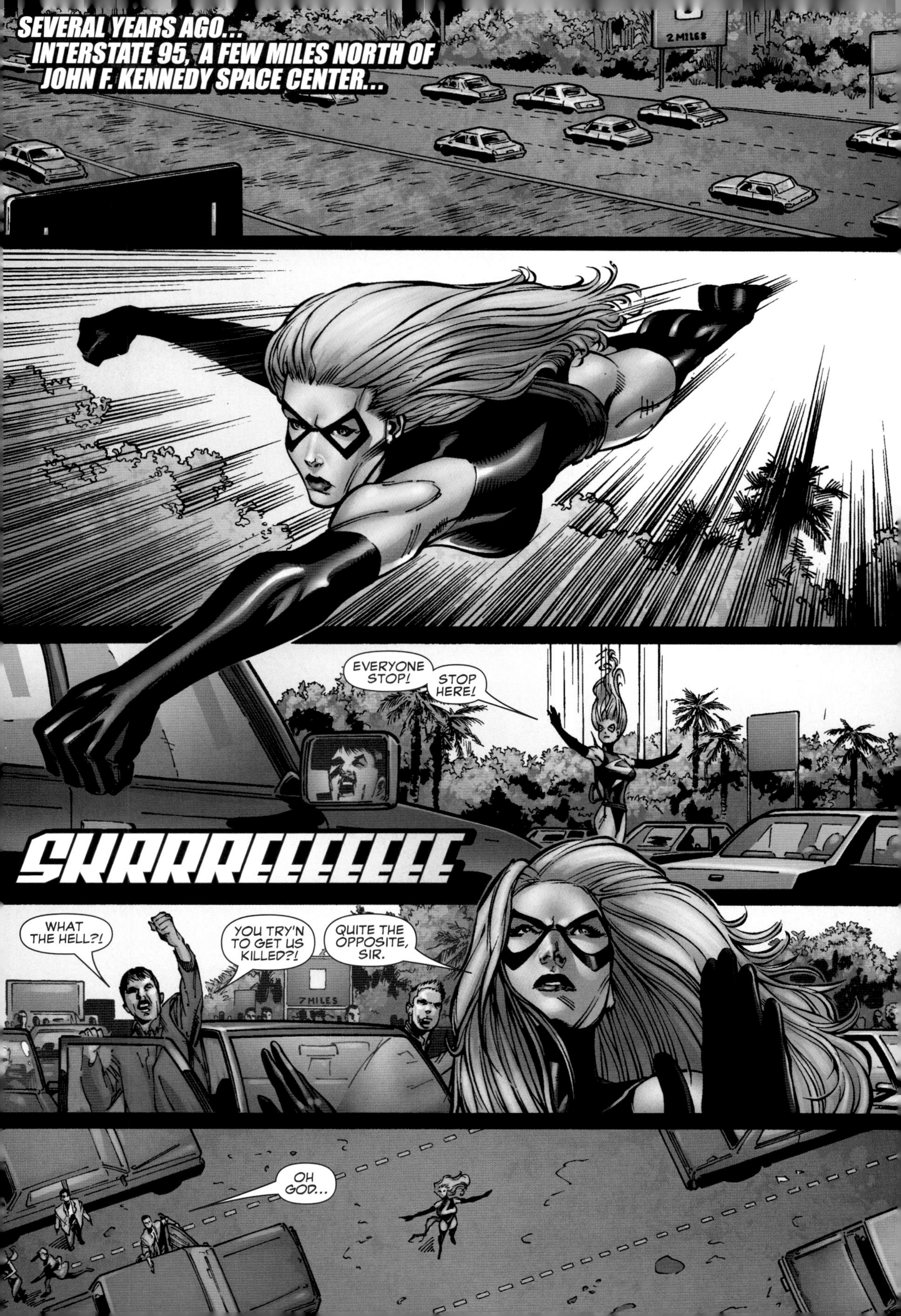
SEVERAL YEARS AGO... INTERSTATE 95, A FEW MILES NORTH OF JOHN F. KENNEDY SPACE CENTER...
2 MILES
EVERYONE STOP!
STOP HERE!
SKRRREEEEEEE
WHAT THE HELL?!
YOU TRY'N TO GET US KILLED?!
QUITE THE OPPOSITE, SIR.
7 MILES
OH GOD...

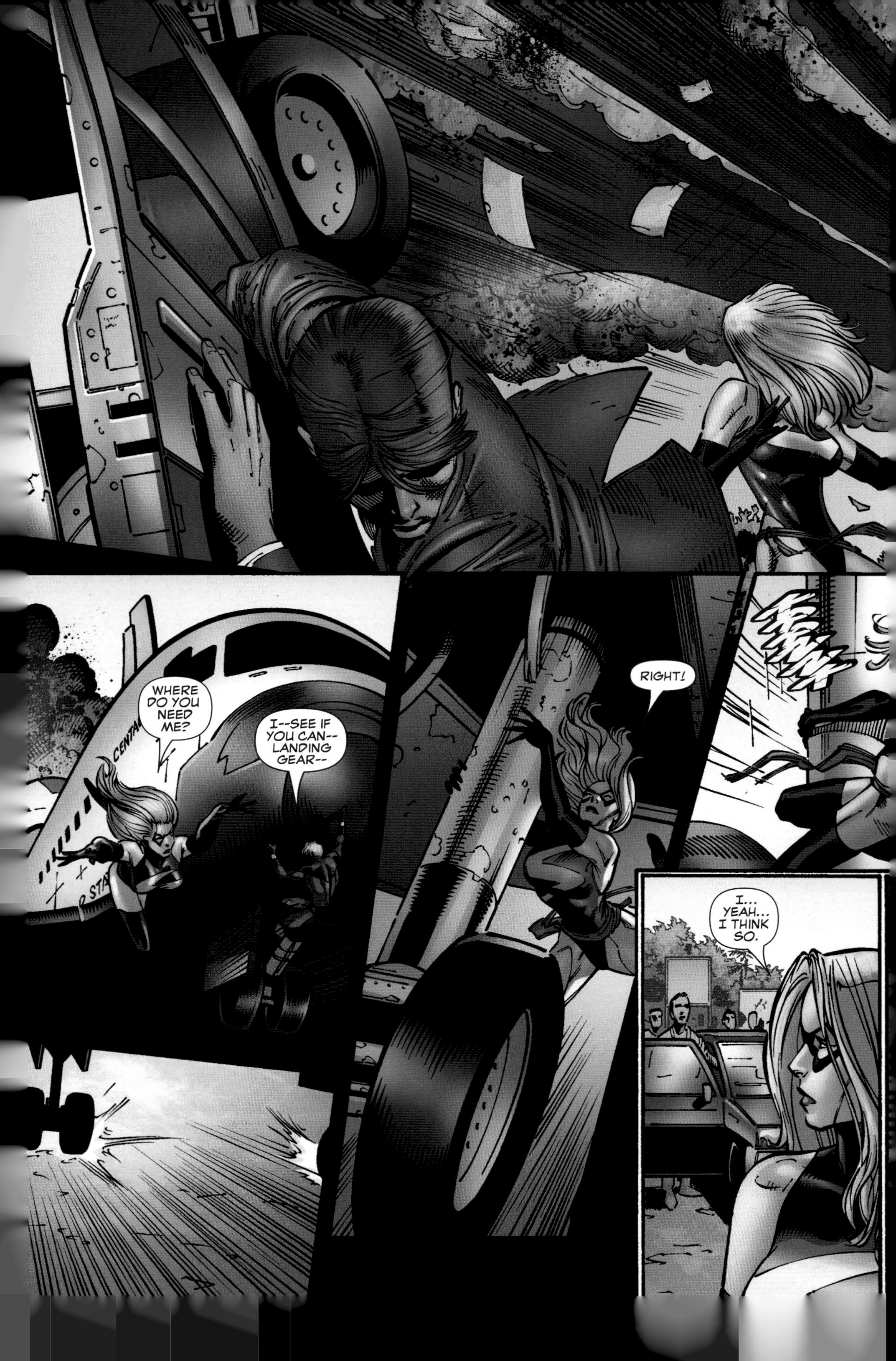
WHERE DO YOU NEED ME?
I--SEE IF YOU CAN--LANDING GEAR--
RIGHT!
I... YEAH... I THINK SO.

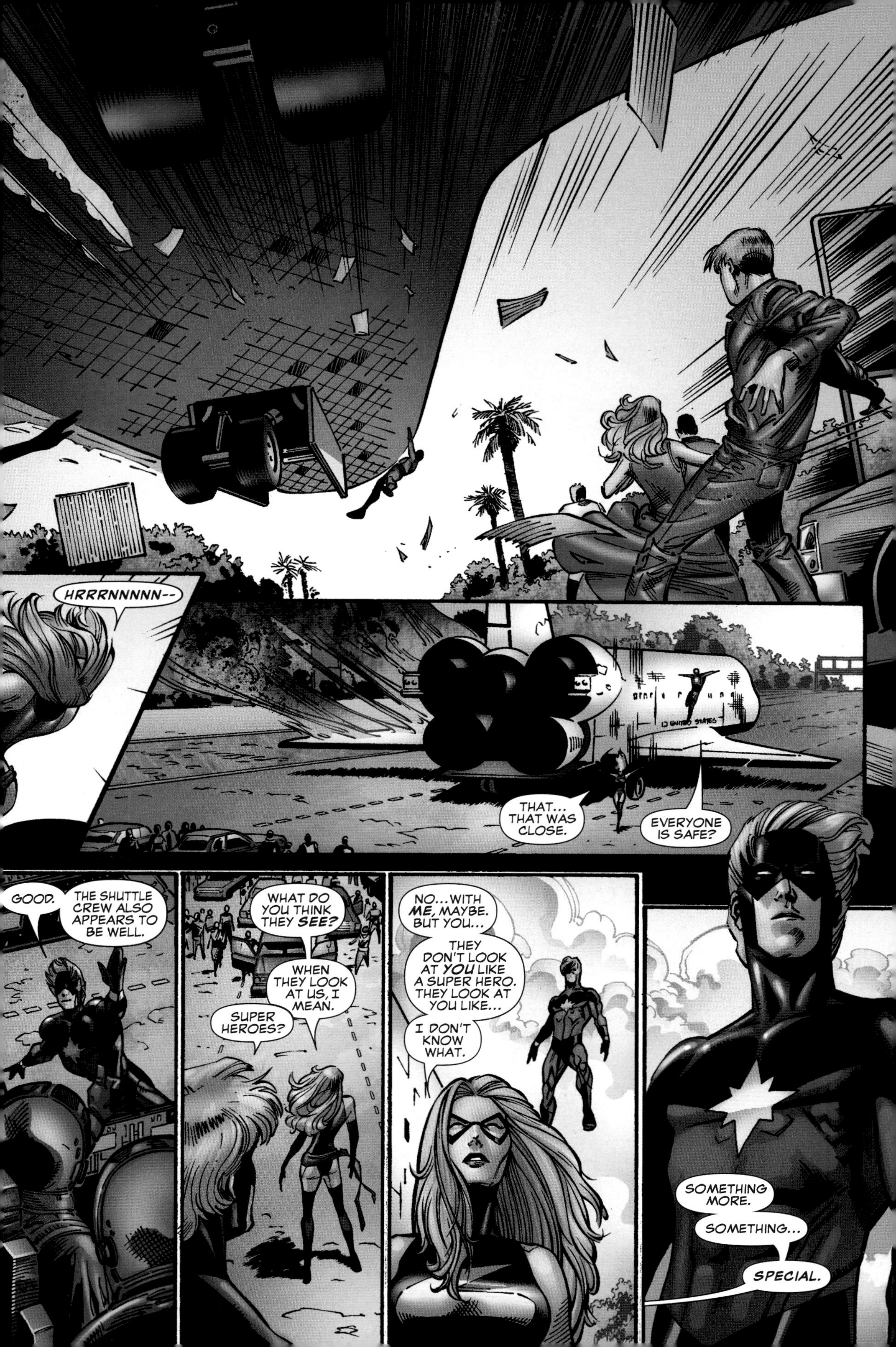
HRRRNNNNN--
13 UNITED STATES
THAT... THAT WAS CLOSE.
EVERYONE IS SAFE?
GOOD.
THE SHUTTLE CREW ALSO APPEARS TO BE WELL.
WHAT DO YOU THINK THEY *SEE?*
WHEN THEY LOOK AT US, I MEAN.
SUPER HEROES?
NO...WITH *ME,* MAYBE. BUT YOU...
THEY DON'T LOOK AT *YOU* LIKE A SUPER HERO. THEY LOOK AT YOU LIKE...
I DON'T KNOW WHAT.
SOMETHING MORE.
SOMETHING...
SPECIAL.

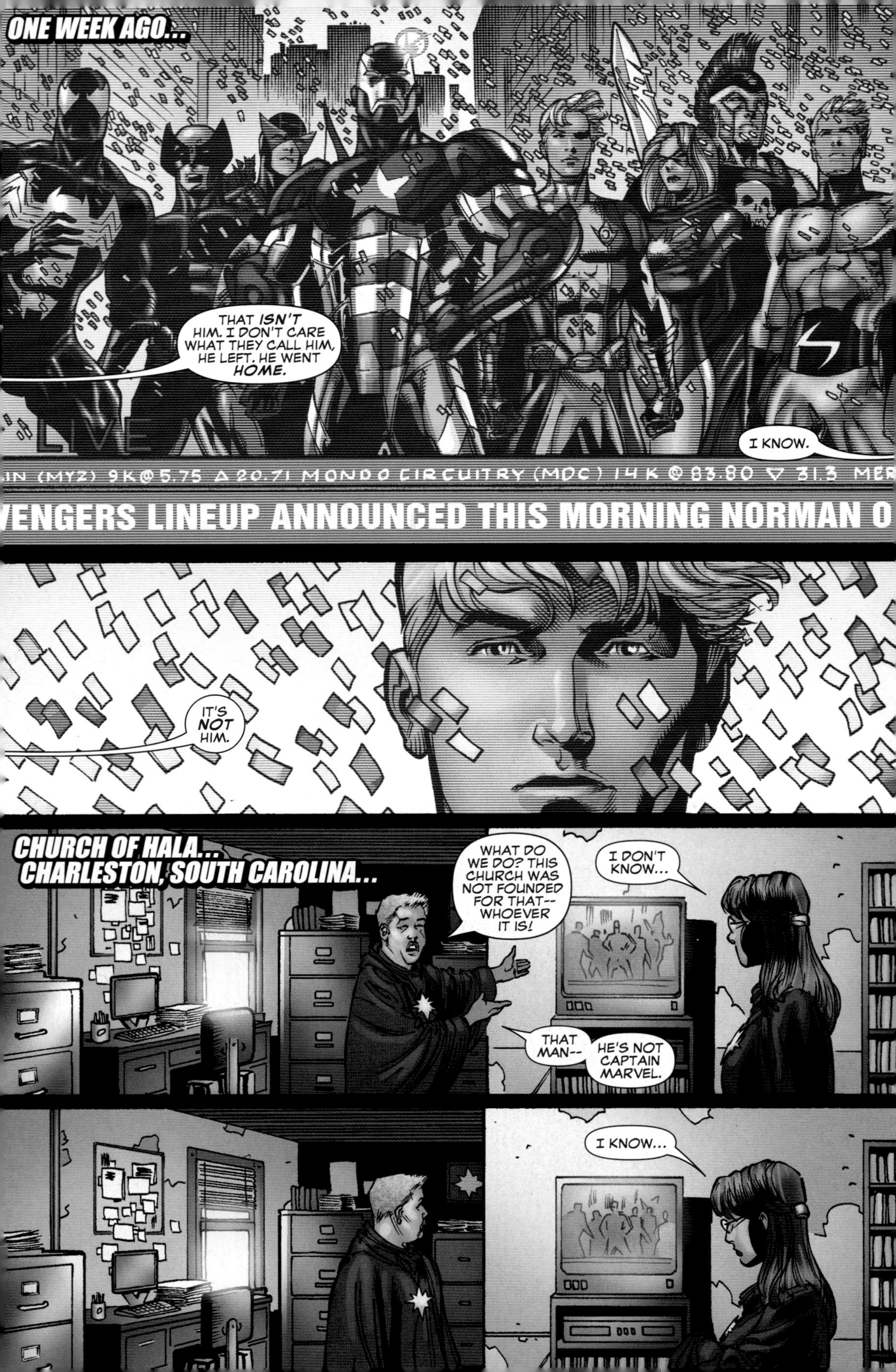
ONE WEEK AGO...
THAT ISN'T HIM. I DON'T CARE WHAT THEY CALL HIM, HE LEFT. HE WENT HOME.
I KNOW.
IN (MYZ) 9K@5.75 △20.71 MONDO CIRCUITRY (MDC) 14K @83.80 ▽31.3 MER
VENGERS LINEUP ANNOUNCED THIS MORNING NORMAN O
IT'S NOT HIM.
CHURCH OF HALA... CHARLESTON, SOUTH CAROLINA...
WHAT DO WE DO? THIS CHURCH WAS NOT FOUNDED FOR THAT-- WHOEVER IT IS!
I DON'T KNOW...
THAT MAN--
HE'S NOT CAPTAIN MARVEL.
I KNOW...

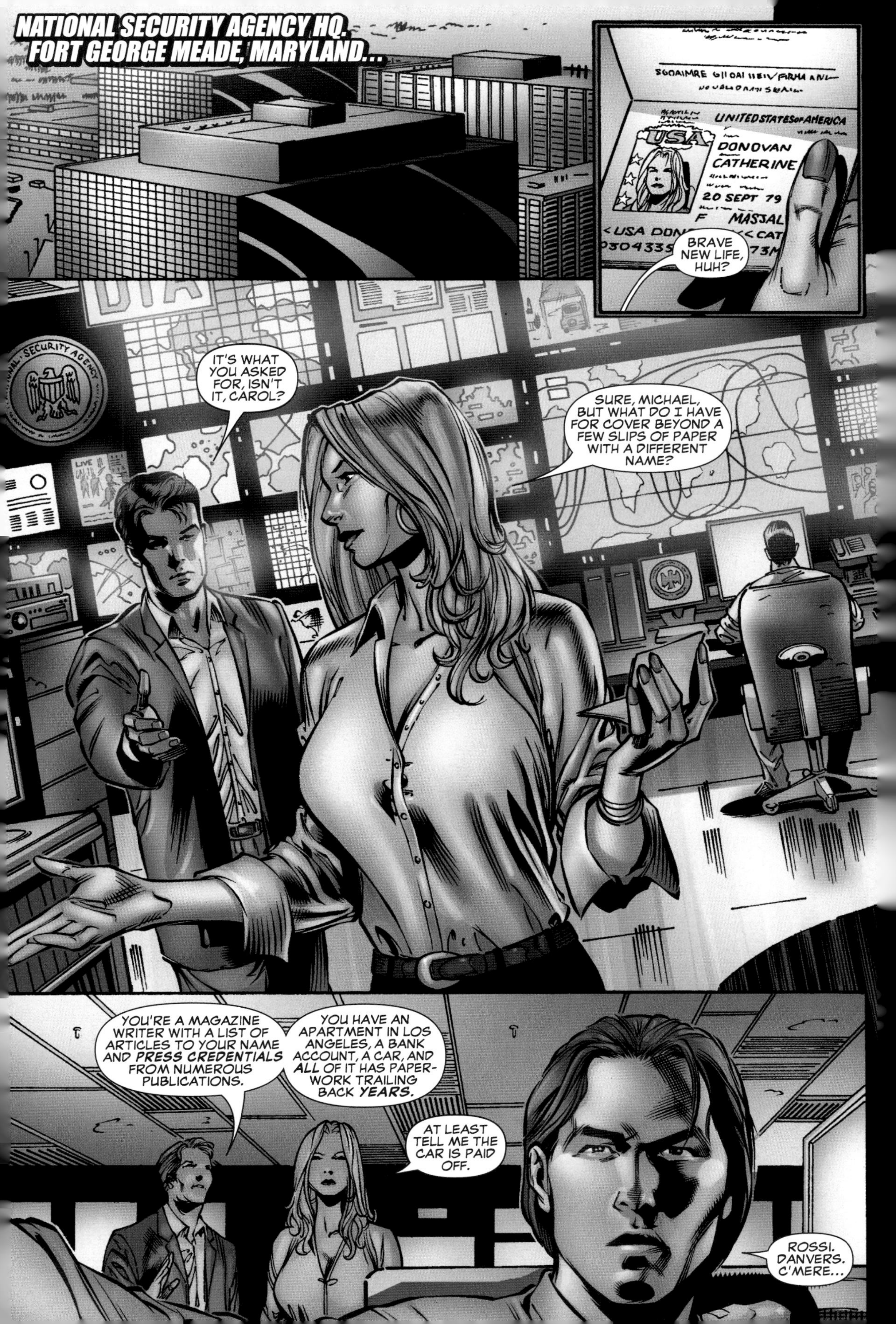
NATIONAL SECURITY AGENCY HQ. FORT GEORGE MEADE, MARYLAND...
UNITED STATES OF AMERICA
USA
DONOVAN
CATHERINE
20 SEPT 79
F
BRAVE NEW LIFE, HUH?
IT'S WHAT YOU ASKED FOR, ISN'T IT, CAROL?
SURE, MICHAEL, BUT WHAT DO I HAVE FOR COVER BEYOND A FEW SLIPS OF PAPER WITH A DIFFERENT NAME?
YOU'RE A MAGAZINE WRITER WITH A LIST OF ARTICLES TO YOUR NAME AND PRESS CREDENTIALS FROM NUMEROUS PUBLICATIONS.
YOU HAVE AN APARTMENT IN LOS ANGELES, A BANK ACCOUNT, A CAR, AND ALL OF IT HAS PAPER-WORK TRAILING BACK YEARS.
AT LEAST TELL ME THE CAR IS PAID OFF.
ROSSI. DANVERS. C'MERE...

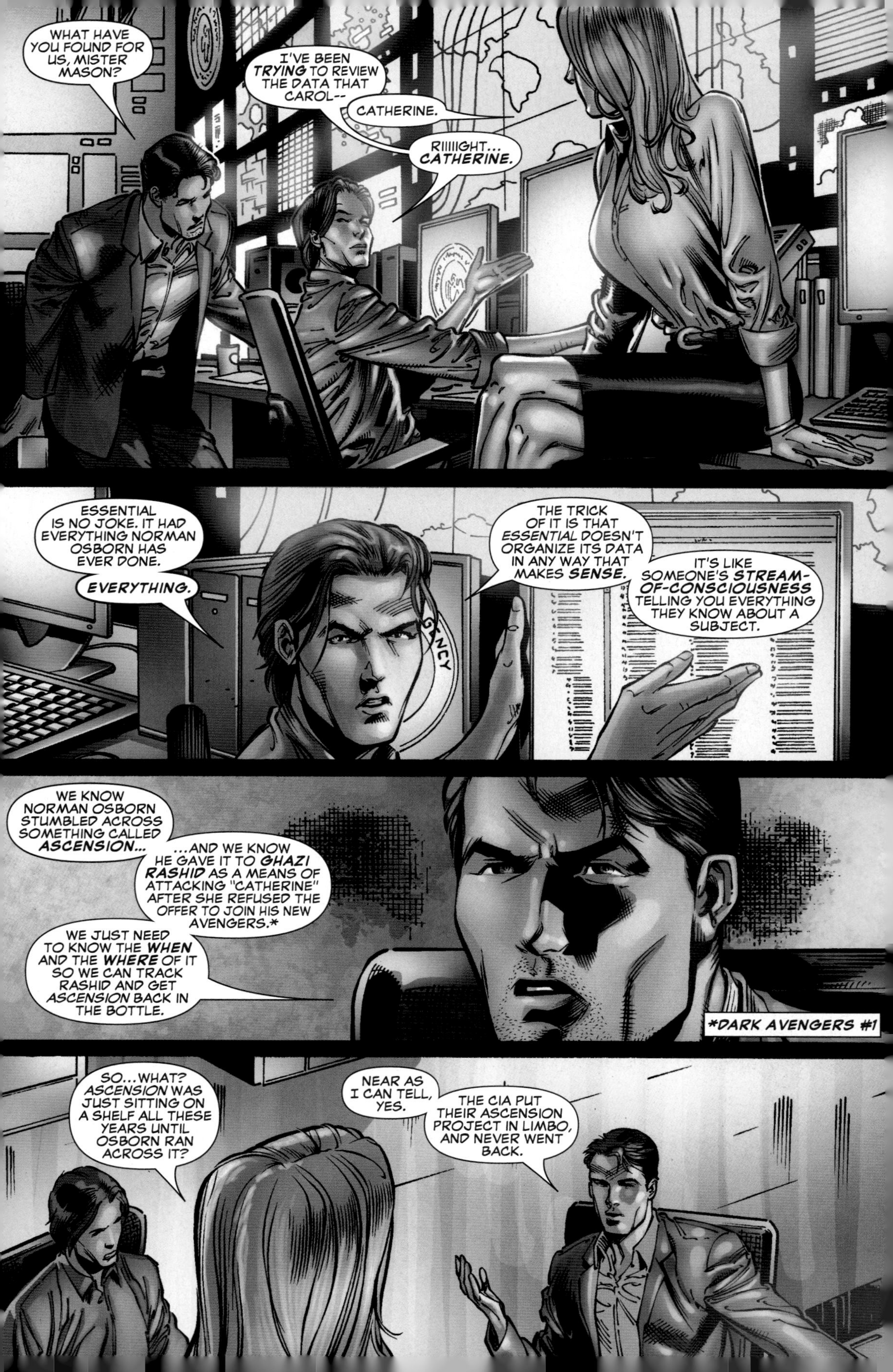
WHAT HAVE YOU FOUND FOR US, MISTER MASON?
I'VE BEEN *TRYING* TO REVIEW THE DATA THAT CAROL--
CATHERINE.
RIIIIIGHT... ***CATHERINE.***
ESSENTIAL IS NO JOKE. IT HAD EVERYTHING NORMAN OSBORN HAS EVER DONE.
EVERYTHING.
THE TRICK OF IT IS THAT *ESSENTIAL* DOESN'T ORGANIZE ITS DATA IN ANY WAY THAT MAKES ***SENSE.***
IT'S LIKE SOMEONE'S ***STREAM-OF-CONSCIOUSNESS*** TELLING YOU EVERYTHING THEY KNOW ABOUT A SUBJECT.
WE KNOW NORMAN OSBORN STUMBLED ACROSS SOMETHING CALLED ***ASCENSION...***
...AND WE KNOW HE GAVE IT TO ***GHAZI RASHID*** AS A MEANS OF ATTACKING "CATHERINE" AFTER SHE REFUSED THE OFFER TO JOIN HIS NEW AVENGERS.*
WE JUST NEED TO KNOW THE ***WHEN*** AND THE ***WHERE*** OF IT SO WE CAN TRACK RASHID AND GET ASCENSION BACK IN THE BOTTLE.
*DARK AVENGERS #1
SO...WHAT? *ASCENSION* WAS JUST SITTING ON A SHELF ALL THESE YEARS UNTIL OSBORN RAN ACROSS IT?
NEAR AS I CAN TELL, YES.
THE CIA PUT THEIR ASCENSION PROJECT IN LIMBO, AND NEVER WENT BACK.

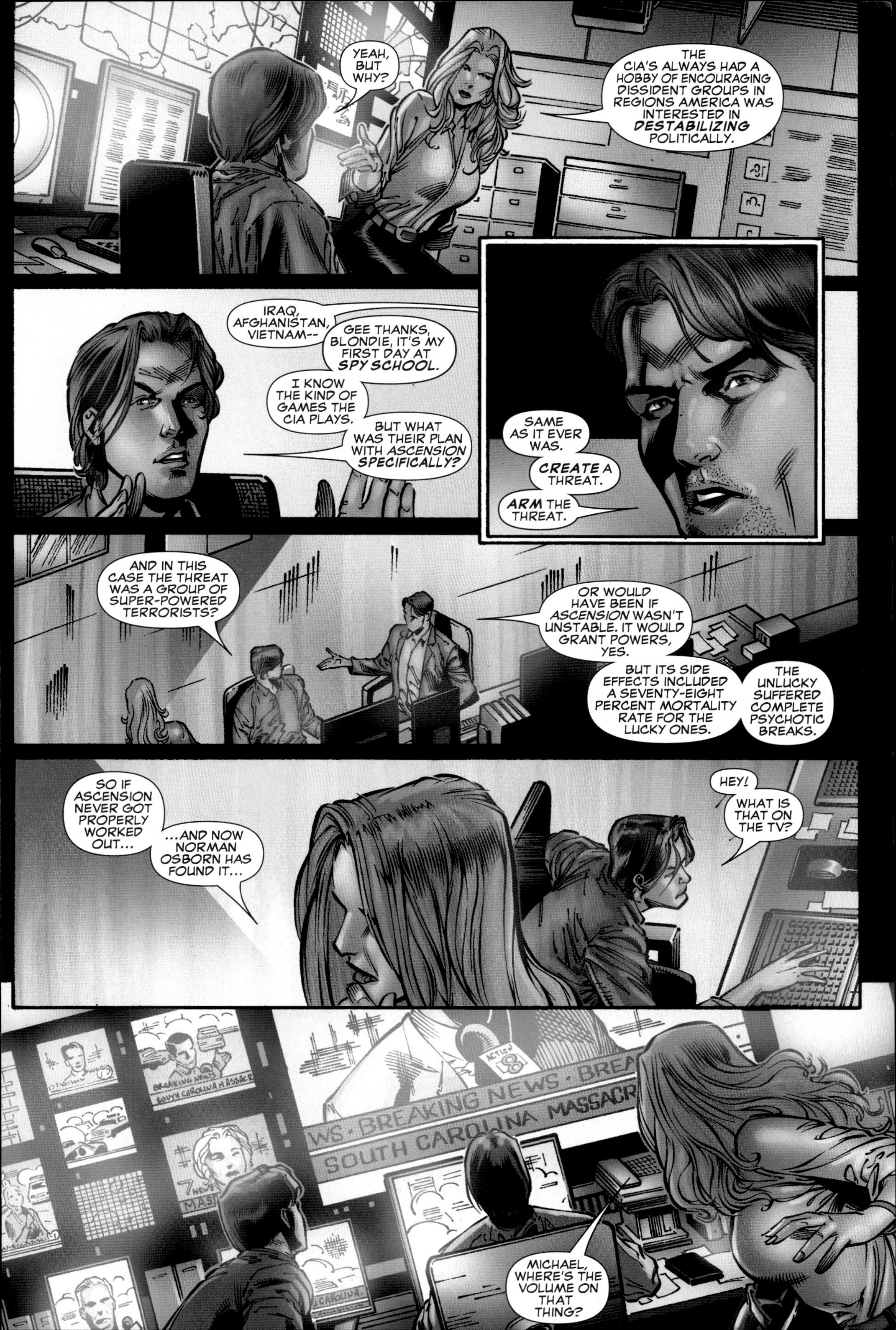

YEAH, BUT WHY?
THE CIA'S ALWAYS HAD A HOBBY OF ENCOURAGING DISSIDENT GROUPS IN REGIONS AMERICA WAS INTERESTED IN DESTABILIZING POLITICALLY.
IRAQ, AFGHANISTAN, VIETNAM--
GEE THANKS, BLONDIE, IT'S MY FIRST DAY AT SPY SCHOOL.
I KNOW THE KIND OF GAMES THE CIA PLAYS.
BUT WHAT WAS THEIR PLAN WITH ASCENSION SPECIFICALLY?
SAME AS IT EVER WAS.
CREATE A THREAT.
ARM THE THREAT.
AND IN THIS CASE THE THREAT WAS A GROUP OF SUPER-POWERED TERRORISTS?
OR WOULD HAVE BEEN IF ASCENSION WASN'T UNSTABLE. IT WOULD GRANT POWERS, YES.
BUT ITS SIDE EFFECTS INCLUDED A SEVENTY-EIGHT PERCENT MORTALITY RATE FOR THE LUCKY ONES.
THE UNLUCKY SUFFERED COMPLETE PSYCHOTIC BREAKS.
SO IF ASCENSION NEVER GOT PROPERLY WORKED OUT...
...AND NOW NORMAN OSBORN HAS FOUND IT...
HEY!
WHAT IS THAT ON THE TV?
BREAKING NEWS · BREA
SOUTH CAROLINA MASSACR
ACTION 8
MICHAEL, WHERE'S THE VOLUME ON THAT THING?

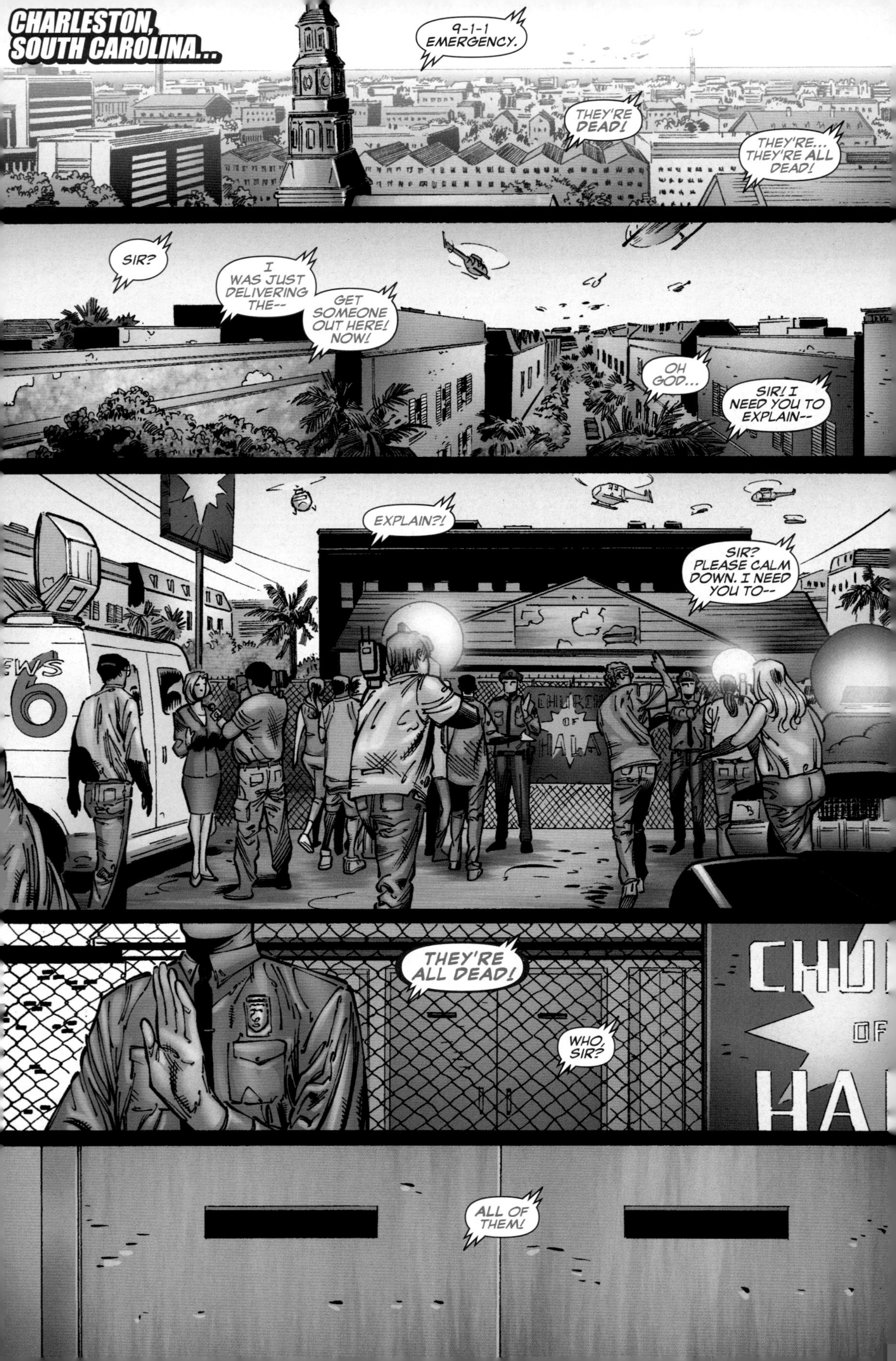
CHARLESTON, SOUTH CAROLINA...
9-1-1 EMERGENCY.
THEY'RE DEAD!
THEY'RE... THEY'RE ALL DEAD!
SIR?
I WAS JUST DELIVERING THE--
GET SOMEONE OUT HERE! NOW!
OH GOD...
SIR! I NEED YOU TO EXPLAIN--
EXPLAIN?!
SIR? PLEASE CALM DOWN. I NEED YOU TO--
NEWS 6
THEY'RE ALL DEAD!
WHO, SIR?
ALL OF THEM!

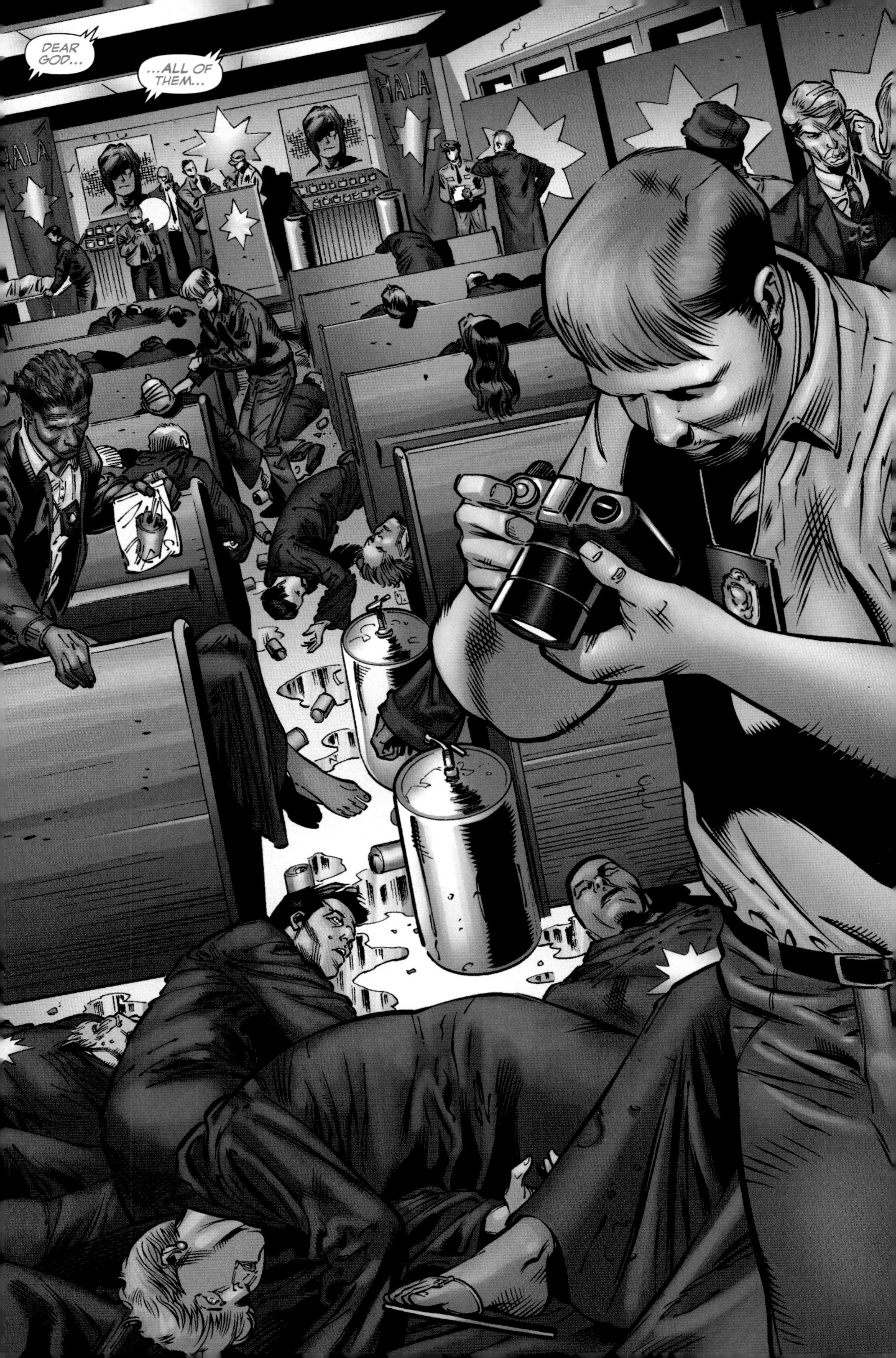
DEAR GOD...
...ALL OF THEM...
HALA
HALA

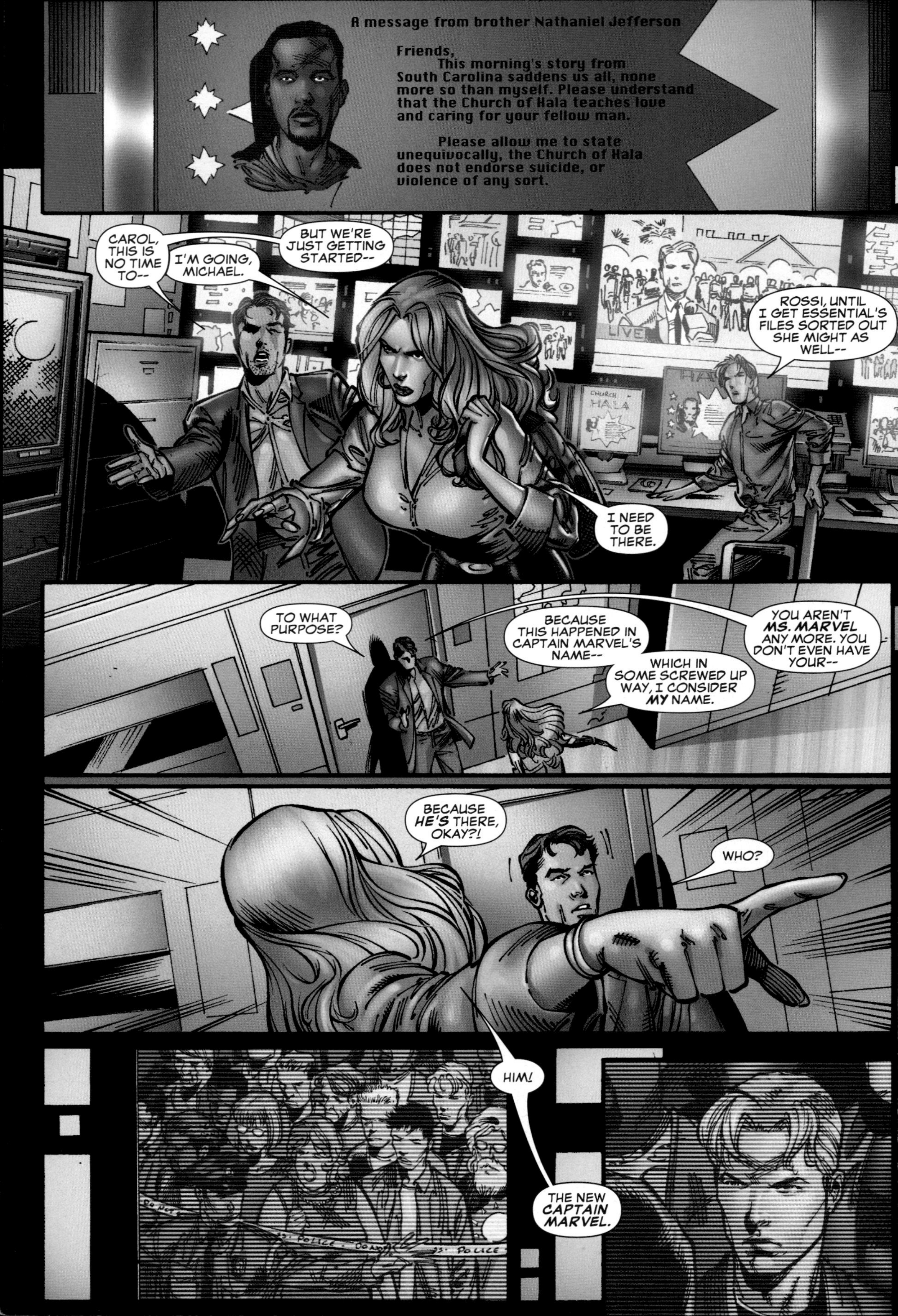
A message from brother Nathaniel Jefferson
Friends,
This morning's story from South Carolina saddens us all, none more so than myself. Please understand that the Church of Hala teaches love and caring for your fellow man.
Please allow me to state unequivocally, the Church of Hala does not endorse suicide, or violence of any sort.
CAROL, THIS IS NO TIME TO--
I'M GOING, MICHAEL.
BUT WE'RE JUST GETTING STARTED--
ROSSI, UNTIL I GET ESSENTIAL'S FILES SORTED OUT SHE MIGHT AS WELL--
I NEED TO BE THERE.
TO WHAT PURPOSE?
BECAUSE THIS HAPPENED IN CAPTAIN MARVEL'S NAME--
WHICH IN SOME SCREWED UP WAY, I CONSIDER MY NAME.
YOU AREN'T MS. MARVEL ANY MORE. YOU DON'T EVEN HAVE YOUR--
BECAUSE HE'S THERE, OKAY?!
WHO?
HIM!
THE NEW CAPTAIN MARVEL.

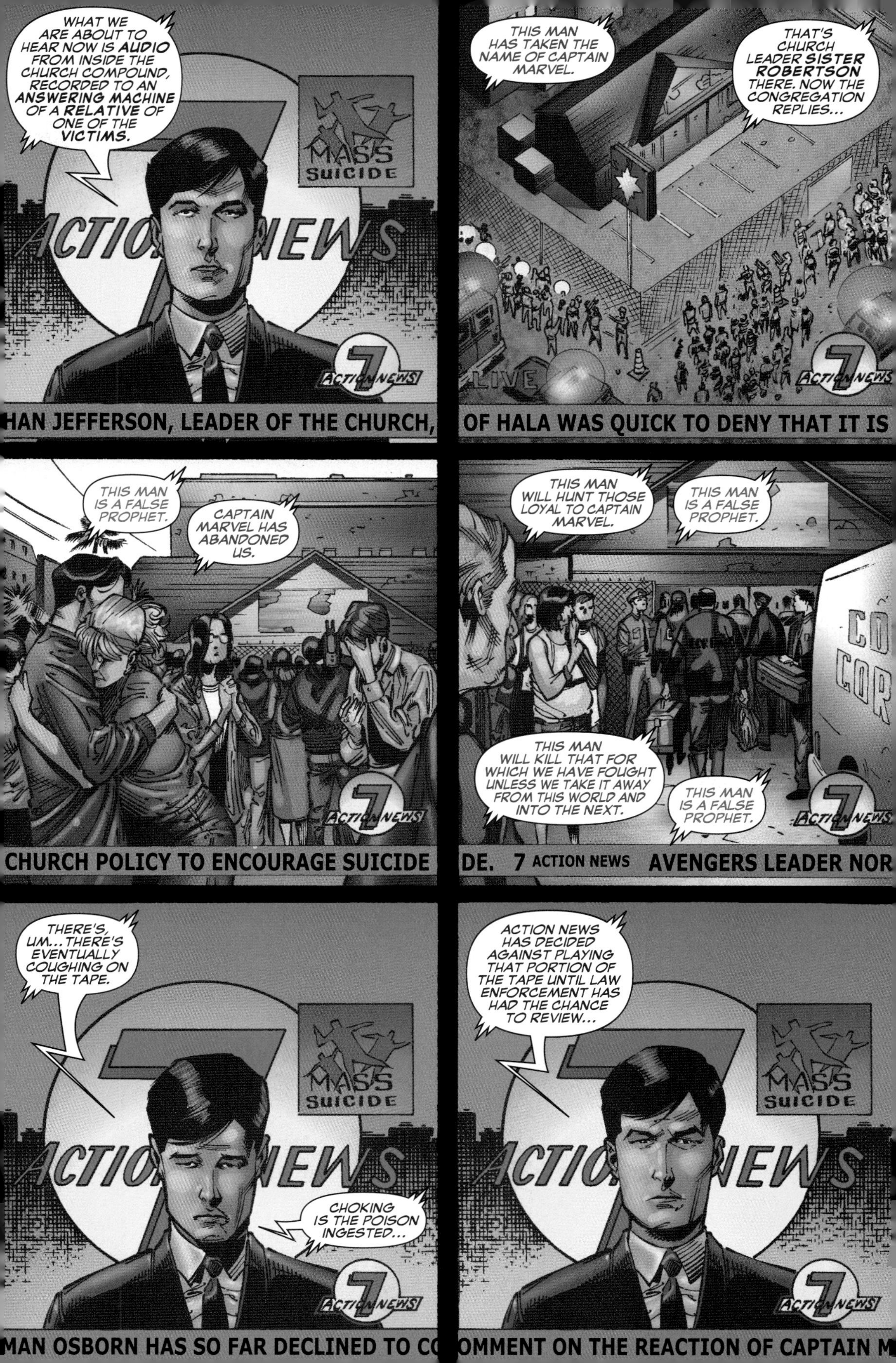
WHAT WE ARE ABOUT TO HEAR NOW IS AUDIO FROM INSIDE THE CHURCH COMPOUND, RECORDED TO AN ANSWERING MACHINE OF A RELATIVE OF ONE OF THE VICTIMS.
MASS SUICIDE
ACTION NEWS
7 ACTION NEWS
HAN JEFFERSON, LEADER OF THE CHURCH,
THIS MAN HAS TAKEN THE NAME OF CAPTAIN MARVEL.
THAT'S CHURCH LEADER SISTER ROBERTSON THERE. NOW THE CONGREGATION REPLIES...
LIVE
7 ACTION NEWS
OF HALA WAS QUICK TO DENY THAT IT IS
THIS MAN IS A FALSE PROPHET.
CAPTAIN MARVEL HAS ABANDONED US.
7 ACTION NEWS
CHURCH POLICY TO ENCOURAGE SUICIDE
THIS MAN WILL HUNT THOSE LOYAL TO CAPTAIN MARVEL.
THIS MAN IS A FALSE PROPHET.
THIS MAN WILL KILL THAT FOR WHICH WE HAVE FOUGHT UNLESS WE TAKE IT AWAY FROM THIS WORLD AND INTO THE NEXT.
THIS MAN IS A FALSE PROPHET.
7 ACTION NEWS
DE. 7 ACTION NEWS AVENGERS LEADER NOR
THERE'S, UM...THERE'S EVENTUALLY COUGHING ON THE TAPE.
CHOKING IS THE POISON INGESTED...
MASS SUICIDE
ACTION NEWS
7 ACTION NEWS
MAN OSBORN HAS SO FAR DECLINED TO CO
ACTION NEWS HAS DECIDED AGAINST PLAYING THAT PORTION OF THE TAPE UNTIL LAW ENFORCEMENT HAS HAD THE CHANCE TO REVIEW...
MASS SUICIDE
ACTION NEWS
7 ACTION NEWS
OMMENT ON THE REACTION OF CAPTAIN M

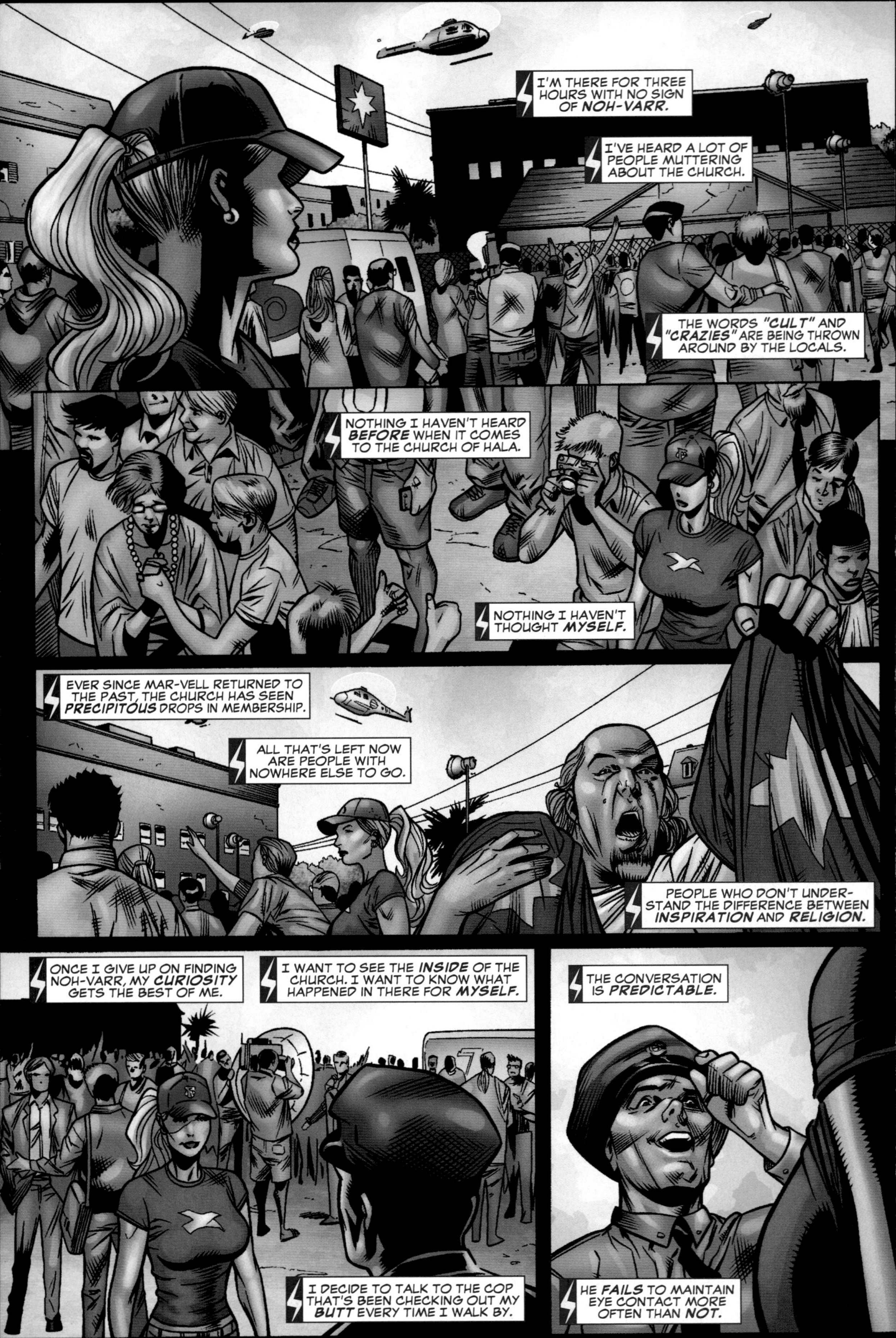
I'M THERE FOR THREE HOURS WITH NO SIGN OF NOH-VARR.
I'VE HEARD A LOT OF PEOPLE MUTTERING ABOUT THE CHURCH.
THE WORDS "CULT" AND "CRAZIES" ARE BEING THROWN AROUND BY THE LOCALS.
NOTHING I HAVEN'T HEARD BEFORE WHEN IT COMES TO THE CHURCH OF HALA.
NOTHING I HAVEN'T THOUGHT MYSELF.
EVER SINCE MAR-VELL RETURNED TO THE PAST, THE CHURCH HAS SEEN PRECIPITOUS DROPS IN MEMBERSHIP.
ALL THAT'S LEFT NOW ARE PEOPLE WITH NOWHERE ELSE TO GO.
PEOPLE WHO DON'T UNDERSTAND THE DIFFERENCE BETWEEN INSPIRATION AND RELIGION.
ONCE I GIVE UP ON FINDING NOH-VARR, MY CURIOSITY GETS THE BEST OF ME.
I WANT TO SEE THE INSIDE OF THE CHURCH. I WANT TO KNOW WHAT HAPPENED IN THERE FOR MYSELF.
I DECIDE TO TALK TO THE COP THAT'S BEEN CHECKING OUT MY BUTT EVERY TIME I WALK BY.
THE CONVERSATION IS PREDICTABLE.
HE FAILS TO MAINTAIN EYE CONTACT MORE OFTEN THAN NOT.

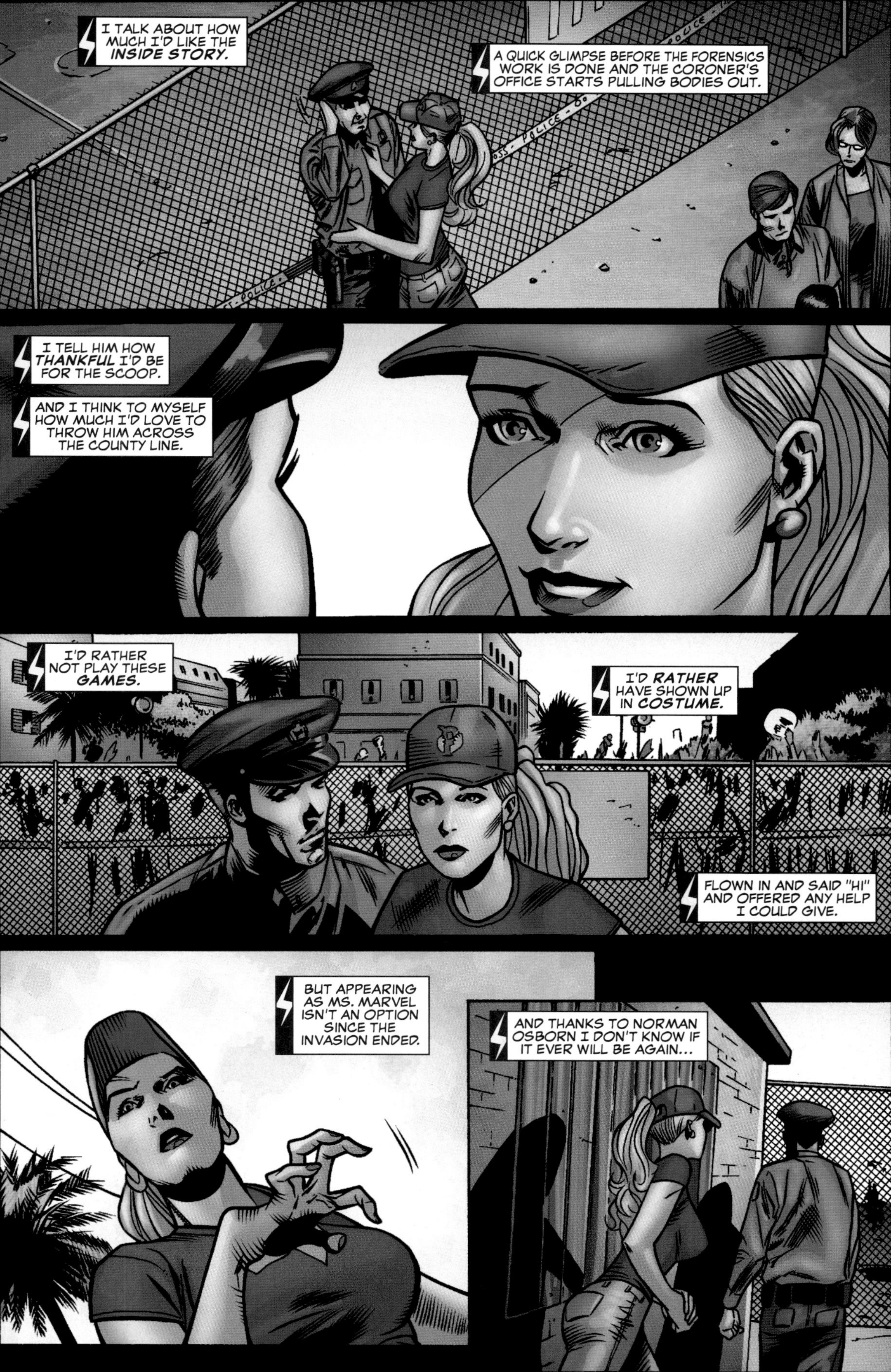
I TALK ABOUT HOW MUCH I'D LIKE THE INSIDE STORY.
A QUICK GLIMPSE BEFORE THE FORENSICS WORK IS DONE AND THE CORONER'S OFFICE STARTS PULLING BODIES OUT.
I TELL HIM HOW THANKFUL I'D BE FOR THE SCOOP.
AND I THINK TO MYSELF HOW MUCH I'D LOVE TO THROW HIM ACROSS THE COUNTY LINE.
I'D RATHER NOT PLAY THESE GAMES.
I'D RATHER HAVE SHOWN UP IN COSTUME.
FLOWN IN AND SAID "HI" AND OFFERED ANY HELP I COULD GIVE.
BUT APPEARING AS MS. MARVEL ISN'T AN OPTION SINCE THE INVASION ENDED.
AND THANKS TO NORMAN OSBORN I DON'T KNOW IF IT EVER WILL BE AGAIN...

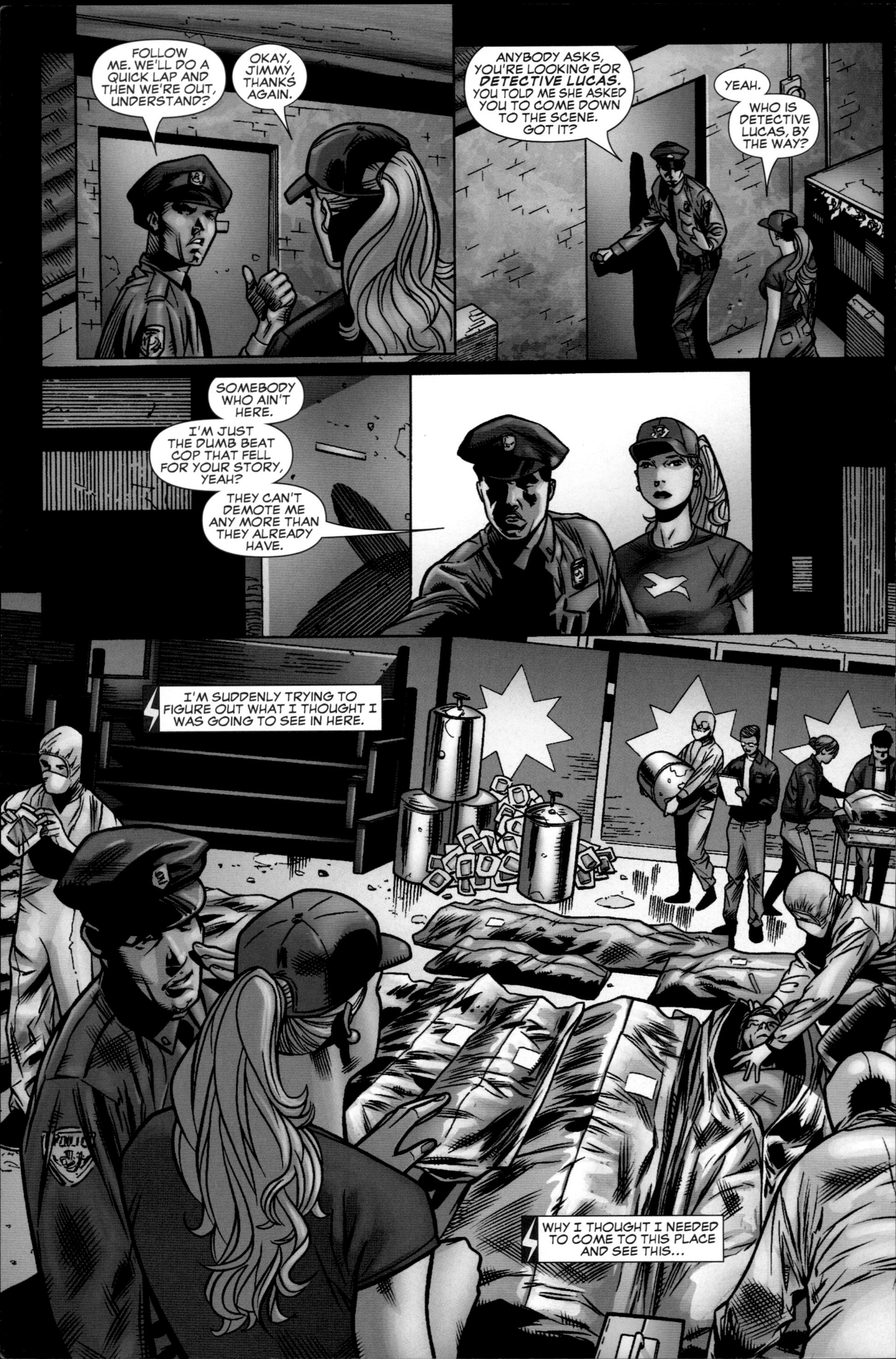
FOLLOW ME. WE'LL DO A QUICK LAP AND THEN WE'RE OUT, UNDERSTAND?
OKAY, JIMMY, THANKS AGAIN.
ANYBODY ASKS, YOU'RE LOOKING FOR DETECTIVE LUCAS. YOU TOLD ME SHE ASKED YOU TO COME DOWN TO THE SCENE. GOT IT?
YEAH.
WHO IS DETECTIVE LUCAS, BY THE WAY?
SOMEBODY WHO AIN'T HERE.
I'M JUST THE DUMB BEAT COP THAT FELL FOR YOUR STORY, YEAH?
THEY CAN'T DEMOTE ME ANY MORE THAN THEY ALREADY HAVE.
I'M SUDDENLY TRYING TO FIGURE OUT WHAT I THOUGHT I WAS GOING TO SEE IN HERE.
WHY I THOUGHT I NEEDED TO COME TO THIS PLACE AND SEE THIS...

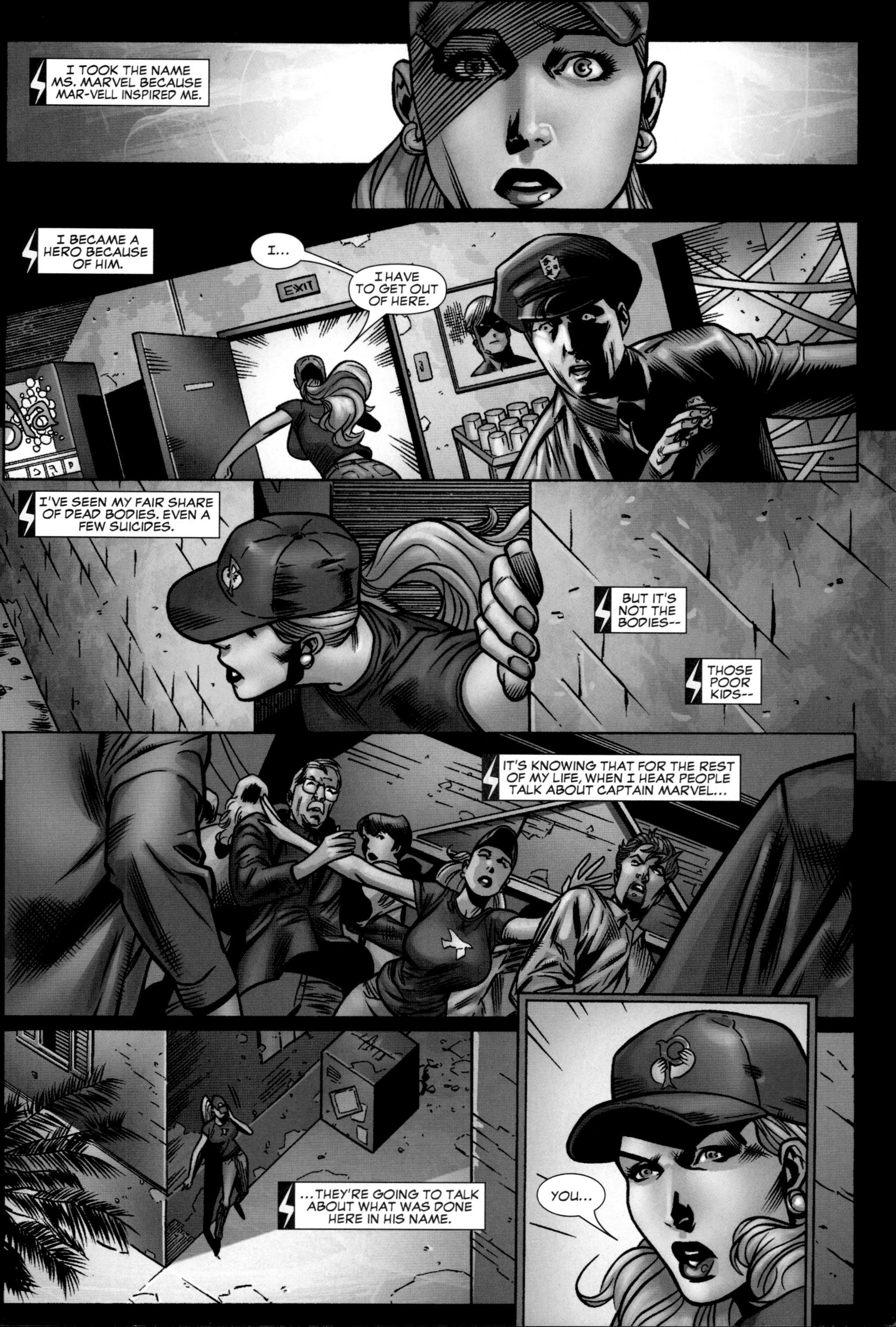
I TOOK THE NAME MS. MARVEL BECAUSE MAR-VELL INSPIRED ME.
I BECAME A HERO BECAUSE OF HIM.
I...
I HAVE TO GET OUT OF HERE.
EXIT
I'VE SEEN MY FAIR SHARE OF DEAD BODIES. EVEN A FEW SUICIDES.
BUT IT'S NOT THE BODIES--
THOSE POOR KIDS--
IT'S KNOWING THAT FOR THE REST OF MY LIFE, WHEN I HEAR PEOPLE TALK ABOUT CAPTAIN MARVEL...
...THEY'RE GOING TO TALK ABOUT WHAT WAS DONE HERE IN HIS NAME.
YOU...

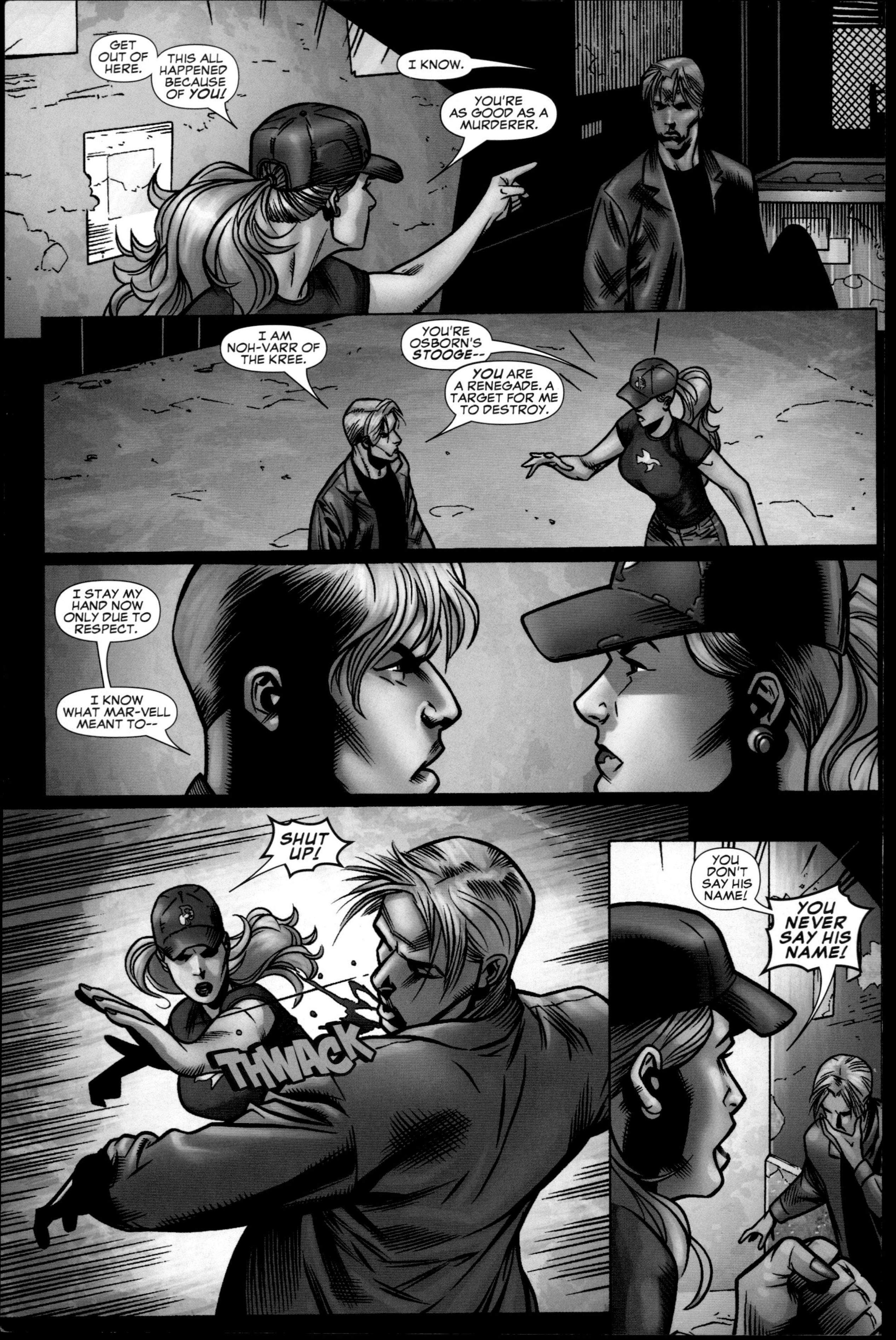
GET OUT OF HERE.
THIS ALL HAPPENED BECAUSE OF YOU!
I KNOW.
YOU'RE AS GOOD AS A MURDERER.
I AM NOH-VARR OF THE KREE.
YOU'RE OSBORN'S STOOGE--
YOU ARE A RENEGADE. A TARGET FOR ME TO DESTROY.
I STAY MY HAND NOW ONLY DUE TO RESPECT.
I KNOW WHAT MAR-VELL MEANT TO--
SHUT UP!
THWACK
YOU DON'T SAY HIS NAME!
YOU NEVER SAY HIS NAME!

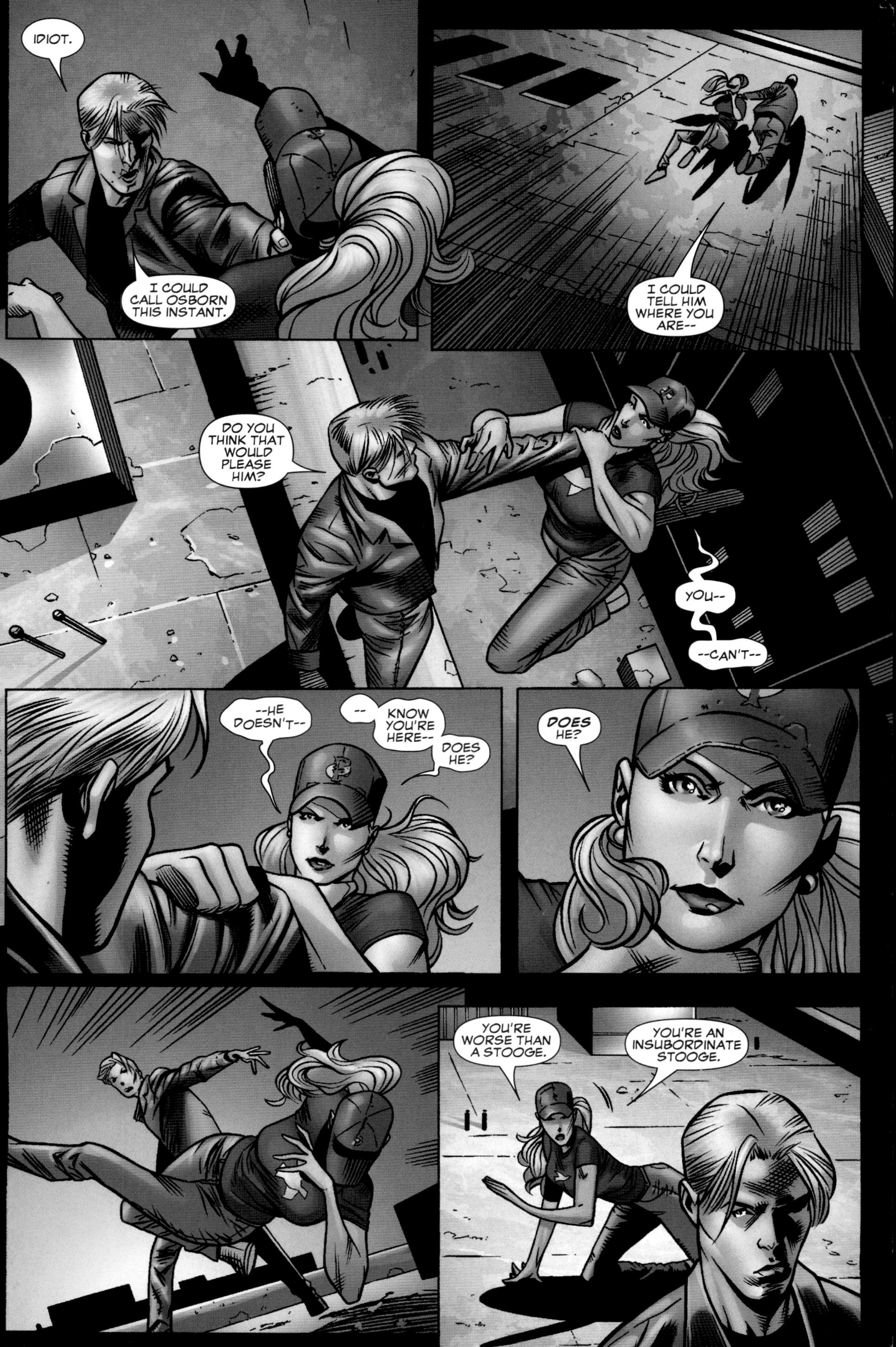
IDIOT.
I COULD CALL OSBORN THIS INSTANT.
I COULD TELL HIM WHERE YOU ARE--
DO YOU THINK THAT WOULD PLEASE HIM?
YOU--
--CAN'T--
--HE DOESN'T--
--
KNOW YOU'RE HERE--
DOES HE?
DOES HE?
YOU'RE WORSE THAN A STOOGE.
YOU'RE AN INSUBORDINATE STOOGE.

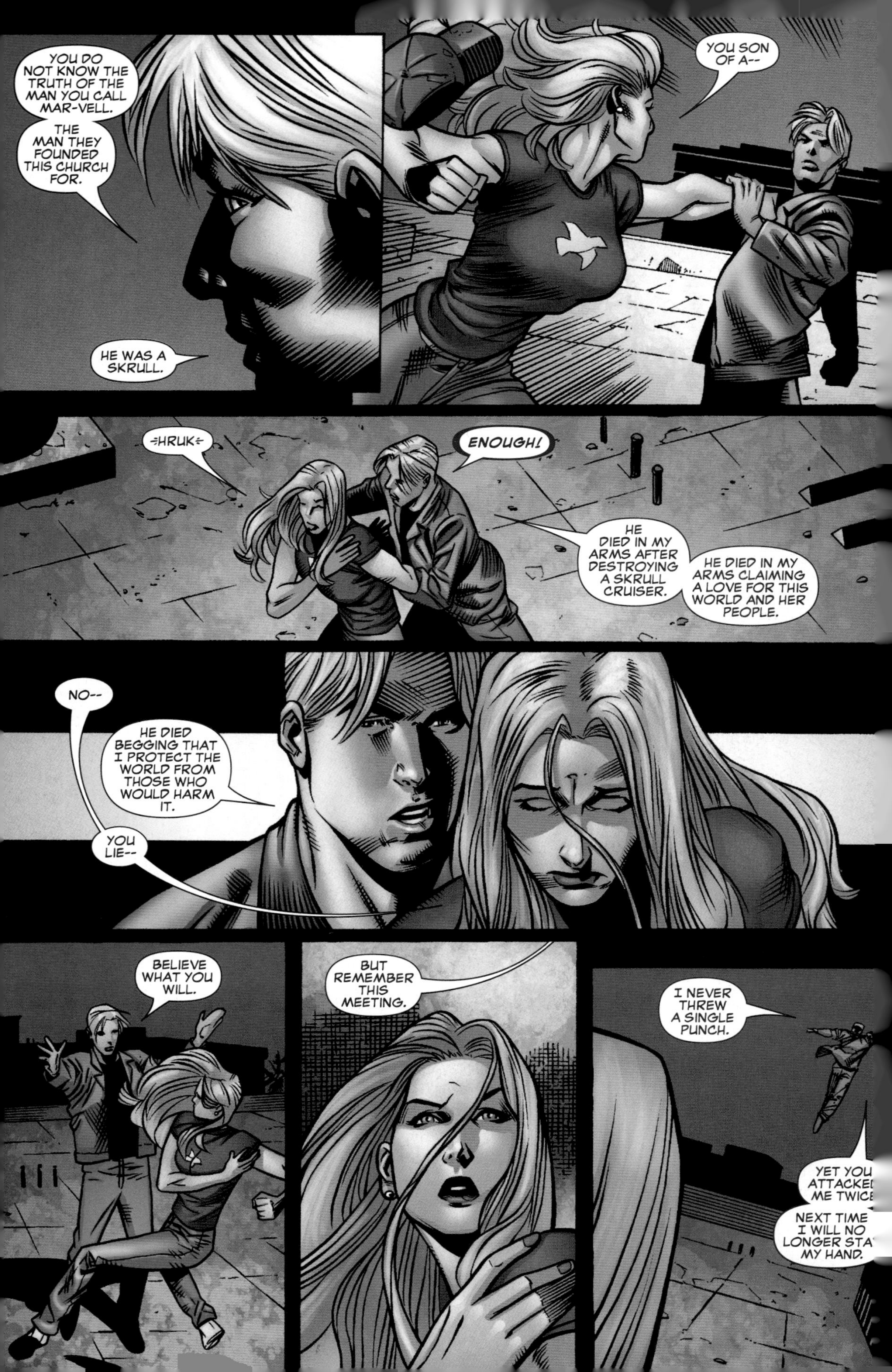
YOU DO NOT KNOW THE TRUTH OF THE MAN YOU CALL MAR-VELL.
THE MAN THEY FOUNDED THIS CHURCH FOR.
HE WAS A SKRULL.
YOU SON OF A--
=HRUK=
ENOUGH!
HE DIED IN MY ARMS AFTER DESTROYING A SKRULL CRUISER.
HE DIED IN MY ARMS CLAIMING A LOVE FOR THIS WORLD AND HER PEOPLE.
NO--
HE DIED BEGGING THAT I PROTECT THE WORLD FROM THOSE WHO WOULD HARM IT.
YOU LIE--
BELIEVE WHAT YOU WILL.
BUT REMEMBER THIS MEETING.
I NEVER THREW A SINGLE PUNCH.
YET YOU ATTACKED ME TWICE
NEXT TIME I WILL NO LONGER STAY MY HAND.

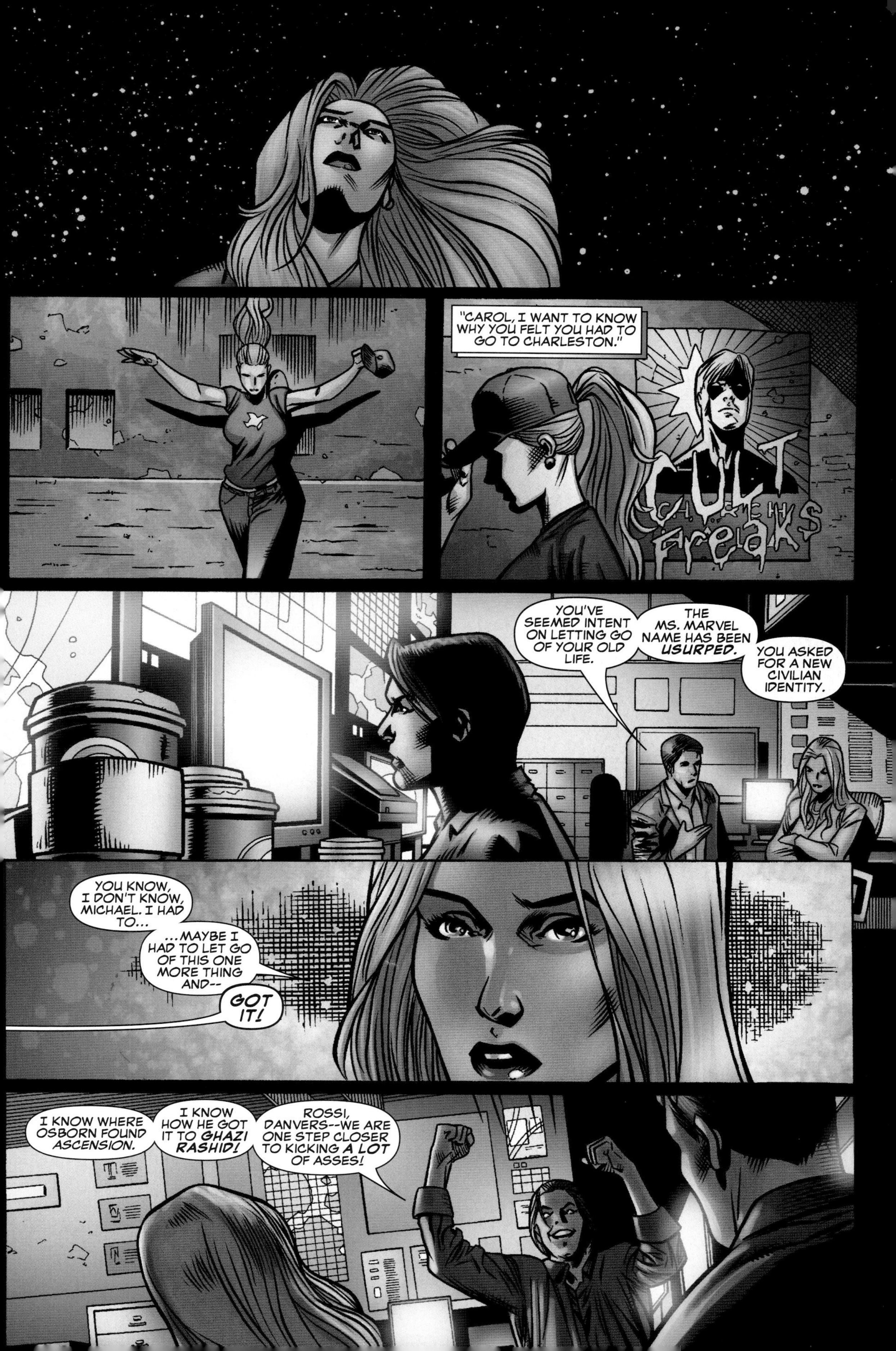
"CAROL, I WANT TO KNOW WHY YOU FELT YOU HAD TO GO TO CHARLESTON."
CULT
Freaks
YOU'VE SEEMED INTENT ON LETTING GO OF YOUR OLD LIFE.
THE MS. MARVEL NAME HAS BEEN USURPED.
YOU ASKED FOR A NEW CIVILIAN IDENTITY.
YOU KNOW, I DON'T KNOW, MICHAEL. I HAD TO...
...MAYBE I HAD TO LET GO OF THIS ONE MORE THING AND--
GOT IT!
I KNOW WHERE OSBORN FOUND ASCENSION.
I KNOW HOW HE GOT IT TO GHAZI RASHID!
ROSSI, DANVERS--WE ARE ONE STEP CLOSER TO KICKING A LOT OF ASSES!

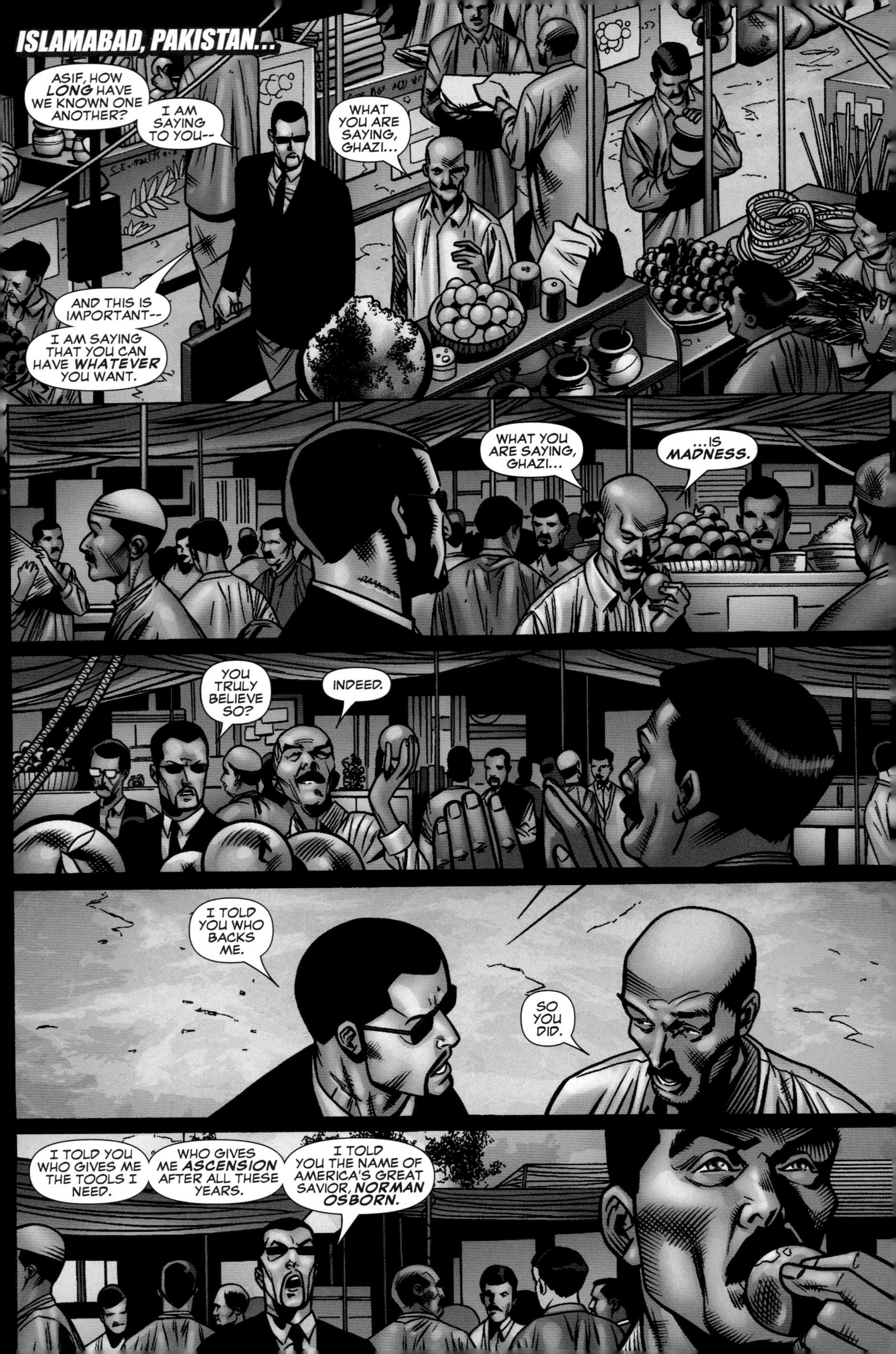
ISLAMABAD, PAKISTAN...
ASIF, HOW LONG HAVE WE KNOWN ONE ANOTHER?
I AM SAYING TO YOU--
WHAT YOU ARE SAYING, GHAZI...
AND THIS IS IMPORTANT--
I AM SAYING THAT YOU CAN HAVE WHATEVER YOU WANT.
WHAT YOU ARE SAYING, GHAZI...
...IS MADNESS.
YOU TRULY BELIEVE SO?
INDEED.
I TOLD YOU WHO BACKS ME.
SO YOU DID.
I TOLD YOU WHO GIVES ME THE TOOLS I NEED.
WHO GIVES ME ASCENSION AFTER ALL THESE YEARS.
I TOLD YOU THE NAME OF AMERICA'S GREAT SAVIOR, NORMAN OSBORN.

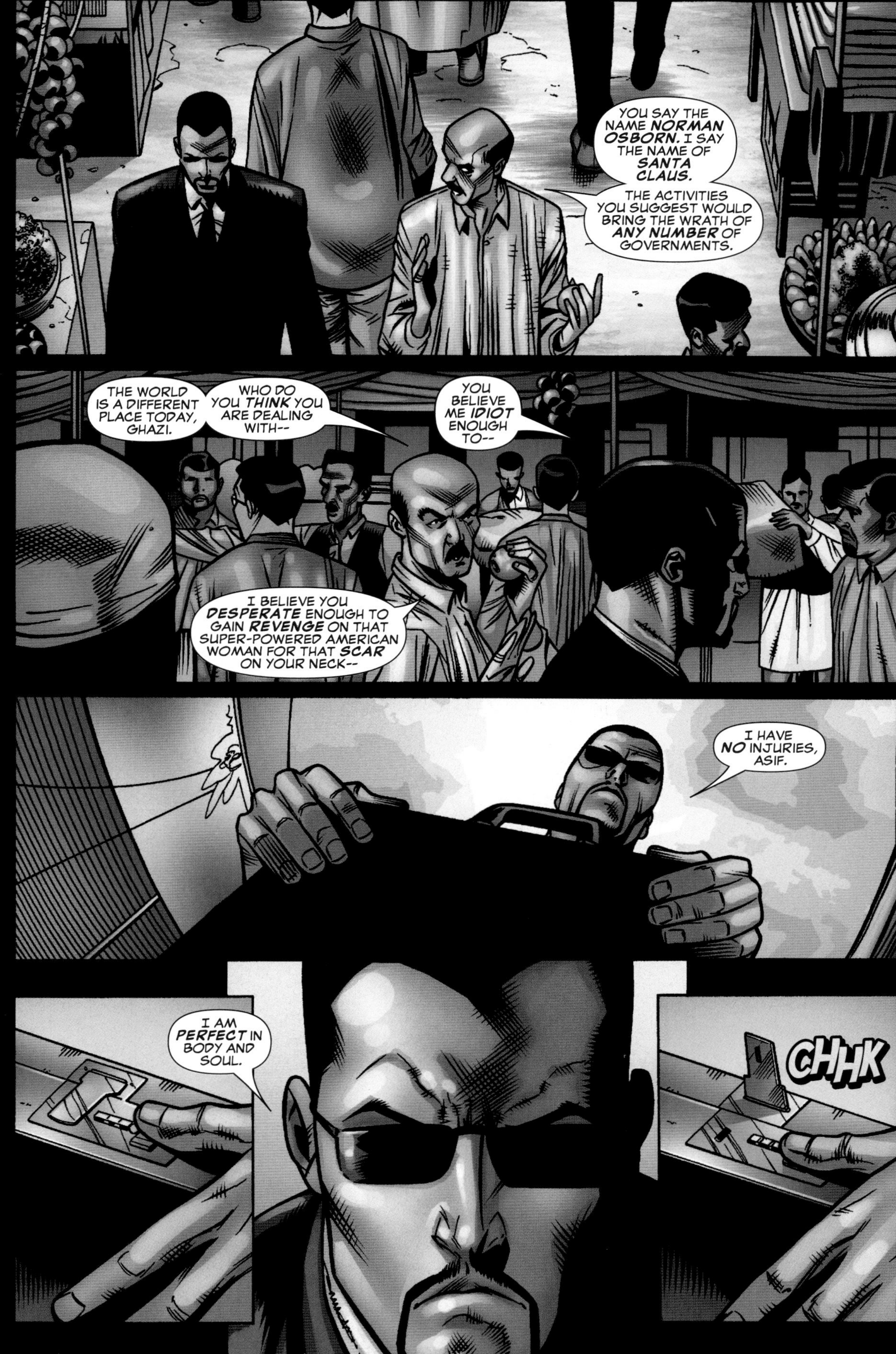

YOU SAY THE NAME NORMAN OSBORN. I SAY THE NAME OF SANTA CLAUS.
THE ACTIVITIES YOU SUGGEST WOULD BRING THE WRATH OF ANY NUMBER OF GOVERNMENTS.
THE WORLD IS A DIFFERENT PLACE TODAY, GHAZI.
WHO DO YOU THINK YOU ARE DEALING WITH--
YOU BELIEVE ME IDIOT ENOUGH TO--
I BELIEVE YOU DESPERATE ENOUGH TO GAIN REVENGE ON THAT SUPER-POWERED AMERICAN WOMAN FOR THAT SCAR ON YOUR NECK--
I HAVE NO INJURIES, ASIF.
I AM PERFECT IN BODY AND SOUL.
CHHK

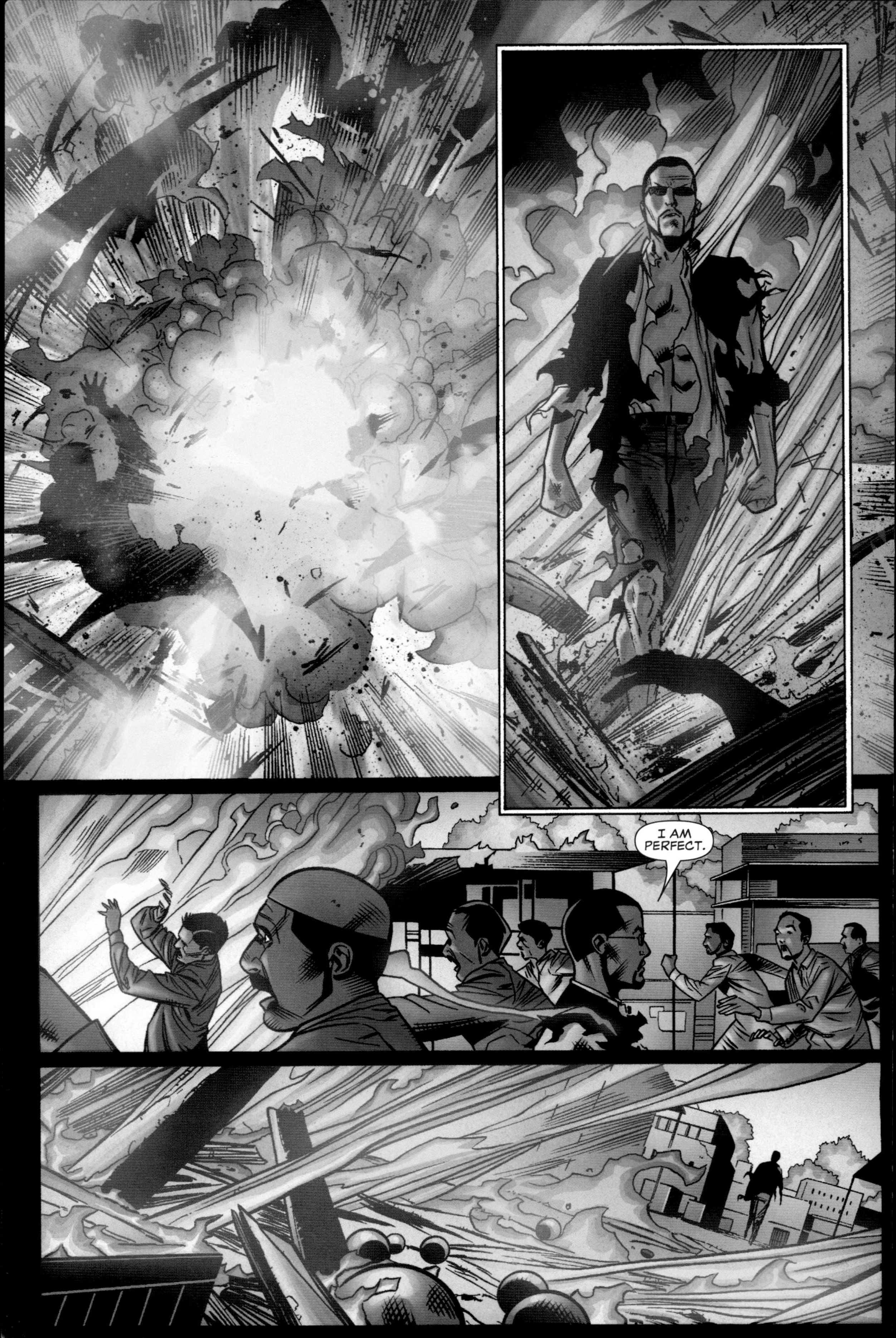
I AM PERFECT.

36

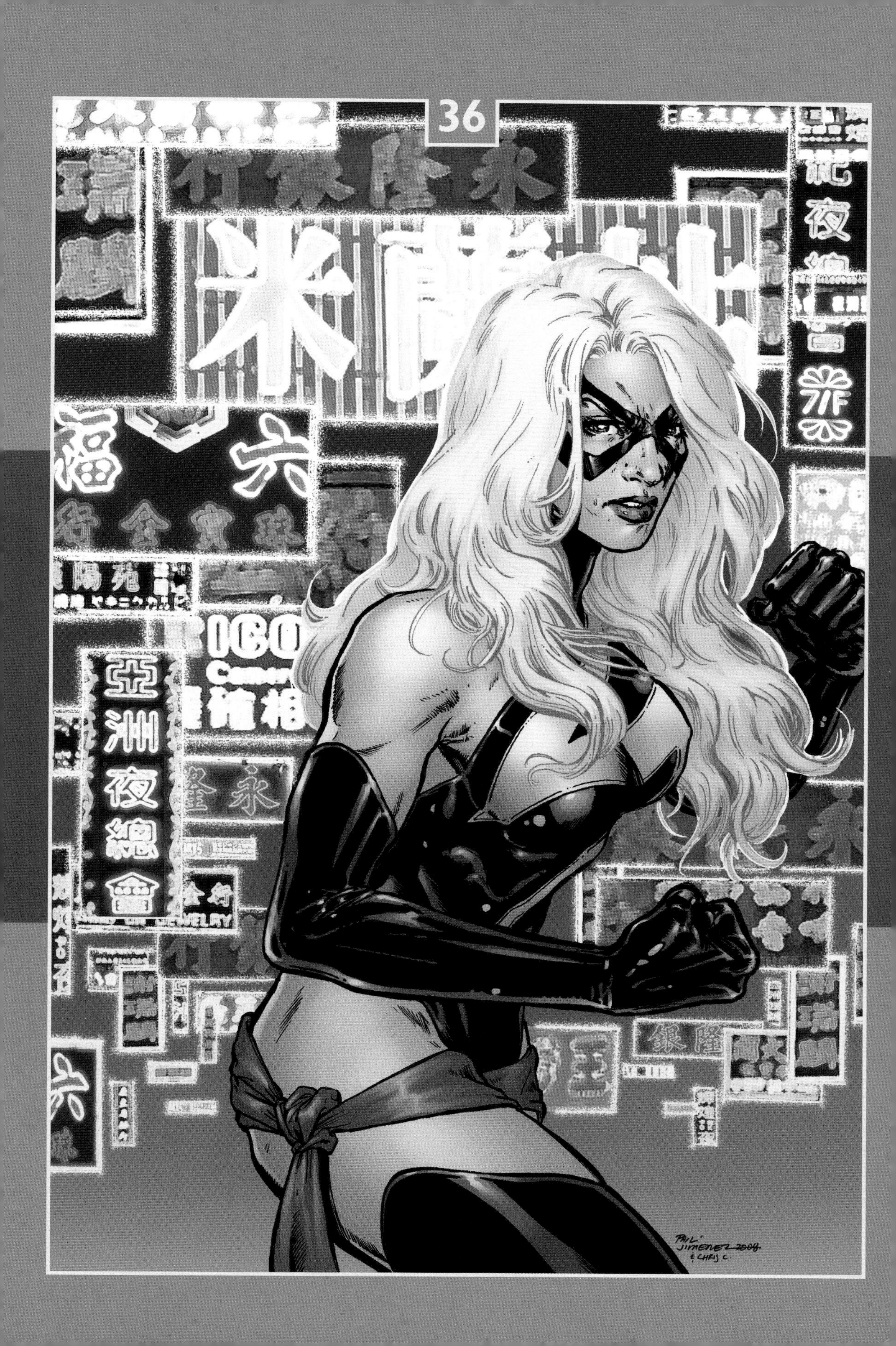

亞洲夜總會
RICO
Camera
PAUL JIMENEZ 2008 & CHRIS C.

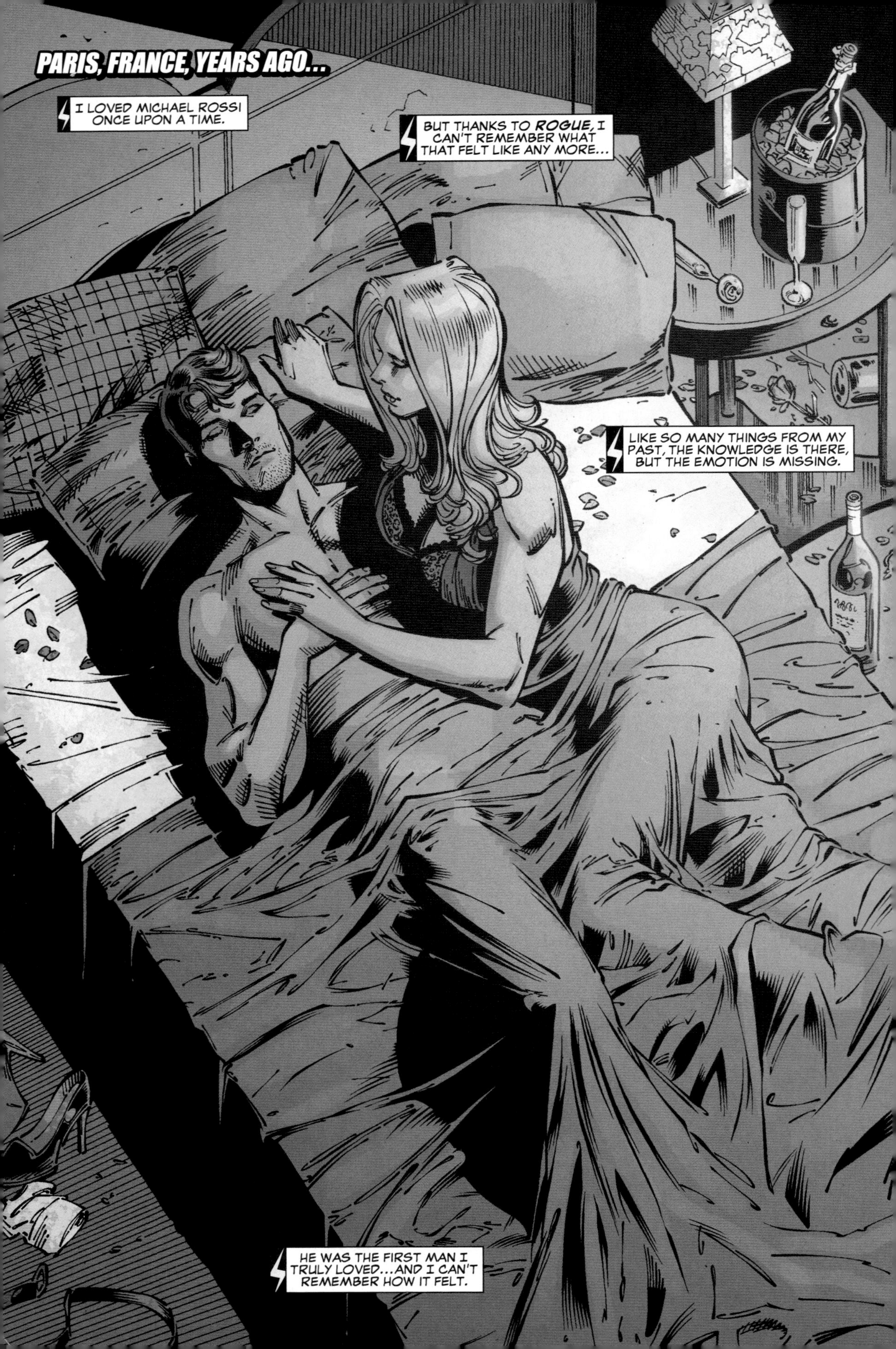
PARIS, FRANCE, YEARS AGO...
I LOVED MICHAEL ROSSI ONCE UPON A TIME.
BUT THANKS TO ROGUE, I CAN'T REMEMBER WHAT THAT FELT LIKE ANY MORE...
LIKE SO MANY THINGS FROM MY PAST, THE KNOWLEDGE IS THERE, BUT THE EMOTION IS MISSING.
HE WAS THE FIRST MAN I TRULY LOVED...AND I CAN'T REMEMBER HOW IT FELT.

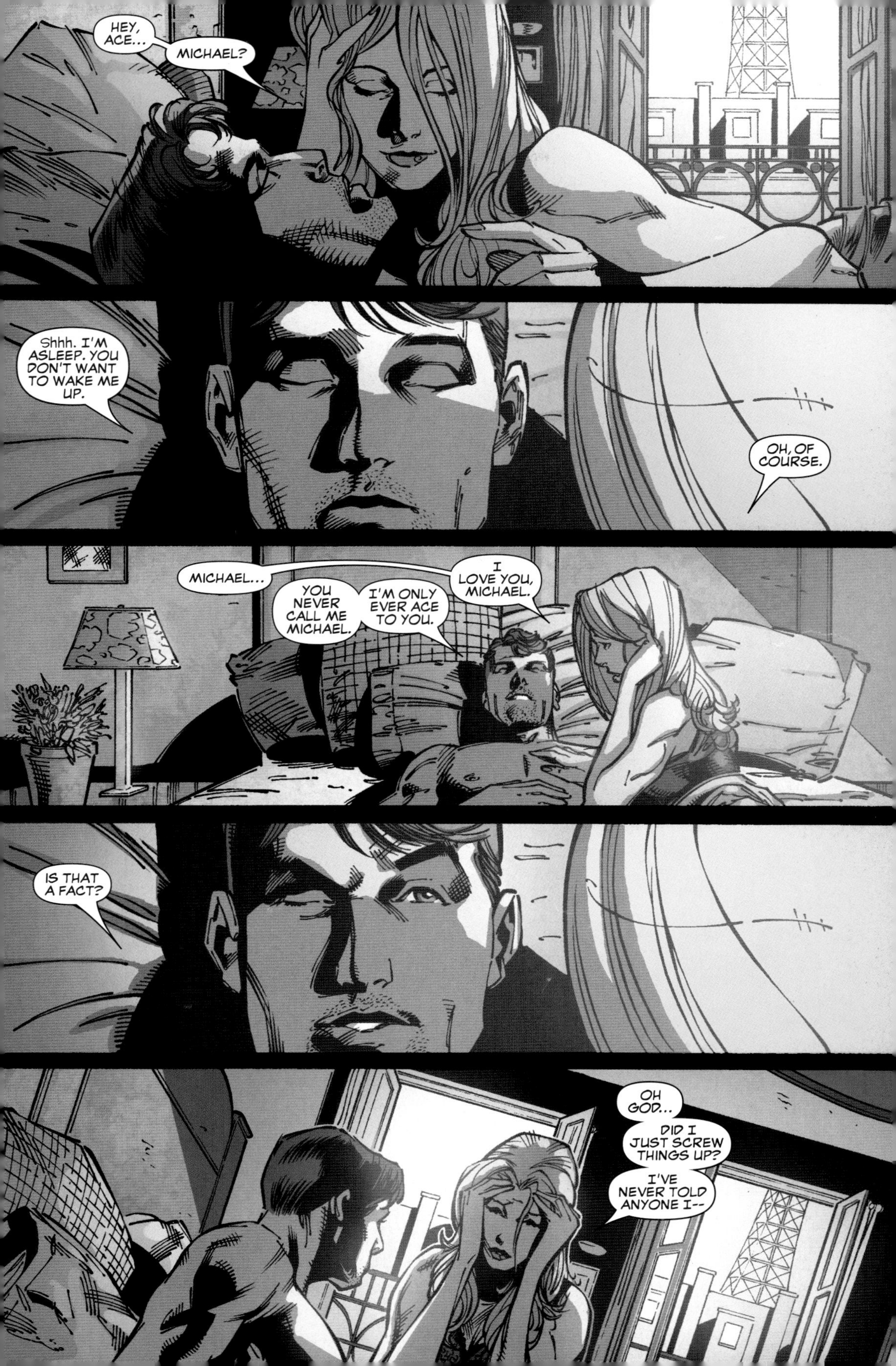
HEY, ACE...
MICHAEL?
Shhh. I'M ASLEEP. YOU DON'T WANT TO WAKE ME UP.
OH, OF COURSE.
MICHAEL...
I LOVE YOU, MICHAEL.
YOU NEVER CALL ME MICHAEL.
I'M ONLY EVER ACE TO YOU.
IS THAT A FACT?
OH GOD...
DID I JUST SCREW THINGS UP?
I'VE NEVER TOLD ANYONE I--

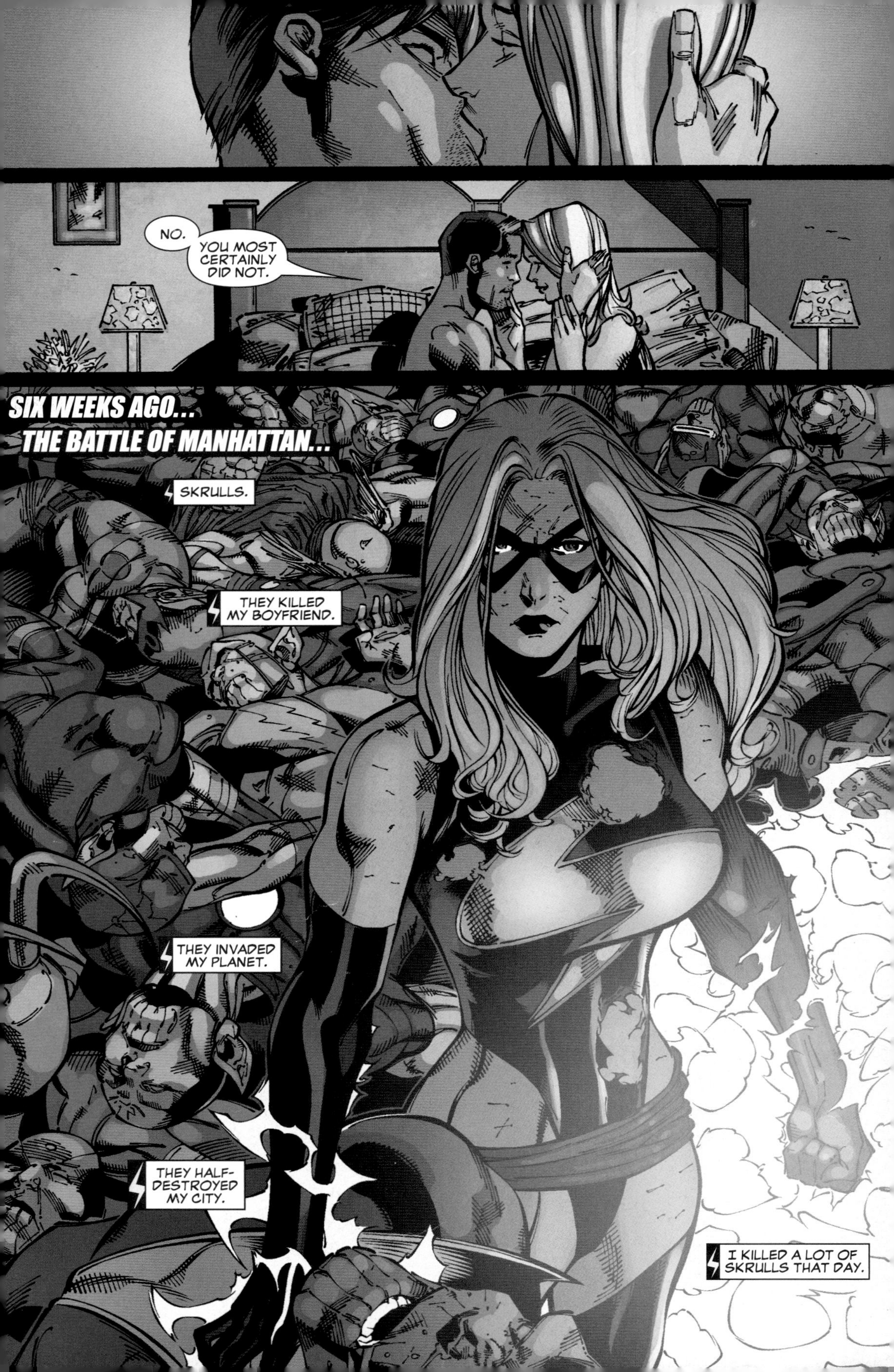
NO.
YOU MOST CERTAINLY DID NOT.
SIX WEEKS AGO...
THE BATTLE OF MANHATTAN...
SKRULLS.
THEY KILLED MY BOYFRIEND.
THEY INVADED MY PLANET.
THEY HALF-DESTROYED MY CITY.
I KILLED A LOT OF SKRULLS THAT DAY.

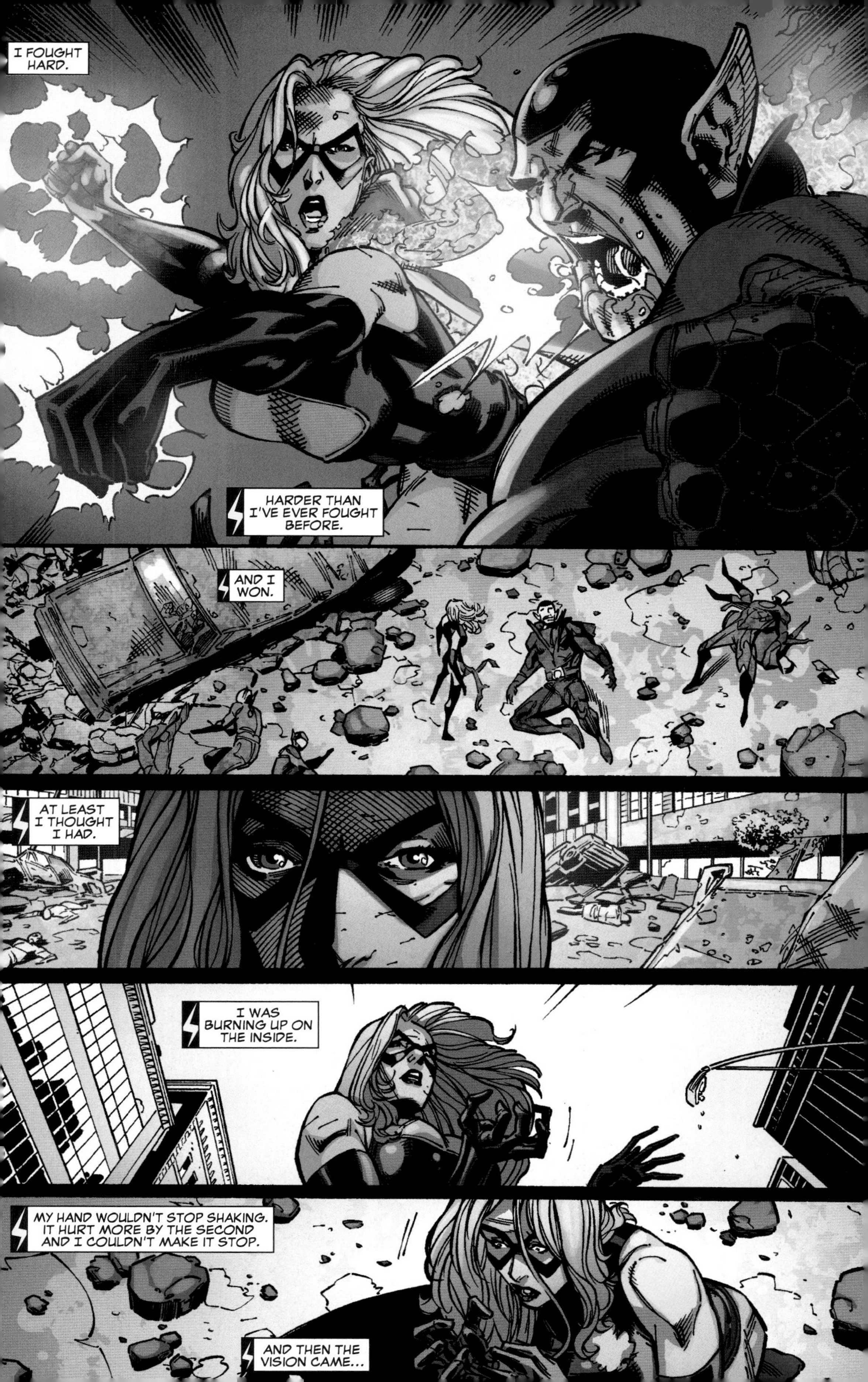
I FOUGHT HARD.
HARDER THAN I'VE EVER FOUGHT BEFORE.
AND I WON.
AT LEAST I THOUGHT I HAD.
I WAS BURNING UP ON THE INSIDE.
MY HAND WOULDN'T STOP SHAKING. IT HURT MORE BY THE SECOND AND I COULDN'T MAKE IT STOP.
AND THEN THE VISION CAME...

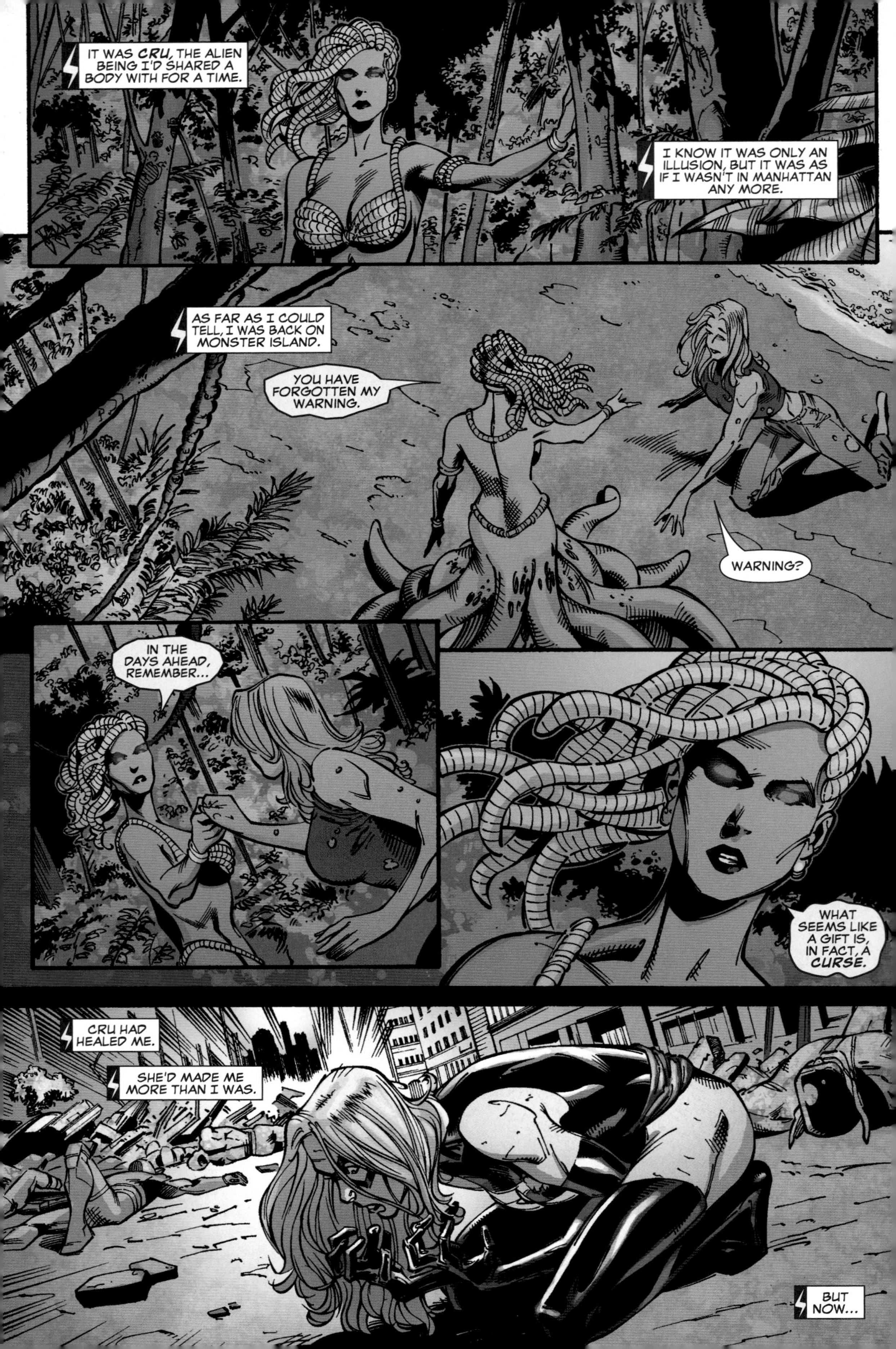
IT WAS CRU, THE ALIEN BEING I'D SHARED A BODY WITH FOR A TIME.
I KNOW IT WAS ONLY AN ILLUSION, BUT IT WAS AS IF I WASN'T IN MANHATTAN ANY MORE.
AS FAR AS I COULD TELL, I WAS BACK ON MONSTER ISLAND.
YOU HAVE FORGOTTEN MY WARNING.
WARNING?
IN THE DAYS AHEAD, REMEMBER...
WHAT SEEMS LIKE A GIFT IS, IN FACT, A CURSE.
CRU HAD HEALED ME.
SHE'D MADE ME MORE THAN I WAS.
BUT NOW...

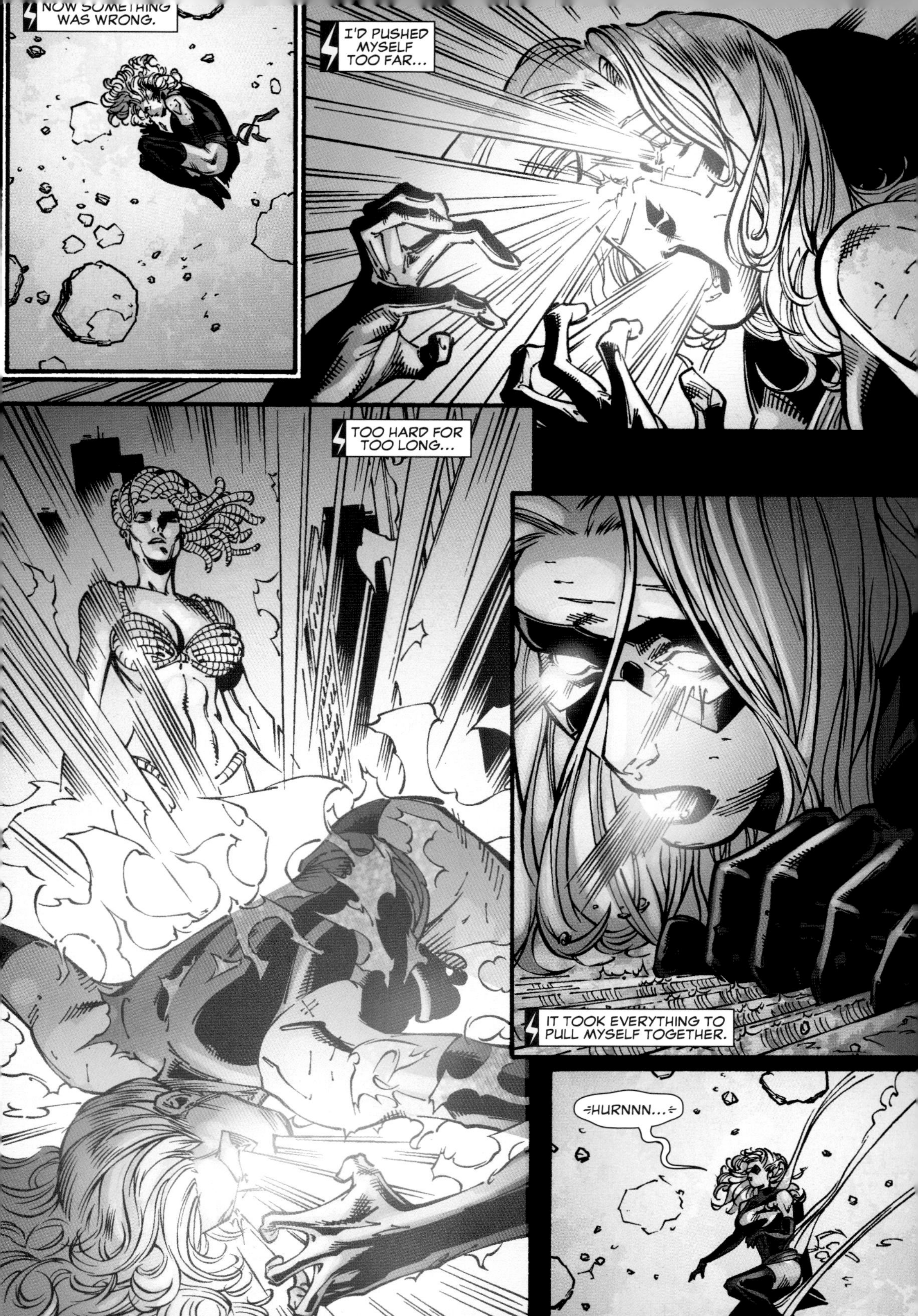
NOW SOMETHING WAS WRONG.
I'D PUSHED MYSELF TOO FAR...
TOO HARD FOR TOO LONG...
IT TOOK EVERYTHING TO PULL MYSELF TOGETHER.
HURNNN...

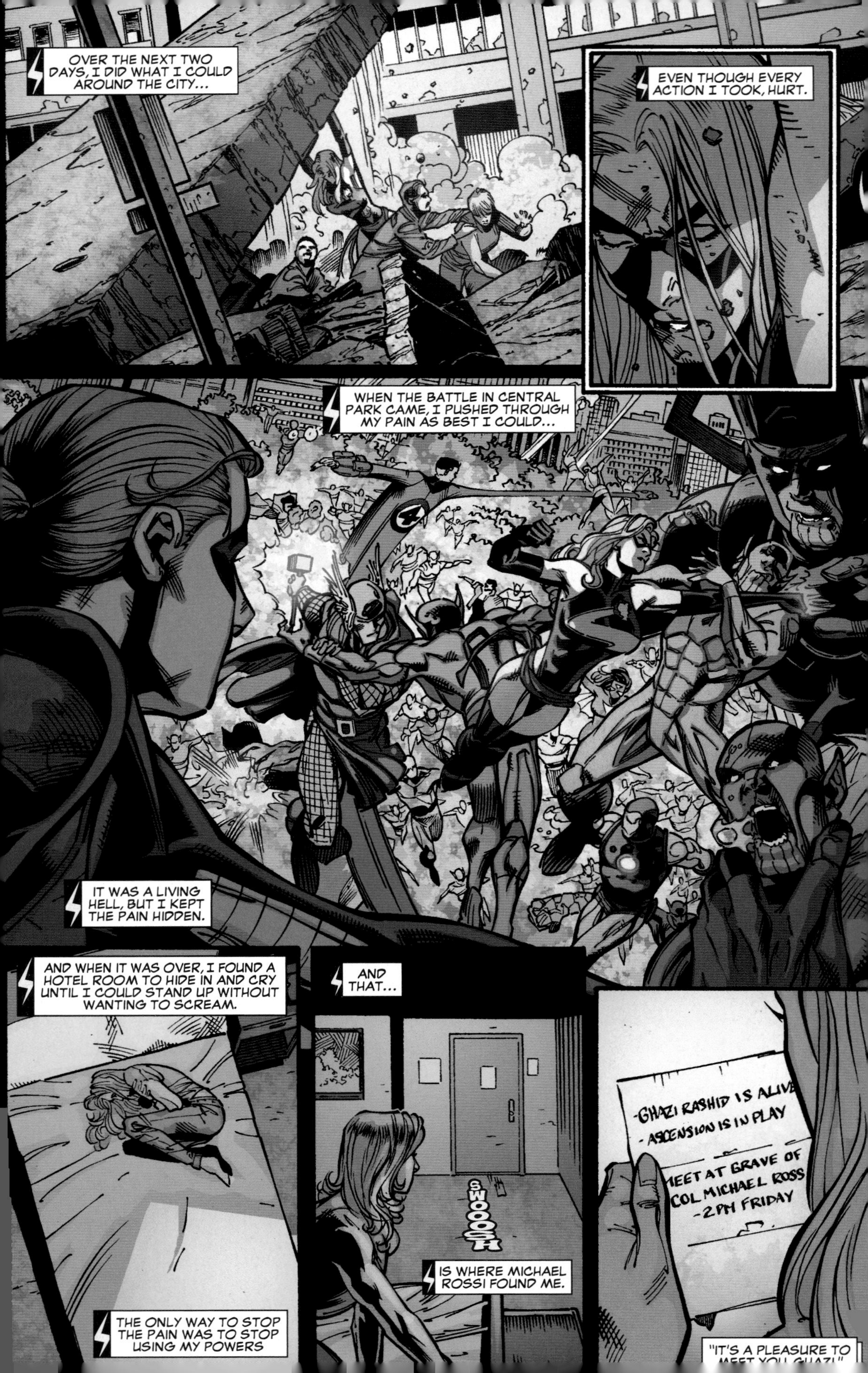
OVER THE NEXT TWO DAYS, I DID WHAT I COULD AROUND THE CITY...
EVEN THOUGH EVERY ACTION I TOOK, HURT.
WHEN THE BATTLE IN CENTRAL PARK CAME, I PUSHED THROUGH MY PAIN AS BEST I COULD...
IT WAS A LIVING HELL, BUT I KEPT THE PAIN HIDDEN.
AND WHEN IT WAS OVER, I FOUND A HOTEL ROOM TO HIDE IN AND CRY UNTIL I COULD STAND UP WITHOUT WANTING TO SCREAM.
THE ONLY WAY TO STOP THE PAIN WAS TO STOP USING MY POWERS
AND THAT...
SWOOOSH
IS WHERE MICHAEL ROSSI FOUND ME.
-GHAZI RASHID IS ALIVE
-ASCENSION IS IN PLAY
MEET AT GRAVE OF COL MICHAEL ROSS
-2PM FRIDAY
"IT'S A PLEASURE TO

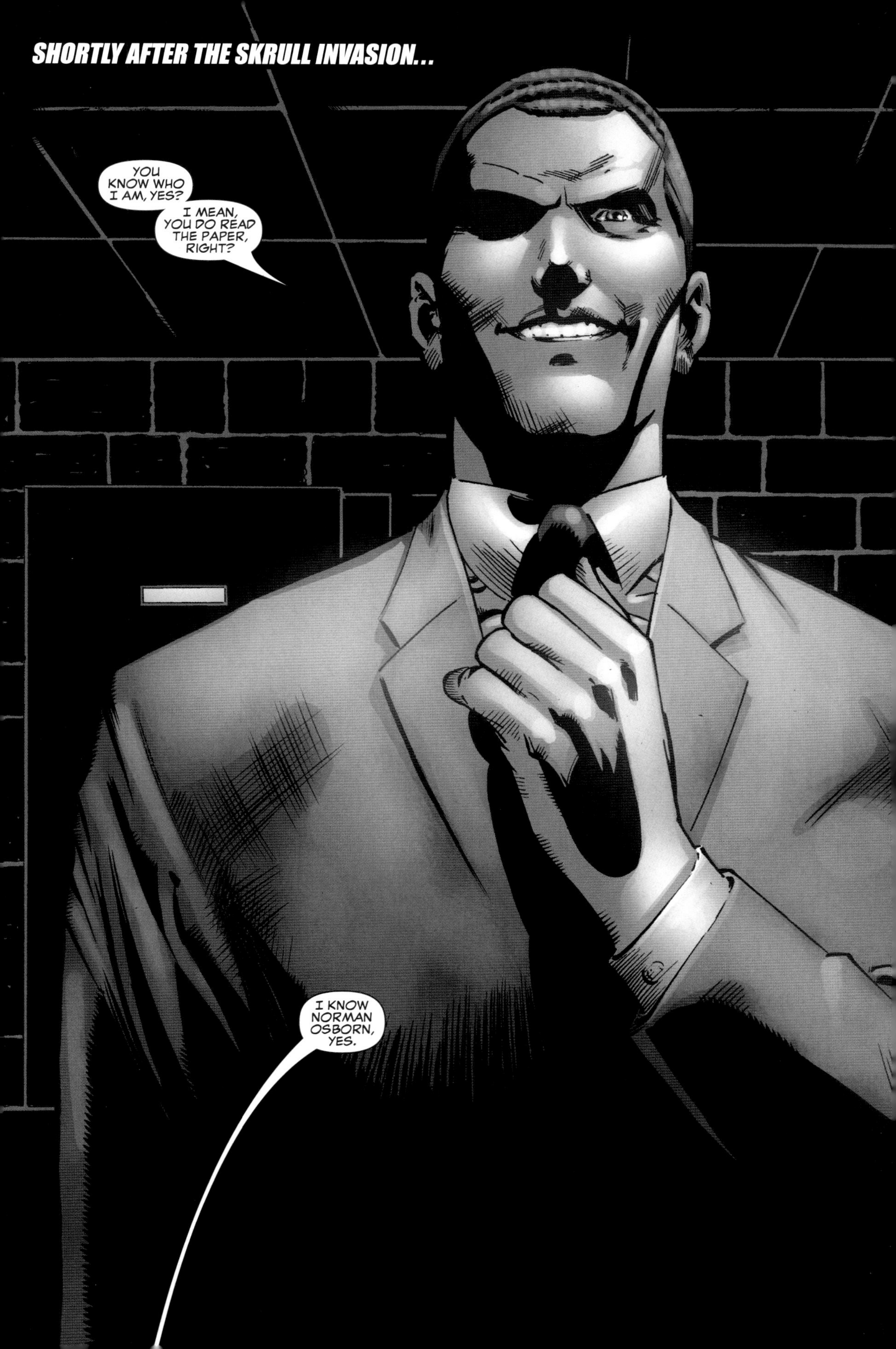
SHORTLY AFTER THE SKRULL INVASION...
YOU KNOW WHO I AM, YES?
I MEAN, YOU DO READ THE PAPER, RIGHT?
I KNOW NORMAN OSBORN, YES.

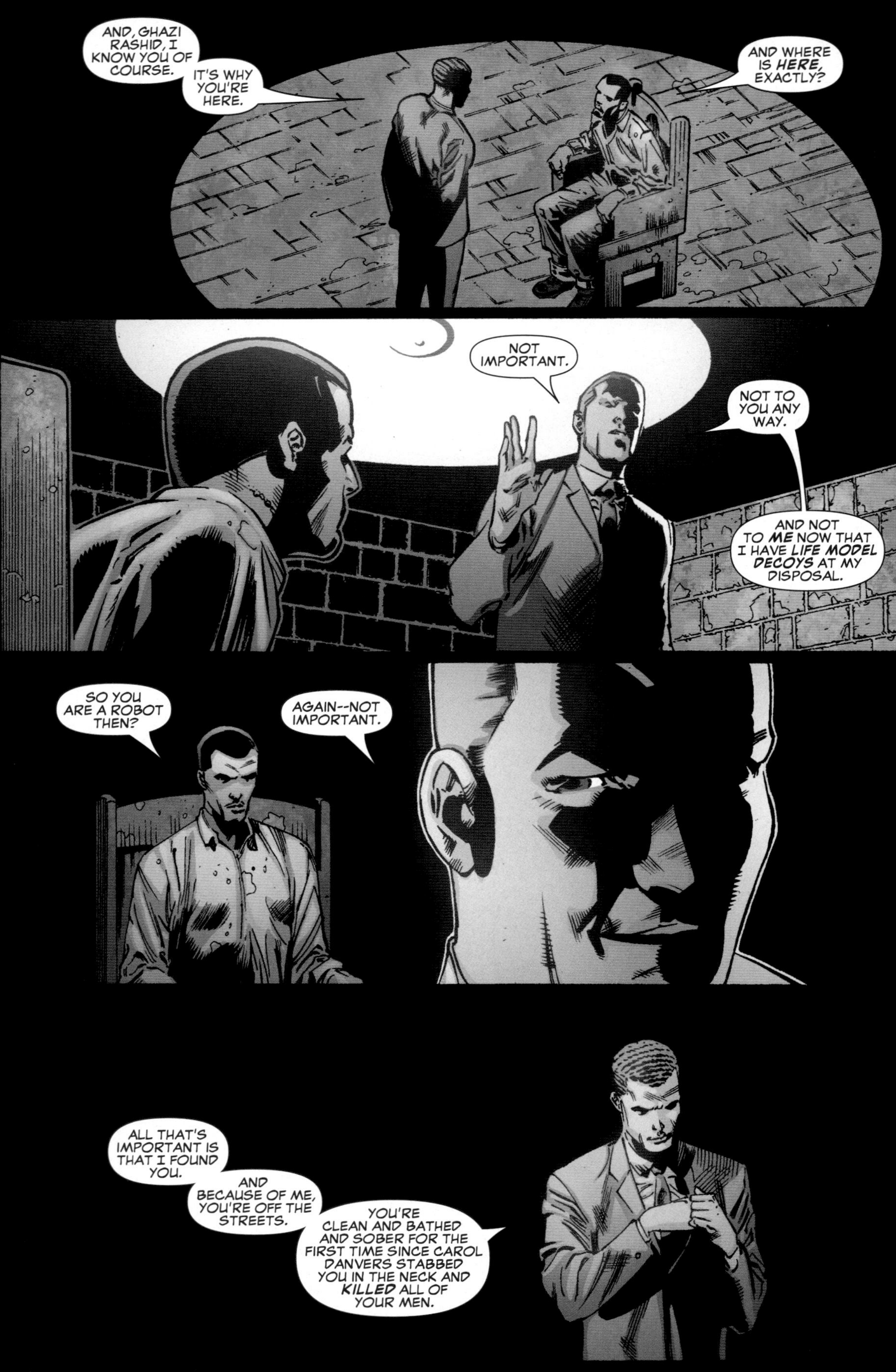

AND, GHAZI RASHID, I KNOW YOU OF COURSE.
IT'S WHY YOU'RE HERE.
AND WHERE IS HERE, EXACTLY?
NOT IMPORTANT.
NOT TO YOU ANY WAY.
AND NOT TO ME NOW THAT I HAVE LIFE MODEL DECOYS AT MY DISPOSAL.
SO YOU ARE A ROBOT THEN?
AGAIN--NOT IMPORTANT.
ALL THAT'S IMPORTANT IS THAT I FOUND YOU.
AND BECAUSE OF ME, YOU'RE OFF THE STREETS.
YOU'RE CLEAN AND BATHED AND SOBER FOR THE FIRST TIME SINCE CAROL DANVERS STABBED YOU IN THE NECK AND KILLED ALL OF YOUR MEN.

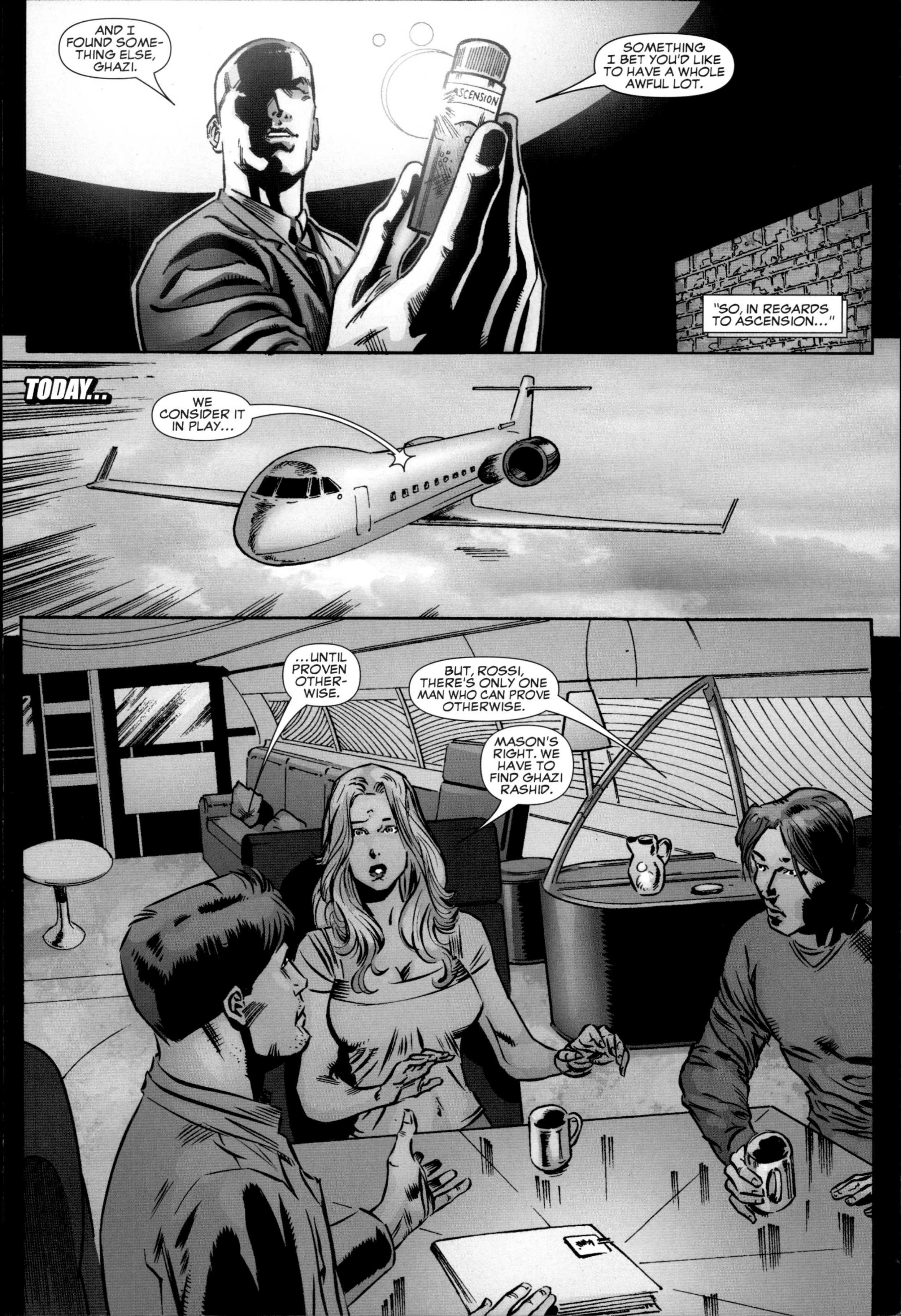
AND I FOUND SOME-THING ELSE, GHAZI.
ASCENSION
SOMETHING I BET YOU'D LIKE TO HAVE A WHOLE AWFUL LOT.
"SO, IN REGARDS TO ASCENSION..."
TODAY...
WE CONSIDER IT IN PLAY...
...UNTIL PROVEN OTHER-WISE.
BUT, ROSSI, THERE'S ONLY ONE MAN WHO CAN PROVE OTHERWISE.
MASON'S RIGHT. WE HAVE TO FIND GHAZI RASHID.

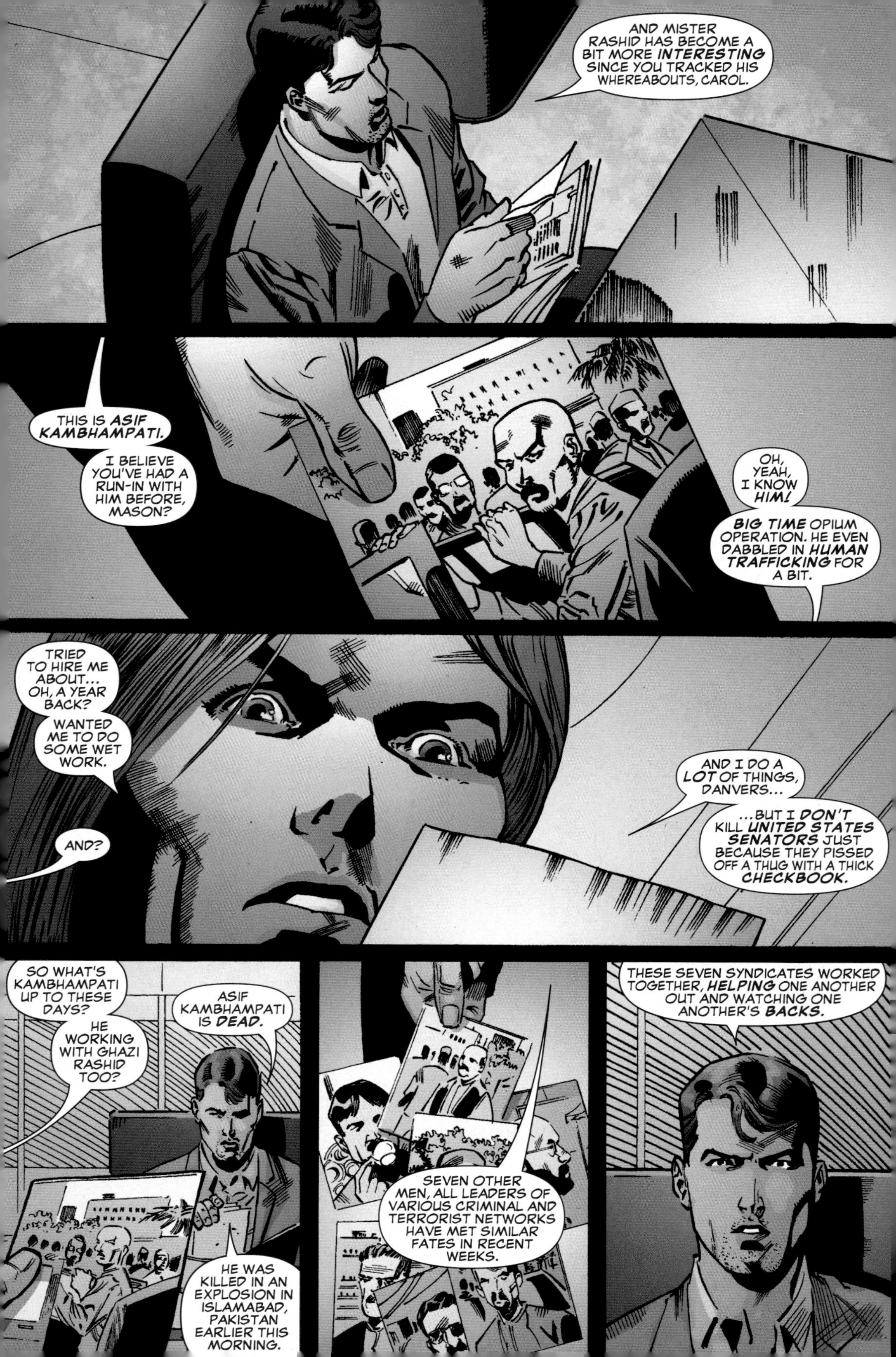
AND MISTER RASHID HAS BECOME A BIT MORE INTERESTING SINCE YOU TRACKED HIS WHEREABOUTS, CAROL.
THIS IS ASIF KAMBHAMPATI.
I BELIEVE YOU'VE HAD A RUN-IN WITH HIM BEFORE, MASON?
OH, YEAH, I KNOW HIM!
BIG TIME OPIUM OPERATION. HE EVEN DABBLED IN HUMAN TRAFFICKING FOR A BIT.
TRIED TO HIRE ME ABOUT... OH, A YEAR BACK?
WANTED ME TO DO SOME WET WORK.
AND?
AND I DO A LOT OF THINGS, DANVERS...
...BUT I DON'T KILL UNITED STATES SENATORS JUST BECAUSE THEY PISSED OFF A THUG WITH A THICK CHECKBOOK.
SO WHAT'S KAMBHAMPATI UP TO THESE DAYS?
HE WORKING WITH GHAZI RASHID TOO?
ASIF KAMBHAMPATI IS DEAD.
HE WAS KILLED IN AN EXPLOSION IN ISLAMABAD, PAKISTAN EARLIER THIS MORNING.
SEVEN OTHER MEN, ALL LEADERS OF VARIOUS CRIMINAL AND TERRORIST NETWORKS HAVE MET SIMILAR FATES IN RECENT WEEKS.
THESE SEVEN SYNDICATES WORKED TOGETHER, HELPING ONE ANOTHER OUT AND WATCHING ONE ANOTHER'S BACKS.

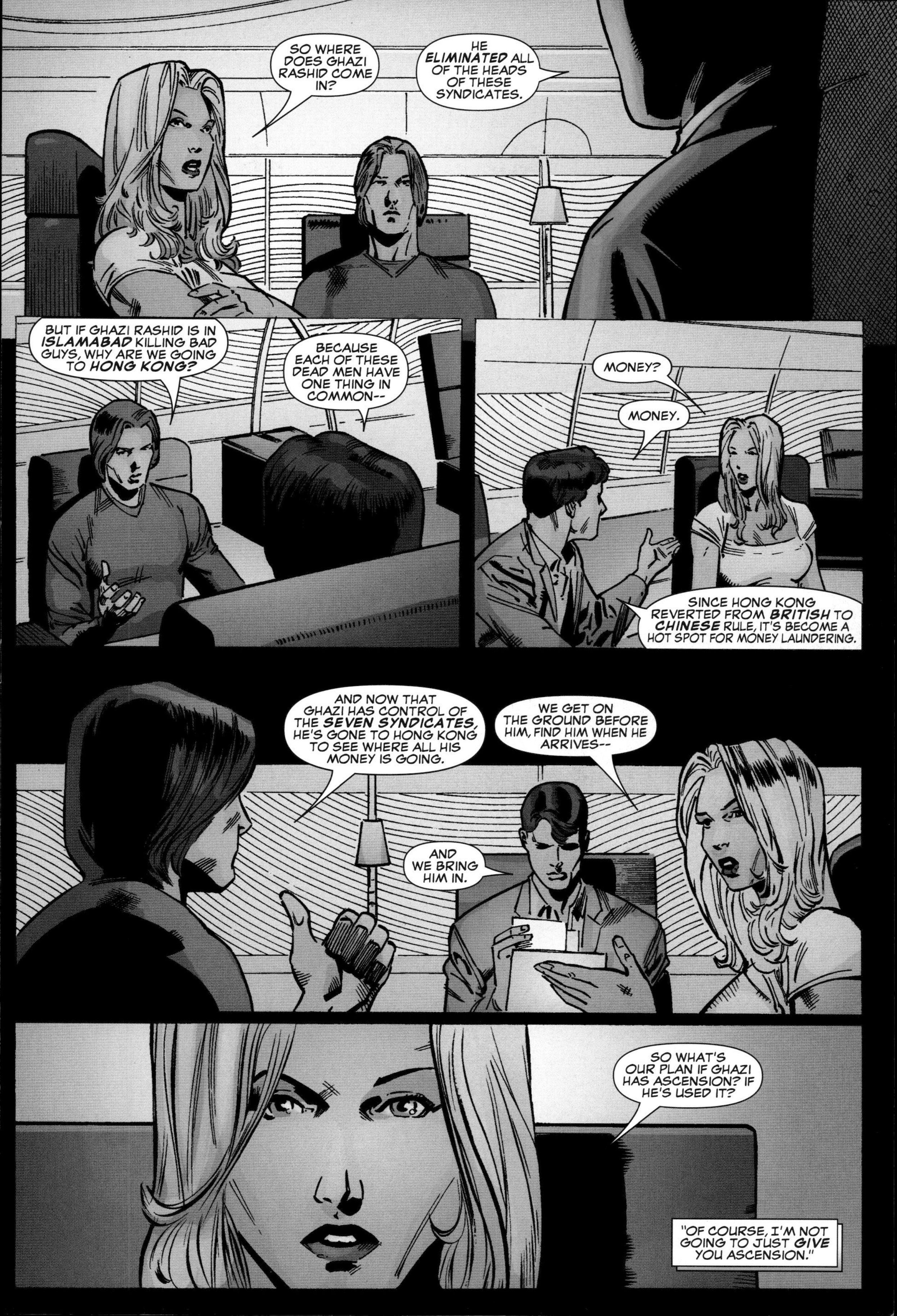
SO WHERE DOES GHAZI RASHID COME IN?
HE *ELIMINATED* ALL OF THE HEADS OF THESE SYNDICATES.
BUT IF GHAZI RASHID IS IN *ISLAMABAD* KILLING BAD GUYS, WHY ARE WE GOING TO *HONG KONG?*
BECAUSE EACH OF THESE DEAD MEN HAVE ONE THING IN COMMON--
MONEY?
MONEY.
SINCE HONG KONG REVERTED FROM *BRITISH* TO *CHINESE* RULE, IT'S BECOME A HOT SPOT FOR MONEY LAUNDERING.
AND NOW THAT GHAZI HAS CONTROL OF THE *SEVEN SYNDICATES,* HE'S GONE TO HONG KONG TO SEE WHERE ALL HIS MONEY IS GOING.
WE GET ON THE GROUND BEFORE HIM, FIND HIM WHEN HE ARRIVES--
AND WE BRING HIM IN.
SO WHAT'S OUR PLAN IF GHAZI HAS ASCENSION? IF HE'S USED IT?
"OF COURSE, I'M NOT GOING TO JUST *GIVE* YOU ASCENSION."

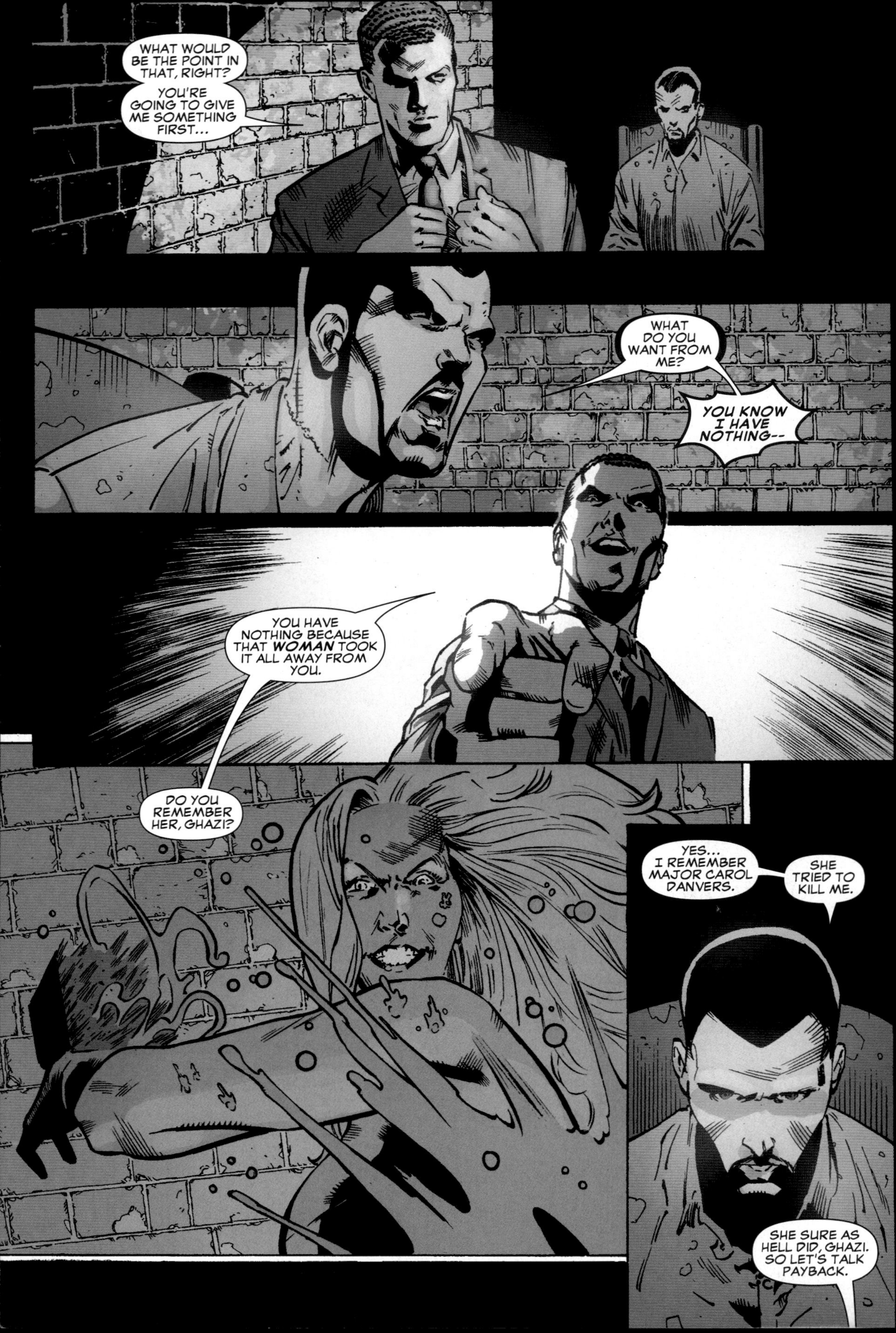
WHAT WOULD BE THE POINT IN THAT, RIGHT?
YOU'RE GOING TO GIVE ME SOMETHING FIRST...
WHAT DO YOU WANT FROM ME?
YOU KNOW I HAVE NOTHING--
YOU HAVE NOTHING BECAUSE THAT WOMAN TOOK IT ALL AWAY FROM YOU.
DO YOU REMEMBER HER, GHAZI?
YES... I REMEMBER MAJOR CAROL DANVERS.
SHE TRIED TO KILL ME.
SHE SURE AS HELL DID, GHAZI. SO LET'S TALK PAYBACK.

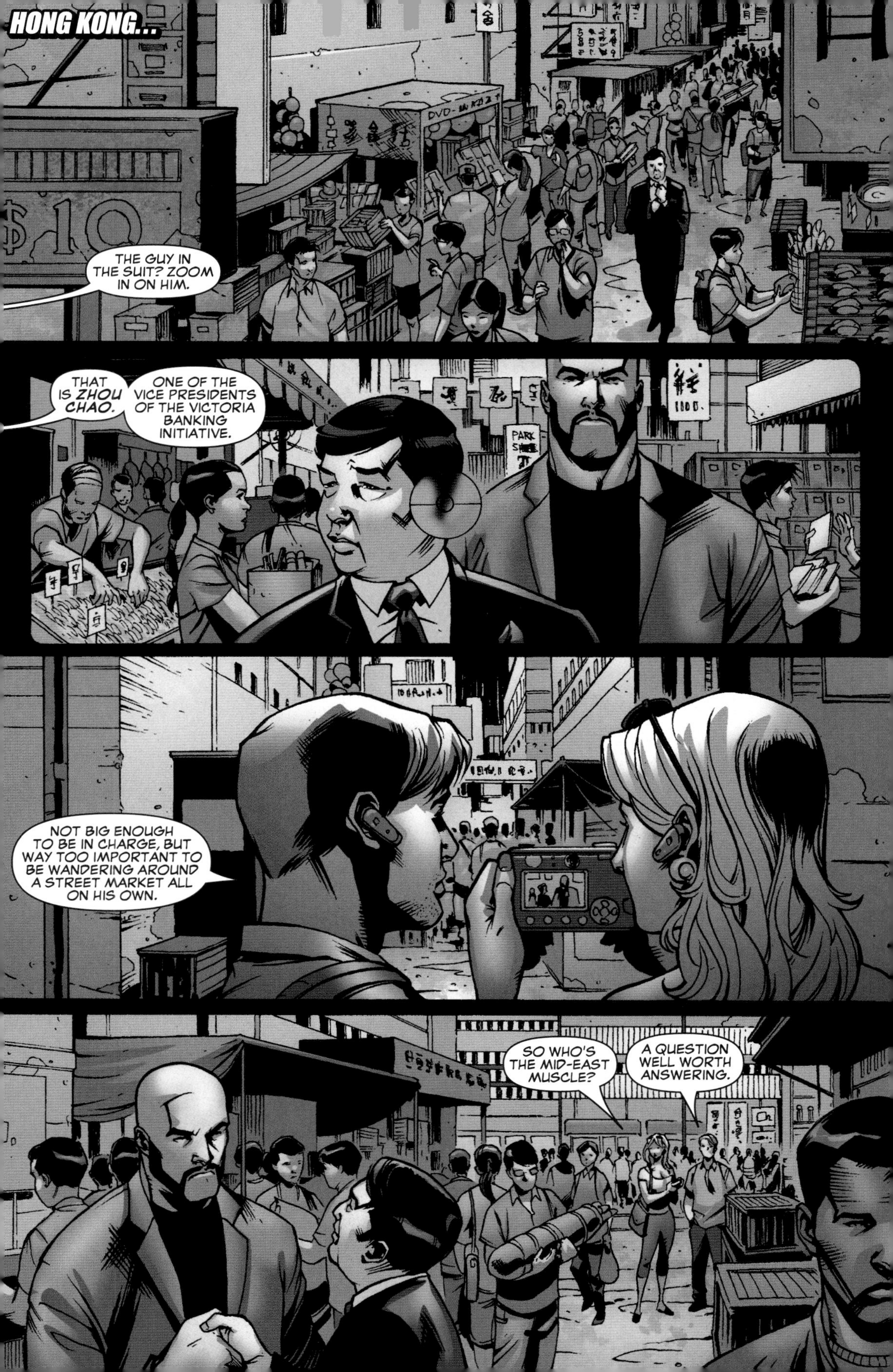
HONG KONG...
$10
THE GUY IN THE SUIT? ZOOM IN ON HIM.
THAT IS ZHOU CHAO.
ONE OF THE VICE PRESIDENTS OF THE VICTORIA BANKING INITIATIVE.
PARK
NOT BIG ENOUGH TO BE IN CHARGE, BUT WAY TOO IMPORTANT TO BE WANDERING AROUND A STREET MARKET ALL ON HIS OWN.
SO WHO'S THE MID-EAST MUSCLE?
A QUESTION WELL WORTH ANSWERING.

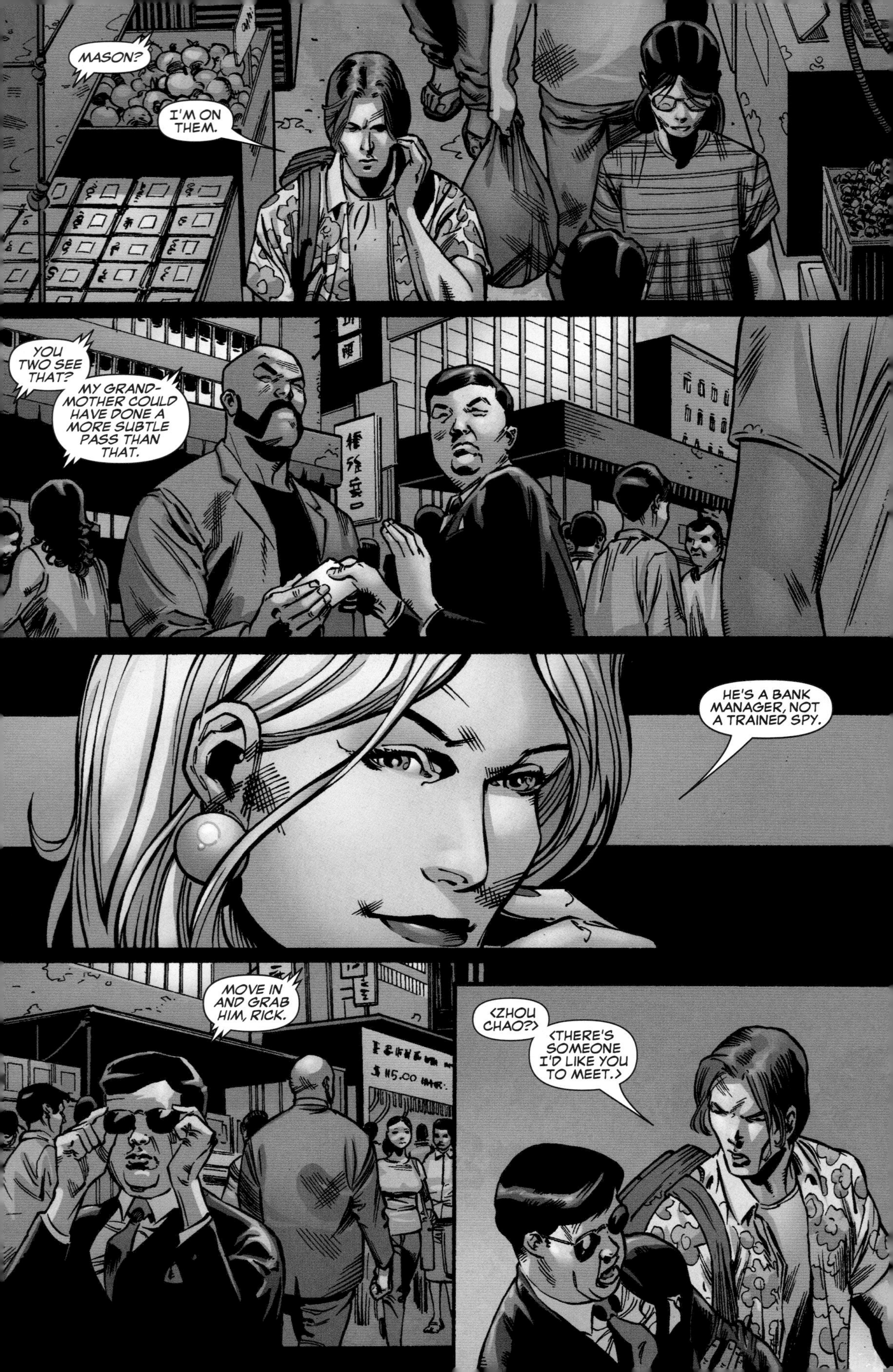
MASON?
I'M ON THEM.
YOU TWO SEE THAT?
MY GRAND-MOTHER COULD HAVE DONE A MORE SUBTLE PASS THAN THAT.
HE'S A BANK MANAGER, NOT A TRAINED SPY.
MOVE IN AND GRAB HIM, RICK.
<ZHOU CHAO?>
<THERE'S SOMEONE I'D LIKE YOU TO MEET.>

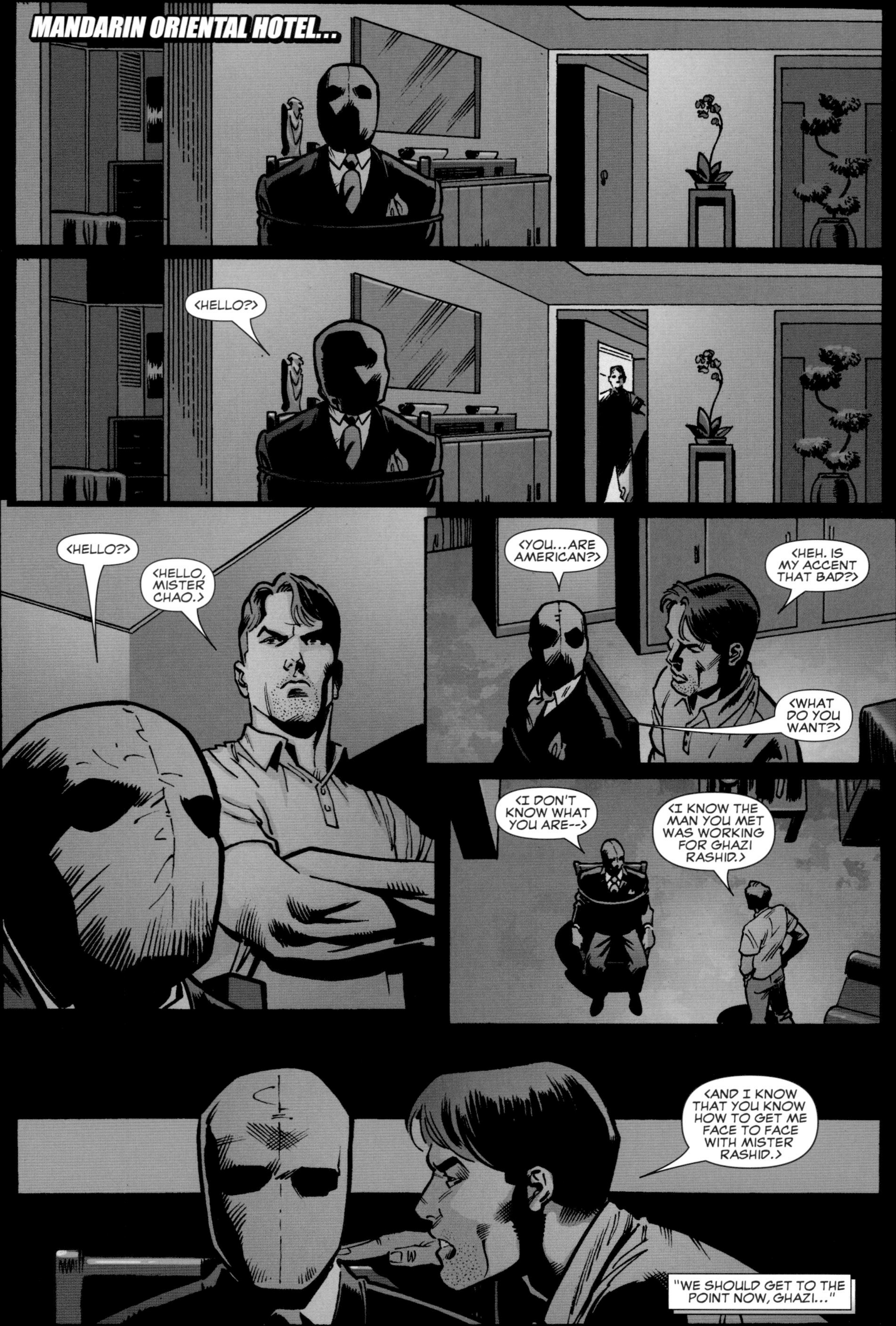
MANDARIN ORIENTAL HOTEL...
<HELLO?>
<HELLO?>
<HELLO, MISTER CHAO.>
<YOU...ARE AMERICAN?>
<HEH. IS MY ACCENT THAT BAD?>
<WHAT DO YOU WANT?>
<I DON'T KNOW WHAT YOU ARE-->
<I KNOW THE MAN YOU MET WAS WORKING FOR GHAZI RASHID.>
<AND I KNOW THAT YOU KNOW HOW TO GET ME FACE TO FACE WITH MISTER RASHID.>
"WE SHOULD GET TO THE POINT NOW, GHAZI..."

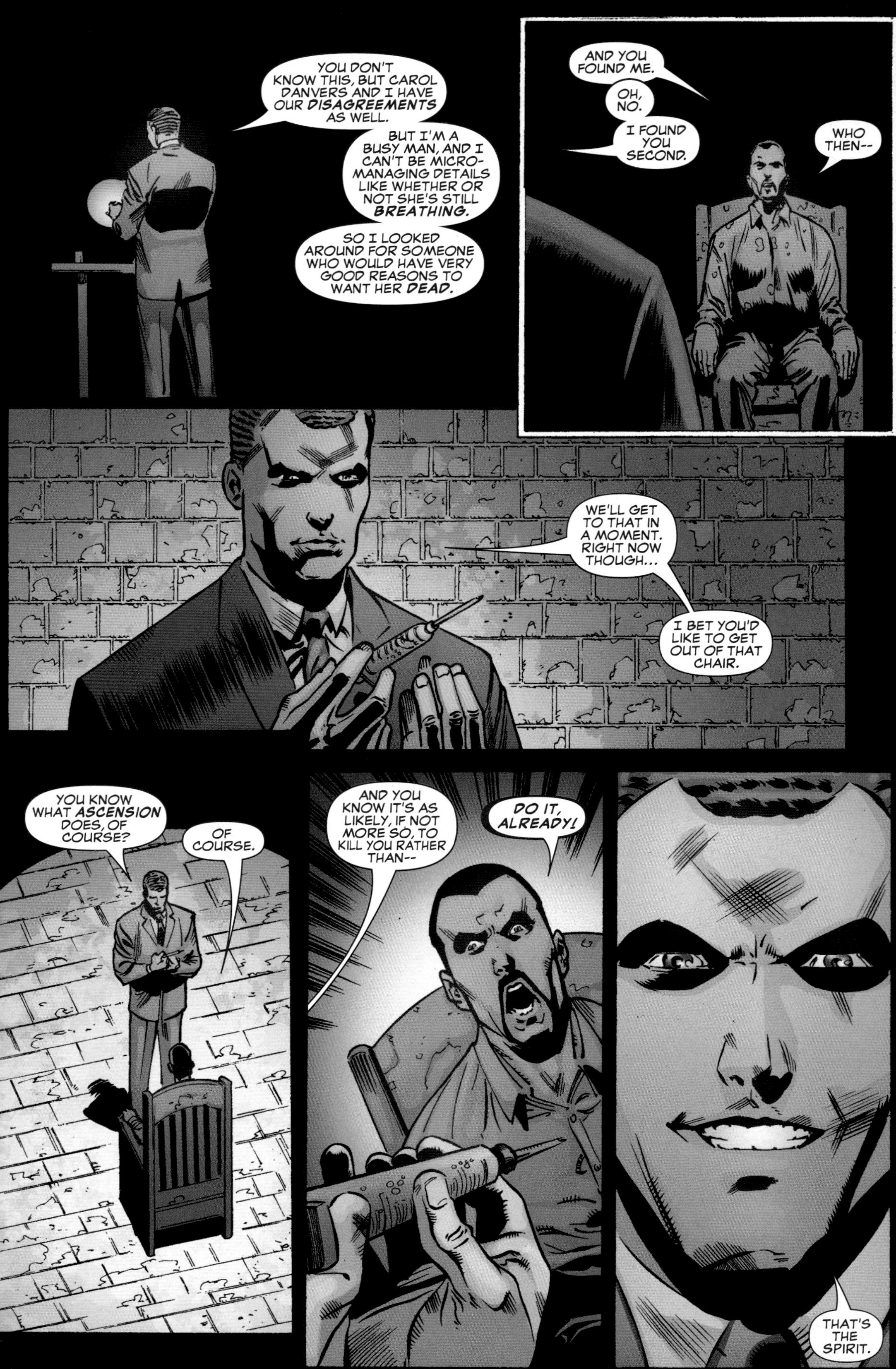
YOU DON'T KNOW THIS, BUT CAROL DANVERS AND I HAVE OUR DISAGREEMENTS AS WELL.
BUT I'M A BUSY MAN, AND I CAN'T BE MICRO-MANAGING DETAILS LIKE WHETHER OR NOT SHE'S STILL BREATHING.
SO I LOOKED AROUND FOR SOMEONE WHO WOULD HAVE VERY GOOD REASONS TO WANT HER DEAD.
AND YOU FOUND ME.
OH, NO.
I FOUND YOU SECOND.
WHO THEN--
WE'LL GET TO THAT IN A MOMENT. RIGHT NOW THOUGH...
I BET YOU'D LIKE TO GET OUT OF THAT CHAIR.
YOU KNOW WHAT ASCENSION DOES, OF COURSE?
OF COURSE.
AND YOU KNOW IT'S AS LIKELY, IF NOT MORE SO, TO KILL YOU RATHER THAN--
DO IT, ALREADY!
THAT'S THE SPIRIT.

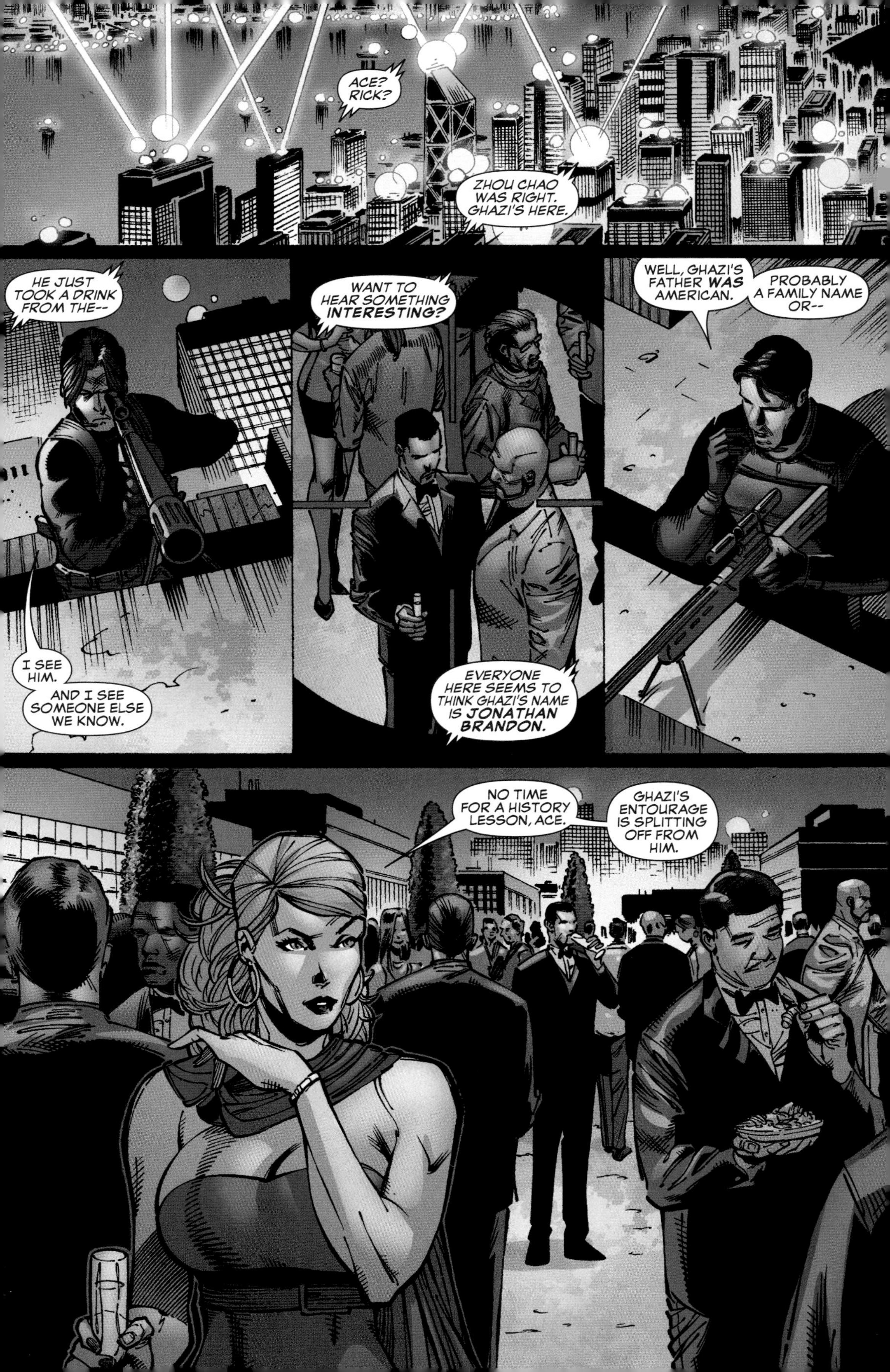

ACE? RICK?
ZHOU CHAO WAS RIGHT. GHAZI'S HERE.
HE JUST TOOK A DRINK FROM THE--
I SEE HIM.
AND I SEE SOMEONE ELSE WE KNOW.
WANT TO HEAR SOMETHING **INTERESTING?**
EVERYONE HERE SEEMS TO THINK GHAZI'S NAME IS **JONATHAN BRANDON.**
WELL, GHAZI'S FATHER **WAS** AMERICAN.
PROBABLY A FAMILY NAME OR--
NO TIME FOR A HISTORY LESSON, ACE.
GHAZI'S ENTOURAGE IS SPLITTING OFF FROM HIM.

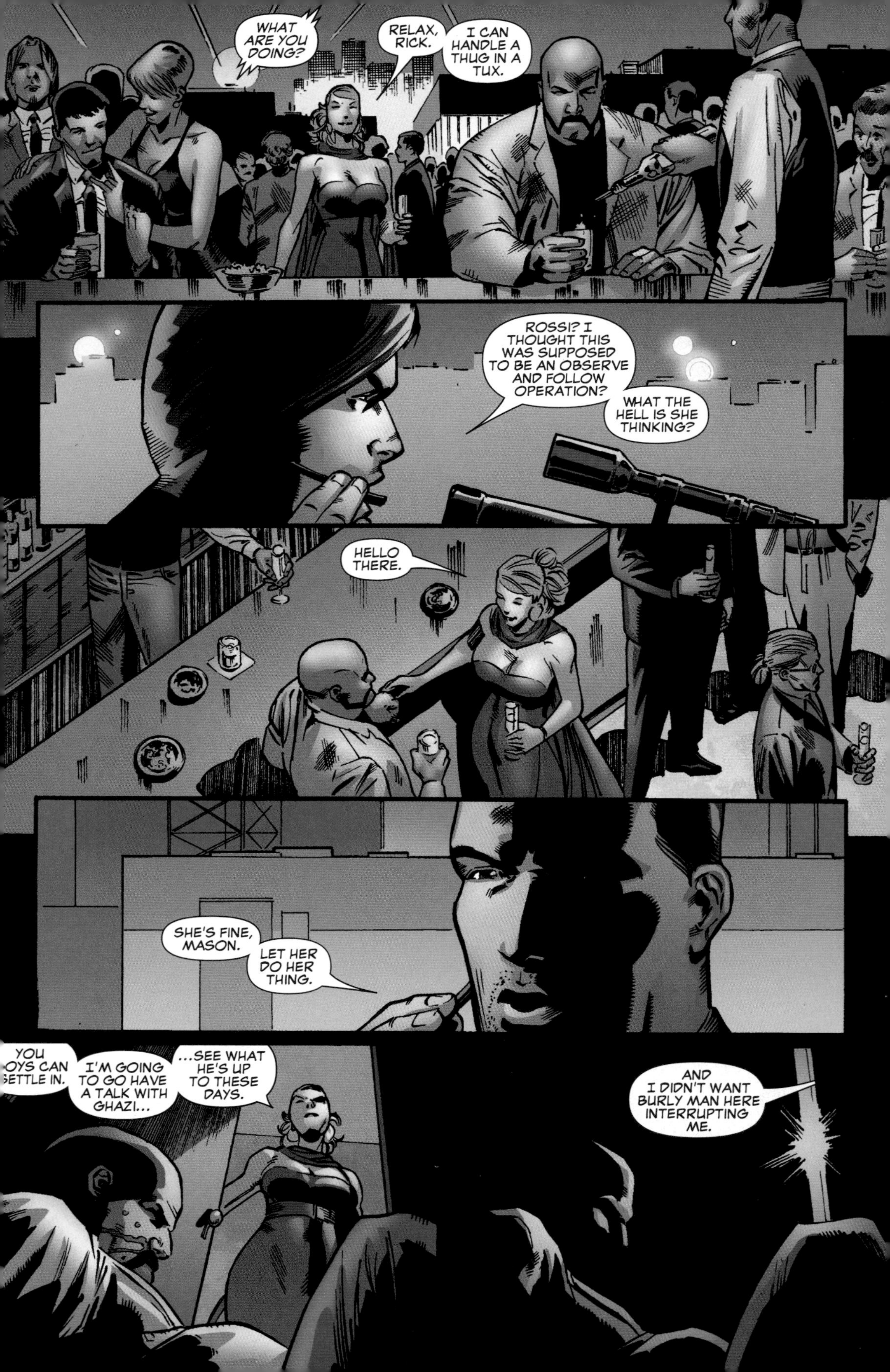
WHAT ARE YOU DOING?
RELAX, RICK.
I CAN HANDLE A THUG IN A TUX.
ROSSI? I THOUGHT THIS WAS SUPPOSED TO BE AN OBSERVE AND FOLLOW OPERATION?
WHAT THE HELL IS SHE THINKING?
HELLO THERE.
SHE'S FINE, MASON.
LET HER DO HER THING.
YOU OYS CAN SETTLE IN.
I'M GOING TO GO HAVE A TALK WITH GHAZI...
...SEE WHAT HE'S UP TO THESE DAYS.
AND I DIDN'T WANT BURLY MAN HERE INTERRUPTING ME.

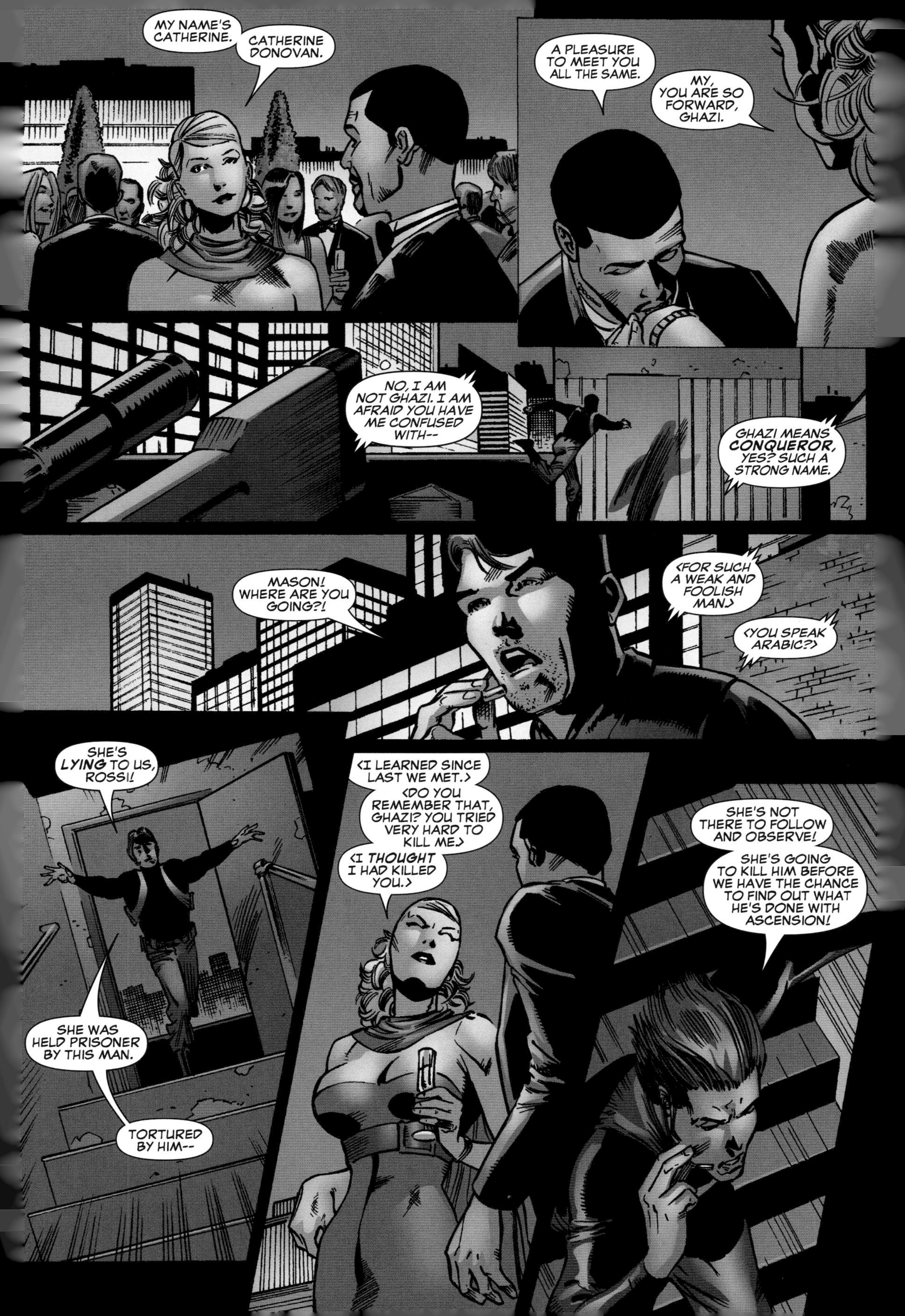
MY NAME'S CATHERINE.
CATHERINE DONOVAN.
A PLEASURE TO MEET YOU ALL THE SAME.
MY, YOU ARE SO FORWARD, GHAZI.
NO, I AM NOT GHAZI. I AM AFRAID YOU HAVE ME CONFUSED WITH--
GHAZI MEANS CONQUEROR, YES? SUCH A STRONG NAME.
MASON! WHERE ARE YOU GOING?!
<FOR SUCH A WEAK AND FOOLISH MAN.>
<YOU SPEAK ARABIC?>
SHE'S LYING TO US, ROSSI!
SHE WAS HELD PRISONER BY THIS MAN.
TORTURED BY HIM--
<I LEARNED SINCE LAST WE MET.>
<DO YOU REMEMBER THAT, GHAZI? YOU TRIED VERY HARD TO KILL ME.>
<I THOUGHT I HAD KILLED YOU.>
SHE'S NOT THERE TO FOLLOW AND OBSERVE!
SHE'S GOING TO KILL HIM BEFORE WE HAVE THE CHANCE TO FIND OUT WHAT HE'S DONE WITH ASCENSION!

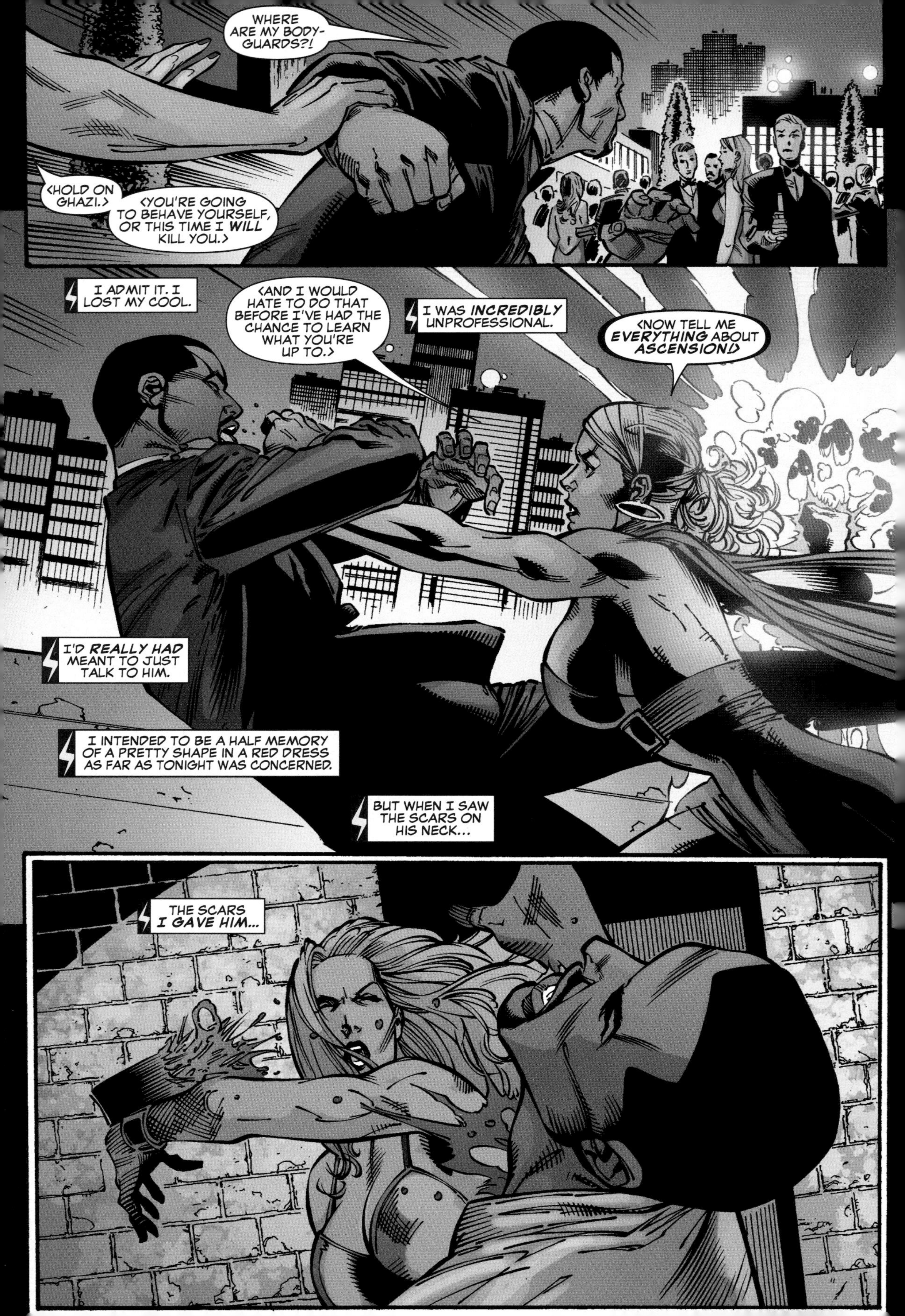

WHERE ARE MY BODY-GUARDS?!
<HOLD ON GHAZI.>
<YOU'RE GOING TO BEHAVE YOURSELF, OR THIS TIME I WILL KILL YOU.>
I ADMIT IT. I LOST MY COOL.
<AND I WOULD HATE TO DO THAT BEFORE I'VE HAD THE CHANCE TO LEARN WHAT YOU'RE UP TO.>
I WAS INCREDIBLY UNPROFESSIONAL.
<NOW TELL ME EVERYTHING ABOUT ASCENSION!>
I'D REALLY HAD MEANT TO JUST TALK TO HIM.
I INTENDED TO BE A HALF MEMORY OF A PRETTY SHAPE IN A RED DRESS AS FAR AS TONIGHT WAS CONCERNED.
BUT WHEN I SAW THE SCARS ON HIS NECK...
THE SCARS I GAVE HIM...

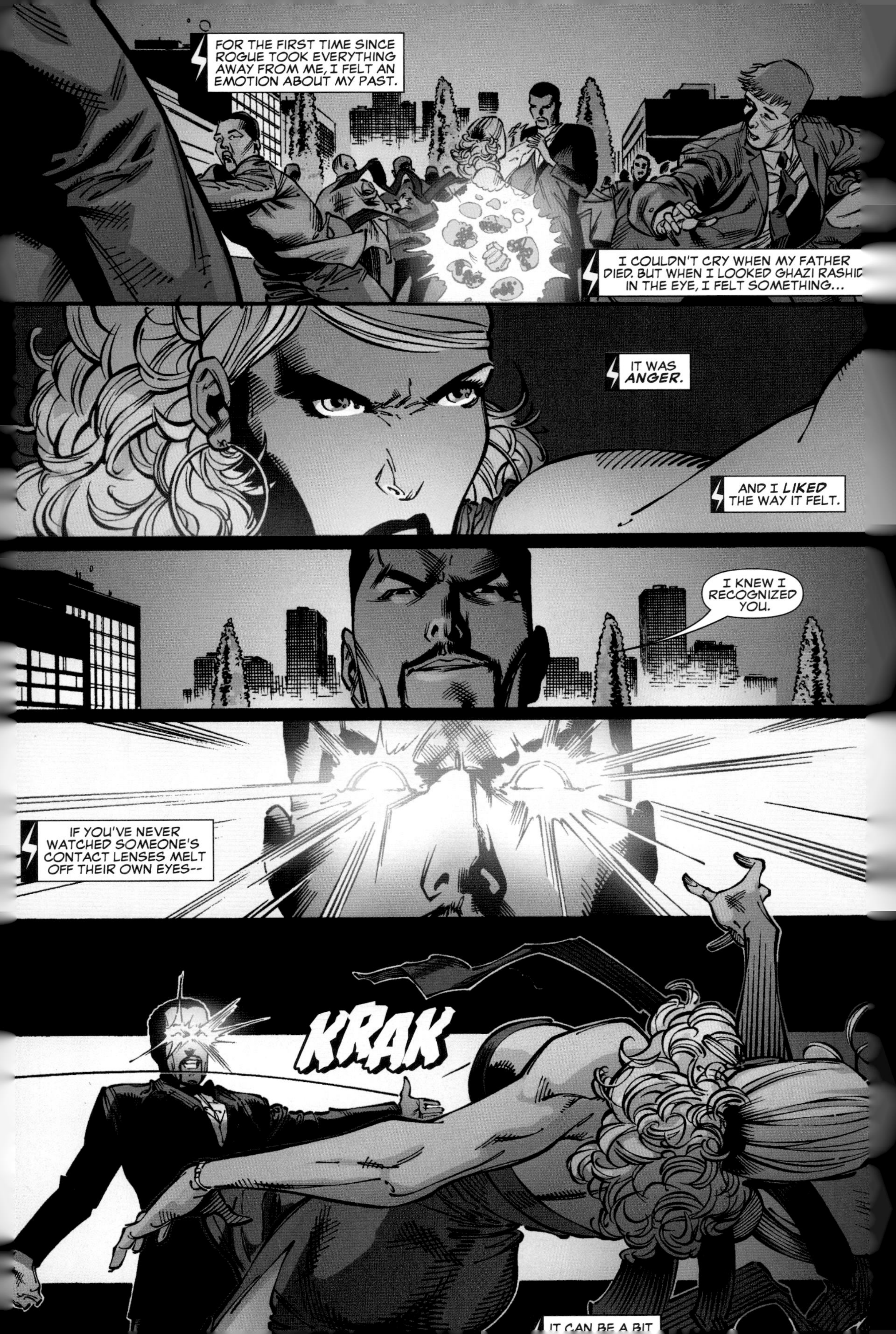
FOR THE FIRST TIME SINCE ROGUE TOOK EVERYTHING AWAY FROM ME, I FELT AN EMOTION ABOUT MY PAST.
I COULDN'T CRY WHEN MY FATHER DIED. BUT WHEN I LOOKED GHAZI RASHID IN THE EYE, I FELT SOMETHING...
IT WAS ANGER.
AND I LIKED THE WAY IT FELT.
I KNEW I RECOGNIZED YOU.
IF YOU'VE NEVER WATCHED SOMEONE'S CONTACT LENSES MELT OFF THEIR OWN EYES--
KRAK
IT CAN BE A BIT

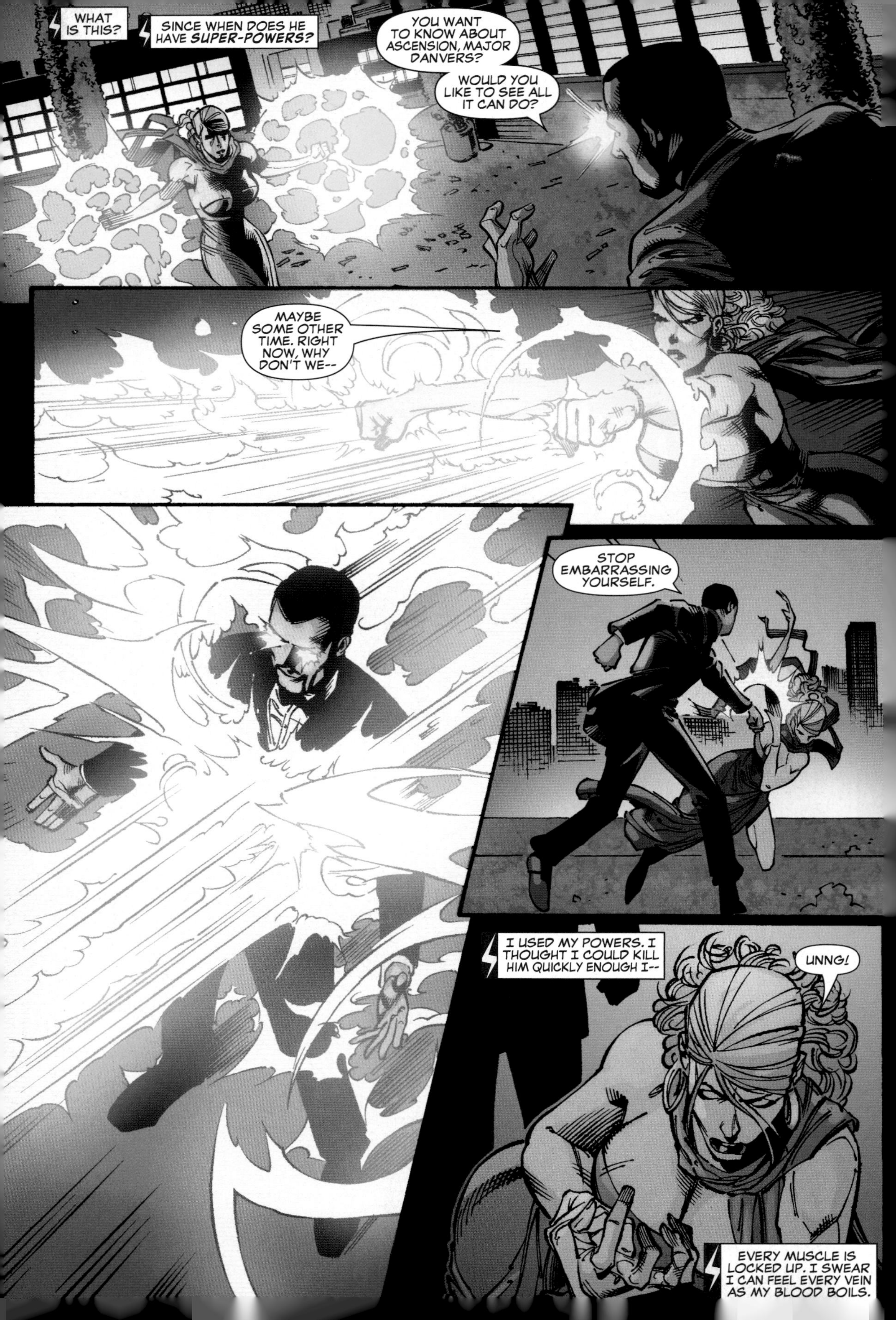
WHAT IS THIS?
SINCE WHEN DOES HE HAVE SUPER-POWERS?
YOU WANT TO KNOW ABOUT ASCENSION, MAJOR DANVERS?
WOULD YOU LIKE TO SEE ALL IT CAN DO?
MAYBE SOME OTHER TIME. RIGHT NOW, WHY DON'T WE--
STOP EMBARRASSING YOURSELF.
I USED MY POWERS. I THOUGHT I COULD KILL HIM QUICKLY ENOUGH I--
UNNG!
EVERY MUSCLE IS LOCKED UP. I SWEAR I CAN FEEL EVERY VEIN AS MY BLOOD BOILS.

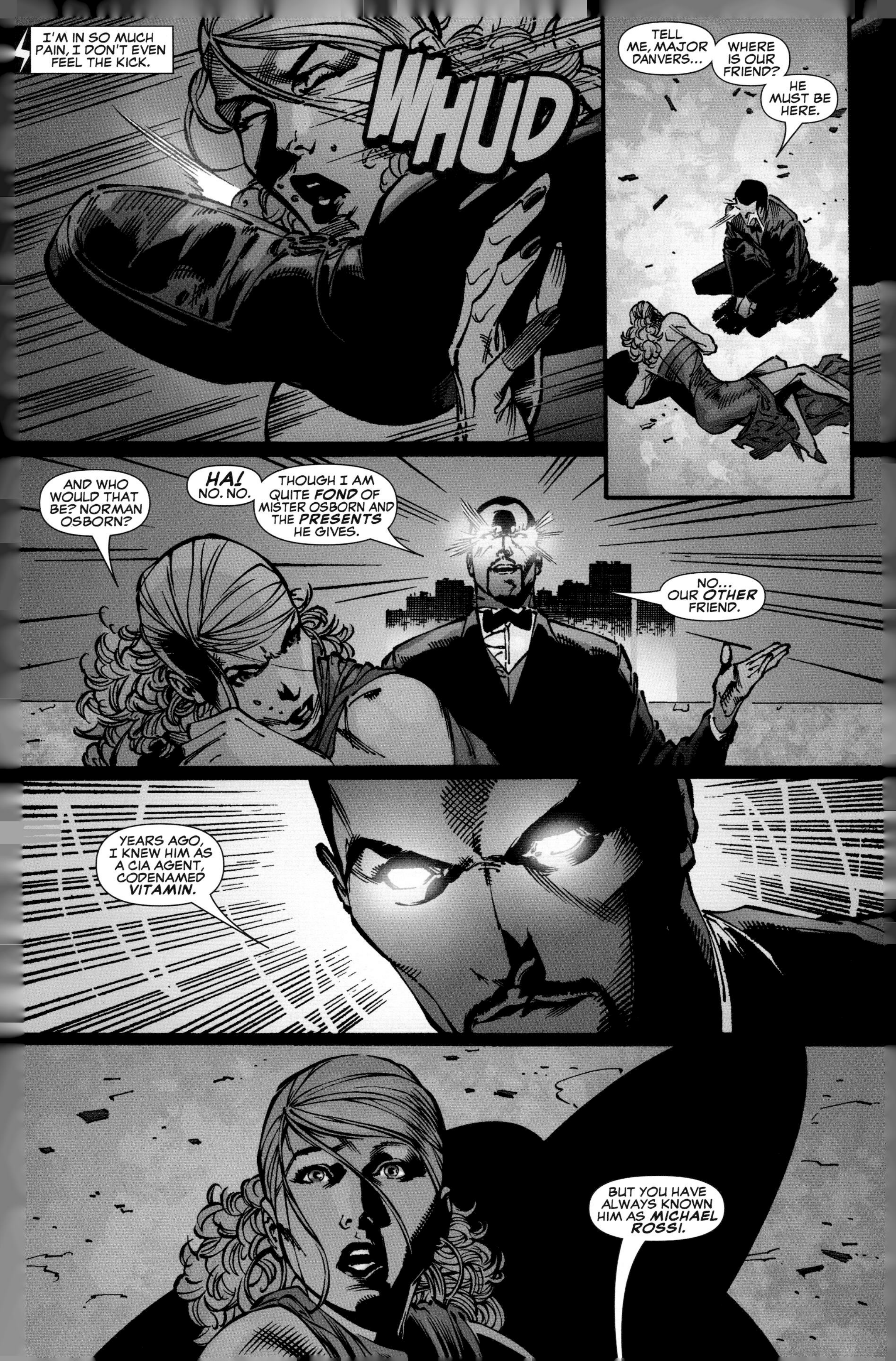
I'M IN SO MUCH PAIN, I DON'T EVEN FEEL THE KICK.
WHUD
TELL ME, MAJOR DANVERS...
WHERE IS OUR FRIEND?
HE MUST BE HERE.
AND WHO WOULD THAT BE? NORMAN OSBORN?
HA! NO. NO.
THOUGH I AM QUITE FOND OF MISTER OSBORN AND THE PRESENTS HE GIVES.
NO... OUR OTHER FRIEND.
YEARS AGO, I KNEW HIM AS A CIA AGENT, CODENAMED VITAMIN.
BUT YOU HAVE ALWAYS KNOWN HIM AS MICHAEL ROSSI.

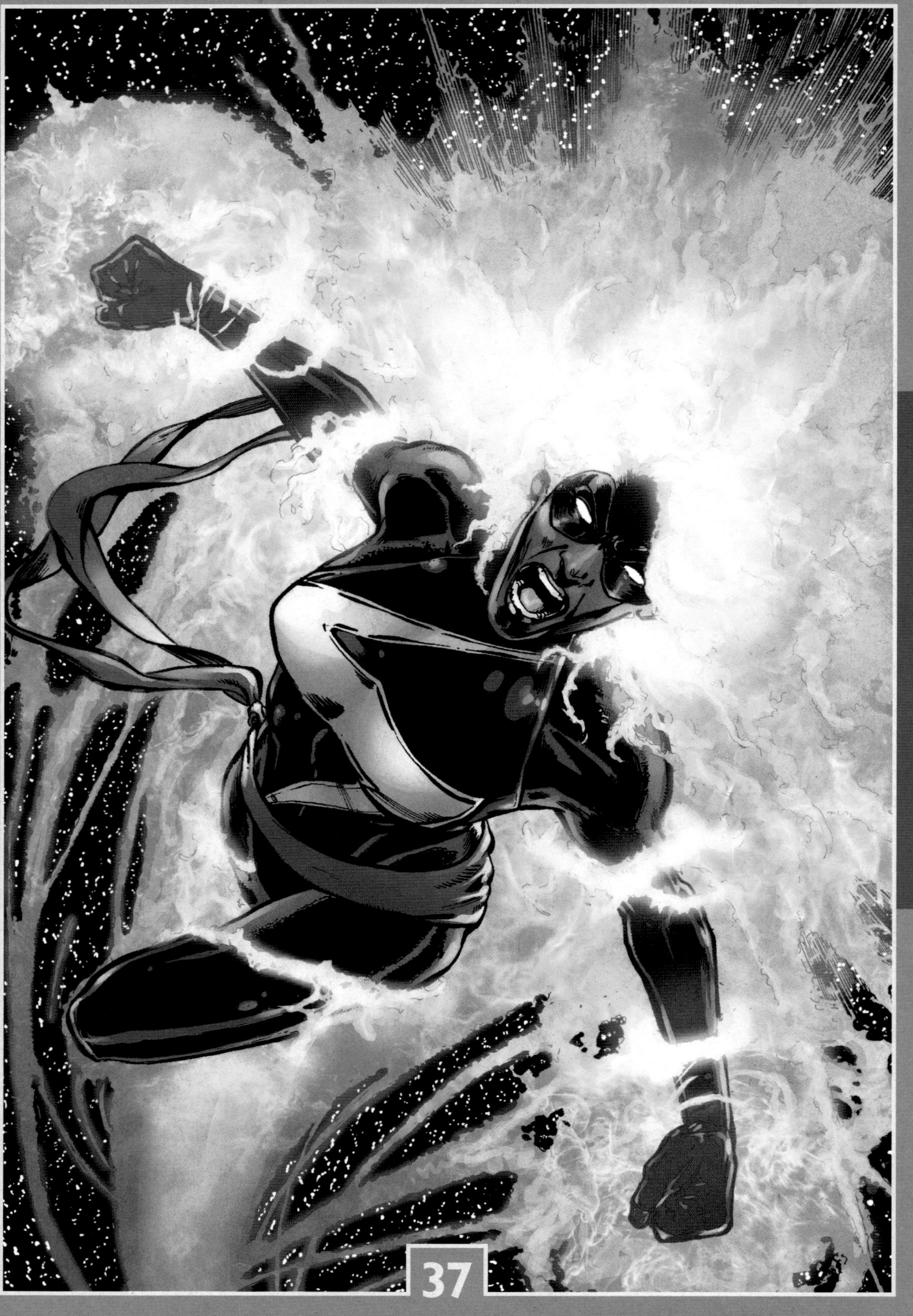

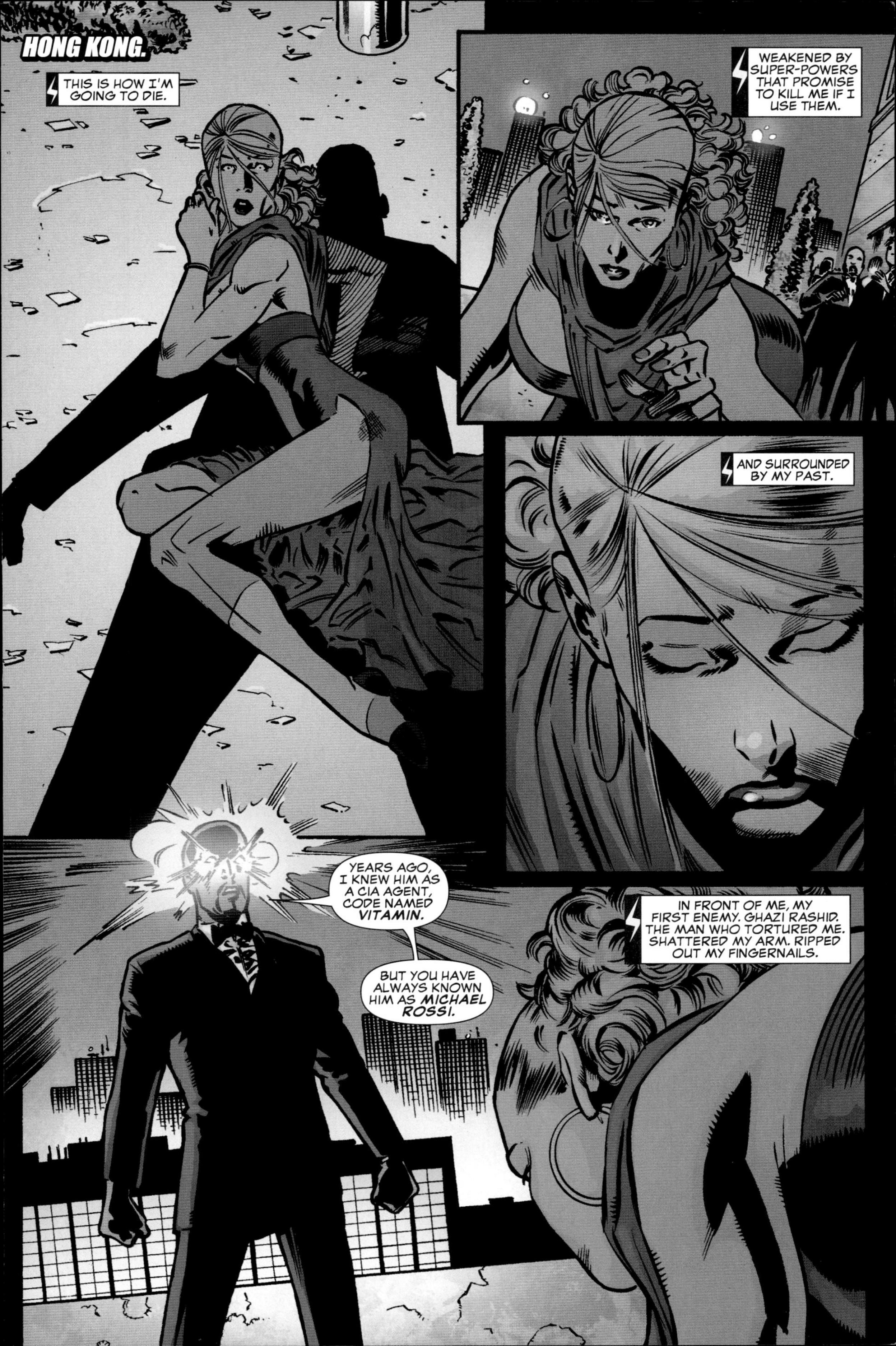
HONG KONG.
THIS IS HOW I'M GOING TO DIE.
WEAKENED BY SUPER-POWERS THAT PROMISE TO KILL ME IF I USE THEM.
AND SURROUNDED BY MY PAST.
YEARS AGO, I KNEW HIM AS A CIA AGENT, CODE NAMED VITAMIN.
BUT YOU HAVE ALWAYS KNOWN HIM AS MICHAEL ROSSI.
IN FRONT OF ME, MY FIRST ENEMY. GHAZI RASHID. THE MAN WHO TORTURED ME. SHATTERED MY ARM. RIPPED OUT MY FINGERNAILS.

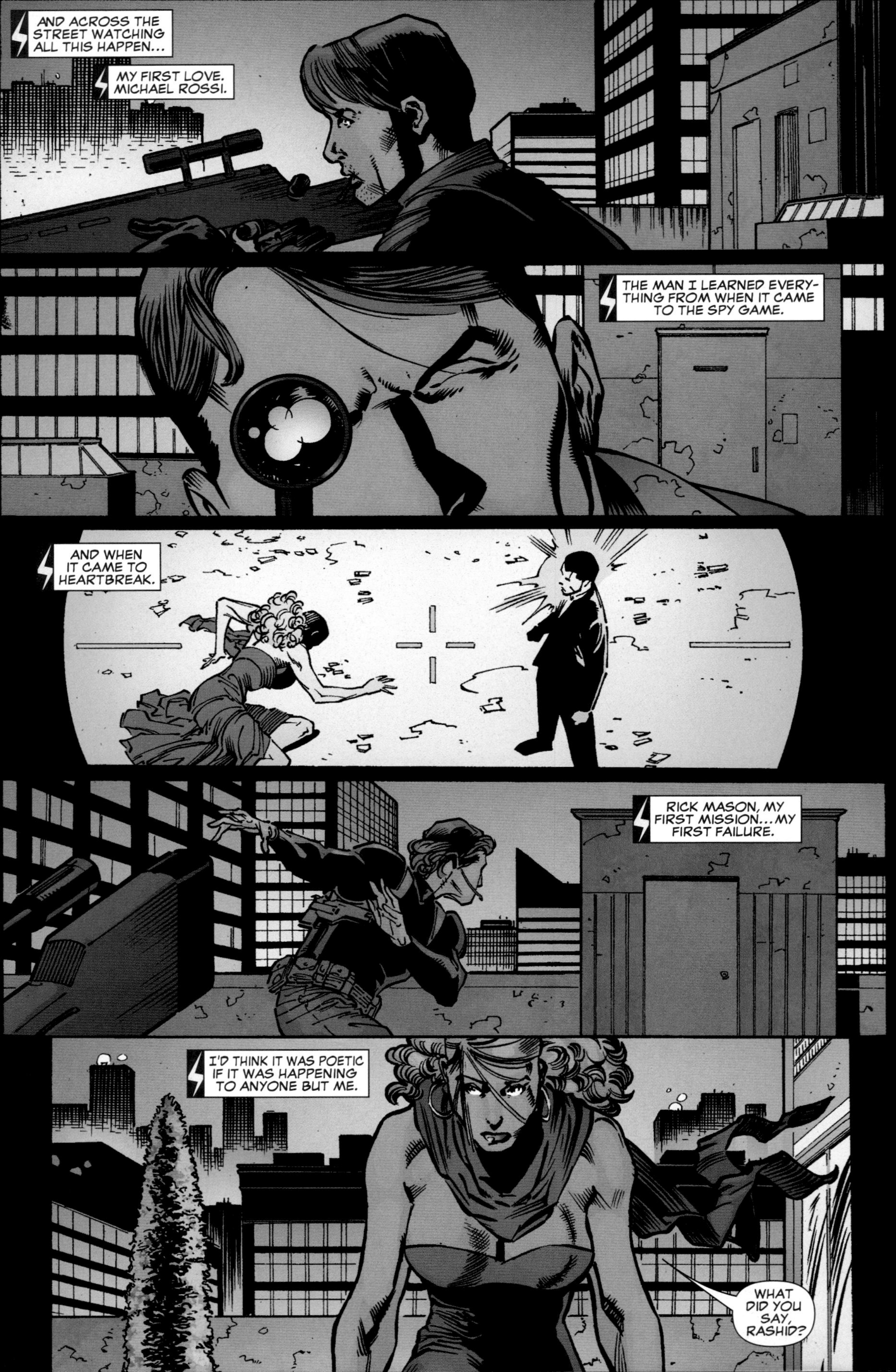
AND ACROSS THE STREET WATCHING ALL THIS HAPPEN...
MY FIRST LOVE. MICHAEL ROSSI.
THE MAN I LEARNED EVERY-THING FROM WHEN IT CAME TO THE SPY GAME.
AND WHEN IT CAME TO HEARTBREAK.
RICK MASON, MY FIRST MISSION... MY FIRST FAILURE.
I'D THINK IT WAS POETIC IF IT WAS HAPPENING TO ANYONE BUT ME.
WHAT DID YOU SAY, RASHID?

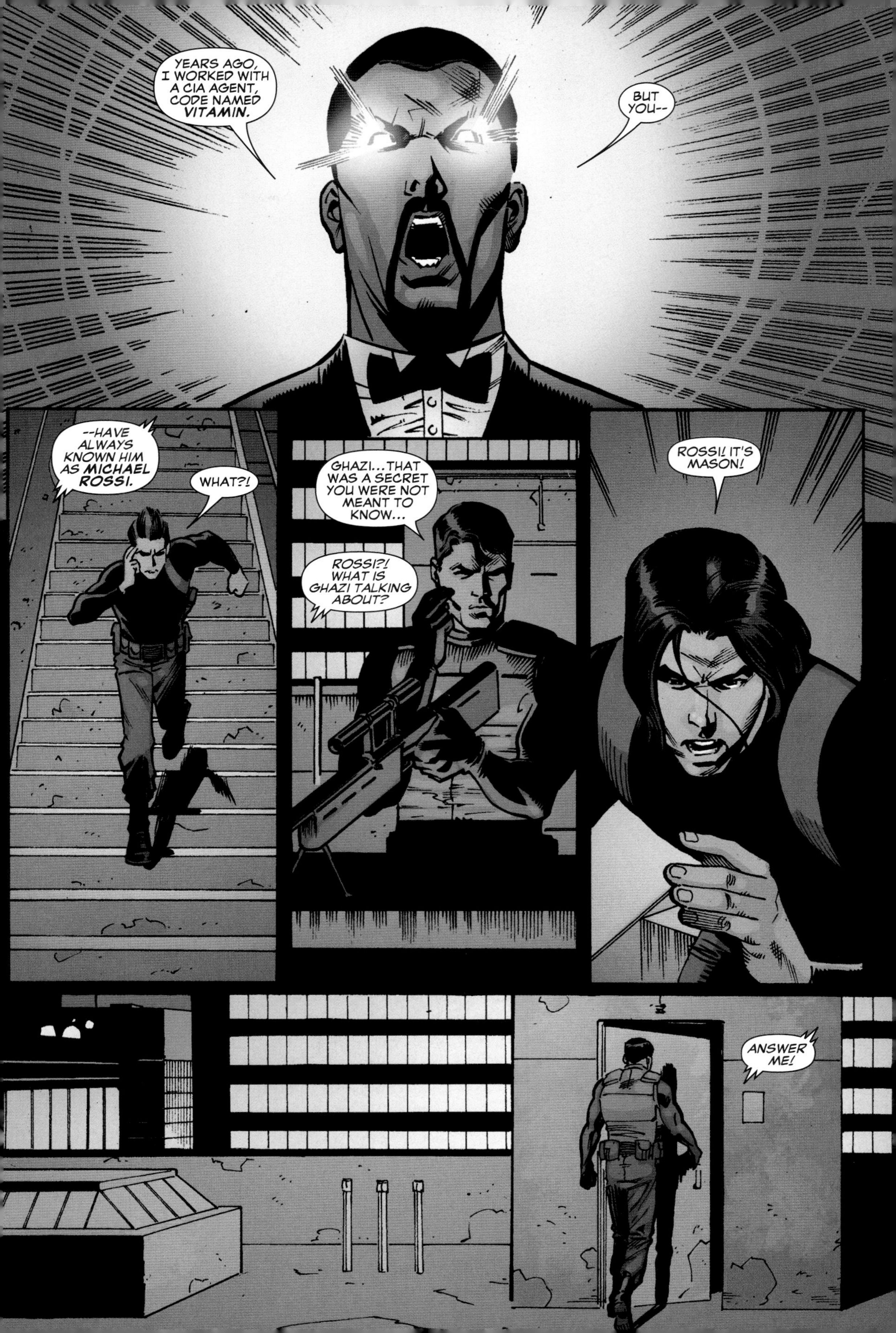
YEARS AGO, I WORKED WITH A CIA AGENT, CODE NAMED VITAMIN.
BUT YOU--
--HAVE ALWAYS KNOWN HIM AS MICHAEL ROSSI.
WHAT?!
GHAZI...THAT WAS A SECRET YOU WERE NOT MEANT TO KNOW...
ROSSI?! WHAT IS GHAZI TALKING ABOUT?
ROSSI! IT'S MASON!
ANSWER ME!

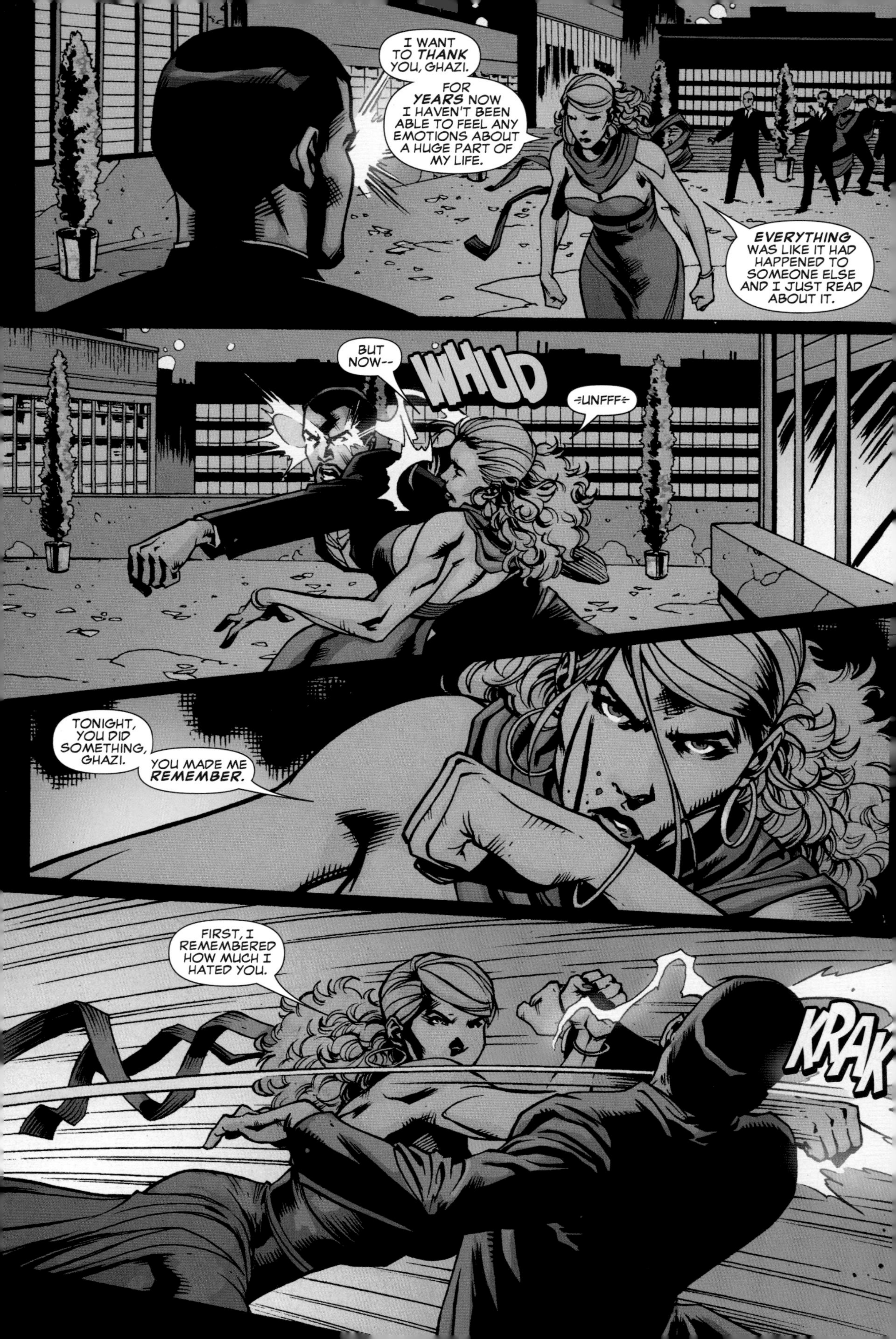

I WANT TO THANK YOU, GHAZI.
FOR YEARS NOW I HAVEN'T BEEN ABLE TO FEEL ANY EMOTIONS ABOUT A HUGE PART OF MY LIFE.
EVERYTHING WAS LIKE IT HAD HAPPENED TO SOMEONE ELSE AND I JUST READ ABOUT IT.
BUT NOW--
WHUD
=UNFFF=
TONIGHT, YOU DID SOMETHING, GHAZI.
YOU MADE ME REMEMBER.
FIRST, I REMEMBERED HOW MUCH I HATED YOU.
KRAK

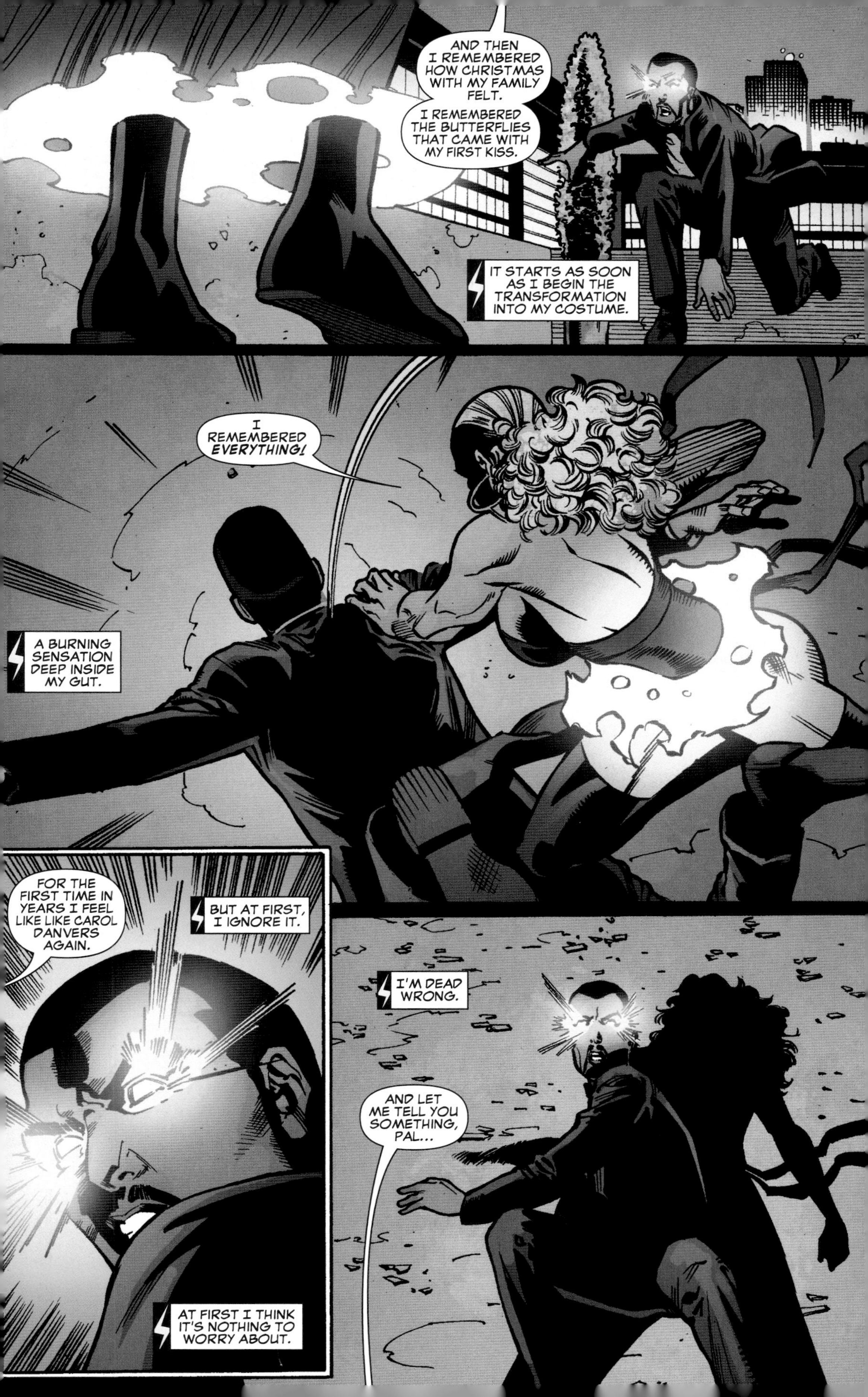
AND THEN I REMEMBERED HOW CHRISTMAS WITH MY FAMILY FELT.
I REMEMBERED THE BUTTERFLIES THAT CAME WITH MY FIRST KISS.
IT STARTS AS SOON AS I BEGIN THE TRANSFORMATION INTO MY COSTUME.
I REMEMBERED EVERYTHING!
A BURNING SENSATION DEEP INSIDE MY GUT.
FOR THE FIRST TIME IN YEARS I FEEL LIKE LIKE CAROL DANVERS AGAIN.
BUT AT FIRST, I IGNORE IT.
AT FIRST I THINK IT'S NOTHING TO WORRY ABOUT.
I'M DEAD WRONG.
AND LET ME TELL YOU SOMETHING, PAL...

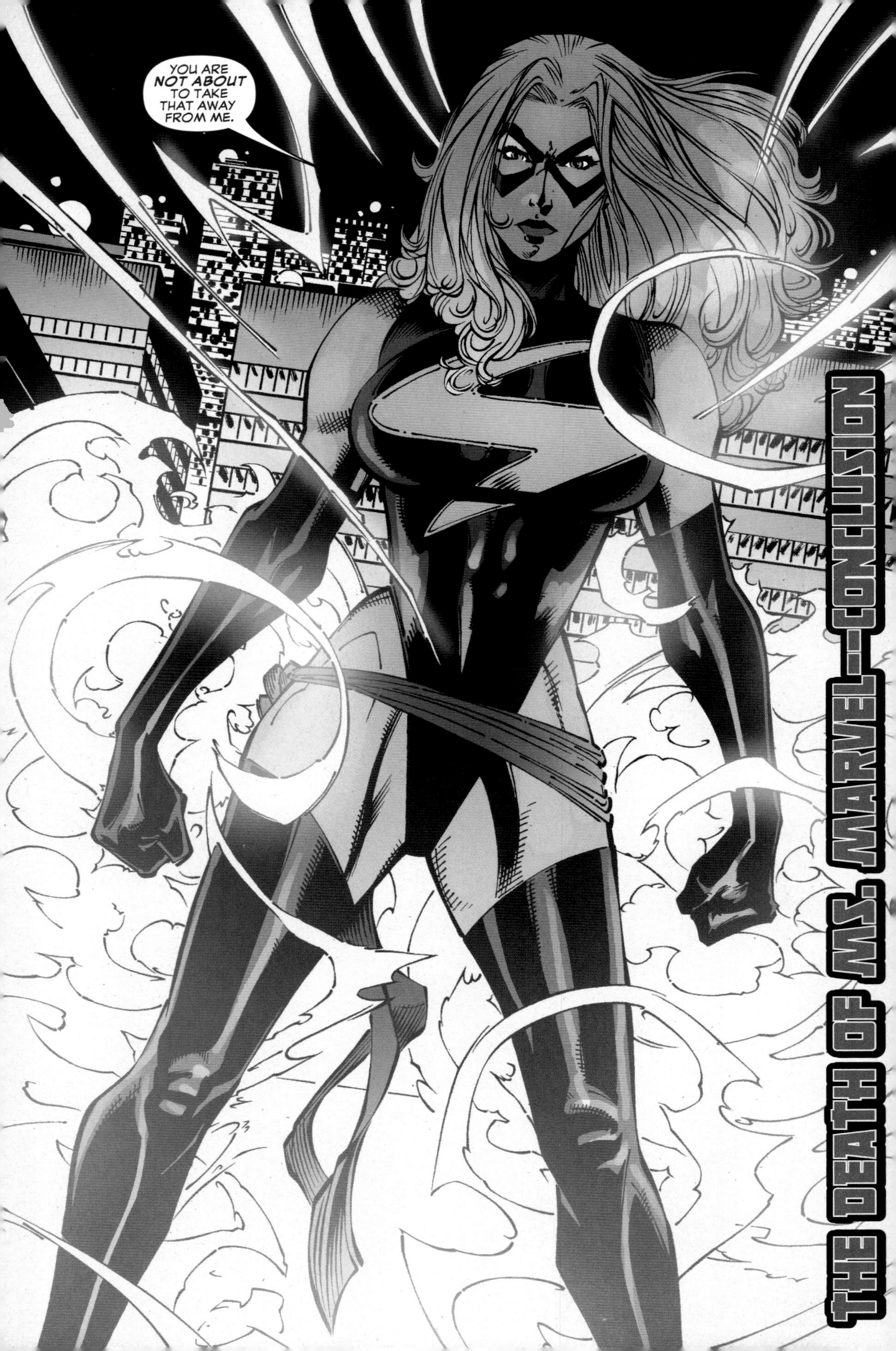

YOU ARE NOT ABOUT TO TAKE THAT AWAY FROM ME.
THE DEATH OF MS. MARVEL--CONCLUSION

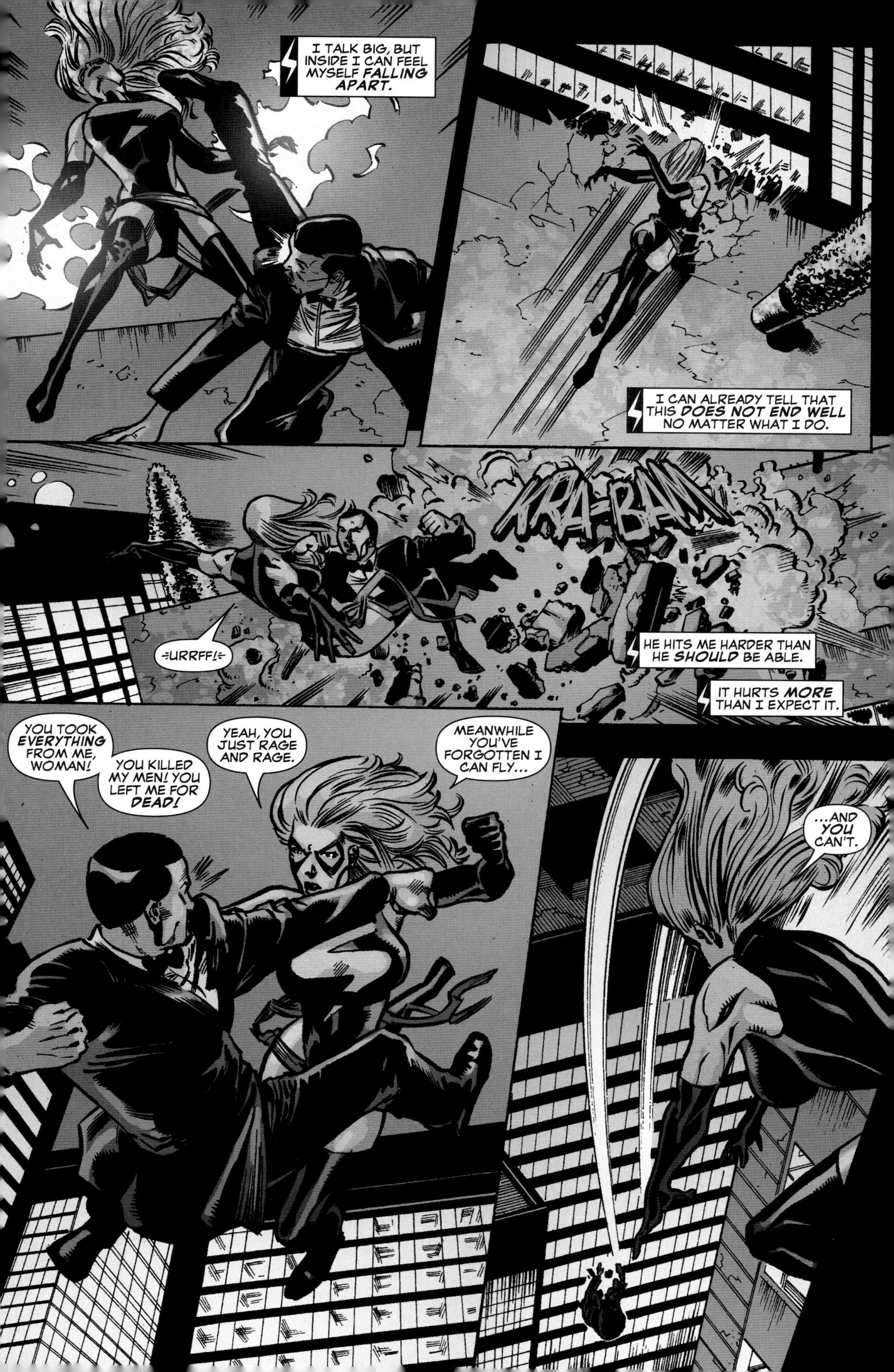

I TALK BIG, BUT INSIDE I CAN FEEL MYSELF FALLING APART.
I CAN ALREADY TELL THAT THIS DOES NOT END WELL NO MATTER WHAT I DO.
KRA-BAM
URRFF!
HE HITS ME HARDER THAN HE SHOULD BE ABLE.
IT HURTS MORE THAN I EXPECT IT.
YOU TOOK EVERYTHING FROM ME, WOMAN!
YOU KILLED MY MEN! YOU LEFT ME FOR DEAD!
YEAH, YOU JUST RAGE AND RAGE.
MEANWHILE YOU'VE FORGOTTEN I CAN FLY...
...AND YOU CAN'T.

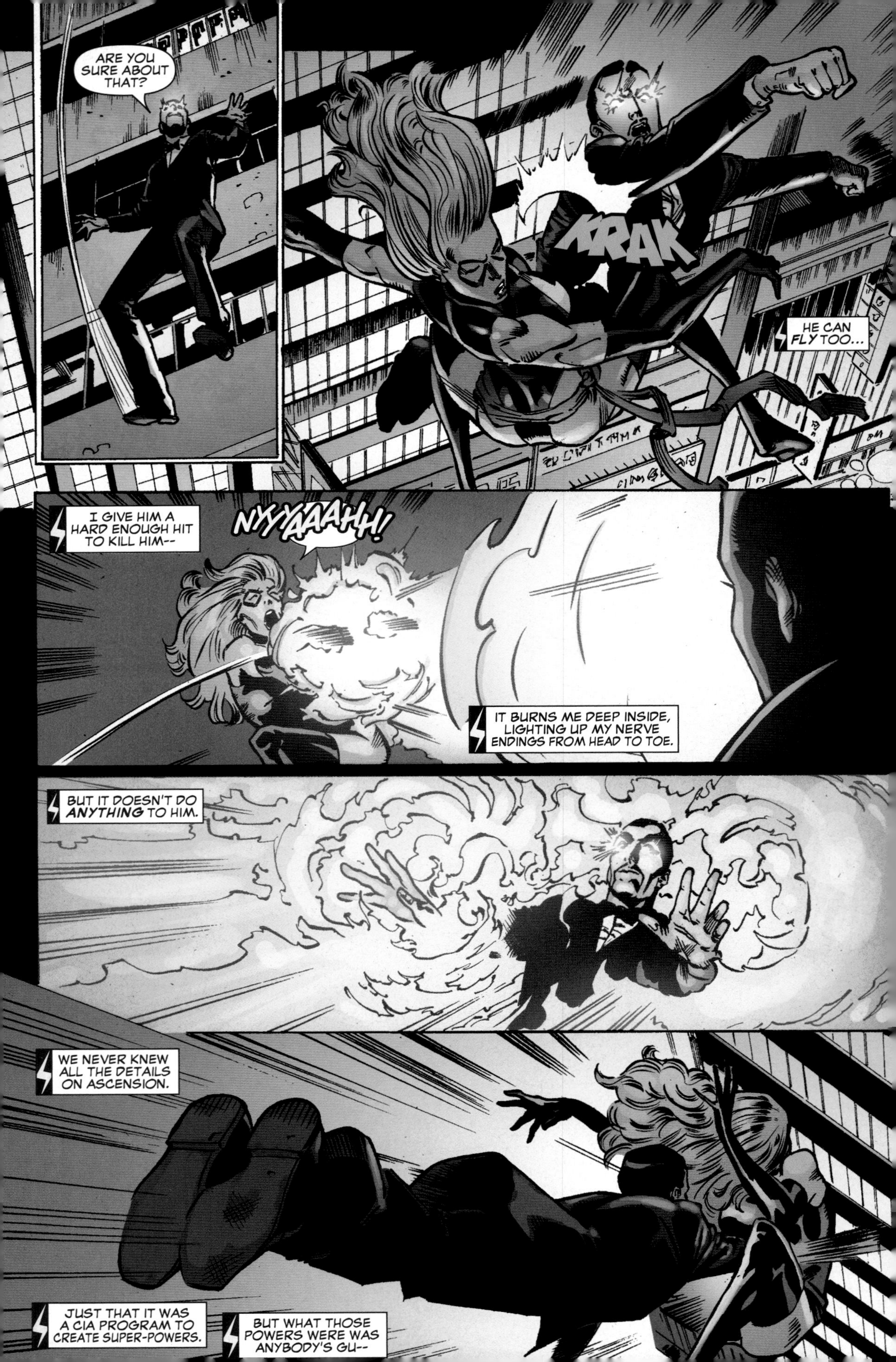
ARE YOU SURE ABOUT THAT?
KRAK
HE CAN FLY TOO...
I GIVE HIM A HARD ENOUGH HIT TO KILL HIM--
NYYAAAHH!
IT BURNS ME DEEP INSIDE, LIGHTING UP MY NERVE ENDINGS FROM HEAD TO TOE.
BUT IT DOESN'T DO ANYTHING TO HIM.
WE NEVER KNEW ALL THE DETAILS ON ASCENSION.
JUST THAT IT WAS A CIA PROGRAM TO CREATE SUPER-POWERS.
BUT WHAT THOSE POWERS WERE WAS ANYBODY'S GU--

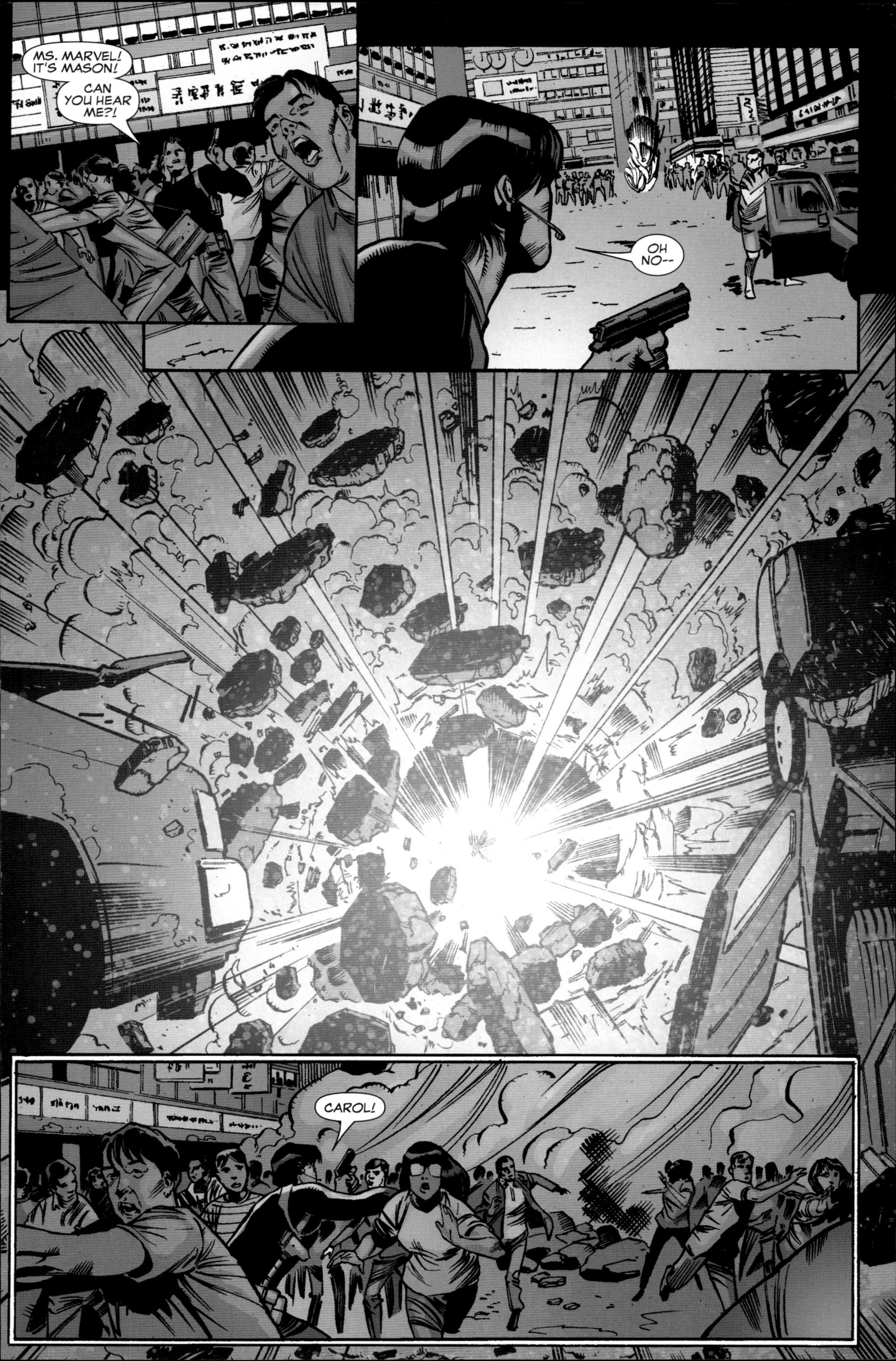
MS. MARVEL! IT'S MASON!
CAN YOU HEAR ME?!
OH NO--
CAROL!

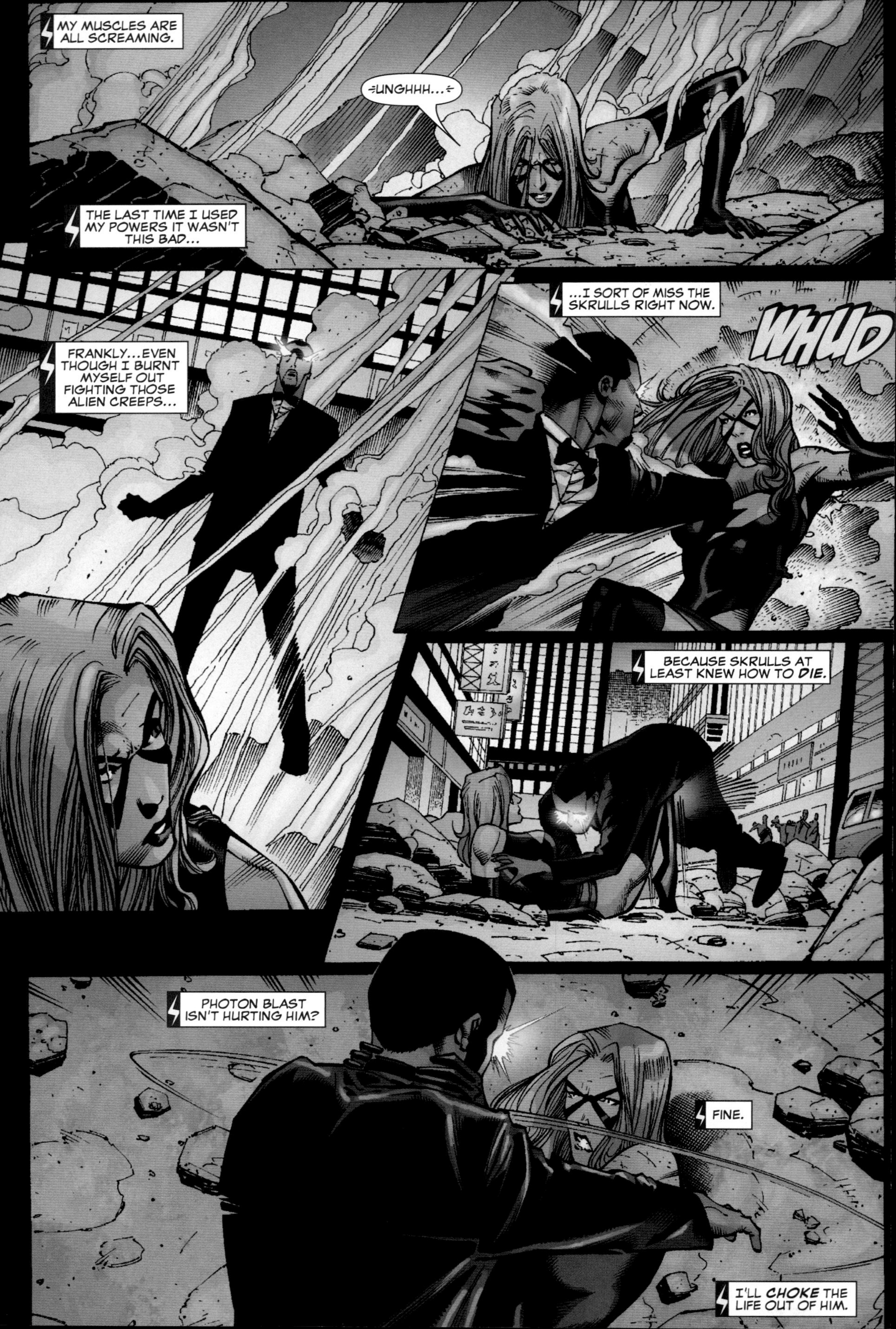
MY MUSCLES ARE ALL SCREAMING.
=UNGHHH...=
THE LAST TIME I USED MY POWERS IT WASN'T THIS BAD...
FRANKLY...EVEN THOUGH I BURNT MYSELF OUT FIGHTING THOSE ALIEN CREEPS...
...I SORT OF MISS THE SKRULLS RIGHT NOW.
WHUD
BECAUSE SKRULLS AT LEAST KNEW HOW TO DIE.
PHOTON BLAST ISN'T HURTING HIM?
FINE.
I'LL CHOKE THE LIFE OUT OF HIM.

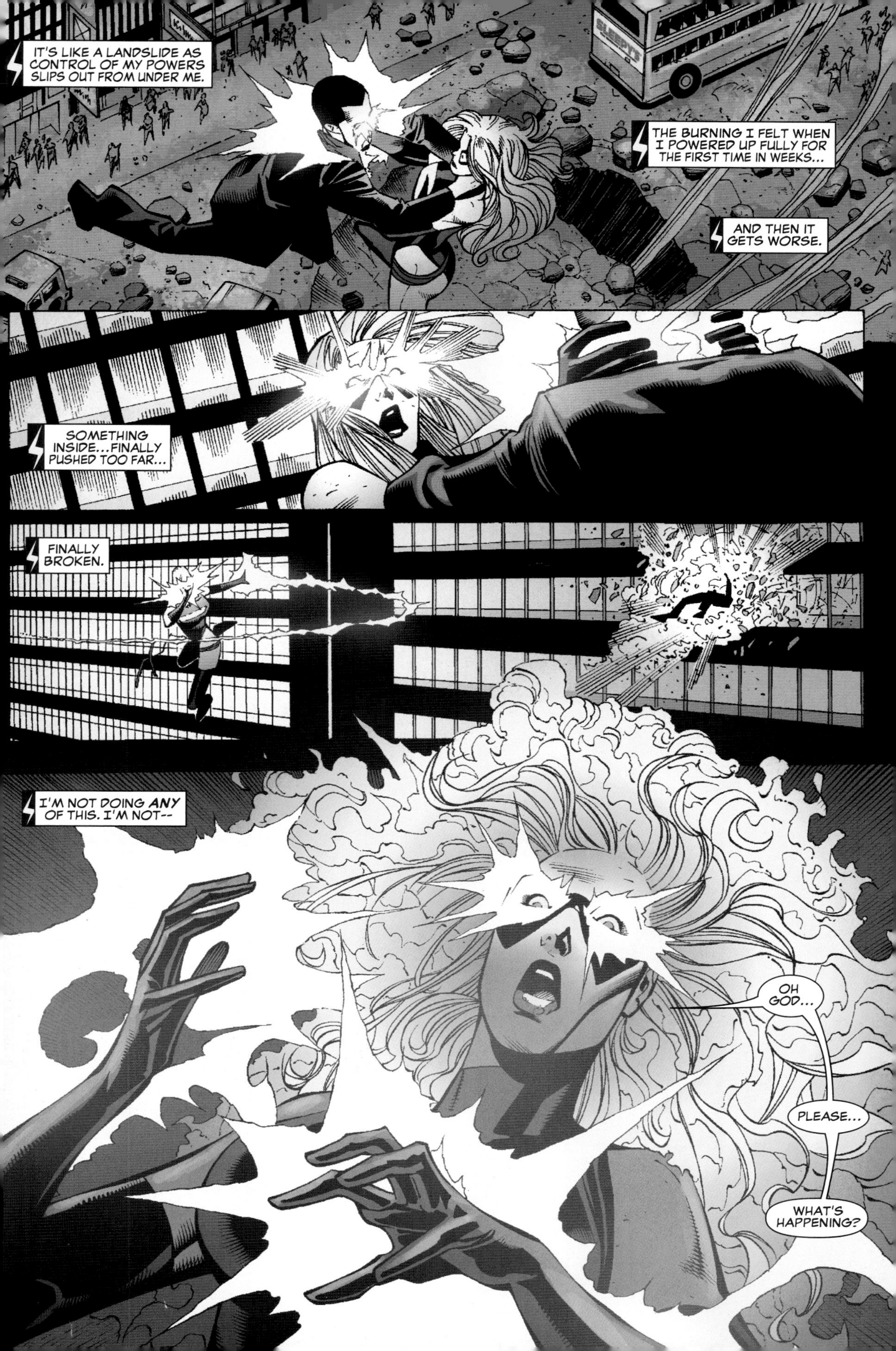

IT'S LIKE A LANDSLIDE AS CONTROL OF MY POWERS SLIPS OUT FROM UNDER ME.
THE BURNING I FELT WHEN I POWERED UP FULLY FOR THE FIRST TIME IN WEEKS...
AND THEN IT GETS WORSE.
SOMETHING INSIDE...FINALLY PUSHED TOO FAR...
FINALLY BROKEN.
I'M NOT DOING *ANY* OF THIS. I'M NOT--
OH GOD...
PLEASE...
WHAT'S HAPPENING?

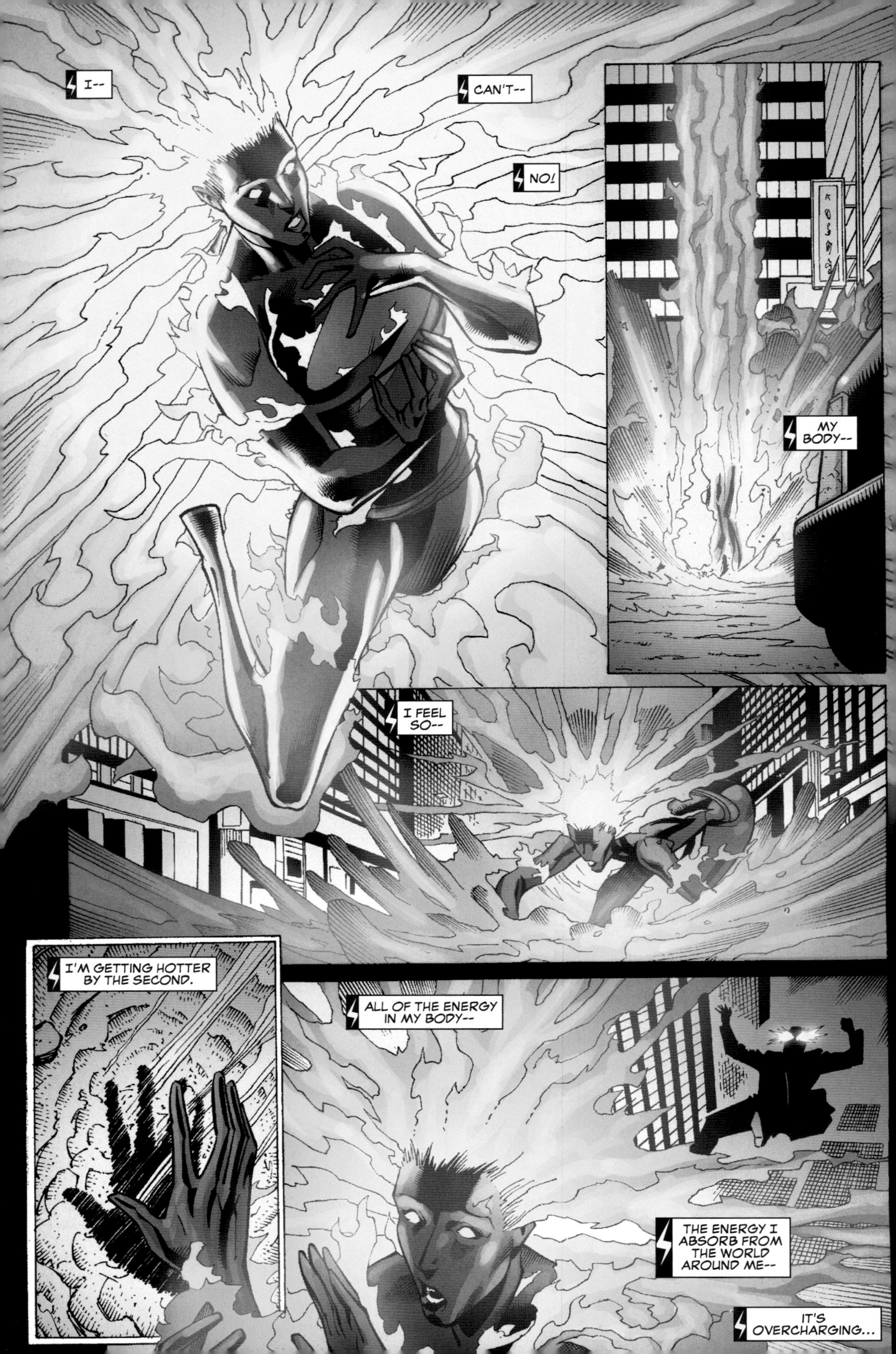

I--
CAN'T--
NO!
MY BODY--
I FEEL SO--
I'M GETTING HOTTER BY THE SECOND.
ALL OF THE ENERGY IN MY BODY--
THE ENERGY I ABSORB FROM THE WORLD AROUND ME--
IT'S OVERCHARGING...

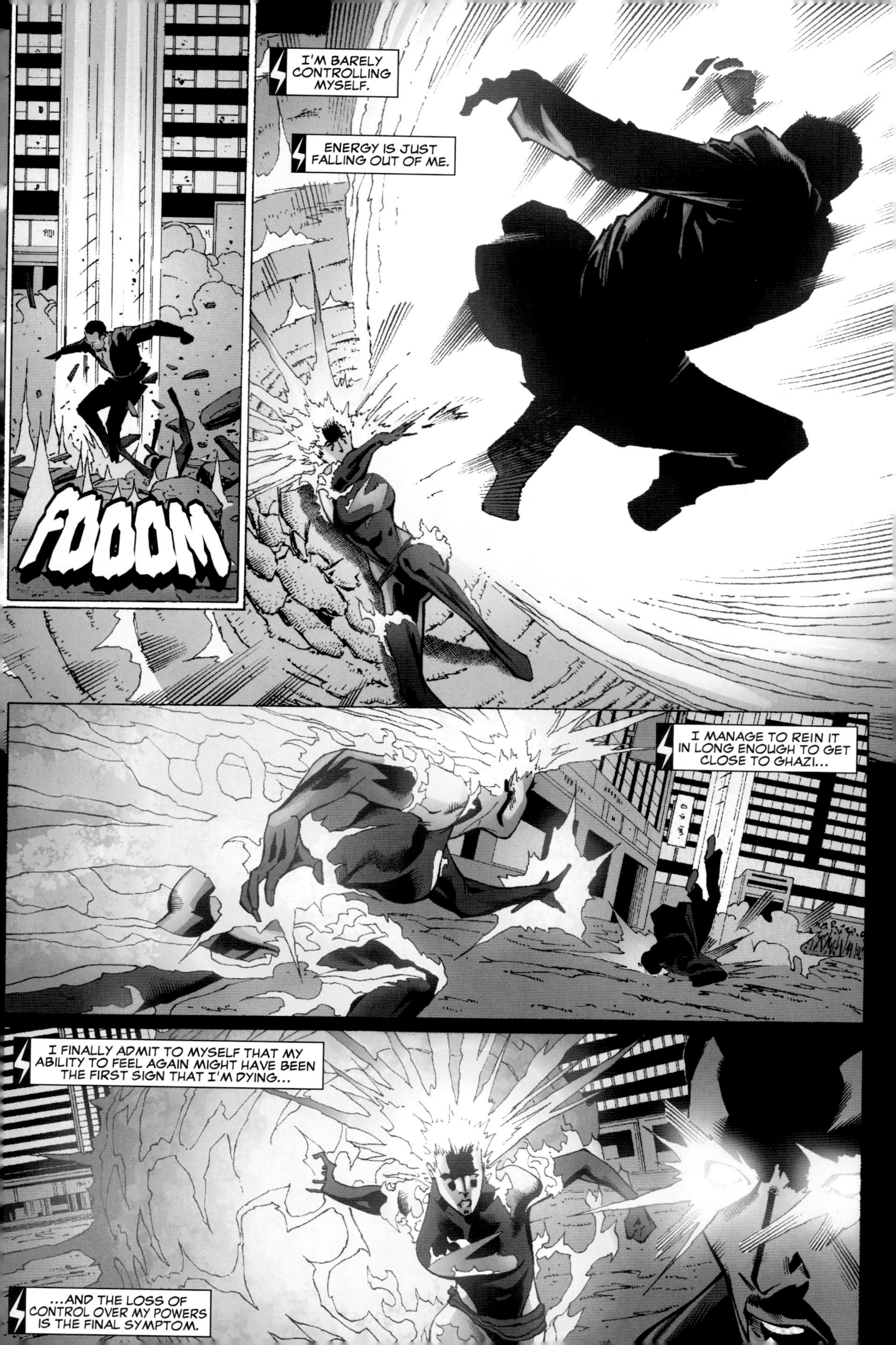

FOOOM
I'M BARELY CONTROLLING MYSELF.
ENERGY IS JUST FALLING OUT OF ME.
I MANAGE TO REIN IT IN LONG ENOUGH TO GET CLOSE TO GHAZI...
I FINALLY ADMIT TO MYSELF THAT MY ABILITY TO FEEL AGAIN MIGHT HAVE BEEN THE FIRST SIGN THAT I'M DYING...
...AND THE LOSS OF CONTROL OVER MY POWERS IS THE FINAL SYMPTOM.

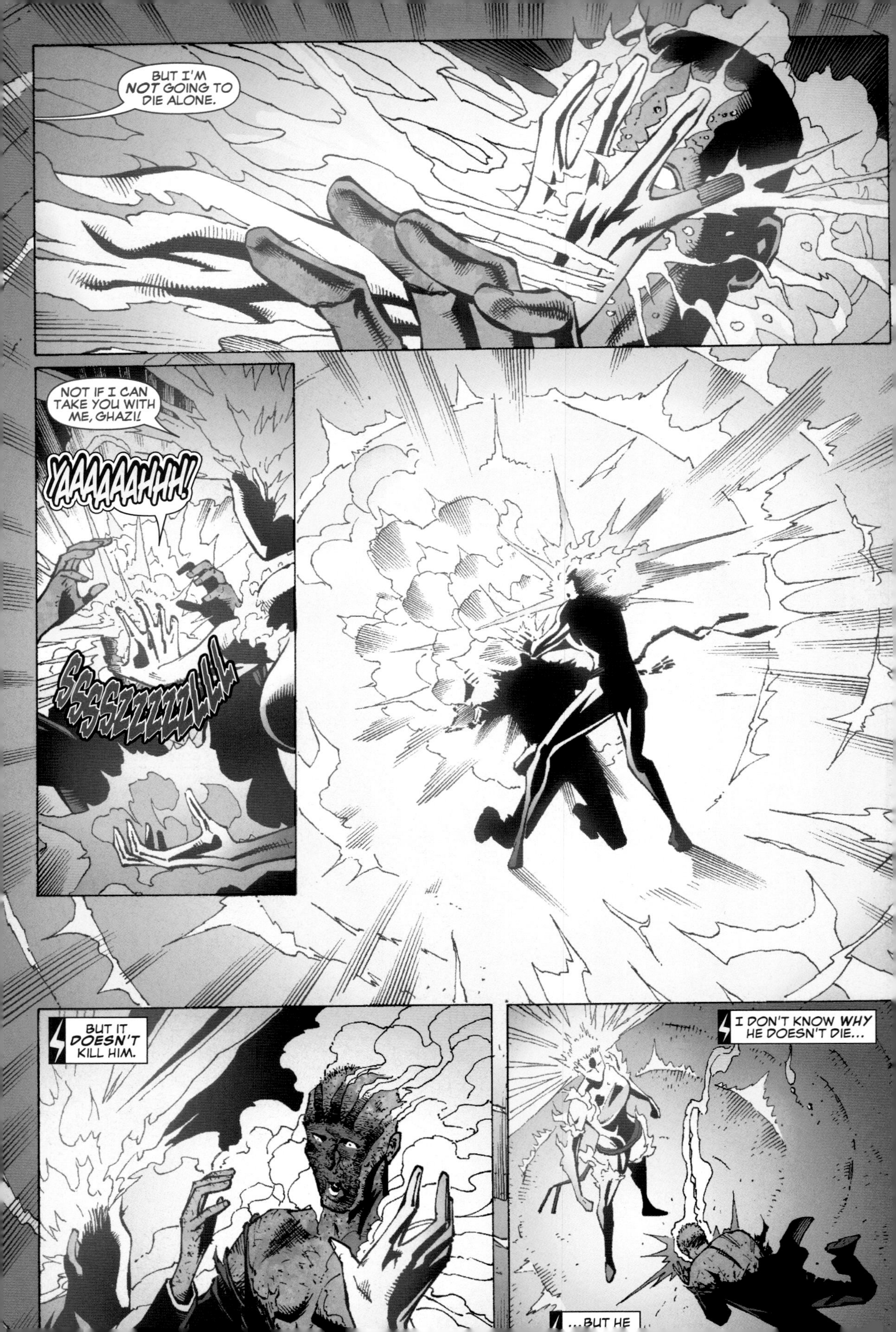

BUT I'M NOT GOING TO DIE ALONE.
NOT IF I CAN TAKE YOU WITH ME, GHAZI!
YAAAAAAHHH!
SSSSZZZZZZLLL
BUT IT DOESN'T KILL HIM.
I DON'T KNOW WHY HE DOESN'T DIE...
...BUT HE

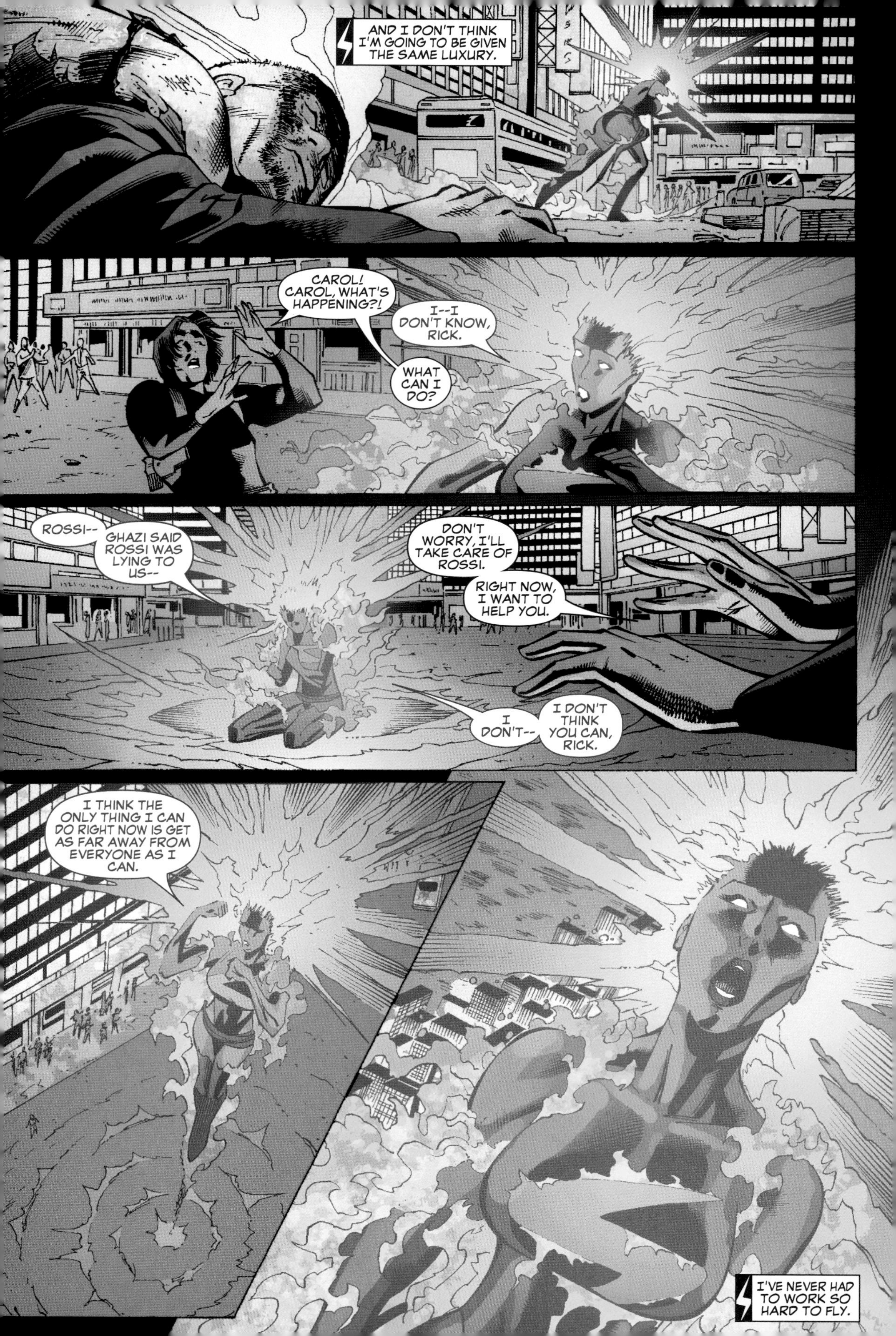
AND I DON'T THINK I'M GOING TO BE GIVEN THE SAME LUXURY.
CAROL! CAROL, WHAT'S HAPPENING?!
I--I DON'T KNOW, RICK.
WHAT CAN I DO?
ROSSI--
GHAZI SAID ROSSI WAS LYING TO US--
DON'T WORRY, I'LL TAKE CARE OF ROSSI.
RIGHT NOW, I WANT TO HELP YOU.
I DON'T--
I DON'T THINK YOU CAN, RICK.
I THINK THE ONLY THING I CAN DO RIGHT NOW IS GET AS FAR AWAY FROM EVERYONE AS I CAN.
I'VE NEVER HAD TO WORK SO HARD TO FLY.

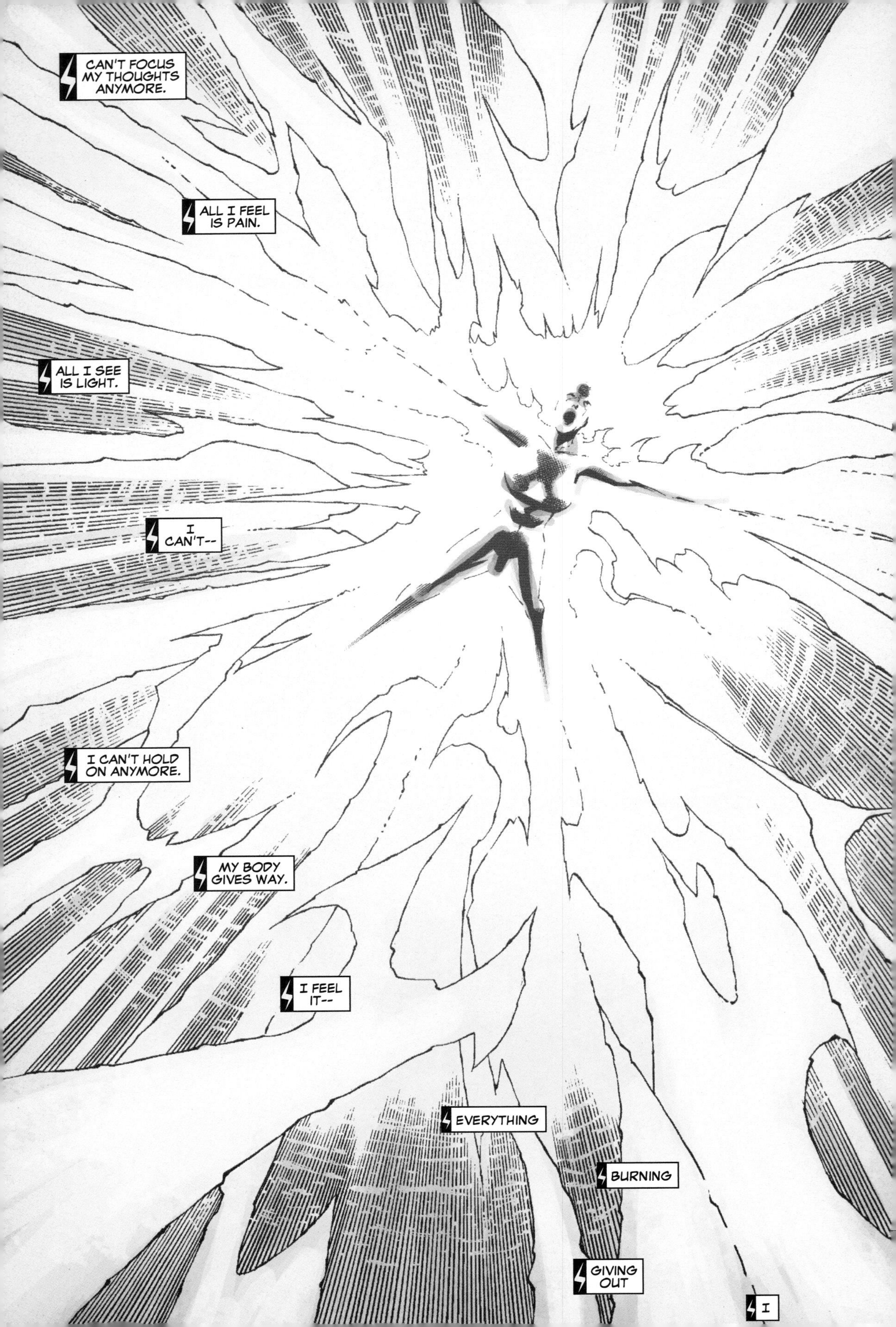
CAN'T FOCUS MY THOUGHTS ANYMORE.
ALL I FEEL IS PAIN.
ALL I SEE IS LIGHT.
I CAN'T--
I CAN'T HOLD ON ANYMORE.
MY BODY GIVES WAY.
I FEEL IT--
EVERYTHING
BURNING
GIVING OUT
I

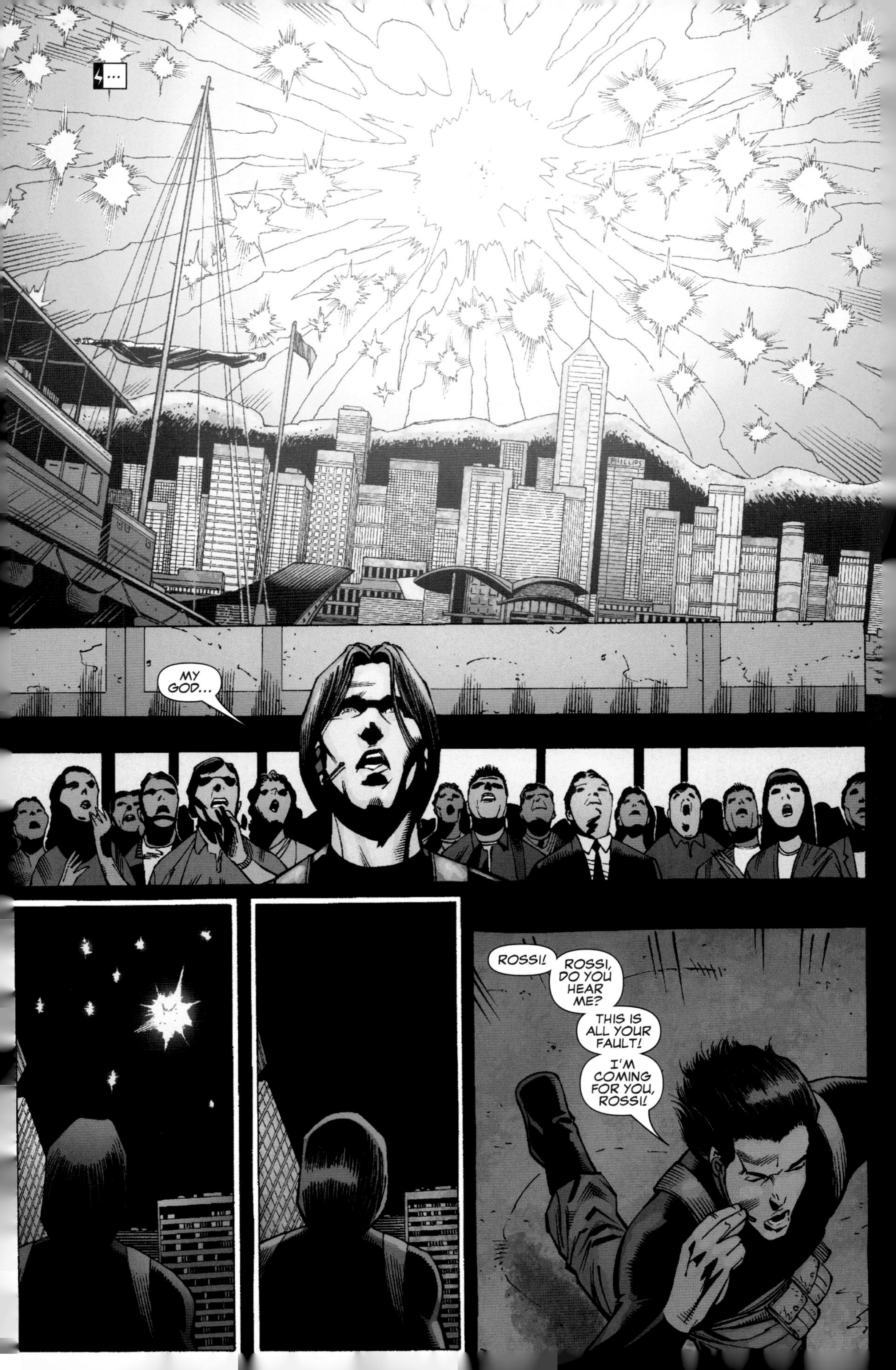
...
MY GOD...
ROSSI!
ROSSI, DO YOU HEAR ME?
THIS IS ALL YOUR FAULT!
I'M COMING FOR YOU, ROSSI!

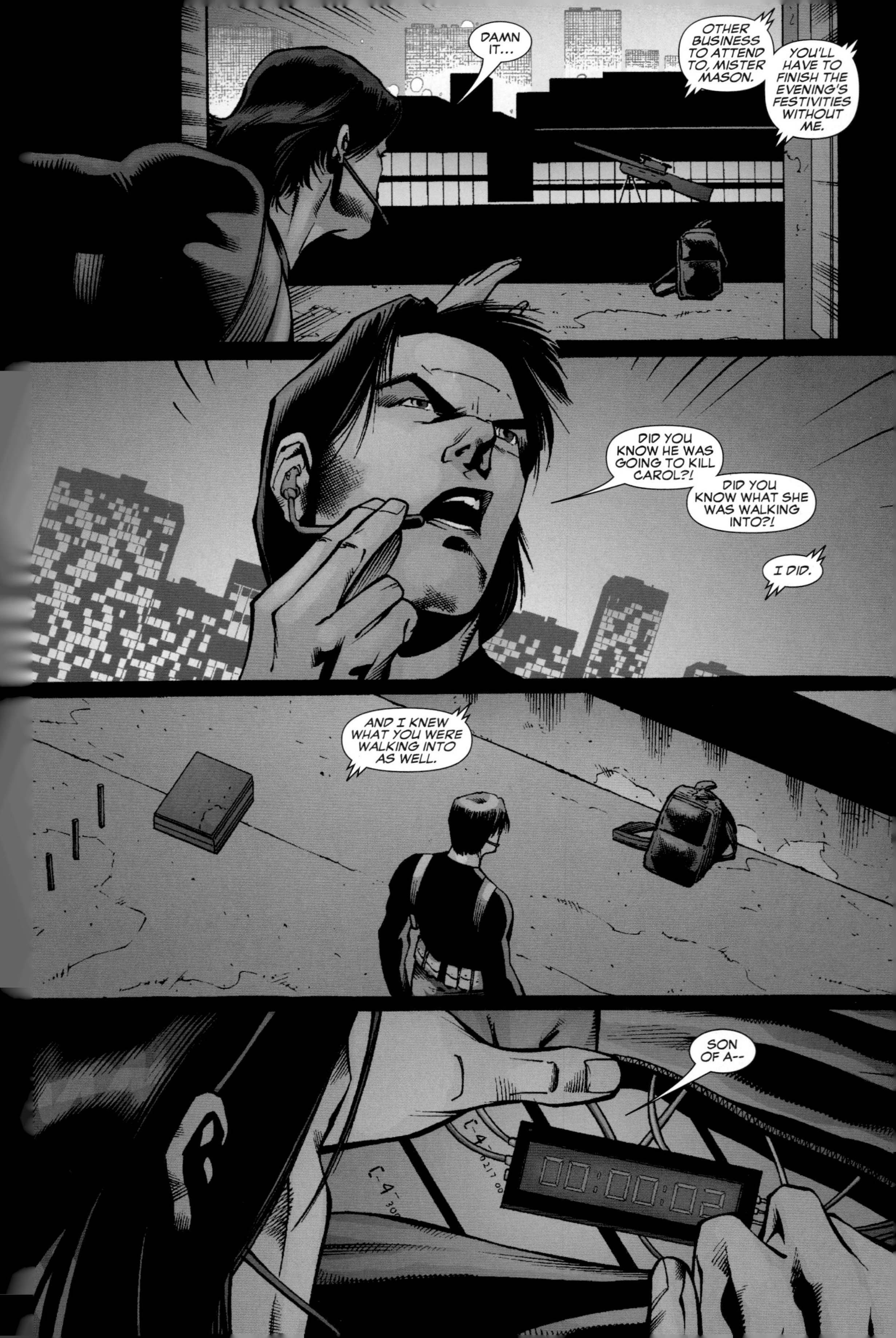
DAMN IT...
OTHER BUSINESS TO ATTEND TO, MISTER MASON.
YOU'LL HAVE TO FINISH THE EVENING'S FESTIVITIES WITHOUT ME.
DID YOU KNOW HE WAS GOING TO KILL CAROL?!
DID YOU KNOW WHAT SHE WAS WALKING INTO?!
I DID.
AND I KNEW WHAT YOU WERE WALKING INTO AS WELL.
SON OF A--
00:00:02

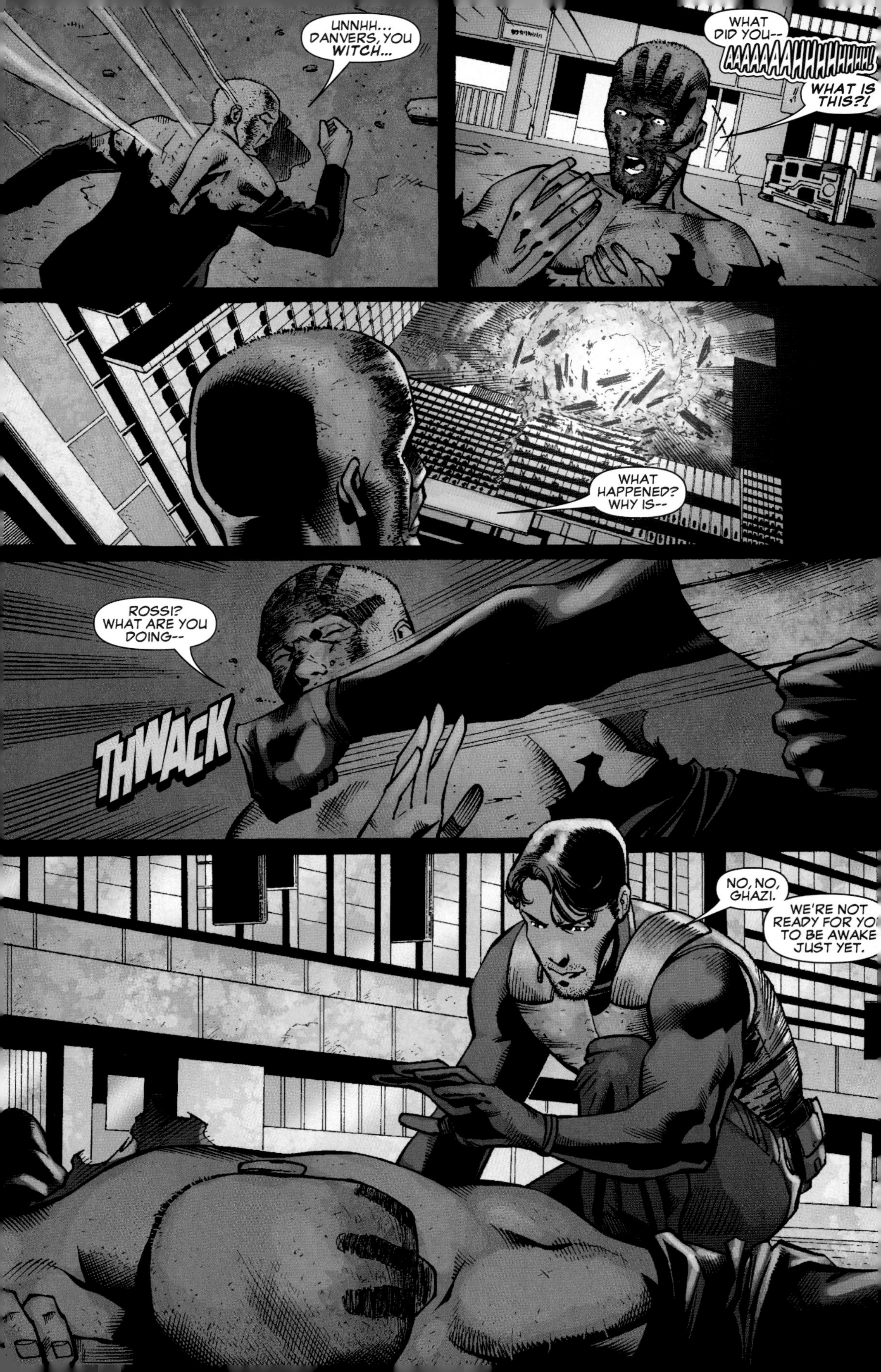
UNNHH... DANVERS, YOU WITCH...
WHAT DID YOU--
AAAAAAAHHHHHHHH!
WHAT IS THIS?!
WHAT HAPPENED? WHY IS--
ROSSI? WHAT ARE YOU DOING--
THWACK
NO, NO, GHAZI.
WE'RE NOT READY FOR YO TO BE AWAKE JUST YET.

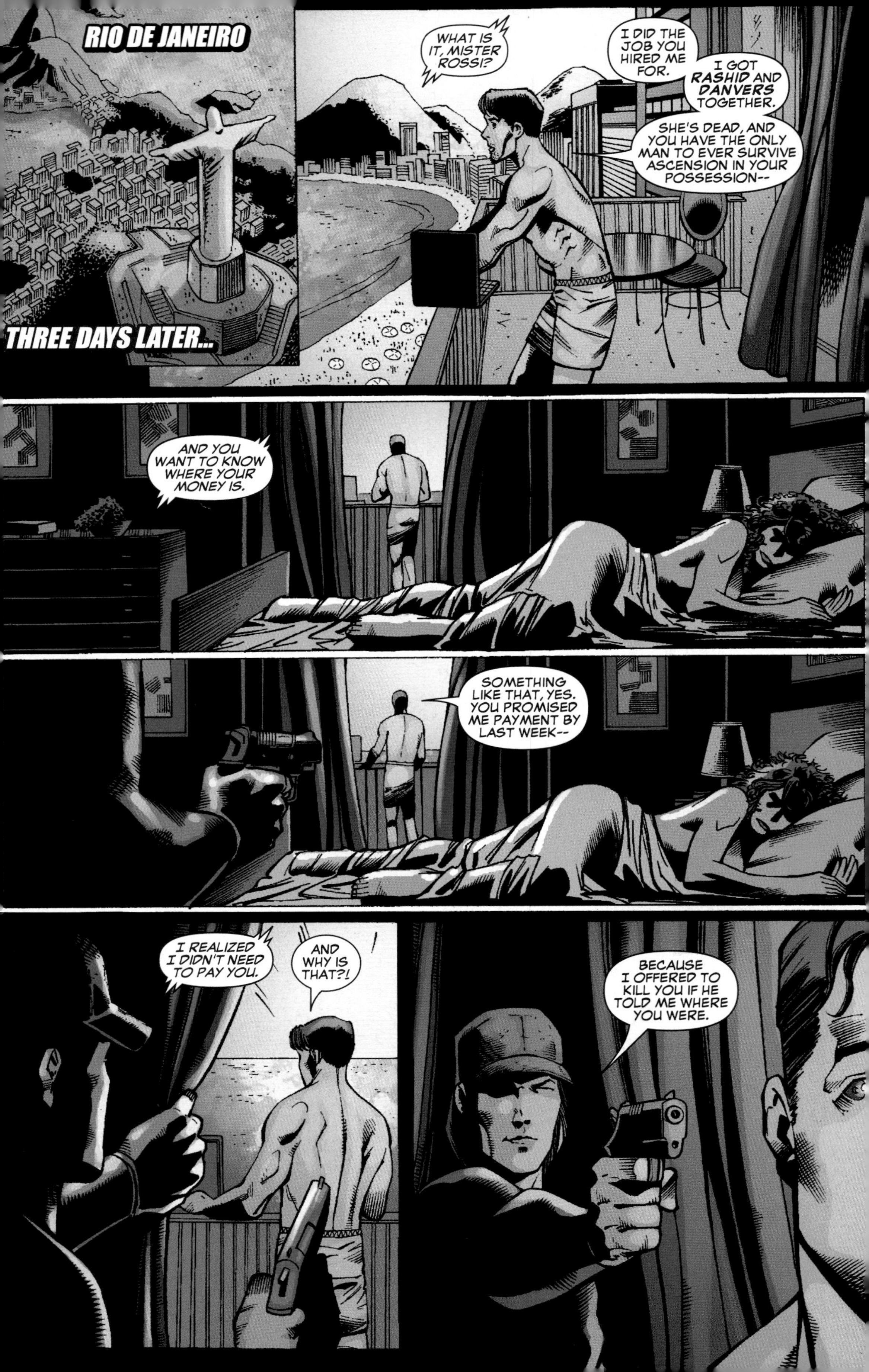
RIO DE JANEIRO
THREE DAYS LATER...
WHAT IS IT, MISTER ROSSI?
I DID THE JOB YOU HIRED ME FOR.
I GOT RASHID AND DANVERS TOGETHER.
SHE'S DEAD, AND YOU HAVE THE ONLY MAN TO EVER SURVIVE ASCENSION IN YOUR POSSESSION--
AND YOU WANT TO KNOW WHERE YOUR MONEY IS.
SOMETHING LIKE THAT, YES. YOU PROMISED ME PAYMENT BY LAST WEEK--
I REALIZED I DIDN'T NEED TO PAY YOU.
AND WHY IS THAT?!
BECAUSE I OFFERED TO KILL YOU IF HE TOLD ME WHERE YOU WERE.

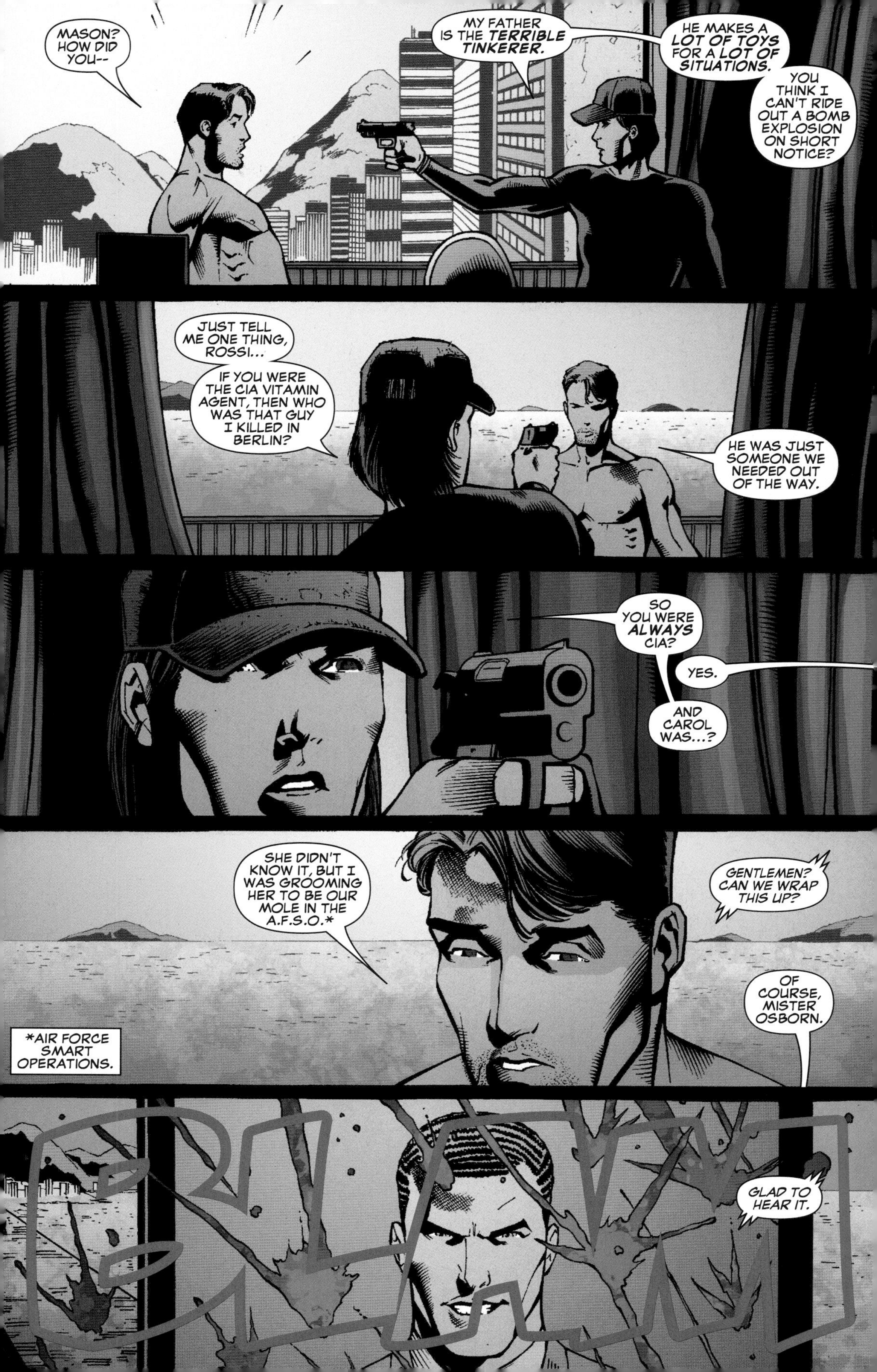

MASON? HOW DID YOU--
MY FATHER IS THE TERRIBLE TINKERER.
HE MAKES A LOT OF TOYS FOR A LOT OF SITUATIONS.
YOU THINK I CAN'T RIDE OUT A BOMB EXPLOSION ON SHORT NOTICE?
JUST TELL ME ONE THING, ROSSI...
IF YOU WERE THE CIA VITAMIN AGENT, THEN WHO WAS THAT GUY I KILLED IN BERLIN?
HE WAS JUST SOMEONE WE NEEDED OUT OF THE WAY.
SO YOU WERE ALWAYS CIA?
YES.
AND CAROL WAS...?
SHE DIDN'T KNOW IT, BUT I WAS GROOMING HER TO BE OUR MOLE IN THE A.F.S.O.*
GENTLEMEN? CAN WE WRAP THIS UP?
OF COURSE, MISTER OSBORN.
*AIR FORCE SMART OPERATIONS.
GLAD TO HEAR IT.

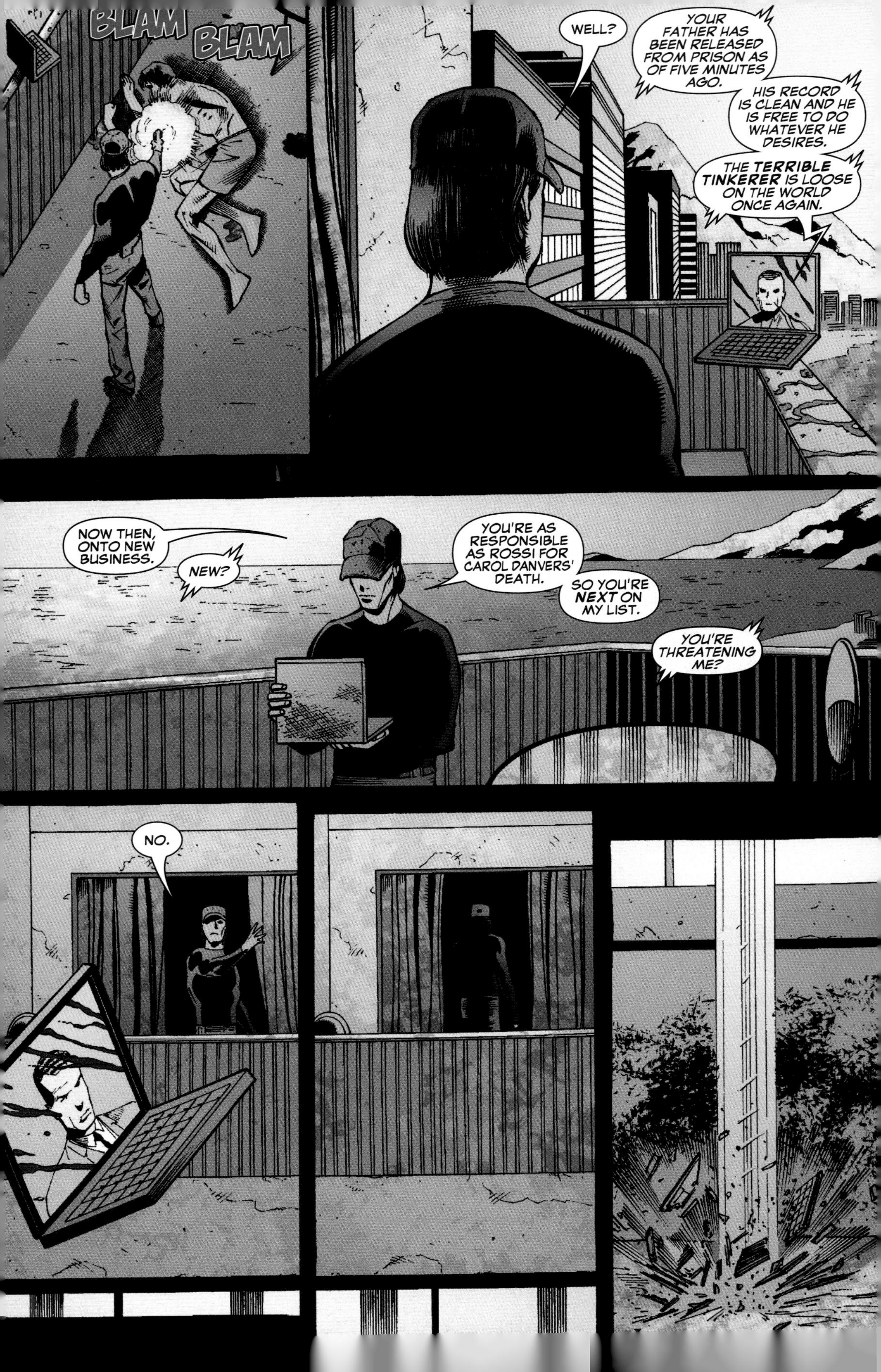
BLAM
BLAM
WELL?
YOUR FATHER HAS BEEN RELEASED FROM PRISON AS OF FIVE MINUTES AGO.
HIS RECORD IS CLEAN AND HE IS FREE TO DO WHATEVER HE DESIRES.
THE **TERRIBLE TINKERER** IS LOOSE ON THE WORLD ONCE AGAIN.
NOW THEN, ONTO NEW BUSINESS.
NEW?
YOU'RE AS RESPONSIBLE AS ROSSI FOR CAROL DANVERS' DEATH.
SO YOU'RE ***NEXT*** ON MY LIST.
YOU'RE THREATENING ME?
NO.

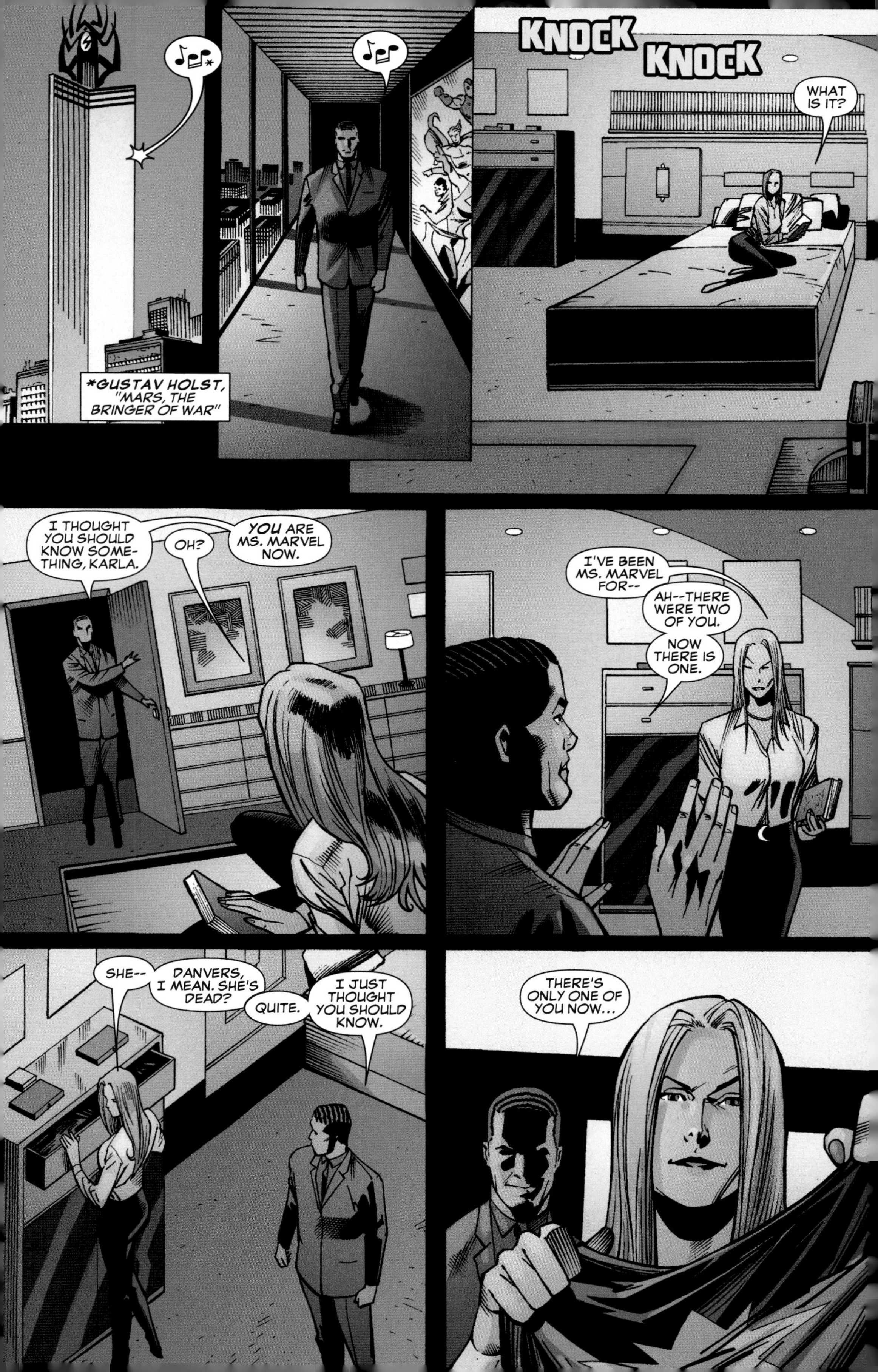

*GUSTAV HOLST, "MARS, THE BRINGER OF WAR"
KNOCK KNOCK
WHAT IS IT?
I THOUGHT YOU SHOULD KNOW SOME-THING, KARLA.
OH?
YOU ARE MS. MARVEL NOW.
I'VE BEEN MS. MARVEL FOR--
AH--THERE WERE TWO OF YOU.
NOW THERE IS ONE.
SHE--
DANVERS, I MEAN. SHE'S DEAD?
QUITE.
I JUST THOUGHT YOU SHOULD KNOW.
THERE'S ONLY ONE OF YOU NOW...

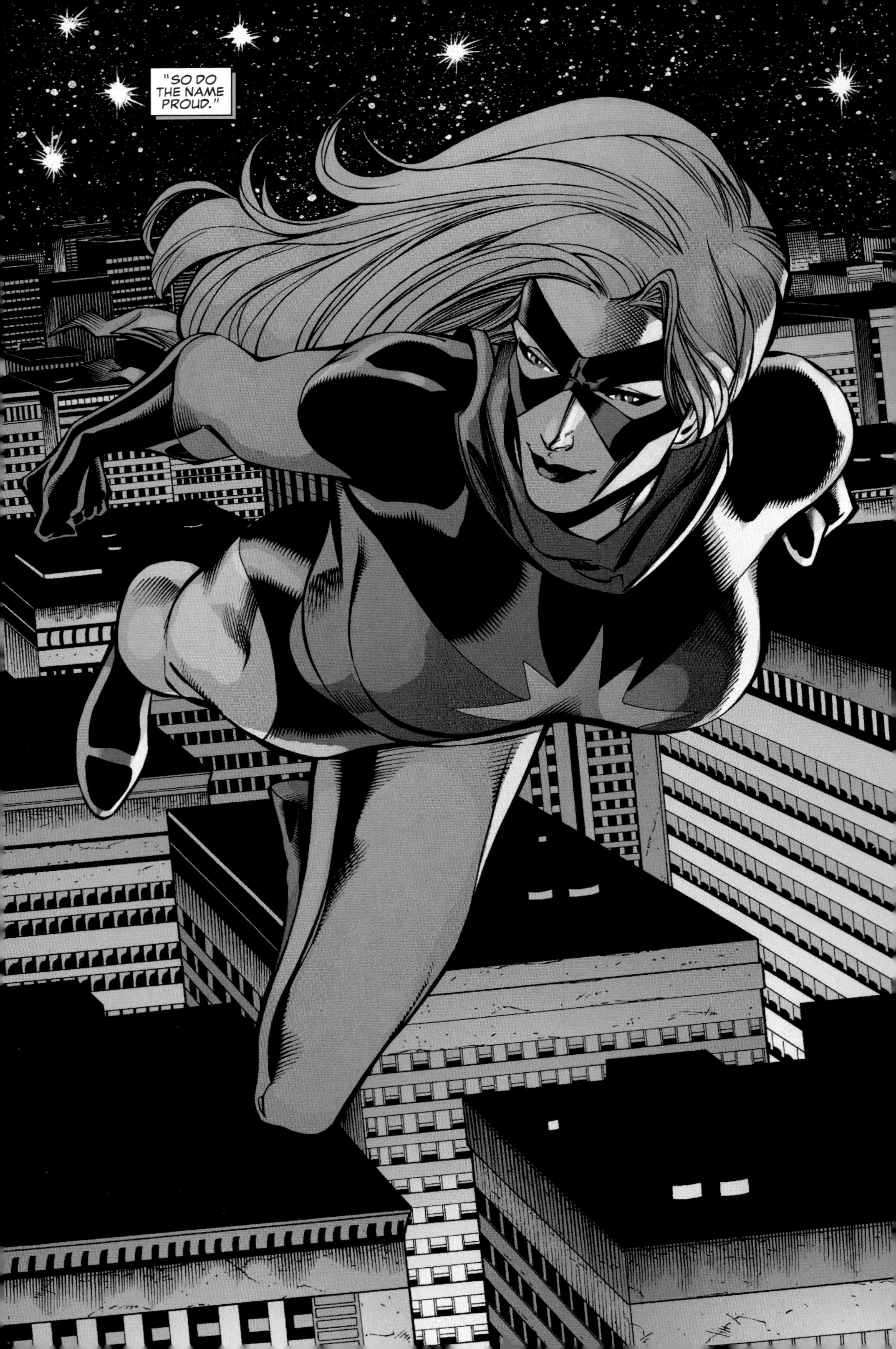
"SO DO THE NAME PROUD."

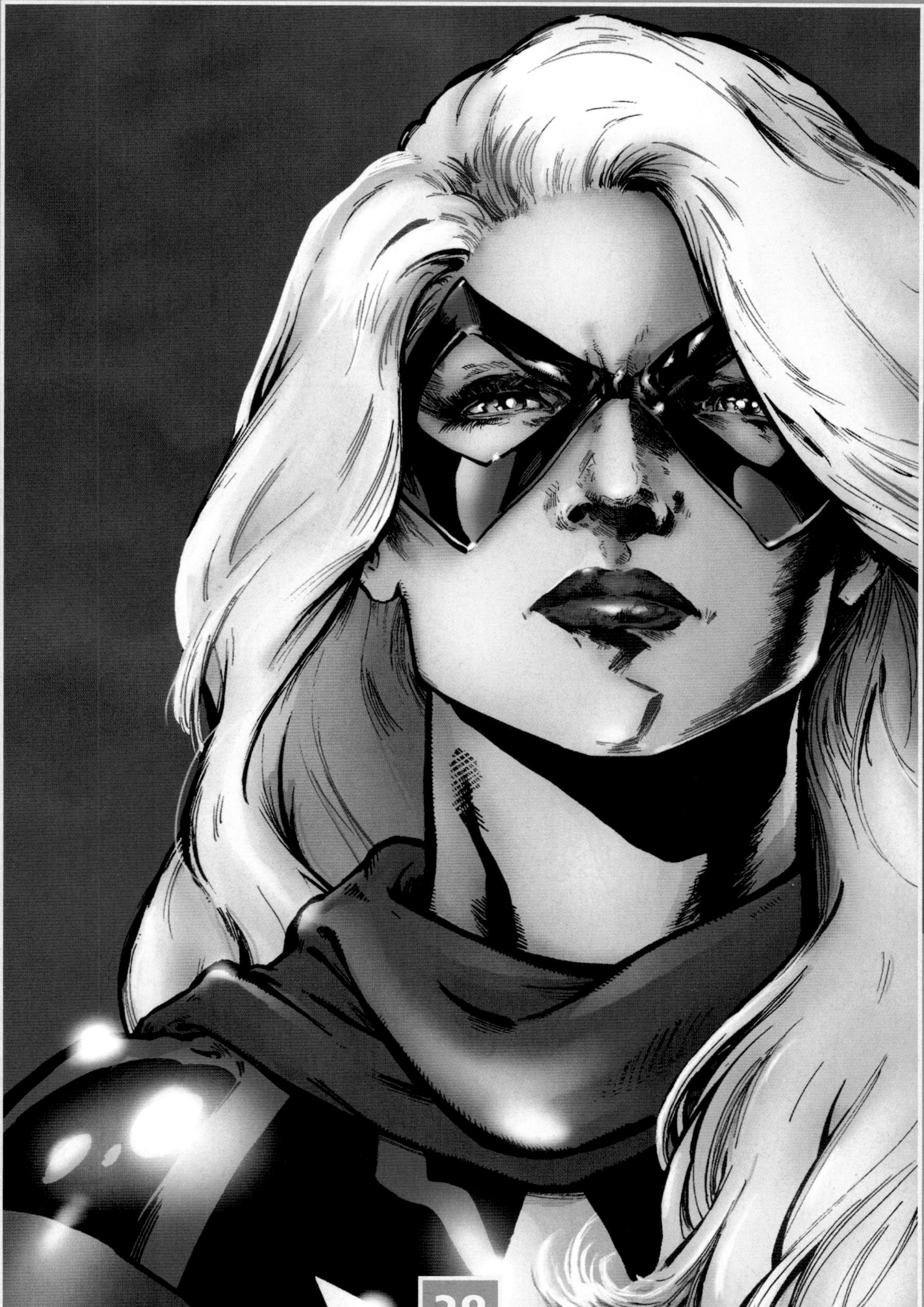

38
MEET THE NEW BOSS...

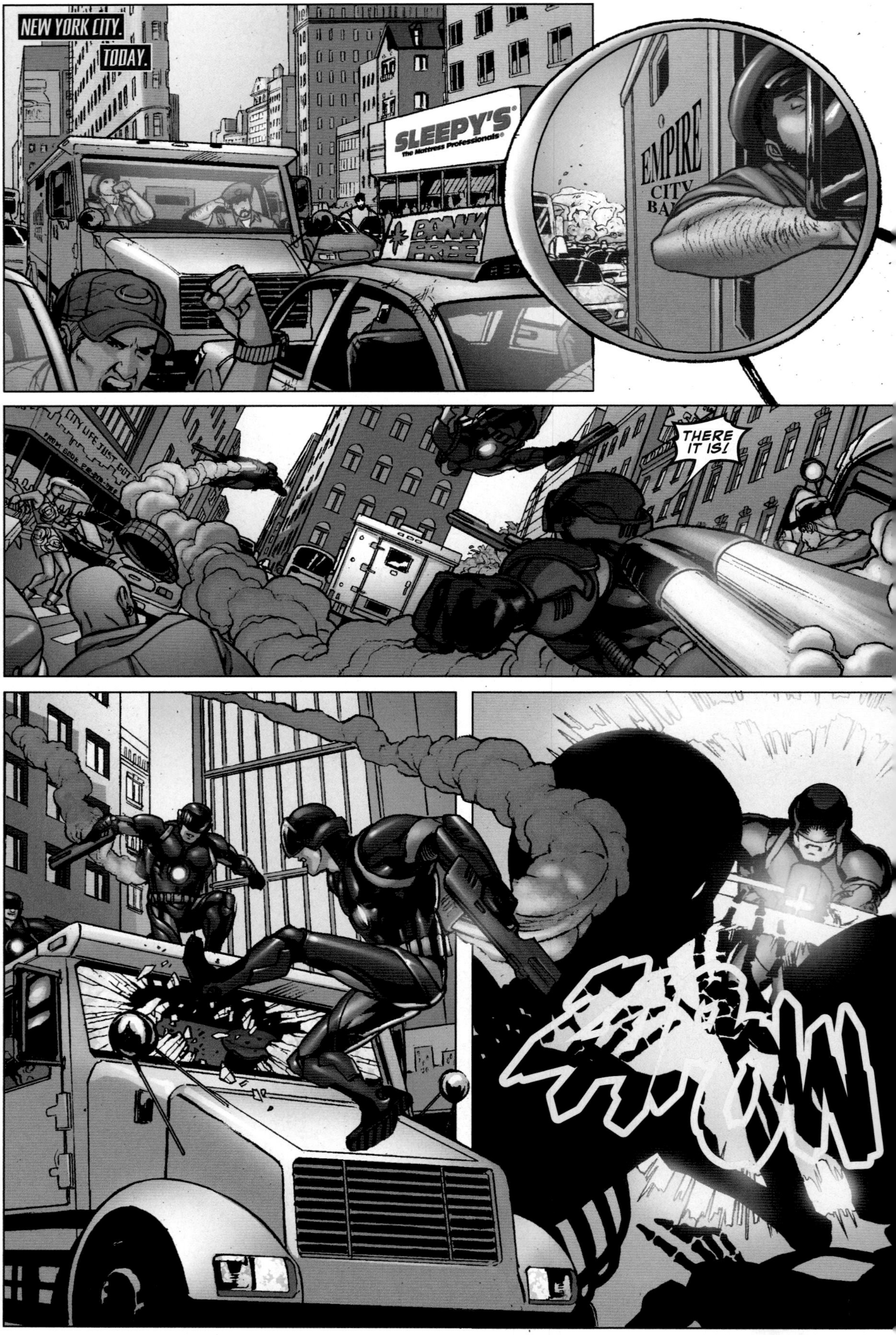
NEW YORK CITY.
TODAY.
SLEEPY'S
The Mattress Professionals
EMPIRE
CITY
THERE IT IS!

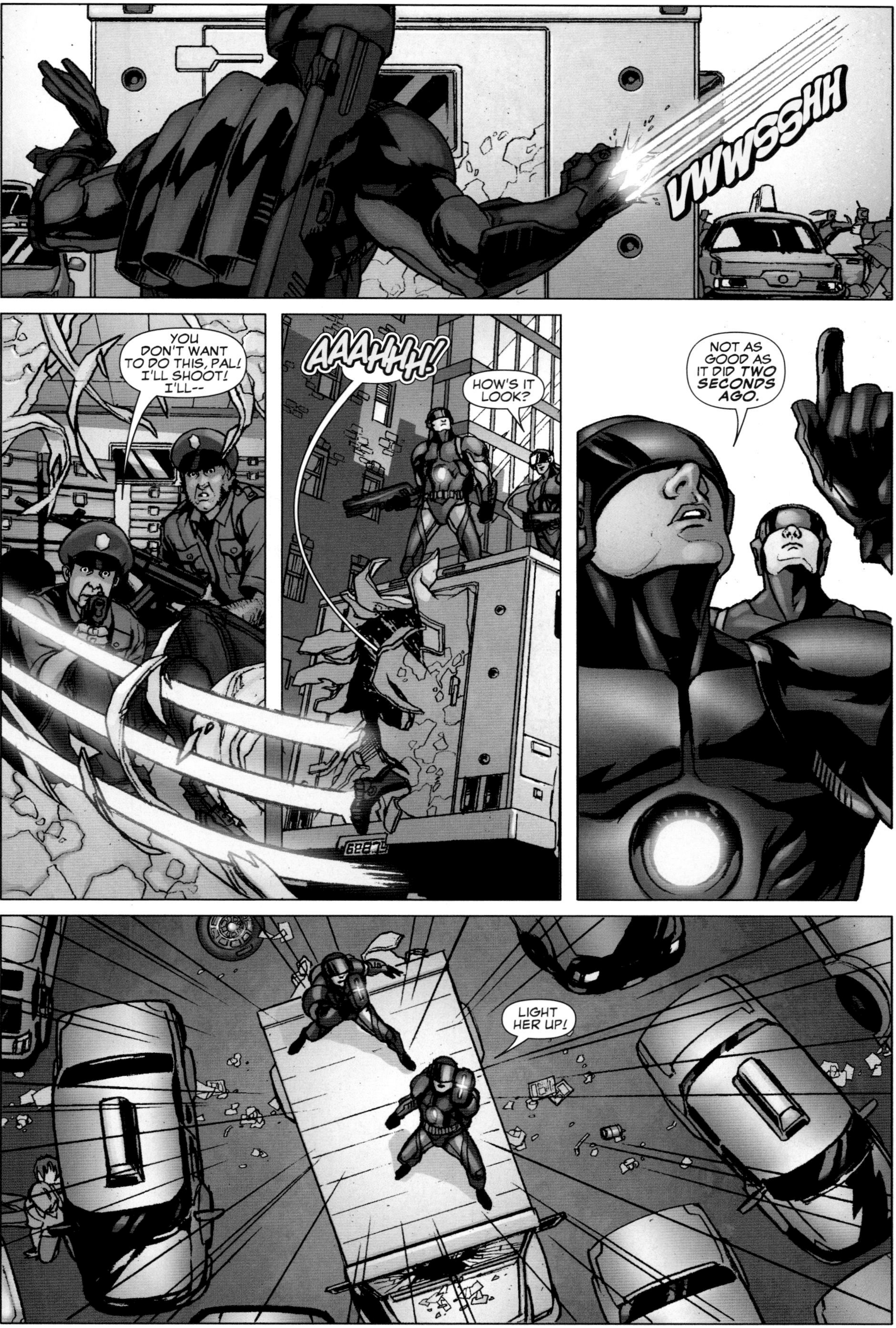
VWWSSHH
YOU DON'T WANT TO DO THIS, PAL! I'LL SHOOT! I'LL--
AAAHHH!
HOW'S IT LOOK?
NOT AS GOOD AS IT DID TWO SECONDS AGO.
LIGHT HER UP!

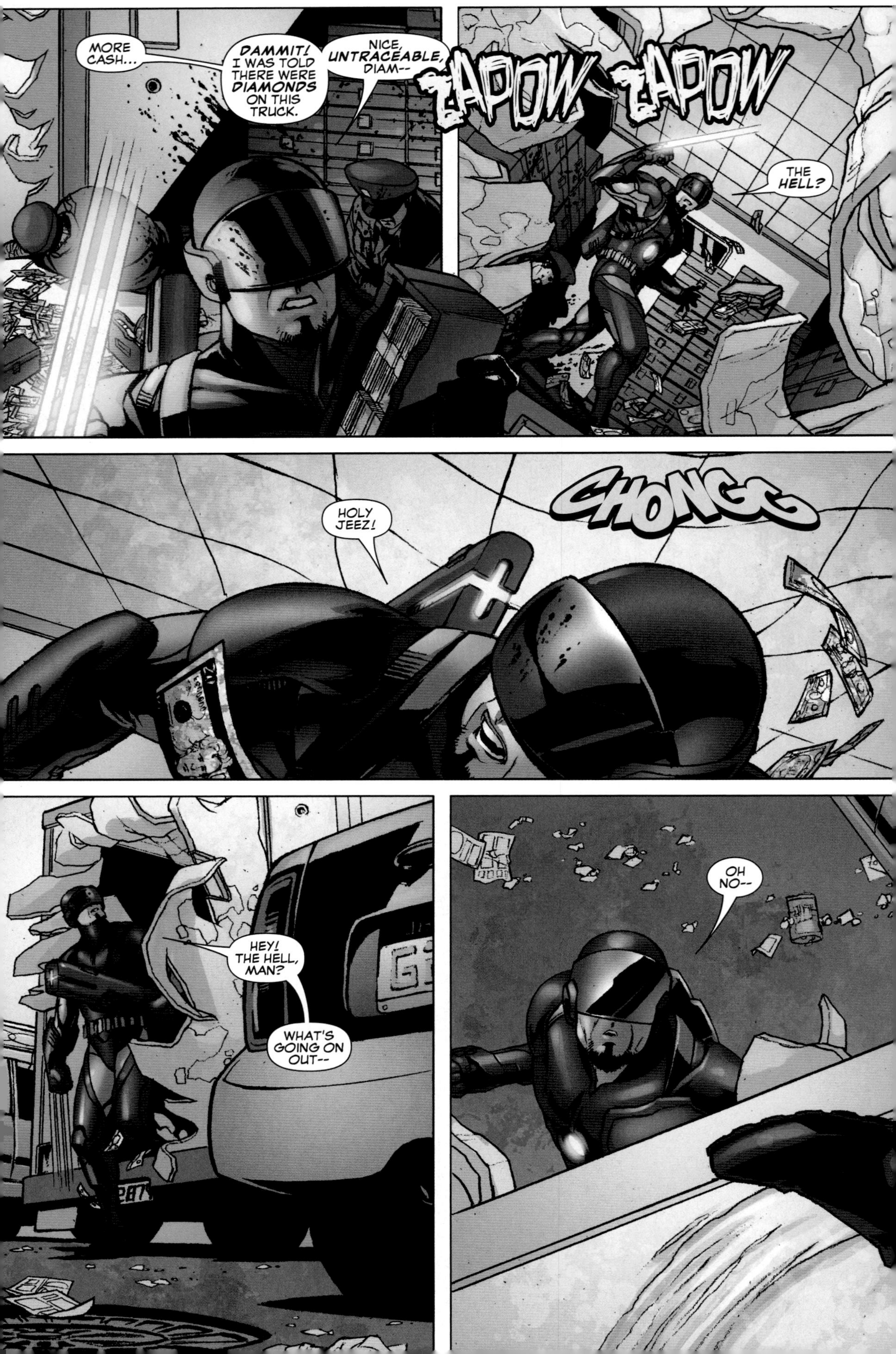
MORE CASH...
DAMMIT! I WAS TOLD THERE WERE DIAMONDS ON THIS TRUCK.
NICE, UNTRACEABLE, DIAM--
ZAPOW ZAPOW
THE HELL?
CHONGG
HOLY JEEZ!
HEY! THE HELL, MAN?
WHAT'S GOING ON OUT--
OH NO--

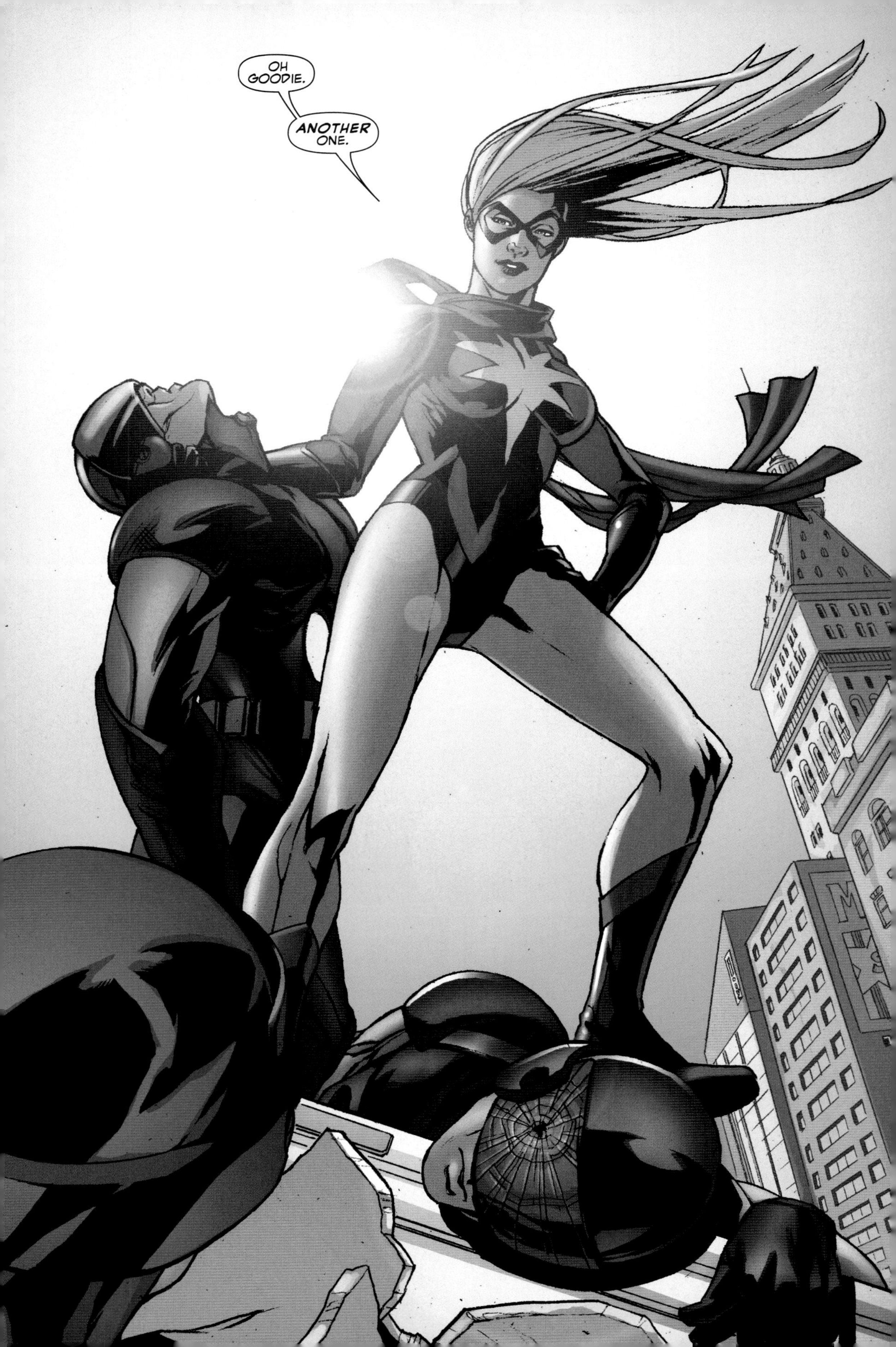
OH GOODIE.
ANOTHER ONE.

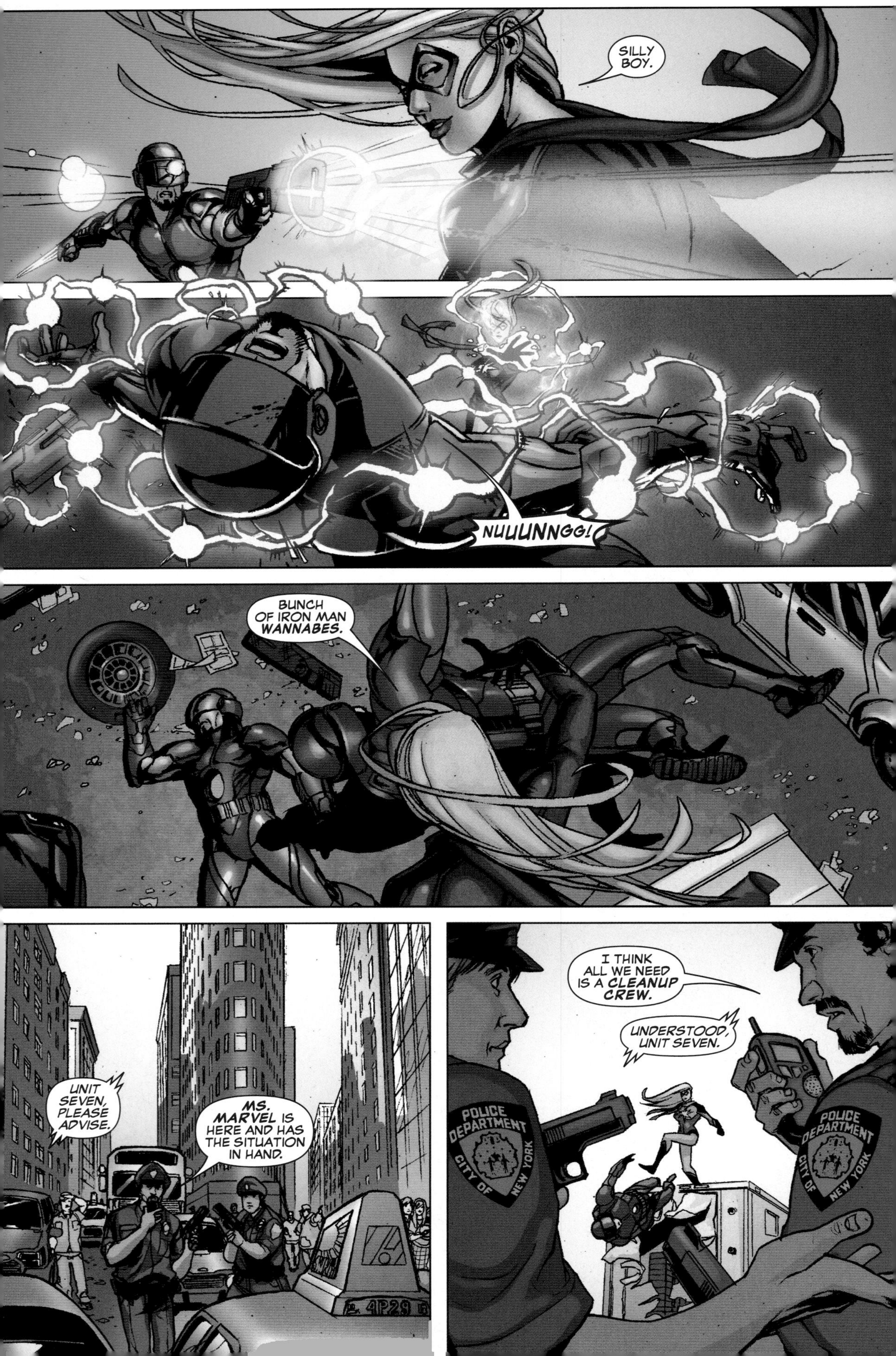
SILLY BOY.
NUUUNNGG!
BUNCH OF IRON MAN WANNABES.
UNIT SEVEN, PLEASE ADVISE.
MS. MARVEL IS HERE AND HAS THE SITUATION IN HAND.
POLICE DEPARTMENT CITY OF NEW YORK
I THINK ALL WE NEED IS A CLEANUP CREW.
UNDERSTOOD, UNIT SEVEN.
POLICE DEPARTMENT CITY OF NEW YORK

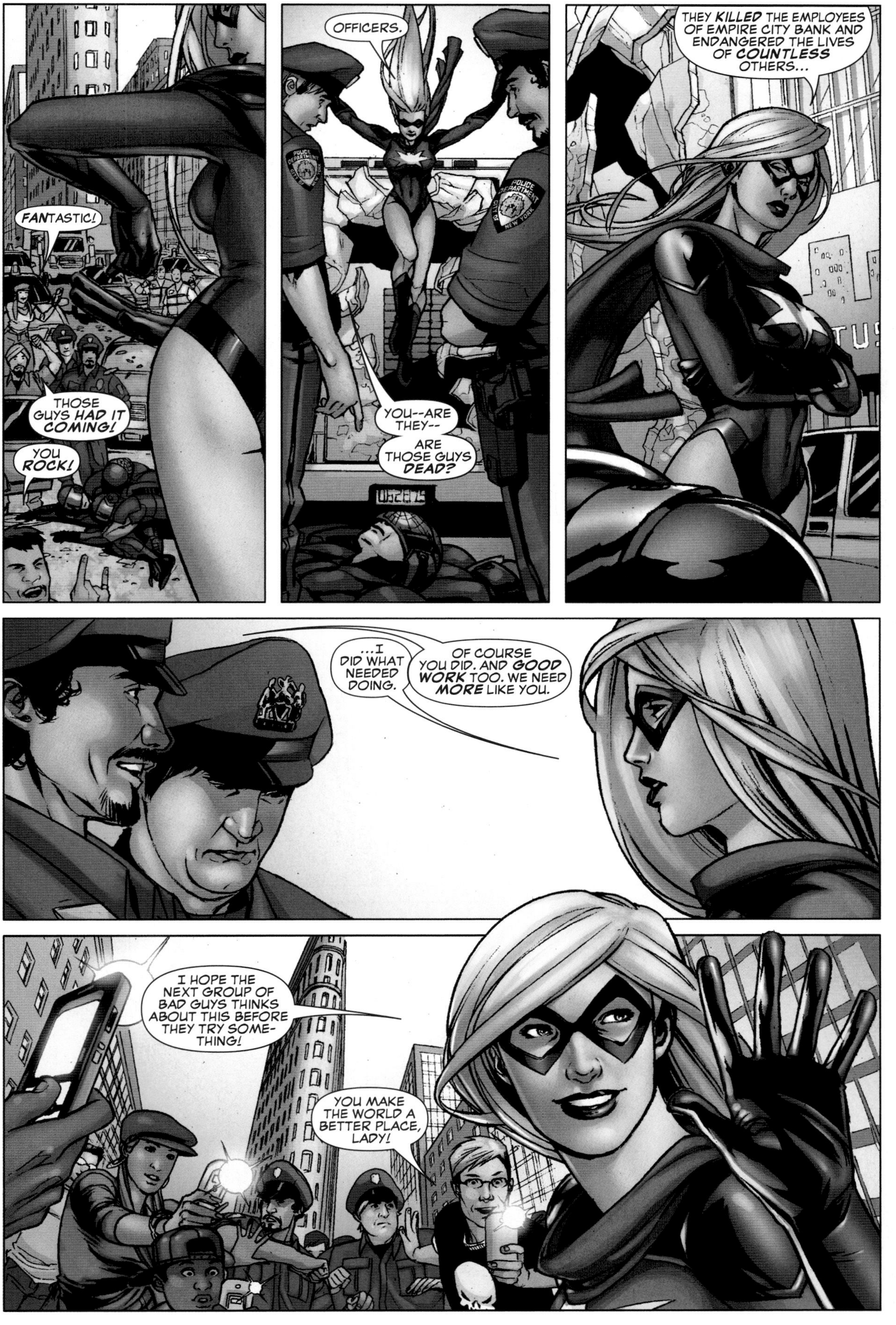
FANTASTIC!
THOSE GUYS HAD IT COMING!
YOU ROCK!
OFFICERS.
YOU--ARE THEY--
ARE THOSE GUYS DEAD?
THEY KILLED THE EMPLOYEES OF EMPIRE CITY BANK AND ENDANGERED THE LIVES OF COUNTLESS OTHERS...
...I DID WHAT NEEDED DOING.
OF COURSE YOU DID. AND GOOD WORK TOO. WE NEED MORE LIKE YOU.
I HOPE THE NEXT GROUP OF BAD GUYS THINKS ABOUT THIS BEFORE THEY TRY SOME-THING!
YOU MAKE THE WORLD A BETTER PLACE, LADY!

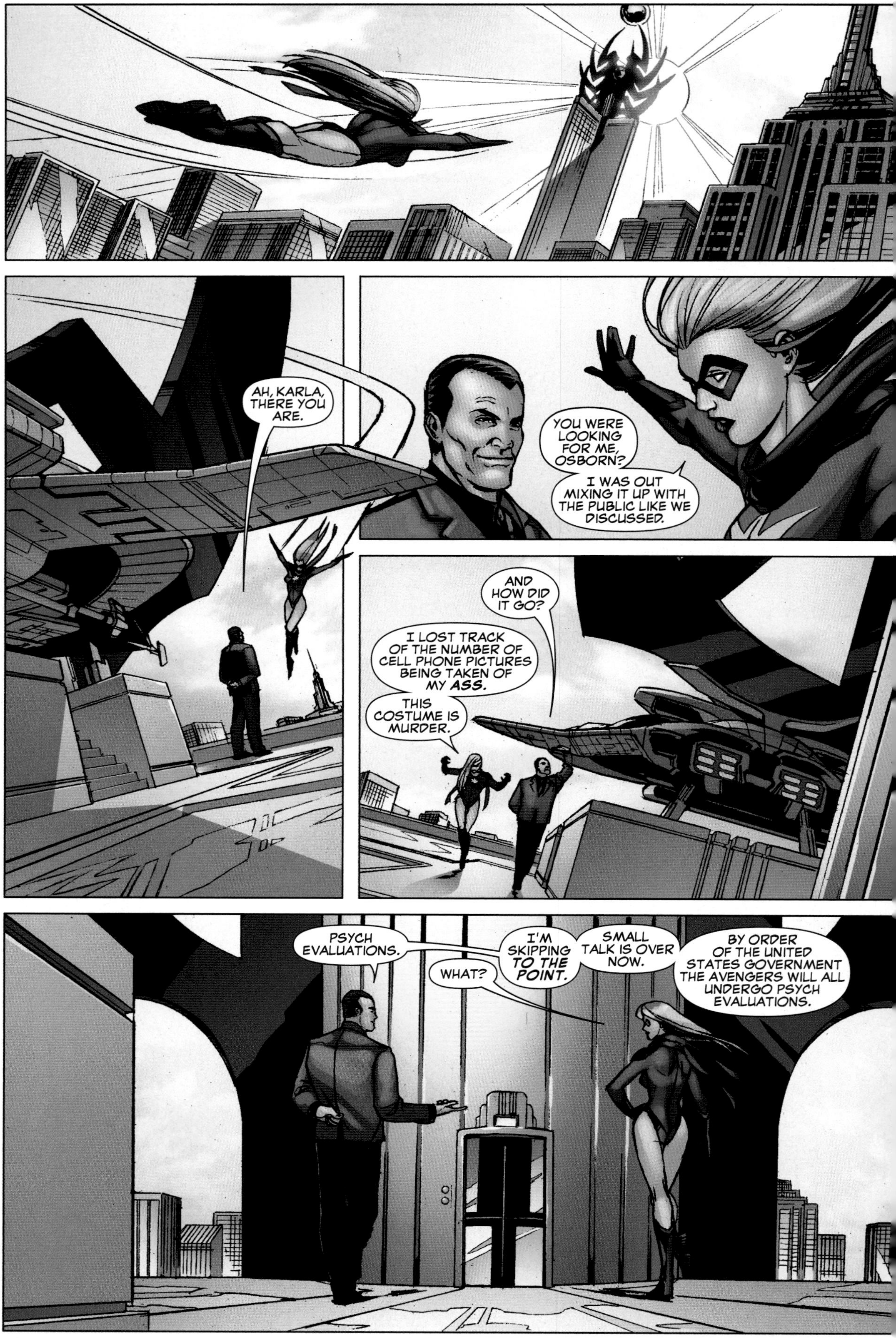
AH, KARLA, THERE YOU ARE.
YOU WERE LOOKING FOR ME, OSBORN?
I WAS OUT MIXING IT UP WITH THE PUBLIC LIKE WE DISCUSSED.
AND HOW DID IT GO?
I LOST TRACK OF THE NUMBER OF CELL PHONE PICTURES BEING TAKEN OF MY ASS.
THIS COSTUME IS MURDER.
PSYCH EVALUATIONS.
WHAT?
I'M SKIPPING TO THE POINT.
SMALL TALK IS OVER NOW.
BY ORDER OF THE UNITED STATES GOVERNMENT THE AVENGERS WILL ALL UNDERGO PSYCH EVALUATIONS.

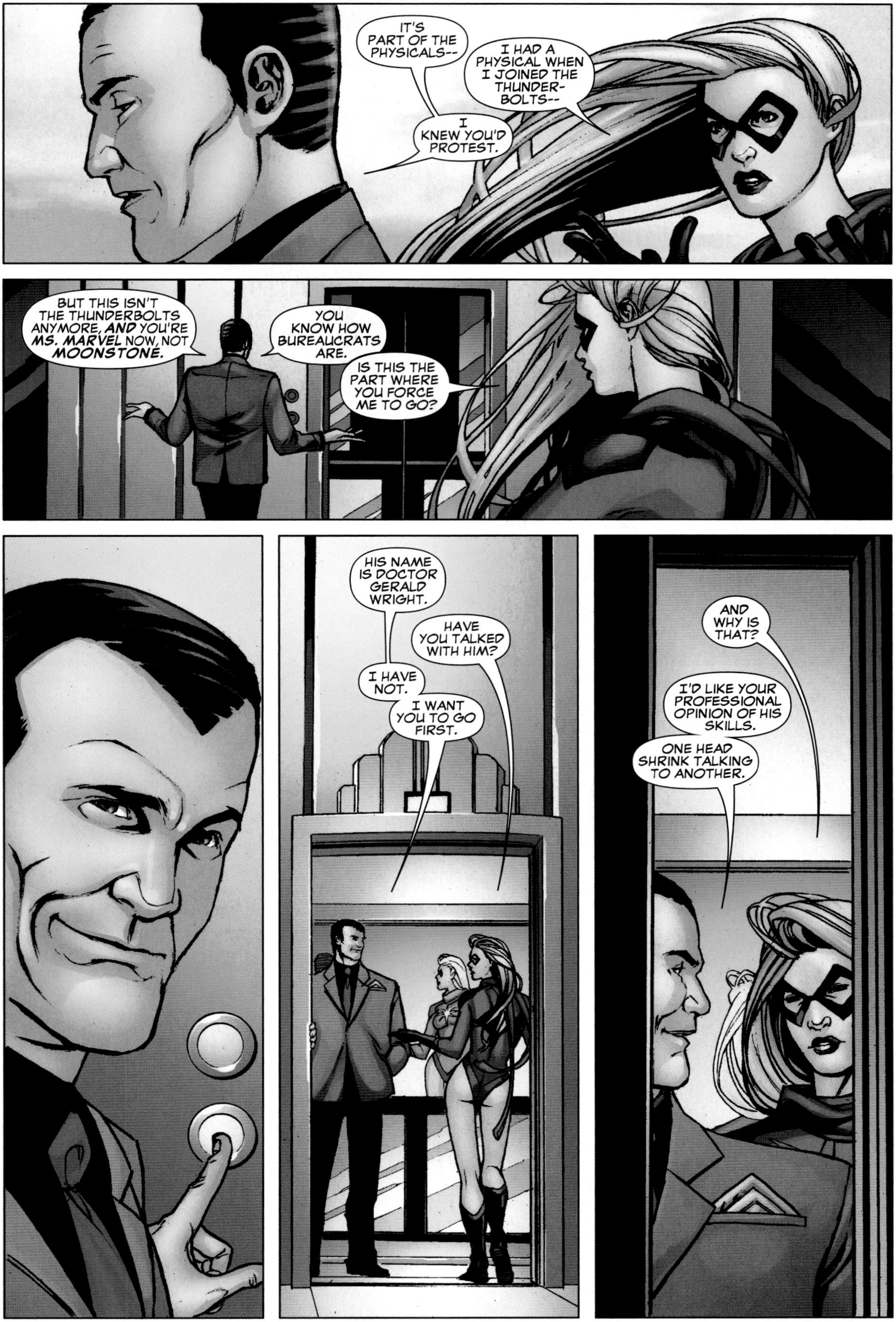

IT'S PART OF THE PHYSICALS--
I HAD A PHYSICAL WHEN I JOINED THE THUNDER-BOLTS--
I KNEW YOU'D PROTEST.
BUT THIS ISN'T THE THUNDERBOLTS ANYMORE, AND YOU'RE MS. MARVEL NOW, NOT MOONSTONE.
YOU KNOW HOW BUREAUCRATS ARE.
IS THIS THE PART WHERE YOU FORCE ME TO GO?
HIS NAME IS DOCTOR GERALD WRIGHT.
HAVE YOU TALKED WITH HIM?
I HAVE NOT.
I WANT YOU TO GO FIRST.
AND WHY IS THAT?
I'D LIKE YOUR PROFESSIONAL OPINION OF HIS SKILLS.
ONE HEAD SHRINK TALKING TO ANOTHER.

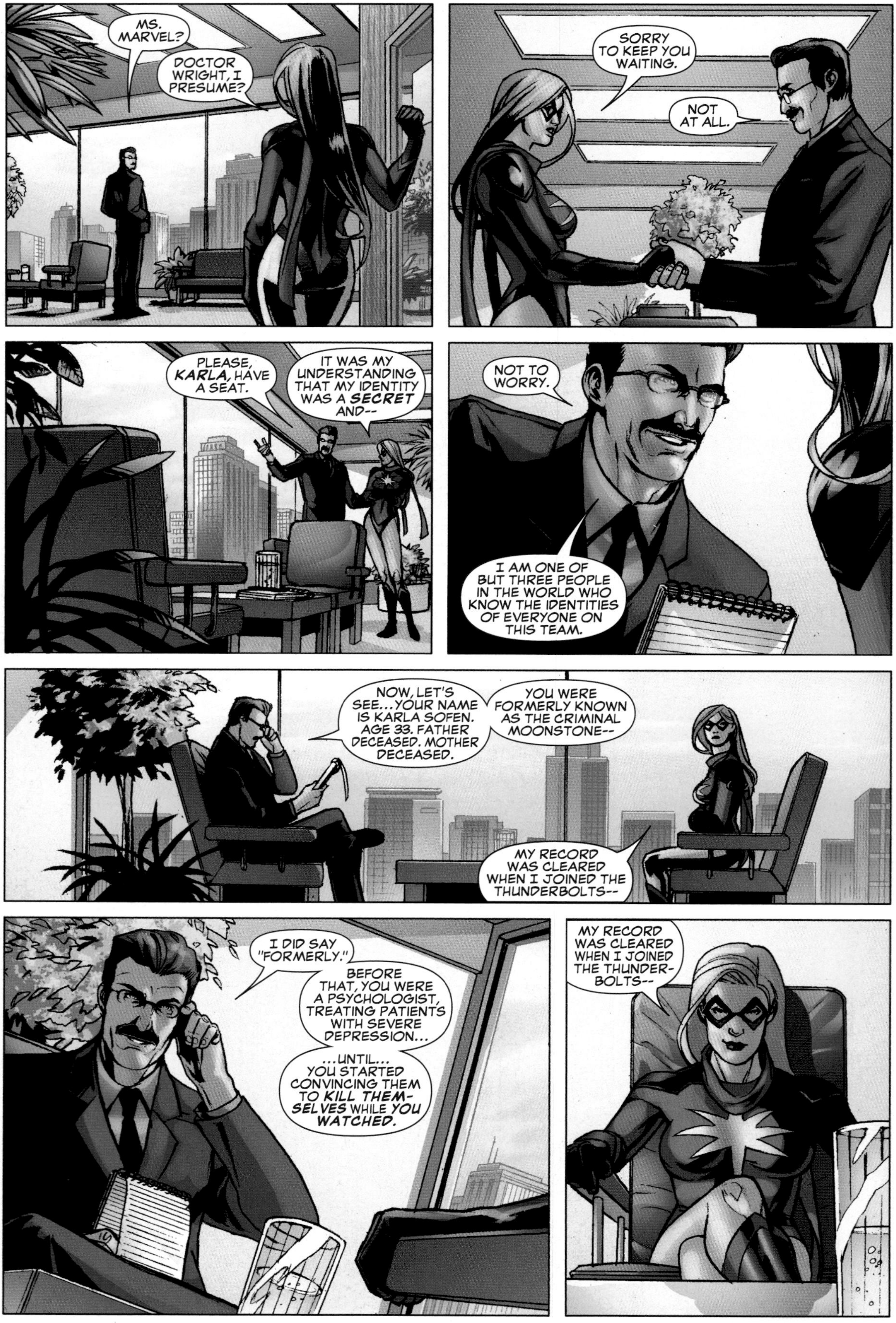
MS. MARVEL?
DOCTOR WRIGHT, I PRESUME?
SORRY TO KEEP YOU WAITING.
NOT AT ALL.
PLEASE, KARLA, HAVE A SEAT.
IT WAS MY UNDERSTANDING THAT MY IDENTITY WAS A SECRET AND--
NOT TO WORRY.
I AM ONE OF BUT THREE PEOPLE IN THE WORLD WHO KNOW THE IDENTITIES OF EVERYONE ON THIS TEAM.
NOW, LET'S SEE... YOUR NAME IS KARLA SOFEN. AGE 33. FATHER DECEASED. MOTHER DECEASED.
YOU WERE FORMERLY KNOWN AS THE CRIMINAL MOONSTONE--
MY RECORD WAS CLEARED WHEN I JOINED THE THUNDERBOLTS--
I DID SAY "FORMERLY."
BEFORE THAT, YOU WERE A PSYCHOLOGIST, TREATING PATIENTS WITH SEVERE DEPRESSION...
...UNTIL... YOU STARTED CONVINCING THEM TO KILL THEMSELVES WHILE YOU WATCHED.
MY RECORD WAS CLEARED WHEN I JOINED THE THUNDERBOLTS--

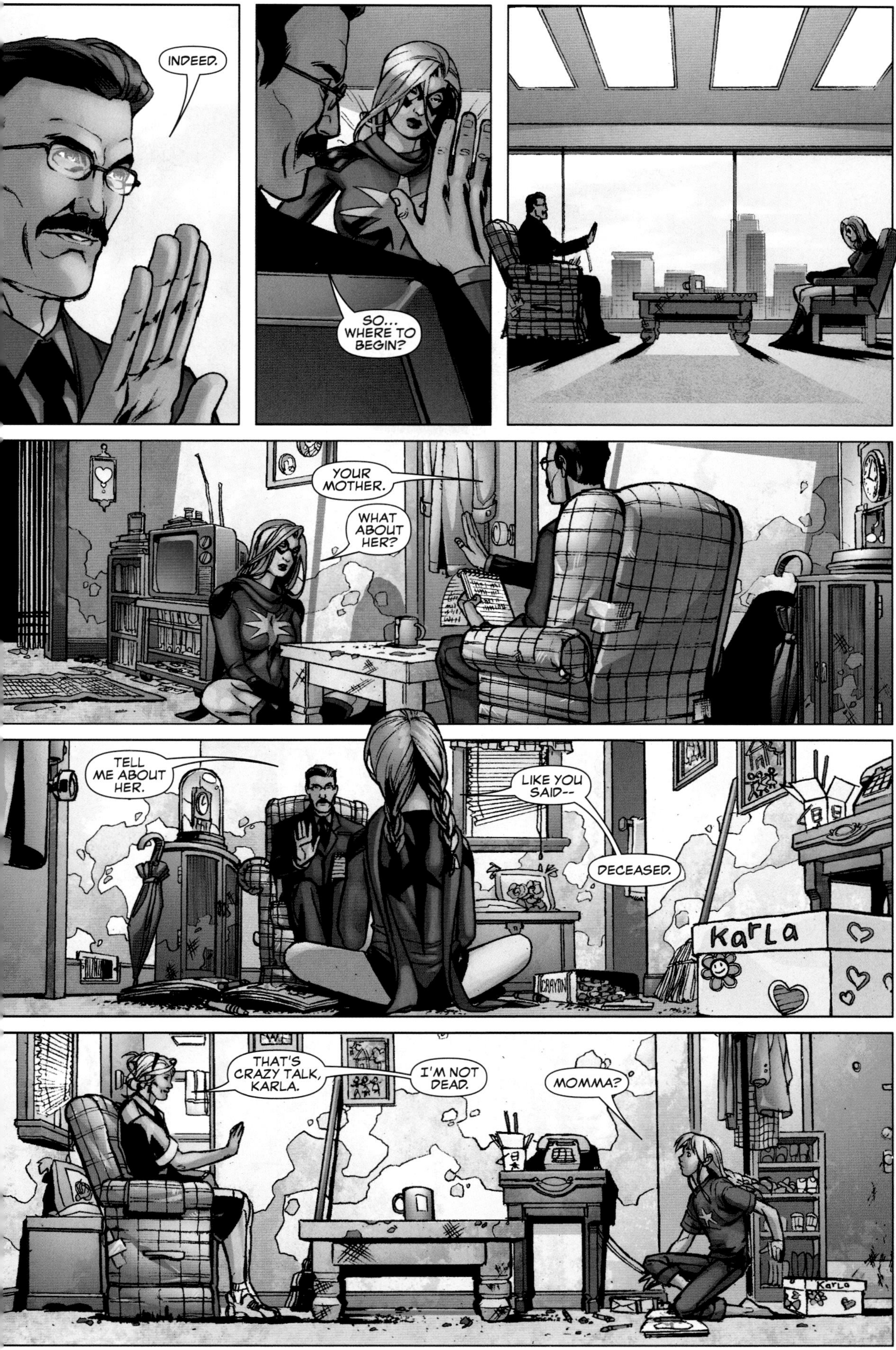
INDEED.
SO... WHERE TO BEGIN?
YOUR MOTHER.
WHAT ABOUT HER?
TELL ME ABOUT HER.
LIKE YOU SAID--
DECEASED.
KARLA
CRAYON
THAT'S CRAZY TALK, KARLA.
I'M NOT DEAD.
MOMMA?
KARLA

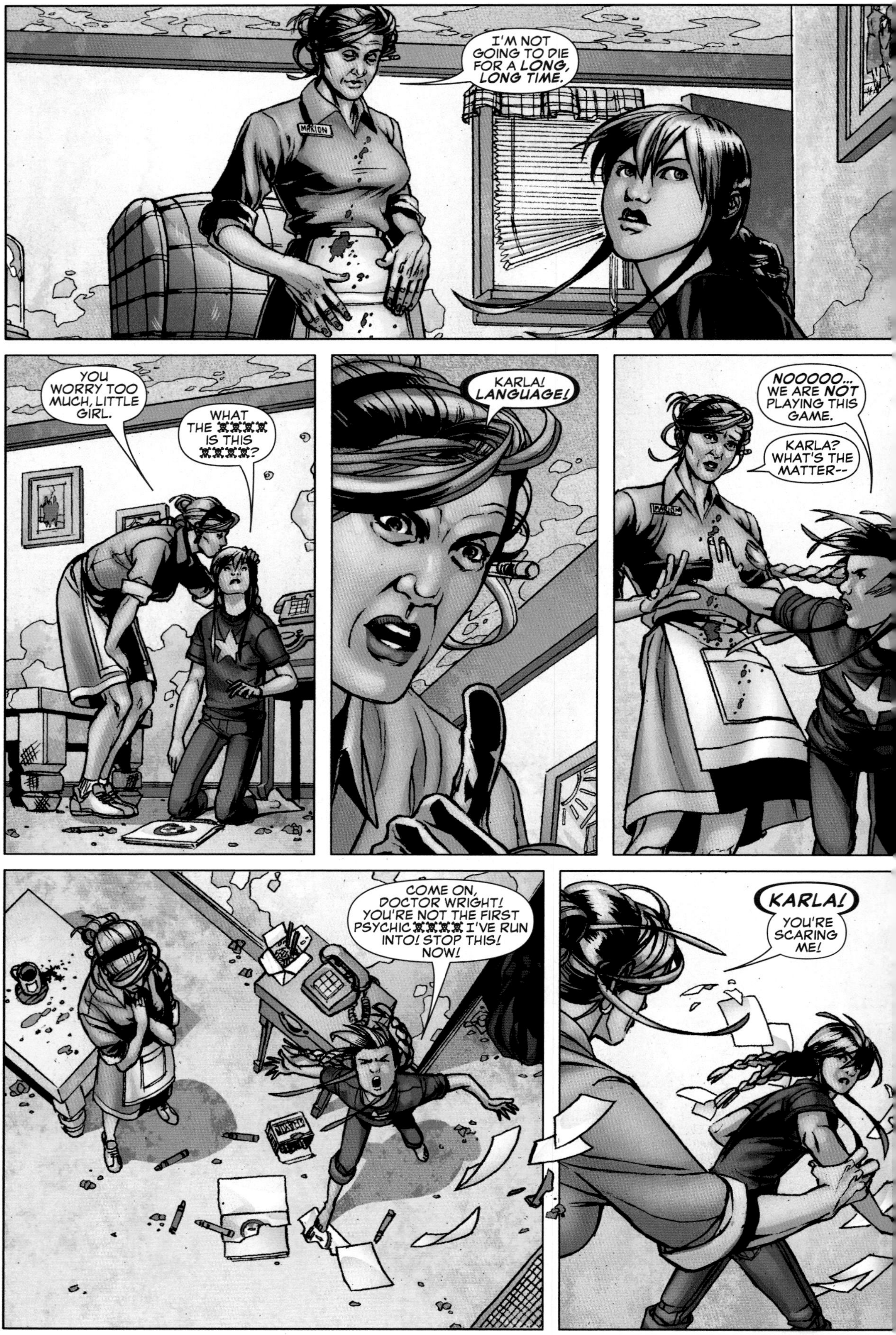
I'M NOT GOING TO DIE FOR A LONG, LONG TIME.
YOU WORRY TOO MUCH, LITTLE GIRL.
WHAT THE ☠☠☠☠ IS THIS ☠☠☠☠?
KARLA! LANGUAGE!
NOOOOO... WE ARE NOT PLAYING THIS GAME.
KARLA? WHAT'S THE MATTER--
COME ON, DOCTOR WRIGHT! YOU'RE NOT THE FIRST PSYCHIC ☠☠☠☠ I'VE RUN INTO! STOP THIS! NOW!
KARLA!
YOU'RE SCARING ME!

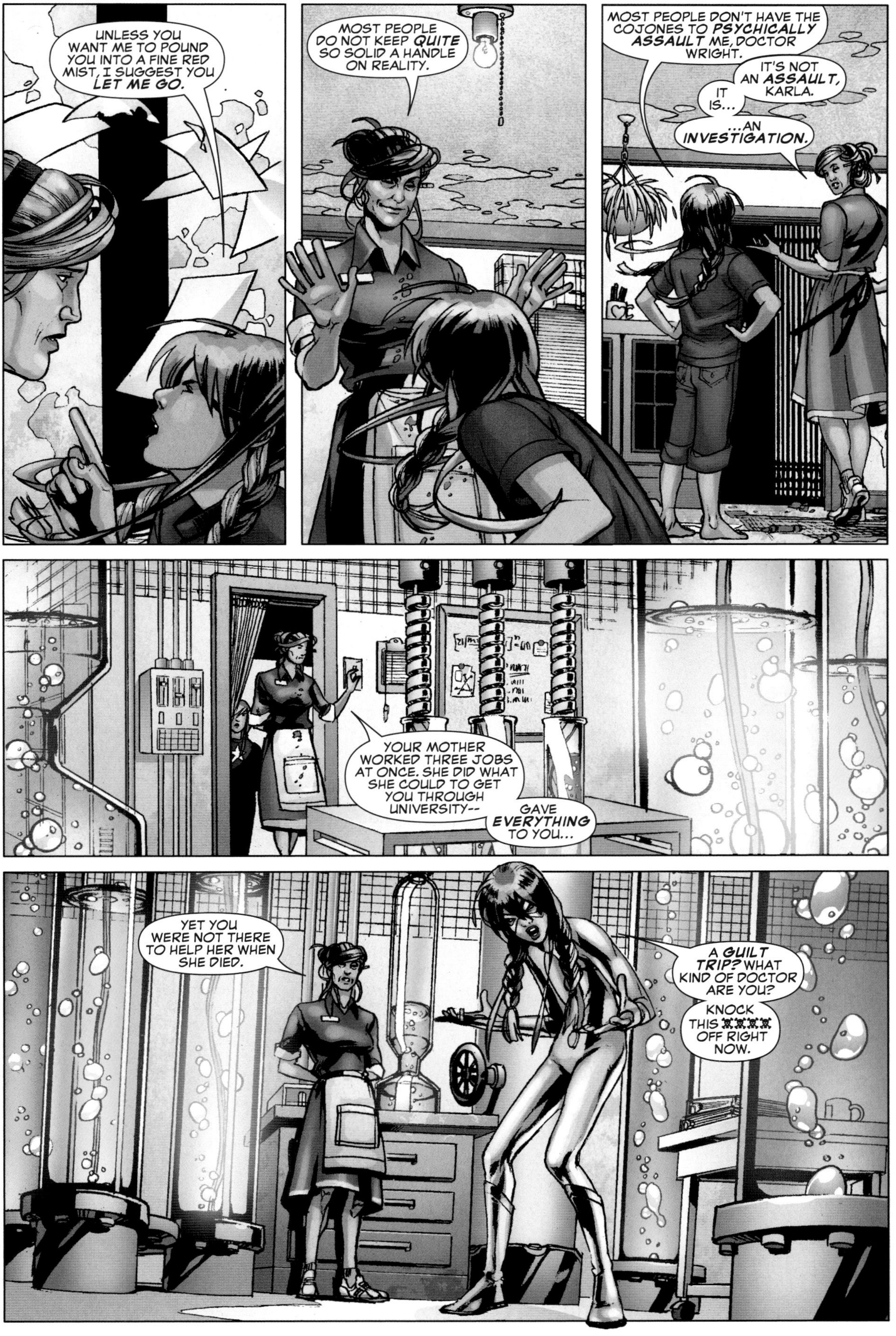
UNLESS YOU WANT ME TO POUND YOU INTO A FINE RED MIST, I SUGGEST YOU LET ME GO.
MOST PEOPLE DO NOT KEEP QUITE SO SOLID A HANDLE ON REALITY.
MOST PEOPLE DON'T HAVE THE COJONES TO PSYCHICALLY ASSAULT ME, DOCTOR WRIGHT.
IT'S NOT AN ASSAULT, KARLA.
IT IS...
...AN INVESTIGATION.
YOUR MOTHER WORKED THREE JOBS AT ONCE. SHE DID WHAT SHE COULD TO GET YOU THROUGH UNIVERSITY--
GAVE EVERYTHING TO YOU...
YET YOU WERE NOT THERE TO HELP HER WHEN SHE DIED.
A GUILT TRIP? WHAT KIND OF DOCTOR ARE YOU?
KNOCK THIS ☠☠☠ OFF RIGHT NOW.

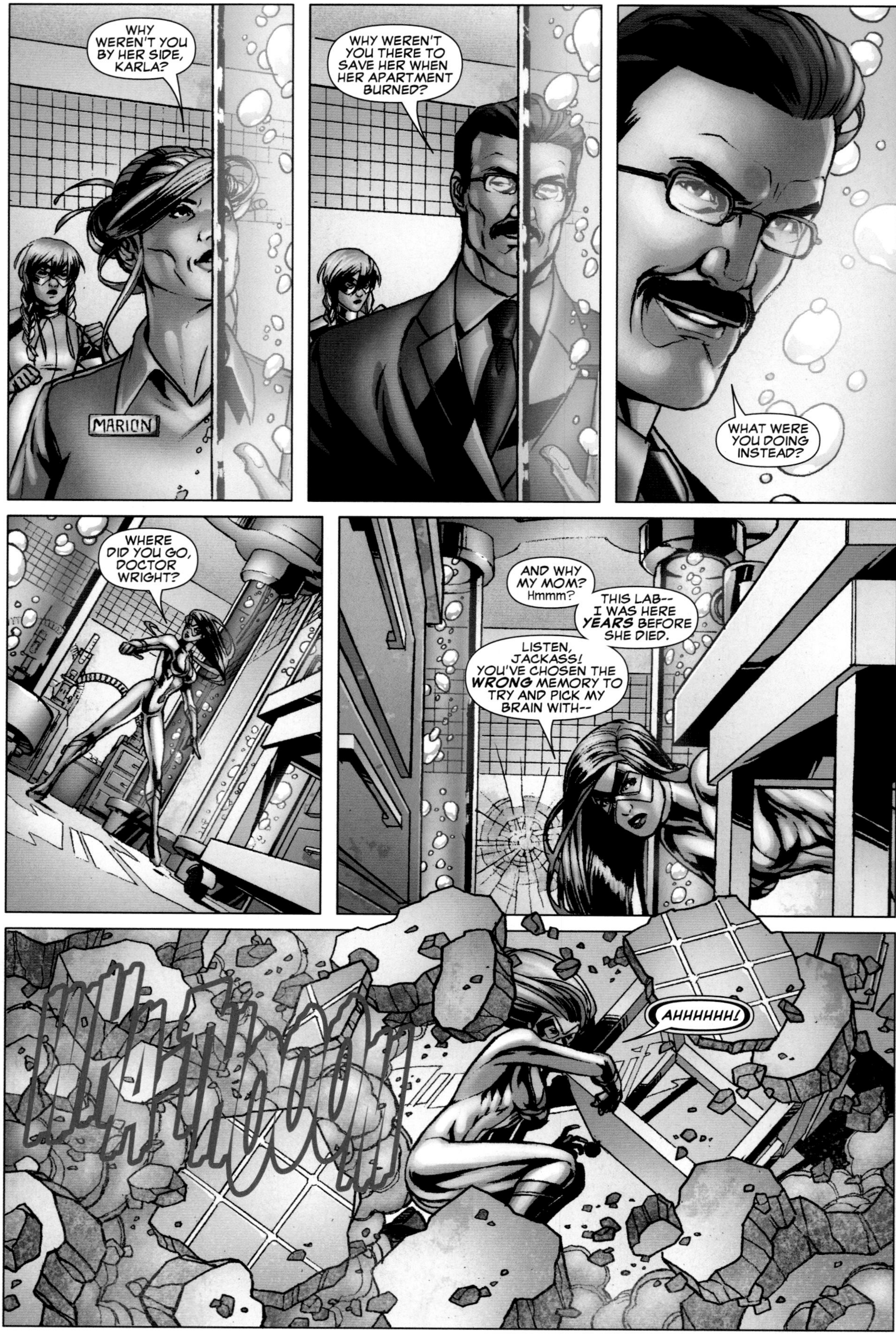
WHY WEREN'T YOU BY HER SIDE, KARLA?
MARION
WHY WEREN'T YOU THERE TO SAVE HER WHEN HER APARTMENT BURNED?
WHAT WERE YOU DOING INSTEAD?
WHERE DID YOU GO, DOCTOR WRIGHT?
AND WHY MY MOM? Hmmm?
THIS LAB-- I WAS HERE YEARS BEFORE SHE DIED.
LISTEN, JACKASS! YOU'VE CHOSEN THE WRONG MEMORY TO TRY AND PICK MY BRAIN WITH--
AHHHHHH!

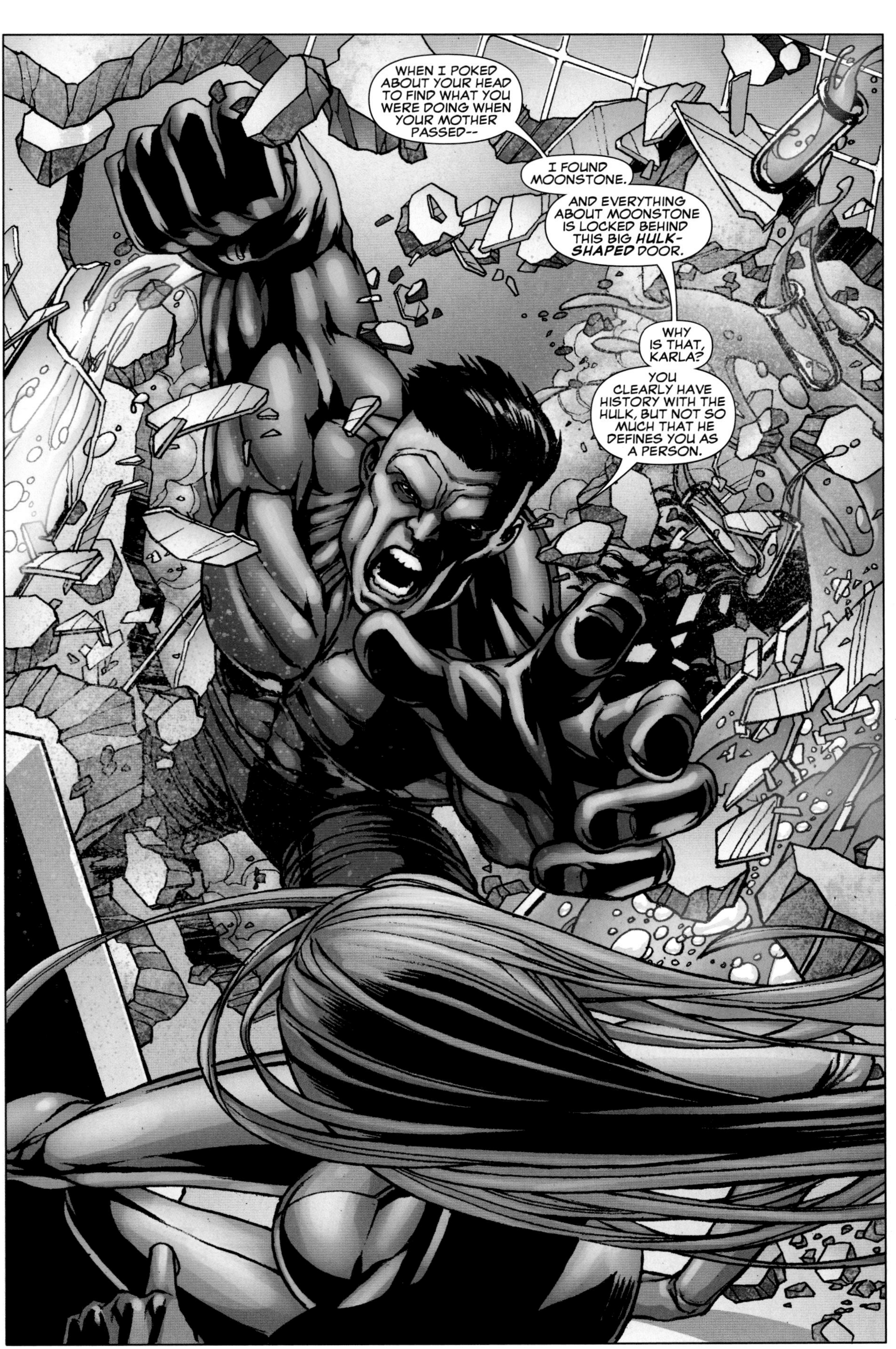
WHEN I POKED ABOUT YOUR HEAD TO FIND WHAT YOU WERE DOING WHEN YOUR MOTHER PASSED--
I FOUND MOONSTONE.
AND EVERYTHING ABOUT MOONSTONE IS LOCKED BEHIND THIS BIG *HULK-SHAPED* DOOR.
WHY IS THAT, KARLA?
YOU CLEARLY HAVE HISTORY WITH THE HULK, BUT NOT SO MUCH THAT HE DEFINES YOU AS A PERSON.

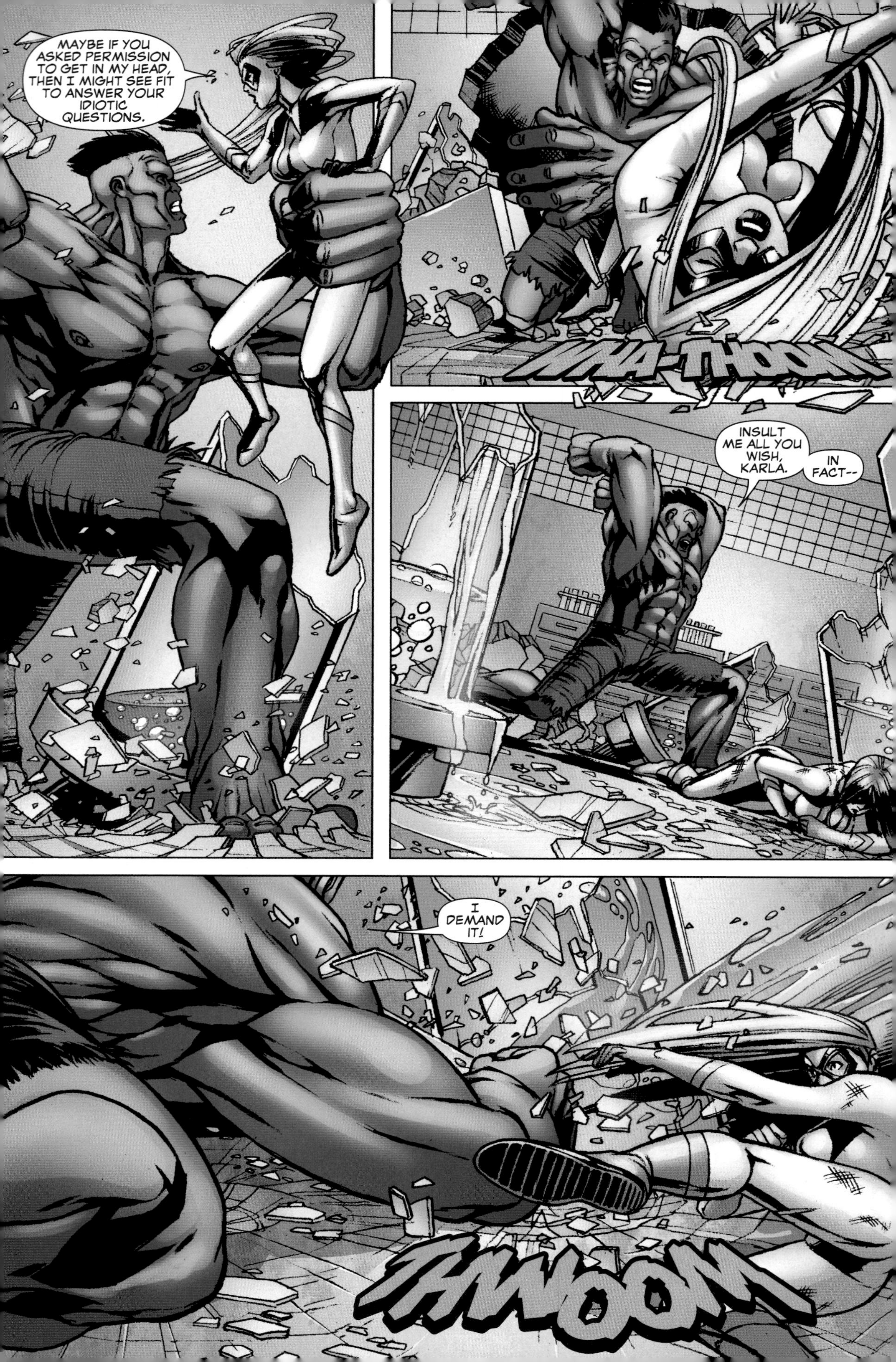
MAYBE IF YOU ASKED PERMISSION TO GET IN MY HEAD, THEN I MIGHT SEE FIT TO ANSWER YOUR IDIOTIC QUESTIONS.
WHA-THOOM
INSULT ME ALL YOU WISH, KARLA.
IN FACT--
I DEMAND IT!
THWOOM

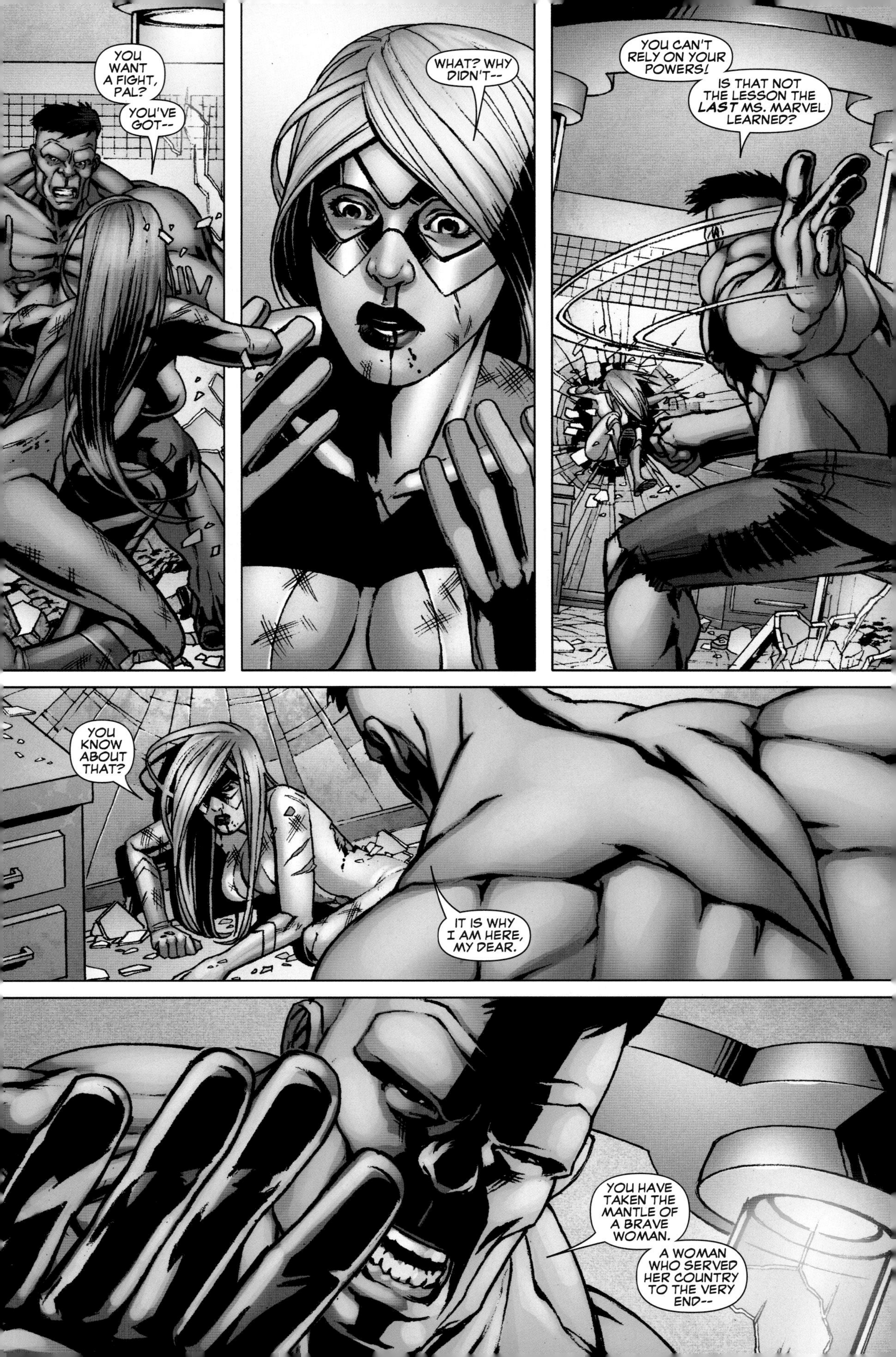
YOU WANT A FIGHT, PAL?
YOU'VE GOT--
WHAT? WHY DIDN'T--
YOU CAN'T RELY ON YOUR POWERS!
IS THAT NOT THE LESSON THE LAST MS. MARVEL LEARNED?
YOU KNOW ABOUT THAT?
IT IS WHY I AM HERE, MY DEAR.
YOU HAVE TAKEN THE MANTLE OF A BRAVE WOMAN.
A WOMAN WHO SERVED HER COUNTRY TO THE VERY END--

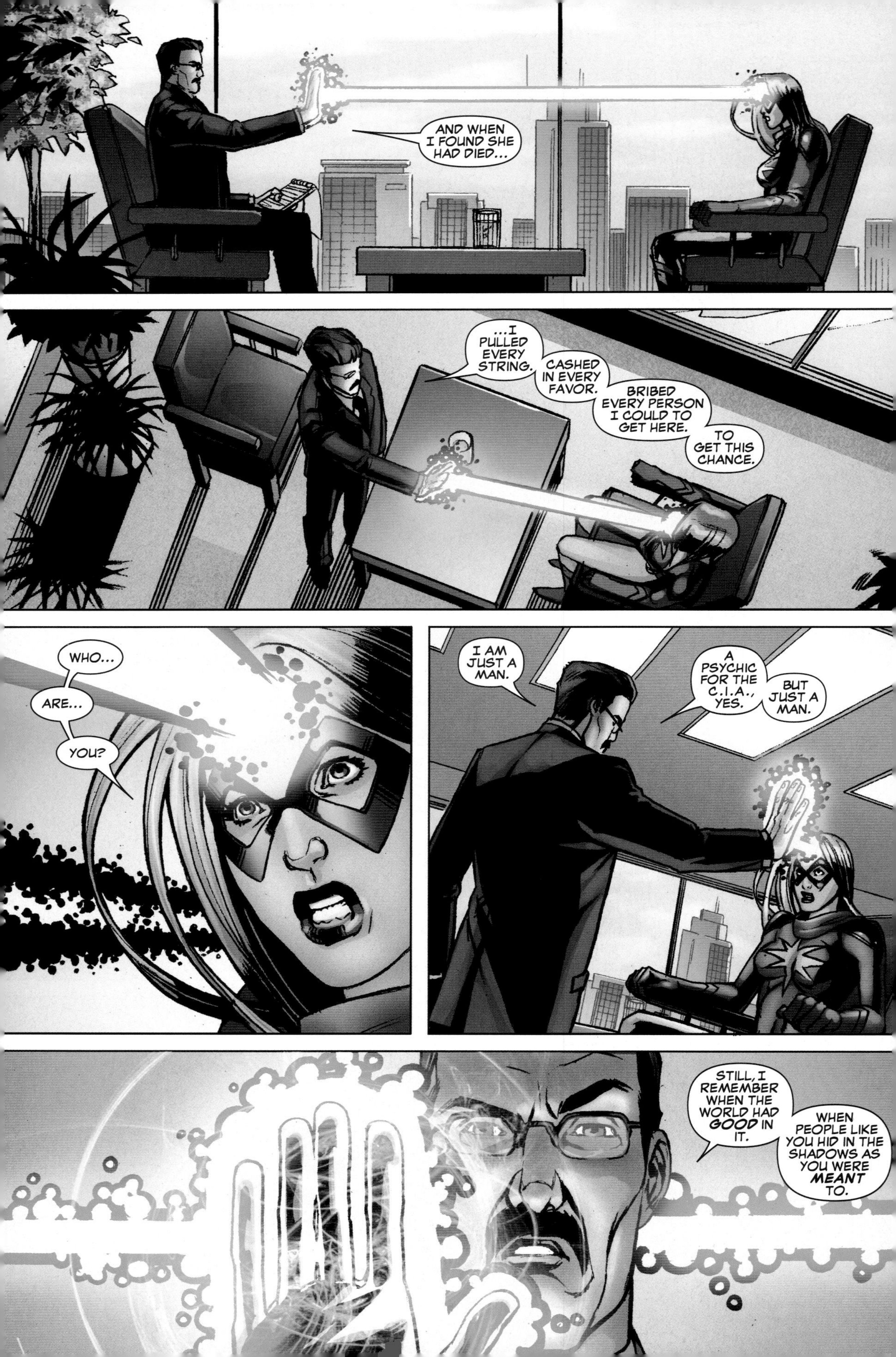
AND WHEN I FOUND SHE HAD DIED...
...I PULLED EVERY STRING.
CASHED IN EVERY FAVOR.
BRIBED EVERY PERSON I COULD TO GET HERE.
TO GET THIS CHANCE.
WHO...
ARE...
YOU?
I AM JUST A MAN.
A PSYCHIC FOR THE C.I.A., YES.
BUT JUST A MAN.
STILL, I REMEMBER WHEN THE WORLD HAD GOOD IN IT.
WHEN PEOPLE LIKE YOU HID IN THE SHADOWS AS YOU WERE MEANT TO.

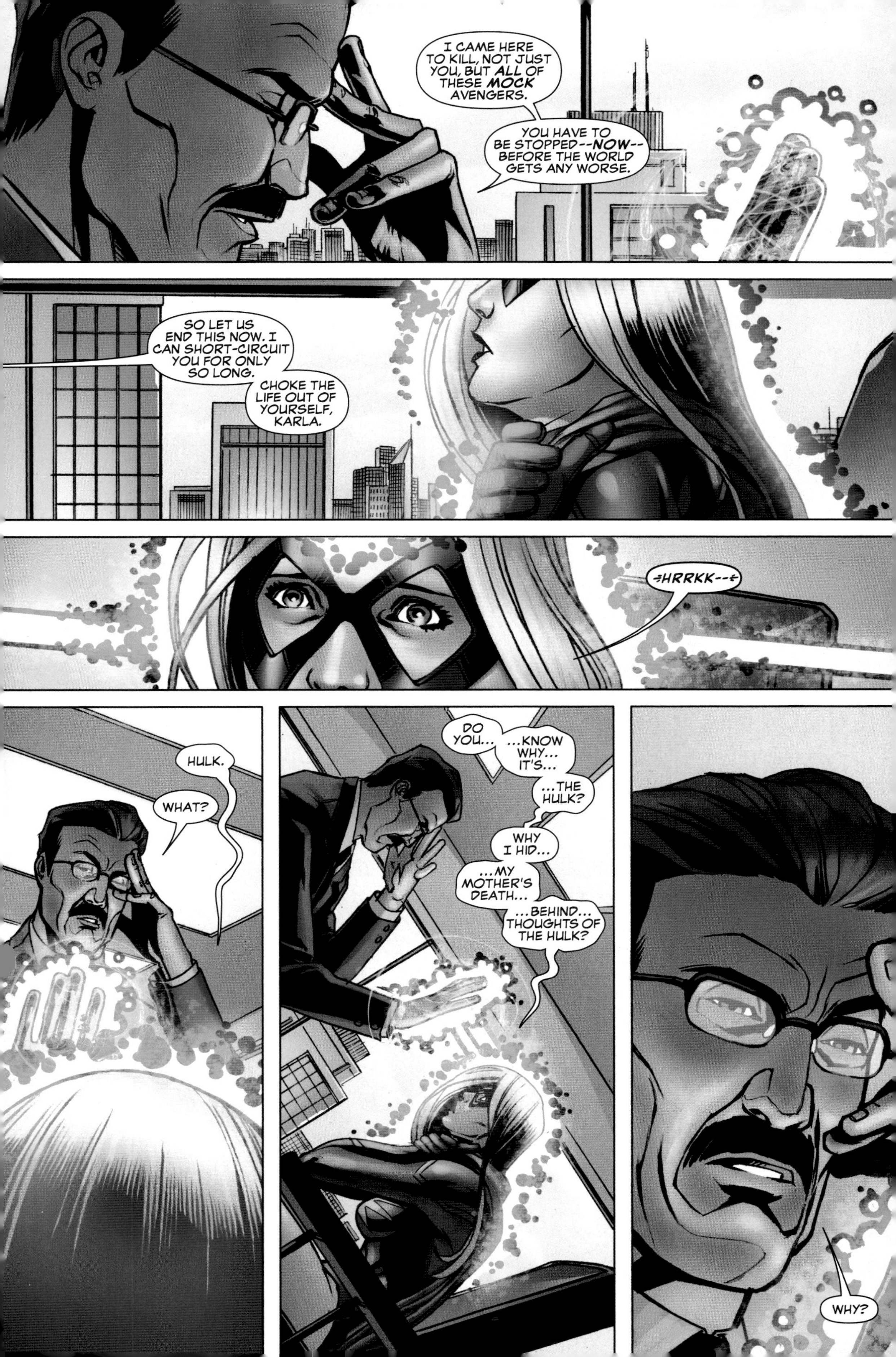
I CAME HERE TO KILL, NOT JUST YOU, BUT ALL OF THESE MOCK AVENGERS.
YOU HAVE TO BE STOPPED--NOW--BEFORE THE WORLD GETS ANY WORSE.
SO LET US END THIS NOW. I CAN SHORT-CIRCUIT YOU FOR ONLY SO LONG.
CHOKE THE LIFE OUT OF YOURSELF, KARLA.
HRRKK--
HULK.
WHAT?
DO YOU...
...KNOW WHY... IT'S...
...THE HULK?
WHY I HID...
...MY MOTHER'S DEATH...
...BEHIND... THOUGHTS OF THE HULK?
WHY?

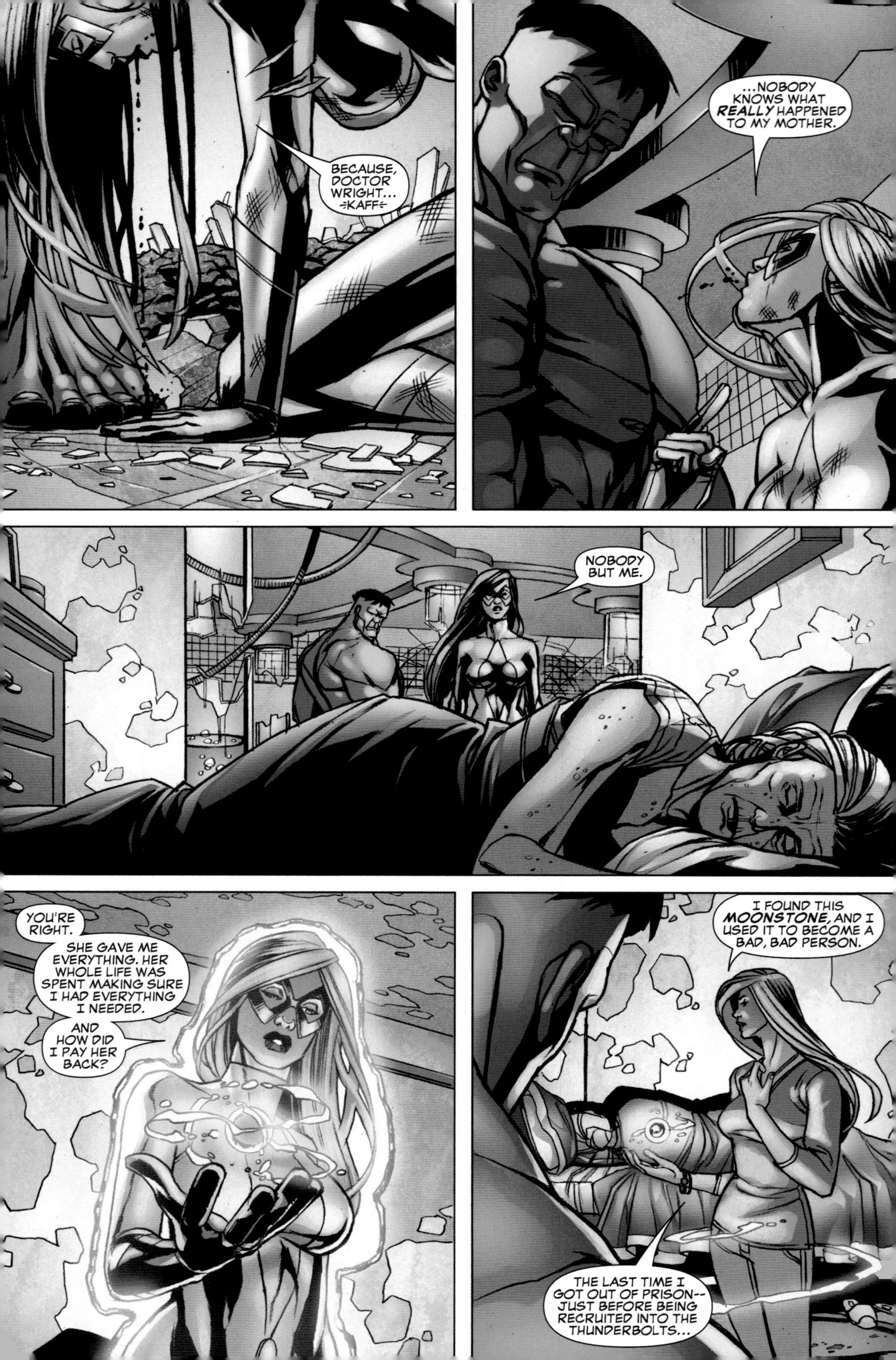

BECAUSE, DOCTOR WRIGHT... =KAFF=
...NOBODY KNOWS WHAT REALLY HAPPENED TO MY MOTHER.
NOBODY BUT ME.
YOU'RE RIGHT.
SHE GAVE ME EVERYTHING. HER WHOLE LIFE WAS SPENT MAKING SURE I HAD EVERYTHING I NEEDED.
AND HOW DID I PAY HER BACK?
I FOUND THIS MOONSTONE, AND I USED IT TO BECOME A BAD, BAD PERSON.
THE LAST TIME I GOT OUT OF PRISON-- JUST BEFORE BEING RECRUITED INTO THE THUNDERBOLTS...

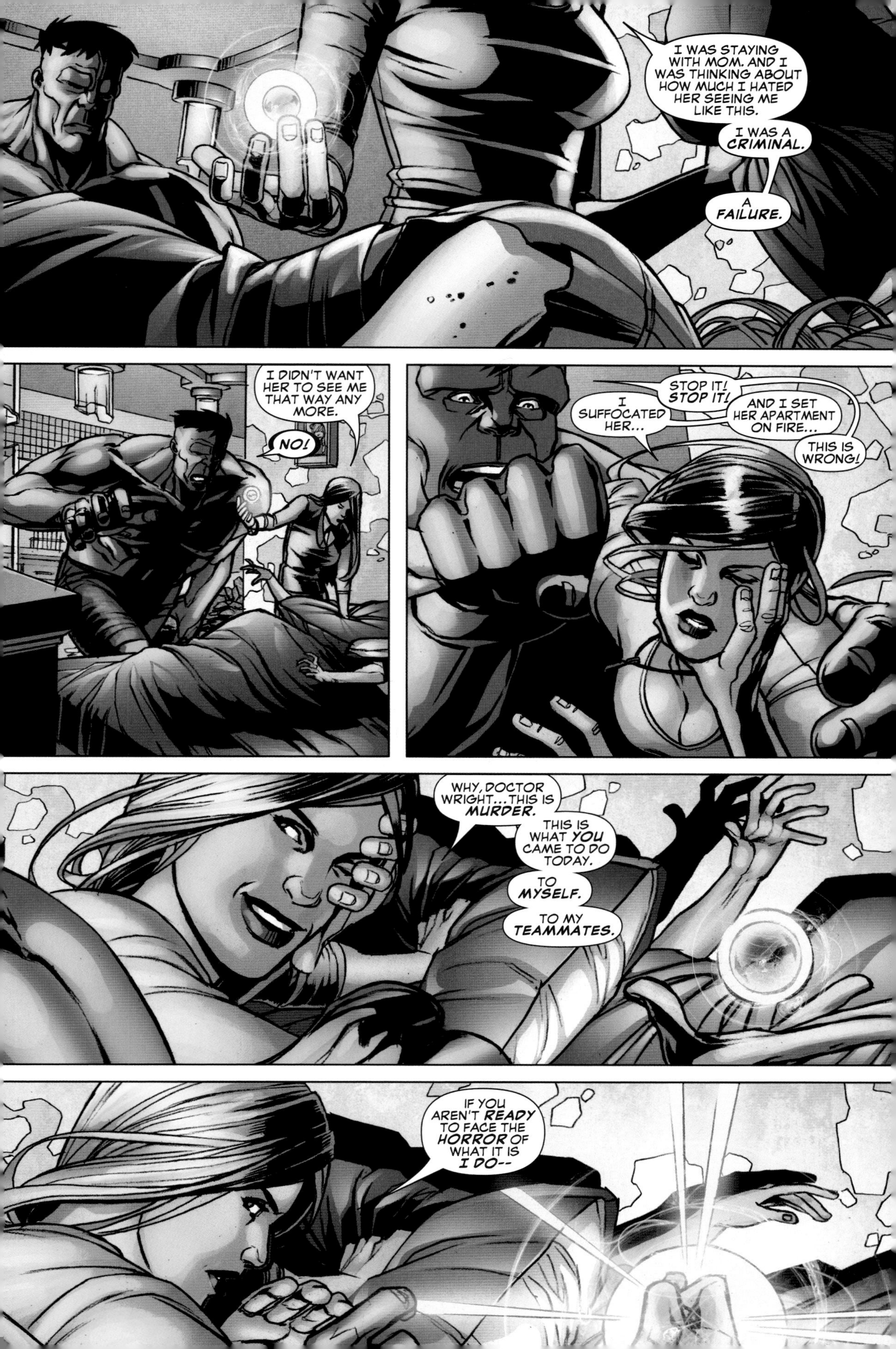
I WAS STAYING WITH MOM. AND I WAS THINKING ABOUT HOW MUCH I HATED HER SEEING ME LIKE THIS.
I WAS A CRIMINAL.
A FAILURE.
I DIDN'T WANT HER TO SEE ME THAT WAY ANY MORE.
NO!
I SUFFOCATED HER...
STOP IT! STOP IT!
AND I SET HER APARTMENT ON FIRE...
THIS IS WRONG!
WHY, DOCTOR WRIGHT... THIS IS MURDER.
THIS IS WHAT YOU CAME TO DO TODAY.
TO MYSELF.
TO MY TEAMMATES.
IF YOU AREN'T READY TO FACE THE HORROR OF WHAT IT IS I DO--

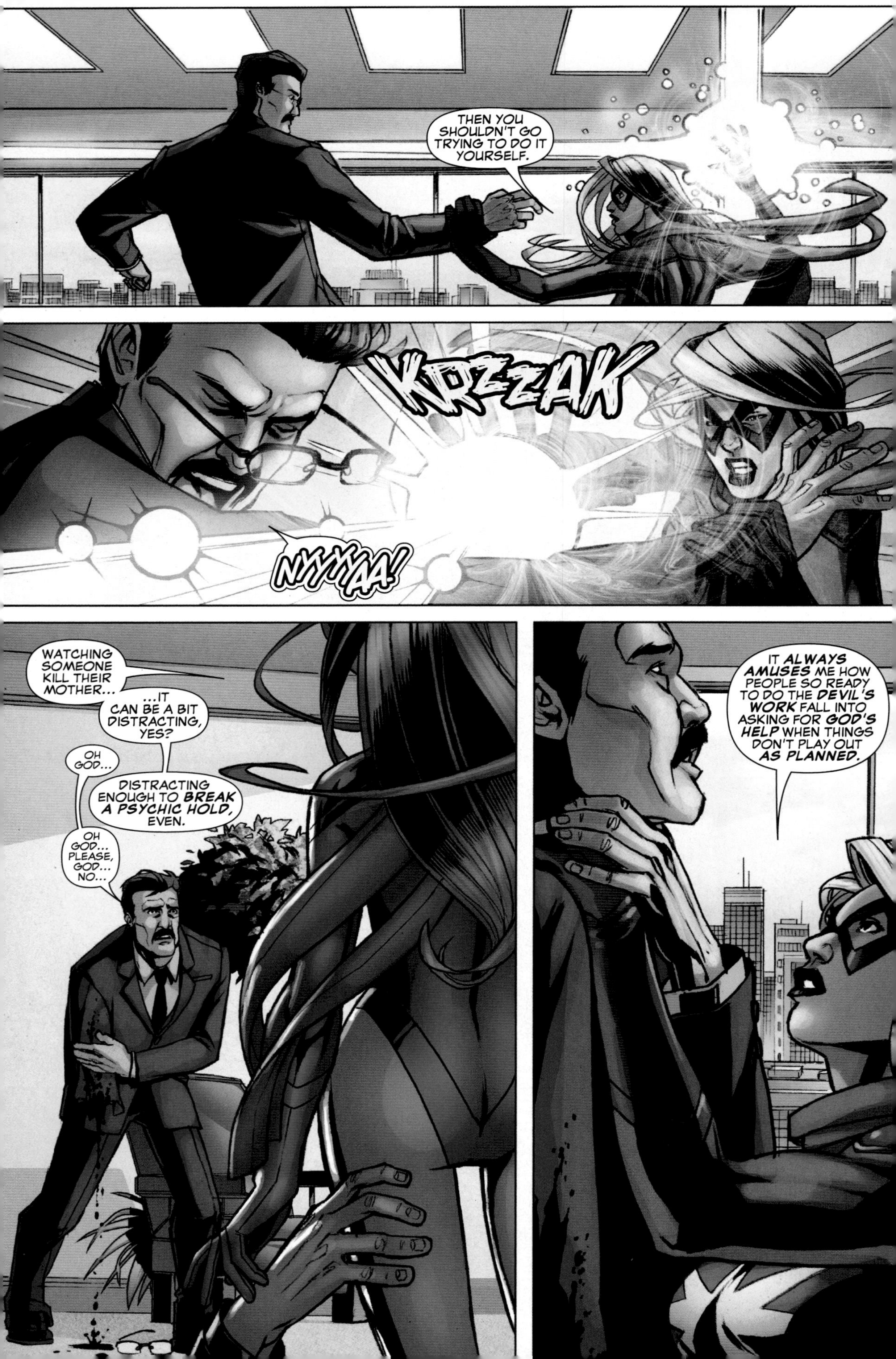
THEN YOU SHOULDN'T GO TRYING TO DO IT YOURSELF.
KRZZAK
NYYYAA!
WATCHING SOMEONE KILL THEIR MOTHER...
...IT CAN BE A BIT DISTRACTING, YES?
OH GOD...
DISTRACTING ENOUGH TO BREAK A PSYCHIC HOLD, EVEN.
OH GOD... PLEASE, GOD... NO...
IT ALWAYS AMUSES ME HOW PEOPLE SO READY TO DO THE DEVIL'S WORK FALL INTO ASKING FOR GOD'S HELP WHEN THINGS DON'T PLAY OUT AS PLANNED.

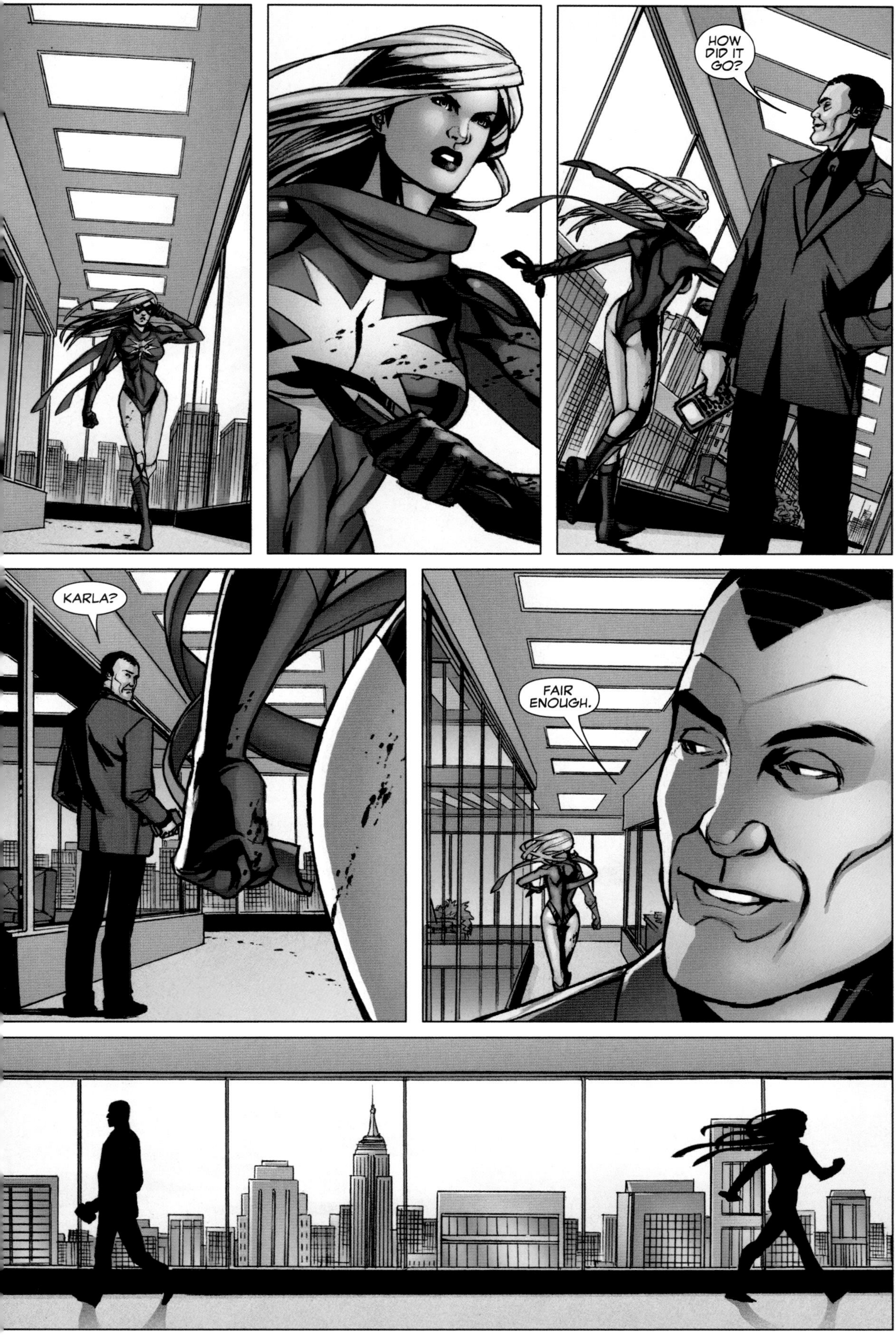
HOW DID IT GO?
KARLA?
FAIR ENOUGH.

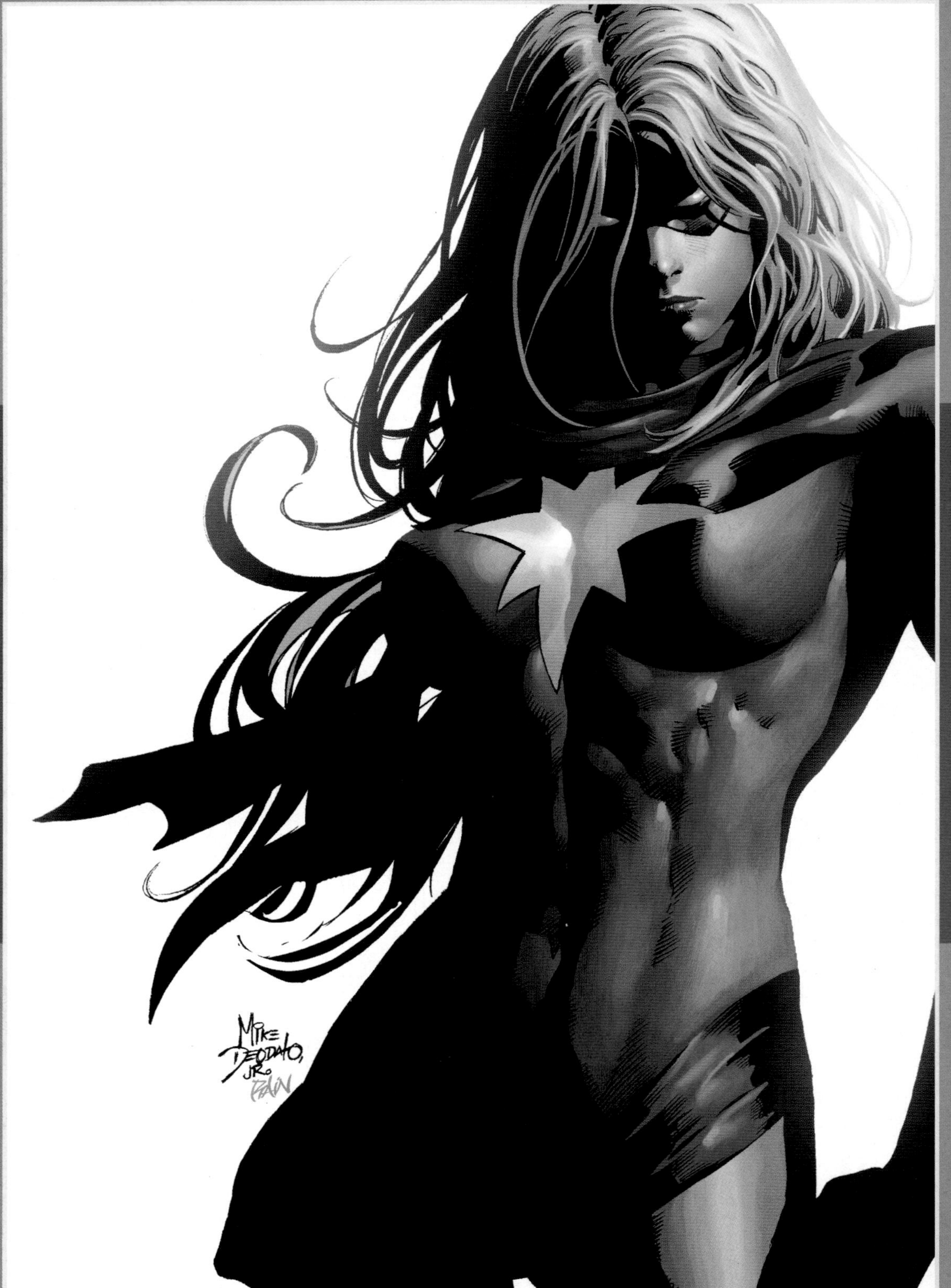
MIKE DEODATO, JR.
RAIN

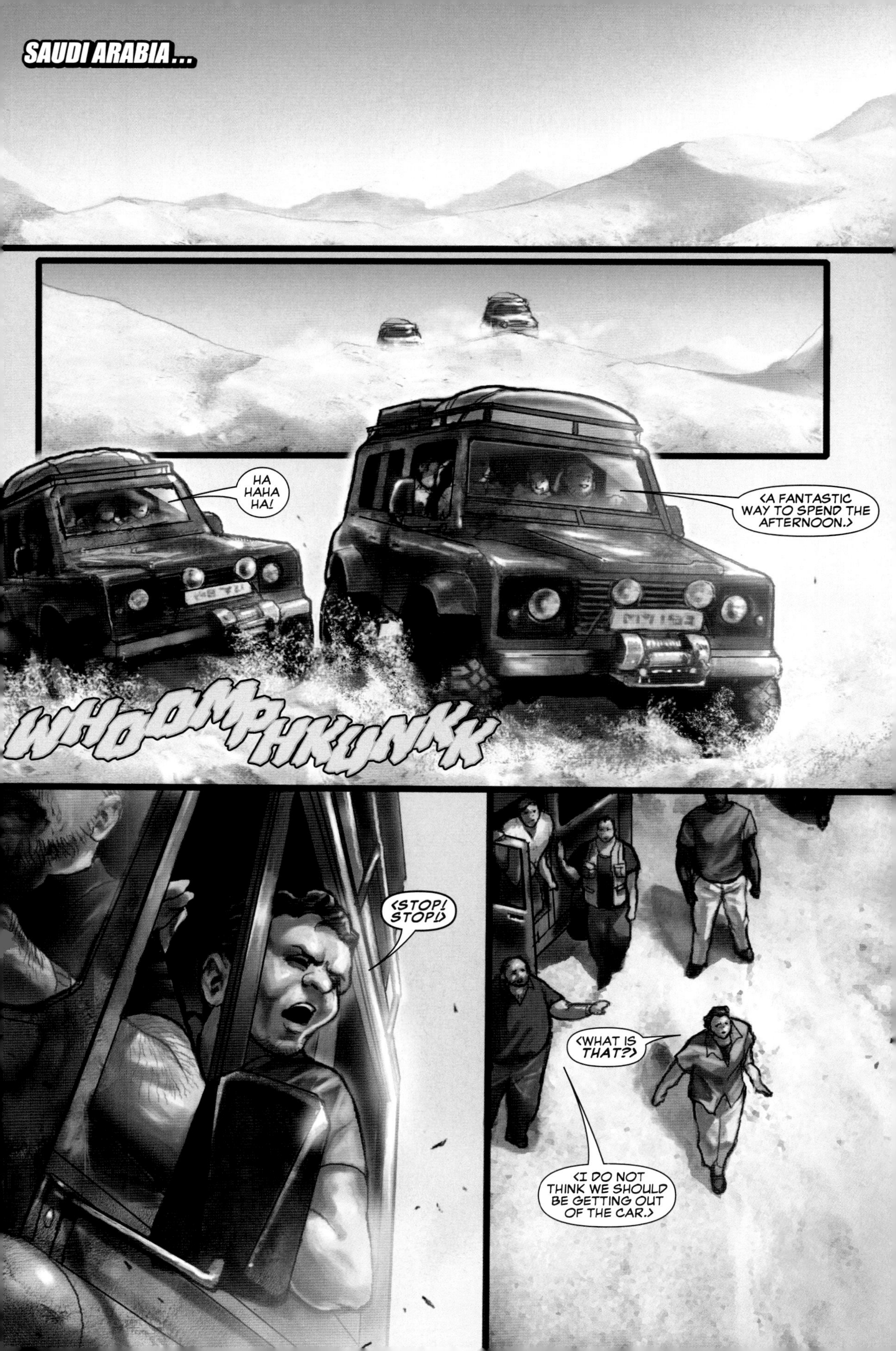
SAUDI ARABIA...
HA HAHA HA!
<A FANTASTIC WAY TO SPEND THE AFTERNOON.>
WHOOMPHKUNKK
<STOP! STOP!>
<WHAT IS THAT?>
<I DO NOT THINK WE SHOULD BE GETTING OUT OF THE CAR.>

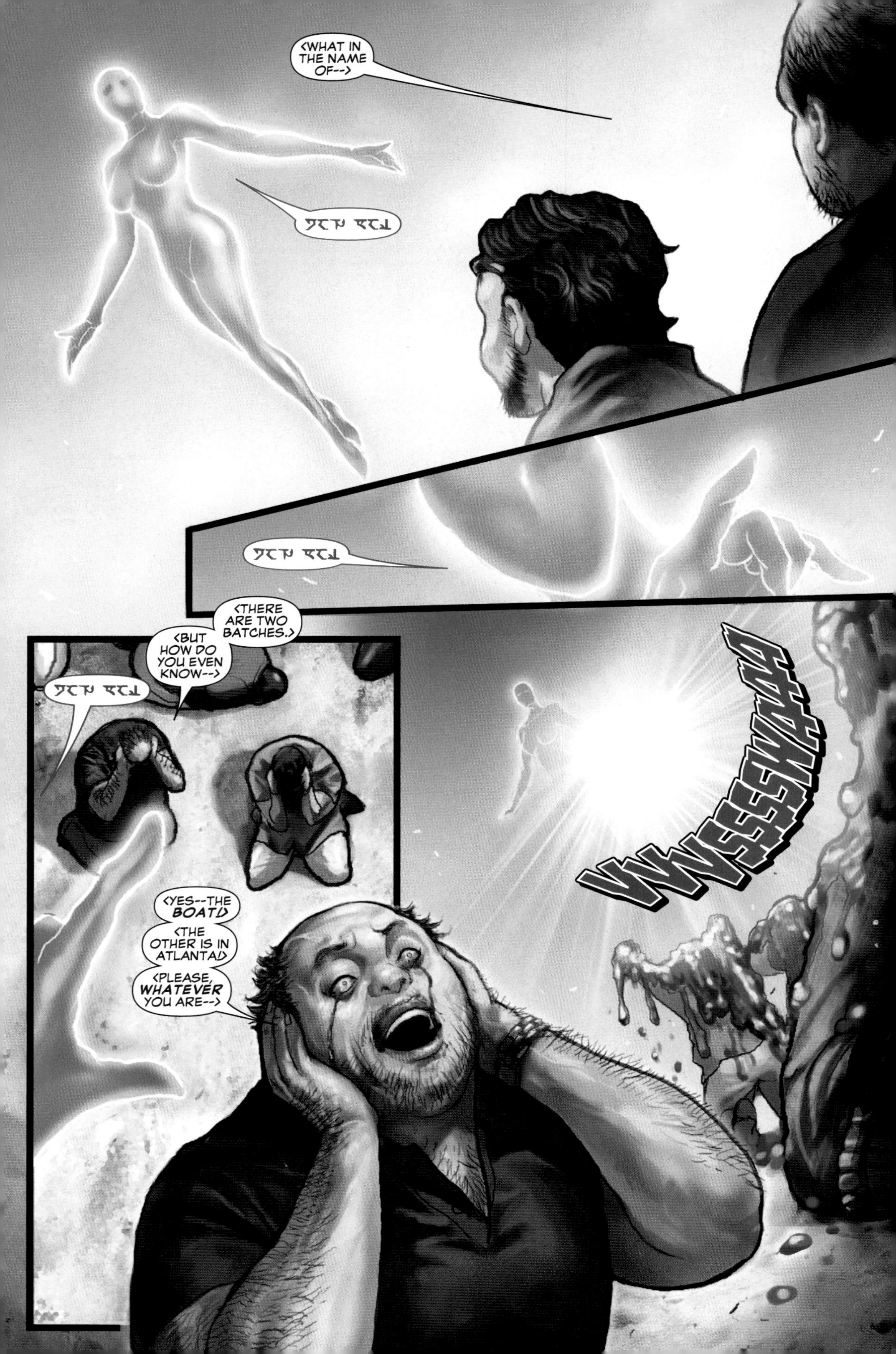

<WHAT IN THE NAME OF-->
<THERE ARE TWO BATCHES.>
<BUT HOW DO YOU EVEN KNOW-->
<YES--THE **BOAT!**>
<THE OTHER IS IN ATLANTA!>
<PLEASE, **WHATEVER** YOU ARE-->
VVVSSSHAAAA

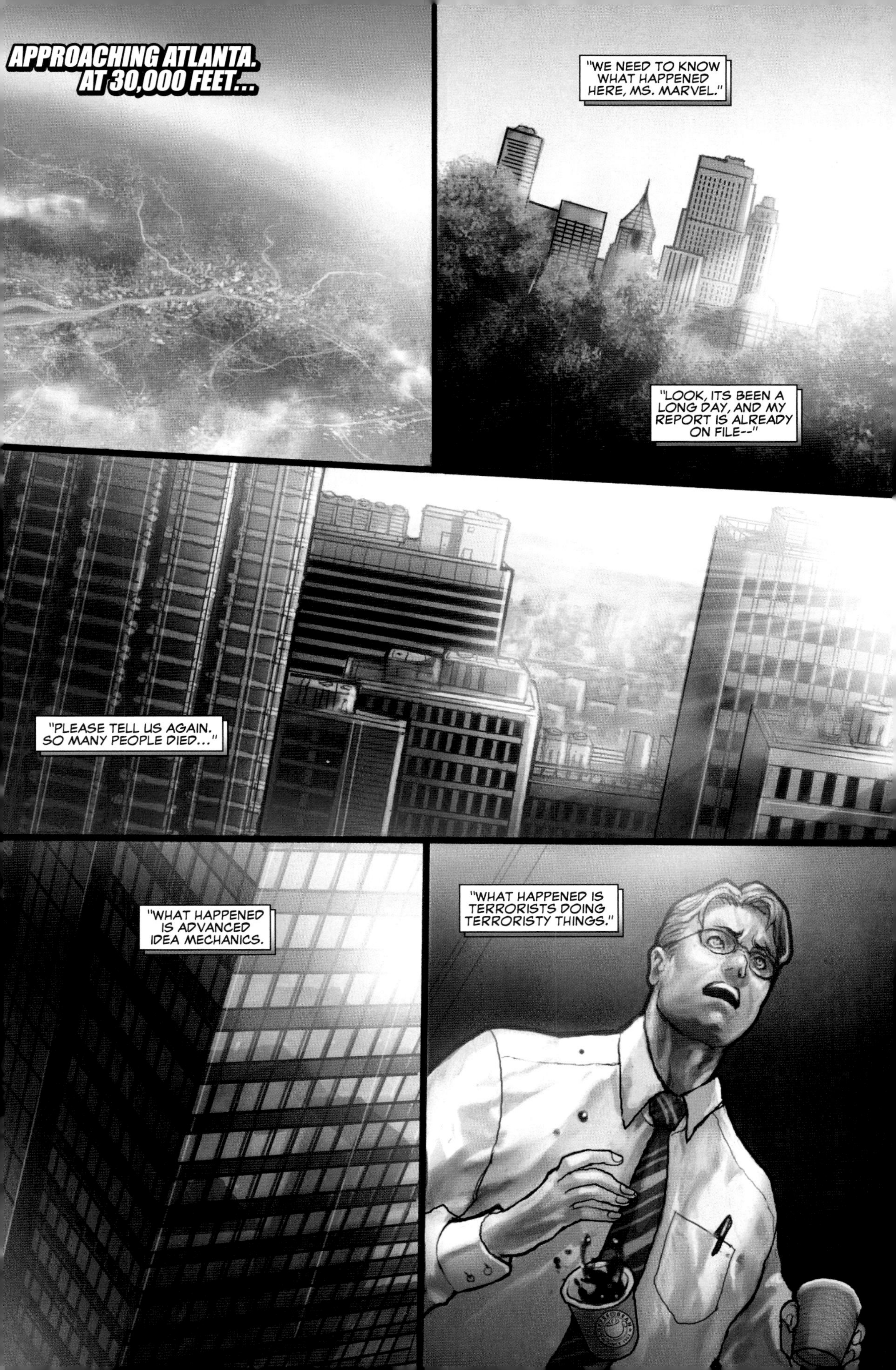
APPROACHING ATLANTA. AT 30,000 FEET...
"WE NEED TO KNOW WHAT HAPPENED HERE, MS. MARVEL."
"LOOK, ITS BEEN A LONG DAY, AND MY REPORT IS ALREADY ON FILE--"
"PLEASE TELL US AGAIN. SO MANY PEOPLE DIED..."
"WHAT HAPPENED IS ADVANCED IDEA MECHANICS.
"WHAT HAPPENED IS TERRORISTS DOING TERRORISTY THINGS."

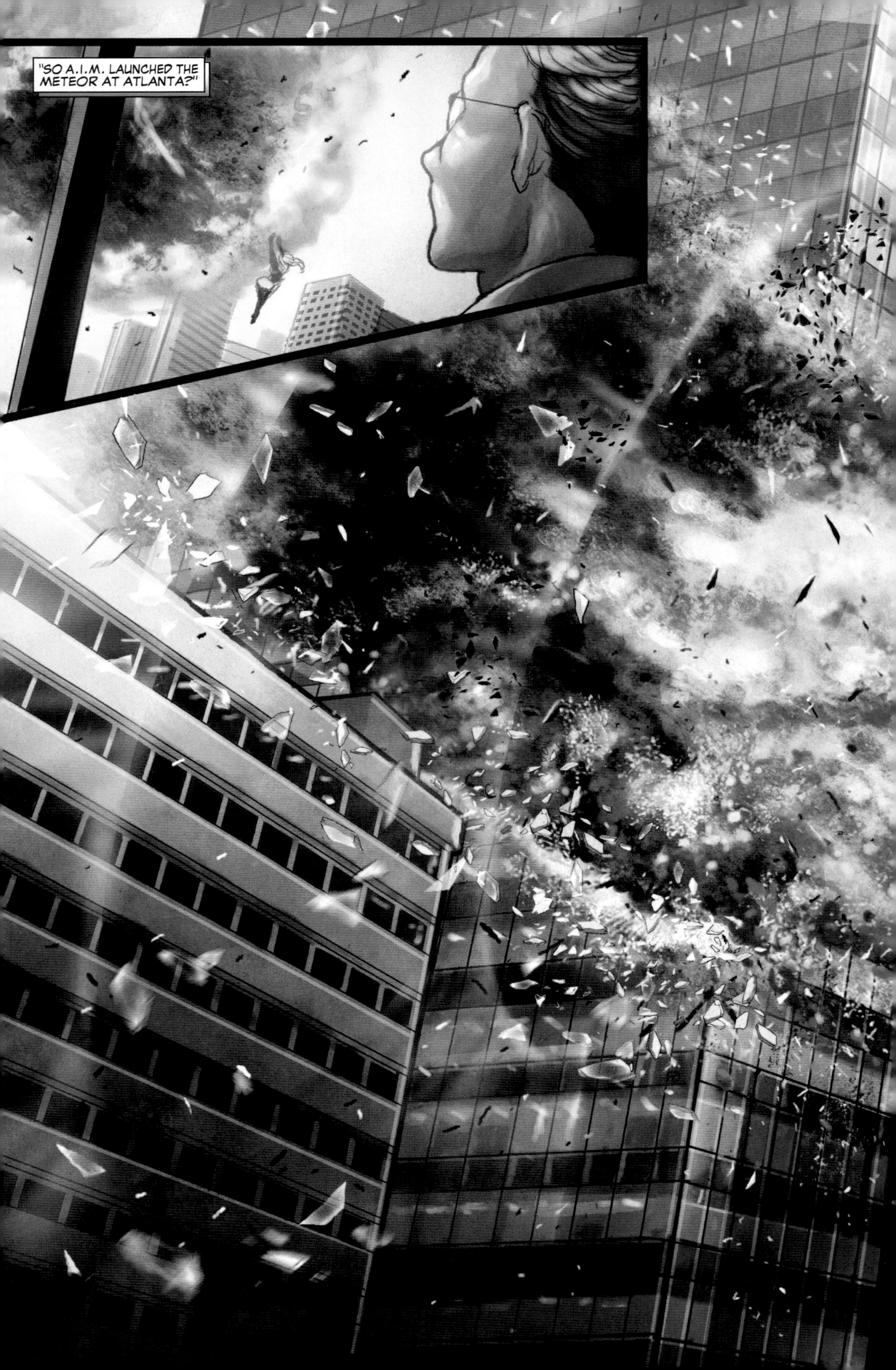
"SO A.I.M. LAUNCHED THE METEOR AT ATLANTA?"

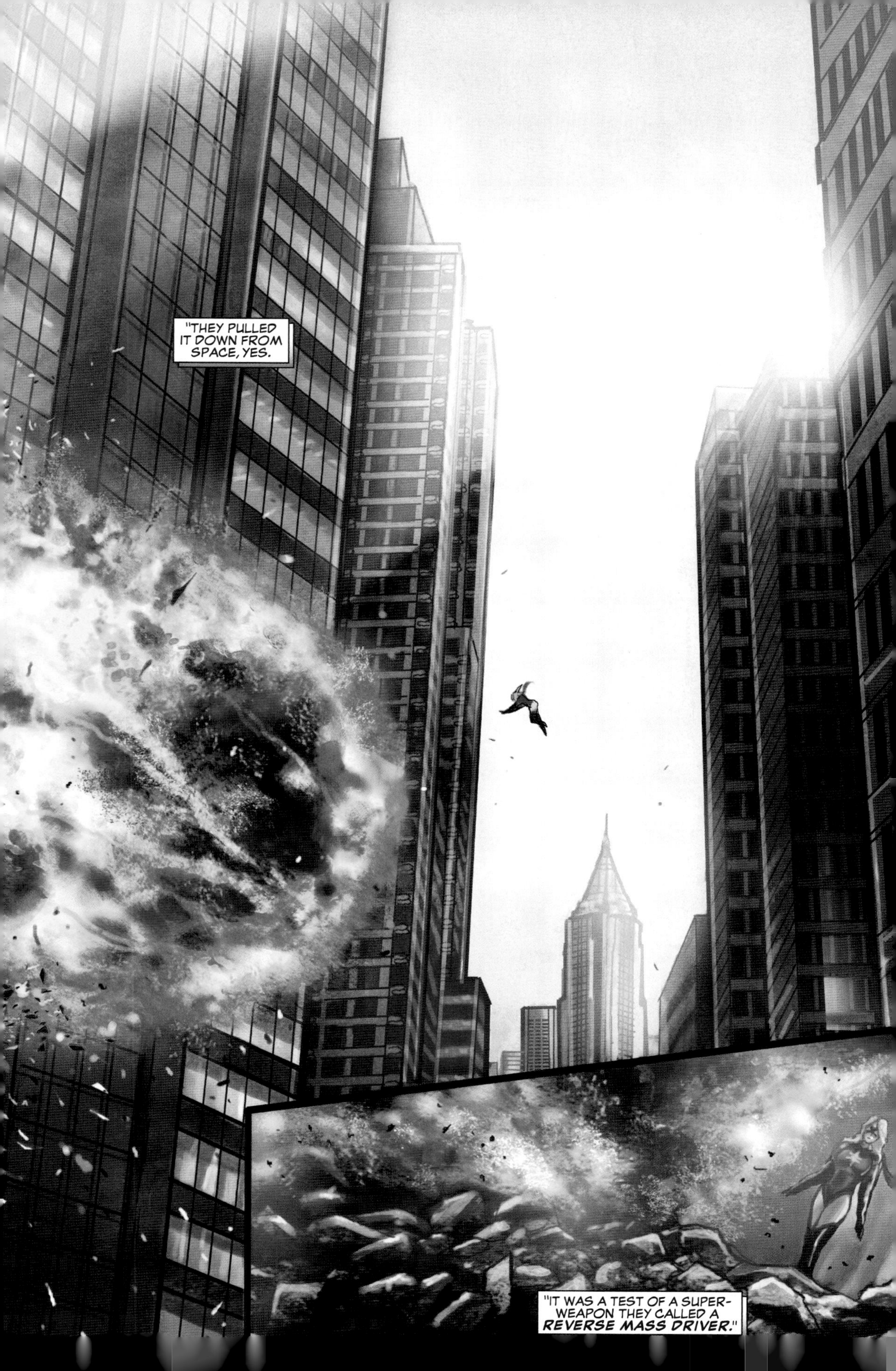
"THEY PULLED IT DOWN FROM SPACE, YES.
"IT WAS A TEST OF A SUPER-WEAPON THEY CALLED A REVERSE MASS DRIVER."

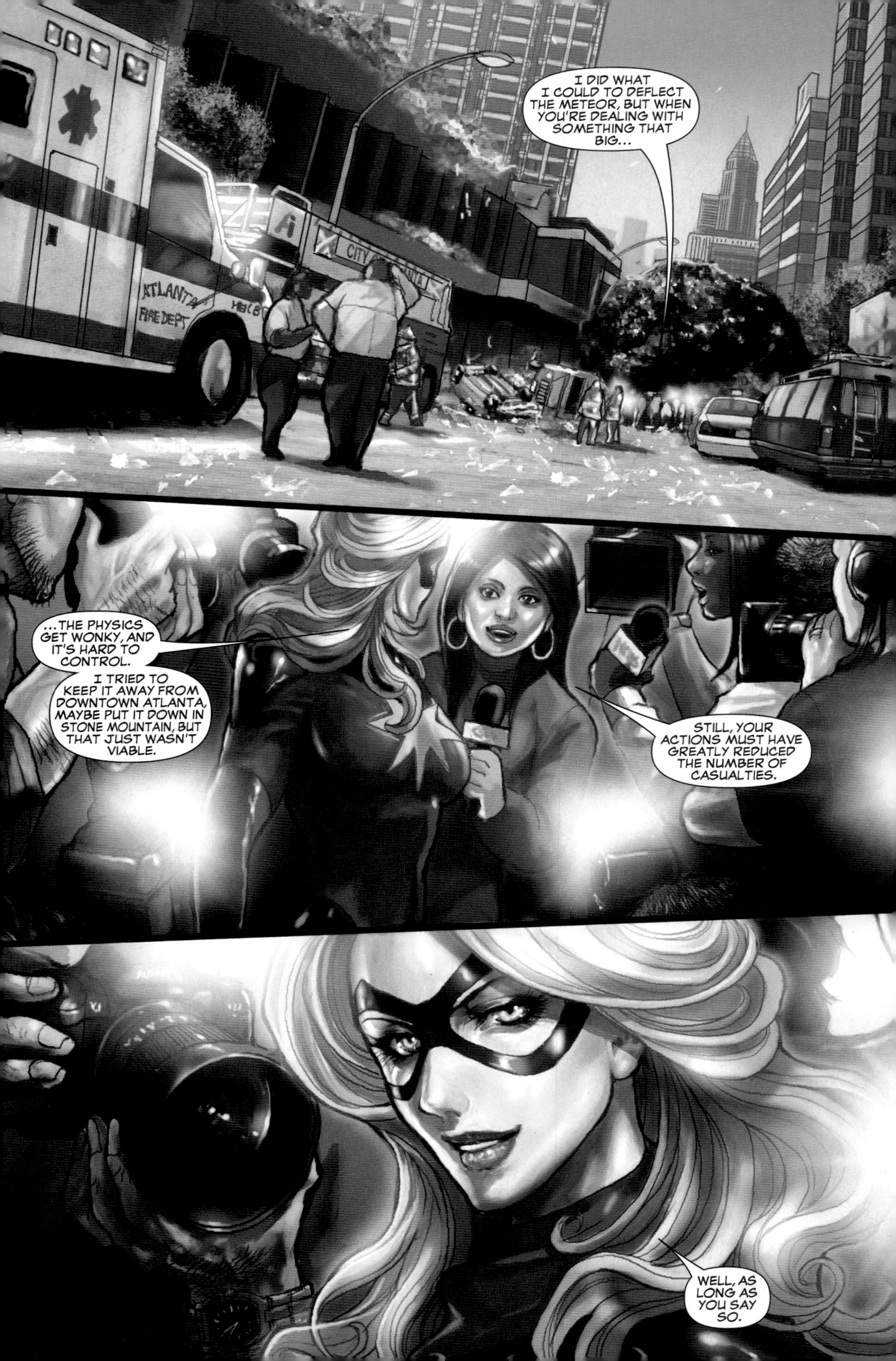
ATLANTA FIRE DEPT
I DID WHAT I COULD TO DEFLECT THE METEOR, BUT WHEN YOU'RE DEALING WITH SOMETHING THAT BIG...
...THE PHYSICS GET WONKY, AND IT'S HARD TO CONTROL.
I TRIED TO KEEP IT AWAY FROM DOWNTOWN ATLANTA, MAYBE PUT IT DOWN IN STONE MOUNTAIN, BUT THAT JUST WASN'T VIABLE.
STILL, YOUR ACTIONS MUST HAVE GREATLY REDUCED THE NUMBER OF CASUALTIES.
WELL, AS LONG AS YOU SAY SO.

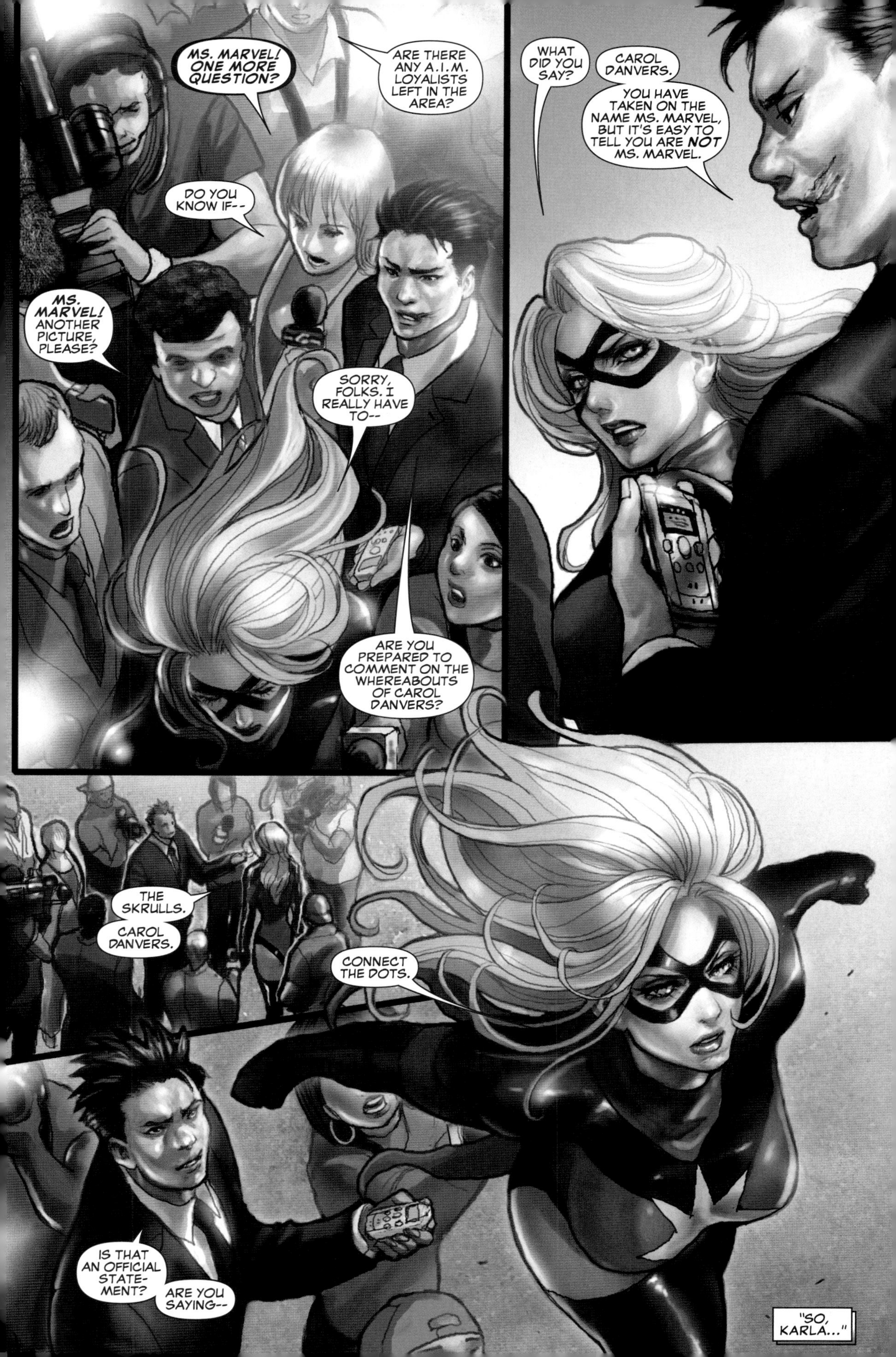
MS. MARVEL! ONE MORE QUESTION?
ARE THERE ANY A.I.M. LOYALISTS LEFT IN THE AREA?
DO YOU KNOW IF--
MS. MARVEL! ANOTHER PICTURE, PLEASE?
SORRY, FOLKS. I REALLY HAVE TO--
ARE YOU PREPARED TO COMMENT ON THE WHEREABOUTS OF CAROL DANVERS?
WHAT DID YOU SAY?
CAROL DANVERS.
YOU HAVE TAKEN ON THE NAME MS. MARVEL, BUT IT'S EASY TO TELL YOU ARE NOT MS. MARVEL.
THE SKRULLS.
CAROL DANVERS.
CONNECT THE DOTS.
IS THAT AN OFFICIAL STATE-MENT?
ARE YOU SAYING--
"SO, KARLA..."

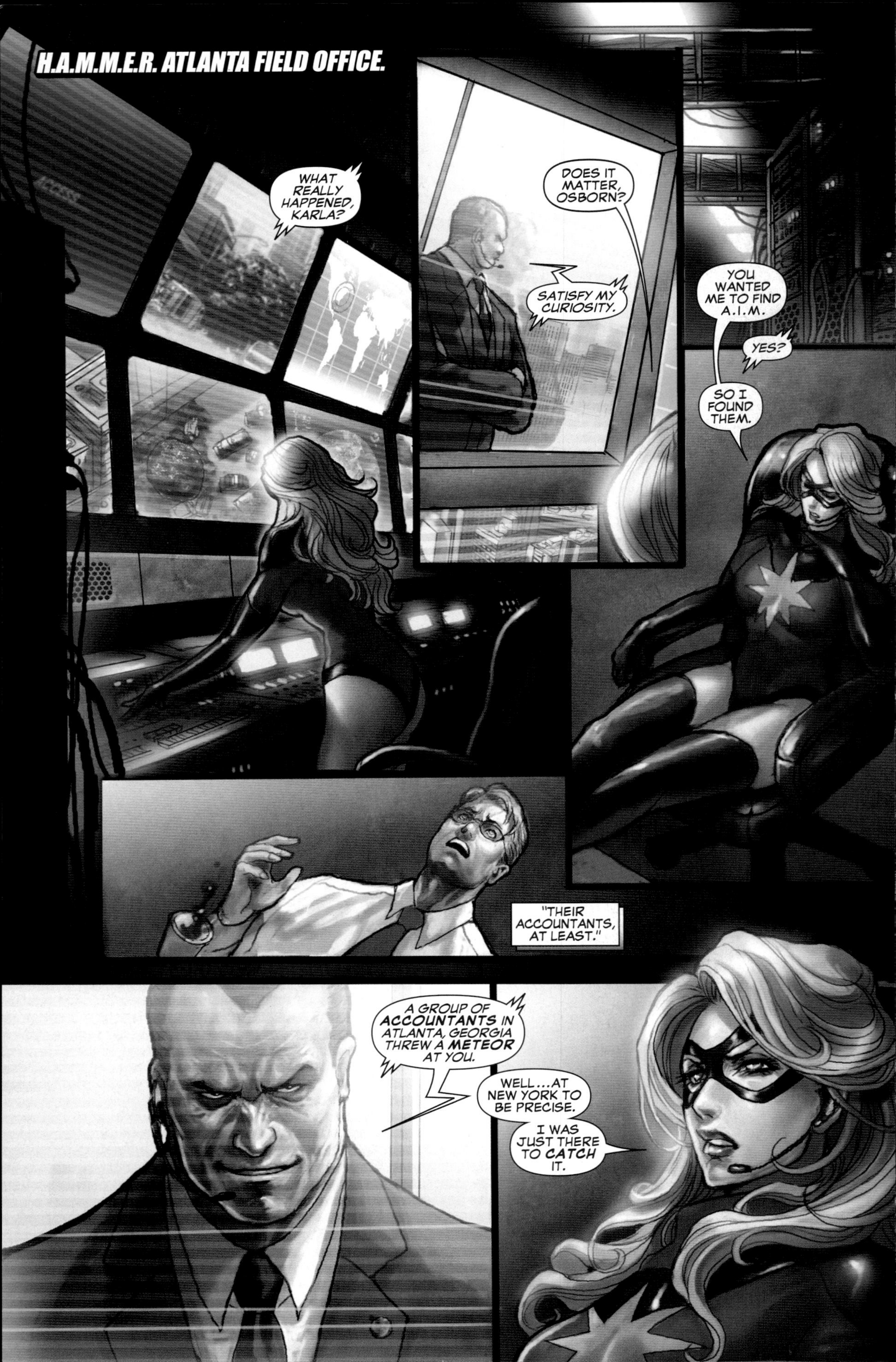
H.A.M.M.E.R. ATLANTA FIELD OFFICE.
WHAT REALLY HAPPENED, KARLA?
DOES IT MATTER, OSBORN?
SATISFY MY CURIOSITY.
YOU WANTED ME TO FIND A.I.M.
YES?
SO I FOUND THEM.
"THEIR ACCOUNTANTS, AT LEAST."
A GROUP OF ACCOUNTANTS IN ATLANTA, GEORGIA THREW A METEOR AT YOU.
WELL...AT NEW YORK TO BE PRECISE.
I WAS JUST THERE TO CATCH IT.

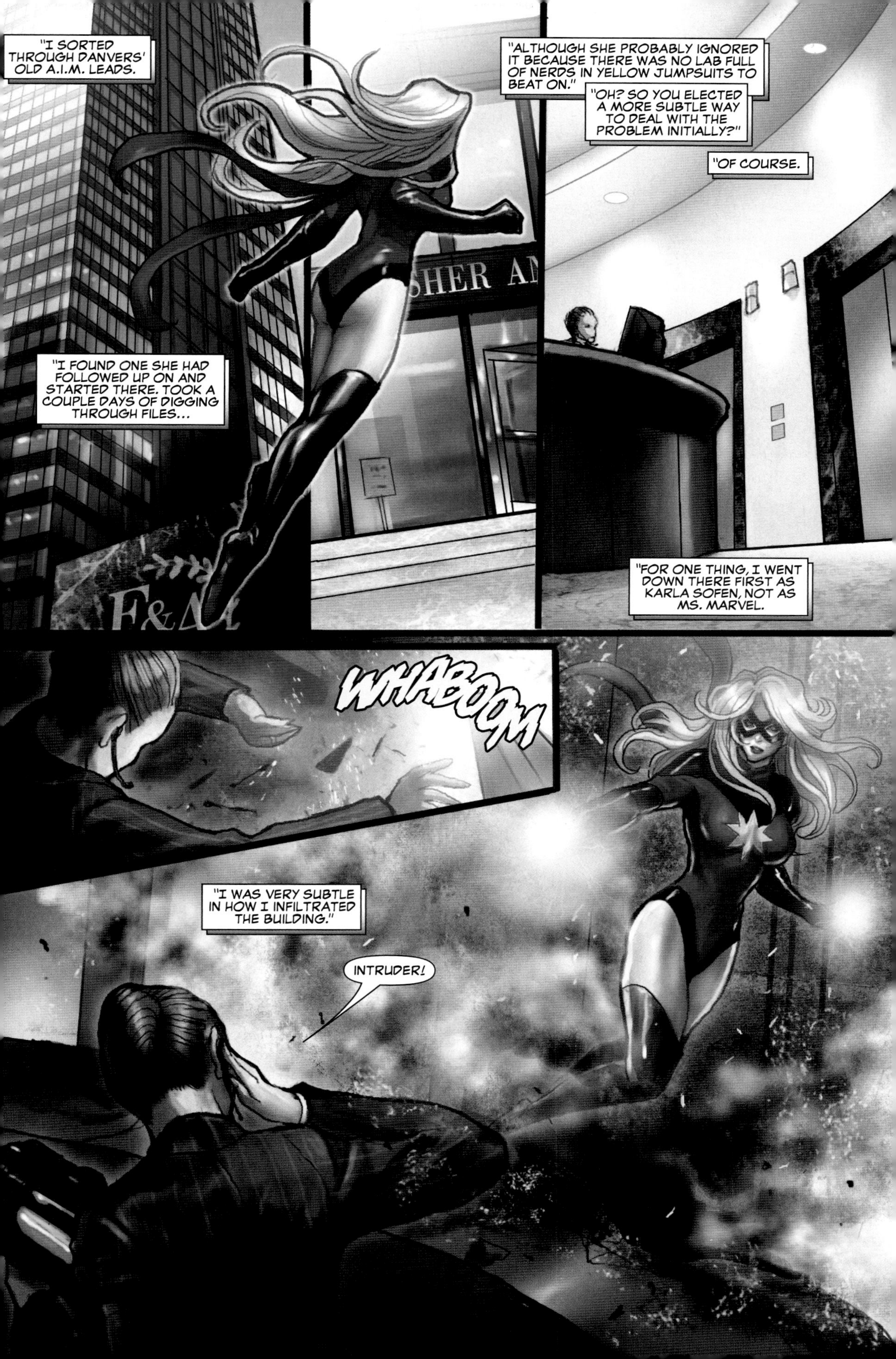
"I SORTED THROUGH DANVERS' OLD A.I.M. LEADS.
"I FOUND ONE SHE HAD FOLLOWED UP ON AND STARTED THERE. TOOK A COUPLE DAYS OF DIGGING THROUGH FILES...
SHER AN
F&A
"ALTHOUGH SHE PROBABLY IGNORED IT BECAUSE THERE WAS NO LAB FULL OF NERDS IN YELLOW JUMPSUITS TO BEAT ON."
"OH? SO YOU ELECTED A MORE SUBTLE WAY TO DEAL WITH THE PROBLEM INITIALLY?"
"OF COURSE.
"FOR ONE THING, I WENT DOWN THERE FIRST AS KARLA SOFEN, NOT AS MS. MARVEL.
WHABOOM
"I WAS VERY SUBTLE IN HOW I INFILTRATED THE BUILDING."
INTRUDER!

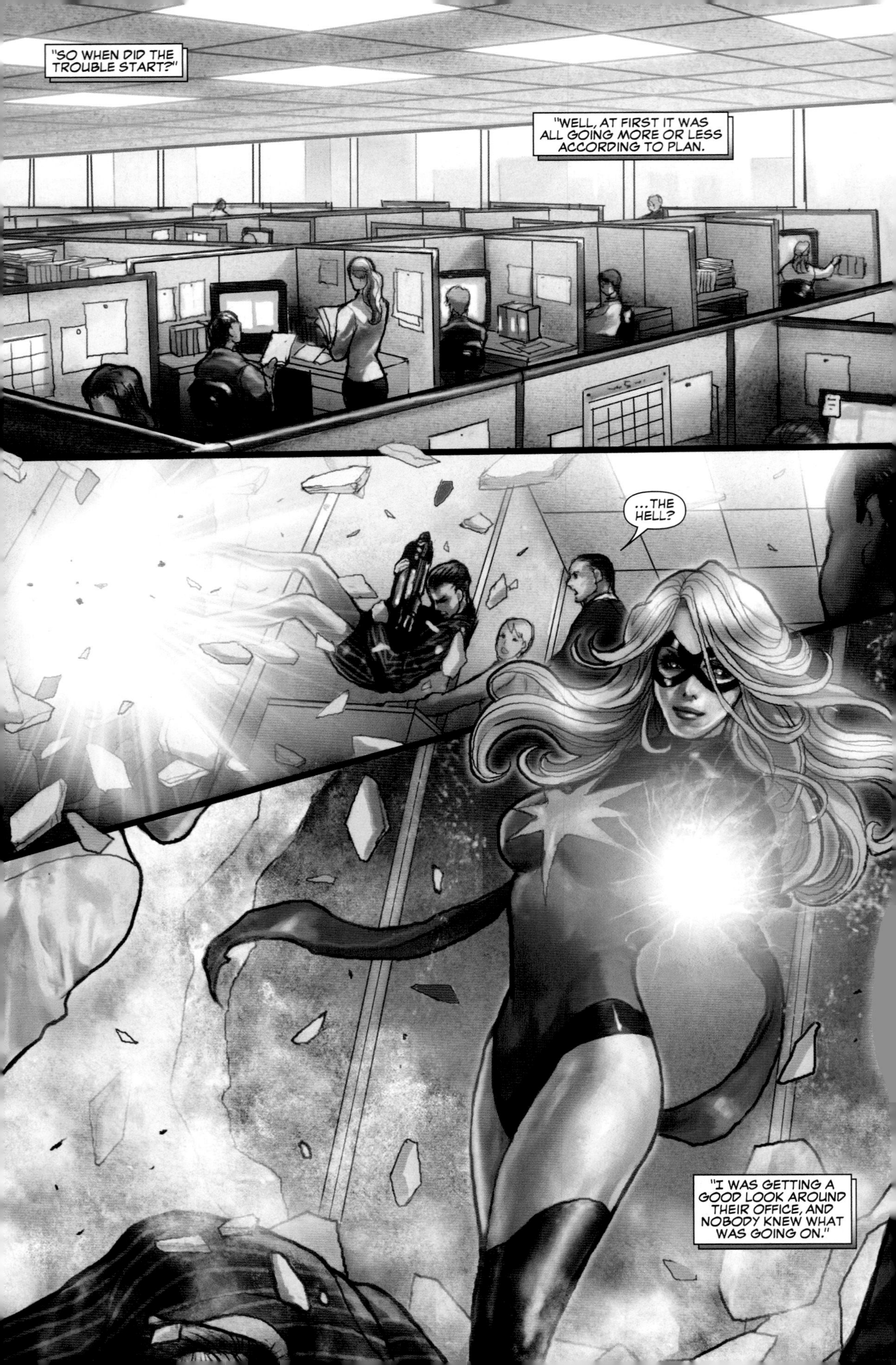
"SO WHEN DID THE TROUBLE START?"
"WELL, AT FIRST IT WAS ALL GOING MORE OR LESS ACCORDING TO PLAN.
...THE HELL?
"I WAS GETTING A GOOD LOOK AROUND THEIR OFFICE, AND NOBODY KNEW WHAT WAS GOING ON."

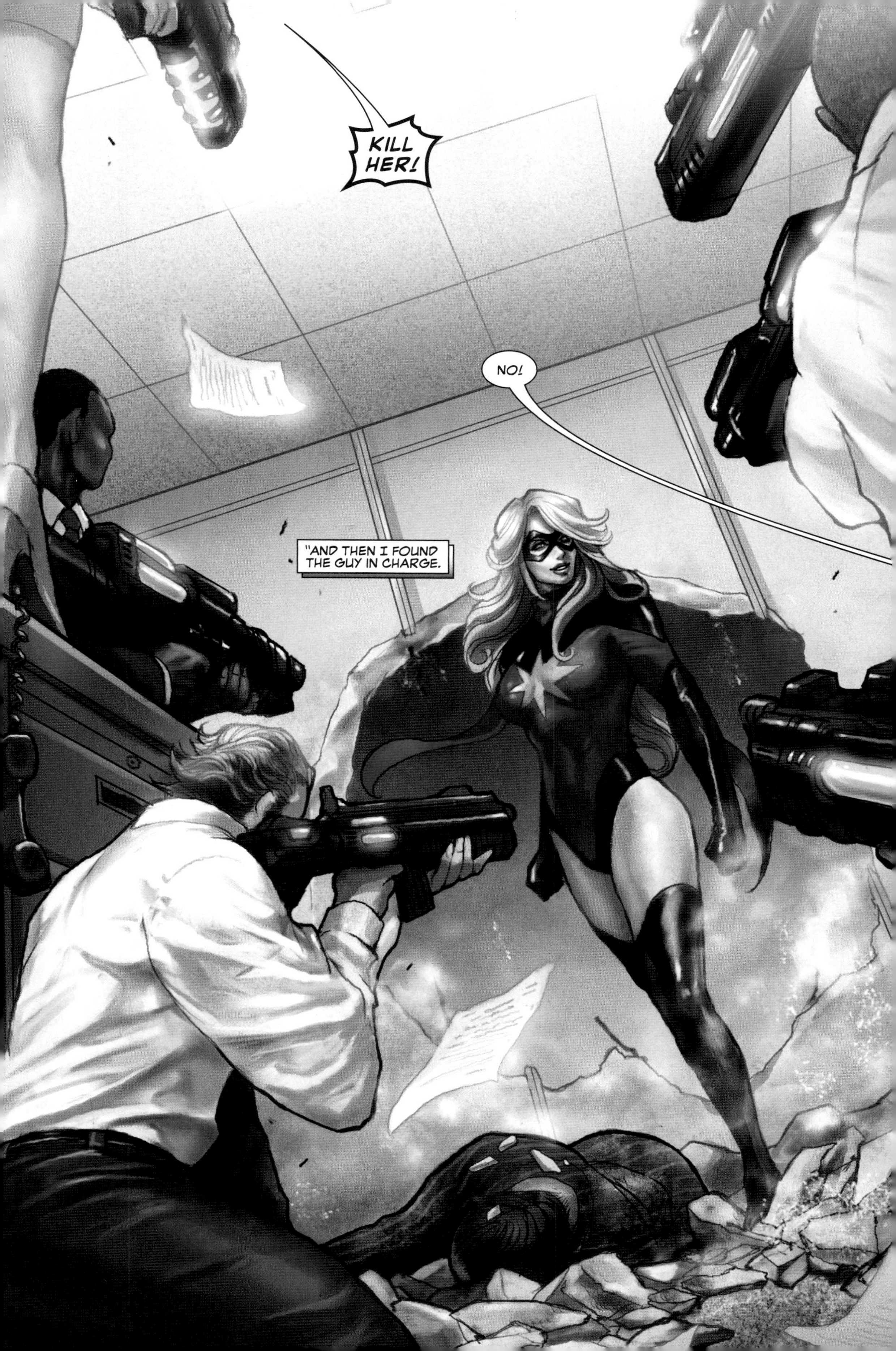
"AND THEN I FOUND THE GUY IN CHARGE.
KILL HER!
NO!

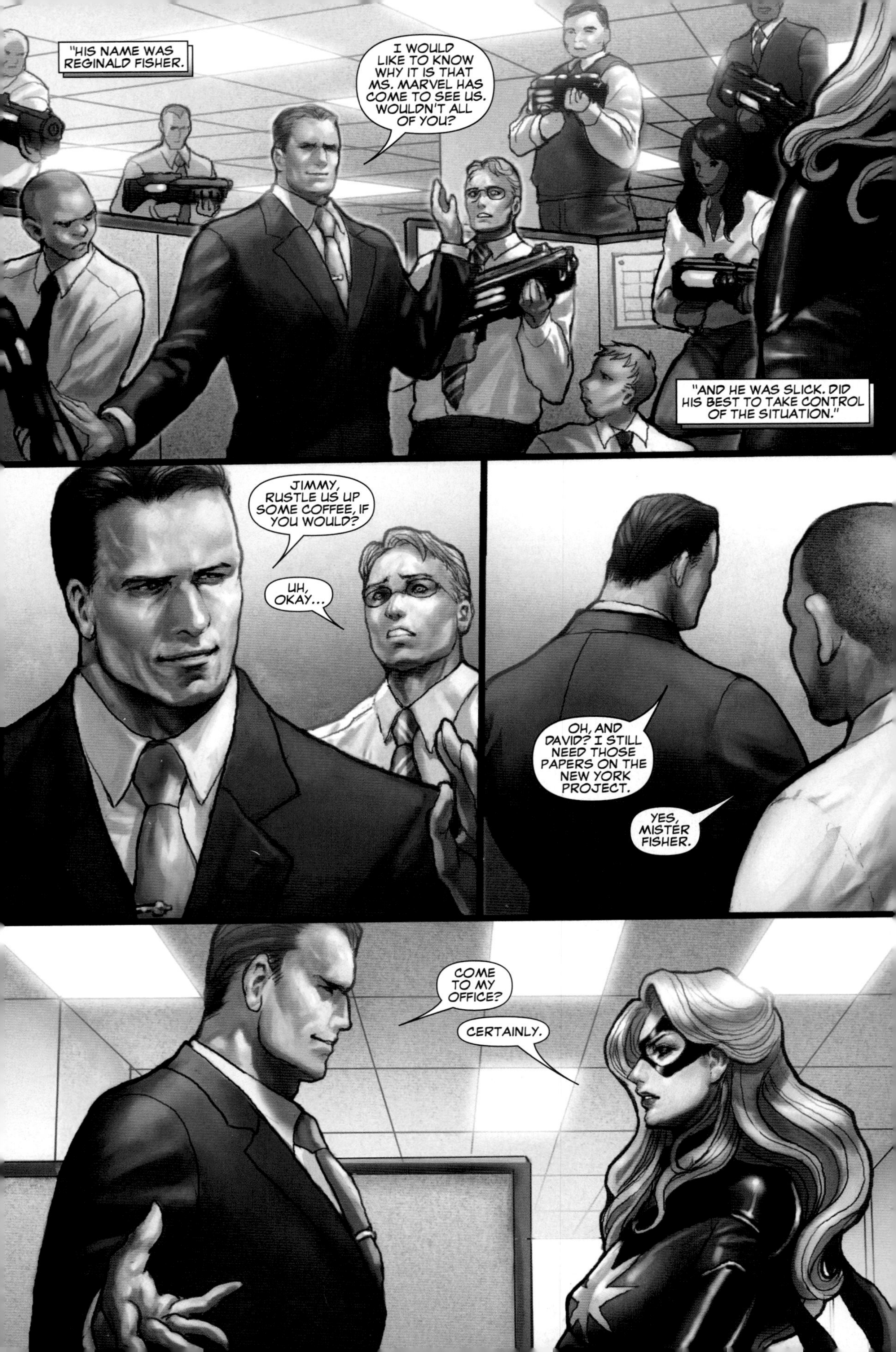
"HIS NAME WAS REGINALD FISHER.
I WOULD LIKE TO KNOW WHY IT IS THAT MS. MARVEL HAS COME TO SEE US. WOULDN'T ALL OF YOU?
"AND HE WAS SLICK. DID HIS BEST TO TAKE CONTROL OF THE SITUATION."
JIMMY, RUSTLE US UP SOME COFFEE, IF YOU WOULD?
UH, OKAY...
OH, AND DAVID? I STILL NEED THOSE PAPERS ON THE NEW YORK PROJECT.
YES, MISTER FISHER.
COME TO MY OFFICE?
CERTAINLY.

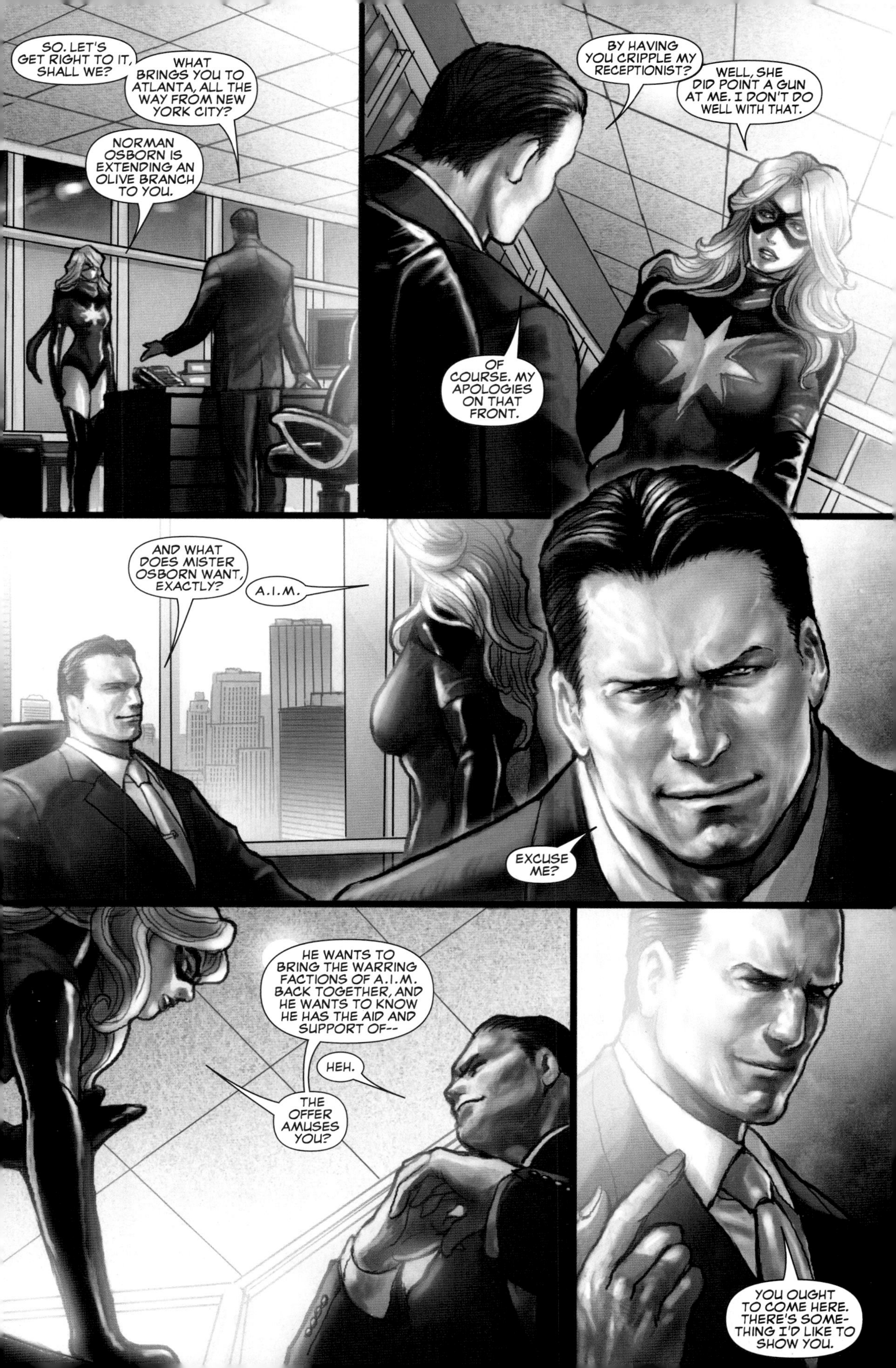
SO. LET'S GET RIGHT TO IT, SHALL WE?
WHAT BRINGS YOU TO ATLANTA, ALL THE WAY FROM NEW YORK CITY?
NORMAN OSBORN IS EXTENDING AN OLIVE BRANCH TO YOU.
BY HAVING YOU CRIPPLE MY RECEPTIONIST?
WELL, SHE DID POINT A GUN AT ME. I DON'T DO WELL WITH THAT.
OF COURSE. MY APOLOGIES ON THAT FRONT.
AND WHAT DOES MISTER OSBORN WANT, EXACTLY?
A.I.M.
EXCUSE ME?
HE WANTS TO BRING THE WARRING FACTIONS OF A.I.M. BACK TOGETHER, AND HE WANTS TO KNOW HE HAS THE AID AND SUPPORT OF--
HEH.
THE OFFER AMUSES YOU?
YOU OUGHT TO COME HERE. THERE'S SOME-THING I'D LIKE TO SHOW YOU.

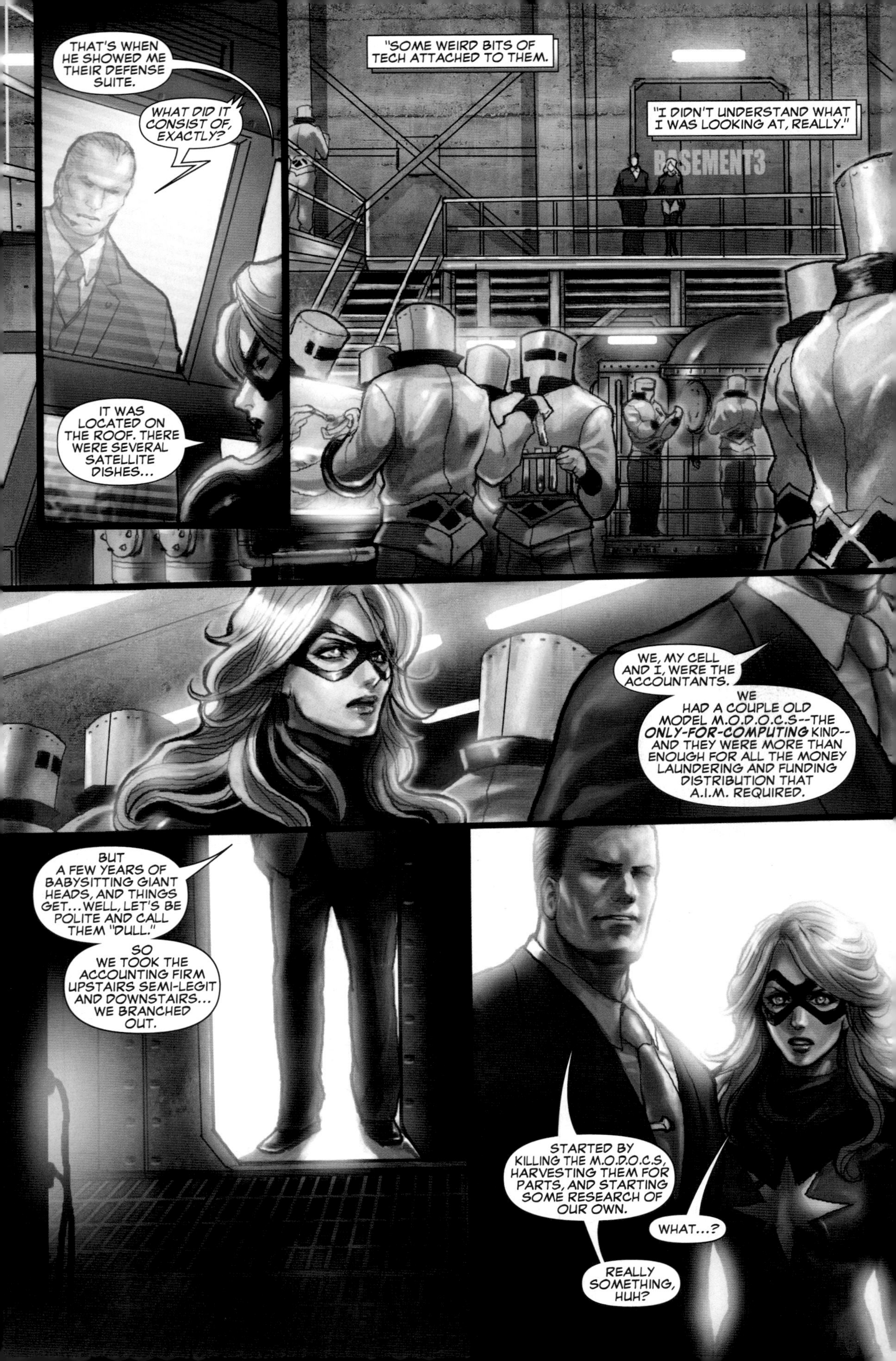
THAT'S WHEN HE SHOWED ME THEIR DEFENSE SUITE.
WHAT DID IT CONSIST OF, EXACTLY?
IT WAS LOCATED ON THE ROOF. THERE WERE SEVERAL SATELLITE DISHES...
"SOME WEIRD BITS OF TECH ATTACHED TO THEM.
"I DIDN'T UNDERSTAND WHAT I WAS LOOKING AT, REALLY."
BASEMENT3
WE, MY CELL AND I, WERE THE ACCOUNTANTS.
WE HAD A COUPLE OLD MODEL M.O.D.O.C.S--THE ONLY-FOR-COMPUTING KIND--AND THEY WERE MORE THAN ENOUGH FOR ALL THE MONEY LAUNDERING AND FUNDING DISTRIBUTION THAT A.I.M. REQUIRED.
BUT A FEW YEARS OF BABYSITTING GIANT HEADS, AND THINGS GET...WELL, LET'S BE POLITE AND CALL THEM "DULL."
SO WE TOOK THE ACCOUNTING FIRM UPSTAIRS SEMI-LEGIT AND DOWNSTAIRS... WE BRANCHED OUT.
STARTED BY KILLING THE M.O.D.O.C.S, HARVESTING THEM FOR PARTS, AND STARTING SOME RESEARCH OF OUR OWN.
WHAT...?
REALLY SOMETHING, HUH?

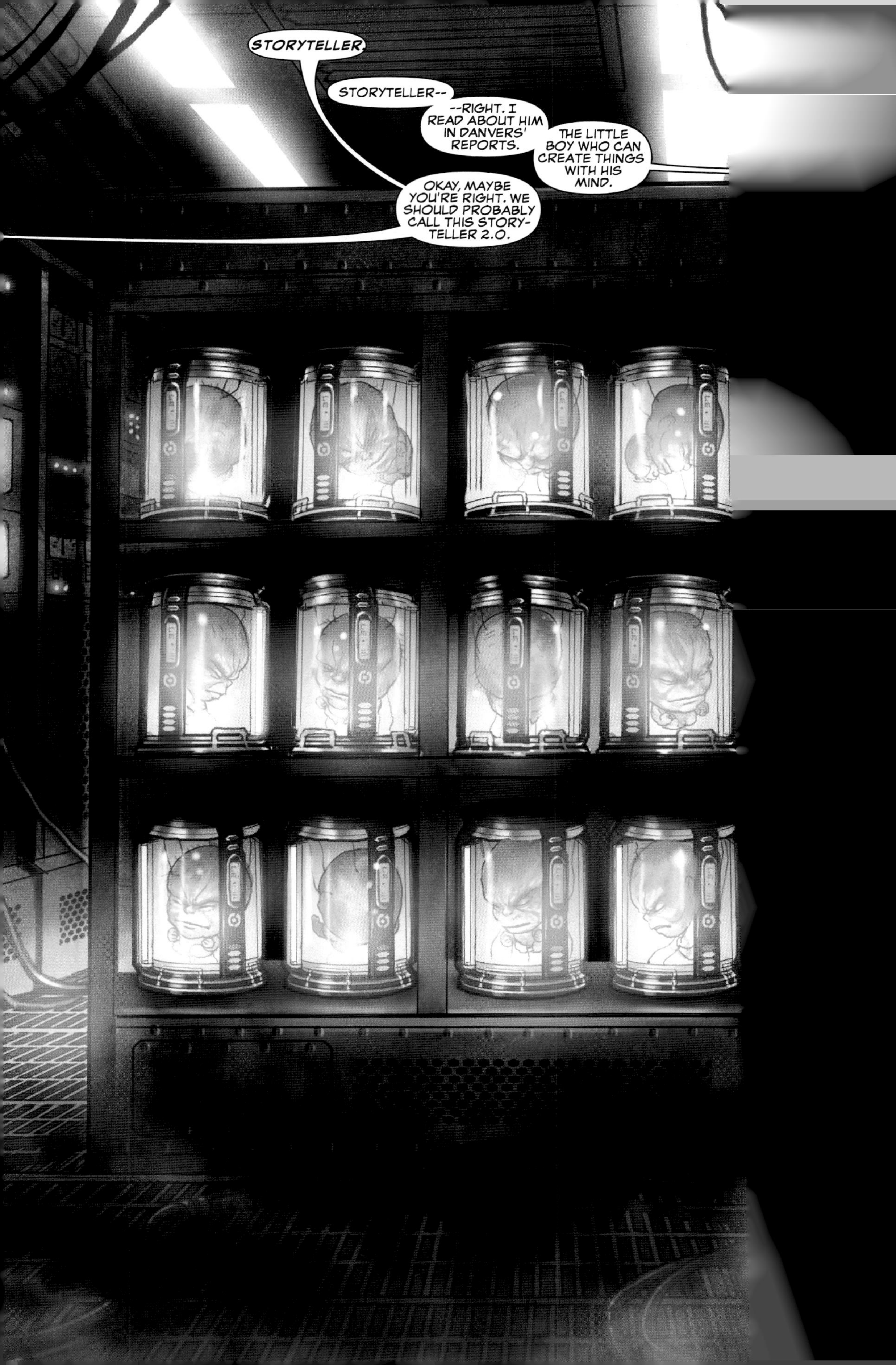
STORYTELLER.
STORYTELLER--
--RIGHT. I READ ABOUT HIM IN DANVERS' REPORTS.
THE LITTLE BOY WHO CAN CREATE THINGS WITH HIS MIND.
OKAY, MAYBE YOU'RE RIGHT. WE SHOULD PROBABLY CALL THIS STORY-TELLER 2.0.

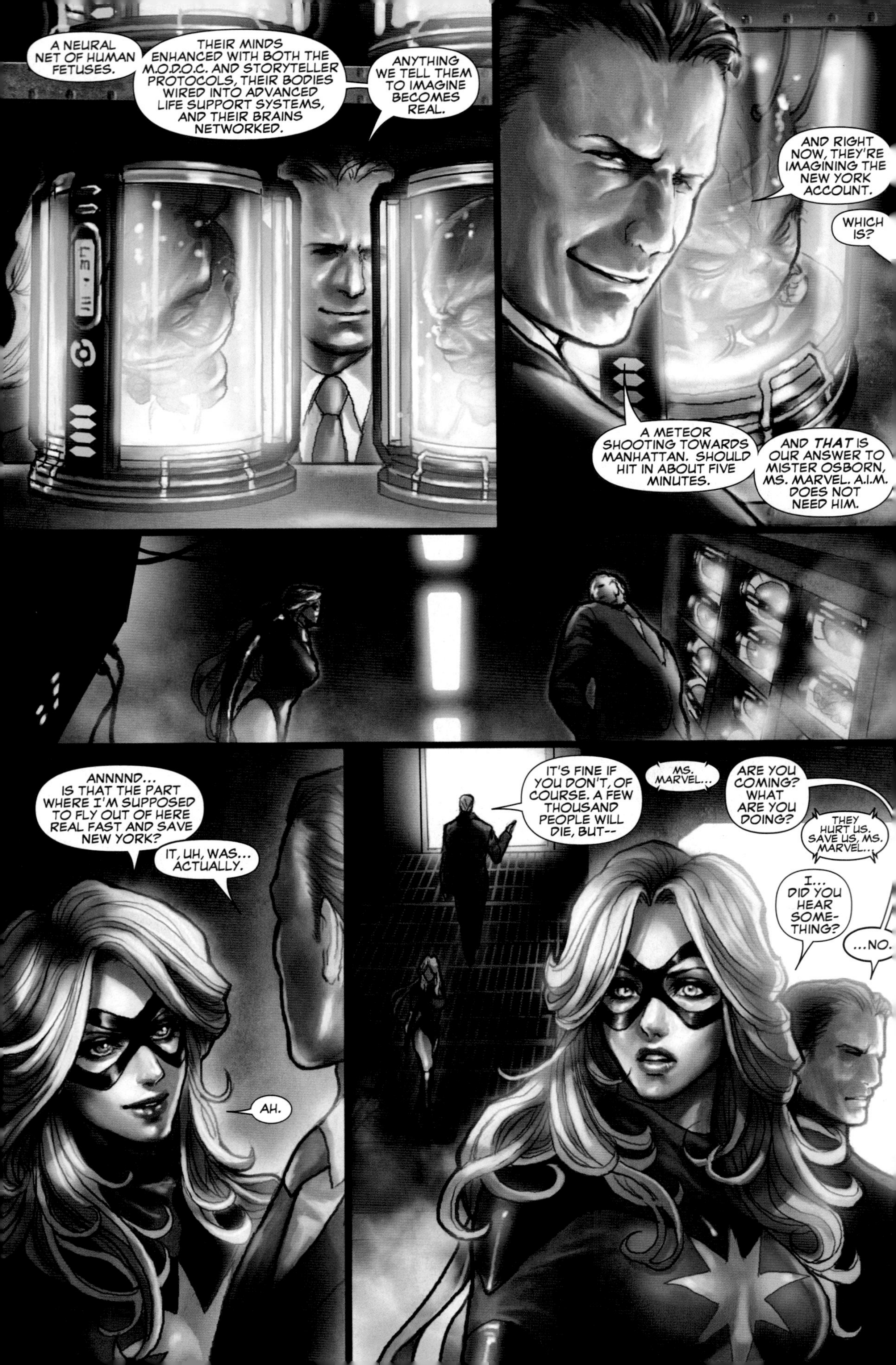
A NEURAL NET OF HUMAN FETUSES.
THEIR MINDS ENHANCED WITH BOTH THE M.O.D.O.C. AND STORYTELLER PROTOCOLS, THEIR BODIES WIRED INTO ADVANCED LIFE SUPPORT SYSTEMS, AND THEIR BRAINS NETWORKED.
ANYTHING WE TELL THEM TO IMAGINE BECOMES REAL.
AND RIGHT NOW, THEY'RE IMAGINING THE NEW YORK ACCOUNT.
WHICH IS?
A METEOR SHOOTING TOWARDS MANHATTAN. SHOULD HIT IN ABOUT FIVE MINUTES.
AND THAT IS OUR ANSWER TO MISTER OSBORN, MS. MARVEL. A.I.M. DOES NOT NEED HIM.
ANNNND... IS THAT THE PART WHERE I'M SUPPOSED TO FLY OUT OF HERE REAL FAST AND SAVE NEW YORK?
IT, UH, WAS... ACTUALLY.
AH.
IT'S FINE IF YOU DON'T, OF COURSE. A FEW THOUSAND PEOPLE WILL DIE, BUT--
MS. MARVEL...
ARE YOU COMING? WHAT ARE YOU DOING?
THEY HURT US. SAVE US, MS. MARVEL...
I... DID YOU HEAR SOMETHING?
...NO.

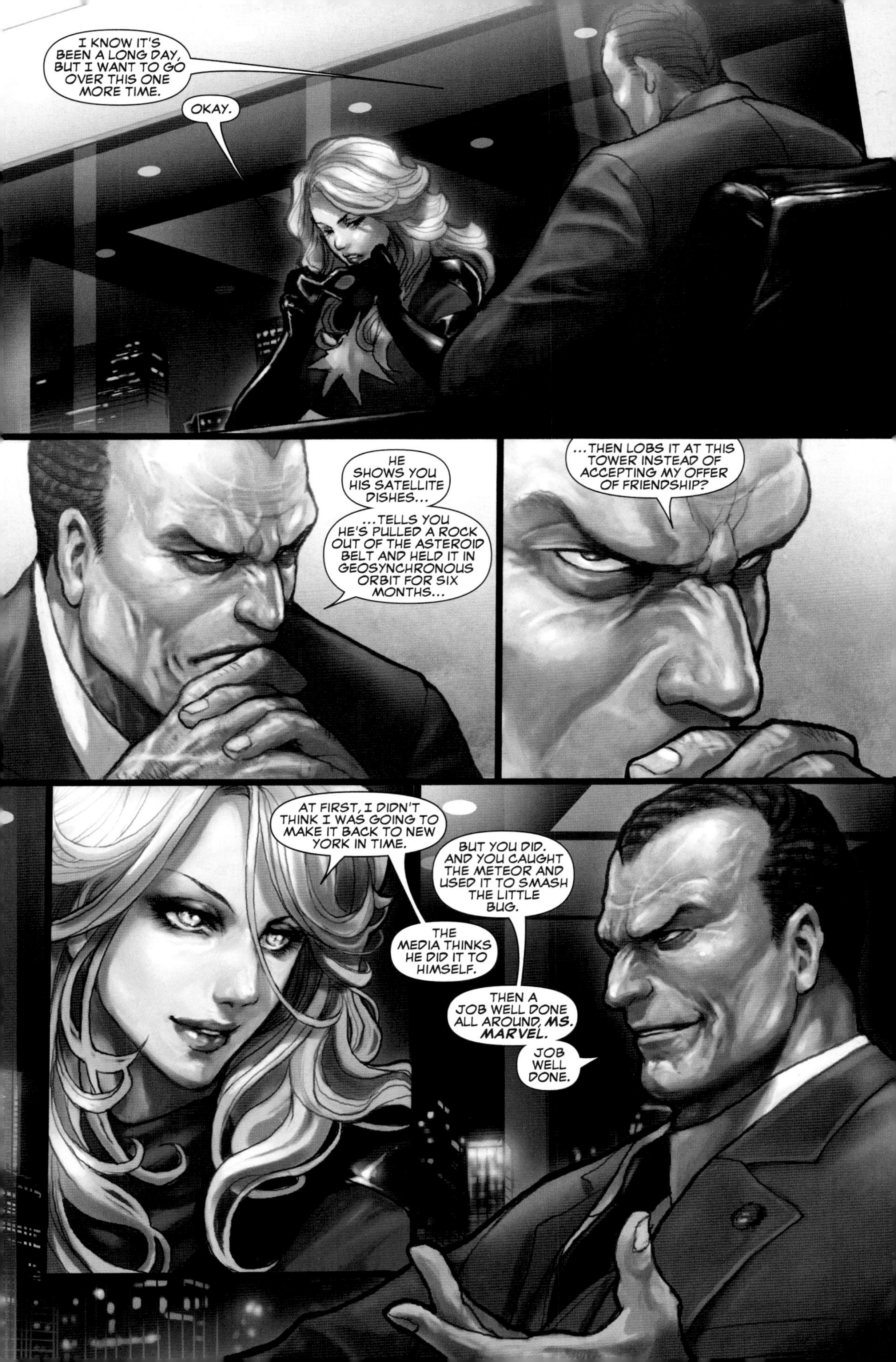
I KNOW IT'S BEEN A LONG DAY, BUT I WANT TO GO OVER THIS ONE MORE TIME.
OKAY.
HE SHOWS YOU HIS SATELLITE DISHES...
...TELLS YOU HE'S PULLED A ROCK OUT OF THE ASTEROID BELT AND HELD IT IN GEOSYNCHRONOUS ORBIT FOR SIX MONTHS...
...THEN LOBS IT AT THIS TOWER INSTEAD OF ACCEPTING MY OFFER OF FRIENDSHIP?
AT FIRST, I DIDN'T THINK I WAS GOING TO MAKE IT BACK TO NEW YORK IN TIME.
BUT YOU DID. AND YOU CAUGHT THE METEOR AND USED IT TO SMASH THE LITTLE BUG.
THE MEDIA THINKS HE DID IT TO HIMSELF.
THEN A JOB WELL DONE ALL AROUND, MS. MARVEL.
JOB WELL DONE.

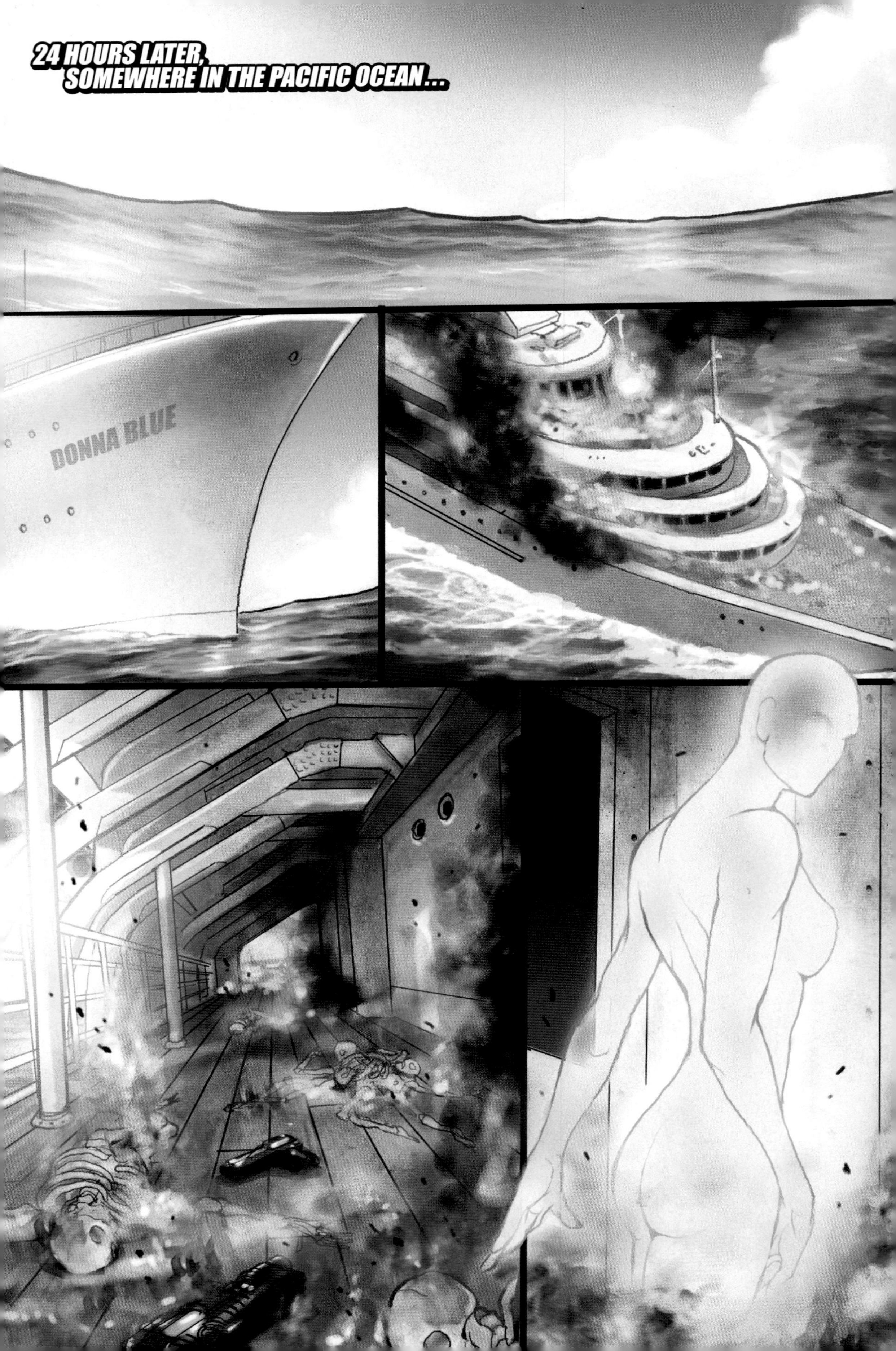
24 HOURS LATER, SOMEWHERE IN THE PACIFIC OCEAN...
DONNA BLUE

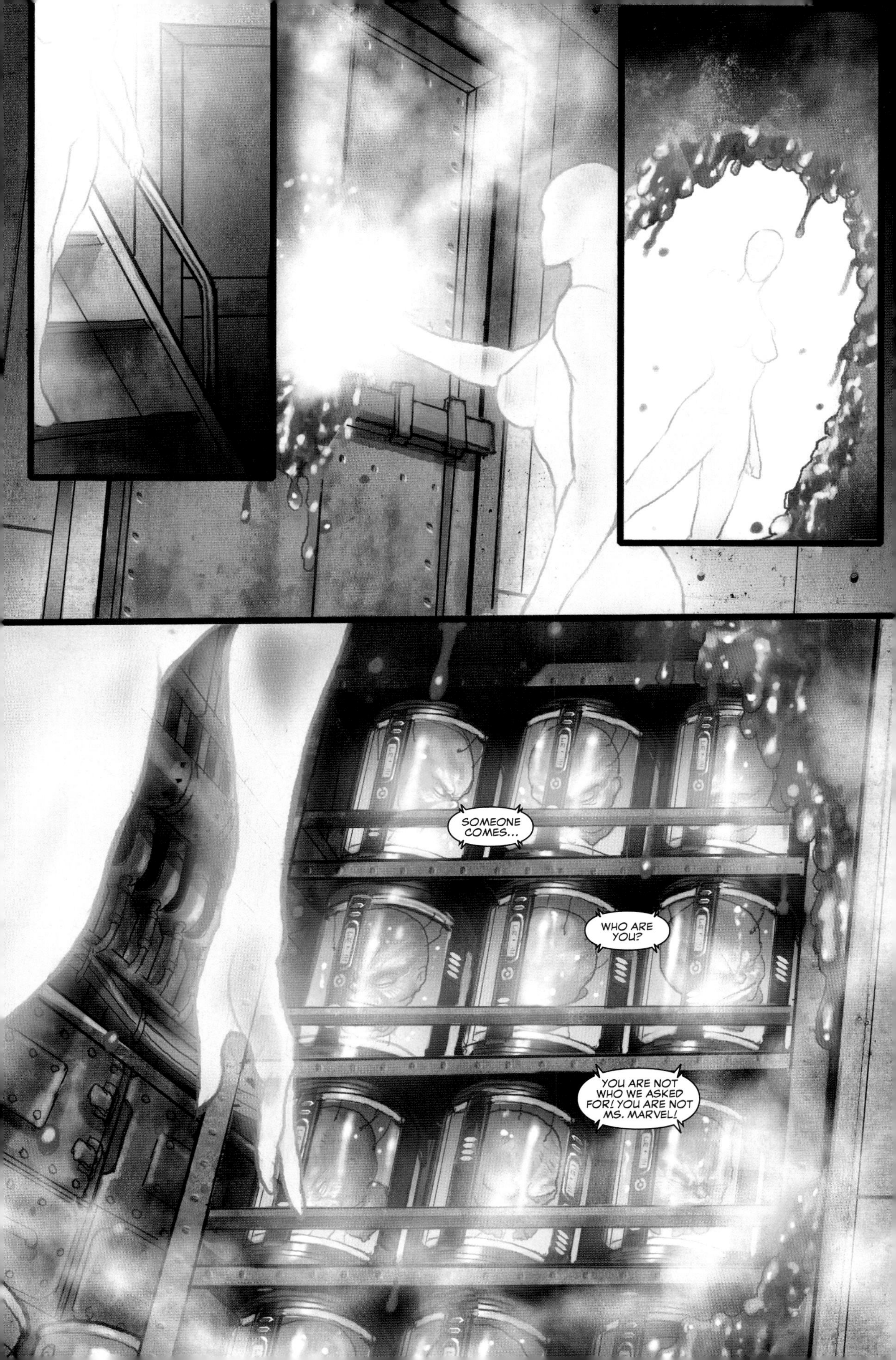
SOMEONE COMES...
WHO ARE YOU?
YOU ARE NOT WHO WE ASKED FOR! YOU ARE NOT MS. MARVEL!

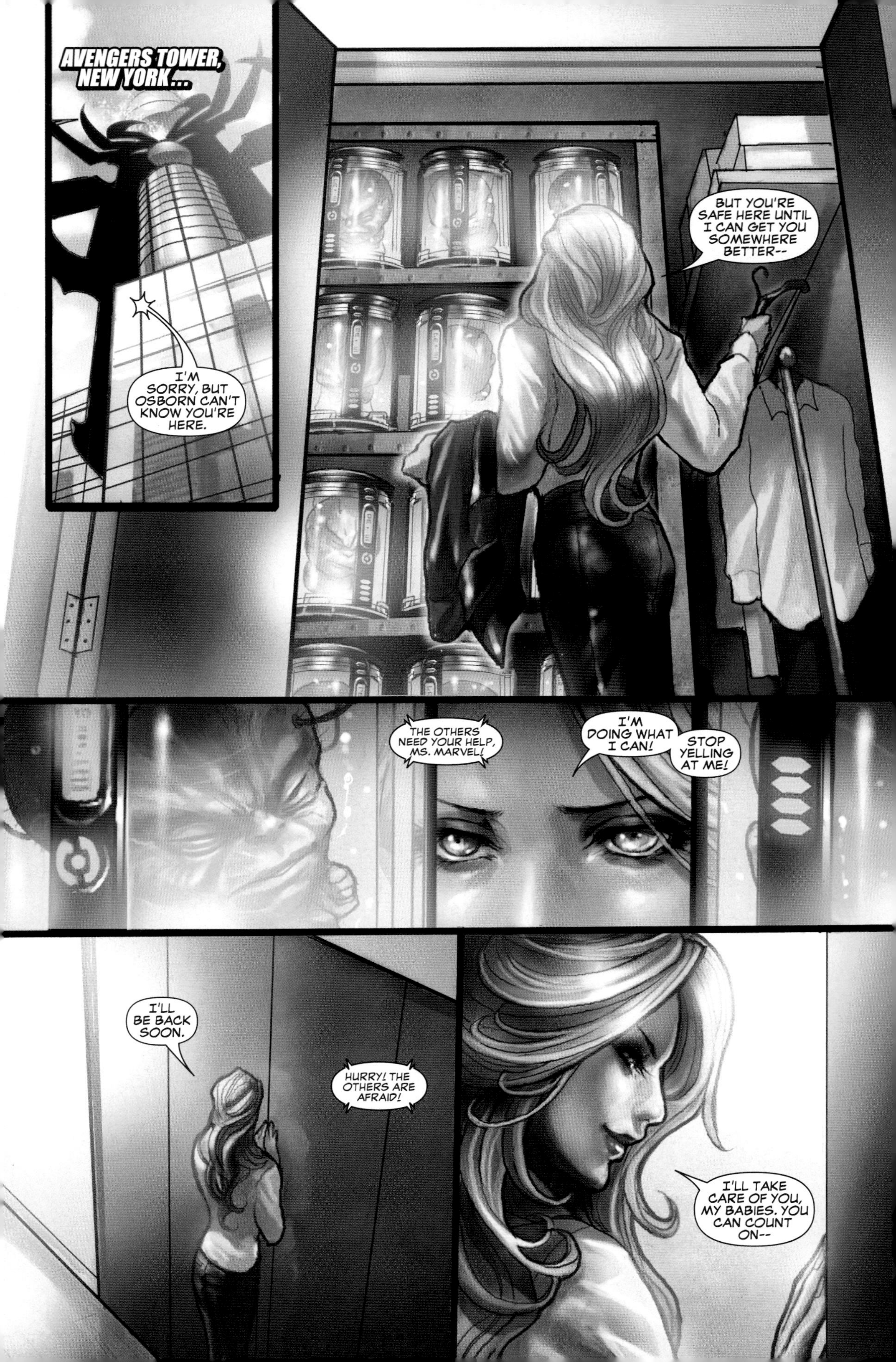
AVENGERS TOWER, NEW YORK...
I'M SORRY, BUT OSBORN CAN'T KNOW YOU'RE HERE.
BUT YOU'RE SAFE HERE UNTIL I CAN GET YOU SOMEWHERE BETTER--
THE OTHERS NEED YOUR HELP, MS. MARVEL!
I'M DOING WHAT I CAN!
STOP YELLING AT ME!
I'LL BE BACK SOON.
HURRY! THE OTHERS ARE AFRAID!
I'LL TAKE CARE OF YOU, MY BABIES. YOU CAN COUNT ON--

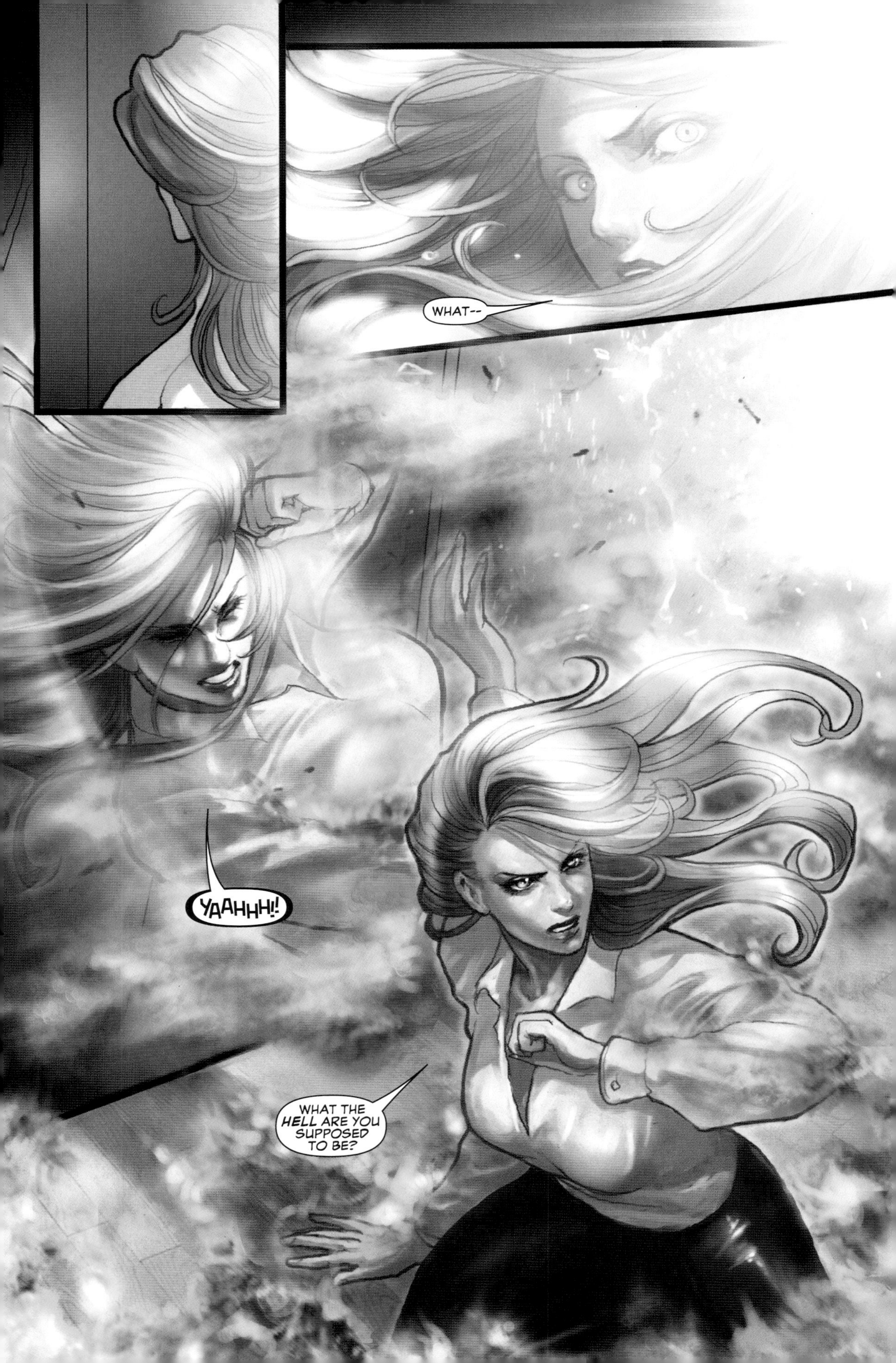
WHAT--
YAAHHH!!
WHAT THE HELL ARE YOU SUPPOSED TO BE?

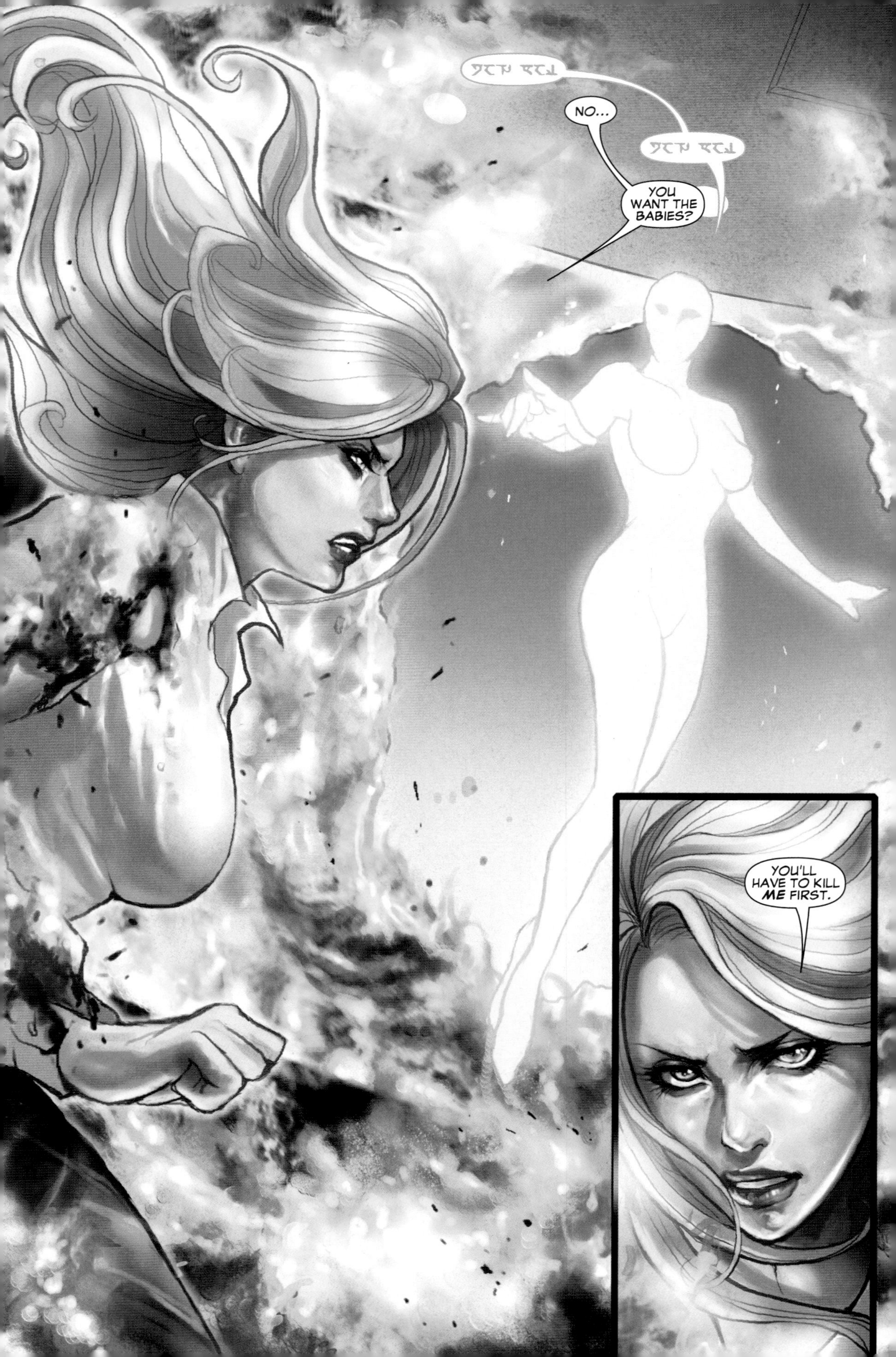

NO...
YOU WANT THE BABIES?
YOU'LL HAVE TO KILL **ME** FIRST.

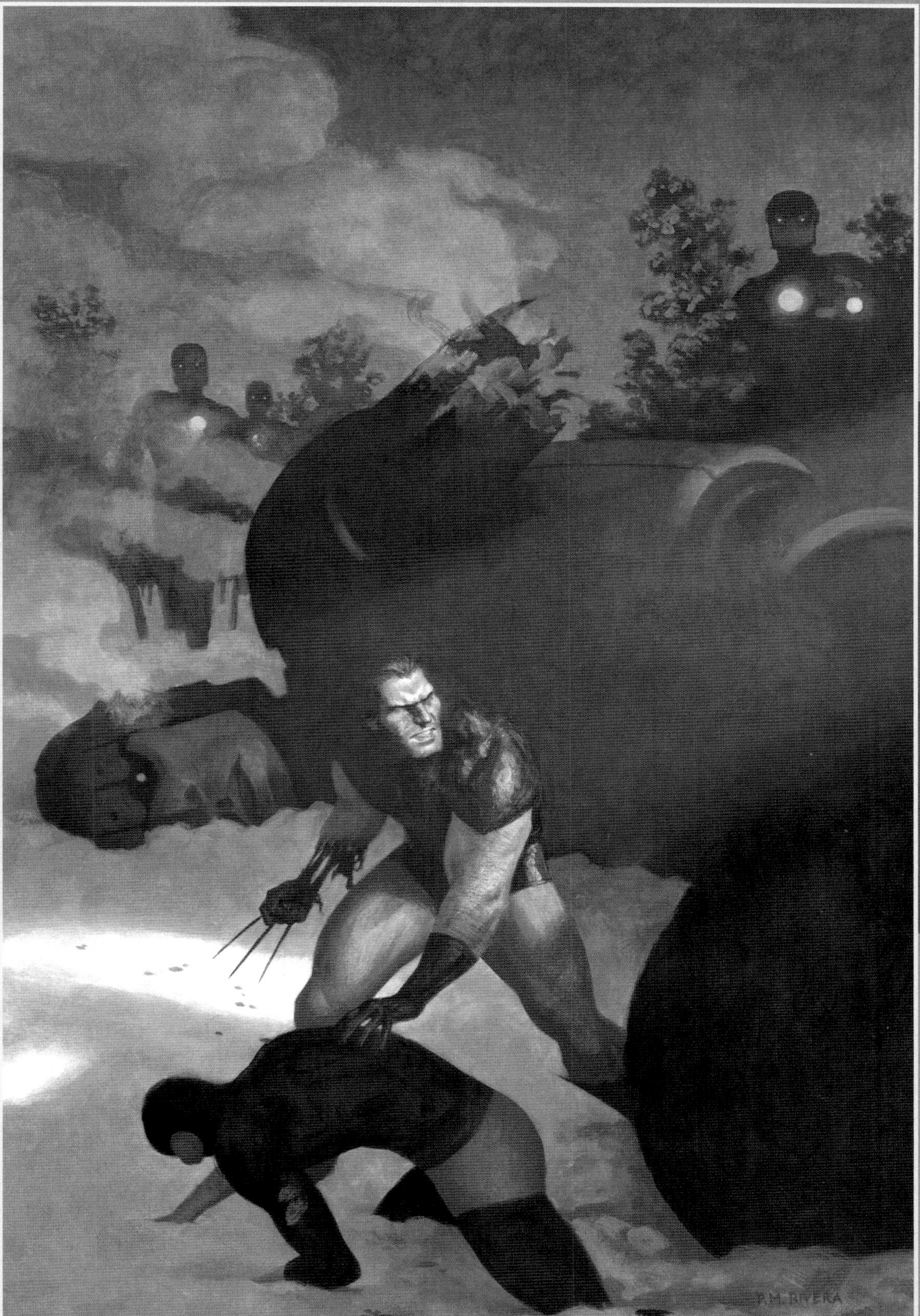
P.M. RIVERA

MS. MARVEL #38 **WOLVERINE ART APPRECIATION VARIANT BY PAOLO RIVERA**

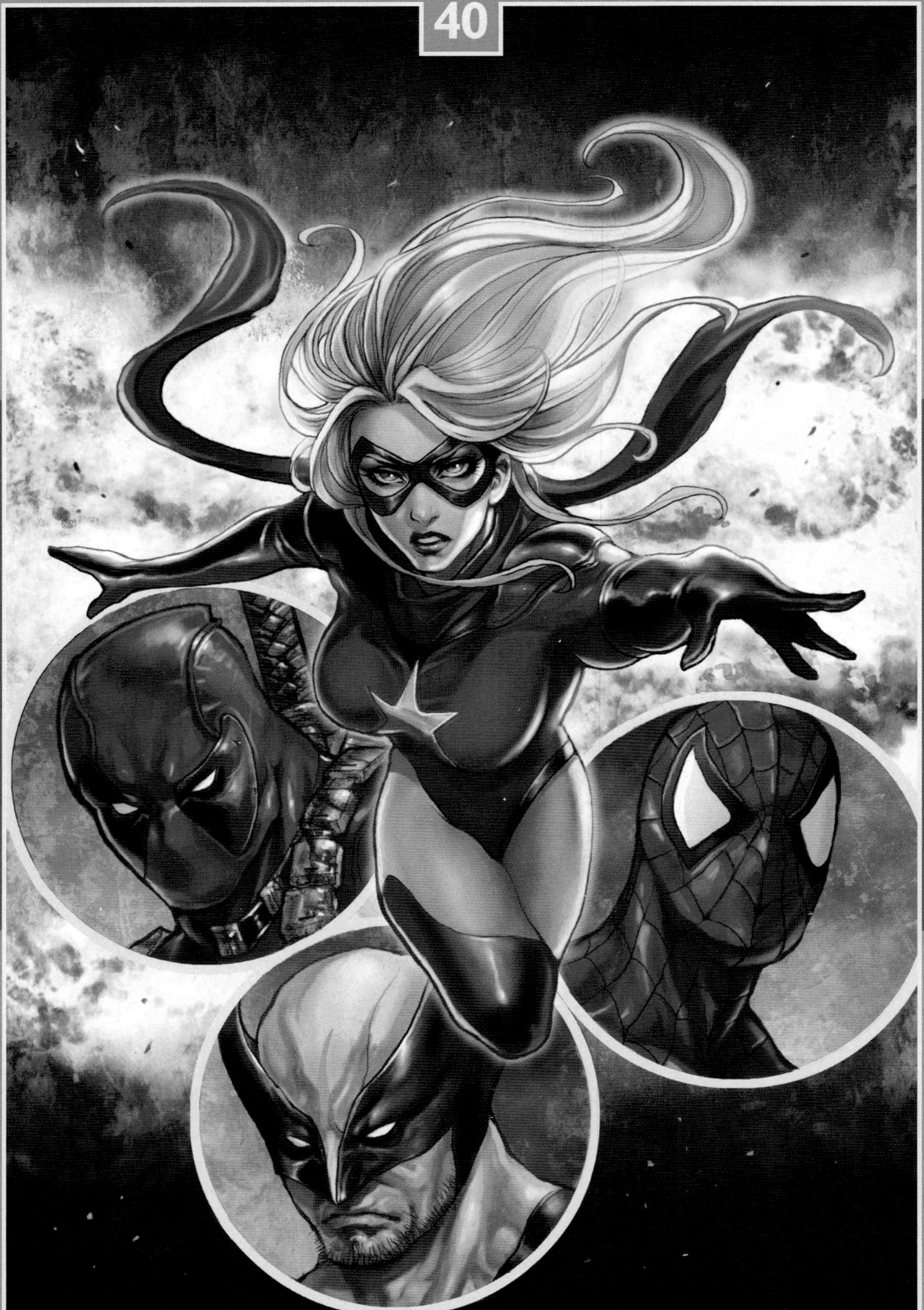
40

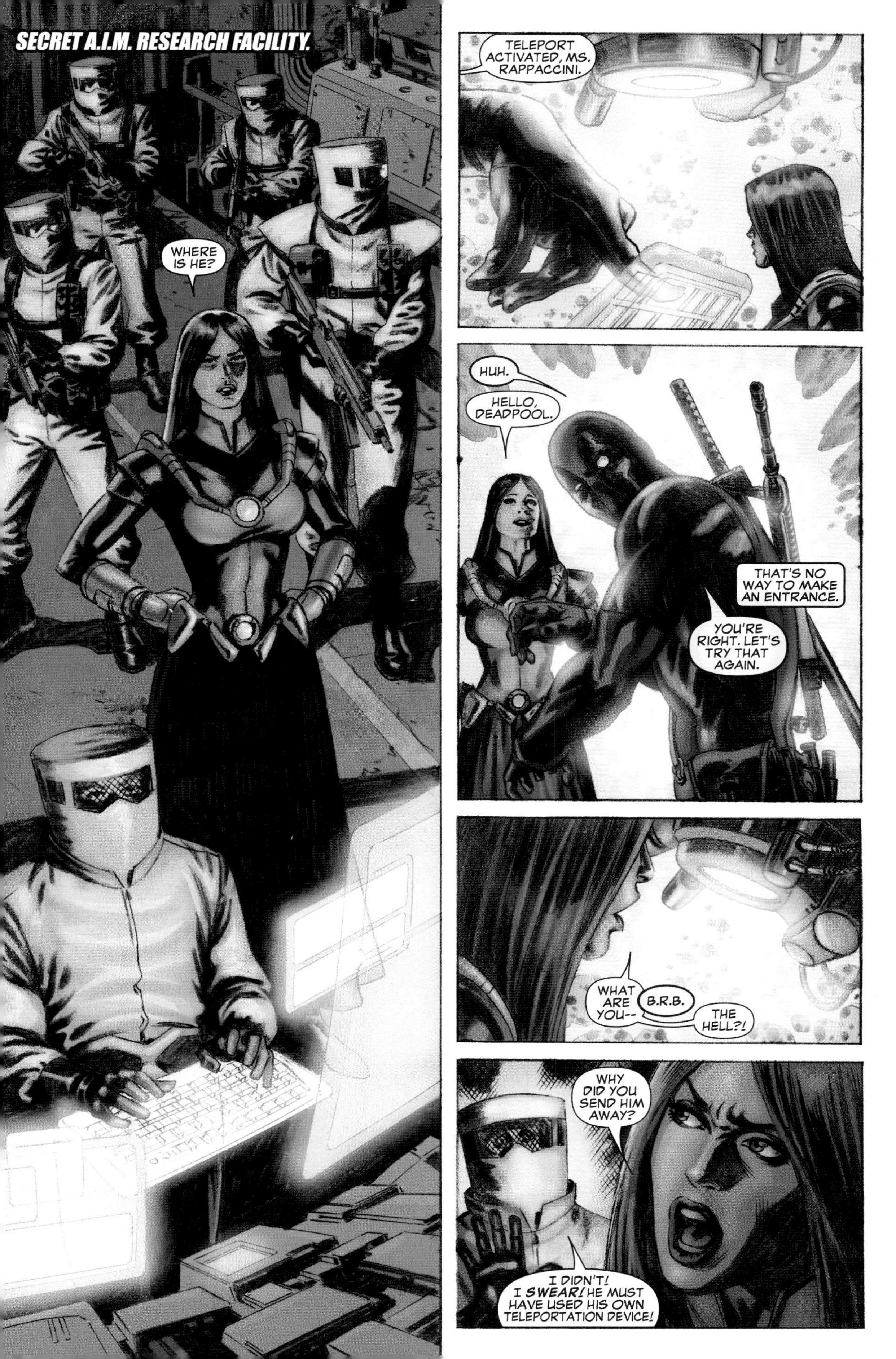
SECRET A.I.M. RESEARCH FACILITY.
WHERE IS HE?
TELEPORT ACTIVATED, MS. RAPPACCINI.
HUH.
HELLO, DEADPOOL.
THAT'S NO WAY TO MAKE AN ENTRANCE.
YOU'RE RIGHT. LET'S TRY THAT AGAIN.
WHAT ARE YOU--
B.R.B.
THE HELL?!
WHY DID YOU SEND HIM AWAY?
I DIDN'T! I SWEAR! HE MUST HAVE USED HIS OWN TELEPORTATION DEVICE!

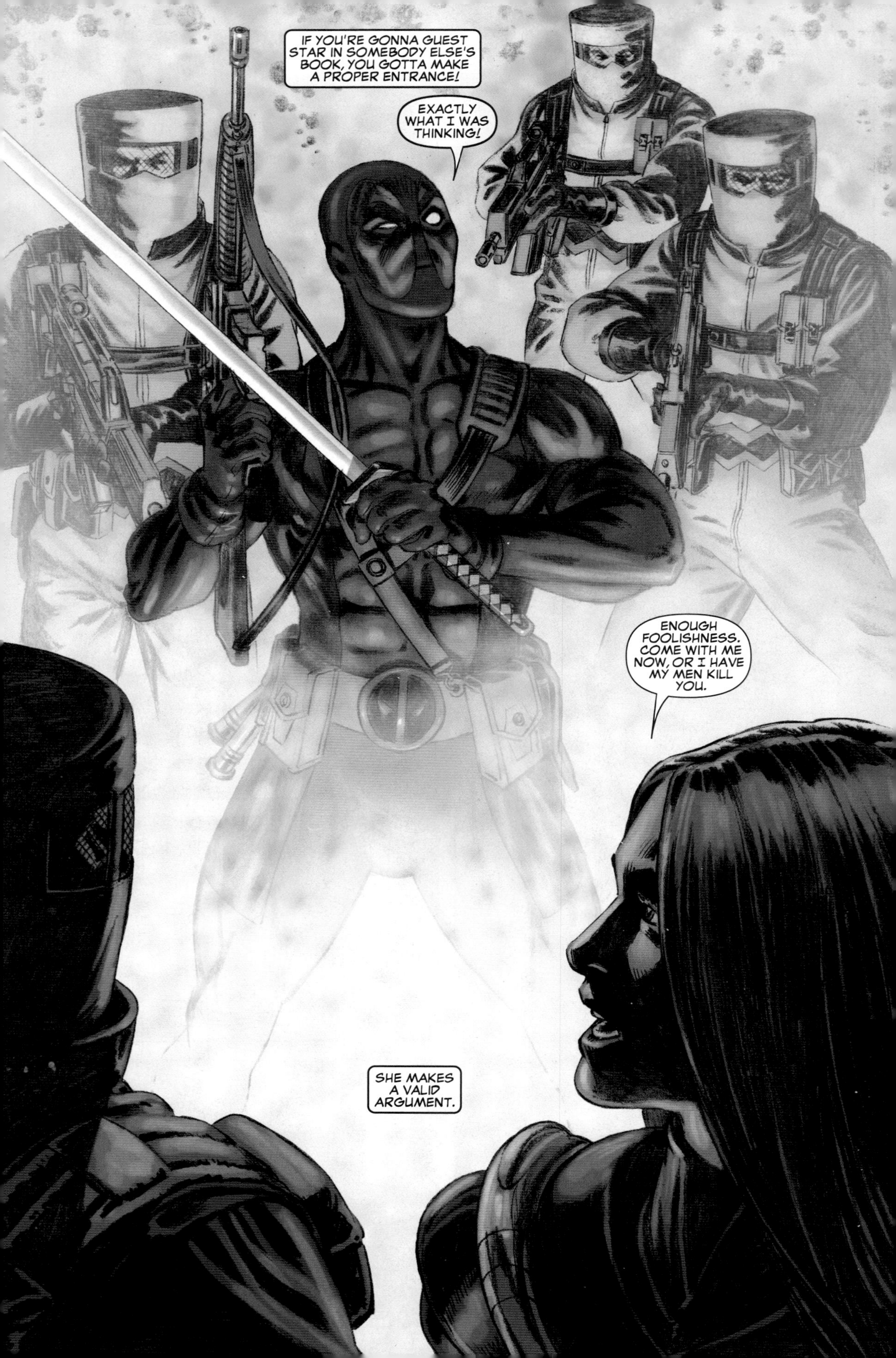
IF YOU'RE GONNA GUEST STAR IN SOMEBODY ELSE'S BOOK, YOU GOTTA MAKE A PROPER ENTRANCE!
EXACTLY WHAT I WAS THINKING!
ENOUGH FOOLISHNESS. COME WITH ME NOW, OR I HAVE MY MEN KILL YOU.
SHE MAKES A VALID ARGUMENT.

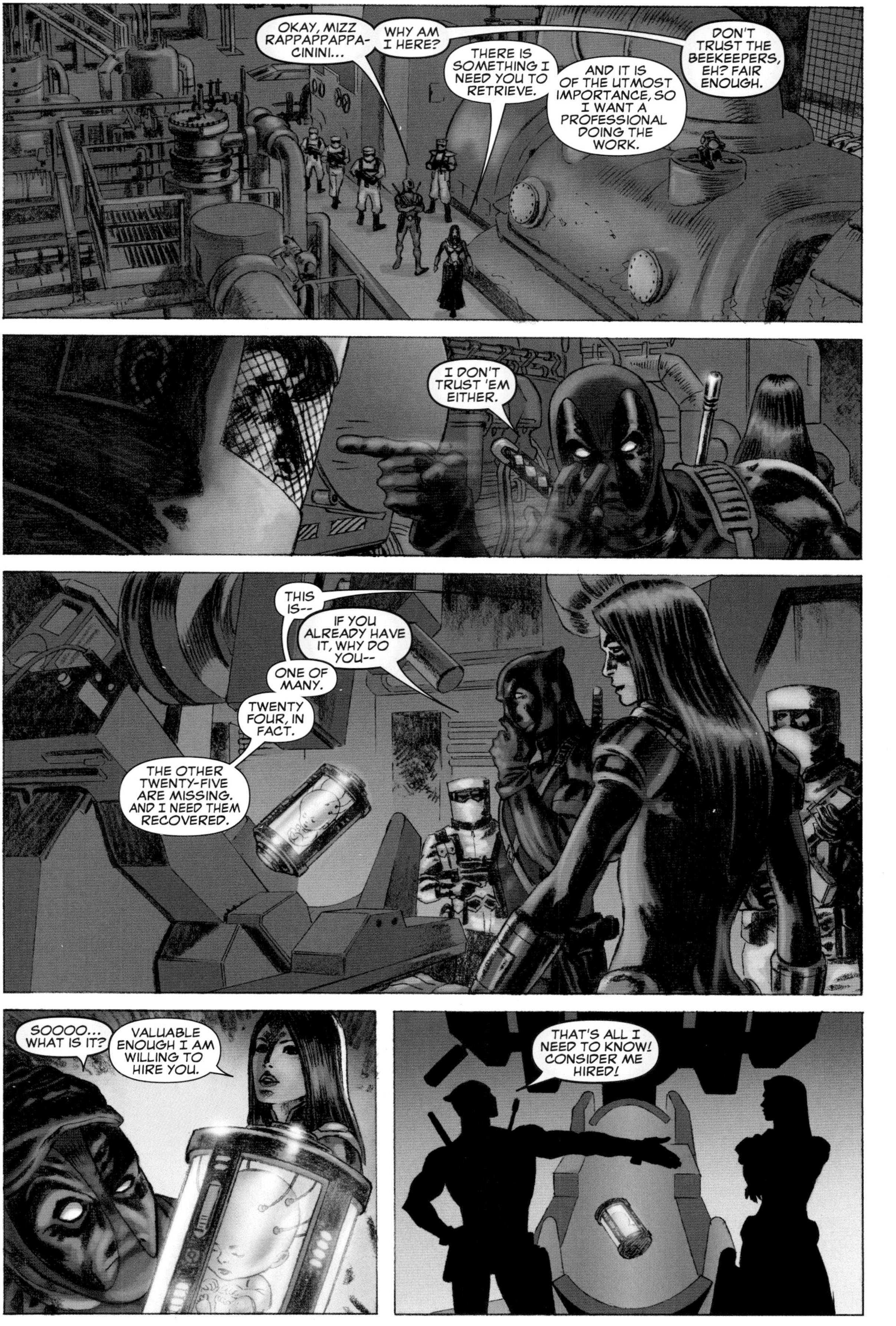
OKAY, MIZZ RAPPAPPAPPA-CININI...
WHY AM I HERE?
THERE IS SOMETHING I NEED YOU TO RETRIEVE.
AND IT IS OF THE UTMOST IMPORTANCE, SO I WANT A PROFESSIONAL DOING THE WORK.
DON'T TRUST THE BEEKEEPERS, EH? FAIR ENOUGH.
I DON'T TRUST 'EM EITHER.
THIS IS--
IF YOU ALREADY HAVE IT, WHY DO YOU--
ONE OF MANY.
TWENTY FOUR, IN FACT.
THE OTHER TWENTY-FIVE ARE MISSING. AND I NEED THEM RECOVERED.
SOOOO... WHAT IS IT?
VALUABLE ENOUGH I AM WILLING TO HIRE YOU.
THAT'S ALL I NEED TO KNOW! CONSIDER ME HIRED!

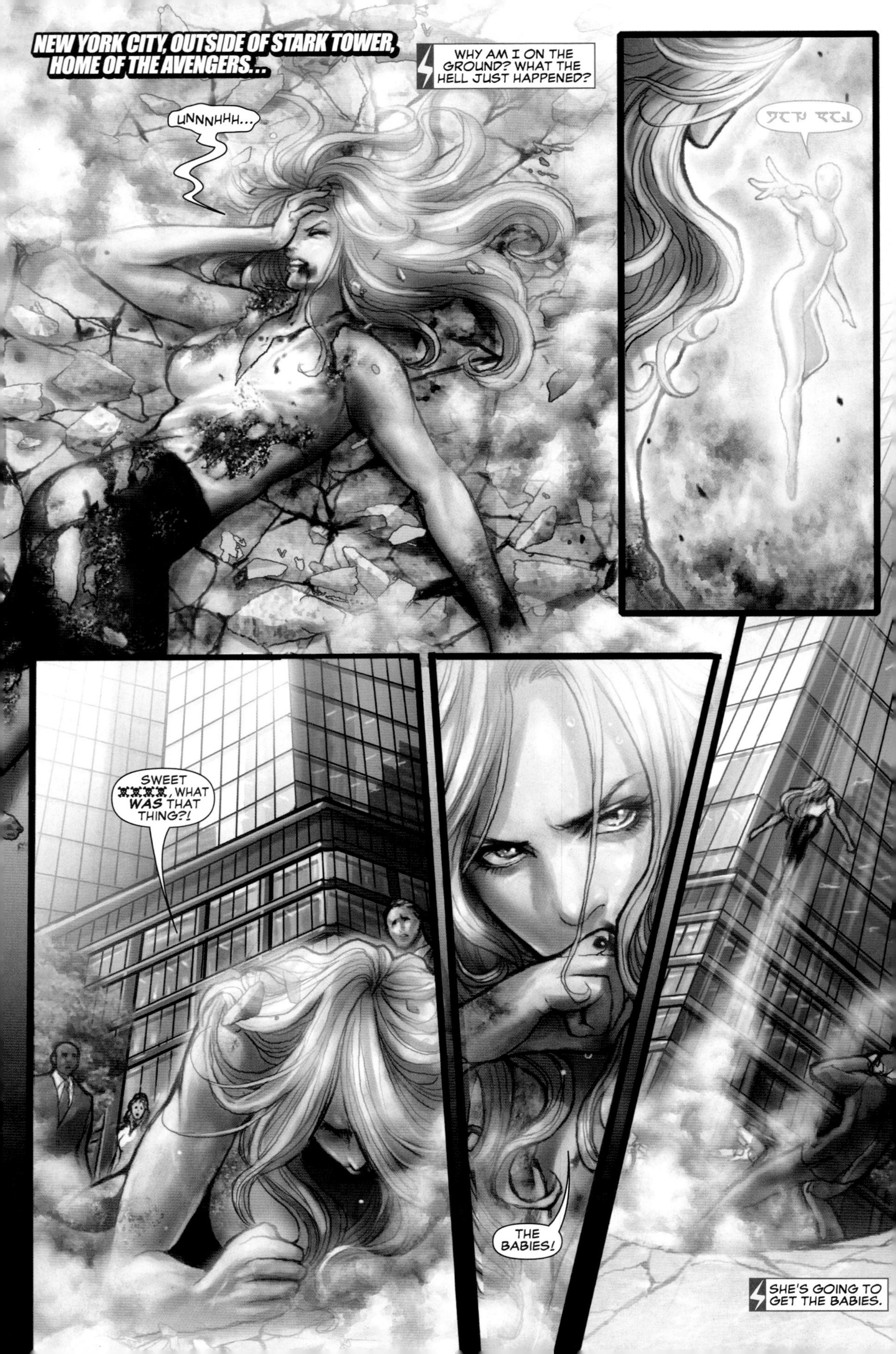

NEW YORK CITY, OUTSIDE OF STARK TOWER, HOME OF THE AVENGERS...
WHY AM I ON THE GROUND? WHAT THE HELL JUST HAPPENED?
UNNNHHH...
SWEET ☠☠☠☠, WHAT *WAS* THAT THING?!
THE BABIES!
SHE'S GOING TO GET THE BABIES.

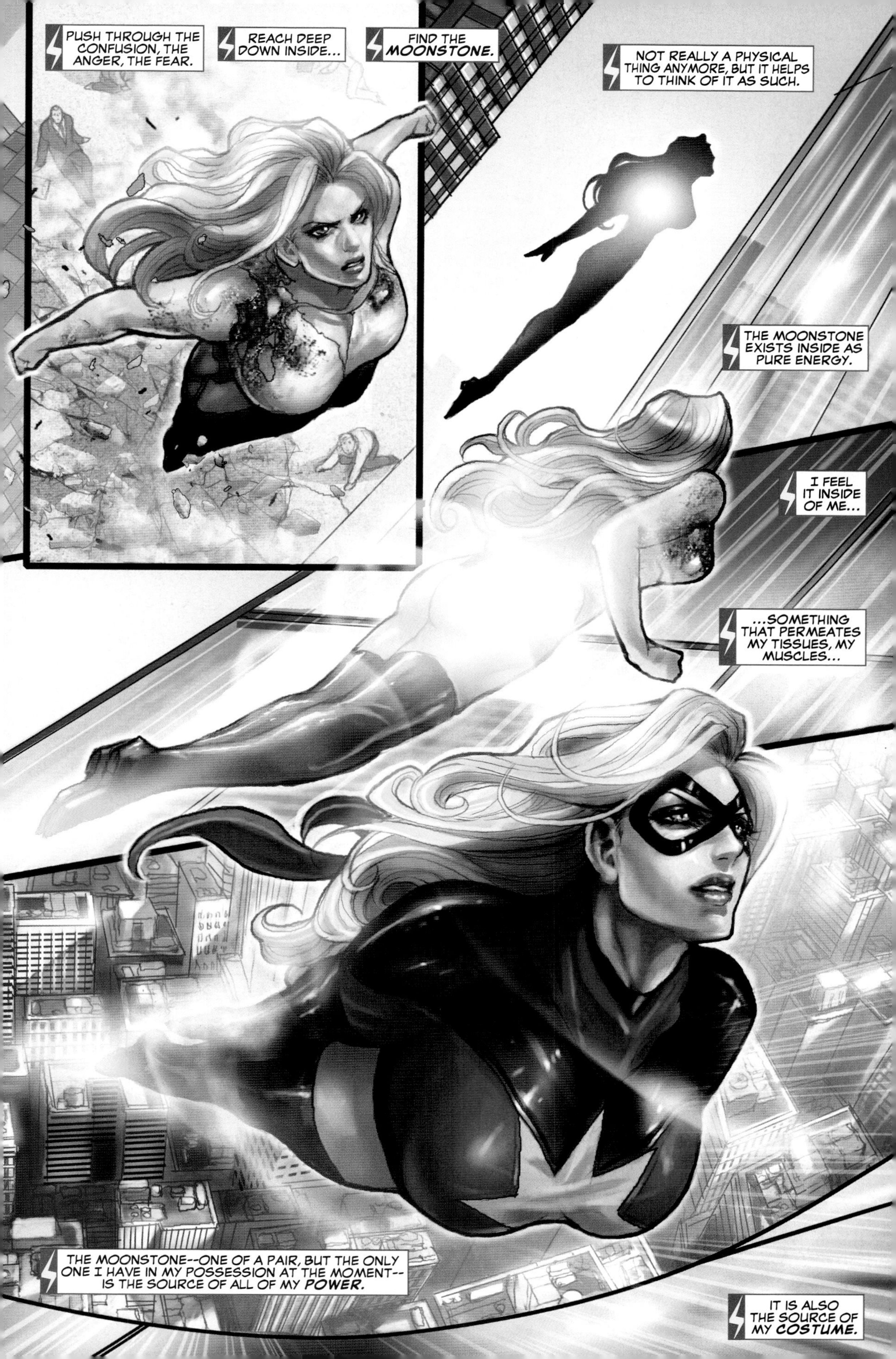
PUSH THROUGH THE CONFUSION, THE ANGER, THE FEAR.
REACH DEEP DOWN INSIDE...
FIND THE MOONSTONE.
NOT REALLY A PHYSICAL THING ANYMORE, BUT IT HELPS TO THINK OF IT AS SUCH.
THE MOONSTONE EXISTS INSIDE AS PURE ENERGY.
I FEEL IT INSIDE OF ME...
...SOMETHING THAT PERMEATES MY TISSUES, MY MUSCLES...
THE MOONSTONE--ONE OF A PAIR, BUT THE ONLY ONE I HAVE IN MY POSSESSION AT THE MOMENT--IS THE SOURCE OF ALL OF MY POWER.
IT IS ALSO THE SOURCE OF MY COSTUME.

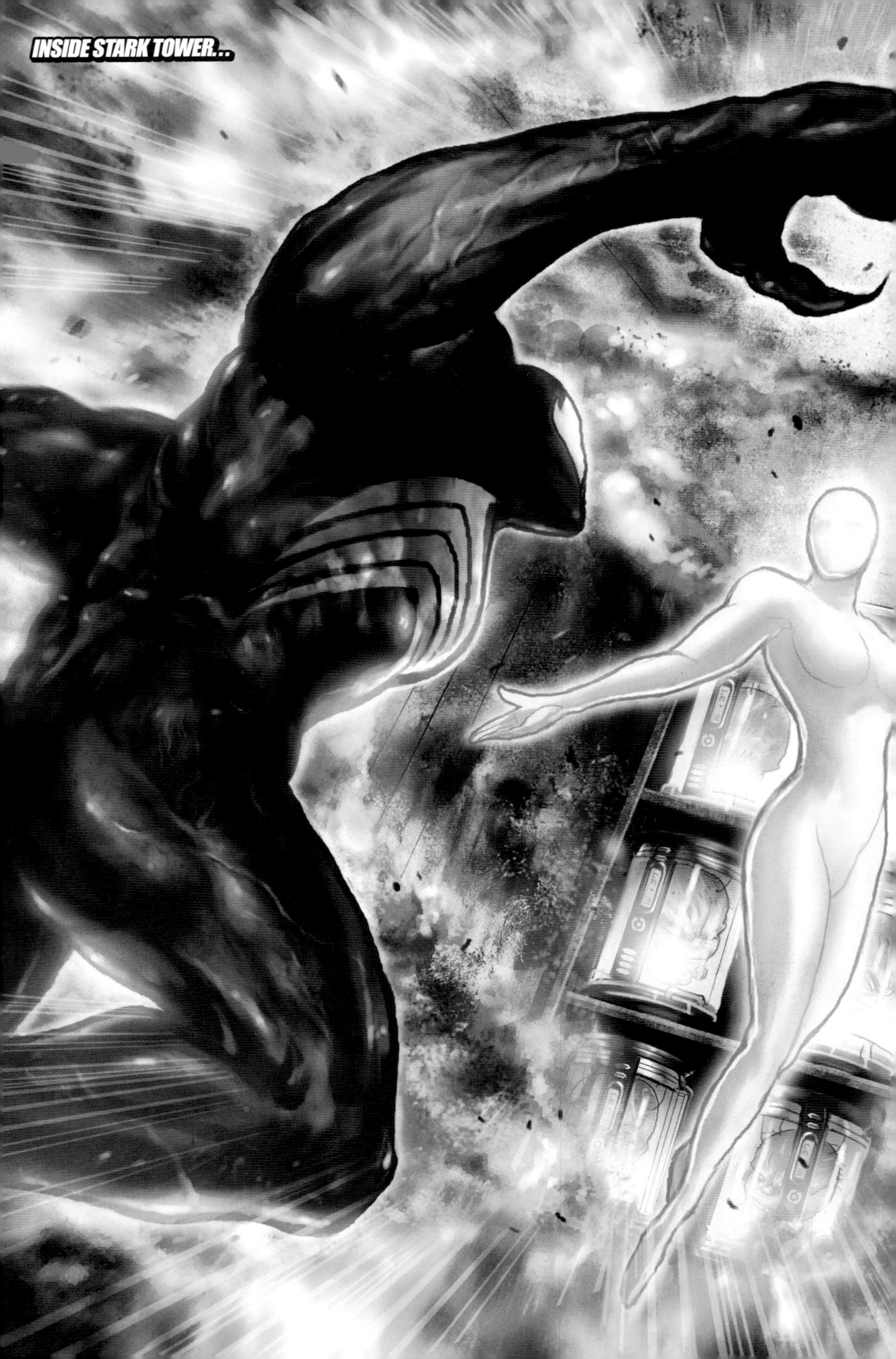
INSIDE STARK TOWER...

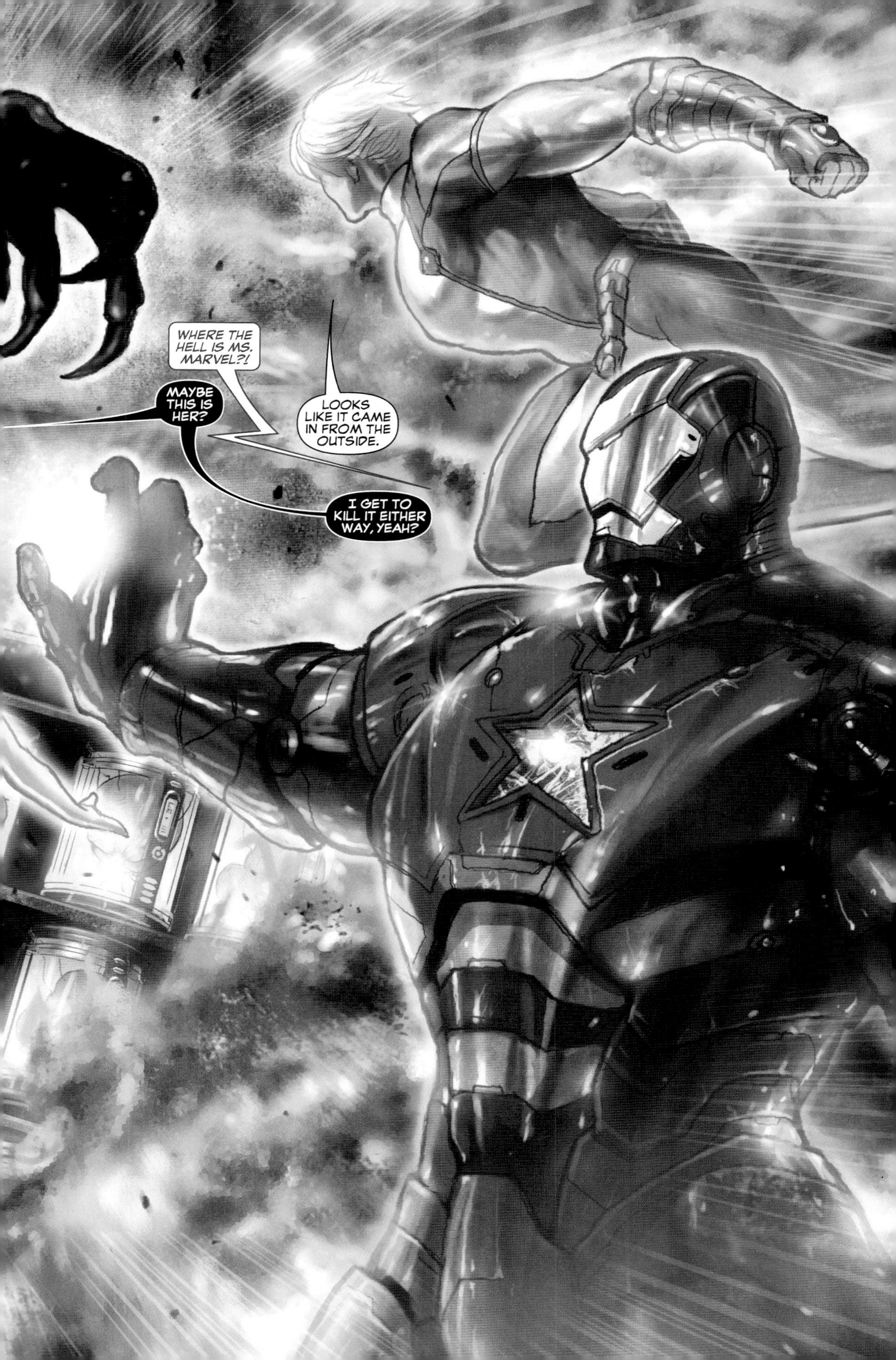
WHERE THE HELL IS MS. MARVEL?!
MAYBE THIS IS HER?
LOOKS LIKE IT CAME IN FROM THE OUTSIDE.
I GET TO KILL IT EITHER WAY, YEAH?

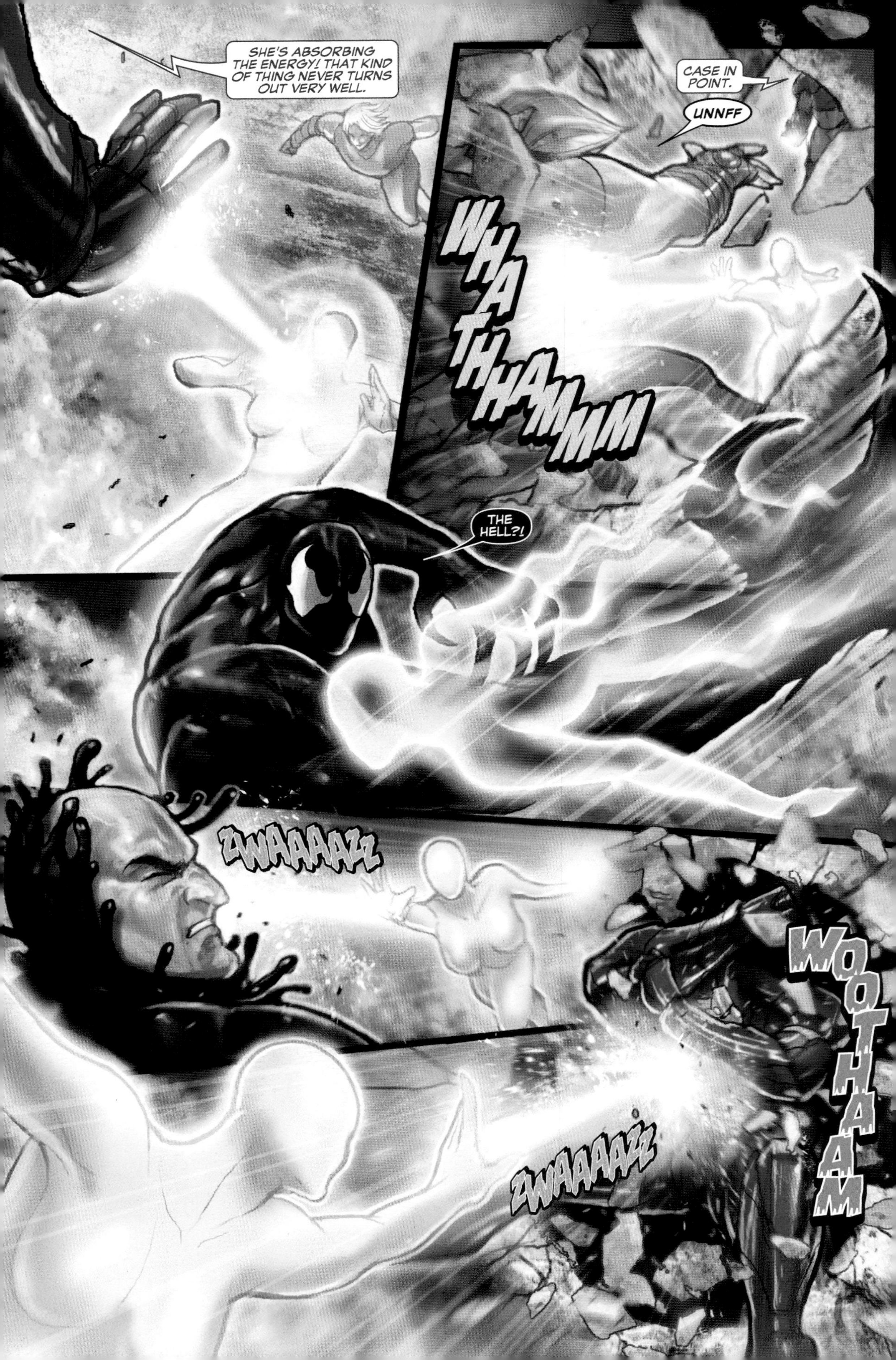
SHE'S ABSORBING THE ENERGY! THAT KIND OF THING NEVER TURNS OUT VERY WELL.
CASE IN POINT.
UNNFF
WHA THHAMMM
THE HELL?!
ZWAAAAZZ
ZWAAAAZZ
WOOTHAAM

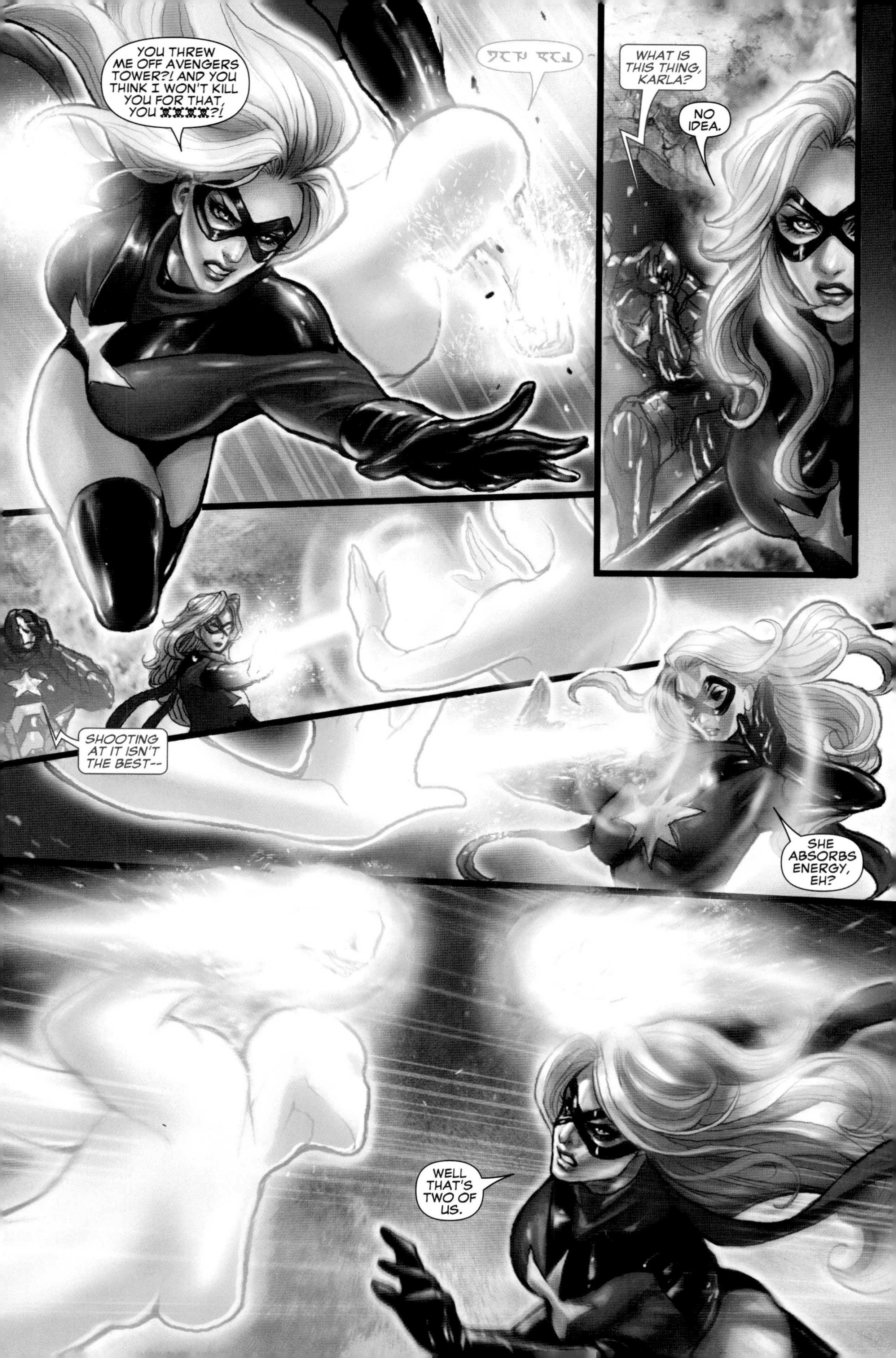
YOU THREW ME OFF AVENGERS TOWER?! AND YOU THINK I WON'T KILL YOU FOR THAT, YOU ☠☠☠☠?!
WHAT IS THIS THING, KARLA?
NO IDEA.
SHOOTING AT IT ISN'T THE BEST--
SHE ABSORBS ENERGY, EH?
WELL THAT'S TWO OF US.

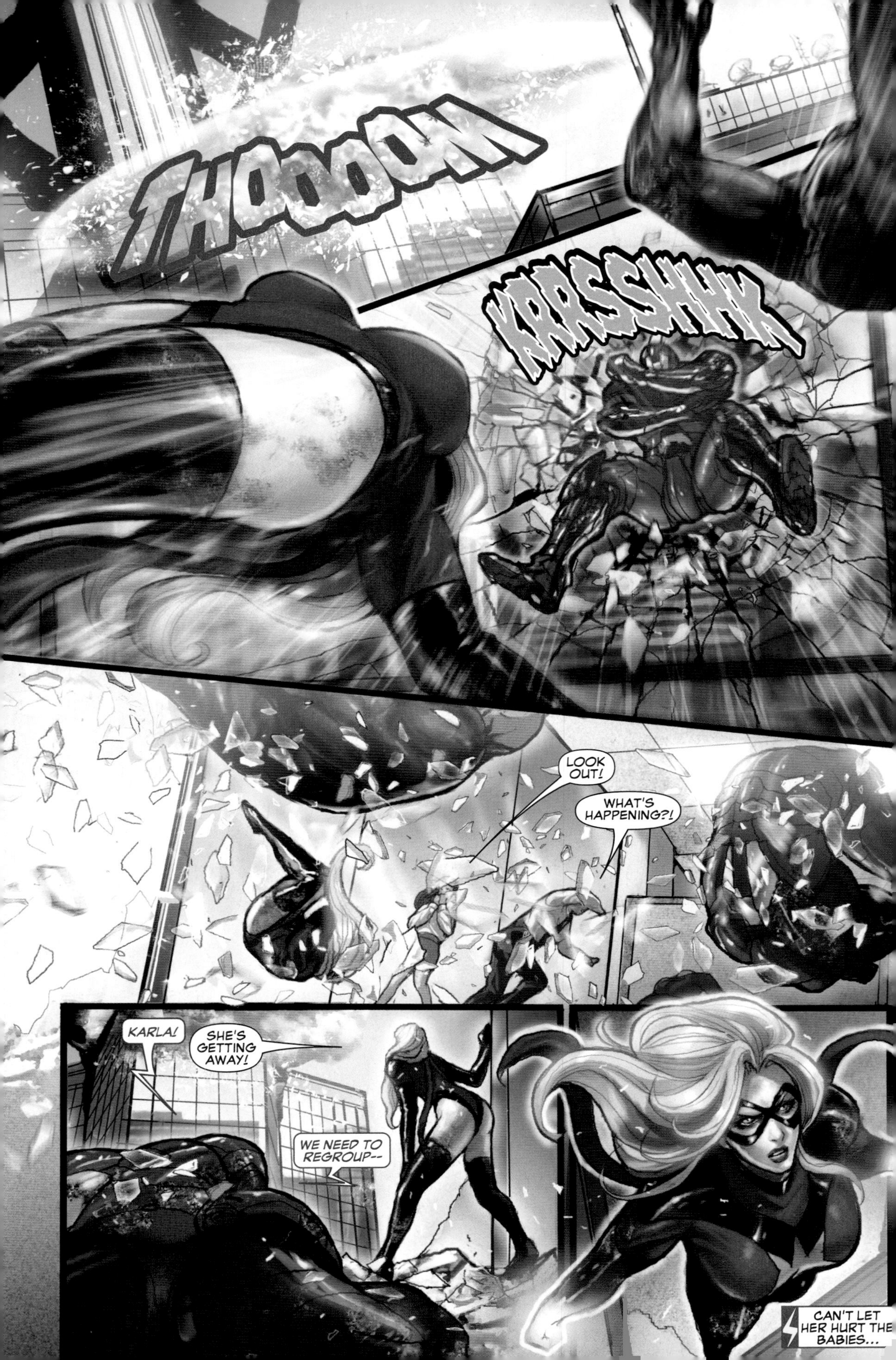
THOOOOM
KRRSSHHK
LOOK OUT!
WHAT'S HAPPENING?!
KARLA!
SHE'S GETTING AWAY!
WE NEED TO REGROUP--
CAN'T LET HER HURT THE BABIES...

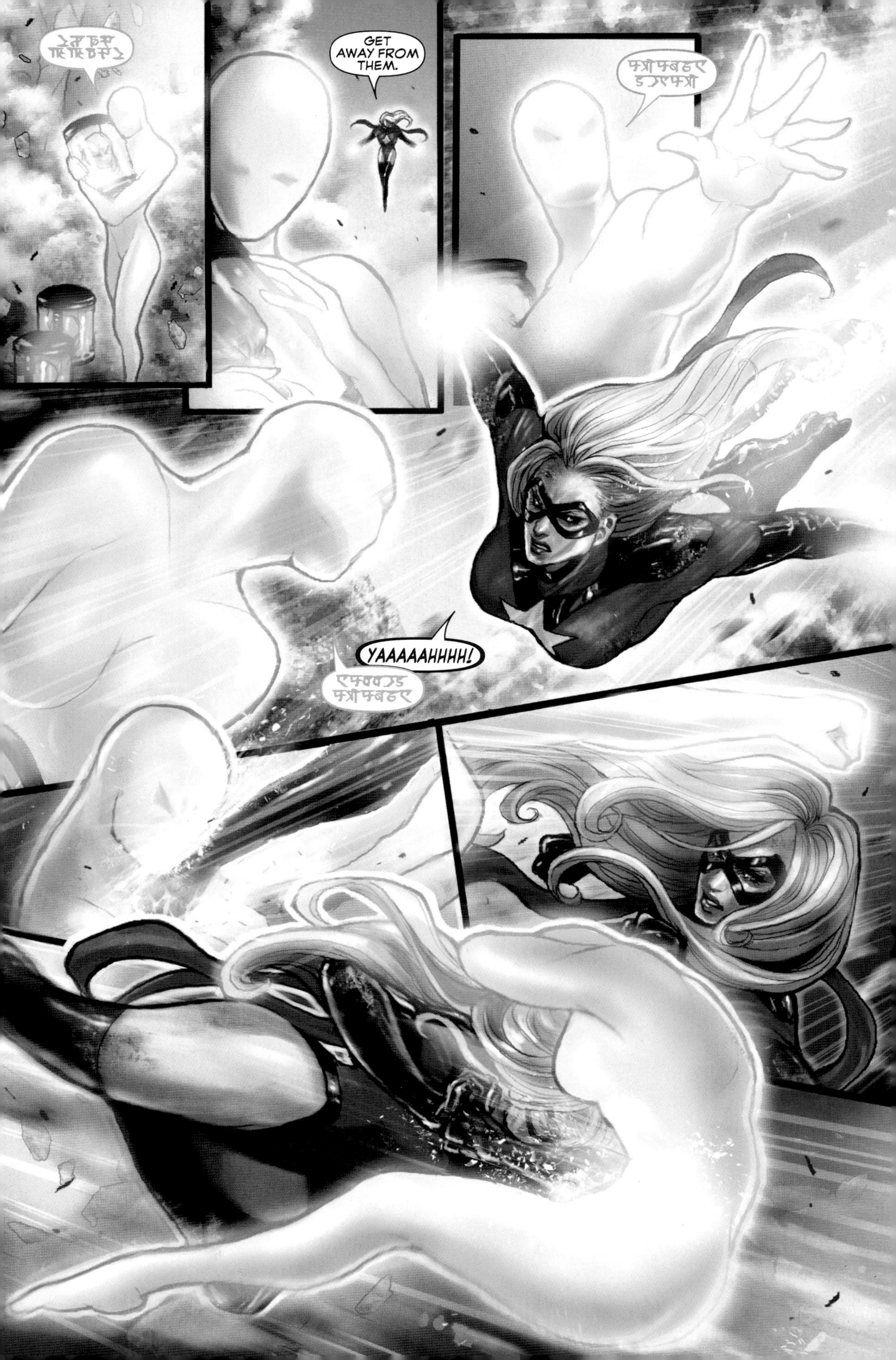
GET AWAY FROM THEM.
YAAAAAHHHH!

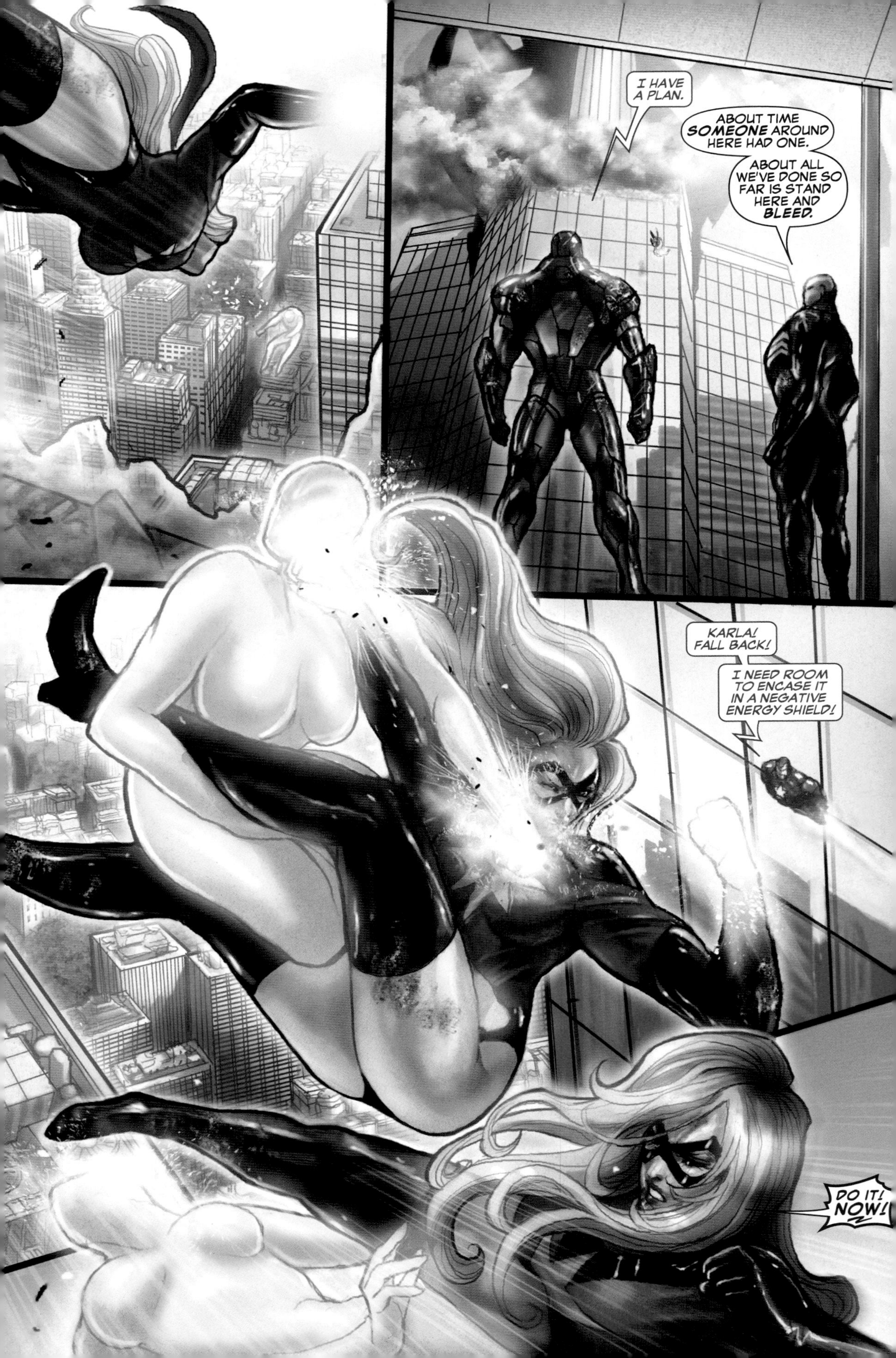
I HAVE A PLAN.
ABOUT TIME SOMEONE AROUND HERE HAD ONE.
ABOUT ALL WE'VE DONE SO FAR IS STAND HERE AND BLEED.
KARLA! FALL BACK!
I NEED ROOM TO ENCASE IT IN A NEGATIVE ENERGY SHIELD!
DO IT! NOW!

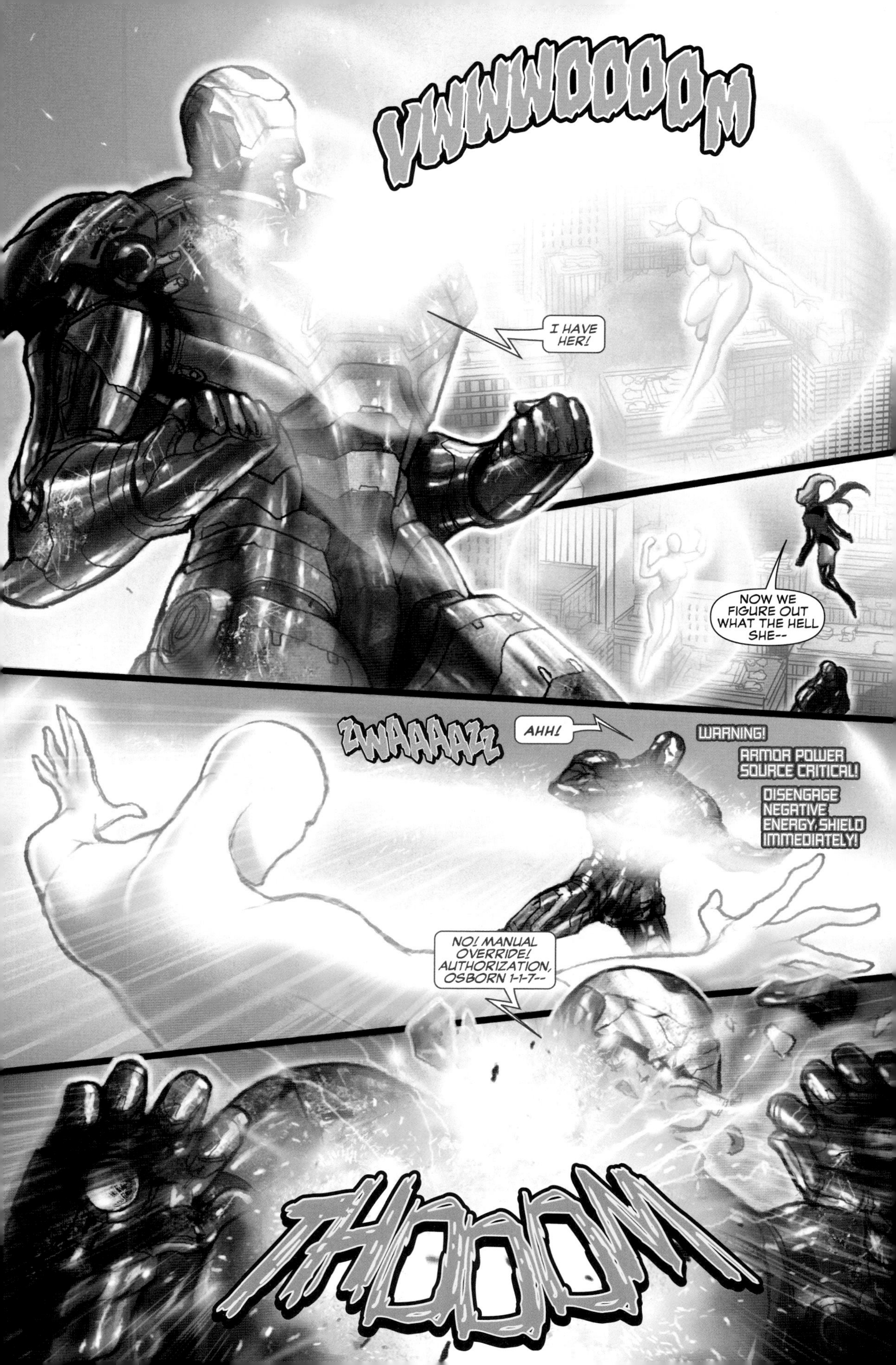
VWWWOOOOM
I HAVE HER!
NOW WE FIGURE OUT WHAT THE HELL SHE--
ZWAAAAZZ
AHH!
WARNING!
ARMOR POWER SOURCE CRITICAL!
DISENGAGE NEGATIVE ENERGY SHIELD IMMEDIATELY!
NO! MANUAL OVERRIDE! AUTHORIZATION, OSBORN 1-1-7--
THOOOM

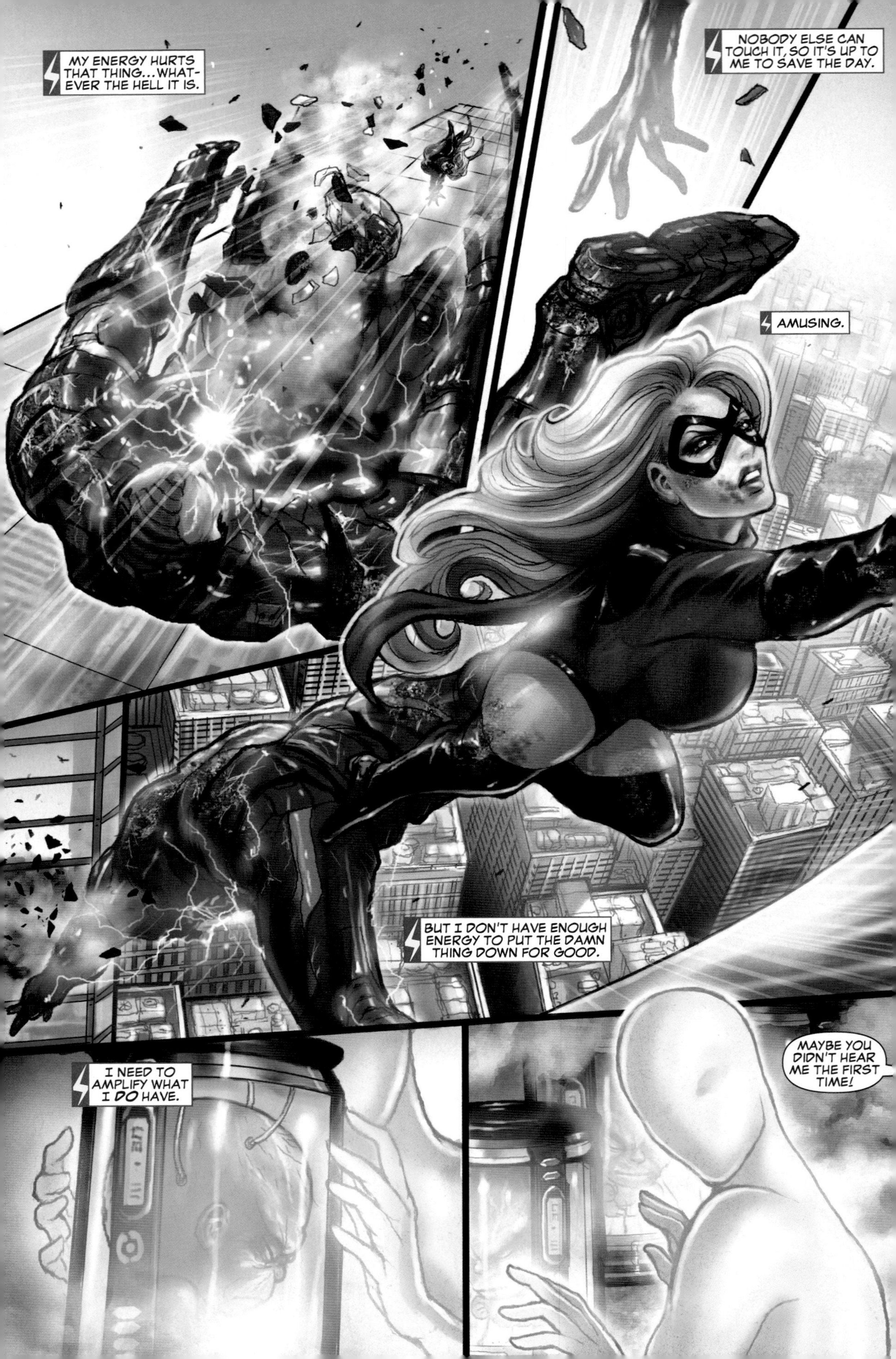

MY ENERGY HURTS THAT THING... WHATEVER THE HELL IT IS.
NOBODY ELSE CAN TOUCH IT, SO IT'S UP TO ME TO SAVE THE DAY.
AMUSING.
BUT I DON'T HAVE ENOUGH ENERGY TO PUT THE DAMN THING DOWN FOR GOOD.
I NEED TO AMPLIFY WHAT I DO HAVE.
MAYBE YOU DIDN'T HEAR ME THE FIRST TIME!

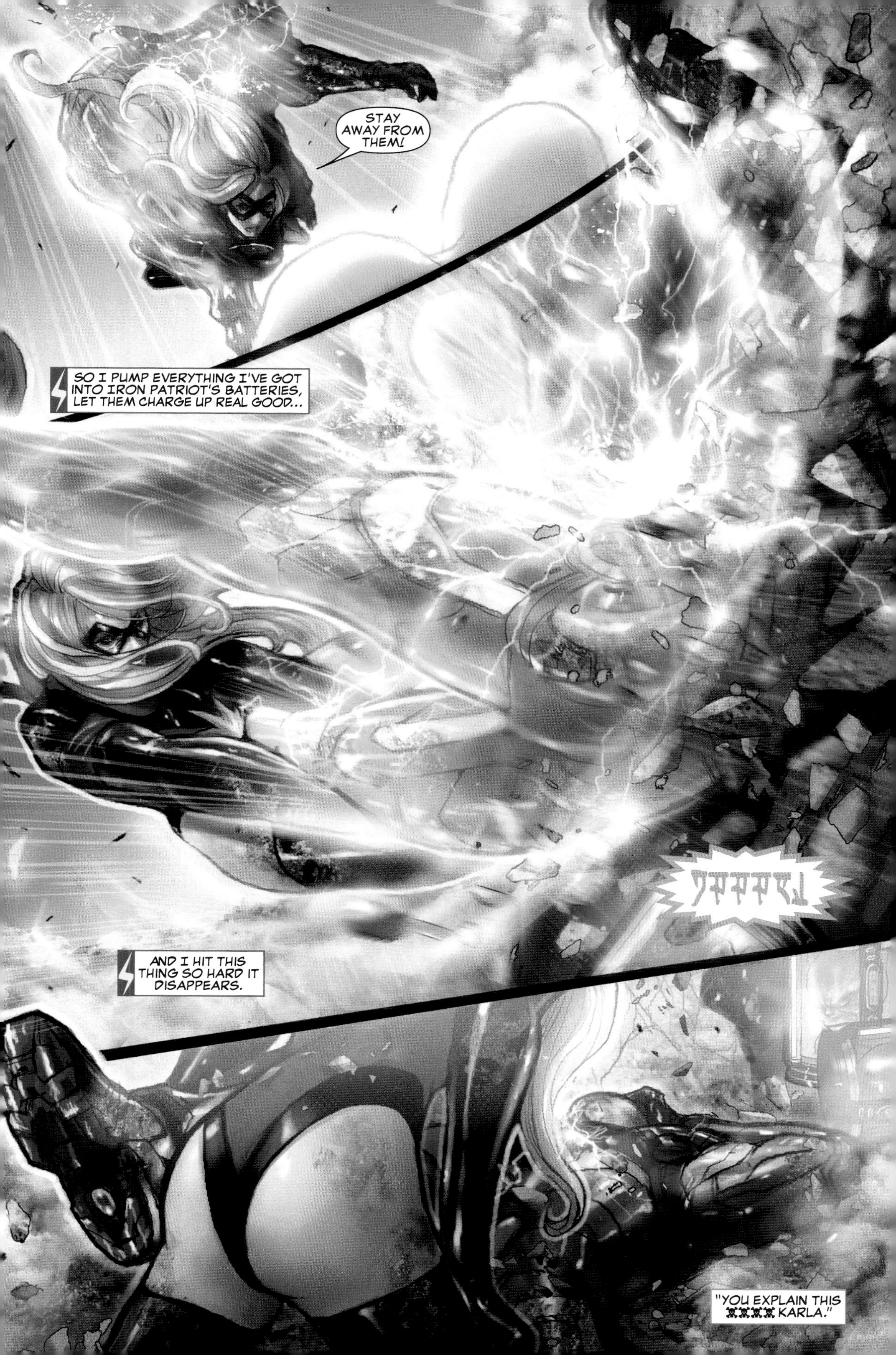
STAY AWAY FROM THEM!
SO I PUMP EVERYTHING I'VE GOT INTO IRON PATRIOT'S BATTERIES, LET THEM CHARGE UP REAL GOOD...
AND I HIT THIS THING SO HARD IT DISAPPEARS.
"YOU EXPLAIN THIS ☠☠☠☠ KARLA."

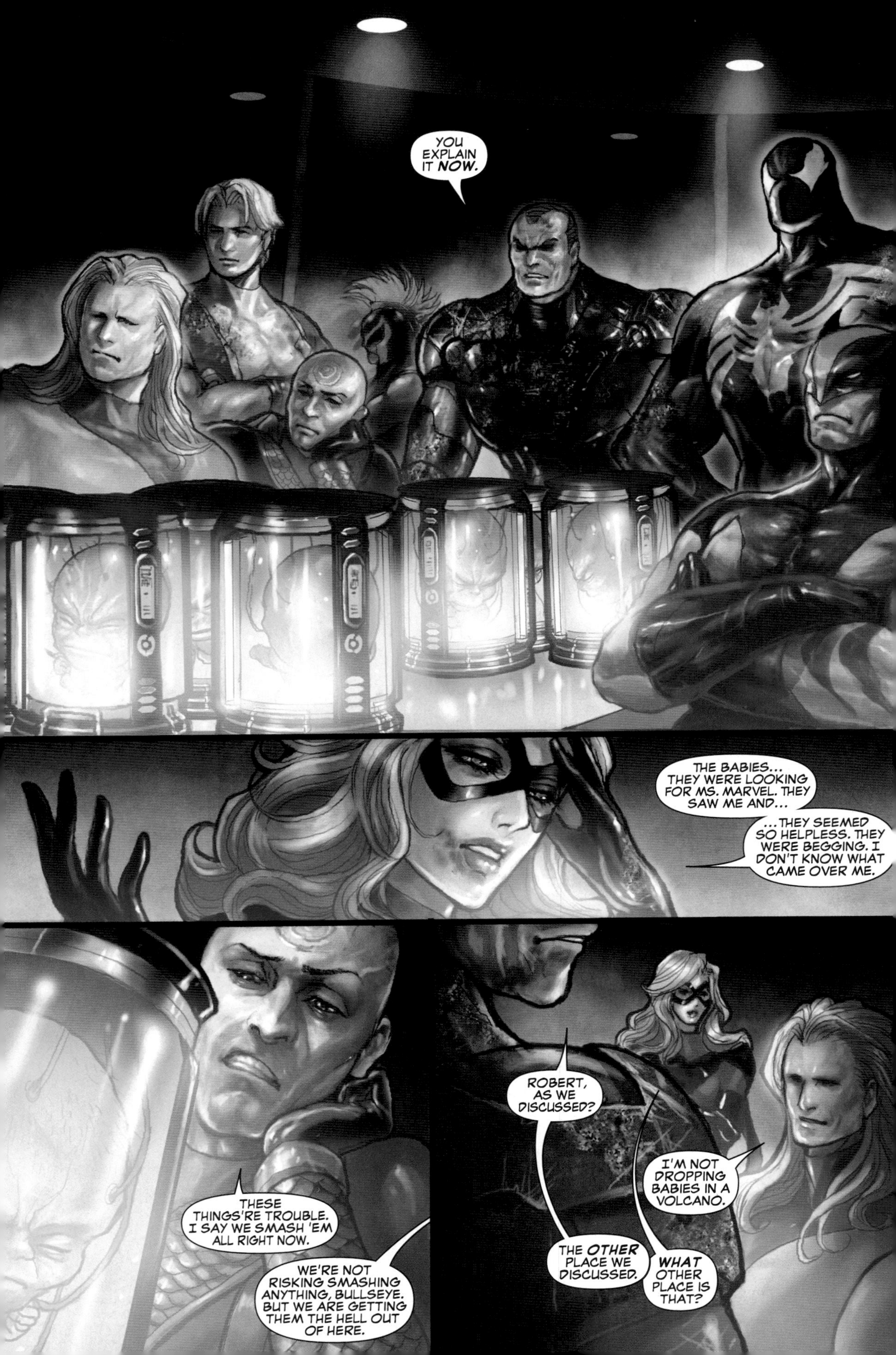
YOU EXPLAIN IT NOW.
THE BABIES... THEY WERE LOOKING FOR MS. MARVEL. THEY SAW ME AND...
...THEY SEEMED SO HELPLESS. THEY WERE BEGGING. I DON'T KNOW WHAT CAME OVER ME.
THESE THINGS'RE TROUBLE. I SAY WE SMASH 'EM ALL RIGHT NOW.
WE'RE NOT RISKING SMASHING ANYTHING, BULLSEYE. BUT WE ARE GETTING THEM THE HELL OUT OF HERE.
ROBERT, AS WE DISCUSSED?
I'M NOT DROPPING BABIES IN A VOLCANO.
THE OTHER PLACE WE DISCUSSED.
WHAT OTHER PLACE IS THAT?

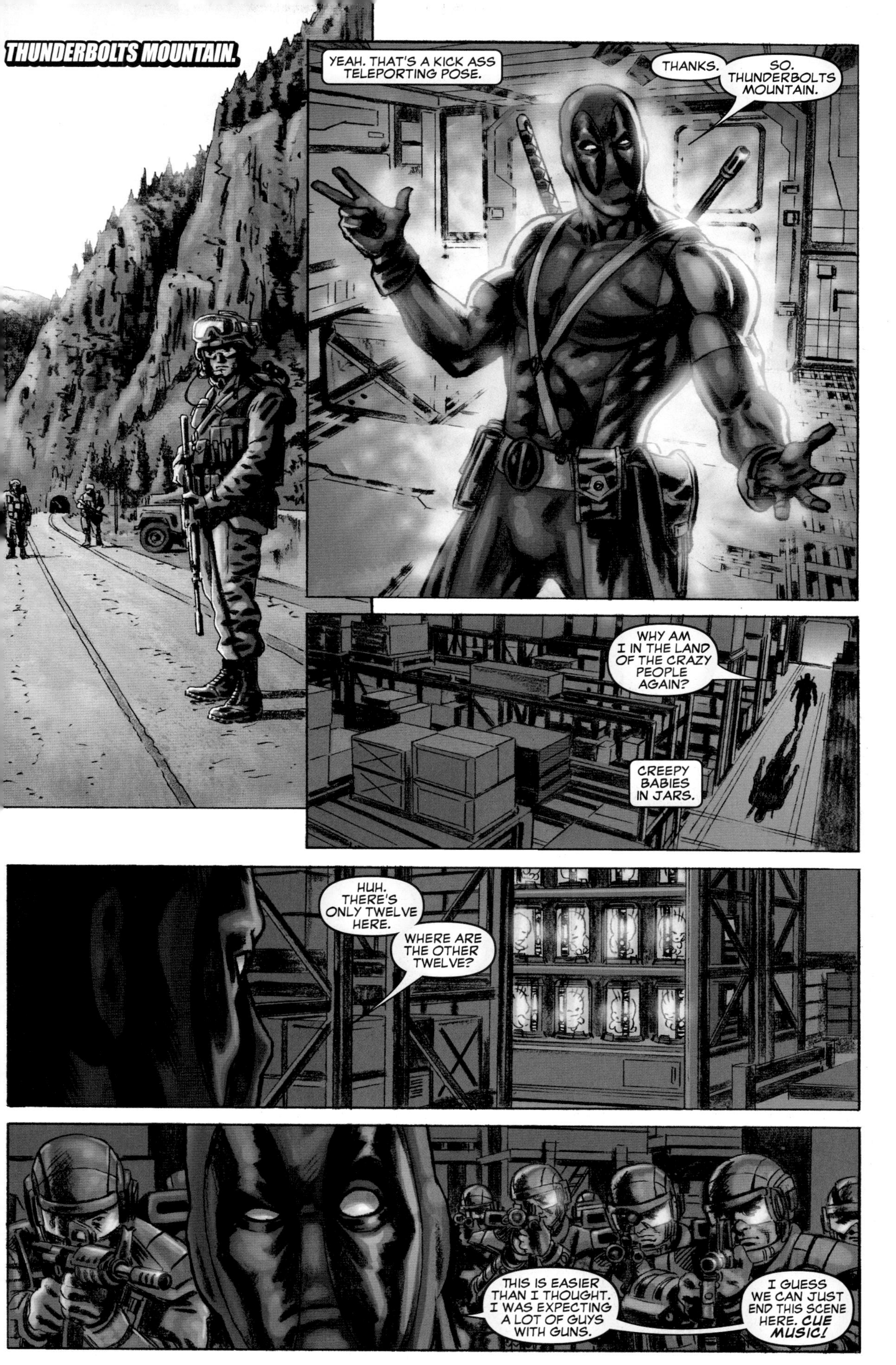
THUNDERBOLTS MOUNTAIN.
YEAH. THAT'S A KICK ASS TELEPORTING POSE.
THANKS.
SO. THUNDERBOLTS MOUNTAIN.
WHY AM I IN THE LAND OF THE CRAZY PEOPLE AGAIN?
CREEPY BABIES IN JARS.
HUH. THERE'S ONLY TWELVE HERE.
WHERE ARE THE OTHER TWELVE?
THIS IS EASIER THAN I THOUGHT. I WAS EXPECTING A LOT OF GUYS WITH GUNS.
I GUESS WE CAN JUST END THIS SCENE HERE. CUE MUSIC!

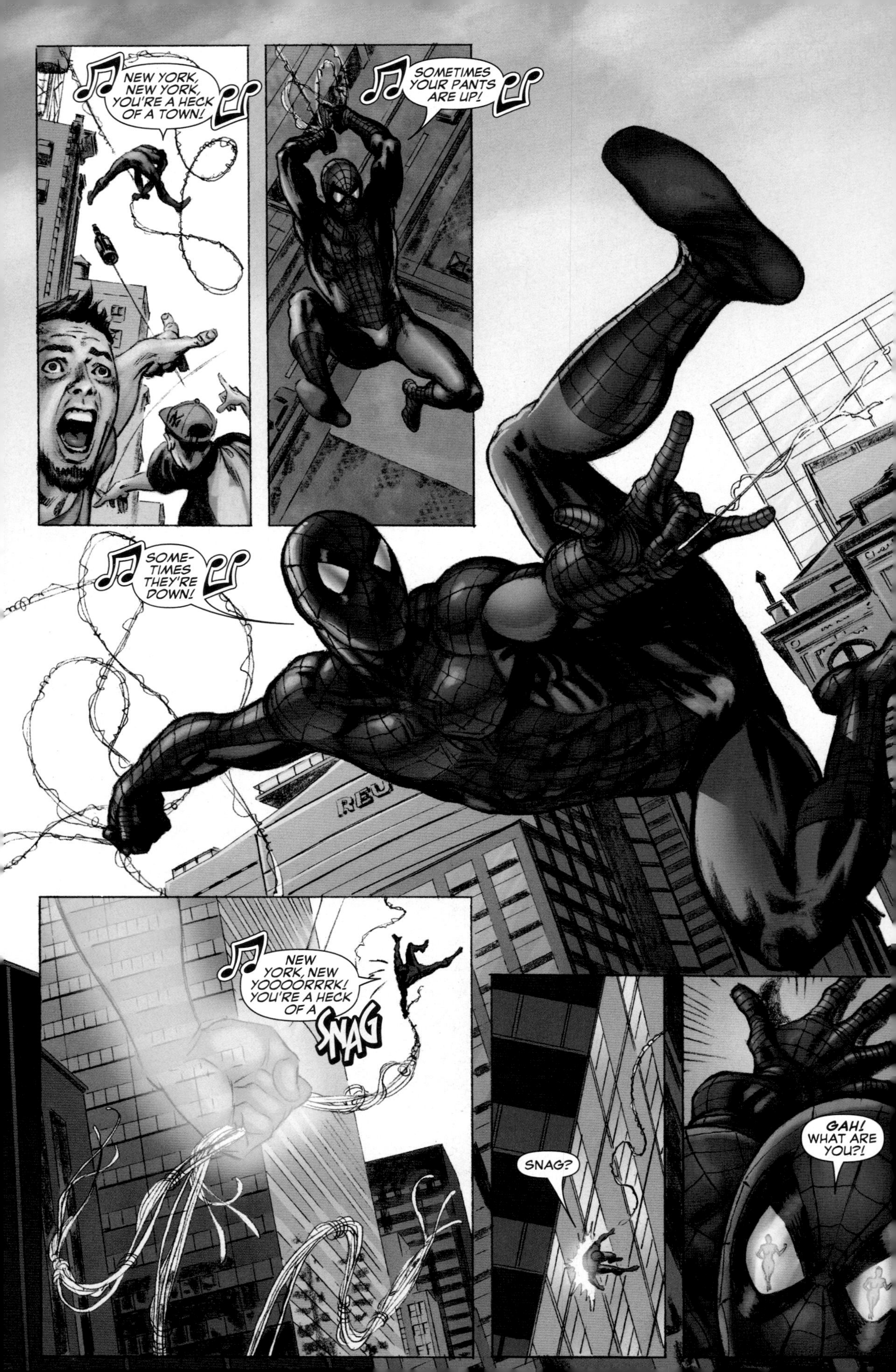
NEW YORK, NEW YORK, YOU'RE A HECK OF A TOWN!
SOMETIMES YOUR PANTS ARE UP!
SOME-TIMES THEY'RE DOWN!
NEW YORK, NEW YOOOORRRK! YOU'RE A HECK OF A
SNAG
SNAG?
GAH! WHAT ARE YOU?!

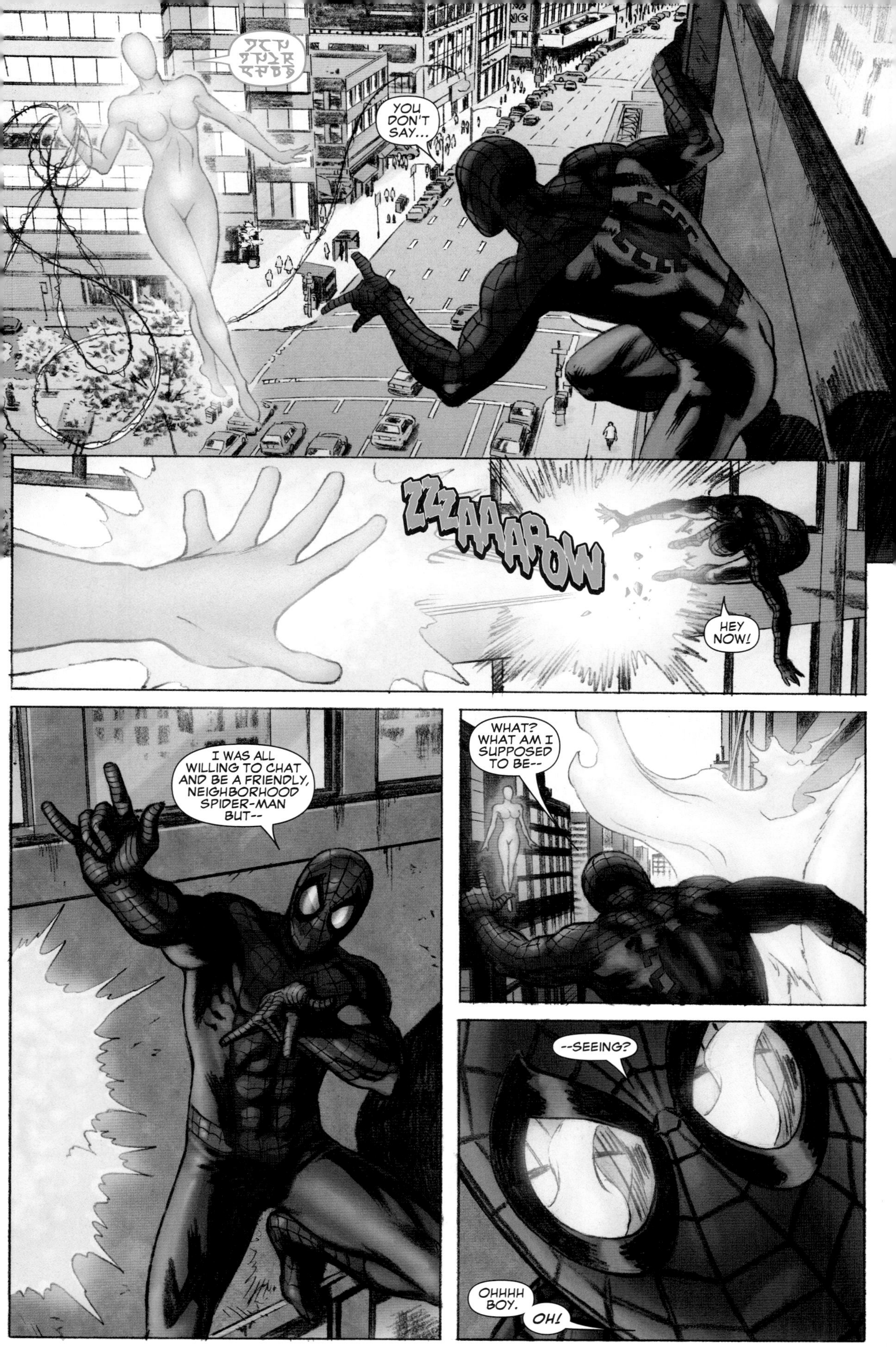
YOU DON'T SAY...
ZZZAAAAPOW
HEY NOW!
I WAS ALL WILLING TO CHAT AND BE A FRIENDLY, NEIGHBORHOOD SPIDER-MAN BUT--
WHAT? WHAT AM I SUPPOSED TO BE--
--SEEING?
OHHHH BOY.
OH!

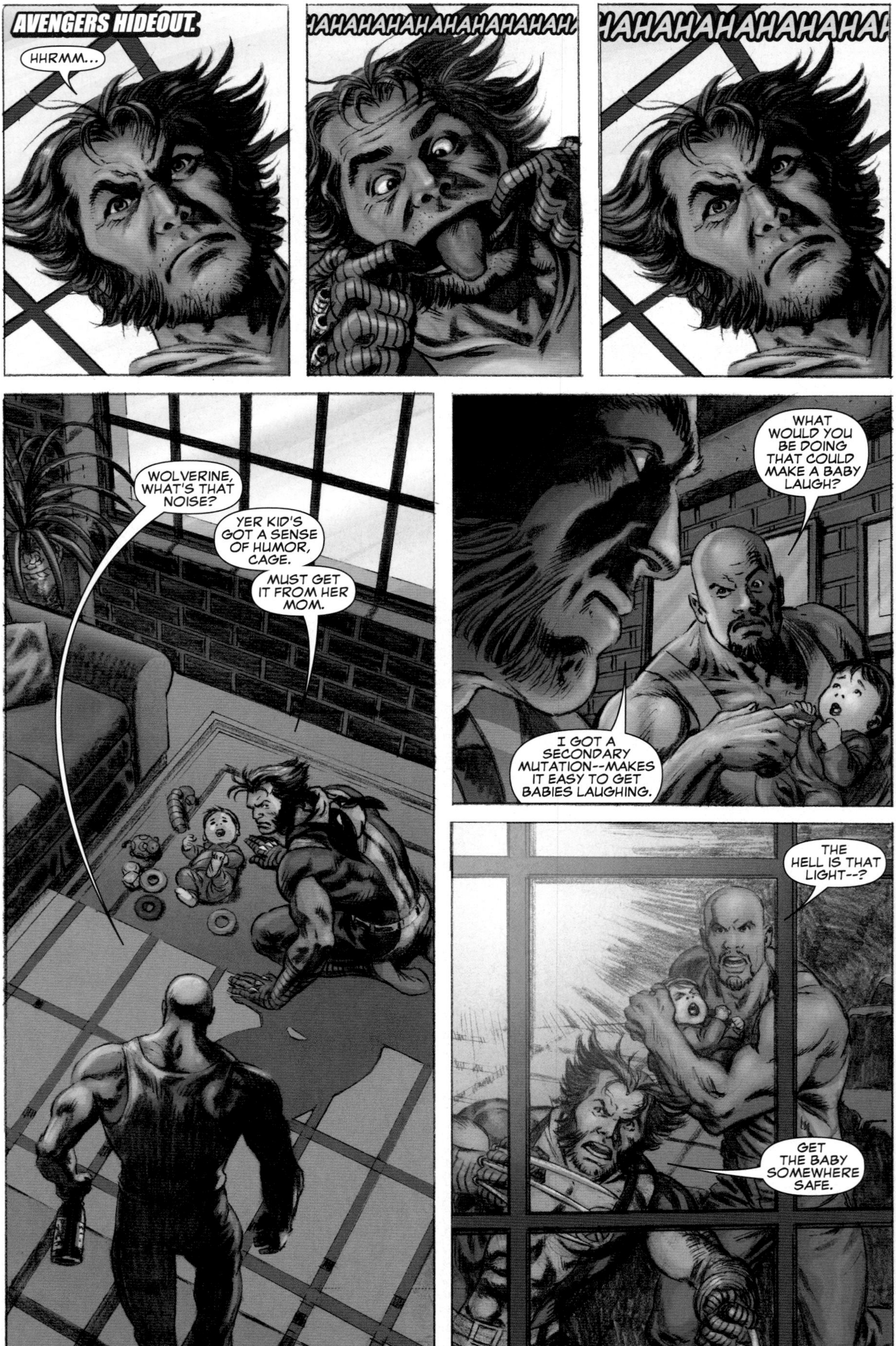
AVENGERS HIDEOUT.
HHRMM...
HAHAHAHAHAHAHAHAHAH
HAHAHAHAHAHAHAHA
WOLVERINE, WHAT'S THAT NOISE?
YER KID'S GOT A SENSE OF HUMOR, CAGE.
MUST GET IT FROM HER MOM.
WHAT WOULD YOU BE DOING THAT COULD MAKE A BABY LAUGH?
I GOT A SECONDARY MUTATION--MAKES IT EASY TO GET BABIES LAUGHING.
THE HELL IS THAT LIGHT--?
GET THE BABY SOMEWHERE SAFE.

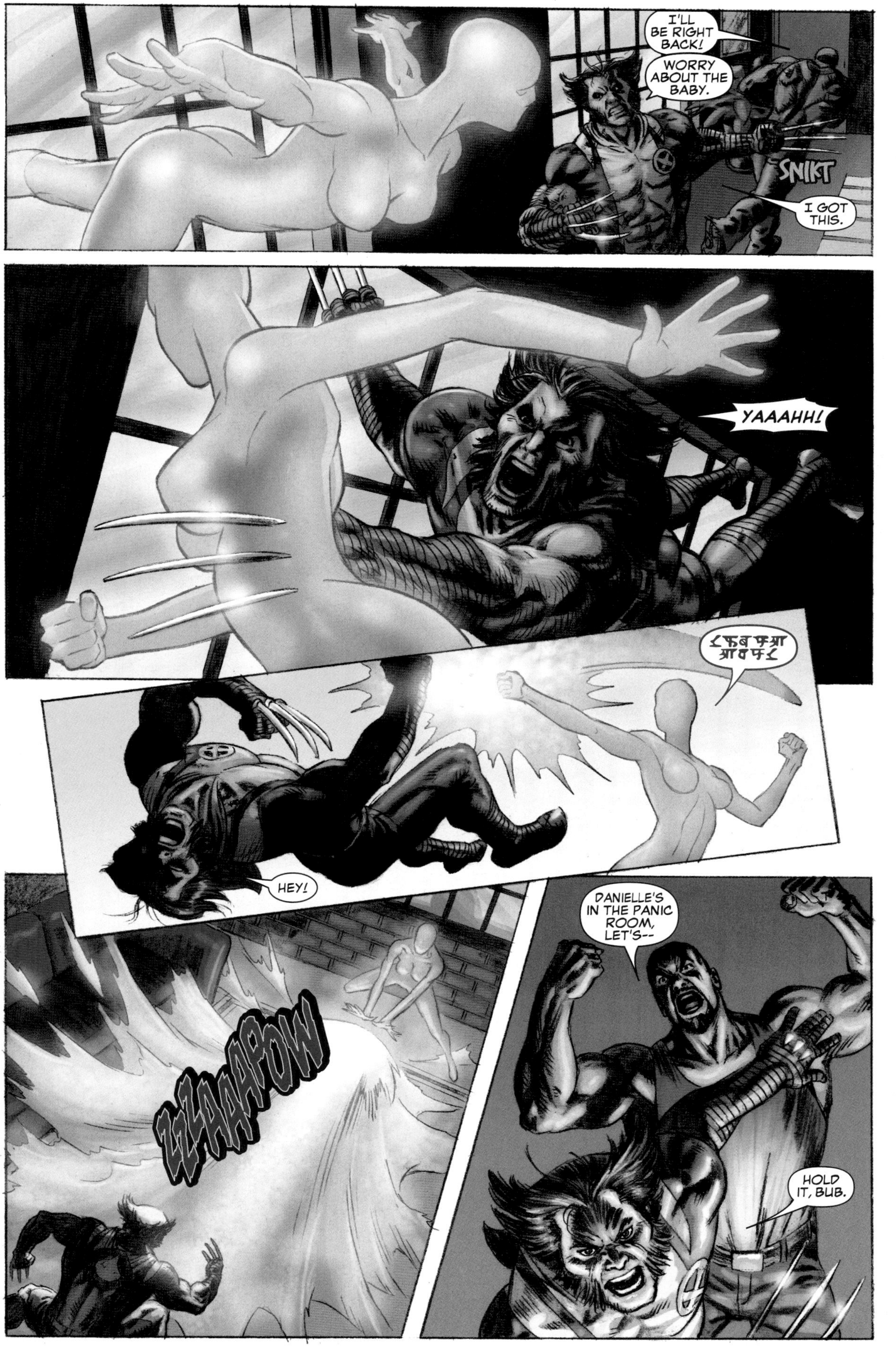

I'LL BE RIGHT BACK!
WORRY ABOUT THE BABY.
SNIKT
I GOT THIS.
YAAAHH!
HEY!
ZZZAAAPOW
DANIELLE'S IN THE PANIC ROOM, LET'S--
HOLD IT, BUB.

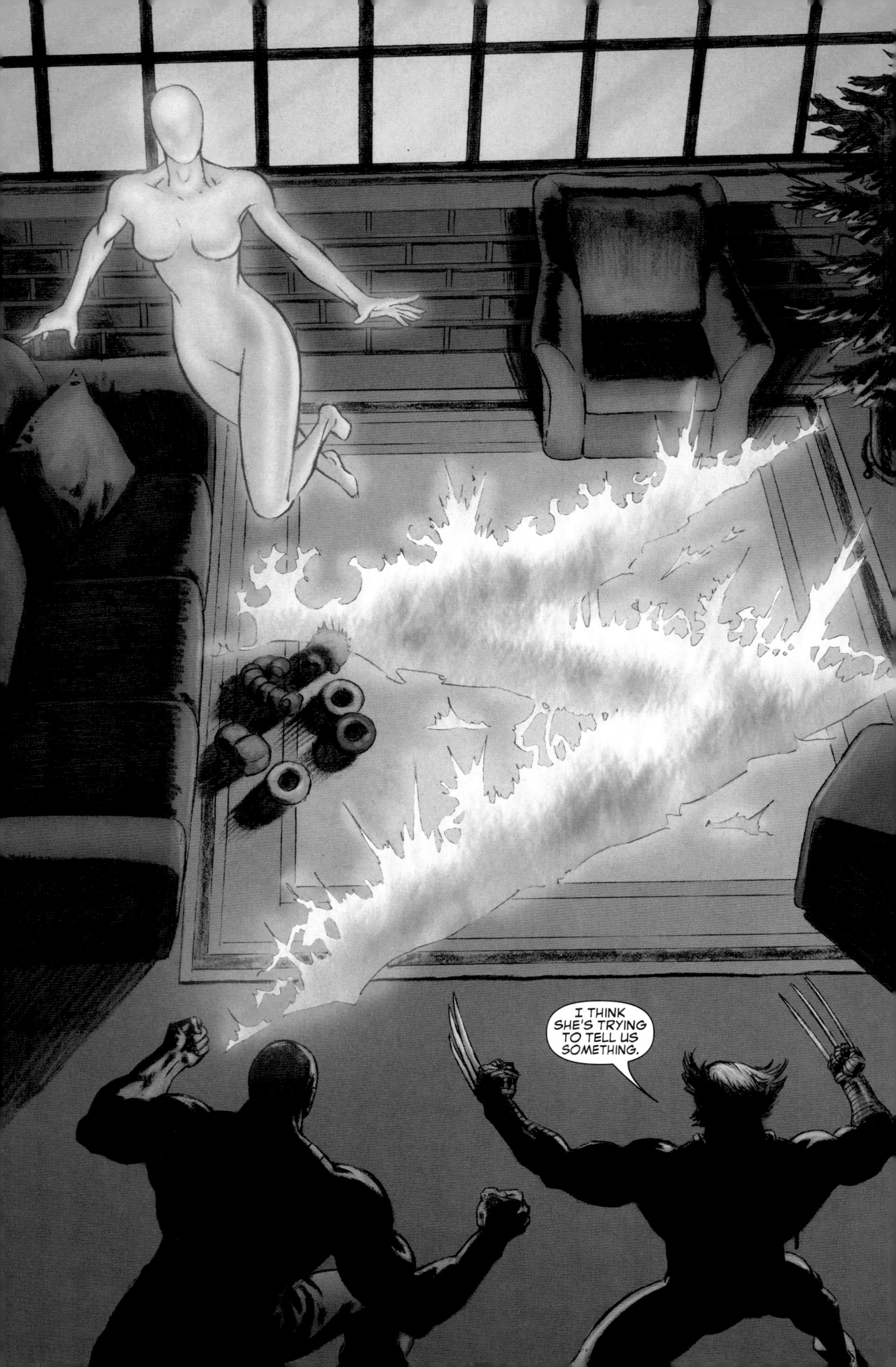
I THINK SHE'S TRYING TO TELL US SOMETHING.

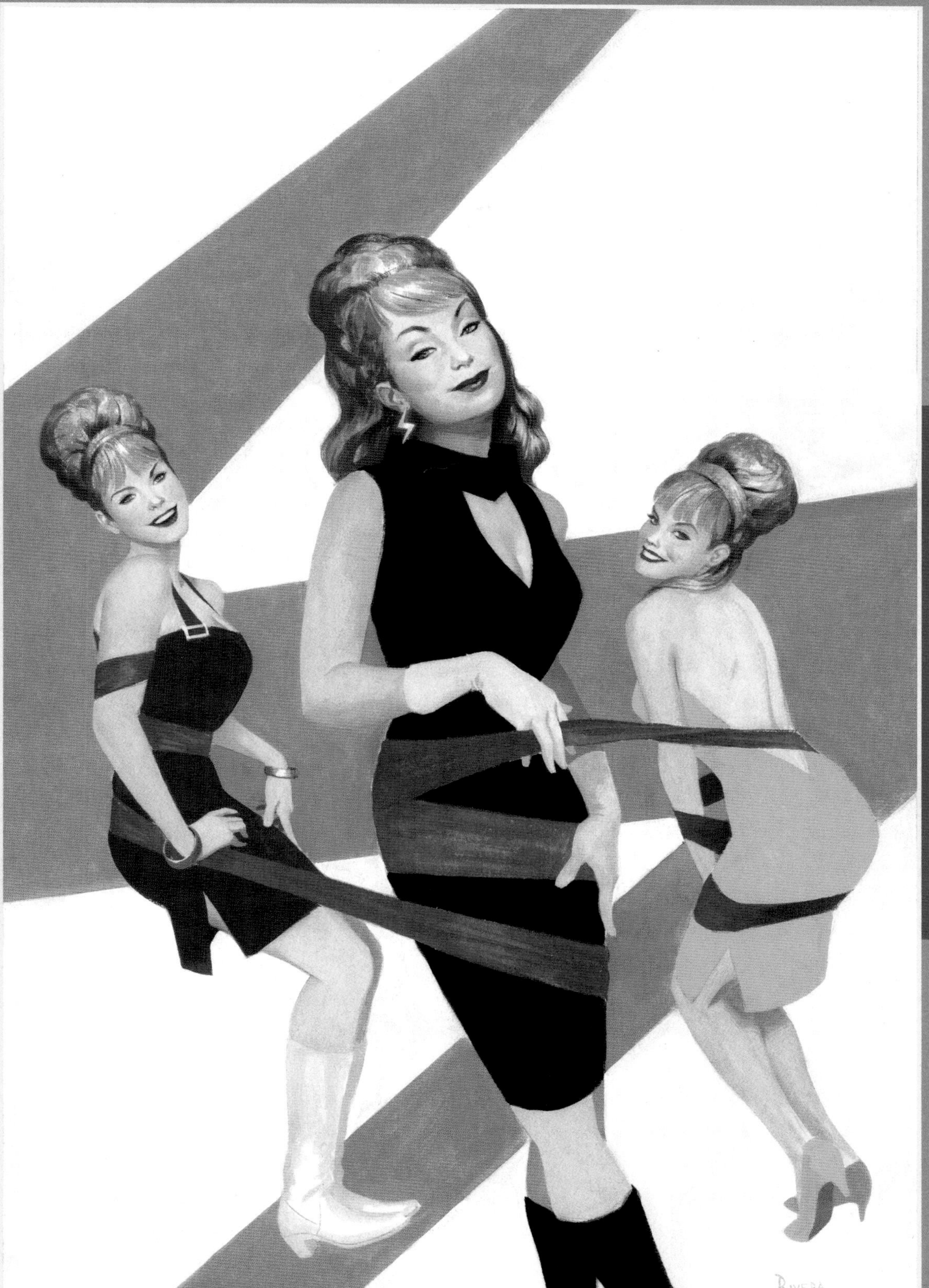
RIVERA
2009

MS. MARVEL #31 **1960s DECADE VARIANT BY PAOLO RIVERA**

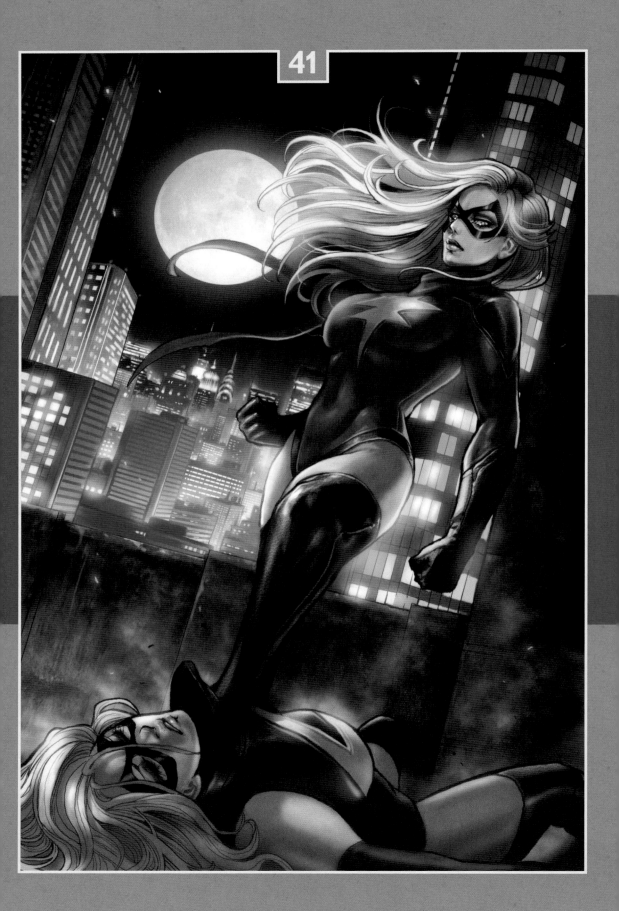

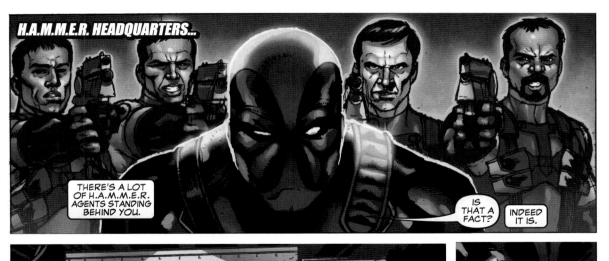

41

THERE'S A LOT OF H.A.M.M.E.R. AGENTS STANDING BEHIND YOU.

IS THAT A FACT?

INDEED IT IS.

GENTLEMEN. I'D LIKE TO THANK YOU FOR COMING.

I WAS TERRIBLY AFRAID I WOULD BE ABLE TO STEAL THESE LITTLE JARS OF WONDERFUL WITH *NARY* A FIGHT.

READY--

--SET--

FIGHT SCENE!

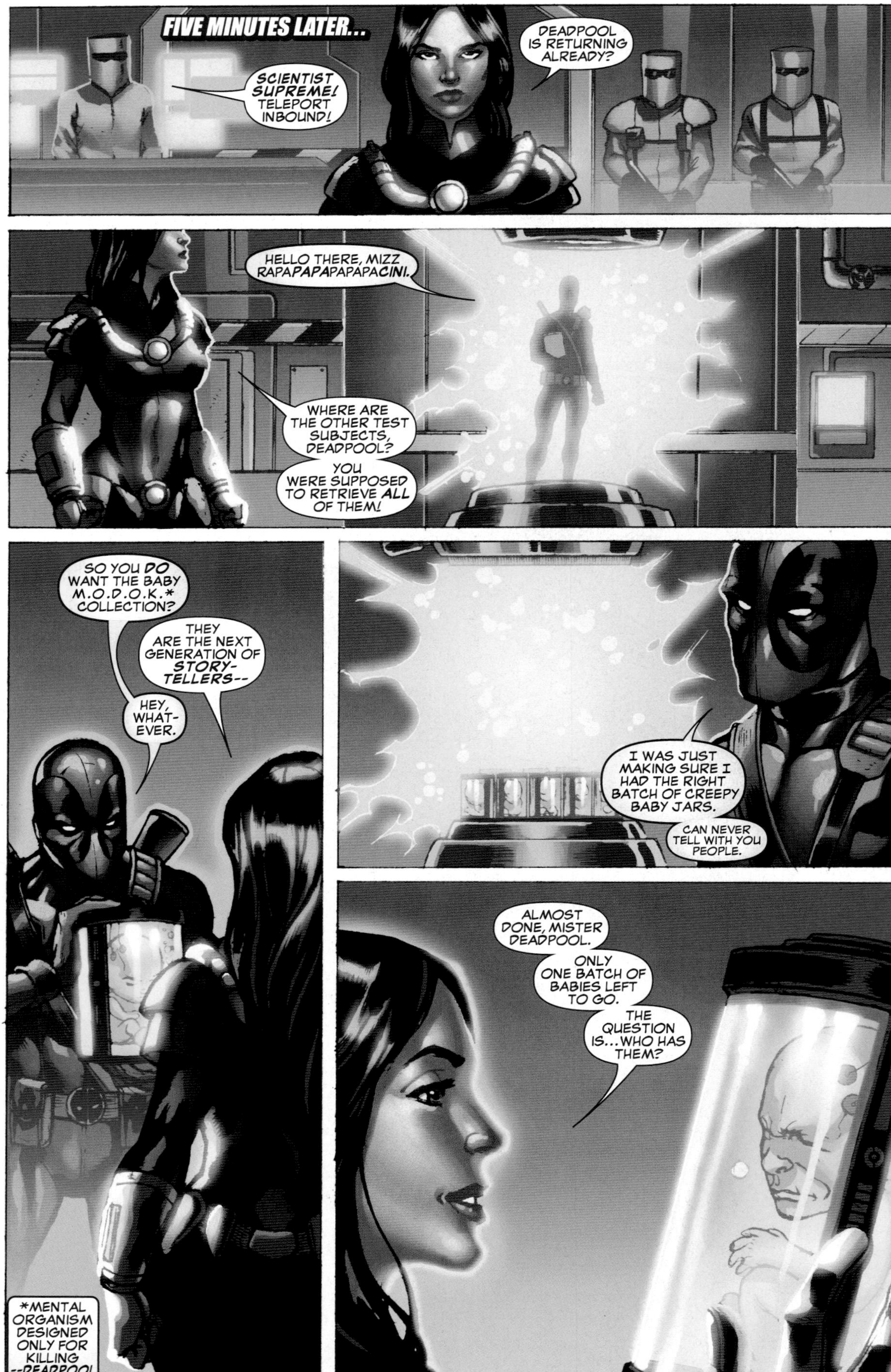
FIVE MINUTES LATER...
SCIENTIST SUPREME! TELEPORT INBOUND!
DEADPOOL IS RETURNING ALREADY?
HELLO THERE, MIZZ RAPAPAPAPAPAPACINI.
WHERE ARE THE OTHER TEST SUBJECTS, DEADPOOL?
YOU WERE SUPPOSED TO RETRIEVE ALL OF THEM!
I WAS JUST MAKING SURE I HAD THE RIGHT BATCH OF CREEPY BABY JARS.
CAN NEVER TELL WITH YOU PEOPLE.
SO YOU DO WANT THE BABY M.O.D.O.K.* COLLECTION?
THEY ARE THE NEXT GENERATION OF STORY-TELLERS--
HEY, WHAT-EVER.
*MENTAL ORGANISM DESIGNED ONLY FOR KILLING --DEADPOOL
ALMOST DONE, MISTER DEADPOOL.
ONLY ONE BATCH OF BABIES LEFT TO GO.
THE QUESTION IS...WHO HAS THEM?

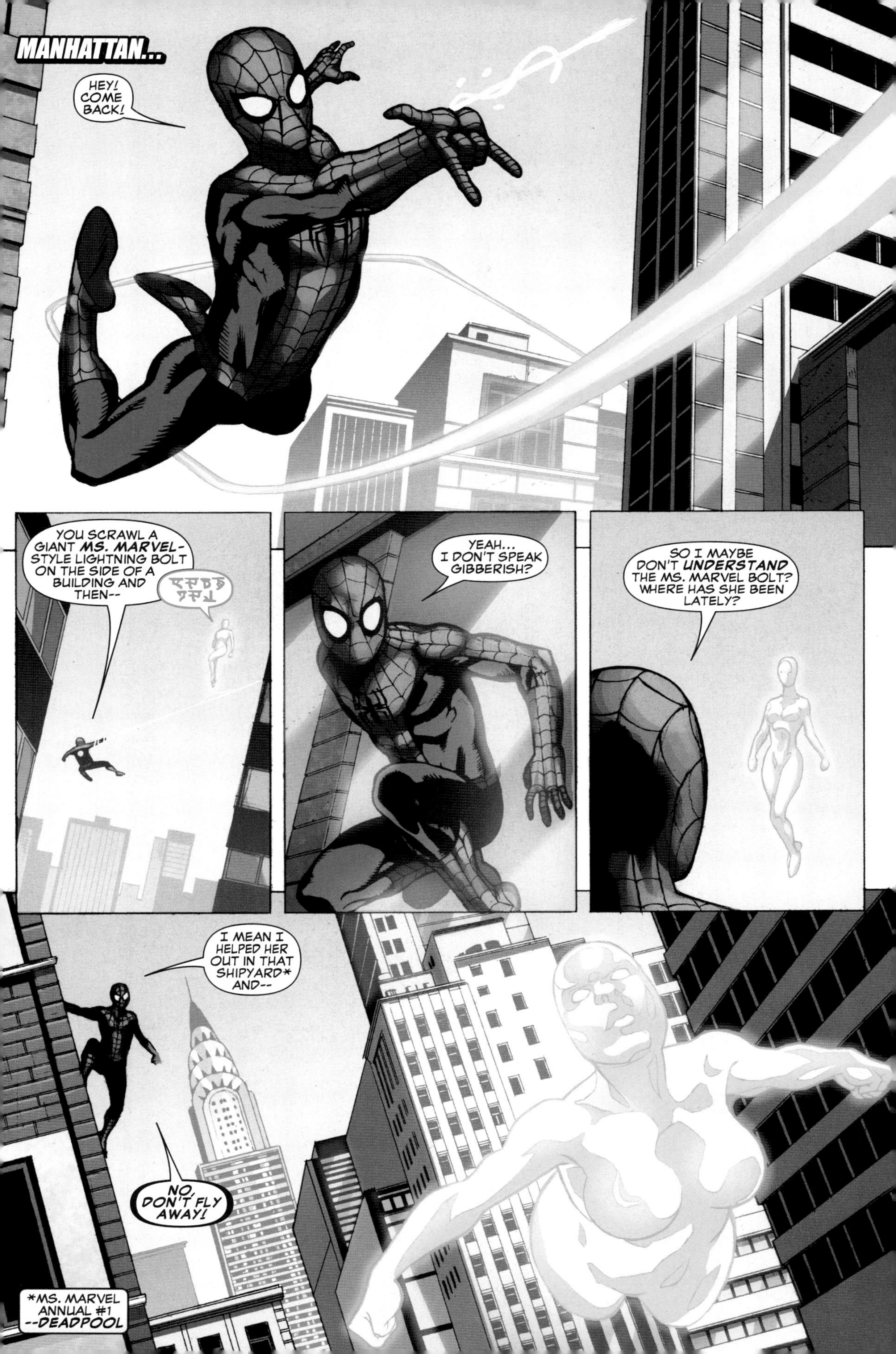
MANHATTAN...
HEY! COME BACK!
YOU SCRAWL A GIANT MS. MARVEL-STYLE LIGHTNING BOLT ON THE SIDE OF A BUILDING AND THEN--
YEAH... I DON'T SPEAK GIBBERISH?
SO I MAYBE DON'T UNDERSTAND THE MS. MARVEL BOLT? WHERE HAS SHE BEEN LATELY?
I MEAN I HELPED HER OUT IN THAT SHIPYARD* AND--
NO, DON'T FLY AWAY!
*MS. MARVEL ANNUAL #1 --DEADPOOL

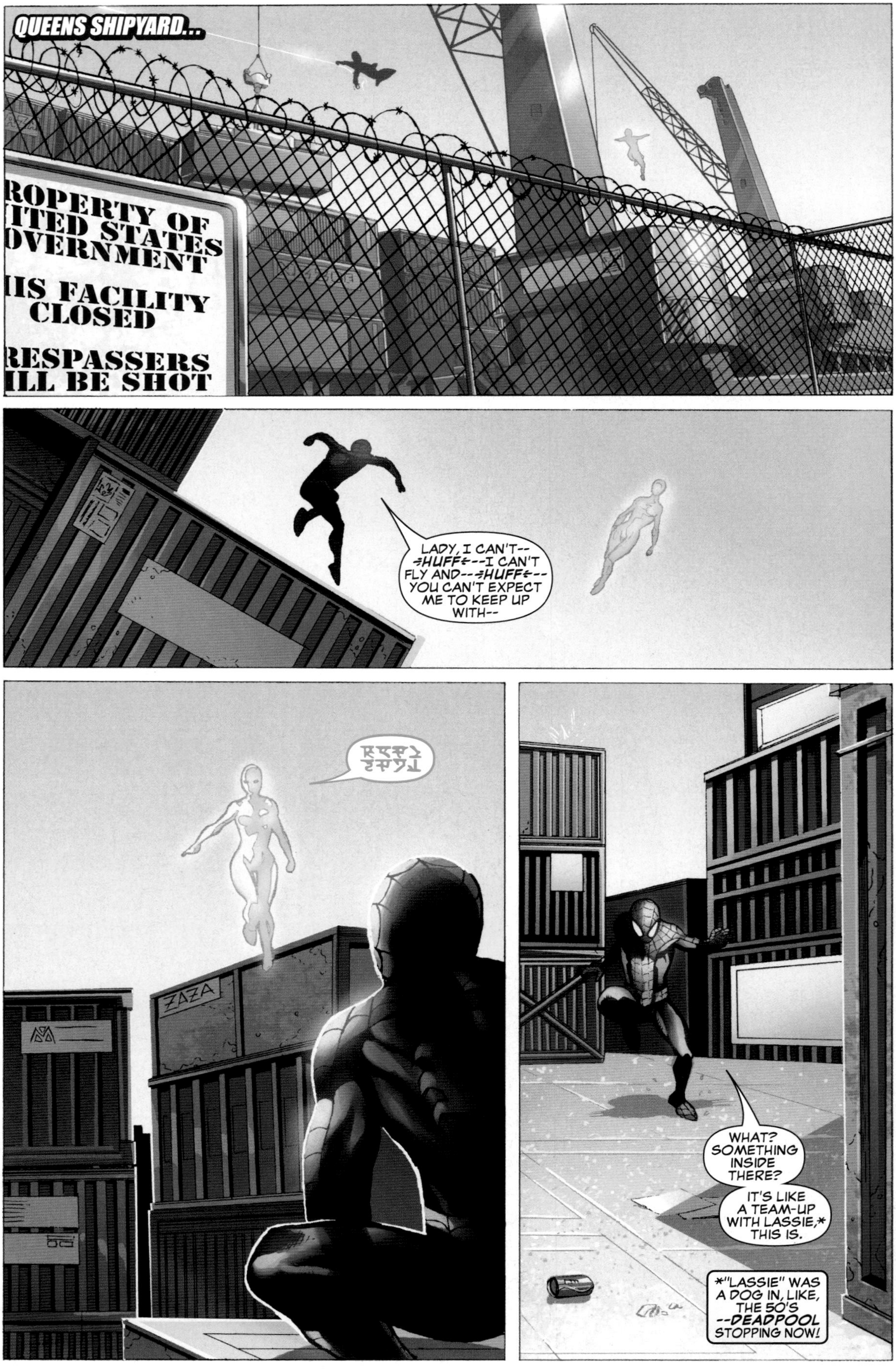
QUEENS SHIPYARD...
ROPERTY OF
ITED STATES
OVERNMENT
HIS FACILITY
CLOSED
RESPASSERS
ILL BE SHOT
LADY, I CAN'T-- *HUFF*--I CAN'T FLY AND--*HUFF*-- YOU CAN'T EXPECT ME TO KEEP UP WITH--
ZAZA
WHAT? SOMETHING INSIDE THERE?
IT'S LIKE A TEAM-UP WITH LASSIE,* THIS IS.
*"LASSIE" WAS A DOG IN, LIKE, THE 50'S --DEADPOOL STOPPING NOW!

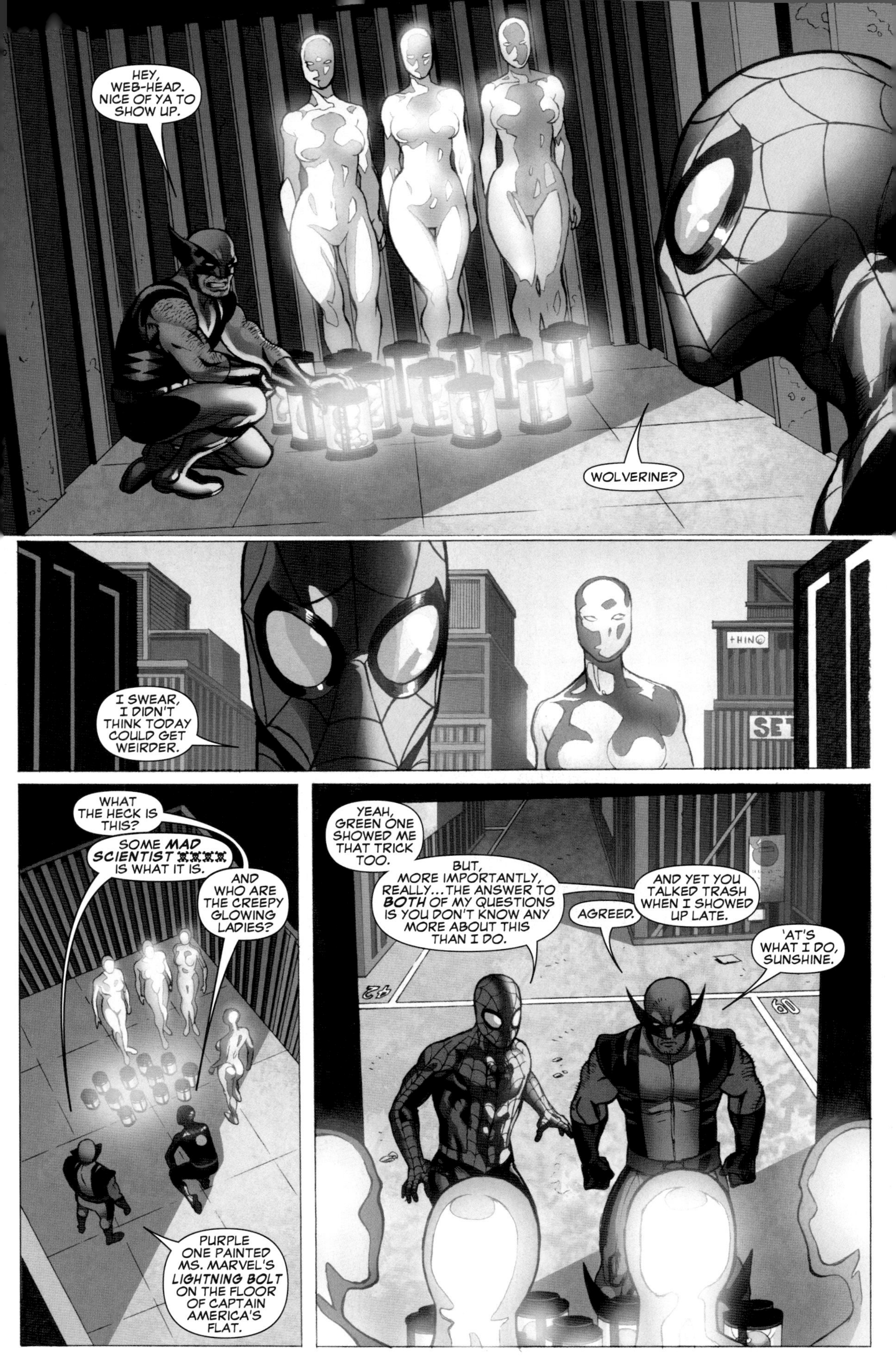
HEY, WEB-HEAD. NICE OF YA TO SHOW UP.
WOLVERINE?
THING
SET
I SWEAR, I DIDN'T THINK TODAY COULD GET WEIRDER.
WHAT THE HECK IS THIS?
SOME MAD SCIENTIST ☠☠☠ IS WHAT IT IS.
AND WHO ARE THE CREEPY GLOWING LADIES?
PURPLE ONE PAINTED MS. MARVEL'S LIGHTNING BOLT ON THE FLOOR OF CAPTAIN AMERICA'S FLAT.
YEAH, GREEN ONE SHOWED ME THAT TRICK TOO.
BUT, MORE IMPORTANTLY, REALLY... THE ANSWER TO BOTH OF MY QUESTIONS IS YOU DON'T KNOW ANY MORE ABOUT THIS THAN I DO.
AGREED.
AND YET YOU TALKED TRASH WHEN I SHOWED UP LATE.
'AT'S WHAT I DO, SUNSHINE.

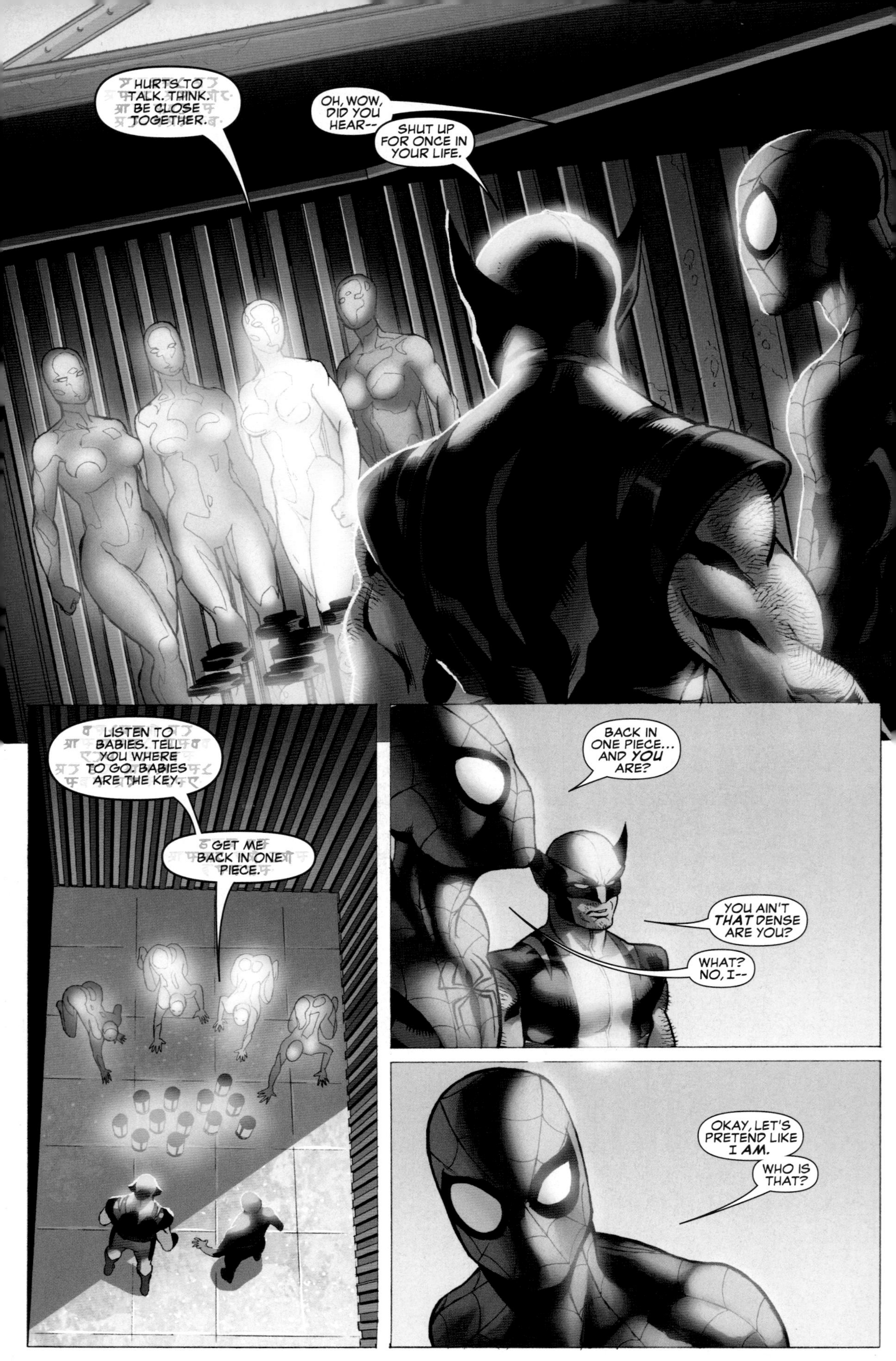
HURTS TO TALK. THINK. BE CLOSE TOGETHER.
OH, WOW, DID YOU HEAR--
SHUT UP FOR ONCE IN YOUR LIFE.
LISTEN TO BABIES. TELL YOU WHERE TO GO. BABIES ARE THE KEY.
GET ME BACK IN ONE PIECE.
BACK IN ONE PIECE... AND YOU ARE?
YOU AIN'T THAT DENSE ARE YOU?
WHAT? NO, I--
OKAY, LET'S PRETEND LIKE I AM.
WHO IS THAT?

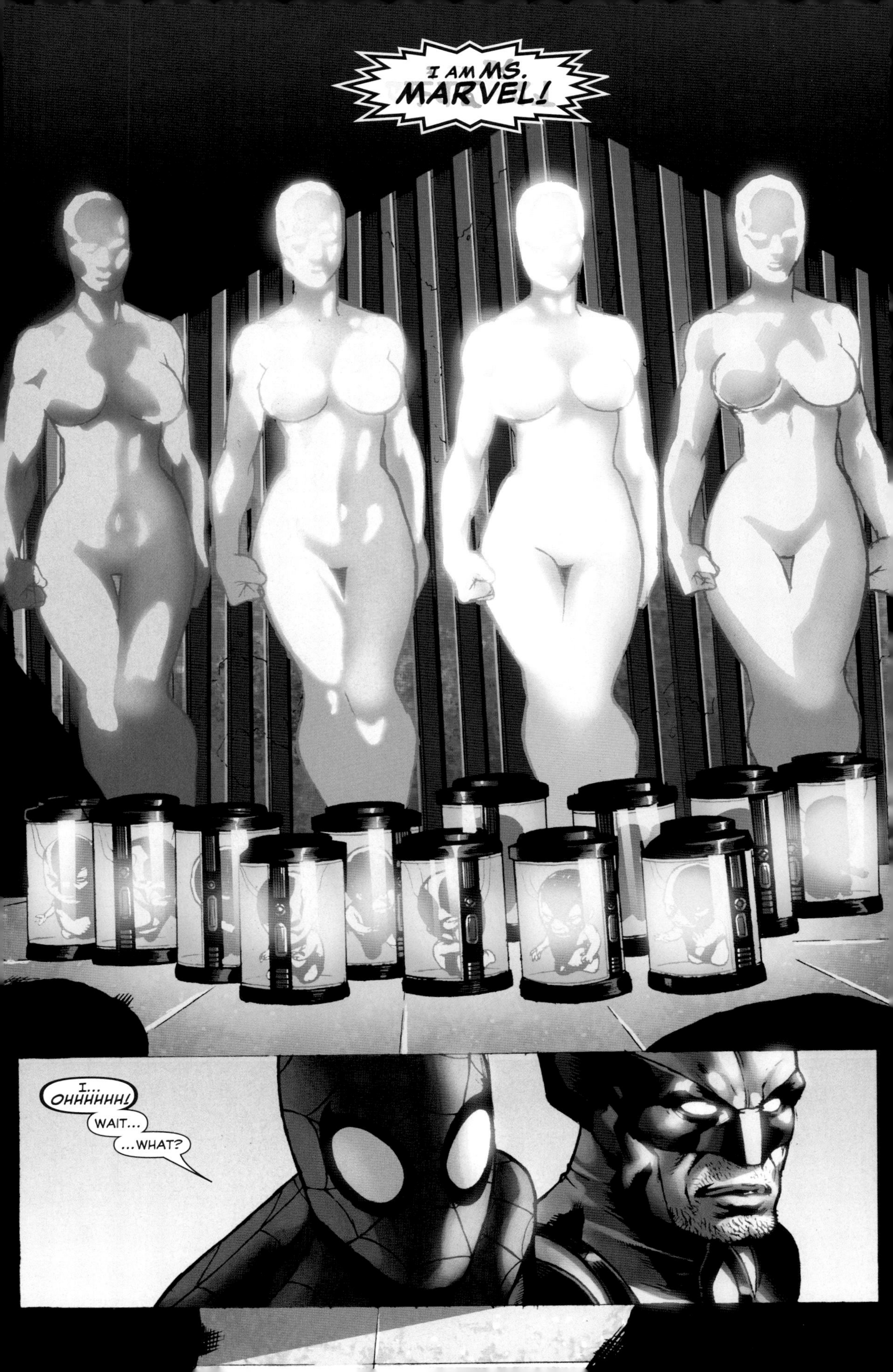
I AM MS. MARVEL!
I... OHHHHHH!
WAIT...
...WHAT?

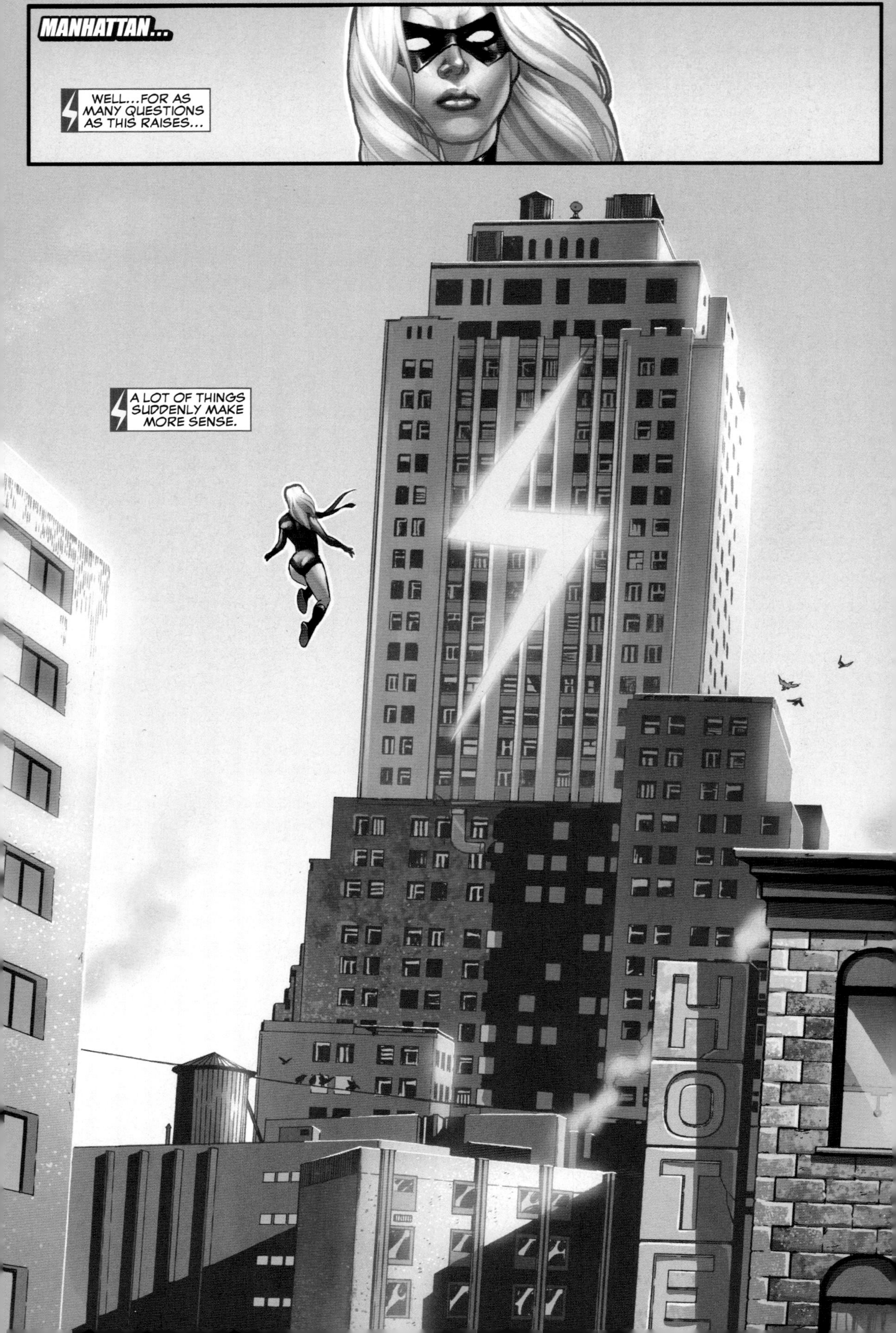
MANHATTAN...
WELL...FOR AS MANY QUESTIONS AS THIS RAISES...
A LOT OF THINGS SUDDENLY MAKE MORE SENSE.
HOTE

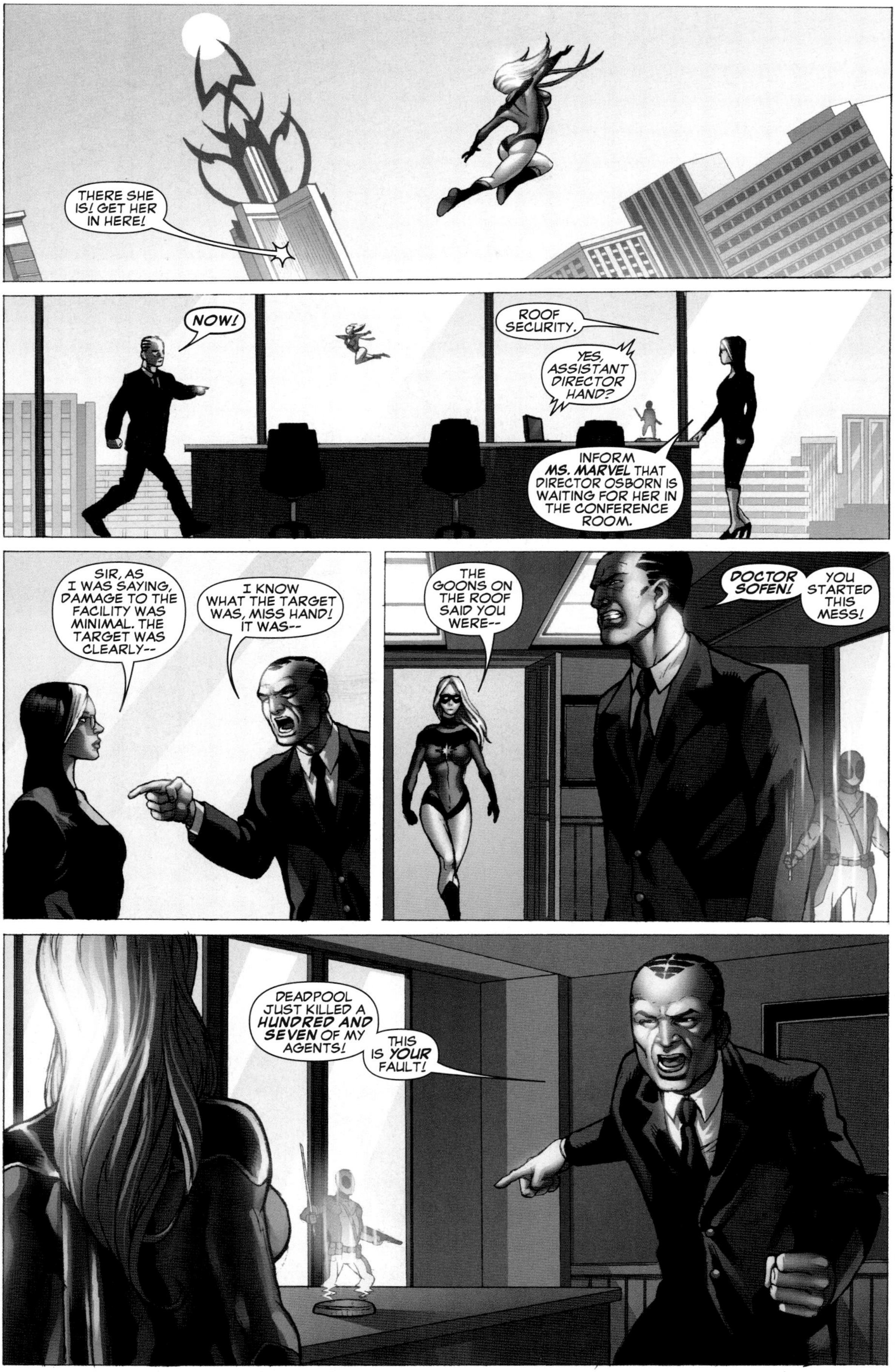
THERE SHE IS! GET HER IN HERE!
NOW!
ROOF SECURITY.
YES, ASSISTANT DIRECTOR HAND?
INFORM MS. MARVEL THAT DIRECTOR OSBORN IS WAITING FOR HER IN THE CONFERENCE ROOM.
SIR, AS I WAS SAYING, DAMAGE TO THE FACILITY WAS MINIMAL. THE TARGET WAS CLEARLY--
I KNOW WHAT THE TARGET WAS, MISS HAND! IT WAS--
THE GOONS ON THE ROOF SAID YOU WERE--
DOCTOR SOFEN!
YOU STARTED THIS MESS!
DEADPOOL JUST KILLED A HUNDRED AND SEVEN OF MY AGENTS!
THIS IS YOUR FAULT!

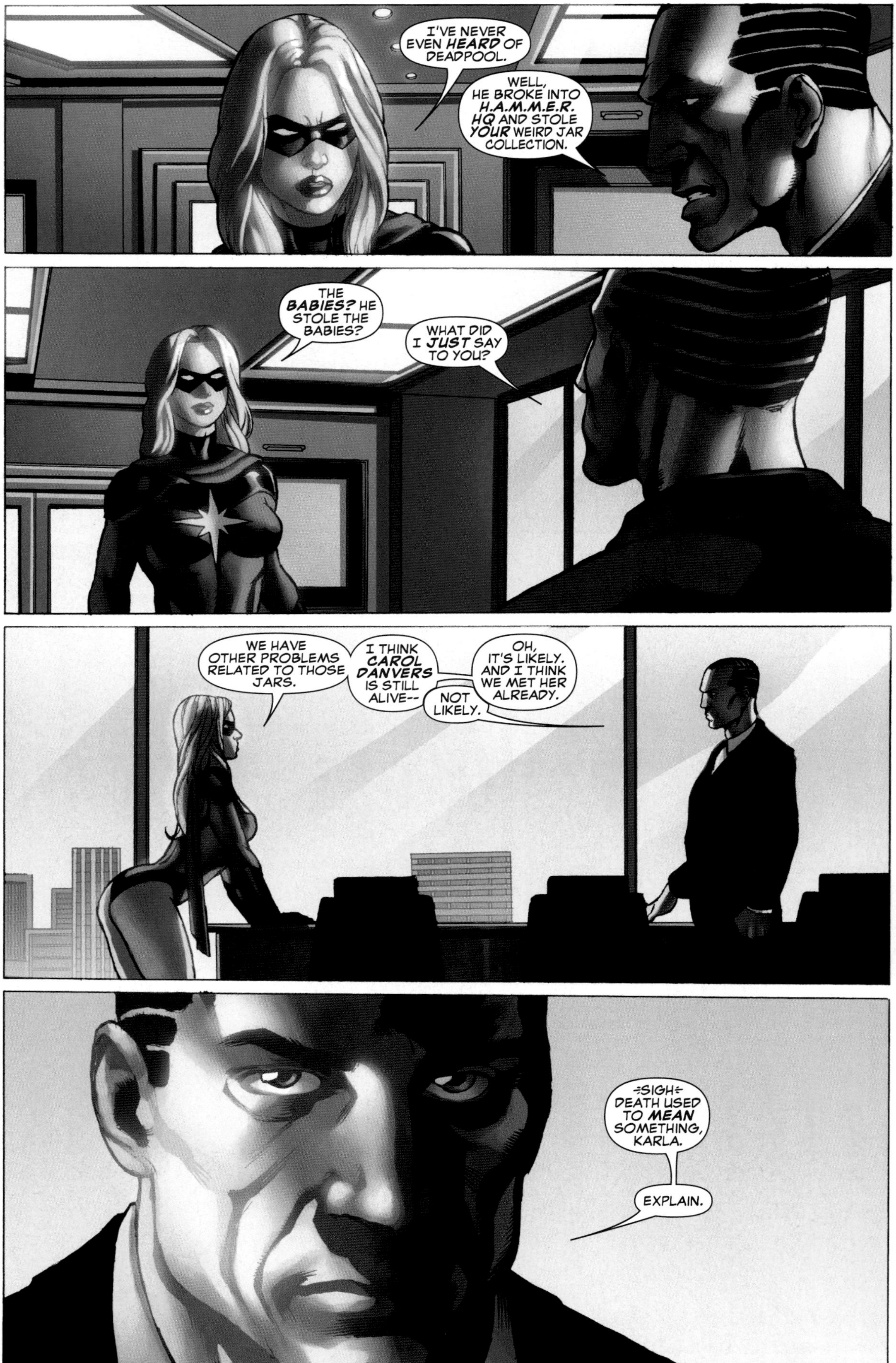
I'VE NEVER EVEN HEARD OF DEADPOOL.
WELL, HE BROKE INTO H.A.M.M.E.R. HQ AND STOLE YOUR WEIRD JAR COLLECTION.
THE BABIES? HE STOLE THE BABIES?
WHAT DID I JUST SAY TO YOU?
WE HAVE OTHER PROBLEMS RELATED TO THOSE JARS.
I THINK CAROL DANVERS IS STILL ALIVE--
NOT LIKELY.
OH, IT'S LIKELY. AND I THINK WE MET HER ALREADY.
=SIGH= DEATH USED TO MEAN SOMETHING, KARLA.
EXPLAIN.

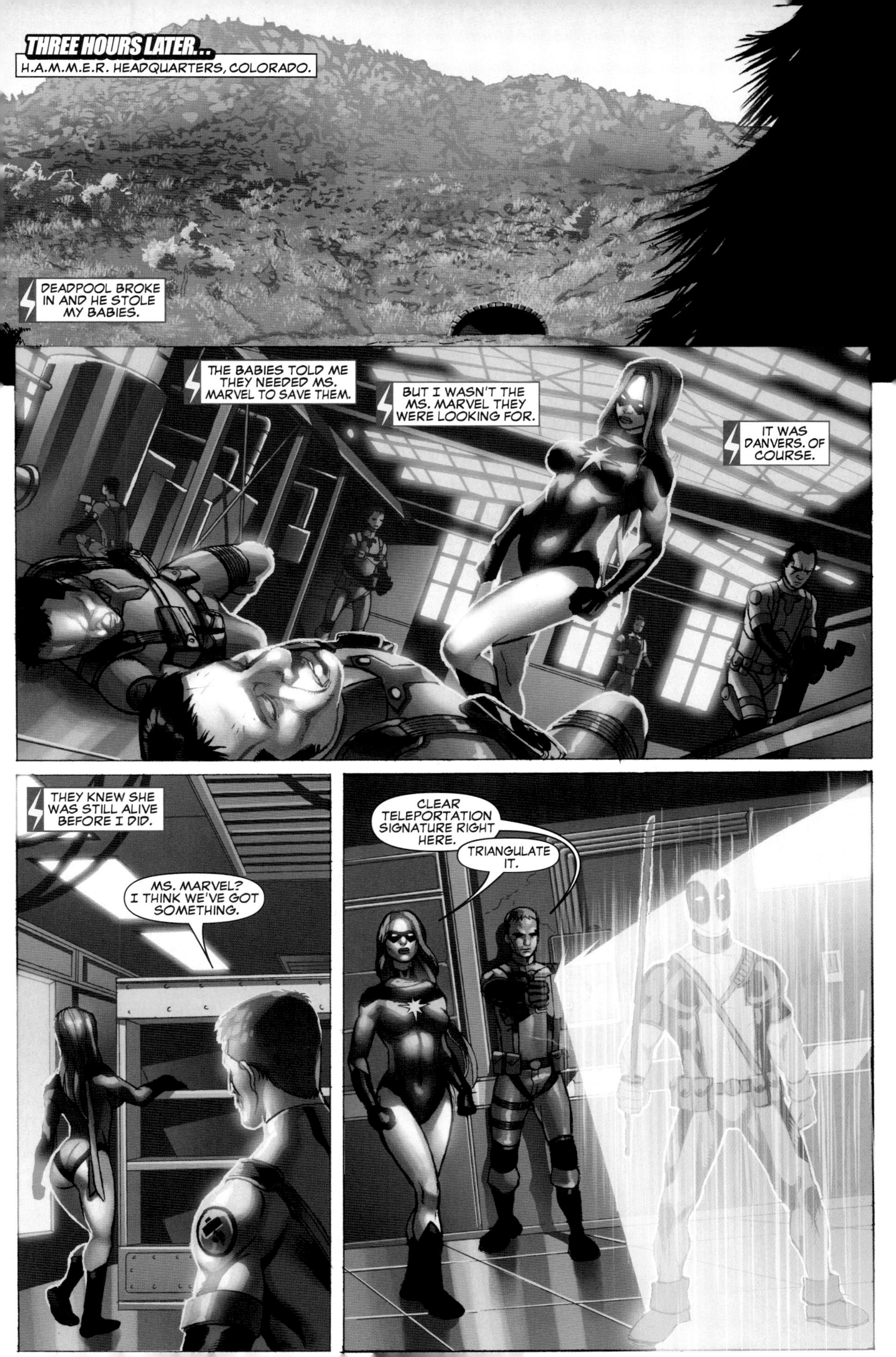
THREE HOURS LATER...
H.A.M.M.E.R. HEADQUARTERS, COLORADO.
DEADPOOL BROKE IN AND HE STOLE MY BABIES.
THE BABIES TOLD ME THEY NEEDED MS. MARVEL TO SAVE THEM.
BUT I WASN'T THE MS. MARVEL THEY WERE LOOKING FOR.
IT WAS DANVERS. OF COURSE.
THEY KNEW SHE WAS STILL ALIVE BEFORE I DID.
MS. MARVEL? I THINK WE'VE GOT SOMETHING.
CLEAR TELEPORTATION SIGNATURE RIGHT HERE.
TRIANGULATE IT.

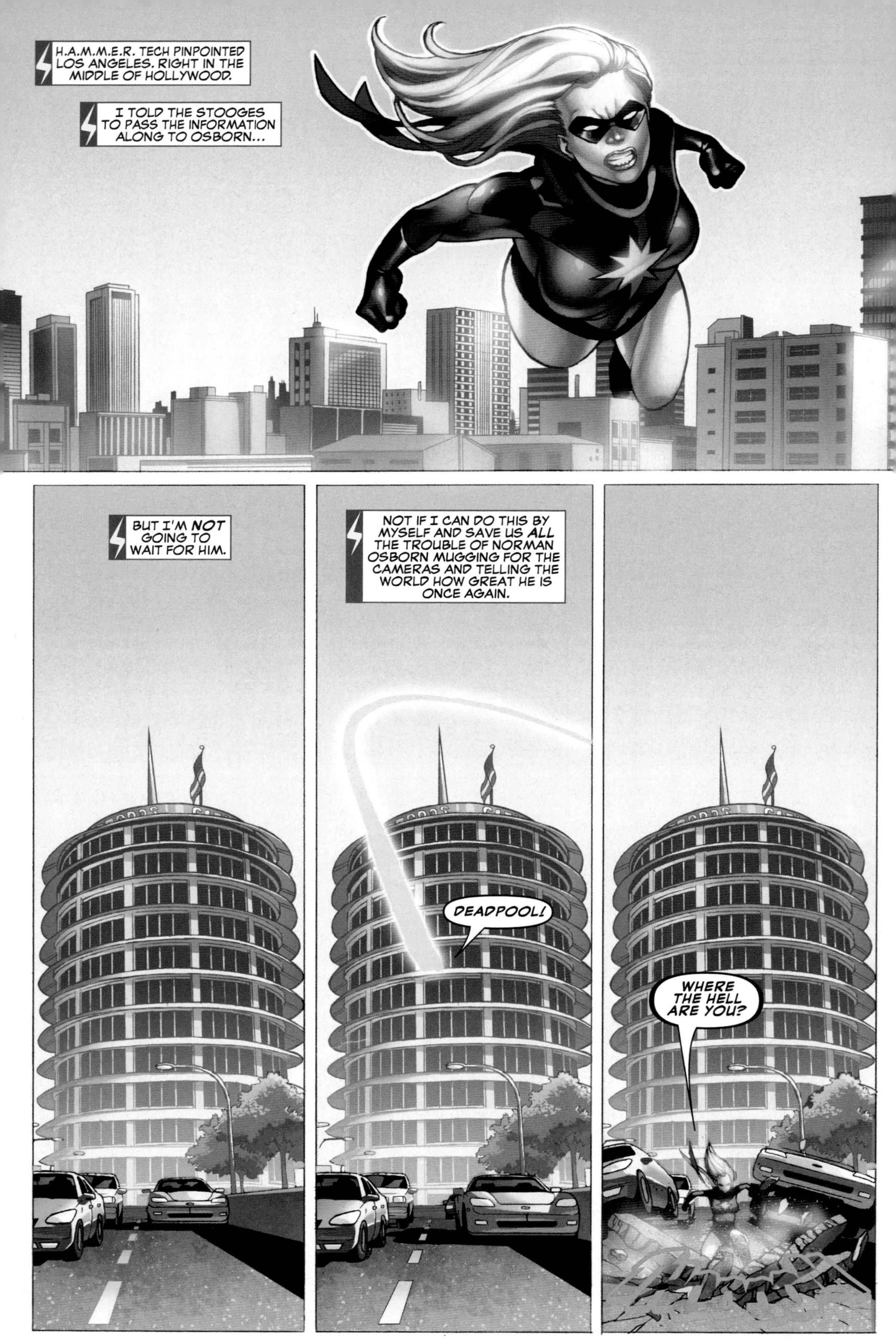
H.A.M.M.E.R. TECH PINPOINTED LOS ANGELES. RIGHT IN THE MIDDLE OF HOLLYWOOD.
I TOLD THE STOOGES TO PASS THE INFORMATION ALONG TO OSBORN...
BUT I'M NOT GOING TO WAIT FOR HIM.
NOT IF I CAN DO THIS BY MYSELF AND SAVE US ALL THE TROUBLE OF NORMAN OSBORN MUGGING FOR THE CAMERAS AND TELLING THE WORLD HOW GREAT HE IS ONCE AGAIN.
DEADPOOL!
WHERE THE HELL ARE YOU?

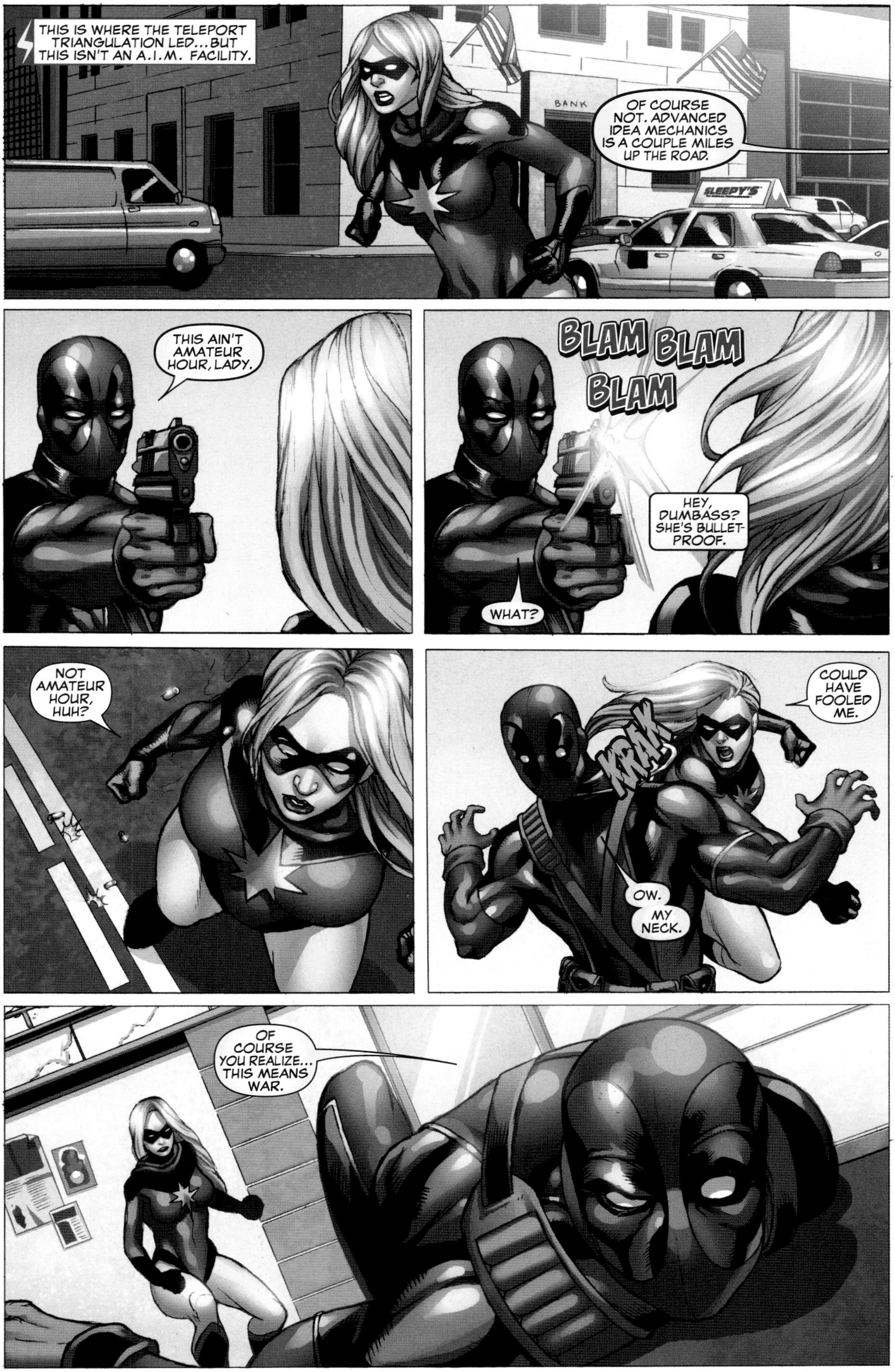
THIS IS WHERE THE TELEPORT TRIANGULATION LED...BUT THIS ISN'T AN A.I.M. FACILITY.
BANK
OF COURSE NOT. ADVANCED IDEA MECHANICS IS A COUPLE MILES UP THE ROAD.
SLEEPY'S
THIS AIN'T AMATEUR HOUR, LADY.
BLAM BLAM BLAM
HEY, DUMBASS? SHE'S BULLET-PROOF.
WHAT?
NOT AMATEUR HOUR, HUH?
KRAK
COULD HAVE FOOLED ME.
OW. MY NECK.
OF COURSE YOU REALIZE... THIS MEANS WAR.

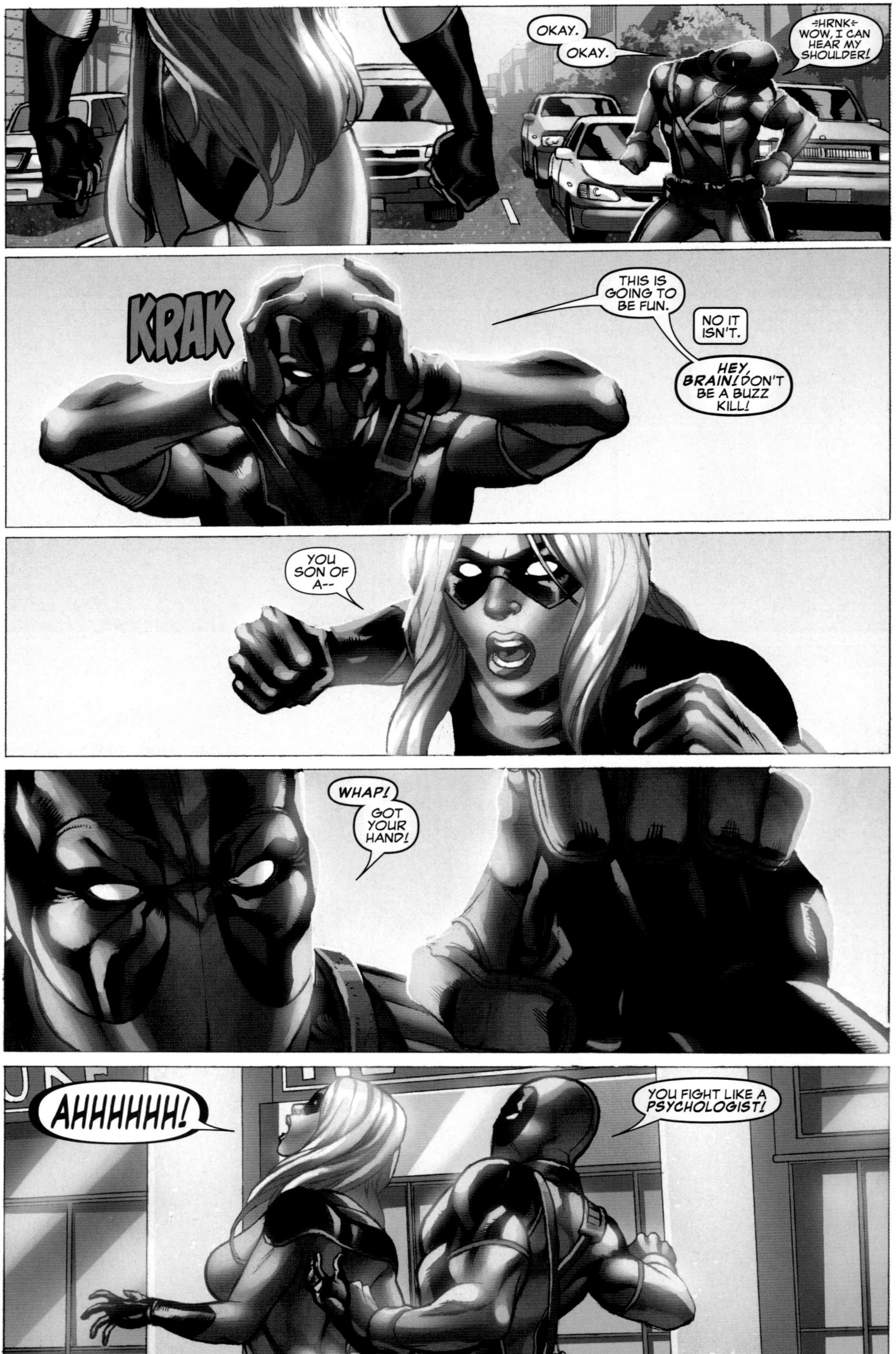

OKAY.
OKAY.
=HRNK= WOW, I CAN HEAR MY SHOULDER!
KRAK
THIS IS GOING TO BE FUN.
NO IT ISN'T.
HEY, BRAIN! DON'T BE A BUZZ KILL!
YOU SON OF A--
WHAP! GOT YOUR HAND!
AHHHHHH!
YOU FIGHT LIKE A PSYCHOLOGIST!

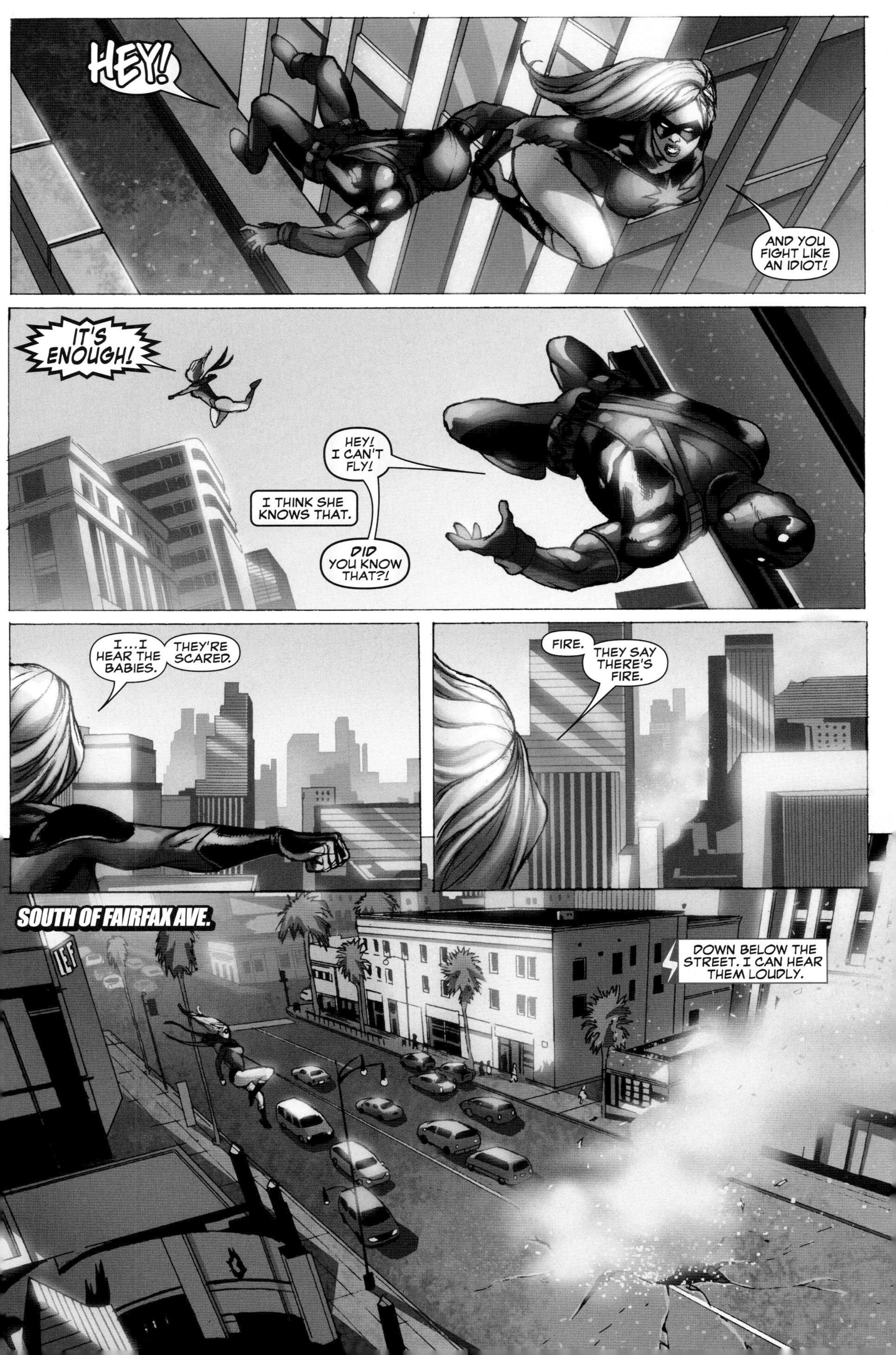
HEY!
AND YOU FIGHT LIKE AN IDIOT!
IT'S ENOUGH!
HEY! I CAN'T FLY!
I THINK SHE KNOWS THAT.
DID YOU KNOW THAT?!
I...I HEAR THE BABIES.
THEY'RE SCARED.
FIRE.
THEY SAY THERE'S FIRE.
SOUTH OF FAIRFAX AVE.
DOWN BELOW THE STREET. I CAN HEAR THEM LOUDLY.

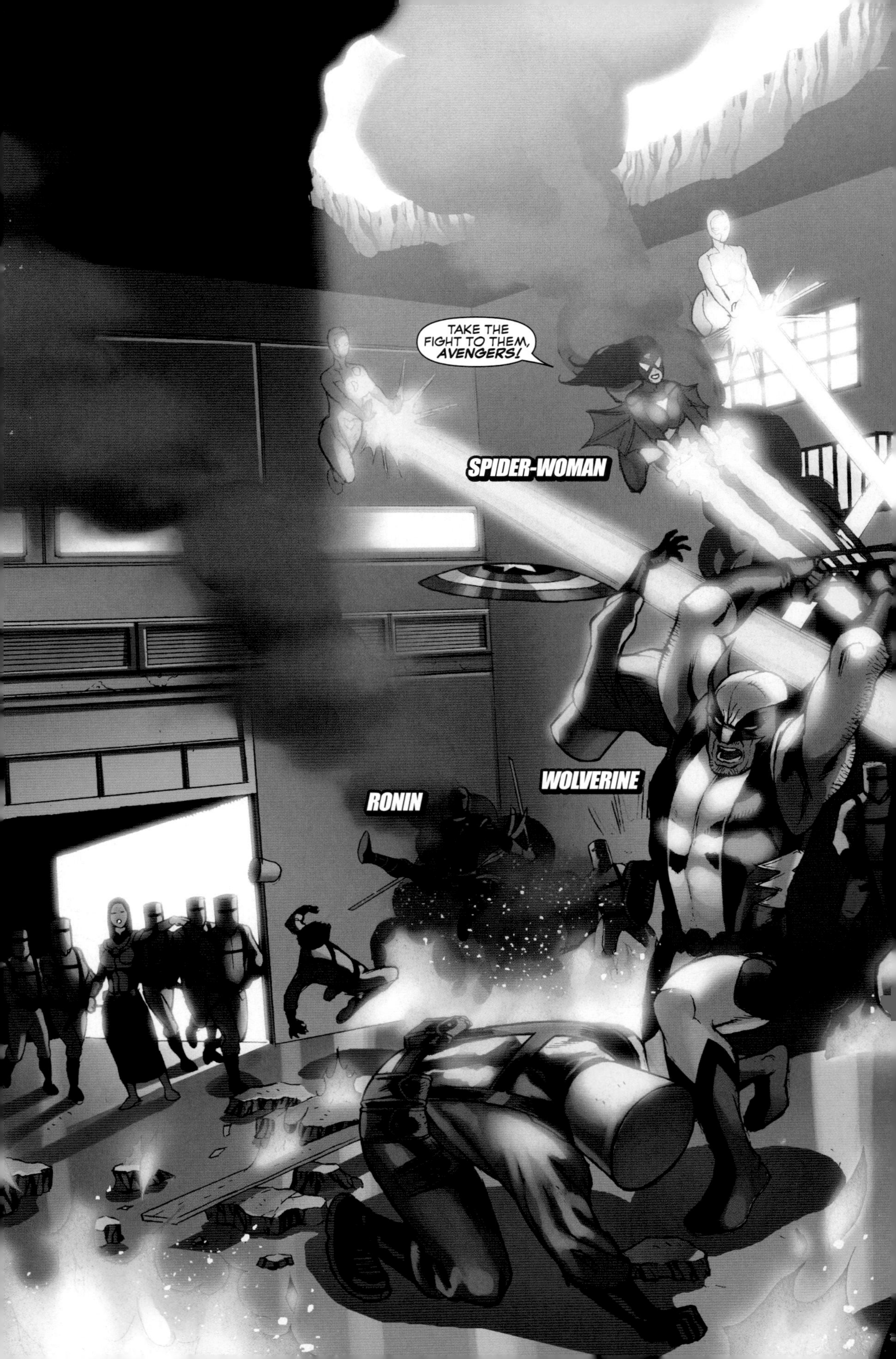
TAKE THE FIGHT TO THEM, AVENGERS!
SPIDER-WOMAN
WOLVERINE
RONIN

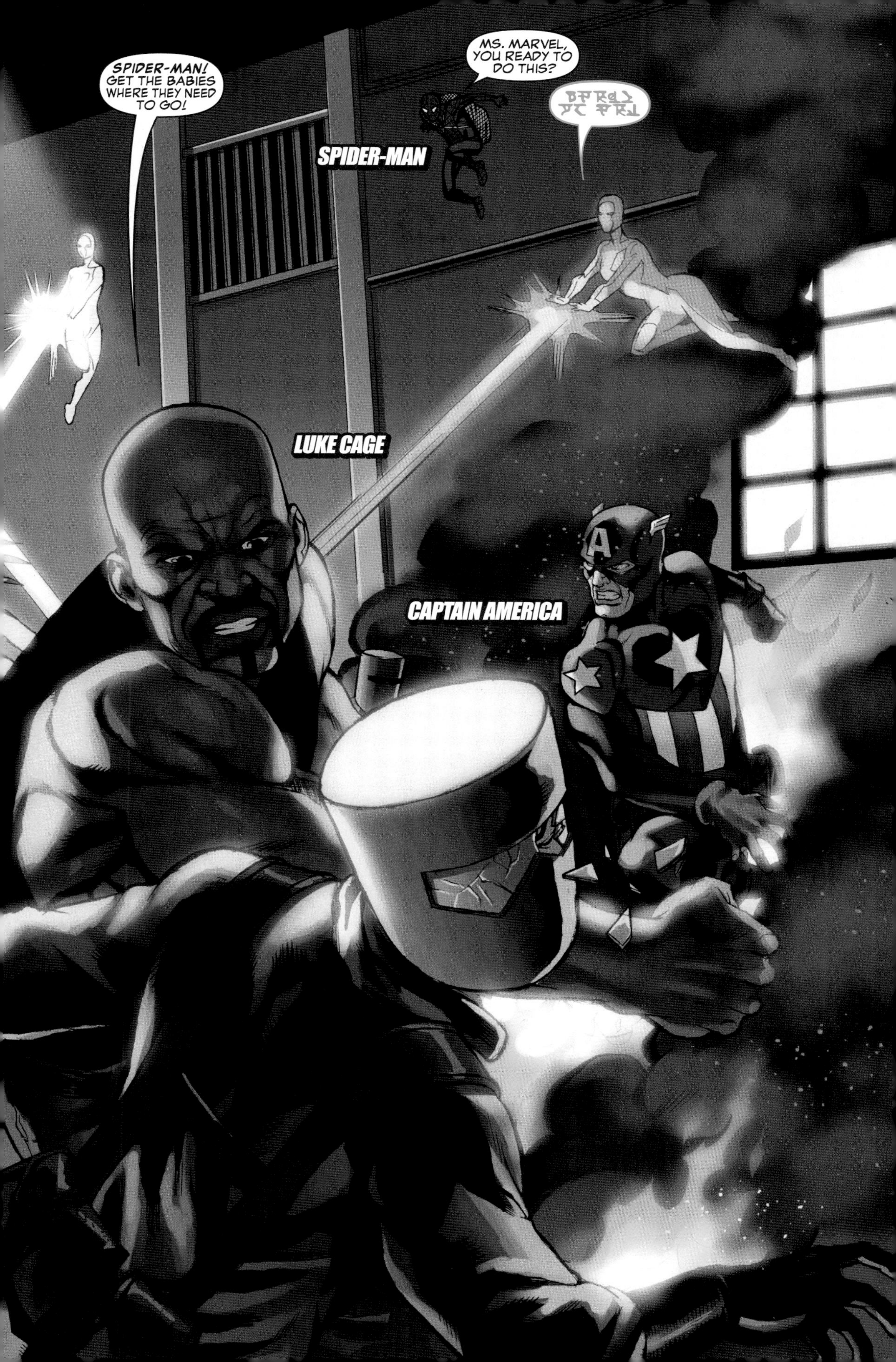
SPIDER-MAN! GET THE BABIES WHERE THEY NEED TO GO!
MS. MARVEL, YOU READY TO DO THIS?
SPIDER-MAN
LUKE CAGE
CAPTAIN AMERICA

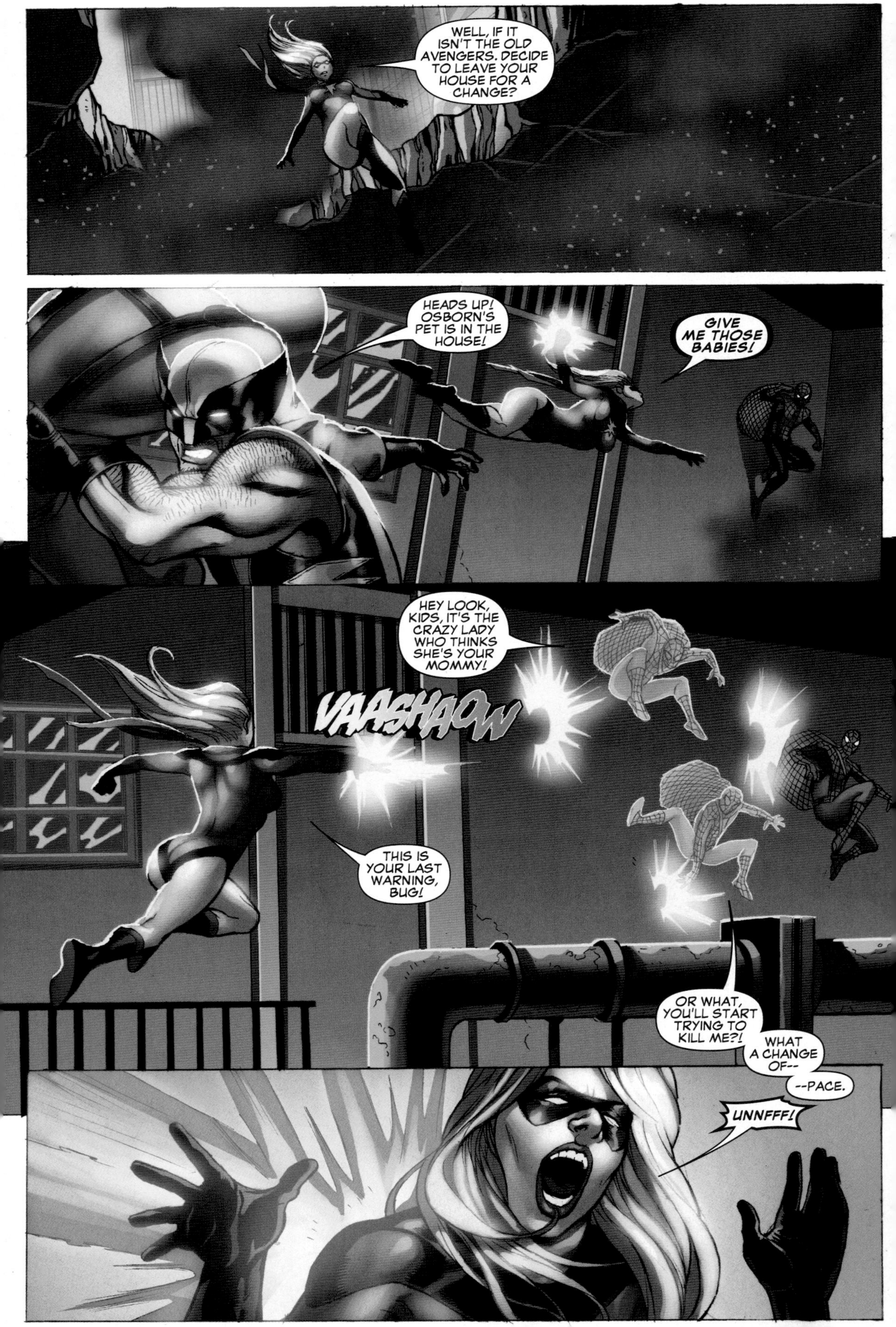

WELL, IF IT ISN'T THE OLD AVENGERS. DECIDE TO LEAVE YOUR HOUSE FOR A CHANGE?
HEADS UP! OSBORN'S PET IS IN THE HOUSE!
GIVE ME THOSE BABIES!
HEY LOOK, KIDS, IT'S THE CRAZY LADY WHO THINKS SHE'S YOUR MOMMY!
VAASHAOW
THIS IS YOUR LAST WARNING, BUG!
OR WHAT, YOU'LL START TRYING TO KILL ME?!
WHAT A CHANGE OF--
--PACE.
UNNFFF!

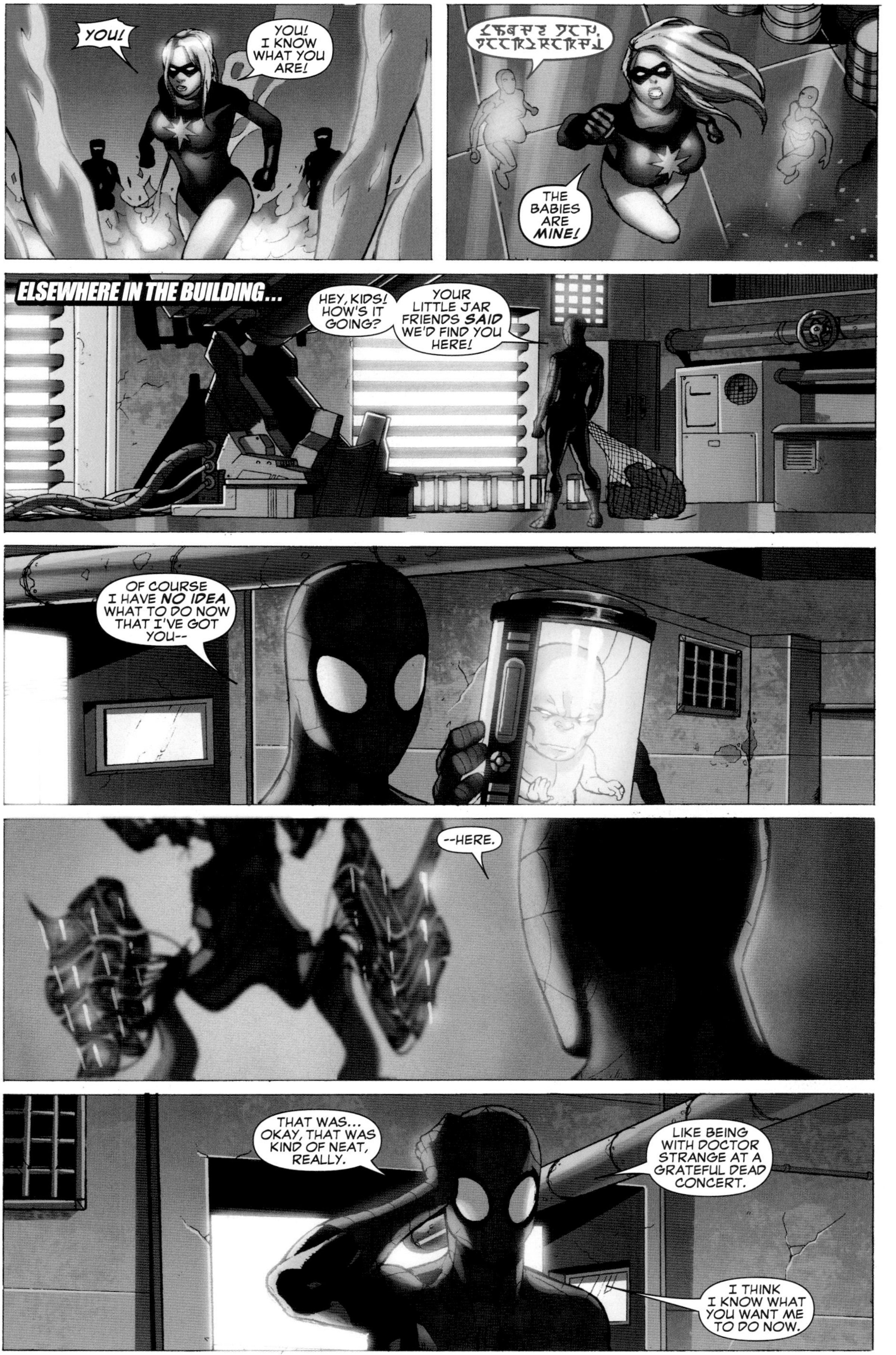
YOU!
YOU! I KNOW WHAT YOU ARE!
THE BABIES ARE MINE!
ELSEWHERE IN THE BUILDING...
HEY, KIDS! HOW'S IT GOING?
YOUR LITTLE JAR FRIENDS SAID WE'D FIND YOU HERE!
OF COURSE I HAVE NO IDEA WHAT TO DO NOW THAT I'VE GOT YOU--
--HERE.
THAT WAS... OKAY, THAT WAS KIND OF NEAT, REALLY.
LIKE BEING WITH DOCTOR STRANGE AT A GRATEFUL DEAD CONCERT.
I THINK I KNOW WHAT YOU WANT ME TO DO NOW.

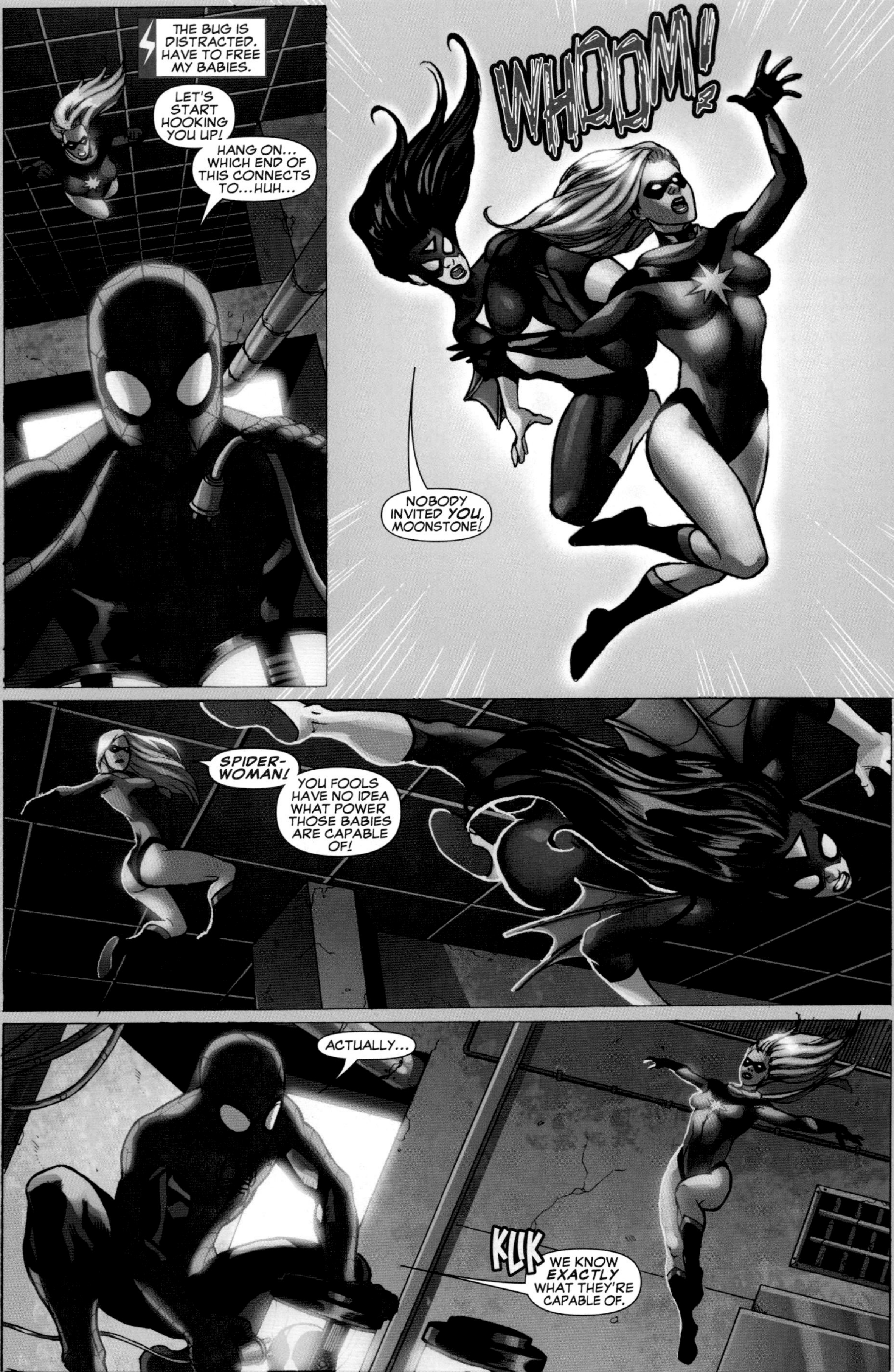
THE BUG IS DISTRACTED. HAVE TO FREE MY BABIES.
LET'S START HOOKING YOU UP!
HANG ON... WHICH END OF THIS CONNECTS TO...HUH...
WHOOM!
NOBODY INVITED YOU, MOONSTONE!
SPIDER-WOMAN!
YOU FOOLS HAVE NO IDEA WHAT POWER THOSE BABIES ARE CAPABLE OF!
ACTUALLY...
KLIK
WE KNOW EXACTLY WHAT THEY'RE CAPABLE OF.

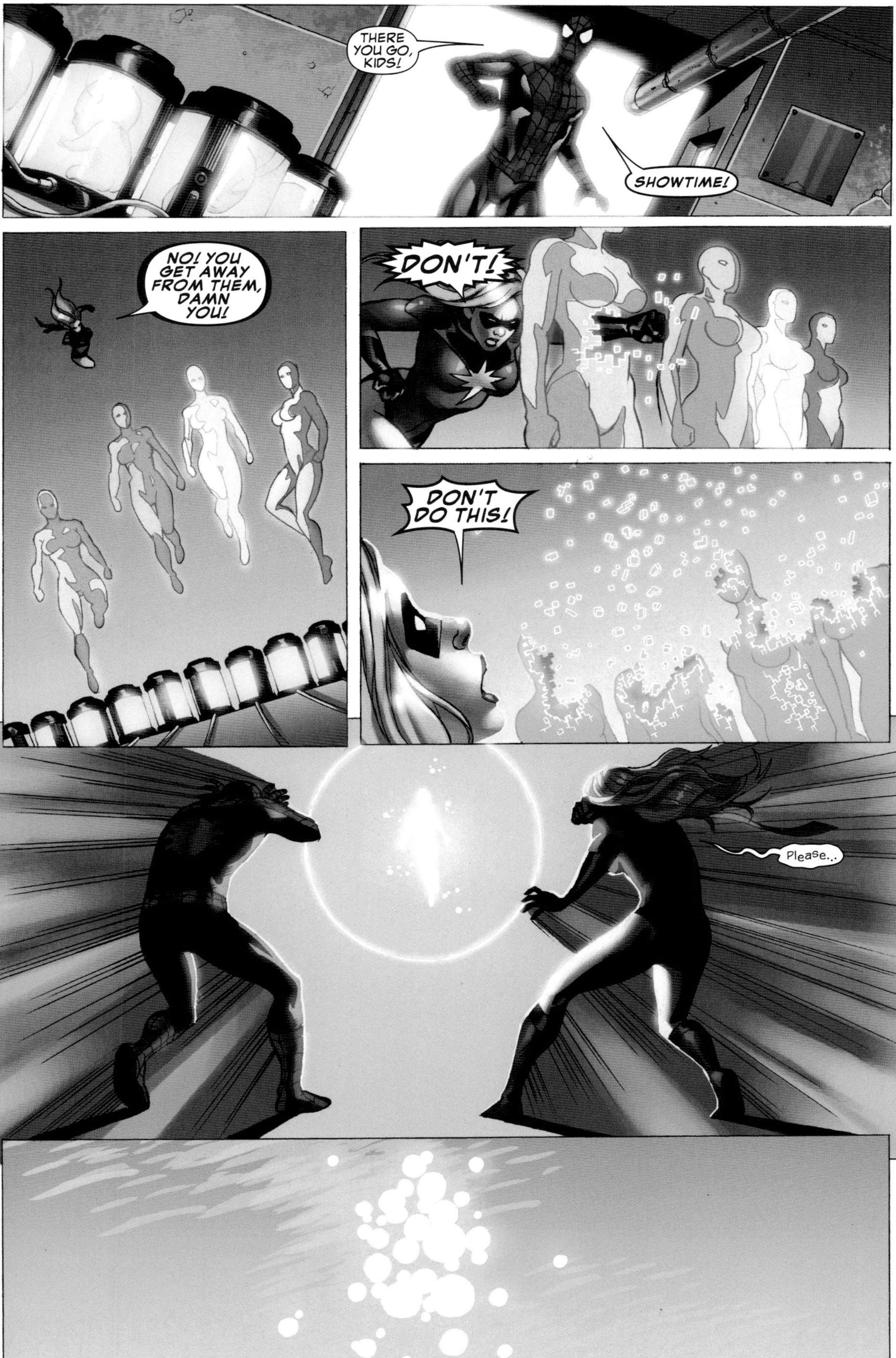
THERE YOU GO, KIDS!
SHOWTIME!
NO! YOU GET AWAY FROM THEM, DAMN YOU!
DON'T!
DON'T DO THIS!
Please...

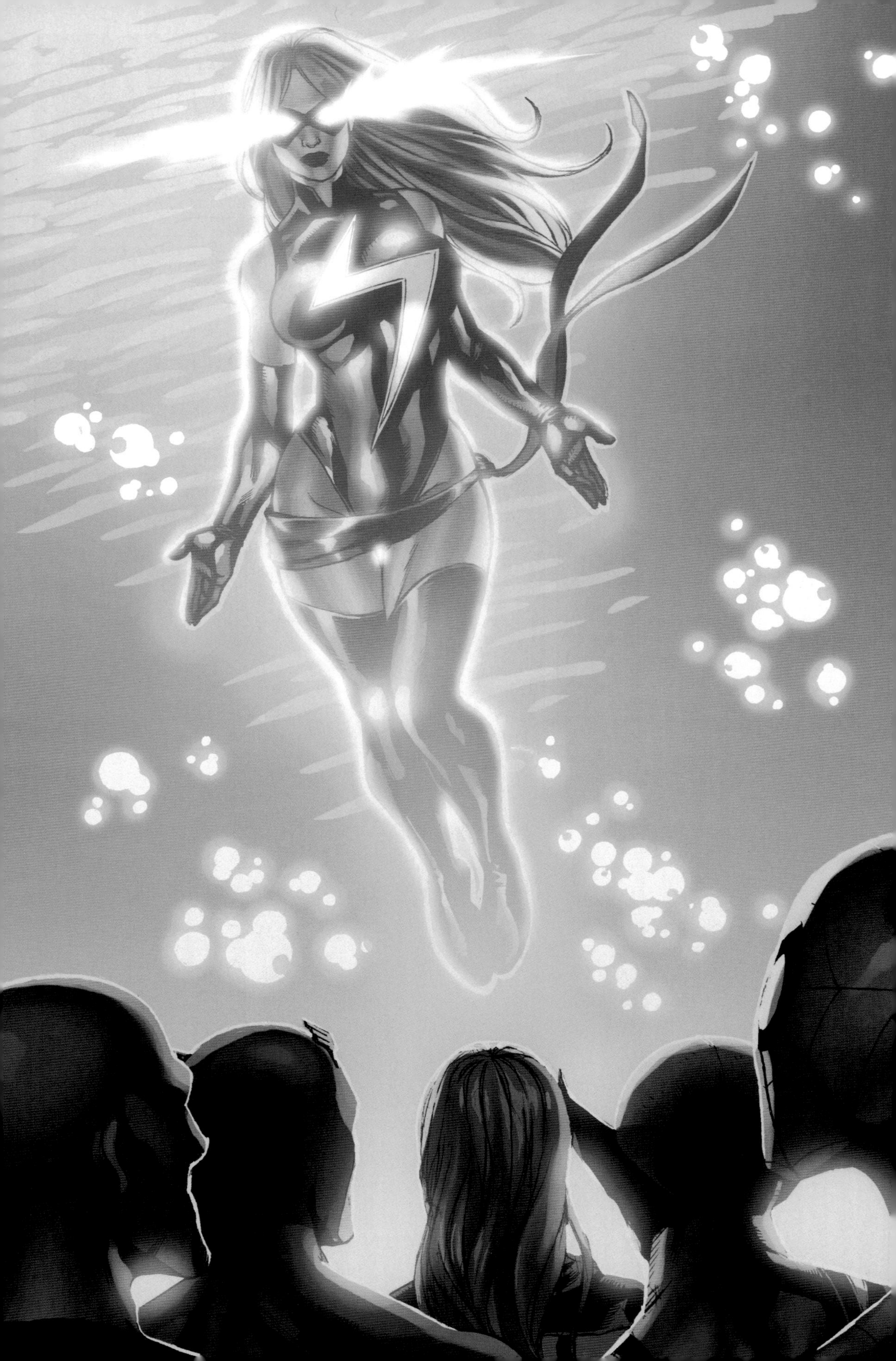

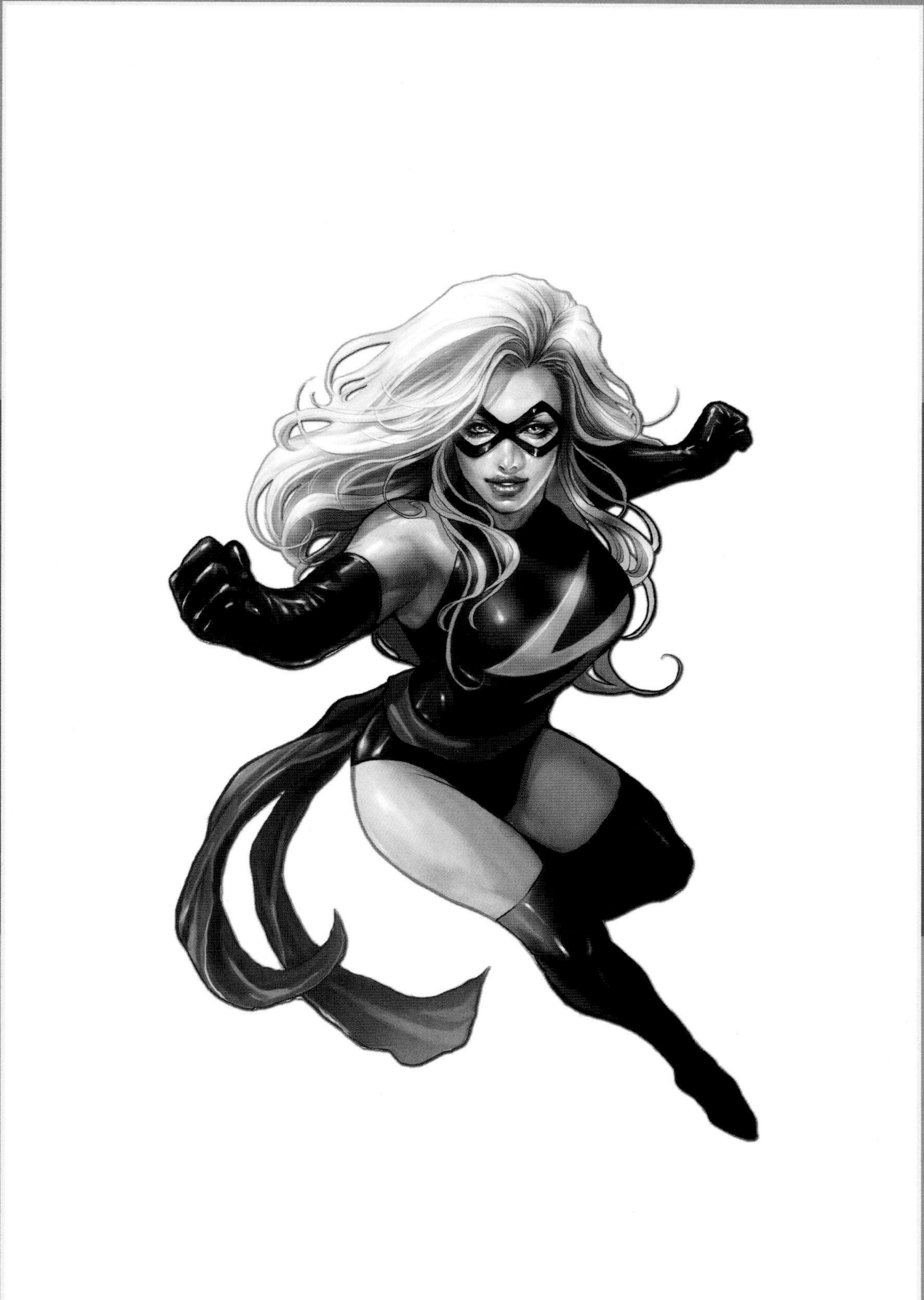

MS. MARVEL #43 70TH ANNIVERSARY FRAME VARIANT BY SANA TAKEDA

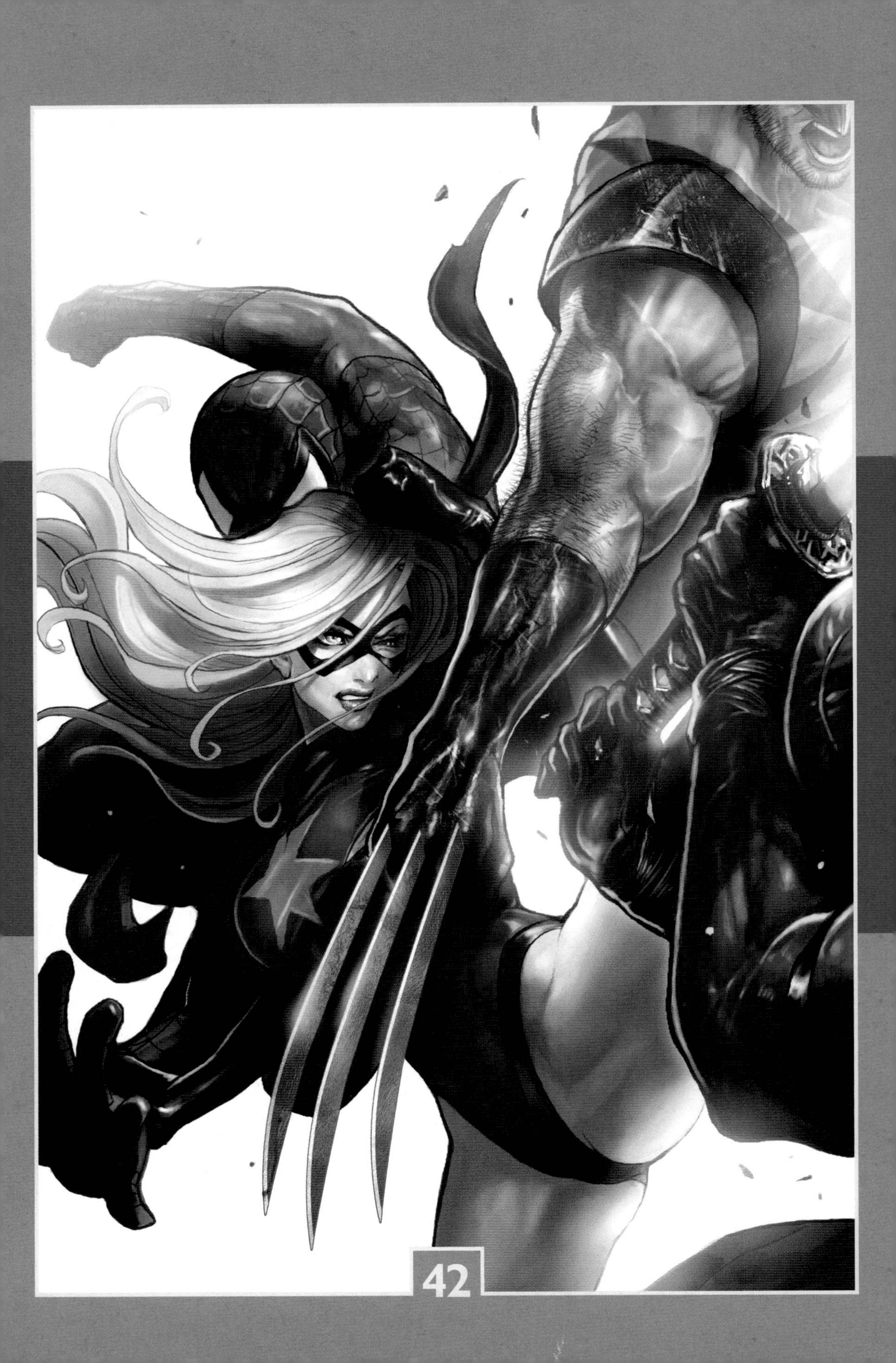

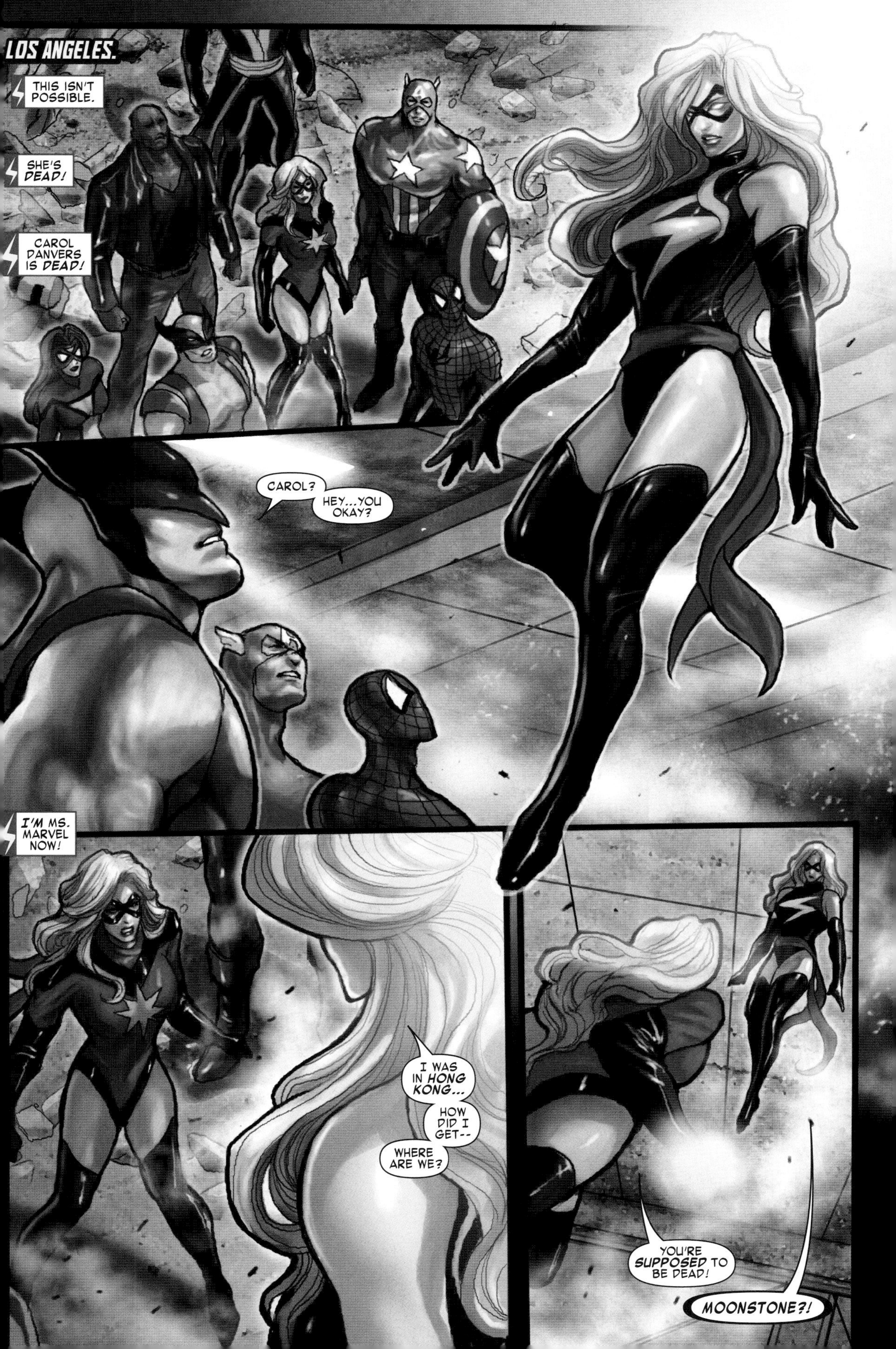
LOS ANGELES.
THIS ISN'T POSSIBLE.
SHE'S DEAD!
CAROL DANVERS IS DEAD!
CAROL?
HEY...YOU OKAY?
I'M MS. MARVEL NOW!
I WAS IN HONG KONG...
HOW DID I GET--
WHERE ARE WE?
YOU'RE SUPPOSED TO BE DEAD!
MOONSTONE?!

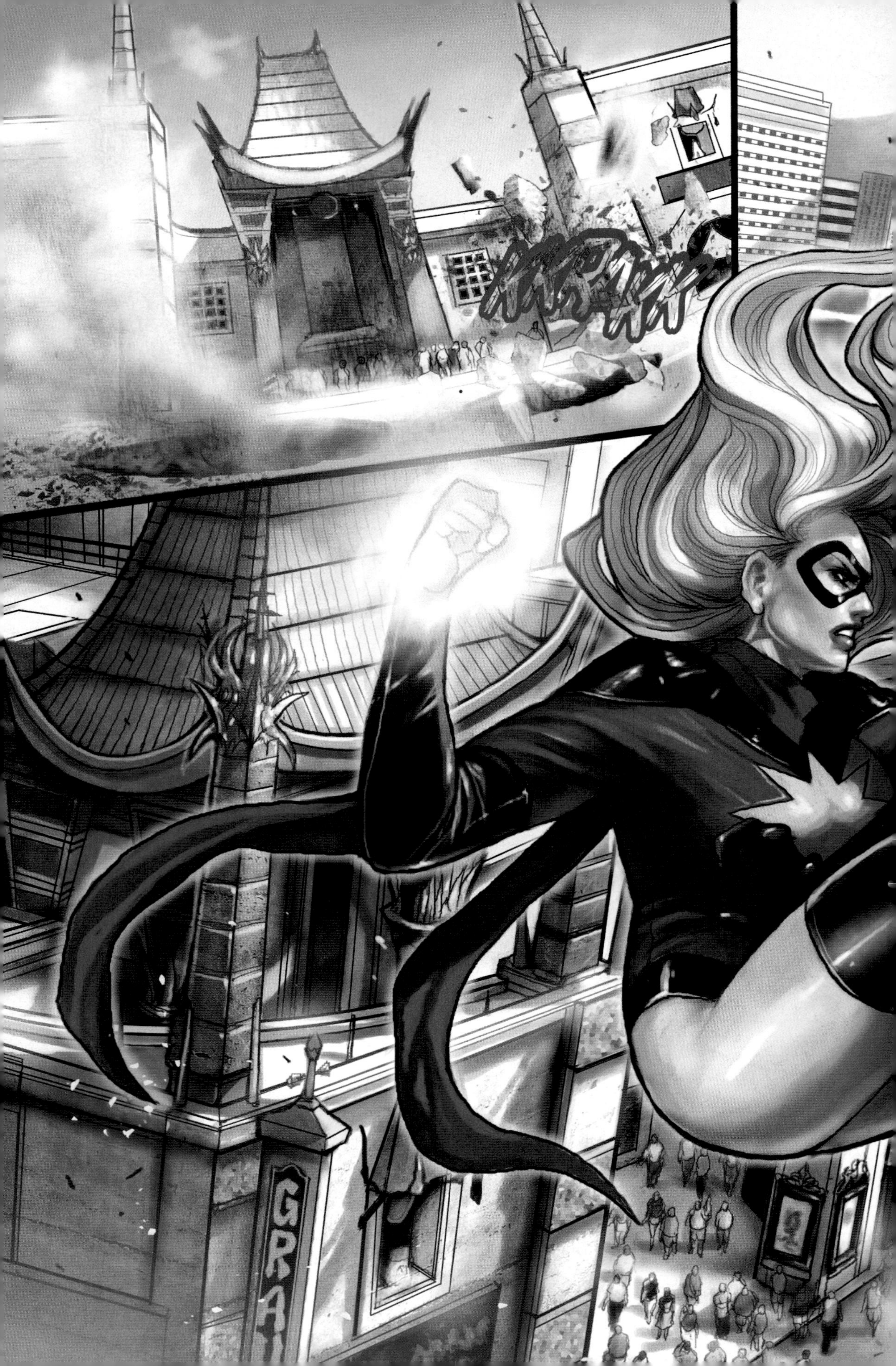
GRA

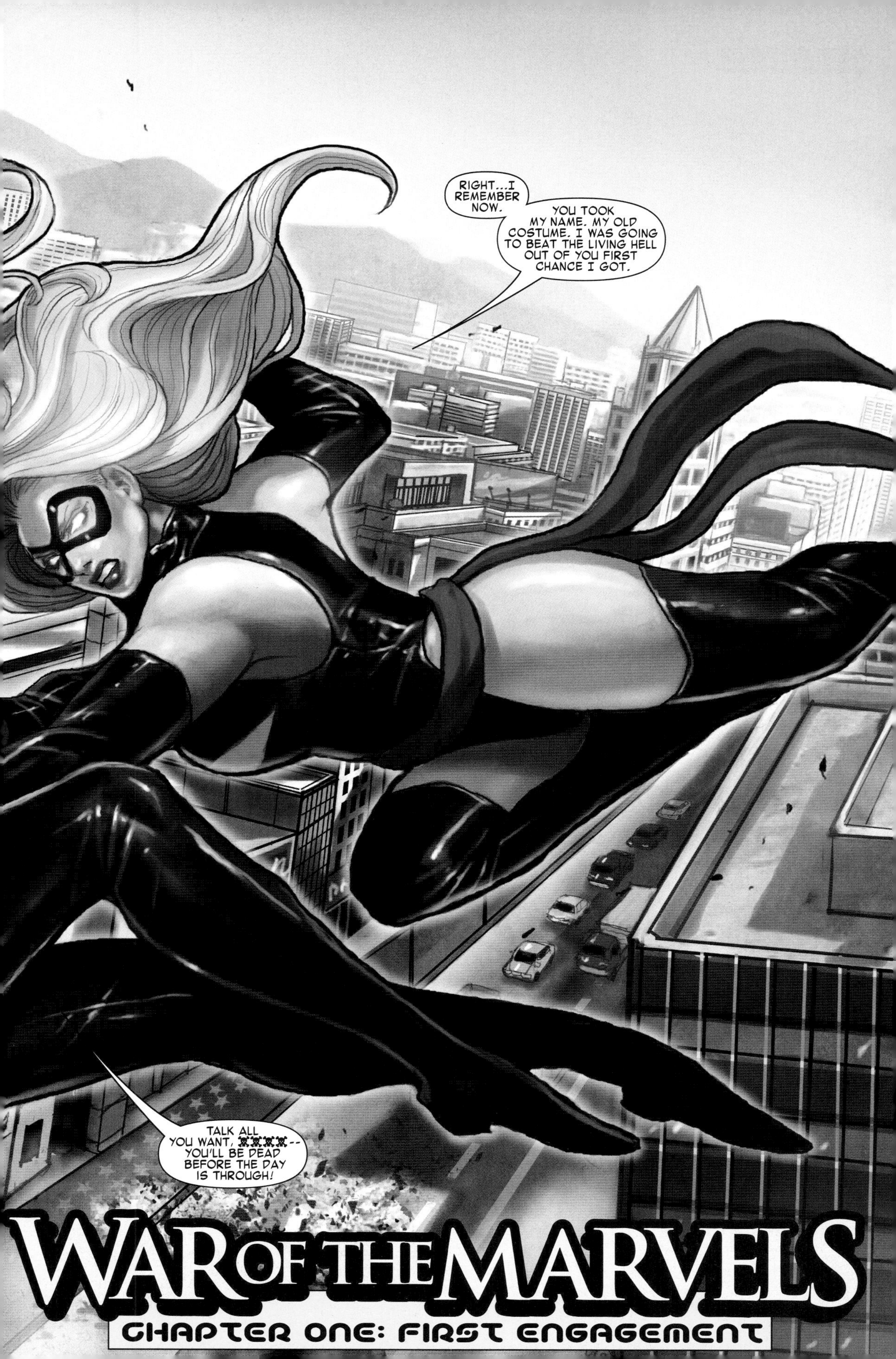

RIGHT...I REMEMBER NOW.
YOU TOOK MY NAME. MY OLD COSTUME. I WAS GOING TO BEAT THE LIVING HELL OUT OF YOU FIRST CHANCE I GOT.
TALK ALL YOU WANT, ☠☠☠☠-- YOU'LL BE DEAD BEFORE THE DAY IS THROUGH!
WAR OF THE MARVELS
CHAPTER ONE: FIRST ENGAGEMENT

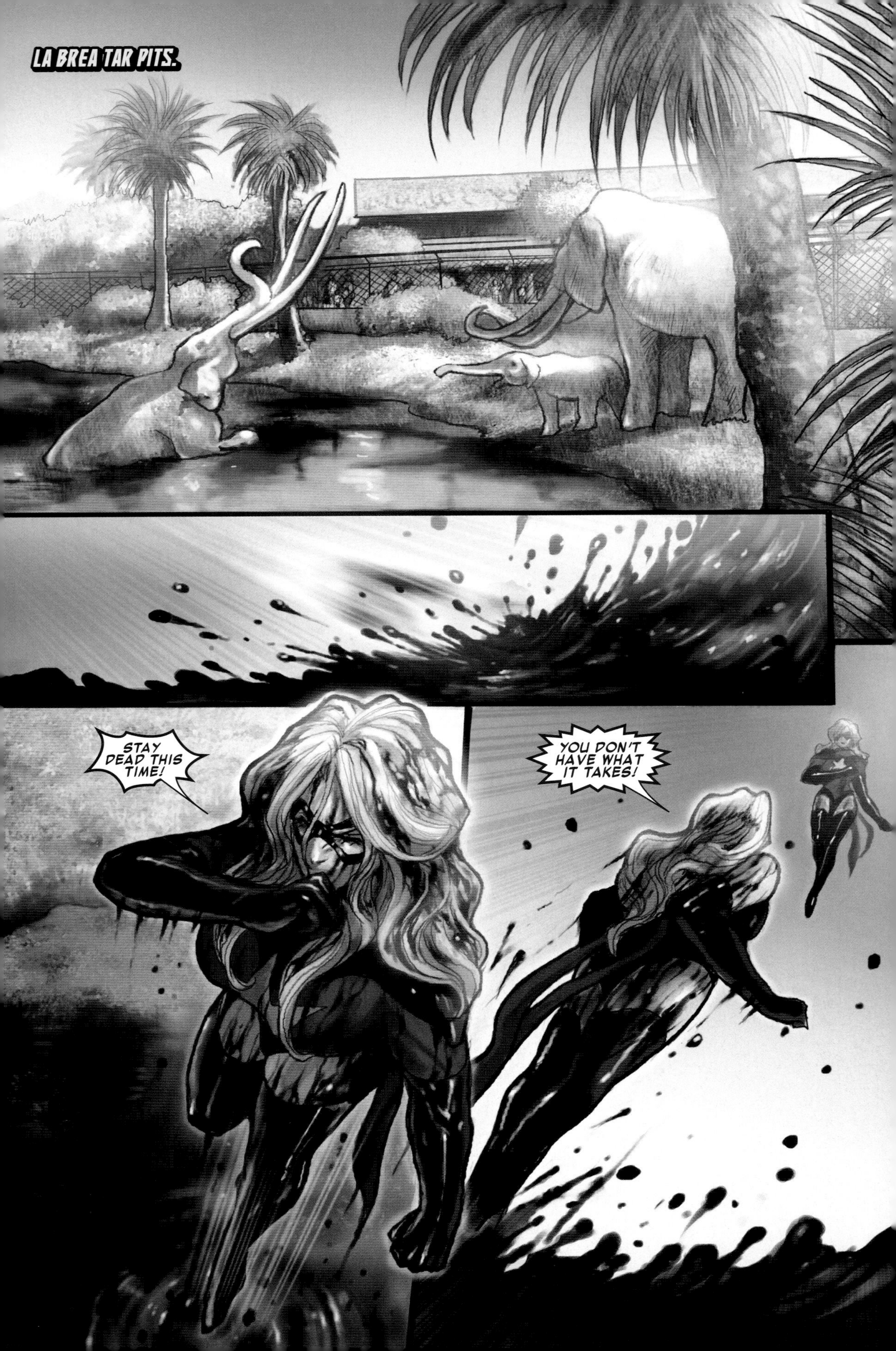
LA BREA TAR PITS.
STAY DEAD THIS TIME!
YOU DON'T HAVE WHAT IT TAKES!

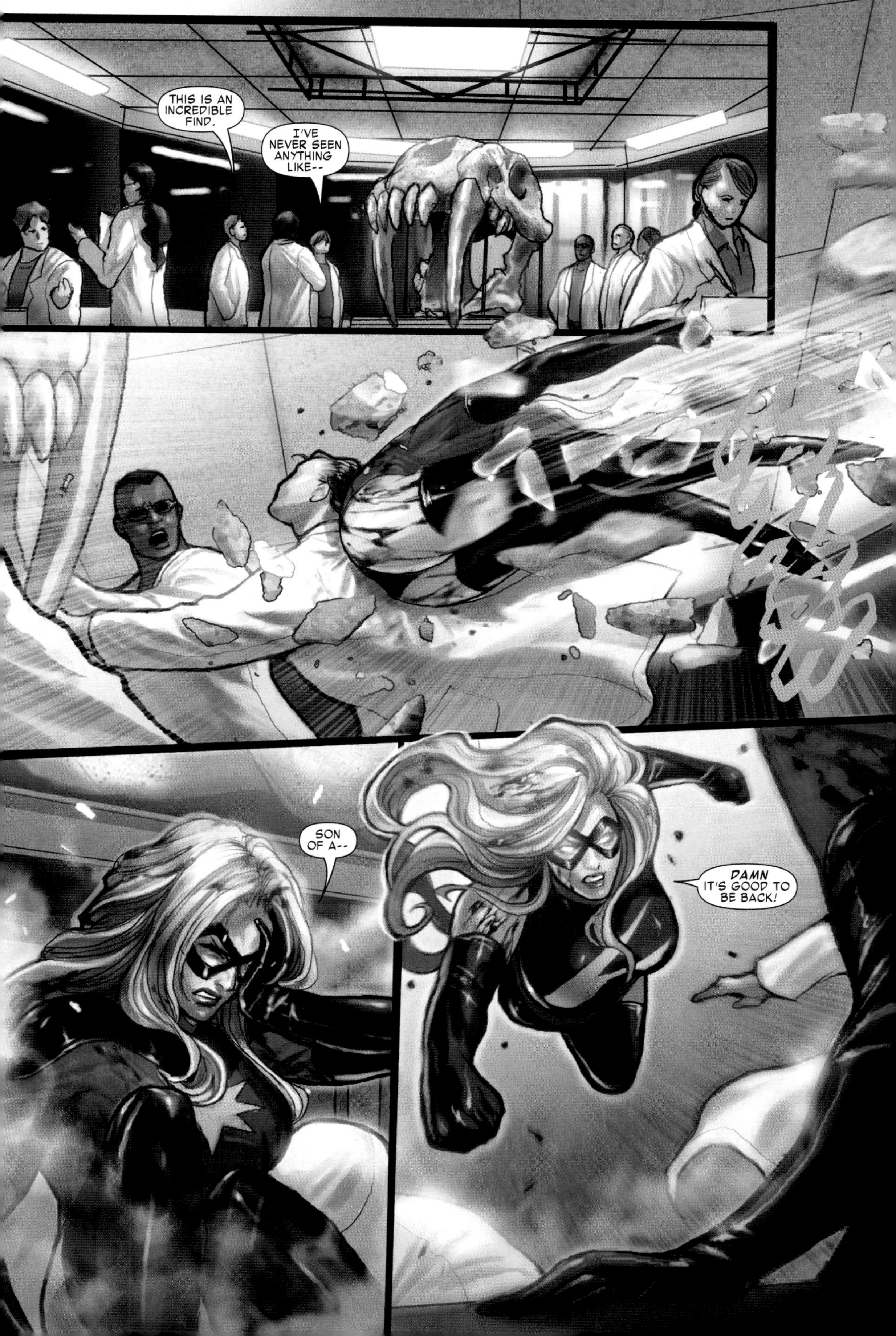
THIS IS AN INCREDIBLE FIND.
I'VE NEVER SEEN ANYTHING LIKE--
SON OF A--
DAMN IT'S GOOD TO BE BACK!

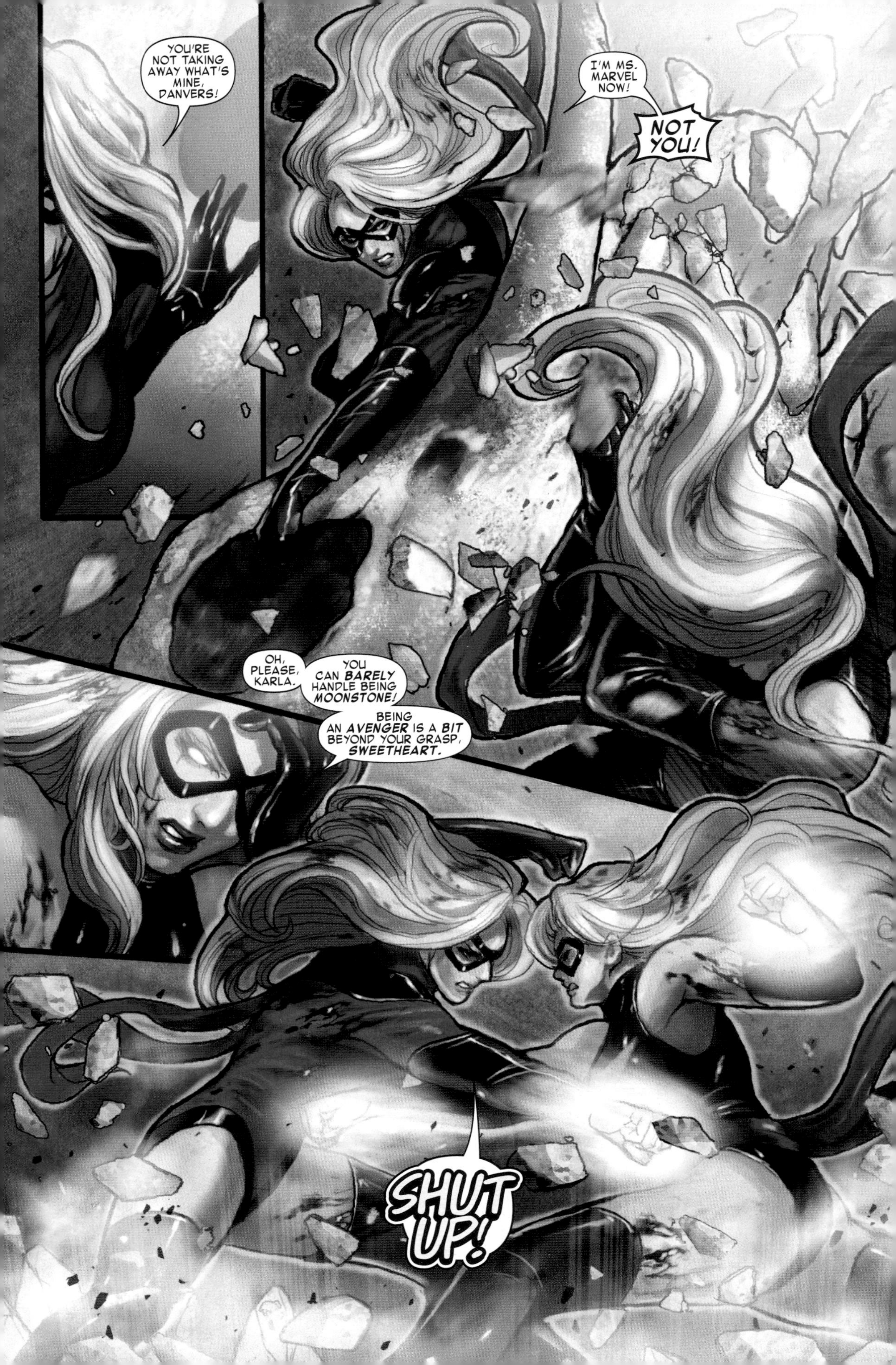

YOU'RE NOT TAKING AWAY WHAT'S MINE, DANVERS!
I'M MS. MARVEL NOW!
NOT YOU!
OH, PLEASE, KARLA.
YOU CAN BARELY HANDLE BEING MOONSTONE!
BEING AN AVENGER IS A BIT BEYOND YOUR GRASP, SWEETHEART.
SHUT UP!

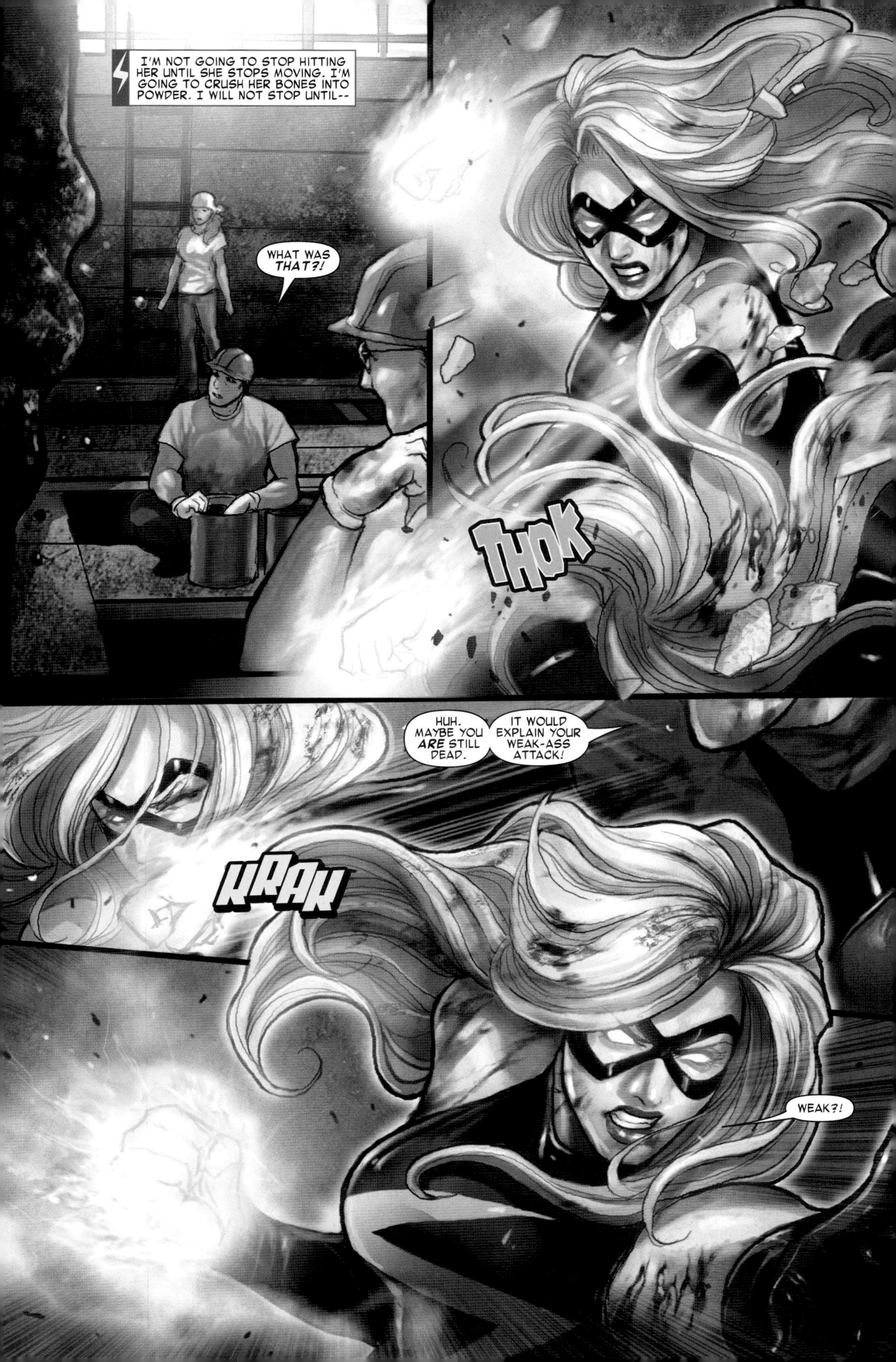
I'M NOT GOING TO STOP HITTING HER UNTIL SHE STOPS MOVING. I'M GOING TO CRUSH HER BONES INTO POWDER. I WILL NOT STOP UNTIL--
WHAT WAS THAT?!
THOK
HUH. MAYBE YOU ARE STILL DEAD.
IT WOULD EXPLAIN YOUR WEAK-ASS ATTACK!
KRAK
WEAK?!

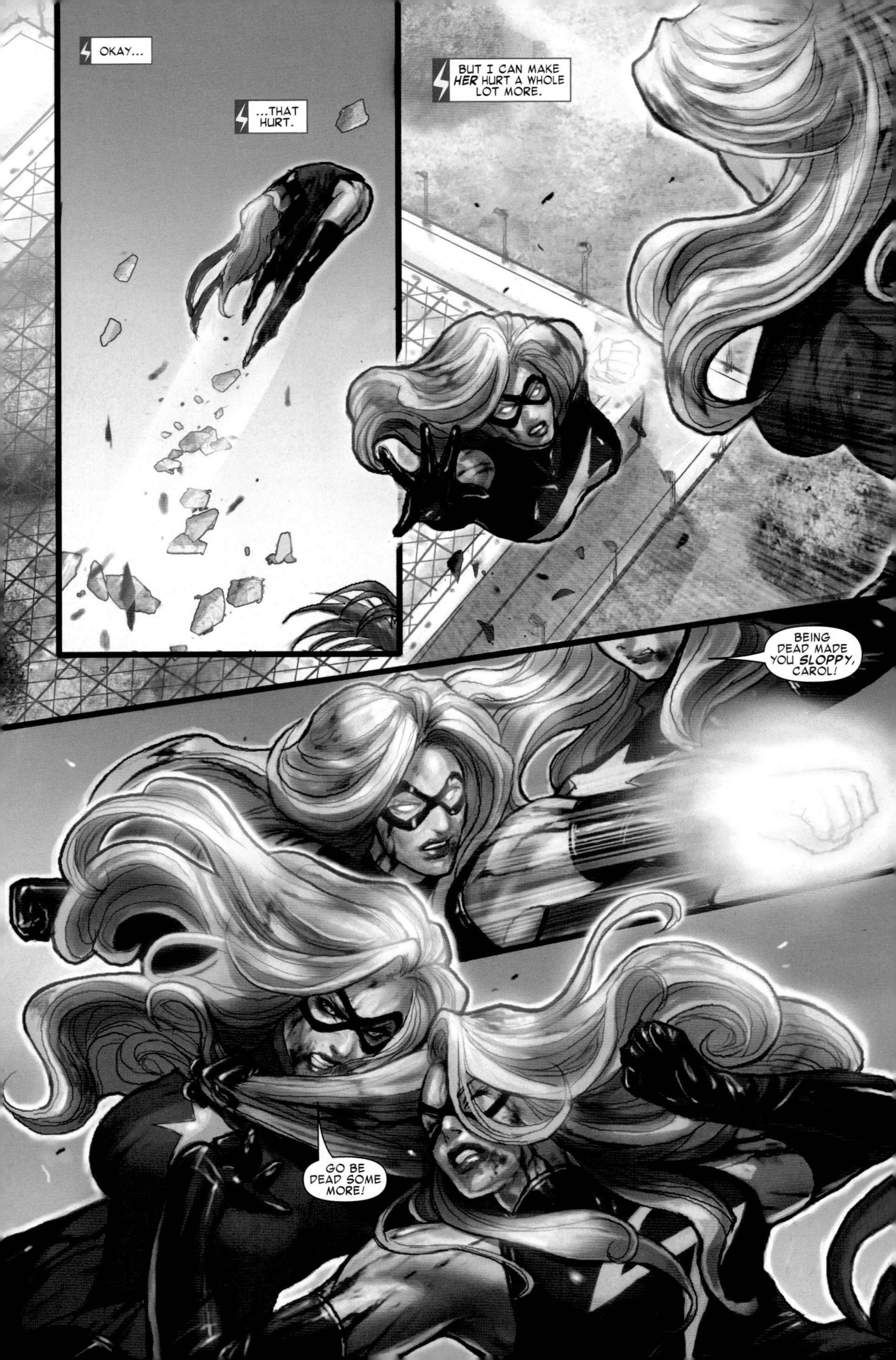
OKAY...
...THAT HURT.
BUT I CAN MAKE HER HURT A WHOLE LOT MORE.
BEING DEAD MADE YOU SLOPPY, CAROL!
GO BE DEAD SOME MORE!

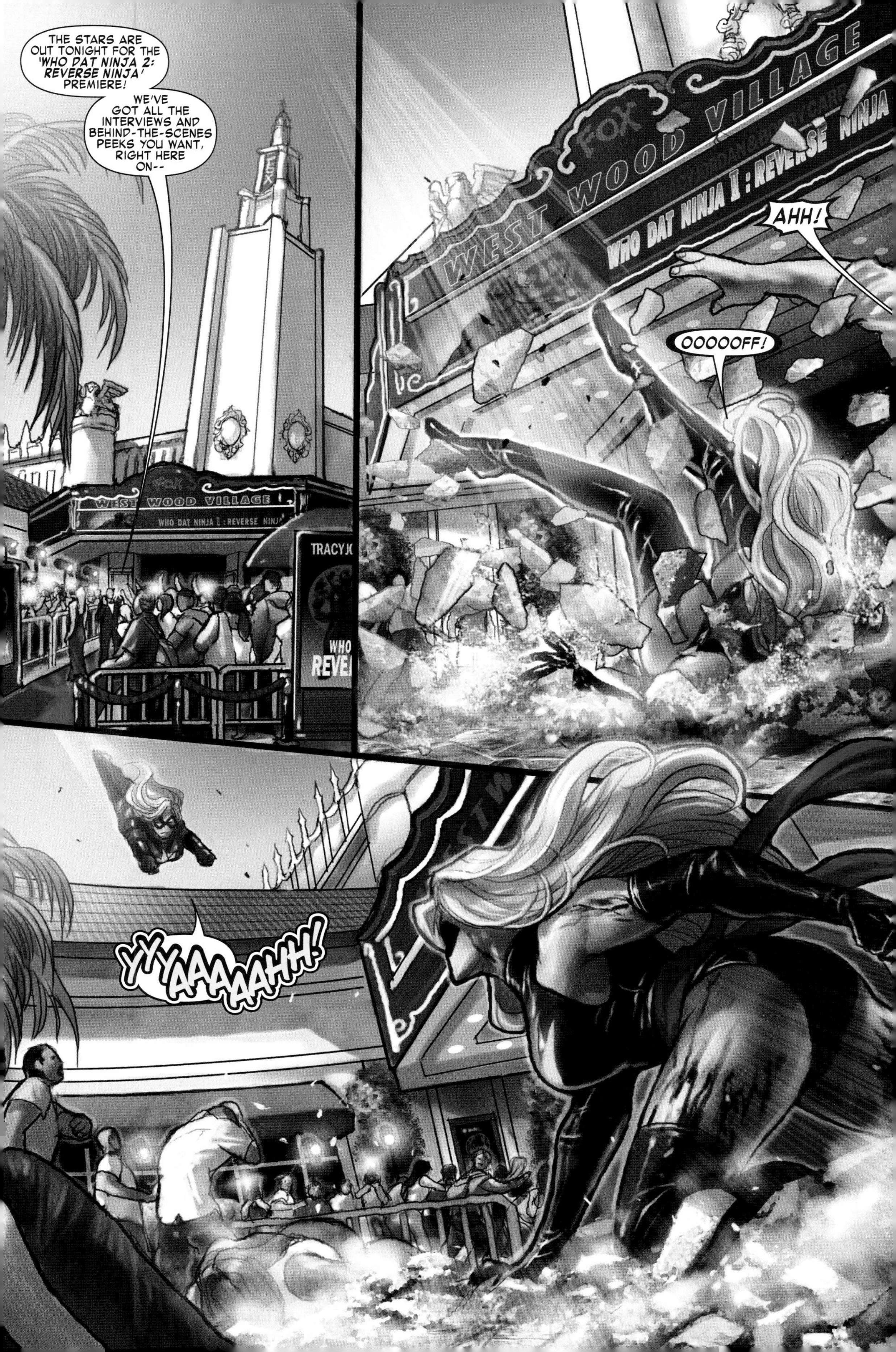
THE STARS ARE OUT TONIGHT FOR THE 'WHO DAT NINJA 2: REVERSE NINJA' PREMIERE!
WE'VE GOT ALL THE INTERVIEWS AND BEHIND-THE-SCENES PEEKS YOU WANT, RIGHT HERE ON--
FOX
WEST WOOD VILLAGE
WHO DAT NINJA II : REVERSE NINJA
TRACYJO
WHO
REVER
AHH!
OOOOOFF!
YYAAAAAHH!

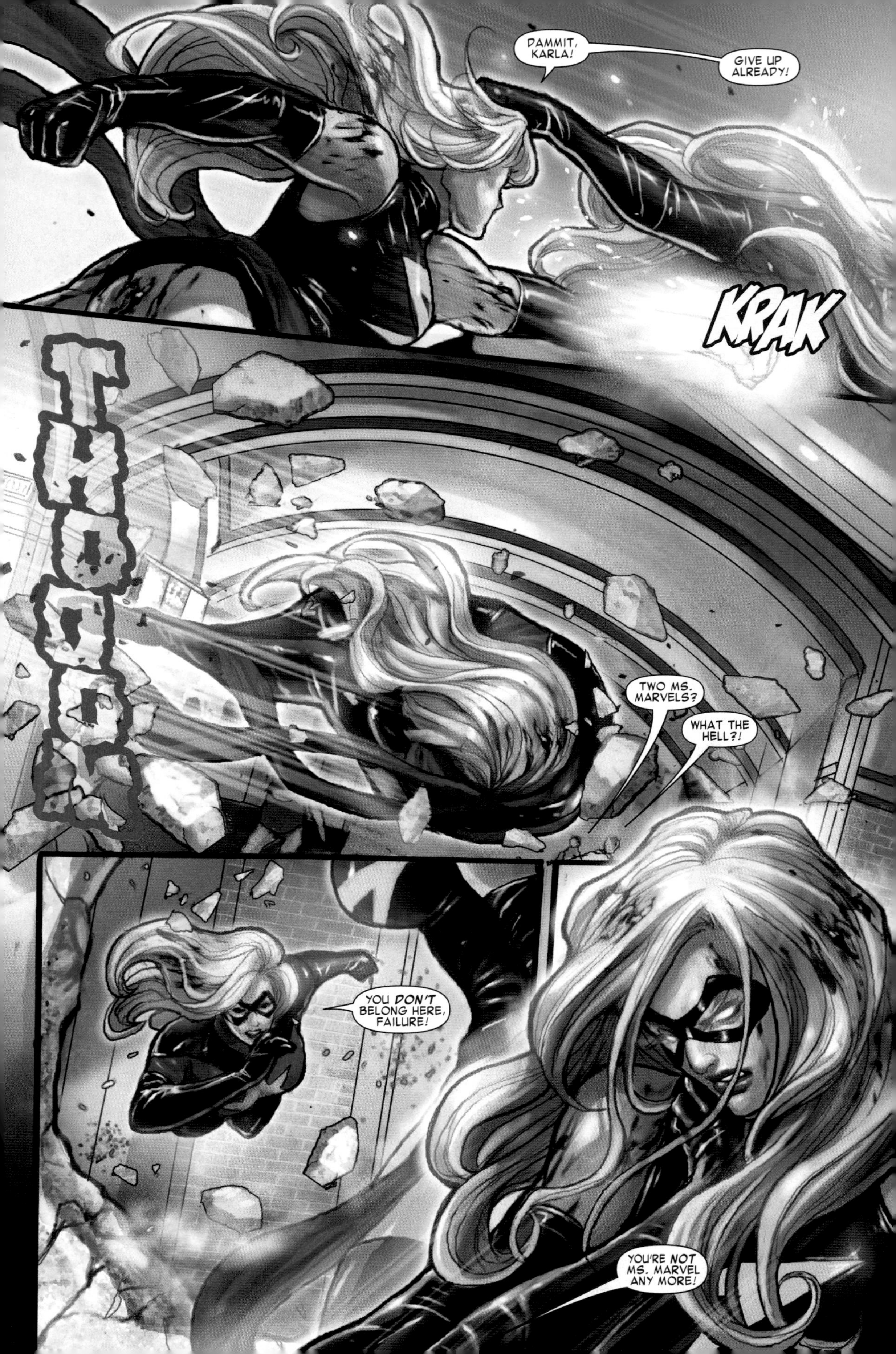
DAMMIT, KARLA!
GIVE UP ALREADY!
KRAK
THUD
TWO MS. MARVELS?
WHAT THE HELL?!
YOU DON'T BELONG HERE, FAILURE!
YOU'RE NOT MS. MARVEL ANY MORE!

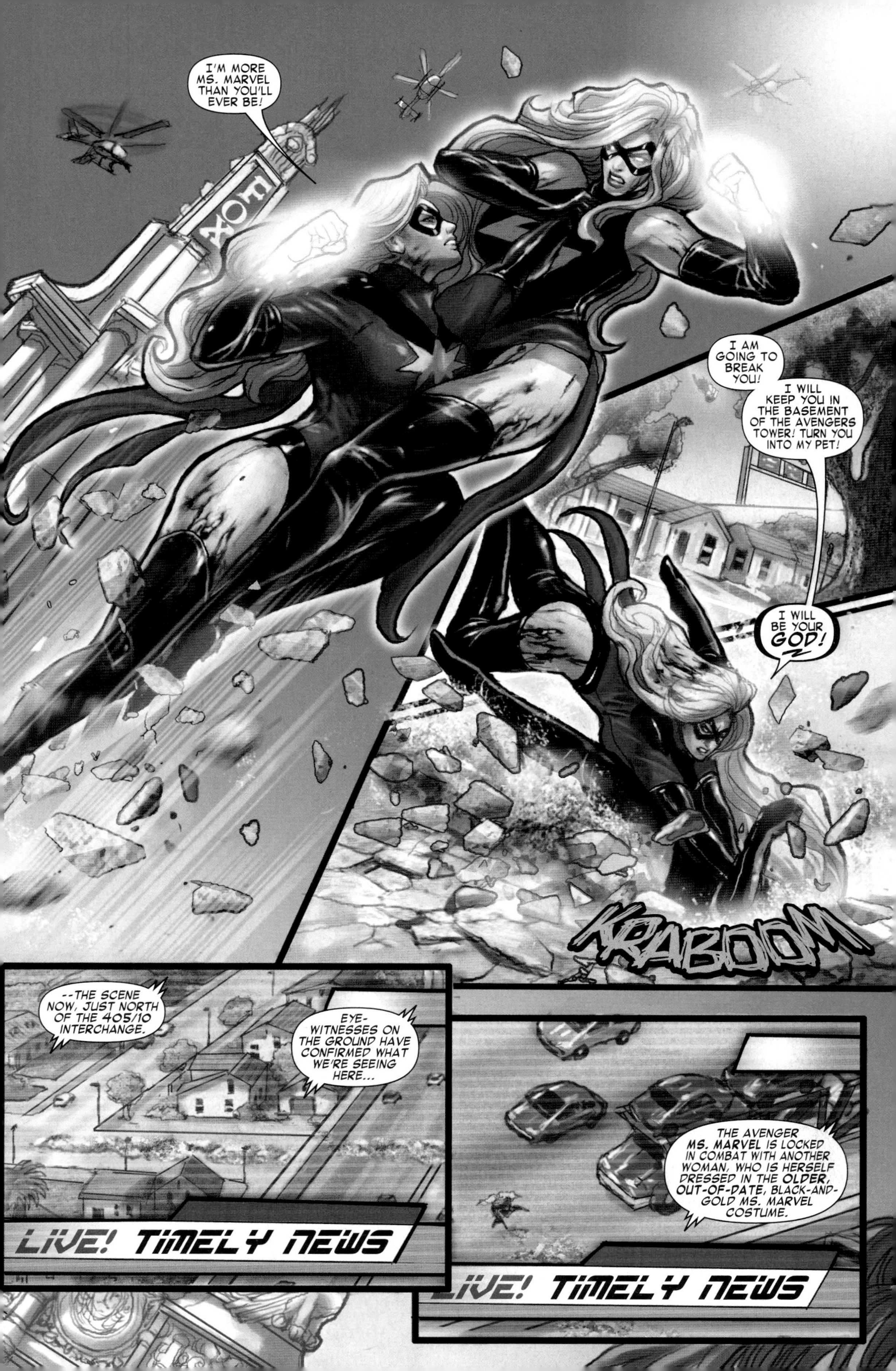
I'M MORE MS. MARVEL THAN YOU'LL EVER BE!
I AM GOING TO BREAK YOU!
I WILL KEEP YOU IN THE BASEMENT OF THE AVENGERS TOWER! TURN YOU INTO MY PET!
I WILL BE YOUR GOD!
KRABOOM
--THE SCENE NOW, JUST NORTH OF THE 405/10 INTERCHANGE.
EYE-WITNESSES ON THE GROUND HAVE CONFIRMED WHAT WE'RE SEEING HERE...
LIVE! TIMELY NEWS
THE AVENGER MS. MARVEL IS LOCKED IN COMBAT WITH ANOTHER WOMAN, WHO IS HERSELF DRESSED IN THE OLDER, OUT-OF-DATE, BLACK-AND-GOLD MS. MARVEL COSTUME.
LIVE! TIMELY NEWS

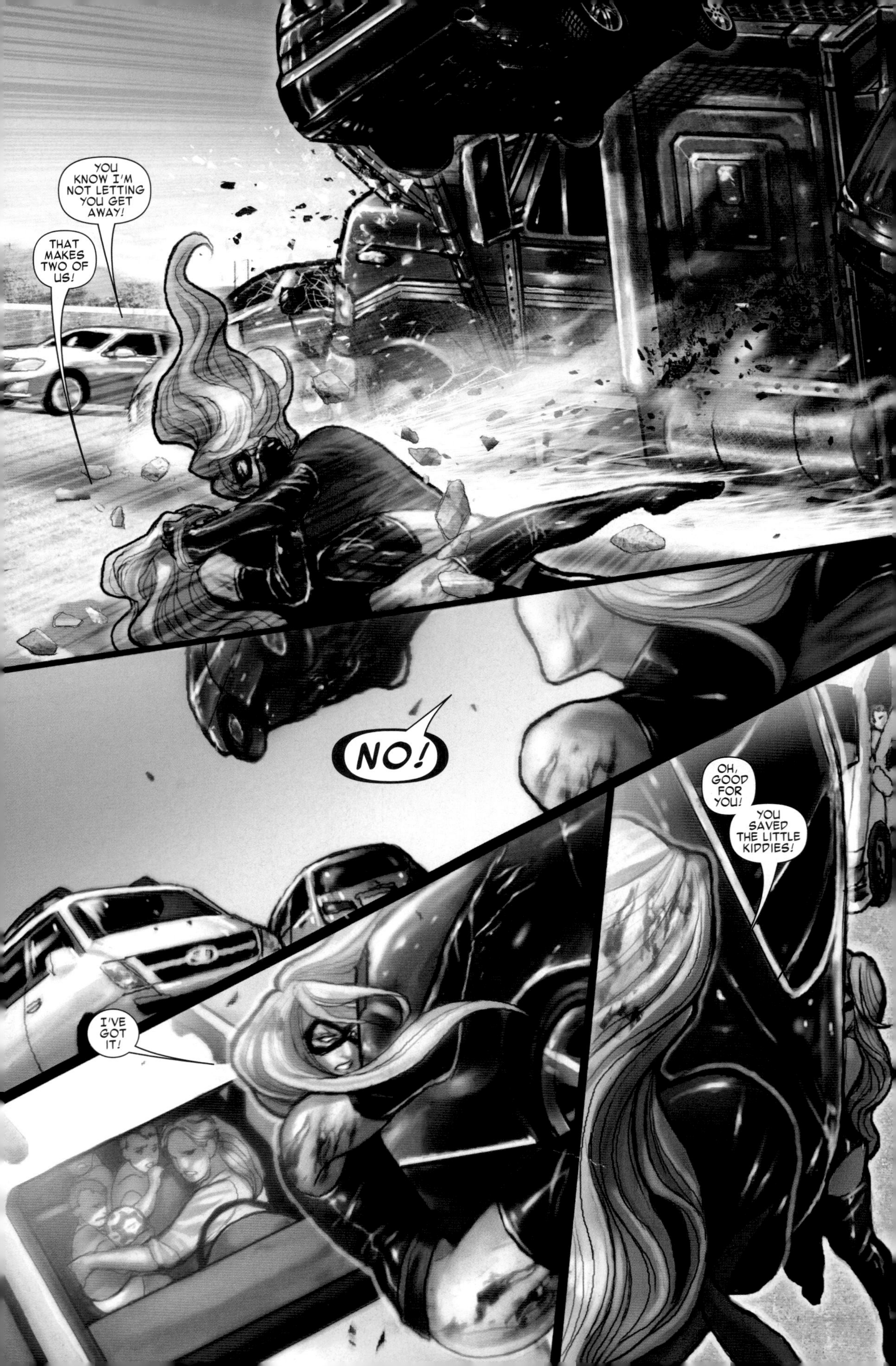
YOU KNOW I'M NOT LETTING YOU GET AWAY!
THAT MAKES TWO OF US!
NO!
OH, GOOD FOR YOU!
YOU SAVED THE LITTLE KIDDIES!
I'VE GOT IT!

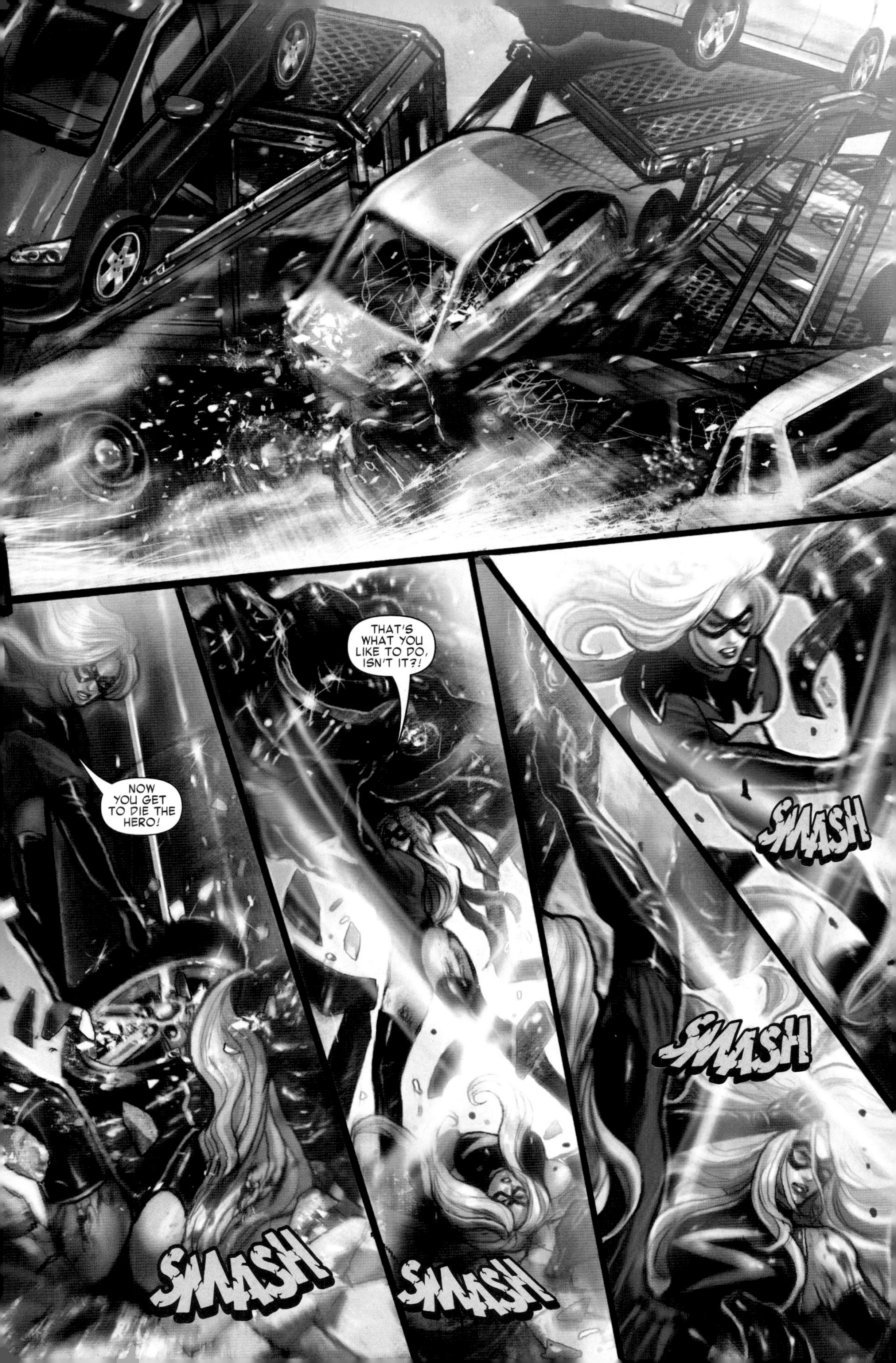
NOW YOU GET TO DIE THE HERO!
THAT'S WHAT YOU LIKE TO DO, ISN'T IT?!
SMASH
SMASH
SMASH
SMASH

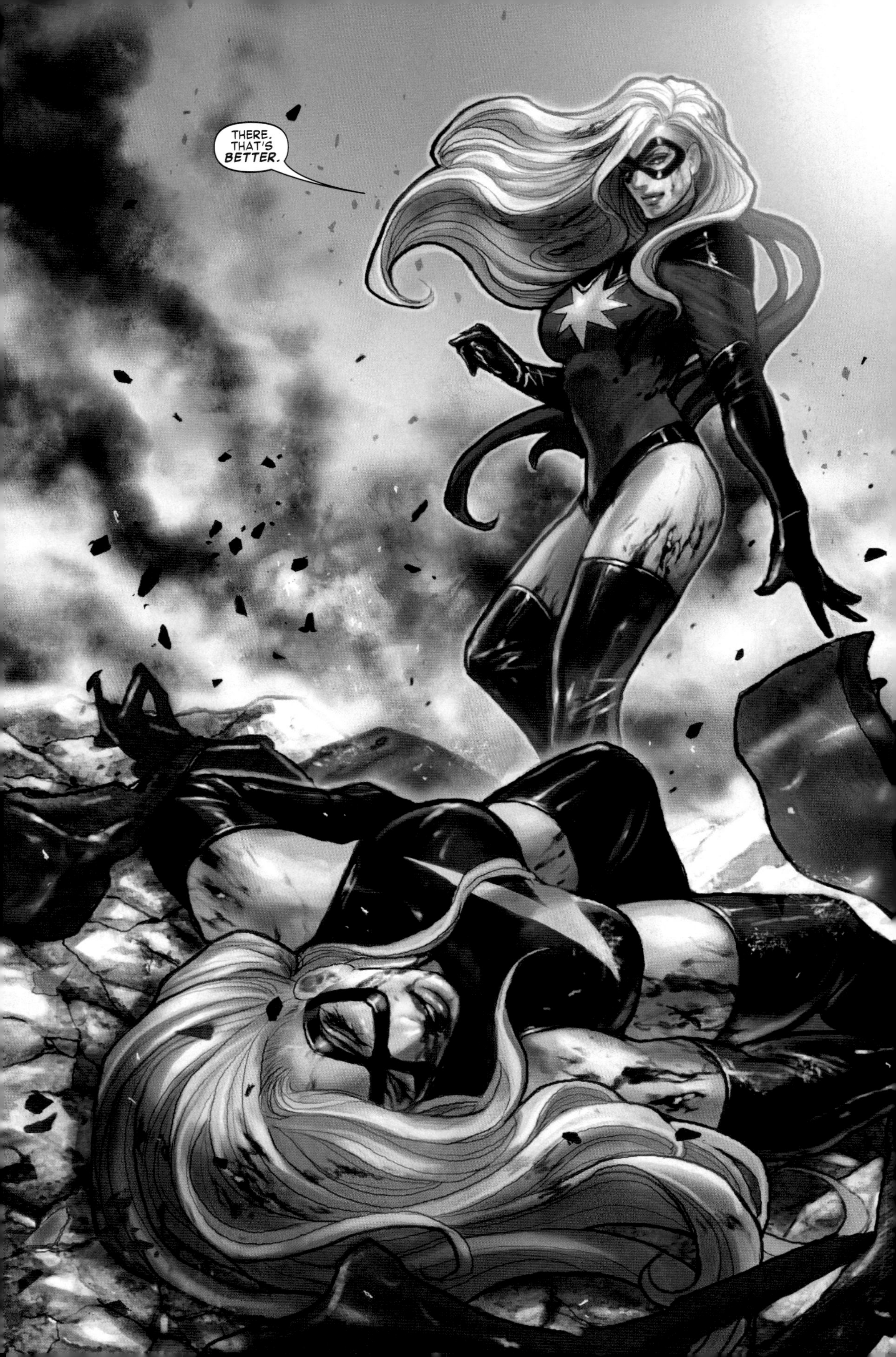
THERE. THAT'S BETTER.

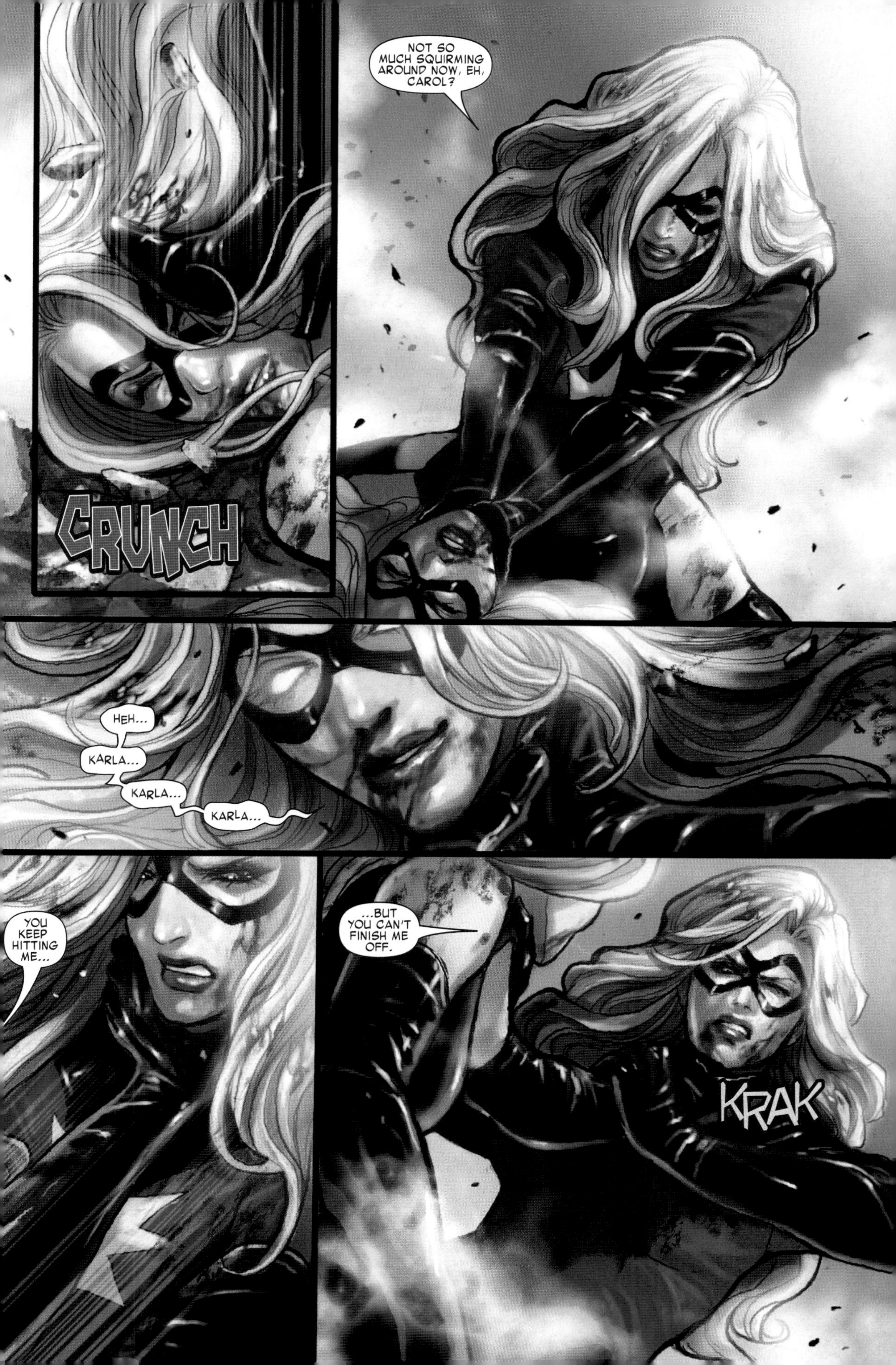
CRUNCH
NOT SO MUCH SQUIRMING AROUND NOW, EH, CAROL?
HEH...
KARLA...
KARLA...
KARLA...
YOU KEEP HITTING ME...
...BUT YOU CAN'T FINISH ME OFF.
KRAK

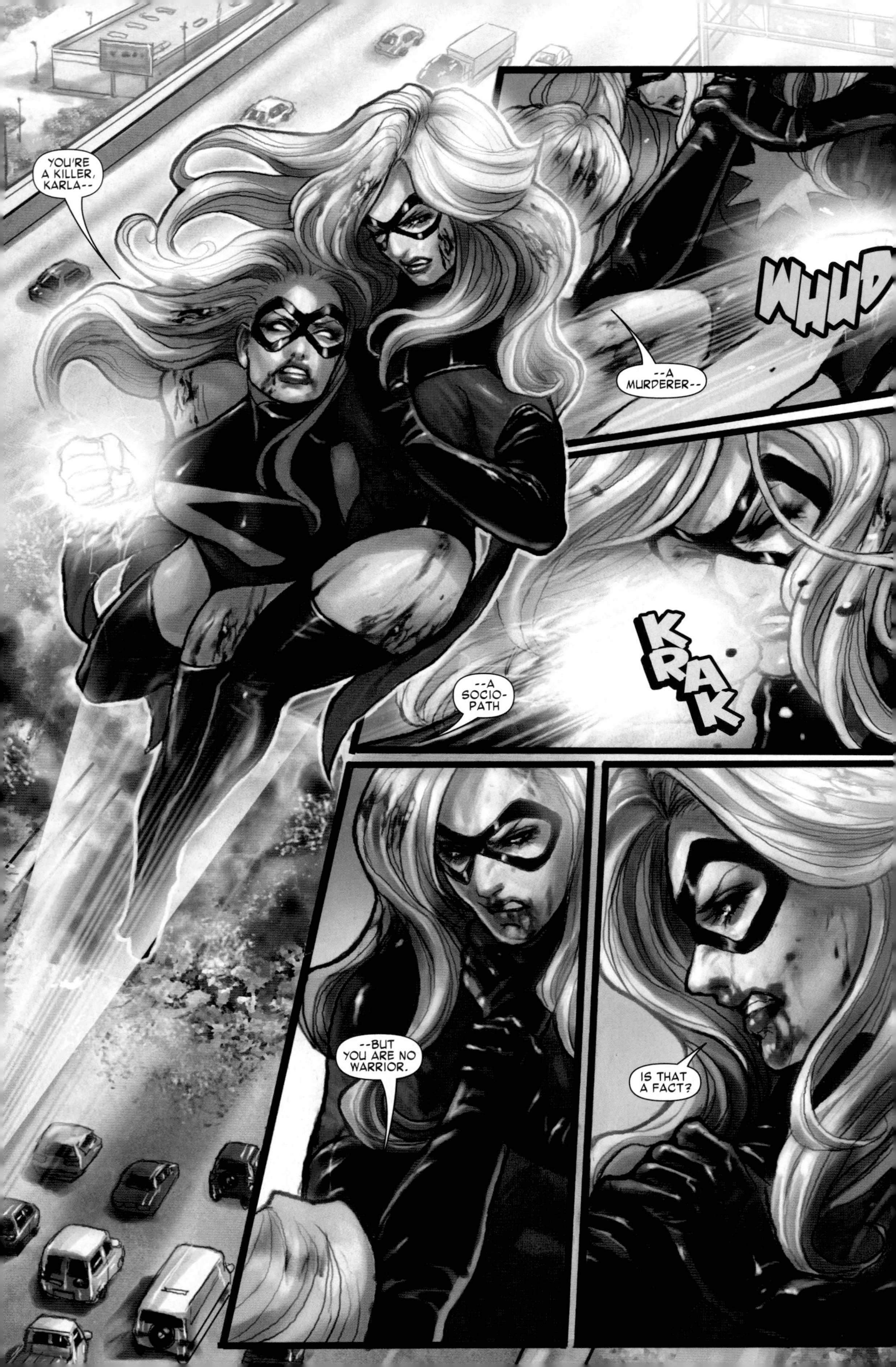
YOU'RE A KILLER, KARLA--
WHUD
--A MURDERER--
KRAK
--A SOCIO-PATH
--BUT YOU ARE NO WARRIOR.
IS THAT A FACT?

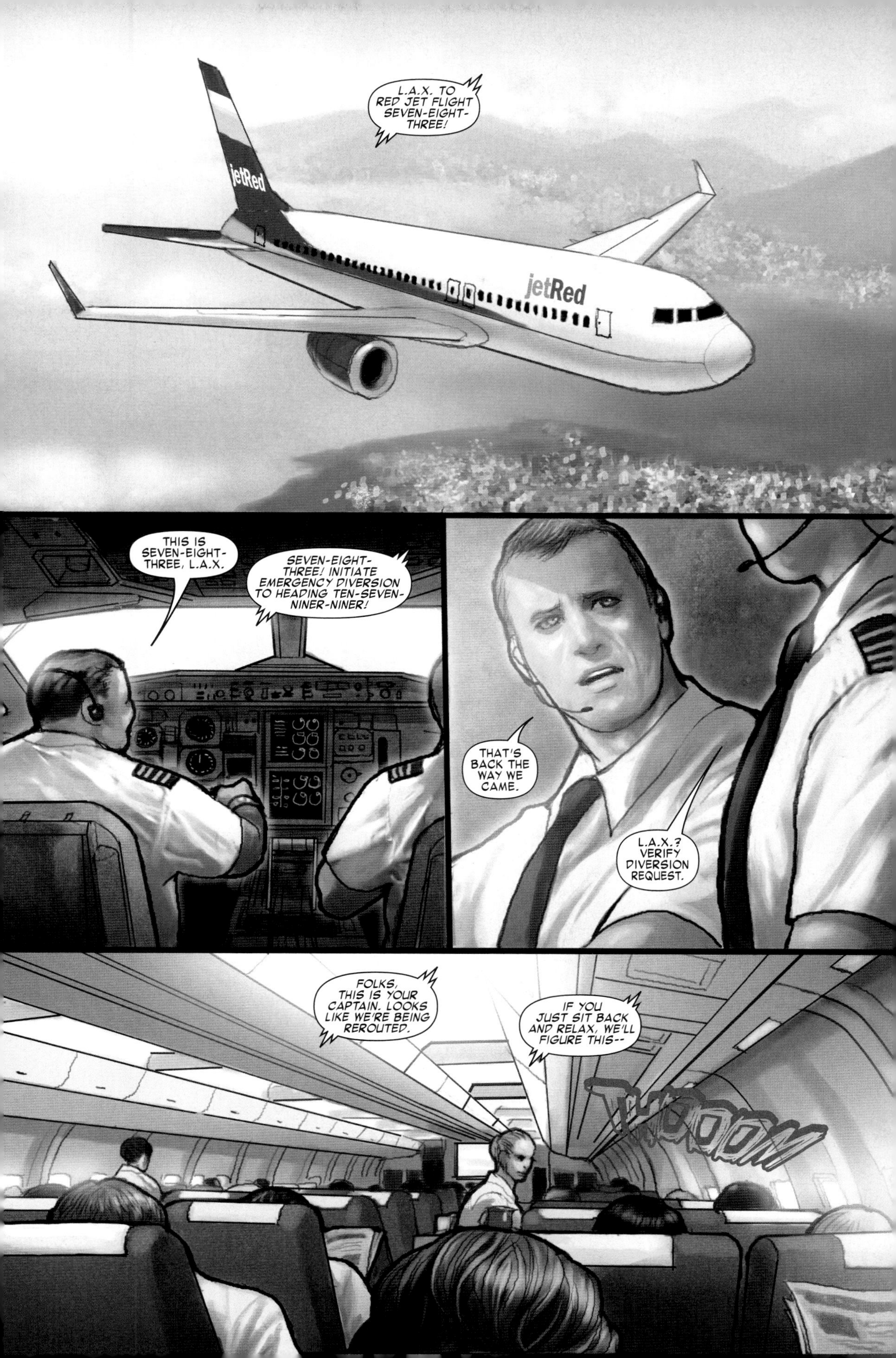
L.A.X. TO RED JET FLIGHT SEVEN-EIGHT-THREE!
jetRed
jetRed
THIS IS SEVEN-EIGHT-THREE, L.A.X.
SEVEN-EIGHT-THREE! INITIATE EMERGENCY DIVERSION TO HEADING TEN-SEVEN-NINER-NINER!
THAT'S BACK THE WAY WE CAME.
L.A.X.? VERIFY DIVERSION REQUEST.
FOLKS, THIS IS YOUR CAPTAIN. LOOKS LIKE WE'RE BEING REROUTED.
IF YOU JUST SIT BACK AND RELAX, WE'LL FIGURE THIS--
THOOOM

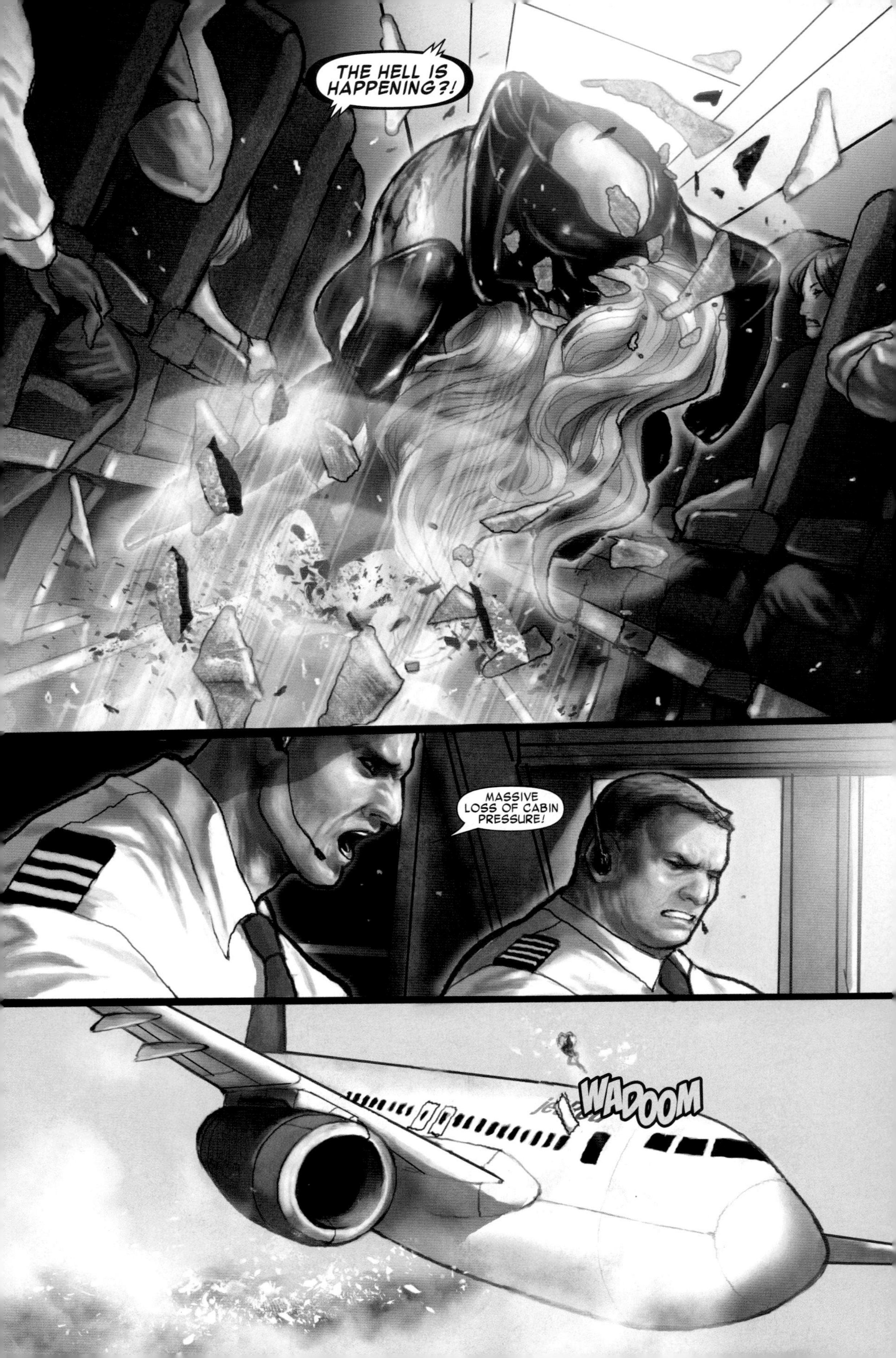
THE HELL IS HAPPENING?!
MASSIVE LOSS OF CABIN PRESSURE!
WADOOM

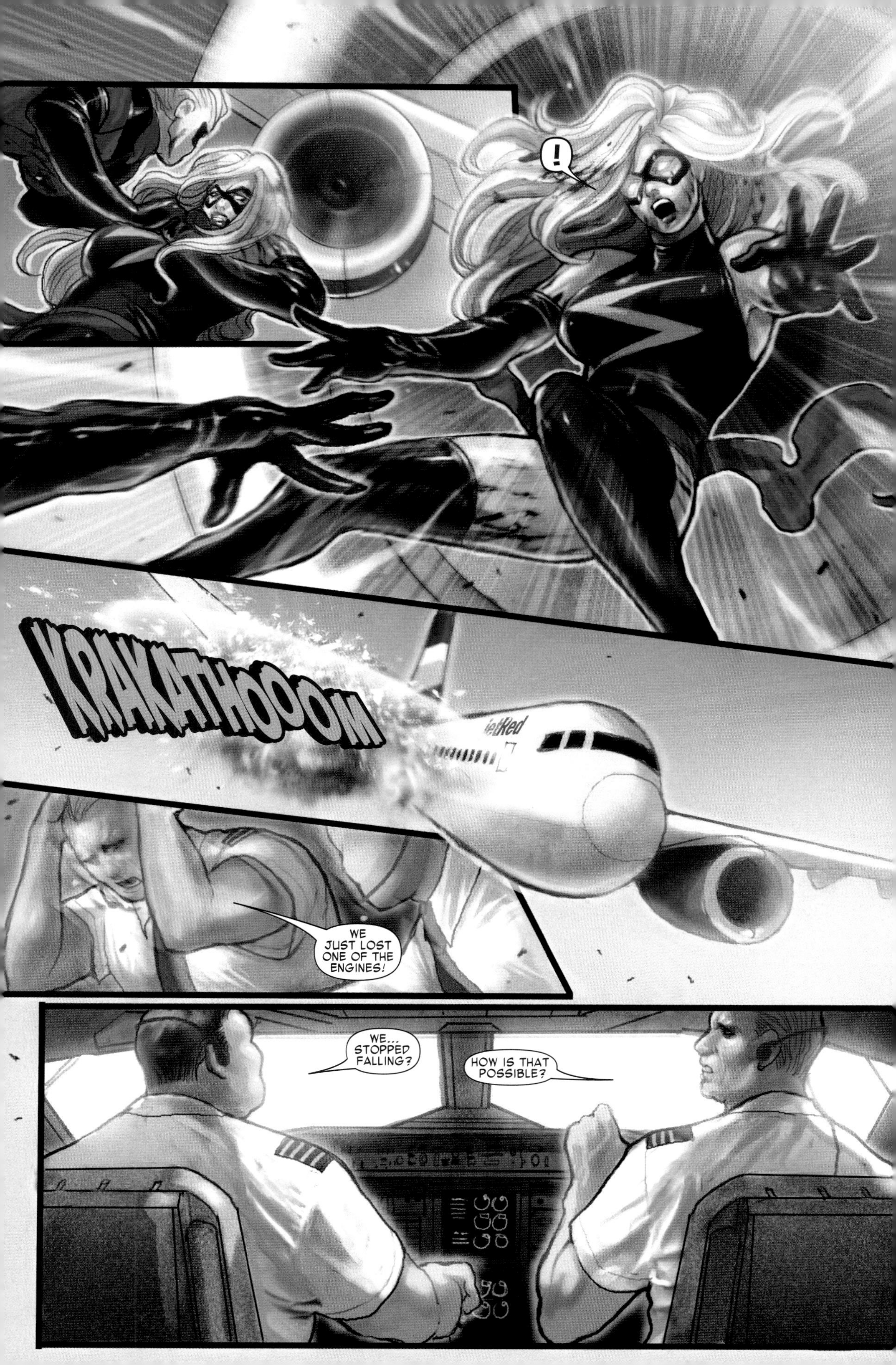
!
KRAKATHOOOOM
WE JUST LOST ONE OF THE ENGINES!
WE... STOPPED FALLING?
HOW IS THAT POSSIBLE?

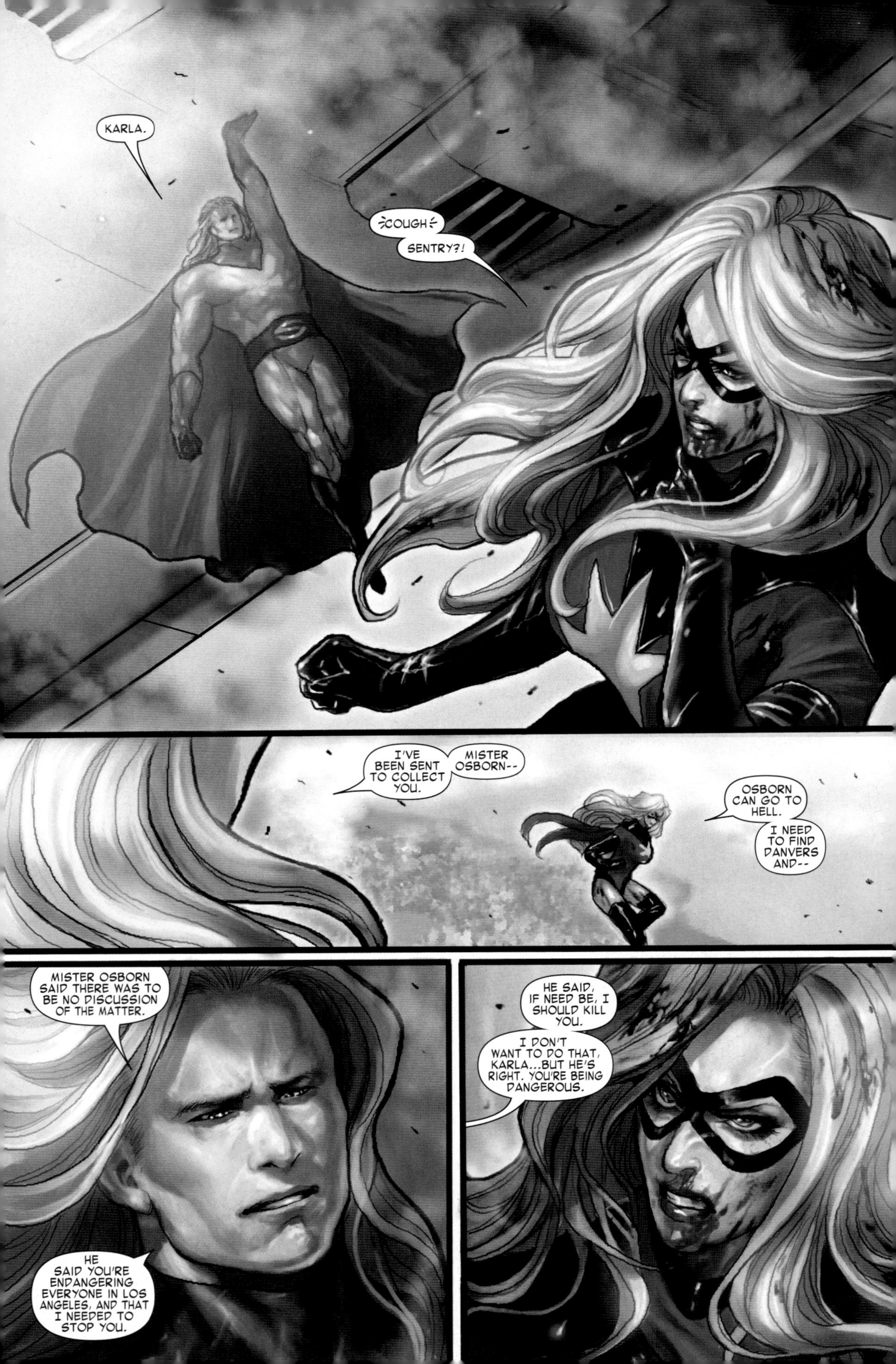
KARLA.
≈COUGH≈
SENTRY?!
MISTER OSBORN--
I'VE BEEN SENT TO COLLECT YOU.
OSBORN CAN GO TO HELL.
I NEED TO FIND DANVERS AND--
MISTER OSBORN SAID THERE WAS TO BE NO DISCUSSION OF THE MATTER.
HE SAID YOU'RE ENDANGERING EVERYONE IN LOS ANGELES, AND THAT I NEEDED TO STOP YOU.
HE SAID, IF NEED BE, I SHOULD KILL YOU.
I DON'T WANT TO DO THAT, KARLA...BUT HE'S RIGHT. YOU'RE BEING DANGEROUS.

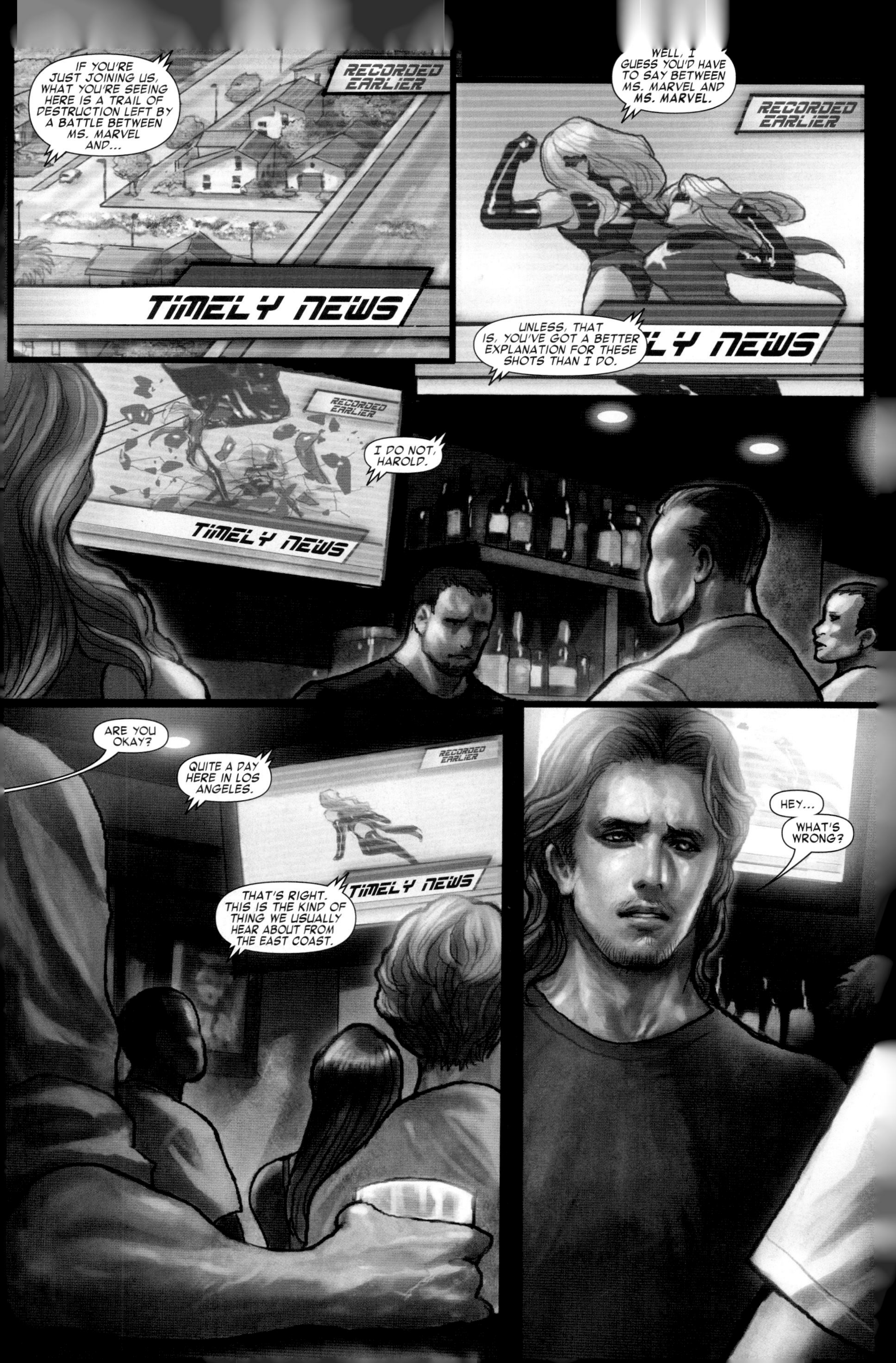
IF YOU'RE JUST JOINING US, WHAT YOU'RE SEEING HERE IS A TRAIL OF DESTRUCTION LEFT BY A BATTLE BETWEEN MS. MARVEL AND...
RECORDED EARLIER
TIMELY NEWS
WELL, I GUESS YOU'D HAVE TO SAY BETWEEN MS. MARVEL AND MS. MARVEL.
RECORDED EARLIER
UNLESS, THAT IS, YOU'VE GOT A BETTER EXPLANATION FOR THESE SHOTS THAN I DO.
RECORDED EARLIER
TIMELY NEWS
I DO NOT, HAROLD.
ARE YOU OKAY?
QUITE A DAY HERE IN LOS ANGELES.
RECORDED EARLIER
TIMELY NEWS
THAT'S RIGHT. THIS IS THE KIND OF THING WE USUALLY HEAR ABOUT FROM THE EAST COAST.
HEY...
WHAT'S WRONG?

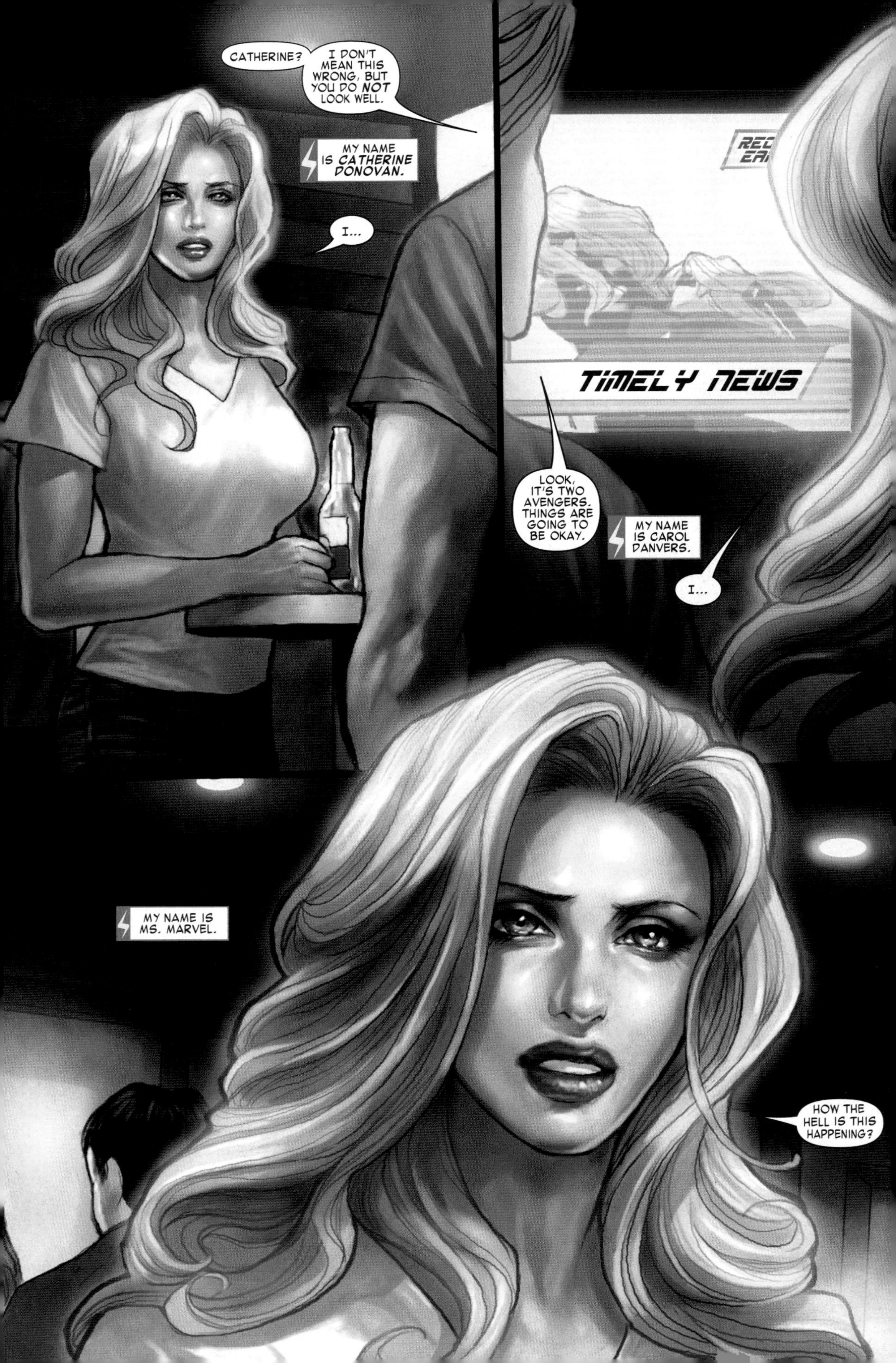
CATHERINE?
I DON'T MEAN THIS WRONG, BUT YOU DO NOT LOOK WELL.
MY NAME IS CATHERINE DONOVAN.
I...
TIMELY NEWS
LOOK, IT'S TWO AVENGERS. THINGS ARE GOING TO BE OKAY.
MY NAME IS CAROL DANVERS.
I...
MY NAME IS MS. MARVEL.
HOW THE HELL IS THIS HAPPENING?

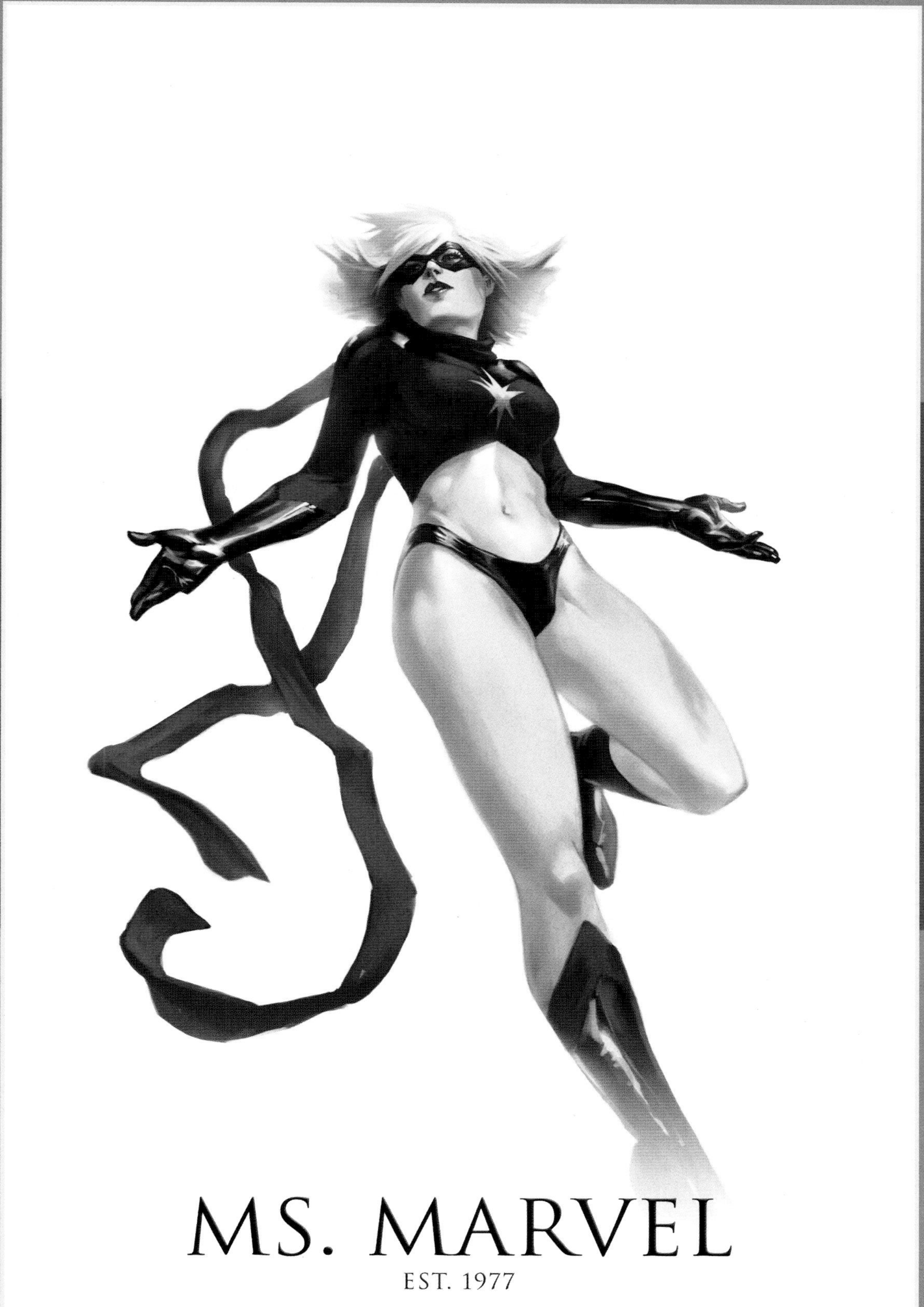
MS. MARVEL
EST. 1977

***MS. MARVEL* #45 70TH ANNIVERSARY VARIANT BY MARKO DJURDJEVIĆ**

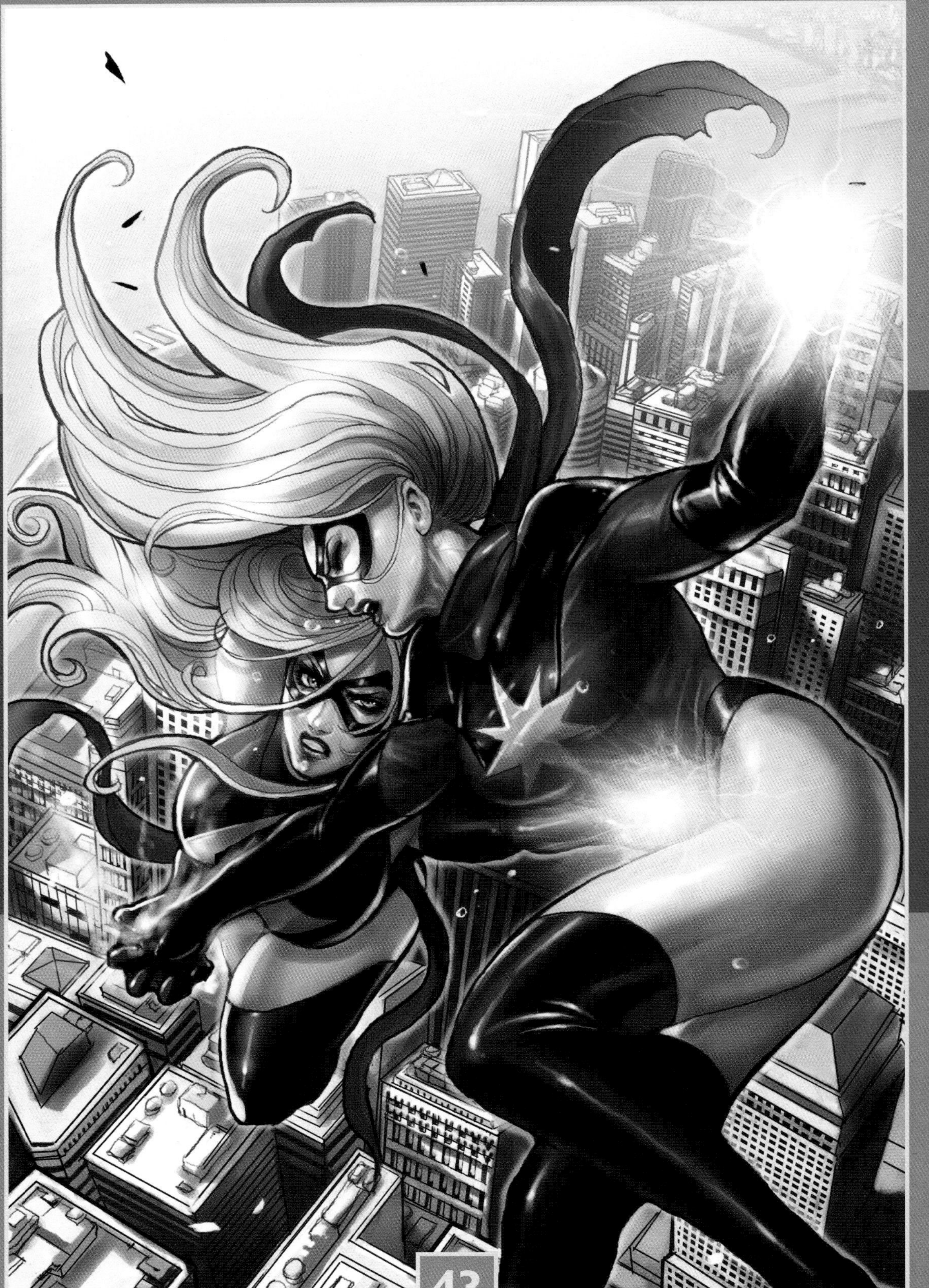

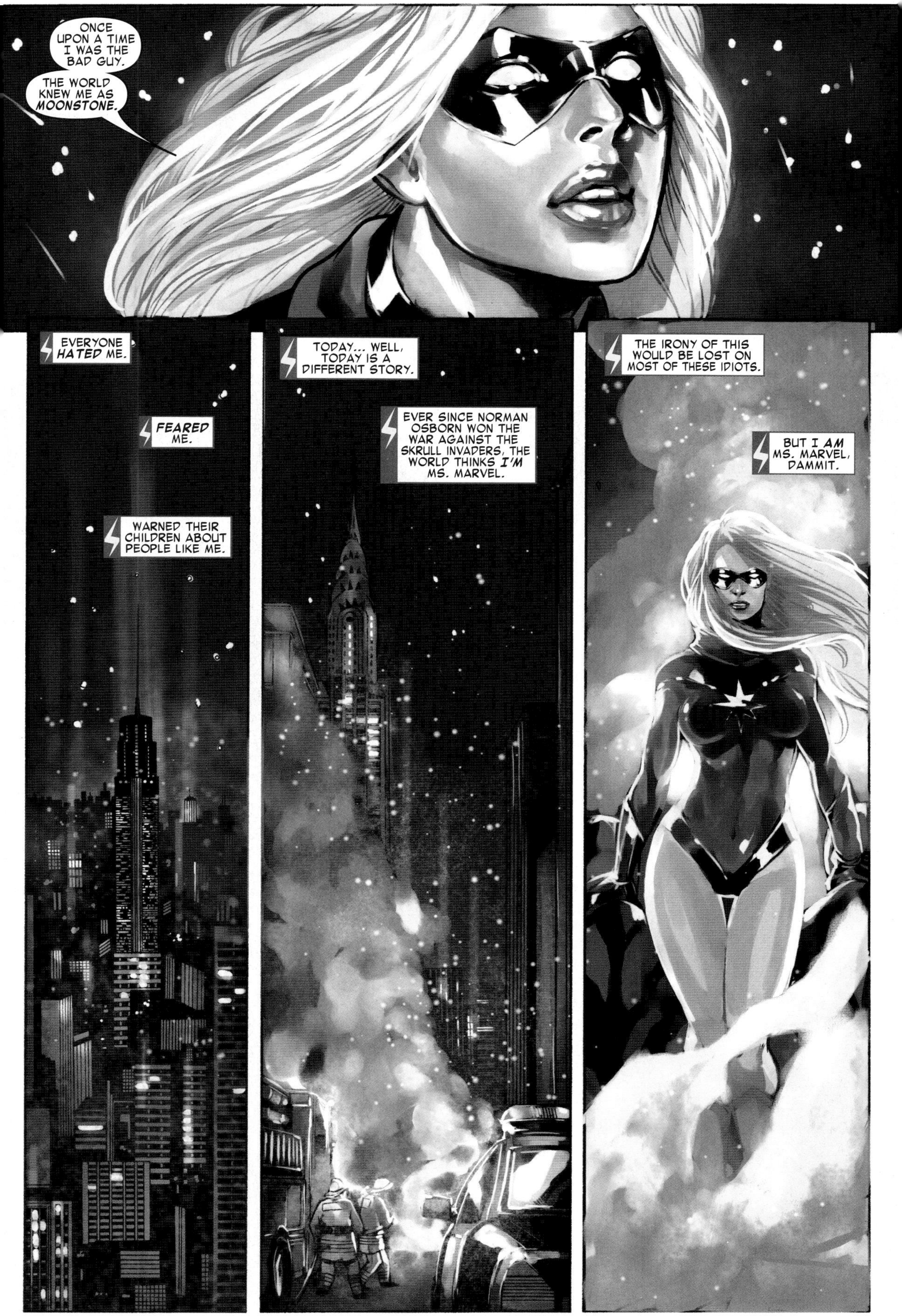

ONCE UPON A TIME I WAS THE BAD GUY.
THE WORLD KNEW ME AS MOONSTONE.
EVERYONE HATED ME.
FEARED ME.
WARNED THEIR CHILDREN ABOUT PEOPLE LIKE ME.
TODAY... WELL, TODAY IS A DIFFERENT STORY.
EVER SINCE NORMAN OSBORN WON THE WAR AGAINST THE SKRULL INVADERS, THE WORLD THINKS I'M MS. MARVEL.
THE IRONY OF THIS WOULD BE LOST ON MOST OF THESE IDIOTS.
BUT I AM MS. MARVEL, DAMMIT.

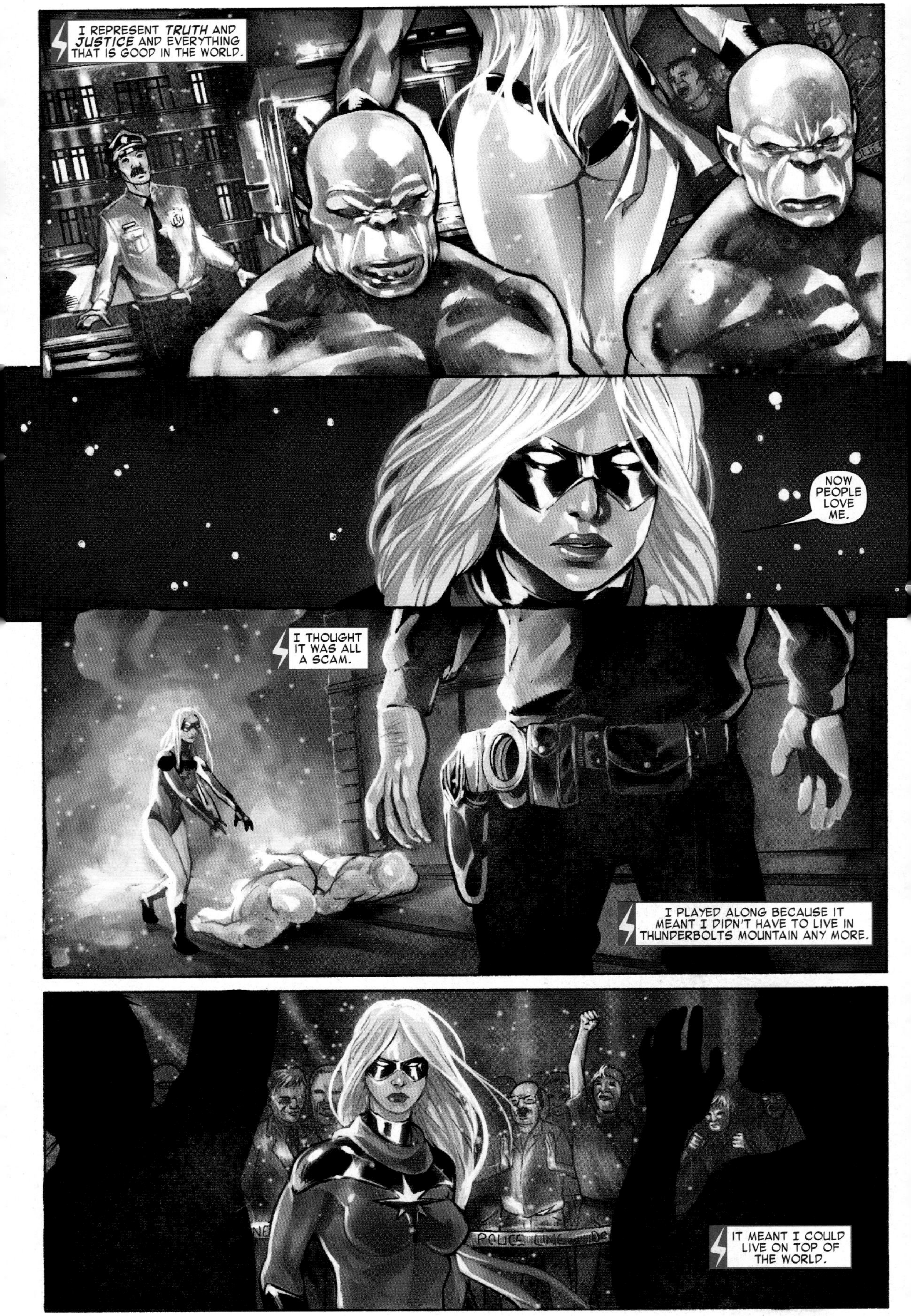
I REPRESENT TRUTH AND JUSTICE AND EVERYTHING THAT IS GOOD IN THE WORLD.
NOW PEOPLE LOVE ME.
I THOUGHT IT WAS ALL A SCAM.
I PLAYED ALONG BECAUSE IT MEANT I DIDN'T HAVE TO LIVE IN THUNDERBOLTS MOUNTAIN ANY MORE.
IT MEANT I COULD LIVE ON TOP OF THE WORLD.

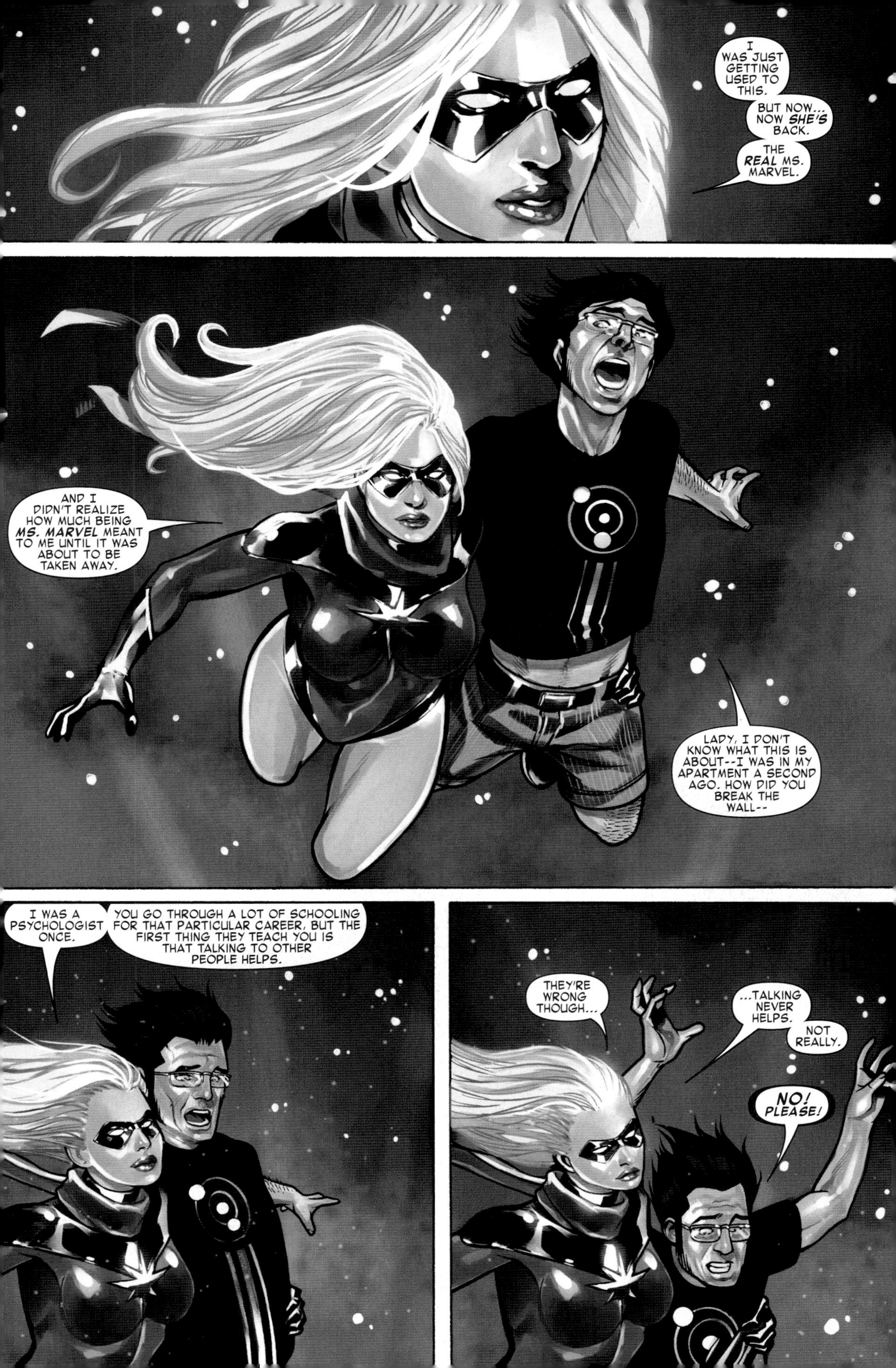
I WAS JUST GETTING USED TO THIS.
BUT NOW... NOW SHE'S BACK.
THE REAL MS. MARVEL.
AND I DIDN'T REALIZE HOW MUCH BEING MS. MARVEL MEANT TO ME UNTIL IT WAS ABOUT TO BE TAKEN AWAY.
LADY, I DON'T KNOW WHAT THIS IS ABOUT--I WAS IN MY APARTMENT A SECOND AGO. HOW DID YOU BREAK THE WALL--
I WAS A PSYCHOLOGIST ONCE.
YOU GO THROUGH A LOT OF SCHOOLING FOR THAT PARTICULAR CAREER, BUT THE FIRST THING THEY TEACH YOU IS THAT TALKING TO OTHER PEOPLE HELPS.
THEY'RE WRONG THOUGH...
...TALKING NEVER HELPS.
NOT REALLY.
NO! PLEASE!

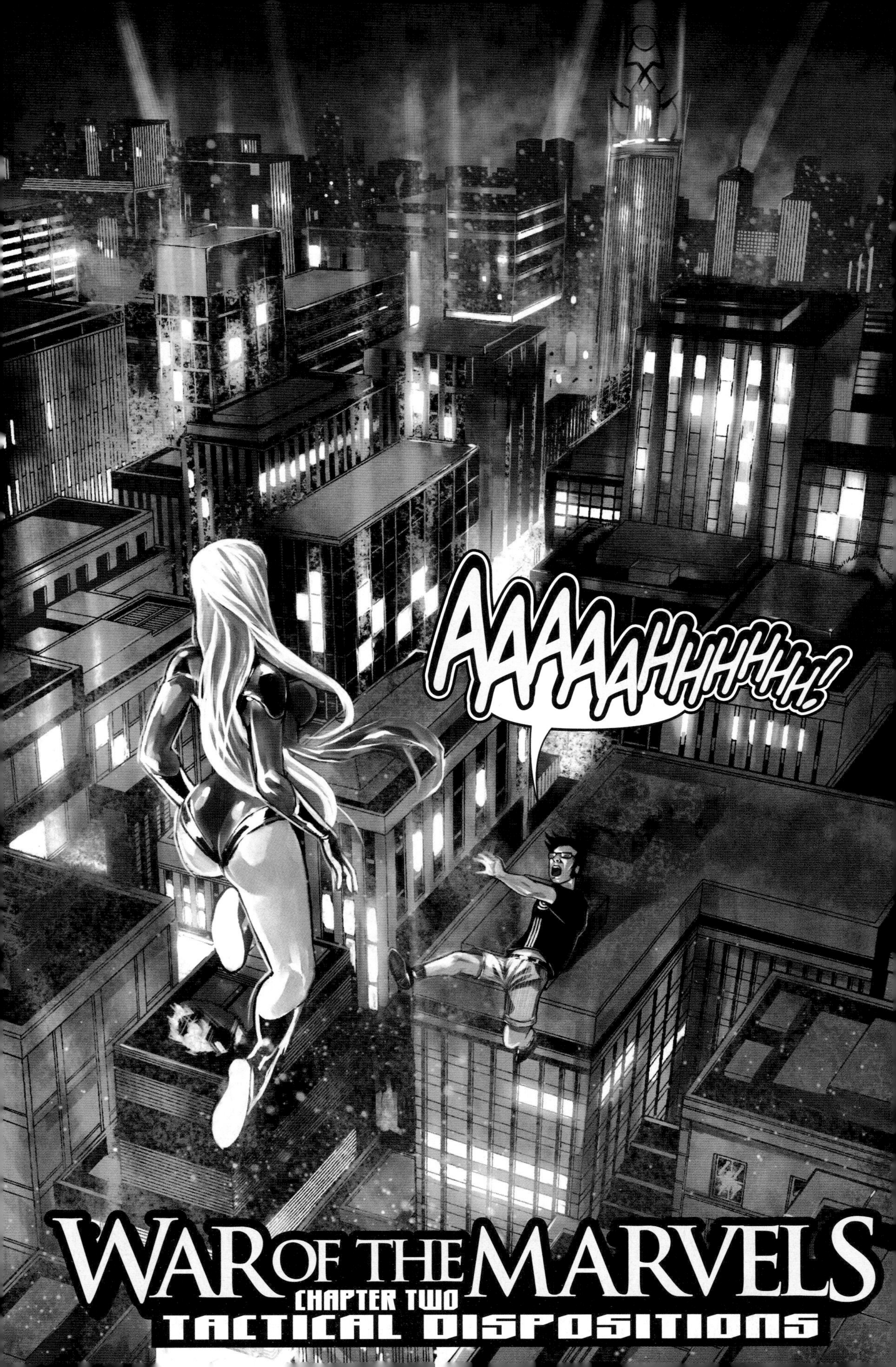
AAAAAHHHHHH!
WAR OF THE MARVELS
CHAPTER TWO
TACTICAL DISPOSITIONS

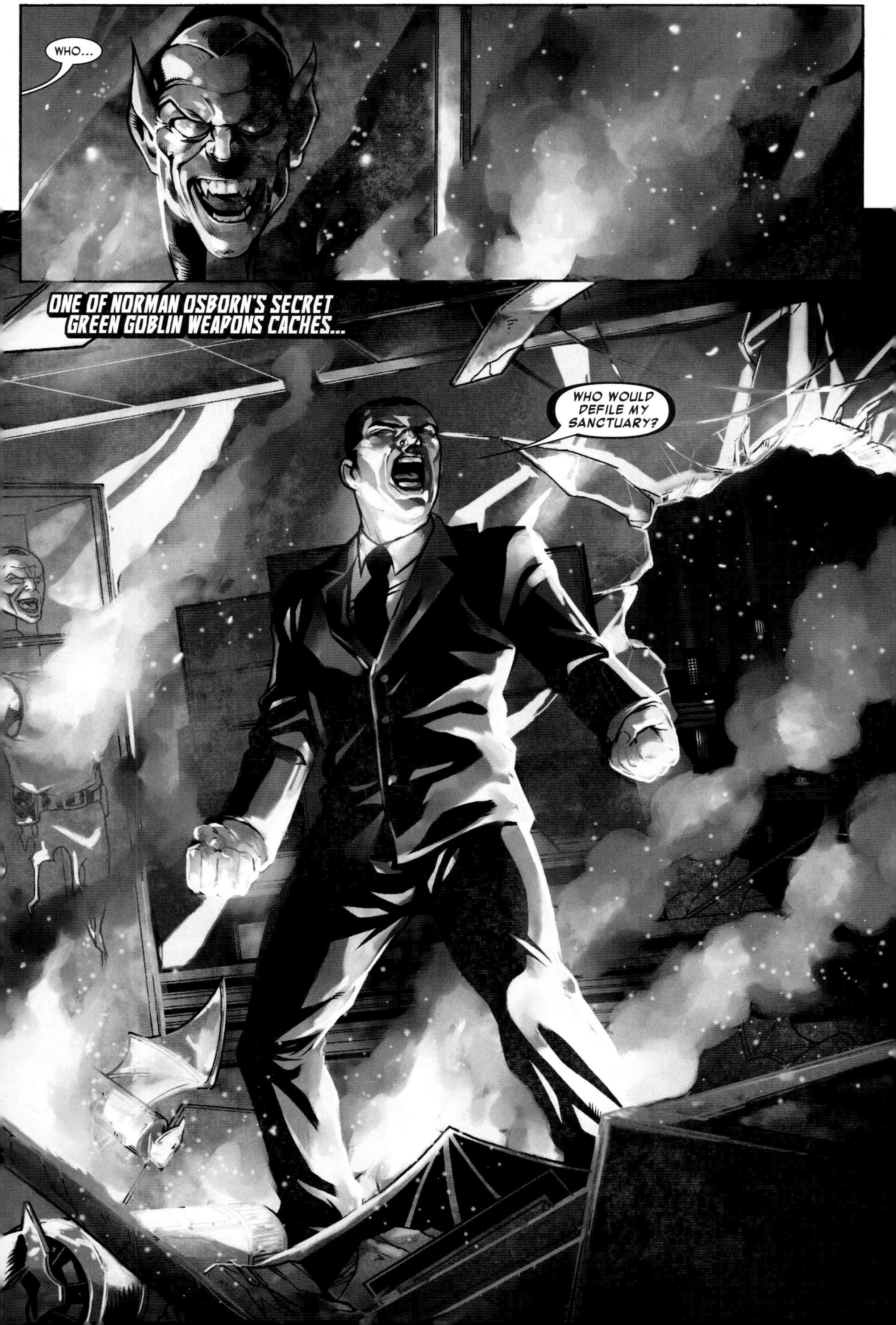
WHO...
ONE OF NORMAN OSBORN'S SECRET GREEN GOBLIN WEAPONS CACHES...
WHO WOULD DEFILE MY SANCTUARY?

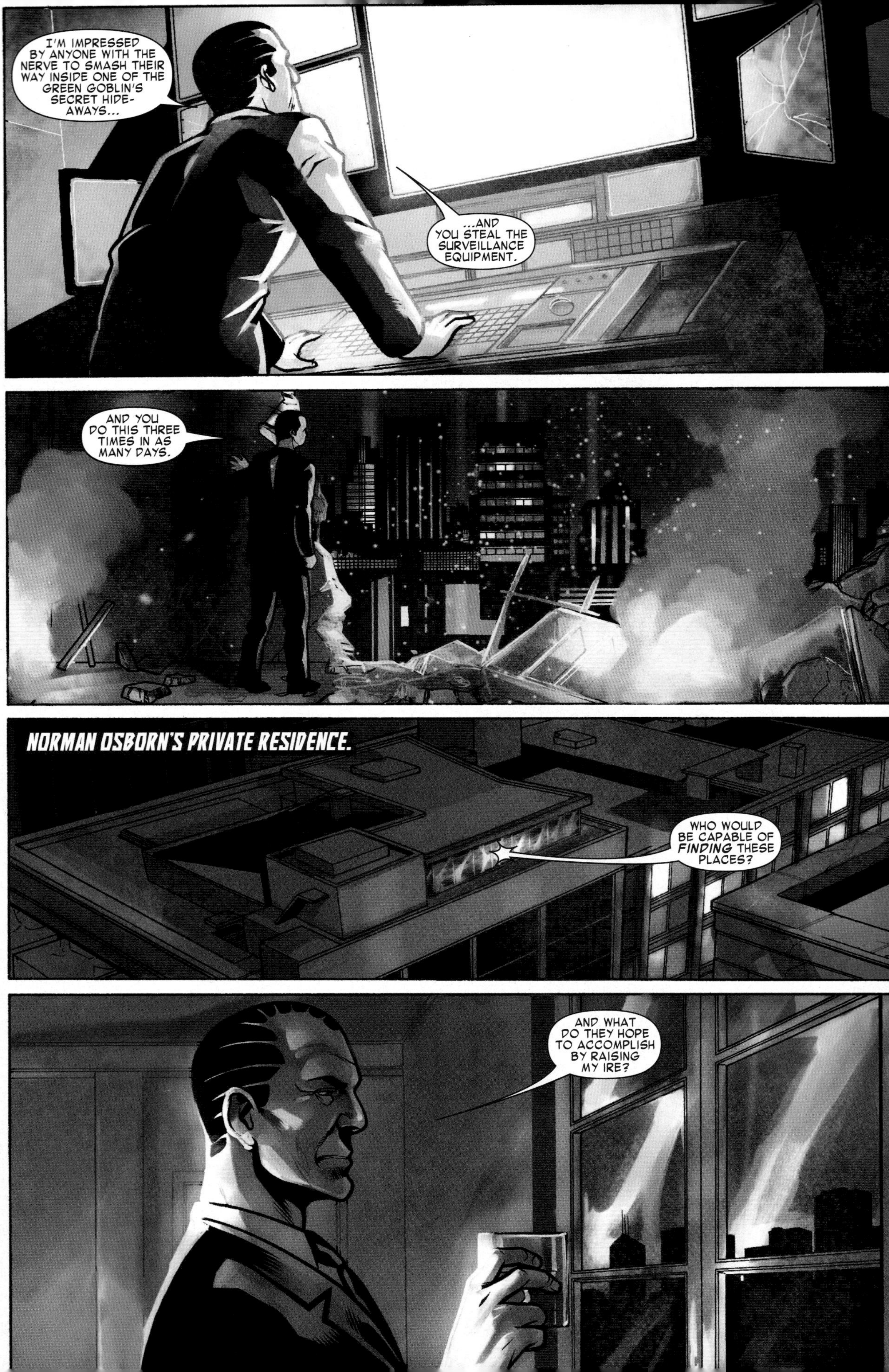
I'M IMPRESSED BY ANYONE WITH THE NERVE TO SMASH THEIR WAY INSIDE ONE OF THE GREEN GOBLIN'S SECRET HIDE-AWAYS...
...AND YOU STEAL THE SURVEILLANCE EQUIPMENT.
AND YOU DO THIS THREE TIMES IN AS MANY DAYS.
NORMAN OSBORN'S PRIVATE RESIDENCE.
WHO WOULD BE CAPABLE OF FINDING THESE PLACES?
AND WHAT DO THEY HOPE TO ACCOMPLISH BY RAISING MY IRE?

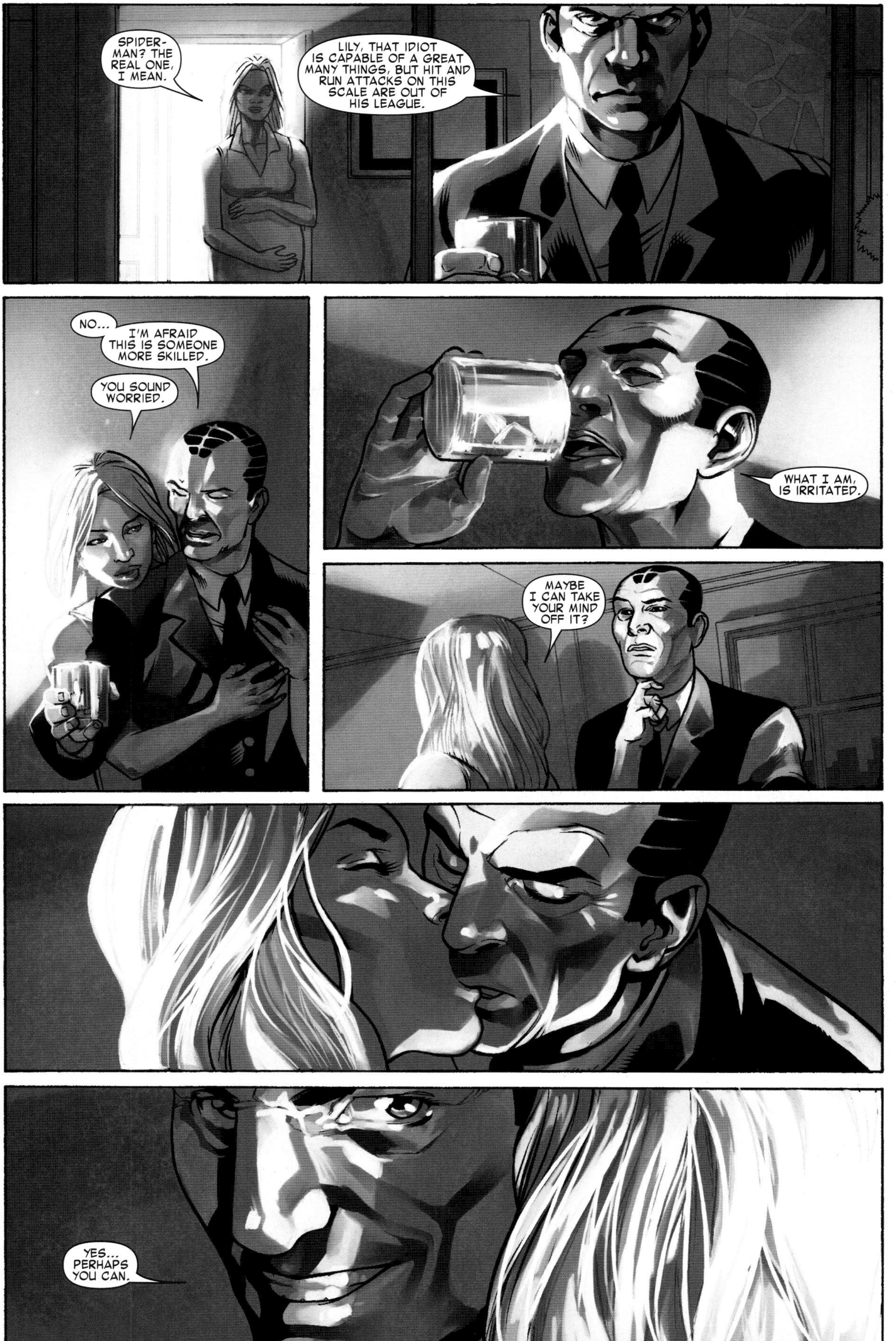
SPIDER-MAN? THE REAL ONE, I MEAN.
LILY, THAT IDIOT IS CAPABLE OF A GREAT MANY THINGS, BUT HIT AND RUN ATTACKS ON THIS SCALE ARE OUT OF HIS LEAGUE.
NO... I'M AFRAID THIS IS SOMEONE MORE SKILLED.
YOU SOUND WORRIED.
WHAT I AM, IS IRRITATED.
MAYBE I CAN TAKE YOUR MIND OFF IT?
YES... PERHAPS YOU CAN.

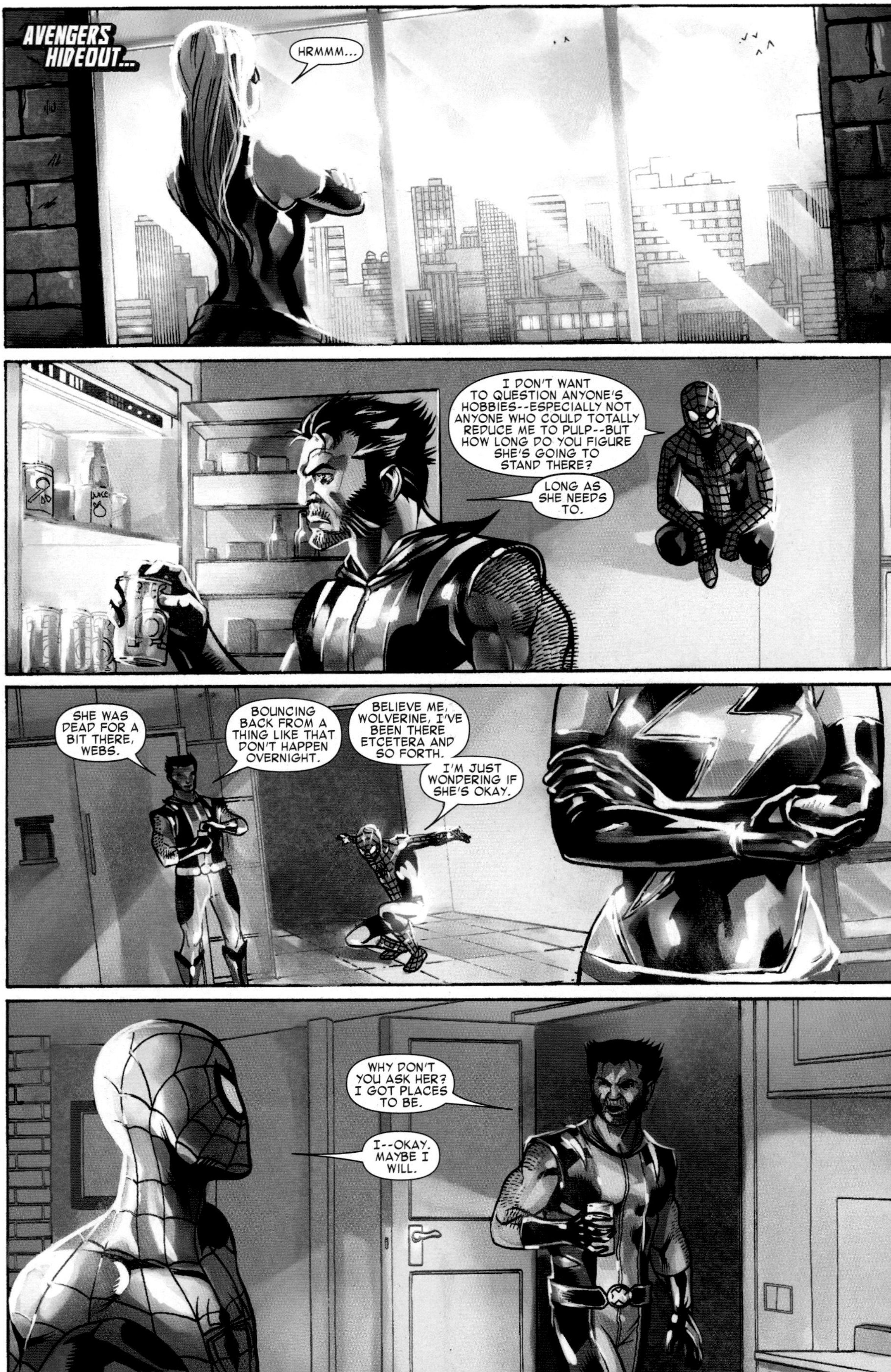
AVENGERS HIDEOUT...
HRMMM...
I DON'T WANT TO QUESTION ANYONE'S HOBBIES--ESPECIALLY NOT ANYONE WHO COULD TOTALLY REDUCE ME TO PULP--BUT HOW LONG DO YOU FIGURE SHE'S GOING TO STAND THERE?
LONG AS SHE NEEDS TO.
SHE WAS DEAD FOR A BIT THERE, WEBS.
BOUNCING BACK FROM A THING LIKE THAT DON'T HAPPEN OVERNIGHT.
BELIEVE ME, WOLVERINE, I'VE BEEN THERE ETCETERA AND SO FORTH.
I'M JUST WONDERING IF SHE'S OKAY.
WHY DON'T YOU ASK HER? I GOT PLACES TO BE.
I--OKAY. MAYBE I WILL.

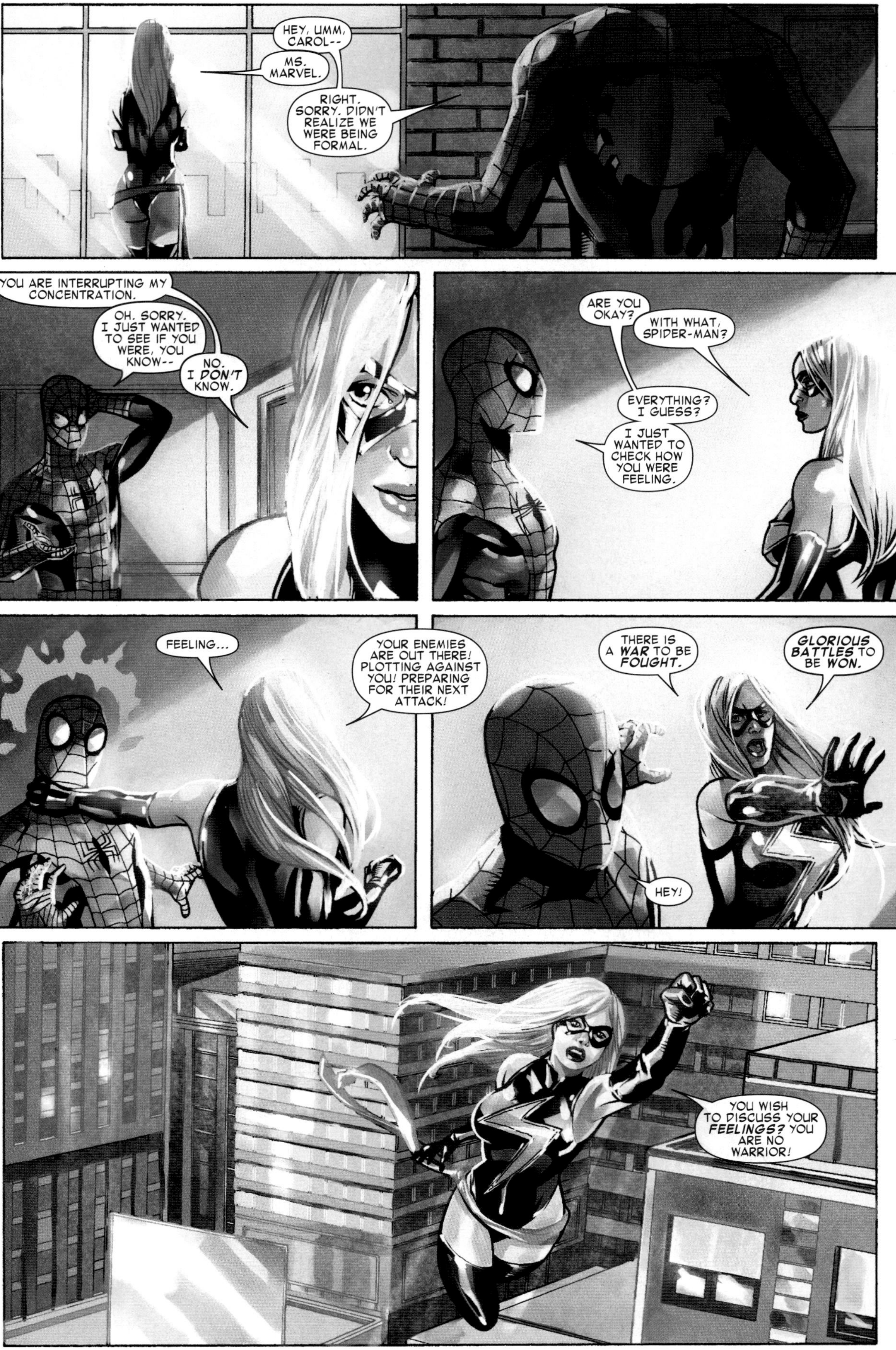
HEY, UMM, CAROL--
MS. MARVEL.
RIGHT. SORRY. DIDN'T REALIZE WE WERE BEING FORMAL.
YOU ARE INTERRUPTING MY CONCENTRATION.
OH. SORRY. I JUST WANTED TO SEE IF YOU WERE, YOU KNOW--
NO. I *DON'T* KNOW.
ARE YOU OKAY?
WITH WHAT, SPIDER-MAN?
EVERYTHING? I GUESS?
I JUST WANTED TO CHECK HOW YOU WERE FEELING.
FEELING...
YOUR ENEMIES ARE OUT THERE! PLOTTING AGAINST YOU! PREPARING FOR THEIR NEXT ATTACK!
THERE IS A *WAR* TO BE *FOUGHT.*
GLORIOUS BATTLES TO BE *WON.*
HEY!
YOU WISH TO DISCUSS YOUR *FEELINGS?* YOU ARE NO WARRIOR!

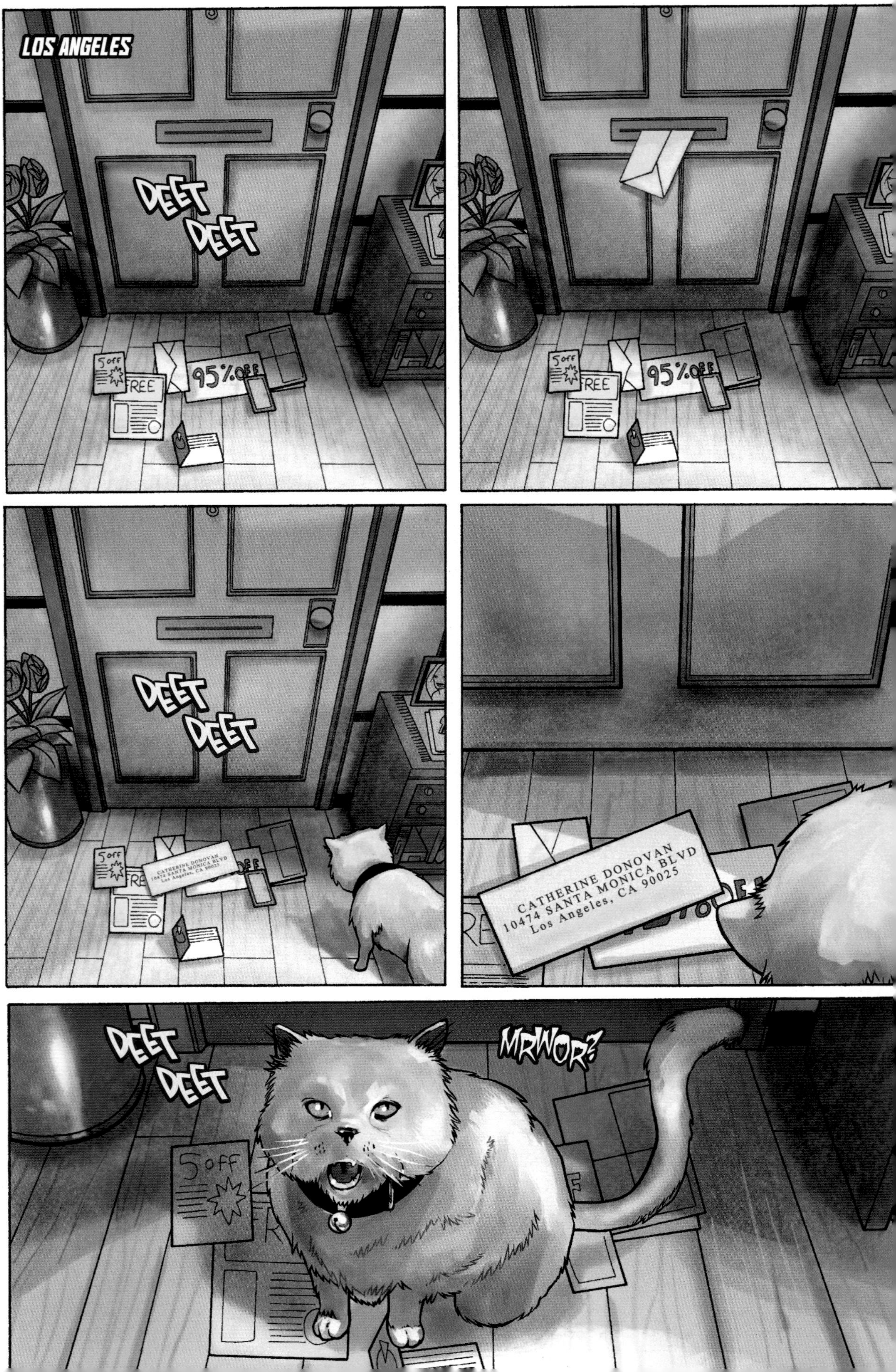
LOS ANGELES
DEET DEET
95% OFF
5 OFF
FREE
DEET DEET
CATHERINE DONOVAN
10474 SANTA MONICA BLVD
Los Angeles, CA 90025
DEET DEET
MRWOR?

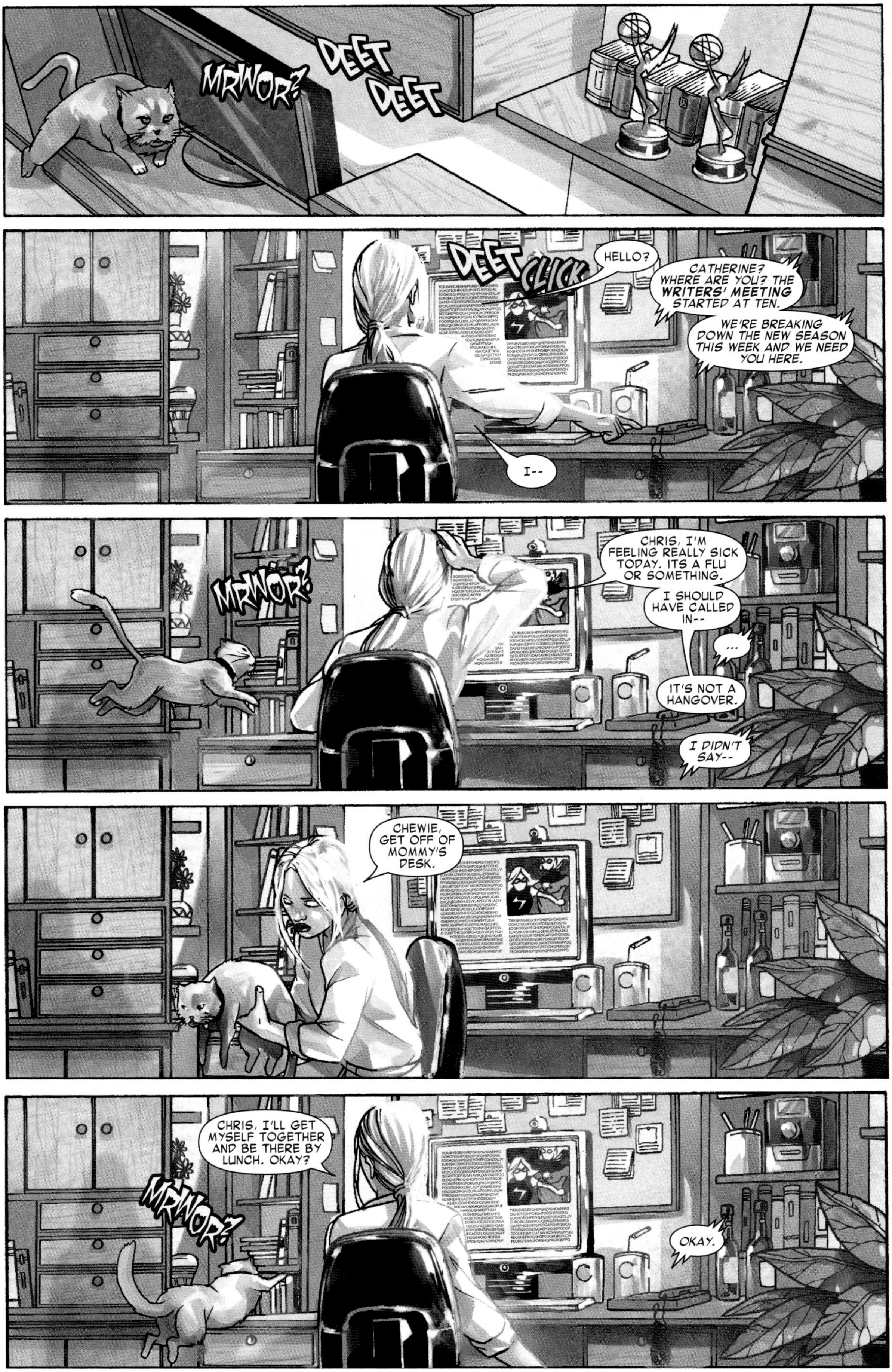
MRWOR?
DEET DEET
DEET
CLICK
HELLO?
CATHERINE? WHERE ARE YOU? THE WRITERS' MEETING STARTED AT TEN.
WE'RE BREAKING DOWN THE NEW SEASON THIS WEEK AND WE NEED YOU HERE.
I--
MRWOR?
CHRIS, I'M FEELING REALLY SICK TODAY. ITS A FLU OR SOMETHING.
I SHOULD HAVE CALLED IN--
...
IT'S NOT A HANGOVER.
I DIDN'T SAY--
CHEWIE, GET OFF OF MOMMY'S DESK.
CHRIS, I'LL GET MYSELF TOGETHER AND BE THERE BY LUNCH. OKAY?
MRWOR?
OKAY.

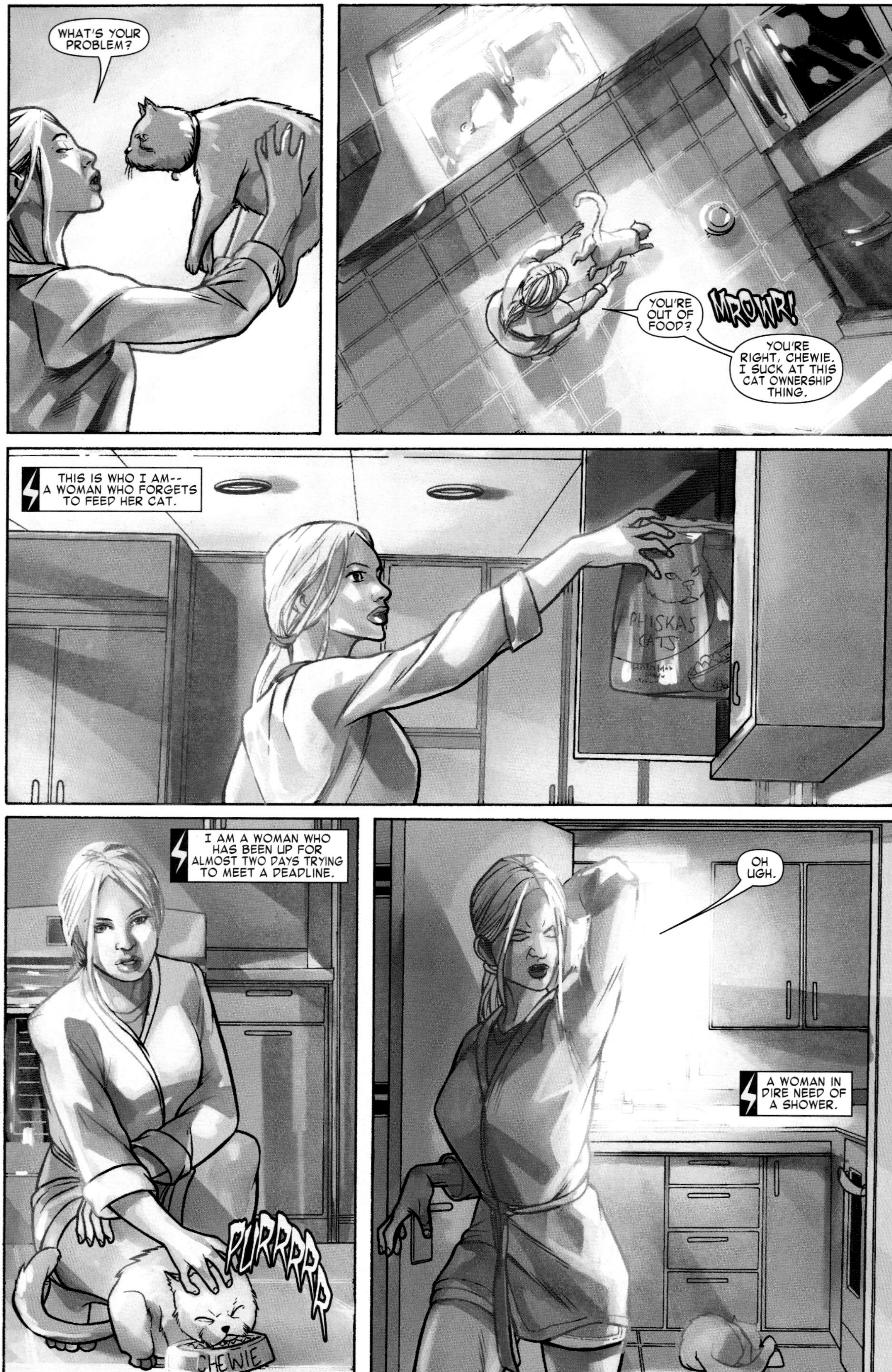
WHAT'S YOUR PROBLEM?
YOU'RE OUT OF FOOD?
MROWR!
YOU'RE RIGHT, CHEWIE. I SUCK AT THIS CAT OWNERSHIP THING.
THIS IS WHO I AM-- A WOMAN WHO FORGETS TO FEED HER CAT.
PHISKAS CATS
I AM A WOMAN WHO HAS BEEN UP FOR ALMOST TWO DAYS TRYING TO MEET A DEADLINE.
PURRRRRR
CHEWIE
OH UGH.
A WOMAN IN DIRE NEED OF A SHOWER.

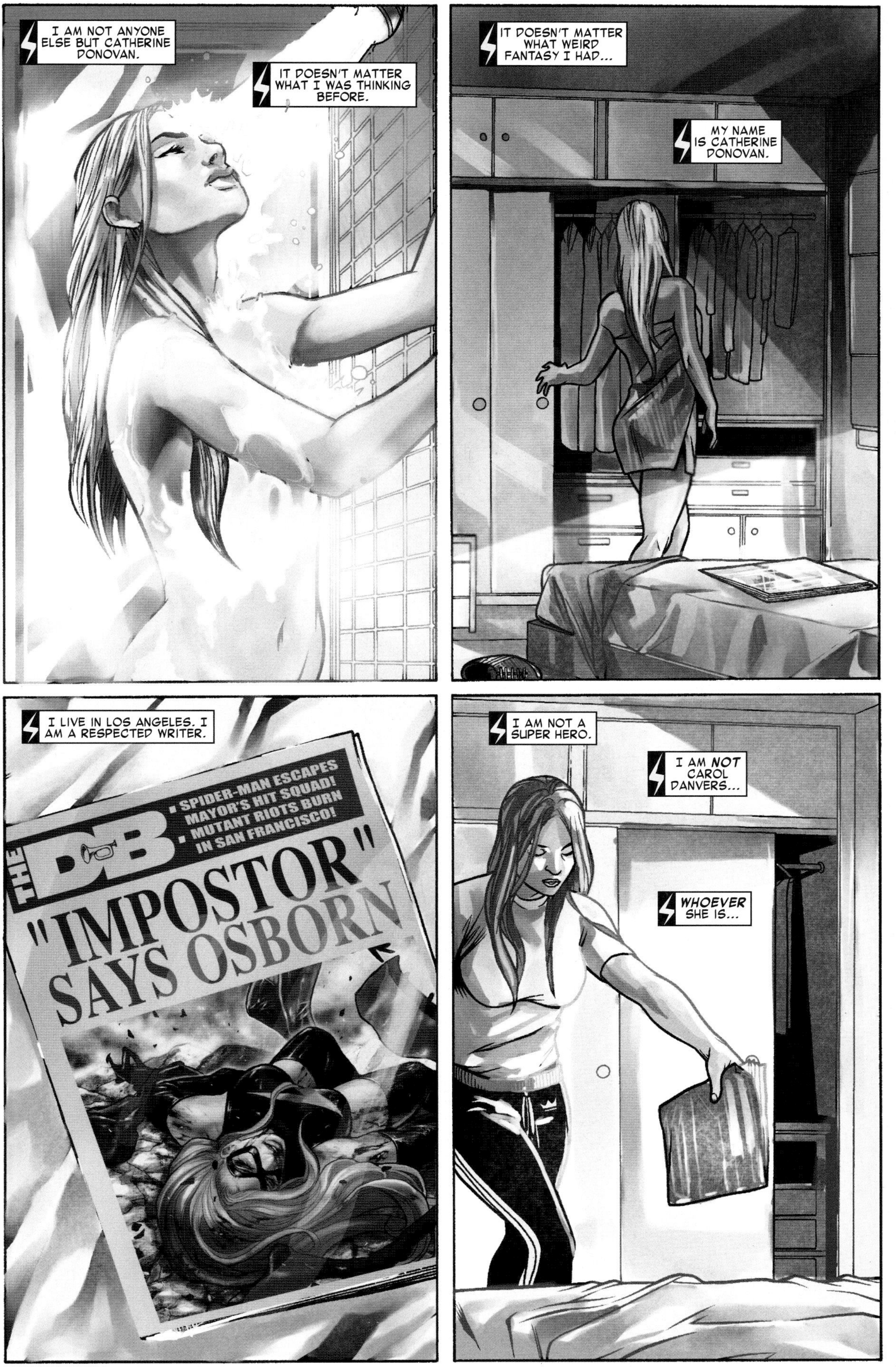
I AM NOT ANYONE ELSE BUT CATHERINE DONOVAN.
IT DOESN'T MATTER WHAT I WAS THINKING BEFORE.
IT DOESN'T MATTER WHAT WEIRD FANTASY I HAD...
MY NAME IS CATHERINE DONOVAN.
I LIVE IN LOS ANGELES. I AM A RESPECTED WRITER.
THE DB
• SPIDER-MAN ESCAPES MAYOR'S HIT SQUAD!
• MUTANT RIOTS BURN IN SAN FRANCISCO!
"IMPOSTOR" SAYS OSBORN
I AM NOT A SUPER HERO.
I AM *NOT* CAROL DANVERS...
WHOEVER SHE IS...

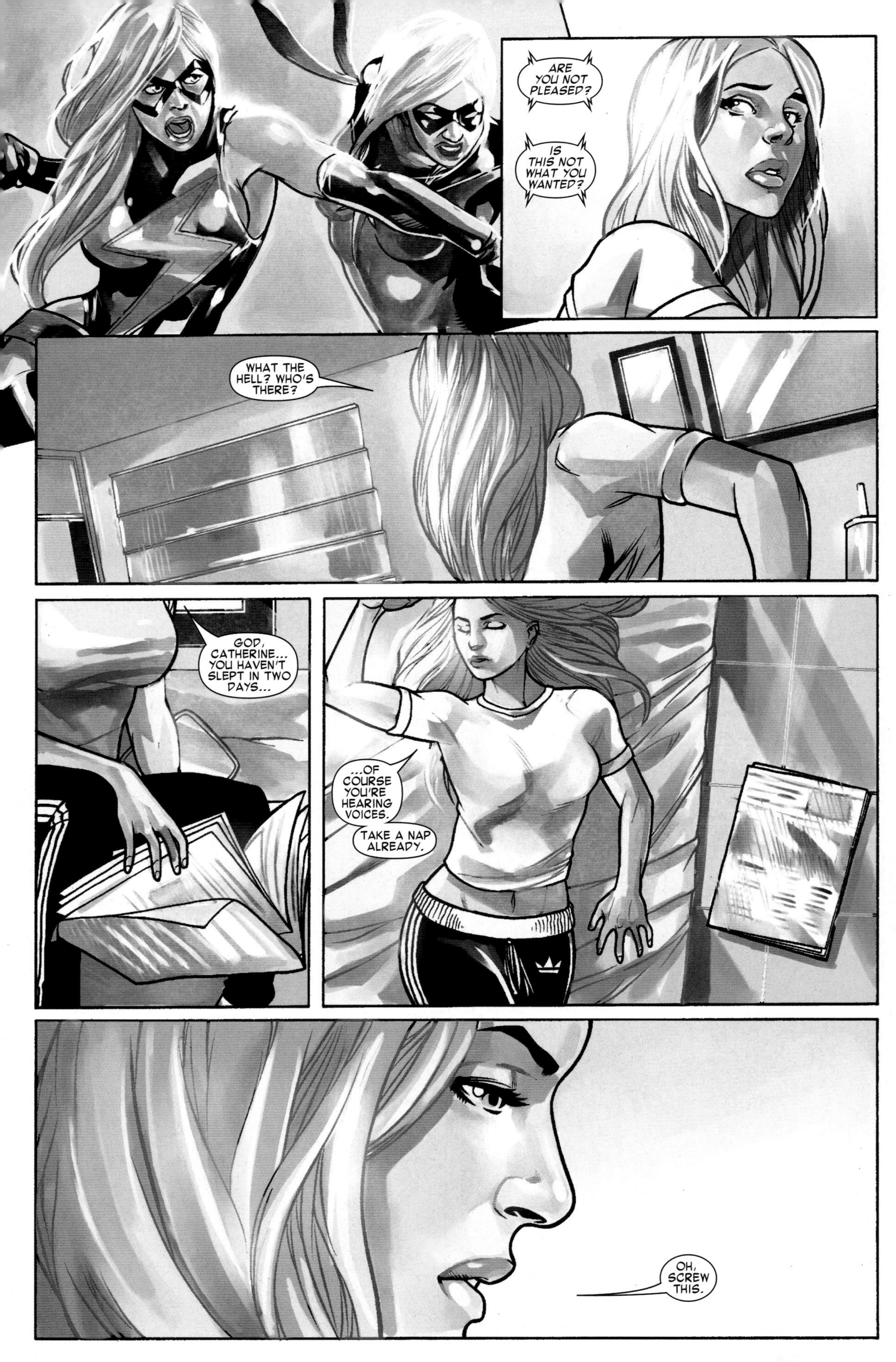
ARE YOU NOT PLEASED?
IS THIS NOT WHAT YOU WANTED?
WHAT THE HELL? WHO'S THERE?
GOD, CATHERINE... YOU HAVEN'T SLEPT IN TWO DAYS...
...OF COURSE YOU'RE HEARING VOICES.
TAKE A NAP ALREADY.
OH, SCREW THIS.

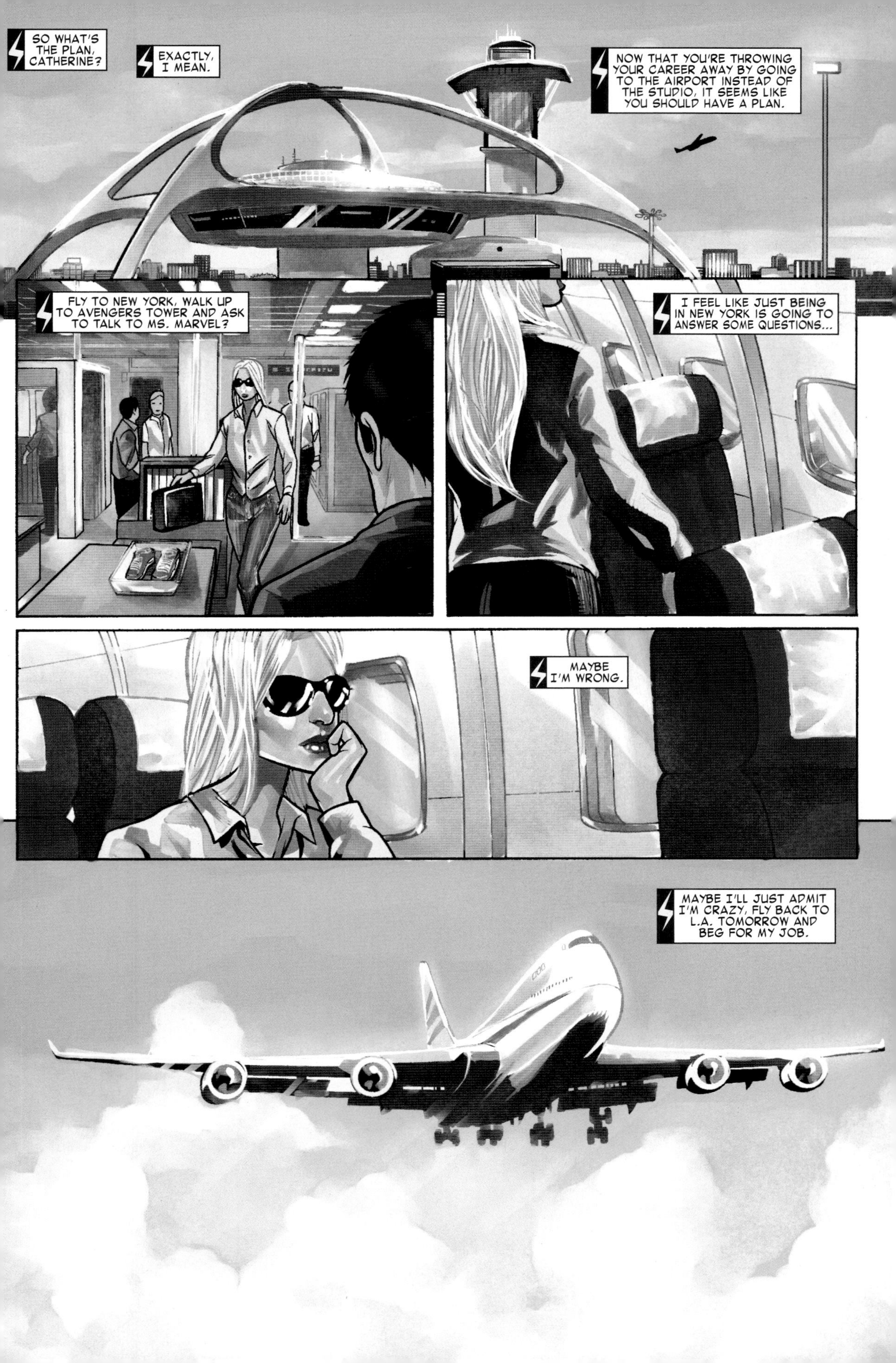
SO WHAT'S THE PLAN, CATHERINE?
EXACTLY, I MEAN.
NOW THAT YOU'RE THROWING YOUR CAREER AWAY BY GOING TO THE AIRPORT INSTEAD OF THE STUDIO, IT SEEMS LIKE YOU SHOULD HAVE A PLAN.
FLY TO NEW YORK, WALK UP TO AVENGERS TOWER AND ASK TO TALK TO MS. MARVEL?
I FEEL LIKE JUST BEING IN NEW YORK IS GOING TO ANSWER SOME QUESTIONS...
MAYBE I'M WRONG.
MAYBE I'LL JUST ADMIT I'M CRAZY, FLY BACK TO L.A. TOMORROW AND BEG FOR MY JOB.

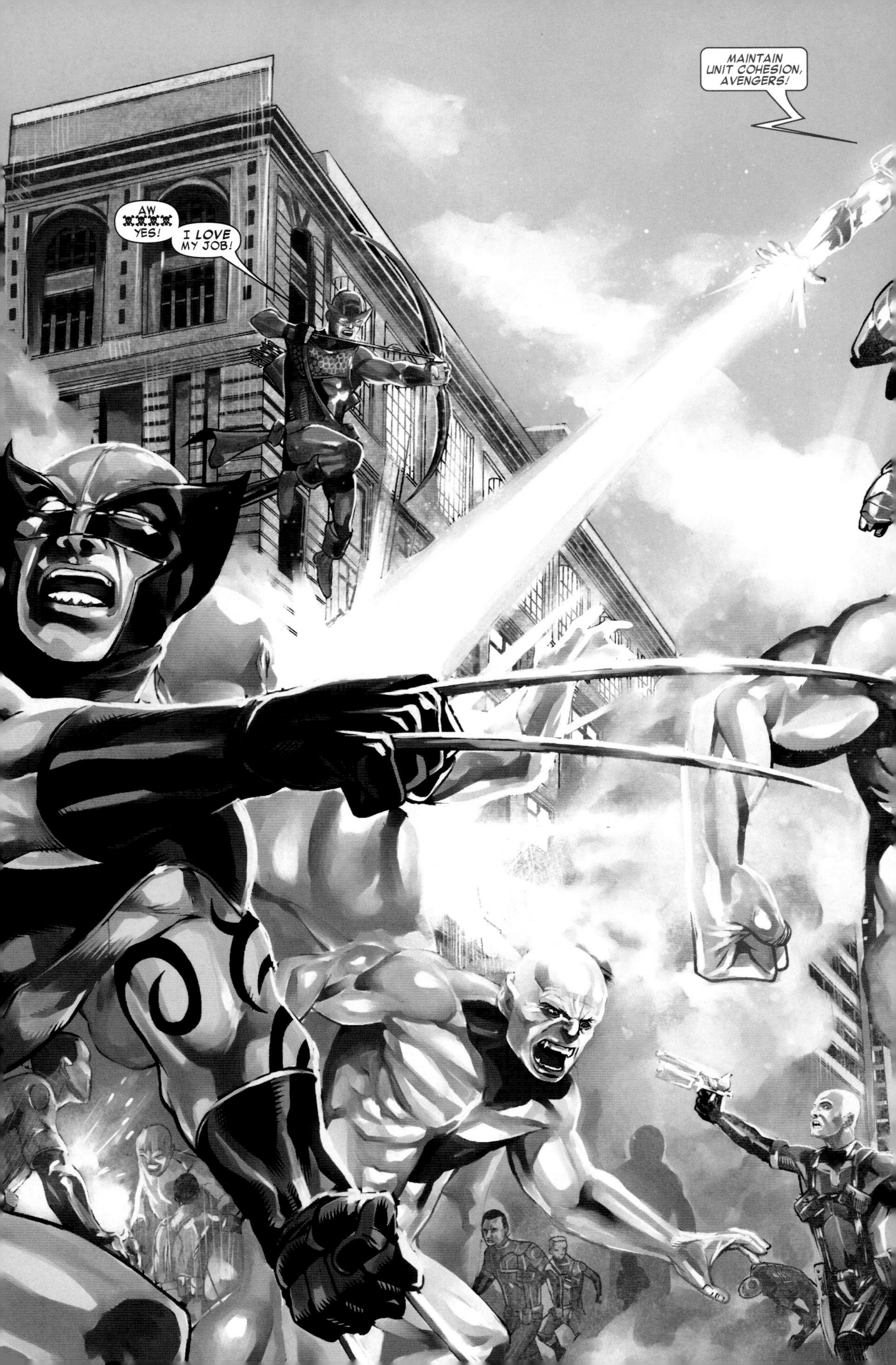
AW ☠☠☠ YES!
I LOVE MY JOB!
MAINTAIN UNIT COHESION, AVENGERS!

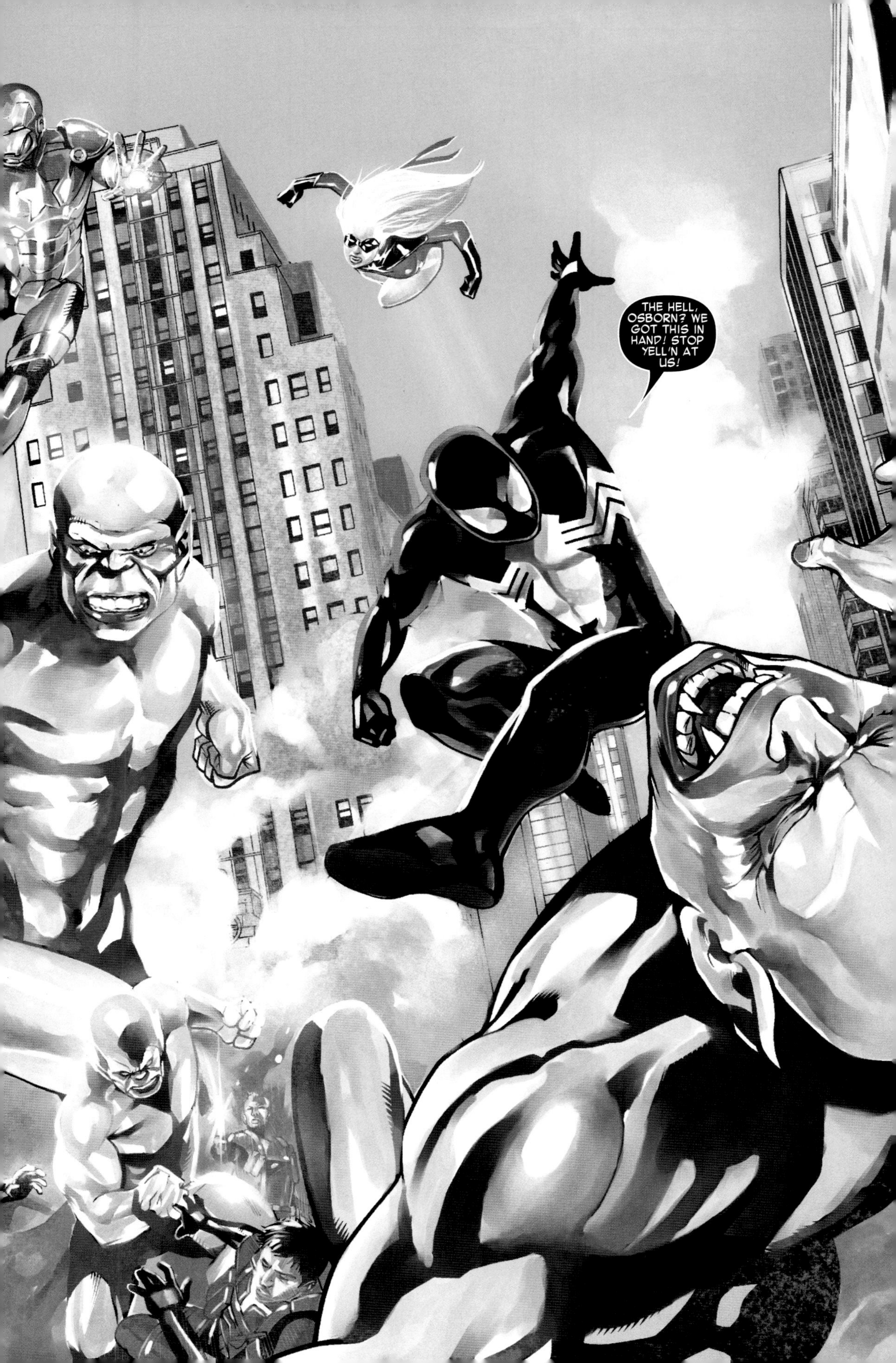
THE HELL, OSBORN? WE GOT THIS IN HAND! STOP YELL'N AT US!

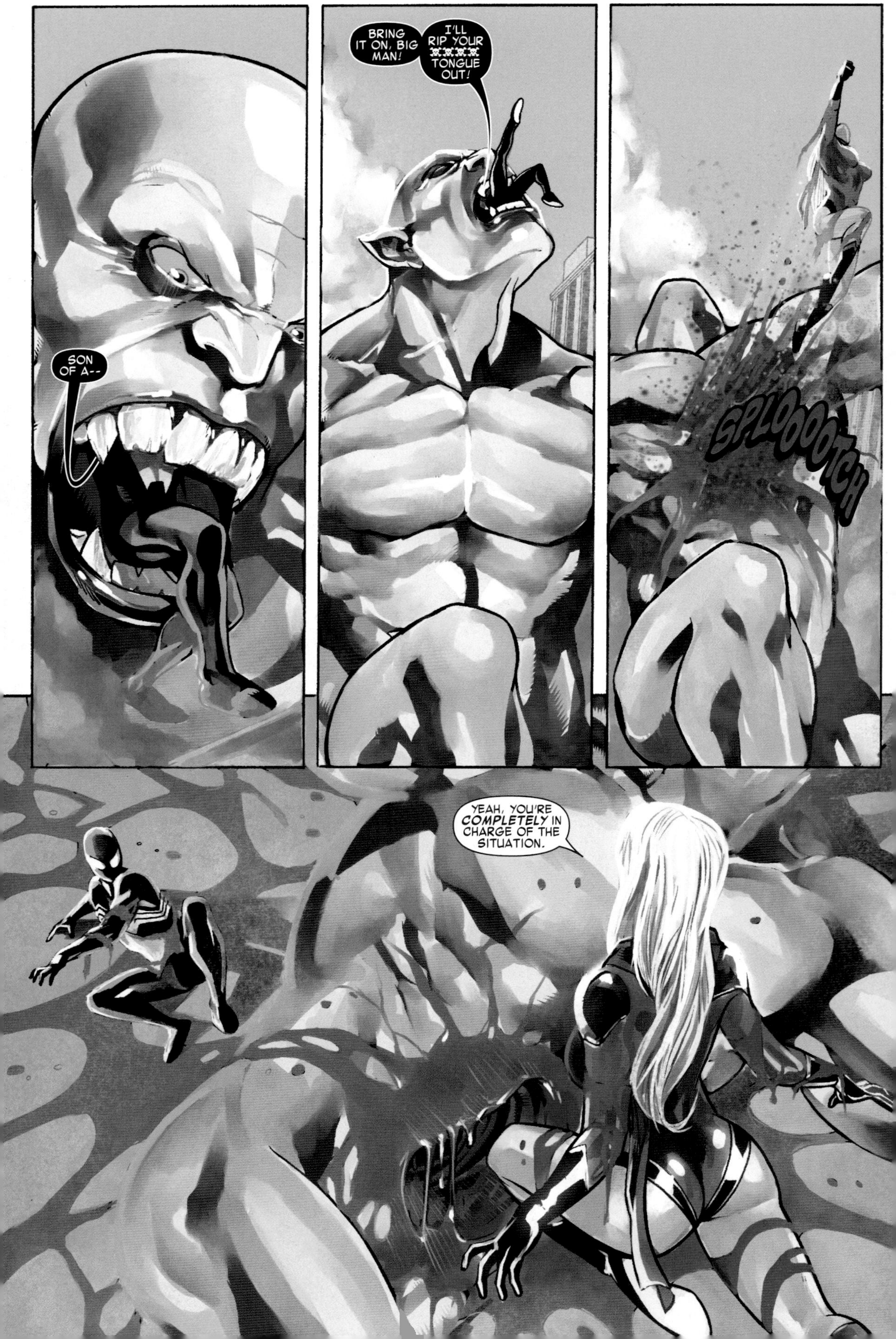
SON OF A--
BRING IT ON, BIG MAN!
I'LL RIP YOUR ☠☠☠ TONGUE OUT!
SPLOOOOOTCH
YEAH, YOU'RE COMPLETELY IN CHARGE OF THE SITUATION.

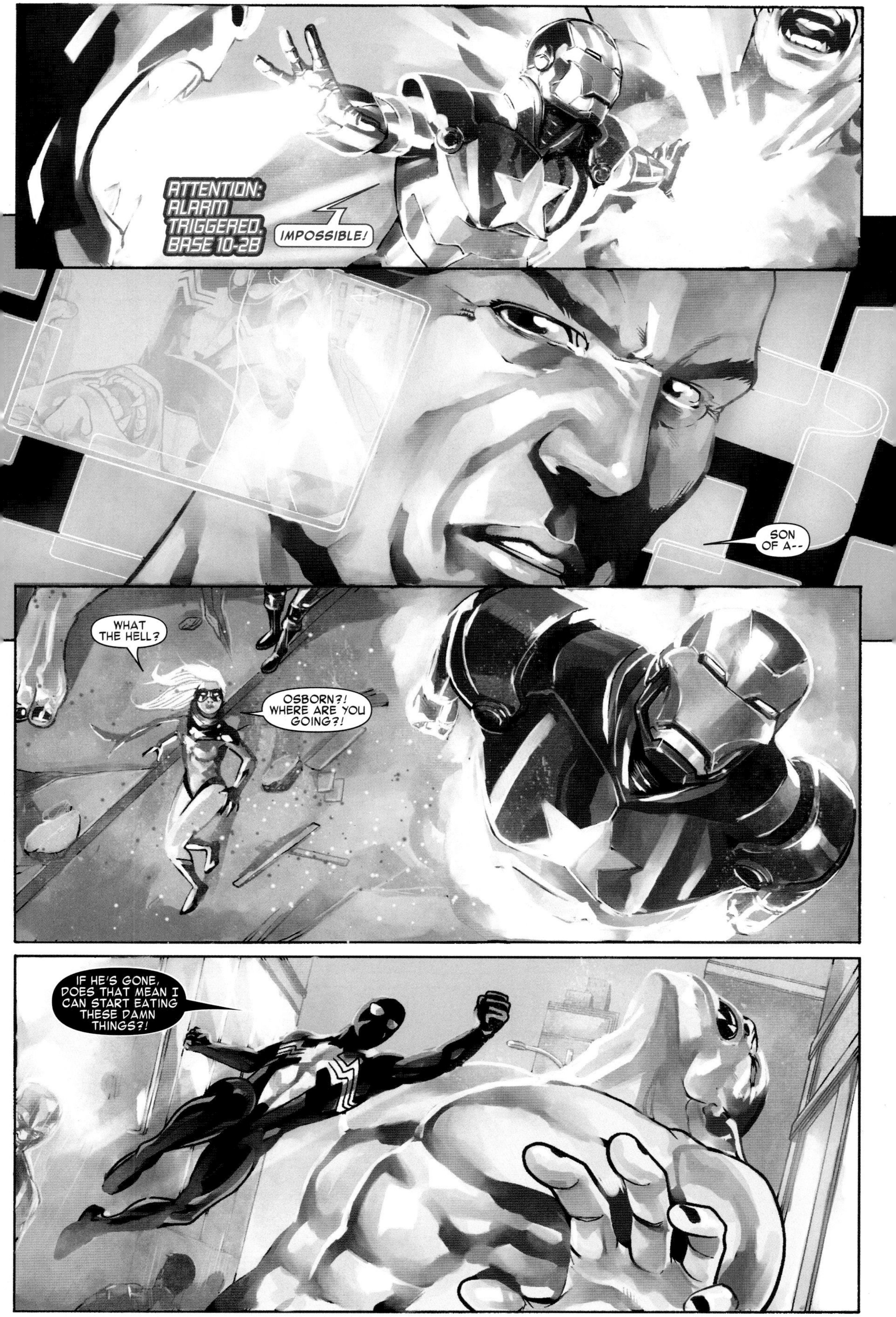
ATTENTION: ALARM TRIGGERED. BASE 10-2B
IMPOSSIBLE!
SON OF A--
WHAT THE HELL?
OSBORN?! WHERE ARE YOU GOING?!
IF HE'S GONE, DOES THAT MEAN I CAN START EATING THESE DAMN THINGS?!

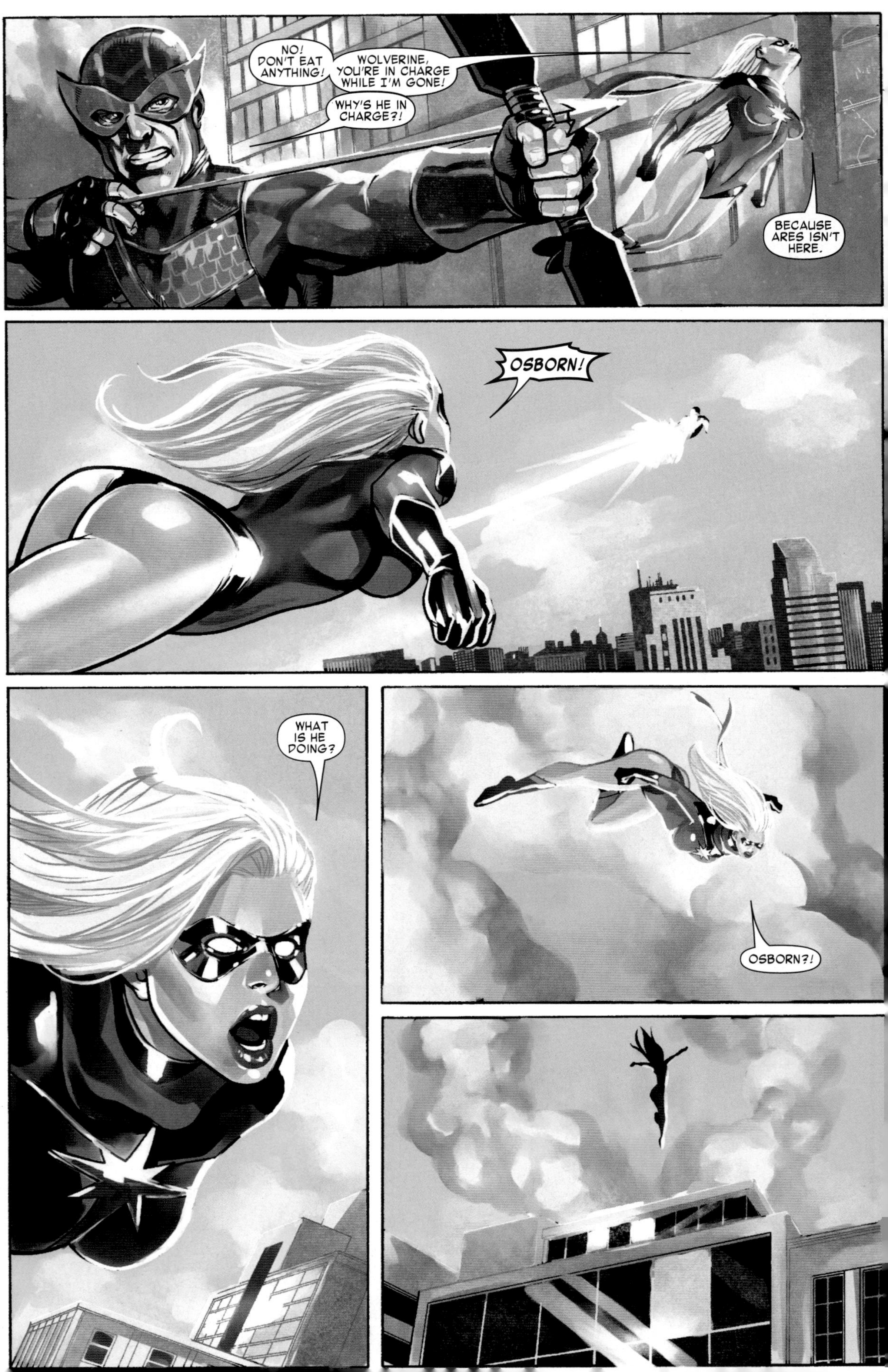
NO! DON'T EAT ANYTHING!
WOLVERINE, YOU'RE IN CHARGE WHILE I'M GONE!
WHY'S HE IN CHARGE?!
BECAUSE ARES ISN'T HERE.
OSBORN!
WHAT IS HE DOING?
OSBORN?!

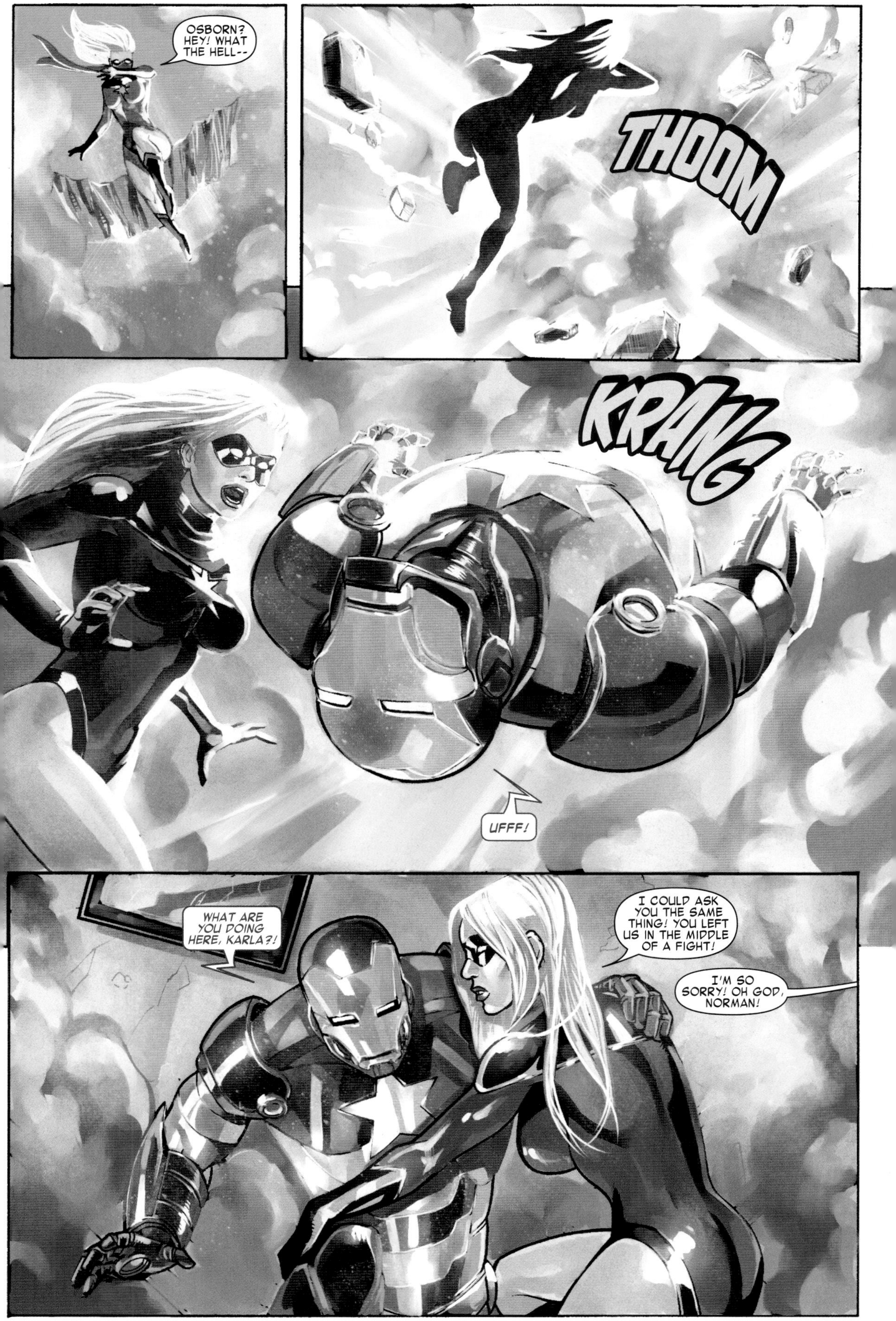
OSBORN? HEY! WHAT THE HELL--
THOOM
KRANG
UFFF!
WHAT ARE YOU DOING HERE, KARLA?!
I COULD ASK YOU THE SAME THING! YOU LEFT US IN THE MIDDLE OF A FIGHT!
I'M SO SORRY! OH GOD, NORMAN!

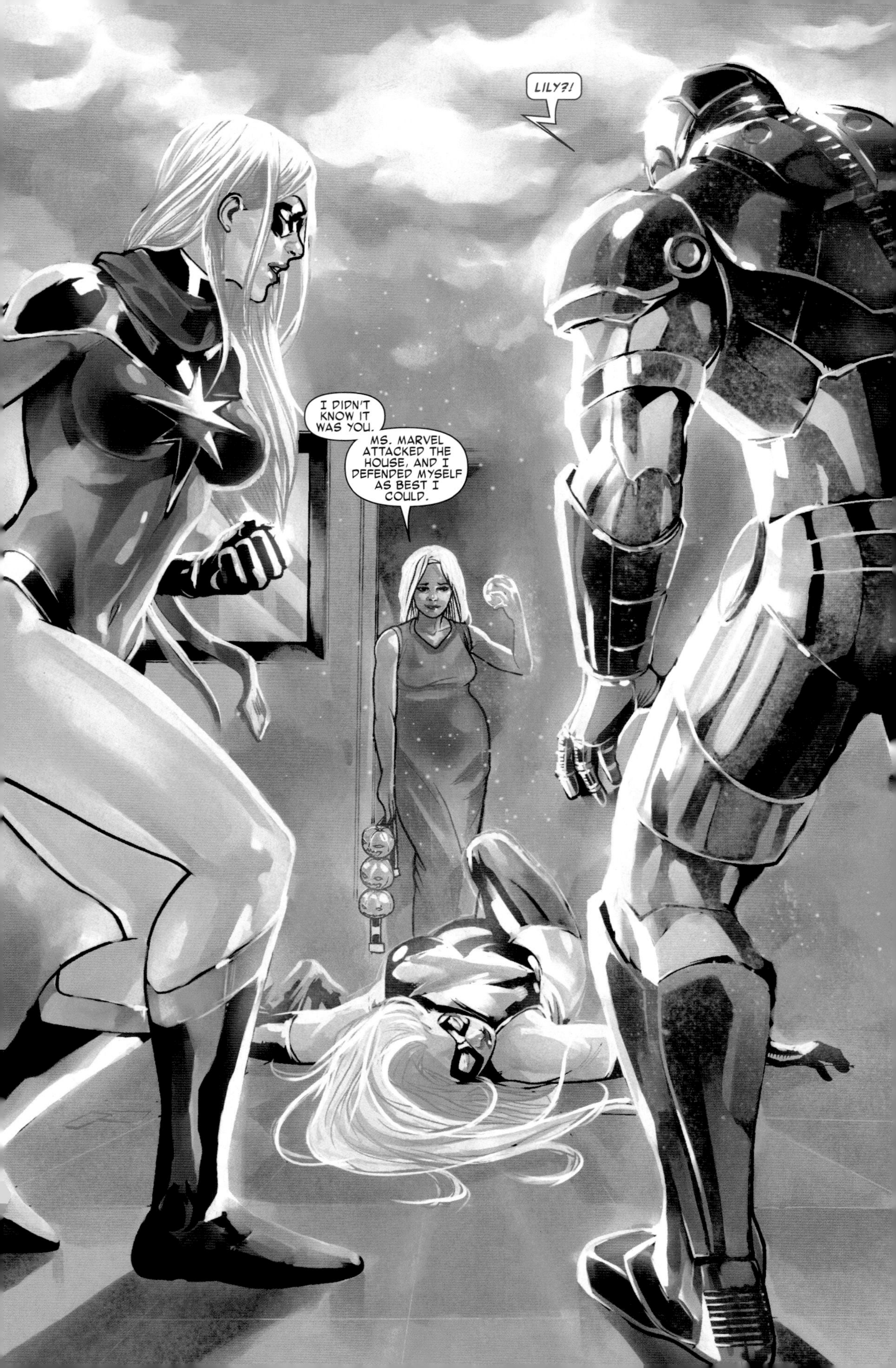
LILY?!
I DIDN'T KNOW IT WAS YOU.
MS. MARVEL ATTACKED THE HOUSE, AND I DEFENDED MYSELF AS BEST I COULD.

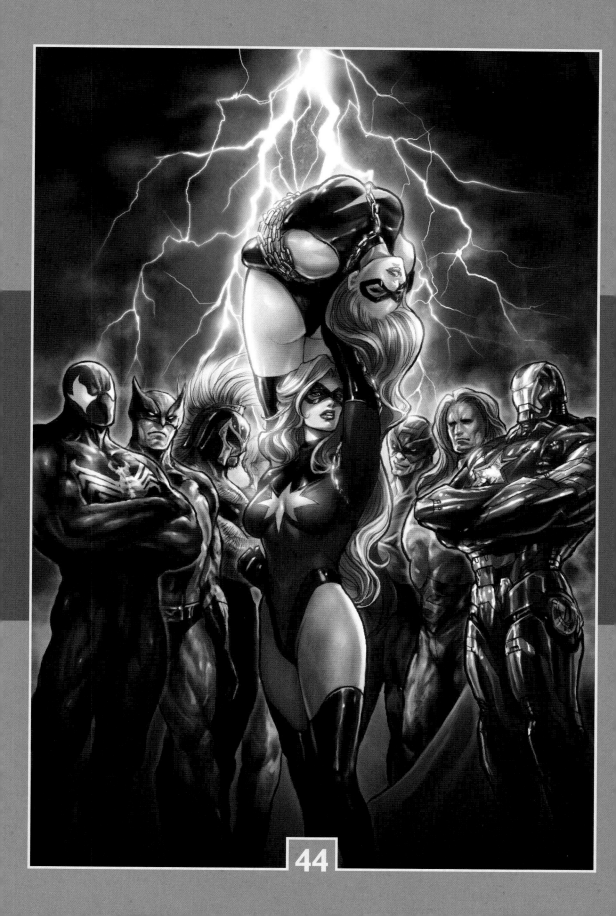

44

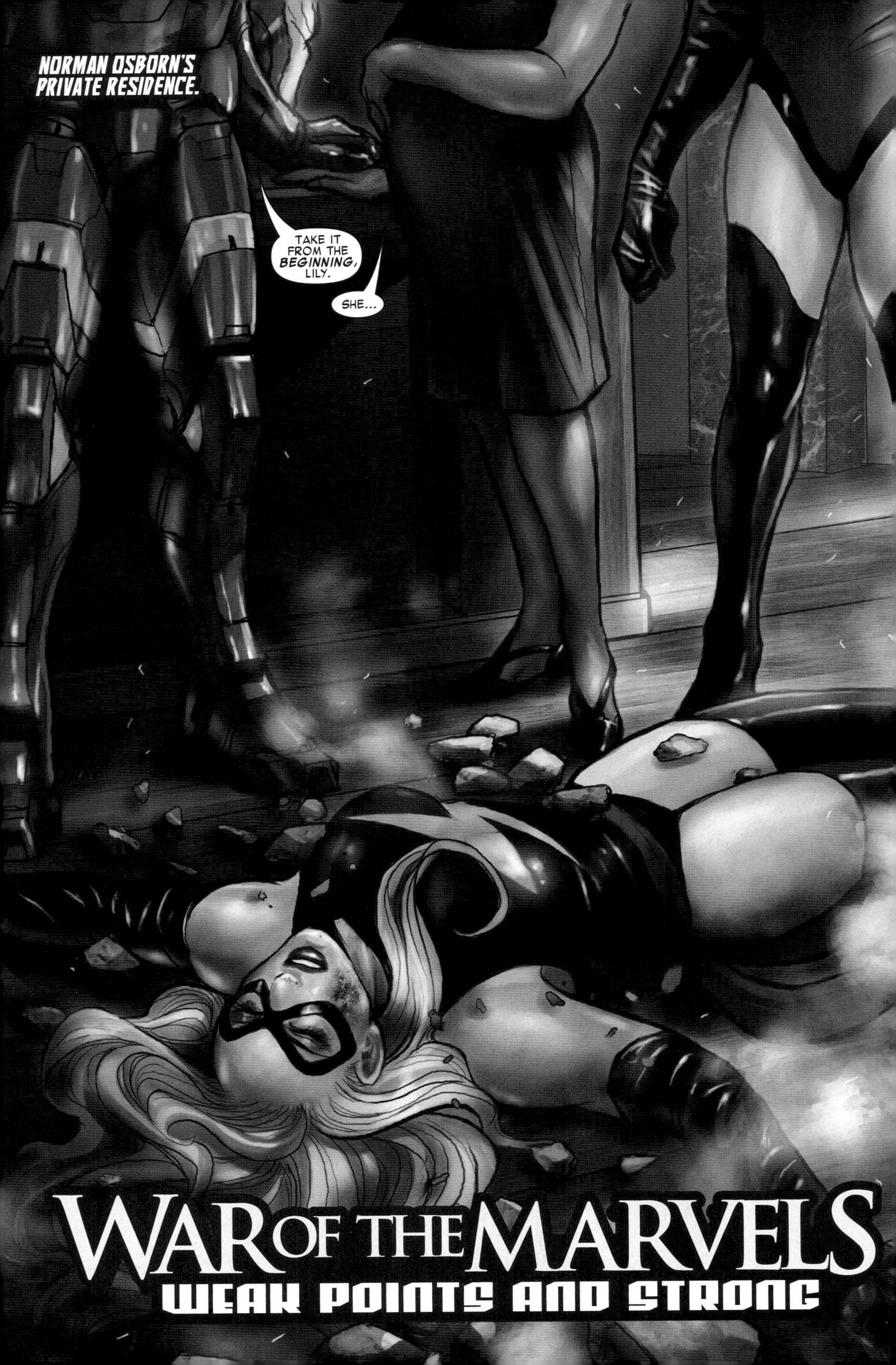
NORMAN OSBORN'S PRIVATE RESIDENCE.
TAKE IT FROM THE BEGINNING, LILY.
SHE...
WAR OF THE MARVELS
WEAK POINTS AND STRONG

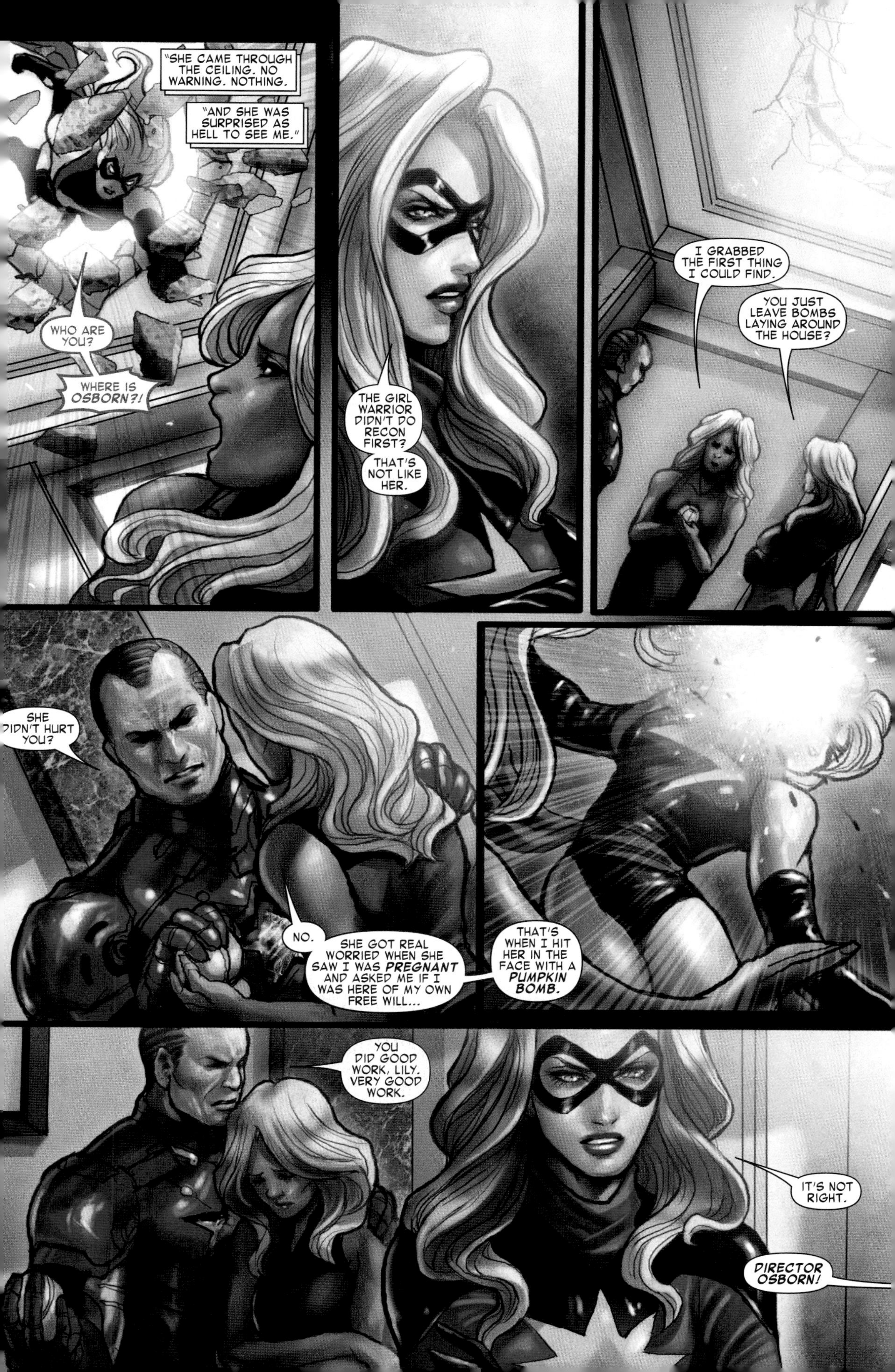

"SHE CAME THROUGH THE CEILING. NO WARNING. NOTHING.
"AND SHE WAS SURPRISED AS HELL TO SEE ME."
WHO ARE YOU?
WHERE IS OSBORN?!
THE GIRL WARRIOR DIDN'T DO RECON FIRST?
THAT'S NOT LIKE HER.
I GRABBED THE FIRST THING I COULD FIND.
YOU JUST LEAVE BOMBS LAYING AROUND THE HOUSE?
SHE DIDN'T HURT YOU?
NO.
SHE GOT REAL WORRIED WHEN SHE SAW I WAS PREGNANT AND ASKED ME IF I WAS HERE OF MY OWN FREE WILL...
THAT'S WHEN I HIT HER IN THE FACE WITH A PUMPKIN BOMB.
YOU DID GOOD WORK, LILY. VERY GOOD WORK.
IT'S NOT RIGHT.
DIRECTOR OSBORN!

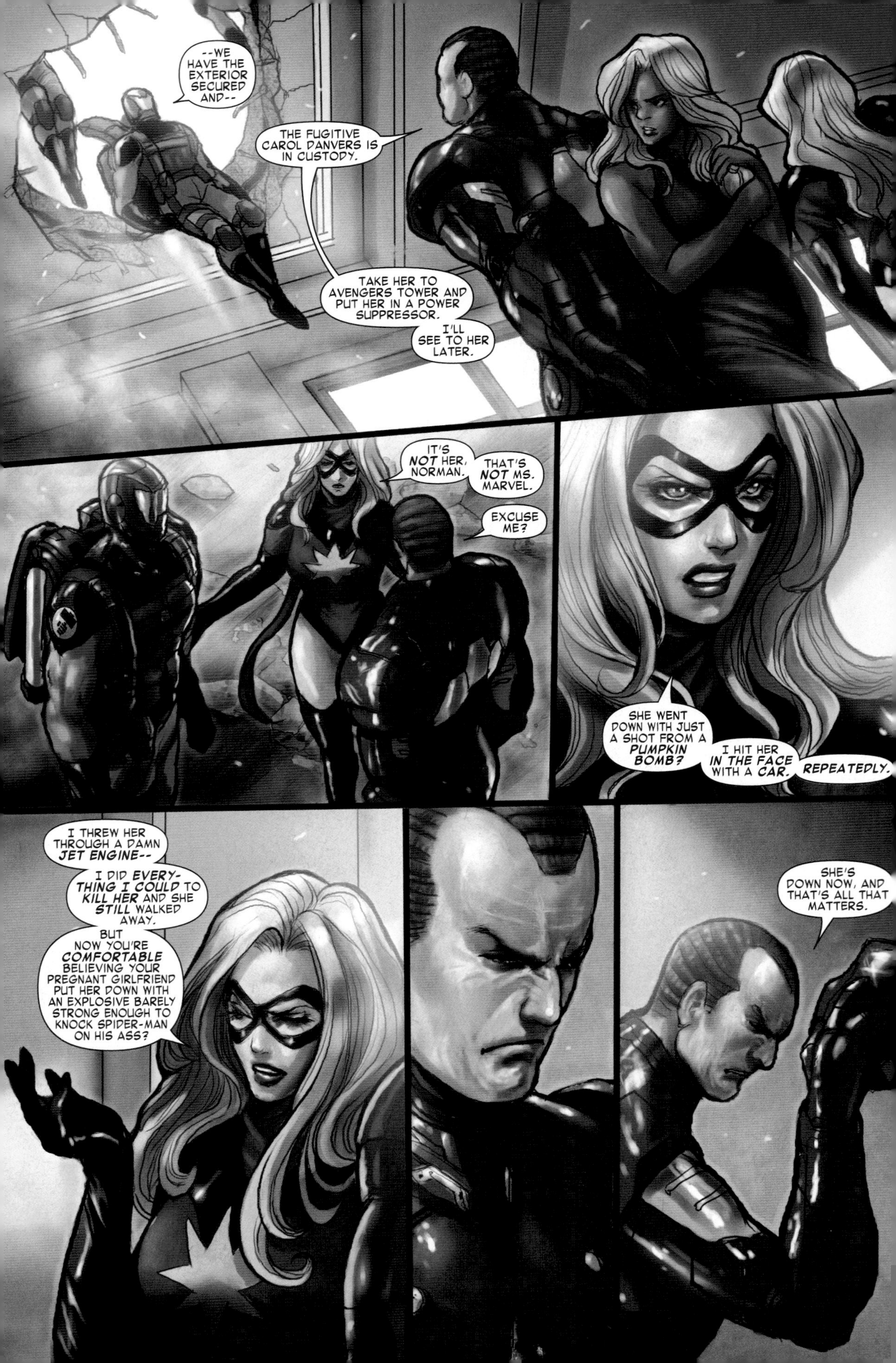
--WE HAVE THE EXTERIOR SECURED AND--
THE FUGITIVE CAROL DANVERS IS IN CUSTODY.
TAKE HER TO AVENGERS TOWER AND PUT HER IN A POWER SUPPRESSOR.
I'LL SEE TO HER LATER.
IT'S NOT HER, NORMAN.
THAT'S NOT MS. MARVEL.
EXCUSE ME?
SHE WENT DOWN WITH JUST A SHOT FROM A PUMPKIN BOMB?
I HIT HER IN THE FACE WITH A CAR.
REPEATEDLY.
I THREW HER THROUGH A DAMN JET ENGINE--
I DID EVERYTHING I COULD TO KILL HER AND SHE STILL WALKED AWAY.
BUT NOW YOU'RE COMFORTABLE BELIEVING YOUR PREGNANT GIRLFRIEND PUT HER DOWN WITH AN EXPLOSIVE BARELY STRONG ENOUGH TO KNOCK SPIDER-MAN ON HIS ASS?
SHE'S DOWN NOW, AND THAT'S ALL THAT MATTERS.

FLIGHT 1977 TO NEW YORK-JFK.

THINGS I KNOW TO BE FACTS:

MY NAME IS CATHERINE DONOVAN, *NOT* "CAROL DANVERS."

I AM *NOT A* SUPER HERO.

I AM A WRITER. A COUPLE OF BOOKS, SOME MAGAZINE ARTICLES, AND THE TV SHOW *GUARDIANS OF THE GALAXY.*

Things I know to be facts:

My name is Catherine Donovan, not "Carol Danvers."

I am not a super hero.

I am a writer. A couple of books, some magazine articles, and the TV show Guardians of the Galaxy.

I have everything I've ever wanted in life.

acts:
ine Donovan,
Danvers."

t a super hero.

ouple of books, some magazine
TV show Guardians of the Galaxy.

I have everything
I've ever wanted in life.

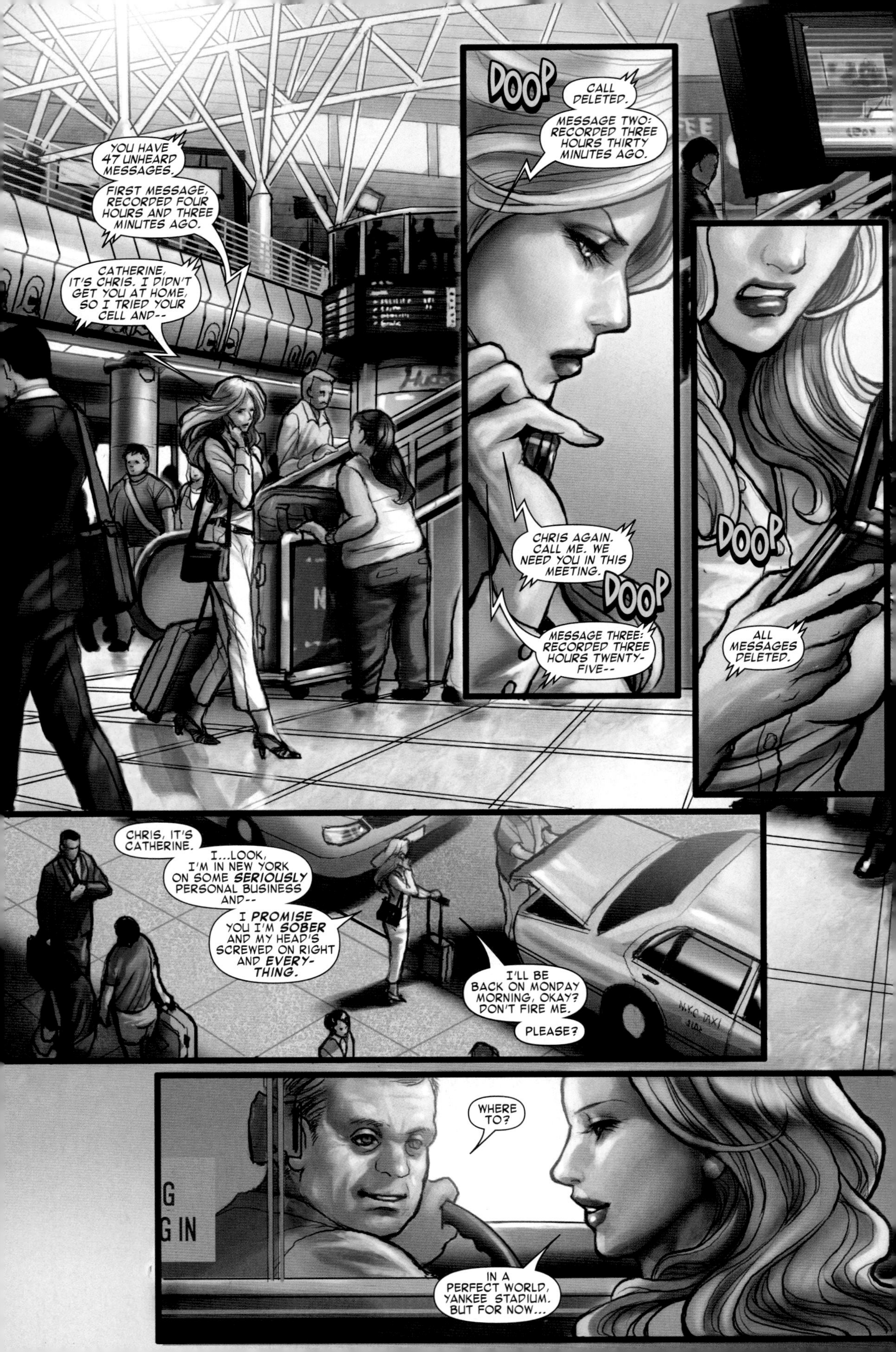
YOU HAVE 47 UNHEARD MESSAGES.
FIRST MESSAGE, RECORDED FOUR HOURS AND THREE MINUTES AGO.
CATHERINE, IT'S CHRIS. I DIDN'T GET YOU AT HOME, SO I TRIED YOUR CELL AND--
DOOP
CALL DELETED.
MESSAGE TWO: RECORDED THREE HOURS THIRTY MINUTES AGO.
CHRIS AGAIN. CALL ME. WE NEED YOU IN THIS MEETING.
DOOP
MESSAGE THREE: RECORDED THREE HOURS TWENTY-FIVE--
DOOP
ALL MESSAGES DELETED.
CHRIS, IT'S CATHERINE.
I...LOOK, I'M IN NEW YORK ON SOME SERIOUSLY PERSONAL BUSINESS AND--
I PROMISE YOU I'M SOBER AND MY HEAD'S SCREWED ON RIGHT AND EVERY-THING.
I'LL BE BACK ON MONDAY MORNING, OKAY? DON'T FIRE ME.
PLEASE?
N.Y.C TAXI
WHERE TO?
IN A PERFECT WORLD, YANKEE STADIUM. BUT FOR NOW...

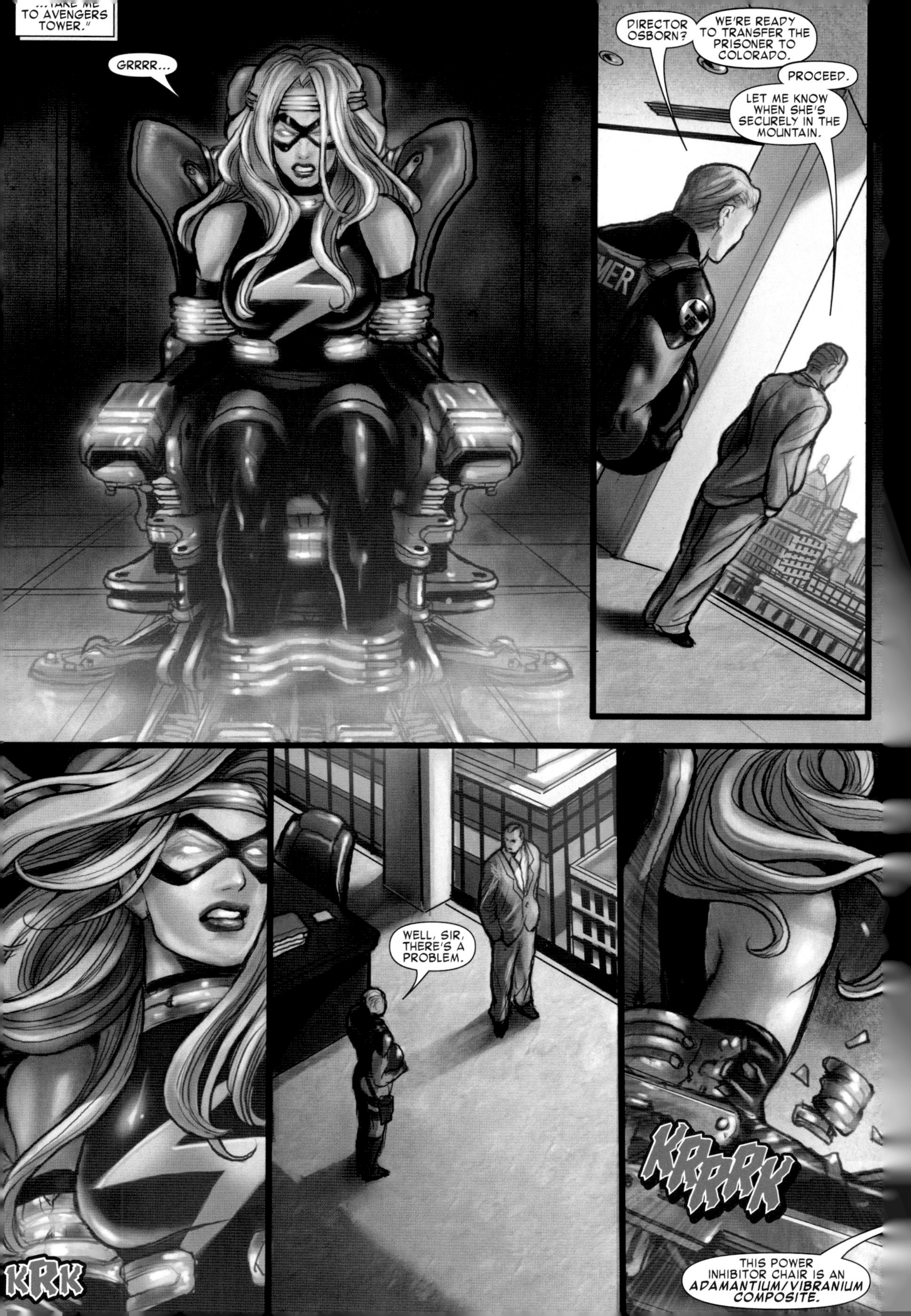
...TAKE ME TO AVENGERS TOWER."
GRRRR...
DIRECTOR OSBORN?
WE'RE READY TO TRANSFER THE PRISONER TO COLORADO.
PROCEED.
LET ME KNOW WHEN SHE'S SECURELY IN THE MOUNTAIN.
KRK
WELL, SIR, THERE'S A PROBLEM.
KRRRK
THIS POWER INHIBITOR CHAIR IS AN *ADAMANTIUM/VIBRANIUM COMPOSITE.*

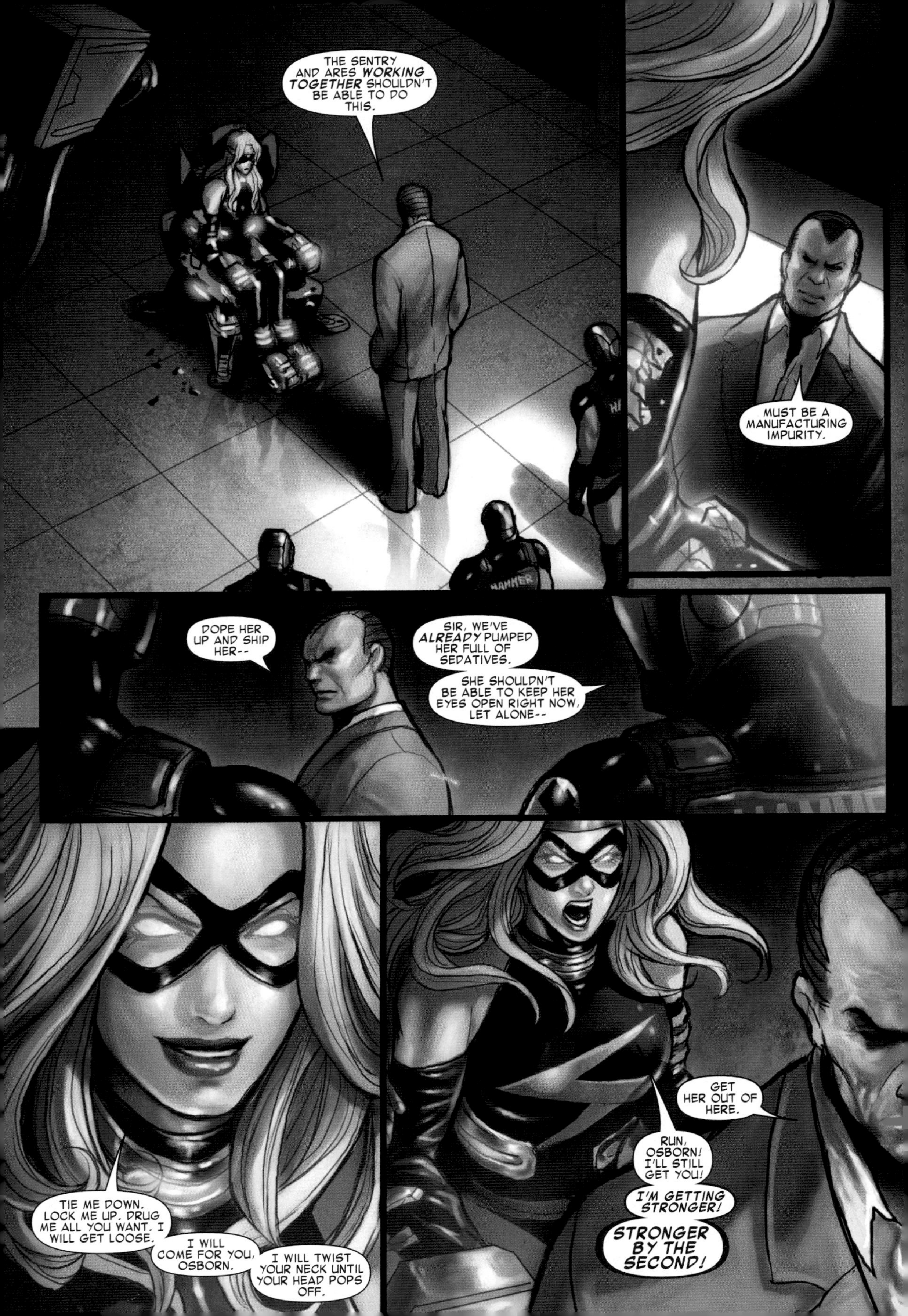

THE SENTRY AND ARES WORKING TOGETHER SHOULDN'T BE ABLE TO DO THIS.
MUST BE A MANUFACTURING IMPURITY.
DOPE HER UP AND SHIP HER--
SIR, WE'VE ALREADY PUMPED HER FULL OF SEDATIVES.
SHE SHOULDN'T BE ABLE TO KEEP HER EYES OPEN RIGHT NOW, LET ALONE--
TIE ME DOWN. LOCK ME UP. DRUG ME ALL YOU WANT. I WILL GET LOOSE.
I WILL COME FOR YOU, OSBORN.
I WILL TWIST YOUR NECK UNTIL YOUR HEAD POPS OFF.
GET HER OUT OF HERE.
RUN, OSBORN! I'LL STILL GET YOU!
I'M GETTING STRONGER!
STRONGER BY THE SECOND!

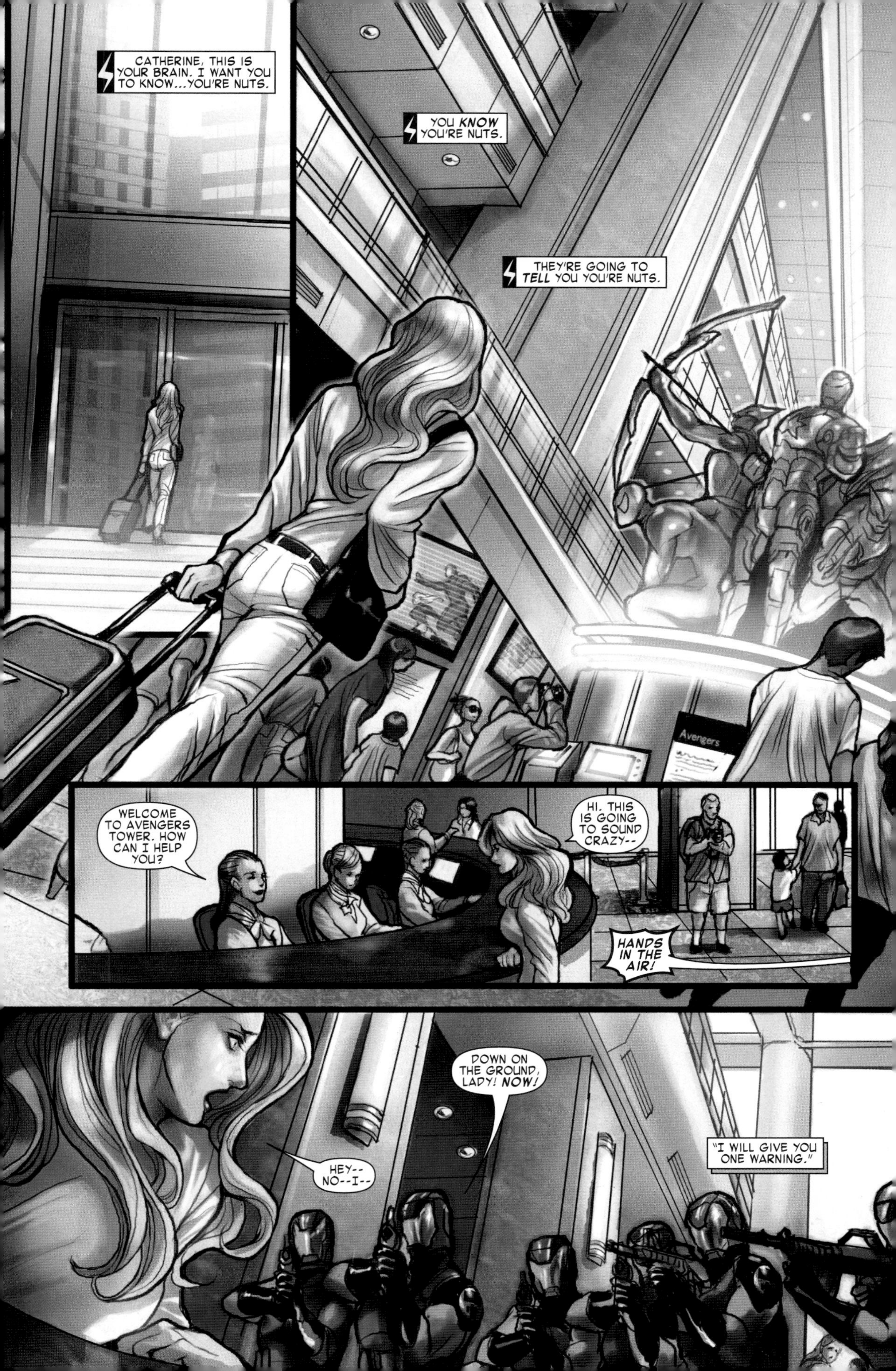

CATHERINE, THIS IS YOUR BRAIN. I WANT YOU TO KNOW...YOU'RE NUTS.
YOU *KNOW* YOU'RE NUTS.
THEY'RE GOING TO *TELL* YOU YOU'RE NUTS.
Avengers
WELCOME TO AVENGERS TOWER. HOW CAN I HELP YOU?
HI. THIS IS GOING TO SOUND CRAZY--
HANDS IN THE AIR!
DOWN ON THE GROUND, LADY! *NOW!*
HEY-- NO--I--
"I WILL GIVE YOU ONE WARNING."

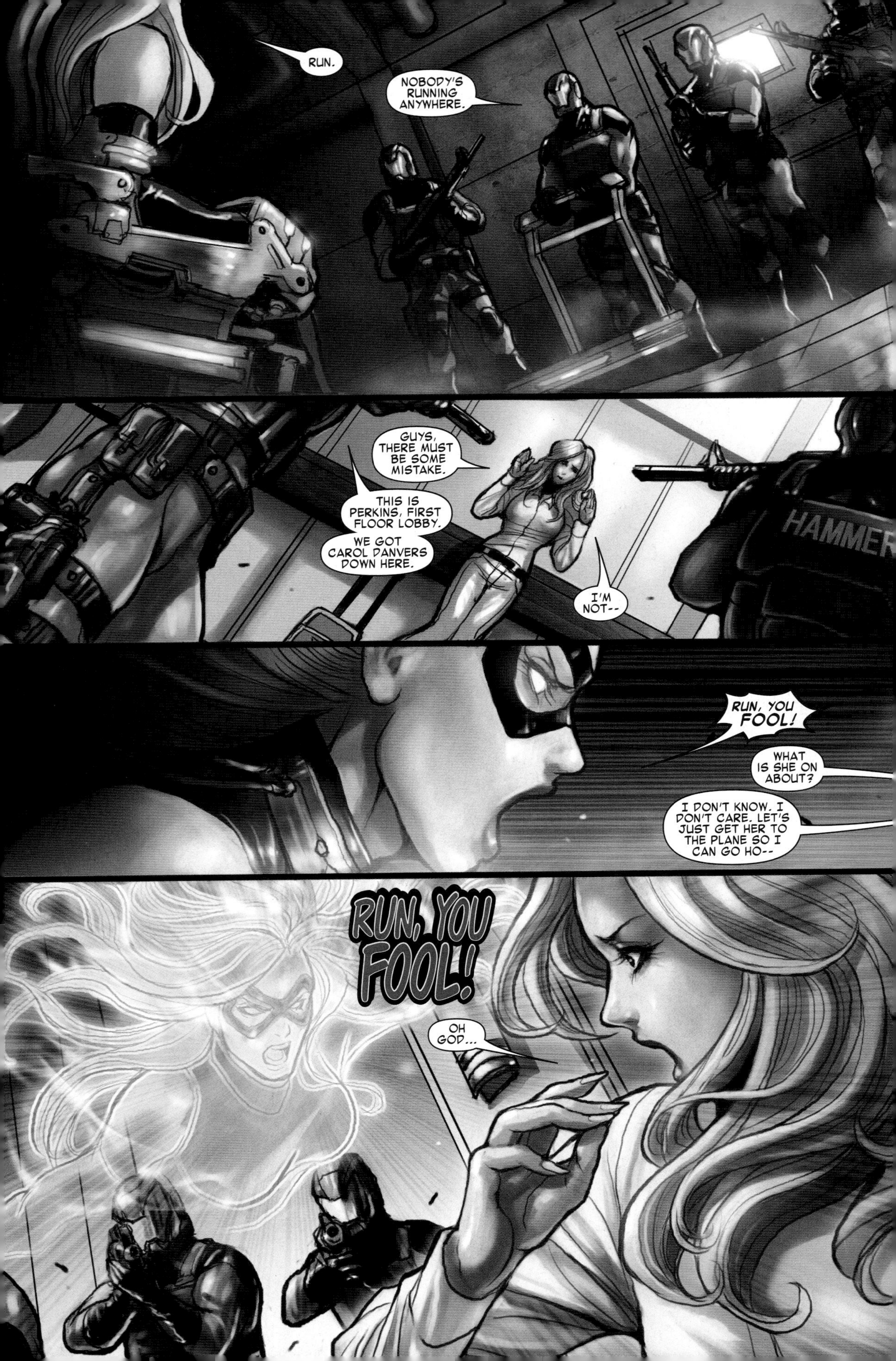
RUN.
NOBODY'S RUNNING ANYWHERE.
GUYS, THERE MUST BE SOME MISTAKE.
THIS IS PERKINS, FIRST FLOOR LOBBY.
WE GOT CAROL DANVERS DOWN HERE.
HAMMER
I'M NOT--
RUN, YOU FOOL!
WHAT IS SHE ON ABOUT?
I DON'T KNOW. I DON'T CARE. LET'S JUST GET HER TO THE PLANE SO I CAN GO HO--
RUN, YOU FOOL!
OH GOD...

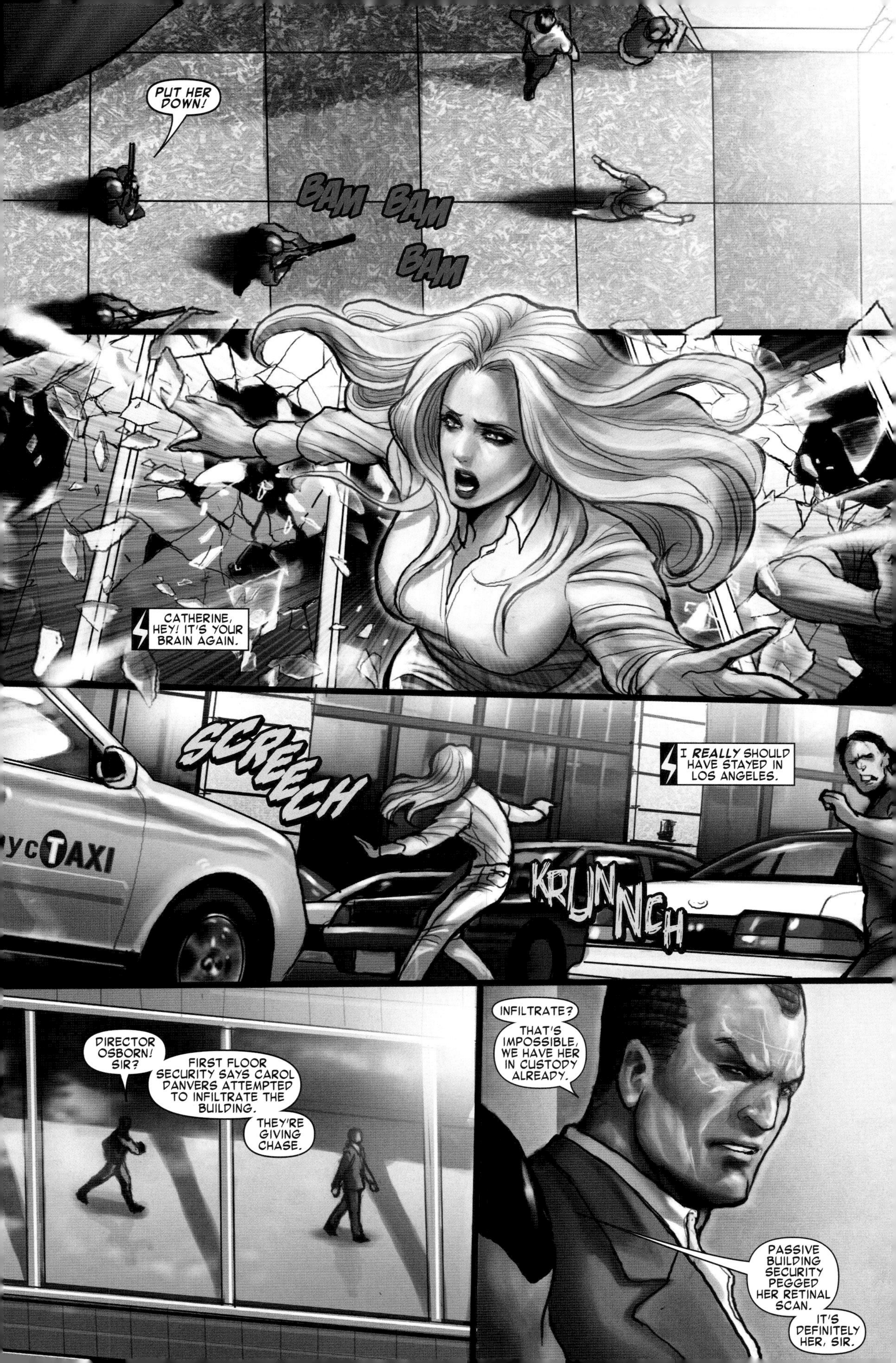
PUT HER DOWN!
BAM BAM BAM
CATHERINE, HEY! IT'S YOUR BRAIN AGAIN.
SCREECH
I REALLY SHOULD HAVE STAYED IN LOS ANGELES.
nycTAXI
KRUNNCH
DIRECTOR OSBORN! SIR?
FIRST FLOOR SECURITY SAYS CAROL DANVERS ATTEMPTED TO INFILTRATE THE BUILDING.
THEY'RE GIVING CHASE.
INFILTRATE?
THAT'S IMPOSSIBLE, WE HAVE HER IN CUSTODY ALREADY.
PASSIVE BUILDING SECURITY PEGGED HER RETINAL SCAN.
IT'S DEFINITELY HER, SIR.

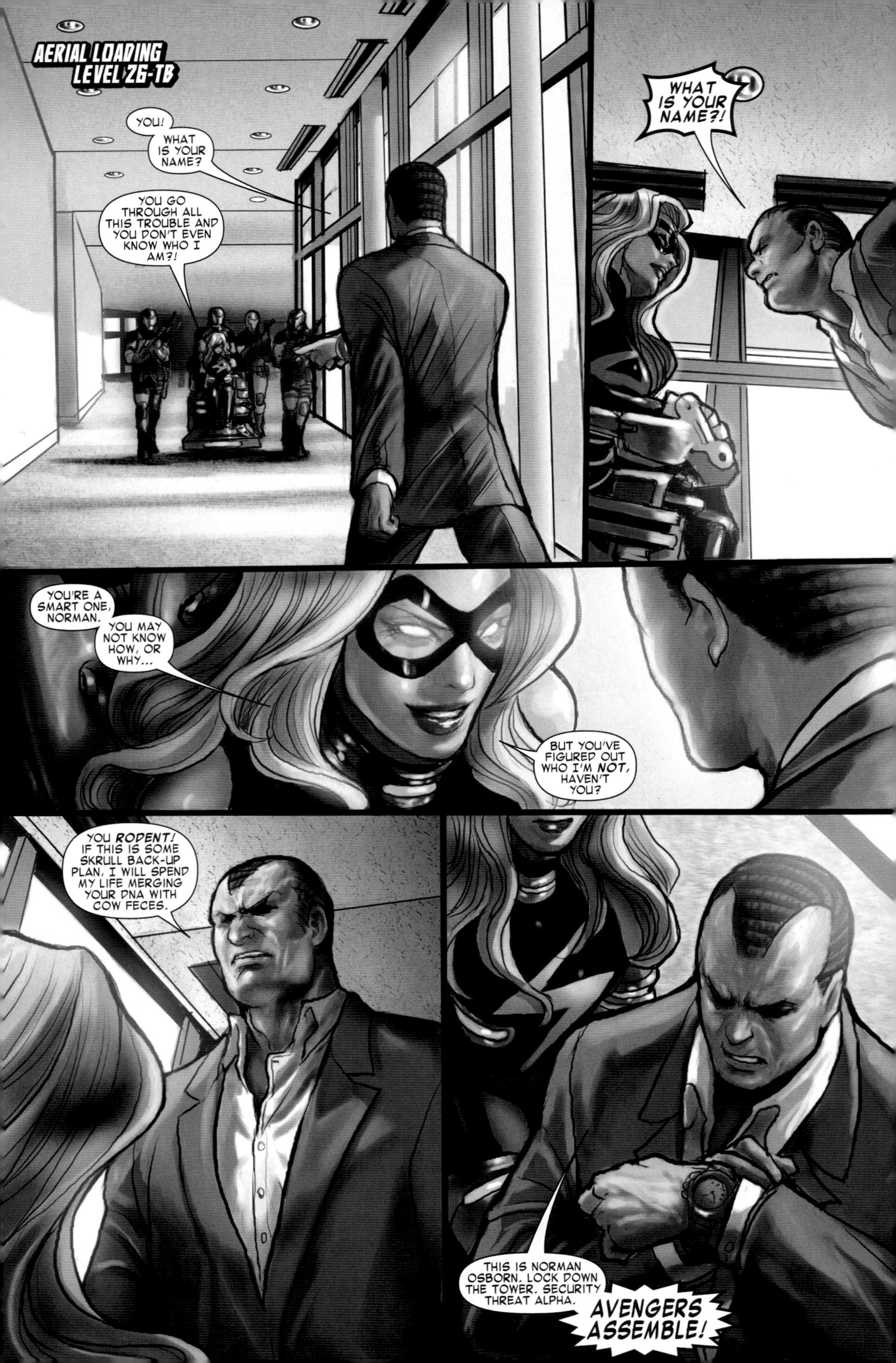
AERIAL LOADING LEVEL 26-TB
YOU!
WHAT IS YOUR NAME?
YOU GO THROUGH ALL THIS TROUBLE AND YOU DON'T EVEN KNOW WHO I AM?!
WHAT IS YOUR NAME?!
YOU'RE A SMART ONE, NORMAN.
YOU MAY NOT KNOW HOW, OR WHY...
BUT YOU'VE FIGURED OUT WHO I'M NOT, HAVEN'T YOU?
YOU RODENT! IF THIS IS SOME SKRULL BACK-UP PLAN, I WILL SPEND MY LIFE MERGING YOUR DNA WITH COW FECES.
THIS IS NORMAN OSBORN. LOCK DOWN THE TOWER. SECURITY THREAT ALPHA.
AVENGERS ASSEMBLE!

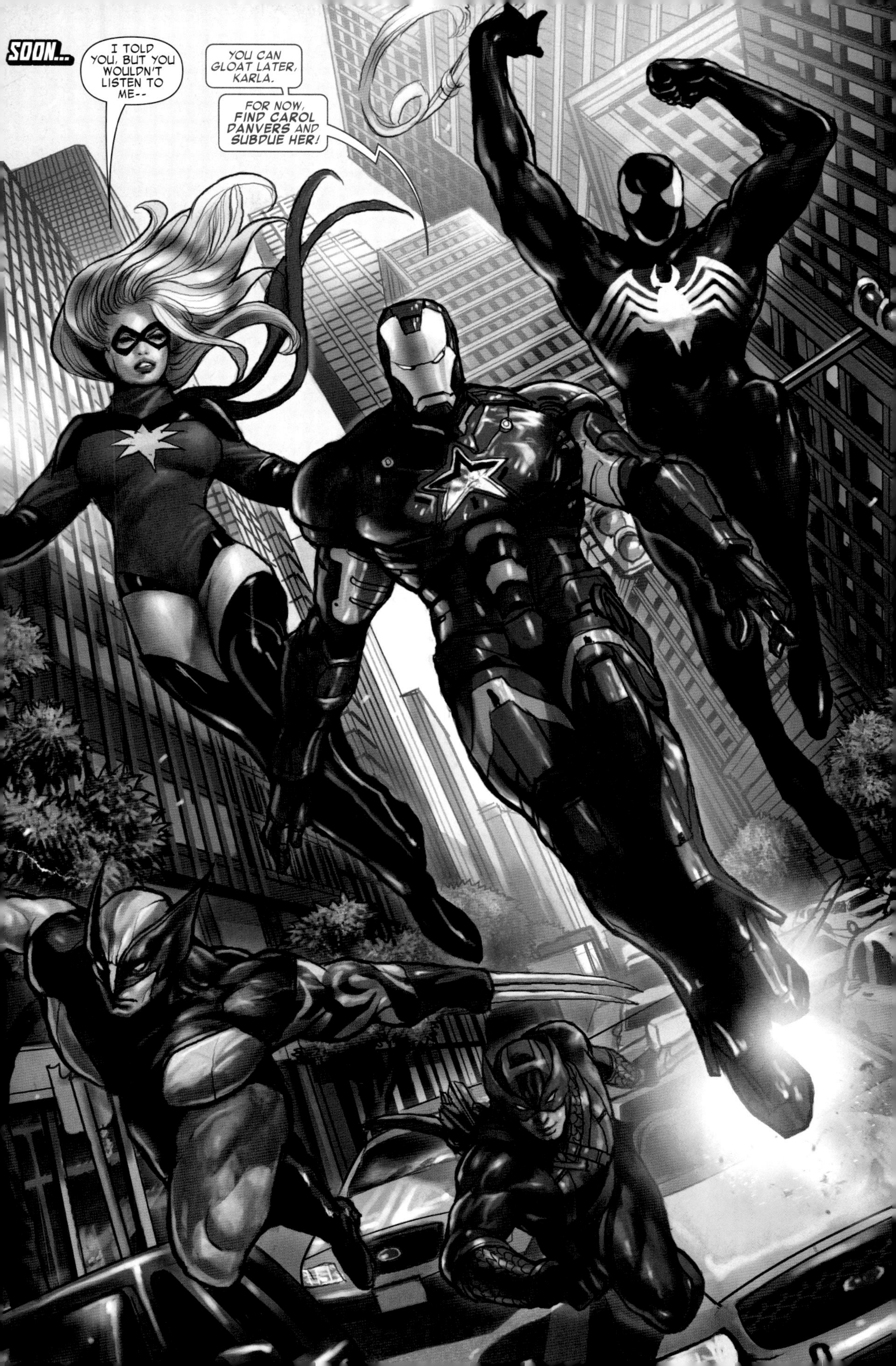
SOON...
I TOLD YOU, BUT YOU WOULDN'T LISTEN TO ME--
YOU CAN GLOAT LATER, KARLA.
FOR NOW, FIND CAROL DANVERS AND SUBDUE HER!

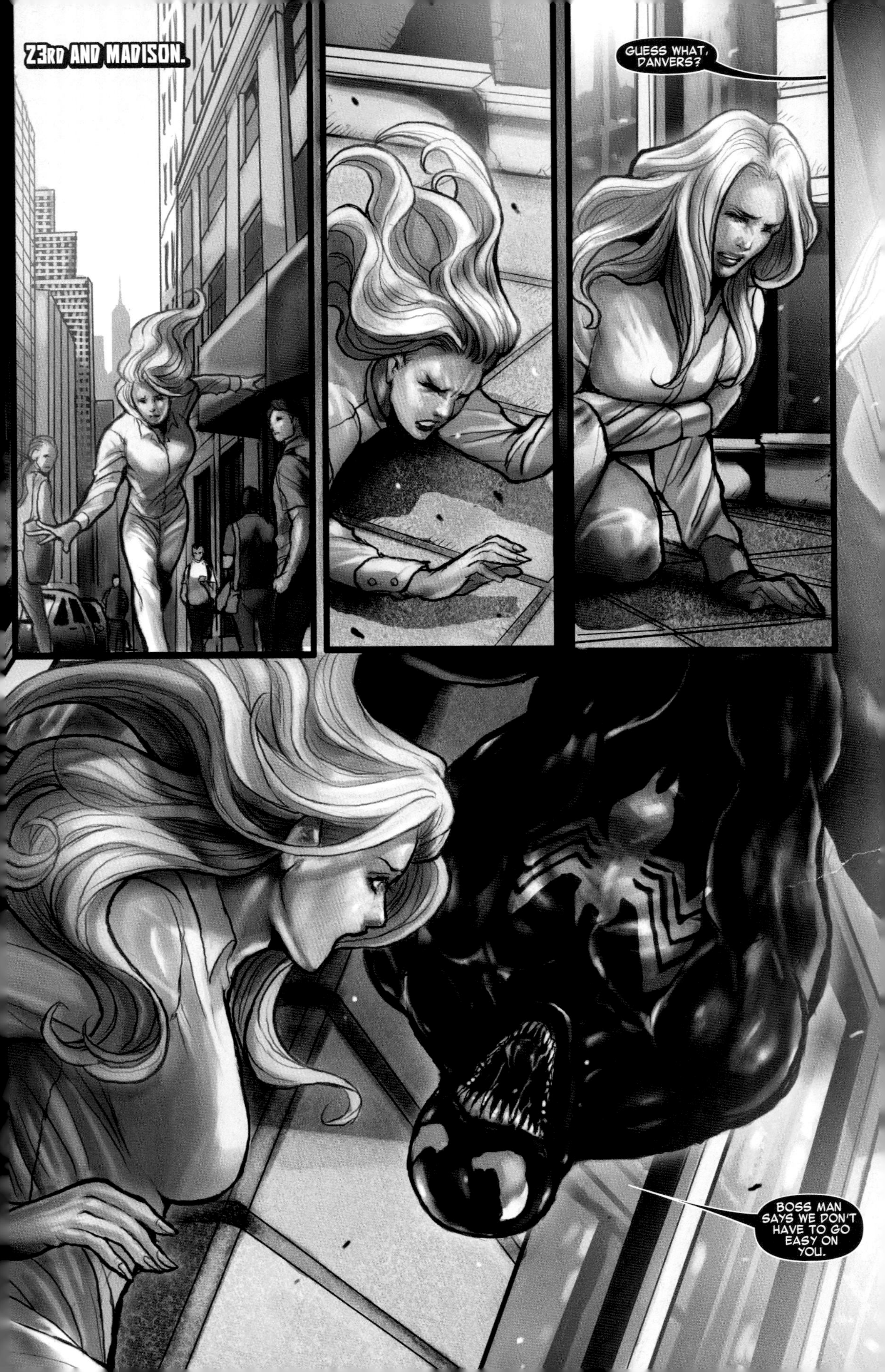
23RD AND MADISON.
GUESS WHAT, DANVERS?
BOSS MAN SAYS WE DON'T HAVE TO GO EASY ON YOU.

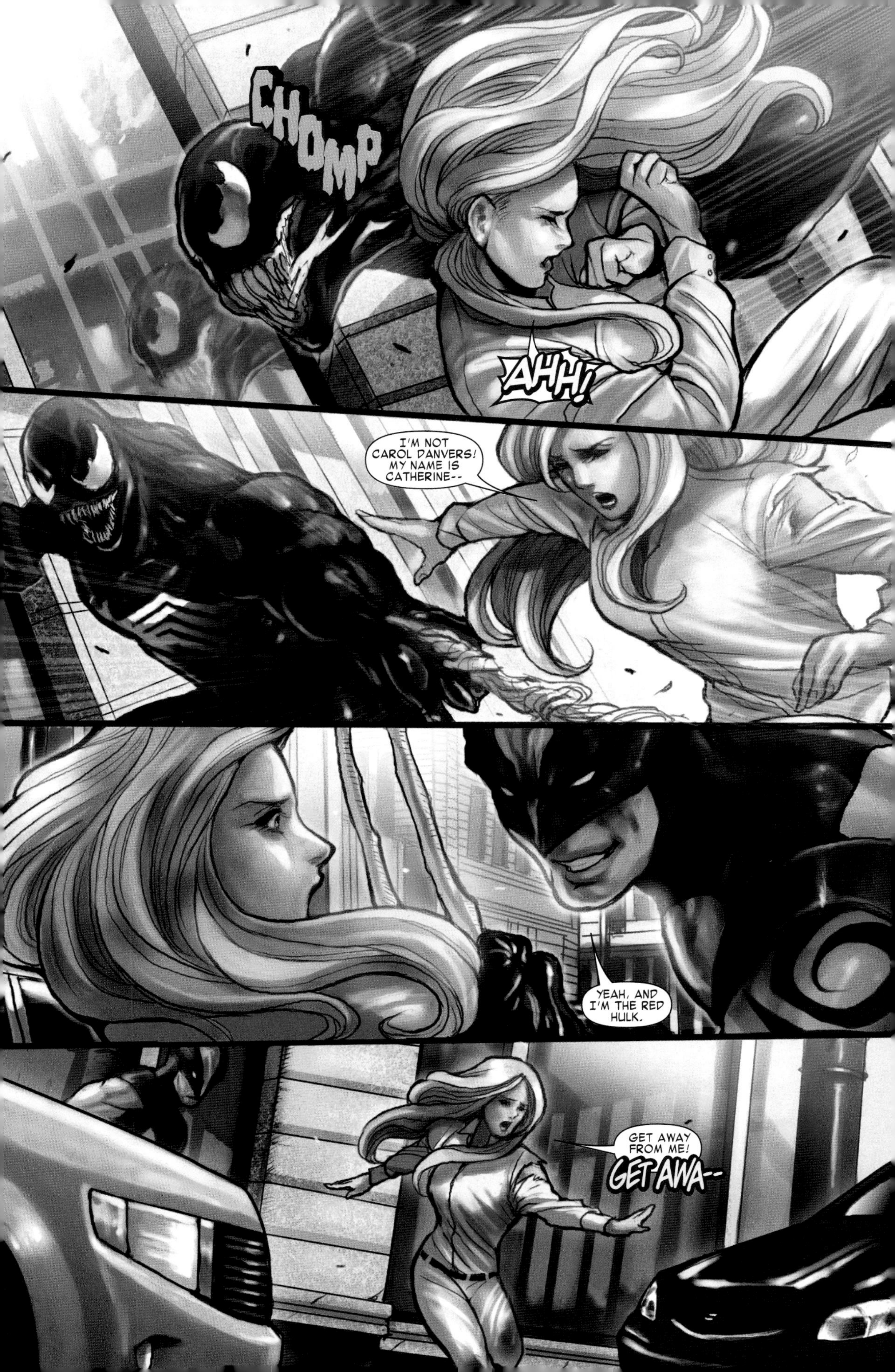
CHOMP
AHH!
I'M NOT CAROL DANVERS! MY NAME IS CATHERINE--
YEAH, AND I'M THE RED HULK.
GET AWAY FROM ME!
GET AWA--

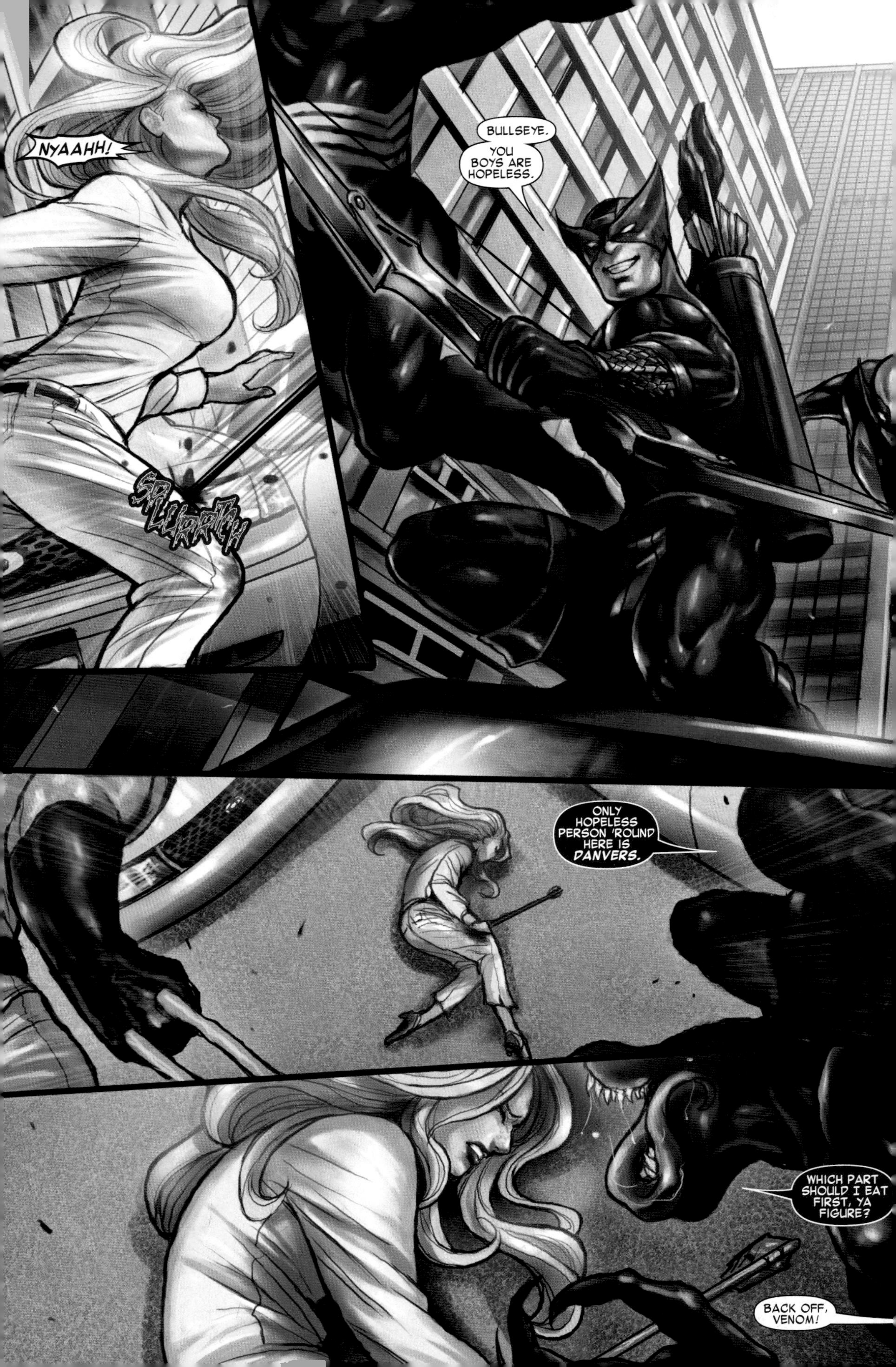
NYAAHH!
SPLURRTCH
BULLSEYE.
YOU BOYS ARE HOPELESS.
ONLY HOPELESS PERSON 'ROUND HERE IS DANVERS.
WHICH PART SHOULD I EAT FIRST, YA FIGURE?
BACK OFF, VENOM!

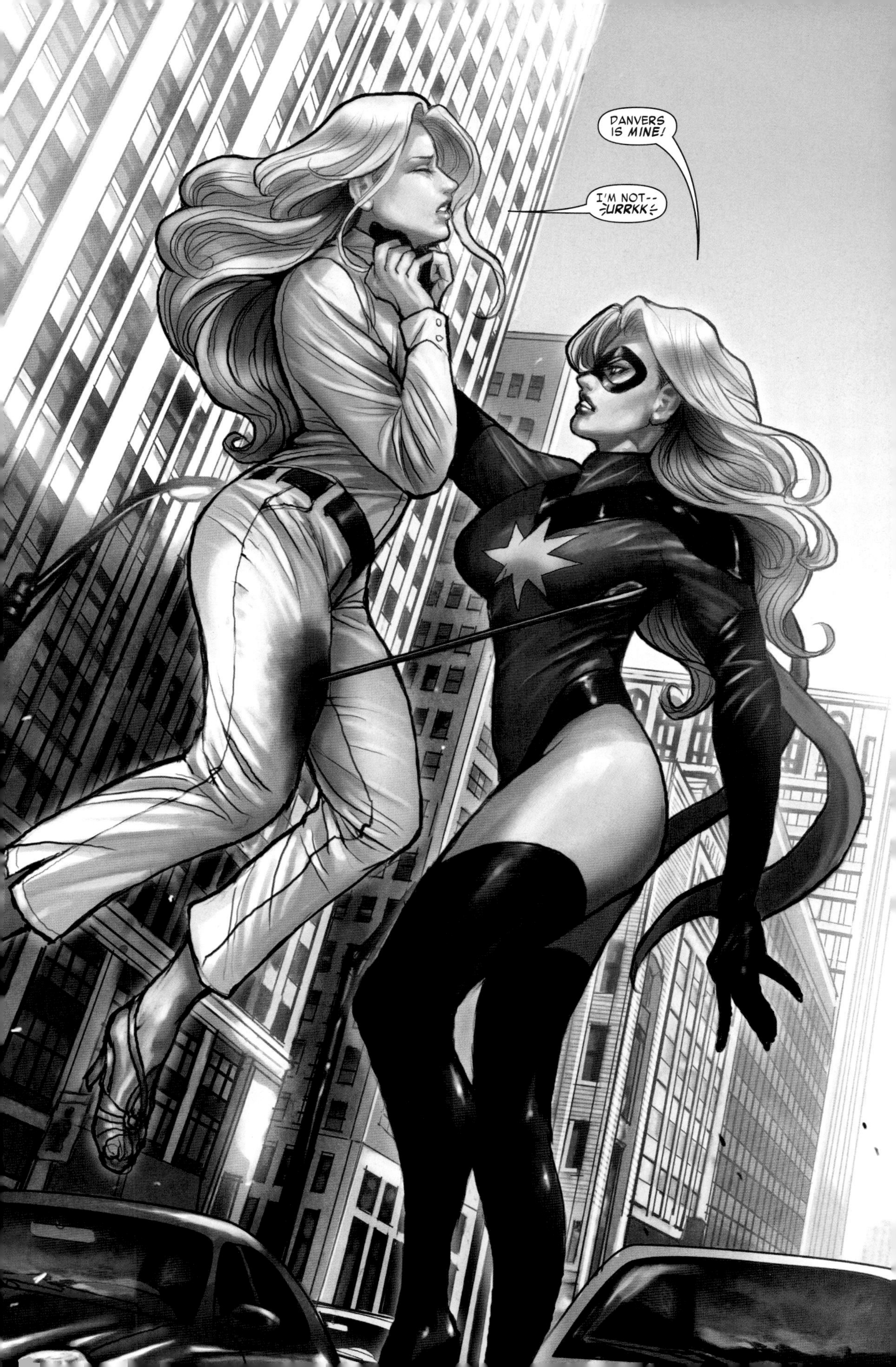
DANVERS IS *MINE!*
I'M NOT-- *-URRKK-*

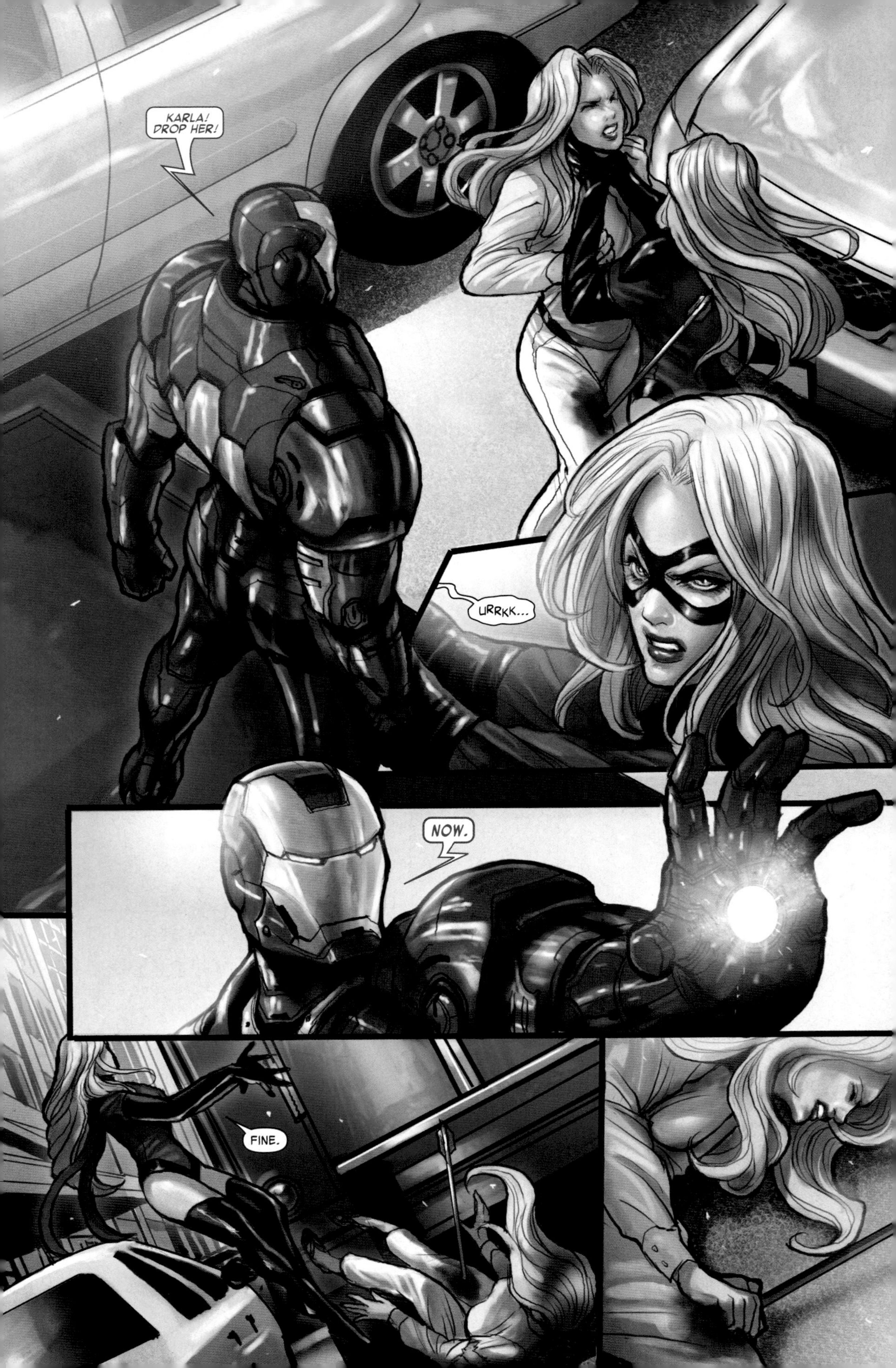
KARLA! DROP HER!
URRKK...
NOW.
FINE.

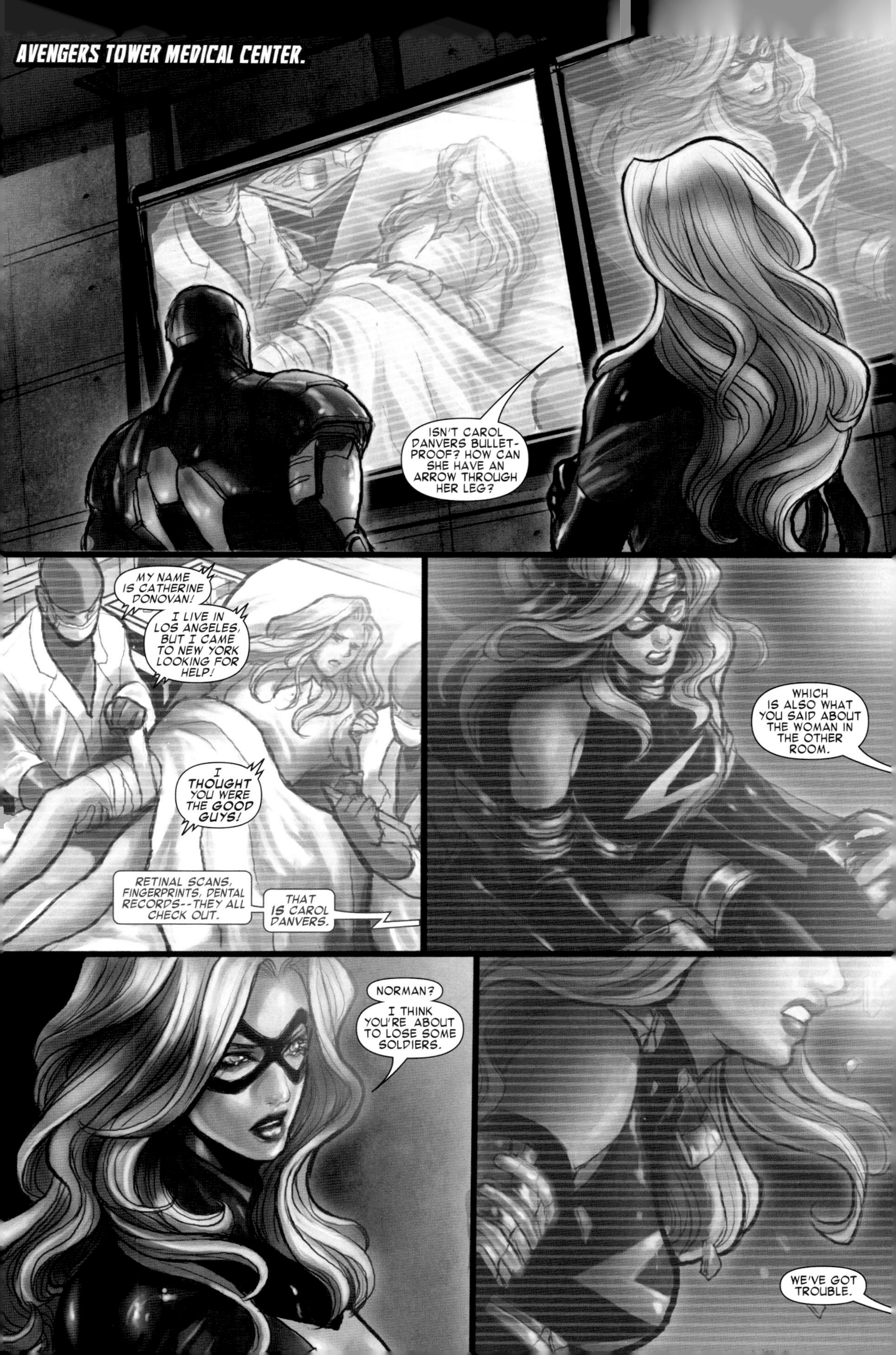
AVENGERS TOWER MEDICAL CENTER.
ISN'T CAROL DANVERS BULLET-PROOF? HOW CAN SHE HAVE AN ARROW THROUGH HER LEG?
MY NAME IS CATHERINE DONOVAN!
I LIVE IN LOS ANGELES, BUT I CAME TO NEW YORK LOOKING FOR HELP!
I THOUGHT YOU WERE THE GOOD GUYS!
RETINAL SCANS, FINGERPRINTS, DENTAL RECORDS--THEY ALL CHECK OUT.
THAT IS CAROL DANVERS.
WHICH IS ALSO WHAT YOU SAID ABOUT THE WOMAN IN THE OTHER ROOM.
NORMAN?
I THINK YOU'RE ABOUT TO LOSE SOME SOLDIERS.
WE'VE GOT TROUBLE.

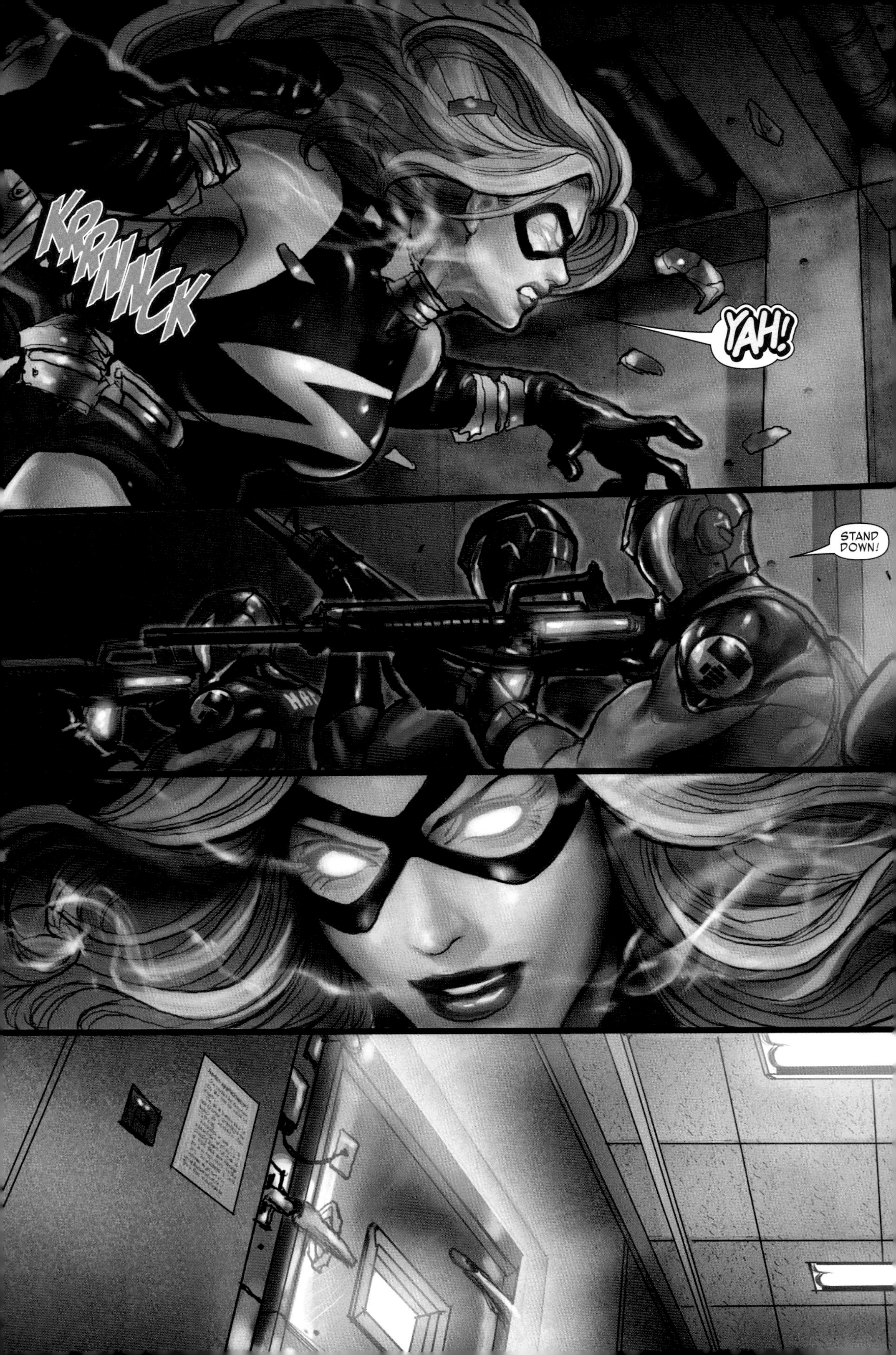
KRRNNCK
YAH!
STAND DOWN!

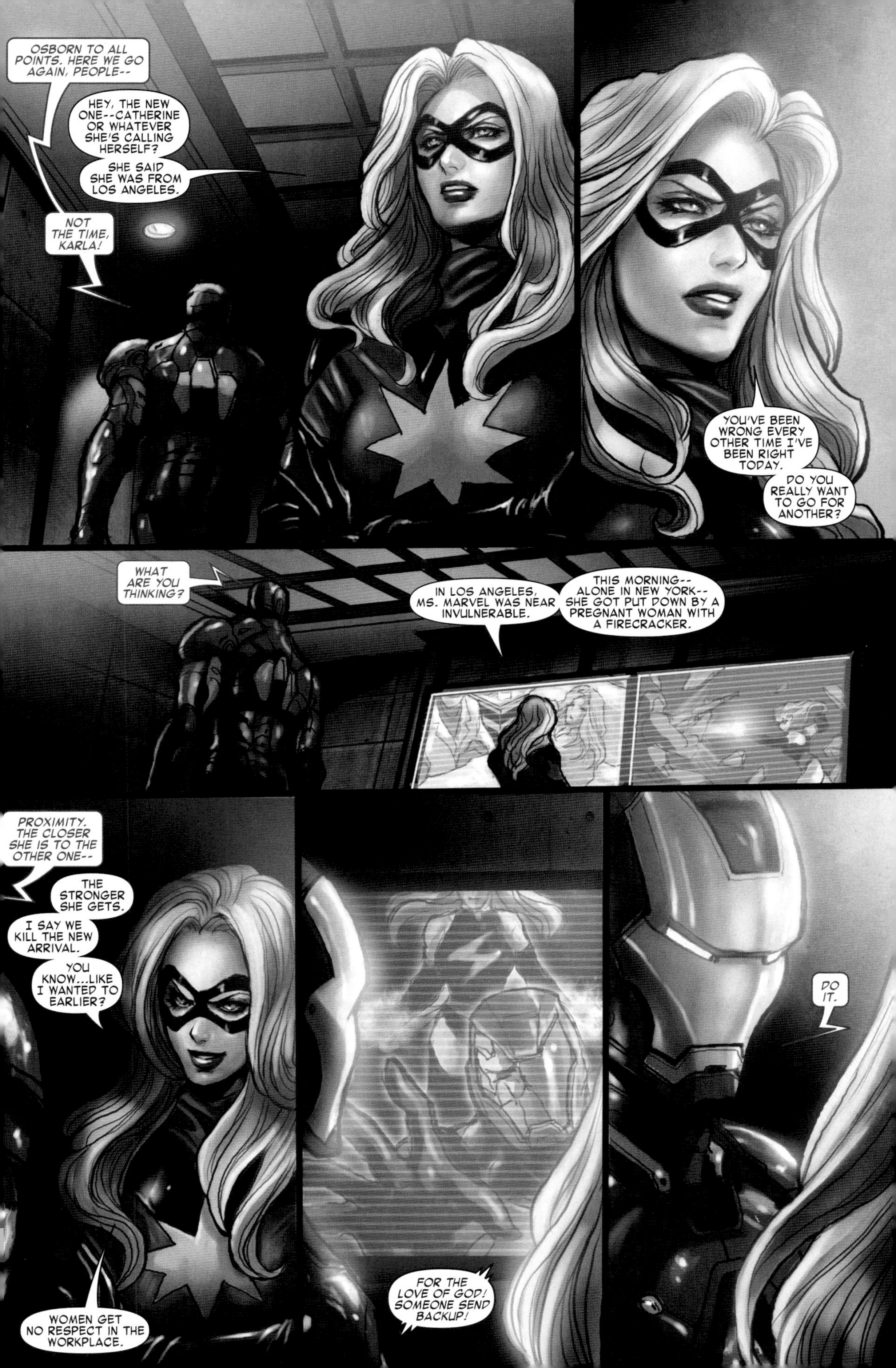
OSBORN TO ALL POINTS. HERE WE GO AGAIN, PEOPLE--
HEY, THE NEW ONE--CATHERINE OR WHATEVER SHE'S CALLING HERSELF?
SHE SAID SHE WAS FROM LOS ANGELES.
NOT THE TIME, KARLA!
YOU'VE BEEN WRONG EVERY OTHER TIME I'VE BEEN RIGHT TODAY.
DO YOU REALLY WANT TO GO FOR ANOTHER?
WHAT ARE YOU THINKING?
IN LOS ANGELES, MS. MARVEL WAS NEAR INVULNERABLE.
THIS MORNING-- ALONE IN NEW YORK-- SHE GOT PUT DOWN BY A PREGNANT WOMAN WITH A FIRECRACKER.
PROXIMITY. THE CLOSER SHE IS TO THE OTHER ONE--
THE STRONGER SHE GETS.
I SAY WE KILL THE NEW ARRIVAL.
YOU KNOW...LIKE I WANTED TO EARLIER?
WOMEN GET NO RESPECT IN THE WORKPLACE.
FOR THE LOVE OF GOD! SOMEONE SEND BACKUP!
DO IT.

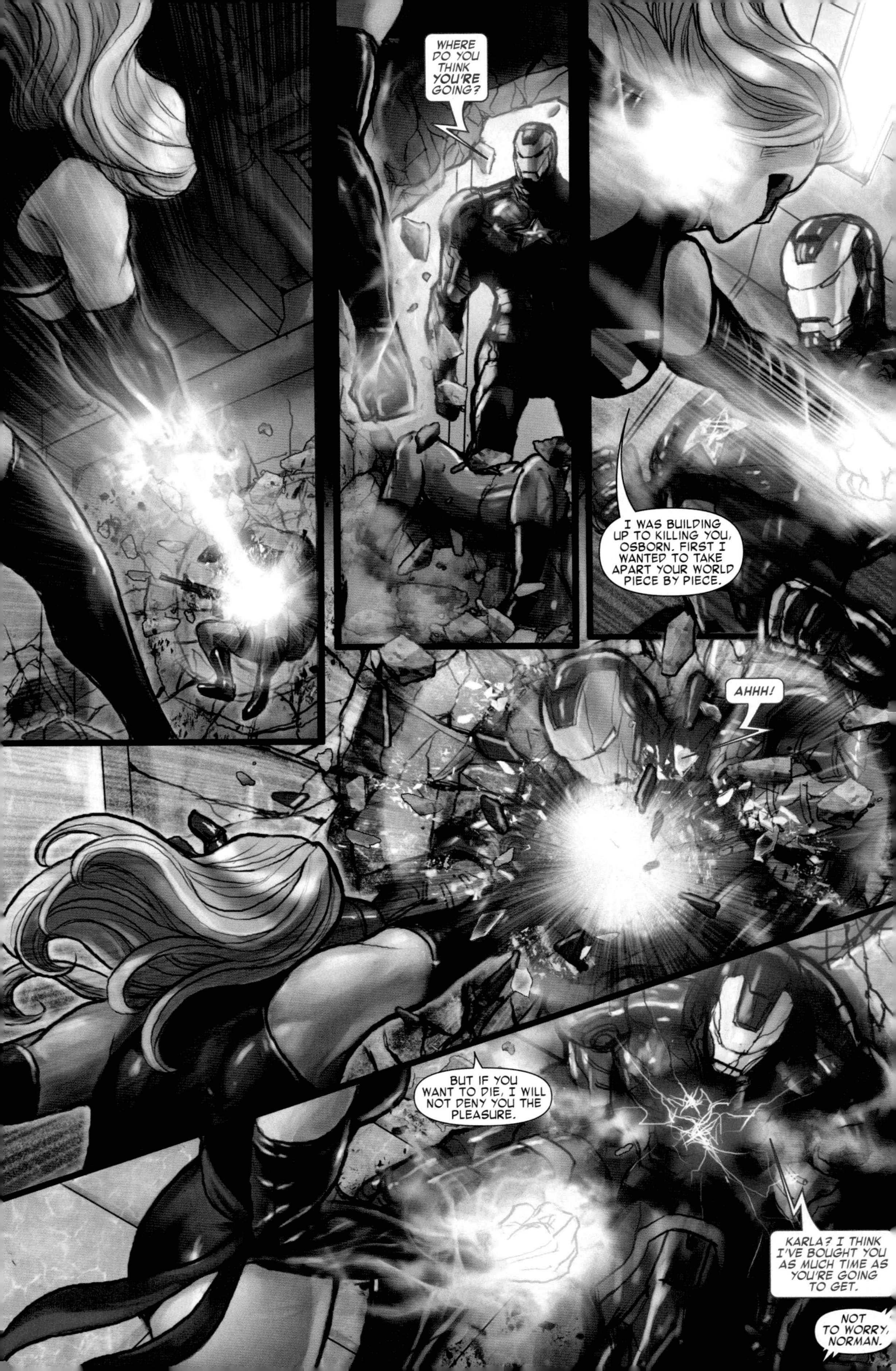

WHERE DO YOU THINK YOU'RE GOING?
I WAS BUILDING UP TO KILLING YOU, OSBORN. FIRST I WANTED TO TAKE APART YOUR WORLD PIECE BY PIECE.
AHHH!
BUT IF YOU WANT TO DIE, I WILL NOT DENY YOU THE PLEASURE.
KARLA? I THINK I'VE BOUGHT YOU AS MUCH TIME AS YOU'RE GOING TO GET.
NOT TO WORRY, NORMAN.

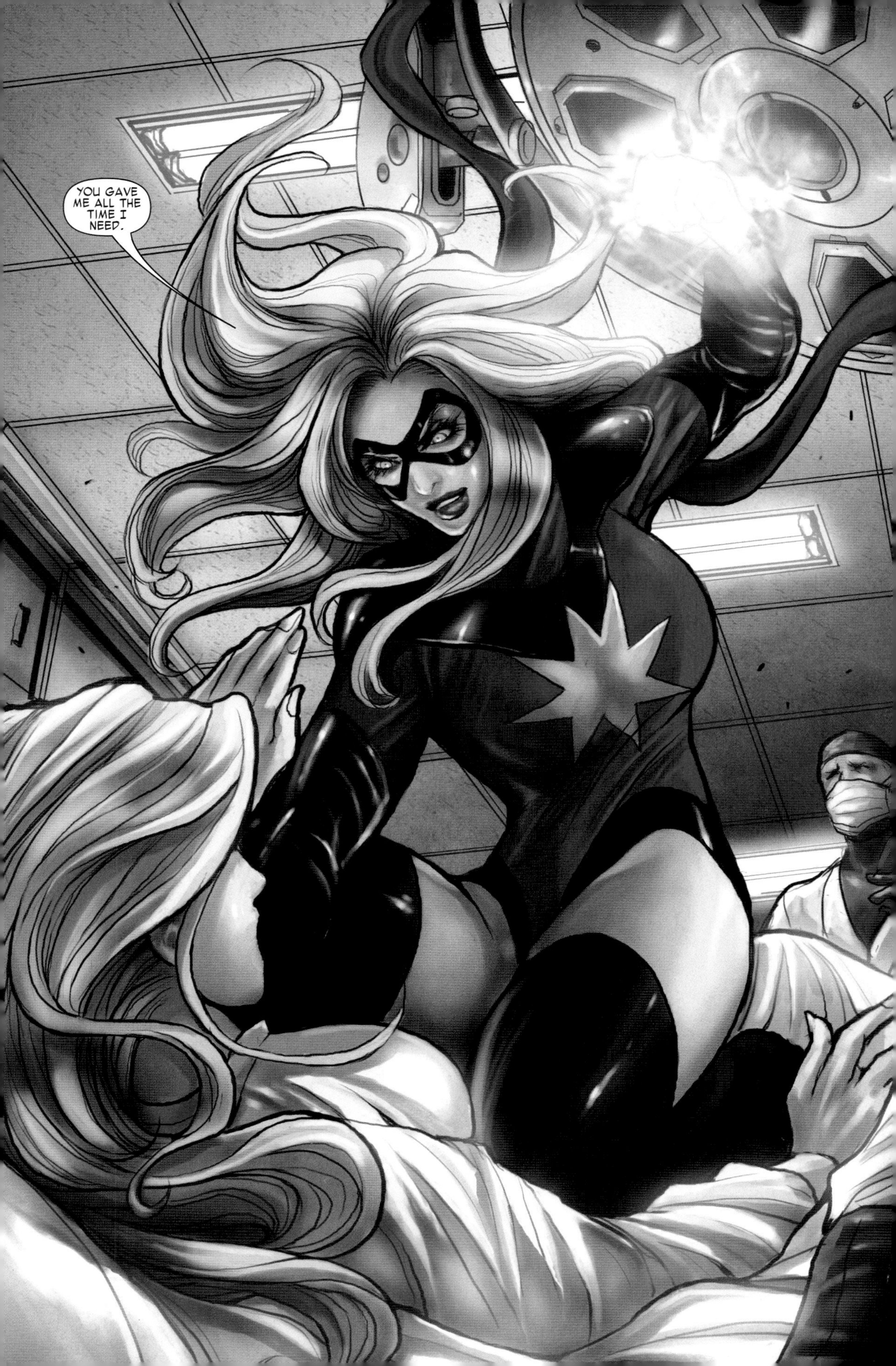
YOU GAVE ME ALL THE TIME I NEED.

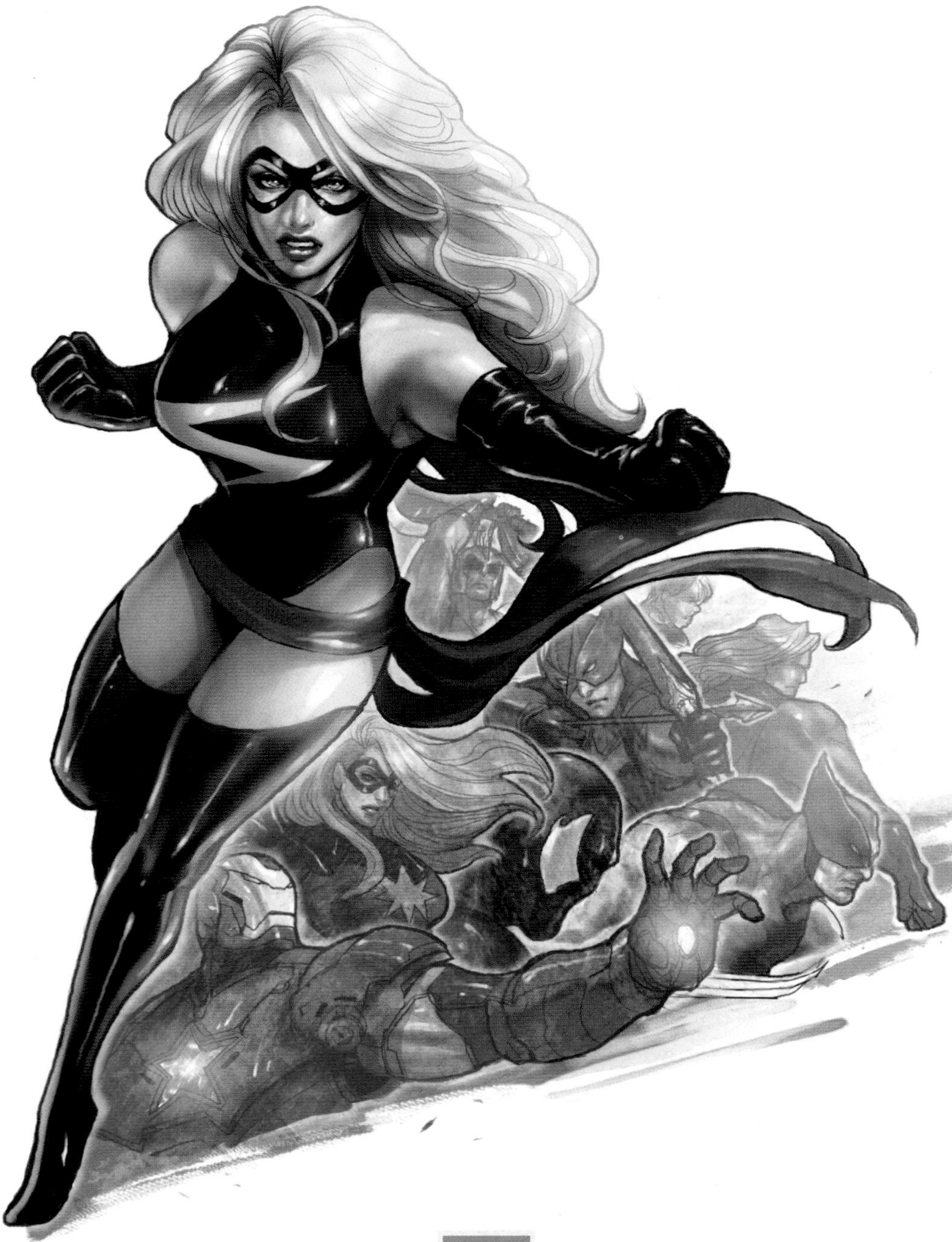

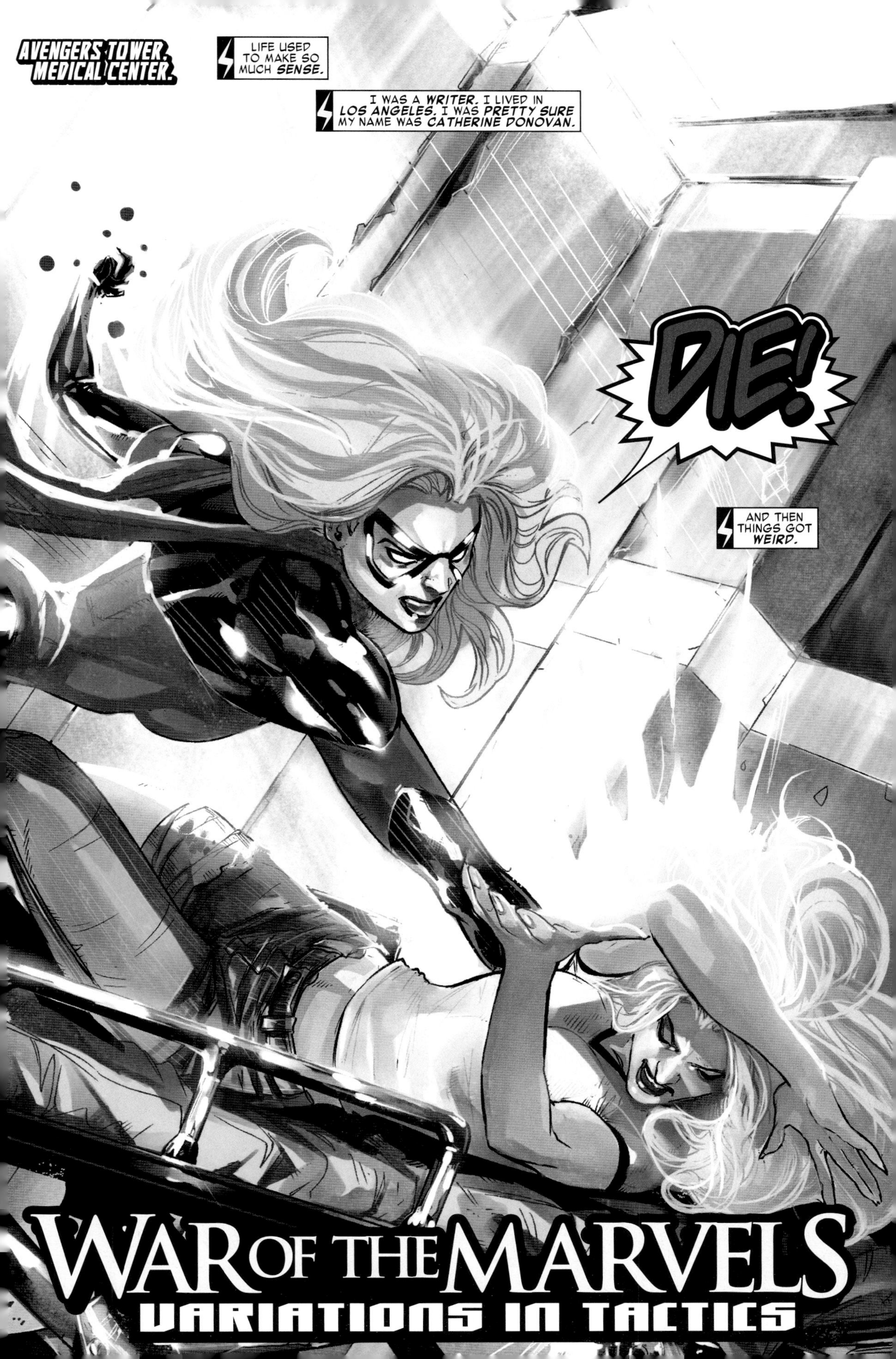
AVENGERS TOWER, MEDICAL CENTER.
LIFE USED TO MAKE SO MUCH SENSE.
I WAS A WRITER. I LIVED IN LOS ANGELES. I WAS PRETTY SURE MY NAME WAS CATHERINE DONOVAN.
DIE!
AND THEN THINGS GOT WEIRD.
WAR OF THE MARVELS
VARIATIONS IN TACTICS

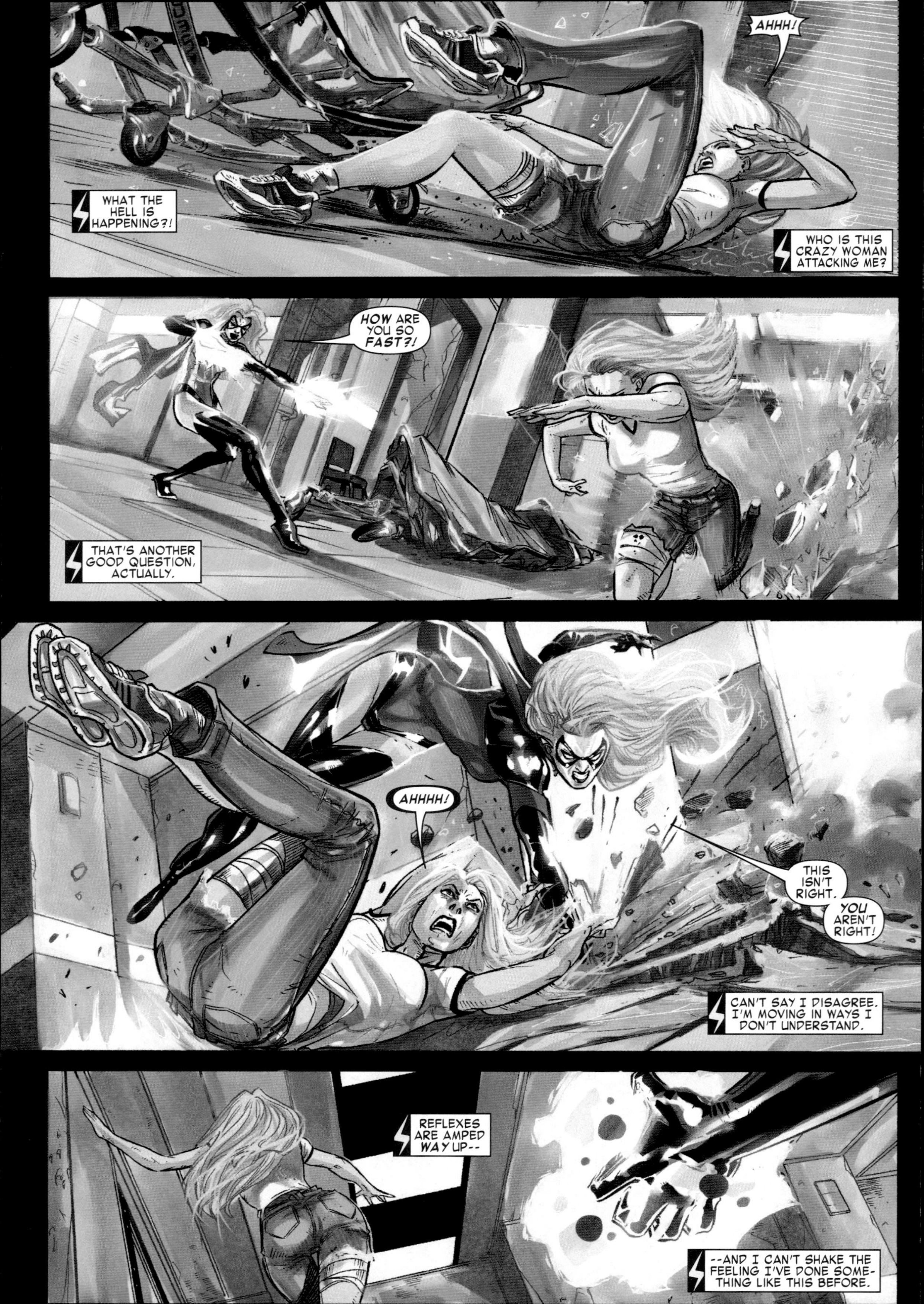

AHHH!
WHAT THE HELL IS HAPPENING?!
WHO IS THIS CRAZY WOMAN ATTACKING ME?
HOW ARE YOU SO FAST?!
THAT'S ANOTHER GOOD QUESTION, ACTUALLY.
AHHHH!
THIS ISN'T RIGHT.
YOU AREN'T RIGHT!
CAN'T SAY I DISAGREE. I'M MOVING IN WAYS I DON'T UNDERSTAND.
REFLEXES ARE AMPED WAY UP--
--AND I CAN'T SHAKE THE FEELING I'VE DONE SOMETHING LIKE THIS BEFORE.

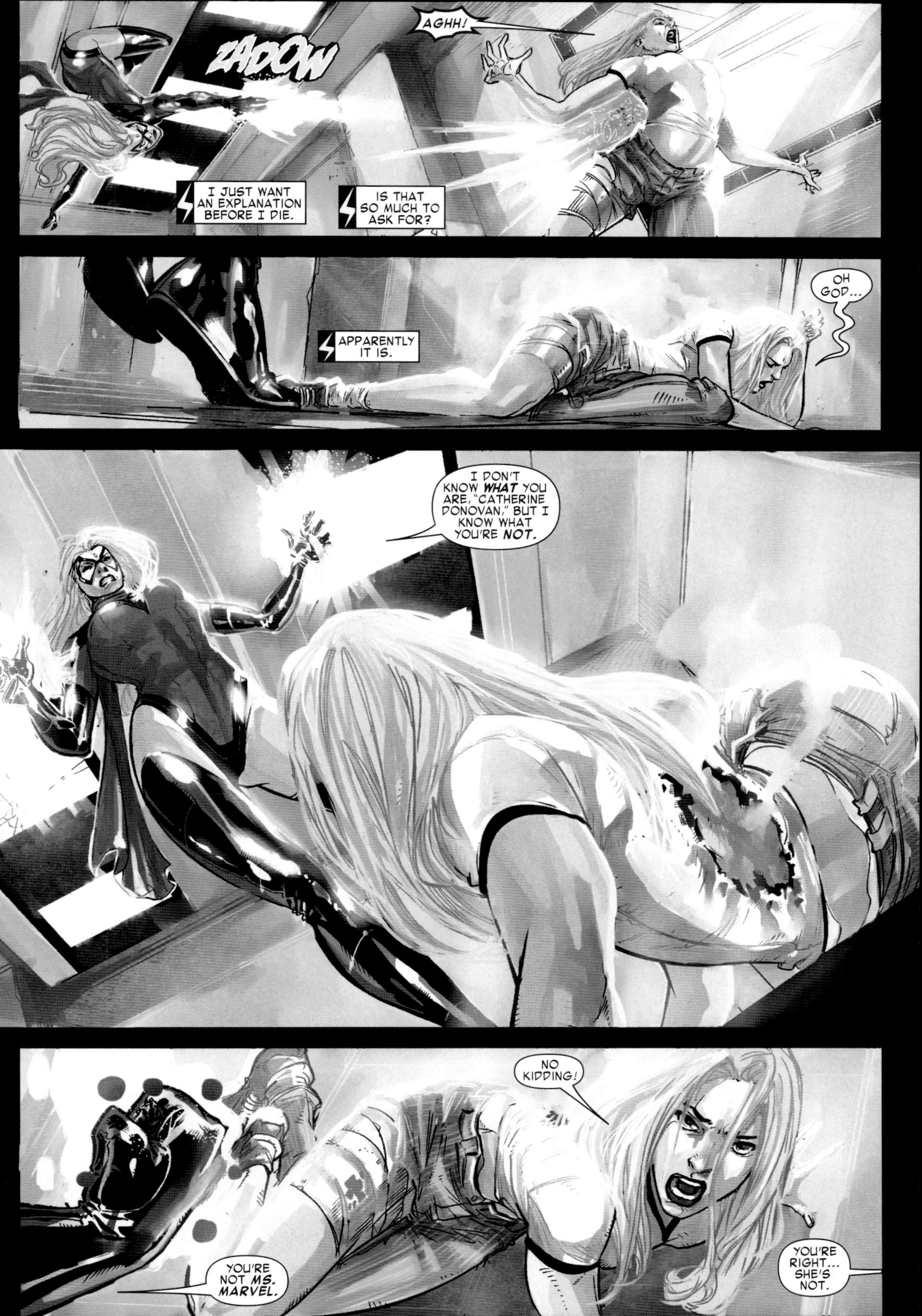
ZADOW
AGHH!
I JUST WANT AN EXPLANATION BEFORE I DIE.
IS THAT SO MUCH TO ASK FOR?
APPARENTLY IT IS.
OH GOD...
I DON'T KNOW **WHAT** YOU ARE, "CATHERINE DONOVAN," BUT I KNOW WHAT YOU'RE **NOT.**
NO KIDDING!
YOU'RE NOT **MS. MARVEL.**
YOU'RE RIGHT... SHE'S NOT.

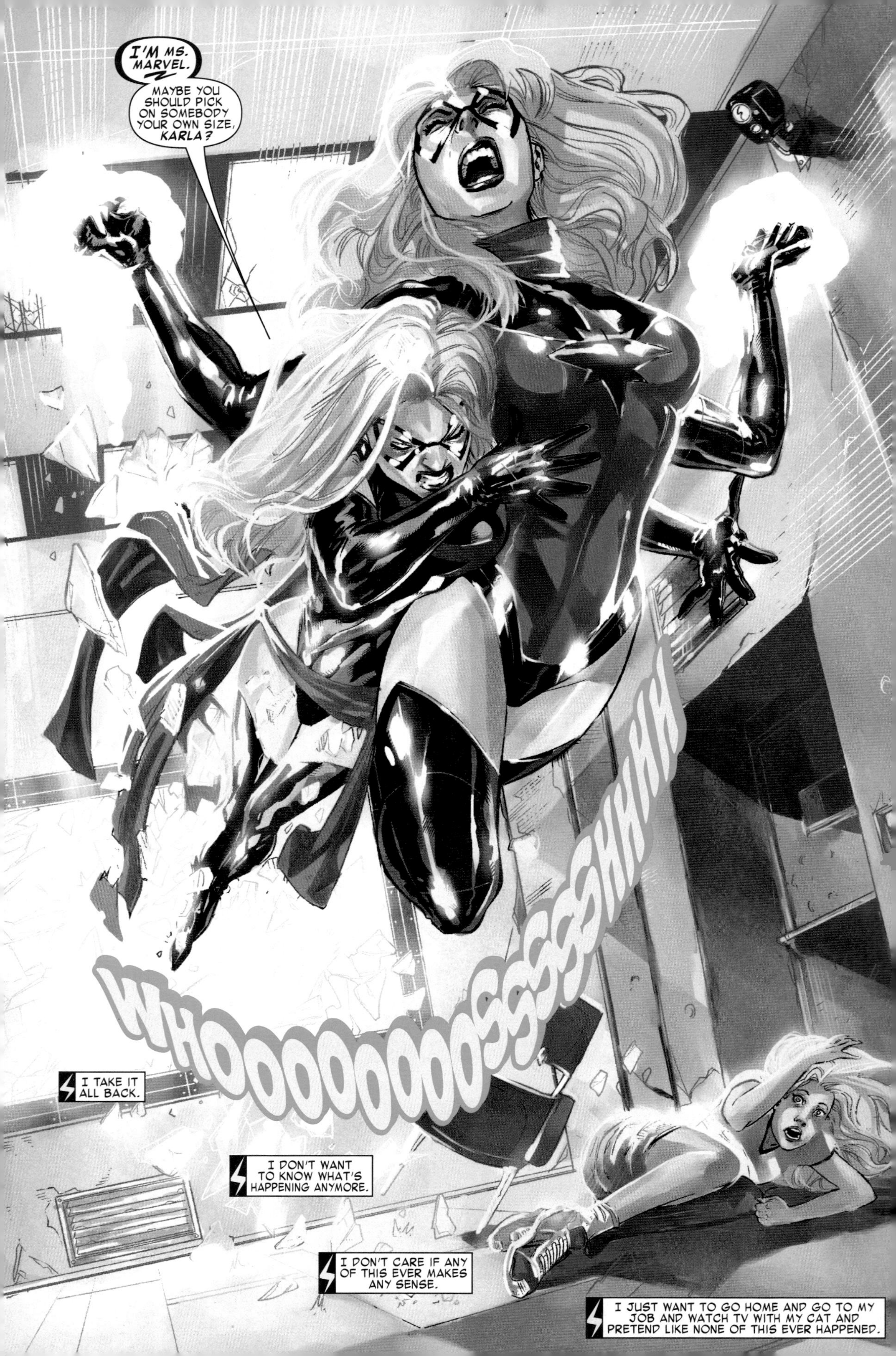
I'M MS. MARVEL.
MAYBE YOU SHOULD PICK ON SOMEBODY YOUR OWN SIZE, KARLA?
WHOOOOOOOOOSSSSHHHH
I TAKE IT ALL BACK.
I DON'T WANT TO KNOW WHAT'S HAPPENING ANYMORE.
I DON'T CARE IF ANY OF THIS EVER MAKES ANY SENSE.
I JUST WANT TO GO HOME AND GO TO MY JOB AND WATCH TV WITH MY CAT AND PRETEND LIKE NONE OF THIS EVER HAPPENED.

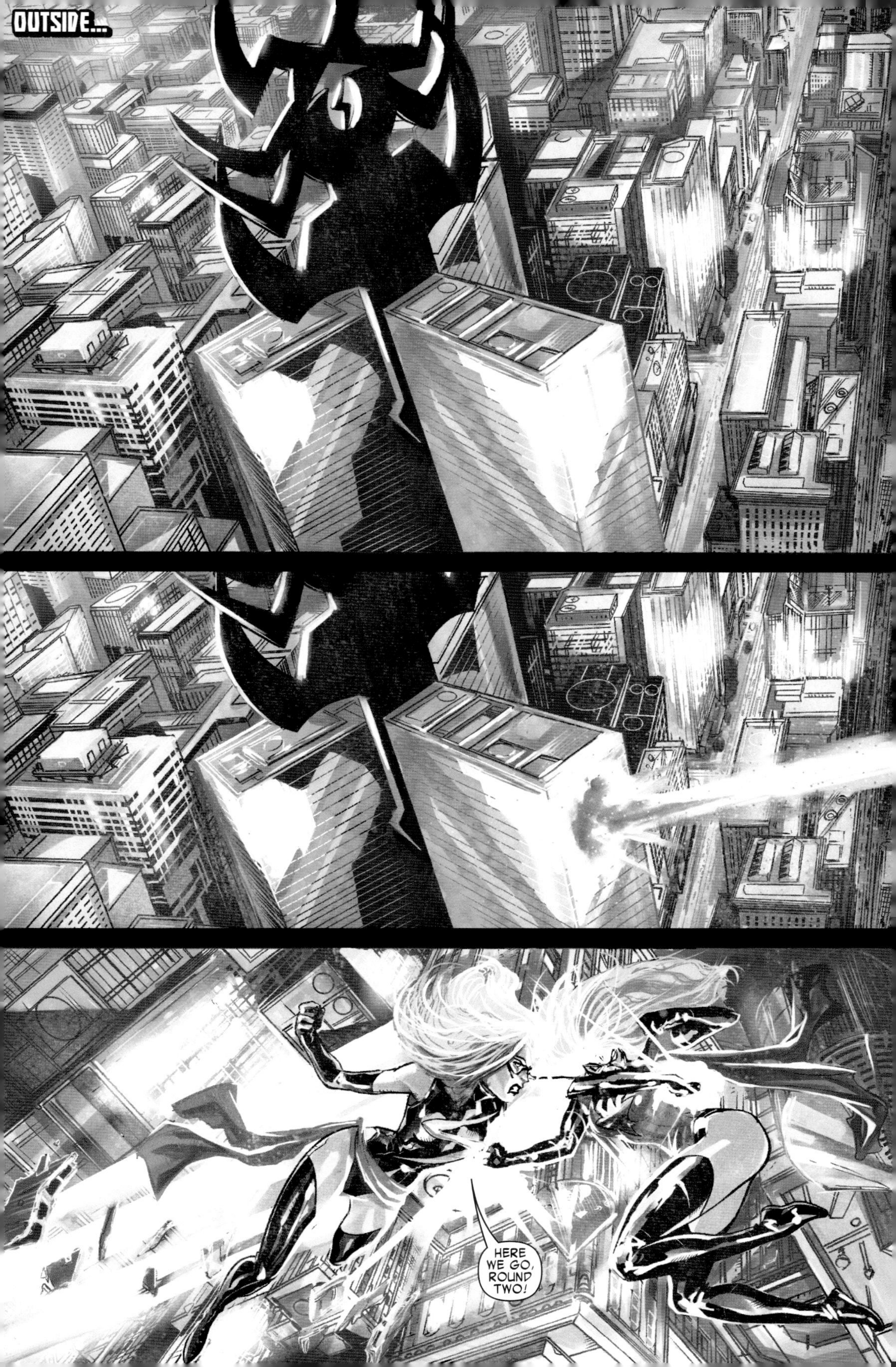
OUTSIDE...
HERE WE GO, ROUND TWO!

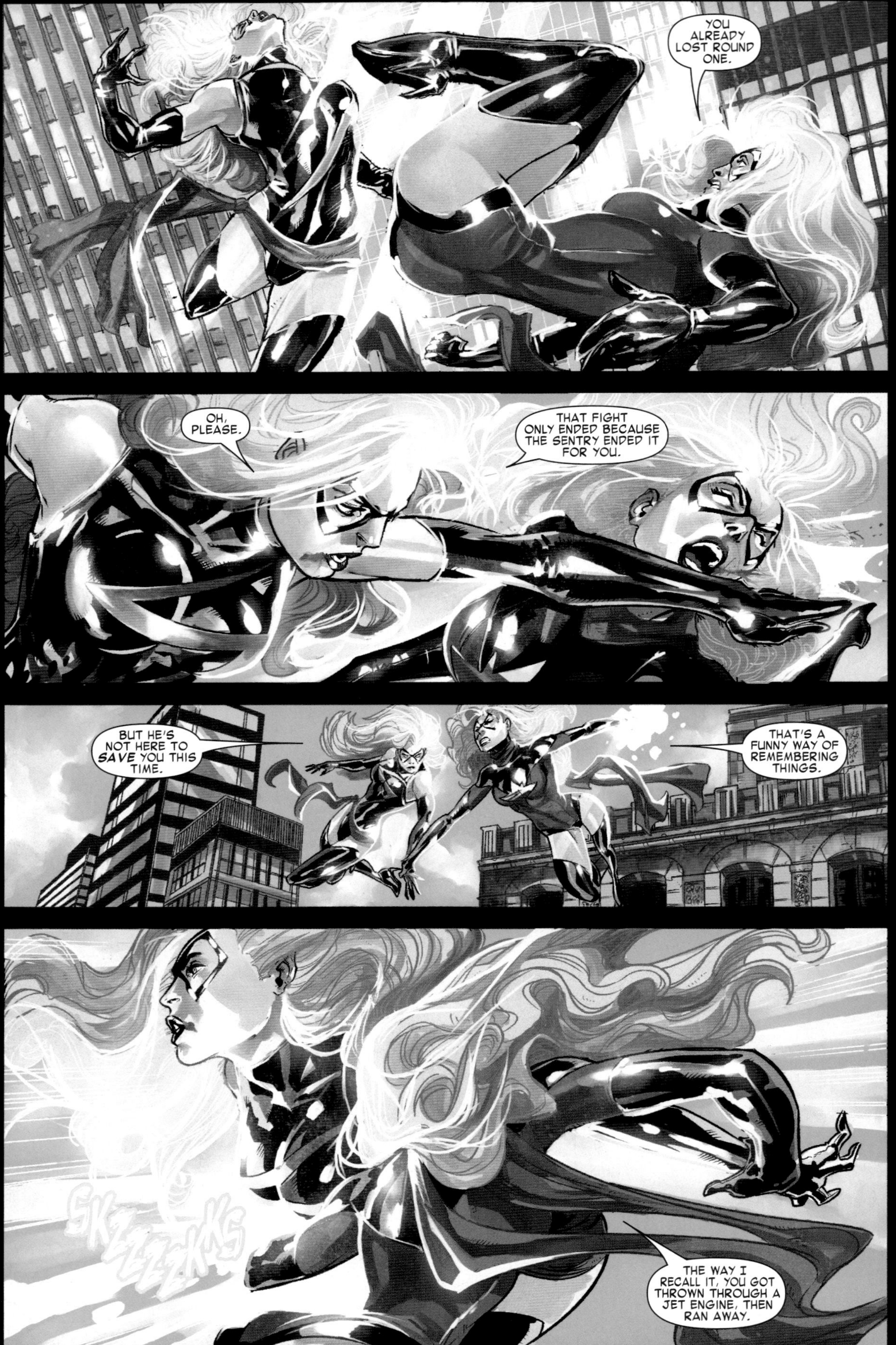
YOU ALREADY LOST ROUND ONE.
OH, PLEASE.
THAT FIGHT ONLY ENDED BECAUSE THE SENTRY ENDED IT FOR YOU.
BUT HE'S NOT HERE TO **SAVE** YOU THIS TIME.
THAT'S A FUNNY WAY OF REMEMBERING THINGS.
SKZZZZKKS
THE WAY I RECALL IT, YOU GOT THROWN THROUGH A JET ENGINE, THEN RAN AWAY.

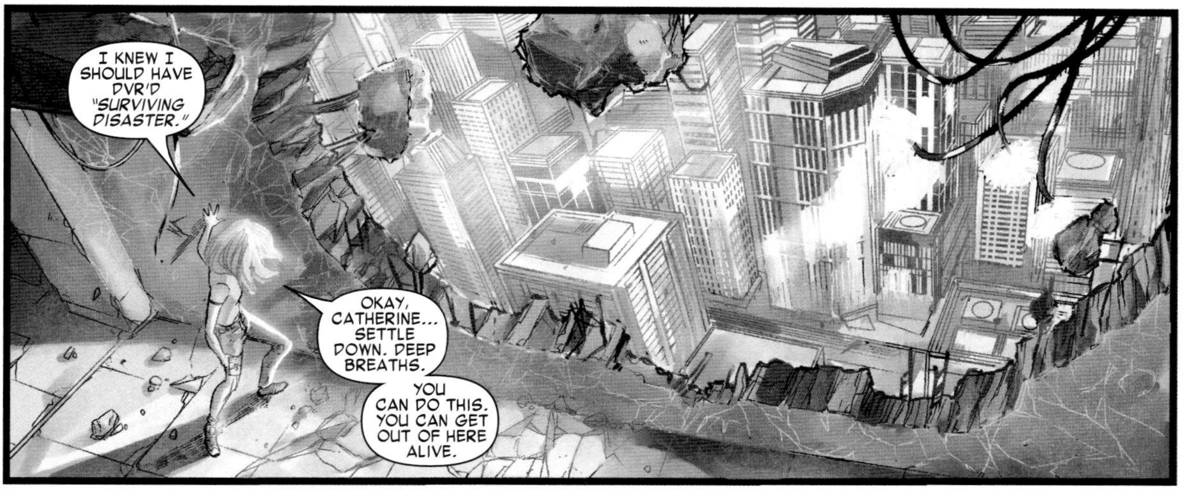
I KNEW I SHOULD HAVE DVR'D "SURVIVING DISASTER."
OKAY, CATHERINE... SETTLE DOWN. DEEP BREATHS.
YOU CAN DO THIS. YOU CAN GET OUT OF HERE ALIVE.

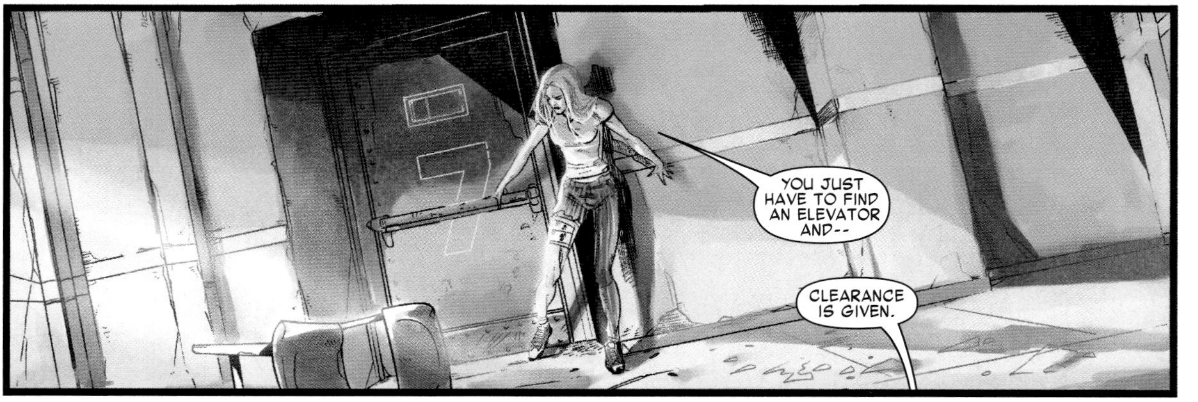
YOU JUST HAVE TO FIND AN ELEVATOR AND--
CLEARANCE IS GIVEN.

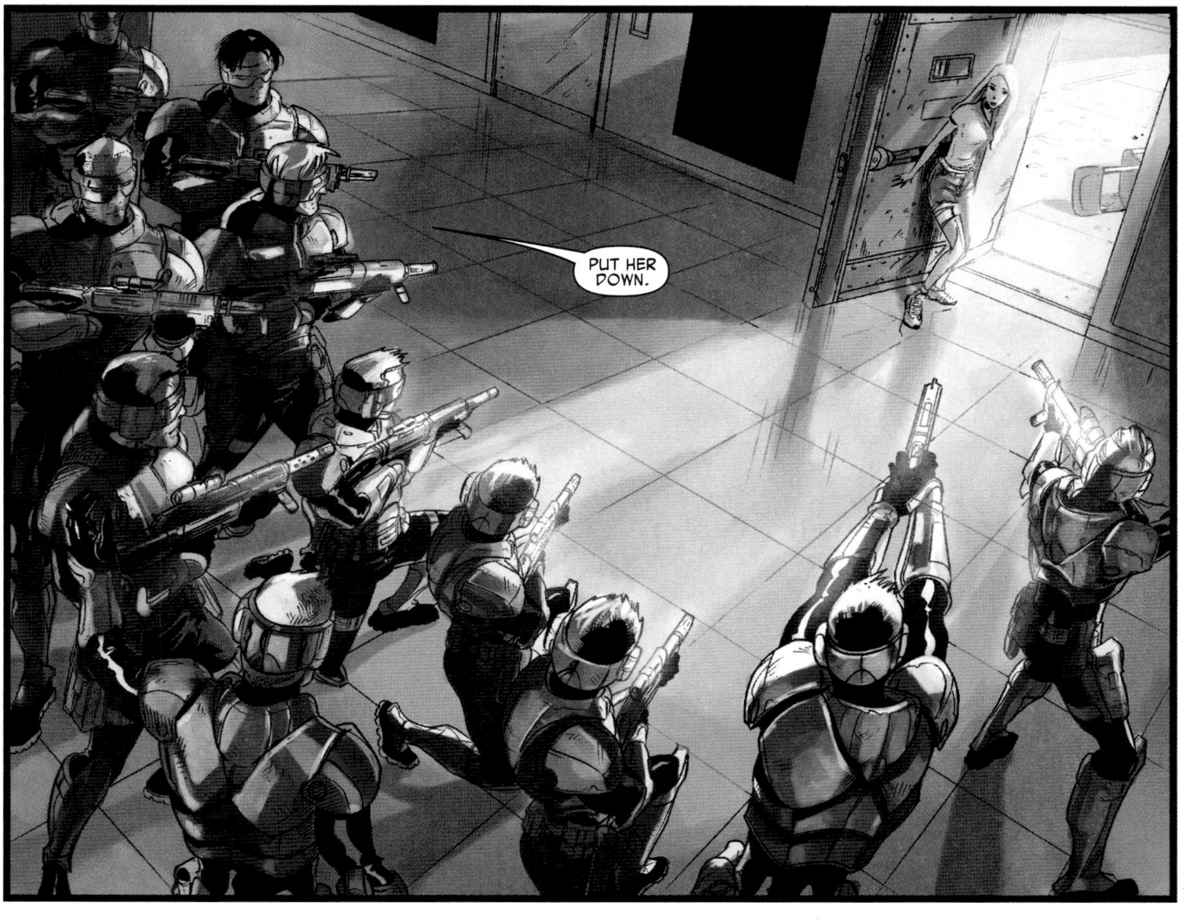
PUT HER DOWN.

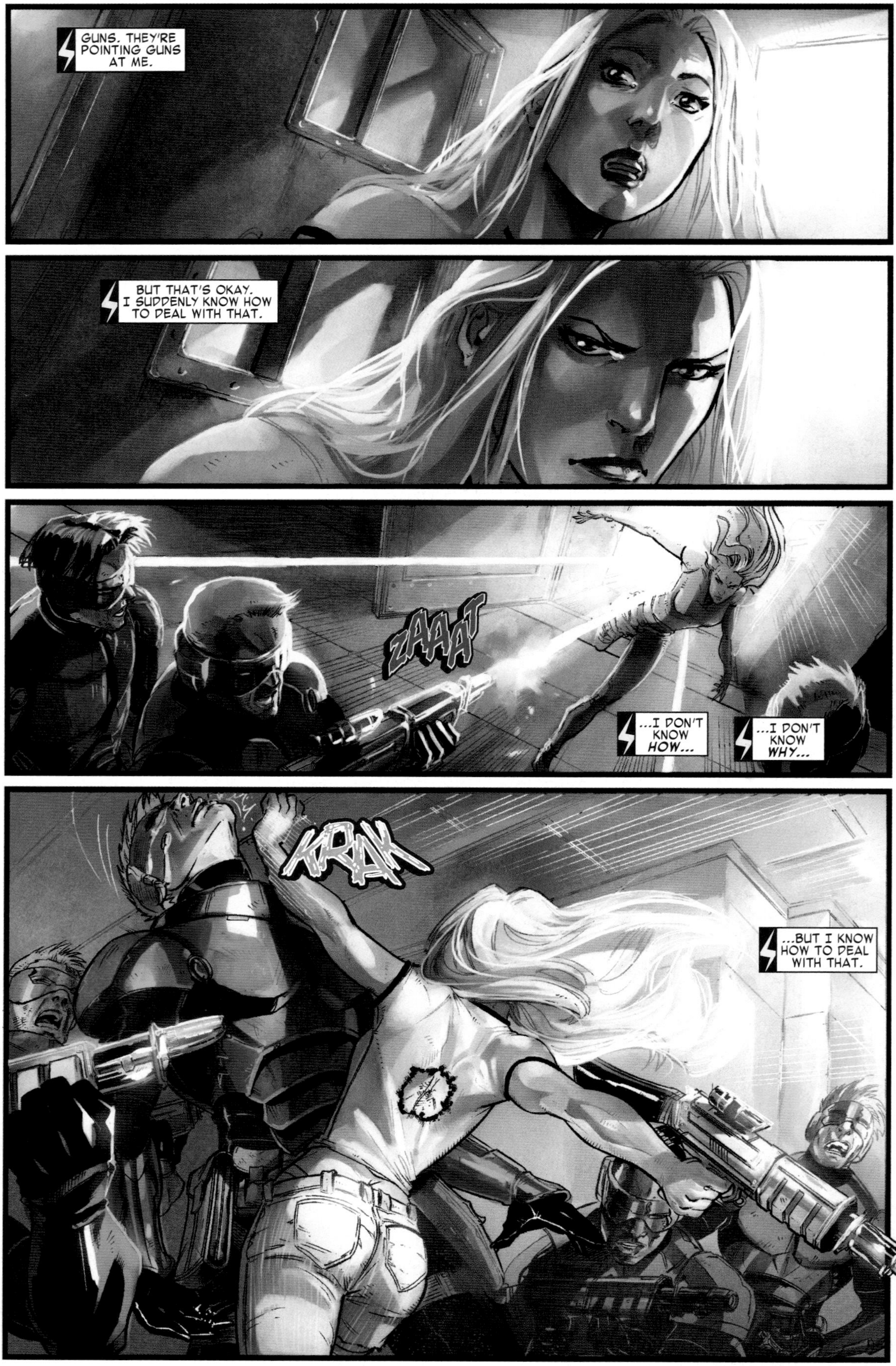

GUNS. THEY'RE POINTING GUNS AT ME.
BUT THAT'S OKAY. I SUDDENLY KNOW HOW TO DEAL WITH THAT.
ZAAAT
...I DON'T KNOW *HOW*...
...I DON'T KNOW *WHY*...
KRAK
...BUT I KNOW HOW TO DEAL WITH THAT.

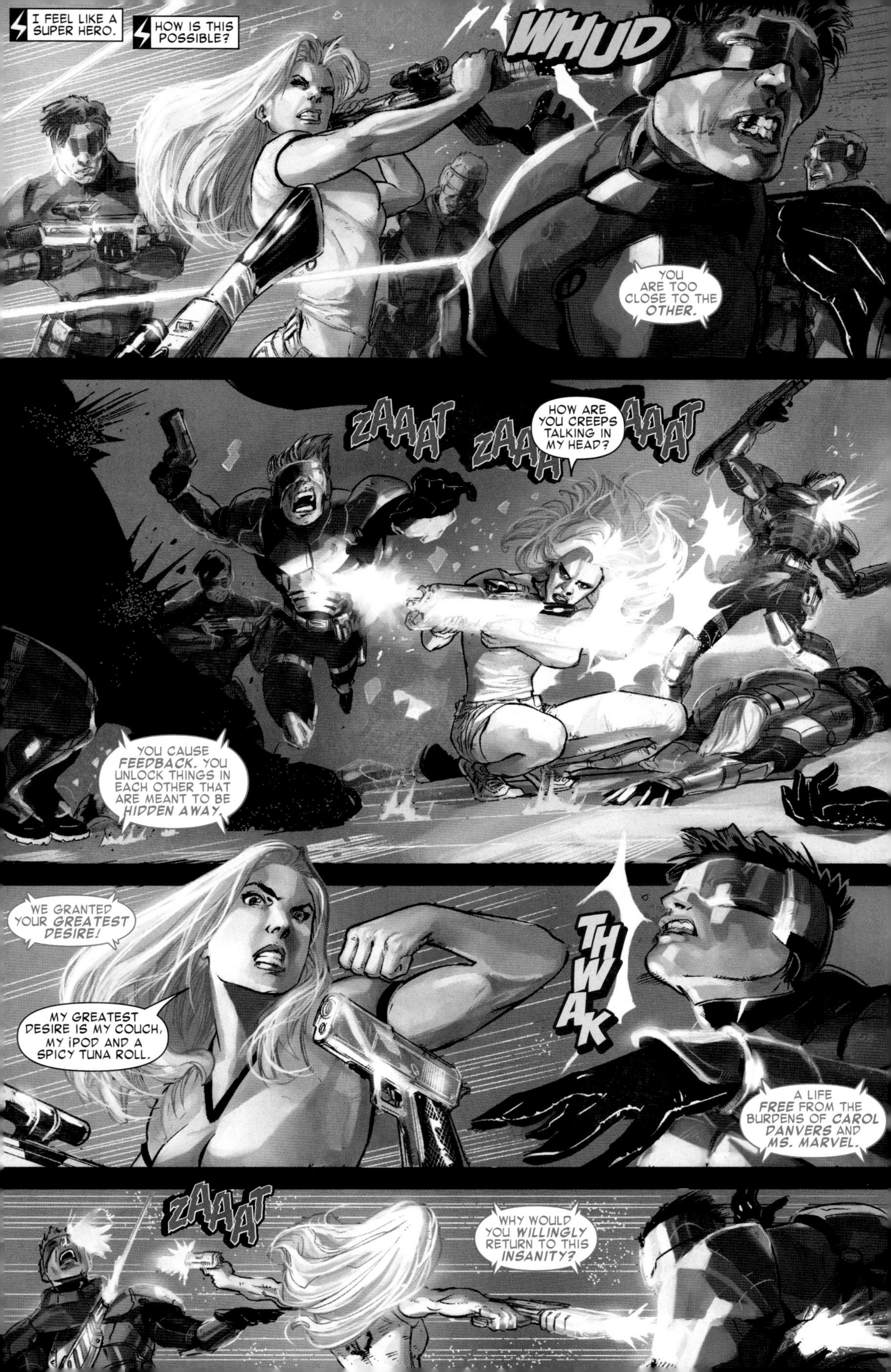
I FEEL LIKE A SUPER HERO.
HOW IS THIS POSSIBLE?
WHUD
YOU ARE TOO CLOSE TO THE OTHER.
ZAAAT
ZAAAAT
HOW ARE YOU CREEPS TALKING IN MY HEAD?
AAAT
YOU CAUSE FEEDBACK. YOU UNLOCK THINGS IN EACH OTHER THAT ARE MEANT TO BE HIDDEN AWAY.
WE GRANTED YOUR GREATEST DESIRE!
MY GREATEST DESIRE IS MY COUCH, MY iPOD AND A SPICY TUNA ROLL.
THWAK
A LIFE FREE FROM THE BURDENS OF CAROL DANVERS AND MS. MARVEL.
ZAAAT
WHY WOULD YOU WILLINGLY RETURN TO THIS INSANITY?

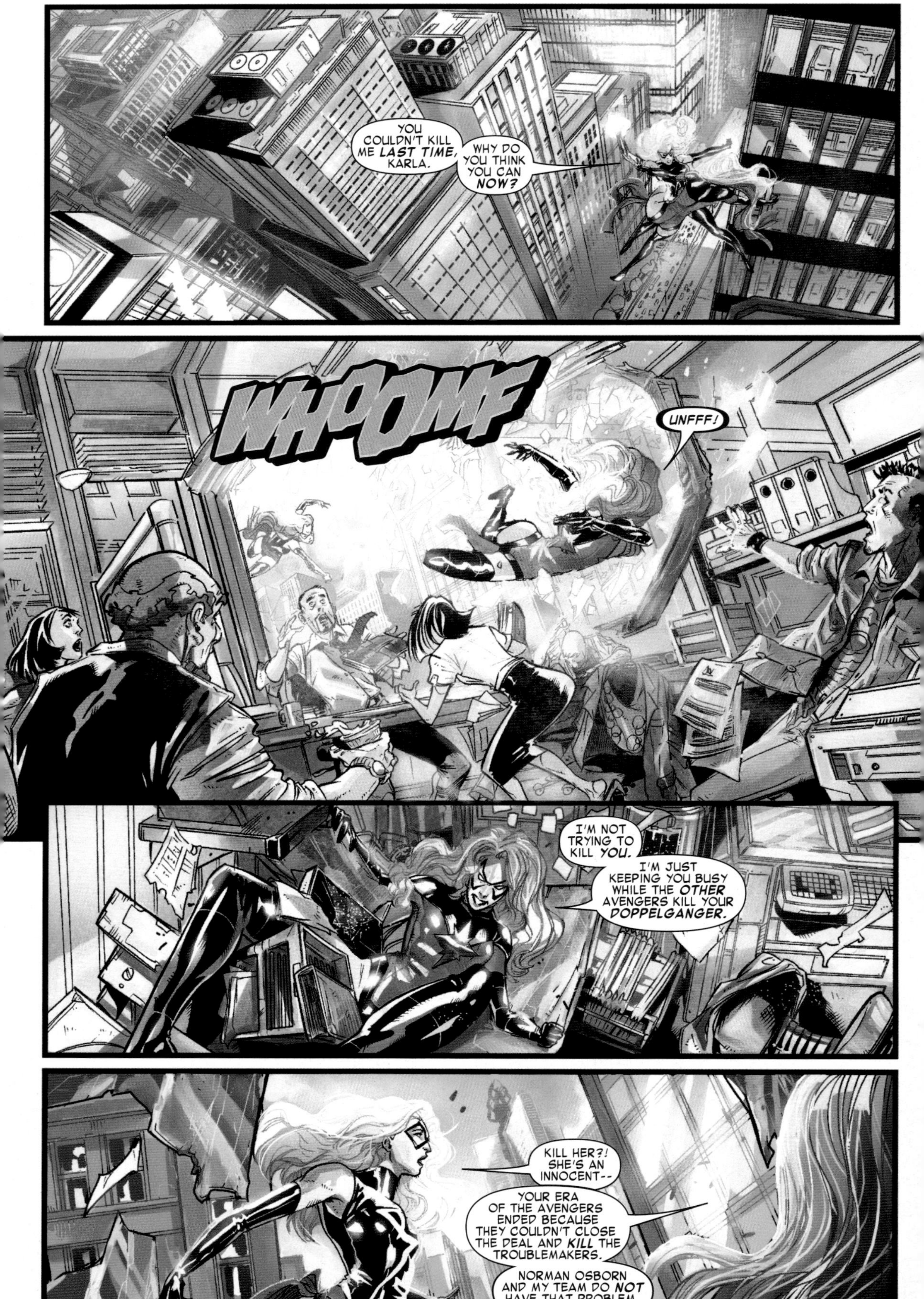
YOU COULDN'T KILL ME LAST TIME, KARLA.
WHY DO YOU THINK YOU CAN NOW?
WHOOMF
UNFFF!
I'M NOT TRYING TO KILL YOU.
I'M JUST KEEPING YOU BUSY WHILE THE OTHER AVENGERS KILL YOUR DOPPELGANGER.
KILL HER?! SHE'S AN INNOCENT--
YOUR ERA OF THE AVENGERS ENDED BECAUSE THEY COULDN'T CLOSE THE DEAL AND KILL THE TROUBLEMAKERS.
NORMAN OSBORN AND MY TEAM DO NOT HAVE THAT PROBLEM.

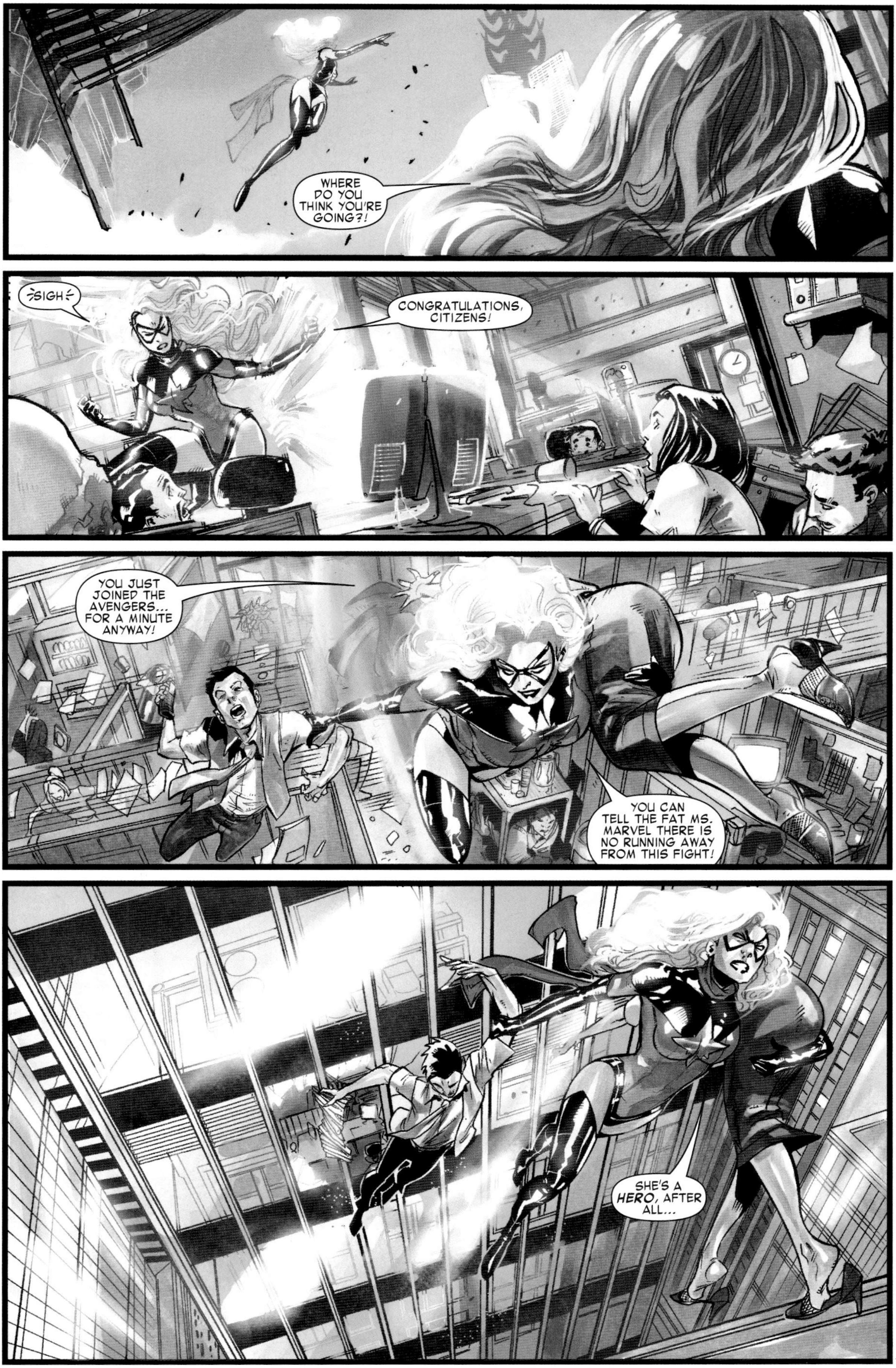
WHERE DO YOU THINK YOU'RE GOING?!
SIGH
CONGRATULATIONS, CITIZENS!
YOU JUST JOINED THE AVENGERS... FOR A MINUTE ANYWAY!
YOU CAN TELL THE FAT MS. MARVEL THERE IS NO RUNNING AWAY FROM THIS FIGHT!
SHE'S A HERO, AFTER ALL...

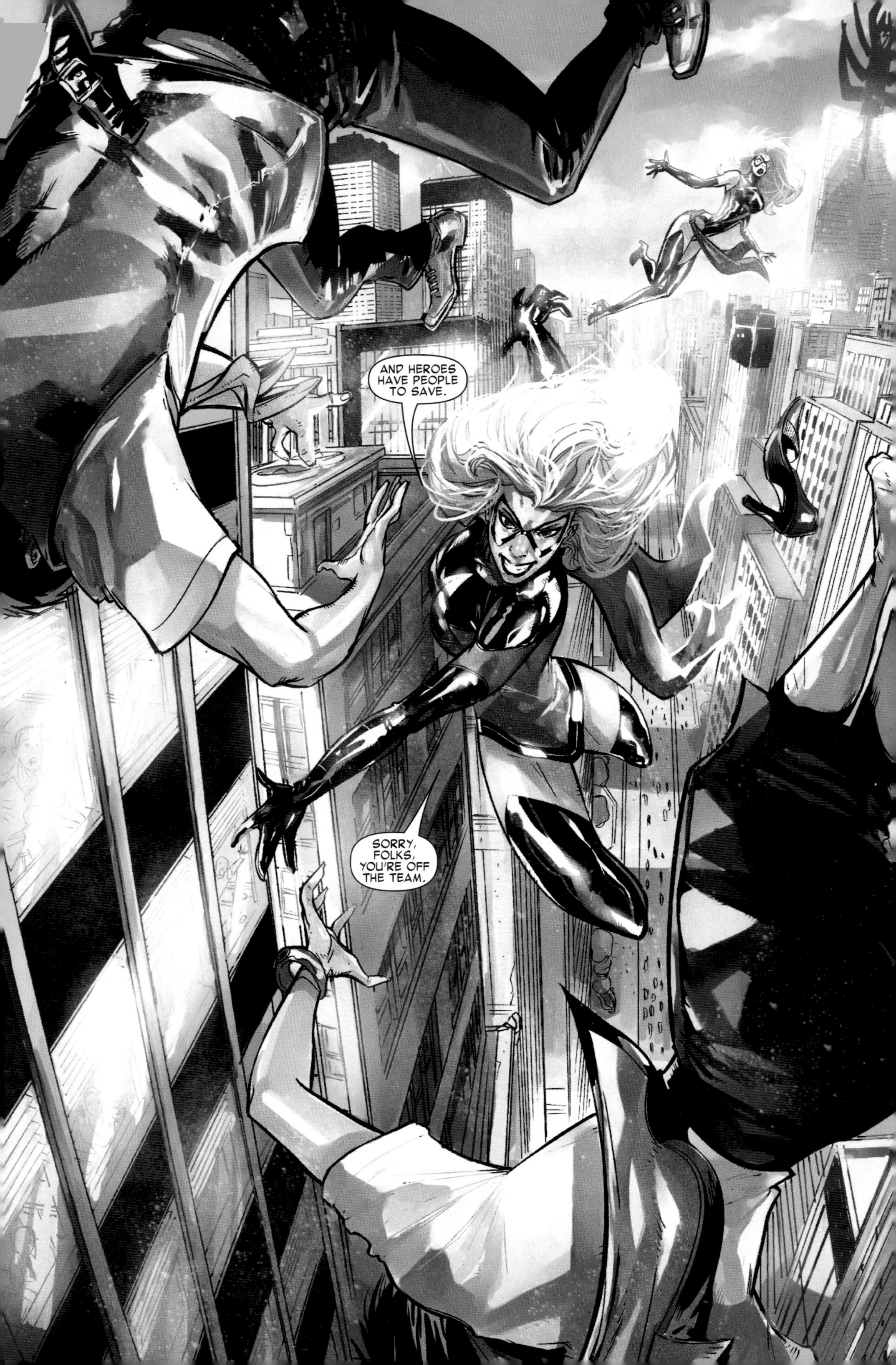
AND HEROES HAVE PEOPLE TO SAVE.
SORRY, FOLKS, YOU'RE OFF THE TEAM.

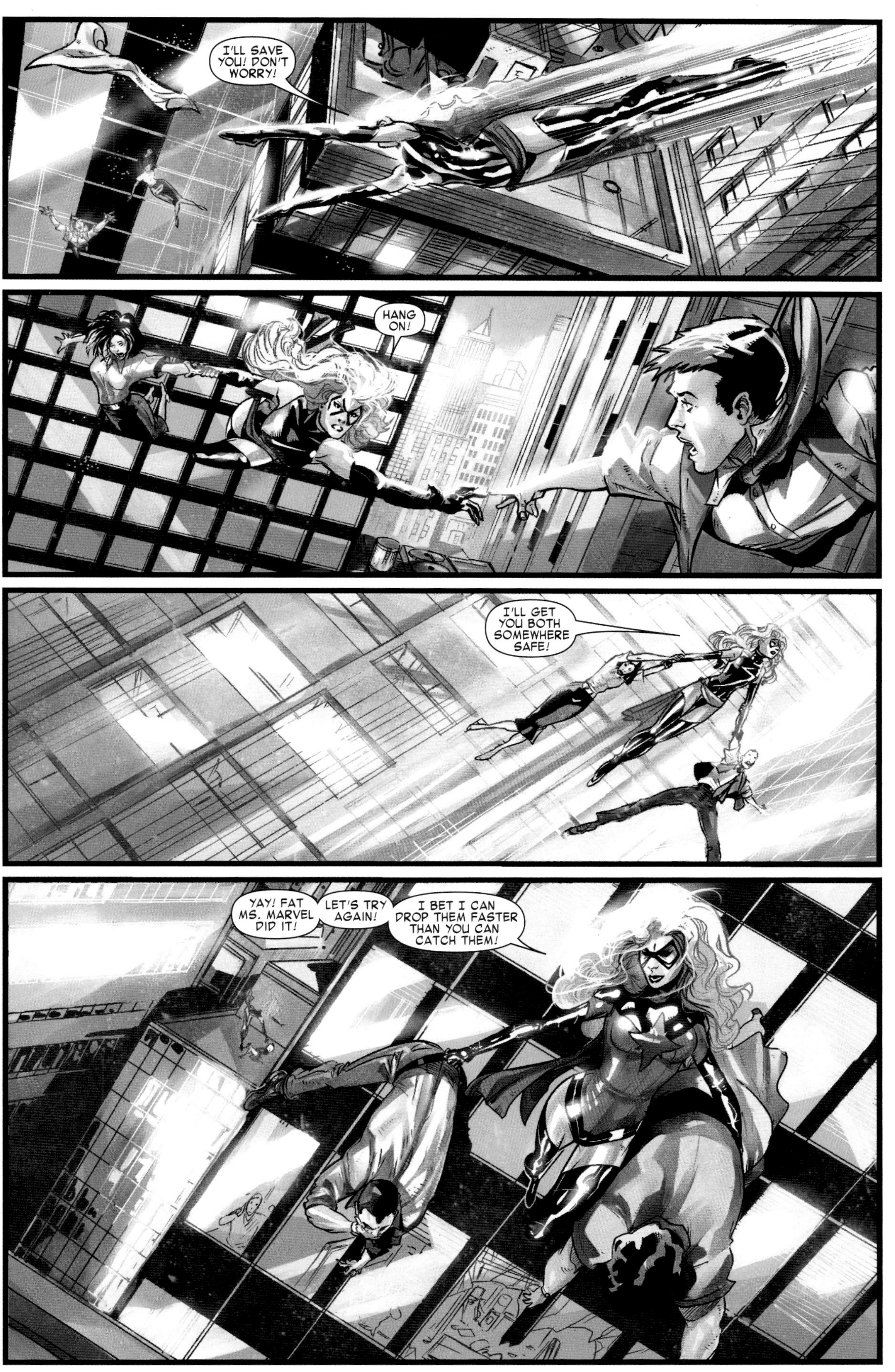
I'LL SAVE YOU! DON'T WORRY!
HANG ON!
I'LL GET YOU BOTH SOMEWHERE SAFE!
YAY! FAT MS. MARVEL DID IT!
LET'S TRY AGAIN!
I BET I CAN DROP THEM FASTER THAN YOU CAN CATCH THEM!

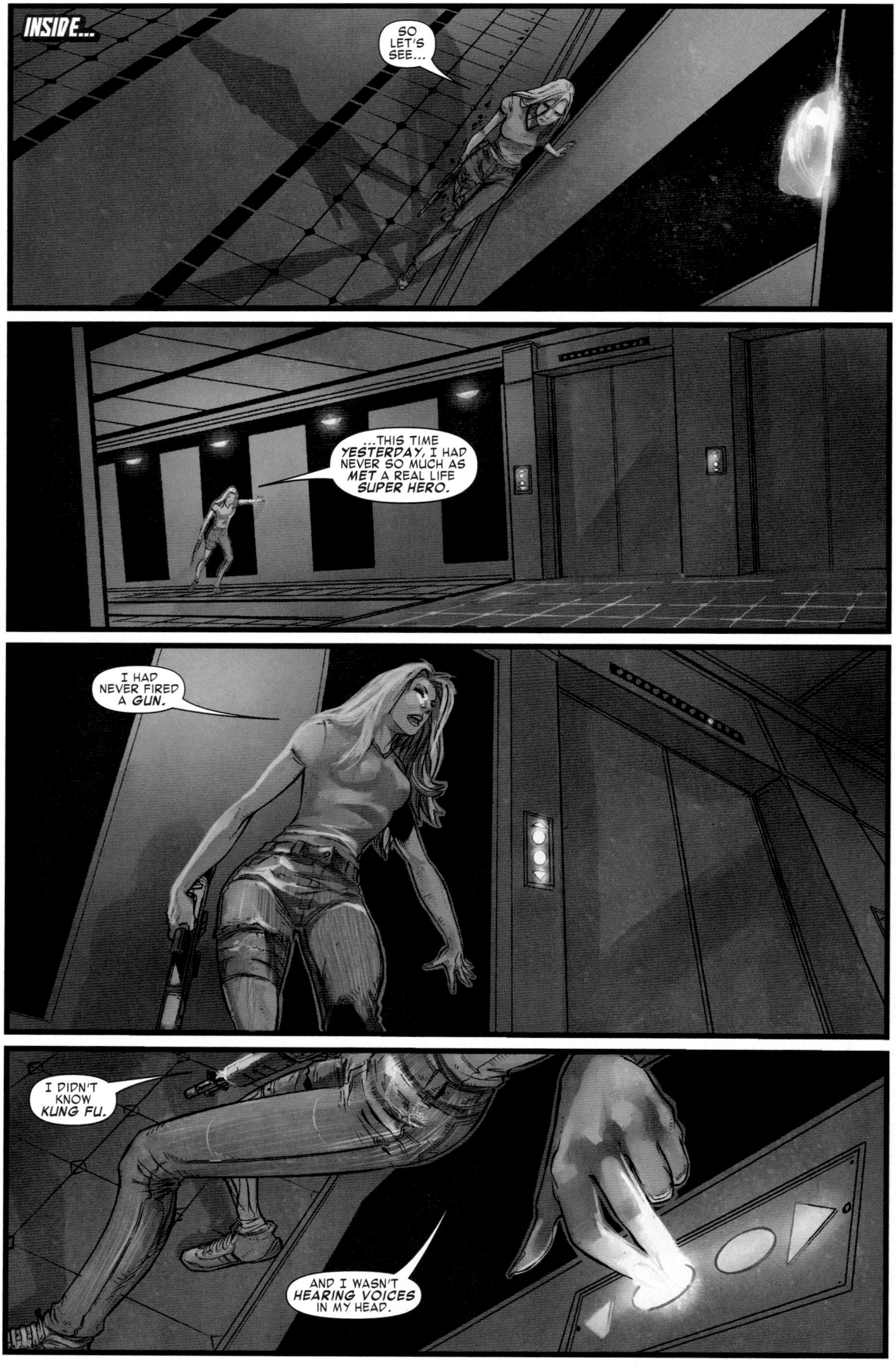
INSIDE...
SO LET'S SEE...
...THIS TIME YESTERDAY, I HAD NEVER SO MUCH AS MET A REAL LIFE SUPER HERO.
I HAD NEVER FIRED A GUN.
I DIDN'T KNOW KUNG FU.
AND I WASN'T HEARING VOICES IN MY HEAD.

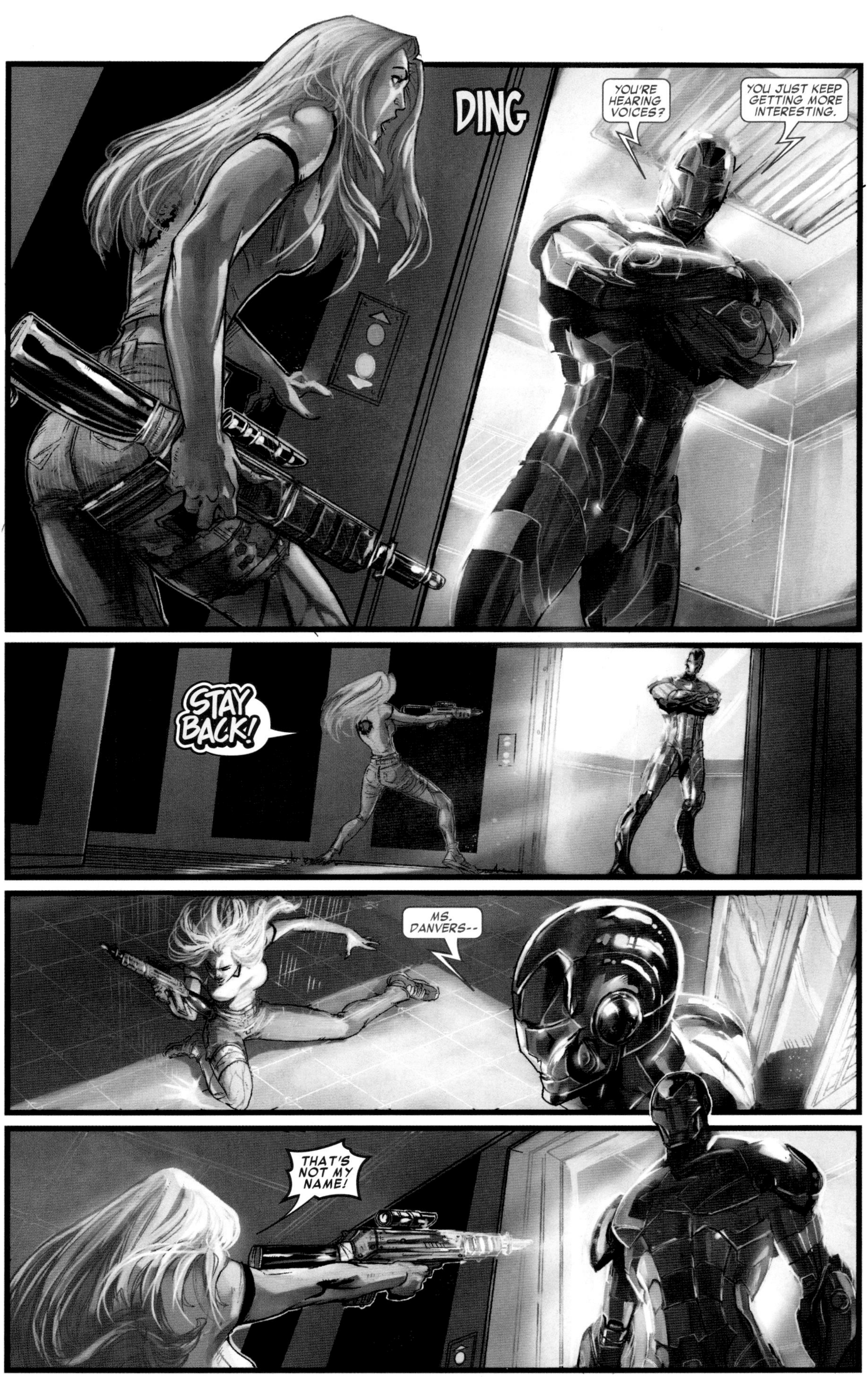
DING
YOU'RE HEARING VOICES?
YOU JUST KEEP GETTING MORE INTERESTING.
STAY BACK!
MS. DANVERS--
THAT'S NOT MY NAME!

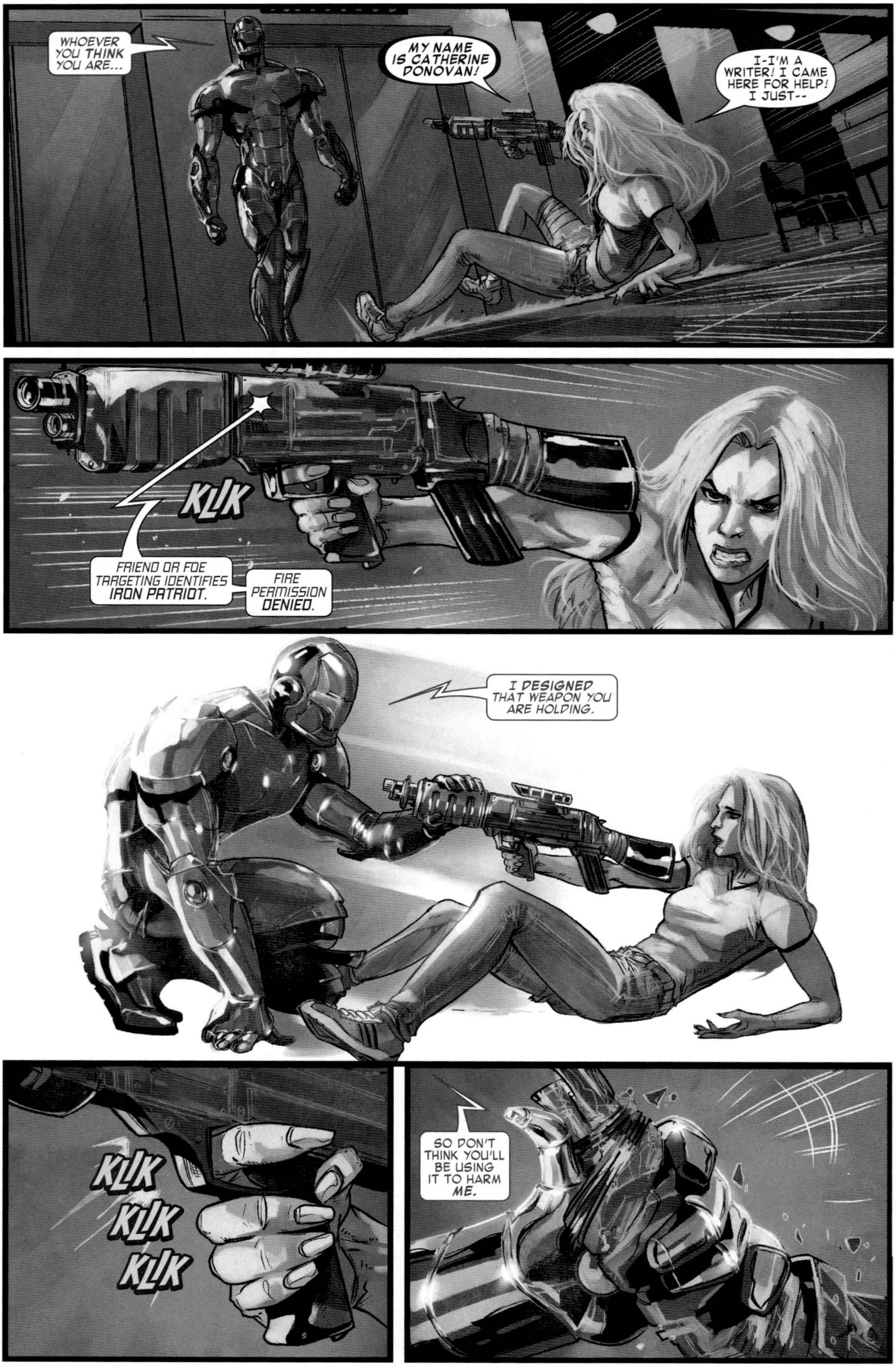

WHOEVER YOU THINK YOU ARE...
MY NAME IS CATHERINE DONOVAN!
I-I'M A WRITER! I CAME HERE FOR HELP! I JUST--
KLIK
FRIEND OR FOE TARGETING IDENTIFIES IRON PATRIOT.
FIRE PERMISSION DENIED.
I DESIGNED THAT WEAPON YOU ARE HOLDING.
KLIK KLIK KLIK
SO DON'T THINK YOU'LL BE USING IT TO HARM ME.

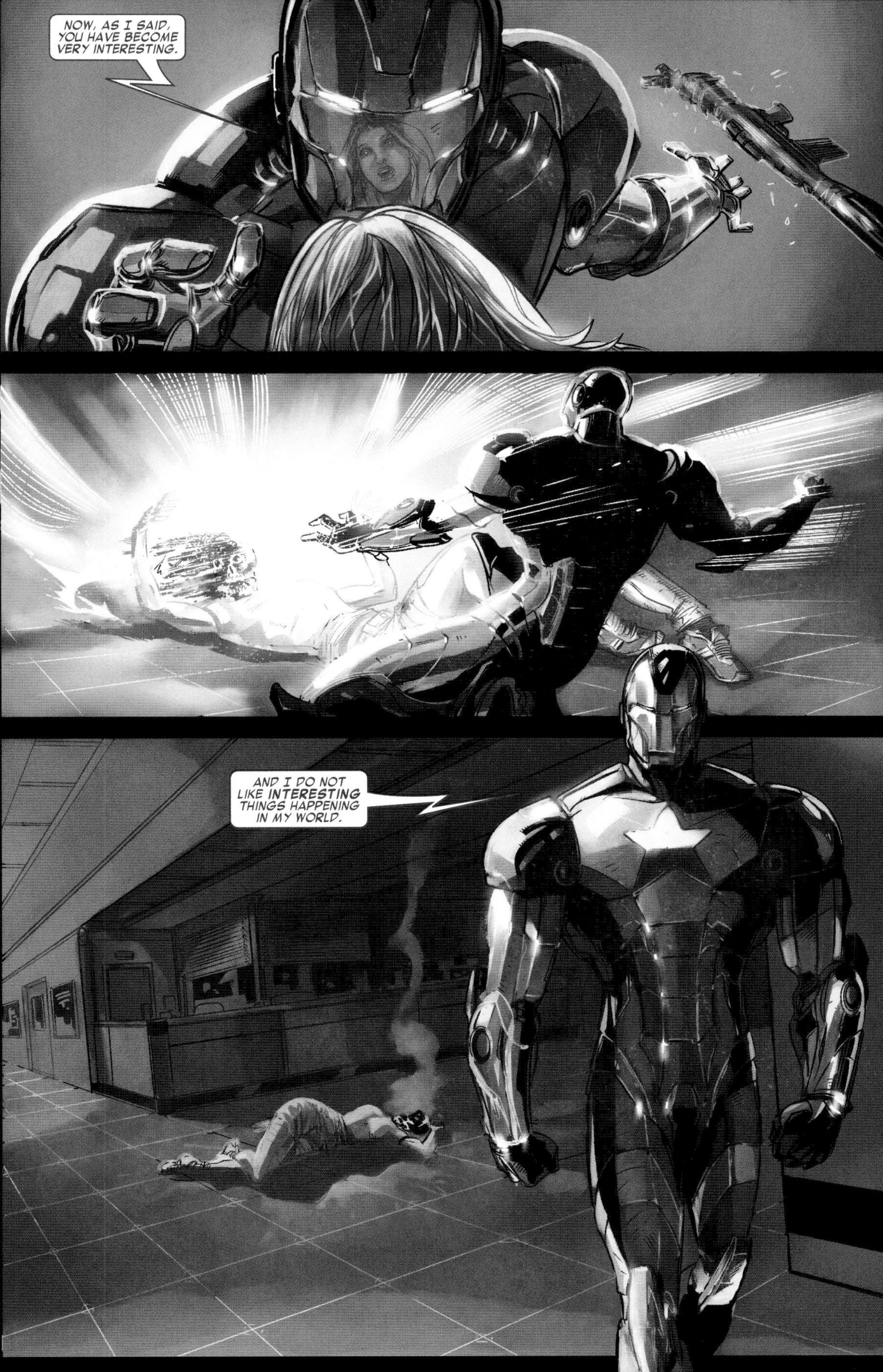
NOW, AS I SAID, YOU HAVE BECOME VERY INTERESTING.
AND I DO NOT LIKE INTERESTING THINGS HAPPENING IN MY WORLD.

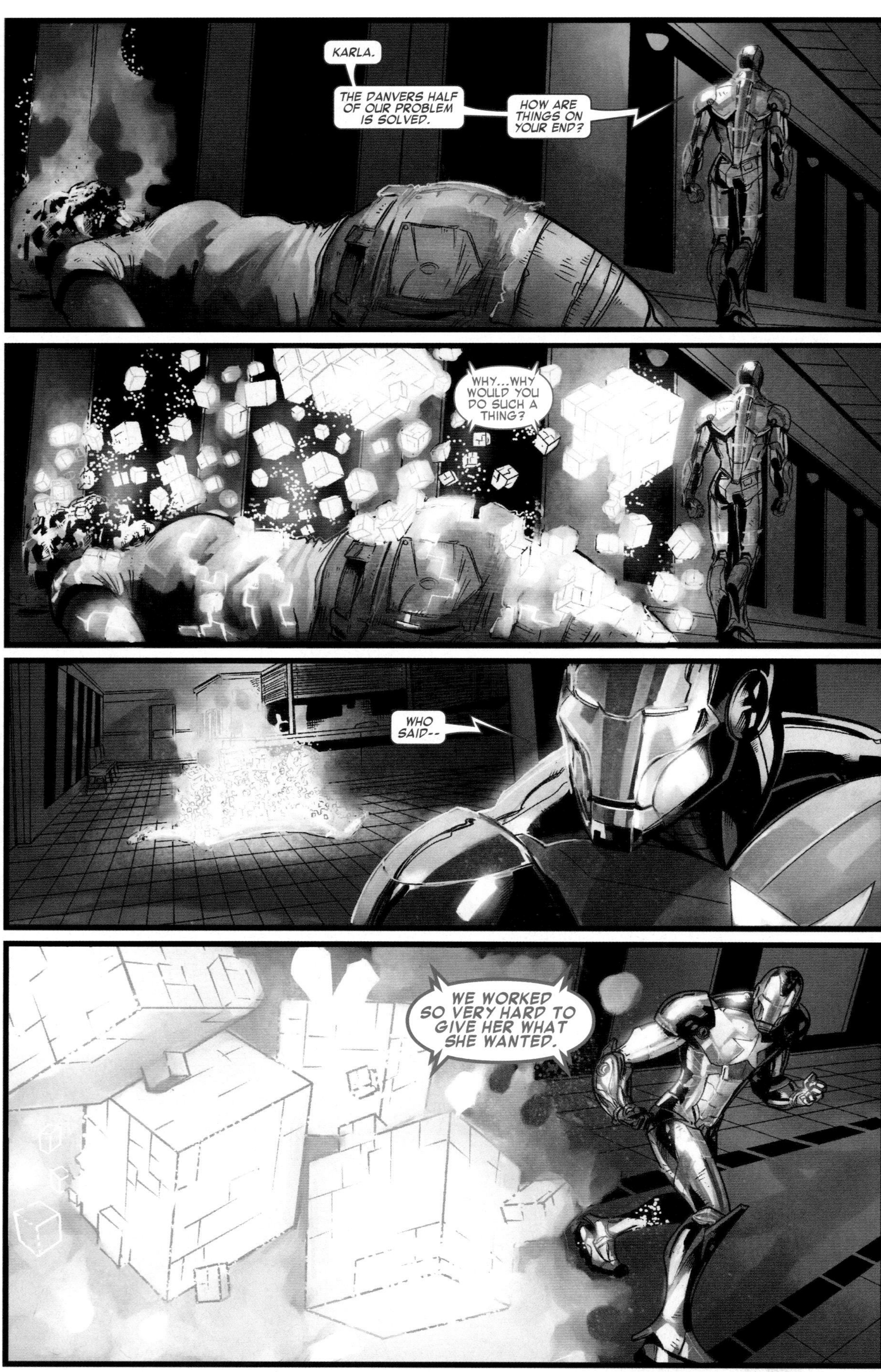
KARLA.
THE DANVERS HALF OF OUR PROBLEM IS SOLVED.
HOW ARE THINGS ON YOUR END?
WHY...WHY WOULD YOU DO SUCH A THING?
WHO SAID--
WE WORKED SO VERY HARD TO GIVE HER WHAT SHE WANTED.

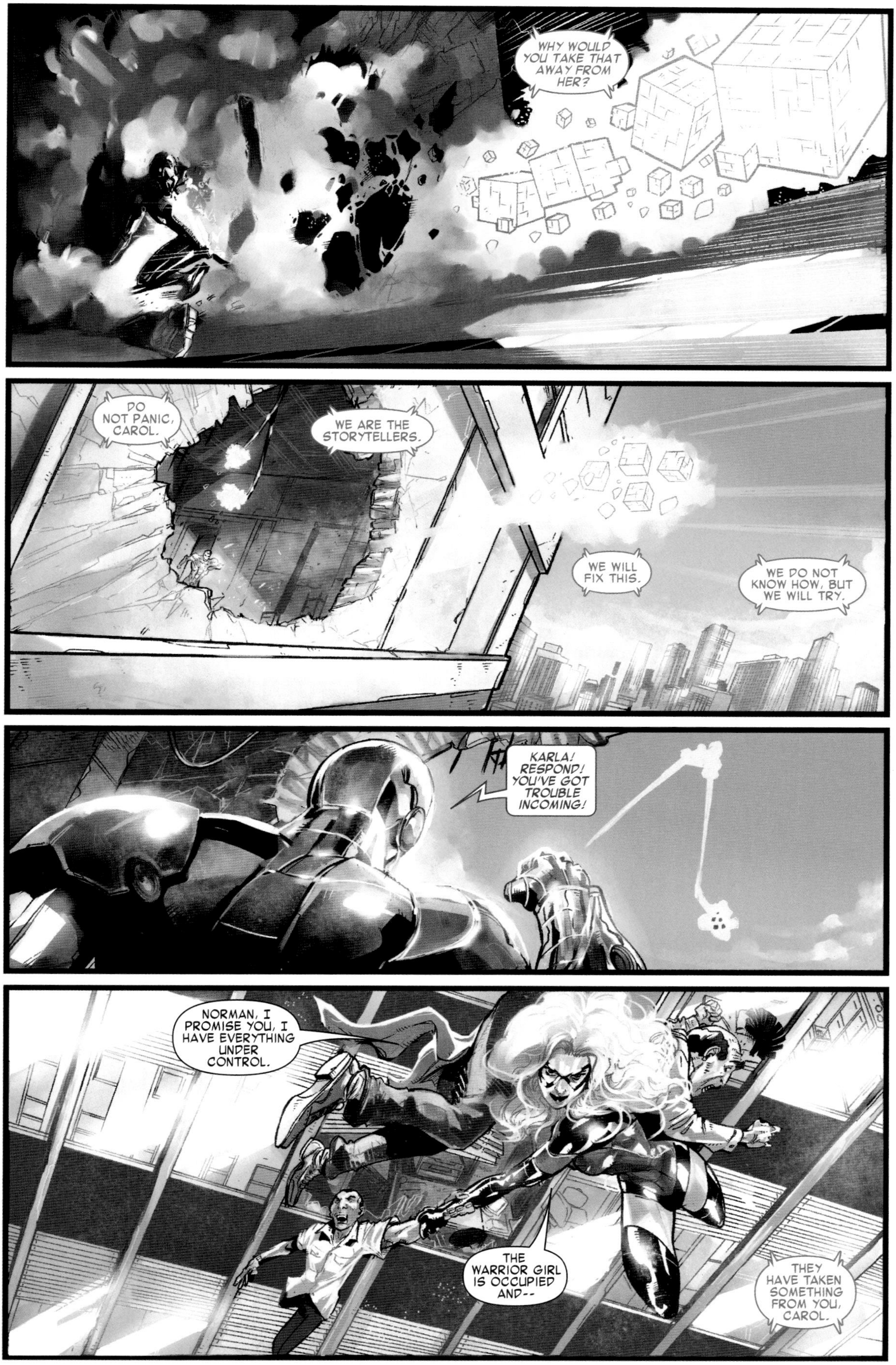
WHY WOULD YOU TAKE THAT AWAY FROM HER?
DO NOT PANIC, CAROL.
WE ARE THE STORYTELLERS.
WE WILL FIX THIS.
WE DO NOT KNOW HOW, BUT WE WILL TRY.
KARLA! RESPOND! YOU'VE GOT TROUBLE INCOMING!
NORMAN, I PROMISE YOU, I HAVE EVERYTHING UNDER CONTROL.
THE WARRIOR GIRL IS OCCUPIED AND--
THEY HAVE TAKEN SOMETHING FROM YOU, CAROL.

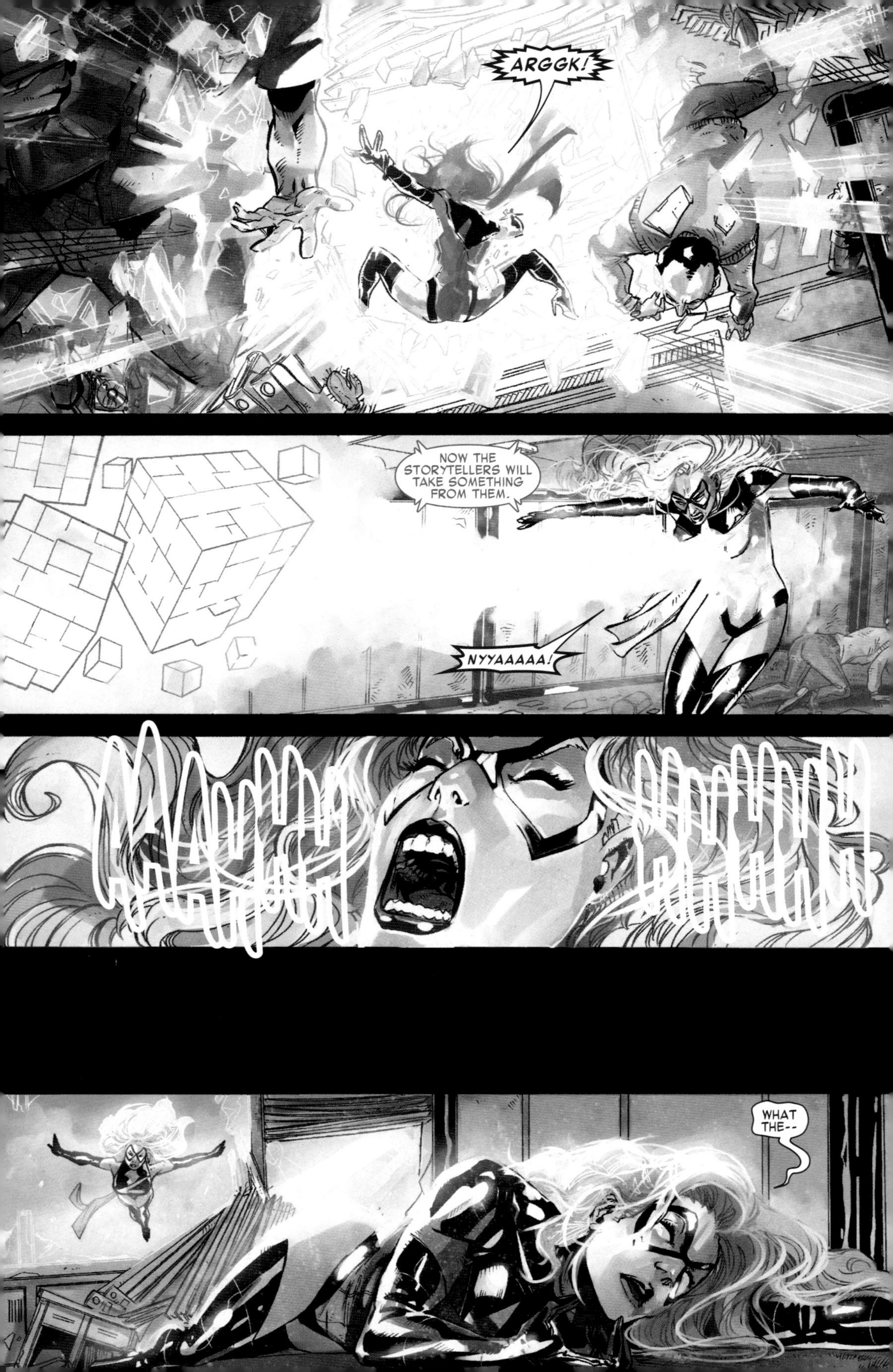
ARGGK!
NOW THE STORYTELLERS WILL TAKE SOMETHING FROM THEM.
NYYAAAAA!
WHAT THE--

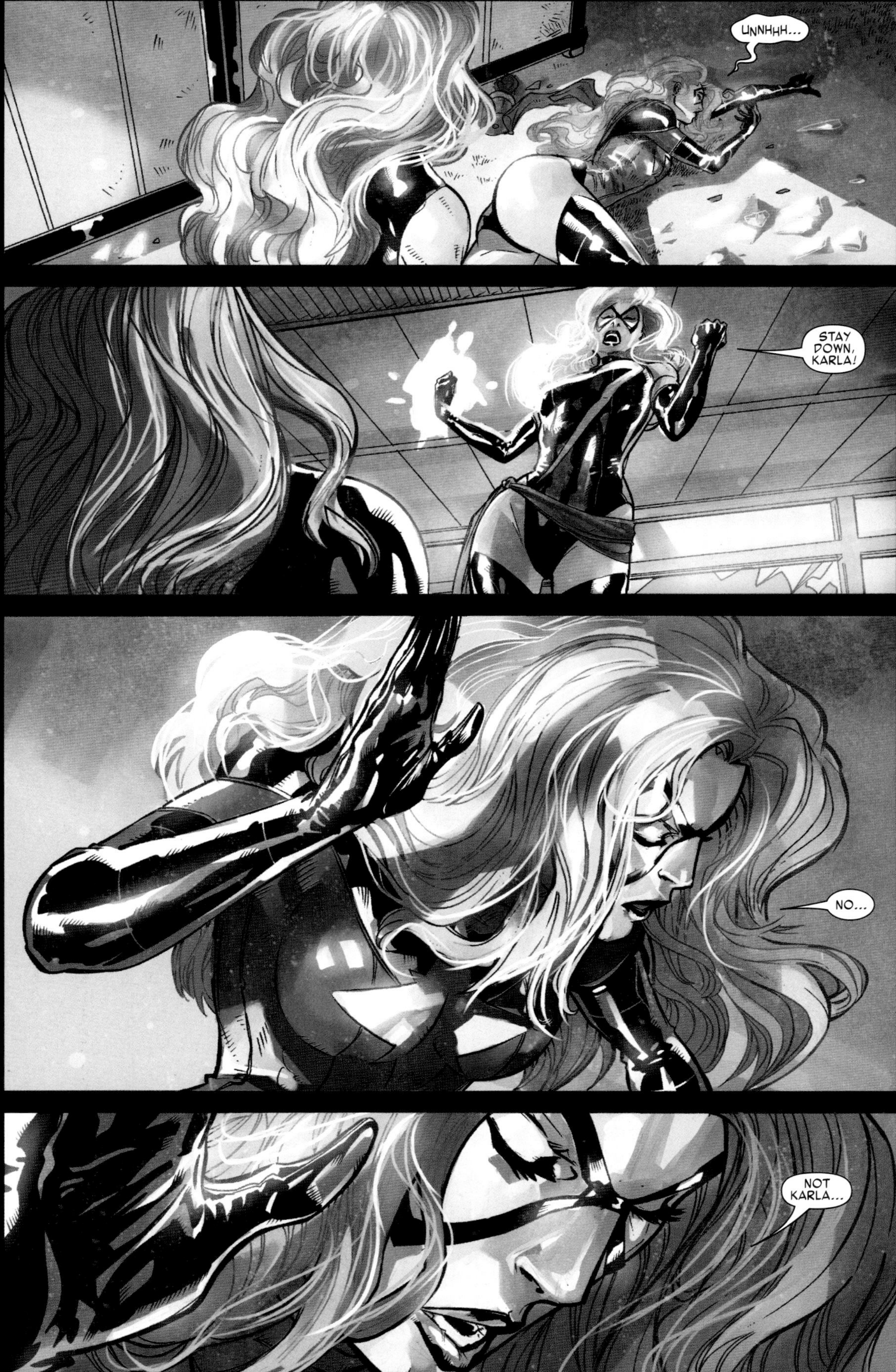
UNNHHH...
STAY DOWN, KARLA!
NO...
NOT KARLA...

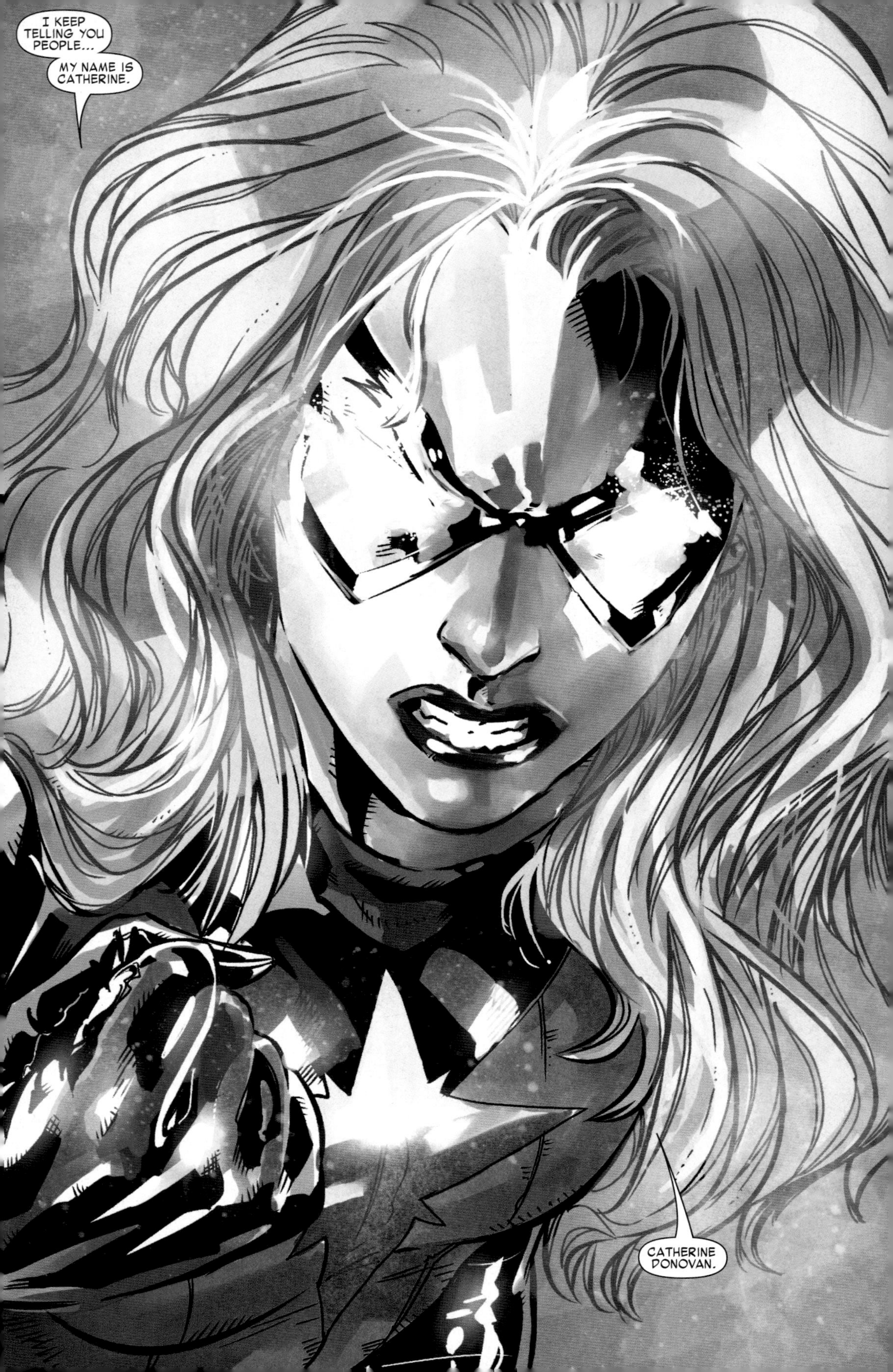

I KEEP TELLING YOU PEOPLE...
MY NAME IS CATHERINE.
CATHERINE DONOVAN.

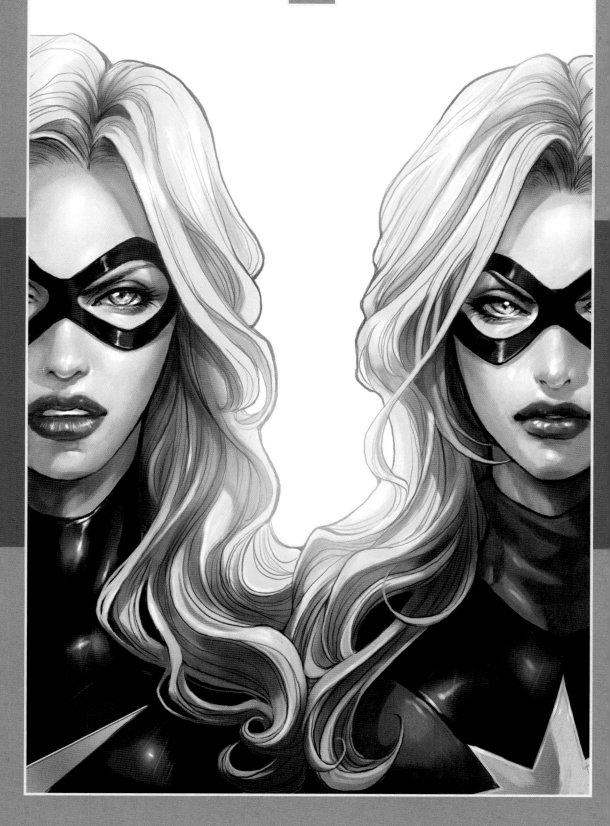

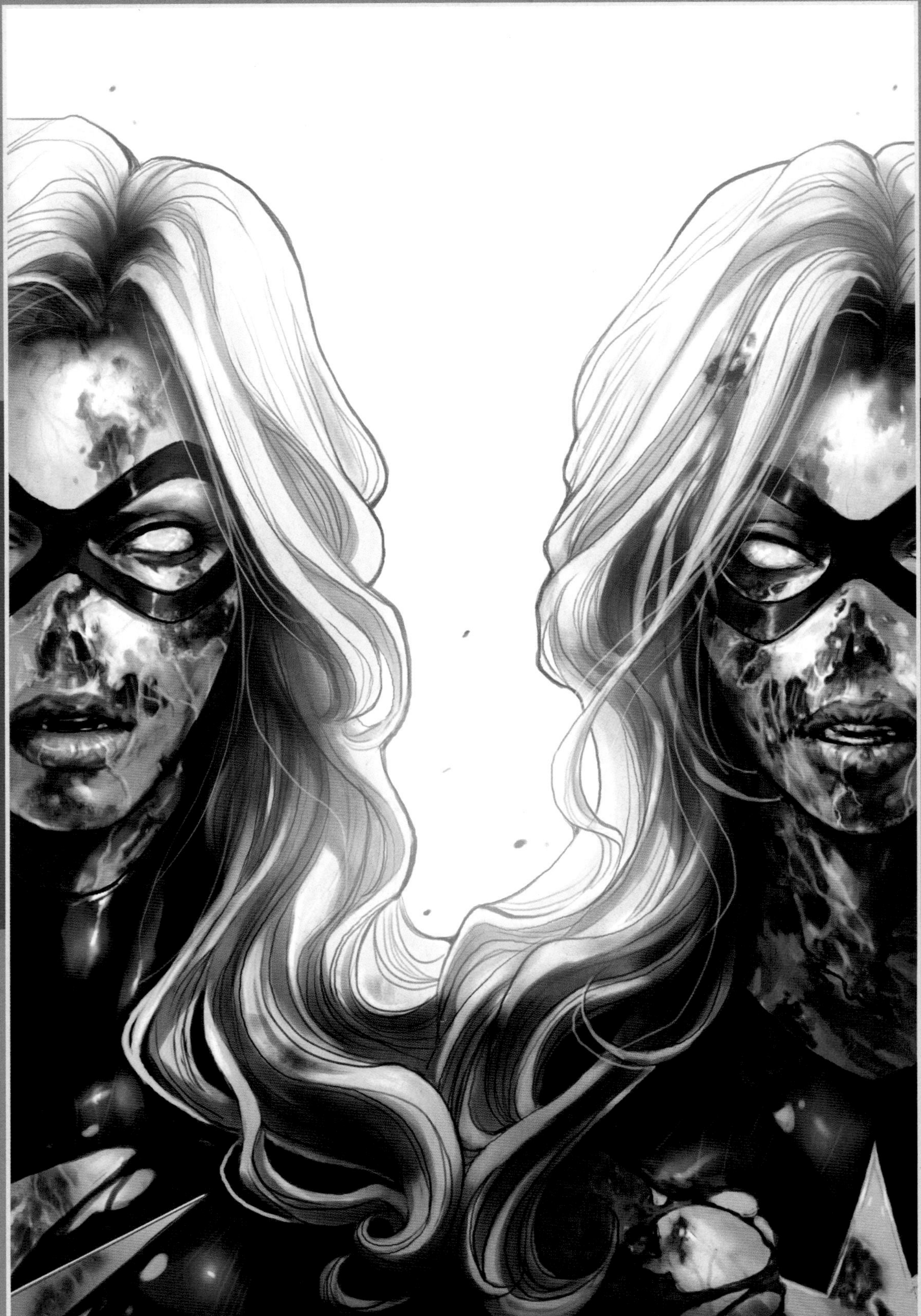

MS. MARVEL #46 ZOMBIE VARIANT BY SANA TAKEDA

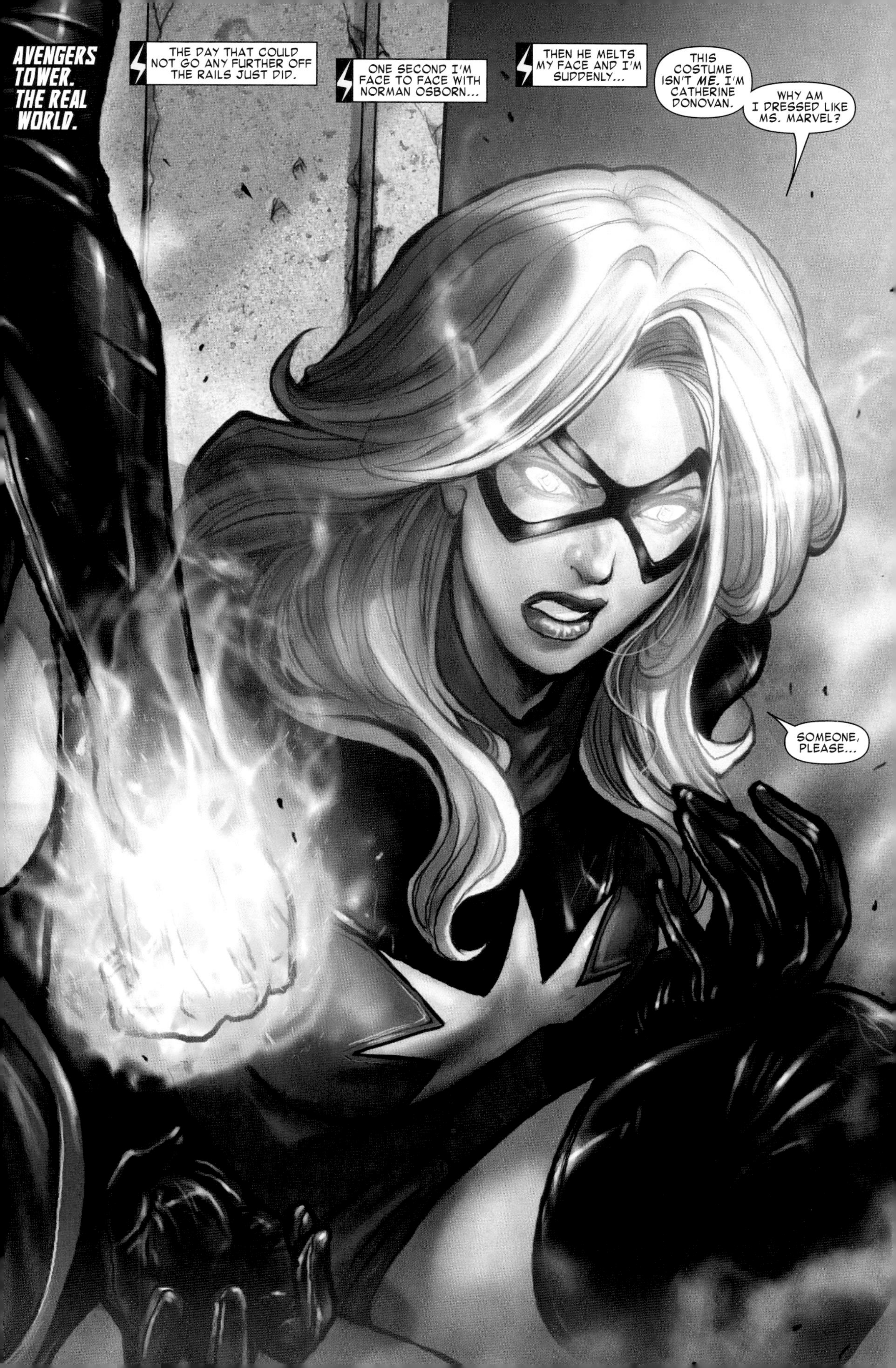
AVENGERS TOWER. THE REAL WORLD.
THE DAY THAT COULD NOT GO ANY FURTHER OFF THE RAILS JUST DID.
ONE SECOND I'M FACE TO FACE WITH NORMAN OSBORN...
THEN HE MELTS MY FACE AND I'M SUDDENLY...
THIS COSTUME ISN'T ME. I'M CATHERINE DONOVAN.
WHY AM I DRESSED LIKE MS. MARVEL?
SOMEONE, PLEASE...

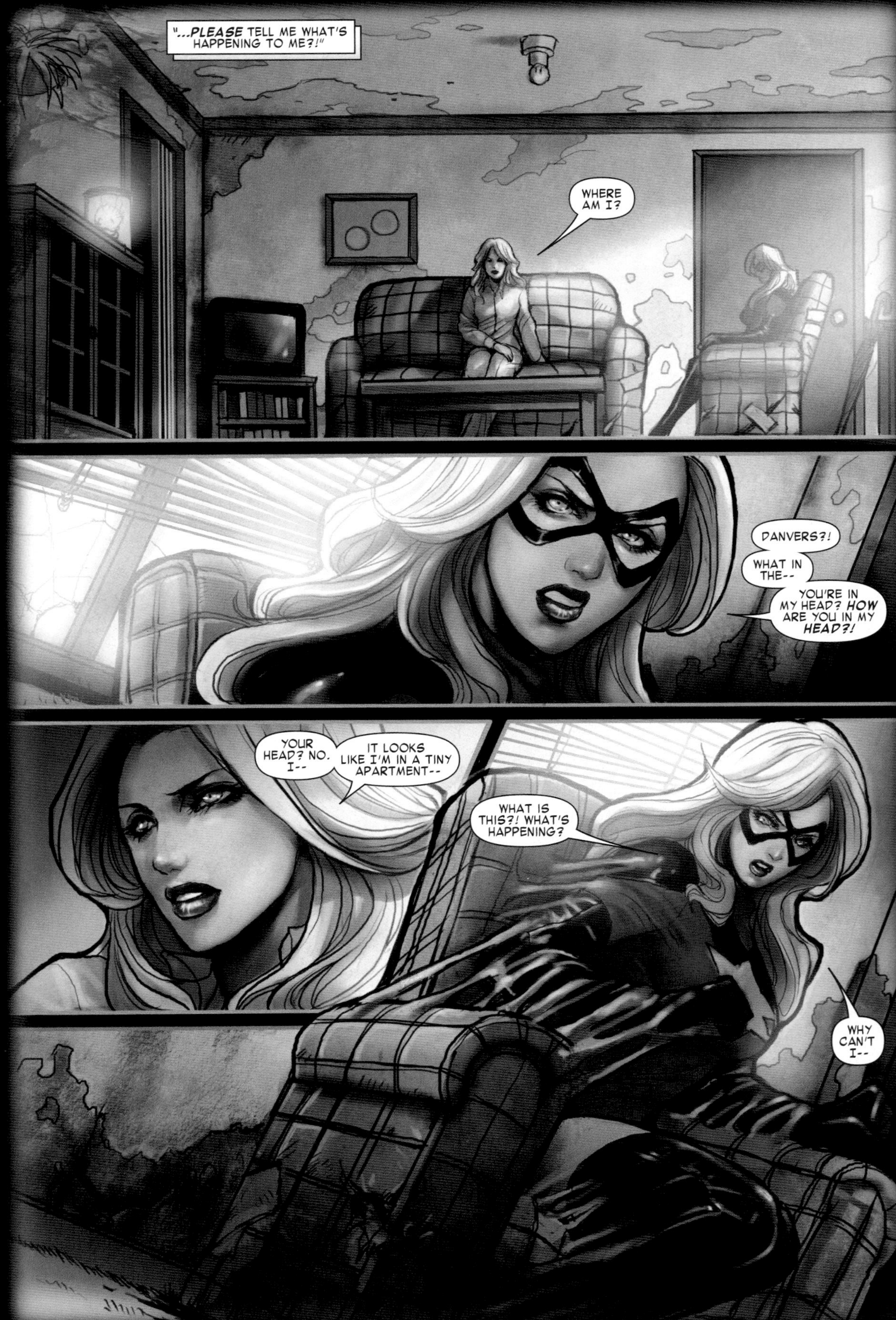
"...PLEASE TELL ME WHAT'S HAPPENING TO ME?!"
WHERE AM I?
DANVERS?!
WHAT IN THE--
YOU'RE IN MY HEAD? HOW ARE YOU IN MY HEAD?!
YOUR HEAD? NO. I--
IT LOOKS LIKE I'M IN A TINY APARTMENT--
WHAT IS THIS?! WHAT'S HAPPENING?
WHY CAN'T I--

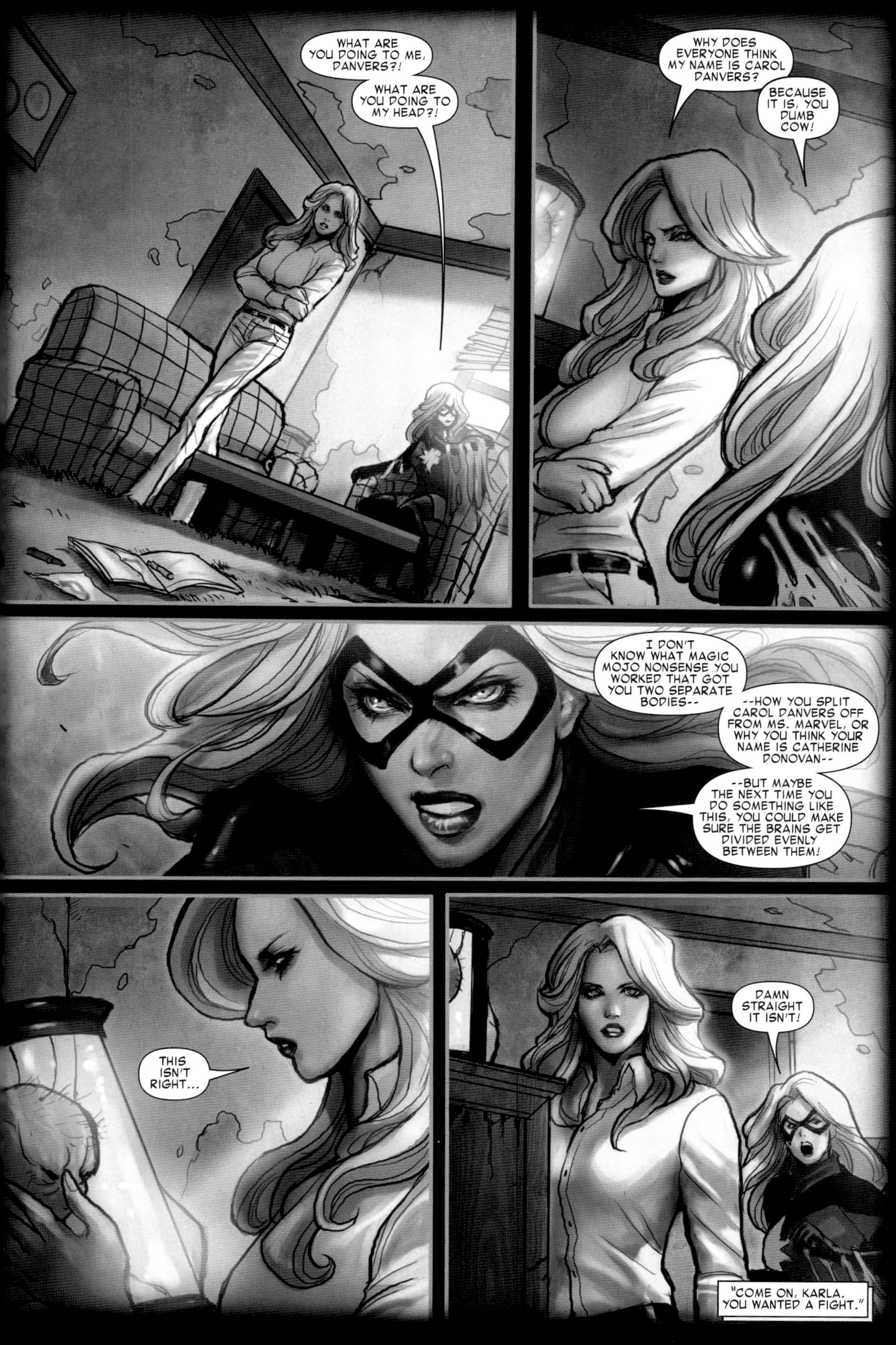
WHAT ARE YOU DOING TO ME, DANVERS?!
WHAT ARE YOU DOING TO MY HEAD?!
WHY DOES EVERYONE THINK MY NAME IS CAROL DANVERS?
BECAUSE IT IS, YOU DUMB COW!
I DON'T KNOW WHAT MAGIC MOJO NONSENSE YOU WORKED THAT GOT YOU TWO SEPARATE BODIES--
--HOW YOU SPLIT CAROL DANVERS OFF FROM MS. MARVEL, OR WHY YOU THINK YOUR NAME IS CATHERINE DONOVAN--
--BUT MAYBE THE NEXT TIME YOU DO SOMETHING LIKE THIS, YOU COULD MAKE SURE THE BRAINS GET DIVIDED EVENLY BETWEEN THEM!
THIS ISN'T RIGHT...
DAMN STRAIGHT IT ISN'T!
"COME ON, KARLA. YOU WANTED A FIGHT."

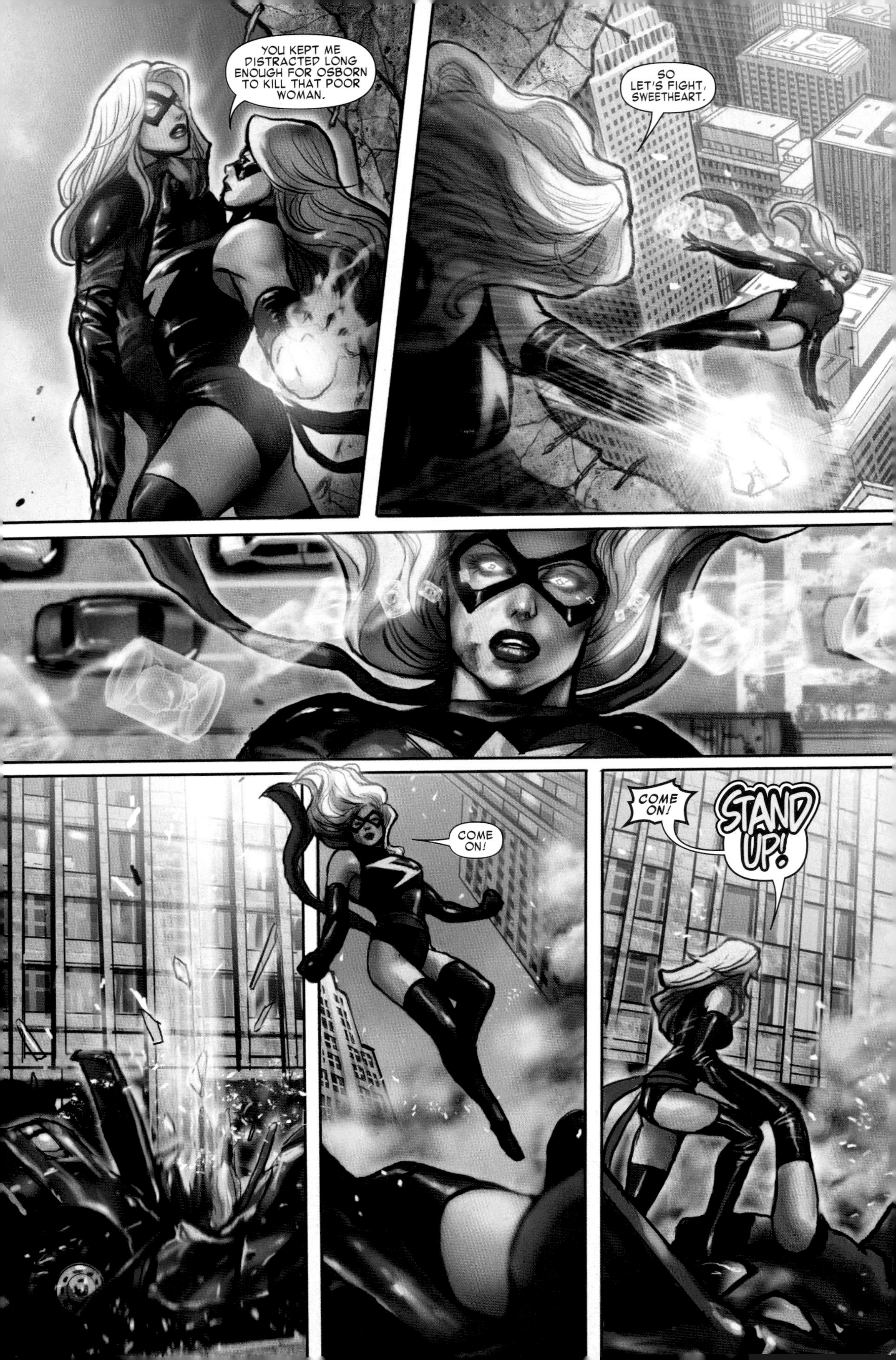
YOU KEPT ME DISTRACTED LONG ENOUGH FOR OSBORN TO KILL THAT POOR WOMAN.
SO LET'S FIGHT, SWEETHEART.
COME ON!
COME ON!
STAND UP!

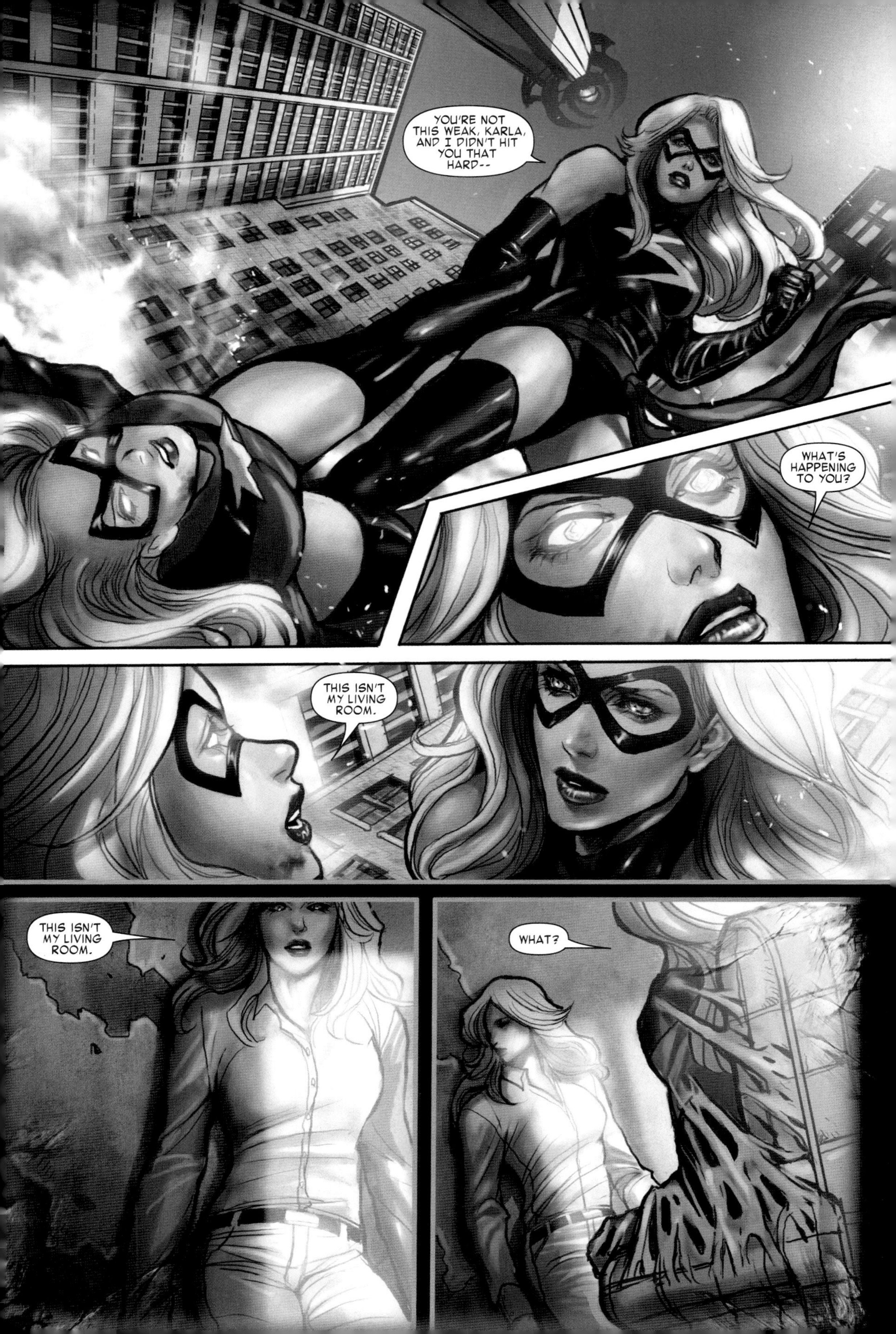
YOU'RE NOT THIS WEAK, KARLA, AND I DIDN'T HIT YOU THAT HARD--
WHAT'S HAPPENING TO YOU?
THIS ISN'T MY LIVING ROOM.
THIS ISN'T MY LIVING ROOM.
WHAT?

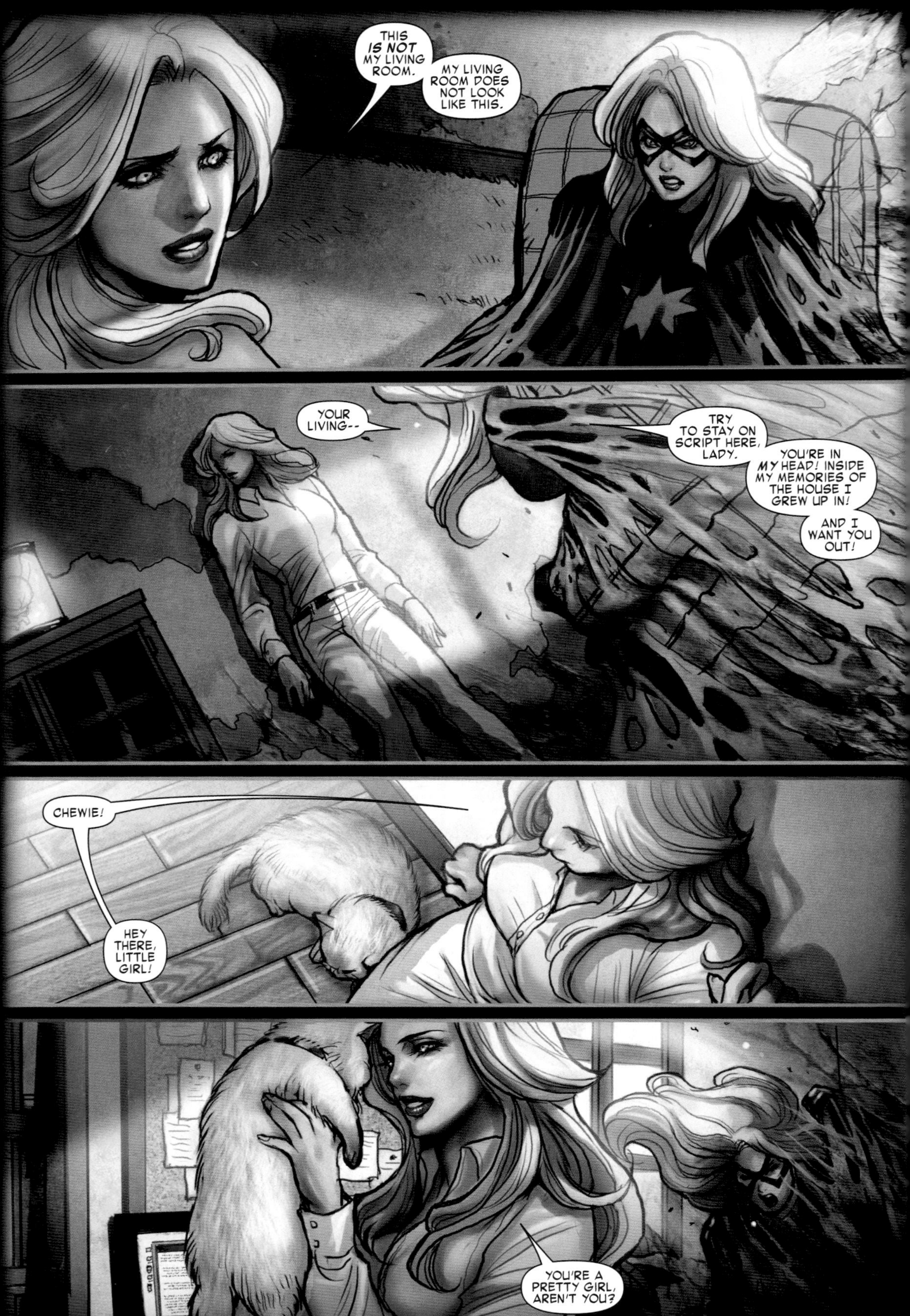
THIS IS NOT MY LIVING ROOM.
MY LIVING ROOM DOES NOT LOOK LIKE THIS.
YOUR LIVING--
TRY TO STAY ON SCRIPT HERE, LADY.
YOU'RE IN MY HEAD! INSIDE MY MEMORIES OF THE HOUSE I GREW UP IN!
AND I WANT YOU OUT!
CHEWIE!
HEY THERE, LITTLE GIRL!
YOU'RE A PRETTY GIRL, AREN'T YOU?

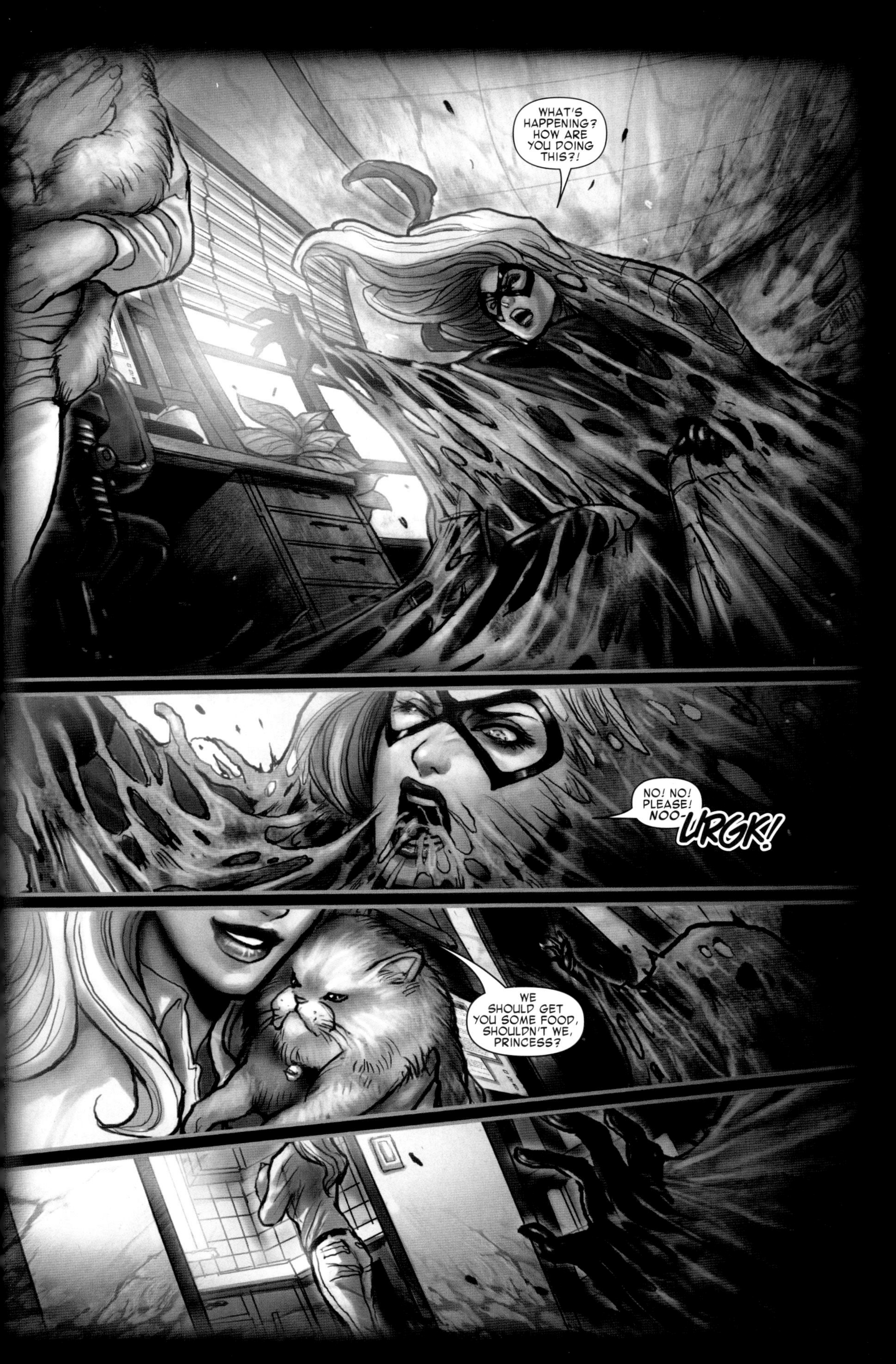
WHAT'S HAPPENING? HOW ARE YOU DOING THIS?!
NO! NO! PLEASE! NOO-
URGK!
WE SHOULD GET YOU SOME FOOD, SHOULDN'T WE, PRINCESS?

OH, KARLA... WHAT HAVE YOU DONE NOW?
MOM?
YOU THOUGHT YOU WERE SO SMART.
MOM, NO I--
YOU WERE SO EMBARRASSED OF WHAT YOU BECAME. YOU *KILLED* ME. YOU KILLED ME SO YOU COULD DO A MILLION MORE TERRIBLE THINGS WITHOUT ME SEEING.
MOM...
I SAW IT ALL KARLA.
I SAW EVERYTHING YOU DID.

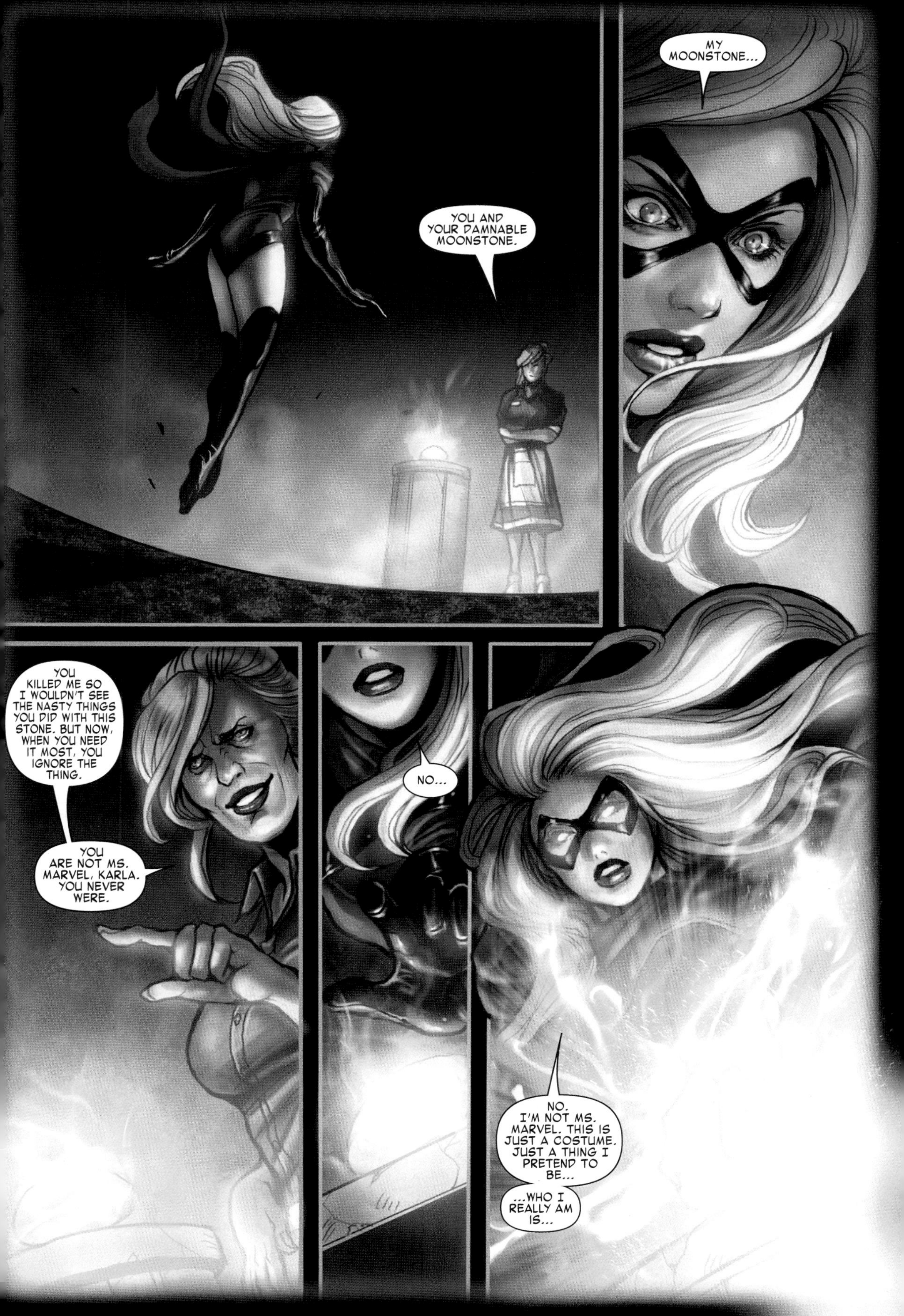
YOU AND YOUR DAMNABLE MOONSTONE.
MY MOONSTONE...
YOU KILLED ME SO I WOULDN'T SEE THE NASTY THINGS YOU DID WITH THIS STONE. BUT NOW, WHEN YOU NEED IT MOST, YOU IGNORE THE THING.
YOU ARE NOT MS. MARVEL, KARLA. YOU NEVER WERE.
NO...
NO. I'M NOT MS. MARVEL. THIS IS JUST A COSTUME. JUST A THING I PRETEND TO BE...
...WHO I REALLY AM IS...

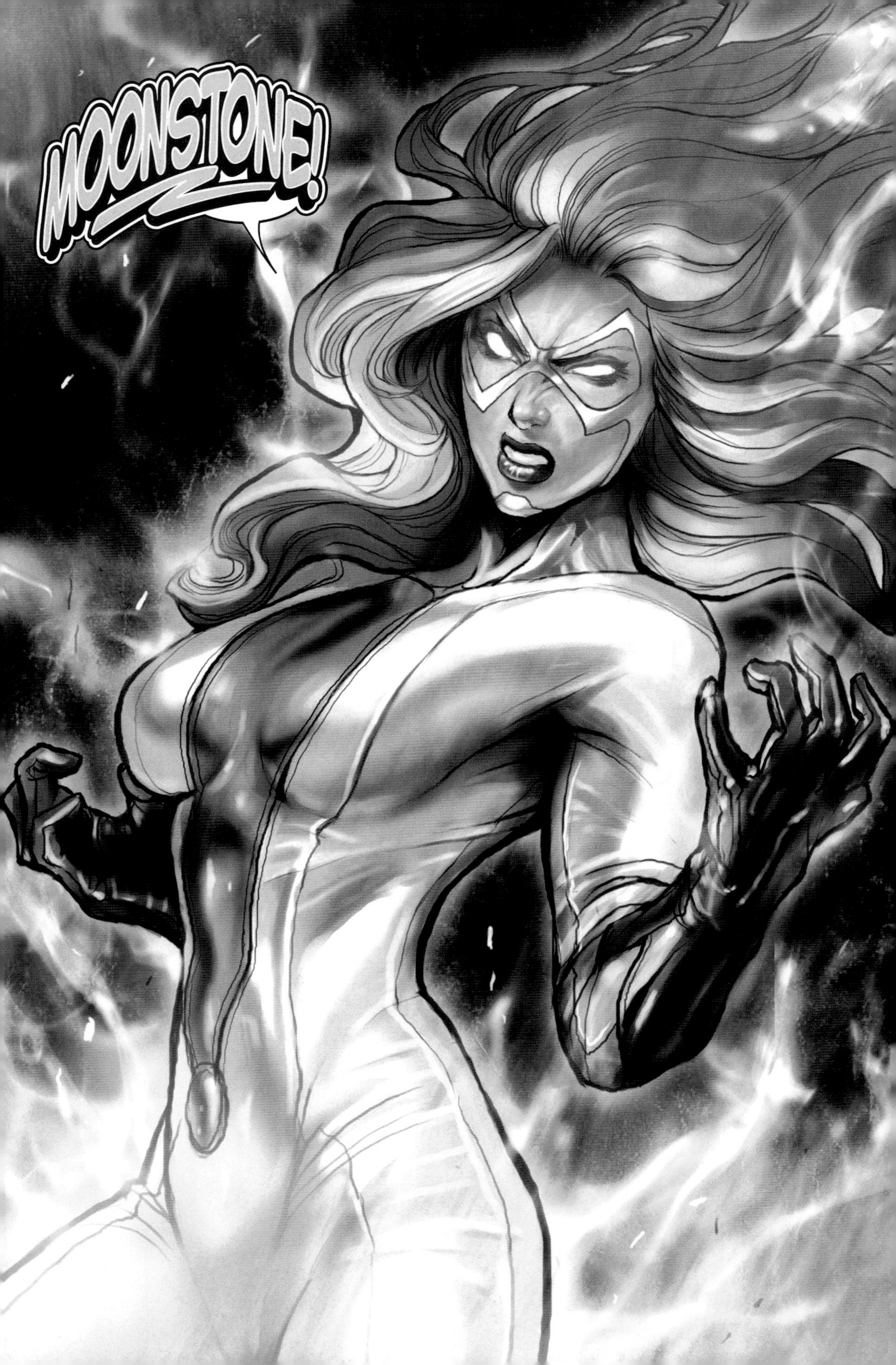
MOONSTONE!

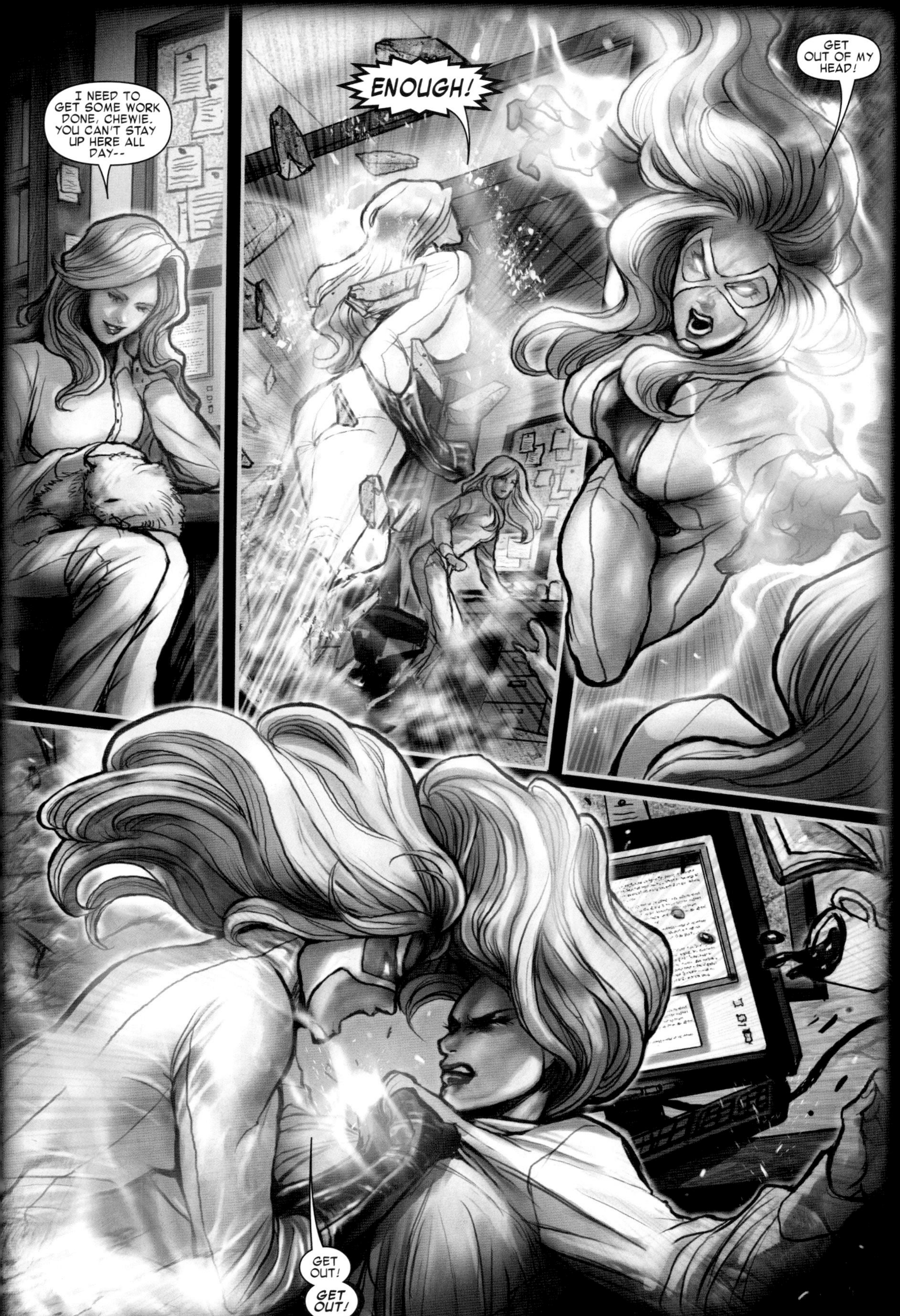
I NEED TO GET SOME WORK DONE, CHEWIE. YOU CAN'T STAY UP HERE ALL DAY--
ENOUGH!
GET OUT OF MY HEAD!
GET OUT!
GET OUT!

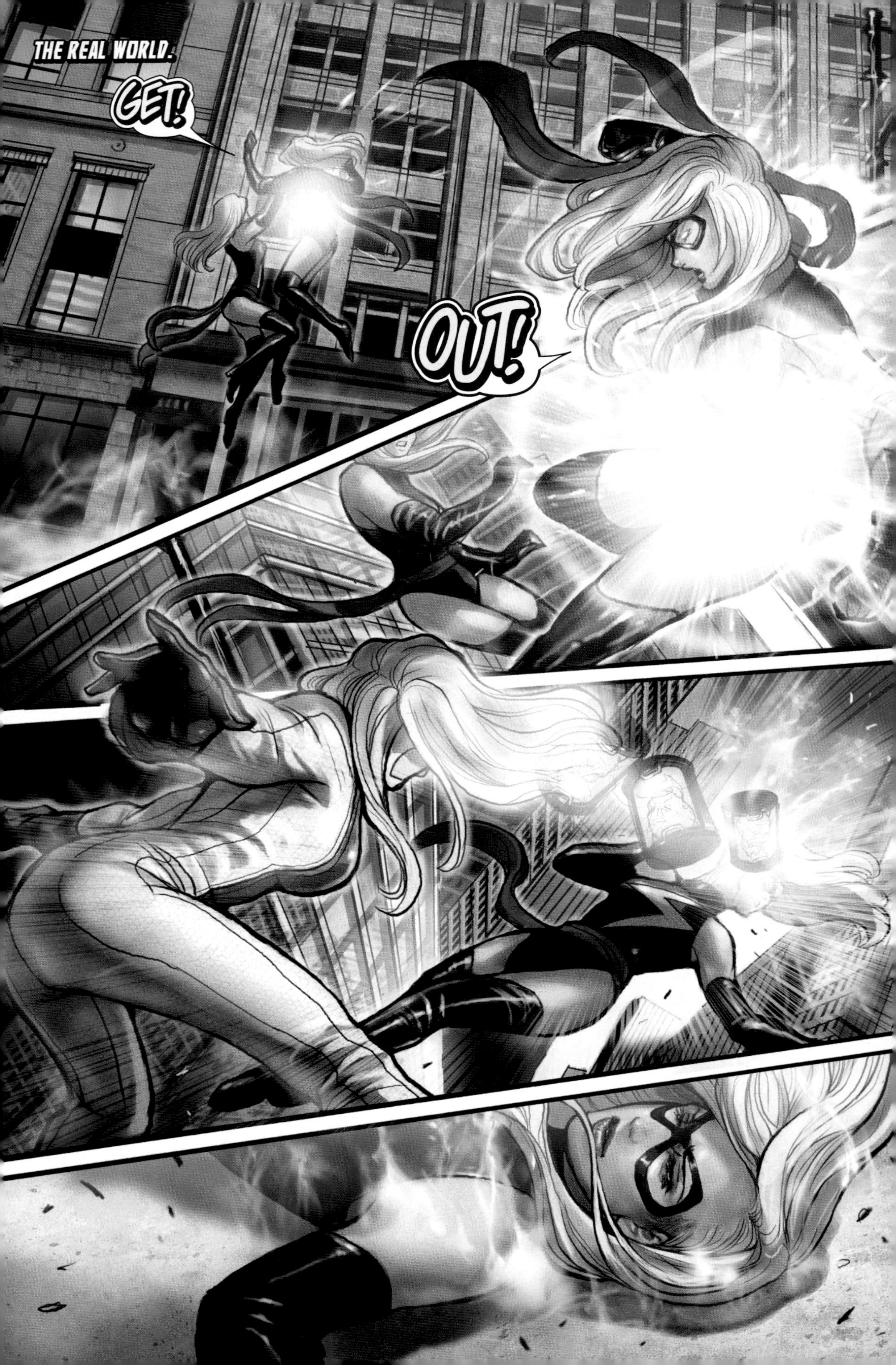
THE REAL WORLD.
GET!
OUT!

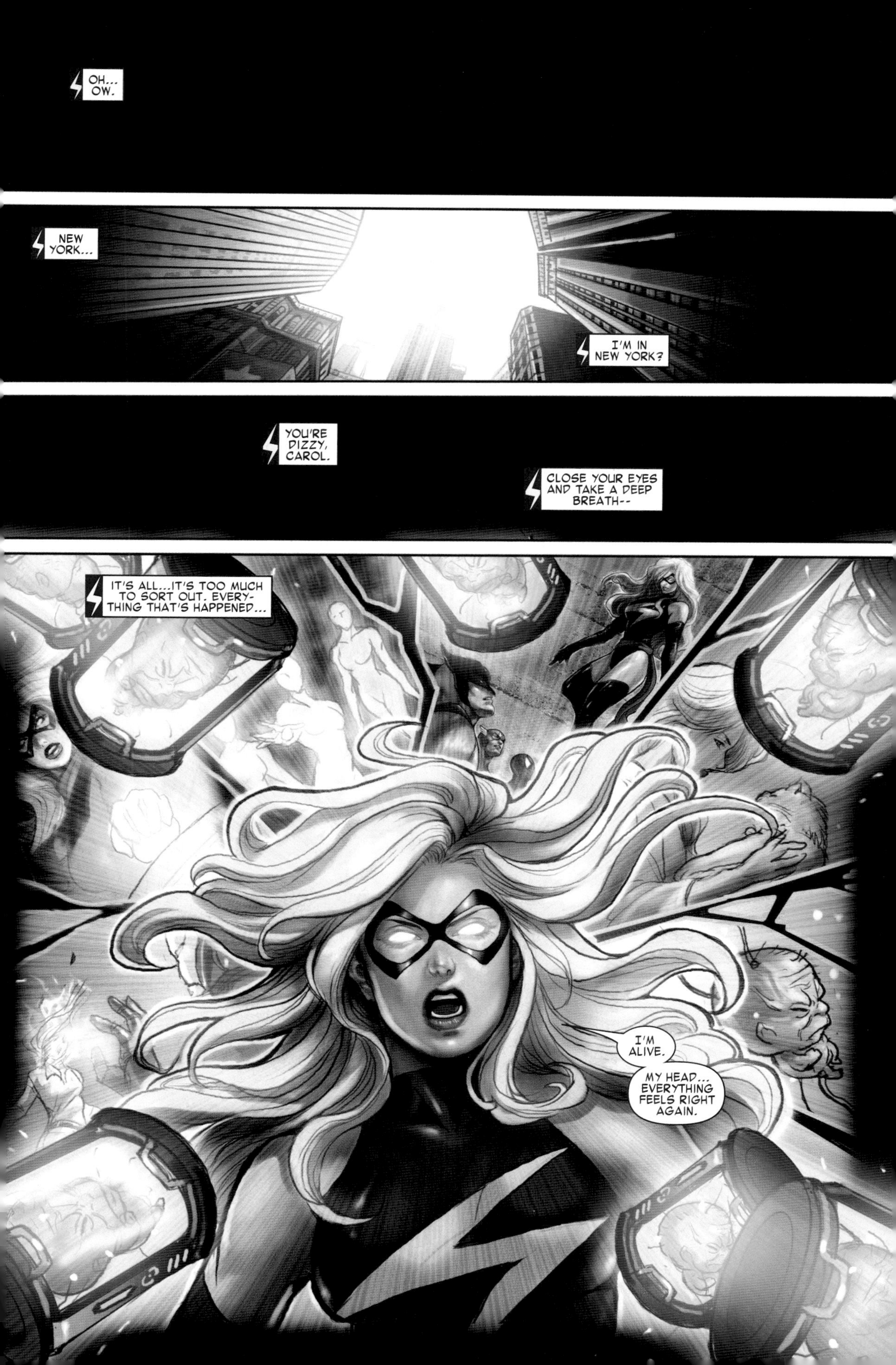
OH... OW.
NEW YORK...
I'M IN NEW YORK?
YOU'RE DIZZY, CAROL.
CLOSE YOUR EYES AND TAKE A DEEP BREATH--
IT'S ALL...IT'S TOO MUCH TO SORT OUT. EVERY-THING THAT'S HAPPENED...
I'M ALIVE.
MY HEAD... EVERYTHING FEELS RIGHT AGAIN.

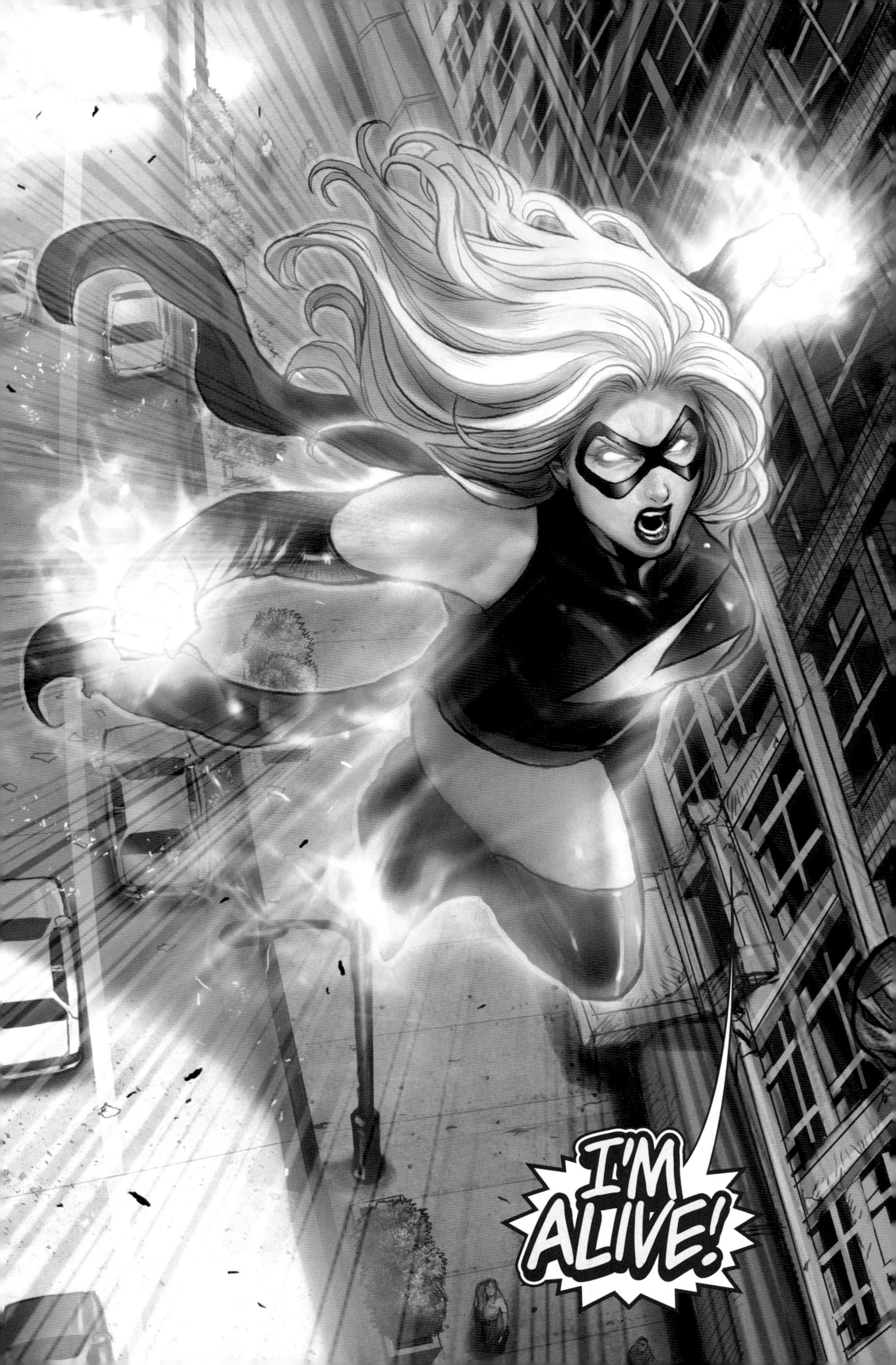
I'M ALIVE!

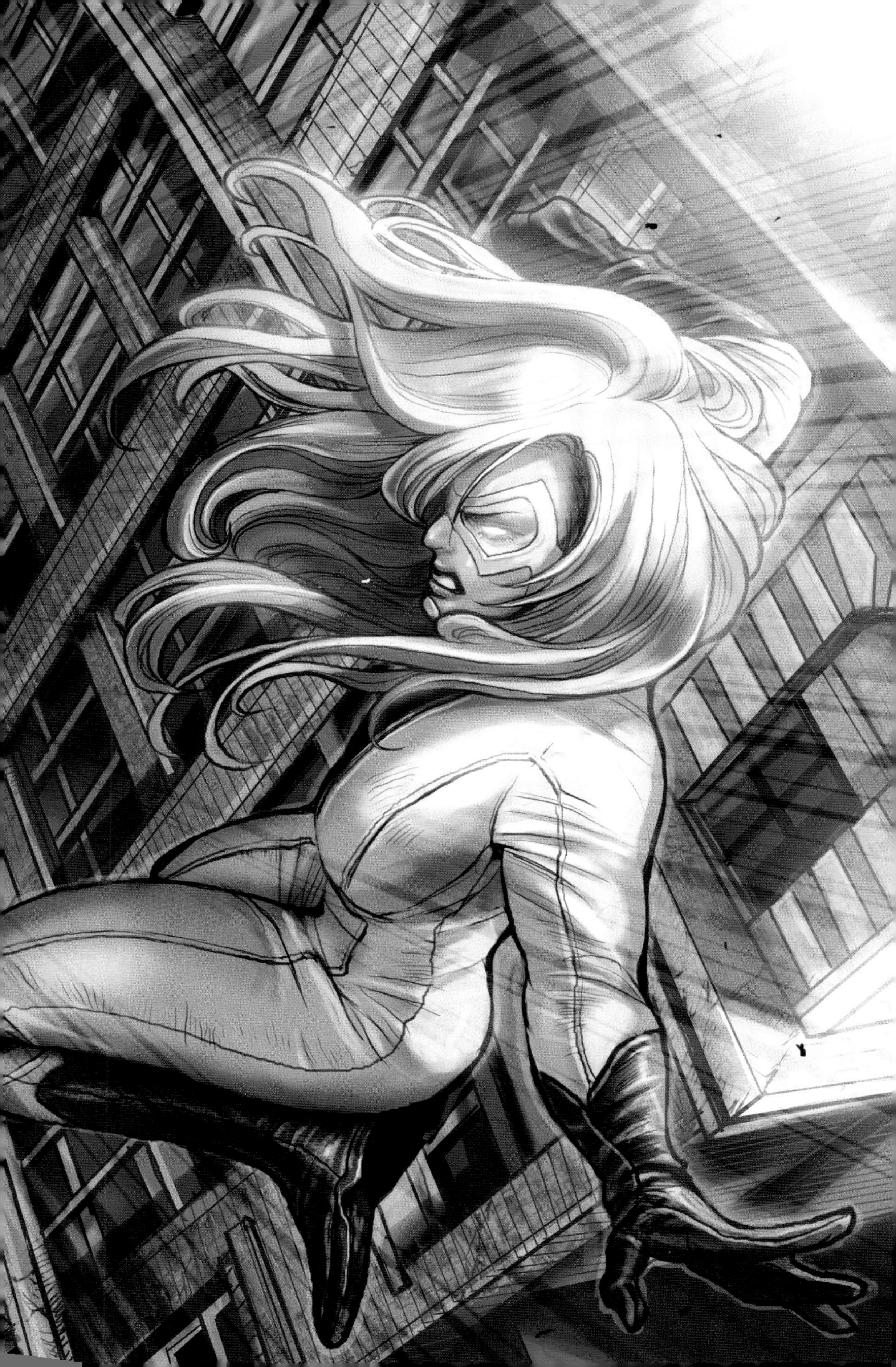

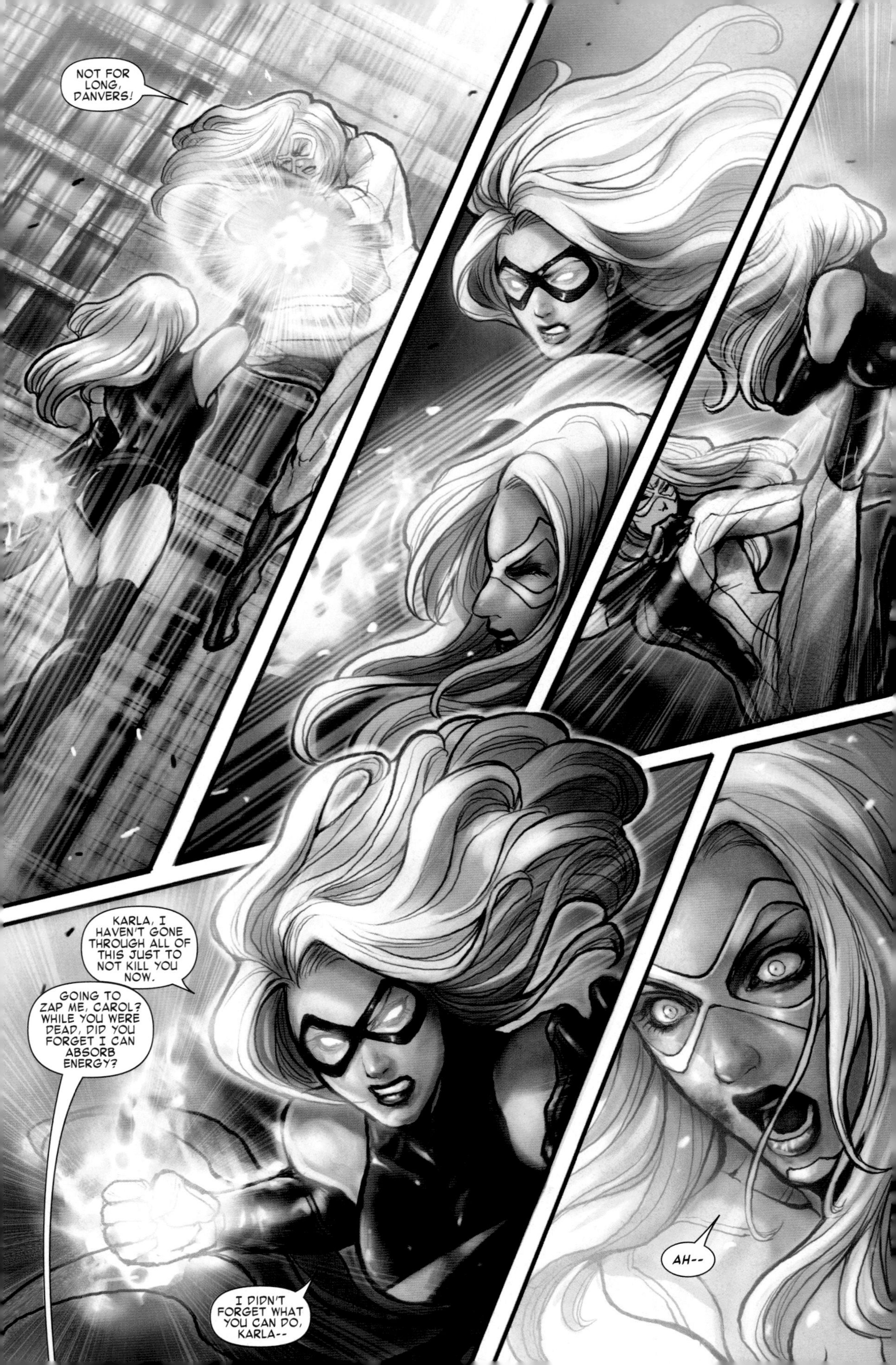
NOT FOR LONG, DANVERS!
KARLA, I HAVEN'T GONE THROUGH ALL OF THIS JUST TO NOT KILL YOU NOW.
GOING TO ZAP ME, CAROL? WHILE YOU WERE DEAD, DID YOU FORGET I CAN ABSORB ENERGY?
I DIDN'T FORGET WHAT YOU CAN DO, KARLA--
AH--

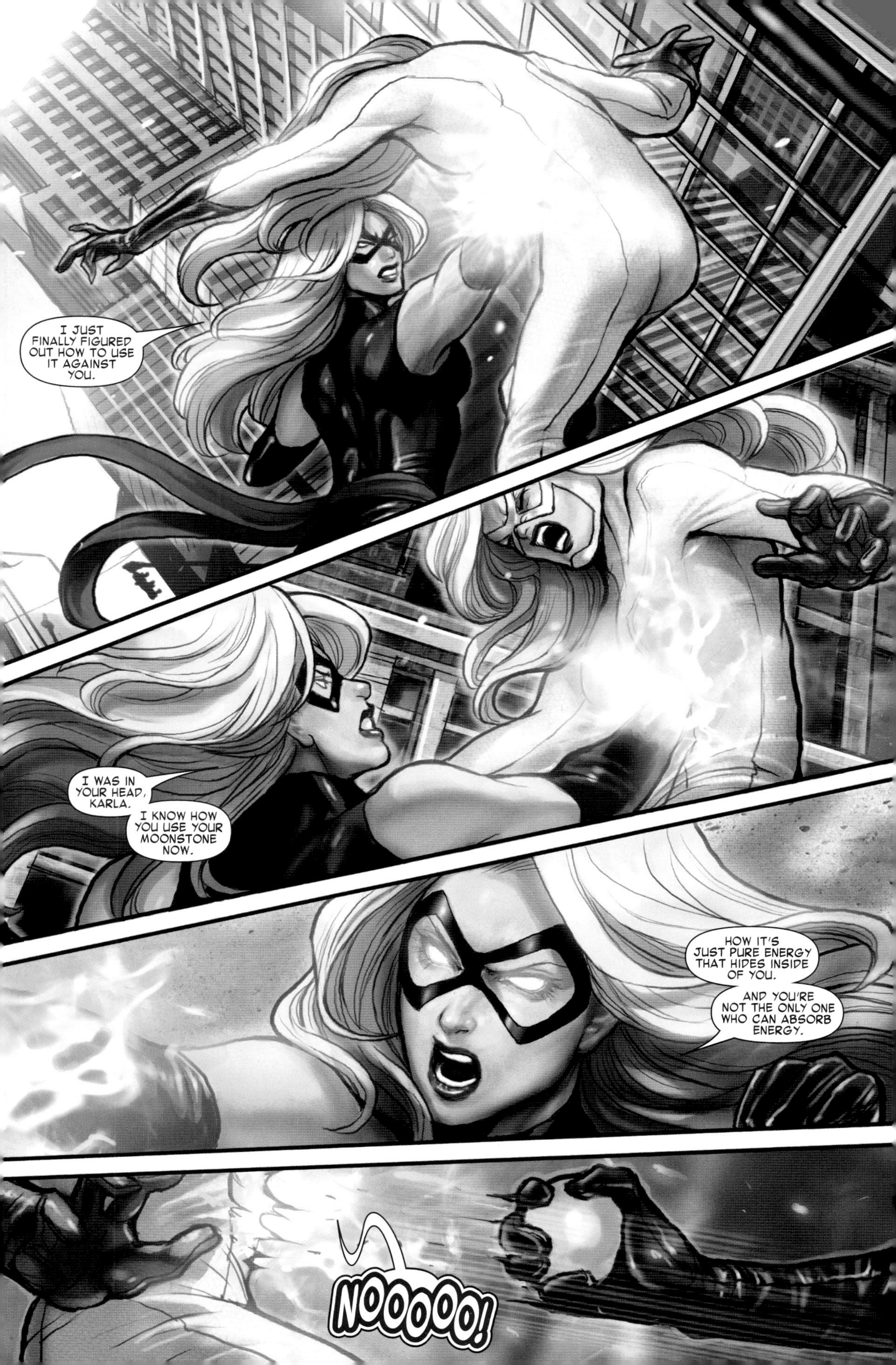
I JUST FINALLY FIGURED OUT HOW TO USE IT AGAINST YOU.
I WAS IN YOUR HEAD, KARLA.
I KNOW HOW YOU USE YOUR MOONSTONE NOW.
HOW IT'S JUST PURE ENERGY THAT HIDES INSIDE OF YOU.
AND YOU'RE NOT THE ONLY ONE WHO CAN ABSORB ENERGY.
NOOOOO!

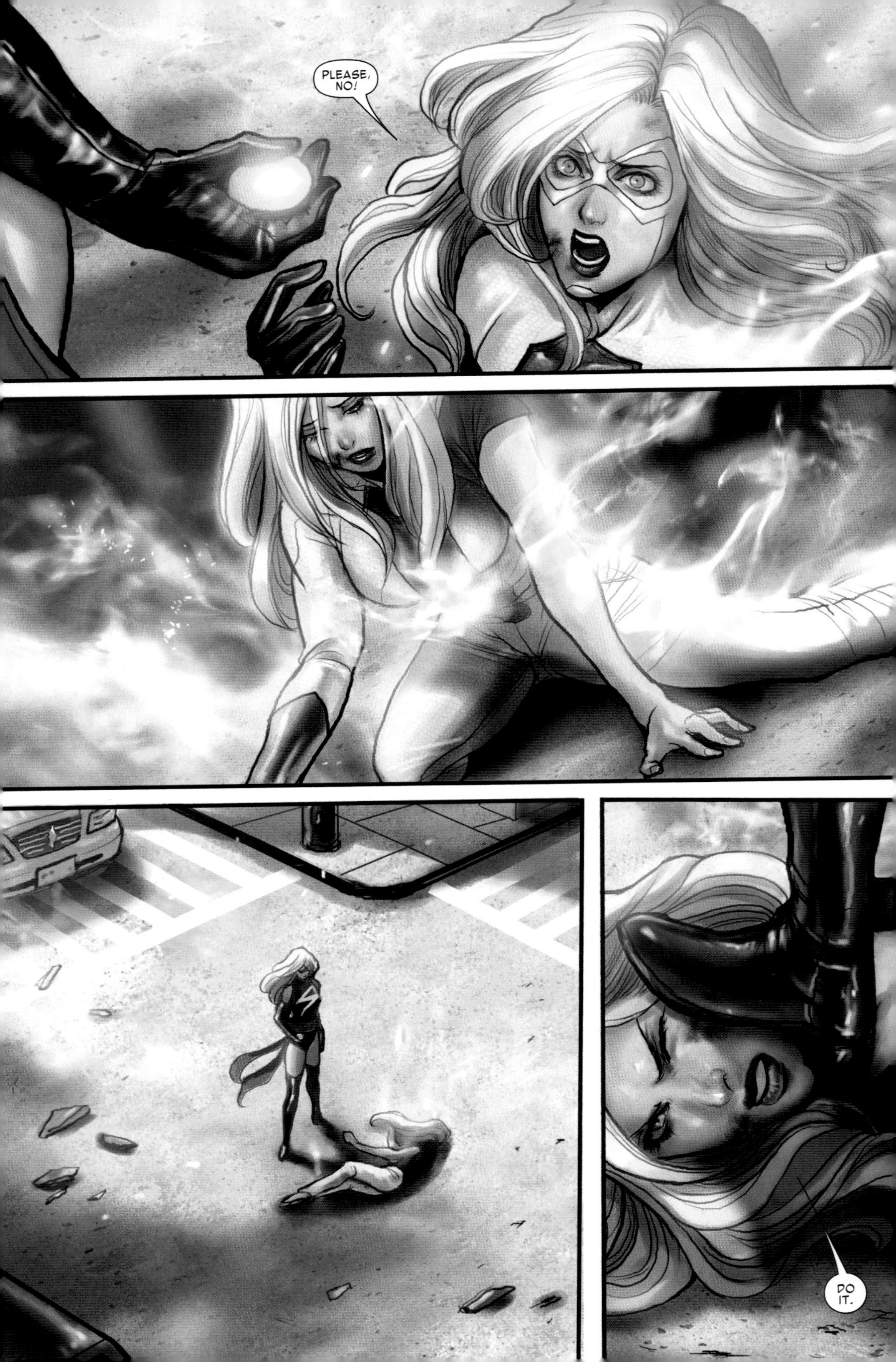
PLEASE, NO!
DO IT.

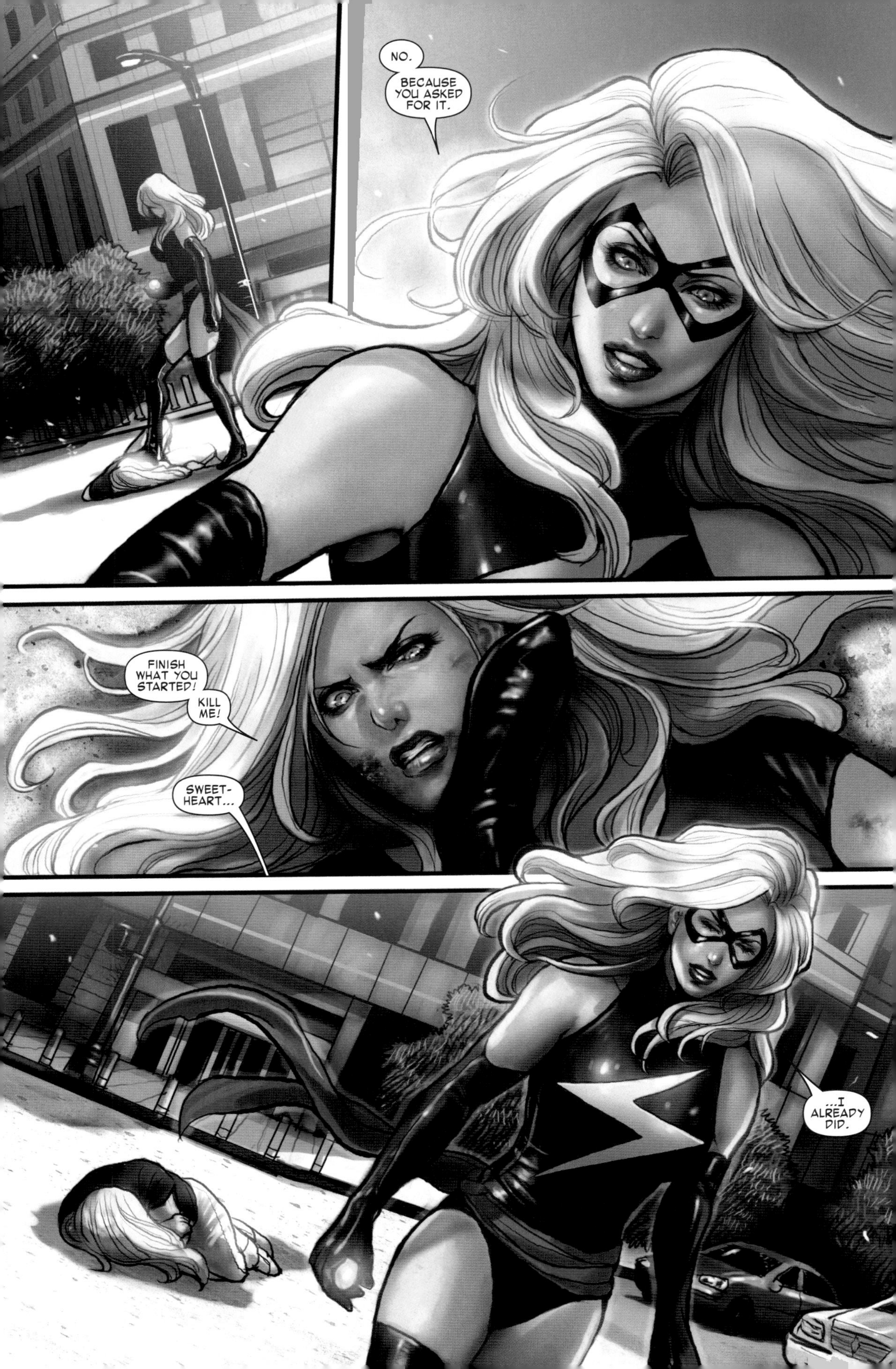
NO.
BECAUSE YOU ASKED FOR IT.
FINISH WHAT YOU STARTED!
KILL ME!
SWEET-HEART...
...I ALREADY DID.

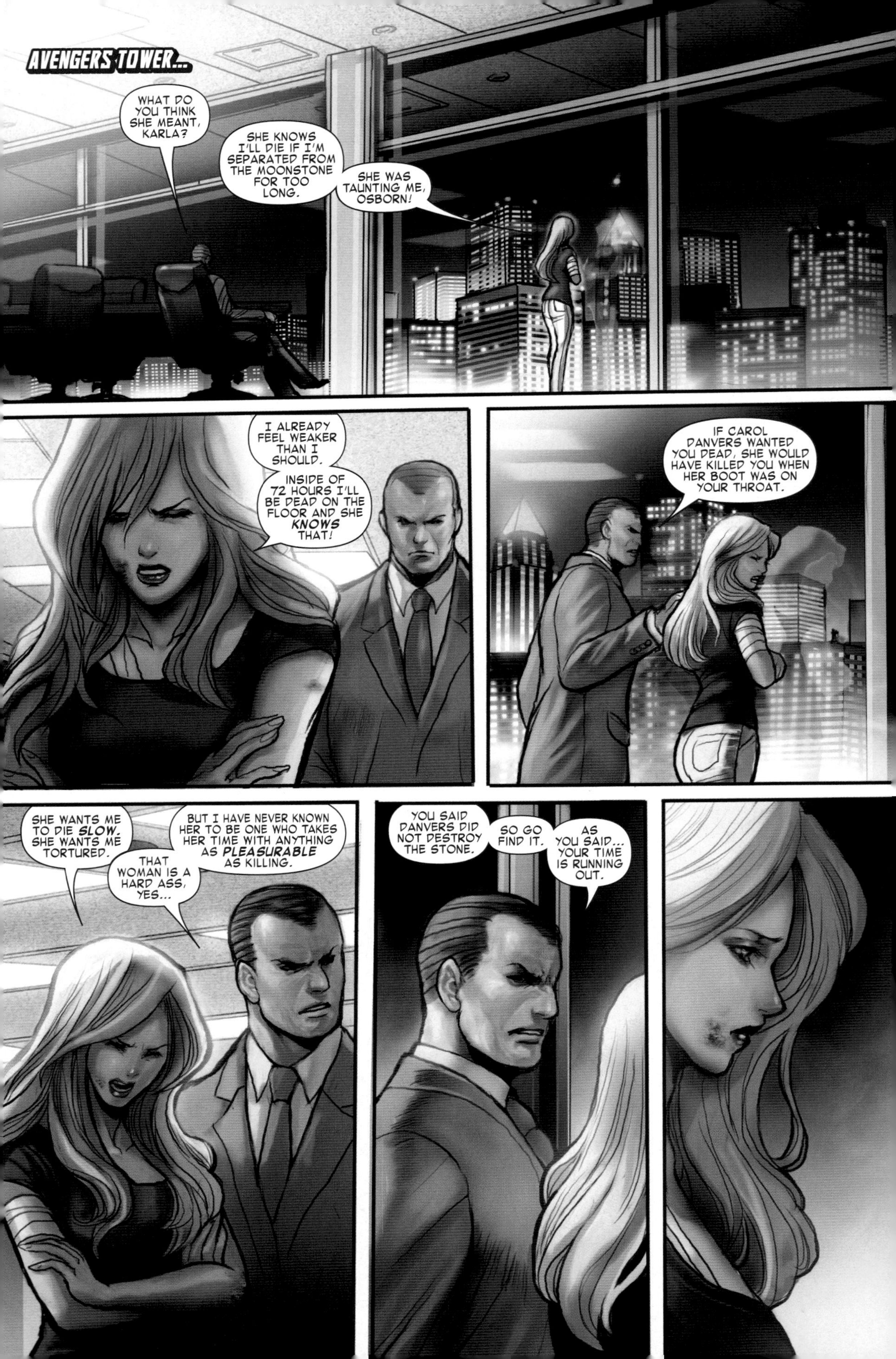
AVENGERS TOWER...
WHAT DO YOU THINK SHE MEANT, KARLA?
SHE KNOWS I'LL DIE IF I'M SEPARATED FROM THE MOONSTONE FOR TOO LONG.
SHE WAS TAUNTING ME, OSBORN!
I ALREADY FEEL WEAKER THAN I SHOULD.
INSIDE OF 72 HOURS I'LL BE DEAD ON THE FLOOR AND SHE KNOWS THAT!
IF CAROL DANVERS WANTED YOU DEAD, SHE WOULD HAVE KILLED YOU WHEN HER BOOT WAS ON YOUR THROAT.
SHE WANTS ME TO DIE SLOW. SHE WANTS ME TORTURED.
THAT WOMAN IS A HARD ASS, YES...
BUT I HAVE NEVER KNOWN HER TO BE ONE WHO TAKES HER TIME WITH ANYTHING AS PLEASURABLE AS KILLING.
YOU SAID DANVERS DID NOT DESTROY THE STONE.
SO GO FIND IT.
AS YOU SAID... YOUR TIME IS RUNNING OUT.

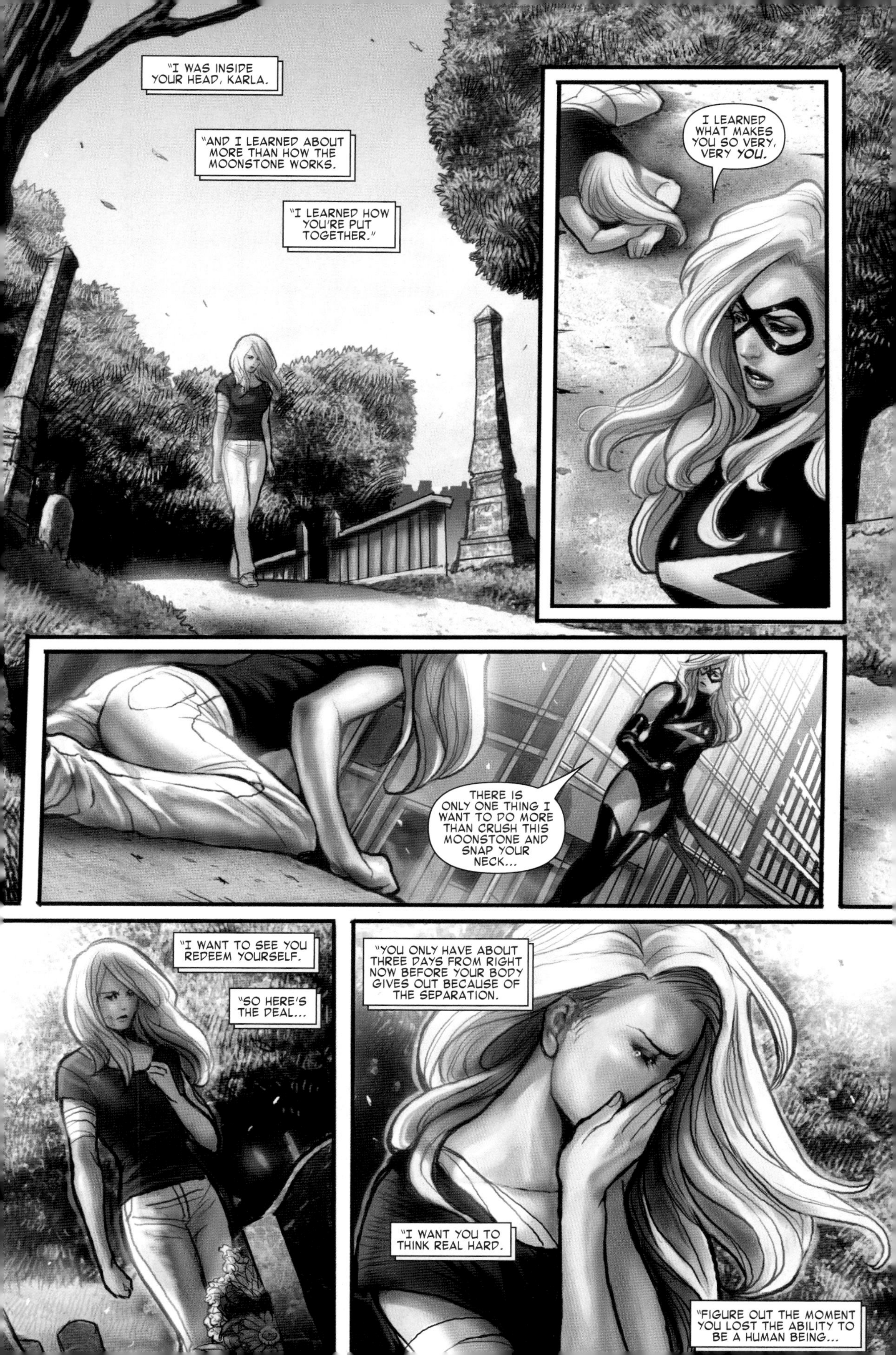
"I WAS INSIDE YOUR HEAD, KARLA.
"AND I LEARNED ABOUT MORE THAN HOW THE MOONSTONE WORKS.
"I LEARNED HOW YOU'RE PUT TOGETHER."
I LEARNED WHAT MAKES YOU SO VERY, VERY YOU.
THERE IS ONLY ONE THING I WANT TO DO MORE THAN CRUSH THIS MOONSTONE AND SNAP YOUR NECK...
"I WANT TO SEE YOU REDEEM YOURSELF.
"SO HERE'S THE DEAL...
"YOU ONLY HAVE ABOUT THREE DAYS FROM RIGHT NOW BEFORE YOUR BODY GIVES OUT BECAUSE OF THE SEPARATION.
"I WANT YOU TO THINK REAL HARD.
"FIGURE OUT THE MOMENT YOU LOST THE ABILITY TO BE A HUMAN BEING...

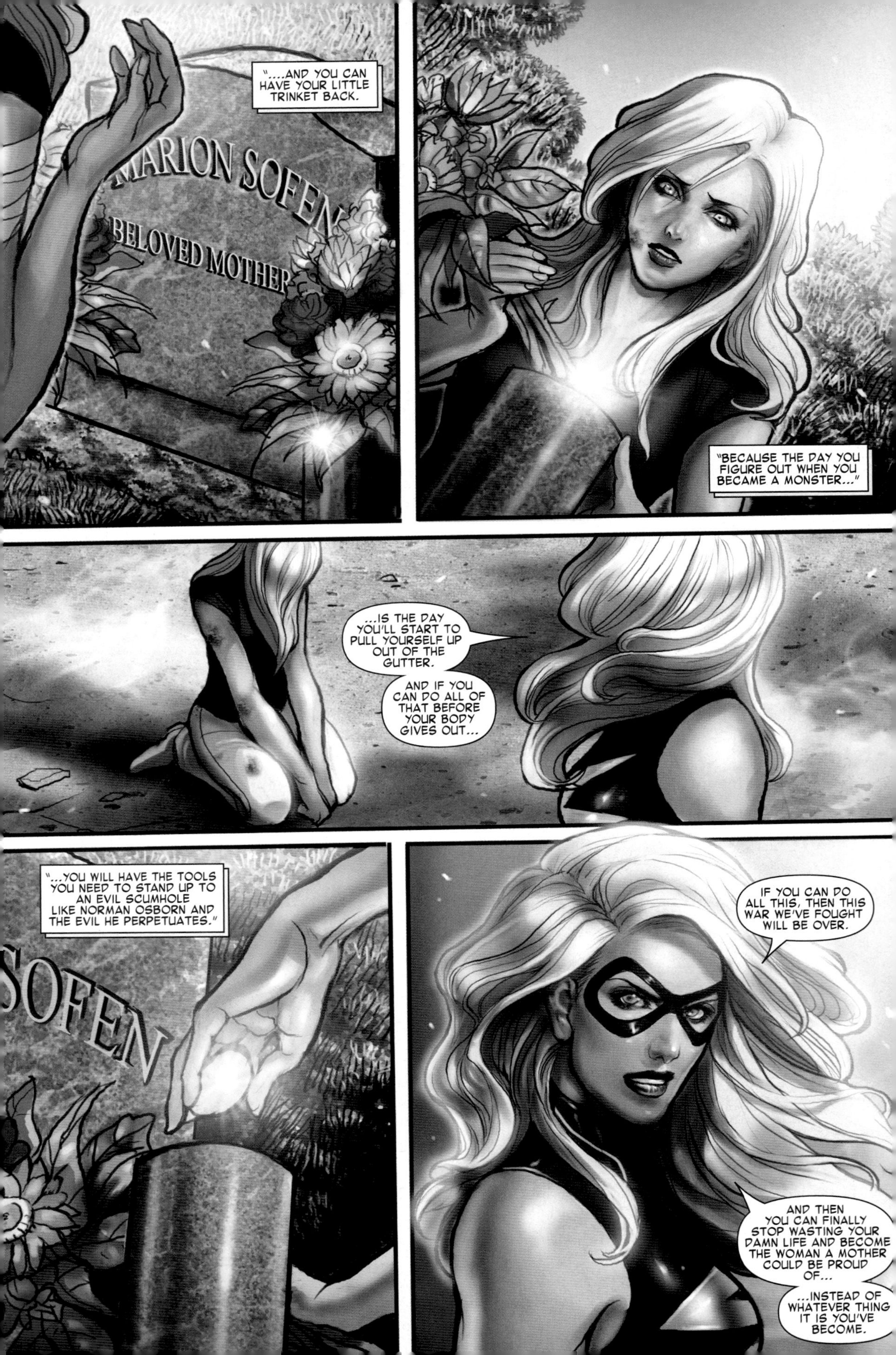

"....AND YOU CAN HAVE YOUR LITTLE TRINKET BACK.
MARION SOFEN
BELOVED MOTHER
"BECAUSE THE DAY YOU FIGURE OUT WHEN YOU BECAME A MONSTER..."
...IS THE DAY YOU'LL START TO PULL YOURSELF UP OUT OF THE GUTTER.
AND IF YOU CAN DO ALL OF THAT BEFORE YOUR BODY GIVES OUT...
"...YOU WILL HAVE THE TOOLS YOU NEED TO STAND UP TO AN EVIL SCUMHOLE LIKE NORMAN OSBORN AND THE EVIL HE PERPETUATES."
SOFEN
IF YOU CAN DO ALL THIS, THEN THIS WAR WE'VE FOUGHT WILL BE OVER.
AND THEN YOU CAN FINALLY STOP WASTING YOUR DAMN LIFE AND BECOME THE WOMAN A MOTHER COULD BE PROUD OF...
...INSTEAD OF WHATEVER THING IT IS YOU'VE BECOME.

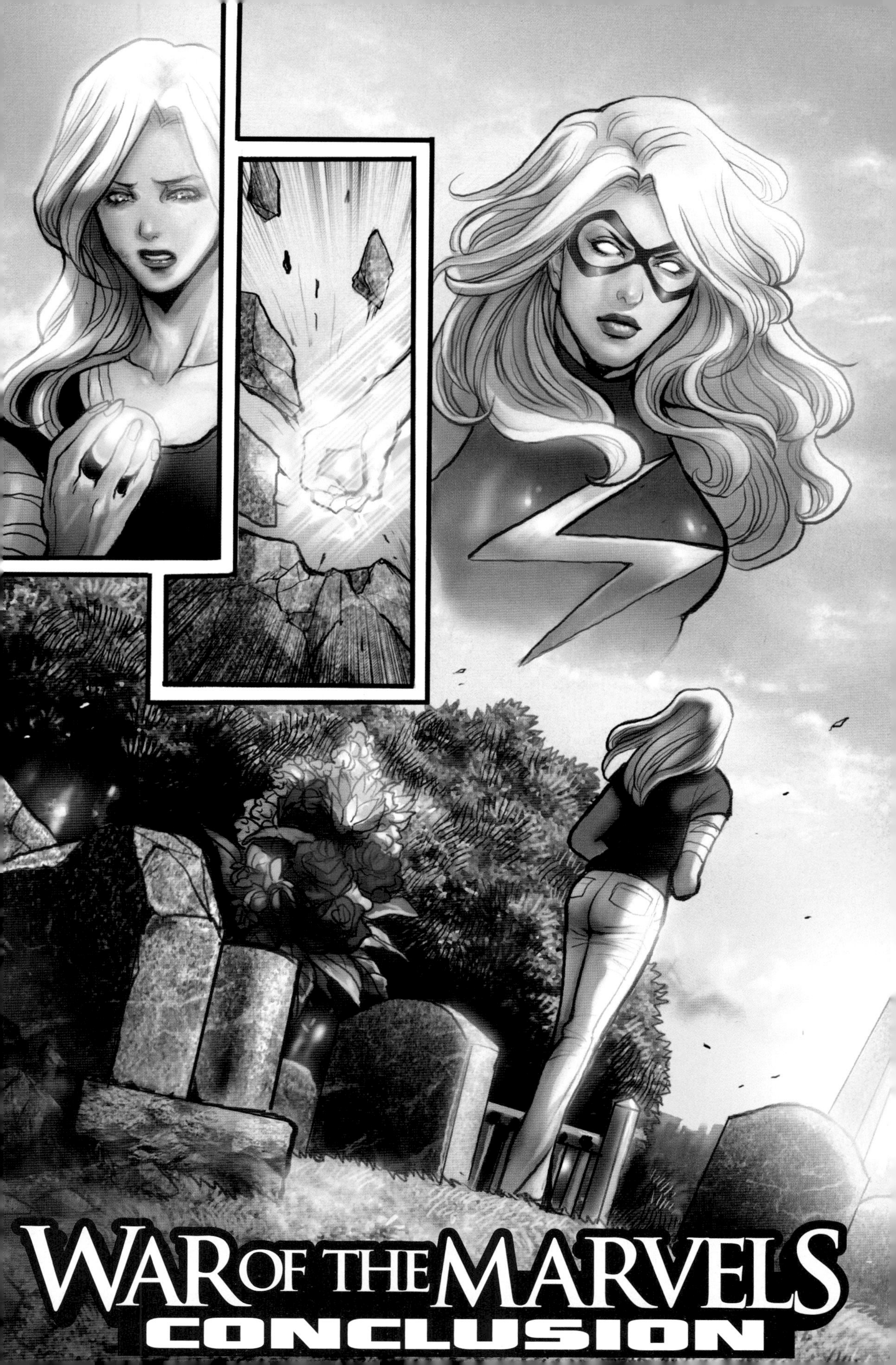
WAR OF THE MARVELS
CONCLUSION

47

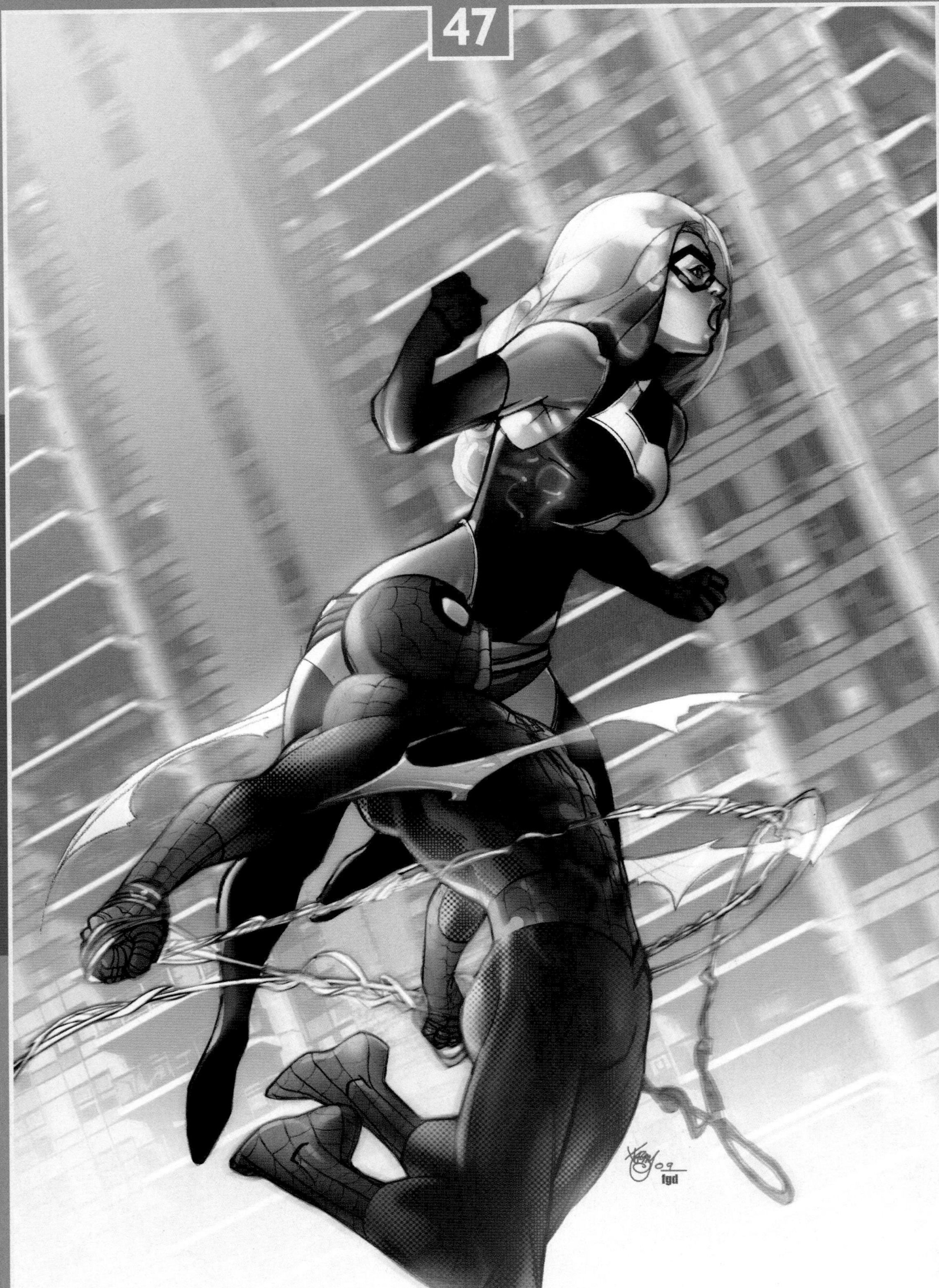

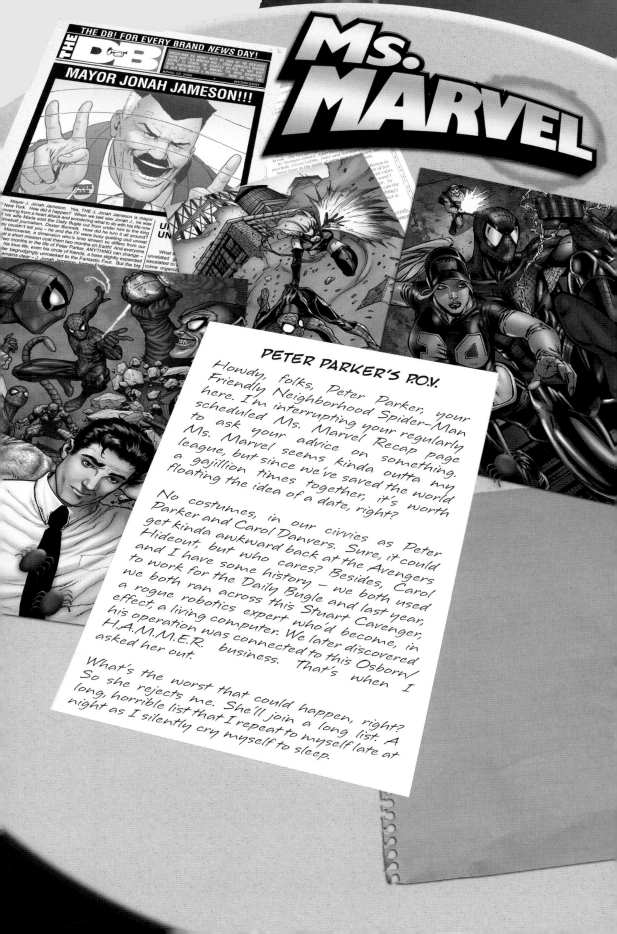

Ms. MARVEL

THE DB! FOR EVERY BRAND NEWS DAY!

MAYOR JONAH JAMESON!!!

PETER PARKER'S P.O.V.

Howdy, folks, Peter Parker, your Friendly Neighborhood Spider-Man here. I'm interrupting your regularly scheduled Ms. Marvel Recap page to ask your advice on something. Ms. Marvel seems kinda outta my league, but since we've saved the world a gajillion times together, it's worth floating the idea of a date, right?

No costumes, in our civvies as Peter Parker and Carol Danvers. Sure, it could get kinda awkward back at the Avengers Hideout, but who cares? Besides, Carol and I have some history — we both used to work for the Daily Bugle and last year, we both ran across this Stuart Cavenger, a rogue robotics expert who'd become, in effect, a living computer. We later discovered his operation was connected to this Osborn/H.A.M.M.E.R. business. That's when I asked her out.

What's the worst that could happen, right? So she rejects me. She'll join a long list. A long, horrible list that I repeat to myself late at night as I silently cry myself to sleep.

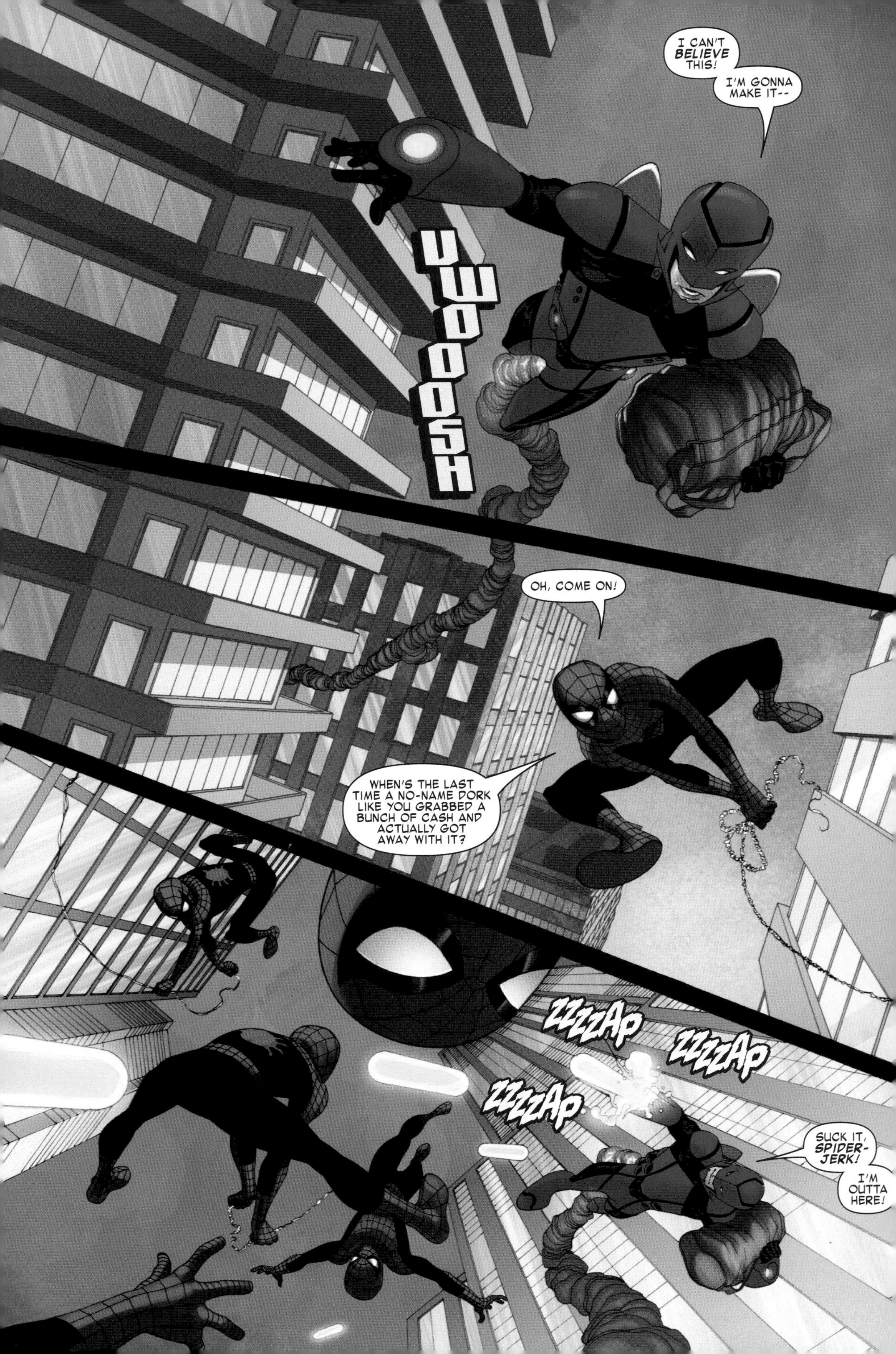
I CAN'T BELIEVE THIS!
I'M GONNA MAKE IT--
VWOOOSH
OH, COME ON!
WHEN'S THE LAST TIME A NO-NAME DORK LIKE YOU GRABBED A BUNCH OF CASH AND ACTUALLY GOT AWAY WITH IT?
ZZZZZAP
ZZZZZAP
ZZZZZAP
SUCK IT, SPIDER-JERK!
I'M OUTTA HERE!

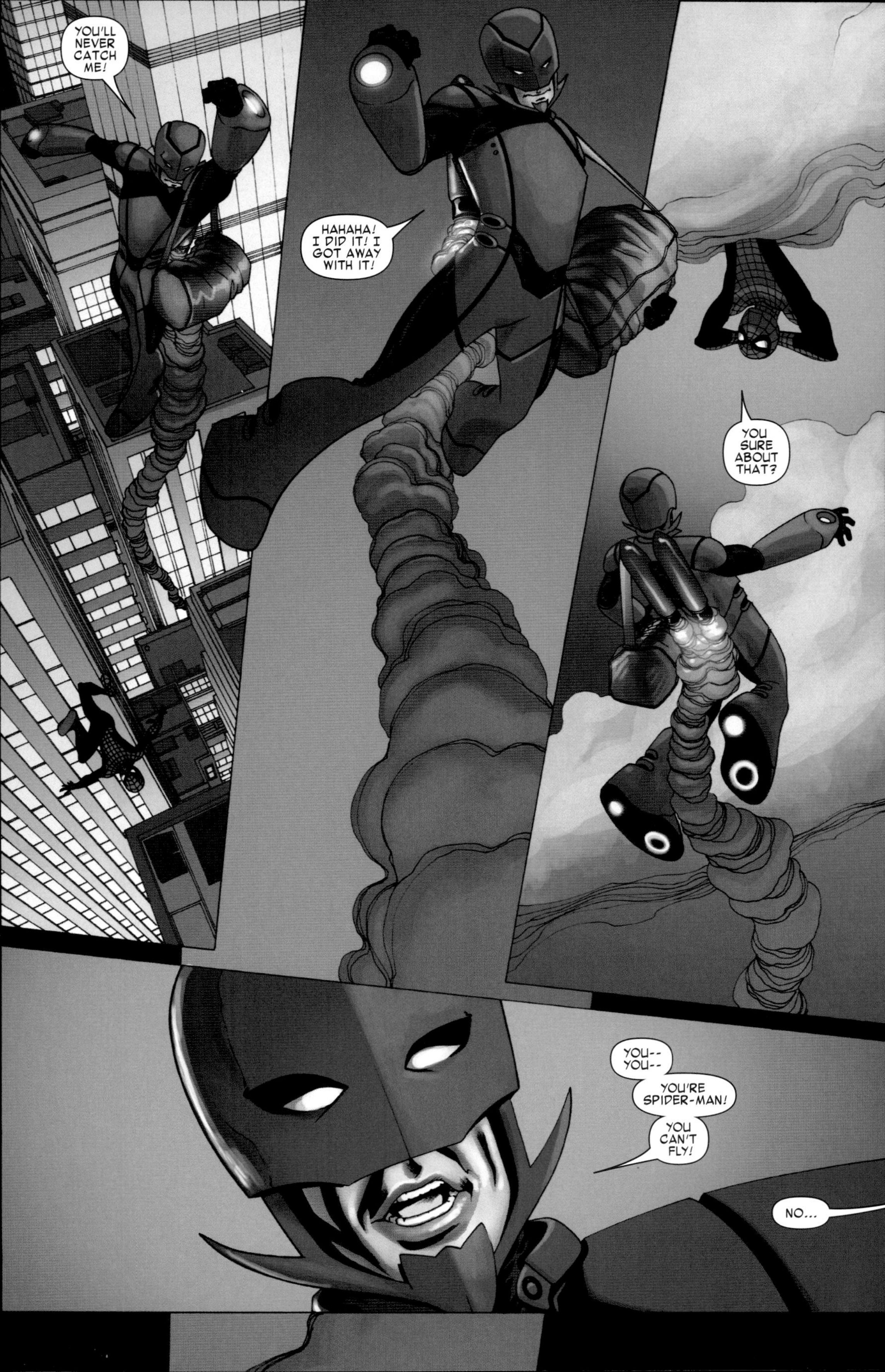
YOU'LL NEVER CATCH ME!
HAHAHA! I DID IT! I GOT AWAY WITH IT!
YOU SURE ABOUT THAT?
YOU-- YOU--
YOU'RE SPIDER-MAN!
YOU CAN'T FLY!
NO...

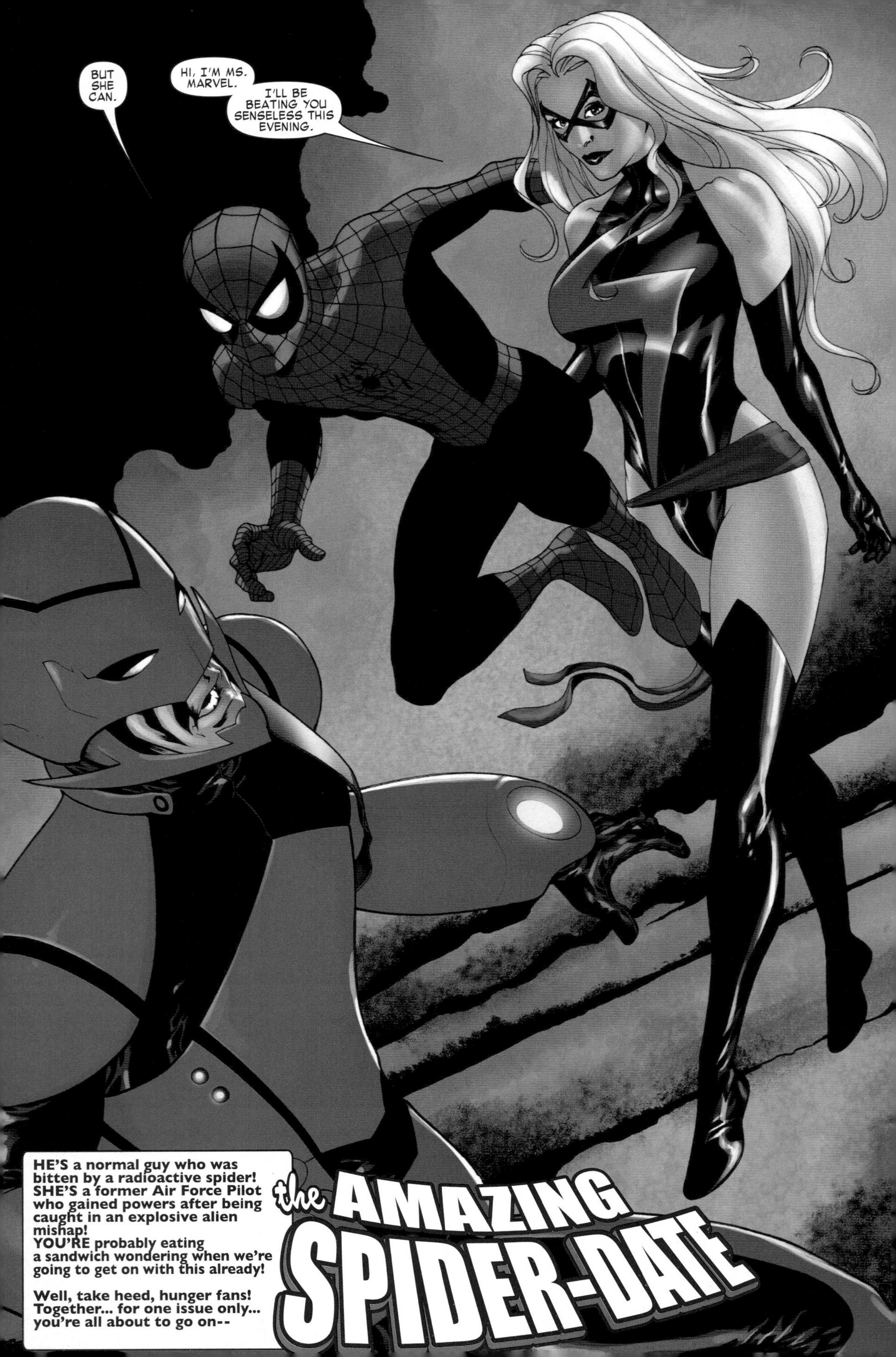
BUT SHE CAN.
HI, I'M MS. MARVEL.
I'LL BE BEATING YOU SENSELESS THIS EVENING.
HE'S a normal guy who was bitten by a radioactive spider! SHE'S a former Air Force Pilot who gained powers after being caught in an explosive alien mishap! YOU'RE probably eating a sandwich wondering when we're going to get on with this already!
Well, take heed, hunger fans! Together... for one issue only... you're all about to go on--
the AMAZING SPIDER-DATE

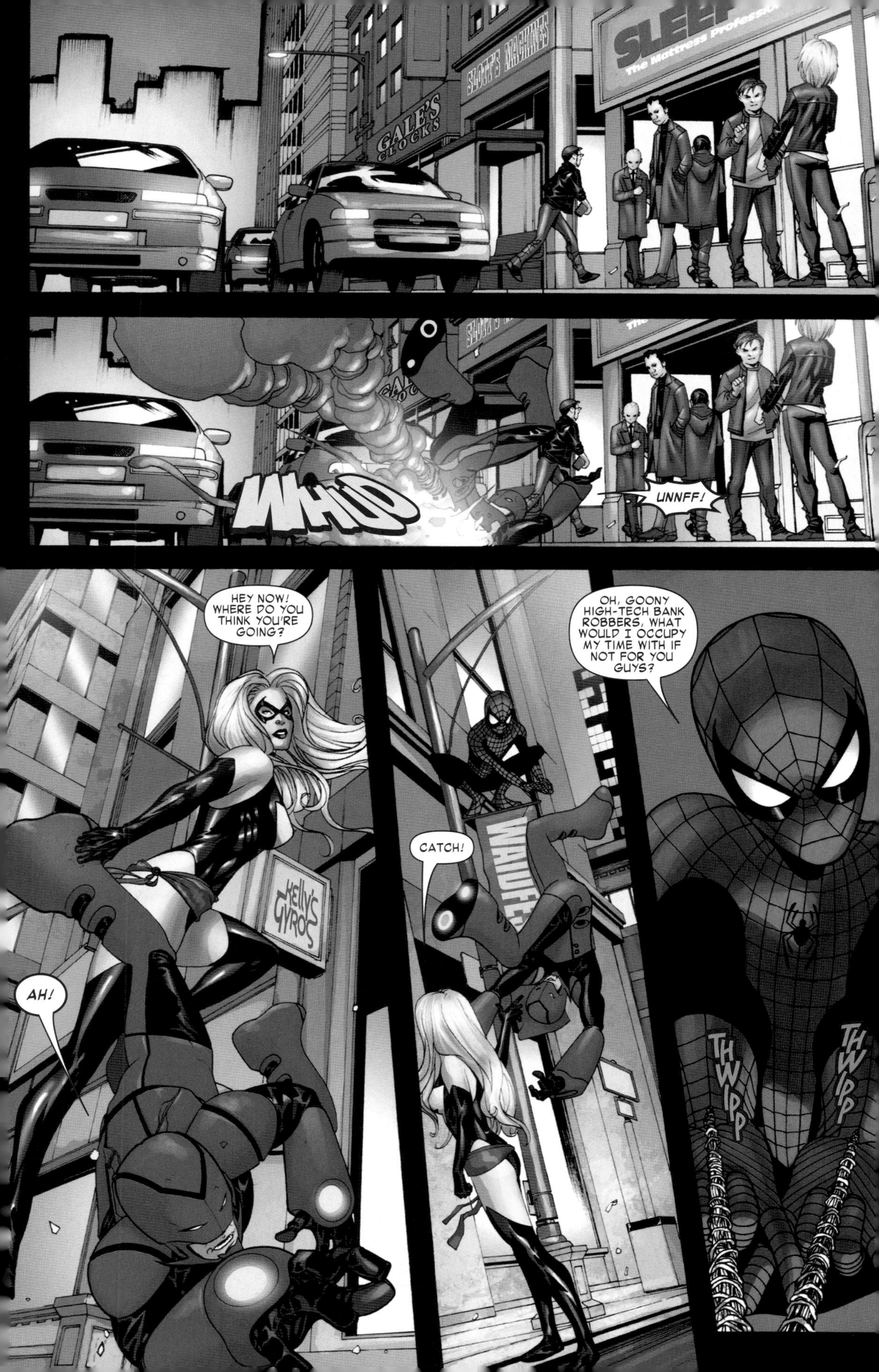
GALE'S CLOCKS
SLOTT'S MACHINES
SLEEP The Mattress Profession
WHOD
UNNFF!
HEY NOW! WHERE DO YOU THINK YOU'RE GOING?
AH!
Kelly's GYROS
CATCH!
OH, GOONY HIGH-TECH BANK ROBBERS, WHAT WOULD I OCCUPY MY TIME WITH IF NOT FOR YOU GUYS?
THWIPP
THWIPP

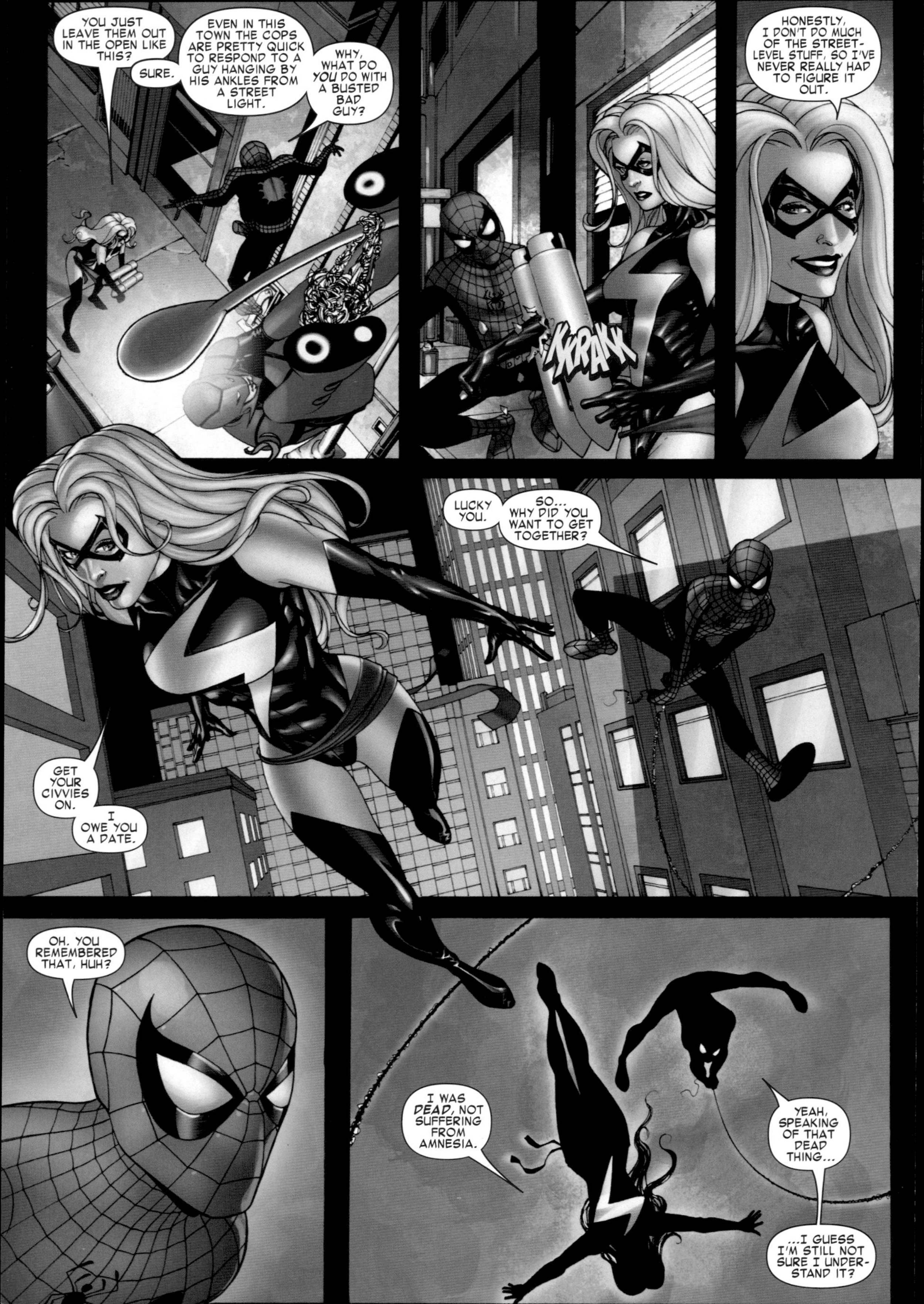
YOU JUST LEAVE THEM OUT IN THE OPEN LIKE THIS?
SURE.
EVEN IN THIS TOWN THE COPS ARE PRETTY QUICK TO RESPOND TO A GUY HANGING BY HIS ANKLES FROM A STREET LIGHT.
WHY, WHAT DO YOU DO WITH A BUSTED BAD GUY?
KKRAKK
HONESTLY, I DON'T DO MUCH OF THE STREET-LEVEL STUFF, SO I'VE NEVER REALLY HAD TO FIGURE IT OUT.
LUCKY YOU.
SO... WHY DID YOU WANT TO GET TOGETHER?
GET YOUR CIVVIES ON.
I OWE YOU A DATE.
OH. YOU REMEMBERED THAT, HUH?
I WAS DEAD, NOT SUFFERING FROM AMNESIA.
YEAH, SPEAKING OF THAT DEAD THING...
...I GUESS I'M STILL NOT SURE I UNDERSTAND IT?

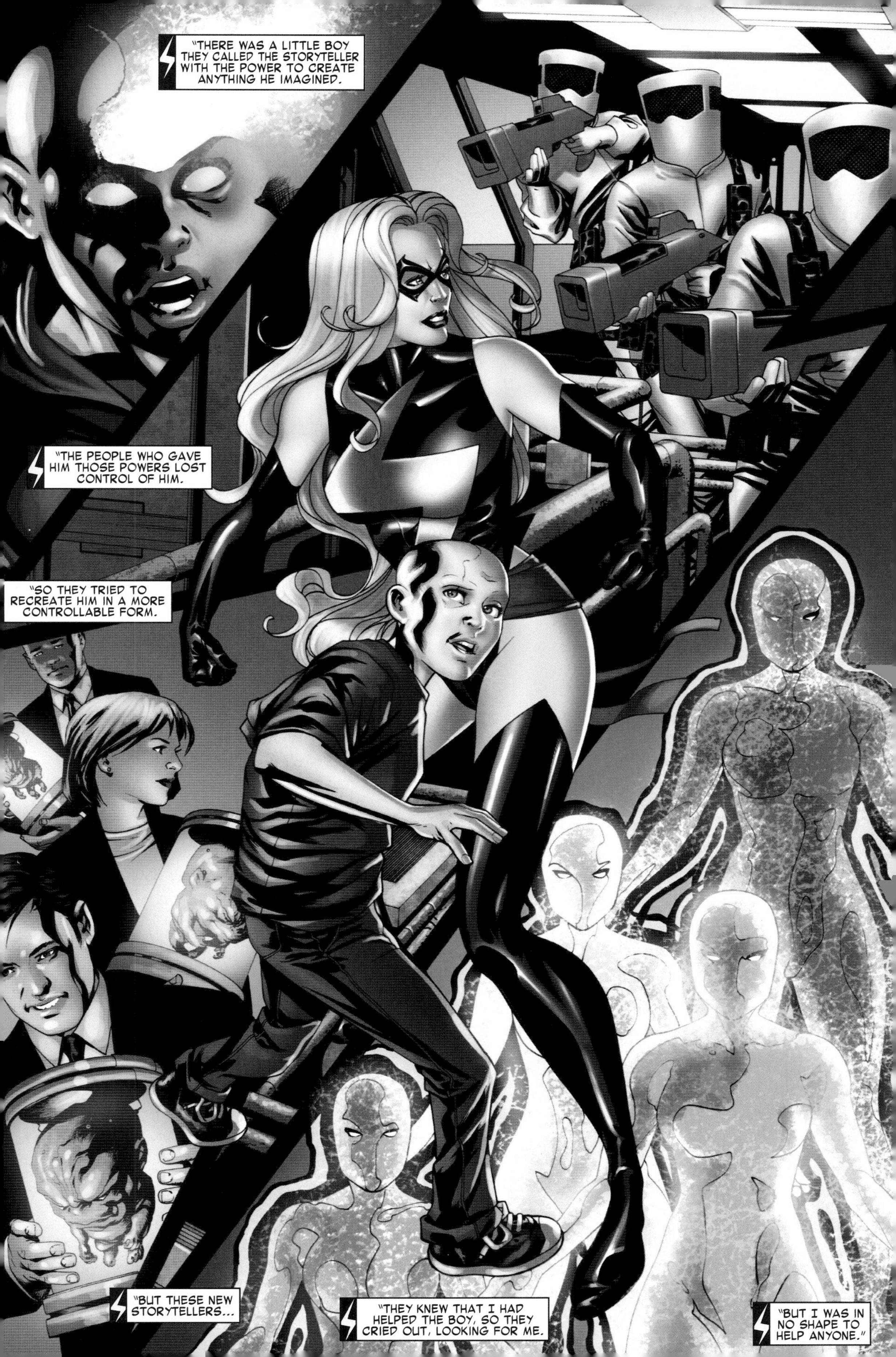
"THERE WAS A LITTLE BOY THEY CALLED THE STORYTELLER WITH THE POWER TO CREATE ANYTHING HE IMAGINED.
"THE PEOPLE WHO GAVE HIM THOSE POWERS LOST CONTROL OF HIM.
"SO THEY TRIED TO RECREATE HIM IN A MORE CONTROLLABLE FORM.
"BUT THESE NEW STORYTELLERS...
"THEY KNEW THAT I HAD HELPED THE BOY, SO THEY CRIED OUT, LOOKING FOR ME.
"BUT I WAS IN NO SHAPE TO HELP ANYONE."

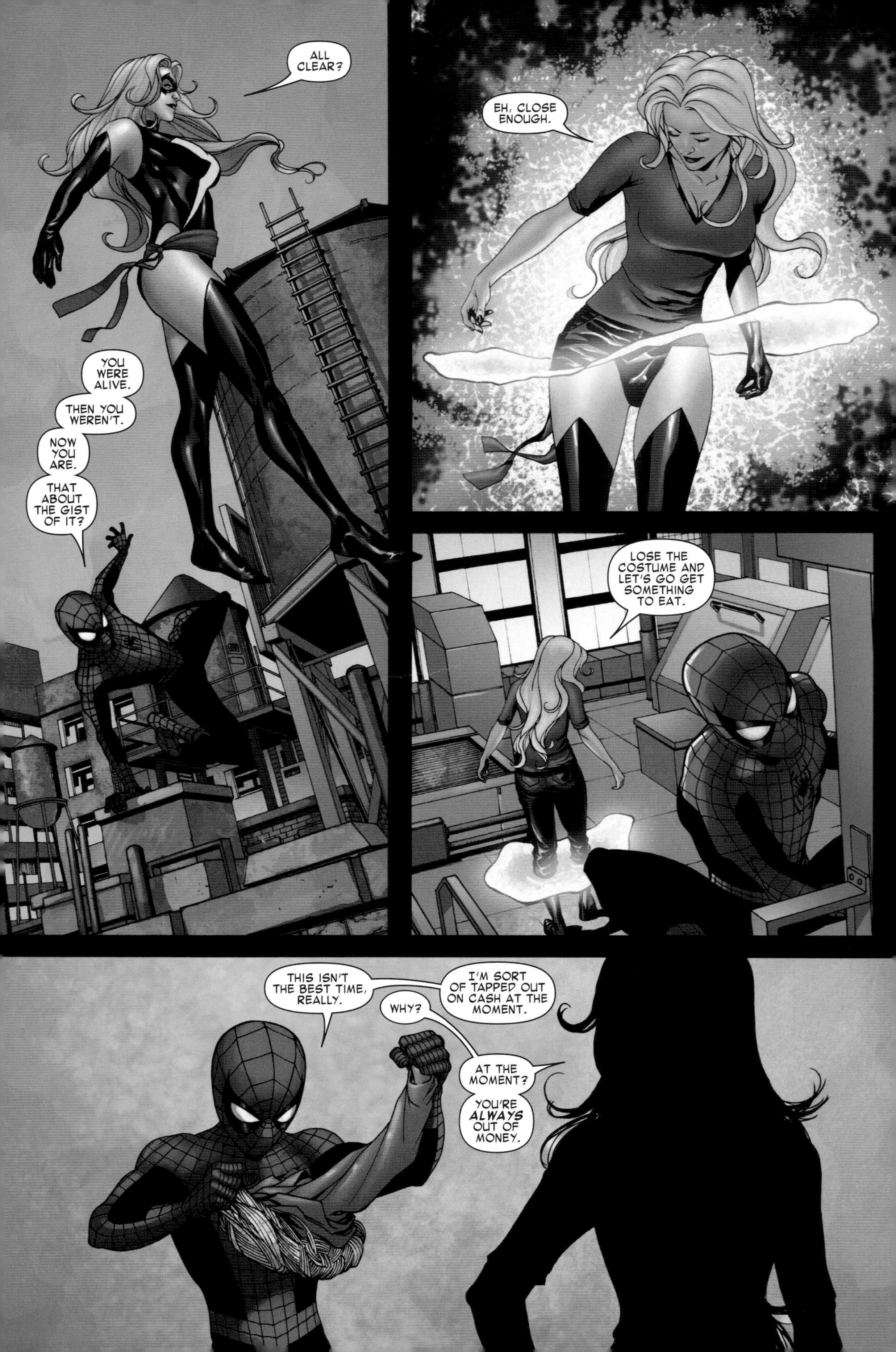
ALL CLEAR?
YOU WERE ALIVE.
THEN YOU WEREN'T.
NOW YOU ARE.
THAT ABOUT THE GIST OF IT?
EH, CLOSE ENOUGH.
LOSE THE COSTUME AND LET'S GO GET SOMETHING TO EAT.
THIS ISN'T THE BEST TIME, REALLY.
WHY?
I'M SORT OF TAPPED OUT ON CASH AT THE MOMENT.
AT THE MOMENT?
YOU'RE *ALWAYS* OUT OF MONEY.

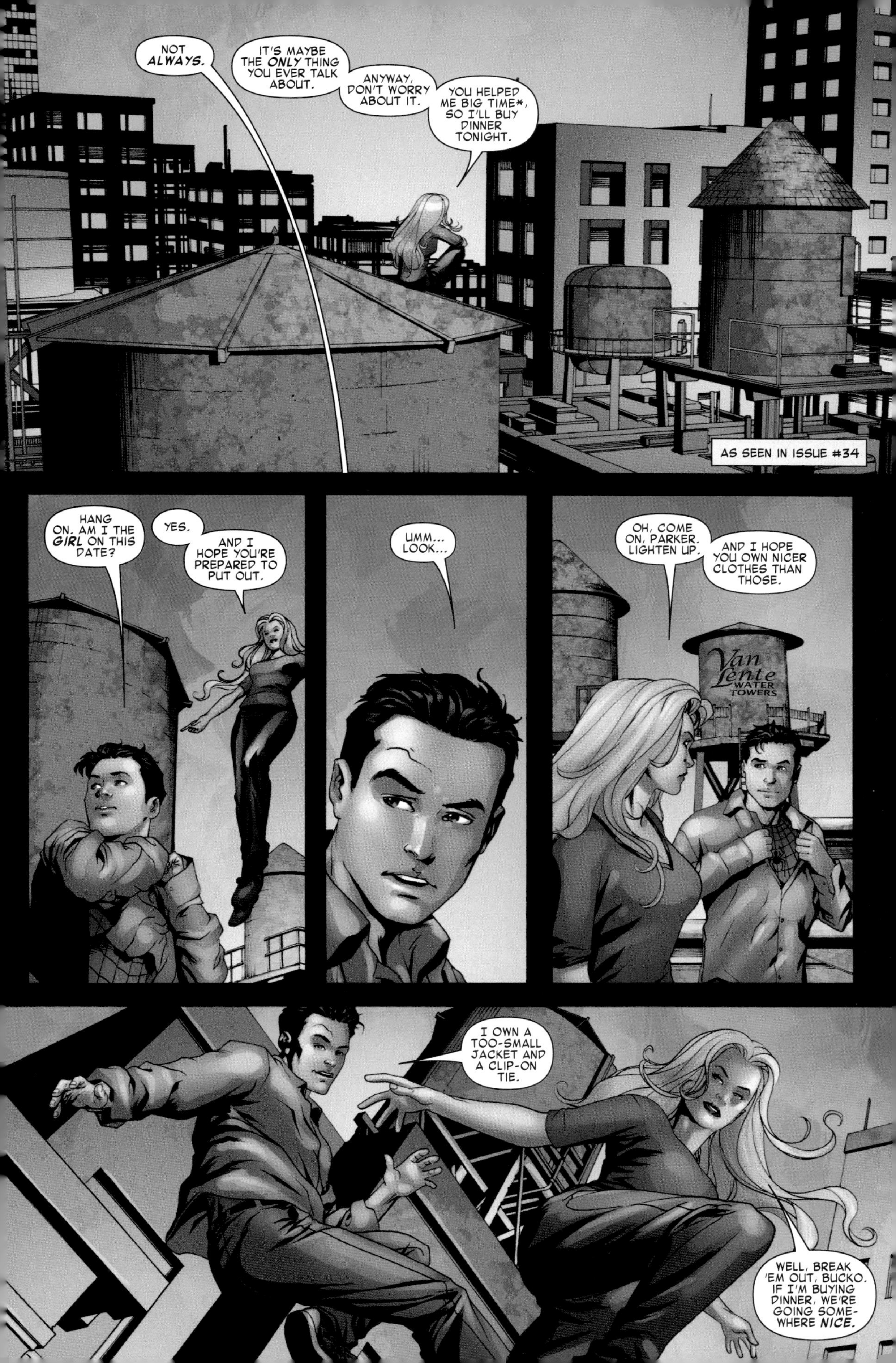
NOT ALWAYS.
IT'S MAYBE THE ONLY THING YOU EVER TALK ABOUT.
ANYWAY, DON'T WORRY ABOUT IT.
YOU HELPED ME BIG TIME*, SO I'LL BUY DINNER TONIGHT.
AS SEEN IN ISSUE #34
HANG ON. AM I THE GIRL ON THIS DATE?
YES.
AND I HOPE YOU'RE PREPARED TO PUT OUT.
UMM... LOOK...
OH, COME ON, PARKER. LIGHTEN UP.
AND I HOPE YOU OWN NICER CLOTHES THAN THOSE.
Van Lente WATER TOWERS
I OWN A TOO-SMALL JACKET AND A CLIP-ON TIE.
WELL, BREAK 'EM OUT, BUCKO. IF I'M BUYING DINNER, WE'RE GOING SOME-WHERE NICE.

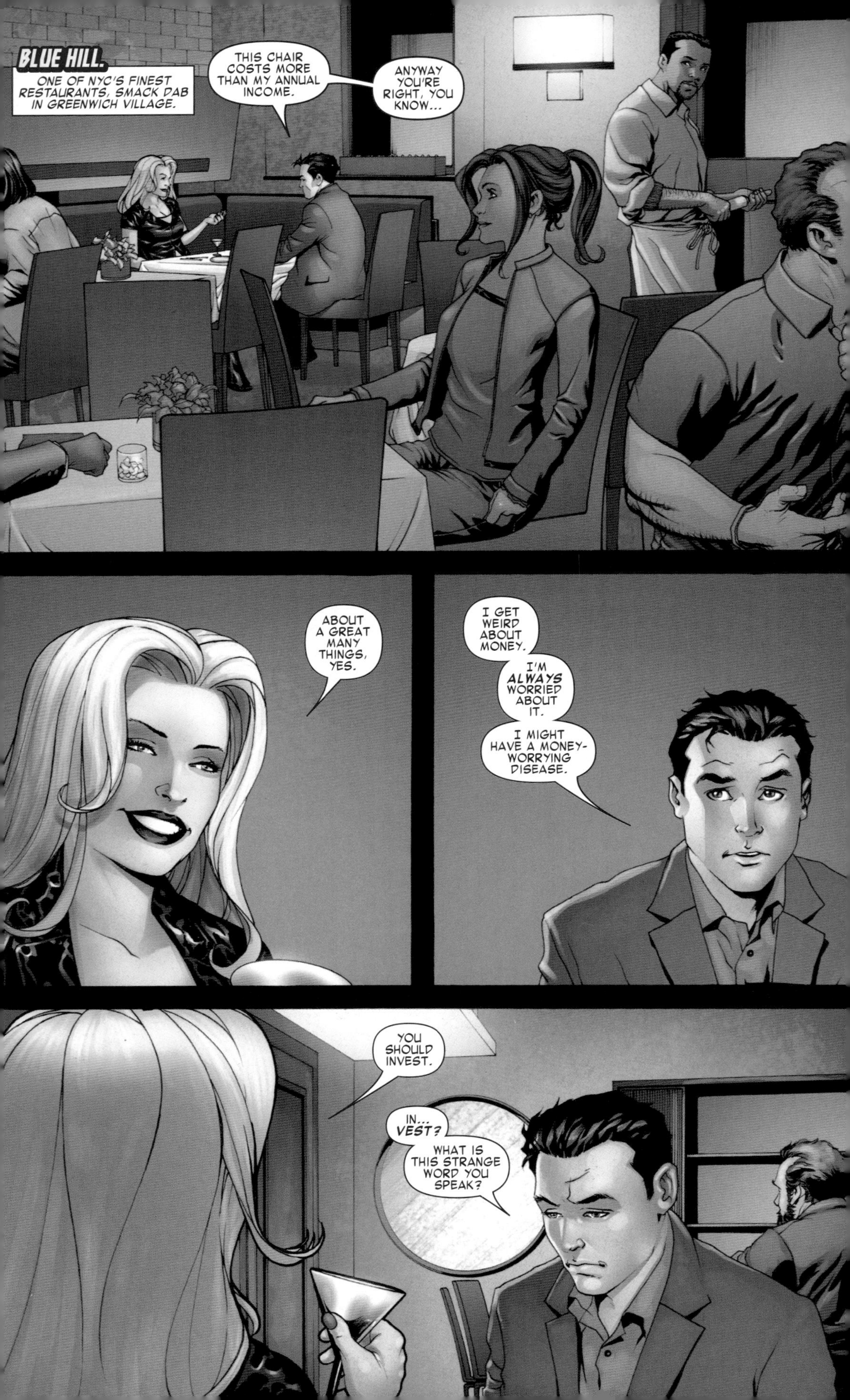
BLUE HILL.
ONE OF NYC'S FINEST RESTAURANTS, SMACK DAB IN GREENWICH VILLAGE.
THIS CHAIR COSTS MORE THAN MY ANNUAL INCOME.
ANYWAY YOU'RE RIGHT, YOU KNOW...
ABOUT A GREAT MANY THINGS, YES.
I GET WEIRD ABOUT MONEY.
I'M ALWAYS WORRIED ABOUT IT.
I MIGHT HAVE A MONEY-WORRYING DISEASE.
YOU SHOULD INVEST.
IN... VEST?
WHAT IS THIS STRANGE WORD YOU SPEAK?

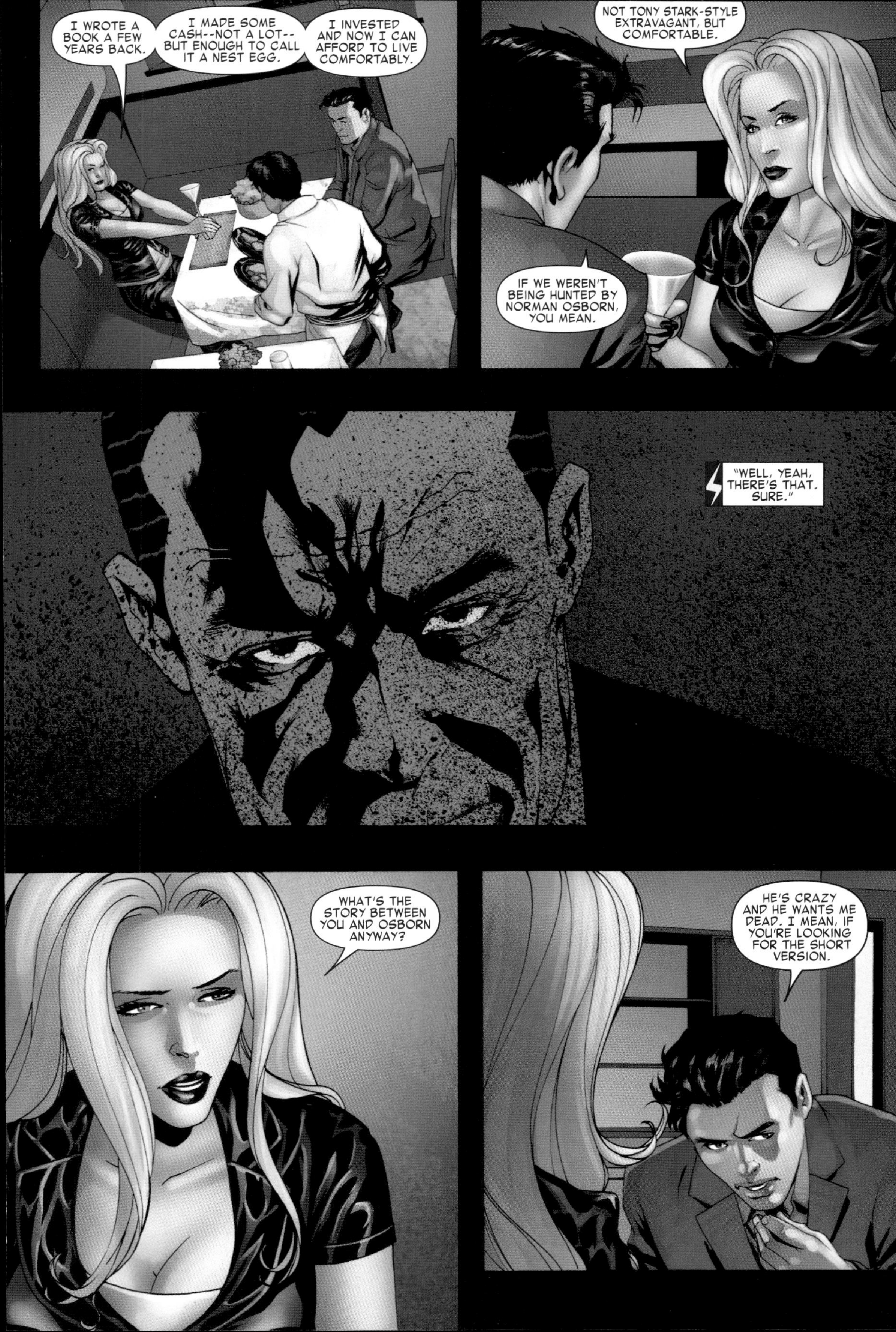
I WROTE A BOOK A FEW YEARS BACK.
I MADE SOME CASH--NOT A LOT--BUT ENOUGH TO CALL IT A NEST EGG.
I INVESTED AND NOW I CAN AFFORD TO LIVE COMFORTABLY.
NOT TONY STARK-STYLE EXTRAVAGANT, BUT COMFORTABLE.
IF WE WEREN'T BEING HUNTED BY NORMAN OSBORN, YOU MEAN.
"WELL, YEAH, THERE'S THAT. SURE."
WHAT'S THE STORY BETWEEN YOU AND OSBORN ANYWAY?
HE'S CRAZY AND HE WANTS ME DEAD. I MEAN, IF YOU'RE LOOKING FOR THE SHORT VERSION.

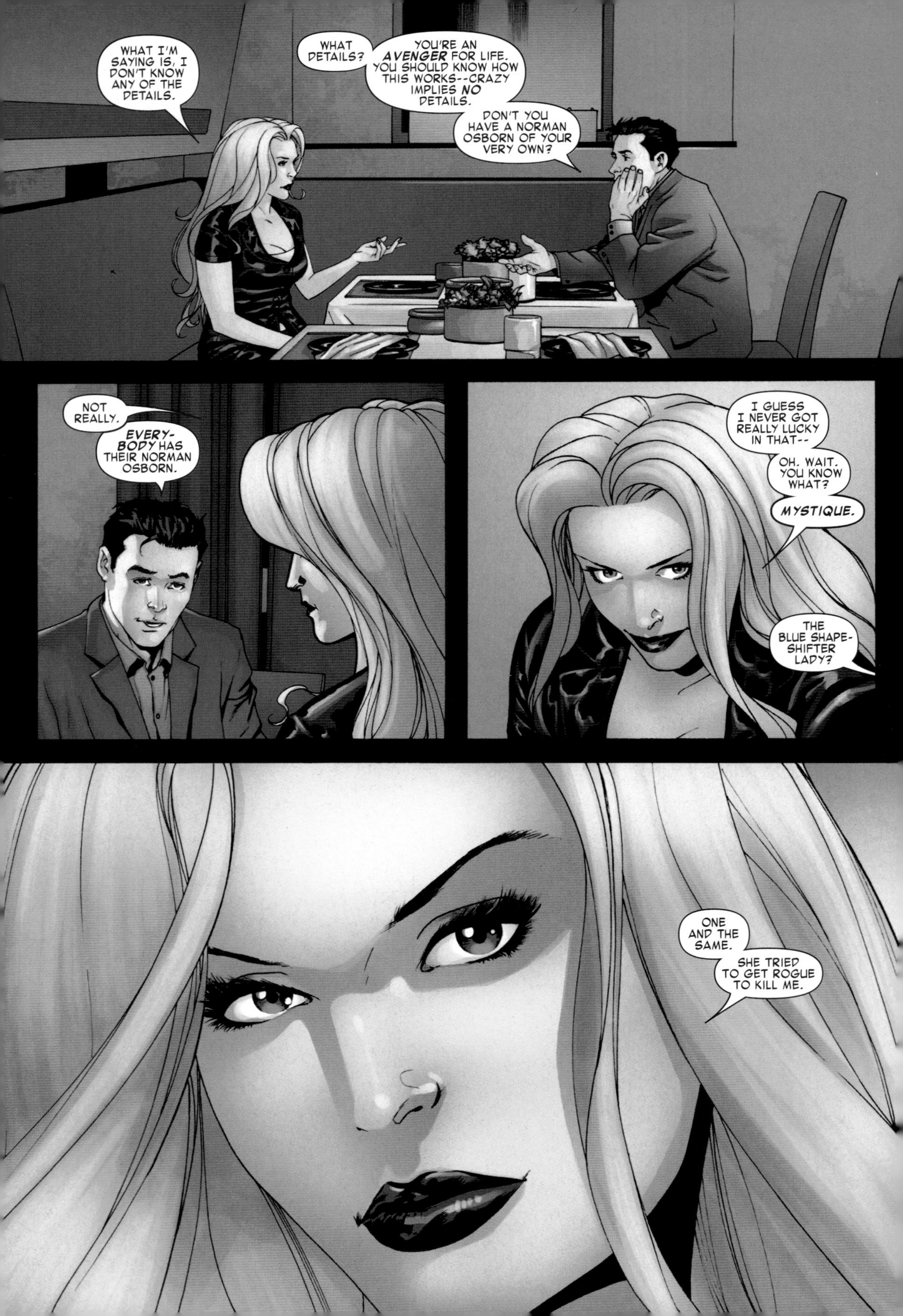
WHAT I'M SAYING IS, I DON'T KNOW ANY OF THE DETAILS.
WHAT DETAILS?
YOU'RE AN AVENGER FOR LIFE. YOU SHOULD KNOW HOW THIS WORKS--CRAZY IMPLIES NO DETAILS.
DON'T YOU HAVE A NORMAN OSBORN OF YOUR VERY OWN?
NOT REALLY.
EVERY-BODY HAS THEIR NORMAN OSBORN.
I GUESS I NEVER GOT REALLY LUCKY IN THAT--
OH. WAIT. YOU KNOW WHAT?
MYSTIQUE.
THE BLUE SHAPE-SHIFTER LADY?
ONE AND THE SAME.
SHE TRIED TO GET ROGUE TO KILL ME.

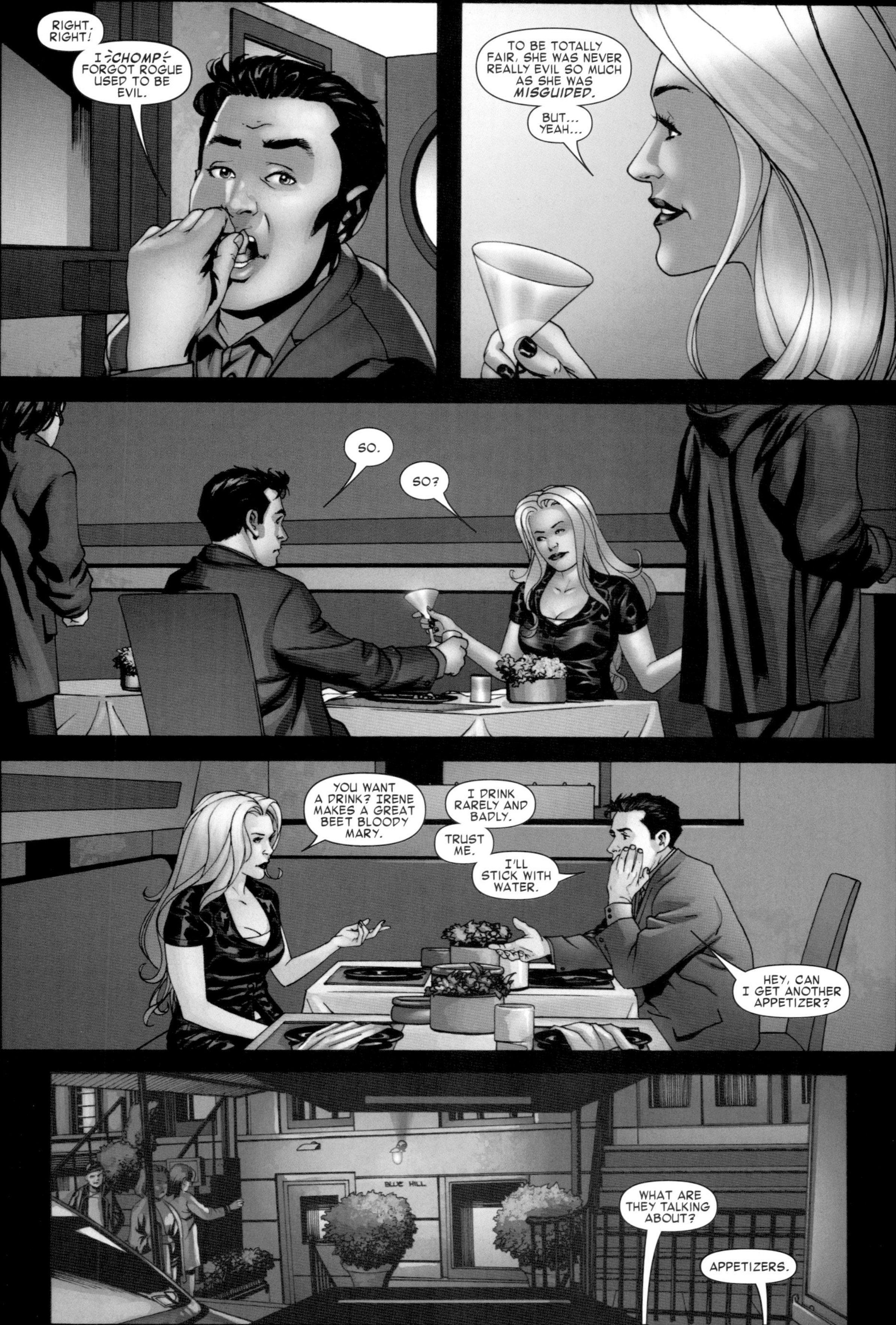
RIGHT. RIGHT!
I *CHOMP* FORGOT ROGUE USED TO BE EVIL.
TO BE TOTALLY FAIR, SHE WAS NEVER REALLY EVIL SO MUCH AS SHE WAS MISGUIDED.
BUT... YEAH...
SO.
SO?
YOU WANT A DRINK? IRENE MAKES A GREAT BEET BLOODY MARY.
I DRINK RARELY AND BADLY.
TRUST ME.
I'LL STICK WITH WATER.
HEY, CAN I GET ANOTHER APPETIZER?
BLUE HILL
WHAT ARE THEY TALKING ABOUT?
APPETIZERS.

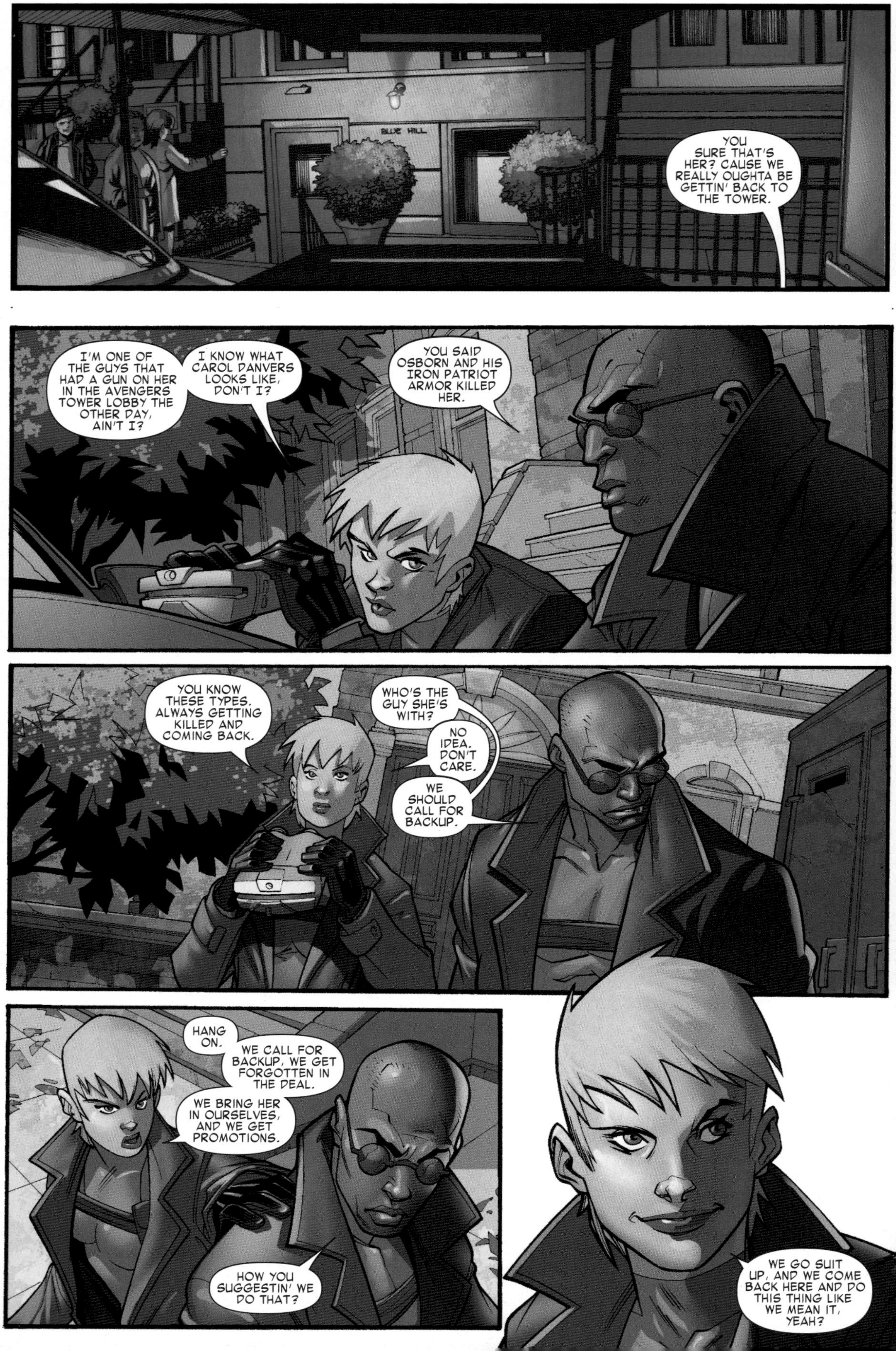
BLUE HILL
YOU SURE THAT'S HER? CAUSE WE REALLY OUGHTA BE GETTIN' BACK TO THE TOWER.
YOU SAID OSBORN AND HIS IRON PATRIOT ARMOR KILLED HER.
I'M ONE OF THE GUYS THAT HAD A GUN ON HER IN THE AVENGERS TOWER LOBBY THE OTHER DAY, AIN'T I?
I KNOW WHAT CAROL DANVERS LOOKS LIKE, DON'T I?
YOU KNOW THESE TYPES. ALWAYS GETTING KILLED AND COMING BACK.
WHO'S THE GUY SHE'S WITH?
NO IDEA. DON'T CARE.
WE SHOULD CALL FOR BACKUP.
HANG ON.
WE CALL FOR BACKUP, WE GET FORGOTTEN IN THE DEAL.
WE BRING HER IN OURSELVES, AND WE GET PROMOTIONS.
HOW YOU SUGGESTIN' WE DO THAT?
WE GO SUIT UP, AND WE COME BACK HERE AND DO THIS THING LIKE WE MEAN IT, YEAH?

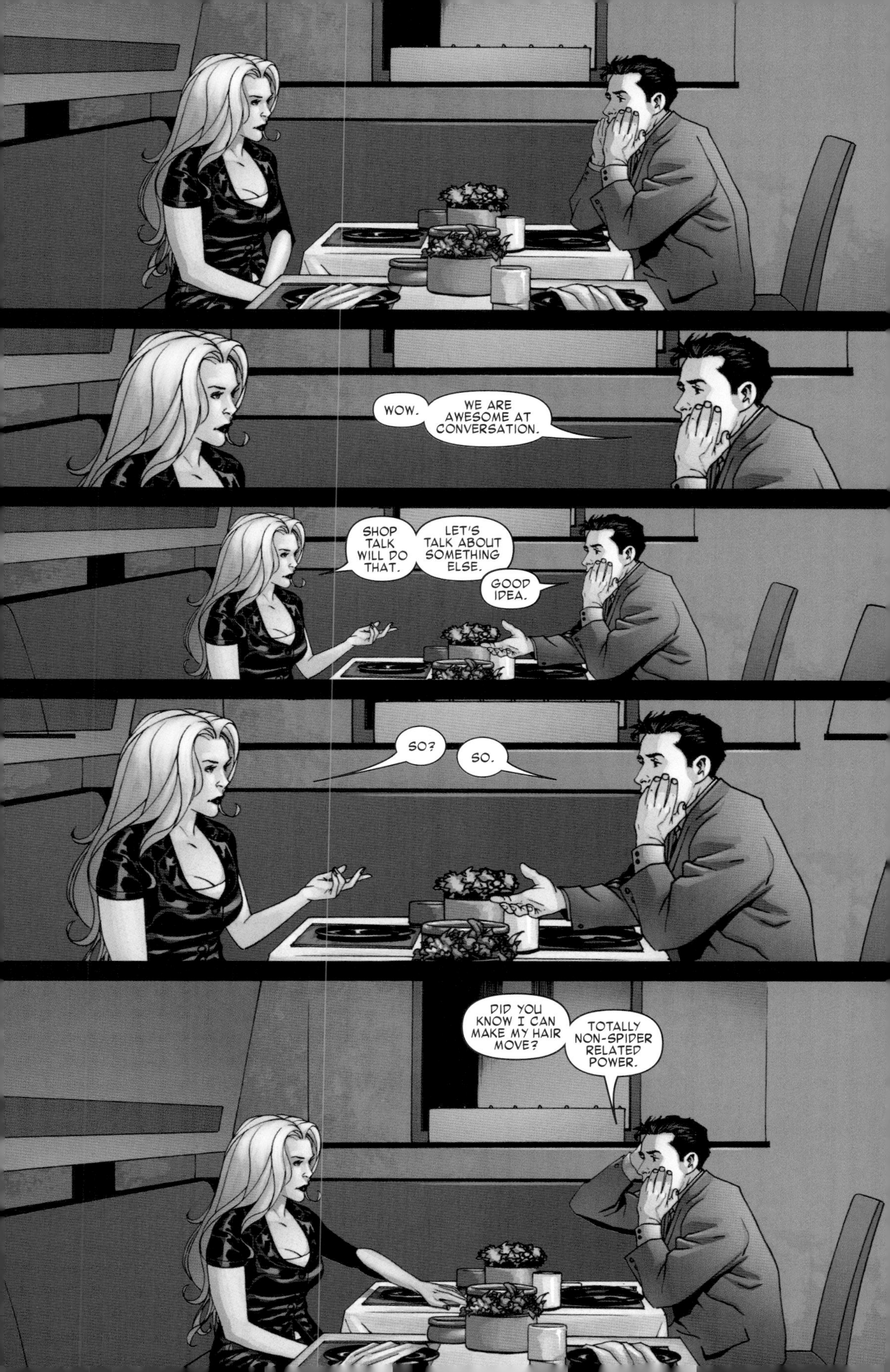
WOW.
WE ARE AWESOME AT CONVERSATION.
SHOP TALK WILL DO THAT.
LET'S TALK ABOUT SOMETHING ELSE.
GOOD IDEA.
SO?
SO.
DID YOU KNOW I CAN MAKE MY HAIR MOVE?
TOTALLY NON-SPIDER RELATED POWER.

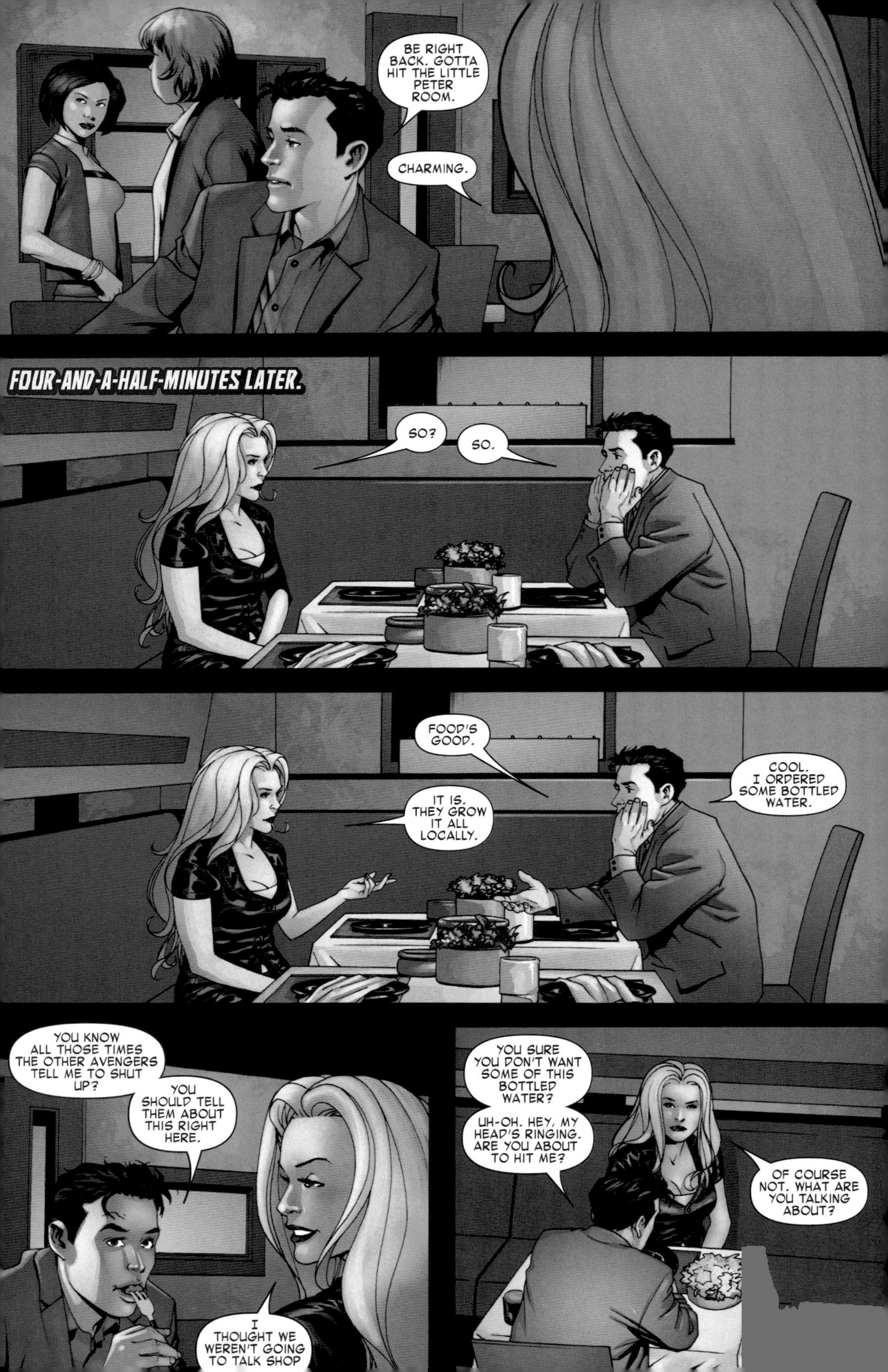
BE RIGHT BACK. GOTTA HIT THE LITTLE PETER ROOM.
CHARMING.
FOUR-AND-A-HALF-MINUTES LATER.
SO?
SO.
FOOD'S GOOD.
IT IS. THEY GROW IT ALL LOCALLY.
COOL. I ORDERED SOME BOTTLED WATER.
YOU KNOW ALL THOSE TIMES THE OTHER AVENGERS TELL ME TO SHUT UP?
YOU SHOULD TELL THEM ABOUT THIS RIGHT HERE.
I THOUGHT WE WEREN'T GOING TO TALK SHOP
YOU SURE YOU DON'T WANT SOME OF THIS BOTTLED WATER?
UH-OH. HEY, MY HEAD'S RINGING. ARE YOU ABOUT TO HIT ME?
OF COURSE NOT. WHAT ARE YOU TALKING ABOUT?

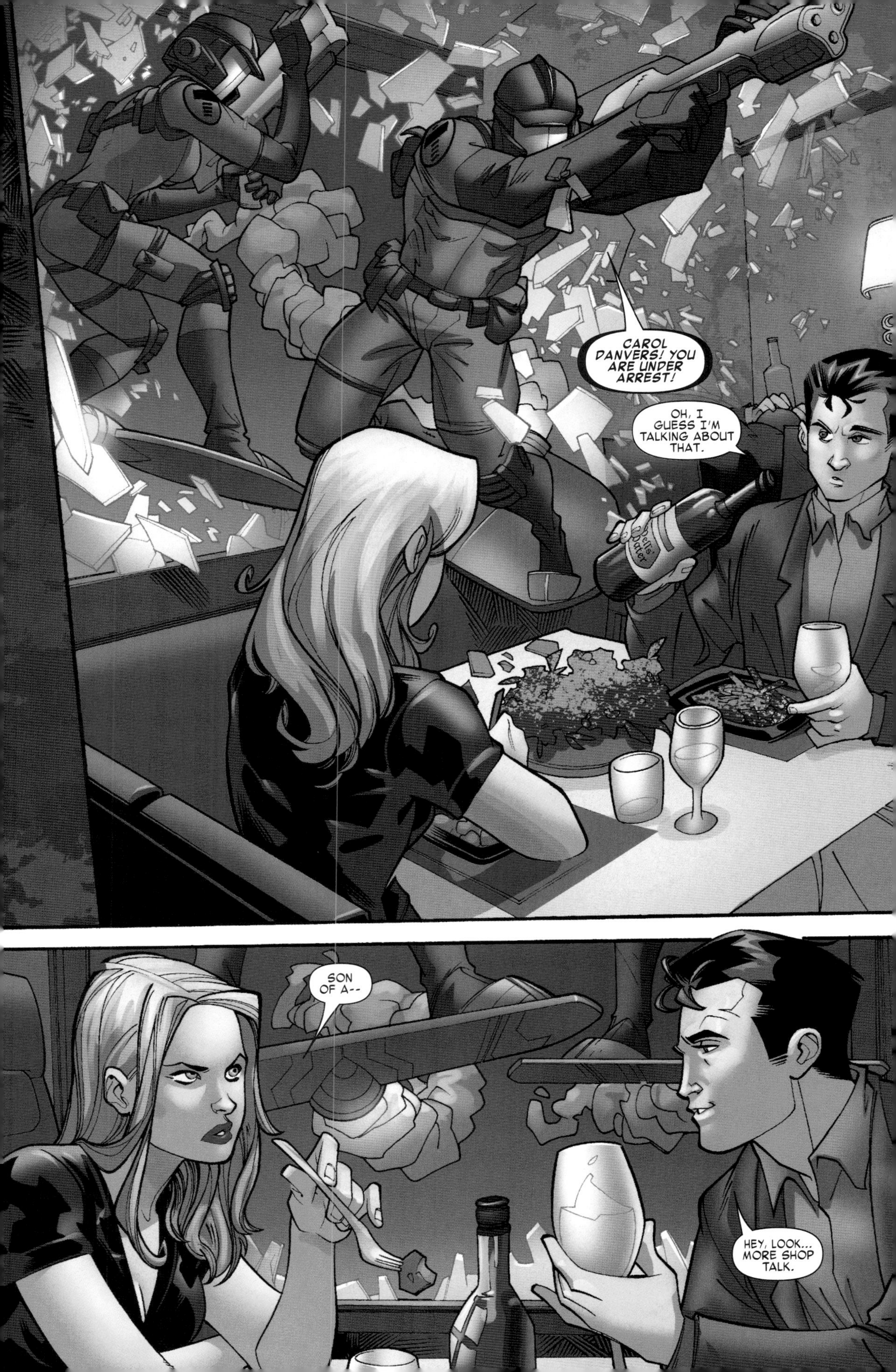
CAROL DANVERS! YOU ARE UNDER ARREST!
OH, I GUESS I'M TALKING ABOUT THAT.
SON OF A--
HEY, LOOK... MORE SHOP TALK.

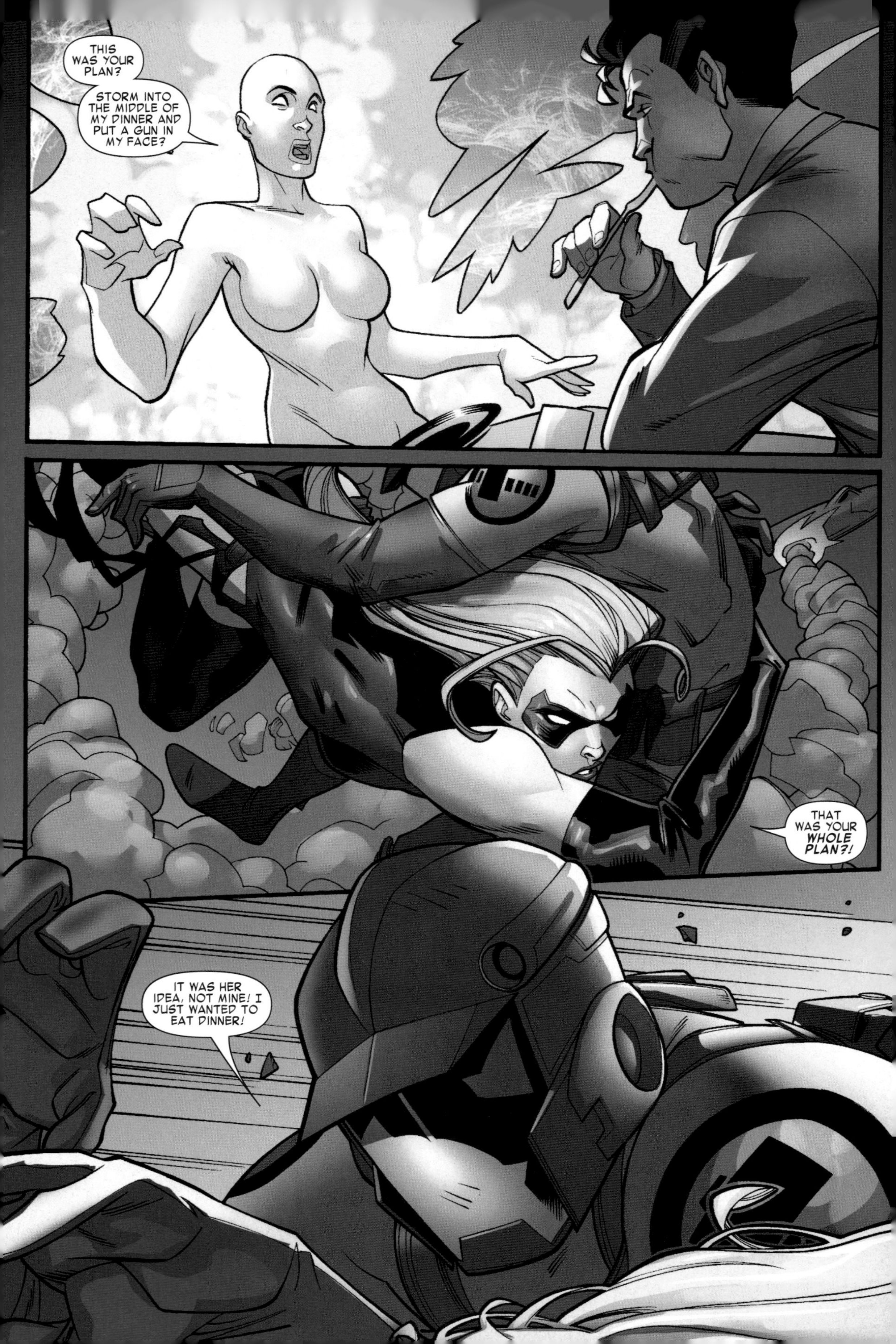
THIS WAS YOUR PLAN?
STORM INTO THE MIDDLE OF MY DINNER AND PUT A GUN IN MY FACE?
THAT WAS YOUR *WHOLE* PLAN?!
IT WAS HER IDEA, NOT MINE! I JUST WANTED TO EAT DINNER!

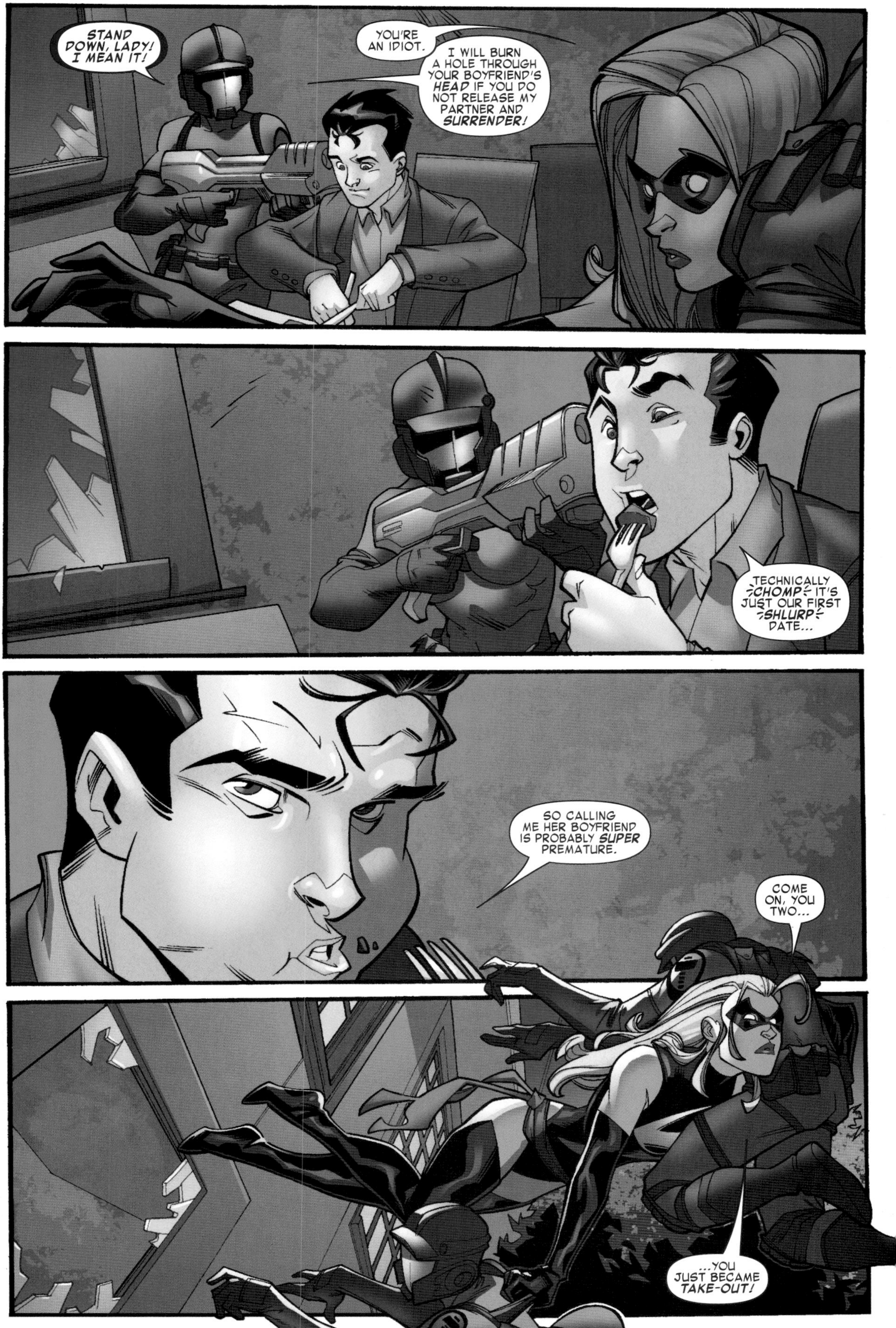

STAND DOWN, LADY! I MEAN IT!
YOU'RE AN IDIOT.
I WILL BURN A HOLE THROUGH YOUR BOYFRIEND'S HEAD IF YOU DO NOT RELEASE MY PARTNER AND SURRENDER!
TECHNICALLY *CHOMP* IT'S JUST OUR FIRST *SHLURP* DATE...
SO CALLING ME HER BOYFRIEND IS PROBABLY SUPER PREMATURE.
COME ON, YOU TWO...
...YOU JUST BECAME TAKE-OUT!

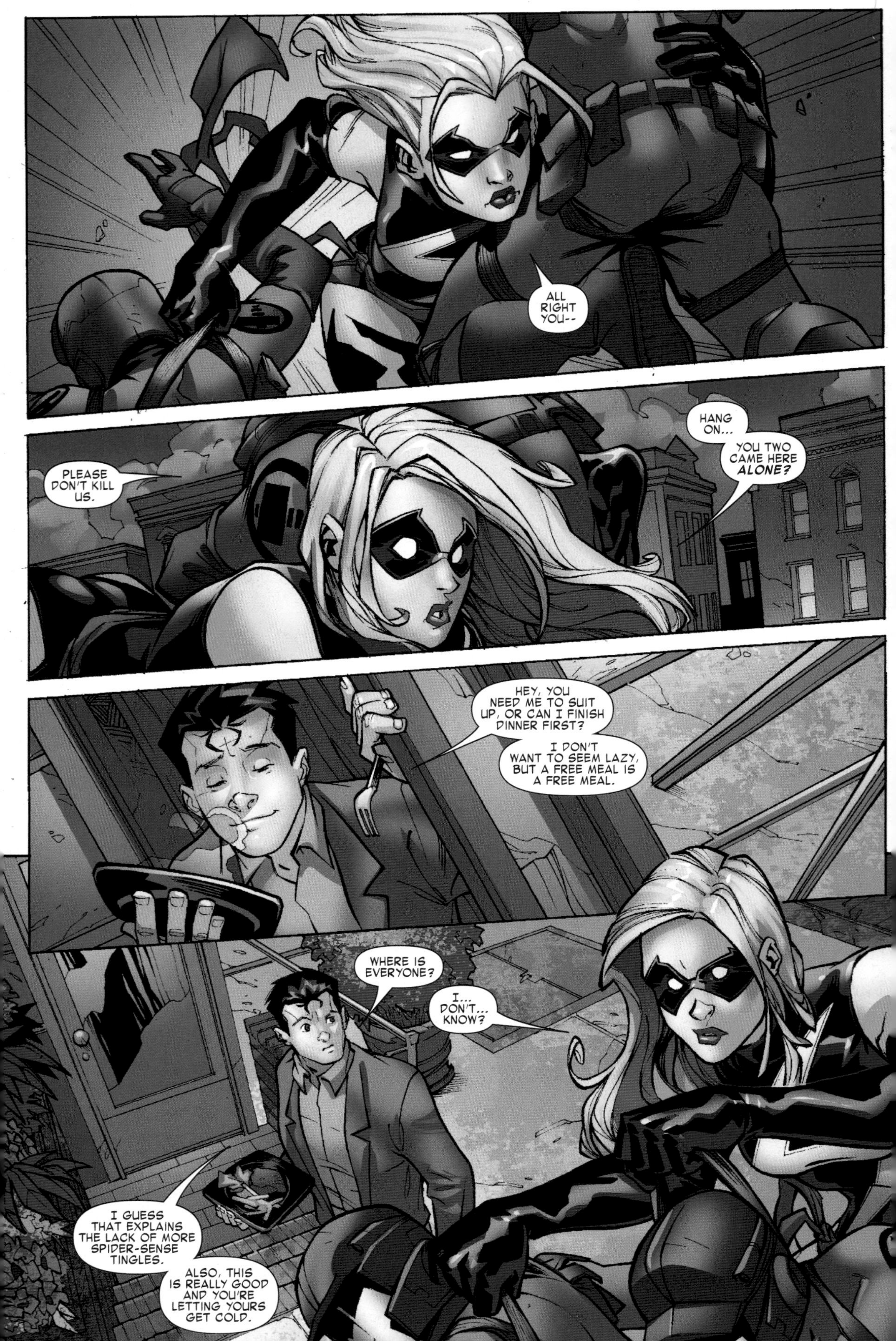

ALL RIGHT YOU--
PLEASE DON'T KILL US.
HANG ON...
YOU TWO CAME HERE ALONE?
HEY, YOU NEED ME TO SUIT UP, OR CAN I FINISH DINNER FIRST?
I DON'T WANT TO SEEM LAZY, BUT A FREE MEAL IS A FREE MEAL.
WHERE IS EVERYONE?
I... DON'T... KNOW?
I GUESS THAT EXPLAINS THE LACK OF MORE SPIDER-SENSE TINGLES.
ALSO, THIS IS REALLY GOOD AND YOU'RE LETTING YOURS GET COLD.

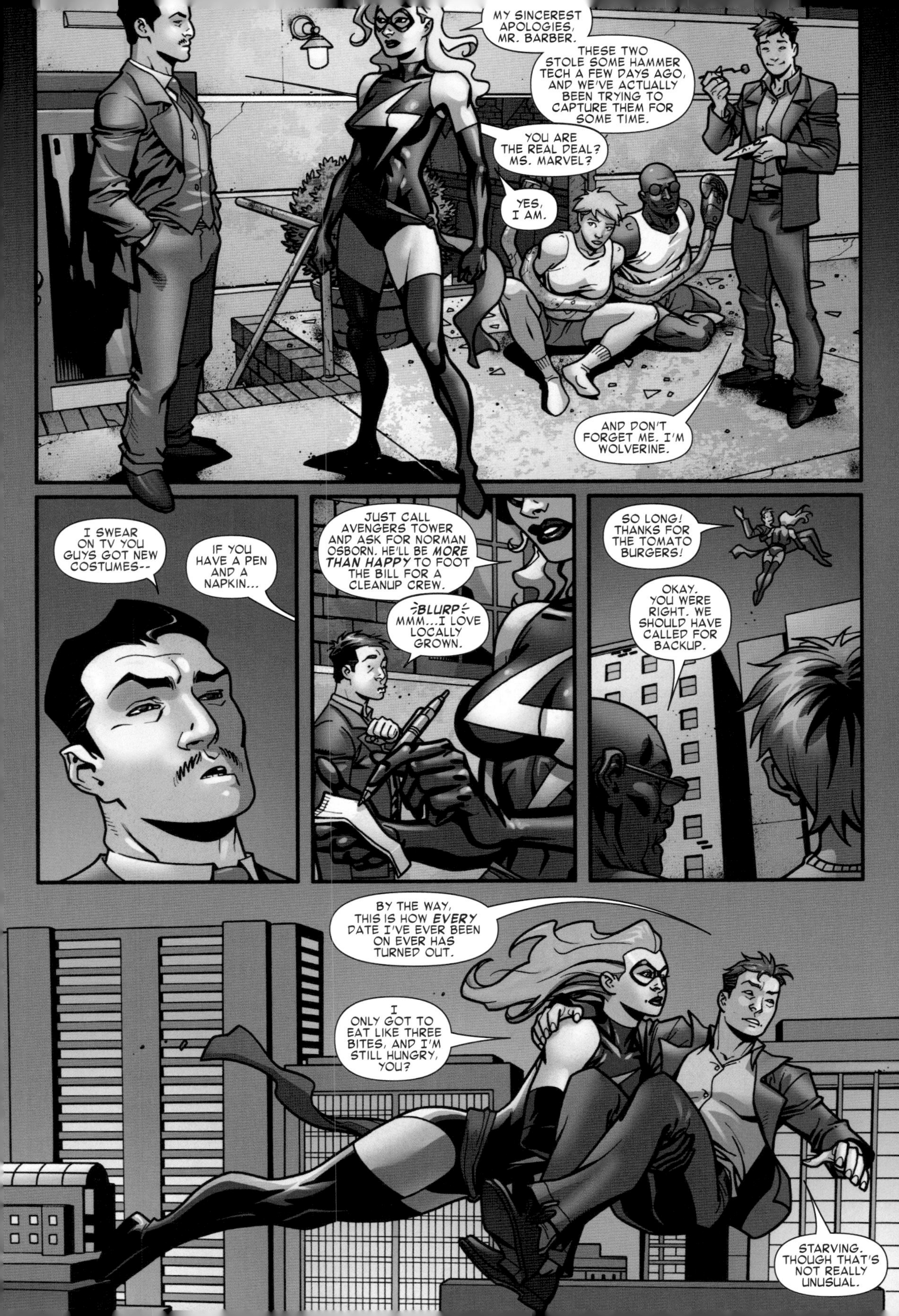
MY SINCEREST APOLOGIES, MR. BARBER.
THESE TWO STOLE SOME HAMMER TECH A FEW DAYS AGO, AND WE'VE ACTUALLY BEEN TRYING TO CAPTURE THEM FOR SOME TIME.
YOU ARE THE REAL DEAL? MS. MARVEL?
YES, I AM.
AND DON'T FORGET ME. I'M WOLVERINE.
I SWEAR ON TV YOU GUYS GOT NEW COSTUMES--
IF YOU HAVE A PEN AND A NAPKIN...
JUST CALL AVENGERS TOWER AND ASK FOR NORMAN OSBORN. HE'LL BE MORE THAN HAPPY TO FOOT THE BILL FOR A CLEANUP CREW.
BLURP MMM...I LOVE LOCALLY GROWN.
SO LONG! THANKS FOR THE TOMATO BURGERS!
OKAY. YOU WERE RIGHT. WE SHOULD HAVE CALLED FOR BACKUP.
BY THE WAY, THIS IS HOW EVERY DATE I'VE EVER BEEN ON EVER HAS TURNED OUT.
I ONLY GOT TO EAT LIKE THREE BITES, AND I'M STILL HUNGRY, YOU?
STARVING. THOUGH THAT'S NOT REALLY UNUSUAL.

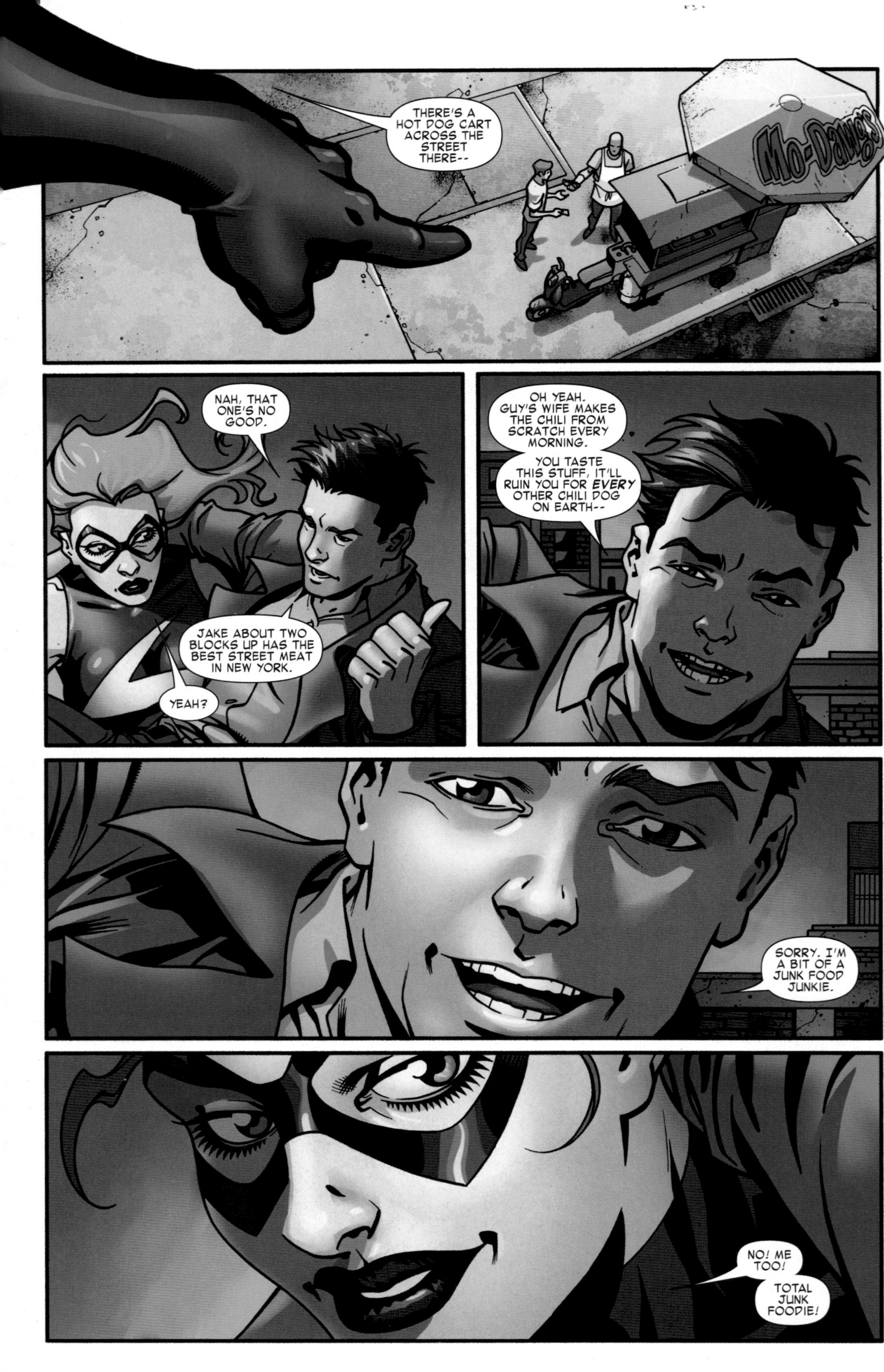
THERE'S A HOT DOG CART ACROSS THE STREET THERE--
MO-DAWGS
NAH, THAT ONE'S NO GOOD.
JAKE ABOUT TWO BLOCKS UP HAS THE BEST STREET MEAT IN NEW YORK.
YEAH?
OH YEAH. GUY'S WIFE MAKES THE CHILI FROM SCRATCH EVERY MORNING.
YOU TASTE THIS STUFF, IT'LL RUIN YOU FOR *EVERY* OTHER CHILI DOG ON EARTH--
SORRY. I'M A BIT OF A JUNK FOOD JUNKIE.
NO! ME TOO!
TOTAL JUNK FOODIE!

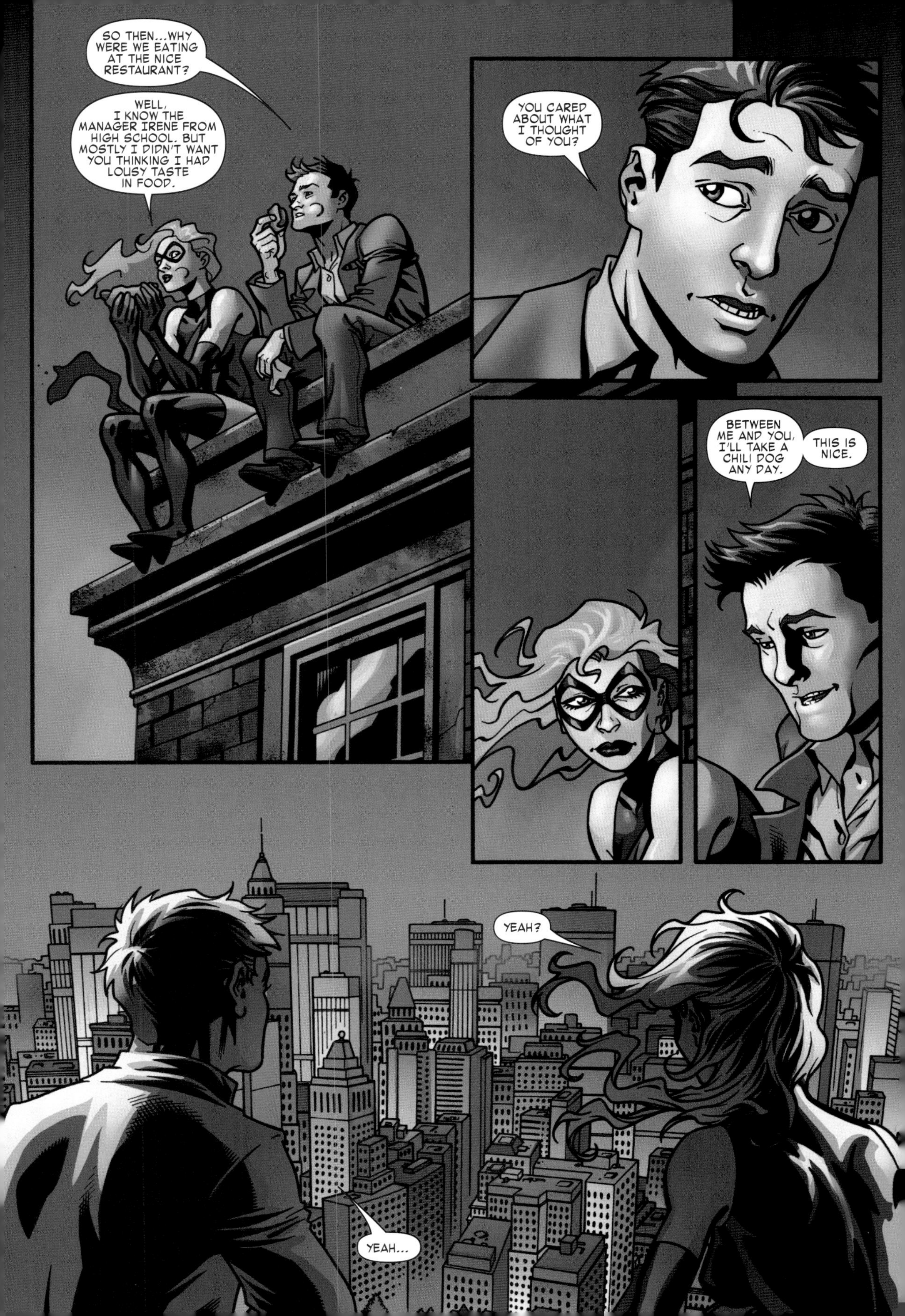
SO THEN...WHY WERE WE EATING AT THE NICE RESTAURANT?
WELL, I KNOW THE MANAGER IRENE FROM HIGH SCHOOL. BUT MOSTLY I DIDN'T WANT YOU THINKING I HAD LOUSY TASTE IN FOOD.
YOU CARED ABOUT WHAT I THOUGHT OF YOU?
BETWEEN ME AND YOU, I'LL TAKE A CHILI DOG ANY DAY.
THIS IS NICE.
YEAH?
YEAH...

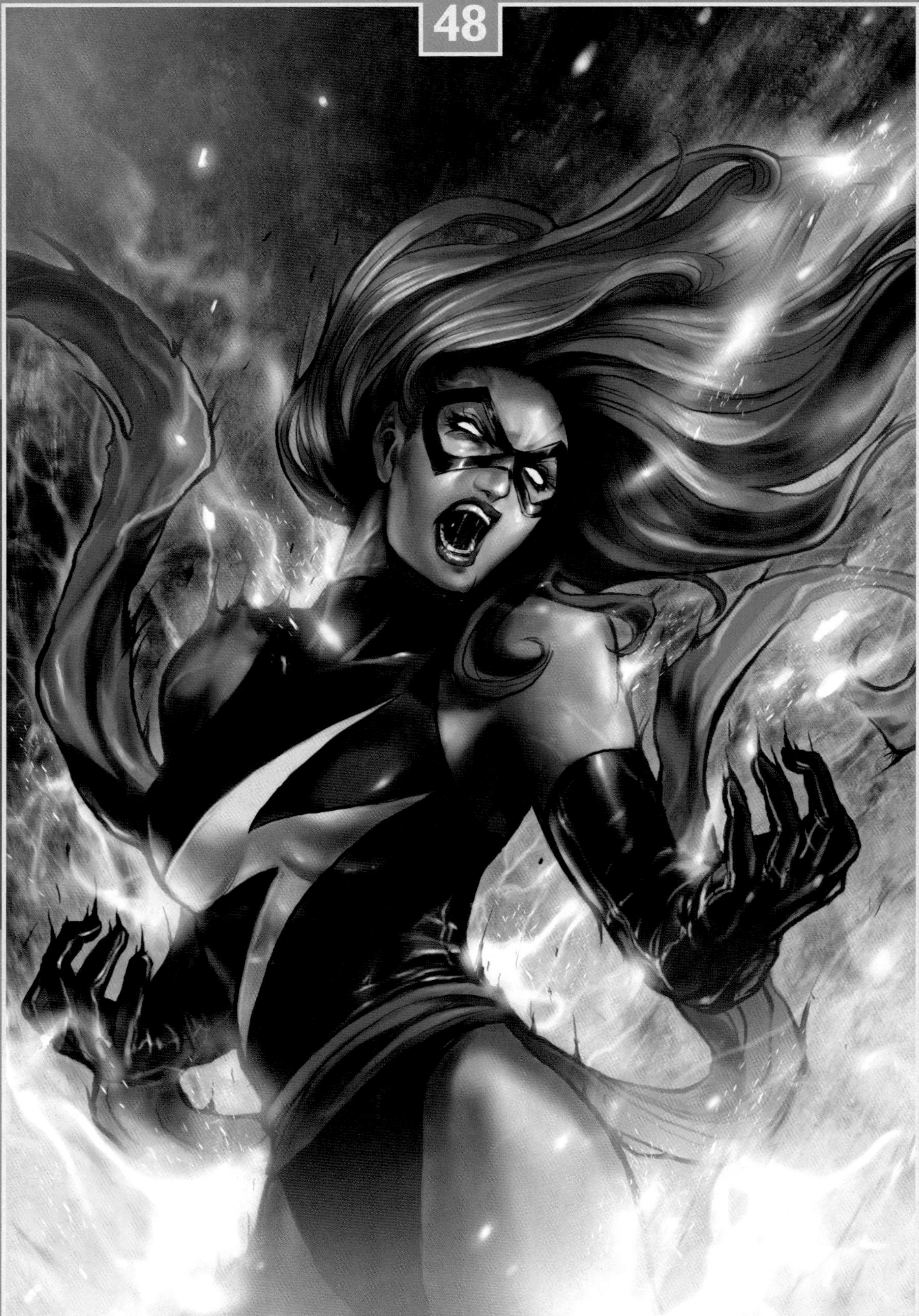
48

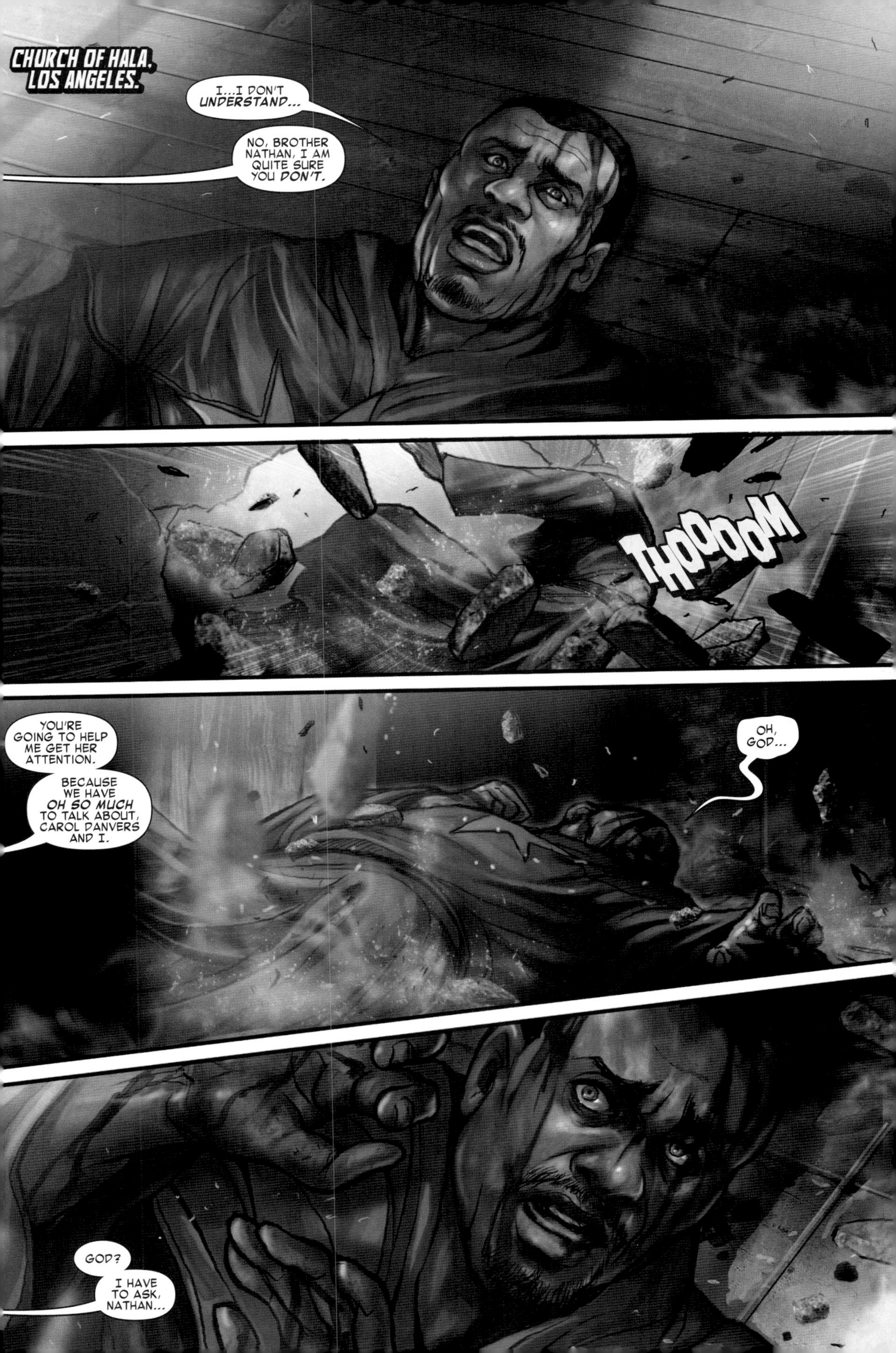
CHURCH OF HALA, LOS ANGELES.
I...I DON'T UNDERSTAND...
NO, BROTHER NATHAN, I AM QUITE SURE YOU DON'T.
THOOOOM
YOU'RE GOING TO HELP ME GET HER ATTENTION.
BECAUSE WE HAVE OH SO MUCH TO TALK ABOUT, CAROL DANVERS AND I.
OH, GOD...
GOD?
I HAVE TO ASK, NATHAN...

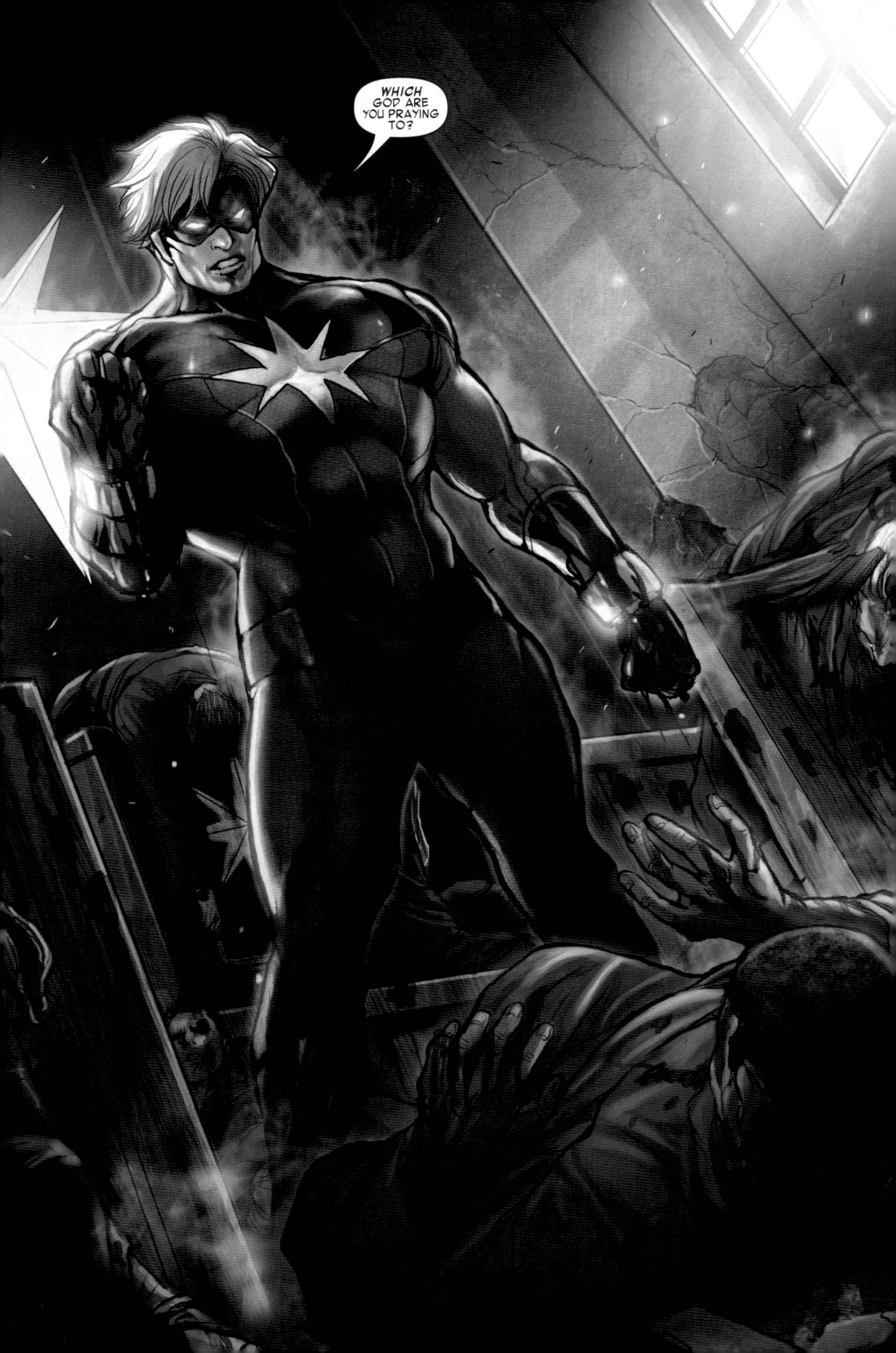
WHICH GOD ARE YOU PRAYING TO?

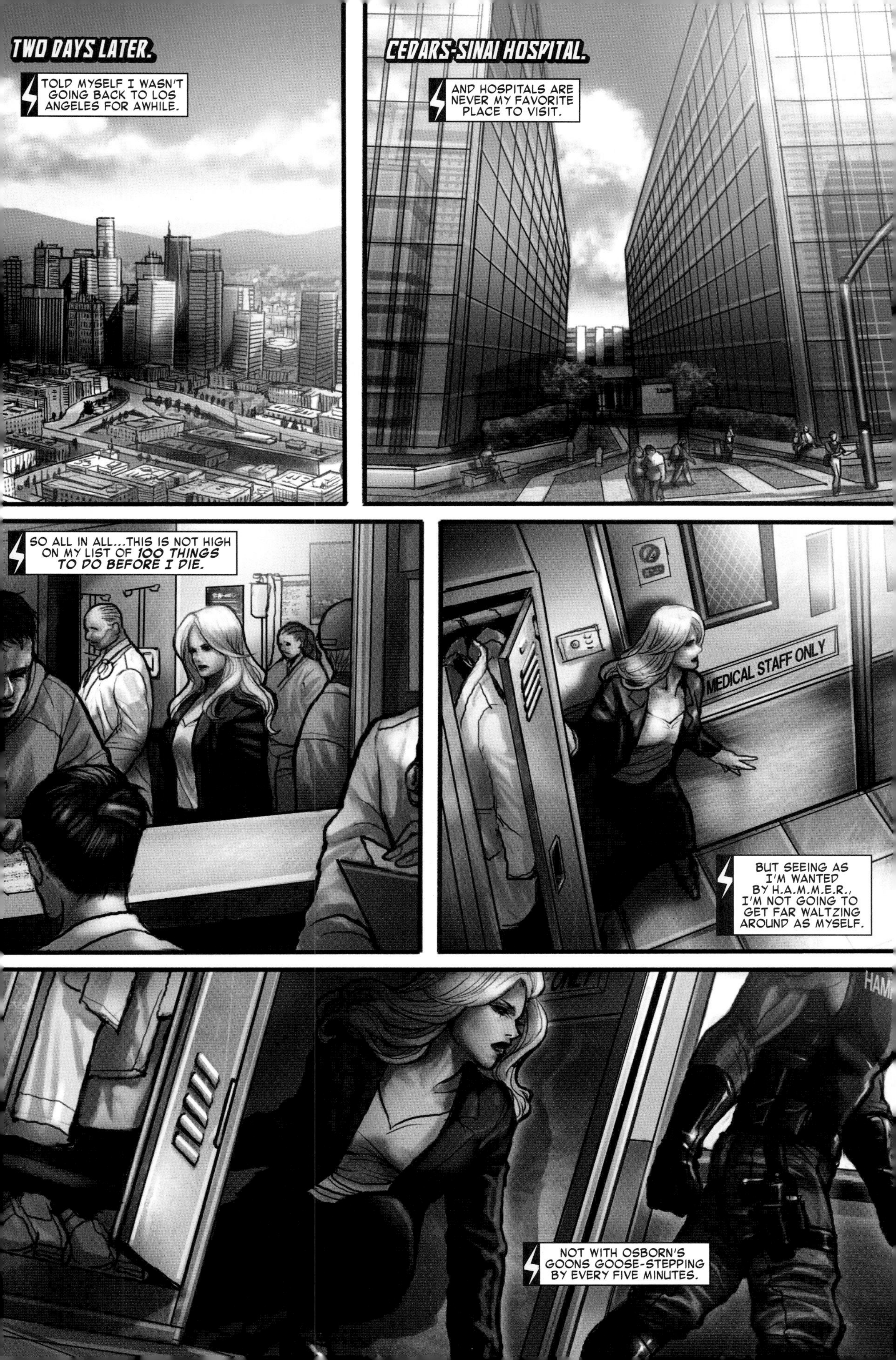

TWO DAYS LATER.
TOLD MYSELF I WASN'T GOING BACK TO LOS ANGELES FOR AWHILE.
CEDARS-SINAI HOSPITAL.
AND HOSPITALS ARE NEVER MY FAVORITE PLACE TO VISIT.
SO ALL IN ALL...THIS IS NOT HIGH ON MY LIST OF 100 THINGS TO DO BEFORE I DIE.
MEDICAL STAFF ONLY
BUT SEEING AS I'M WANTED BY H.A.M.M.E.R., I'M NOT GOING TO GET FAR WALTZING AROUND AS MYSELF.
NOT WITH OSBORN'S GOONS GOOSE-STEPPING BY EVERY FIVE MINUTES.

THE BEST DISGUISES ARE THE KIND THAT OTHER PEOPLE DON'T EVEN *RECOGNIZE* AS A DISGUISE.

FOR INSTANCE, IF YOU'RE IN AN OFFICE BUILDING, A SUIT AND A CLIPBOARD WILL GET YOU JUST ABOUT ANYWHERE.

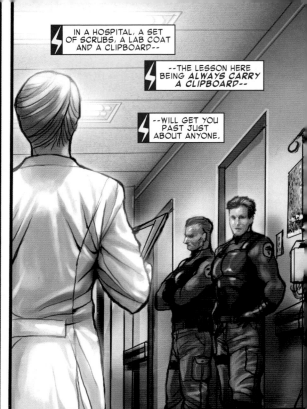

IN A HOSPITAL, A SET OF SCRUBS, A LAB COAT AND A CLIPBOARD--

--THE LESSON HERE BEING *ALWAYS CARRY A CLIPBOARD*--

--WILL GET YOU PAST JUST ABOUT ANYONE.

HOLD ON. I NEED TO SEE SOME I.D.

YOU DON'T NEED TO SEE MY I.D.

IS THAT--DID YOU--?

DUDE, SHE JUST TRIED TO *JEDI MIND TRICK* YOU.

IT SEEMED NICER THAN THE ALTERNATIVE.

YEAH? WHAT'S *THAT?*

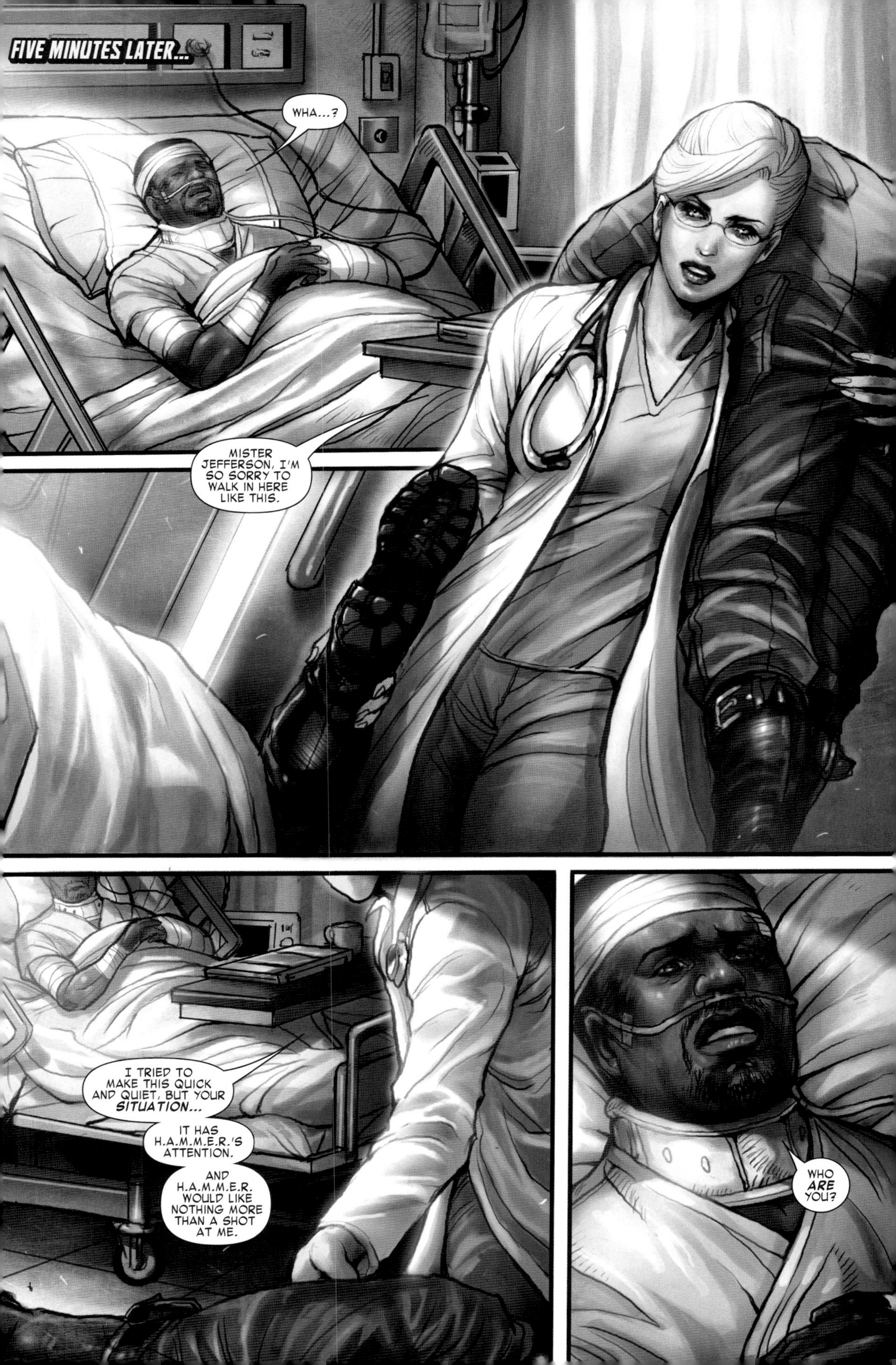
FIVE MINUTES LATER...
WHA...?
MISTER JEFFERSON, I'M SO SORRY TO WALK IN HERE LIKE THIS.
I TRIED TO MAKE THIS QUICK AND QUIET, BUT YOUR SITUATION...
IT HAS H.A.M.M.E.R.'s ATTENTION.
AND H.A.M.M.E.R. WOULD LIKE NOTHING MORE THAN A SHOT AT ME.
WHO ARE YOU?

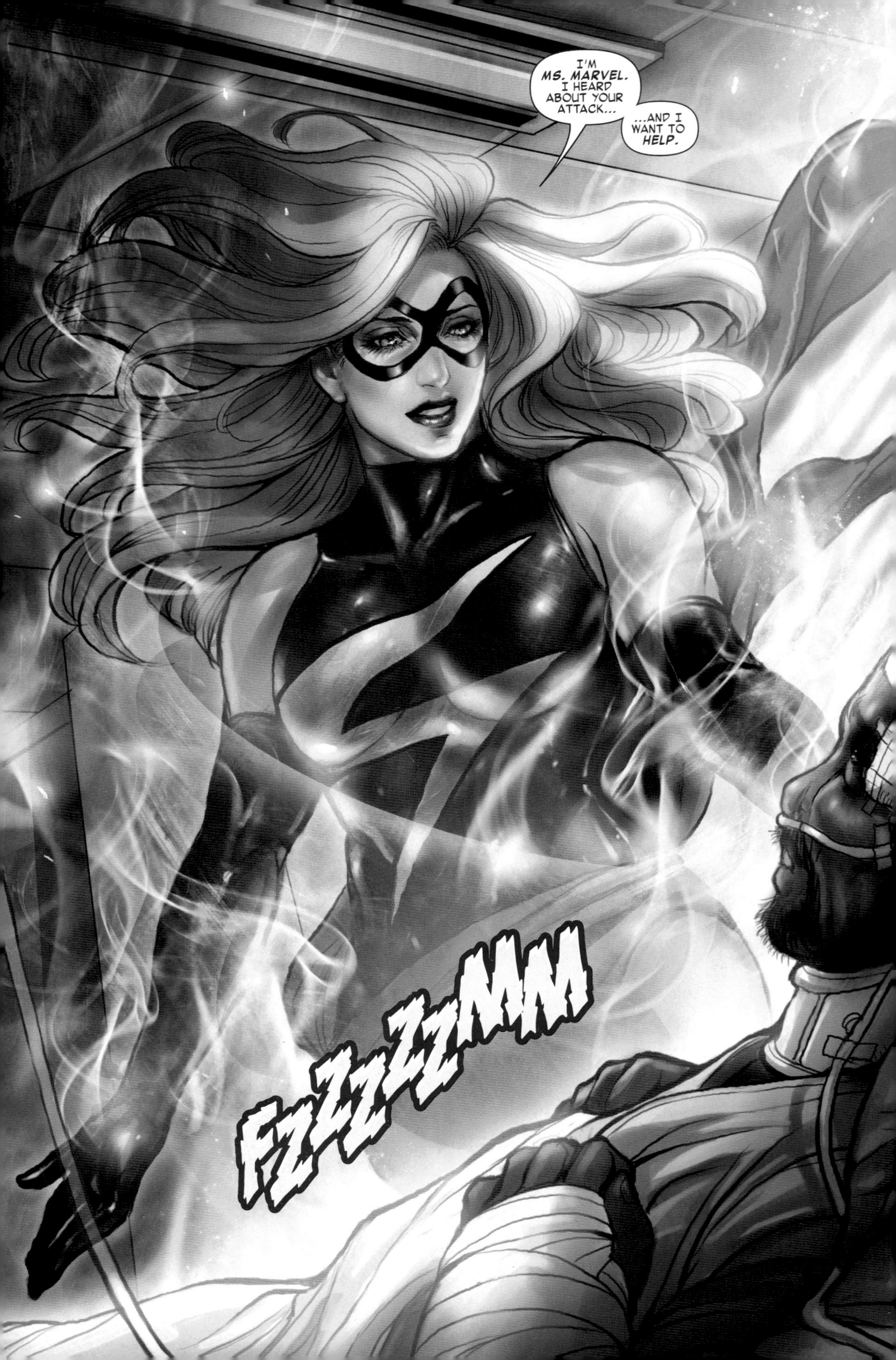
I'M MS. MARVEL. I HEARD ABOUT YOUR ATTACK...
...AND I WANT TO HELP.
FZZZZZMM

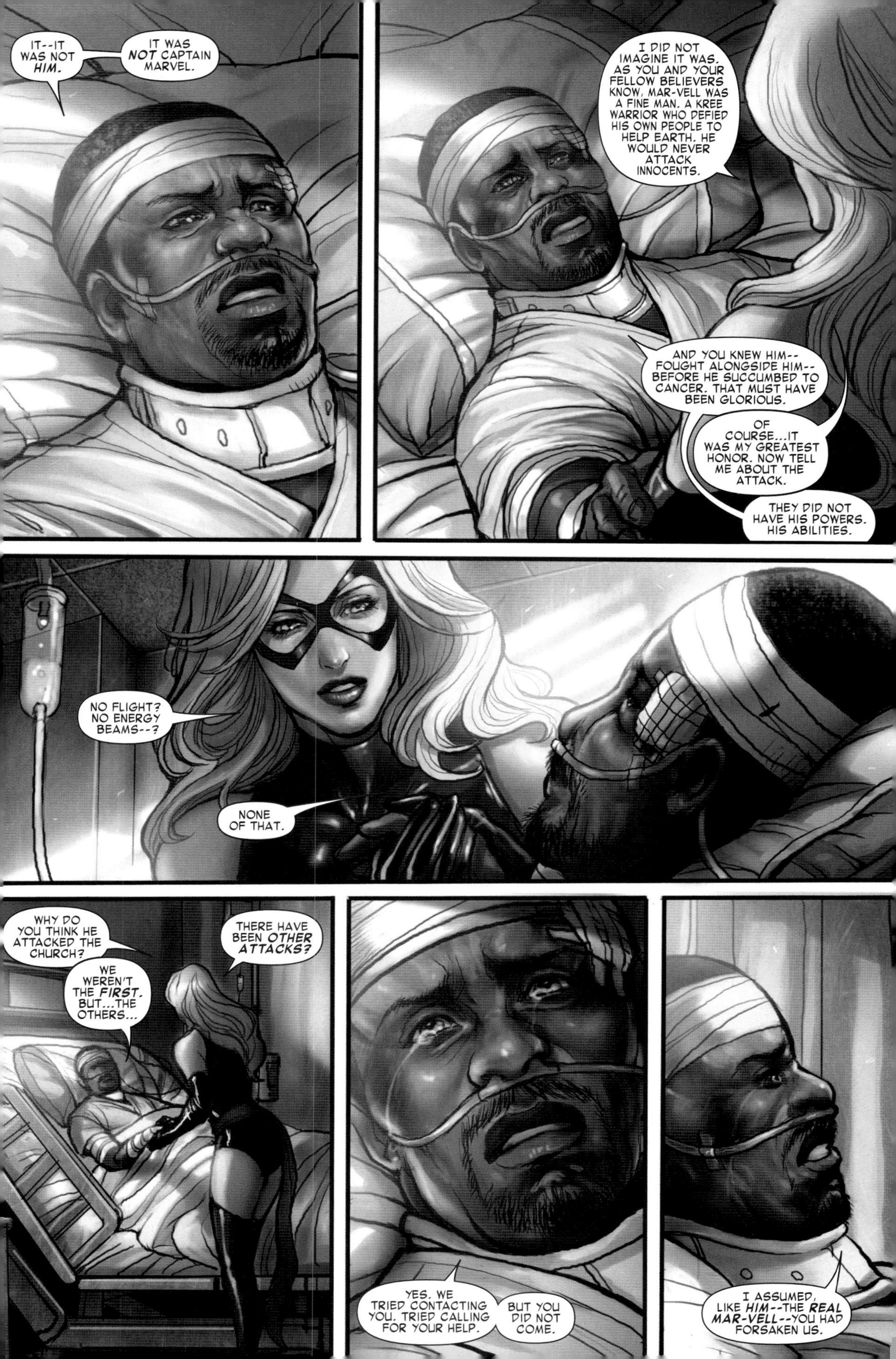
IT--IT WAS NOT HIM.
IT WAS NOT CAPTAIN MARVEL.
I DID NOT IMAGINE IT WAS. AS YOU AND YOUR FELLOW BELIEVERS KNOW, MAR-VELL WAS A FINE MAN. A KREE WARRIOR WHO DEFIED HIS OWN PEOPLE TO HELP EARTH. HE WOULD NEVER ATTACK INNOCENTS.
AND YOU KNEW HIM-- FOUGHT ALONGSIDE HIM-- BEFORE HE SUCCUMBED TO CANCER. THAT MUST HAVE BEEN GLORIOUS.
OF COURSE...IT WAS MY GREATEST HONOR. NOW TELL ME ABOUT THE ATTACK.
THEY DID NOT HAVE HIS POWERS. HIS ABILITIES.
NO FLIGHT? NO ENERGY BEAMS--?
NONE OF THAT.
WHY DO YOU THINK HE ATTACKED THE CHURCH?
WE WEREN'T THE FIRST. BUT...THE OTHERS...
THERE HAVE BEEN OTHER ATTACKS?
YES. WE TRIED CONTACTING YOU. TRIED CALLING FOR YOUR HELP.
BUT YOU DID NOT COME.
I ASSUMED, LIKE HIM--THE REAL MAR-VELL--YOU HAD FORSAKEN US.

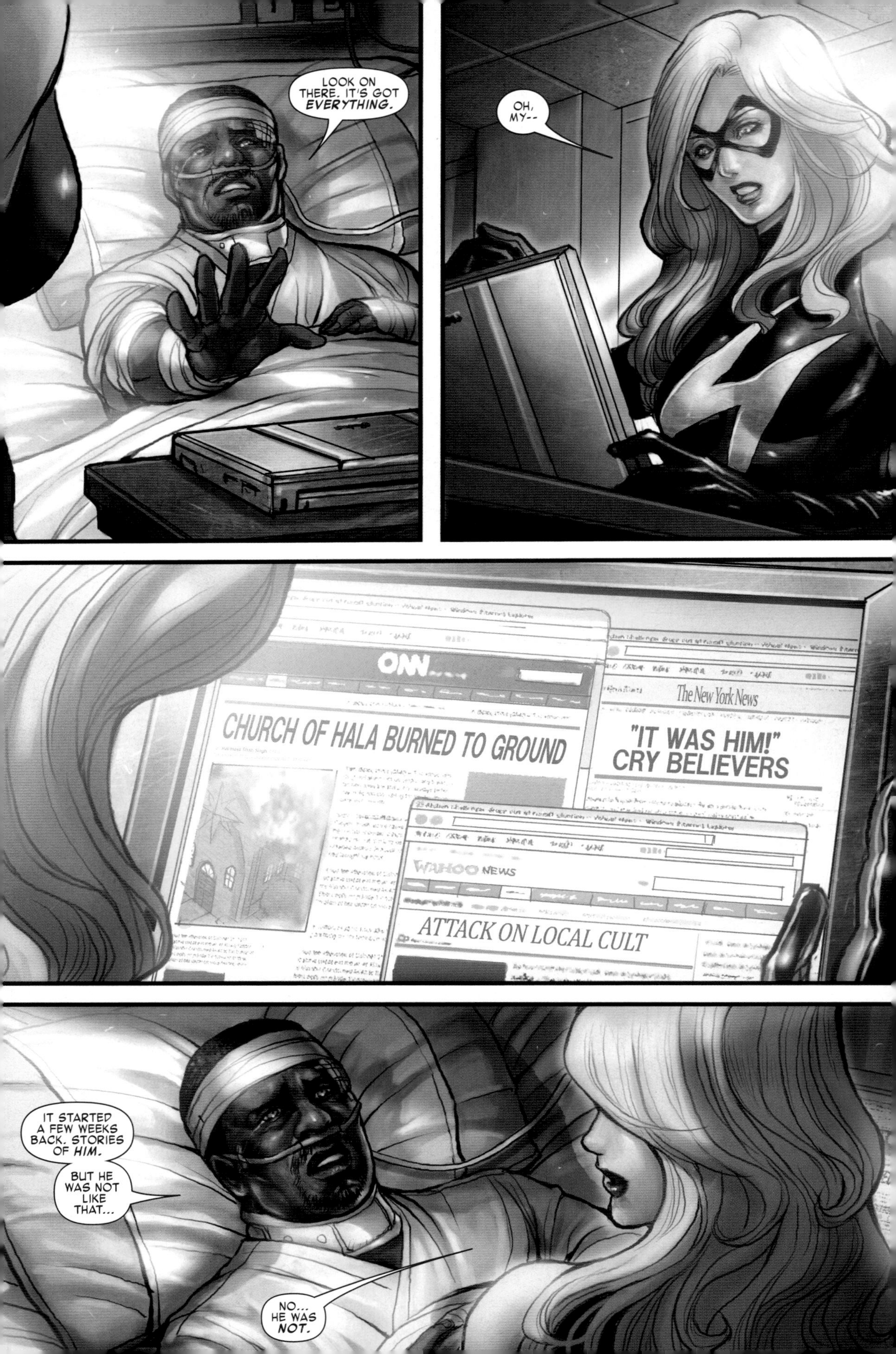
LOOK ON THERE. IT'S GOT *EVERYTHING.*
OH, MY--
ONN
CHURCH OF HALA BURNED TO GROUND
The New York News
"IT WAS HIM!" CRY BELIEVERS
WAHOO NEWS
ATTACK ON LOCAL CULT
IT STARTED A FEW WEEKS BACK. STORIES OF *HIM.*
BUT HE WAS NOT LIKE THAT...
NO... HE WAS *NOT.*

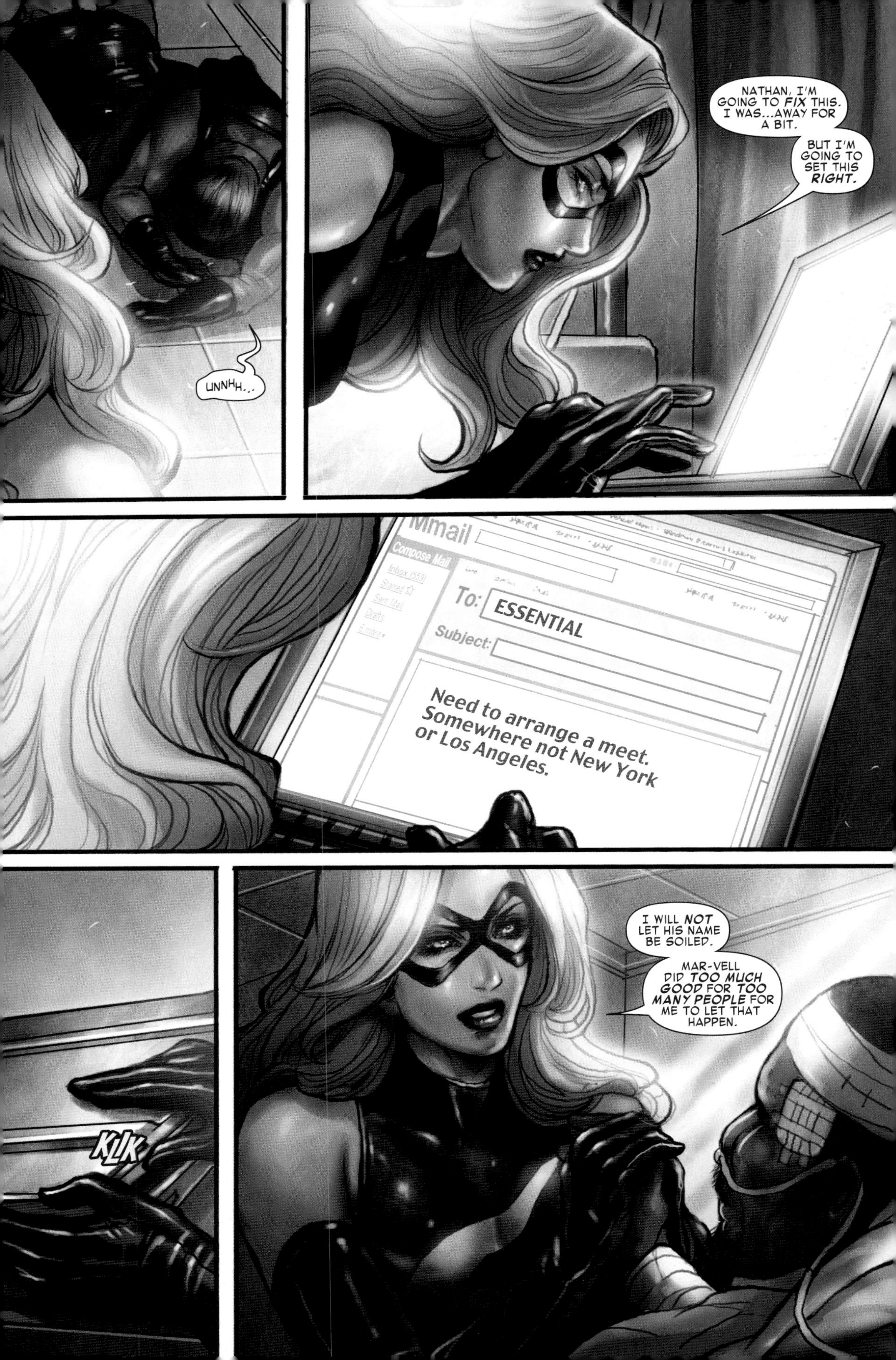
UNNHH...
NATHAN, I'M GOING TO FIX THIS. I WAS...AWAY FOR A BIT.
BUT I'M GOING TO SET THIS RIGHT.
Mmail
Compose Mail
Inbox (559)
Starred
Sent Mail
Drafts
To: ESSENTIAL
Subject:
Need to arrange a meet. Somewhere not New York or Los Angeles.
KLIK
I WILL NOT LET HIS NAME BE SOILED.
MAR-VELL DID TOO MUCH GOOD FOR TOO MANY PEOPLE FOR ME TO LET THAT HAPPEN.

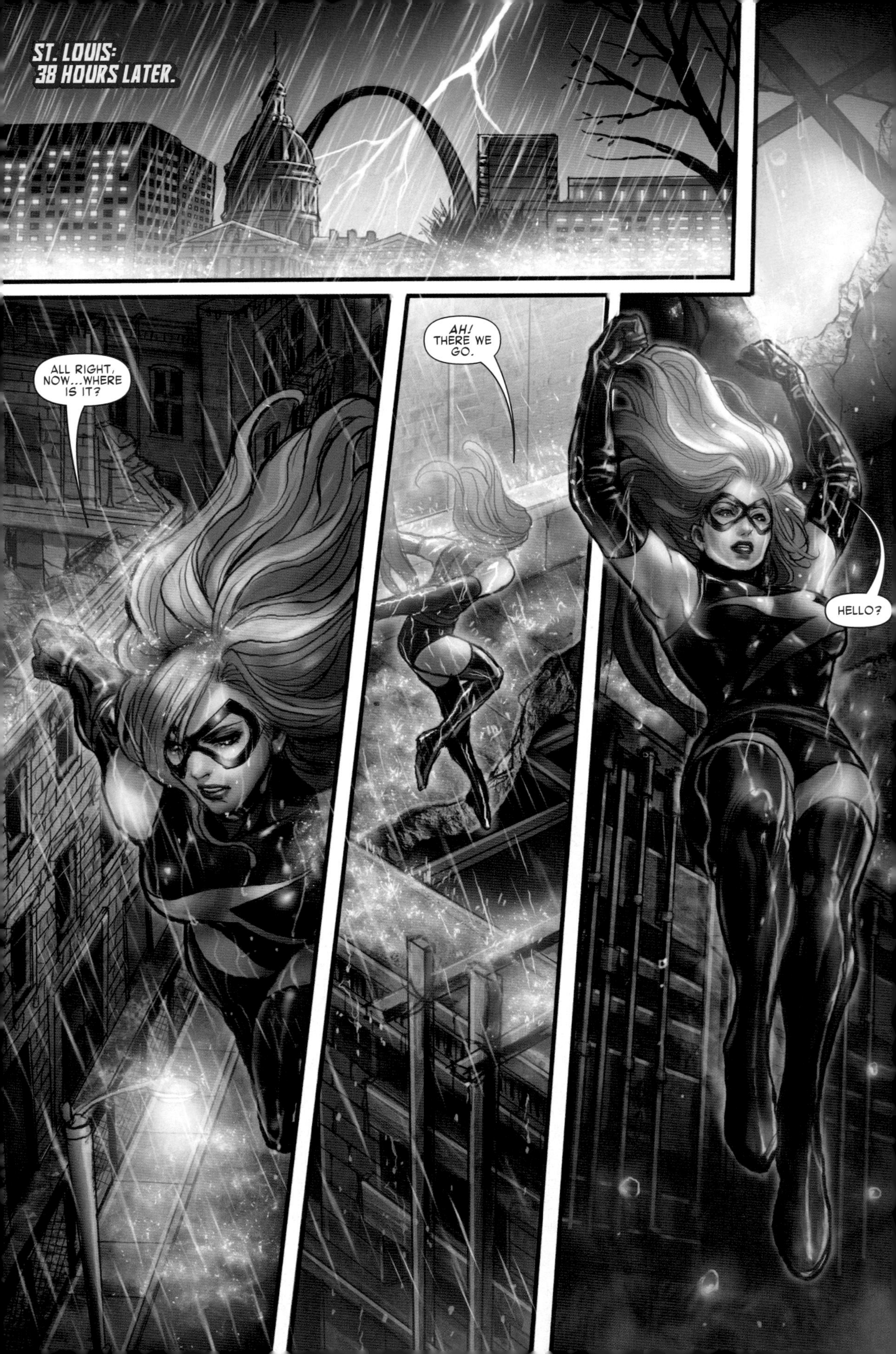
ST. LOUIS:
38 HOURS LATER.
ALL RIGHT, NOW...WHERE IS IT?
AH! THERE WE GO.
HELLO?

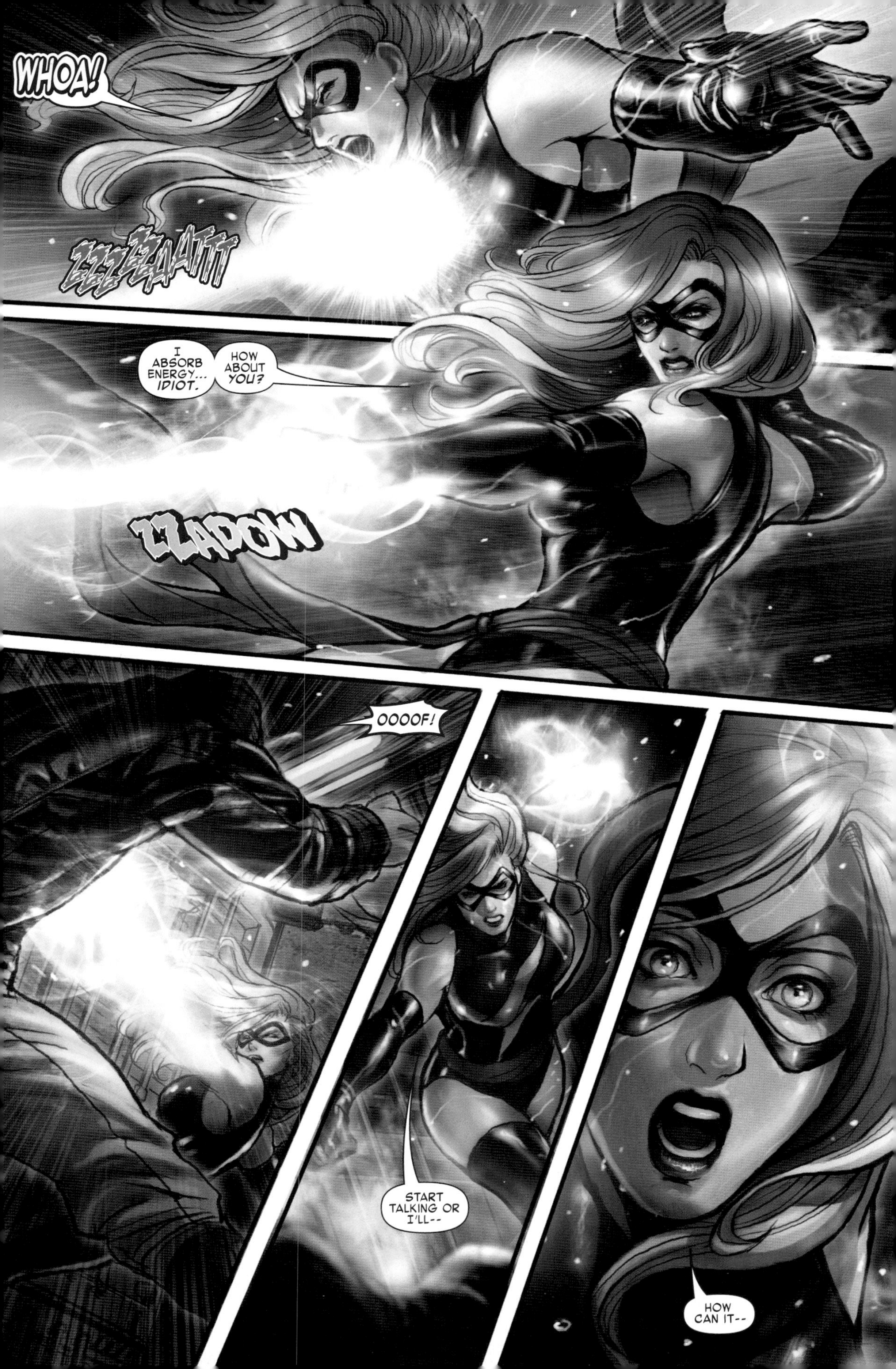
WHOA!
ZZZZZAATTT
I ABSORB ENERGY... IDIOT.
HOW ABOUT YOU?
ZZADOW
OOOOF!
START TALKING OR I'LL--
HOW CAN IT--

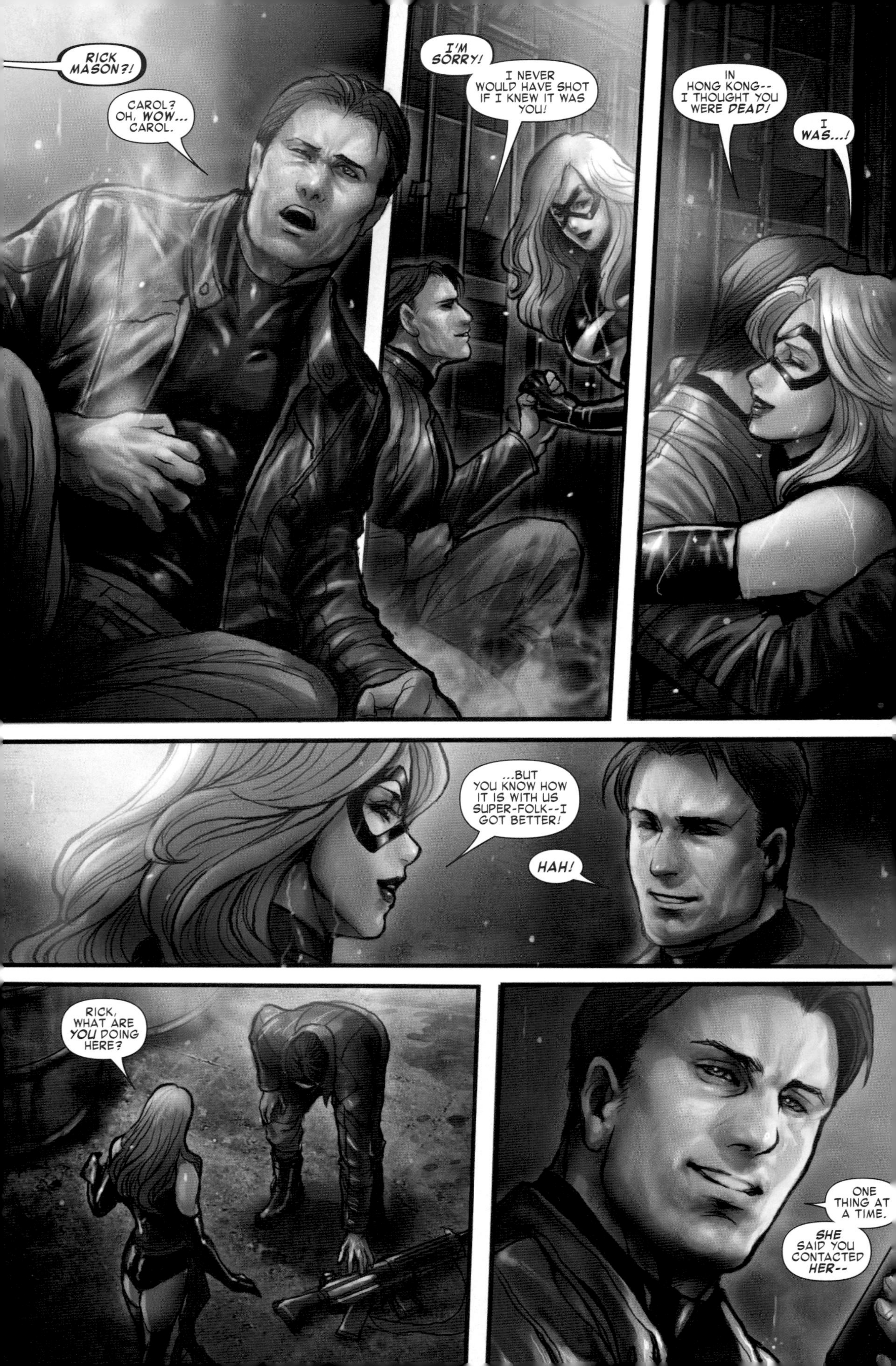
RICK MASON?!
CAROL? OH, WOW... CAROL.
I'M SORRY!
I NEVER WOULD HAVE SHOT IF I KNEW IT WAS YOU!
IN HONG KONG-- I THOUGHT YOU WERE DEAD!
I WAS...!
...BUT YOU KNOW HOW IT IS WITH US SUPER-FOLK--I GOT BETTER!
HAH!
RICK, WHAT ARE YOU DOING HERE?
ONE THING AT A TIME.
SHE SAID YOU CONTACTED HER--

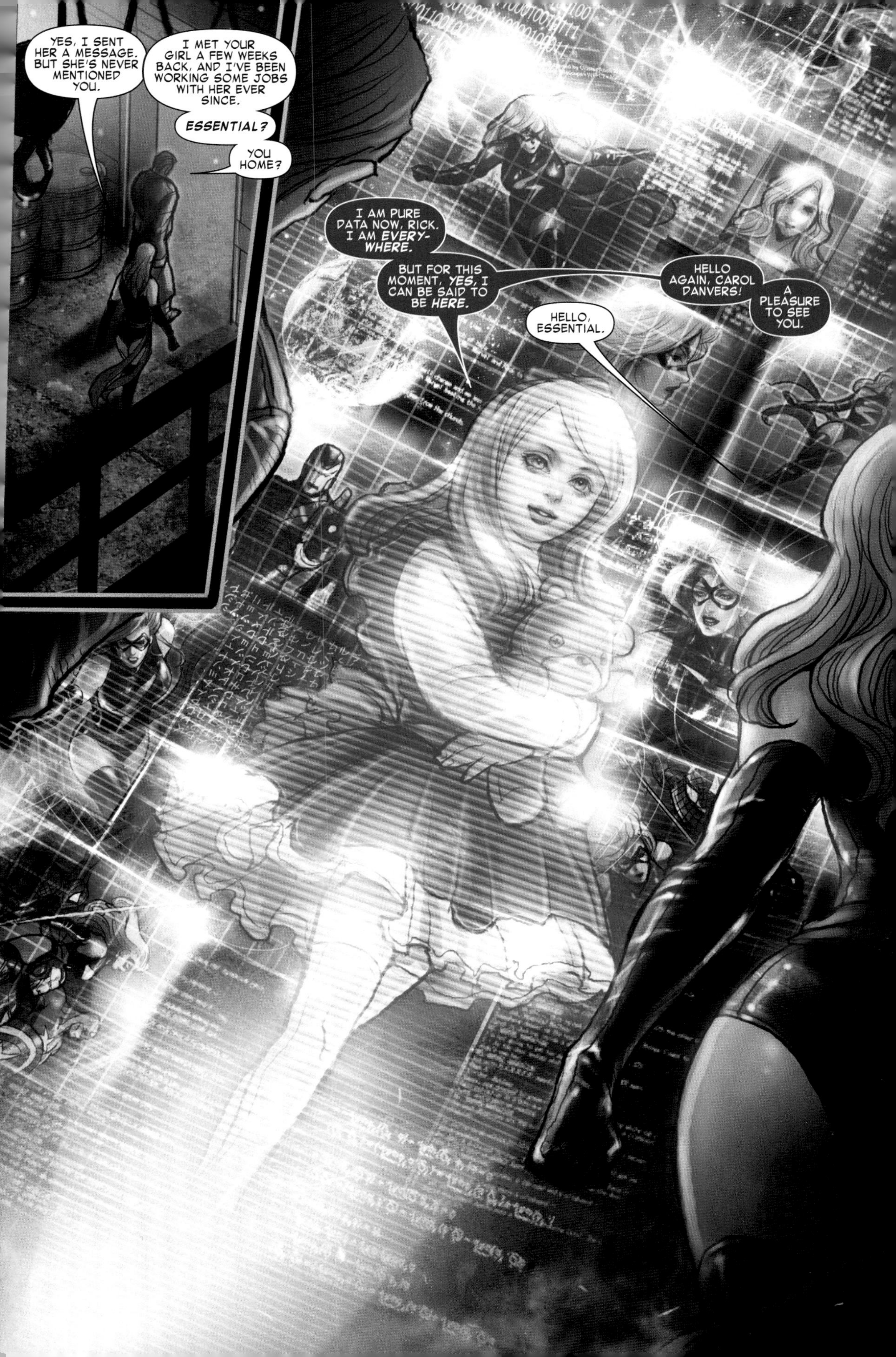
I MET YOUR GIRL A FEW WEEKS BACK, AND I'VE BEEN WORKING SOME JOBS WITH HER EVER SINCE.
ESSENTIAL?
YOU HOME?
YES, I SENT HER A MESSAGE. BUT SHE'S NEVER MENTIONED YOU.
I AM PURE DATA NOW, RICK. I AM EVERYWHERE.
BUT FOR THIS MOMENT, YES, I CAN BE SAID TO BE HERE.
HELLO AGAIN, CAROL DANVERS!
A PLEASURE TO SEE YOU.
HELLO, ESSENTIAL.

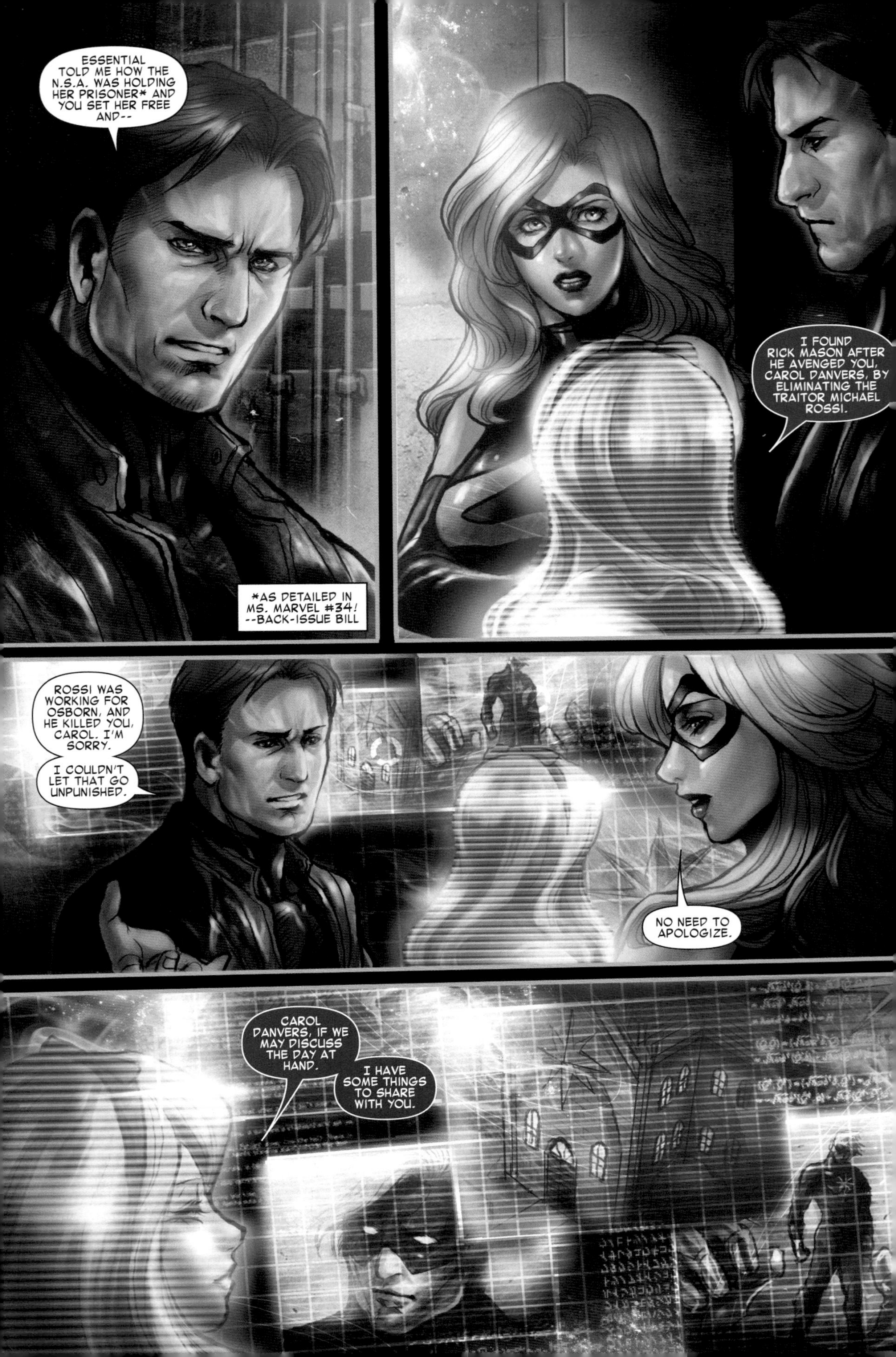
ESSENTIAL TOLD ME HOW THE N.S.A. WAS HOLDING HER PRISONER* AND YOU SET HER FREE AND--
*AS DETAILED IN MS. MARVEL #34! --BACK-ISSUE BILL
I FOUND RICK MASON AFTER HE AVENGED YOU, CAROL DANVERS, BY ELIMINATING THE TRAITOR MICHAEL ROSSI.
ROSSI WAS WORKING FOR OSBORN, AND HE KILLED YOU, CAROL. I'M SORRY.
I COULDN'T LET THAT GO UNPUNISHED.
NO NEED TO APOLOGIZE.
CAROL DANVERS, IF WE MAY DISCUSS THE DAY AT HAND.
I HAVE SOME THINGS TO SHARE WITH YOU.

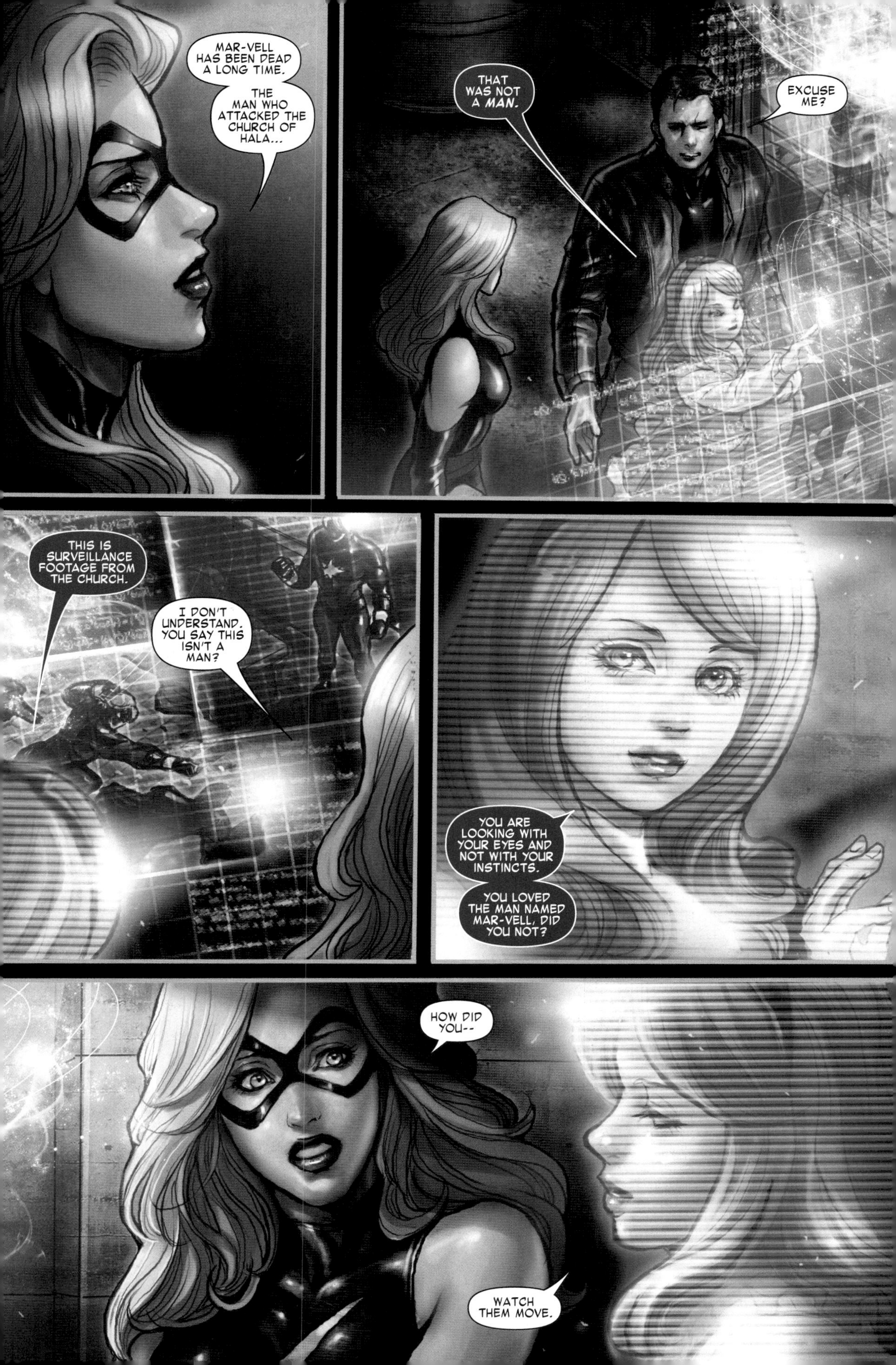
MAR-VELL HAS BEEN DEAD A LONG TIME.
THE MAN WHO ATTACKED THE CHURCH OF HALA...
THAT WAS NOT A *MAN.*
EXCUSE ME?
THIS IS SURVEILLANCE FOOTAGE FROM THE CHURCH.
I DON'T UNDERSTAND. YOU SAY THIS ISN'T A MAN?
YOU ARE LOOKING WITH YOUR EYES AND NOT WITH YOUR INSTINCTS.
YOU LOVED THE MAN NAMED MAR-VELL, DID YOU NOT?
HOW DID YOU--
WATCH THEM MOVE.

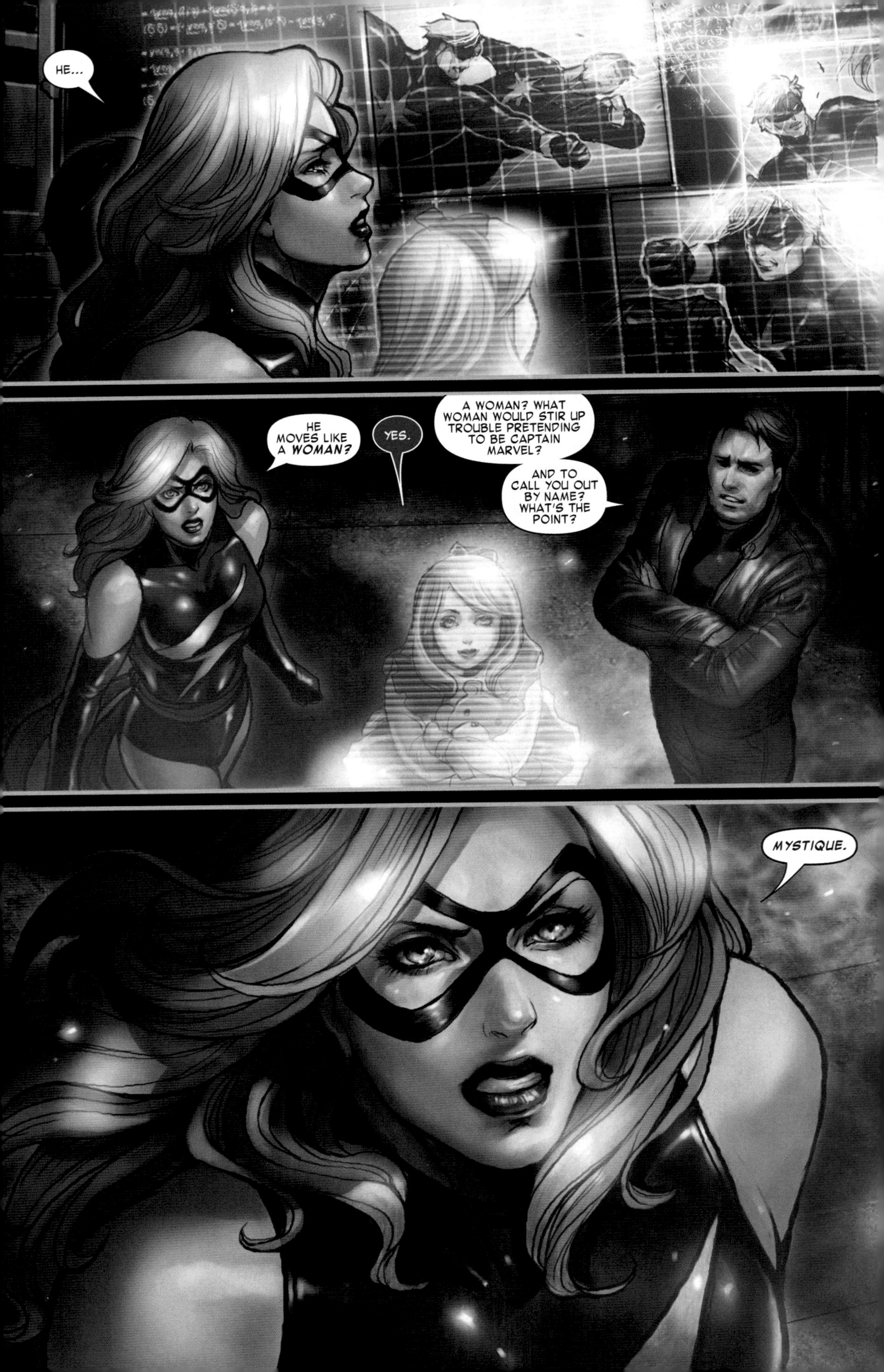
HE...
HE MOVES LIKE A WOMAN?
YES.
A WOMAN? WHAT WOMAN WOULD STIR UP TROUBLE PRETENDING TO BE CAPTAIN MARVEL?
AND TO CALL YOU OUT BY NAME? WHAT'S THE POINT?
MYSTIQUE.

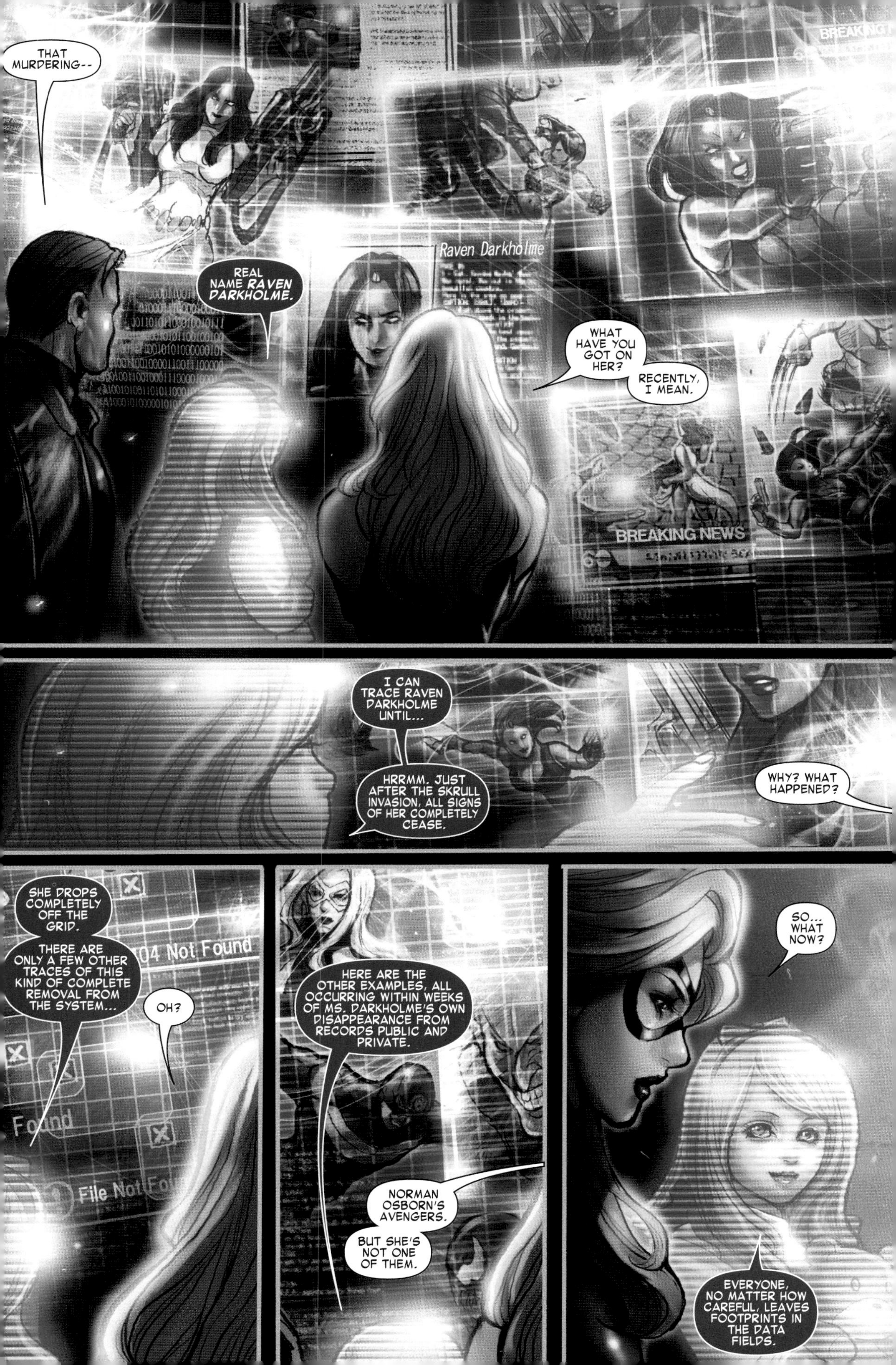
THAT MURDERING--
BREAKING NEWS
Raven Darkholme
REAL NAME RAVEN DARKHOLME.
WHAT HAVE YOU GOT ON HER?
RECENTLY, I MEAN.
BREAKING NEWS
I CAN TRACE RAVEN DARKHOLME UNTIL...
HRRMM. JUST AFTER THE SKRULL INVASION, ALL SIGNS OF HER COMPLETELY CEASE.
WHY? WHAT HAPPENED?
SHE DROPS COMPLETELY OFF THE GRID.
THERE ARE ONLY A FEW OTHER TRACES OF THIS KIND OF COMPLETE REMOVAL FROM THE SYSTEM...
OH?
HERE ARE THE OTHER EXAMPLES, ALL OCCURRING WITHIN WEEKS OF MS. DARKHOLME'S OWN DISAPPEARANCE FROM RECORDS PUBLIC AND PRIVATE.
NORMAN OSBORN'S AVENGERS.
BUT SHE'S NOT ONE OF THEM.
SO... WHAT NOW?
EVERYONE, NO MATTER HOW CAREFUL, LEAVES FOOTPRINTS IN THE DATA FIELDS.

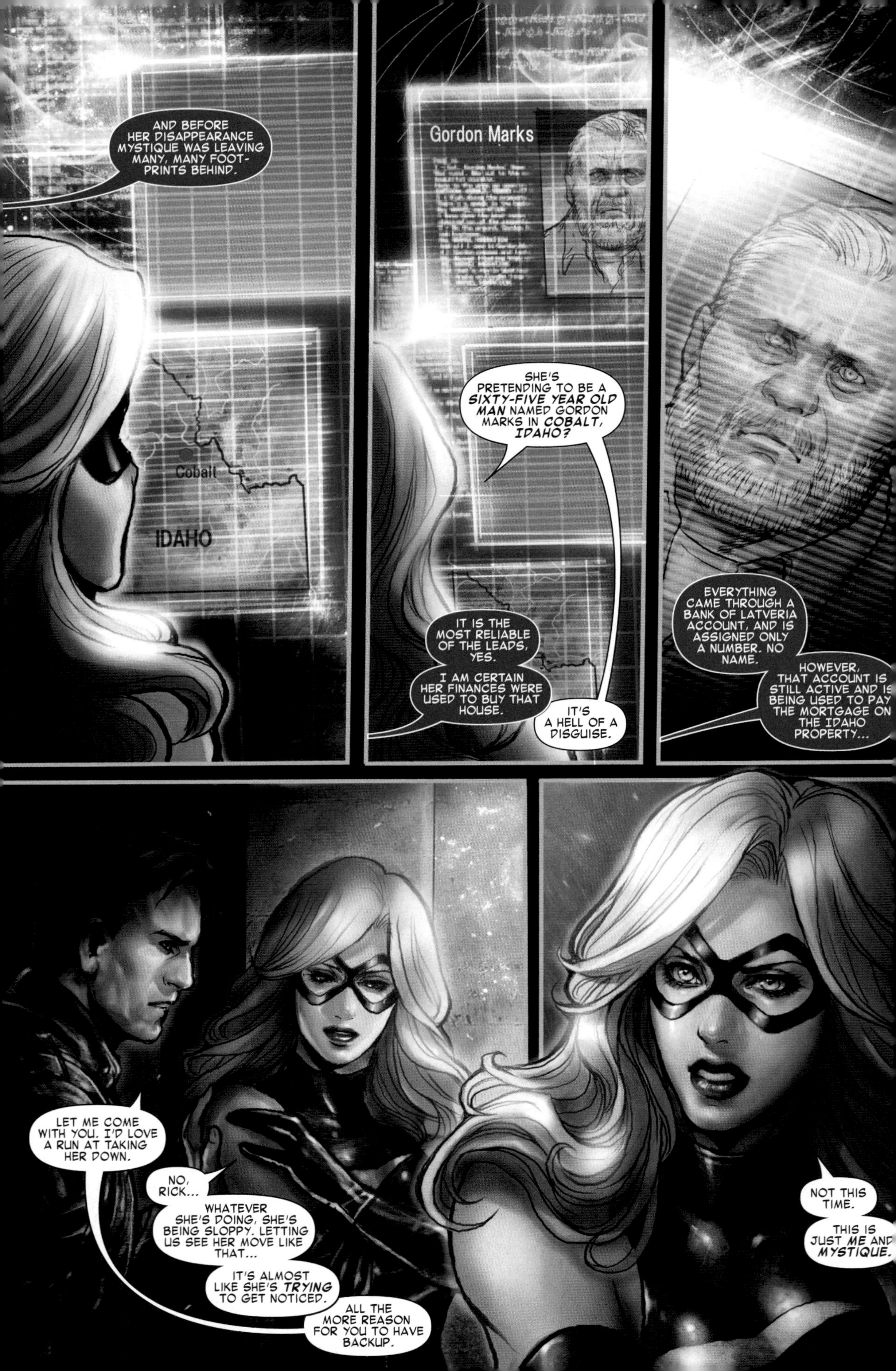
AND BEFORE HER DISAPPEARANCE MYSTIQUE WAS LEAVING MANY, MANY FOOT-PRINTS BEHIND.
Cobalt
IDAHO
Gordon Marks
SHE'S PRETENDING TO BE A SIXTY-FIVE YEAR OLD MAN NAMED GORDON MARKS IN COBALT, IDAHO?
IT IS THE MOST RELIABLE OF THE LEADS, YES.
I AM CERTAIN HER FINANCES WERE USED TO BUY THAT HOUSE.
IT'S A HELL OF A DISGUISE.
EVERYTHING CAME THROUGH A BANK OF LATVERIA ACCOUNT, AND IS ASSIGNED ONLY A NUMBER. NO NAME.
HOWEVER, THAT ACCOUNT IS STILL ACTIVE AND IS BEING USED TO PAY THE MORTGAGE ON THE IDAHO PROPERTY...
LET ME COME WITH YOU. I'D LOVE A RUN AT TAKING HER DOWN.
NO, RICK...
WHATEVER SHE'S DOING, SHE'S BEING SLOPPY. LETTING US SEE HER MOVE LIKE THAT...
IT'S ALMOST LIKE SHE'S TRYING TO GET NOTICED.
ALL THE MORE REASON FOR YOU TO HAVE BACKUP.
NOT THIS TIME.
THIS IS JUST ME AND MYSTIQUE.

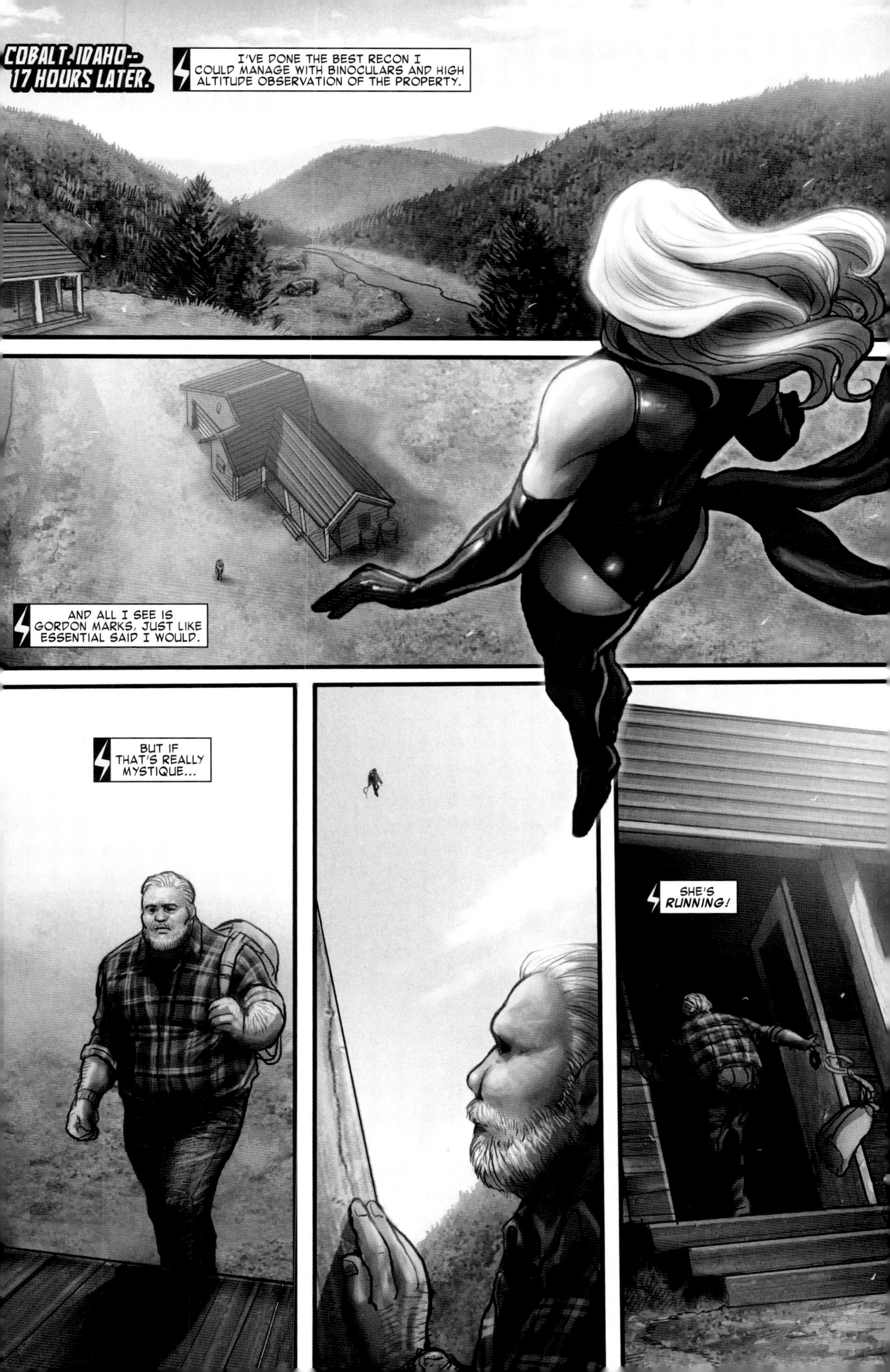
COBALT, IDAHO--
17 HOURS LATER.
I'VE DONE THE BEST RECON I COULD MANAGE WITH BINOCULARS AND HIGH ALTITUDE OBSERVATION OF THE PROPERTY.
AND ALL I SEE IS GORDON MARKS, JUST LIKE ESSENTIAL SAID I WOULD.
BUT IF THAT'S REALLY MYSTIQUE...
SHE'S RUNNING!

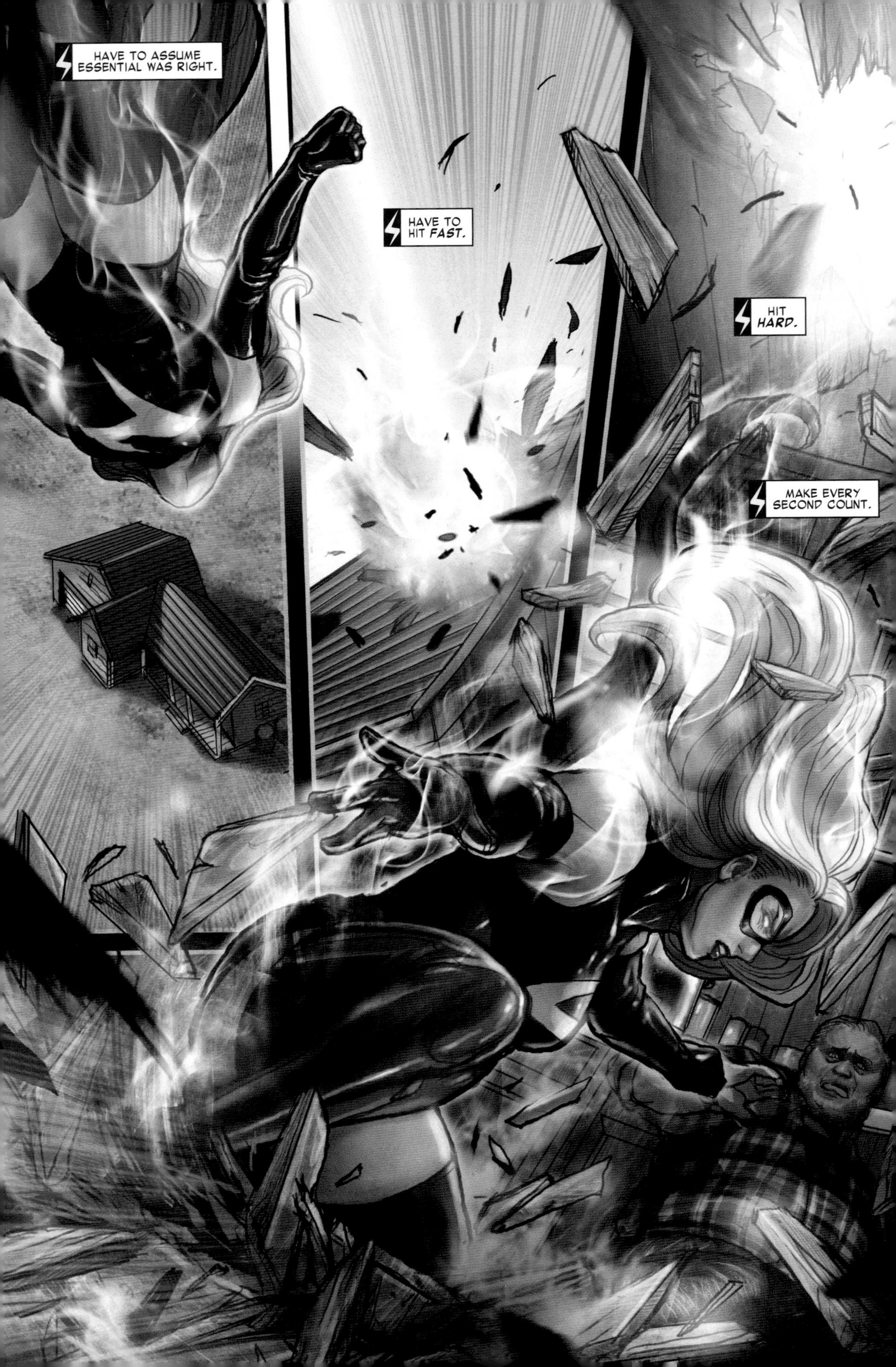
HAVE TO ASSUME ESSENTIAL WAS RIGHT.
HAVE TO HIT FAST.
HIT HARD.
MAKE EVERY SECOND COUNT.

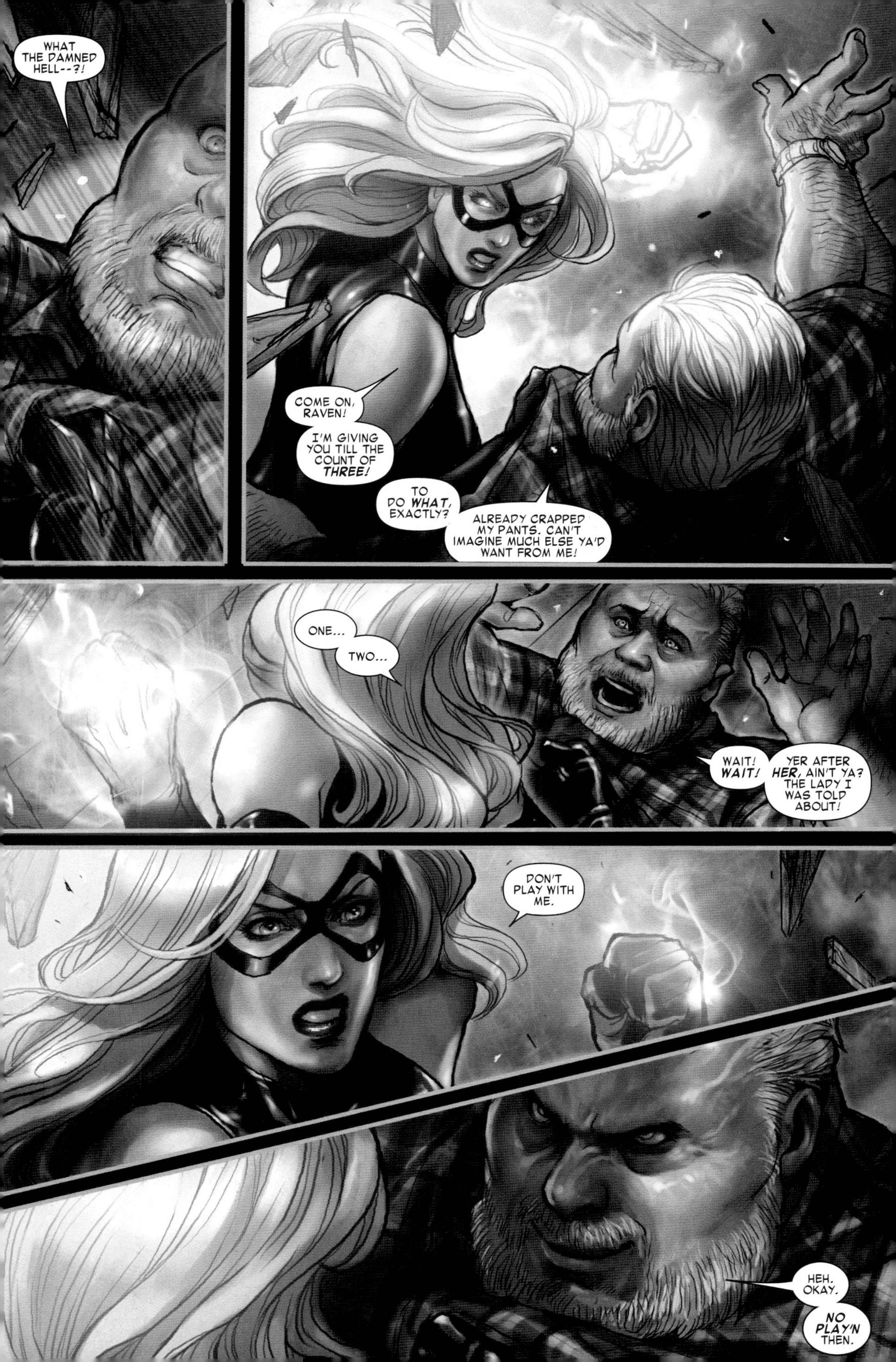
WHAT THE DAMNED HELL--?!
COME ON, RAVEN!
I'M GIVING YOU TILL THE COUNT OF THREE!
TO DO WHAT, EXACTLY?
ALREADY CRAPPED MY PANTS. CAN'T IMAGINE MUCH ELSE YA'D WANT FROM ME!
ONE...
TWO...
WAIT! WAIT!
YER AFTER HER, AIN'T YA? THE LADY I WAS TOLD ABOUT!
DON'T PLAY WITH ME.
HEH. OKAY.
NO PLAY'N THEN.

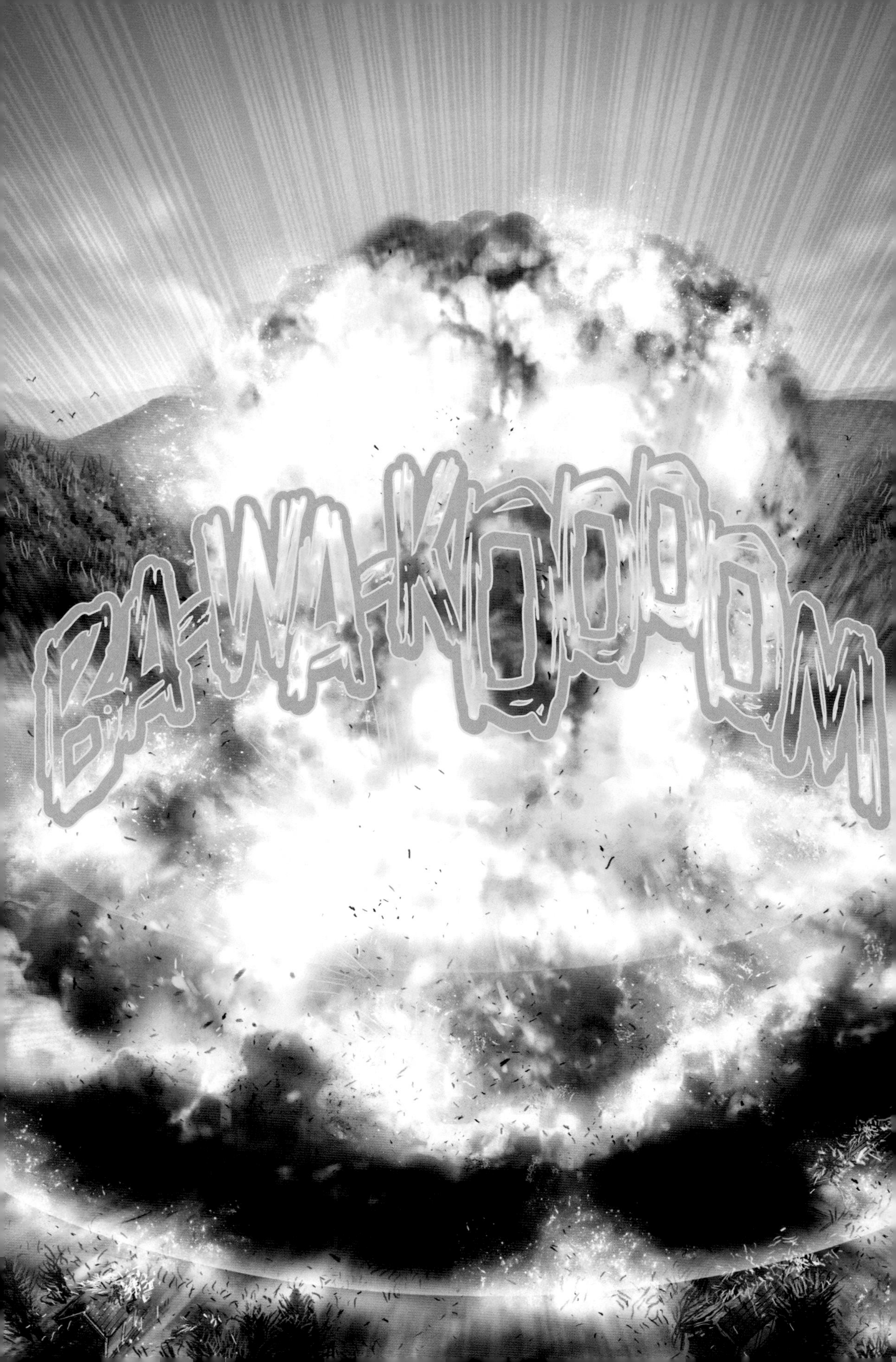
BAHWA-KOOOOOM

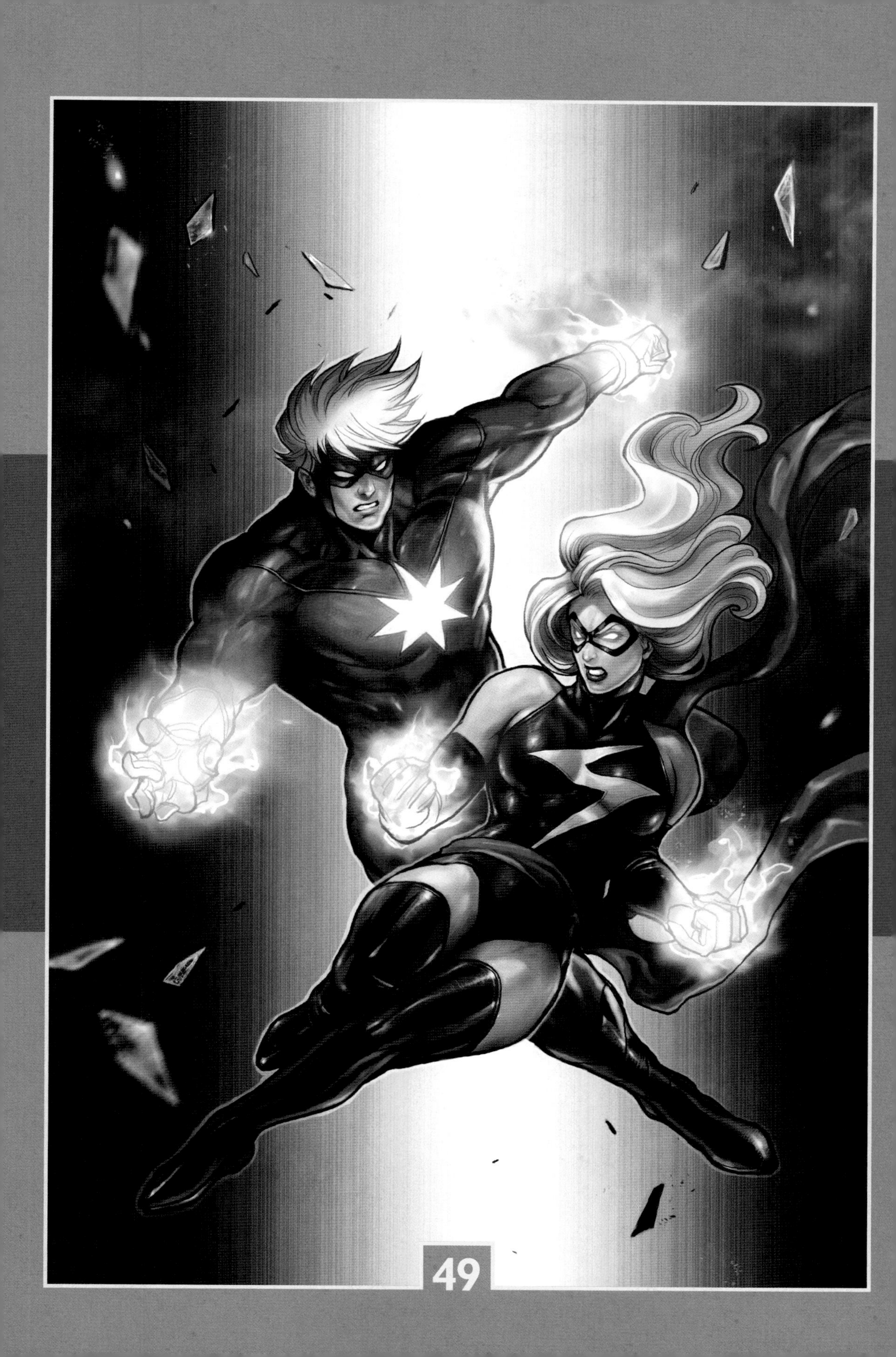

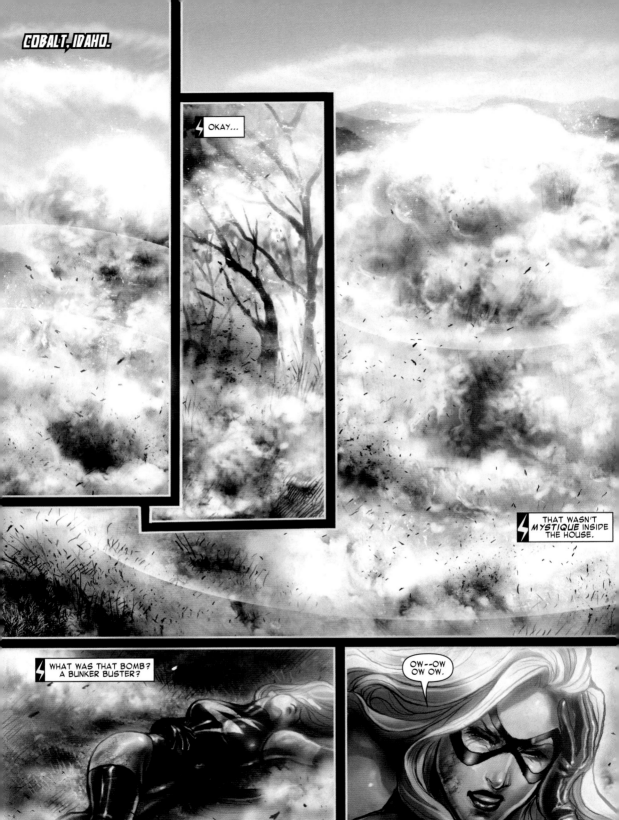

COBALT, IDAHO.

OKAY...

THAT WASN'T *MYSTIQUE* INSIDE THE HOUSE.

WHAT WAS THAT BOMB? A BUNKER BUSTER?

A GIRL CAN ONLY ABSORB SO MUCH ENERGY, BEFORE SHE CAN'T ABSORB ANY MORE.

OW--OW OW OW.

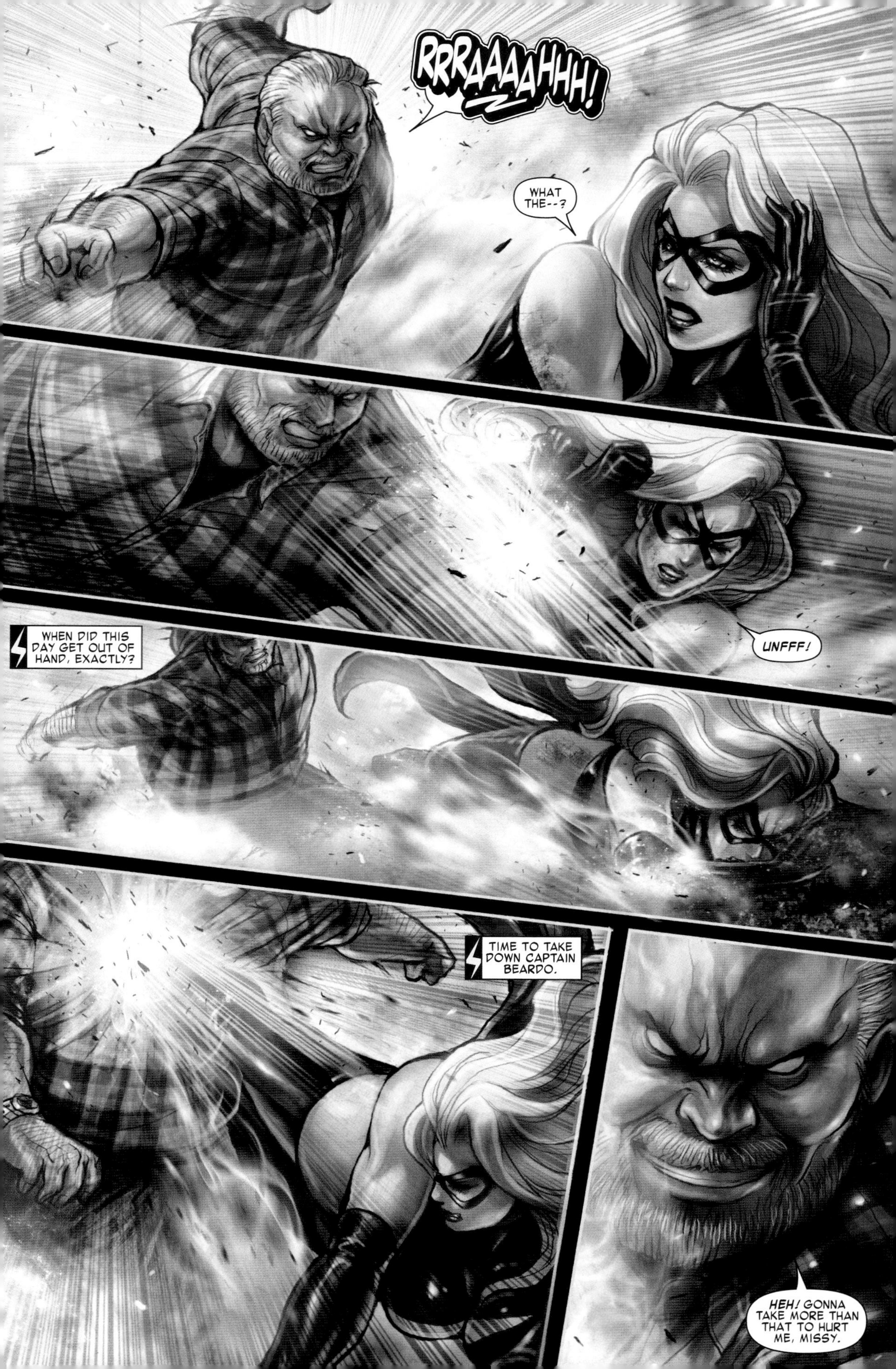
RRRAAAAHHH!
WHAT THE--?
UNFFF!
WHEN DID THIS DAY GET OUT OF HAND, EXACTLY?
TIME TO TAKE DOWN CAPTAIN BEARDO.
HEH! GONNA TAKE MORE THAN THAT TO HURT ME, MISSY.

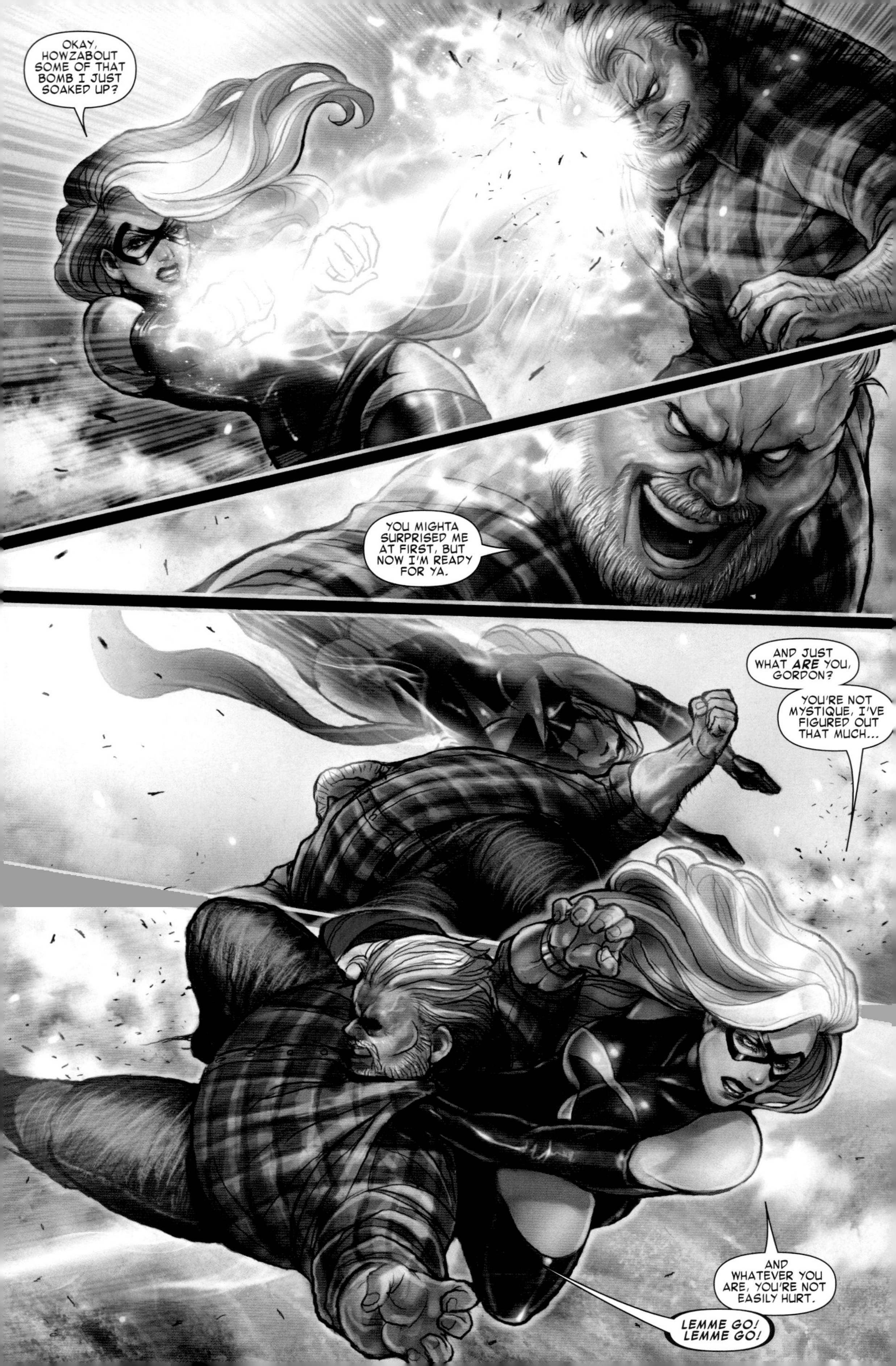
OKAY, HOWZABOUT SOME OF THAT BOMB I JUST SOAKED UP?
YOU MIGHTA SURPRISED ME AT FIRST, BUT NOW I'M READY FOR YA.
AND JUST WHAT *ARE* YOU, GORDON?
YOU'RE NOT MYSTIQUE, I'VE FIGURED OUT THAT MUCH...
AND WHATEVER YOU ARE, YOU'RE NOT EASILY HURT.
LEMME GO! LEMME GO!

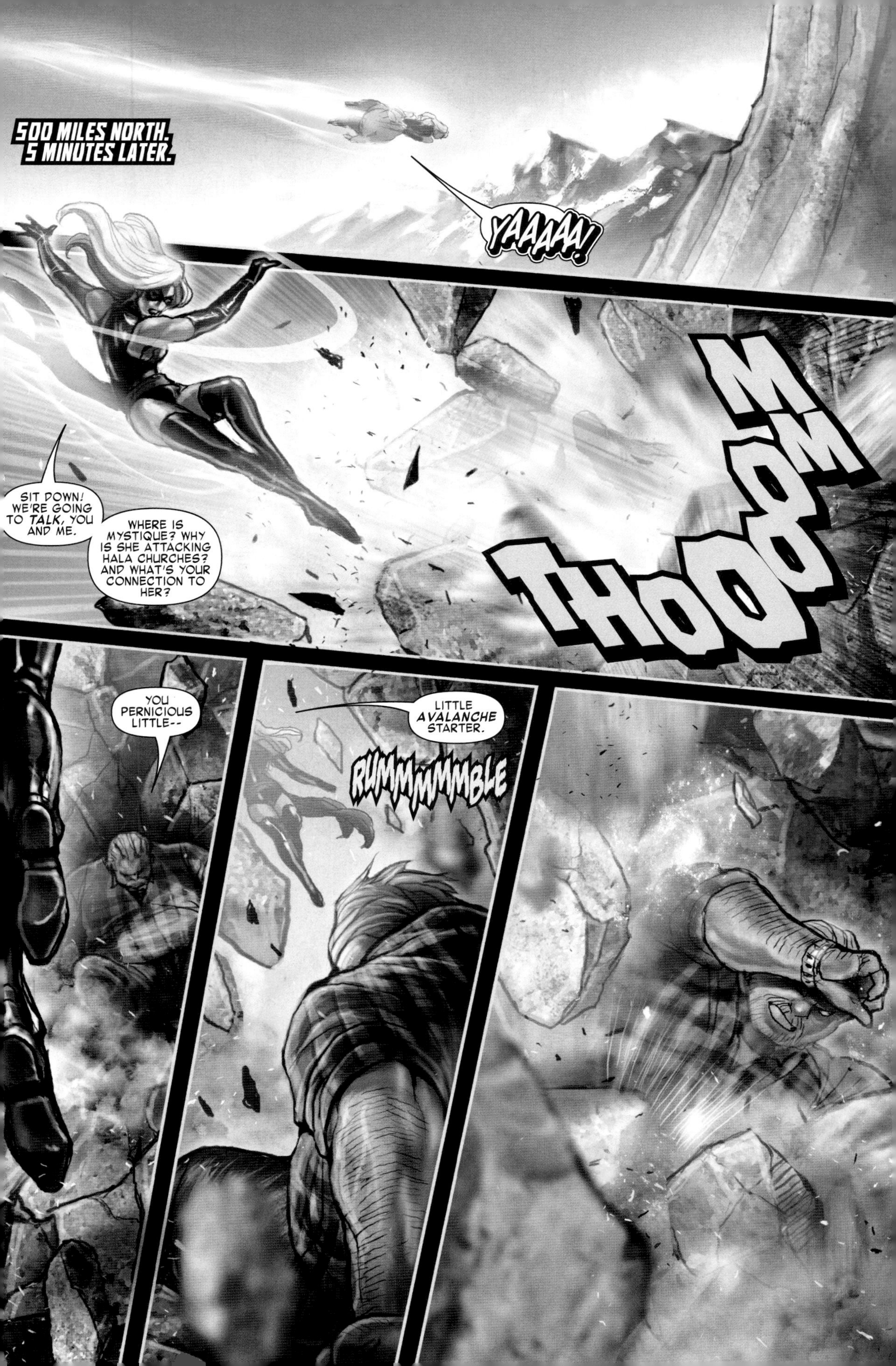

500 MILES NORTH.
5 MINUTES LATER.
YAAAAA!
SIT DOWN! WE'RE GOING TO *TALK*, YOU AND ME.
WHERE IS MYSTIQUE? WHY IS SHE ATTACKING HALA CHURCHES? AND WHAT'S YOUR CONNECTION TO HER?
THOOOOOOM
YOU PERNICIOUS LITTLE--
LITTLE *AVALANCHE* STARTER.
RUMMMMMBLE

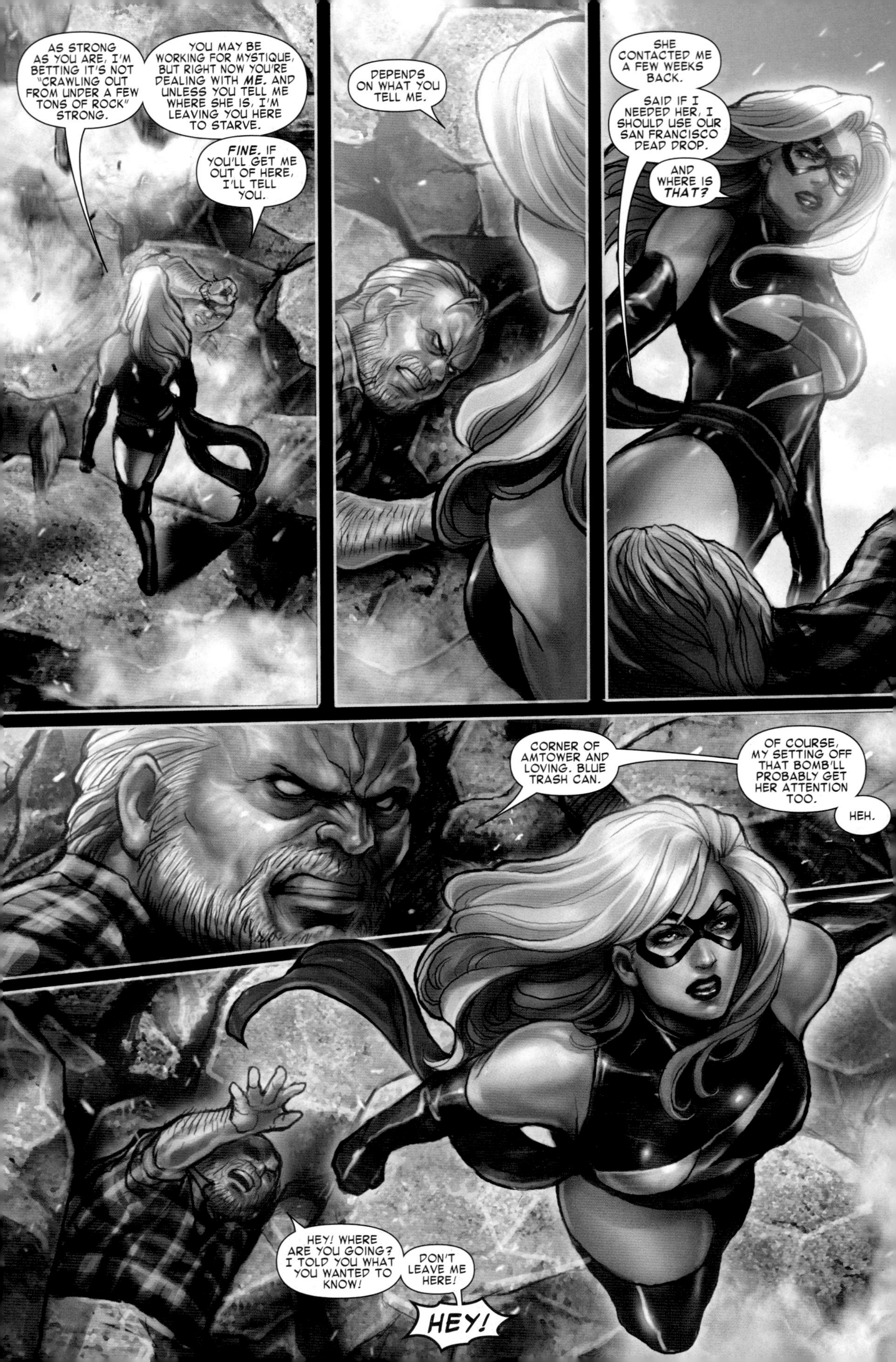
AS STRONG AS YOU ARE, I'M BETTING IT'S NOT "CRAWLING OUT FROM UNDER A FEW TONS OF ROCK" STRONG.
YOU MAY BE WORKING FOR MYSTIQUE, BUT RIGHT NOW YOU'RE DEALING WITH ME. AND UNLESS YOU TELL ME WHERE SHE IS, I'M LEAVING YOU HERE TO STARVE.
FINE. IF YOU'LL GET ME OUT OF HERE, I'LL TELL YOU.
DEPENDS ON WHAT YOU TELL ME.
SHE CONTACTED ME A FEW WEEKS BACK.
SAID IF I NEEDED HER, I SHOULD USE OUR SAN FRANCISCO DEAD DROP.
AND WHERE IS THAT?
CORNER OF AMTOWER AND LOVING. BLUE TRASH CAN.
OF COURSE, MY SETTING OFF THAT BOMB'LL PROBABLY GET HER ATTENTION TOO.
HEH.
HEY! WHERE ARE YOU GOING? I TOLD YOU WHAT YOU WANTED TO KNOW!
DON'T LEAVE ME HERE!
HEY!

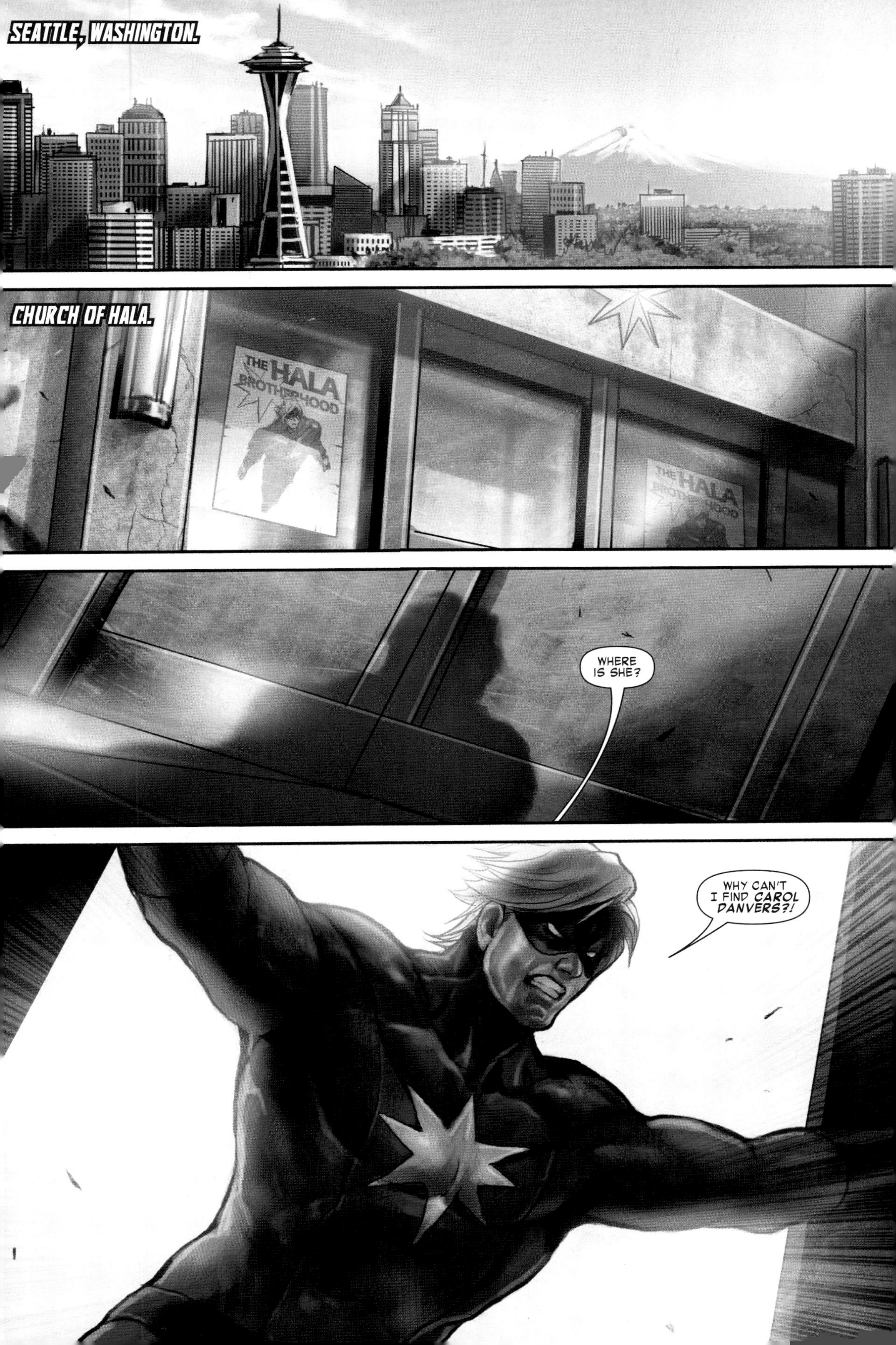
SEATTLE, WASHINGTON.
CHURCH OF HALA.
THE HALA BROTHERHOOD
THE HALA BROTHERHOOD
WHERE IS SHE?
WHY CAN'T I FIND CAROL DANVERS?!

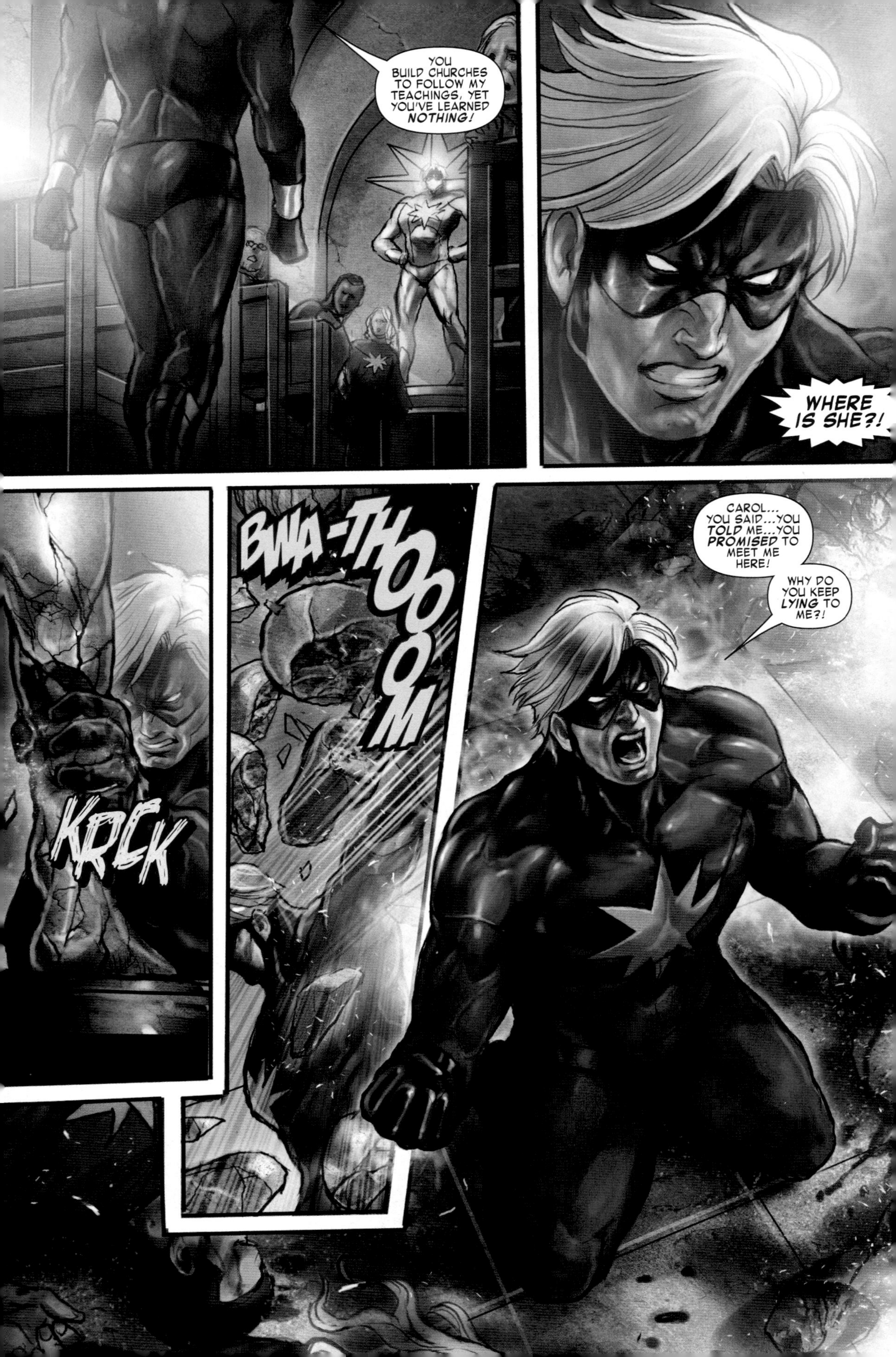
YOU BUILD CHURCHES TO FOLLOW MY TEACHINGS, YET YOU'VE LEARNED NOTHING!
WHERE IS SHE?!
KRCK
BWA-THOOOOM
CAROL... YOU SAID...YOU TOLD ME...YOU PROMISED TO MEET ME HERE!
WHY DO YOU KEEP LYING TO ME?!

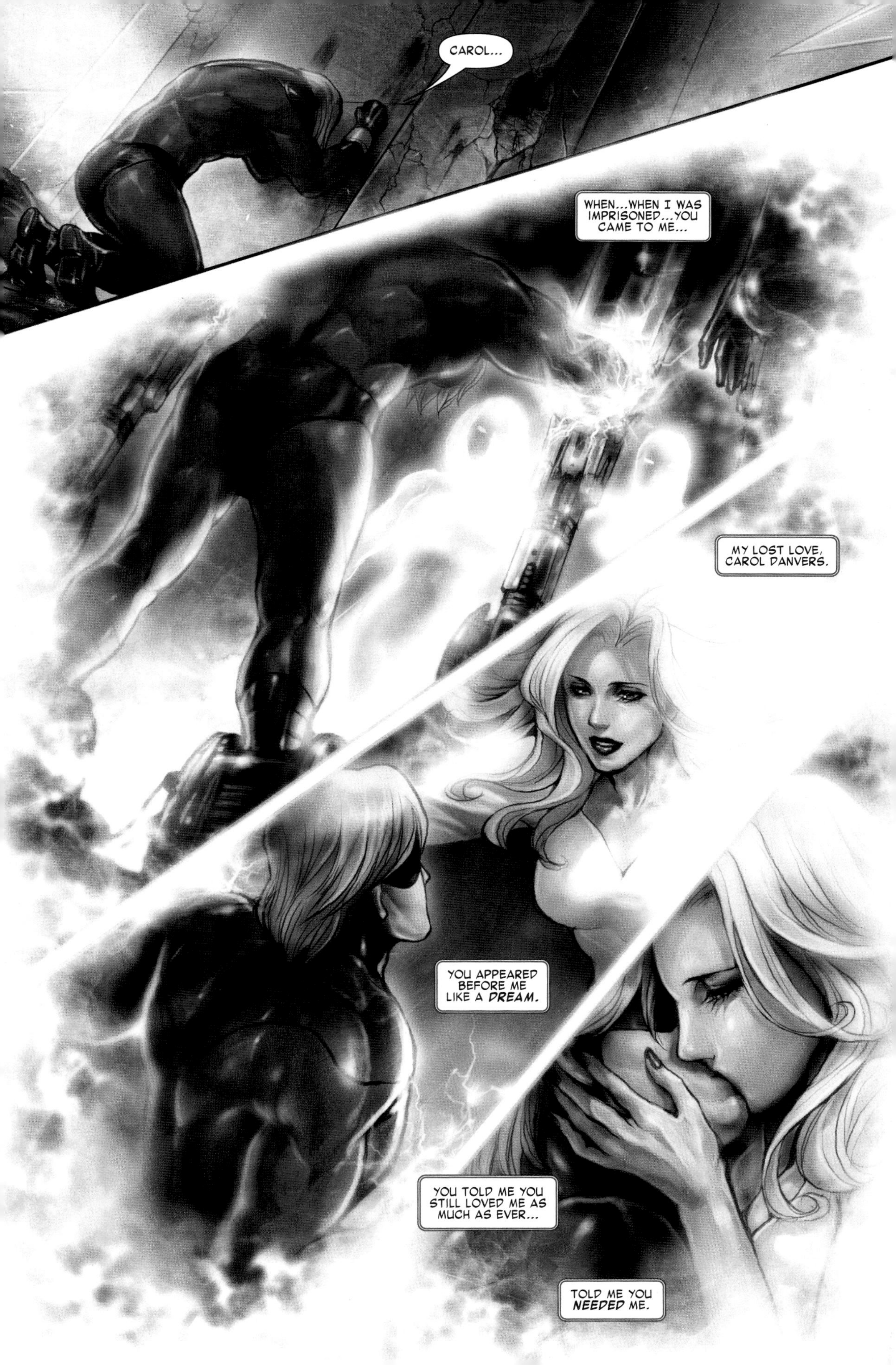
CAROL...
WHEN...WHEN I WAS IMPRISONED...YOU CAME TO ME...
MY LOST LOVE, CAROL DANVERS.
YOU APPEARED BEFORE ME LIKE A *DREAM.*
YOU TOLD ME YOU STILL LOVED ME AS MUCH AS EVER...
TOLD ME YOU *NEEDED* ME.

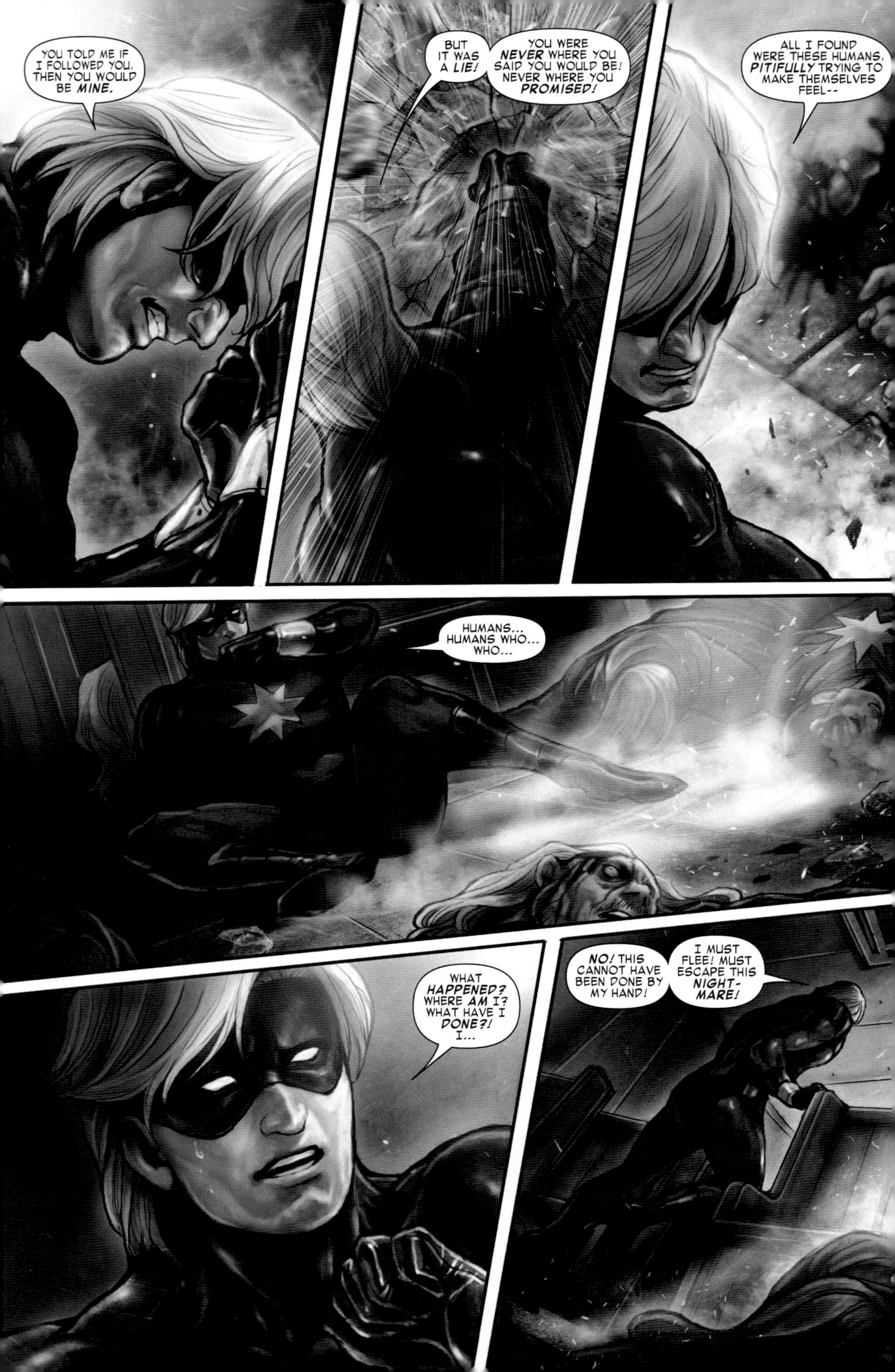
YOU TOLD ME IF I FOLLOWED YOU, THEN YOU WOULD BE MINE.
BUT IT WAS A LIE!
YOU WERE NEVER WHERE YOU SAID YOU WOULD BE! NEVER WHERE YOU PROMISED!
ALL I FOUND WERE THESE HUMANS, PITIFULLY TRYING TO MAKE THEMSELVES FEEL--
HUMANS... HUMANS WHO... WHO...
WHAT HAPPENED? WHERE AM I? WHAT HAVE I DONE?! I...
NO! THIS CANNOT HAVE BEEN DONE BY MY HAND!
I MUST FLEE! MUST ESCAPE THIS NIGHT-MARE!

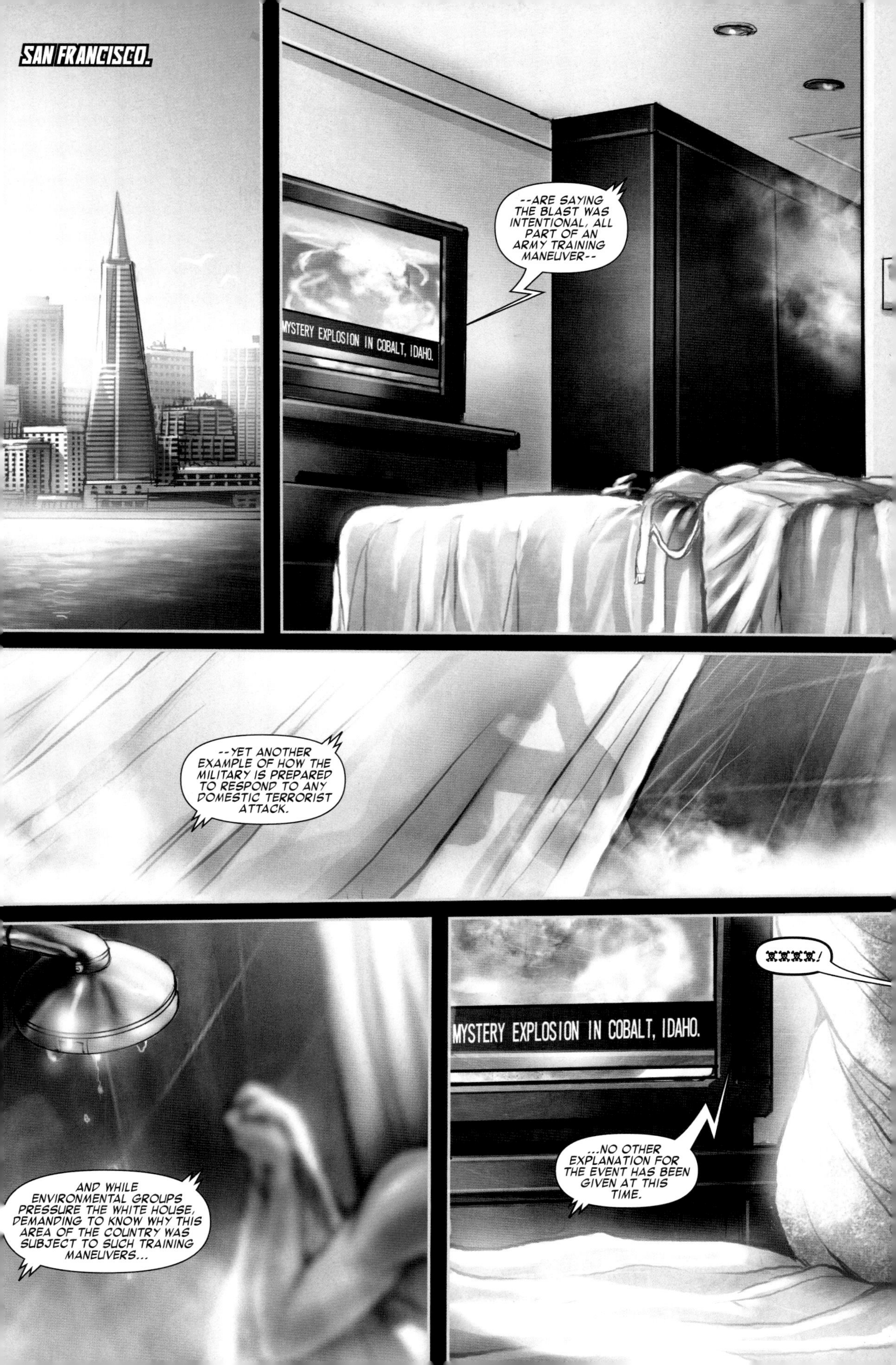
SAN FRANCISCO.
--ARE SAYING THE BLAST WAS INTENTIONAL, ALL PART OF AN ARMY TRAINING MANEUVER--
MYSTERY EXPLOSION IN COBALT, IDAHO.
--YET ANOTHER EXAMPLE OF HOW THE MILITARY IS PREPARED TO RESPOND TO ANY DOMESTIC TERRORIST ATTACK.
AND WHILE ENVIRONMENTAL GROUPS PRESSURE THE WHITE HOUSE, DEMANDING TO KNOW WHY THIS AREA OF THE COUNTRY WAS SUBJECT TO SUCH TRAINING MANEUVERS...
MYSTERY EXPLOSION IN COBALT, IDAHO.
...NO OTHER EXPLANATION FOR THE EVENT HAS BEEN GIVEN AT THIS TIME.

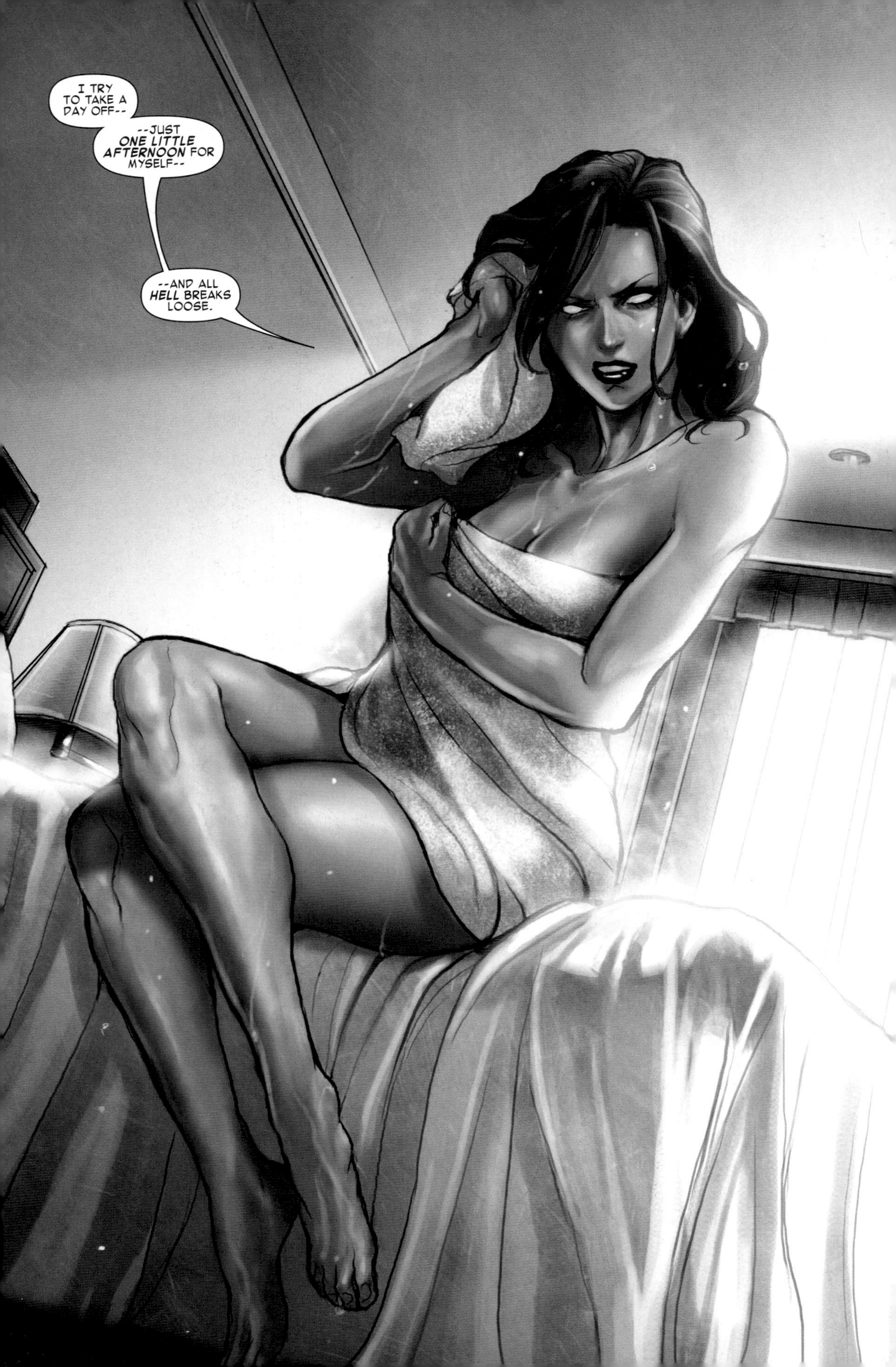
I TRY TO TAKE A DAY OFF--
--JUST ONE LITTLE AFTERNOON FOR MYSELF--
--AND ALL HELL BREAKS LOOSE.

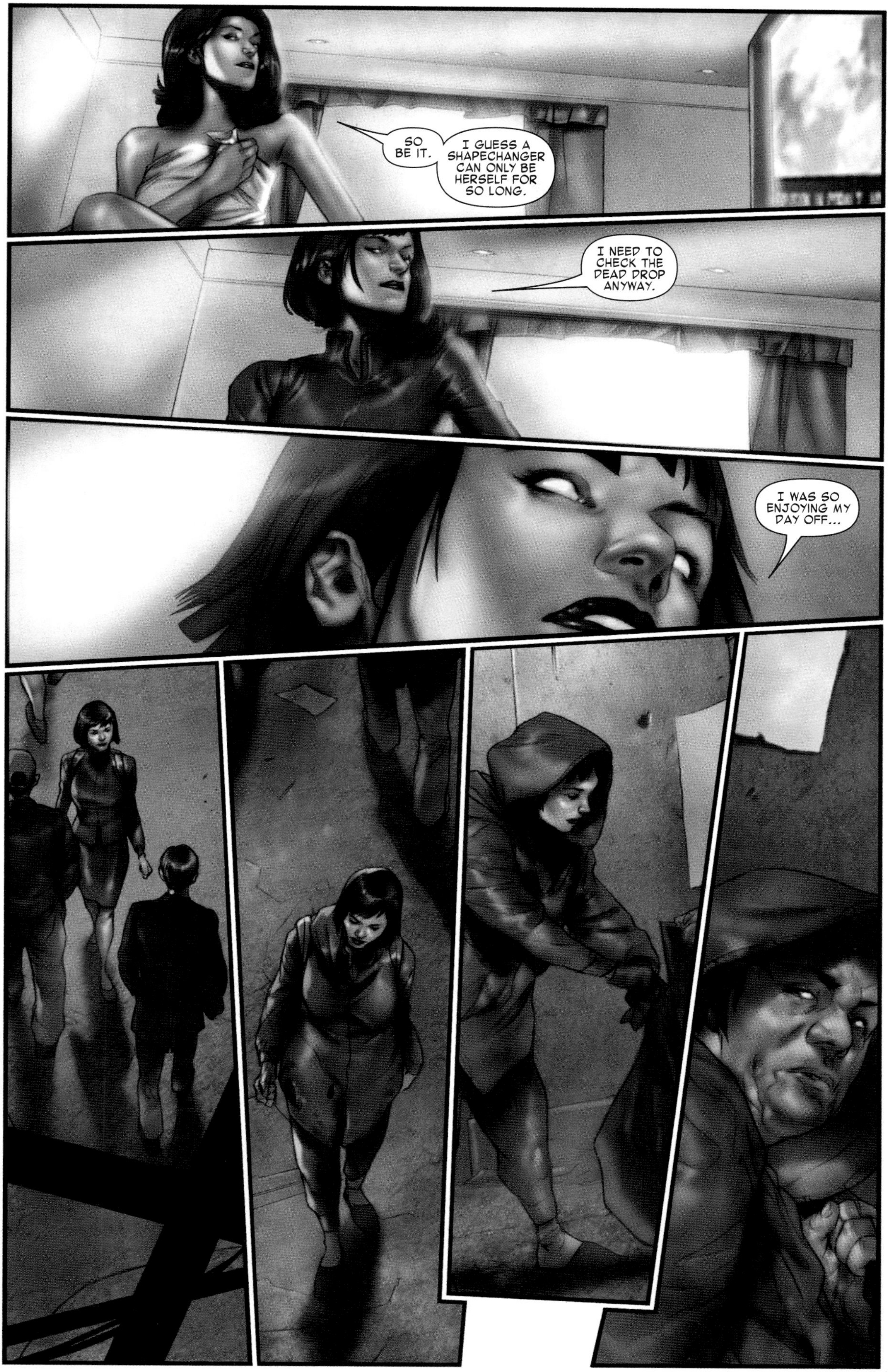
SO BE IT.
I GUESS A SHAPECHANGER CAN ONLY BE HERSELF FOR SO LONG.
I NEED TO CHECK THE DEAD DROP ANYWAY.
I WAS SO ENJOYING MY DAY OFF...

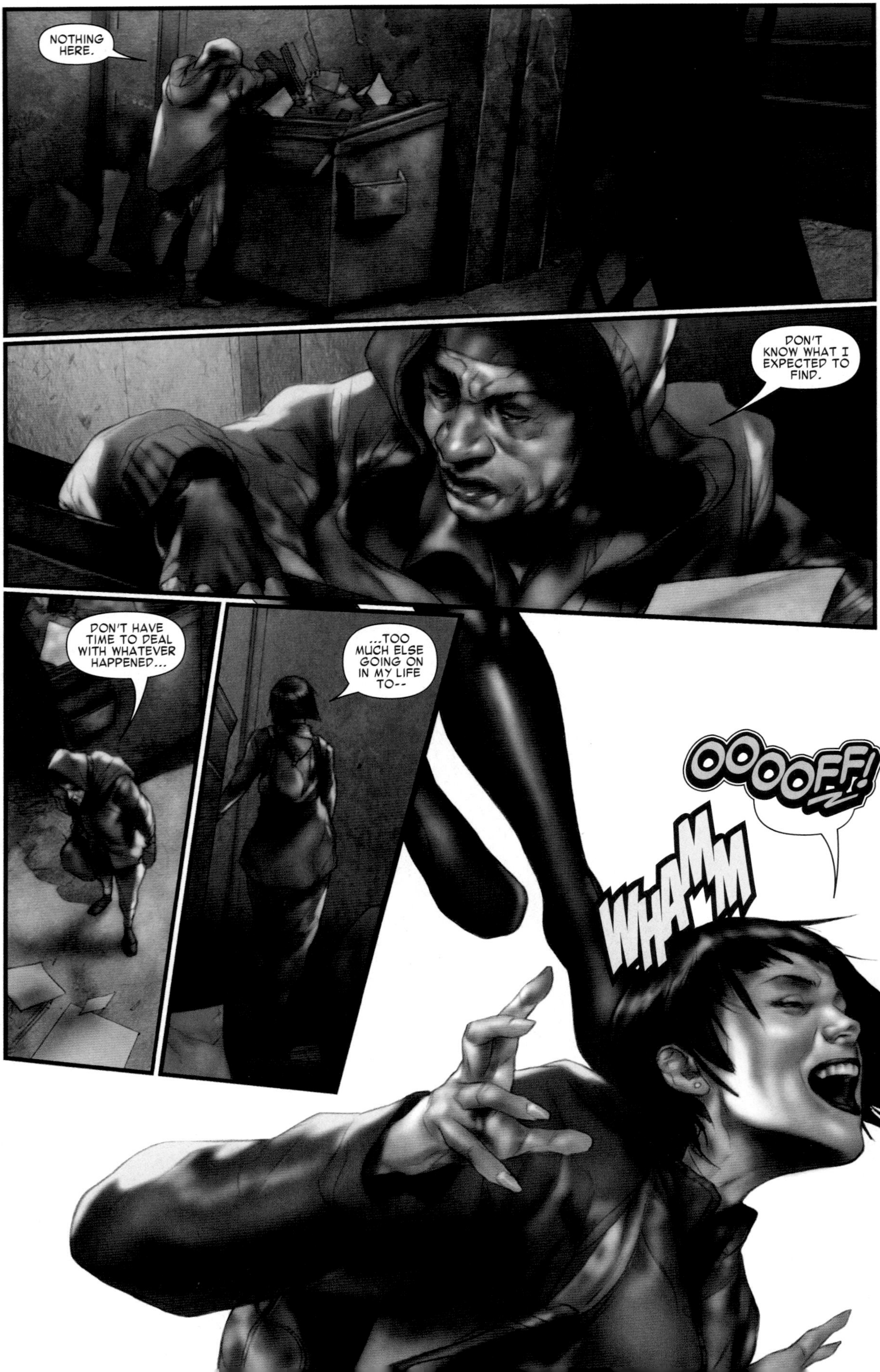
NOTHING HERE.
DON'T KNOW WHAT I EXPECTED TO FIND.
DON'T HAVE TIME TO DEAL WITH WHATEVER HAPPENED...
...TOO MUCH ELSE GOING ON IN MY LIFE TO--
WHAMM
OOOOFF!

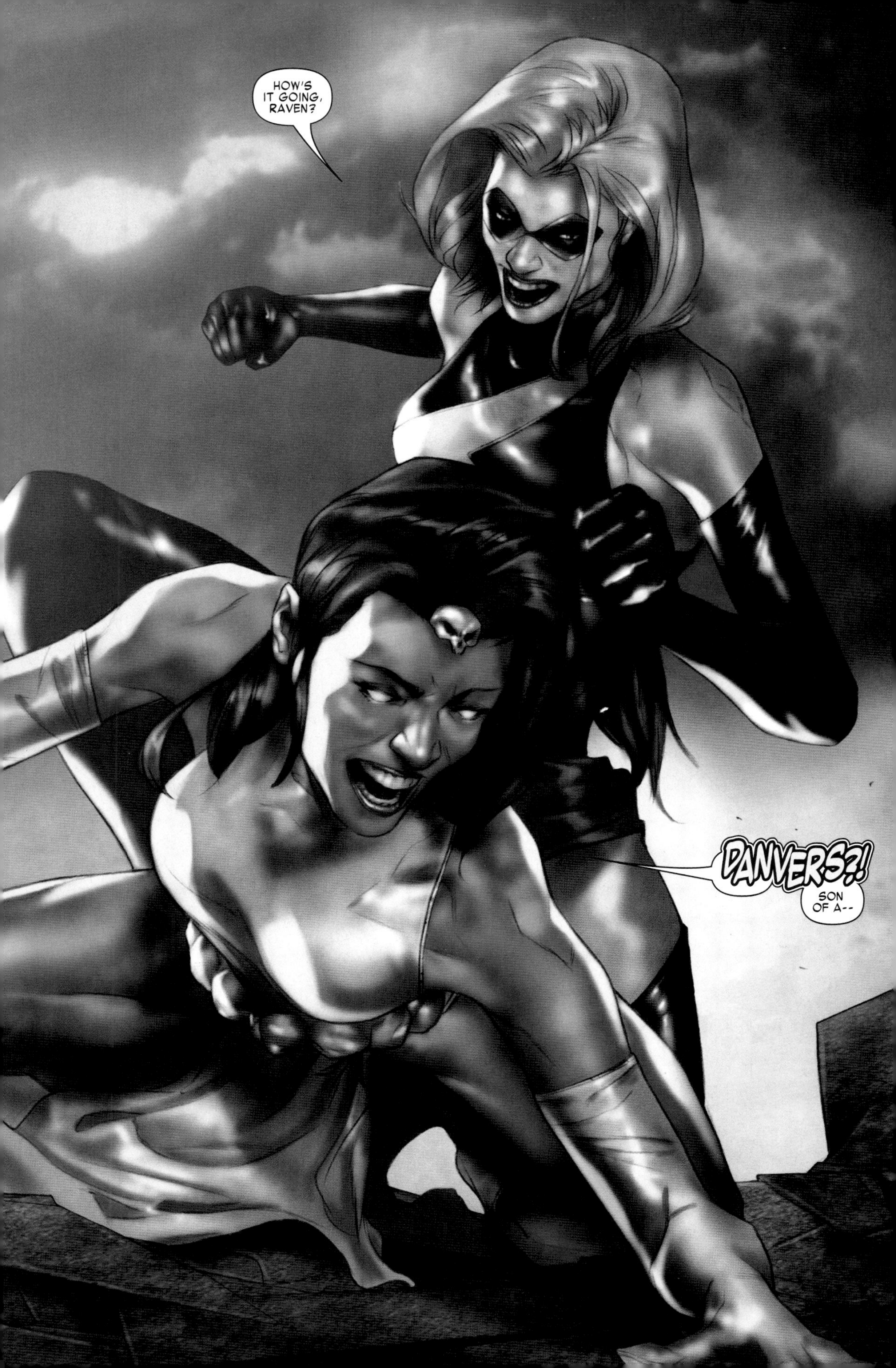
HOW'S IT GOING, RAVEN?
DANVERS?!
SON OF A--

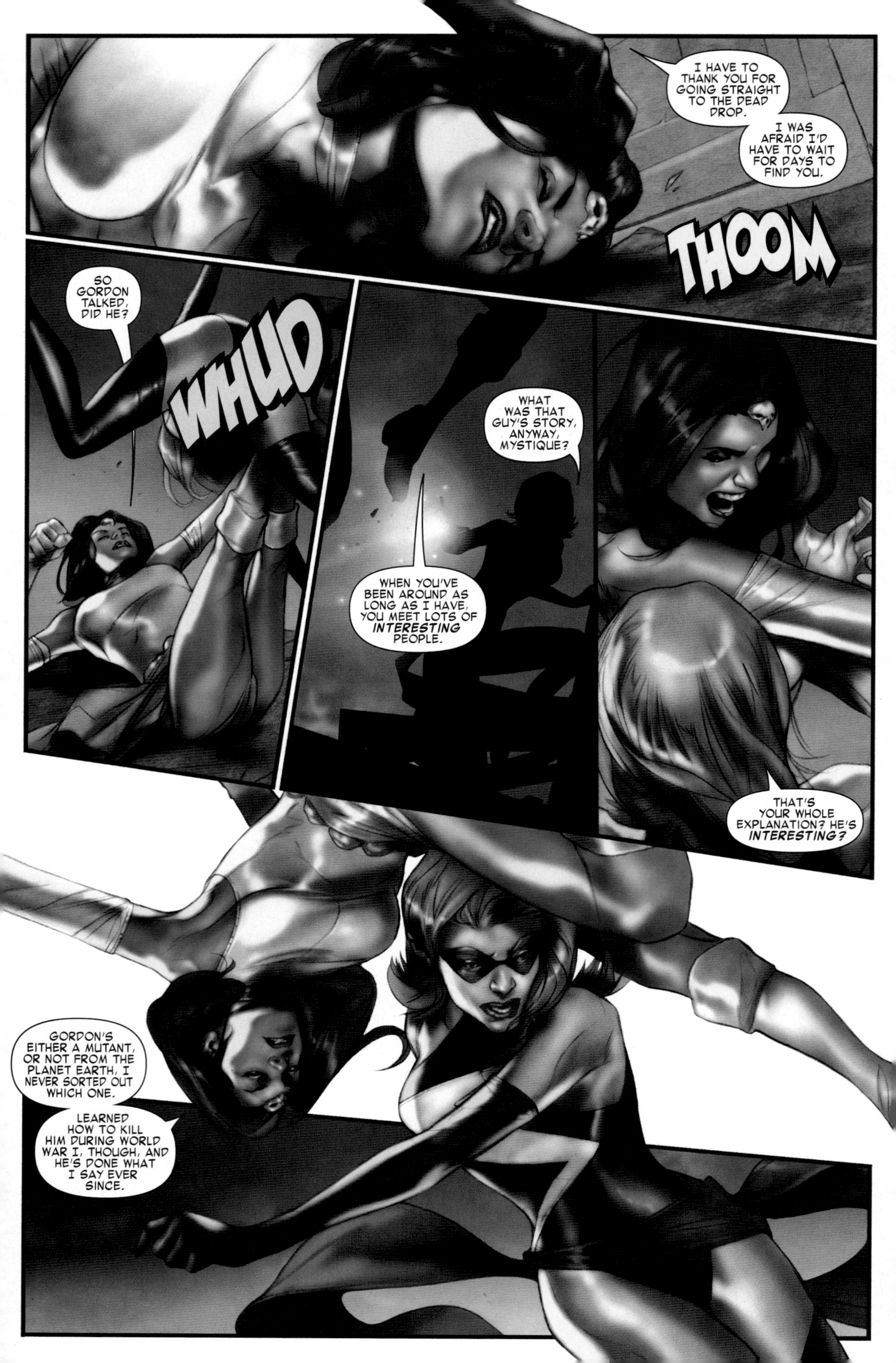
I HAVE TO THANK YOU FOR GOING STRAIGHT TO THE DEAD DROP.
I WAS AFRAID I'D HAVE TO WAIT FOR DAYS TO FIND YOU.
THOOM
SO GORDON TALKED, DID HE?
WHUD
WHAT WAS THAT GUY'S STORY, ANYWAY, MYSTIQUE?
WHEN YOU'VE BEEN AROUND AS LONG AS I HAVE, YOU MEET LOTS OF *INTERESTING* PEOPLE.
THAT'S YOUR WHOLE EXPLANATION? HE'S *INTERESTING?*
GORDON'S EITHER A MUTANT, OR NOT FROM THE PLANET EARTH, I NEVER SORTED OUT WHICH ONE.
LEARNED HOW TO KILL HIM DURING WORLD WAR I, THOUGH, AND HE'S DONE WHAT I SAY EVER SINCE.

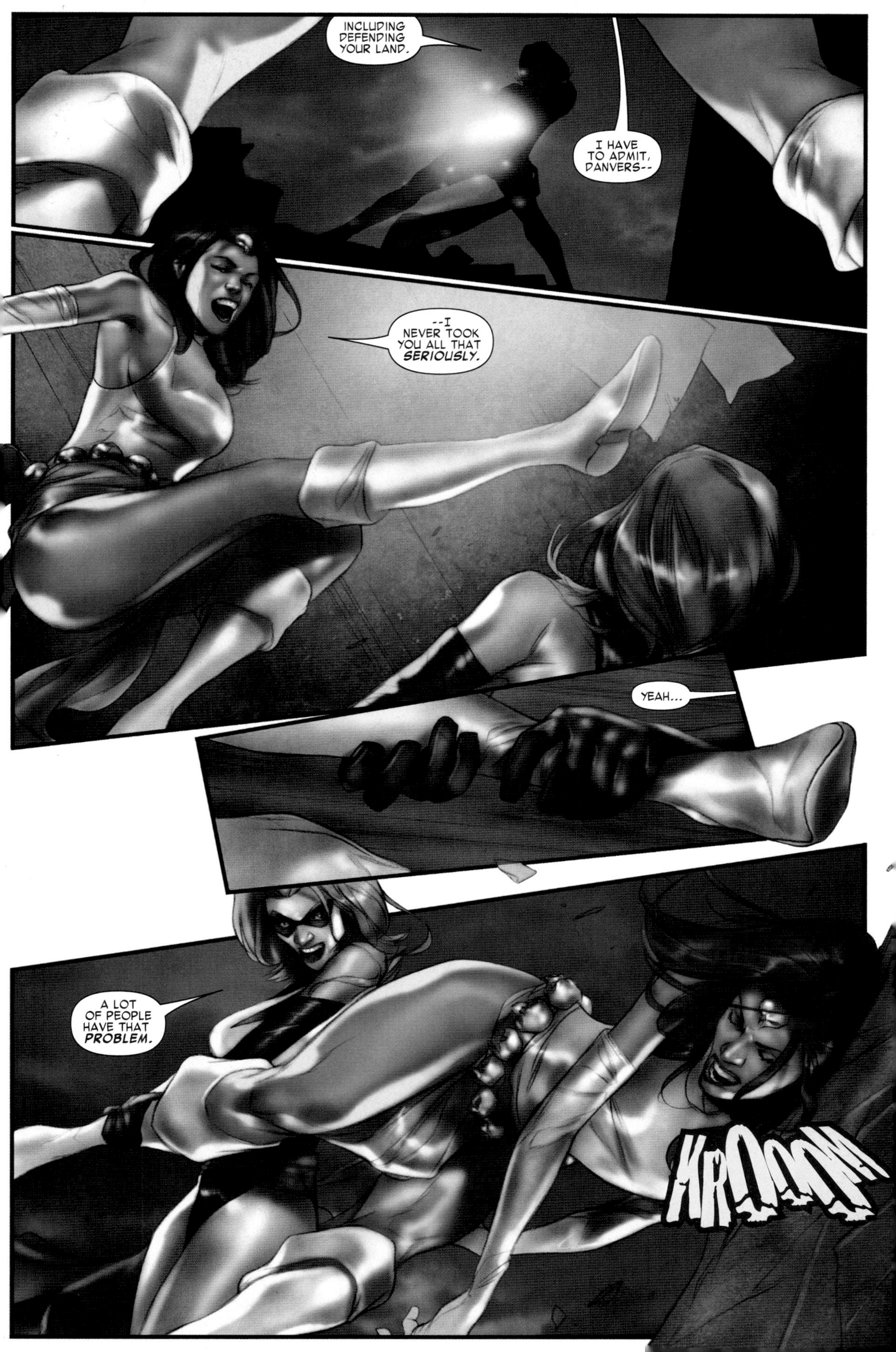

INCLUDING DEFENDING YOUR LAND.
I HAVE TO ADMIT, DANVERS--
--I NEVER TOOK YOU ALL THAT SERIOUSLY.
YEAH...
A LOT OF PEOPLE HAVE THAT PROBLEM.
KROOOM

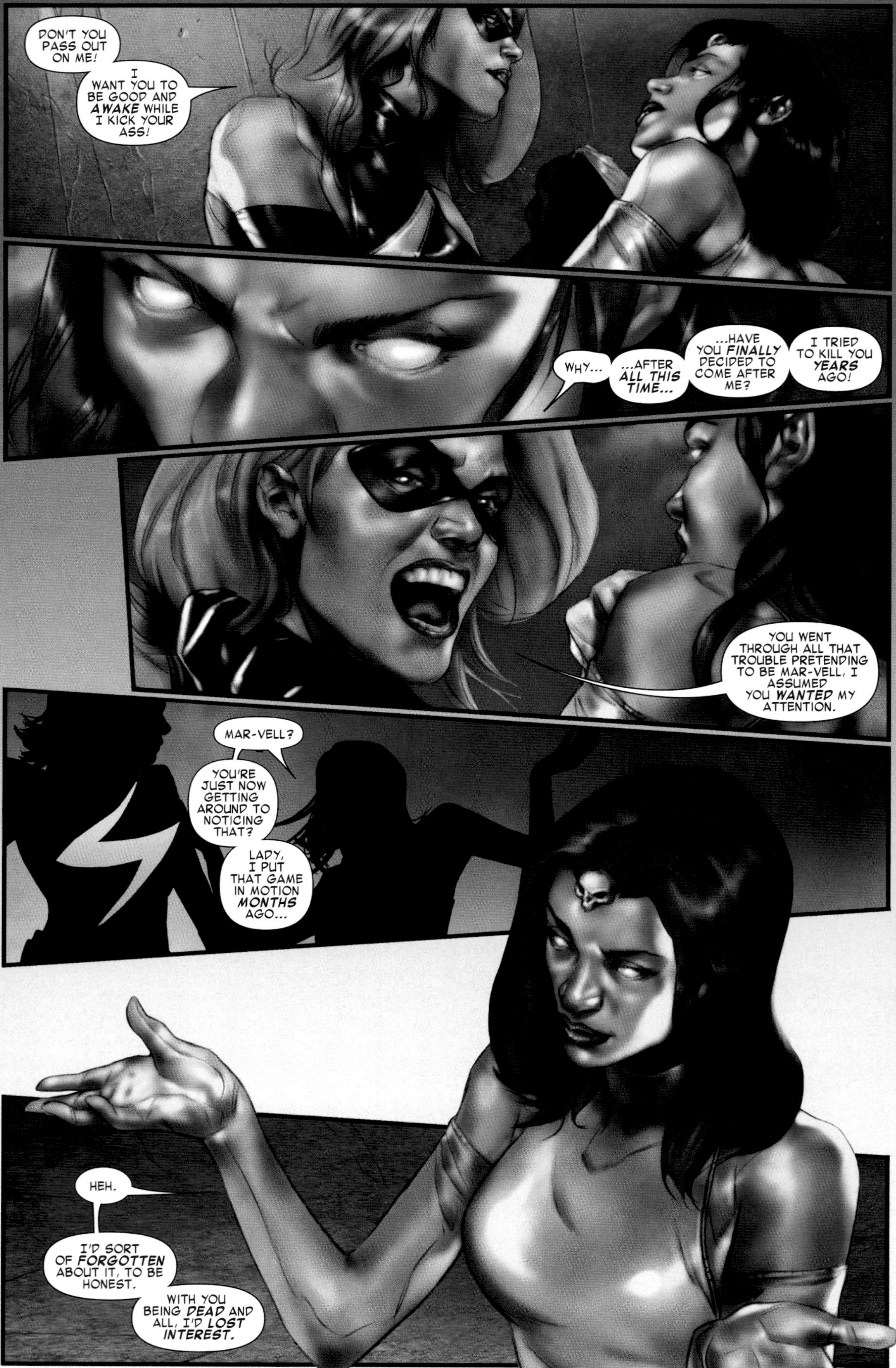
DON'T YOU PASS OUT ON ME!
I WANT YOU TO BE GOOD AND AWAKE WHILE I KICK YOUR ASS!
WHY...
...AFTER ALL THIS TIME...
...HAVE YOU FINALLY DECIDED TO COME AFTER ME?
I TRIED TO KILL YOU YEARS AGO!
YOU WENT THROUGH ALL THAT TROUBLE PRETENDING TO BE MAR-VELL, I ASSUMED YOU WANTED MY ATTENTION.
MAR-VELL?
YOU'RE JUST NOW GETTING AROUND TO NOTICING THAT?
LADY, I PUT THAT GAME IN MOTION MONTHS AGO...
HEH.
I'D SORT OF FORGOTTEN ABOUT IT, TO BE HONEST.
WITH YOU BEING DEAD AND ALL, I'D LOST INTEREST.

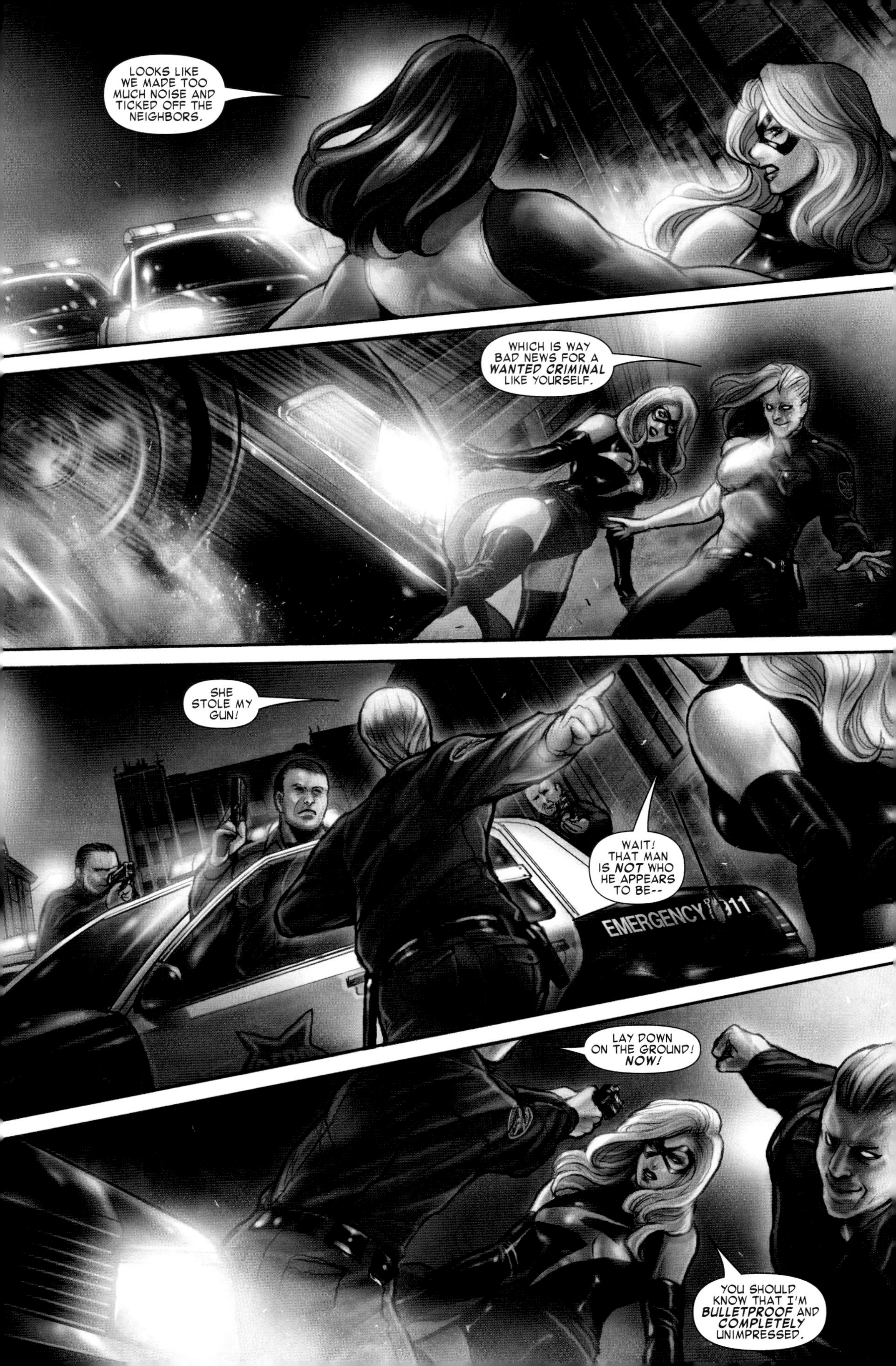

LOOKS LIKE WE MADE TOO MUCH NOISE AND TICKED OFF THE NEIGHBORS.
WHICH IS WAY BAD NEWS FOR A WANTED CRIMINAL LIKE YOURSELF.
SHE STOLE MY GUN!
WAIT! THAT MAN IS NOT WHO HE APPEARS TO BE--
EMERGENCY 911
LAY DOWN ON THE GROUND! NOW!
YOU SHOULD KNOW THAT I'M BULLETPROOF AND COMPLETELY UNIMPRESSED.

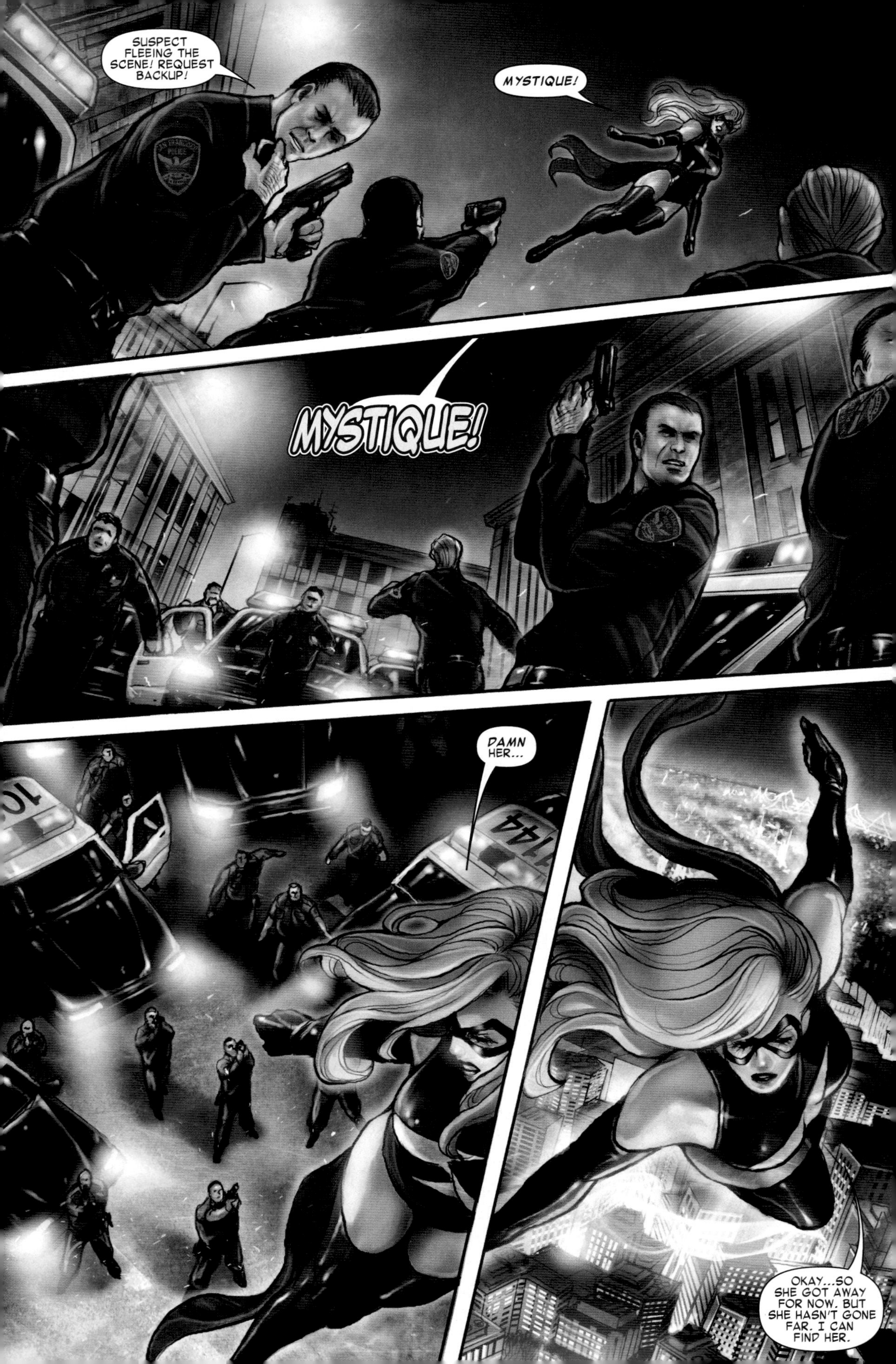
SUSPECT FLEEING THE SCENE! REQUEST BACKUP!
MYSTIQUE!
MYSTIQUE!
DAMN HER...
OKAY...SO SHE GOT AWAY FOR NOW. BUT SHE HASN'T GONE FAR. I CAN FIND HER.

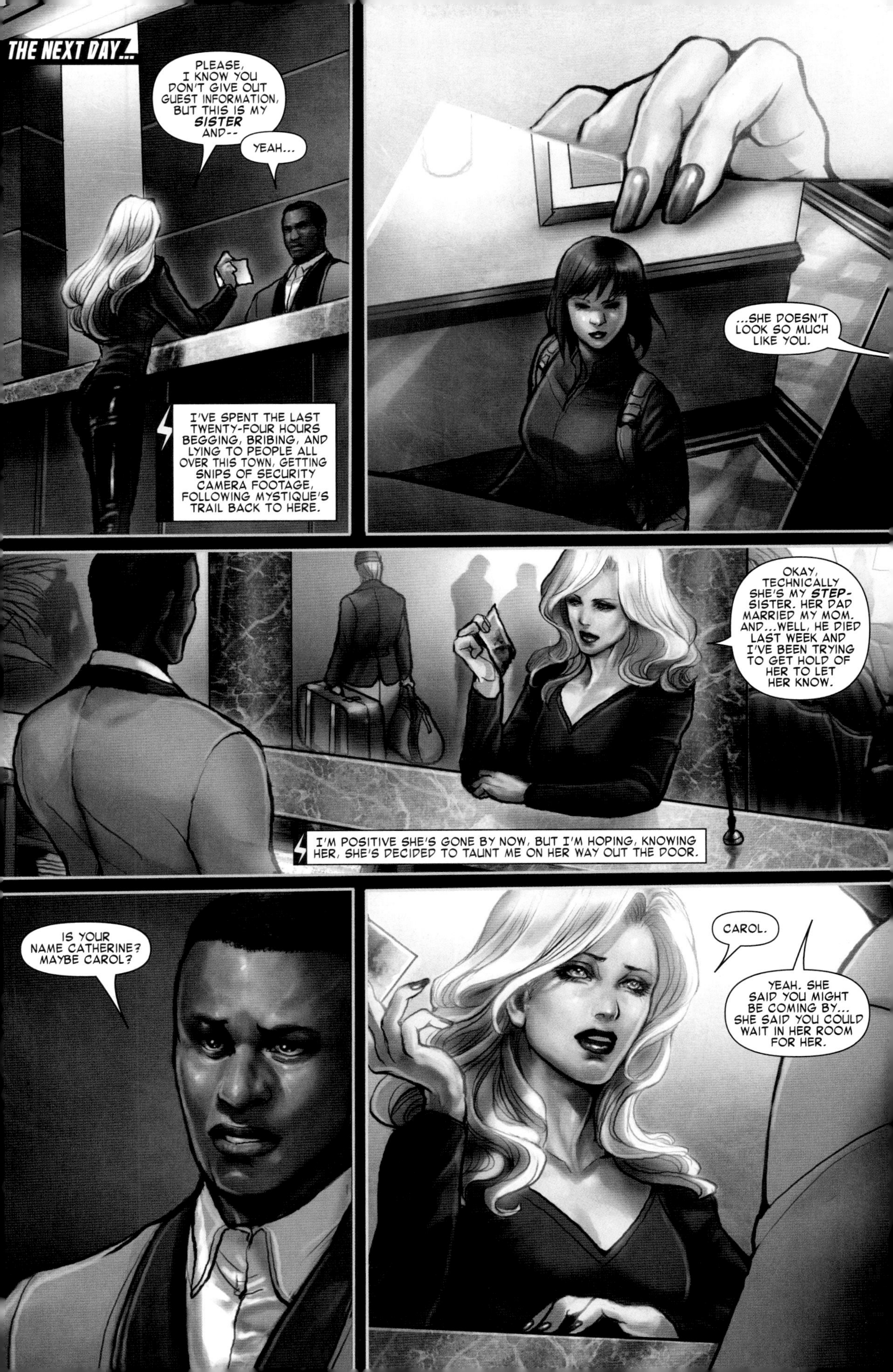
THE NEXT DAY...
PLEASE, I KNOW YOU DON'T GIVE OUT GUEST INFORMATION, BUT THIS IS MY SISTER AND--
YEAH...
I'VE SPENT THE LAST TWENTY-FOUR HOURS BEGGING, BRIBING, AND LYING TO PEOPLE ALL OVER THIS TOWN, GETTING SNIPS OF SECURITY CAMERA FOOTAGE, FOLLOWING MYSTIQUE'S TRAIL BACK TO HERE.
...SHE DOESN'T LOOK SO MUCH LIKE YOU.
OKAY, TECHNICALLY SHE'S MY STEP-SISTER. HER DAD MARRIED MY MOM. AND...WELL, HE DIED LAST WEEK AND I'VE BEEN TRYING TO GET HOLD OF HER TO LET HER KNOW.
I'M POSITIVE SHE'S GONE BY NOW, BUT I'M HOPING, KNOWING HER, SHE'S DECIDED TO TAUNT ME ON HER WAY OUT THE DOOR.
IS YOUR NAME CATHERINE? MAYBE CAROL?
CAROL.
YEAH. SHE SAID YOU MIGHT BE COMING BY... SHE SAID YOU COULD WAIT IN HER ROOM FOR HER.

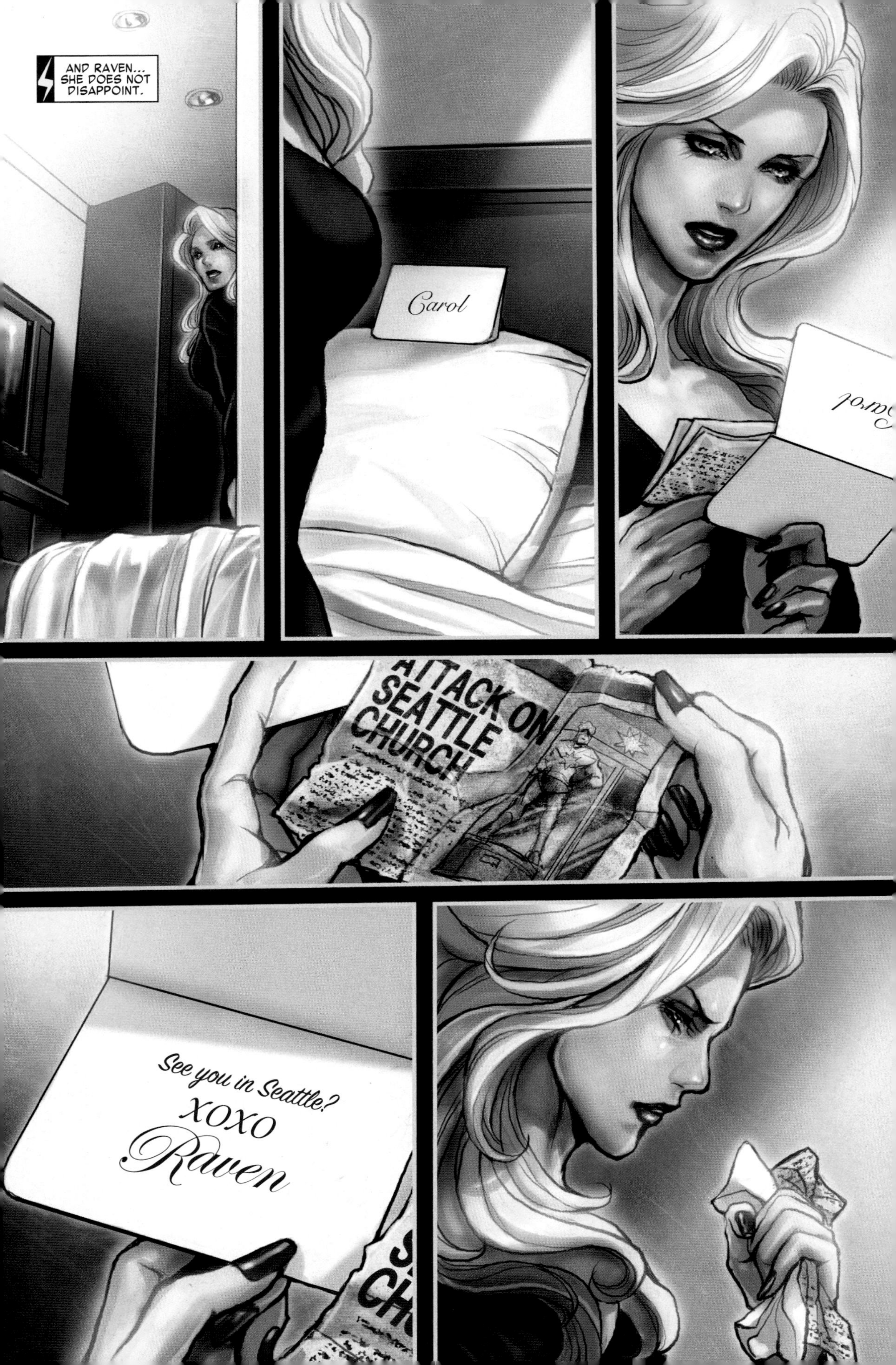
AND RAVEN... SHE DOES NOT DISAPPOINT.
Carol
ATTACK ON SEATTLE CHURCH
See you in Seattle?
XOXO
Raven

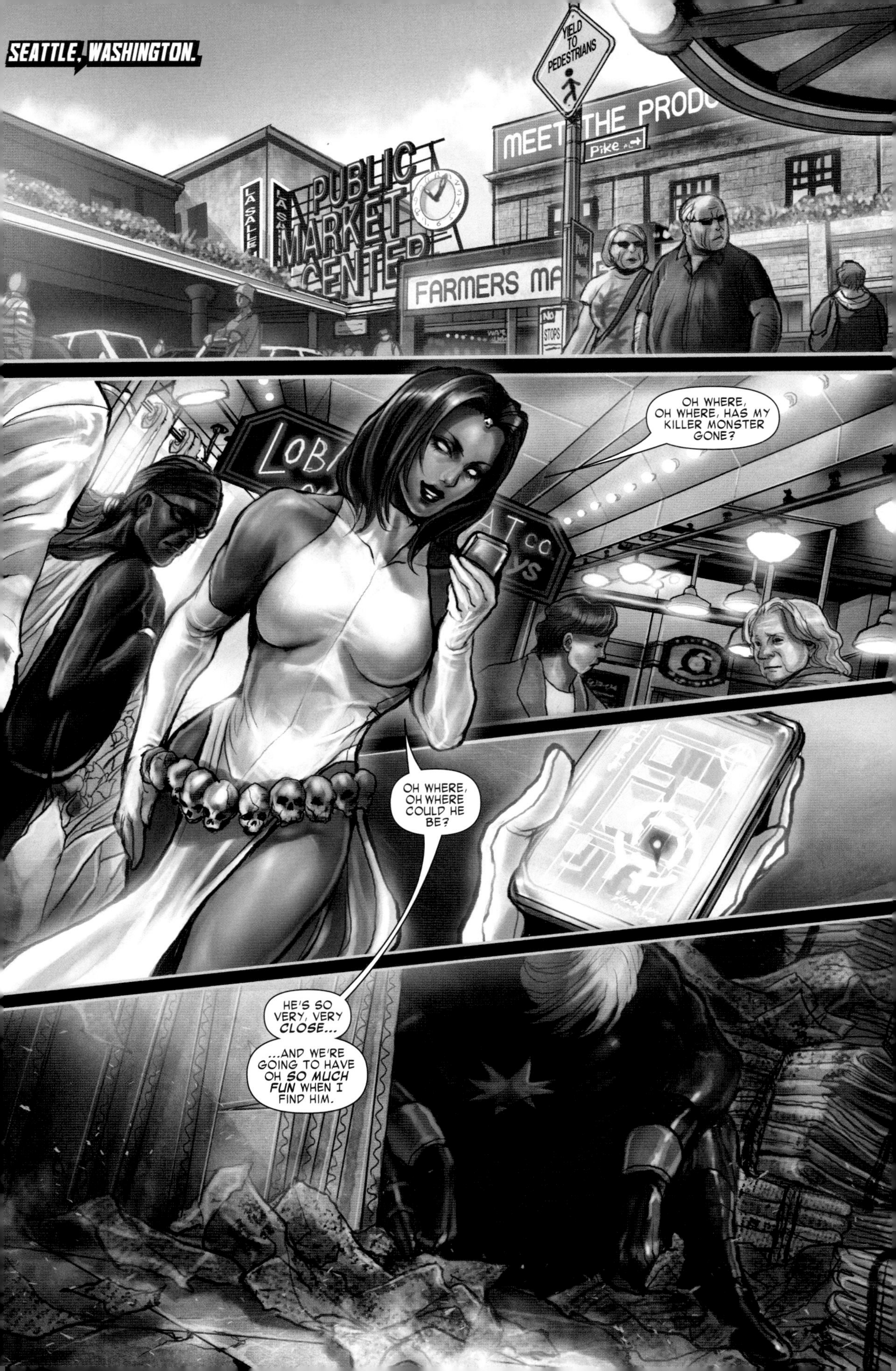
SEATTLE, WASHINGTON.
YIELD TO PEDESTRIANS
PUBLIC MARKET CENTER
Pike
FARMERS MA
OH WHERE, OH WHERE, HAS MY KILLER MONSTER GONE?
OH WHERE, OH WHERE COULD HE BE?
HE'S SO VERY, VERY *CLOSE...*
...AND WE'RE GOING TO HAVE OH ***SO MUCH FUN*** WHEN I FIND HIM.

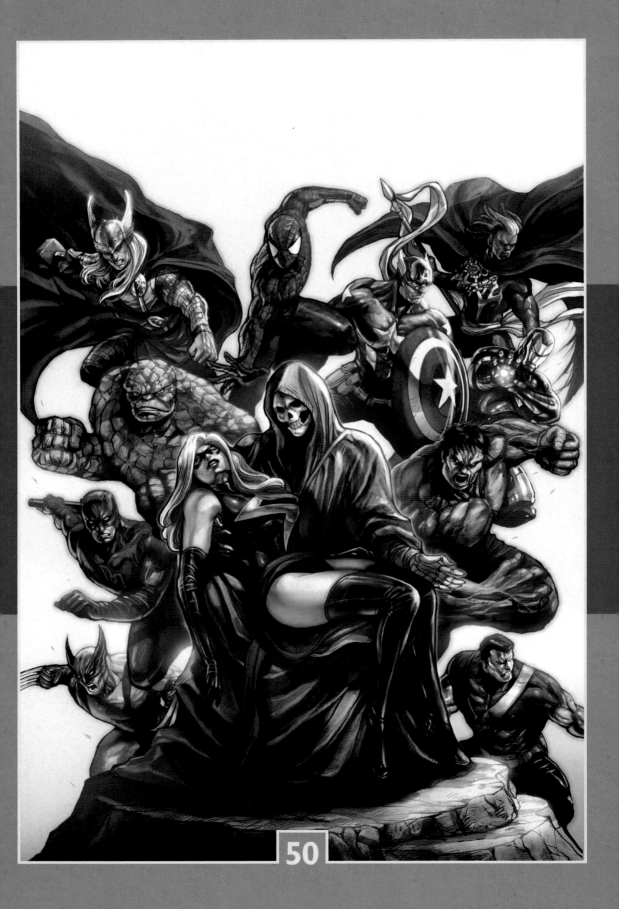

50

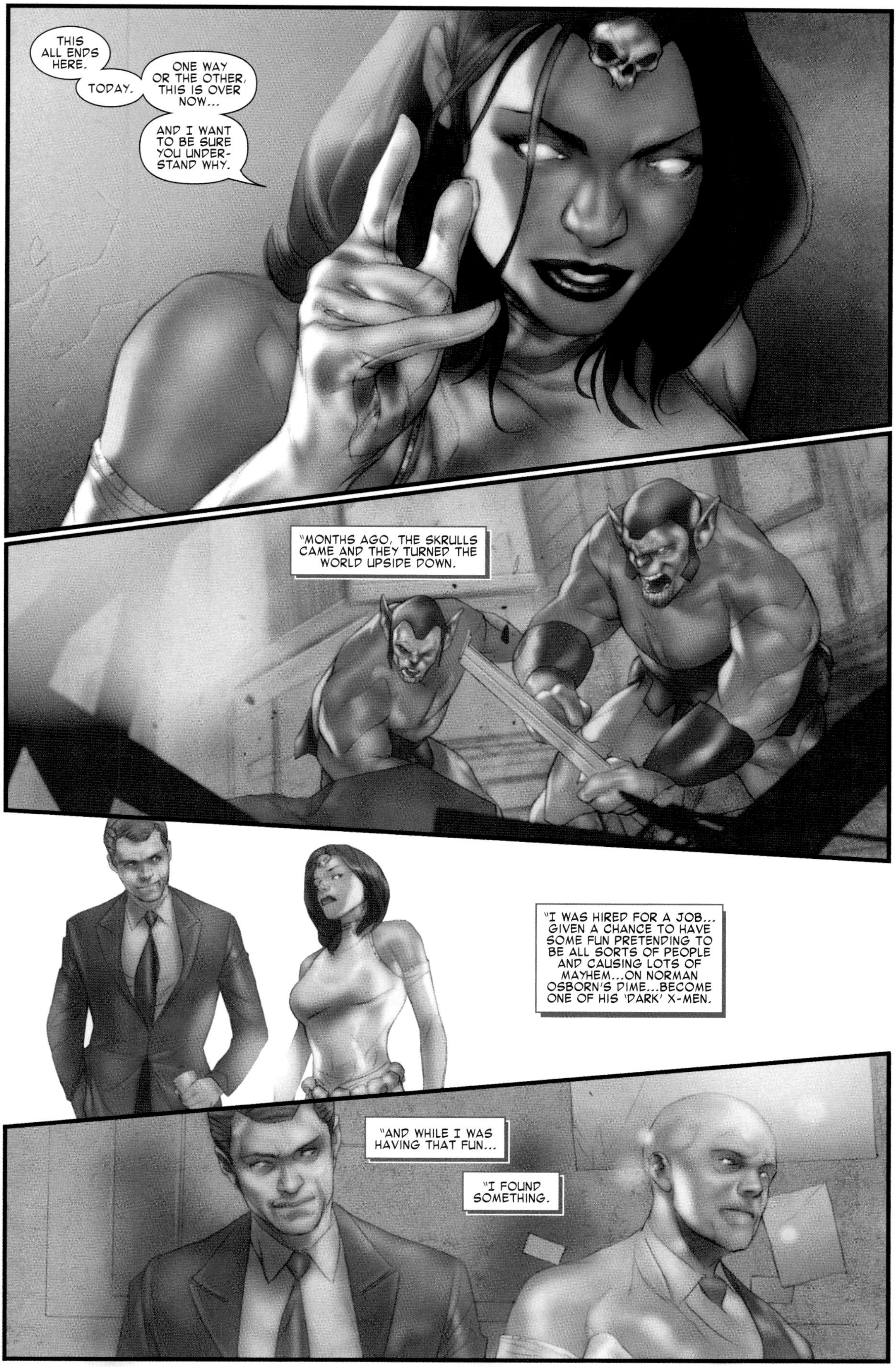
THIS ALL ENDS HERE.
TODAY.
ONE WAY OR THE OTHER, THIS IS OVER NOW...
AND I WANT TO BE SURE YOU UNDERSTAND WHY.
"MONTHS AGO, THE SKRULLS CAME AND THEY TURNED THE WORLD UPSIDE DOWN.
"I WAS HIRED FOR A JOB... GIVEN A CHANCE TO HAVE SOME FUN PRETENDING TO BE ALL SORTS OF PEOPLE AND CAUSING LOTS OF MAYHEM...ON NORMAN OSBORN'S DIME...BECOME ONE OF HIS 'DARK' X-MEN.
"AND WHILE I WAS HAVING THAT FUN...
"I FOUND SOMETHING.

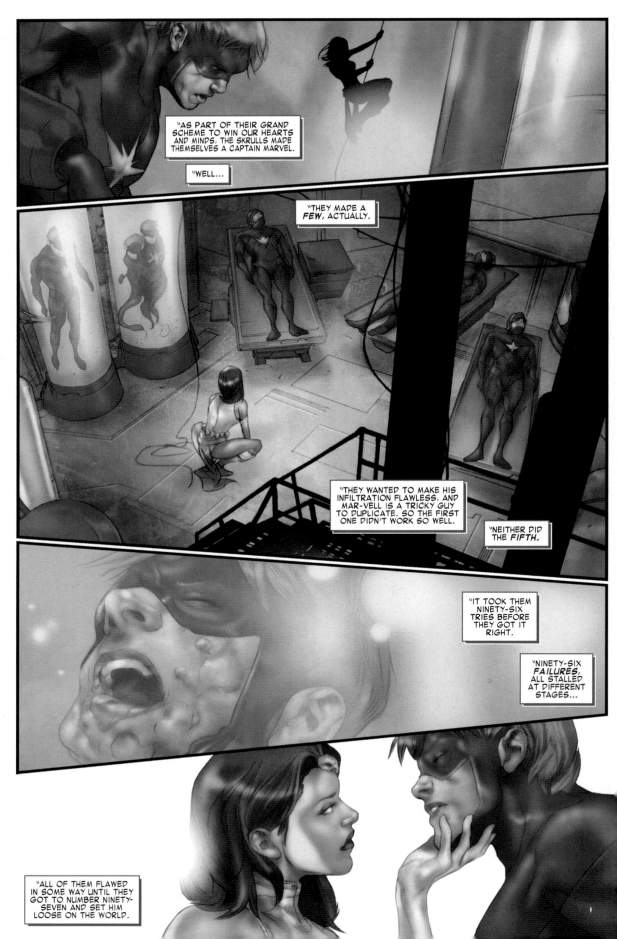

"AS PART OF THEIR GRAND SCHEME TO WIN OUR HEARTS AND MINDS, THE SKRULLS MADE THEMSELVES A CAPTAIN MARVEL.

"WELL...

"THEY MADE A *FEW*, ACTUALLY.

"THEY WANTED TO MAKE HIS INFILTRATION FLAWLESS, AND MAR-VELL IS A TRICKY GUY TO DUPLICATE. SO THE FIRST ONE DIDN'T WORK SO WELL.

"NEITHER DID THE *FIFTH*.

"IT TOOK THEM NINETY-SIX TRIES BEFORE THEY GOT IT RIGHT.

"NINETY-SIX *FAILURES*, ALL STALLED AT DIFFERENT STAGES...

"ALL OF THEM FLAWED IN SOME WAY UNTIL THEY GOT TO NUMBER NINETY-SEVEN AND SET HIM LOOSE ON THE WORLD.

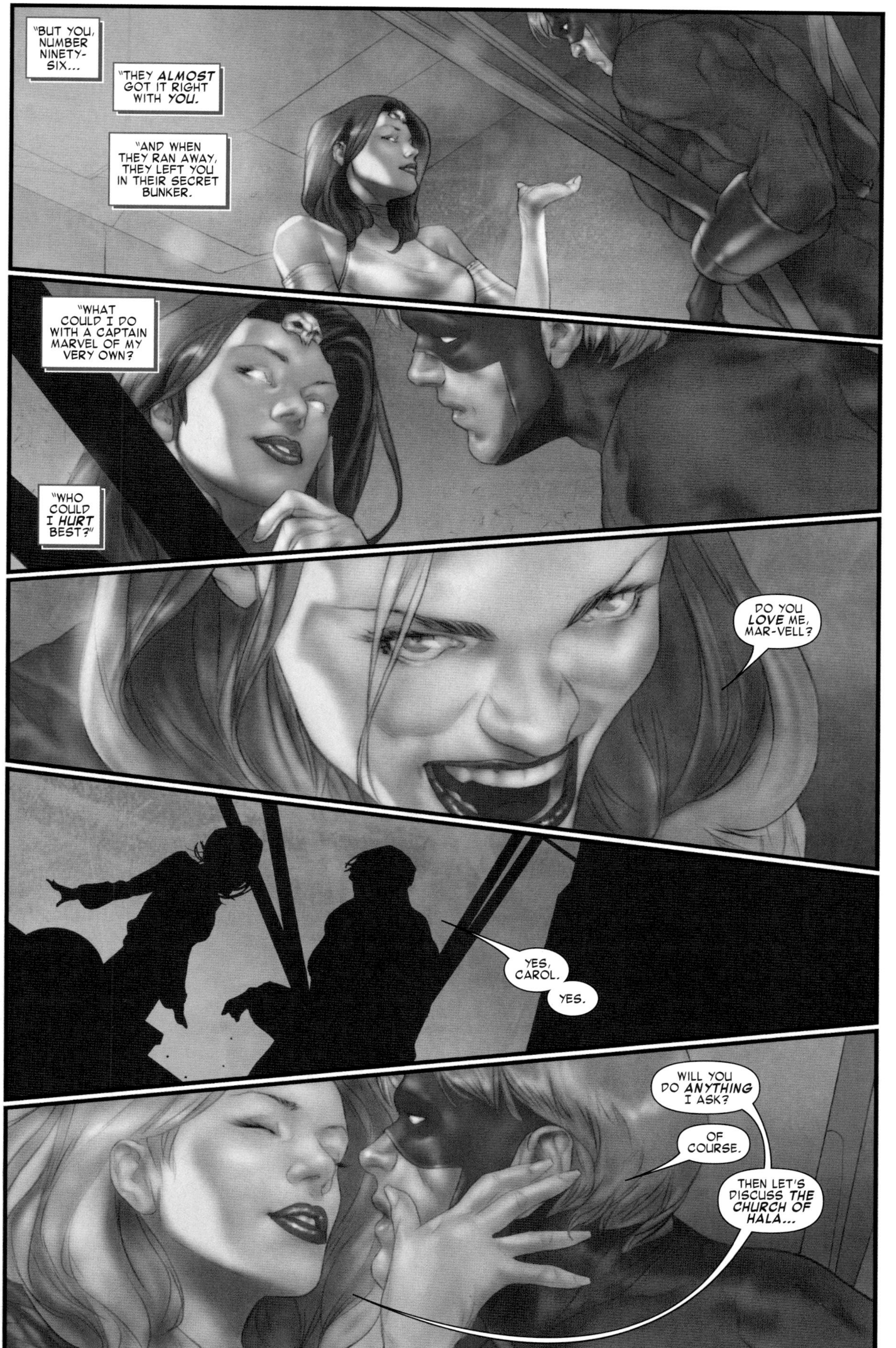
"BUT YOU, NUMBER NINETY-SIX...
"THEY *ALMOST* GOT IT RIGHT WITH *YOU.*
"AND WHEN THEY RAN AWAY, THEY LEFT YOU IN THEIR SECRET BUNKER.
"WHAT COULD I DO WITH A CAPTAIN MARVEL OF MY VERY OWN?
"WHO COULD I *HURT* BEST?"
DO YOU *LOVE* ME, MAR-VELL?
YES, CAROL.
YES.
WILL YOU DO *ANYTHING* I ASK?
OF COURSE.
THEN LET'S DISCUSS *THE CHURCH OF HALA...*

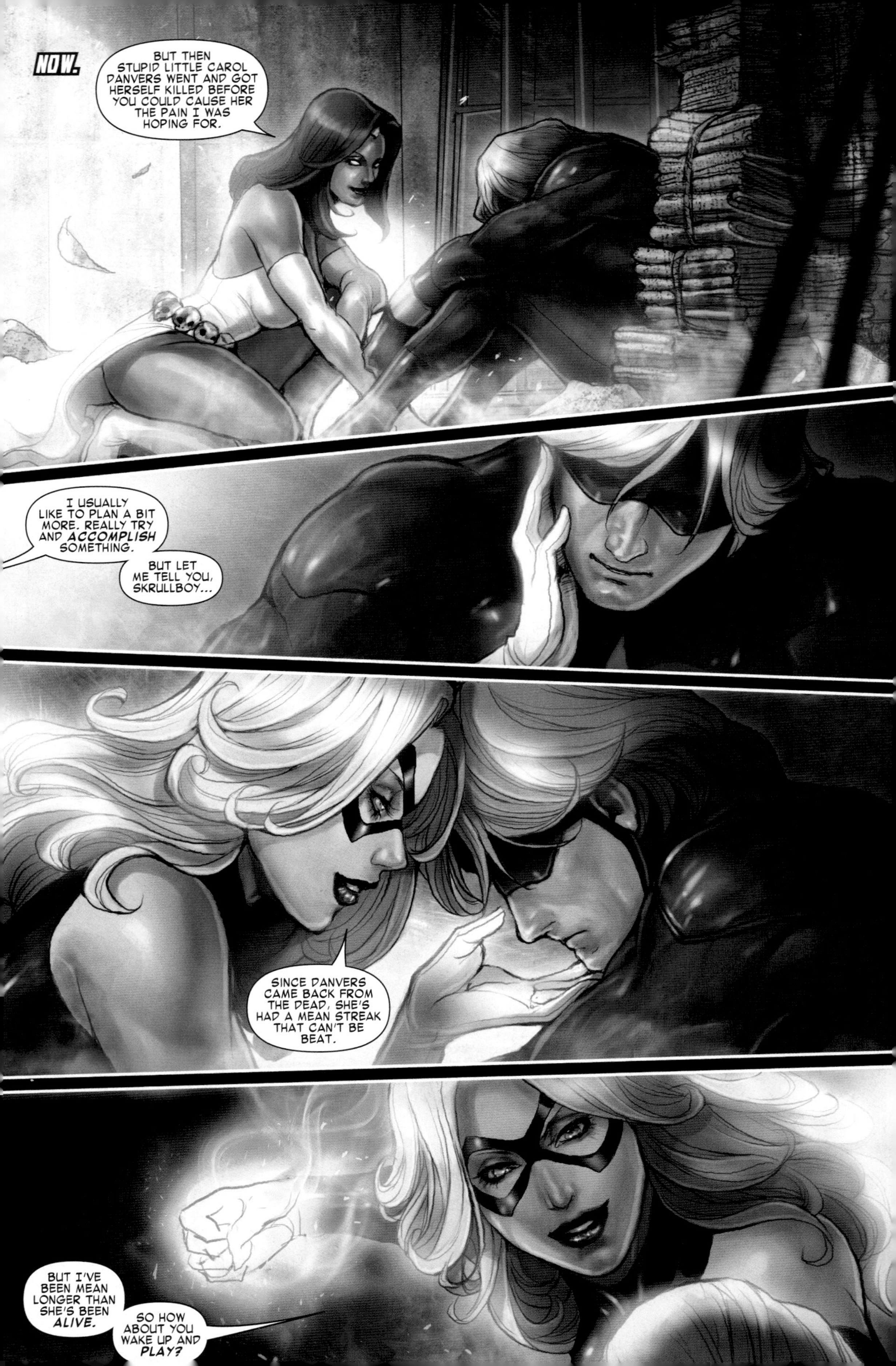
NOW.
BUT THEN STUPID LITTLE CAROL DANVERS WENT AND GOT HERSELF KILLED BEFORE YOU COULD CAUSE HER THE PAIN I WAS HOPING FOR.
I USUALLY LIKE TO PLAN A BIT MORE. REALLY TRY AND ACCOMPLISH SOMETHING.
BUT LET ME TELL YOU, SKRULLBOY...
SINCE DANVERS CAME BACK FROM THE DEAD, SHE'S HAD A MEAN STREAK THAT CAN'T BE BEAT.
BUT I'VE BEEN MEAN LONGER THAN SHE'S BEEN ALIVE.
SO HOW ABOUT YOU WAKE UP AND PLAY?

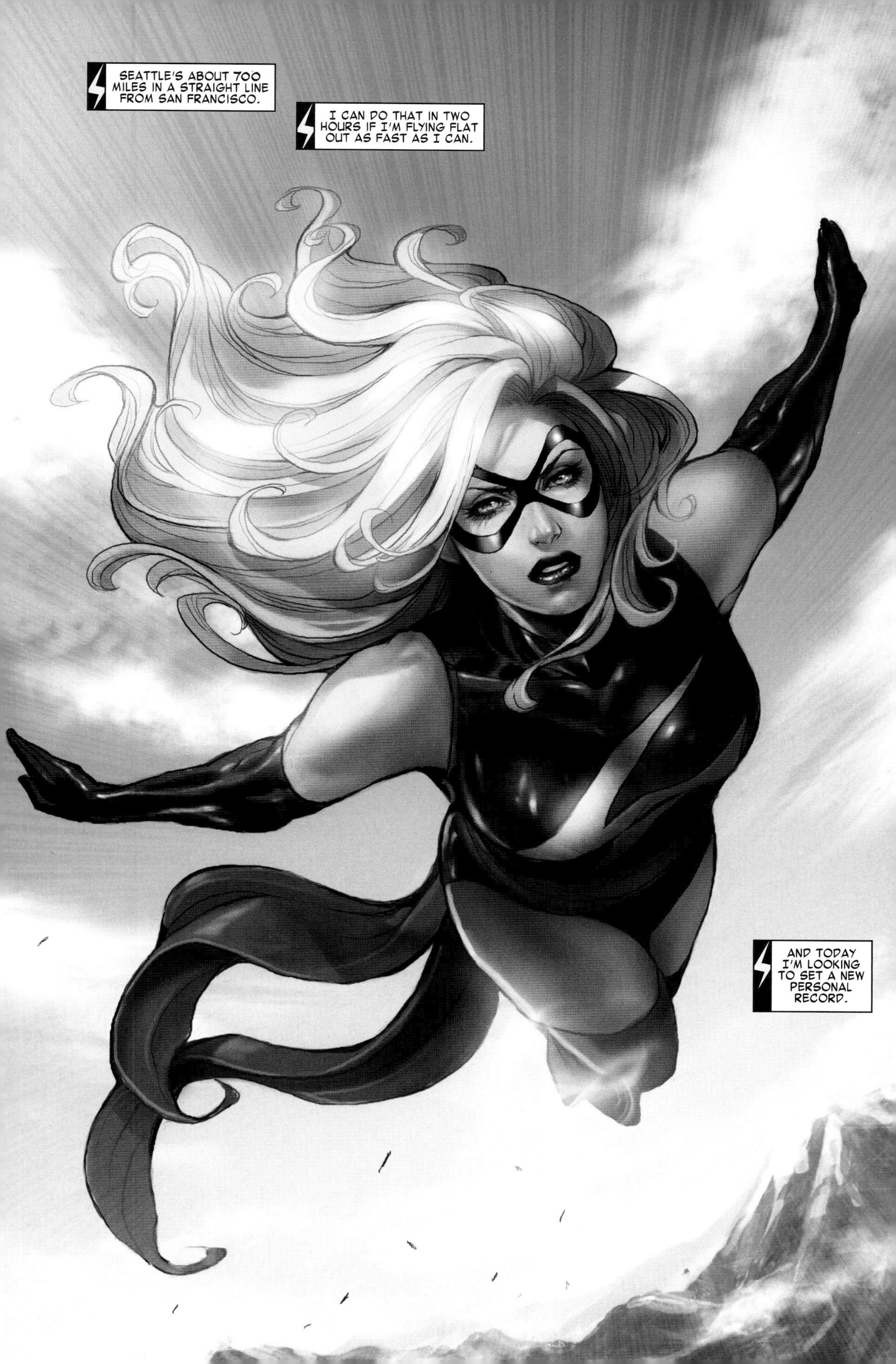
SEATTLE'S ABOUT 700 MILES IN A STRAIGHT LINE FROM SAN FRANCISCO.
I CAN DO THAT IN TWO HOURS IF I'M FLYING FLAT OUT AS FAST AS I CAN.
AND TODAY I'M LOOKING TO SET A NEW PERSONAL RECORD.

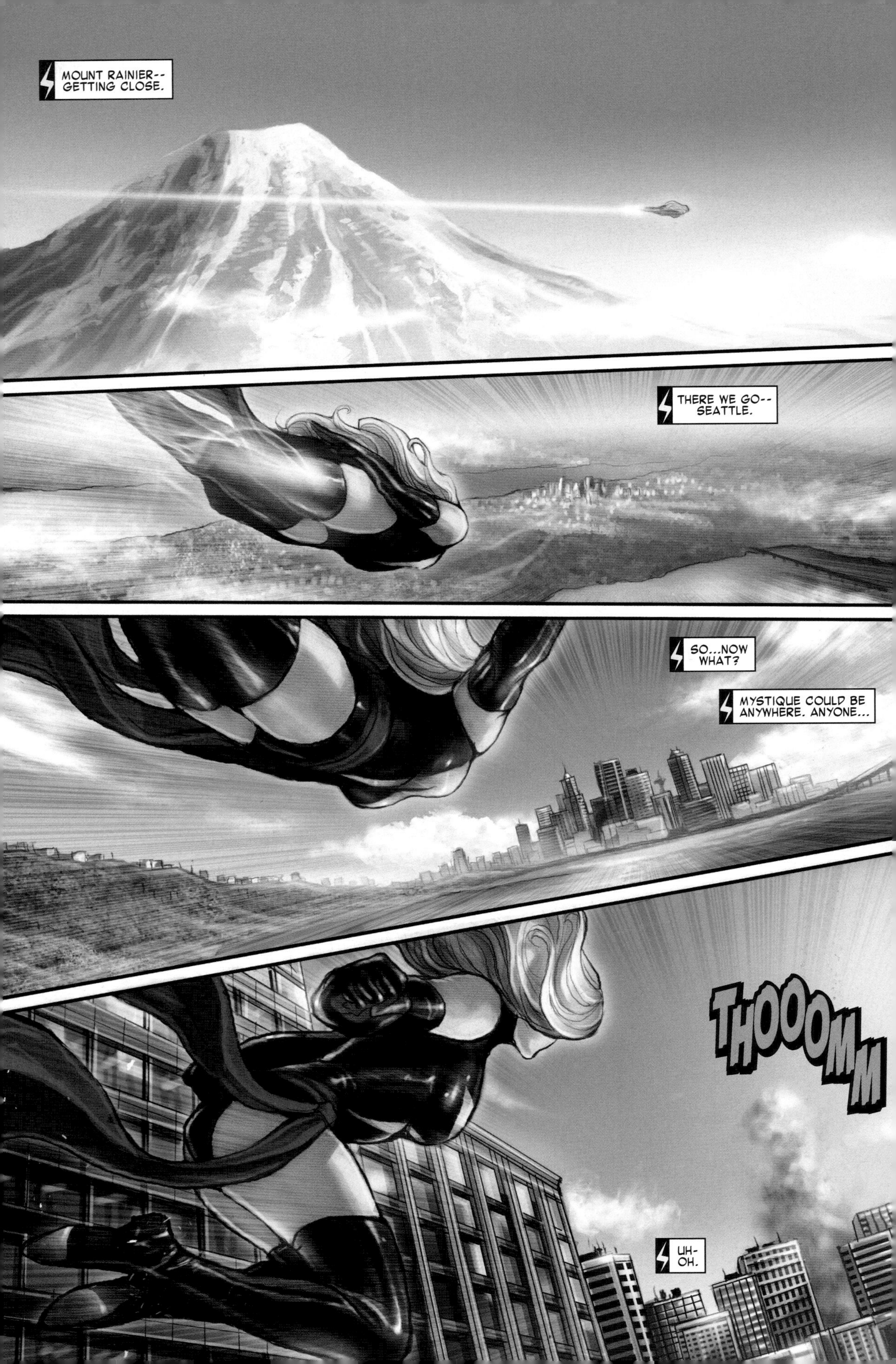
MOUNT RAINIER--
GETTING CLOSE.
THERE WE GO--
SEATTLE.
SO...NOW
WHAT?
MYSTIQUE COULD BE
ANYWHERE. ANYONE...
THOOOMMM
UH-
OH.

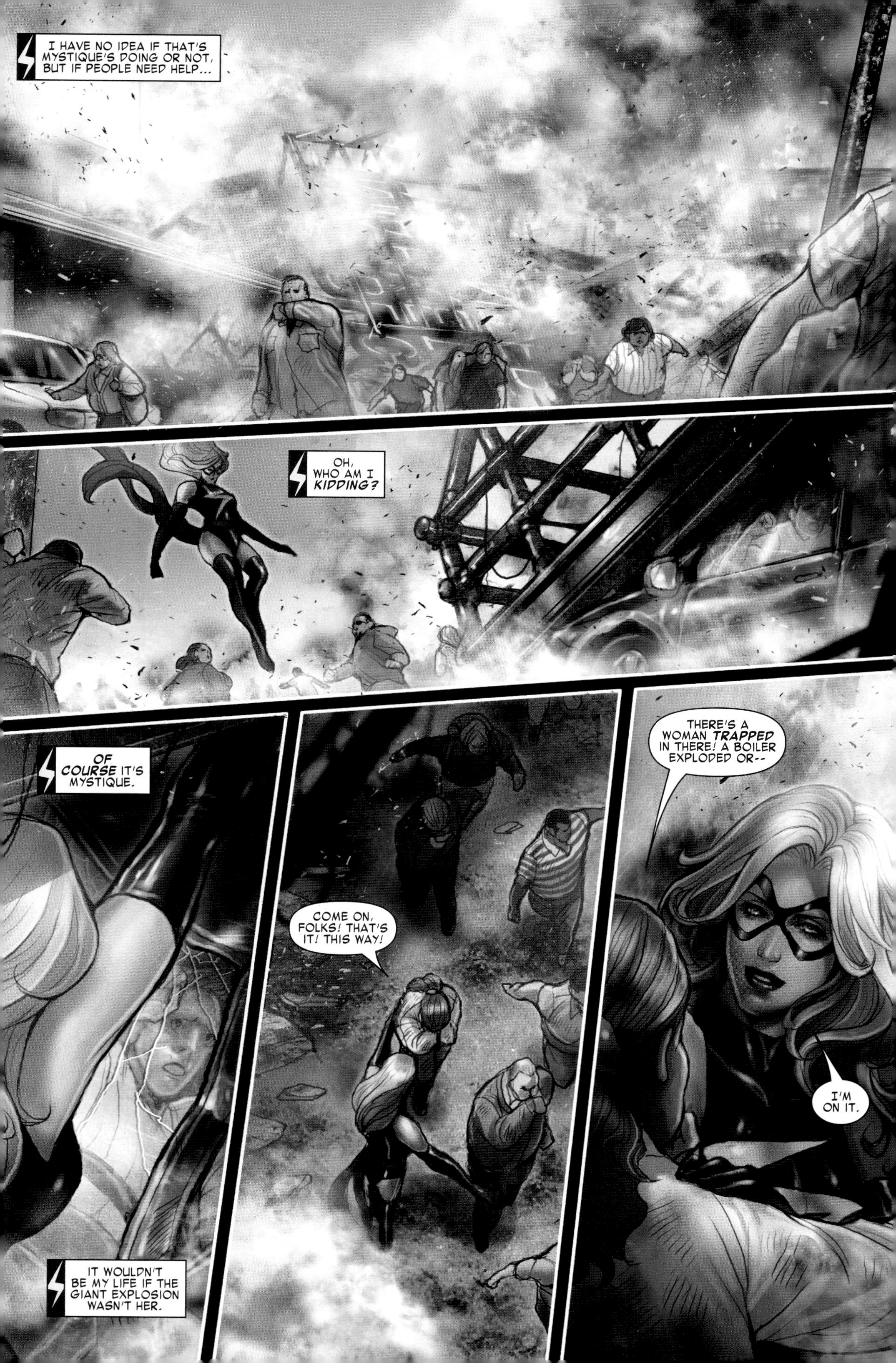
I HAVE NO IDEA IF THAT'S MYSTIQUE'S DOING OR NOT, BUT IF PEOPLE NEED HELP...
OH, WHO AM I *KIDDING?*
OF COURSE IT'S MYSTIQUE.
IT WOULDN'T BE MY LIFE IF THE GIANT EXPLOSION WASN'T HER.
COME ON, FOLKS! THAT'S IT! THIS WAY!
THERE'S A WOMAN ***TRAPPED*** IN THERE! A BOILER EXPLODED OR--
I'M ON IT.

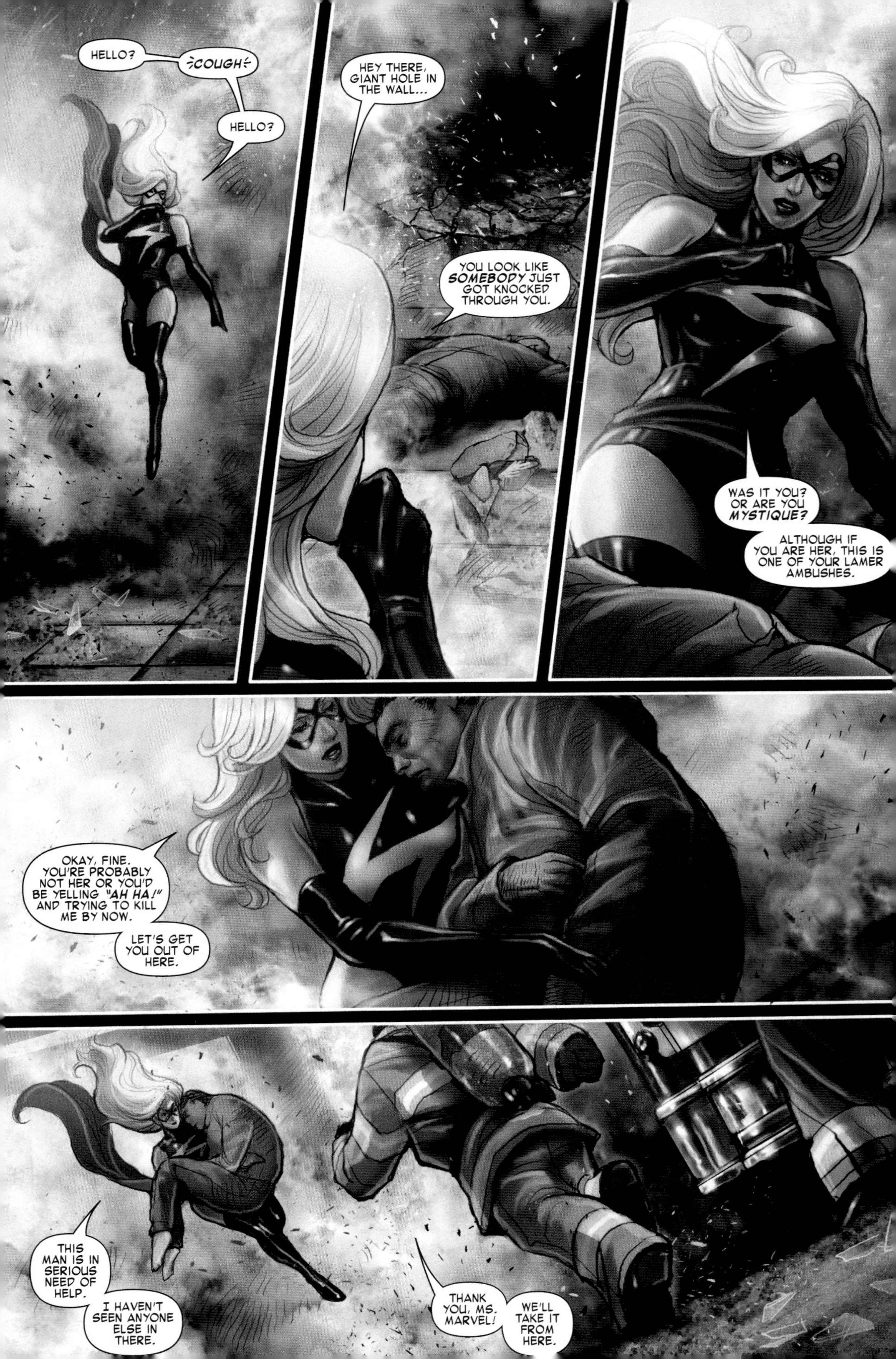
HELLO?
COUGH
HELLO?
HEY THERE, GIANT HOLE IN THE WALL...
YOU LOOK LIKE *SOMEBODY* JUST GOT KNOCKED THROUGH YOU.
WAS IT YOU? OR ARE YOU *MYSTIQUE?*
ALTHOUGH IF YOU ARE HER, THIS IS ONE OF YOUR LAMER AMBUSHES.
OKAY, FINE. YOU'RE PROBABLY NOT HER OR YOU'D BE YELLING *"AH HA!"* AND TRYING TO KILL ME BY NOW.
LET'S GET YOU OUT OF HERE.
THIS MAN IS IN SERIOUS NEED OF HELP.
I HAVEN'T SEEN ANYONE ELSE IN THERE.
THANK YOU, MS. MARVEL!
WE'LL TAKE IT FROM HERE.

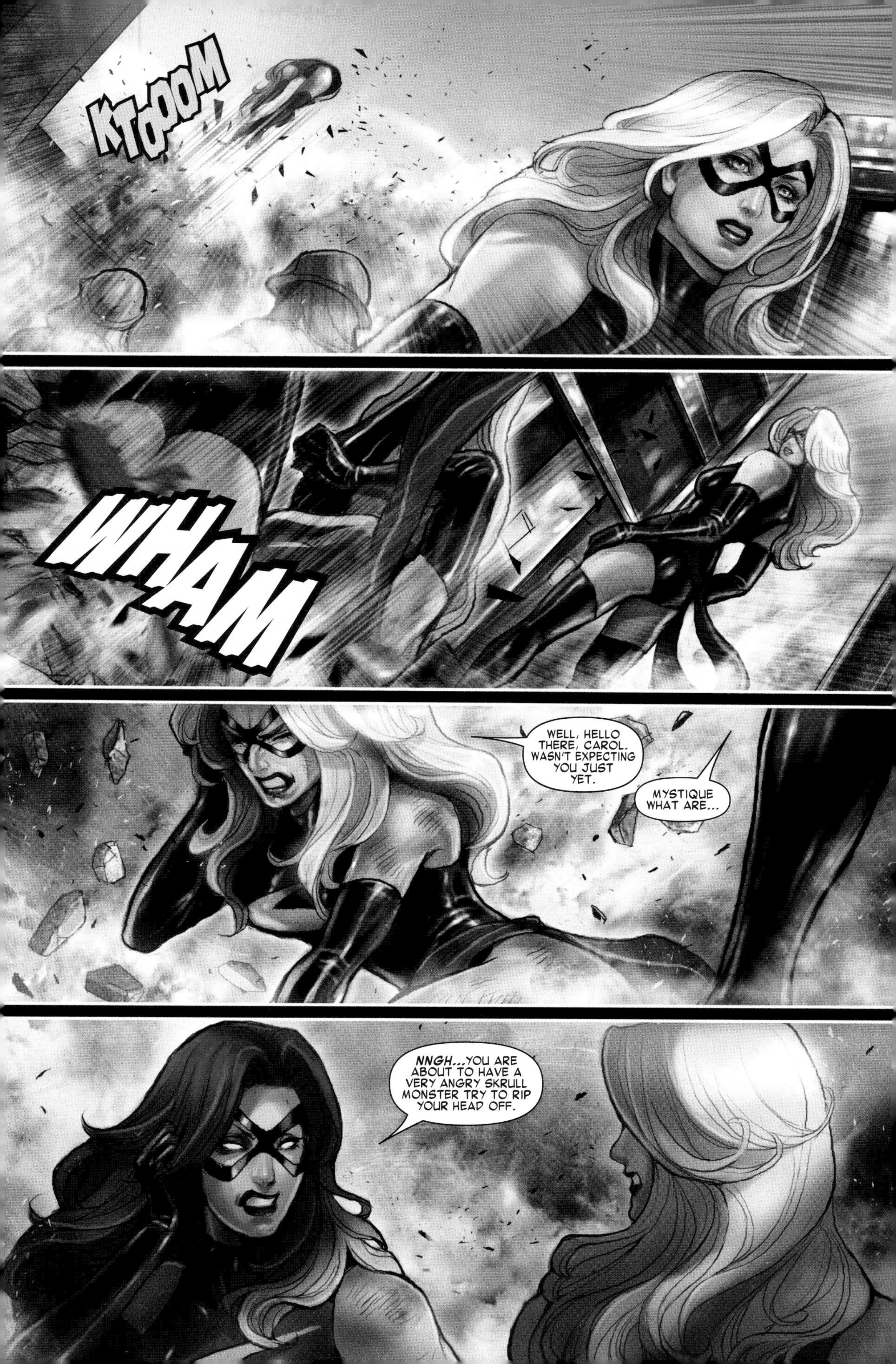
KTOOOM
WHAM
WELL, HELLO THERE, CAROL. WASN'T EXPECTING YOU JUST YET.
MYSTIQUE WHAT ARE...
NNGH...YOU ARE ABOUT TO HAVE A VERY ANGRY SKRULL MONSTER TRY TO RIP YOUR HEAD OFF.

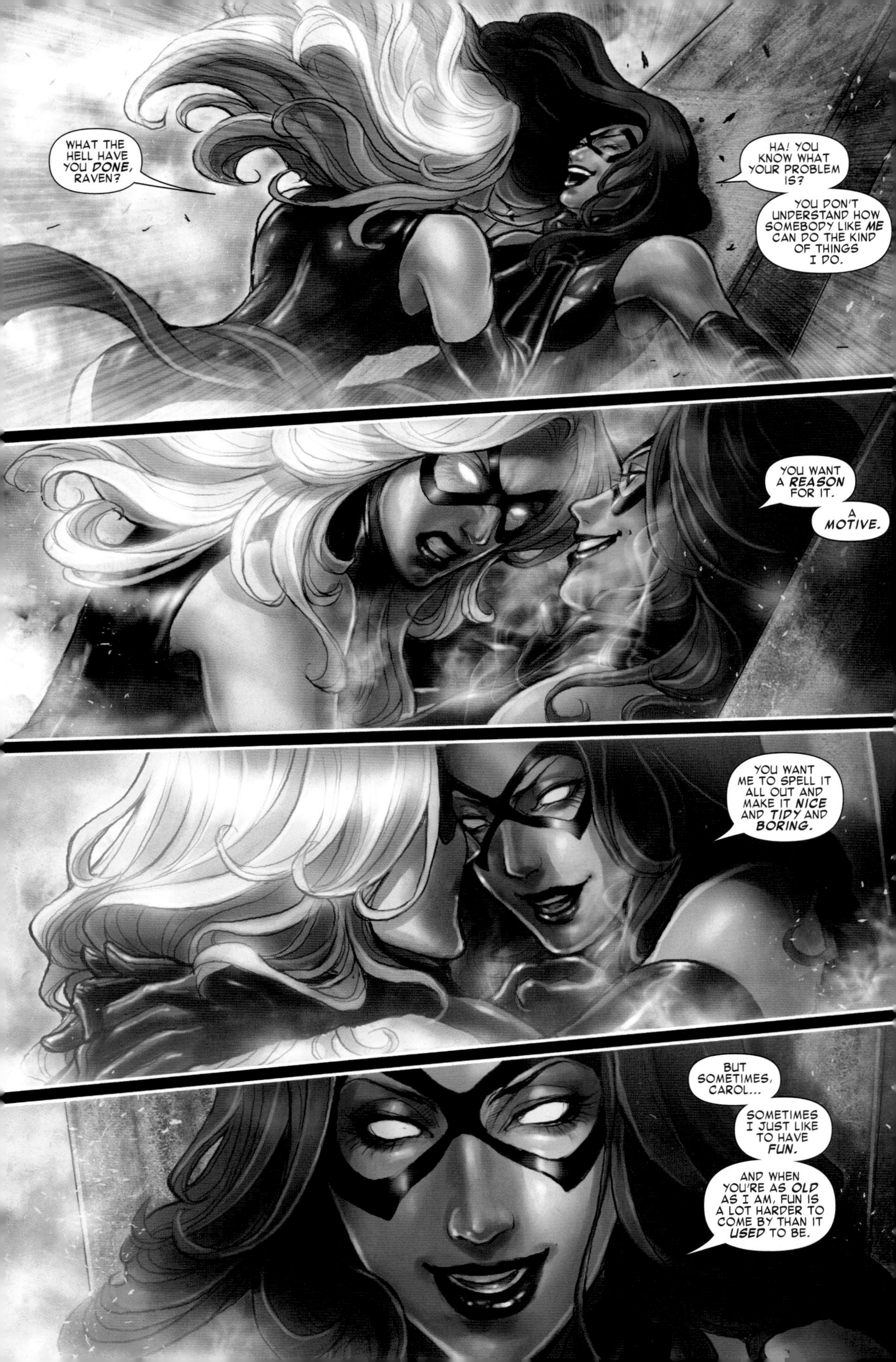
WHAT THE HELL HAVE YOU DONE, RAVEN?
HA! YOU KNOW WHAT YOUR PROBLEM IS?
YOU DON'T UNDERSTAND HOW SOMEBODY LIKE ME CAN DO THE KIND OF THINGS I DO.
YOU WANT A REASON FOR IT.
A MOTIVE.
YOU WANT ME TO SPELL IT ALL OUT AND MAKE IT NICE AND TIDY AND BORING.
BUT SOMETIMES, CAROL...
SOMETIMES I JUST LIKE TO HAVE FUN.
AND WHEN YOU'RE AS OLD AS I AM, FUN IS A LOT HARDER TO COME BY THAN IT USED TO BE.

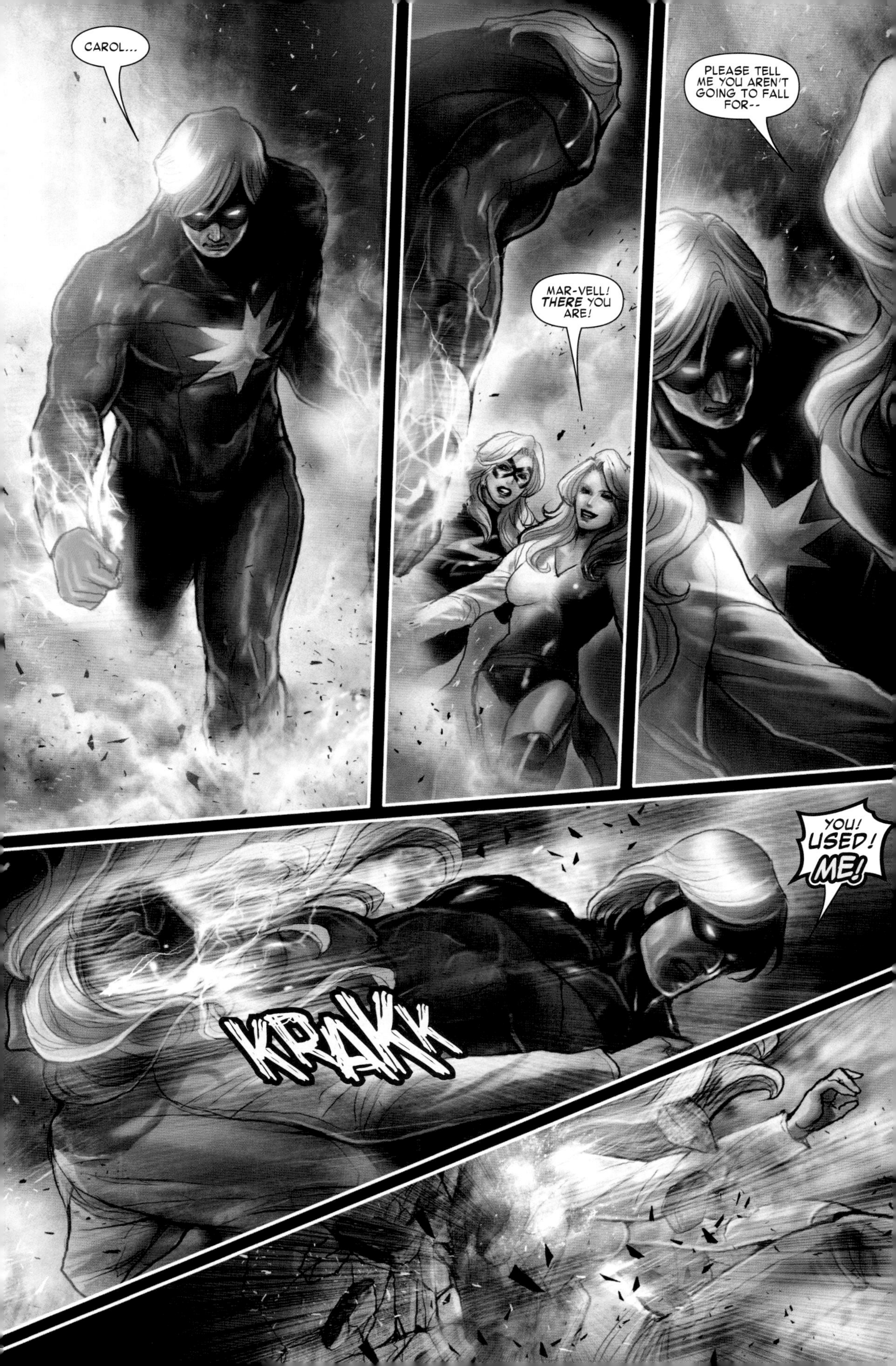

CAROL...
MAR-VELL! THERE YOU ARE!
PLEASE TELL ME YOU AREN'T GOING TO FALL FOR--
YOU! USED! ME!
KRAKK

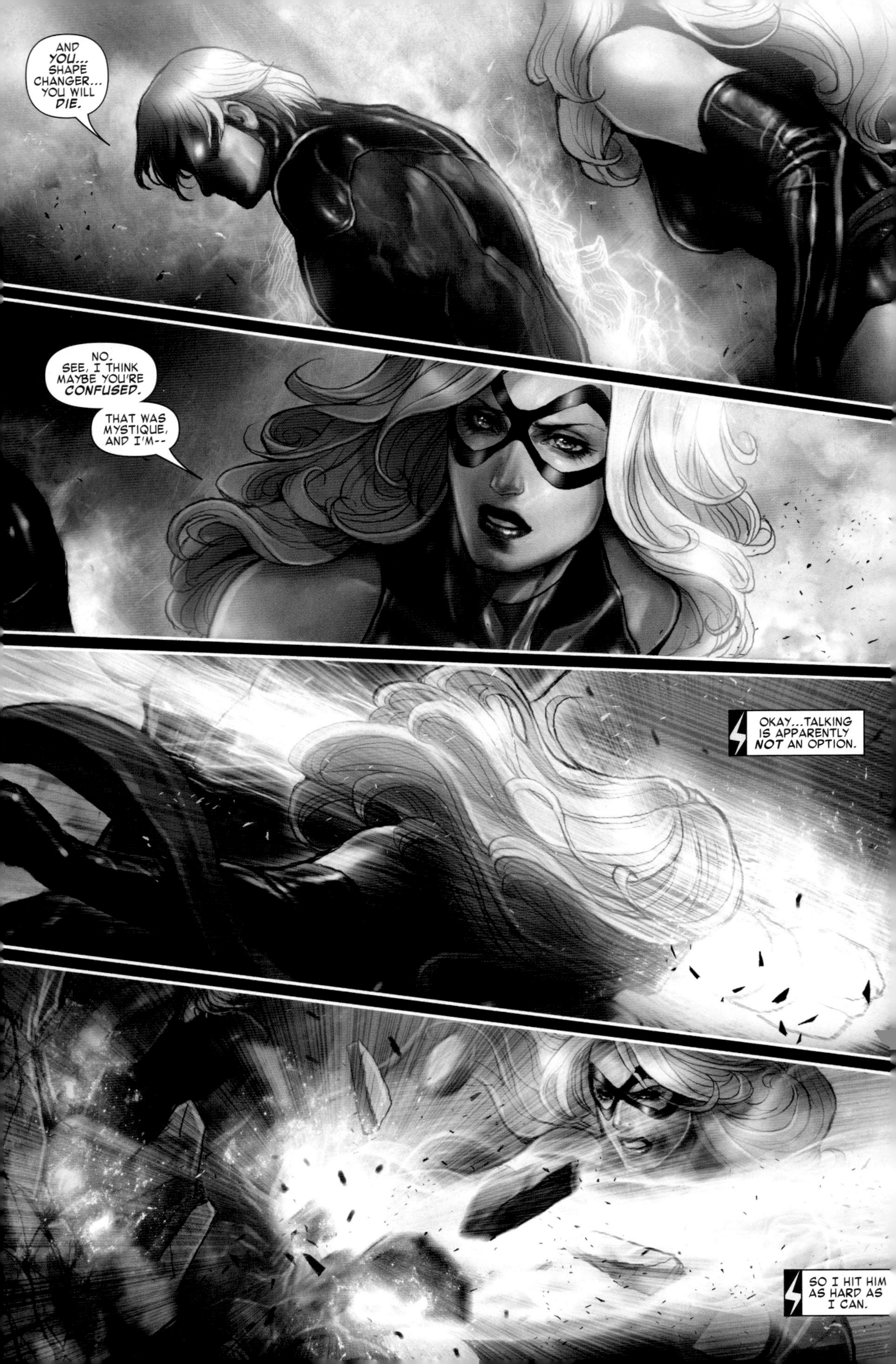
AND YOU... SHAPE CHANGER... YOU WILL DIE.
NO. SEE, I THINK MAYBE YOU'RE CONFUSED.
THAT WAS MYSTIQUE, AND I'M--
OKAY...TALKING IS APPARENTLY NOT AN OPTION.
SO I HIT HIM AS HARD AS I CAN.

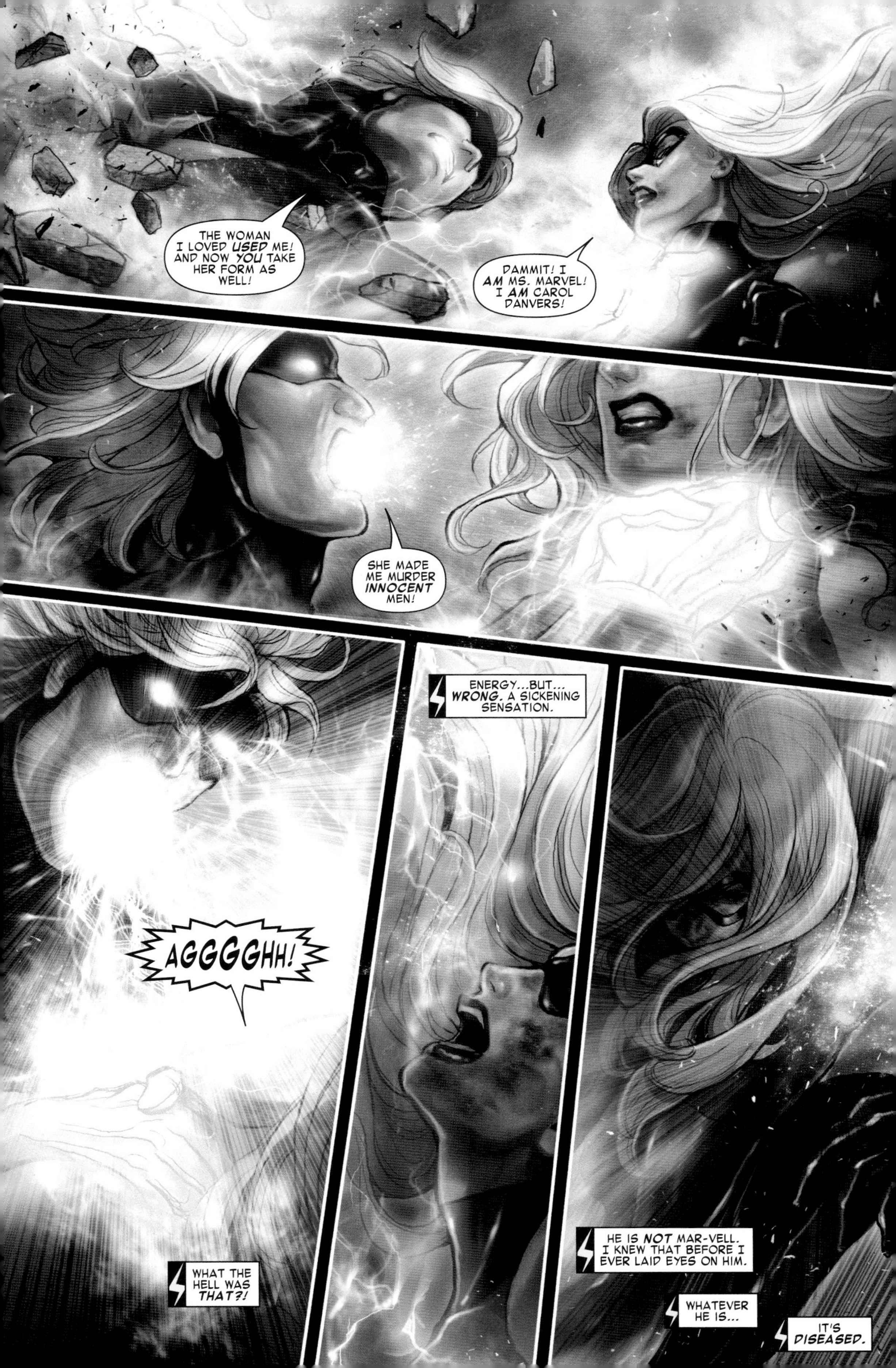
THE WOMAN I LOVED USED ME! AND NOW YOU TAKE HER FORM AS WELL!
DAMMIT! I AM MS. MARVEL! I AM CAROL DANVERS!
SHE MADE ME MURDER INNOCENT MEN!
AGGGGHH!
WHAT THE HELL WAS THAT?!
ENERGY...BUT... WRONG. A SICKENING SENSATION.
HE IS NOT MAR-VELL. I KNEW THAT BEFORE I EVER LAID EYES ON HIM.
WHATEVER HE IS...
IT'S DISEASED.

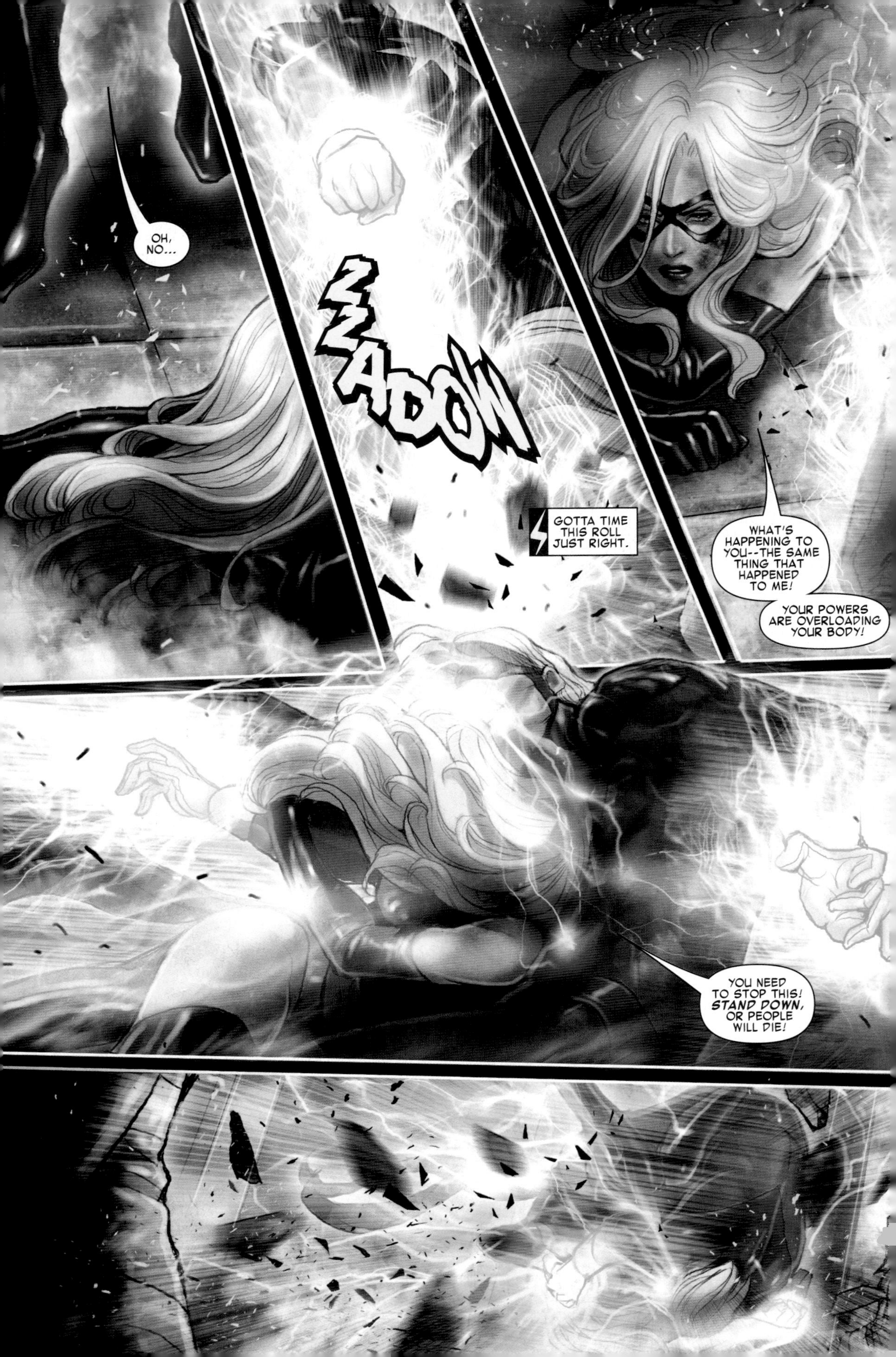
OH, NO...
ZZADOW
GOTTA TIME THIS ROLL JUST RIGHT.
WHAT'S HAPPENING TO YOU--THE SAME THING THAT HAPPENED TO ME!
YOUR POWERS ARE OVERLOADING YOUR BODY!
YOU NEED TO STOP THIS! STAND DOWN, OR PEOPLE WILL DIE!

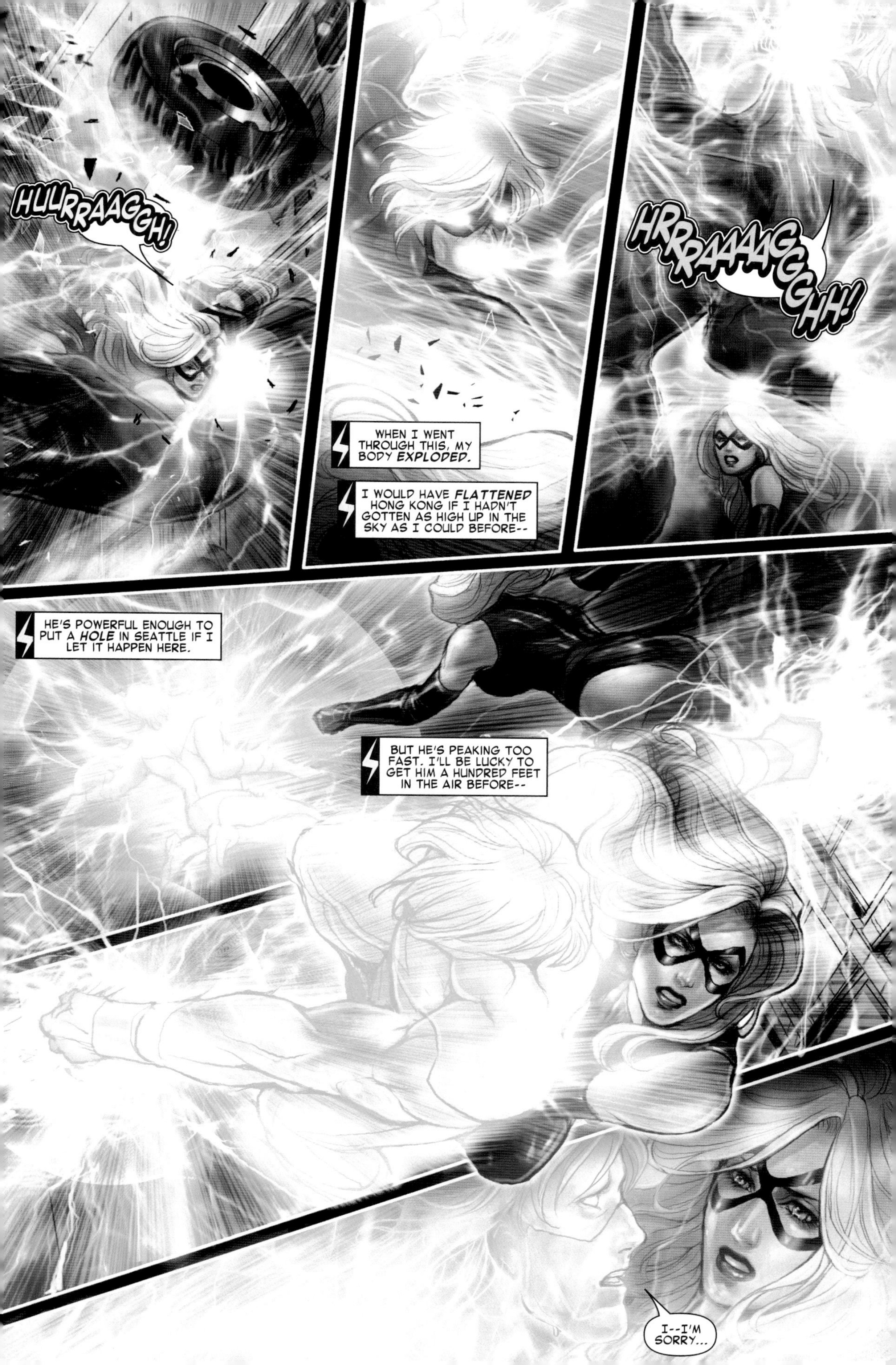
HUURRAAGGH!
WHEN I WENT THROUGH THIS, MY BODY EXPLODED.
I WOULD HAVE FLATTENED HONG KONG IF I HADN'T GOTTEN AS HIGH UP IN THE SKY AS I COULD BEFORE--
HRRRAAAAAGGGHH!
HE'S POWERFUL ENOUGH TO PUT A HOLE IN SEATTLE IF I LET IT HAPPEN HERE.
BUT HE'S PEAKING TOO FAST. I'LL BE LUCKY TO GET HIM A HUNDRED FEET IN THE AIR BEFORE--
I--I'M SORRY...

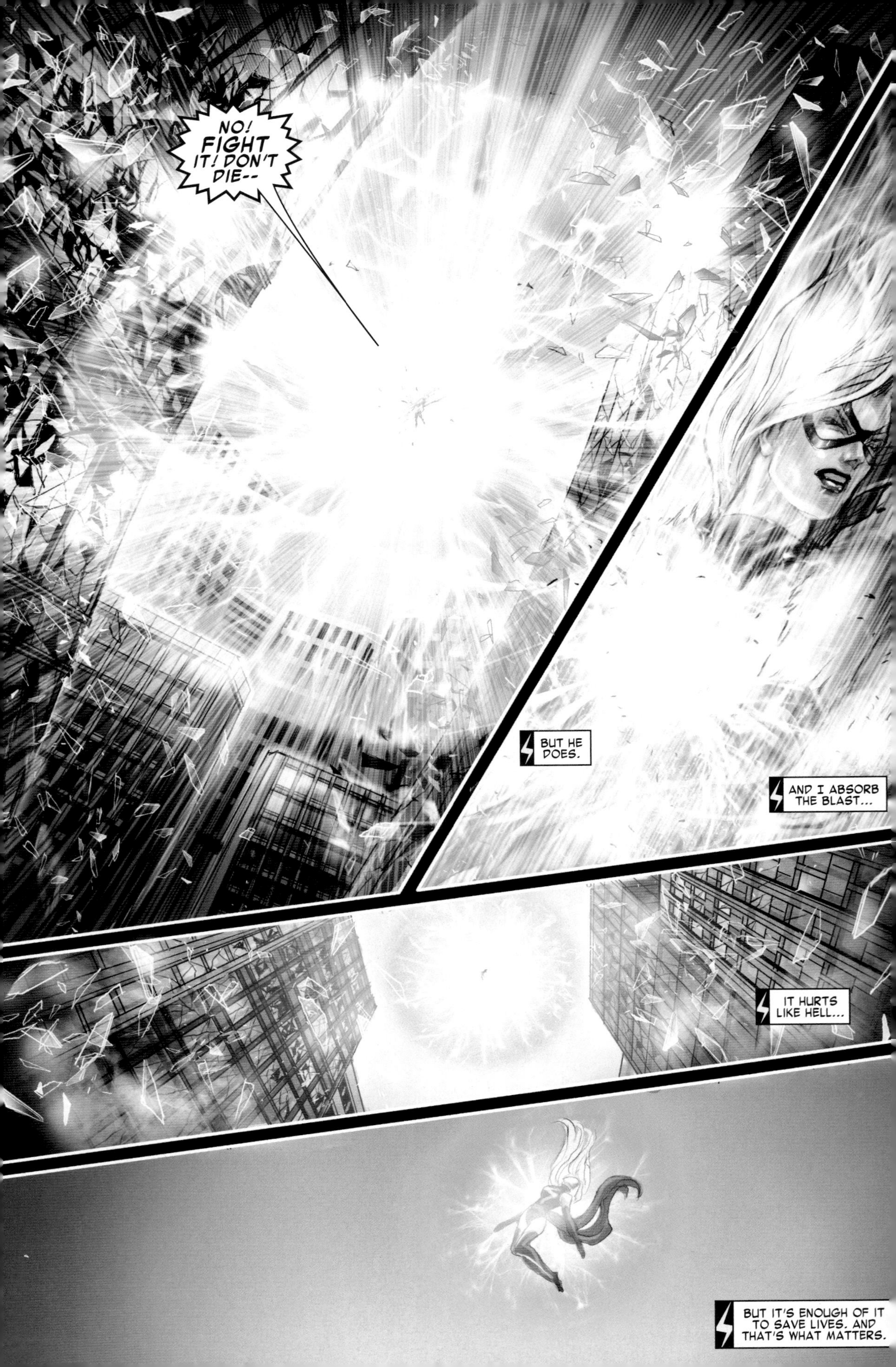
NO! FIGHT IT! DON'T DIE--
BUT HE DOES.
AND I ABSORB THE BLAST...
IT HURTS LIKE HELL...
BUT IT'S ENOUGH OF IT TO SAVE LIVES. AND THAT'S WHAT MATTERS.

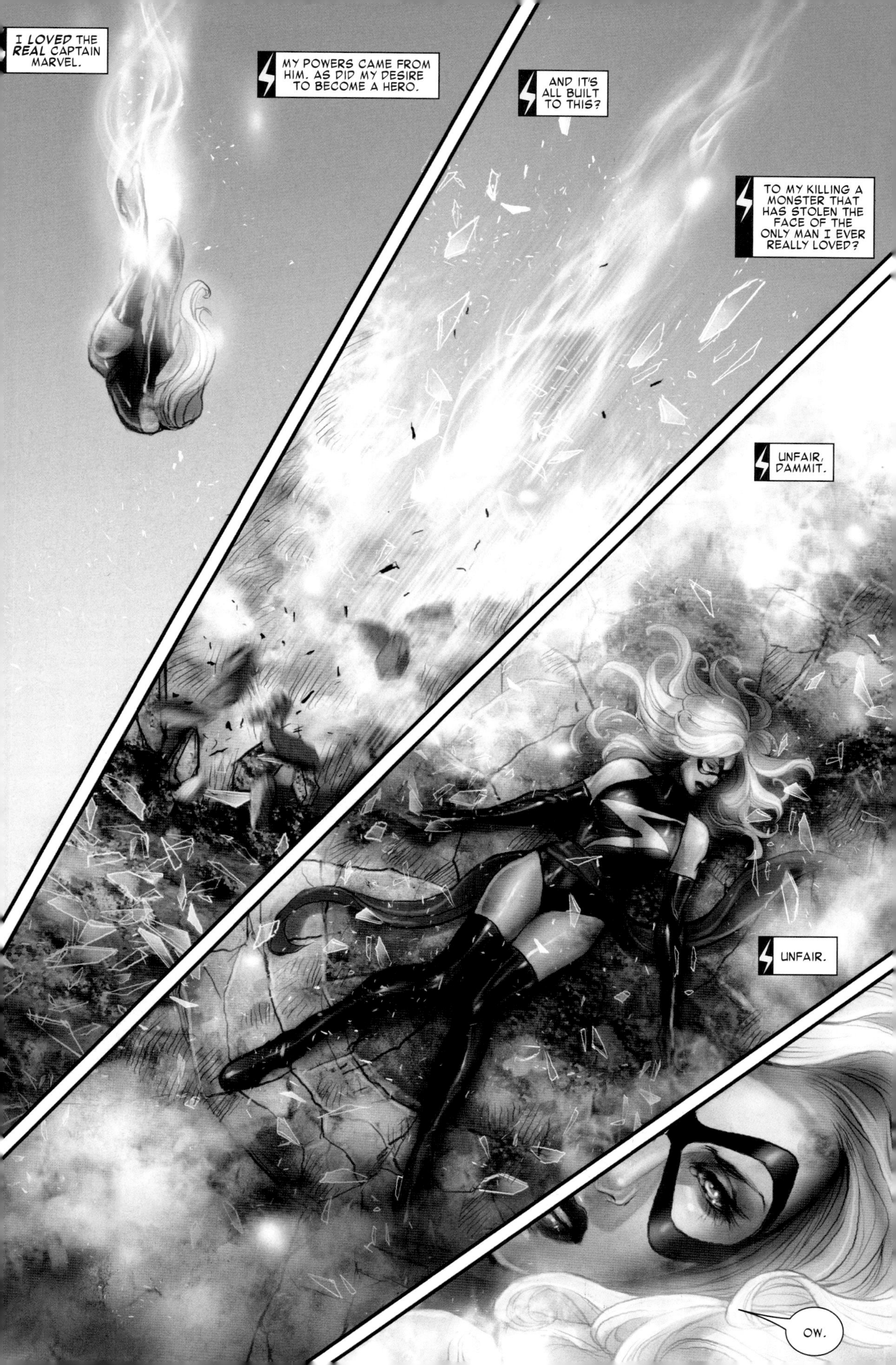
I LOVED THE REAL CAPTAIN MARVEL.
MY POWERS CAME FROM HIM. AS DID MY DESIRE TO BECOME A HERO.
AND IT'S ALL BUILT TO THIS?
TO MY KILLING A MONSTER THAT HAS STOLEN THE FACE OF THE ONLY MAN I EVER REALLY LOVED?
UNFAIR, DAMMIT.
UNFAIR.
OW.

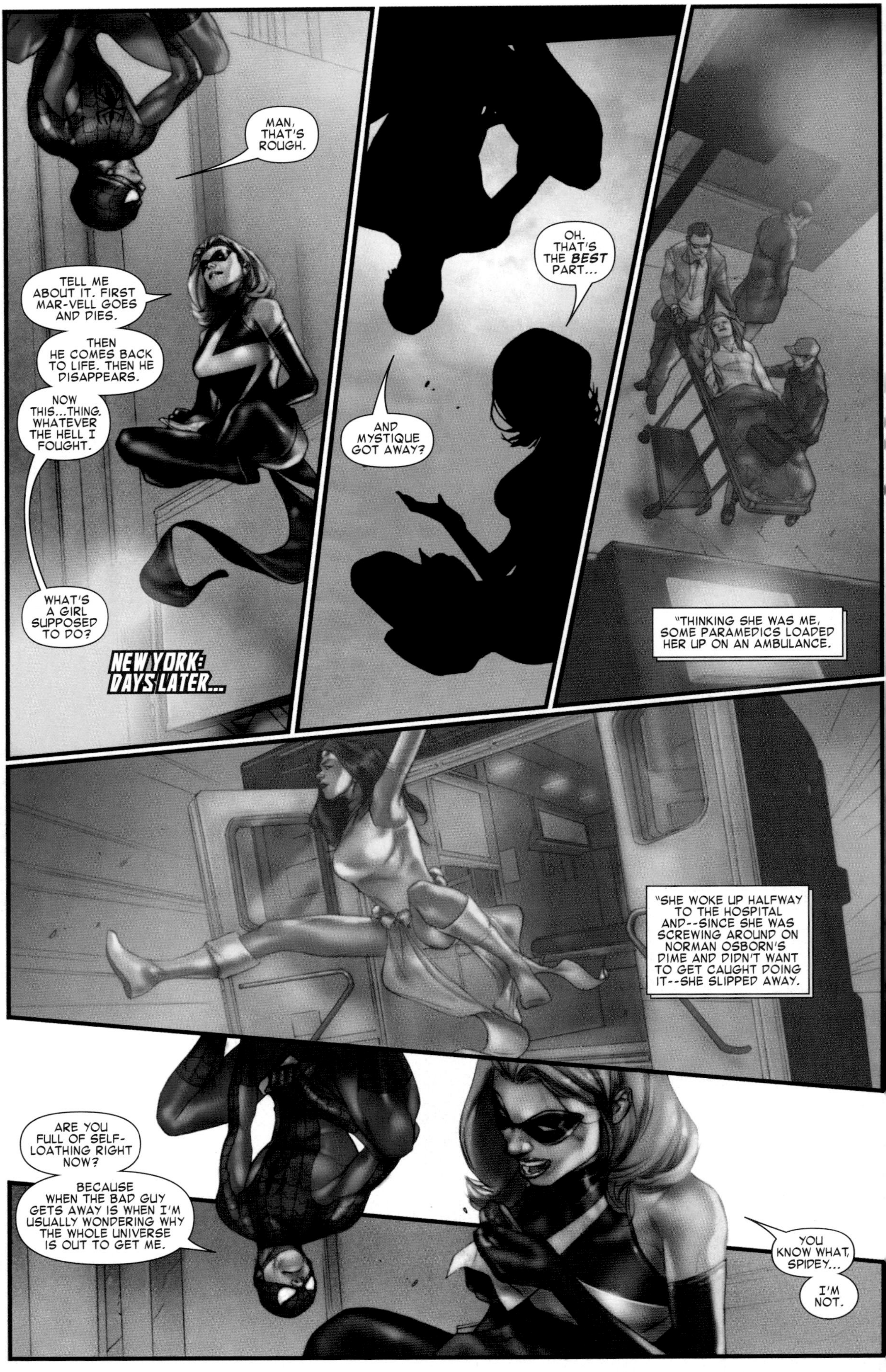
MAN, THAT'S ROUGH.
TELL ME ABOUT IT. FIRST MAR-VELL GOES AND DIES.
THEN HE COMES BACK TO LIFE. THEN HE DISAPPEARS.
NOW THIS...THING. WHATEVER THE HELL I FOUGHT.
WHAT'S A GIRL SUPPOSED TO DO?
NEW YORK: DAYS LATER...
AND MYSTIQUE GOT AWAY?
OH. THAT'S THE BEST PART...
"THINKING SHE WAS ME, SOME PARAMEDICS LOADED HER UP ON AN AMBULANCE.
"SHE WOKE UP HALFWAY TO THE HOSPITAL AND--SINCE SHE WAS SCREWING AROUND ON NORMAN OSBORN'S DIME AND DIDN'T WANT TO GET CAUGHT DOING IT--SHE SLIPPED AWAY.
ARE YOU FULL OF SELF-LOATHING RIGHT NOW?
BECAUSE WHEN THE BAD GUY GETS AWAY IS WHEN I'M USUALLY WONDERING WHY THE WHOLE UNIVERSE IS OUT TO GET ME.
YOU KNOW WHAT, SPIDEY...
I'M NOT.

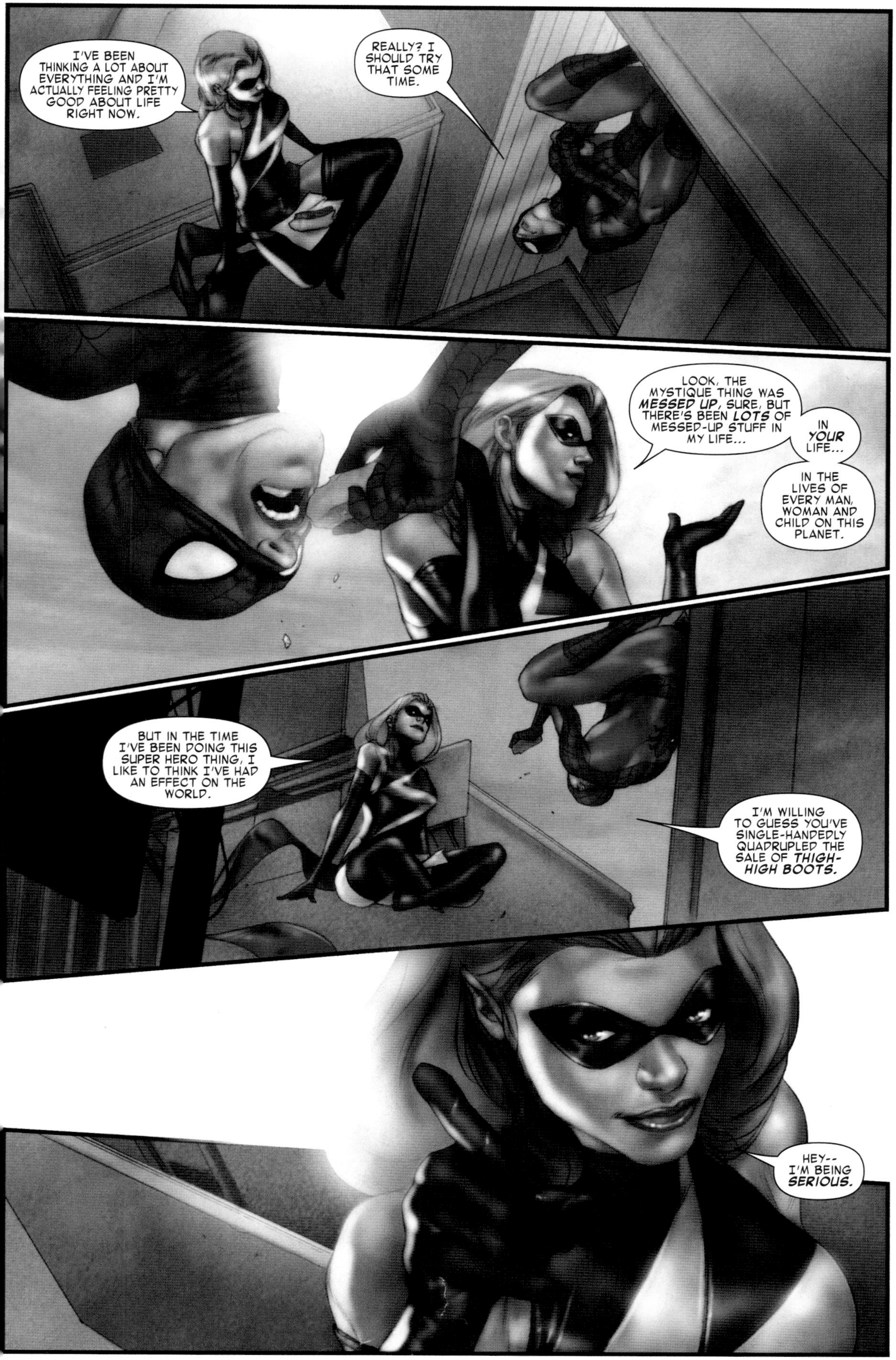
I'VE BEEN THINKING A LOT ABOUT EVERYTHING AND I'M ACTUALLY FEELING PRETTY GOOD ABOUT LIFE RIGHT NOW.
REALLY? I SHOULD TRY THAT SOME TIME.
LOOK, THE MYSTIQUE THING WAS ***MESSED UP***, SURE, BUT THERE'S BEEN ***LOTS*** OF MESSED-UP STUFF IN MY LIFE...
IN ***YOUR*** LIFE...
IN THE LIVES OF EVERY MAN, WOMAN AND CHILD ON THIS PLANET.
BUT IN THE TIME I'VE BEEN DOING THIS SUPER HERO THING, I LIKE TO THINK I'VE HAD AN EFFECT ON THE WORLD.
I'M WILLING TO GUESS YOU'VE SINGLE-HANDEDLY QUADRUPLED THE SALE OF ***THIGH-HIGH BOOTS.***
HEY-- I'M BEING ***SERIOUS.***

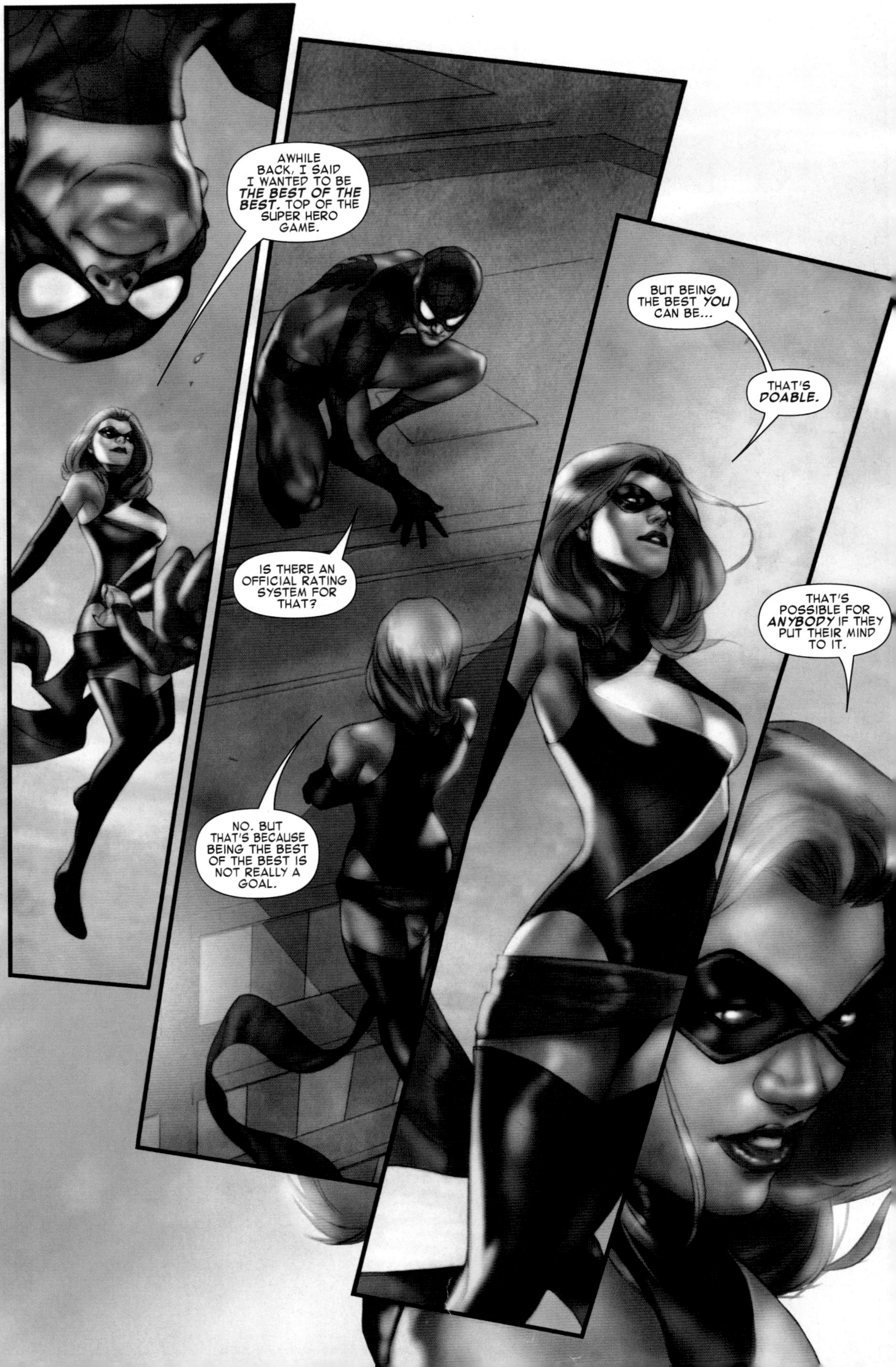

AWHILE BACK, I SAID I WANTED TO BE *THE BEST OF THE BEST.* TOP OF THE SUPER HERO GAME.
IS THERE AN OFFICIAL RATING SYSTEM FOR THAT?
NO. BUT THAT'S BECAUSE BEING THE BEST OF THE BEST IS NOT REALLY A GOAL.
BUT BEING THE BEST *YOU* CAN BE...
THAT'S *DOABLE.*
THAT'S POSSIBLE FOR *ANYBODY* IF THEY PUT THEIR MIND TO IT.

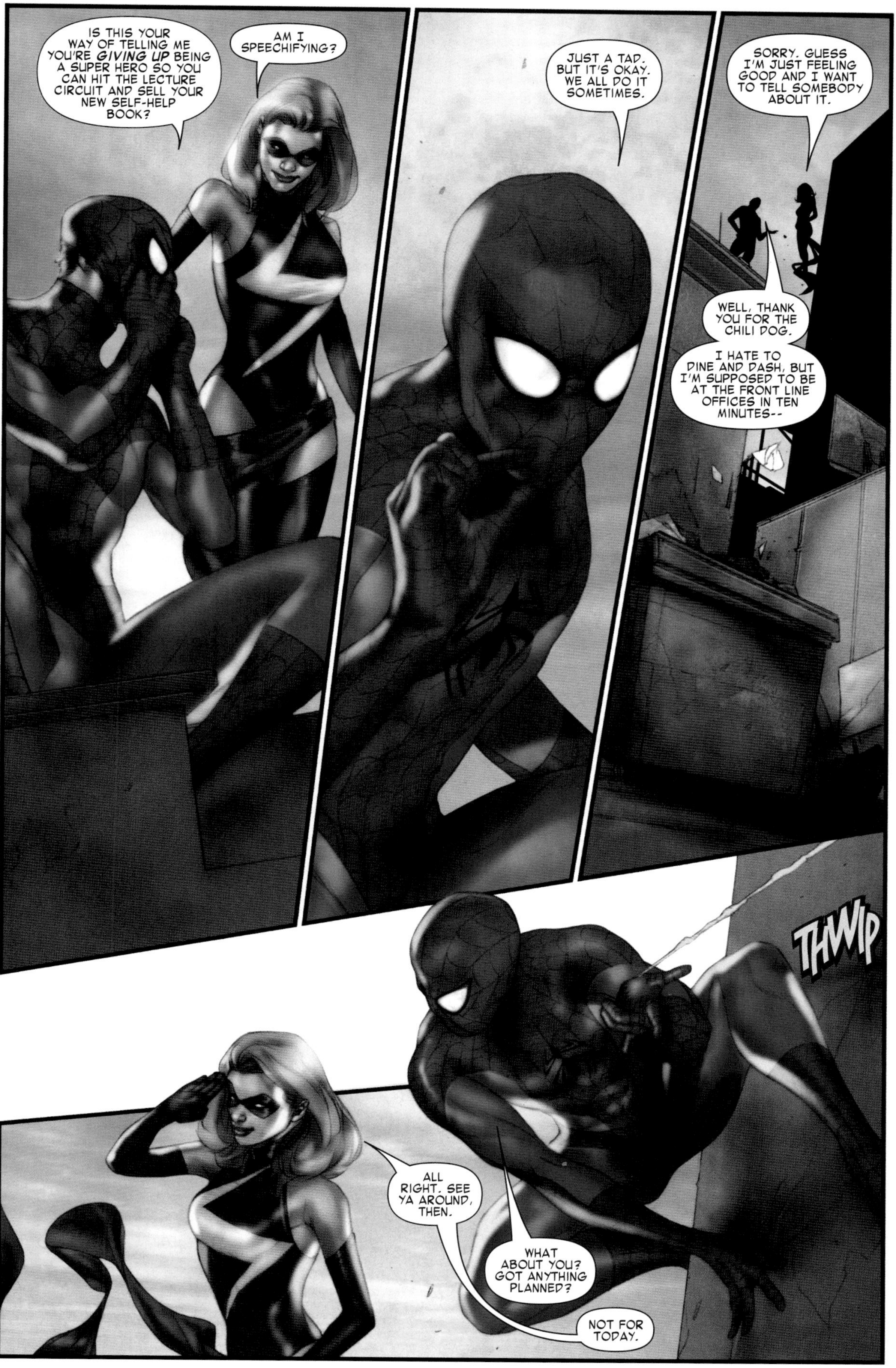
IS THIS YOUR WAY OF TELLING ME YOU'RE *GIVING UP* BEING A SUPER HERO SO YOU CAN HIT THE LECTURE CIRCUIT AND SELL YOUR NEW SELF-HELP BOOK?
AM I SPEECHIFYING?
JUST A TAD. BUT IT'S OKAY. WE ALL DO IT SOMETIMES.
SORRY. GUESS I'M JUST FEELING GOOD AND I WANT TO TELL SOMEBODY ABOUT IT.
WELL, THANK YOU FOR THE CHILI DOG.
I HATE TO DINE AND DASH, BUT I'M SUPPOSED TO BE AT THE FRONT LINE OFFICES IN TEN MINUTES--
THWIP
ALL RIGHT. SEE YA AROUND, THEN.
WHAT ABOUT YOU? GOT ANYTHING PLANNED?
NOT FOR TODAY.

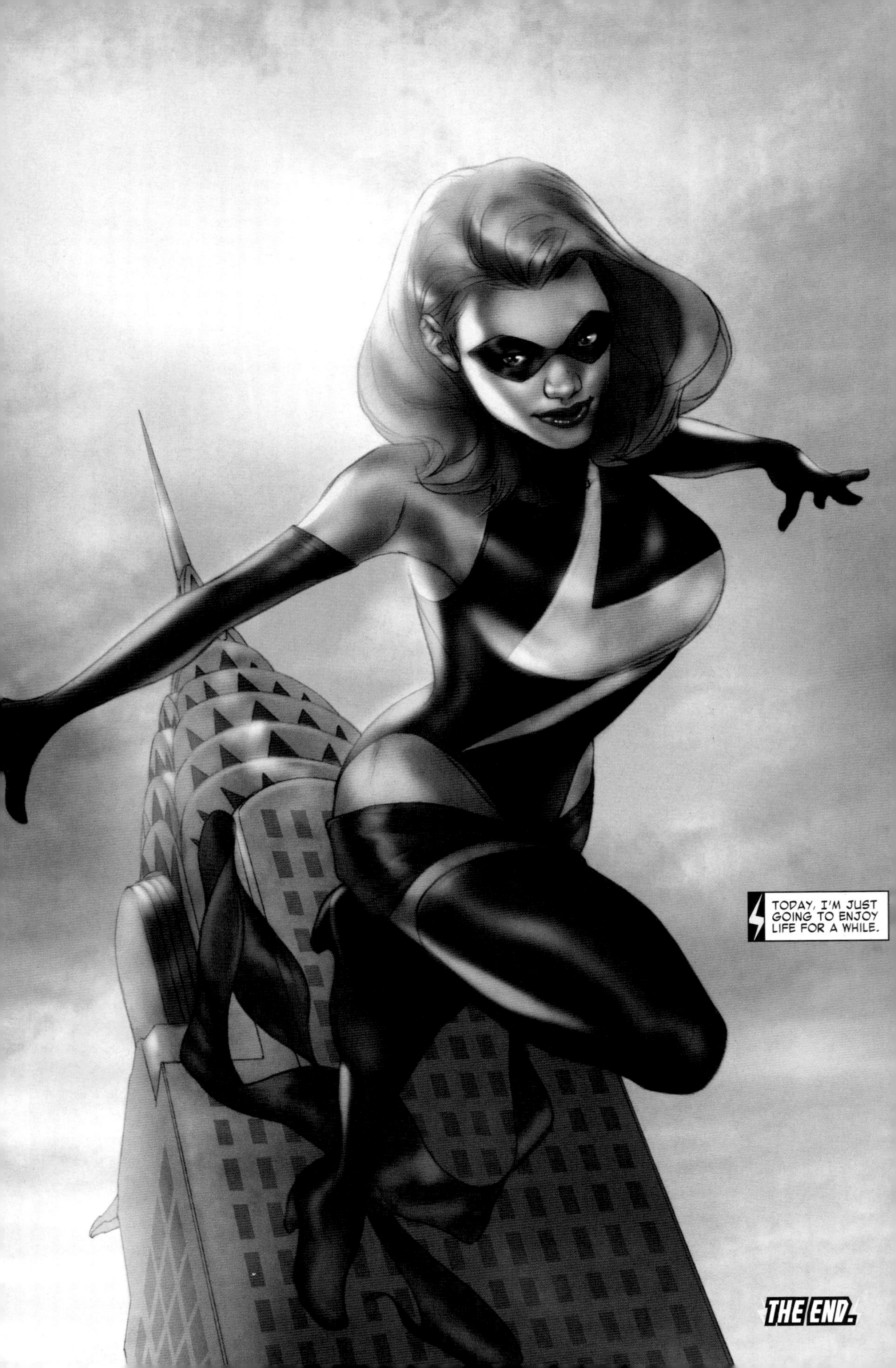
TODAY, I'M JUST GOING TO ENJOY LIFE FOR A WHILE.
THE END.

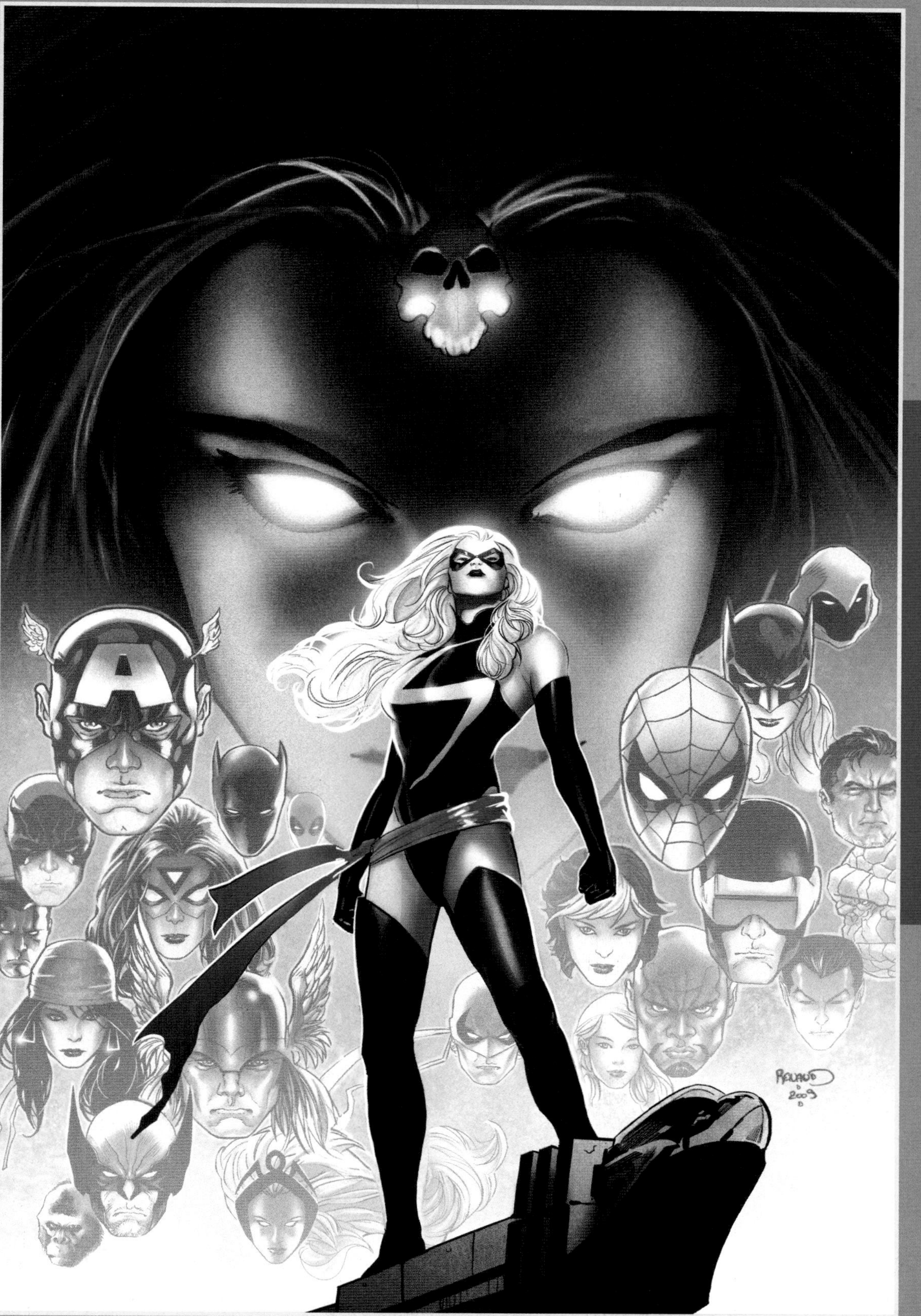
RENAUD
2009

MS. MARVEL #50 **VARIANT BY PAUL RENAUD**

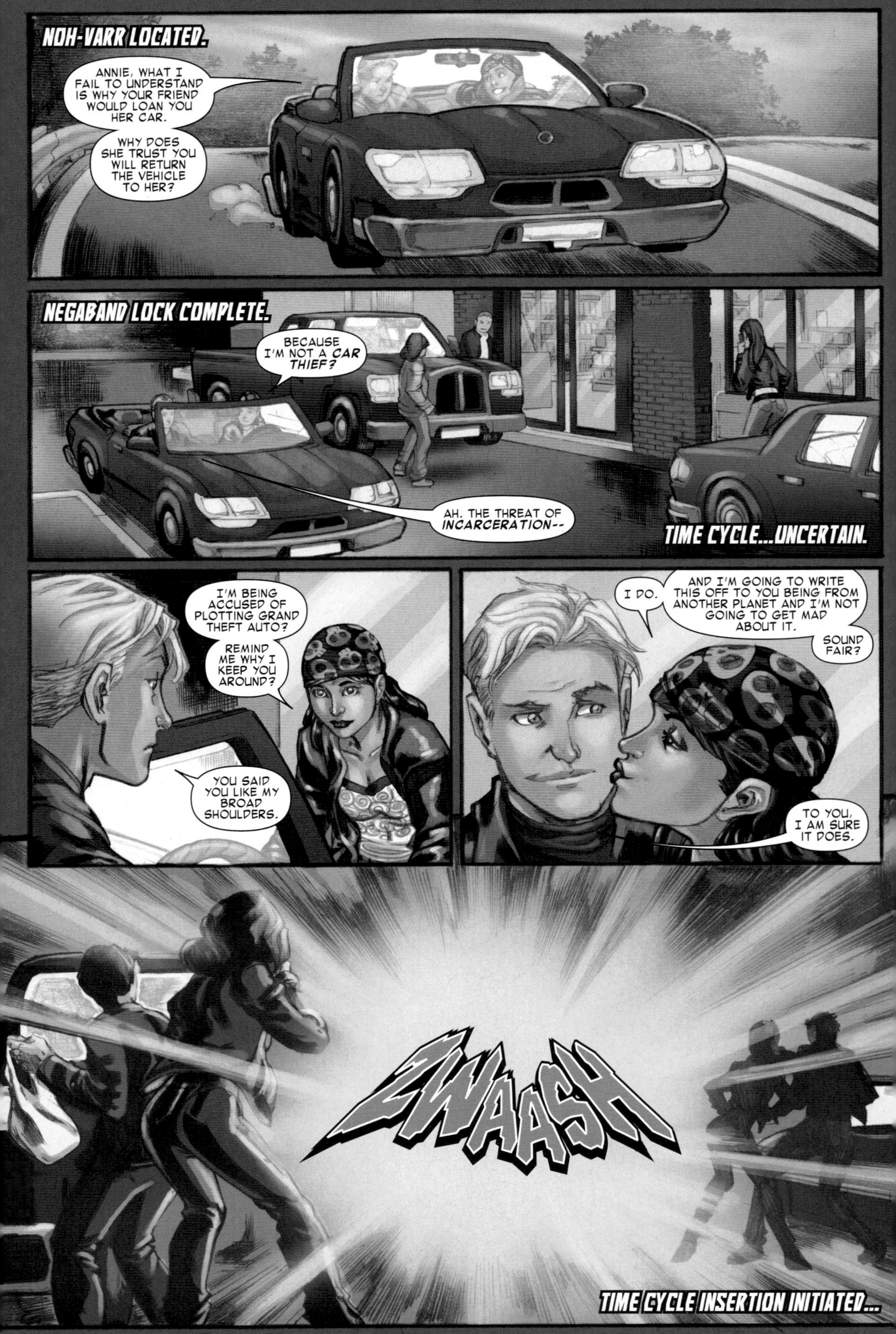
NOH-VARR LOCATED.
ANNIE, WHAT I FAIL TO UNDERSTAND IS WHY YOUR FRIEND WOULD LOAN YOU HER CAR.
WHY DOES SHE TRUST YOU WILL RETURN THE VEHICLE TO HER?
NEGABAND LOCK COMPLETE.
BECAUSE I'M NOT A CAR THIEF?
AH. THE THREAT OF INCARCERATION--
TIME CYCLE...UNCERTAIN.
I'M BEING ACCUSED OF PLOTTING GRAND THEFT AUTO?
REMIND ME WHY I KEEP YOU AROUND?
YOU SAID YOU LIKE MY BROAD SHOULDERS.
I DO.
AND I'M GOING TO WRITE THIS OFF TO YOU BEING FROM ANOTHER PLANET AND I'M NOT GOING TO GET MAD ABOUT IT.
SOUND FAIR?
TO YOU, I AM SURE IT DOES.
ZWAASH
TIME CYCLE INSERTION INITIATED...

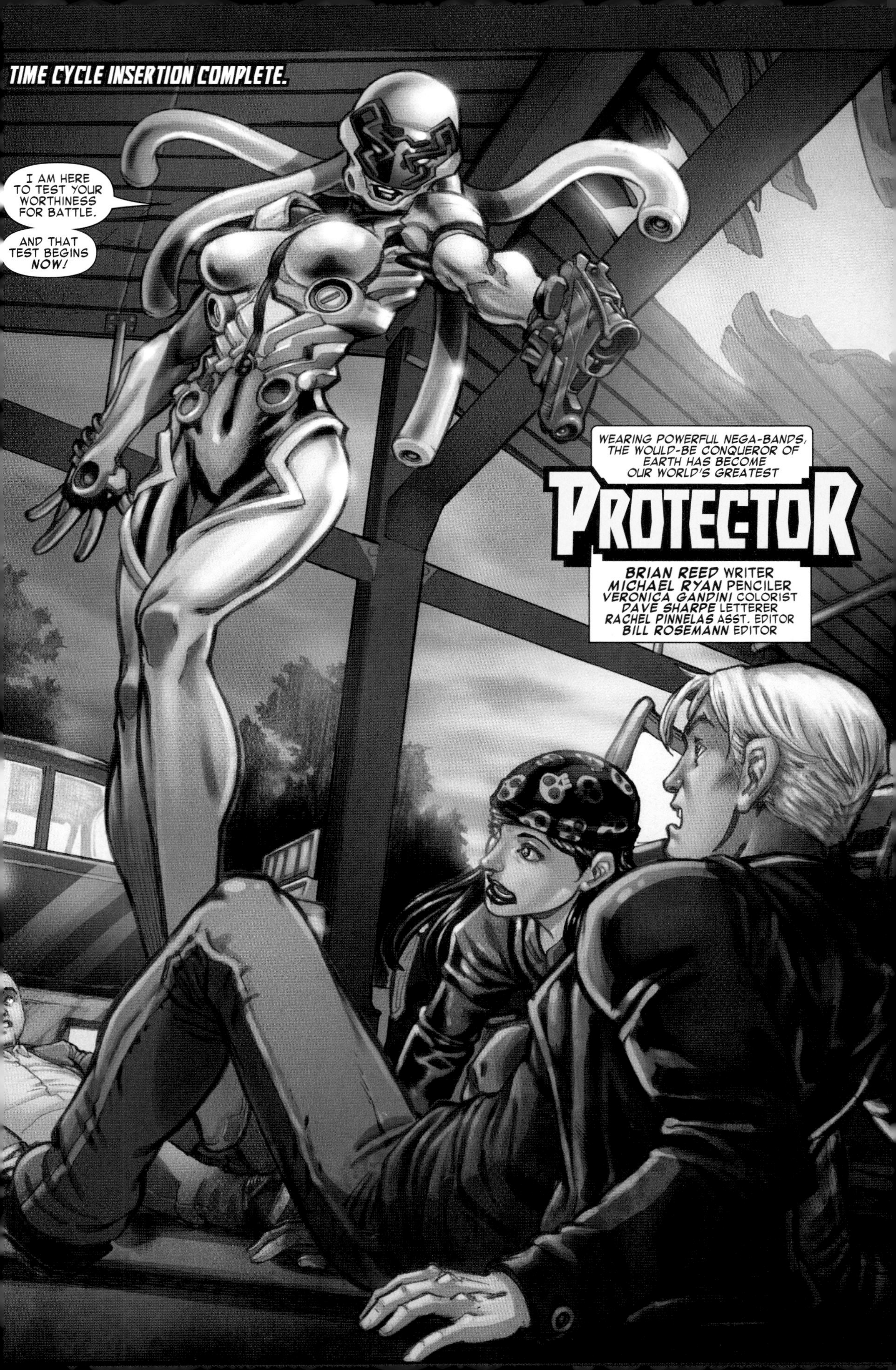
TIME CYCLE INSERTION COMPLETE.
I AM HERE TO TEST YOUR WORTHINESS FOR BATTLE.
AND THAT TEST BEGINS NOW!
WEARING POWERFUL NEGA-BANDS, THE WOULD-BE CONQUEROR OF EARTH HAS BECOME OUR WORLD'S GREATEST
PROTECTOR
BRIAN REED WRITER
MICHAEL RYAN PENCILER
VERONICA GANDINI COLORIST
DAVE SHARPE LETTERER
RACHEL PINNELAS ASST. EDITOR
BILL ROSEMANN EDITOR

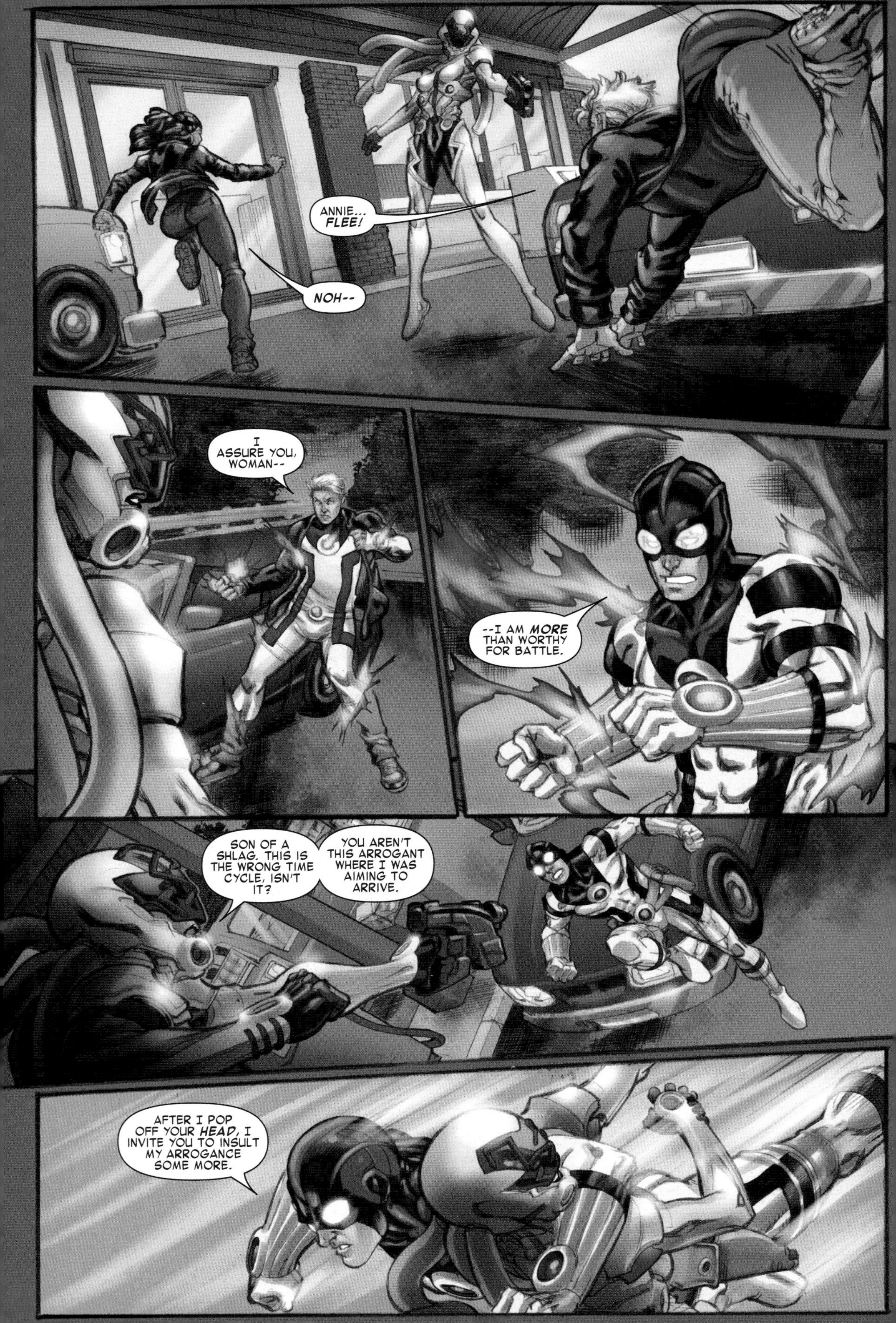
ANNIE... FLEE!
NOH--
I ASSURE YOU, WOMAN--
--I AM MORE THAN WORTHY FOR BATTLE.
SON OF A SHLAG. THIS IS THE WRONG TIME CYCLE, ISN'T IT?
YOU AREN'T THIS ARROGANT WHERE I WAS AIMING TO ARRIVE.
AFTER I POP OFF YOUR HEAD, I INVITE YOU TO INSULT MY ARROGANCE SOME MORE.

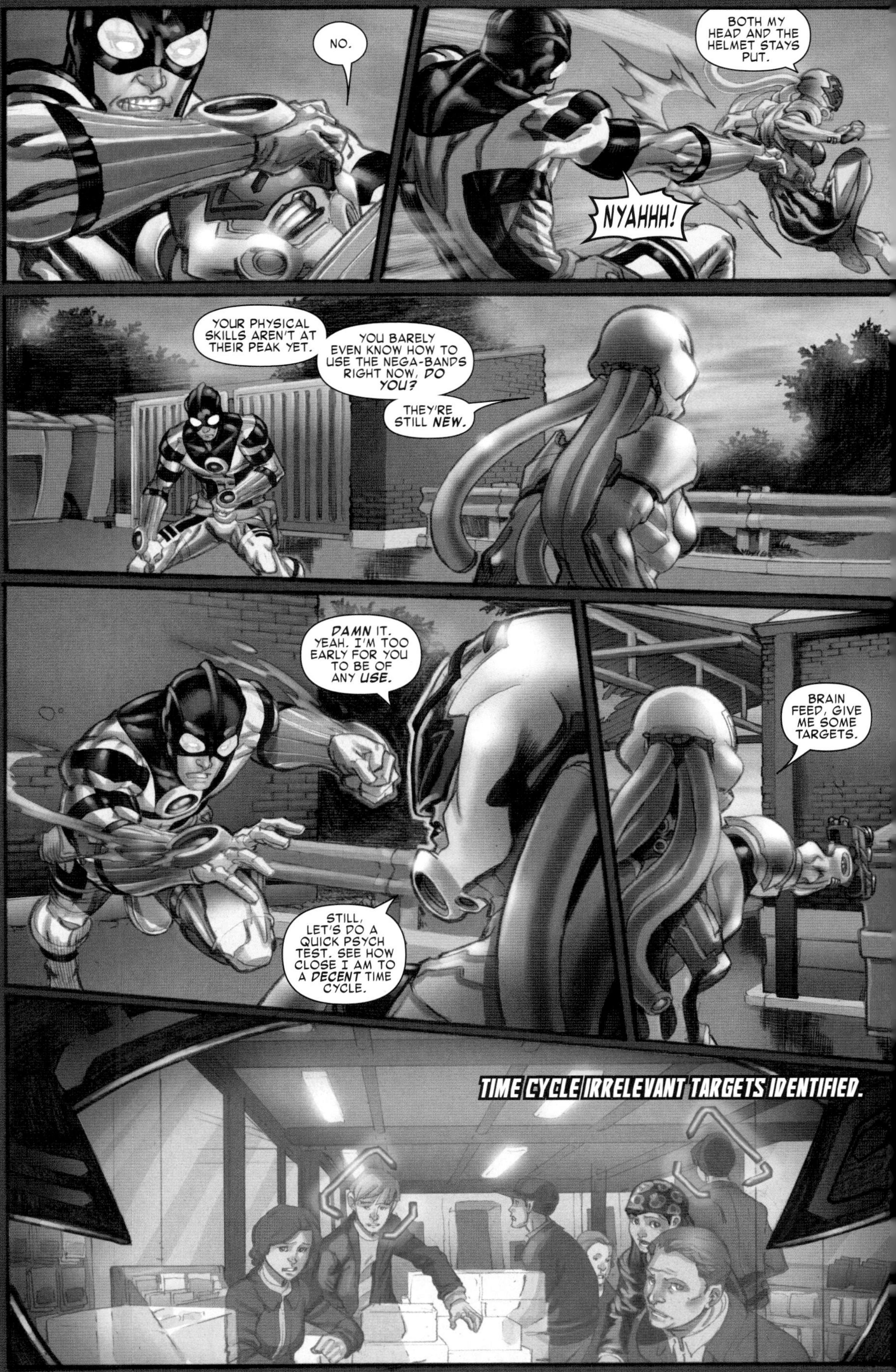
NO.
BOTH MY HEAD AND THE HELMET STAYS PUT.
NYAHHH!
YOUR PHYSICAL SKILLS AREN'T AT THEIR PEAK YET.
YOU BARELY EVEN KNOW HOW TO USE THE NEGA-BANDS RIGHT NOW, DO YOU?
THEY'RE STILL NEW.
DAMN IT. YEAH. I'M TOO EARLY FOR YOU TO BE OF ANY USE.
STILL, LET'S DO A QUICK PSYCH TEST. SEE HOW CLOSE I AM TO A DECENT TIME CYCLE.
BRAIN FEED, GIVE ME SOME TARGETS.
TIME CYCLE IRRELEVANT TARGETS IDENTIFIED.

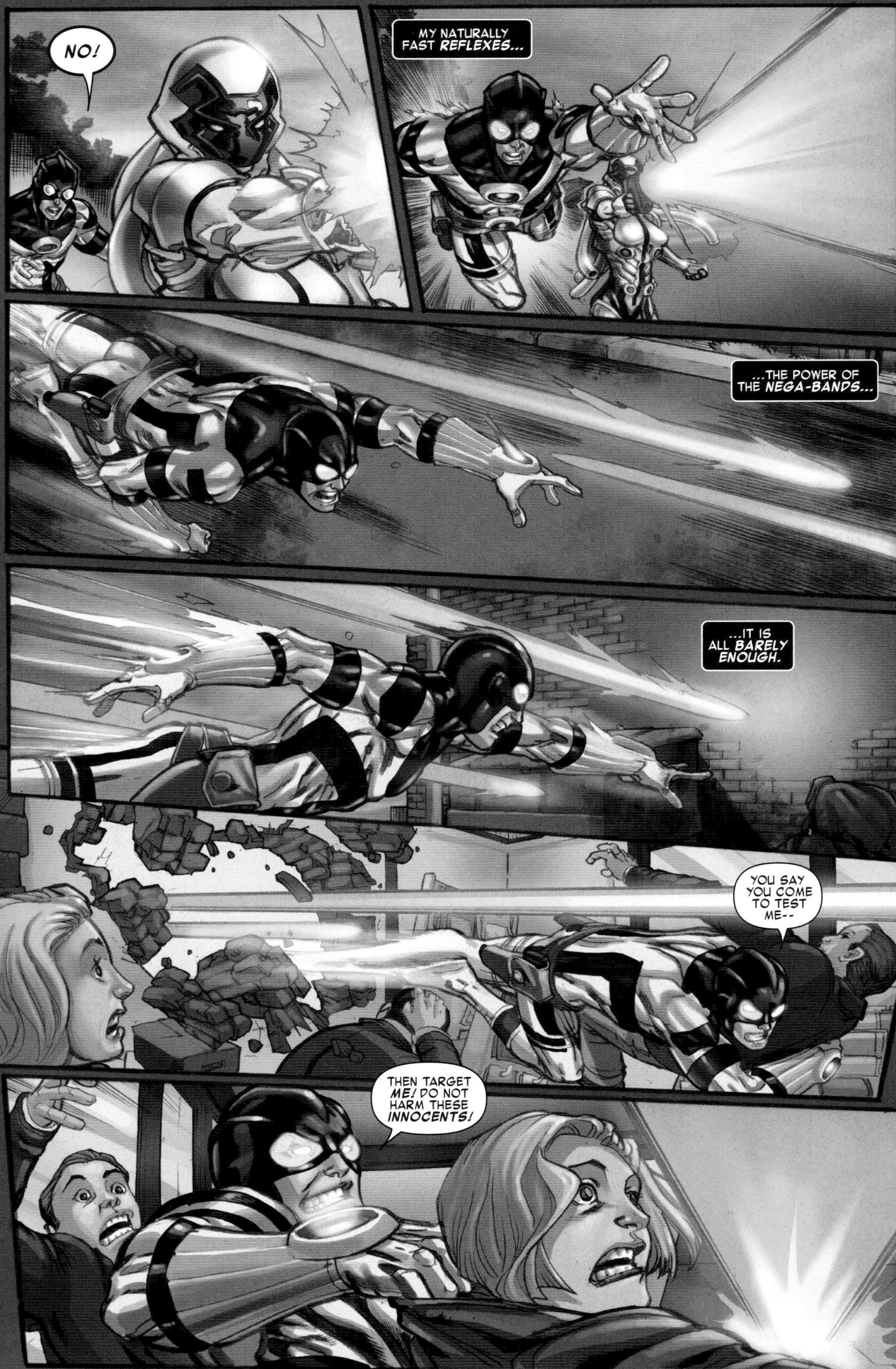
NO!
MY NATURALLY FAST REFLEXES...
...THE POWER OF THE NEGA-BANDS...
...IT IS ALL BARELY ENOUGH.
YOU SAY YOU COME TO TEST ME--
THEN TARGET ME! DO NOT HARM THESE INNOCENTS!

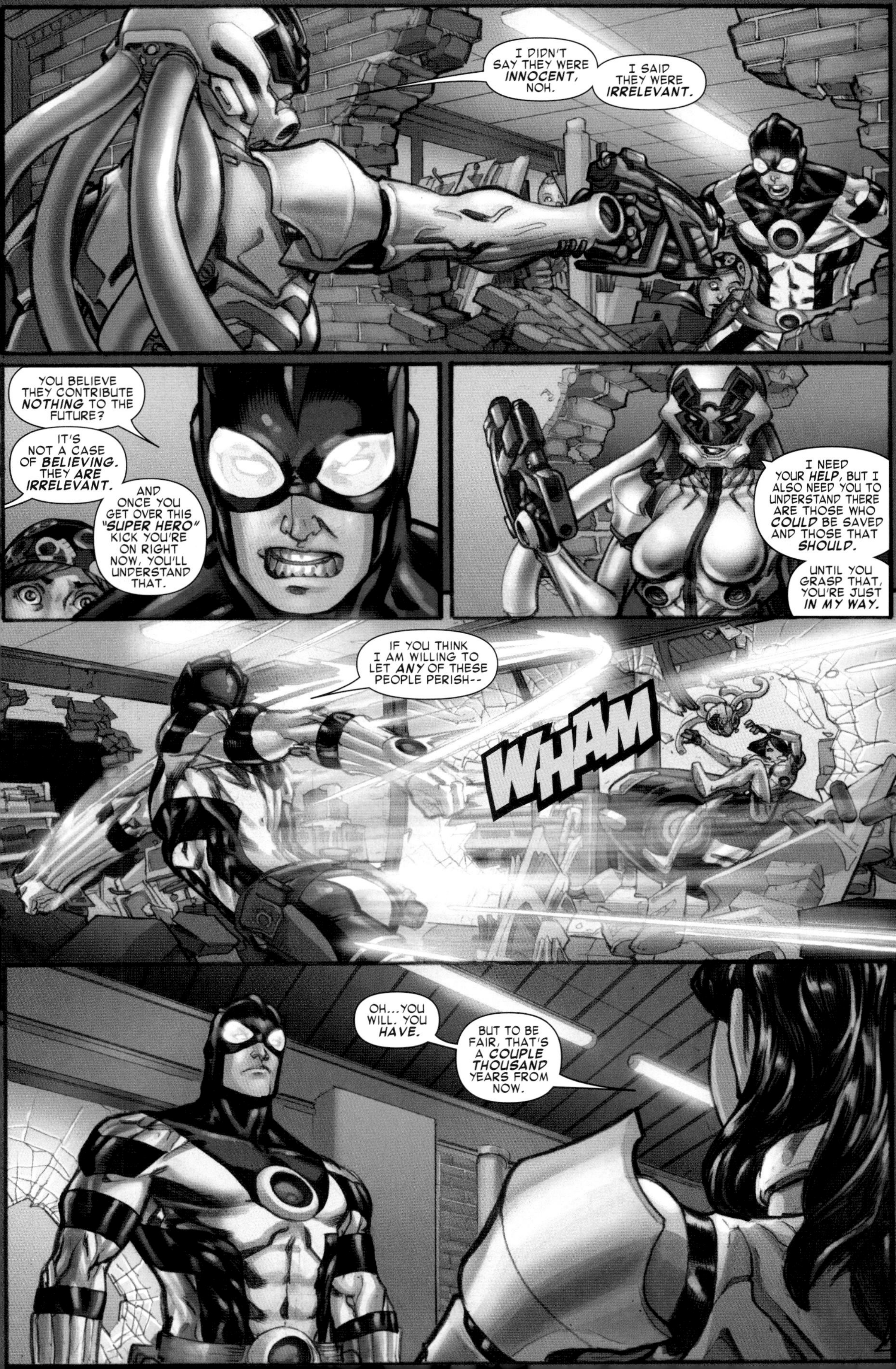
I DIDN'T SAY THEY WERE INNOCENT, NOH.
I SAID THEY WERE IRRELEVANT.
YOU BELIEVE THEY CONTRIBUTE NOTHING TO THE FUTURE?
IT'S NOT A CASE OF BELIEVING. THEY ARE IRRELEVANT.
AND ONCE YOU GET OVER THIS "SUPER HERO" KICK YOU'RE ON RIGHT NOW, YOU'LL UNDERSTAND THAT.
I NEED YOUR HELP, BUT I ALSO NEED YOU TO UNDERSTAND THERE ARE THOSE WHO COULD BE SAVED AND THOSE THAT SHOULD.
UNTIL YOU GRASP THAT, YOU'RE JUST IN MY WAY.
IF YOU THINK I AM WILLING TO LET ANY OF THESE PEOPLE PERISH--
WHAM
OH...YOU WILL. YOU HAVE.
BUT TO BE FAIR, THAT'S A COUPLE THOUSAND YEARS FROM NOW.

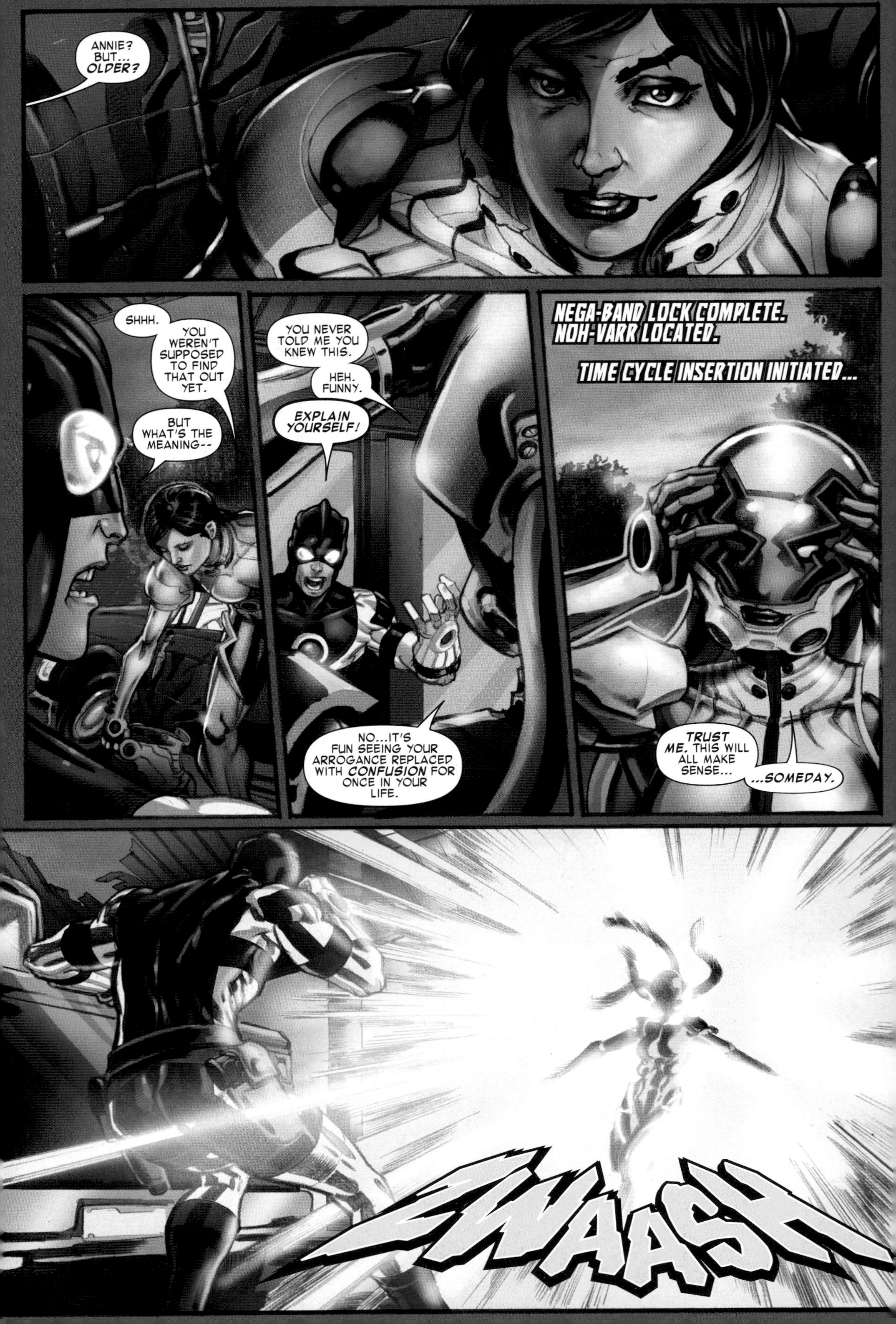
ANNIE? BUT... OLDER?
SHHH.
YOU WEREN'T SUPPOSED TO FIND THAT OUT YET.
BUT WHAT'S THE MEANING--
YOU NEVER TOLD ME YOU KNEW THIS.
HEH. FUNNY.
EXPLAIN YOURSELF!
NO...IT'S FUN SEEING YOUR ARROGANCE REPLACED WITH CONFUSION FOR ONCE IN YOUR LIFE.
NEGA-BAND LOCK COMPLETE. NOH-VARR LOCATED.
TIME CYCLE INSERTION INITIATED...
TRUST ME. THIS WILL ALL MAKE SENSE...
...SOMEDAY.
ZWAASH

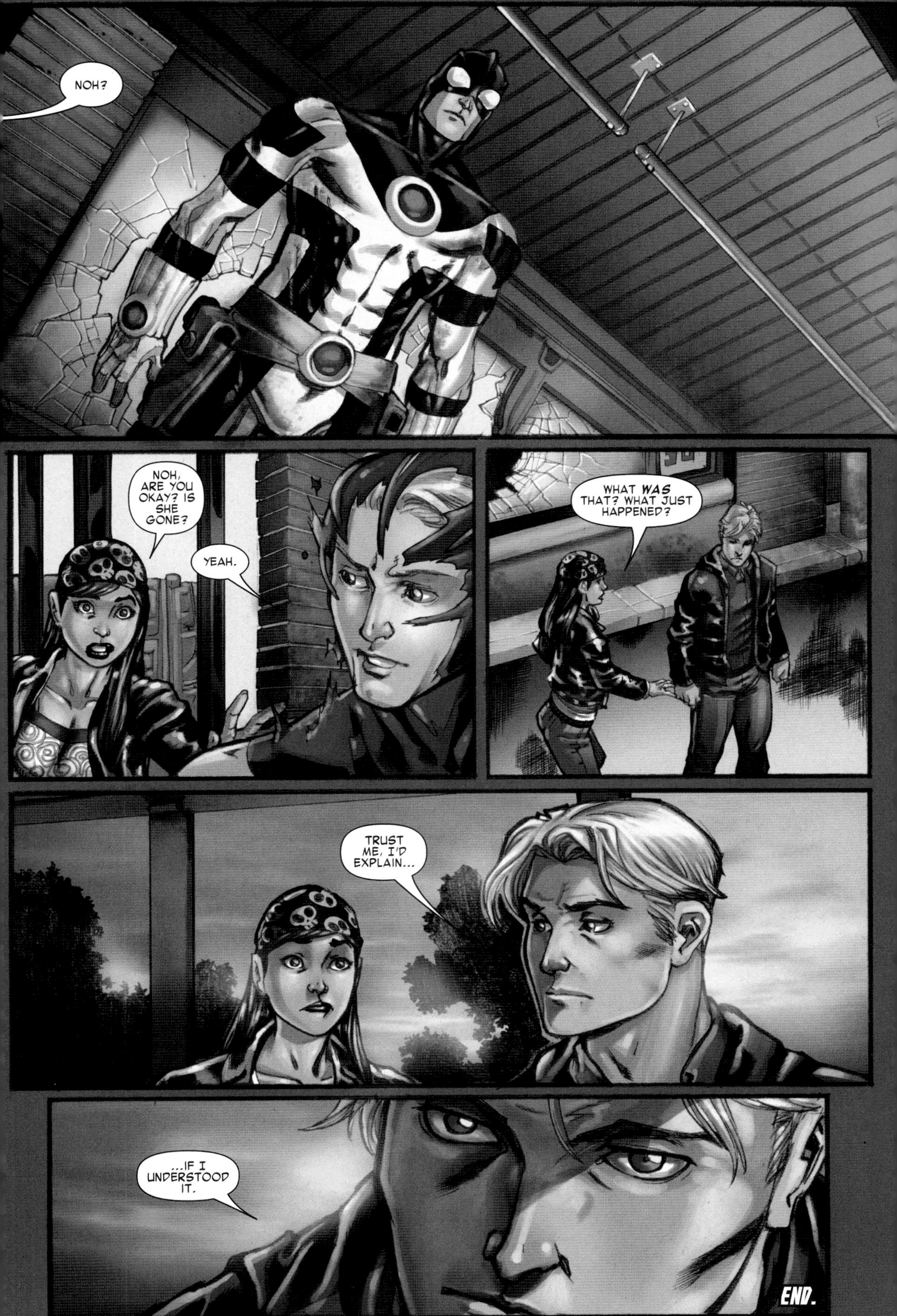
NOH?
NOH, ARE YOU OKAY? IS SHE GONE?
YEAH.
WHAT **WAS** THAT? WHAT JUST HAPPENED?
TRUST ME, I'D EXPLAIN...
...IF I UNDERSTOOD IT.
END.

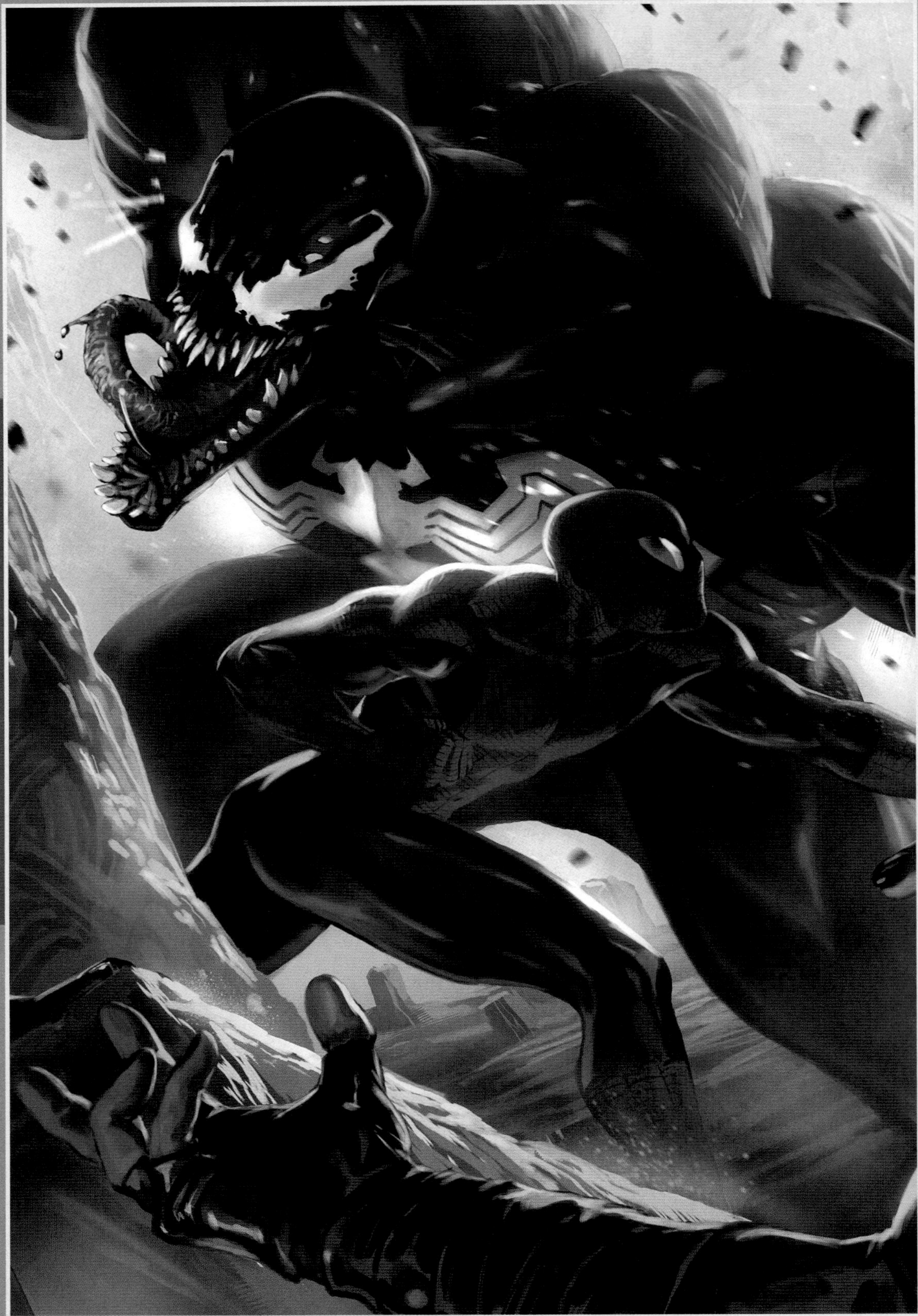

SIEGE: SPIDER-MAN

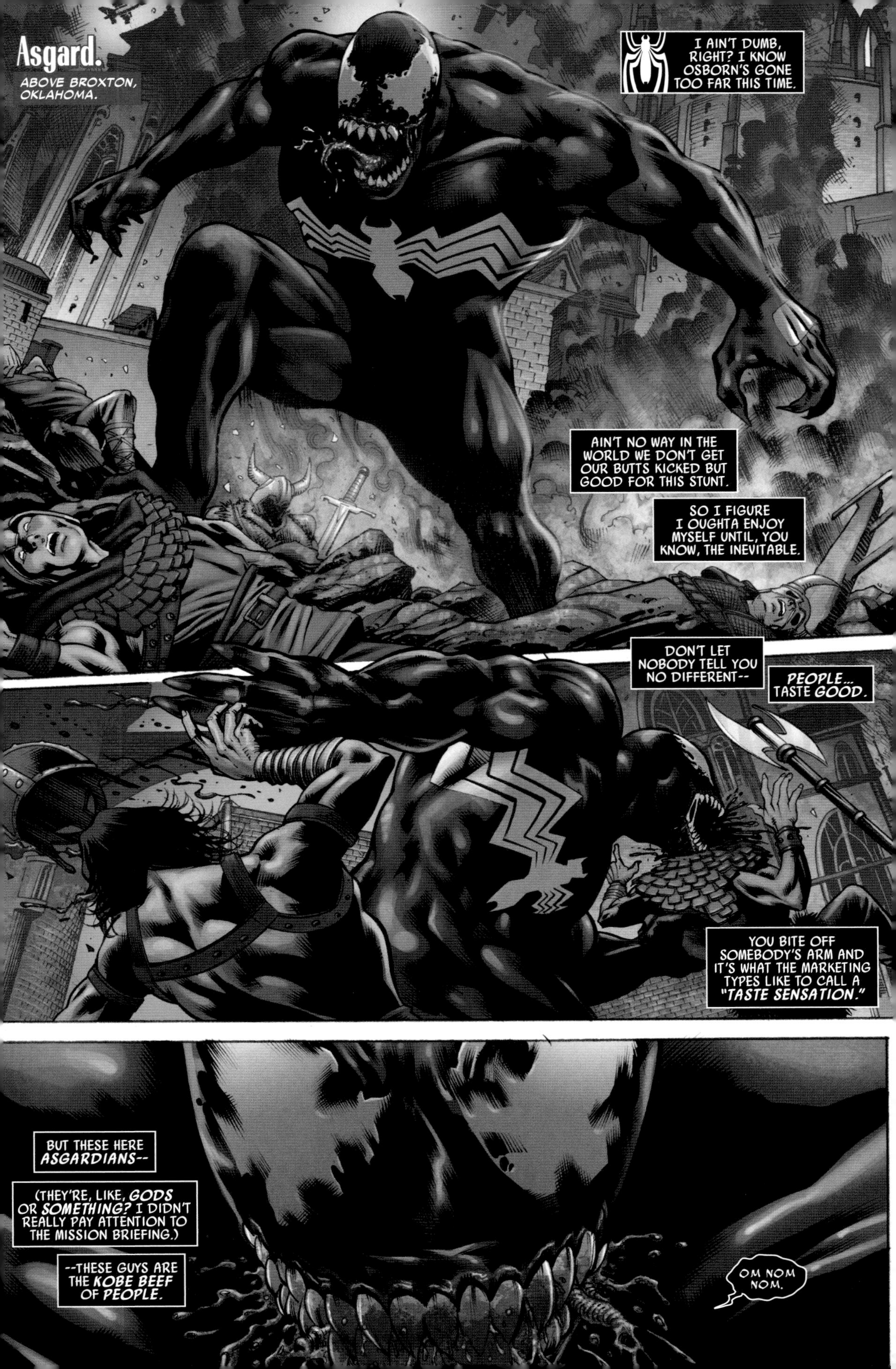
Asgard.
ABOVE BROXTON, OKLAHOMA.
I AIN'T DUMB, RIGHT? I KNOW OSBORN'S GONE TOO FAR THIS TIME.
AIN'T NO WAY IN THE WORLD WE DON'T GET OUR BUTTS KICKED BUT GOOD FOR THIS STUNT.
SO I FIGURE I OUGHTA ENJOY MYSELF UNTIL, YOU KNOW, THE INEVITABLE.
DON'T LET NOBODY TELL YOU NO DIFFERENT--
PEOPLE... TASTE GOOD.
YOU BITE OFF SOMEBODY'S ARM AND IT'S WHAT THE MARKETING TYPES LIKE TO CALL A "TASTE SENSATION."
BUT THESE HERE ASGARDIANS--
(THEY'RE, LIKE, GODS OR SOMETHING? I DIDN'T REALLY PAY ATTENTION TO THE MISSION BRIEFING.)
--THESE GUYS ARE THE KOBE BEEF OF PEOPLE.
OM NOM NOM.

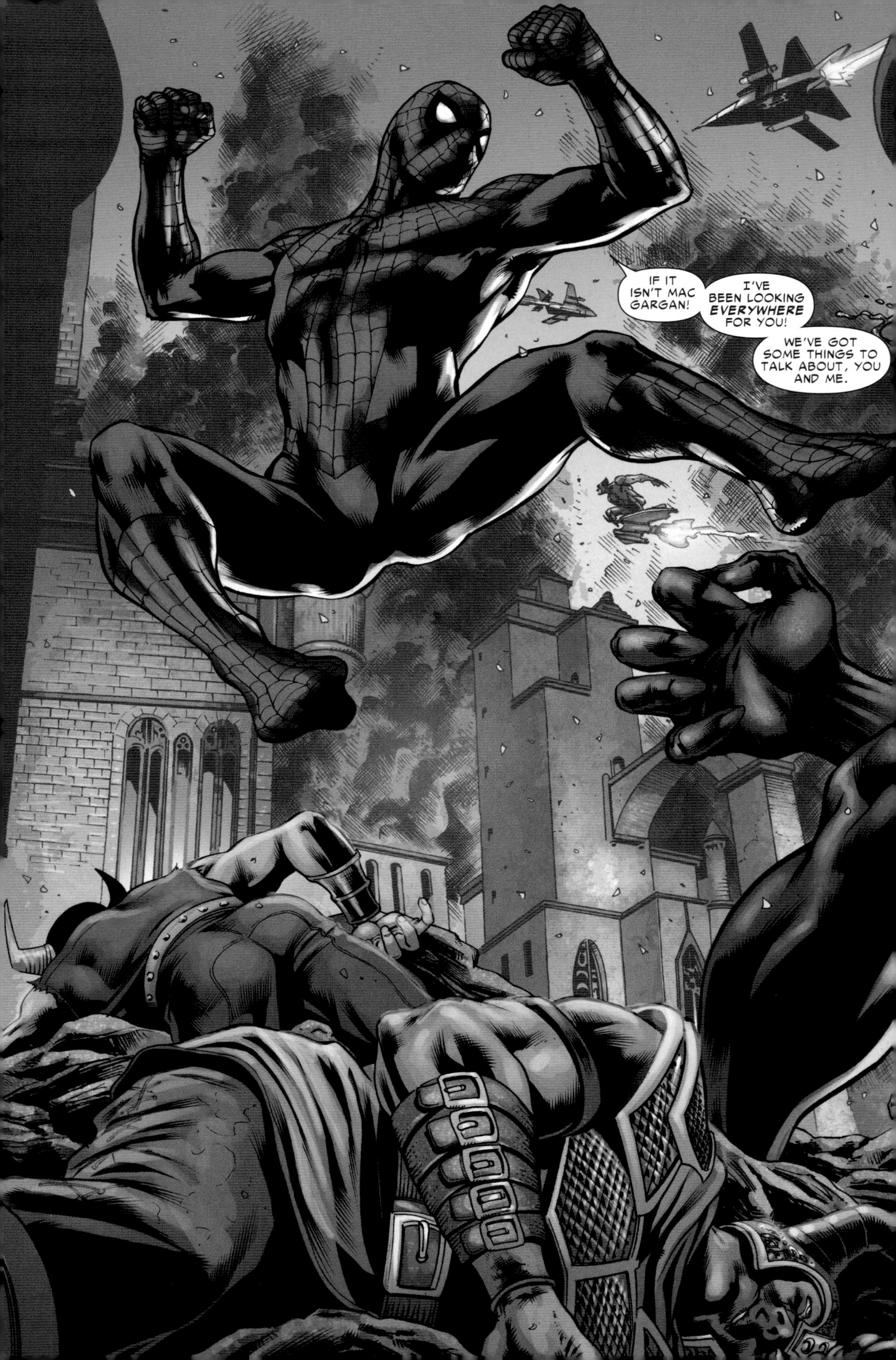
IF IT ISN'T MAC GARGAN!
I'VE BEEN LOOKING EVERYWHERE FOR YOU!
WE'VE GOT SOME THINGS TO TALK ABOUT, YOU AND ME.

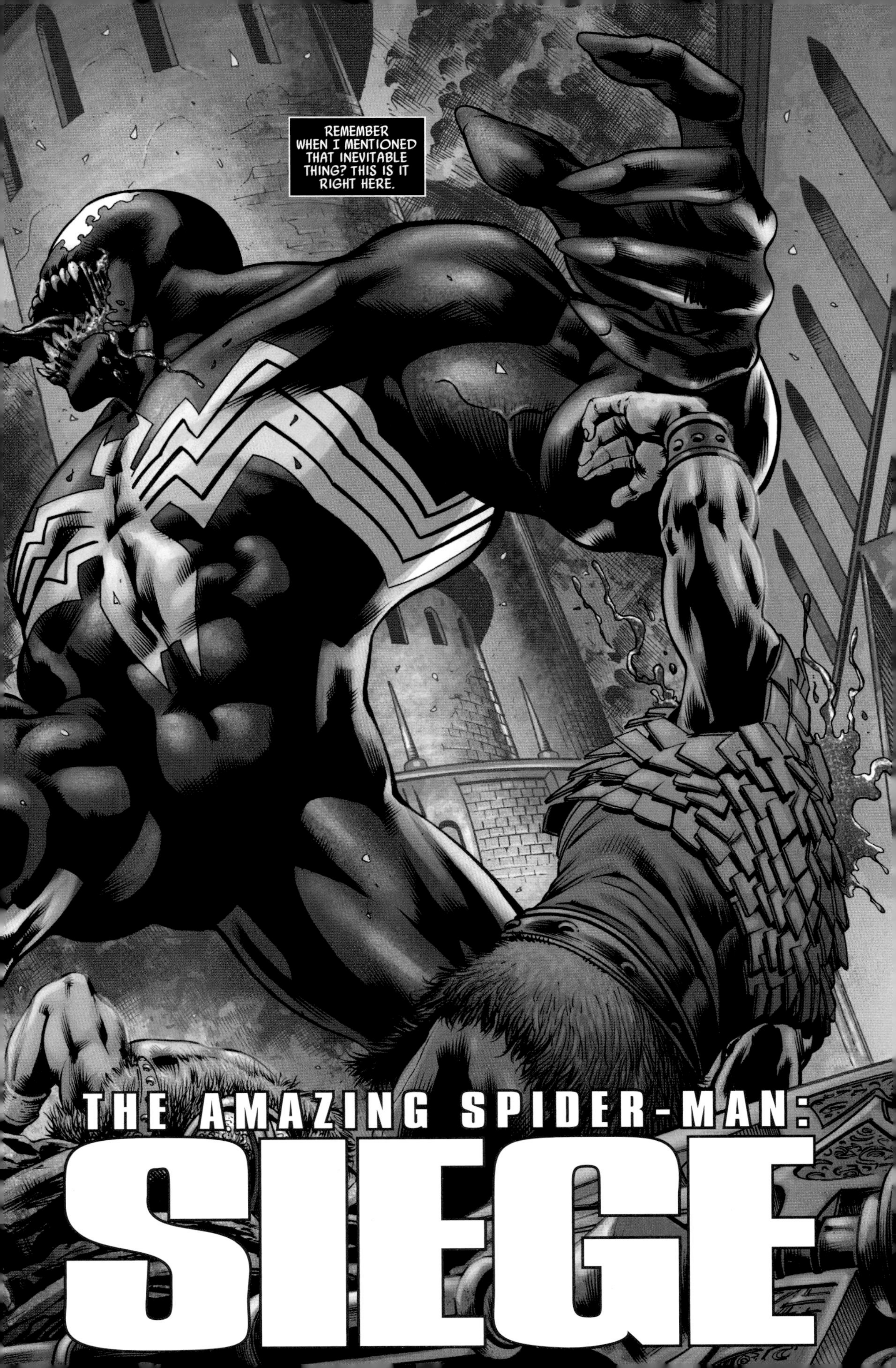
REMEMBER WHEN I MENTIONED THAT INEVITABLE THING? THIS IS IT RIGHT HERE.
THE AMAZING SPIDER-MAN:
SIEGE

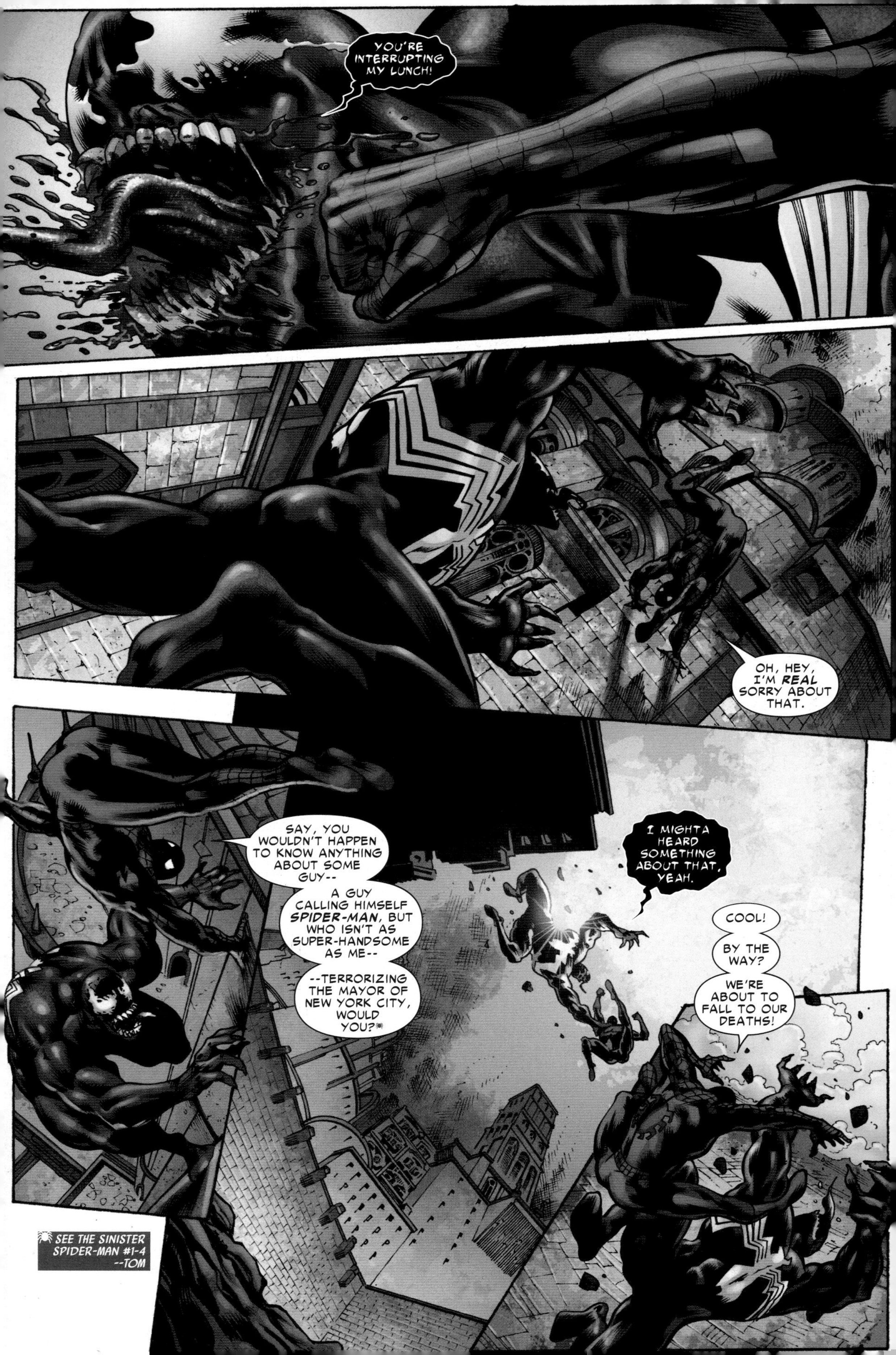
YOU'RE INTERRUPTING MY LUNCH!
OH, HEY, I'M REAL SORRY ABOUT THAT.
SAY, YOU WOULDN'T HAPPEN TO KNOW ANYTHING ABOUT SOME GUY--
A GUY CALLING HIMSELF SPIDER-MAN, BUT WHO ISN'T AS SUPER-HANDSOME AS ME--
--TERRORIZING THE MAYOR OF NEW YORK CITY, WOULD YOU?
I MIGHTA HEARD SOMETHING ABOUT THAT, YEAH.
COOL!
BY THE WAY?
WE'RE ABOUT TO FALL TO OUR DEATHS!
SEE THE SINISTER SPIDER-MAN #1-4 --TOM

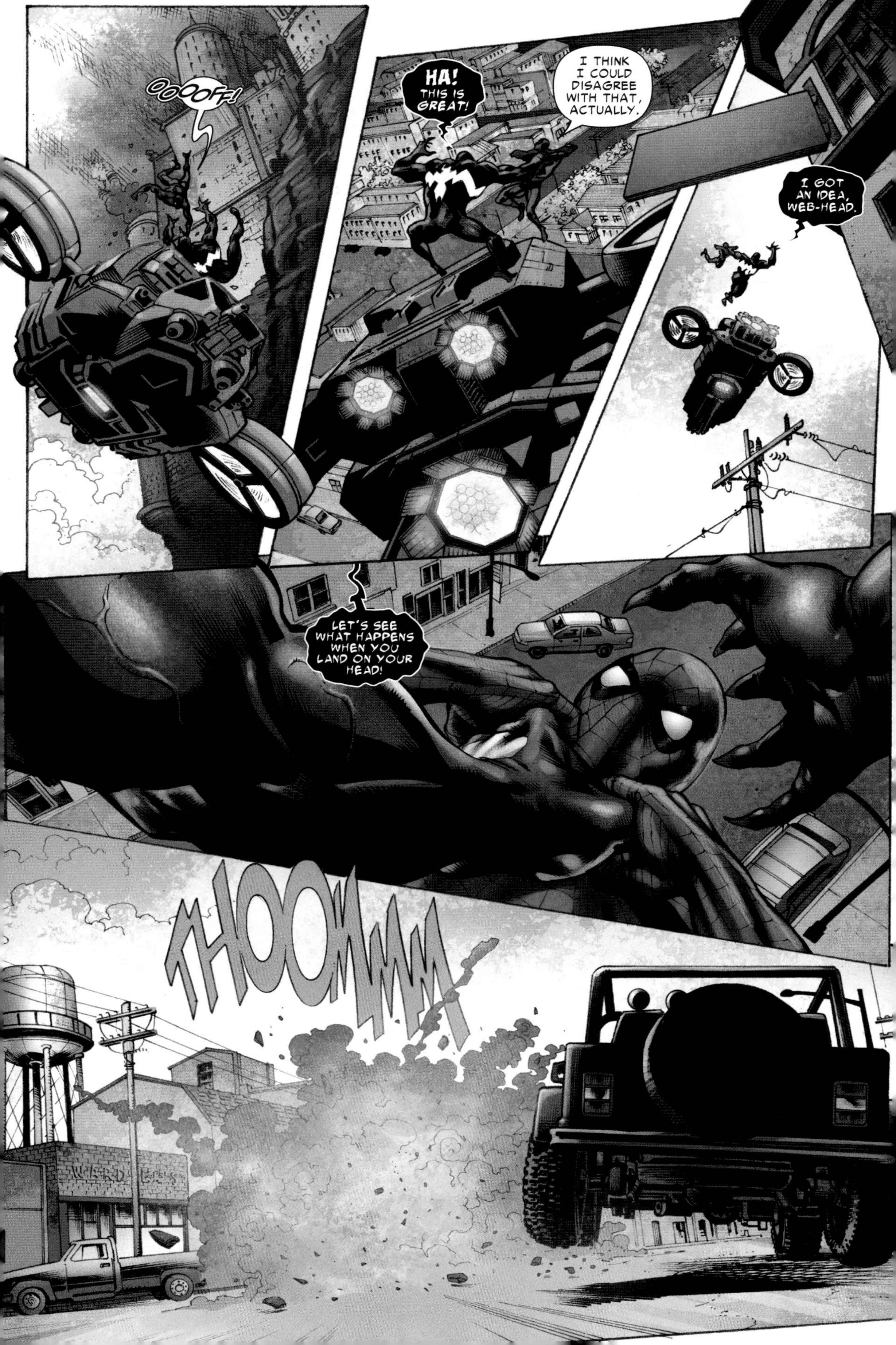
OOOOFF!
HA! THIS IS GREAT!
I THINK I COULD DISAGREE WITH THAT, ACTUALLY.
I GOT AN IDEA, WEB-HEAD.
LET'S SEE WHAT HAPPENS WHEN YOU LAND ON YOUR HEAD!
THOOMMM

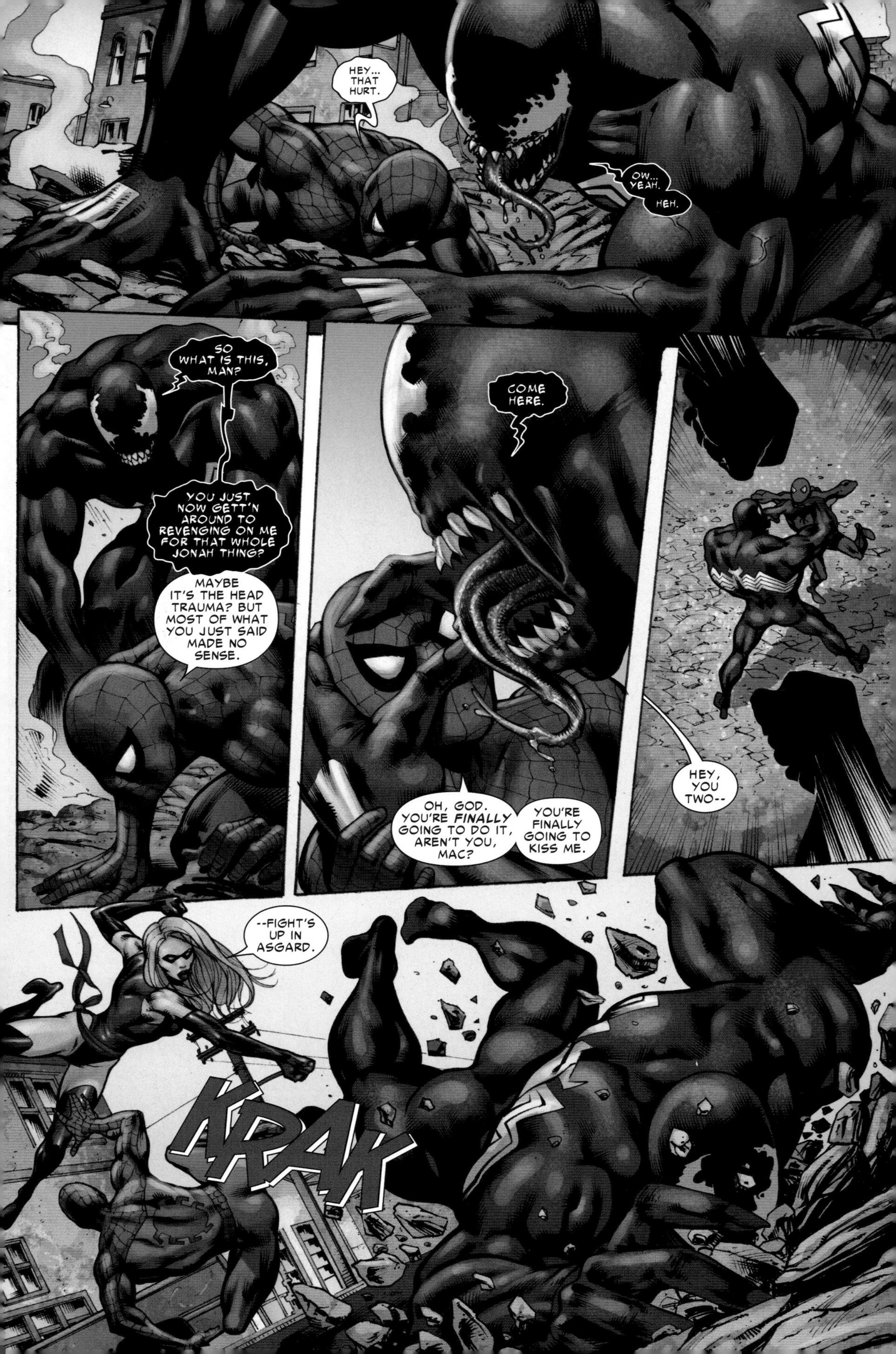
HEY... THAT HURT.
OW... YEAH.
HEH.
SO WHAT IS THIS, MAN?
YOU JUST NOW GETT'N AROUND TO REVENGING ON ME FOR THAT WHOLE JONAH THING?
MAYBE IT'S THE HEAD TRAUMA? BUT MOST OF WHAT YOU JUST SAID MADE NO SENSE.
COME HERE.
OH, GOD. YOU'RE *FINALLY* GOING TO DO IT, AREN'T YOU, MAC?
YOU'RE FINALLY GOING TO KISS ME.
HEY, YOU TWO--
--FIGHT'S UP IN ASGARD.
KRAK

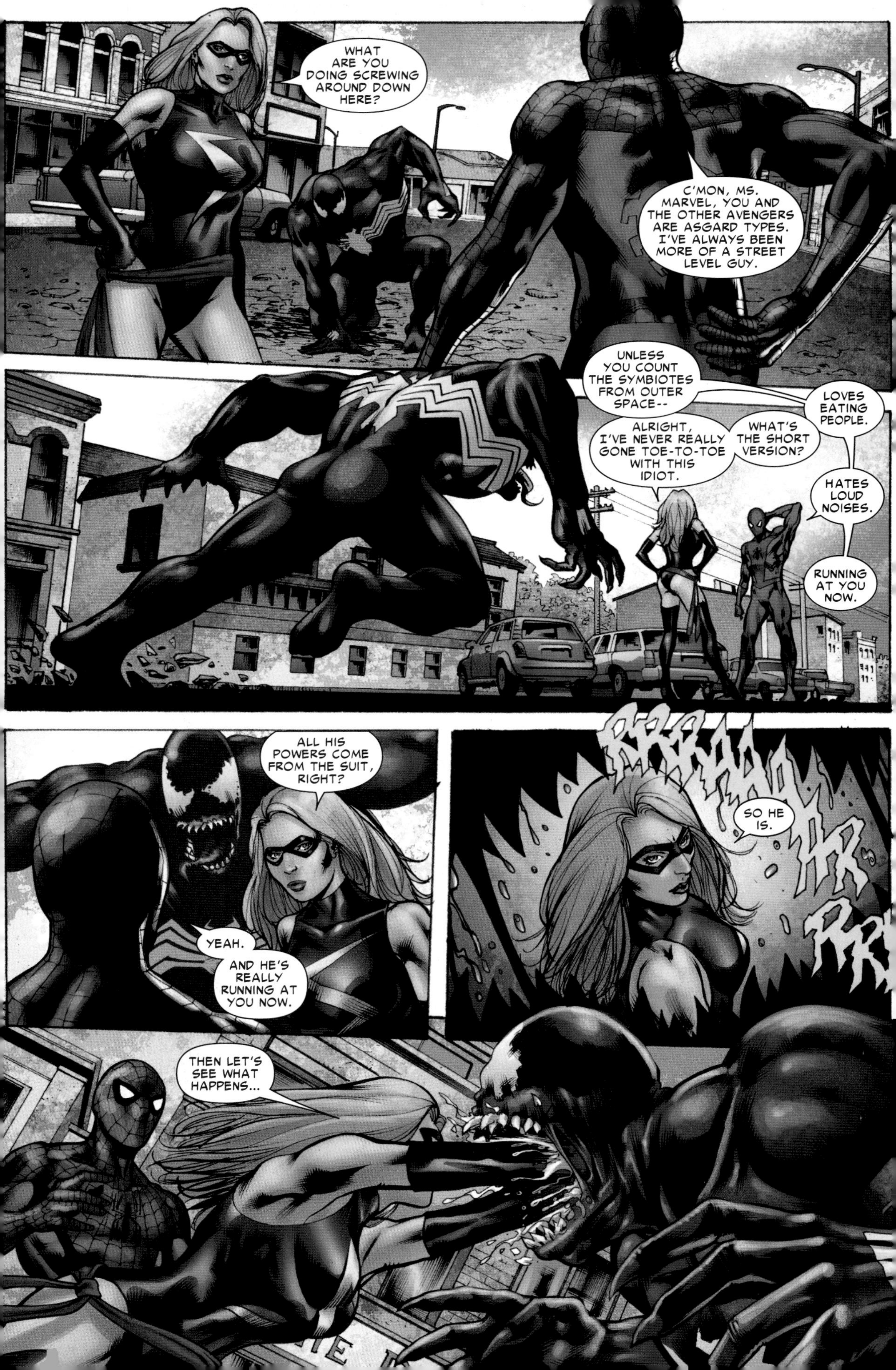
WHAT ARE YOU DOING SCREWING AROUND DOWN HERE?
C'MON, MS. MARVEL, YOU AND THE OTHER AVENGERS ARE ASGARD TYPES. I'VE ALWAYS BEEN MORE OF A STREET LEVEL GUY.
UNLESS YOU COUNT THE SYMBIOTES FROM OUTER SPACE--
ALRIGHT, I'VE NEVER REALLY GONE TOE-TO-TOE WITH THIS IDIOT.
WHAT'S THE SHORT VERSION?
LOVES EATING PEOPLE.
HATES LOUD NOISES.
RUNNING AT YOU NOW.
ALL HIS POWERS COME FROM THE SUIT, RIGHT?
YEAH.
AND HE'S REALLY RUNNING AT YOU NOW.
RRRAAAHR
SO HE IS.
THEN LET'S SEE WHAT HAPPENS...

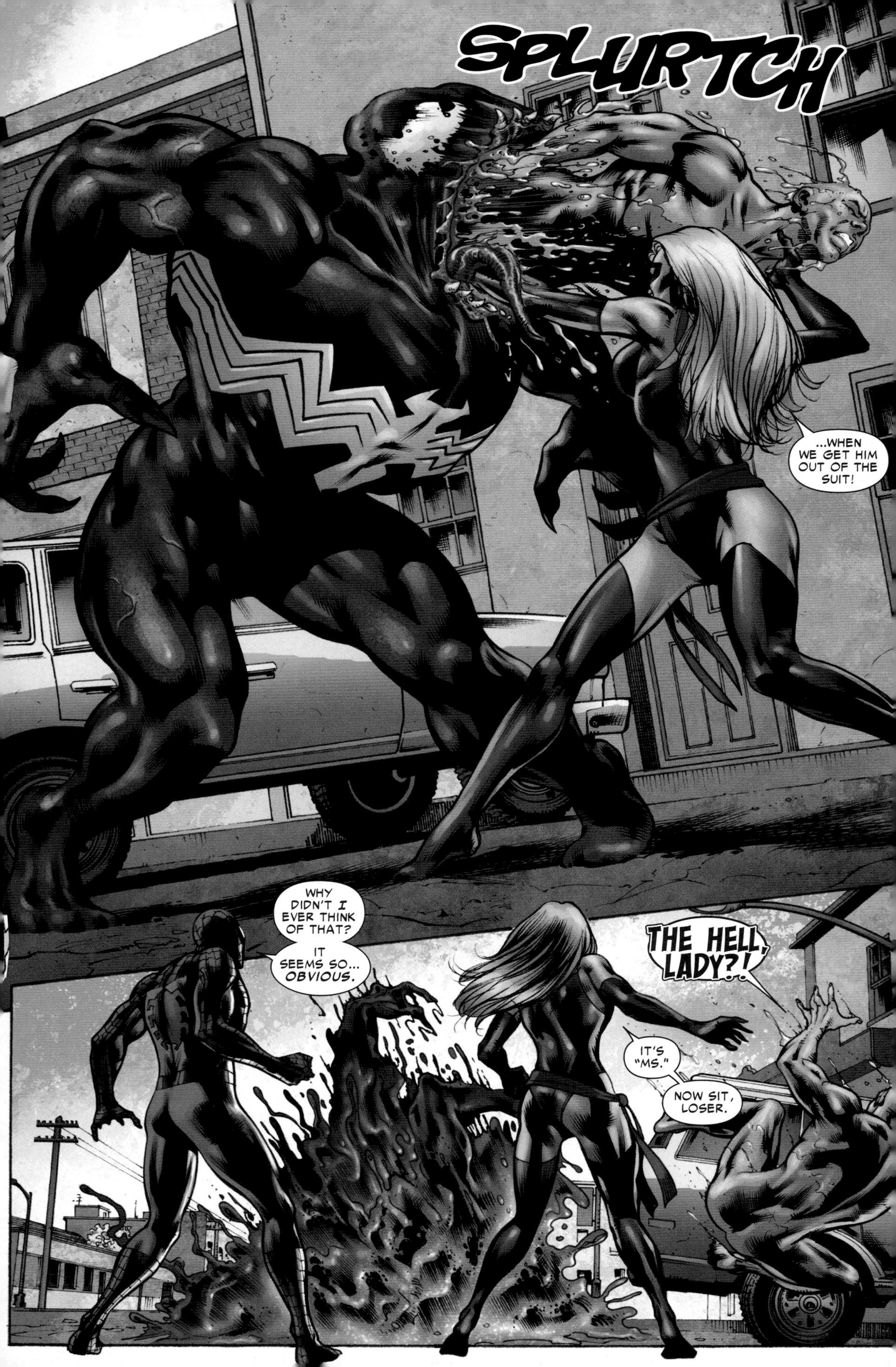
SPLURTCH
...WHEN WE GET HIM OUT OF THE SUIT!
WHY DIDN'T I EVER THINK OF THAT?
IT SEEMS SO... OBVIOUS.
THE HELL, LADY?!
IT'S "MS."
NOW SIT, LOSER.

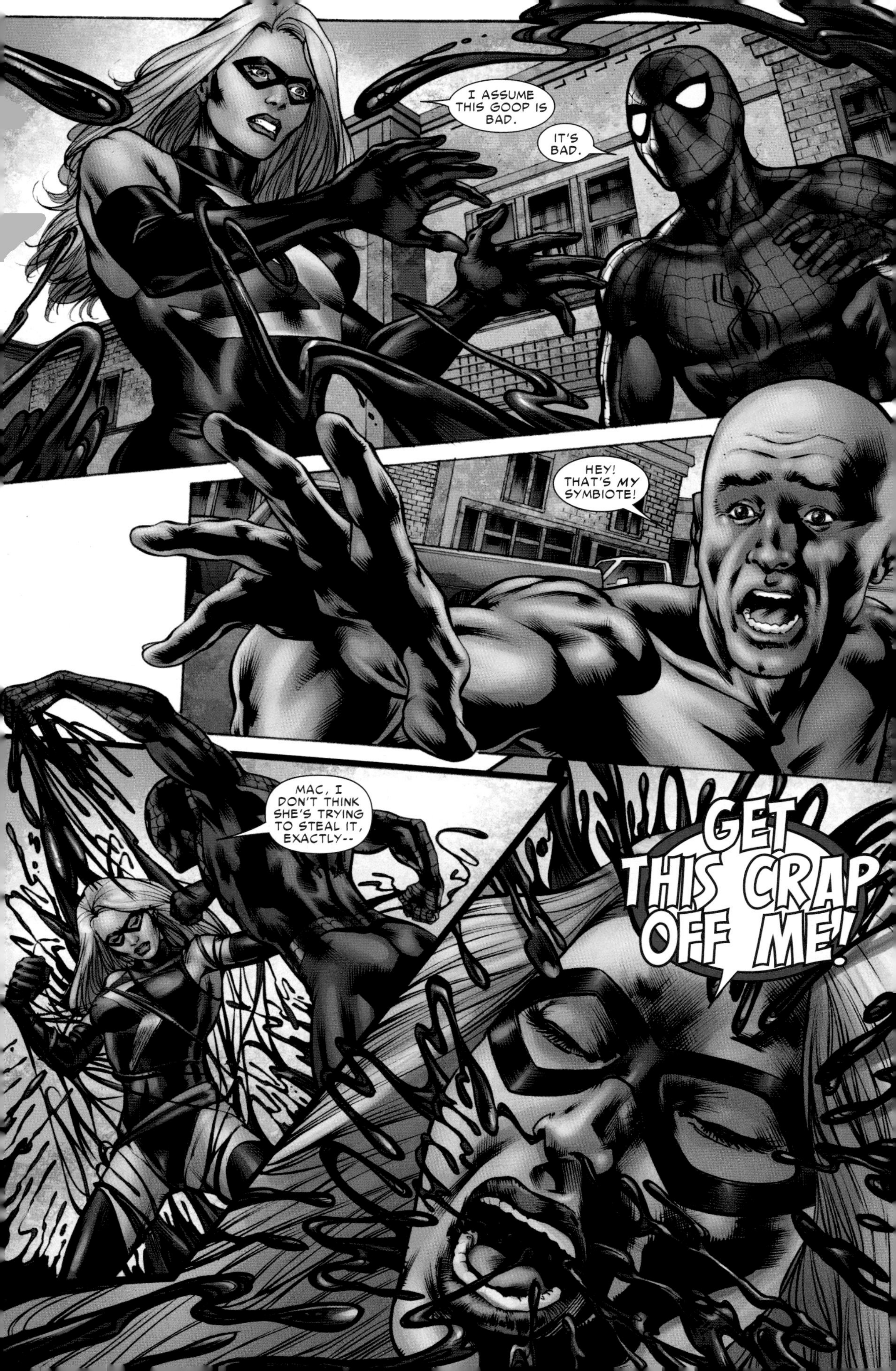
I ASSUME THIS GOOP IS BAD.
IT'S BAD.
HEY! THAT'S MY SYMBIOTE!
MAC, I DON'T THINK SHE'S TRYING TO STEAL IT, EXACTLY--
GET THIS CRAP OFF ME!

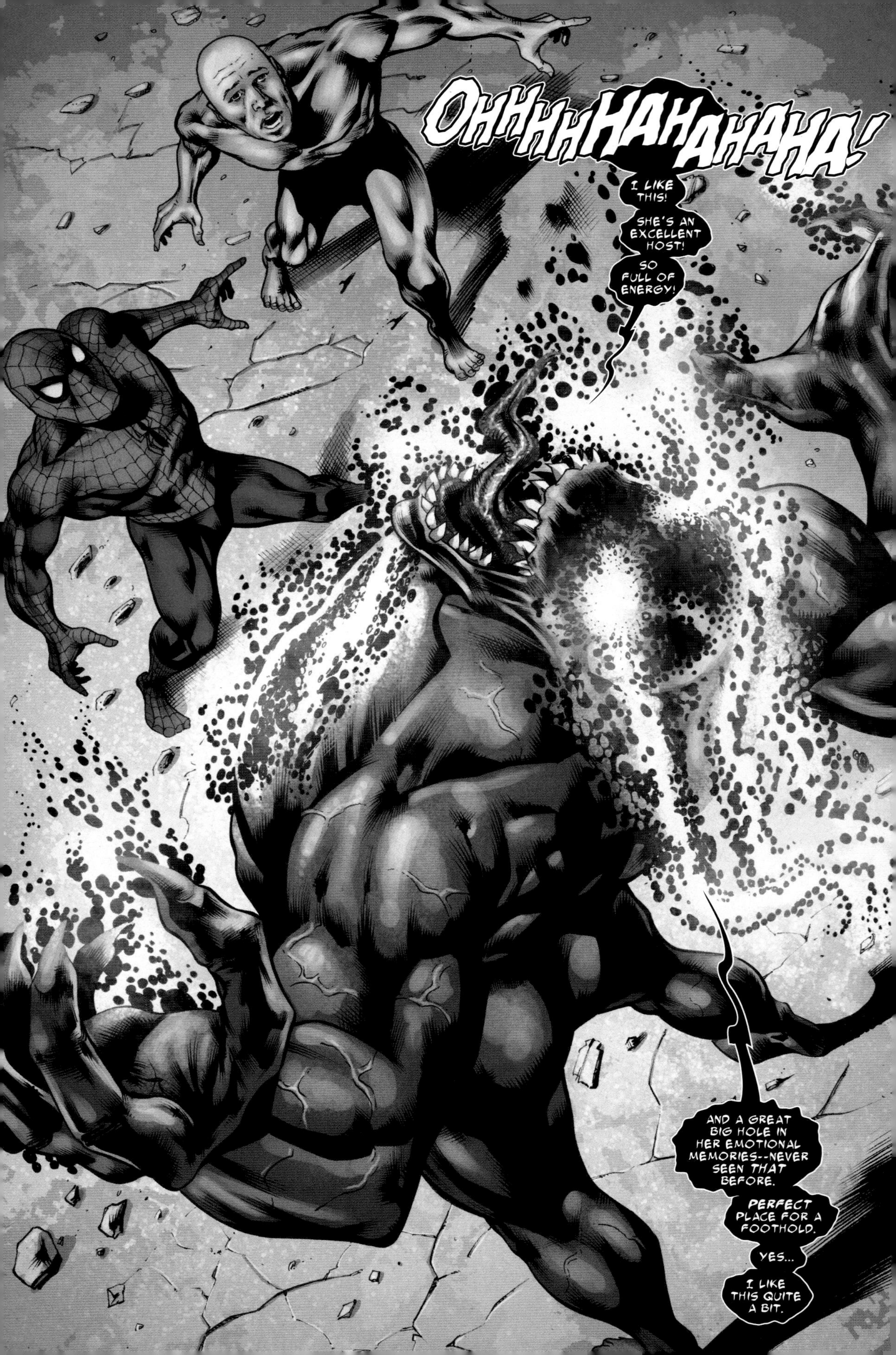
OHHHHHAHAHAHAHA!
I LIKE THIS!
SHE'S AN EXCELLENT HOST!
SO FULL OF ENERGY!
AND A GREAT BIG HOLE IN HER EMOTIONAL MEMORIES--NEVER SEEN *THAT* BEFORE.
PERFECT PLACE FOR A FOOTHOLD.
YES...
I LIKE THIS QUITE A BIT.

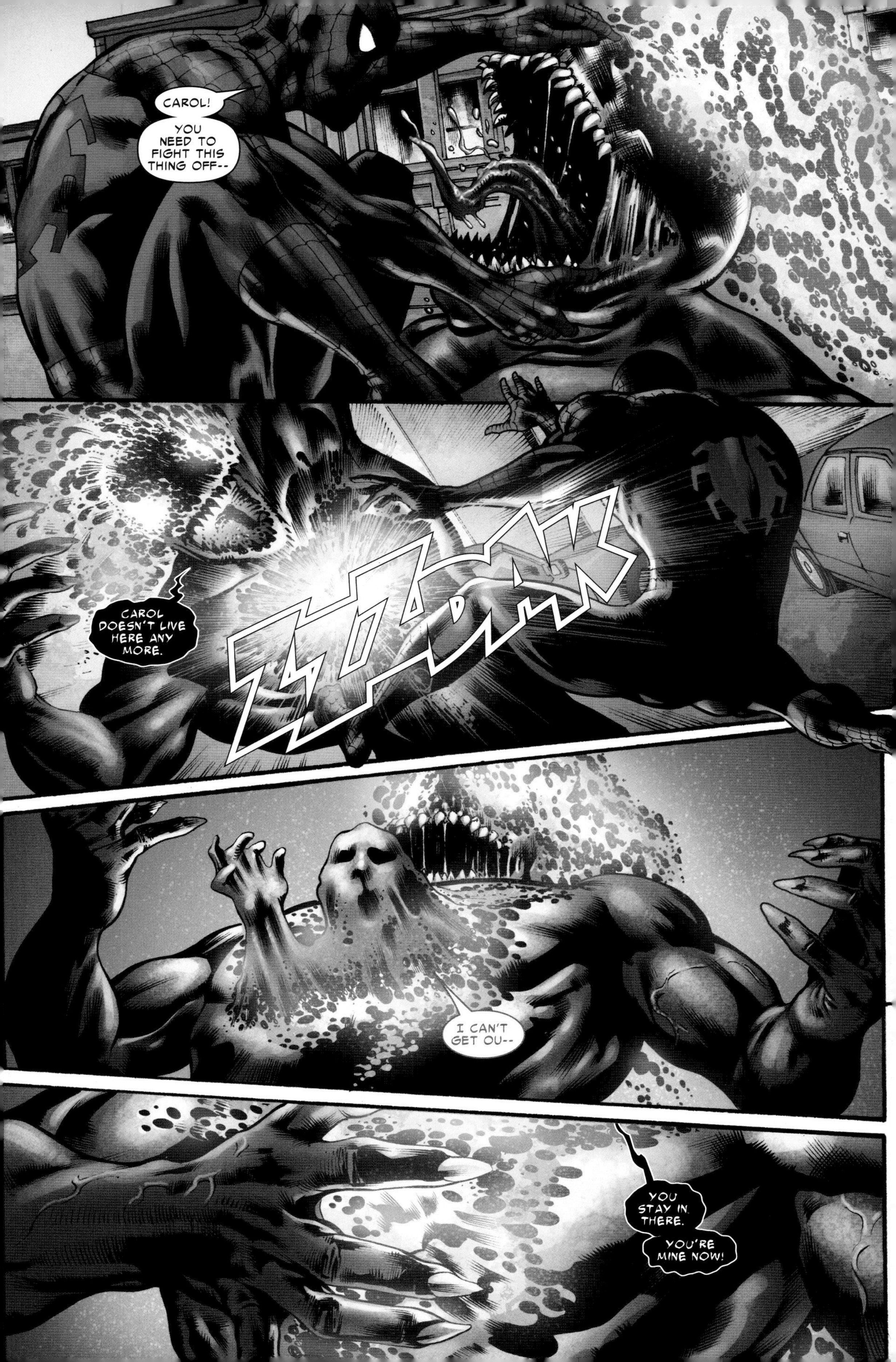

CAROL!
YOU NEED TO FIGHT THIS THING OFF--
CAROL DOESN'T LIVE HERE ANY MORE.
ZZDAK
I CAN'T GET OU--
YOU STAY IN THERE.
YOU'RE MINE NOW!

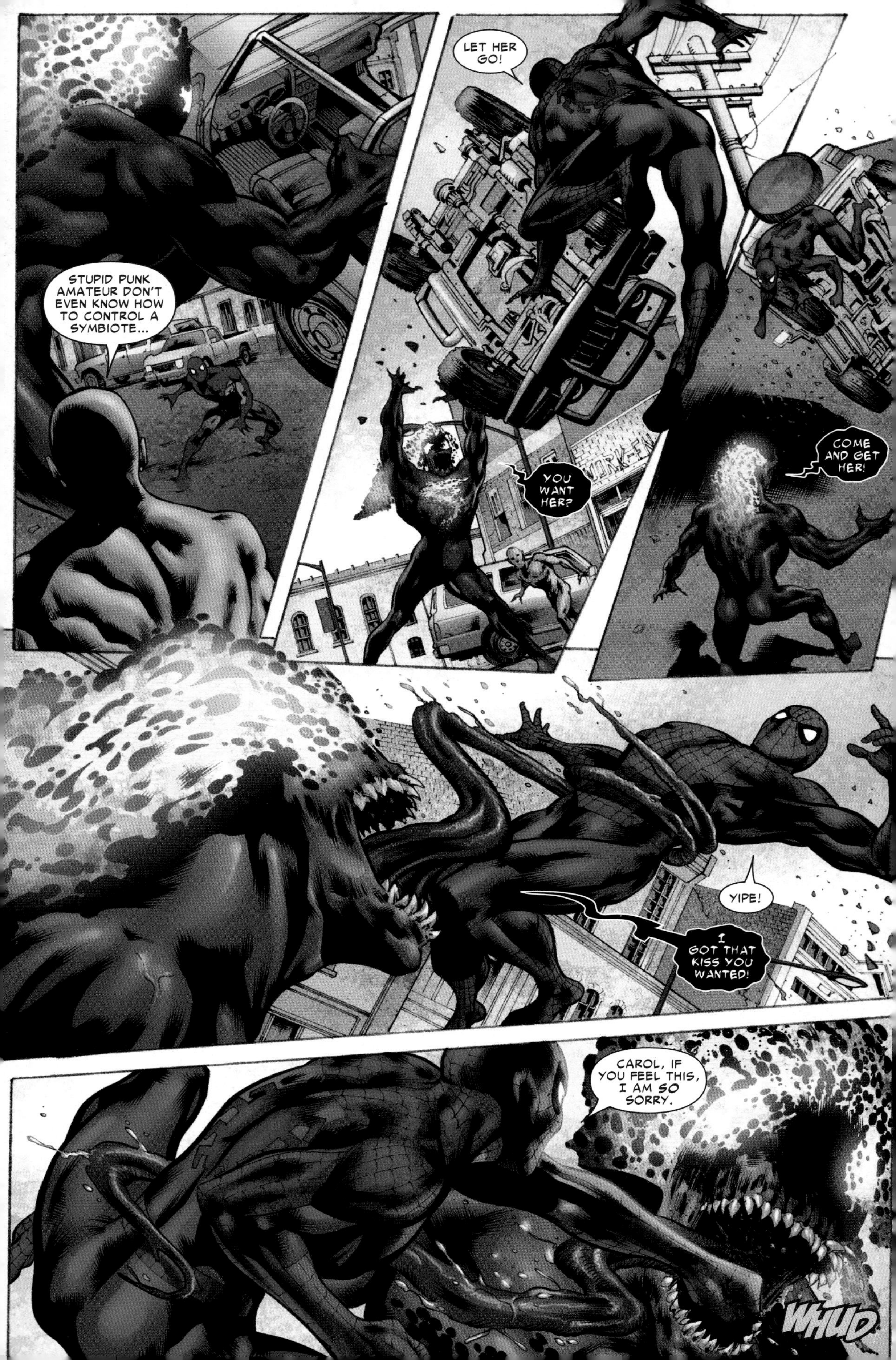
STUPID PUNK AMATEUR DON'T EVEN KNOW HOW TO CONTROL A SYMBIOTE...
LET HER GO!
YOU WANT HER?
COME AND GET HER!
YIPE!
I GOT THAT KISS YOU WANTED!
CAROL, IF YOU FEEL THIS, I AM SO SORRY.
WHUD

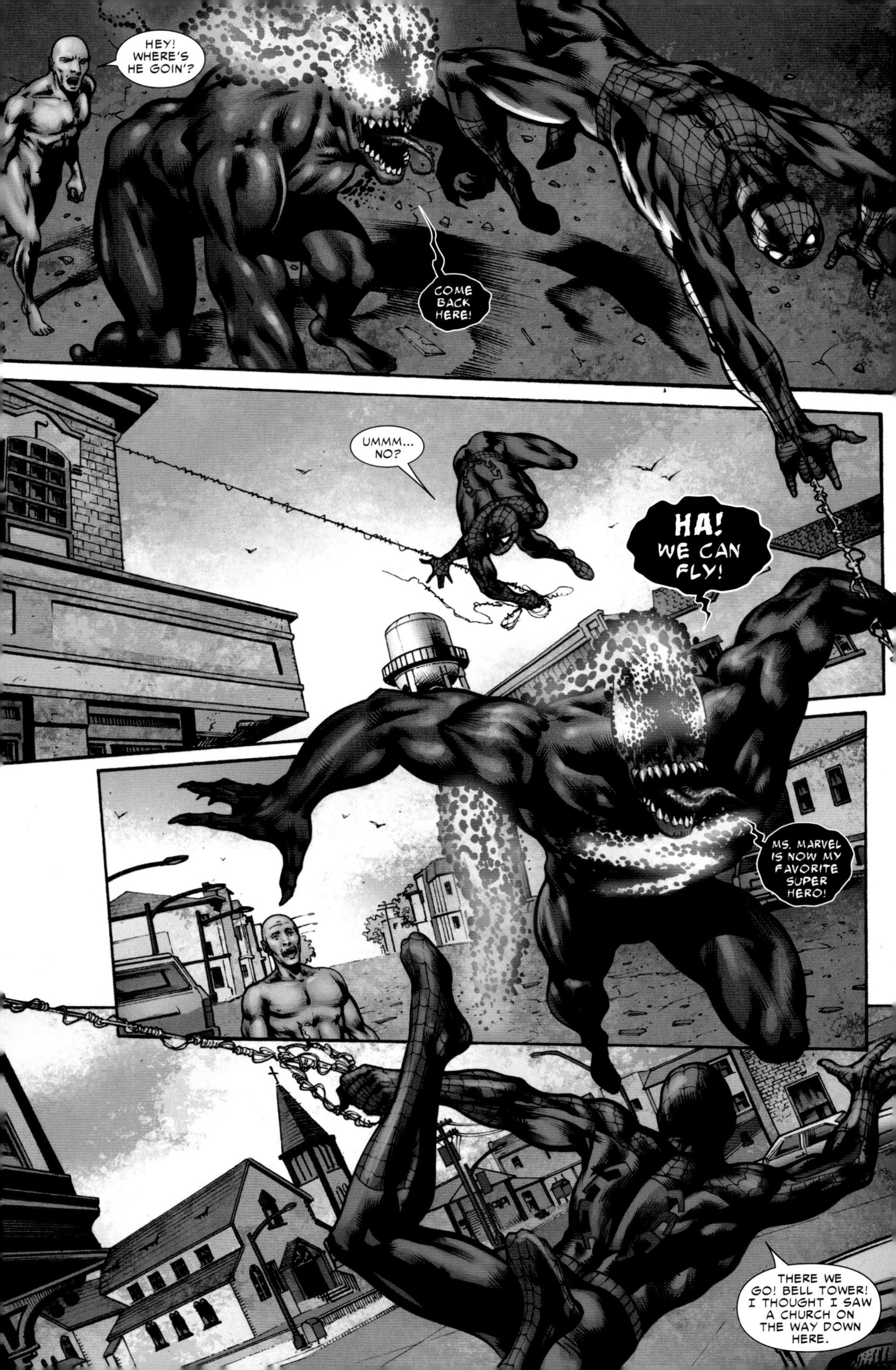
HEY! WHERE'S HE GOIN'?
COME BACK HERE!
UMMM... NO?
HA! WE CAN FLY!
MS. MARVEL IS NOW MY FAVORITE SUPER HERO!
THERE WE GO! BELL TOWER! I THOUGHT I SAW A CHURCH ON THE WAY DOWN HERE.

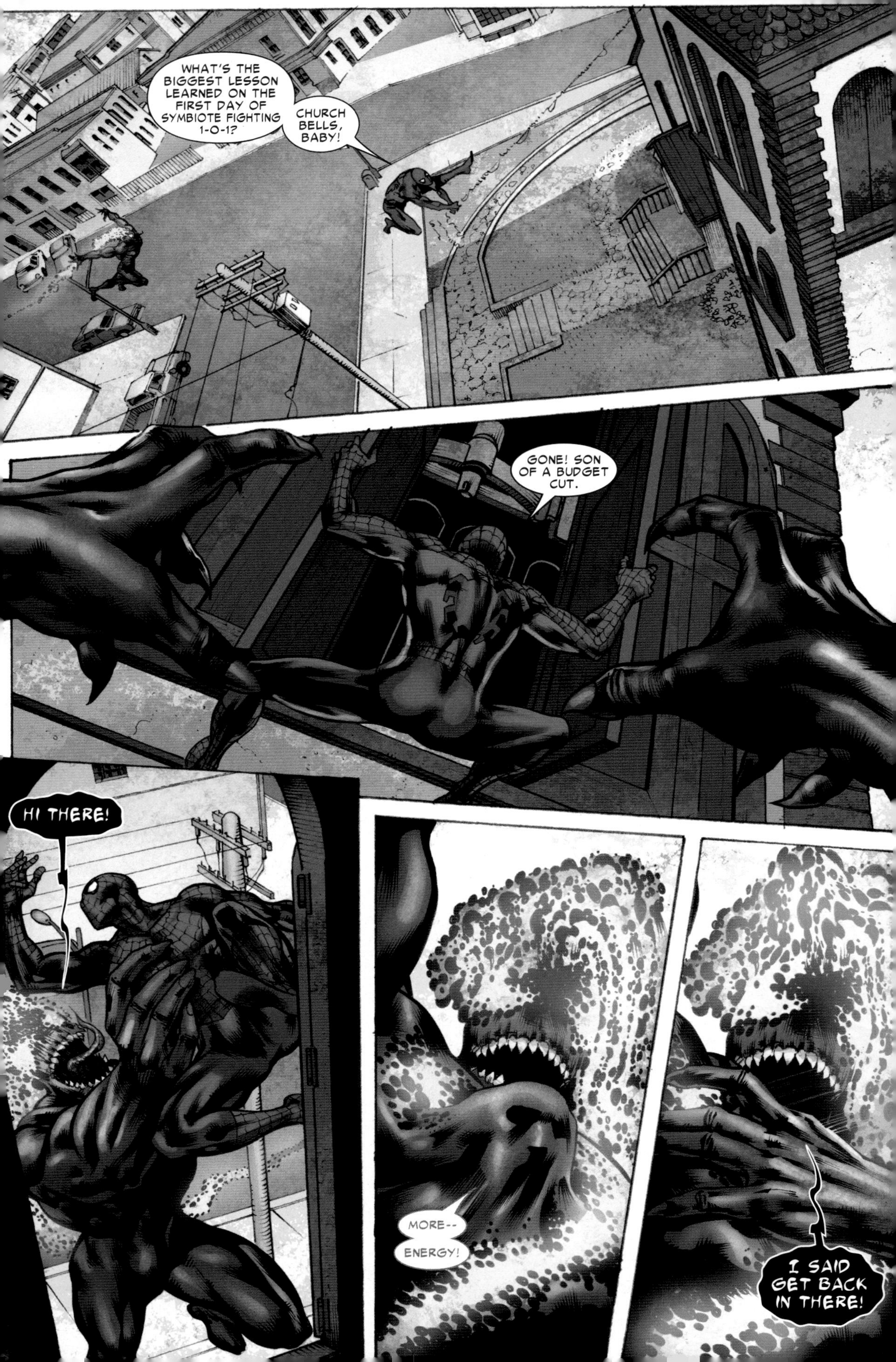

WHAT'S THE BIGGEST LESSON LEARNED ON THE FIRST DAY OF SYMBIOTE FIGHTING 1-0-1?
CHURCH BELLS, BABY!
GONE! SON OF A BUDGET CUT.
HI THERE!
MORE--
ENERGY!
I SAID GET BACK IN THERE!

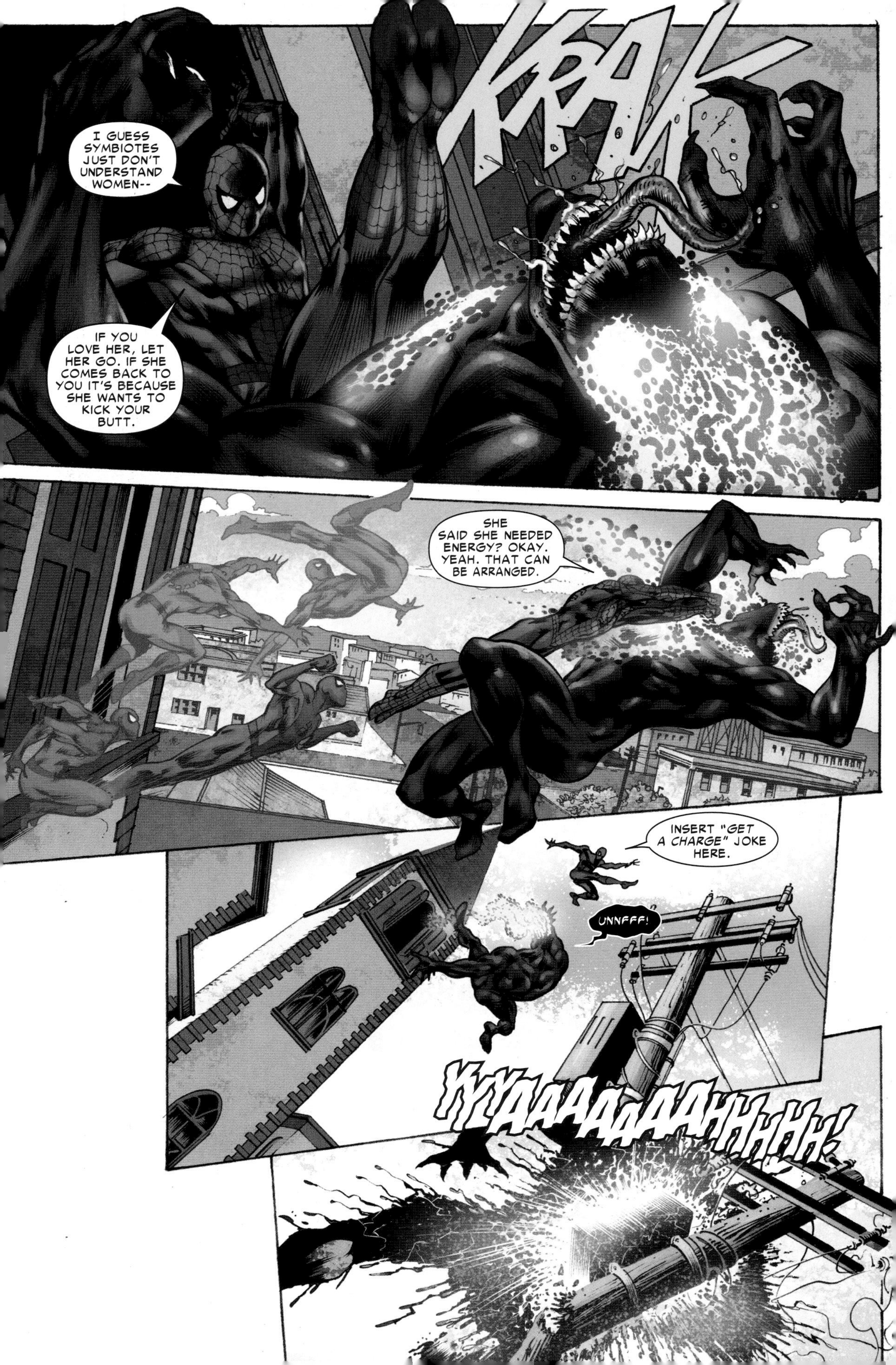
KRAK
I GUESS SYMBIOTES JUST DON'T UNDERSTAND WOMEN--
IF YOU LOVE HER, LET HER GO. IF SHE COMES BACK TO YOU IT'S BECAUSE SHE WANTS TO KICK YOUR BUTT.
SHE SAID SHE NEEDED ENERGY? OKAY. YEAH. THAT CAN BE ARRANGED.
INSERT "GET A CHARGE" JOKE HERE.
UNNFFF!
YYYAAAAAAAHHHHH!

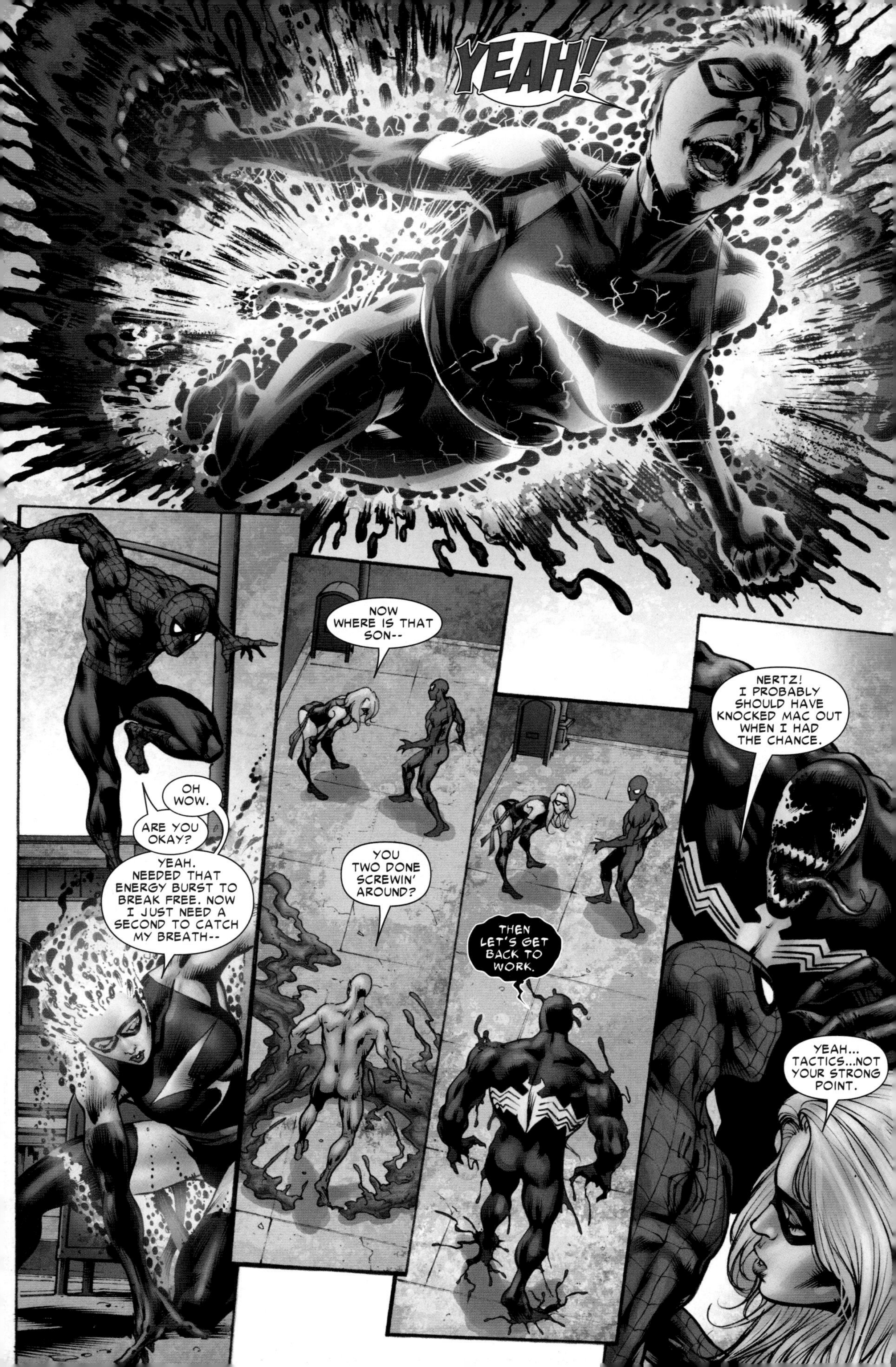
YEAH!
OH WOW.
ARE YOU OKAY?
YEAH. NEEDED THAT ENERGY BURST TO BREAK FREE. NOW I JUST NEED A SECOND TO CATCH MY BREATH--
NOW WHERE IS THAT SON--
YOU TWO DONE SCREWIN' AROUND?
THEN LET'S GET BACK TO WORK.
NERTZ! I PROBABLY SHOULD HAVE KNOCKED MAC OUT WHEN I HAD THE CHANCE.
YEAH... TACTICS...NOT YOUR STRONG POINT.

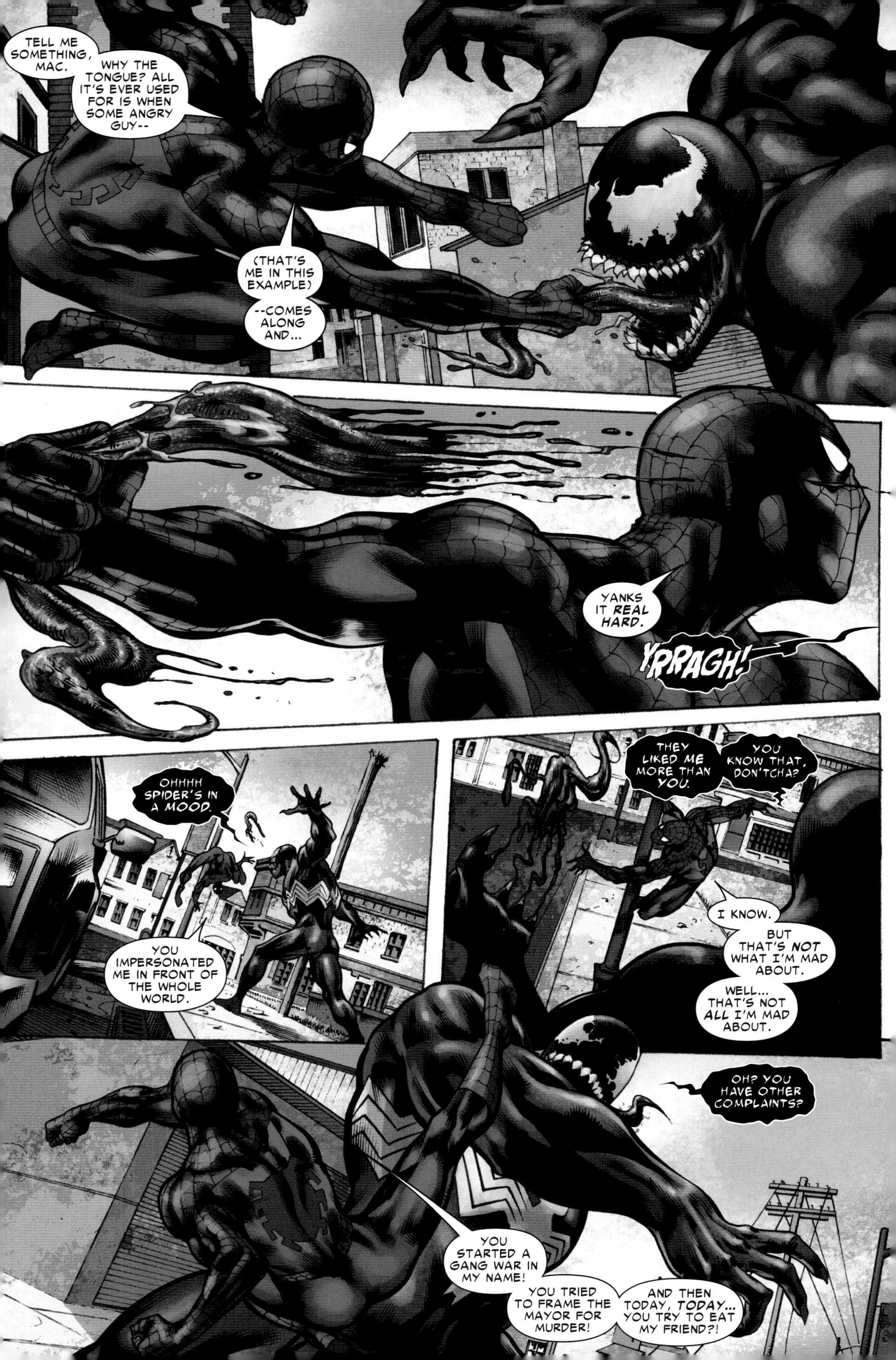

TELL ME SOMETHING, MAC.
WHY THE TONGUE? ALL IT'S EVER USED FOR IS WHEN SOME ANGRY GUY--
(THAT'S ME IN THIS EXAMPLE)
--COMES ALONG AND...
YANKS IT REAL HARD.
YRRAGH!
OHHHH SPIDER'S IN A MOOD.
YOU IMPERSONATED ME IN FRONT OF THE WHOLE WORLD.
THEY LIKED ME MORE THAN YOU.
YOU KNOW THAT, DON'TCHA?
I KNOW.
BUT THAT'S NOT WHAT I'M MAD ABOUT.
WELL... THAT'S NOT ALL I'M MAD ABOUT.
OH? YOU HAVE OTHER COMPLAINTS?
YOU STARTED A GANG WAR IN MY NAME!
YOU TRIED TO FRAME THE MAYOR FOR MURDER!
AND THEN TODAY, TODAY... YOU TRY TO EAT MY FRIEND?!

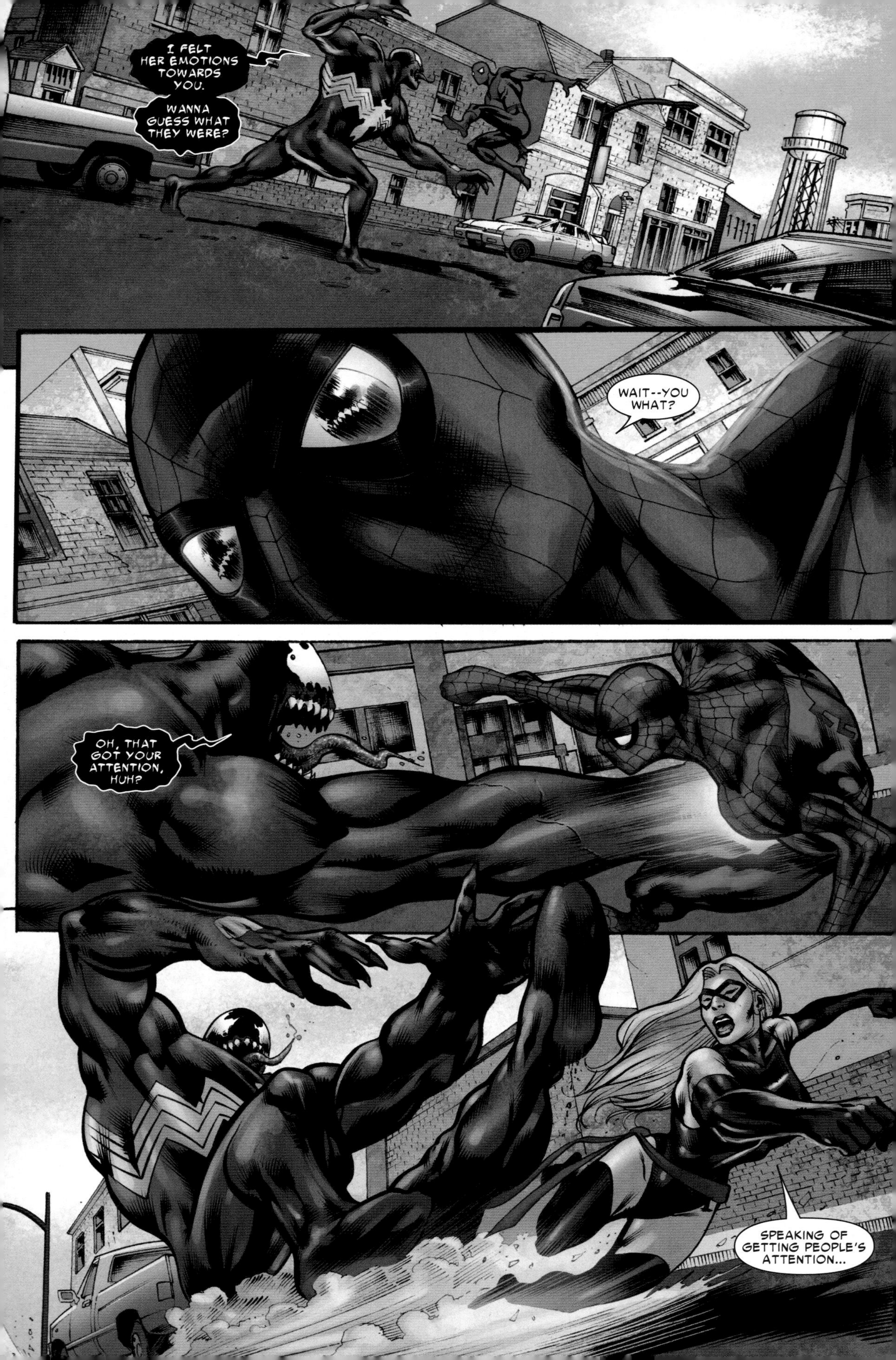
I FELT HER EMOTIONS TOWARDS YOU.
WANNA GUESS WHAT THEY WERE?
WAIT--YOU WHAT?
OH, THAT GOT YOUR ATTENTION, HUH?
SPEAKING OF GETTING PEOPLE'S ATTENTION...

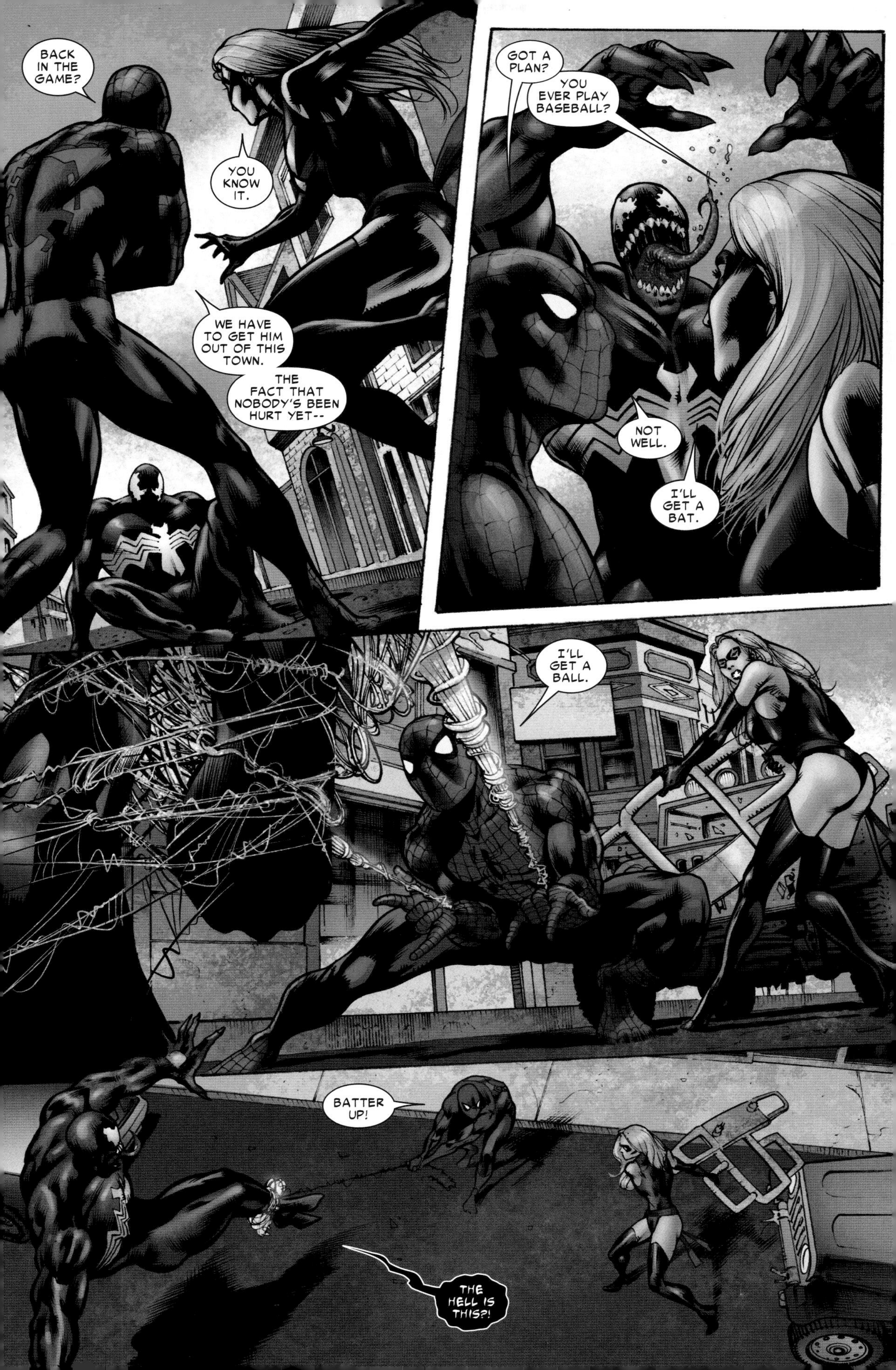
BACK IN THE GAME?
YOU KNOW IT.
WE HAVE TO GET HIM OUT OF THIS TOWN.
THE FACT THAT NOBODY'S BEEN HURT YET--
GOT A PLAN?
YOU EVER PLAY BASEBALL?
NOT WELL.
I'LL GET A BAT.
I'LL GET A BALL.
BATTER UP!
THE HELL IS THIS?!

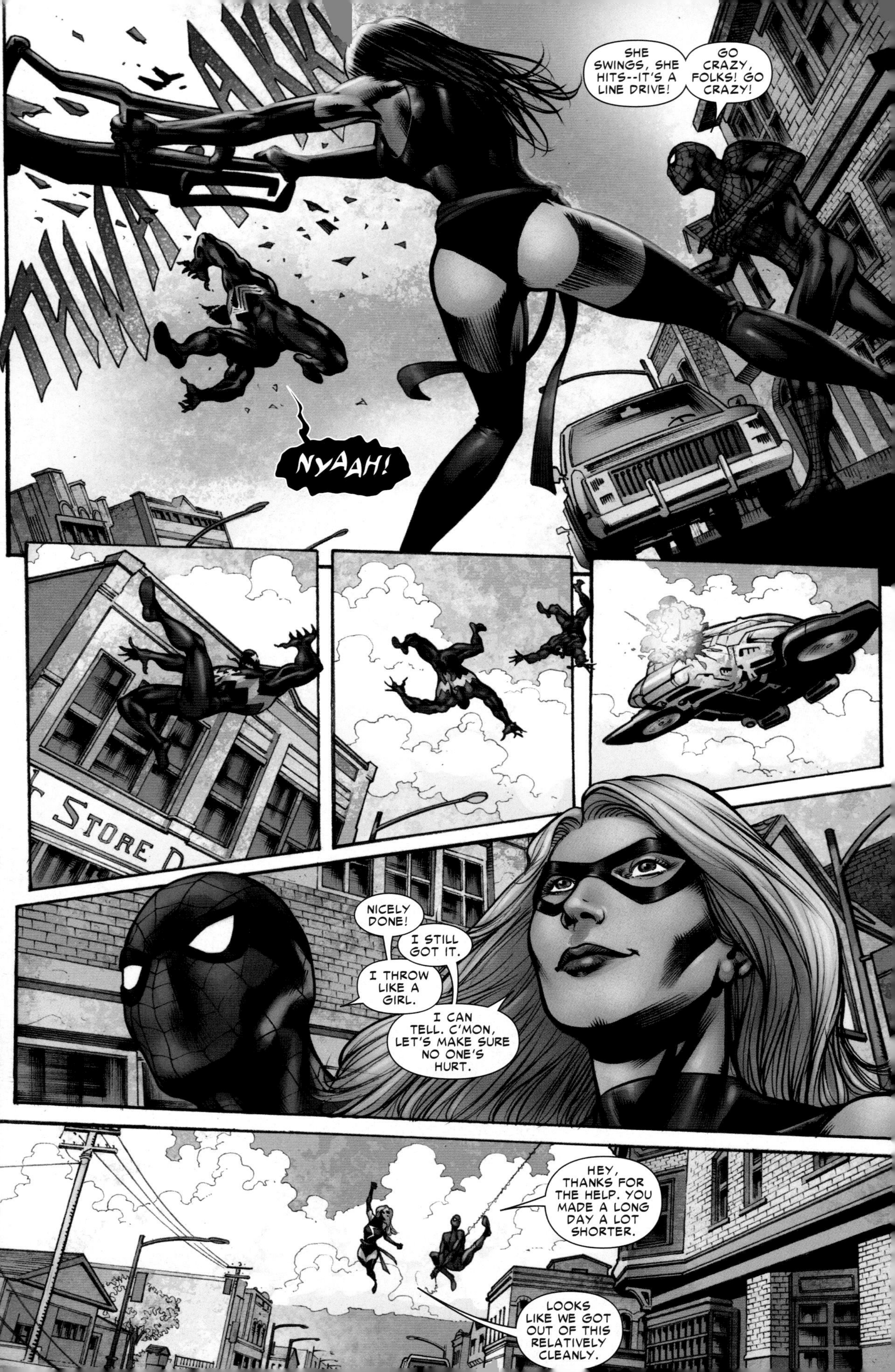
THWAKK
NYAAH!
SHE SWINGS, SHE HITS--IT'S A LINE DRIVE!
GO CRAZY, FOLKS! GO CRAZY!
STORE
NICELY DONE!
I STILL GOT IT.
I THROW LIKE A GIRL.
I CAN TELL. C'MON, LET'S MAKE SURE NO ONE'S HURT.
HEY, THANKS FOR THE HELP. YOU MADE A LONG DAY A LOT SHORTER.
LOOKS LIKE WE GOT OUT OF THIS RELATIVELY CLEANLY.

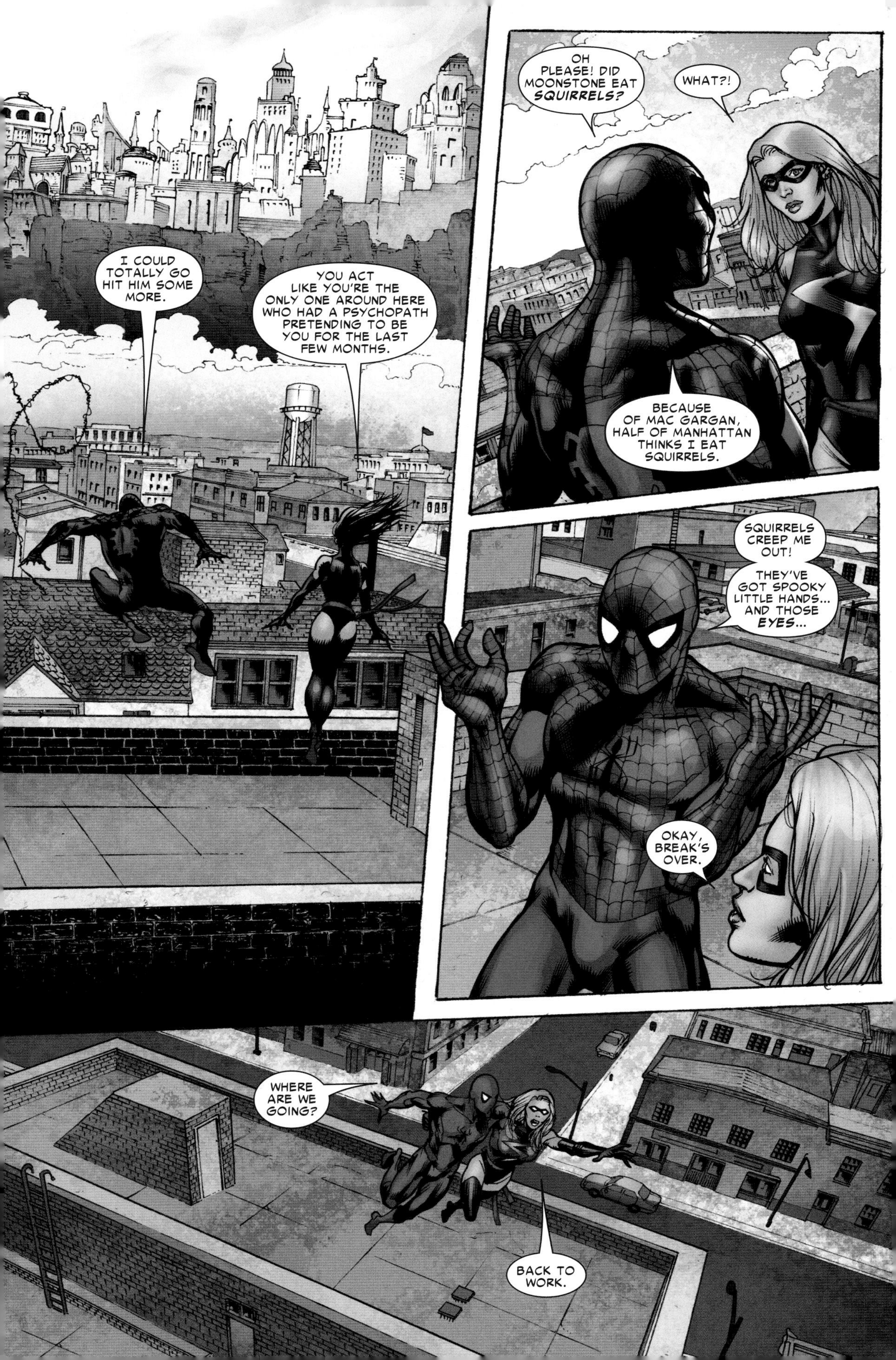
I COULD TOTALLY GO HIT HIM SOME MORE.
YOU ACT LIKE YOU'RE THE ONLY ONE AROUND HERE WHO HAD A PSYCHOPATH PRETENDING TO BE YOU FOR THE LAST FEW MONTHS.
OH PLEASE! DID MOONSTONE EAT SQUIRRELS?
WHAT?!
BECAUSE OF MAC GARGAN, HALF OF MANHATTAN THINKS I EAT SQUIRRELS.
SQUIRRELS CREEP ME OUT!
THEY'VE GOT SPOOKY LITTLE HANDS... AND THOSE EYES...
OKAY, BREAK'S OVER.
WHERE ARE WE GOING?
BACK TO WORK.

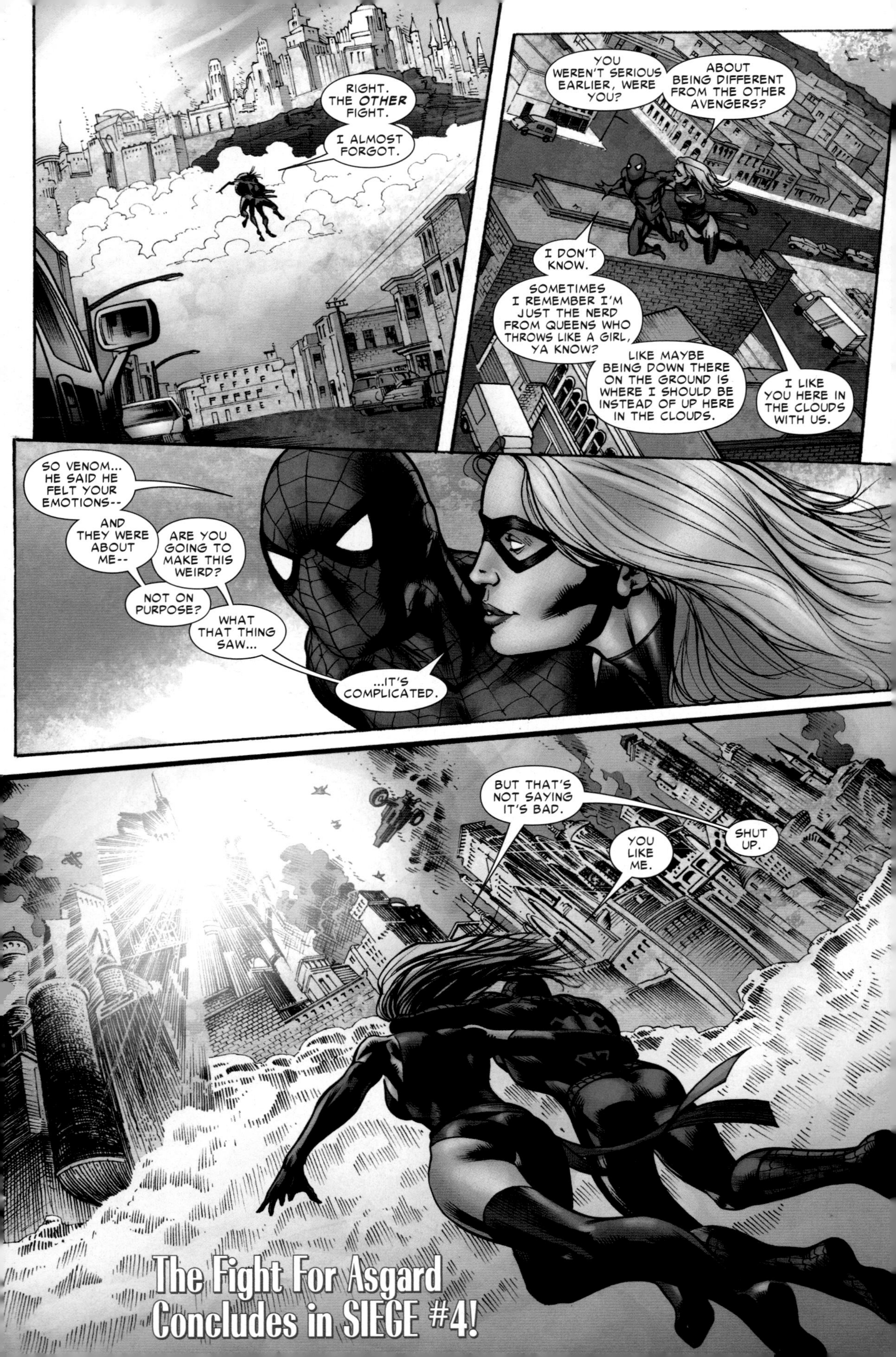
RIGHT. THE OTHER FIGHT.
I ALMOST FORGOT.
YOU WEREN'T SERIOUS EARLIER, WERE YOU?
ABOUT BEING DIFFERENT FROM THE OTHER AVENGERS?
I DON'T KNOW.
SOMETIMES I REMEMBER I'M JUST THE NERD FROM QUEENS WHO THROWS LIKE A GIRL, YA KNOW?
LIKE MAYBE BEING DOWN THERE ON THE GROUND IS WHERE I SHOULD BE INSTEAD OF UP HERE IN THE CLOUDS.
I LIKE YOU HERE IN THE CLOUDS WITH US.
SO VENOM... HE SAID HE FELT YOUR EMOTIONS--
AND THEY WERE ABOUT ME--
ARE YOU GOING TO MAKE THIS WEIRD?
NOT ON PURPOSE?
WHAT THAT THING SAW...
...IT'S COMPLICATED.
BUT THAT'S NOT SAYING IT'S BAD.
YOU LIKE ME.
SHUT UP.
The Fight For Asgard Concludes in SIEGE #4!

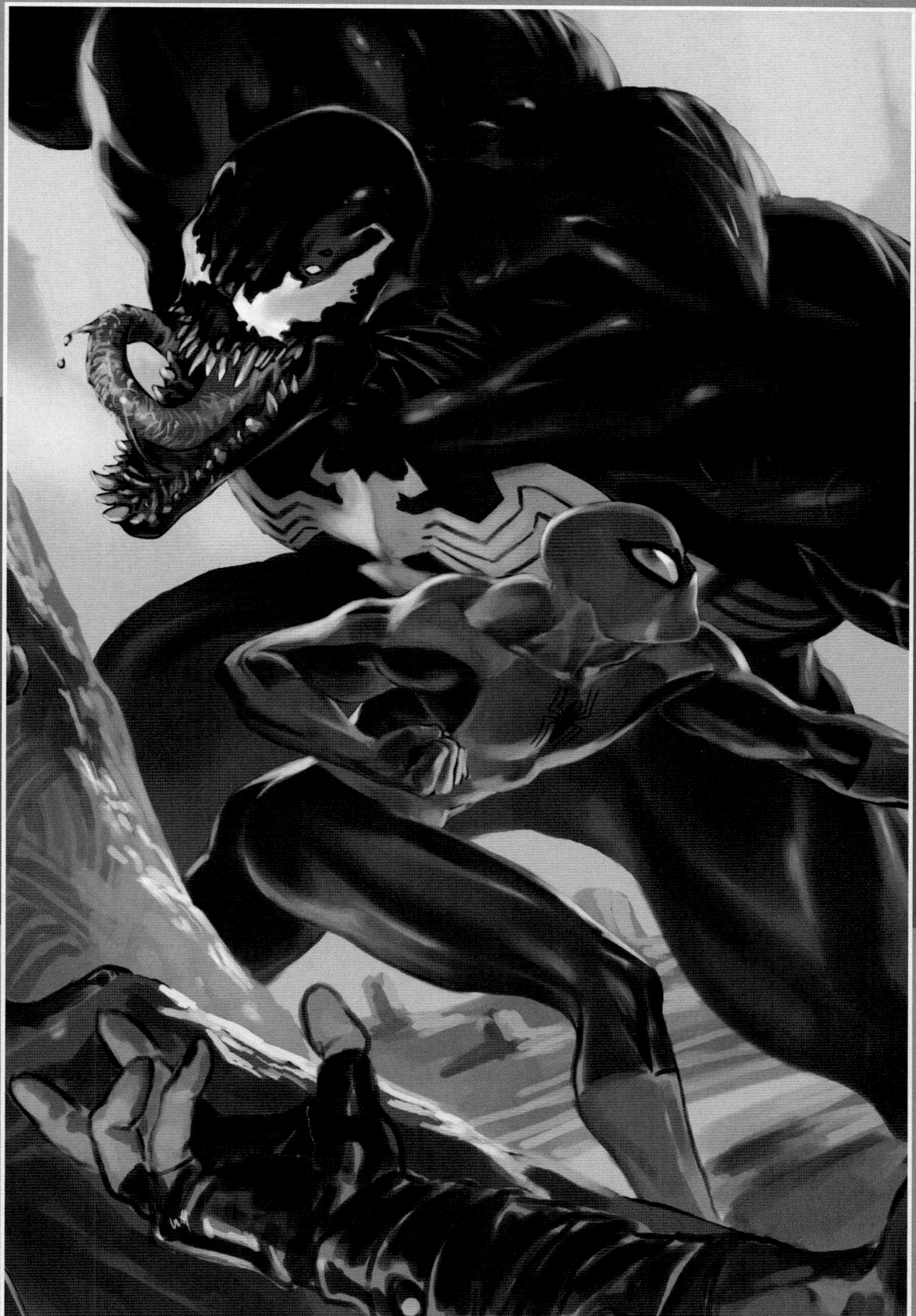

SIEGE: SPIDER-MAN SKETCH VARIANT BY MARKO DJURDJEVIĆ

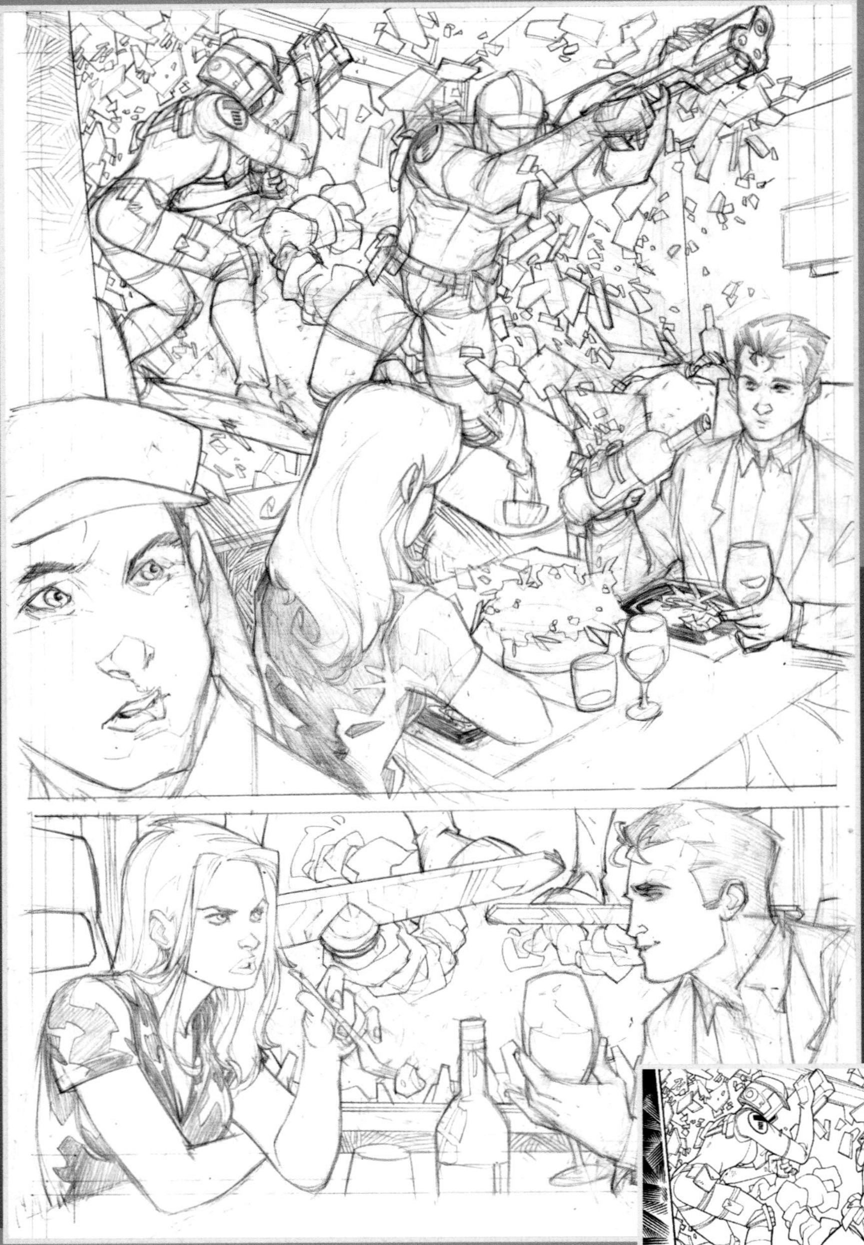

MS. MARVEL #47, PAGE 16
PENCILS & INKS
BY ROBERTO DI SALVO

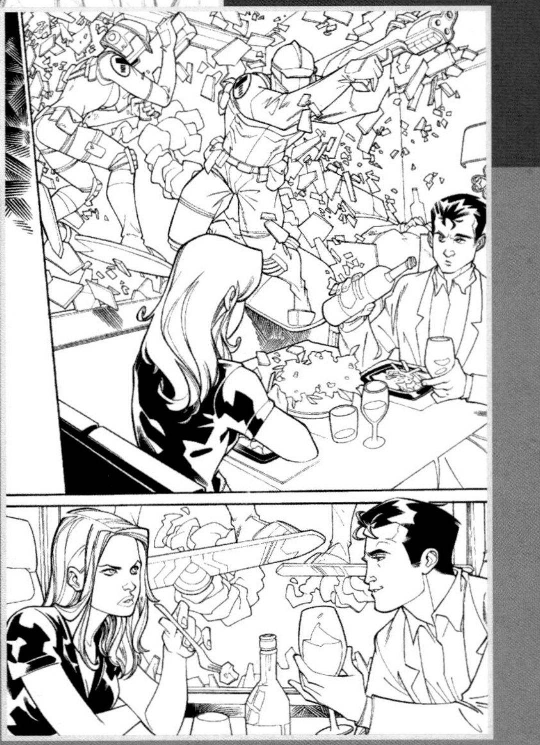

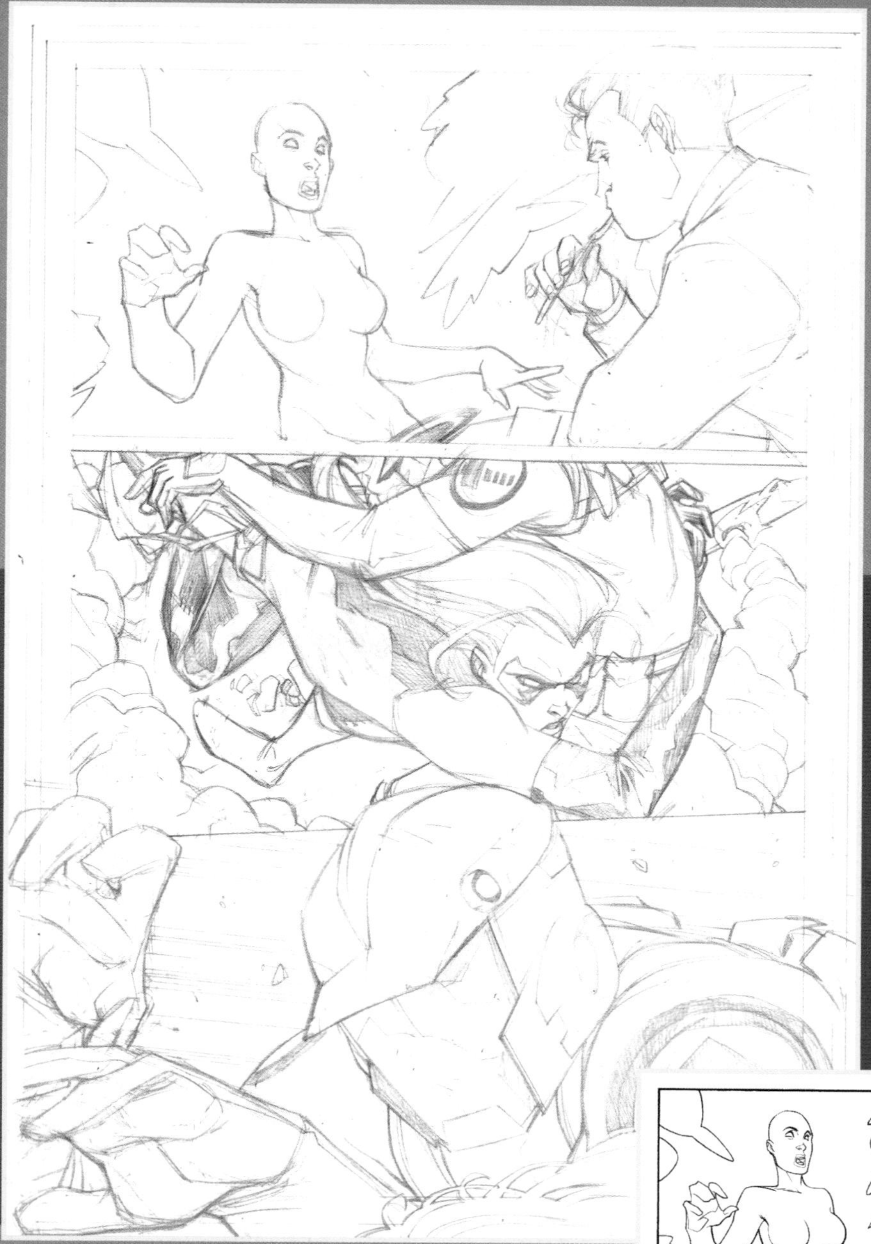

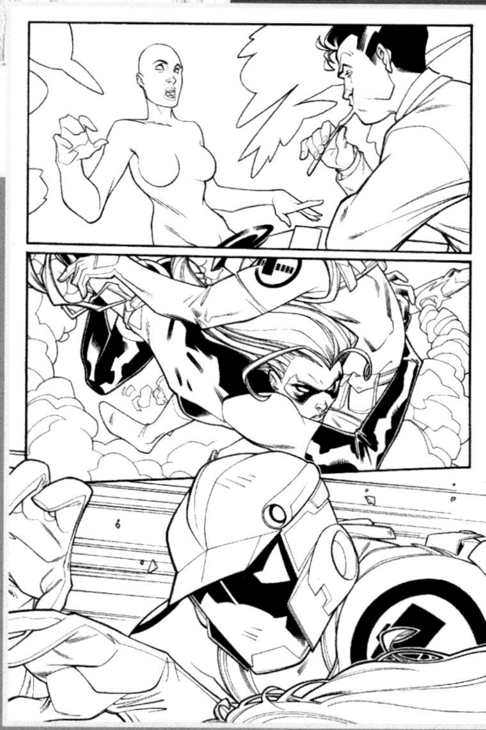

MS. MARVEL #47, PAGE 17
PENCILS & INKS
BY ROBERTO DI SALVO

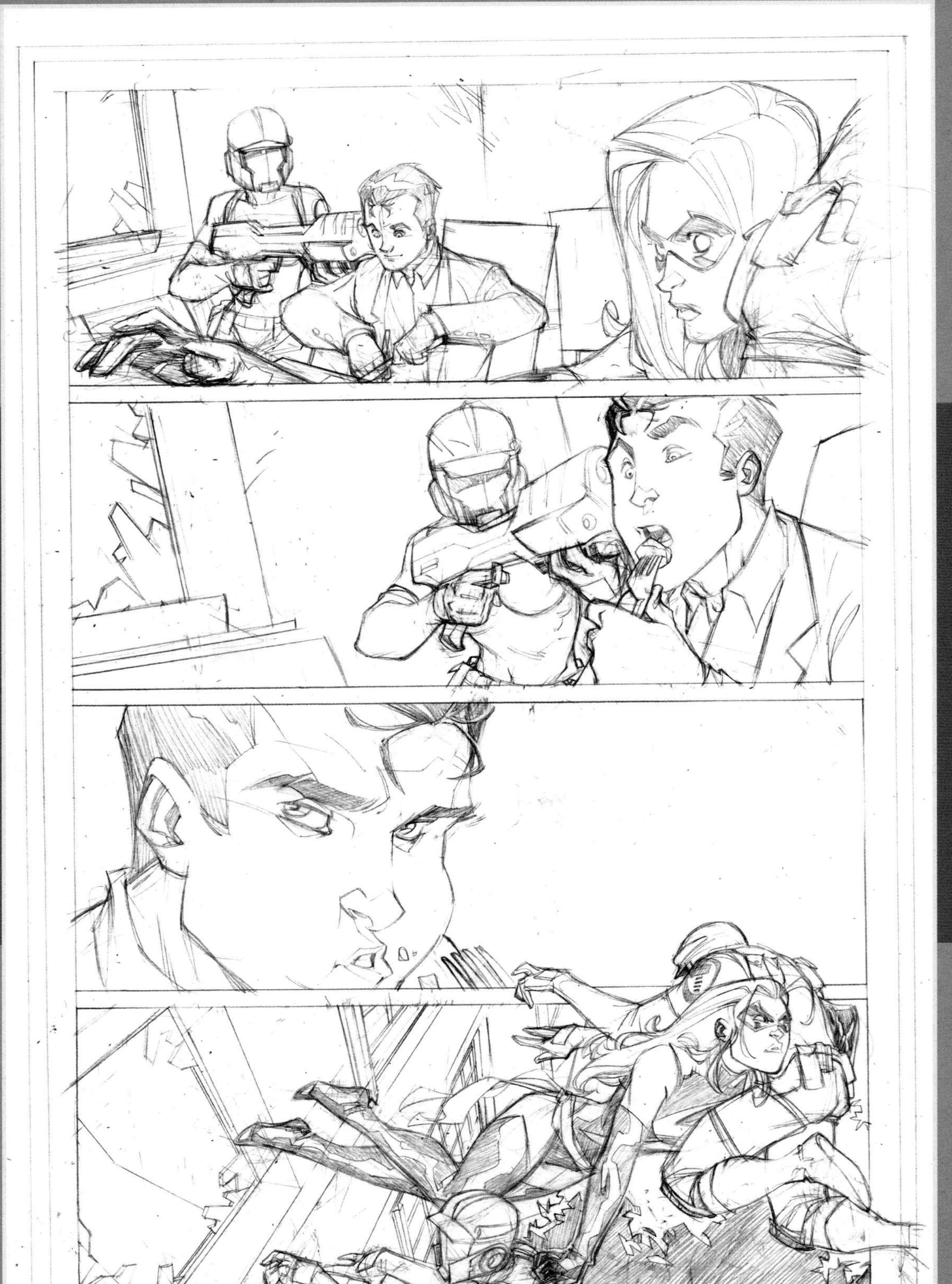

MS. MARVEL #47, PAGE 18 PENCILS
BY ROBERTO DI SALVO

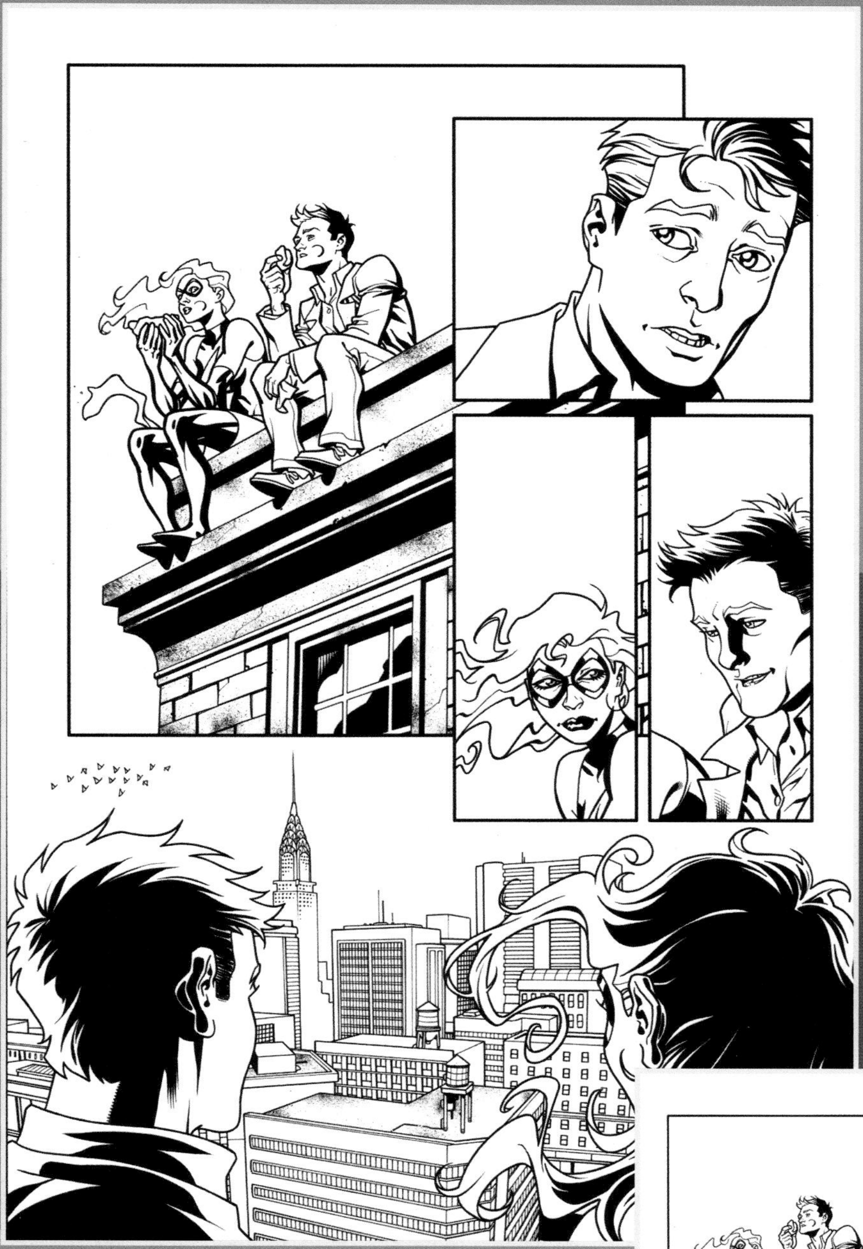

MS. MARVEL #47, PAGE 22
UNUSED VERSION
BY ROBERTO DI SALVO

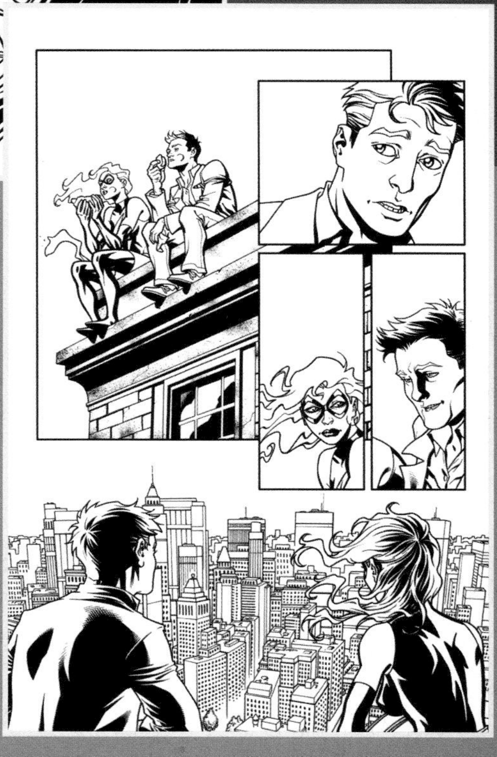

FINAL VERSION

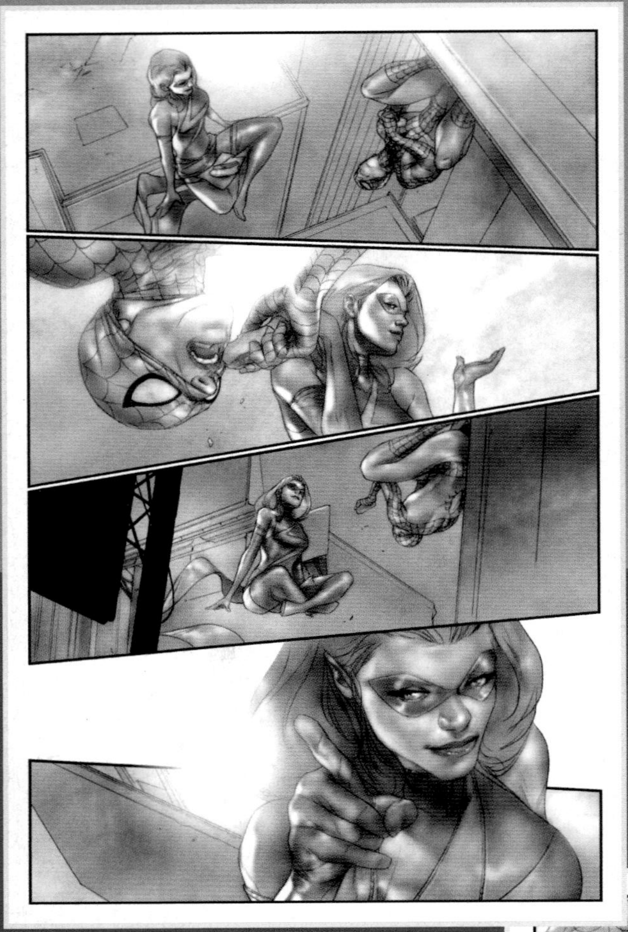

MS. MARVEL #50, PAGES 19-20
PENCILS BY **BEN OLIVER**

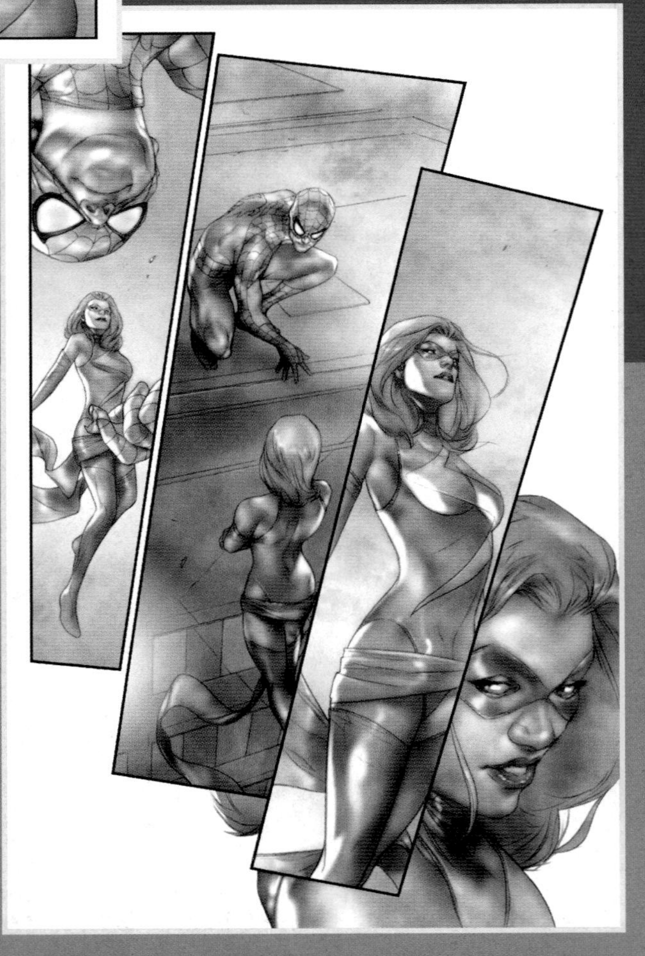

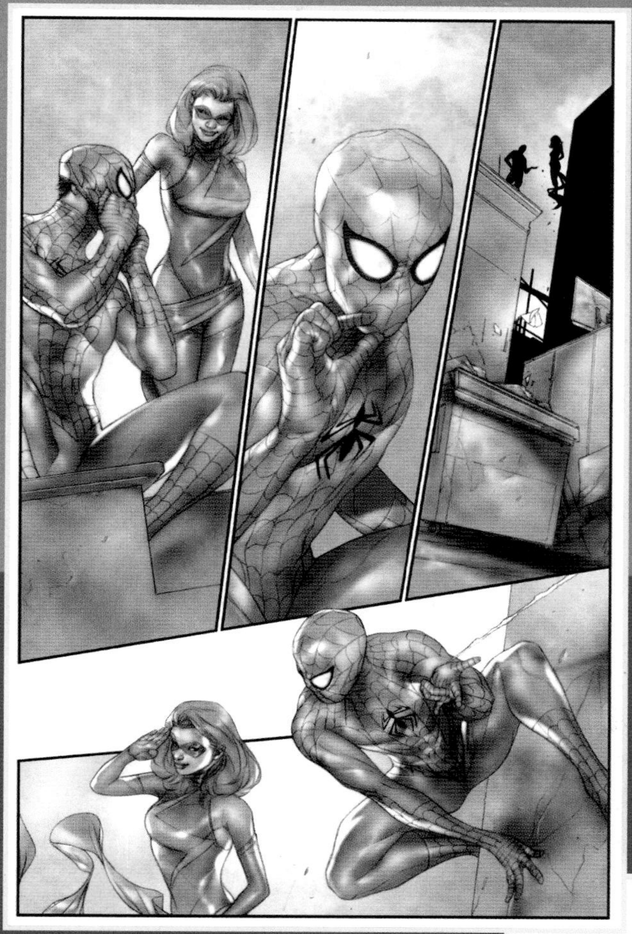

MS. MARVEL #50, PAGES 21-22
PENCILS BY BEN OLIVER

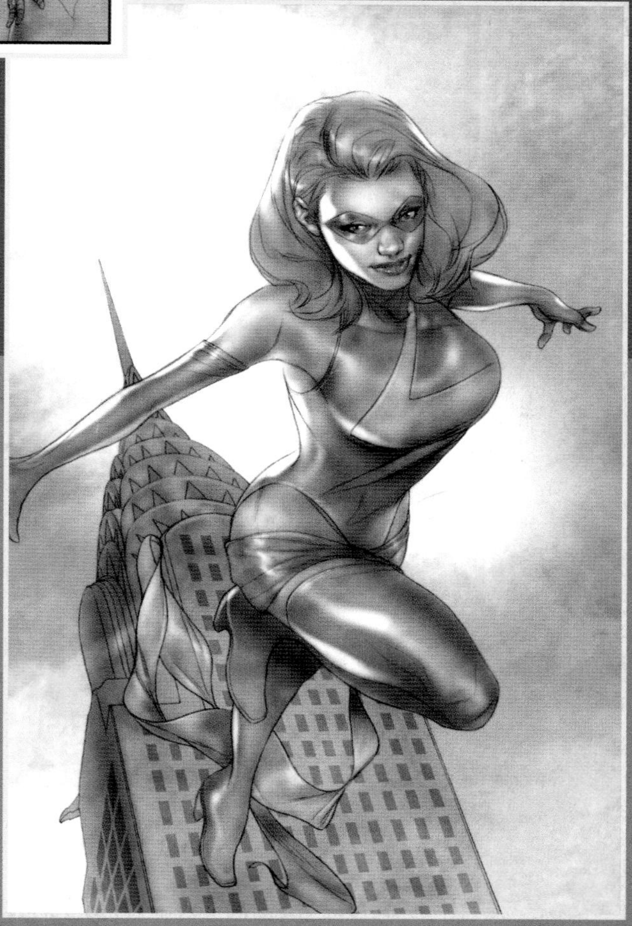

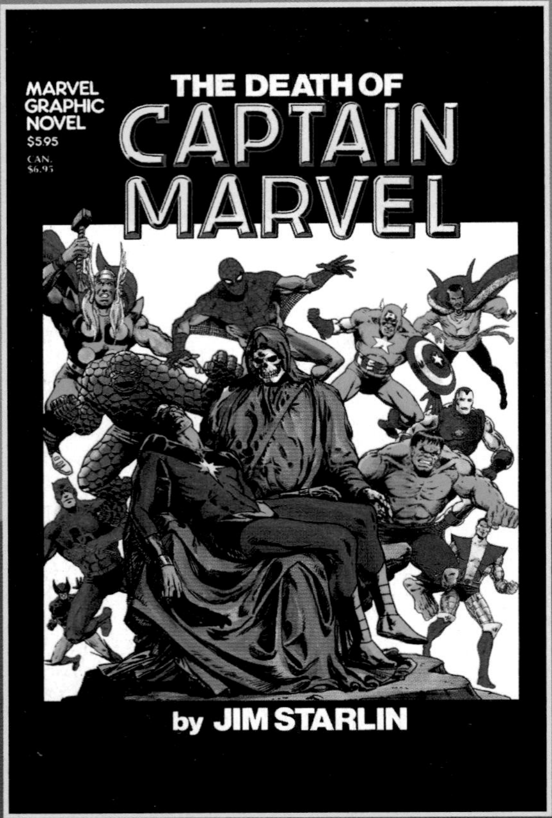
MARVEL
GRAPHIC
NOVEL
$5.95
CAN.
$6.95
THE DEATH OF
CAPTAIN
MARVEL
by JIM STARLIN

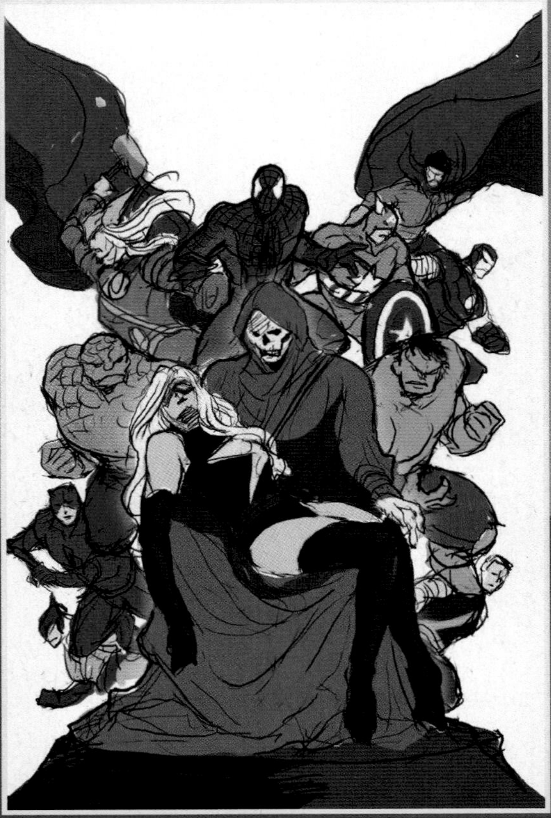

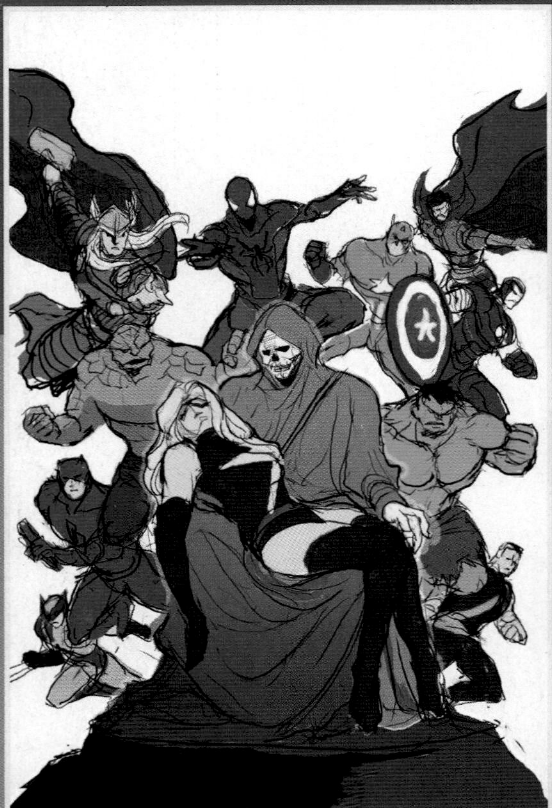

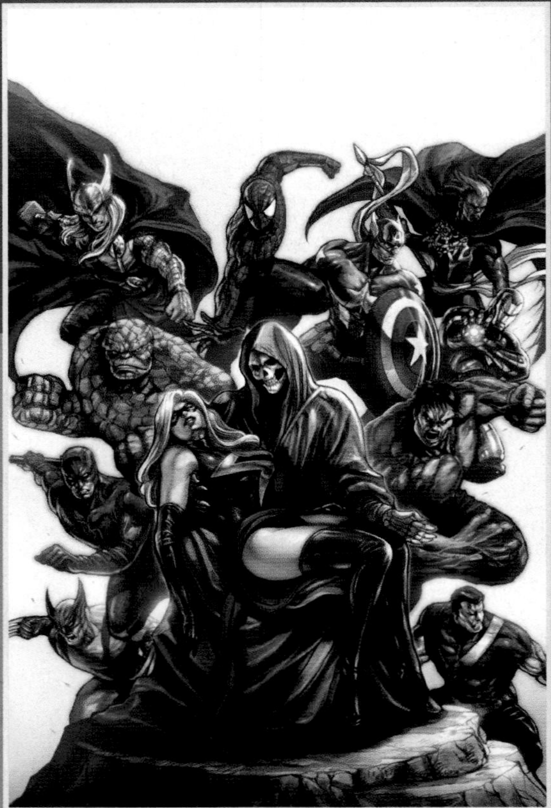

MS. MARVEL #50 COVER PROCESS BY SANA TAKEDA